THE

Novel

Edited by Franco Moretti

Editorial Board: Ernesto Franco, Fredric Jameson, Abdelfattah Kilito,
Pier Vincenzo Mengaldo, and Mario Vargas Llosa

VOLUME 1
HISTORY, GEOGRAPHY, AND CULTURE

VOLUME 2
FORMS AND THEMES

THE

Novel

VOLUME 2

FORMS AND THEMES

EDITED BY
Franco Moretti

Princeton University Press

PRINCETON AND OXFORD

Published by Princeton University Press, 41 William Street,
Princeton, New Jersey 08540
In the United Kingdom: Princeton University Press, 3 Market Place,
Woodstock, Oxfordshire OX20 1SY

This book is a selection from the original five-volume work, published
in Italian under the title *Il romanzo*, copyright © 2001–2003 by Giulio
Einaudi editore s.p.a., Turin. Citations in these essays reflect the
substantive content of those in the Italian edition.

Library of Congress Cataloging-in-Publication Data

Romanzo. English. Selections.
The novel / edited by Franco Moretti.
p. cm.
A selection from the original five-volume work, published in Torino by
G. Einaudi editore, c2001–c2003.
Includes bibliographical references and indexes.
Contents: v. 1. History, geography, and culture — v. 2. Forms and themes.
ISBN-13: 978-0-691-04947-2 (cl : v. 1 : alk. paper)
ISBN-10: 0-691-04947-5 (cl : v. 1 : alk. paper)
ISBN-13: 978-0-691-04948-9 (cl : v. 2 : alk. paper)
ISBN-10: 0-691-04948-3 (cl : v. 2 : alk. paper)
1. Fiction—History and criticism.   I. Moretti, Franco, 1950–   II. Title.

PN3321.R66 2006
809.3—dc22   2005051473

British Library Cataloging-in-Publication Data is available

This book has been composed in Simoncini Garamond

Printed on acid-free paper. ∞

pup.princeton.edu

Printed in the United States of America

1 3 5 7 9 10 8 6 4 2

Contents

2.4. SPACE AND STORY

MIEKE BAL

HANS ULRICH GUMBRECHT

MARGARET COHEN

PHILIP FISHER

Readings: The New Metropolis

2.5. UNCERTAIN BOUNDARIES

ANDREAS GAILUS

FRANCIS MULHERN

On *The Novel*

Countless are the novels of the world. So, how can we speak of them? *The Novel* combines two intersecting perspectives. First, the novel is for us a great anthropological force, which has turned reading into a pleasure and redefined the sense of reality, the meaning of individual existence, the perception of time and of language. The novel as culture, then, but certainly also as form, or rather forms, plural, because in the two thousand years of its history one encounters the strangest creations, and high and low trade places at every opportunity, as the borders of literature are continuously, unpredictably expanded. At times, this endless flexibility borders on chaos. But thanks to it, the novel becomes the first truly planetary form: a phoenix always ready to take flight in a new direction, and to find the right language for the next generation of readers.

———

Two perspectives on the novel, then; and two volumes. *History, Geography, and Culture* is mostly a look from the outside; *Forms and Themes*, from the inside. But like convex and concave in a Borromini façade, inside and outside are here part of the same design, because the novel is always commodity and artwork at once: a major economic investment and an ambitious aesthetic form (for German romanticism, the most universal of all). Don't be surprised, then, if an epistemological analysis of "fiction" slides into a discussion of credit and paper money or if a statistical study of the Japanese book market becomes a reflection on narrative morphology. This is the way of the novel—and of *The Novel*.

———

A history that begins in the Hellenistic world and continues today. A geography that overlaps with the advent of world literature. A morphology that ranges euphorically from war stories, pornography, and melodrama, to syntactic labyrinths, metaphoric prose, and broken plot lines. To make the literary field longer, larger, and deeper: this is, in a nutshell, the project of *The Novel* (and of its Italian five-volume original). And then, project within the project, to take a second look at the new panorama—and estrange it. The essay on the Spanish Golden Age develops its historical argument, and then: "Wait. Why was that magical season so short?" Stating the "facts," then turning them into "problems." At the beginning of the historical arc, we wonder whether to speak of "the" Greek novel—or of a cluster of independent forms. At the opposite end, we explain why it is that the best-known African novels are not written for African readers. And so on. The more we learn about the history of the novel, the stranger it becomes.

———

To make sense of this new history, *The Novel* uses three different registers. Essays, about twenty per volume, are works of abstraction, synthesis, and comparative research: they establish the great periodizations that segment the flow of time, and the conceptual architecture that reveals its unity. "Readings" are shorter pieces, unified by a common question, and devoted to the close analysis of individual texts: *Aethiopica*, *Le Grand Cyrus*, *The War of the Worlds* (and more) as so many prototypes of novelistic subgenres; *Malte Laurids Brigge, Macunaíma, The Making of Americans* (and more) as typical modern experiments. Finally, the sections entitled "Critical Apparatus" study the novel's wider ecosystem, focusing, for instance, on how the semantic field of "narrative" took shape around keywords such as *midrash*, *monogatari, xiaoshuo, qiṣṣa*—and, why not, *romance*.

———

Countless are the novels of the world. We discuss them in two volumes. Quite a few things will be missing, of course. But this is not Noah's ark: it is a collective reflection on the pleasures of storytelling, and their interaction— at times, complicity—with social power. Now more than ever, pleasure and critique should not be divided.

F.M.

The Long Duration

THOMAS PAVEL

The Novel in Search of Itself: A Historical Morphology

ARGUMENT

Like epic and tragedy, the novel tells of the relationships between human beings and the surrounding world. But while epic heroes belong entirely to their cities, and the tragic hero's fate is predetermined, the protagonists of novels are set apart from the world, and their destiny mirrors its contingency. By imposing a breach between characters and their surroundings, the novel is the first genre to reflect on the genesis of the individual and the establishment of a common morality. Most of all, the novel raises, with extraordinary precision, the philosophical question of whether moral ideals are inherent in this world, for, if they are, why do they seem so remote from human behavior, and if they are not, why does their normative value impose itself so clearly on us? For the novel to raise this question is to ask whether, in order to defend their ideals, humans should resist the world, plunge in to try to defend moral order, or concentrate on trying to correct their own frailties. To explore these concerns, the novel has traditionally focused on love and the formation of couples. Whereas epic and tragedy took for granted the links between individuals and their milieu, the novel concentrates on love in order to reflect on the most intimate, interpersonal form taken by these links.

The premodern novel insists on the primacy of an idea that is more important than the observation of the empirical world. This peculiarity influences both the message and the formal features of the highly specific premodern narrative subgenres. Some of these subgenres like the Greek novel, chivalric romance, and the pastoral, presented invincible or, at least, admirable heroes, defending moral norms in a disorderly world. Other subgenres like the elegiac narrative, the picaresque, and the novella, revealed the irremediable imperfection of human beings. During the sixteenth and seventeenth centuries, the dialogue between idealization and denunciation of human frailty took the form of a peaceful coexistence among these subgenres.

The eighteenth- and nineteenth-century novel, by contrast, arising at the confluence of earlier narrative subgenres, sought to merge their different viewpoints and combine an idealizing vision with a keen observation of human imperfection. The eighteenth-century novel, which gave primacy to verisimilitude, asked whether humans are the source of moral law and masters of their own actions. Nineteenth-century novelists concluded that human beings are shaped less by moral norms than by their social and historical milieu. To prove this, they concentrated on scrupulous observation of the social and physical worlds and on the empathetic examination of individual consciences. The genre thus acquired a new scope and power but sacrificed the formal and thematic flexibility of earlier narratives.

At the beginning of the twentieth century, modernists rebelled against both the attempt to imprison human beings in their social milieu and the method of observation and empathy. This rebellion created an unprecedented rupture between, on one side, the individual, liberated from moral concerns and conceived as the site of uncontrollable sensorial and linguistic activity; and, on the other, reality, which came to be seen as mysterious and profoundly disquieting. Modernism gave the novel a new formal dynamism, without however altering its old focus on the individuals and their relation to the surrounding world.

From the Beginnings of the Novel to the End of the Seventeenth Century

Adventure and Idealization: Greek Novels, Chivalric Romance

The Greek idealist novel, which was rediscovered and translated into modern languages in the middle of the sixteenth century, typically relates the story of a couple of lovers whose moral strength gradually conquers the obstacles to happiness. Set apart from the world around them, and guided solely by their requited love, the protagonists endure a long series of ordeals, which symbolize an unjust world. In the end, the tricks of fate are outwitted and the novel concludes with a sacred marriage, highlighting the protagonists' exceptional destiny.

The Greek novel stresses the unity of the human race, living under the protection of providence. In Heliodorus's *Ethiopian Story*, the protagonist Charicleia challenges the particularities of race and milieu from the moment she is born. Of the three men she calls "father," she owes her life of the Ethiopian Hydaspes, her education to the Greek Charicles, and her vocation to the Egyptian Calasiris, the nomadic priest of Memphis. Her true origins are divine, sacred ancestry prevails over human genealogy, and the unity of the world overrides racial specificity.

The concept of a universal humanity not only devalues blood ties but also makes exile imaginable. We noted earlier that epic depicts characters who are strongly rooted in their native land. While tragic heroes sometimes question the duty to one's city in order to affirm the supremacy of religious duties (*Antigone* being the most famous example), tragedies nevertheless depict a world fully circumscribed within the walls of the Greek *polis*. The Greek novel, by contrast, rejects ties of blood as well as love of homeland. Charicleia, born in Ethiopia and raised in Greece, readily leaves the country of her youth to heed a divine call that is stronger than any other duty. Her fiancé Theagenes, a native of Thessaly and descendent of Achilles, also departs without hesitation to follow his beloved into the heart of Africa.

Once the protagonists abandon family and city, they encounter a vast world that is both surprising and hostile. Dangers scattered along the young couple's route combine to form a single, gigantic adversity that torments them without respite. True, Theagenes and Charicleia are endowed with supernatural beauty, a sign of their divine election, but, unhappily, their beauty relentlessly fans the greed, lust, and other evil desires of those around them. Persecuted by men's vile passions, the lovers remain faithful to each other, their virtue being a worldly form of sanctification that links their bodies because a divine aspiration has already united their souls.

Beautiful, chaste, and loyal, the heroes of Greek novels are also unwavering. Shipwrecks, captivity, separation, persecutions, prison, torture, and the funeral pyre have no effect on these beings who are as brilliant as diamonds and as resolute as steel. Their endless misfortunes reveal the world to be a valley of tears, whose injustice must be feared and whose temptations must be fled. Like the stoic sages safely sheltered in their inner fortresses, the couple remains ever impervious to change and suffering. For this reason, it makes no sense to deplore the absence of psychological maturation in Greek novels, as literary critics have sometimes done; the glory of these protagonists is, precisely, their constancy.

The universe of Greek novels unfolds, therefore, between two poles. On one side is providence, separated from the world; on the other, its correlative, the inviolable space within human beings. The cosmic power of divinity is reflected in the steadfastness of the human soul, as if these two spiritual entities had forged a strong alliance against the forces that separate them: the physical universe and human society. Relying on this alliance, the predestined lovers do not fully belong to this world and look on the realm of generation and corruption with a godlike calm and detachment: since they view the human world from a peculiar, unexpected angle—*sub specie divinitatis*—they clearly perceive its contingency. If, therefore, the whims of fortune are so frequently depicted in the Greek novel, this is not because the authors lacked imagination or failed to grasp the concrete diversity of human existence. The random sequence of adventures—shipwrecks, kidnappings, persecutions—reflects the fundamental opposition between a couple that relies on the divinity and a world governed by chance.

Chivalric romances, which were widely read as late as the sixteenth and seventeenth centuries, depend less on a monotheistic conception of the world than Greek novels do and give a lesser role to divinity. The errant knight, in his travels and struggles, draws most of his power from the rigorous norms he follows. Incarnating the *unconditional obligation* to maintain justice, he devotes himself to correcting the world's disorder, and spends his energy in accordance with the laws of chivalry and courtliness he has freely embraced. These laws require an active encounter with the world rather than union with the divine; they demand solidarity with the other members of society, rather than concern for personal salvation.

Chivalric romances in general and *Amadis of Gaul* in particular depict a decentralized society in which local lords exercise their power far away from the king. The ideal governing this system requires the strong to protect the weak, the fortunate to comfort the afflicted, and people of good faith to resist treachery. Applying this ideal to the multitude of social situations is problematic, however, since the fires of violence are continually rekindled in the absence of a permanent central authority. Knights errant frantically cross the country to extinguish these fires and impose the rule of law. The local, limited nature of the infractions favors rapid remedies, but these remedies are always random and piecemeal, never leading to a decisive combat or permanent restoration of order.

Knights thus risk their lives to protect a norm that is perpetually threatened. The instantiation of this threat is called adventure. Day and night, whether in their castles, at the round table, or on the road, knights remain on their guard, waiting to be called. When someone asks for help, the knight's vow obliges him to take instant leave of friends, family, and king, to withdraw from the arms of his beloved, mount his horse and set off to fight. This obligation is doubly rigorous. The knight must safeguard his honor, which the slightest cowardice would forever sully. But, in addition, the knight entertains a mysteriously personal relationship with his adventures. Fate secretly decrees that each adventure belongs to a specific knight, and he alone can and must undertake it.

The episodic, repetitive nature of chivalric tales thus obeys a very different principle from that of Greek novels. In the *Ethiopian Story* the apparently random sequence of adventures ultimately symbolize the separation between the everyday world and the strong souls who dedicate themselves to love and God. In chivalric romances, by contrast, the endless ordeals that await the hero and his companions-in-arms seal a durable alliance between these heroes and the wide world they ceaselessly try to protect in accordance with their moral norms.

In these romances, the power of the couple, signified by *courtly duty*, does not originate in a heavenly call, as in the Greek models. Rather, its source lies inside the couple, more specifically in the power of the lady. This leads to a paradox: on the one hand the image of the beautiful Oriane, Amadis's lady, is that of a true divinity whom the knight invokes whenever he is in danger, but on the other hand, the love between the two characters is the result of a purely human decision between partners who freely choose each other, without consulting any other parties. The lady ensures a warrior's strength by providing him with an ideal goal toward which to aspire. At the same time, by secretly offering herself to her beloved, she seals the couple's independence from any external power.

The knight and his lady thus are invested with a transcendent authority, even as they are required to accomplish specific tasks in society. This means they are at once included in the circuit of earthly adventures, where their humanity subjects them to adversity and desire, and projected as well into a celestial orbit where, invincible and incorruptible, they exert influence over the destiny of other mortals. Exalting the superhuman power of knights and divinizing the lady are effective means of generating transcendence with purely human means. In this way, and despite its symbolic asymmetry, courtly love furthered the norms of chivalry. Together, they established an ideal whose origin was entirely circumscribed within the human realm.

Imperfection and the Everyday World: The Pastoral and the Picaresque

Originally, the pastoral novel did not belong to the family of strongly idealizing works that included Greek and chivalric novels. The first instantiation of the genre, Longus's *Daphnis and Chloe*, is a short narrative set in a modest village rather than in the whole known universe. It features characters who aspire to join, rather than defy, the social world. Kin to the protagonists of comedy, these characters flourish in the grace of idyllic love; they happily discover a balanced sensuality and reject cruelty and violence. Much later, Jacopo Sannazaro's *Arcadia* (1501) and Jorge de Montemayor's *Diana* (1559) added a note of melancholy to the theme of hesitant, graceful maturation.

Very soon, however, the pastoral novel came under the influence of the Greek idealist novel and chivalric romances. Sir Philip Sidney in his *Arcadia* (1580) and Honoré d'Urfé in *Astrea* (1607–27) offered ample syntheses of the elegance of pastorals, on the one hand, and the idealizing power of adventure novels, on the other. These works depict at the same time the energetic affirmation of transcendent ideals and gradual self-discovery through love. *Astrea*, in particular, is not a mere pastoral, but an original synthesis between the pastoral depiction of human frailty and the idealism that governs the life of Greek and chivalric heroes.

Astrea's plot is triggered by a misunderstanding between the two main protagonists, Celadon and Astrea, a fight that underscores the fragility of love. Even the most devoted love, like the one between Celadon and Astrea, is as subject to whim as the most capricious, fleeting feelings. *Astrea* and the entire pastoral universe are governed by the inevitable disparity between ideal love and the behavior of individual couples. Here, the two lovers are separated through their own fault, and the main plot narrates the final triumph of their true sentiments. By forcing the young shepherds to expiate their imperfections, Love distills a pure celestial substance from their imperfection. The base metal changed into gold remains matter, of course, but the transformed substance becomes symbolically incorruptible.

Whereas Greek idealist novels conceived the individual as an utterly steadfast self allied with an omnipotent divinity, pastorals crafted a more nuanced portrait of interiority, focusing on the division of the self and its gradual healing in the course of the character's maturation. The pastoral's shepherds, unskilled at reading themselves or understanding their loved ones, waver between the force of their desires and the ideal they aspire to embody. Their love fills them with a desire for perfection even as it blinds them to the means of achieving it. Only when Celadon is brought to disguise himself as a young woman does he finally rise above his self-involvement and see the world with new eyes. By forgetting himself and scrupulously playing the role of a woman, he succeeds in mastering his passion. Not unlike the disguised lovers in Shakespeare's comedies of the same period, Celadon learns to free himself from his own instincts and passions and follow a general rule that is, and must remain, alien to him. He learns, in short, to follow norms.

It is important not to exaggerate the resemblance between *Astrea* and the modern bildungsroman, nor to neglect another less common premodern subgenre, also devoted to the development of personality: the narrative of the princely education, on the model of Xenophon's *Cyropaedia*. In all their guises, pastoral novels nevertheless meditate about the process of personal maturation and the apprenticeship of community norms. As these novels endlessly insist, the self is prepared to accept a rule of conduct that comes from the community, as long as he or she can seek it freely.

The picaresque novel is the most corrosive of the genres devoted to human imperfection. It belongs to a tradition that dates back to Petronius's *Satyricon* and Apuleius's *Golden Ass*, and was renewed in the tales of

Boccaccio, the *fabliaux*, and the *Roman de Renard*. These works provoke laughter by showing the contrast between a powerful ideal and the evident imperfection that contradicts it. Beginning in the midsixteenth century, a new kind of picaresque story gradually freed itself from laughter and viewed human imperfection with the deliberate seriousness that had previously been reserved for the description of human perfection.

The first example of the genre is *The Life of Lazarillo de Tormes*, an anonymous Spanish work published in 1553–54. The young protagonist is an incarnation of the trickster, the solitary, clever, and unscrupulous character who appears in all oral traditions. As for the world around him, it is highly homogenous, not unlike the world described by the Greek idealist novels. Indeed, all Lazarillo's masters are equally wicked, poor, and dishonest. We observed earlier that Greek and medieval novels used an episodic structure, not because the authors somehow did not manage to construct better plots, but because they sought the best means of representing both the homogeneity and hostility of the world. In picaresque novels the succession of episodes fulfills a similar function. Whatever the outcome of a particular incident, the universe always overwhelms Lazarillo with its inexhaustible hostility, as if each of his masters incarnated, in his own way, a universal threat.

In this particular novel, the threat is twofold: it affects the character's immediate survival as well as the trust among human beings. On the plane of survival, *The Life of Lazarillo*, like most picaresque novels, describes an economy of scarcity. The perpetual concern of picaros is to find bed and board. In their fight against abject poverty, they mirror, in reverse, the struggling heroes of Greek novels. In the *Ethiopian Story*, characters cross land and sea in search of celestial food; here, Lazarillo travels through Spain deploying his cunning to get a crust of bread and a swig of wine. But the true tragedy of the picaresque universe is the decay of the moral order and the absence of trust among human beings. In the picaresque novel, it would be impossible to defend a transcendent law with purely human means. The picaro refutes the chivalric ideal.

We can distinguish between two different kinds of picaros. One accepts the amorality of his condition without remorse; the other, the moralizing picaro, deplores his abject life in the name of a higher law that he is unable to respect. In the first case, a character like Lazarillo acts in defiance of moral norms and perceives his exclusion from morality as his natural condition. This amoral picaro is in fact a happy man, who takes pleasure in fooling others and scarcely reflects on the norms that are supposed to govern human existence. The amoral version of the picaresque genre lacks any awareness of transcendence and moral ideals. As a consequence, characters do not fully understand why this world is a place of contingency and betrayal. They neither remember nor lament a better, lost world based on trust and moral strength.

By contrast, the second kind of picaro undertakes adventures just as immoral as those of Lazarillo or of Quevedo's heroes, but, unlike them, does not accept his own abjectness or condone his moral infractions. The puritan Daniel Defoe specialized in describing this type. In *Moll Flanders* (1722) and *Roxana, the Fortunate Mistress* (1724) he examines with unprecedented lucidity the social dimension of the picaros and their world, emphasizes the moral themes of the genre and reinforces the unity, albeit always precarious, of the main characters' destiny.

Moll and Roxana sustain a complicated and often painful relationship with the moral norms they transgress. For Defoe's characters, the desire to obey the norms—which in their case means the aspiration to wedded bliss—is not merely the result of remorse or nostalgia for innocence but becomes one of the most important motives orienting their actions. And yet Moll practices evil not only by necessity but also by inclination, and is surprised to realize the scope of her own corruption. Roxana's imperfection, even more dramatic than Moll's, leads to catastrophe while Roxana's corrupt past comes back to haunt her. Determined to end her career as courtesan (and former mistress to the king) and lead an honest life, Roxana sees her hard-won happiness threatened by the return of a daughter whom she abandoned much earlier in her life. To preserve a semblance of virtue and ensure her husband's respect, Roxana must bury a double secret: the abandonment of her children and her liaison with the king. After a series of hallucinating scenes, she becomes a virtual accomplice in the assassination of her own daughter.

Normally, picaros, buffeted by contingency, manage to survive as long as they are fully adaptable and avoid the trap of moral dignity. In the universe governed by fortune and filled with surprises, in which both picaresque and idealist novels take place, only two strategies are available. One consists in opposing the world in the name of a transcendent norm, either by fleeing or by imposing justice upon it. The other strategy is to adapt to the world at the price of moral independence. Roxana's atypical inner strength and aspiration to autonomy bring the weight of gravity to the lightness of the picaresque world and imbue its random episodes with a new coherence. By insisting on the seriousness of human transgressions and the indelibility of past sins, *Roxana* brings the picaresque genre to its full fruition and at the same time marks its logical end.

Observations on the Ideographic Method

Despite their differences, all types of idealist novels share certain essential traits. They do not derive credibility from portraying settings that are familiar to the reader. Instead, they invite readers to grasp an idea that unifies the imaginary universe: the radical separation between the human world and the hero who understands the transcendence of moral norms. (Readers may then be prompted to wonder whether this idea does not help them to understand better the actual world better.) Based on this theoretical vision, idealist novels laboriously construct a fictional universe that is very different from the everyday world and present it as a coherent whole. According to this method, which we might call *ideographic*, the imaginary world is shaped by a single abstract idea that is relentlessly illustrated in a multitude of episodes.

Because these novels are generated by an abstract idea, they lack verisimilitude. Both their characters and their settings are idealized, with a focus on primary features—the constancy of Charicleia, the generous courage of Amadis, but also the lust and cruelty of Arsace or the evil trickery of Arcalaus the sorcerer—to the detriment of secondary qualities that remain undeveloped. This insistence on essential traits to the exclusion of accidental ones engenders fictional beings whose qualitative richness is relatively weak but whose main attributes are exceptionally intense. Since in idealist novels the main idea unfolds both in time and in space, the plots of such novels are necessarily episodic. This explains the *durational* character of the novels and the *panoramic* nature of their action. Finally, idealist novels are usually narrated in the third person, as if to convey the objective force of their fundamental idea.

In their own way, picaresque novels perpetuate the ideographic tradition in reverse, as it were, since they replace exceptional beings with flawed individuals. Like idealist novels, the picaresque seeks to evoke, through multiple episodes, an abstract idea: the radical separation between the world and those individuals who are incapable of conforming to societal norms. These characters are just as idealized as the exemplary heroes of the Greek, medieval, or pastoral novels, in the sense that their qualities are reduced to salient traits that coincide with the unifying theme of the novel. Picaresque novels, like idealist narratives, are always durational and panoramic, scanning time and space to uncover the exemplary instantiations of their key idea.

The picaresque novel shares these features, but differs from its idealist predecessors in two ways. One is the massive use of *familiar details* from everyday life; the other is the *testimonial character* of the first-person narrative. It is crucial to realize that both of these traits are meant to enhance the ideographic representation of a flawed world rather than to evoke its historical and social specificity. Familiar details in picaresque novels are meant to suggest specific instances of imperfection and place them in the service of the general unifying idea of the novel. The first-person narrative is also a way of highlighting the imperfection of the protagonists, whose actions are so debasing that no one except the character would ever consider narrating them. In the *Ethiopian Story*, the abundance of unexpected adventures and the third-person discourse incite readers to meditate on the general meaning of the human condition. Similarly, in *The Life of Lazarillo* and *Moll Flanders*, the confessional tone and familiar objects exist, not to provide a faithful representation of reality (since picaresque novels are fully as unrealistic as Greek and chivalric novels), but to illustrate an abstract hypothesis about the moral essence of the world.

Elegiac Narratives

Like the ideographic genres, elegiac narratives and novellas concentrate on specific situations in order to emphasize clearly conceived ideas, for example, the vanity of love or the dangers of curiosity. In these subgenres, however, the chosen idea has a more limited scope that is revealed inductively through one exemplary case.

The elegiac narrative, an heir of Ovid's *Heroides* and perhaps also of Saint Augustine's *Confessions*, is a first-person lament about a protagonist's sentimental misfortunes. The best-known examples are Boccaccio's *Elegy of Lady Fiammetta* (1344–45?) and Guilleragues's *Letters from a Portuguese Nun* (1669). The typical plot relates the unhappy love between a single man and a woman who is bound by marriage or religious vows. The complaint of the woman, who is seduced and then abandoned, constitutes the substance of the work. The object of elegiac narratives is human interiority and its singularity, an interiority they evoke through lyric expression. Occupying a small niche in the range of premodern narrative subgenres, the elegiac narrative nevertheless played an important role in the eighteenth-century revalorization of introspection.

Novellas and the Role of Induction

The novella, with its deep roots in oral traditions, flourished in Italy, France, and Spain from the fourteenth to the seventeenth centuries, as evidenced by the collections of prose narratives of the period: Boccaccio's *Decameron* (written after 1350), Matteo Bandello's *Novels* (1554), Marguerite de Navarre's *Heptameron* (1559), Cinzio Giraldi's *Ecatommiti* (1559), and Cervantes' *Exemplary Novels* (1613). Like the picaresque novel, the novella examines human imperfection, but instead of presenting it as a general abstract hypothesis to be demonstrated by a sequence of examples, the novella captures it as a truth that is unexpectedly revealed in the heat of action. The favorite subject of novellas is the chasm between individuals and their milieu, a chasm that does not preexist, as is the case in the picaresque novels. Rather, it results from the behavior of the protagonists, who end up being separated from their communities, either by choice or by expulsion.

In contrast to the durational and panoramic plots of idealist novels, whose readers are allowed to enjoy long-term familiarity with the characters, novellas are organized around a single surprising event located in a setting that is barely sketched but assumed to be real. While idealist novels require the reader's suspension of disbelief, the novella aims at ensuring a rapid, overwhelming sense of reality and claims to present events belonging to the actual world. A believable setting is not merely a reaction to idealist ideography but a necessary condition for a novella's success.

The representation of a singular, striking event against a plausible background can lend itself to comic or serious treatment, depending on the nature of the incident. Clearly, the presumption that their events belong to the actual world helps comic novellas succeed, since comedy is usually associated with a sense of concrete reality. But in serious and tragic novellas, the nobility of the topic often favors idealization and the depiction of a fictional world that looks quite different from concrete reality. For this reason, some serious novellas whose topic is the arbitrary cruelty of destiny and the unwavering virtue of the characters, (e.g., Griselda's story in Boccaccio's *Decameron*, 10.10), look very much like shortened idealist novels. This resemblance underscores the main challenge faced by serious and tragic novellas: how to ensure verisimilitude while avoiding the techniques of both comic literature and idealist novels.

It is therefore important to distinguish between two means of creating an impression of verisimilitude. This impression can, on the one hand, be obtained at the level of content; it then comes from the resemblance between the depicted universe and the world we take to be real. *Moral realism*, as in serious novellas, and *social realism*, as in nineteenth-century novels, generate this kind of verisimilitude. On the other hand, the effect of verisimilitude may come from specific details that suggest a vividly perceptible fictional universe. *Descriptive realism* offers readers a sense of immersion into the world of the work. Obviously, a mythological subject as distant as possible from our experience can be narrated in a rich, sensual, detailed language that helps produce an effect of immersion. Conversely, a subject ostensibly drawn from the everyday world and written according to the precepts of moral realism can be treated in an austere style that carefully avoids concrete sensory details.

The moral realism of the premodern novella captures individuals who are at the same time fully dependent on others and unable to surrender their own passions and interests to the imperious demands of a watchful society. The characters' moral psychology depends on the kind of adversity they face. Sometimes they confront a *visible external adversity*: family opposition to marriage, unfaithful spouses and lovers, the vagaries of fate. In these situations, the characters act as antagonists, opposing the forces that threaten them. Another kind of adversity stalks the victims of trickery. These characters, exemplified by the Moor of Venice, are manipulated from outside by an enemy disguised as an ally. In such cases of *hidden external adversity*, the blinded character unknowingly becomes the agent of evil forces and the instrument of his own downfall. The *visible internal adversity* consists of innocent or guilty passions that place the characters in conflict with their surroundings. Although in preeighteenth-century literature, we do not find real *internal hidden adversity*—passions that agitate the characters without their knowing—the authors of seventeenth-century novellas, notably Cervantes in *The Ill-Advised Curiosity* and Madame de Lafayette in the *Princess of Clèves* (a work we now call a novel, although its contemporaries considered it a novella), plumb the depths of moral realism by exploring a *visible but incomprehensible internal adversity* in the form of a passion whose nature or purpose remains incomprehensible to the protagonist. While Italian and most Spanish novellas represent the inner life of characters according to a grid of universally accepted motivations, and might be called "casuistic" psychological novellas, the novellas that we might designate as "Augustinian" explore the enigmatic force of passions and the terrible plight of self-blindness.

The Eighteenth Century and the Genesis of the Modern Novel

In the course of the eighteenth century, narrative idealism underwent a profound transformation. Moral norms ceased to be perceived as transcendent and were assumed to inhabit the human heart. This interiorization of the ideal was achieved by Samuel Richardson and Jean-Jacques Rousseau in the name of verisimilitude. It aroused strong opposition and indirectly led to a renewal of the skeptic and comic view of human imperfection, as exemplified by Henry Fielding's fiction. The debate between these two visions encouraged the creation of other new narrative formulas, including the ludic and gothic novels, the sentimental novel, and the novel of manners.

Epistolary Novels and the New Idealism

In the eighteenth century, novels and moral philosophy both contributed to creating a new ideal of human perfection: the beautiful soul. This ideal represented a new answer to the age-old axiological question, as well as the origin of a new conception of love. As I have noted above, the axiological question consisted of asking why, if the moral ideal belongs to the human world, it appears so unattainable, and, conversely, if it does not, why everyone feels its normative weight so vividly. The premodern period assumed that moral values originate outside the human domain and placed the ideal far away from the everyday world, in a realm that was both external and superior. Humans could either give in to their own imperfection or behave heroically and model themselves on the ideal. Souls that captured the light of moral norms and intensified it, like a huge reflector, served as models for human excellence.

The eighteenth-century novel revived the axiological question and offered a new answer that inscribed moral ideals within the human heart. The soul, which had long been assumed to follow norms coming from above, came to be seen as containing within itself (and being capable of deciphering) the eternal laws of moral perfection. Through a process that we might call the *interiorization of the ideal* or the *enchantment of interiority*, all human beings, even the most ordinary ones, were deemed capable of seeking inner perfection, the beautiful soul being the one who always succeeds in the search for perfection.

This interiorization of morality meant that one no longer needed to seek virtuous beings in an ideal, imaginary sphere. If moral beings walked the earth, then the everyday world acquired a value commensurate with theirs. In eighteenth-century novels, beautiful souls no longer felt impelled to separate themselves from their fellow human beings: their inner nobility sufficed to set them apart, *in situ* as it were. Since the destiny of these characters was to love, suffer, and shine among their peers, the modern idealist novel had no need for the wanderings and episodic dispersion that characterized the ancient version of the genre. Instead, modern narratives delved into the subjectivity of the characters and described with great precision their social and physical surroundings.

Since serious novellas had already plumbed the depths of morality, the close relation between individuals and society and, in certain cases, their physical surroundings, eighteenth-century novelists found ongoing lessons in this narrative subgenre. Examining personal perfection as well as the objective world, they attempted simultaneously to depict the isolation of perfect individuals in their full splendor (the specialty of ancient novels) and to imagine, as the novella had done, striking dramas with complex psychological causes. Accordingly, they now needed to reckon with unity of action, a technique that had been developed by novellas and that helped differentiate them from long episodic novels.

The first novel to unite successfully in a single plot the nobility of humble beings, the richness of inner life, the physicality of the universe, and unity of action was *Pamela, or Virtue Rewarded* by Samuel Richardson (1741). It achieved a powerful new synthesis of the idealist novel, the picaresque, and the novella. It created a new incarnation of the virtuous heroine, placed her on a trajectory whose many episodes converged toward a single point, and endowed her with an invisible, highly moral consciousness.

A descendent of the heroines of idealist novels, Pamela is an otherworldly creature, protected by providence, with an unbending strength, capable of resisting all adversity. Her origins may be humble, but as in Greek novels, her exceptional beauty is the visible sign of her quasi-divine status. Pamela's unwavering virtue, constancy, and wisdom signal that she does not depend on the setting into which fate placed her. Her roots, like Charicleia's, lie elsewhere. The enchantment of interiority gives its meaning to the first-person narrative. In earlier novels, where the ideal was conceived as external, the impersonal qualities of chastity and inflexibility shone in the distance, while ignominy hid in the depths of the soul. Looking at one's self, one could see only baseness. In Richardson's work, by contrast, where the ideal emanates from within, the heroine's soul spontaneously and secretly radiates moral beauty. Pamela is the only person who can talk about herself, since no outsider could understand or describe the extraordinary sensitivity and strength that lie hidden in her heart.

Presenting all the events from Pamela's point of view heightens the reader's interest in the action, both as a whole and in its myriad individual episodes. One of the great discoveries of *Pamela* is the art of evoking human experience in its immediacy as well as the intimate play of blindness, anticipation, anguish, and hope. For this reason, Richardson's descriptive realism cannot be reduced to a mere testimony about the world, as if readers were a jury examining the available facts in search of convincing evidence. It is also and above all a way of revealing psychology. This kind of realism immerses the reader in the fictional world as the character perceives it, representing her inner life in a way that is all the more effective for being indirect.

Through the enchantment of interiority, everything the character sees, hears, or feels becomes infinitely precious and worthy of interest. This same enchantment lies, albeit obliquely, at the heart of the new descriptive technique. Instead of going directly to the essence of each event, as his predecessors did, Richardson presents what the heroine perceives here and now, rather than what readers might need to know in order to understand the unfolding of the narrative. In a universe where conscience performs roles once played by divinity, the individual perspective sanctifies all it sees, even the most humble objects. For this reason the representation of immediate experience slowly but irresistibly came to dominate the novel, at the expense of intelligibility and concision.

The Human Comedy or the Emergence of the Author

In *Julie, or the New Heloise* (1749) Rousseau continued and radicalized Richardson's representation of modern virtue by almost entirely basing his narrative on the enchanted interiority of the characters. By contrast, Henry Fielding, who openly opposed Richardson's project, vigorously rejected modern idealism. For him, the goal of the novel was not to lend a modern face to the imaginary virtue of ancient heroes but to capture eternal truths about human nature, in particular about its comic imperfection. In Fielding's view, the novel's true ancestor was the mock epic, a genre illustrated by Matteo Boiardo and Ariosto, whose *Orlando Innamorato*, circa 1484, and *Orlando Furioso*, 1516, respectively, poke fun at the medieval epic and chivalric novels. Fielding saw the novel as a mock epic in prose, portraying men and women drawn from everyday life, instead of heroes and princes. Far removed from heroic idealism, this genre nevertheless maintained the high style of mock epic.

In opposing the modern idealist novel, Fielding also took as a model the grand parody of chivalry, Cervantes' *Don Quixote*, which acquired a new importance in the eighteenth century and influenced the evolution of the genre. For a long time after its publication (part 1 in 1605, part 2 in 1615), *Don Quixote* was admired as a prodigiously smart and funny text. Yet its readers would have been quite surprised to learn that it had opened a new era in the history of the novel. The initial public correctly sensed that while *Don*

Quixote's principal target was the idealism of chivalric romances, the book was not simply a comic work but offered a true anthology of the literary and moralist genres of the period, including the pastoral, the novella, the Erasmian dialogue, literary criticism, and moral eloquence, all of which were deemed to be preferable to the obstinate unreality of chivalric narratives. As a man of his time, Cervantes knew how to discern the particular strength of each narrative genre in depicting ideals and imperfections, and he was careful not to dismiss all varieties of idealist novels. On the contrary, the author of *Don Quixote* belonged to that late-sixteenth- and early-seventeenth-century literary group that criticized chivalric tales precisely because it preferred the idealism of the recently rediscovered Greek novels. In fact, Cervantes ended his career with *The Trials of Persiles and Sigismunda* (1617), a Christian adaptation of the *Ethiopian Story* of which he was immensely proud. It is only later, in the eighteenth century, with the rise of the enchantment of interiority and the *new* idealist novel that the adversaries of idealism, notably Fielding and his contemporary Tobias Smollett, conferred on *Don Quixote* the status it has retained as the ancestor of the ironic, skeptical, anti-idealist novel.

Since then, *Don Quixote* has been assumed to teach that human beings cannot withdraw from the world; that our roots do not grow in the heavens of idealist novels but in the earth of our mortal condition; that the otherworldly individual, struggling against universal contingency, and the heroic, energetic righter of wrongs are mere fantasies and bookish fictions; and that the ideal pursued by the Knight of the Sorrowful Countenance is not inspired by gods or by the chivalric code but rather by undigested reading. Richardson's critics, and especially Fielding, understood that the author of *Pamela* was surreptitiously trying to graft the idealist novel onto the everyday world, just as Don Quixote himself had tried to live the life of an errant knight. But while the honest Knight of the Sorrowful Countenance explicitly proclaimed his devotion to the models of Roland and Amadis, the sly Richardson did not warn us that he was forcing Pamela to emulate the heroines of Heliodorus and Madeleine de Scudéry. In Fielding's view, one can hardly avoid concluding that Cervantes refuted *Pamela* long before its publication, showing once and for all that human nature is not capable of sustaining the goals of idealist literature.

Fielding's *Joseph Andrews* (1742) and, even more, *Tom Jones* (1749) defy the subjective perspective and the enchantment of interiority to reclaim their mock heroic and parodic antecedents. Unlike Richardson's plots, which typically have one major thread and are organized around an obsessive structure that subordinates the story to the individual perspective of the character, Fielding's narratives develop multiple plots that are fully understood only by the author and the reader, the characters' narrow field of vision being unable to encompass the full development of the plot. Richardson's solution excels in psychological intensity but fails to deliver what Fielding's can: an objective view of human destiny that is not reducible to the egocentrism of the characters. Fielding's rejection of individual perspective is also apparent in the way his narrator judges the characters, who generally act under the sway of poorly rationalized impulses and try to hide behind unreliable justifications. Unbeknown to everyone, the protagonist navigates between high principles and deplorable conduct. Only the narrator, steeped in the elegant irony that characterizes mock heroic epic, guesses the character's frailty and exposes it indulgently.

Fielding combines in a single powerful role an inventor-narrator who directs the multiple strands of intrigue, a wise commentator who exposes the gap between the characters' boastful speech and their often reprehensible actions, and a literary critic who explains the meaning of the work. As an impartial, bemused observer of characters whose weaknesses he uncovers, Fielding does not refrain from sprinkling his story with wise remarks that are often as ironic as the narration of the episodes themselves. The inventor-narrator-commentator who has a well-defined moral physiognomy and steers the moral course of the story cannot be reduced to the role of a simple narrator, since he does not simply present the story but openly assumes the role of organizer and creator of the narrative. His voice, which converses with equal joviality about the human comedy and the literary trade cannot be designated by any other name except that of *author*: the one who creates and controls the story, structures and comments on it, ensures its moral and artistic balance, and relates it in his own words.

Thus defined, the author has always been present, more or less visibly, in novels. What Fielding achieved was an unprecedented promotion of the role, a true *anointing of the author*, in reaction against the way modern idealist novels enhanced the narrative and moral authority of the characters. Fielding's promotion of the author led to a new relationship between the narrative voice and the fictional universe, and marked the beginning of a long rivalry between author and character. For the next century and a half they would fight for control of the narrative text.

The Multiplication of Narrative Forms

Tristram Shandy (1760–67) by Laurence Sterne and *Jacques the Fatalist and His Master* (1773–75?) by Denis Diderot, benefited from Fielding's lesson, although the roots of these works lie in the tradition of sixteenth- to eighteenth-century parodic and burlesque narratives, which deliberately defy mimetic conventions and maximize the sheer fun of storytelling. François Rabelais, Charles Sorel, and Jonathan Swift are the best-known examples. Within this tradition, one should distinguish between works that are truly unclassifiable both according to genre and mode of representation (*Pantagruel* and *Gulliver's Travels*) and ludic novels, whose goal is precisely to take advantage of various prose techniques in a playful tone, at the expense of narrative clarity (the *Comical History of Francion*). *Tristram Shandy* and *Jacques the Fatalist* belong to the latter category of works, yet they cannot be fully understood outside the debate that pitted the new idealism of Richardson and Rousseau against the ironic skepticism of Fielding.

While Fielding criticized the modern idealist novel for being too unrealistic, the gothic novel rejected it for the opposite reason, claiming that it favored attentive observation of nature and neglected the powers of imagination. Invented by Horace Walpole, whose *Castle of Otranto* (1765) served as a model for Ann Radcliffe, Matthew Lewis, and many other authors, the gothic novel turned away from empirical reality to engage in an open, unabashed celebration of the most extreme kinds of fictional improbability. Seeking to revive chivalric tales, this genre brought back castles, turrets, and dungeons in the hope of impressing readers more directly and powerfully than Richardson or Rousseau ever did. In the name of imagination, the gothic setting called into question the recently acquired objectivity of the social and physical world and gave new life to the earlier symbolic function of the world as a prison-house of the soul.

The gothic novel also fostered a new kind of hero: the demonic character, overwhelmingly malevolent and endowed with boundless energy. This new character was undoubtedly meant as a response to the enchantment of interiority and to the idea that virtue is an unwavering yet passive force. As a result of the clash between modern idealism and the trends that opposed it, the eighteenth-century novel ended up portraying constancy and energy as mutually exclusive. In the early part of the century, the only characters brimming with energy were thieves, scoundrels, and womanizers, like Roderick Random, Tom Jones, and Lovelace. Later, the gothic novel stripped the beautiful souls of the quasi-supernatural power they possessed in idealist works and abandoned them without defense to the evil designs of their enemies.

The novel of manners, following in the lineage of picaresque novels and of Fielding, is linked to Richardson's idealism as well. While Tobias Smollett's *Expedition of Humphry Clinker* is rooted in picaresque irony, Fanny

Burney's *Evelyna* (1778), which presents a critical image of London society, seen through the eyes of an innocent, generous young provincial woman, merges social satire with modern idealism. Another subgenre, the sentimental novel, exemplified by Oliver Goldsmith's *Vicar of Wakefield*, mitigates the improbability of idealism by creating a believable setting, characters who are virtuous but not sublime, situations that are difficult but not tragic, and moral outcomes that are desirable but not dazzling.

In *The Sorrows of Young Werther* (1774), Goethe continues the efforts of earlier writers to reconcile the enchantment of interiority with psychological realism, but he does so by entirely sacrificing the character's force. The inflexibility of Richardson's great heroines, which was downgraded to mere prudence in the sentimental novel, is here reduced to deplorable weakness. Werther's very impotence to act has a crucial narrative role: it provides the story with unity of action and makes possible a synthesis between features of tragic novellas and of elegiac narratives. Like a novella, *Werther* depicts a restricted space, a limited number of characters, and an insoluble conflict between passion and marriage, while the lyrical tone, absence of decisive action, and resignation of the main character remind us of elegiac narratives. In Werther's case, nobility of soul is nothing more than a subjective poetic state, devoid of tangible external consequences. The power of modern idealism thus gives way to the magic of romanticism. This actually heightens the verisimilitude of Werther's story, since it is much more natural to participate in this character's idle daydreaming than it is to believe in the prodigious moral strength of Richardson's and Rousseau's heroines.

The Sorrows of Young Werther signals the rise of a new pessimistic idealism that acknowledges both the greatness of elected souls and the impossibility of reconciling them with the world. Works like Bernardin de Saint-Pierre's *Paul and Virginia* (1787), Friedrich Hölderlin's *Hyperion* (1799), François-René de Chateaubriand's *Atala* (1801), and Madame de Staël's *Corinne* (1807) lament the natural and historical forces that conspire to defeat great yet defenseless souls.

The Nineteenth Century: The Novel Reaches the Height of Its Glory

The nineteenth century kept alive the modern idealist project of reconciling the representation of a beautiful soul with the reality of the world. Novels of this period gave center stage to the social and historical reality of the conflicts they depicted. The eighteenth-century novel had brought the beautiful soul down to earth, while preserving the contrast between the soul's greatness and its surroundings. Nineteenth-century novels, concerned with individuals' rootedness in their community, examined the links between individual and society, depicting these links not merely as general and relatively uniform, but rather as a precise and well-differentiated network of social and historical dependencies.

The attention that almost all nineteenth-century novelists devoted to the social and historical dimensions of the fictional universe did not mean, however, that they turned away from the debate between modern idealism and moral skepticism. Nineteenth-century partisans of idealism worked hard to find a credible place for beautiful souls at the heart of the empirical world. Seeking plausible examples of moral strength and beauty, these authors examined the universe with a fine-toothed comb to discover examples of virtue buried in the foggy past, lost in exotic countries, or trapped in the labyrinth of modern society. Opponents of idealism were equally active. Some portrayed with ironic benevolence the social incarnations of moral imperfection, while others examined with a mixture of sympathy and severity the traps of subjectivity. The fiercest opponents of idealism, claiming that idealism fosters a mirage meant to disguise our moral depravity, sought to dissipate this mirage and reveal the atrocious truth of the human condition. Finally, in the second half of the century a few great writers achieved new syntheses of idealism and anti-idealism.

Idealism, Anti-idealism, and Social Milieu

The idealist tradition, revived by romantic pessimism, finally had to admit the difficulty of situating the ideal within the modern, prosaic world. But rather than accept the inevitable defeat of heroic souls, writers belonging to this tradition set about discovering other societies and periods where heroism had indeed flourished. Walter Scott's historical novels solved an internal problem of the genre—the plausibility of a great soul—by taking advantage of the dramatic development of historiography in the late eighteenth and early nineteenth centuries. Scott's great innovation was to introduce characters who exhibited the constancy and energy required by idealist novels and to make them believable through proper historical justifications. Since, for Scott, nobility of soul emerges from the archaic customs of warrior states, it can rightfully be celebrated in its original setting while also being explicitly detached from the moral demands of the modern world. Beginning with *Waverly* (1814), which contrasts the adventurous spirit of Scottish highlanders and the modern prudence of the main English character, Scott's historical novel won over two opposing constituencies of readers: those who enjoyed the exceptional deeds of admirable characters and those who distrusted fictional exaggerations.

By studying the variations and discontinuities produced by history, geography, and social class, Scott opened up a vast thematic field for prose narrative. After him, novels no longer needed to focus on universal ideal norms but could explore the myriad normative links that govern human communities. This in turn meant that the fundamental axiological question—if the moral code is inherent in our world why is it disregarded so frequently, and if not, why is it so readily recognized—would henceforth have to be asked only in relation to specific communities. As a consequence, Scott's audience, being rooted in a peaceful, prosaic civilization, could readily agree in principle with the heroism of past times, while remaining totally impervious to it.

Since the historical novel had henceforth to accommodate historical variations in mores, customs, and values, writers who wished to paint truly universal greatness had to discover, among the multiplicity of codes that have governed human beings, those that actually transcend specific societies. We owe to Alessandro Manzoni the most successful effort to fit a novelistic plot of universal import into the mold of the modern historical novel. *Betrothed* (1827), a modern "remake" of the *Ethiopian Story*, narrates the vicissitudes of two young lovers whose unwavering fidelity triumphs over all ordeals. Two courageous villagers, Renzo and Lucia, are persecuted by the local lord, but protected, like the heroes of Greek novels, by the divinity and its church. Their story illustrates a version of the liberal Whig theory of history, which credits the advent of modern liberty to a vast providential project imprinted long ago in the virtues taught by Christianity.

The exotic novel follows a similar project as it seeks nobility of soul in areas and nations untouched by modern civilization: the American Indians in the novels of James Fenimore Cooper; the Caucasus of Lermontov and Tolstoy, the Italy of Stendhal and Lamartine; the Spain of Mérimée. Similarly, the regional novel discovers noble souls in poor, isolated areas where archaic innocence secretly survived, as in Adalbert Stifter's novellas or in George Sand's *Devil's Pool, Country Waif,* and *Fadette*. The idealist social novel finds virtue in the midst of the lower classes: in *Les misérables,* Hugo finds true inner beauty in people who emerge from the poorest rungs of society: Jean Valjean, a convict, and Fantine, a prostitute. The novel of childhood portrays an age of moral innocence and strength: in *Oliver Twist,* Dickens exalts the purity of a lost child; in *Little Dorrit,* that of a young girl scarcely out of childhood.

Balzac focused on a different landscape: modern society as a whole. Using Walter Scott's method of dividing humanity into a multitude of different social and historical milieux, he undertook a vast study of human greatness and misery. As a consequence, in Balzac's novels, larger-than-life characters are highly specialized, as it were. There are faithful, resigned lovers, like Madame de Beauséant in *Old Goriot*; do-gooders bubbling with energy in the *History of the Thirteen*; great artists and thinkers, like Joseph Bridau in *La Rabouilleuse* and Daniel d'Arthez in *Lost Illusions*; and philanthropists, like Dr. Benassis in *The Country Doctor*. Force of character develops only in relation to a well-defined social domain. Since Balzac's goal was to represent all varieties of human beings, he also painted fallen angels alongside his heroes, the best-known being Lucien de Rubempré, protagonist of *Lost Illusions*. A multitude of mean, repulsive characters—the abbé Troubert in the *Curé de Tours*, cousin Bette in the novel that bears her name, Baron Hulot in the same story—emerge from the bowels of modern life, which turn out to be particularly fertile in ugliness and stupidity. On the lowest stratum of society reigns the terrifying yet seductive Vautrin, the demon of the *Human Comedy*, brother of the great evildoers of the gothic novel—Mary Shelley's monster, Frankenstein, and Heathcliff, the hero of Emily Brontë's masterpiece *Wuthering Heights*.

The anti-idealist tradition brought together various remote disciples of Fielding, beginning with what could be called the school of irony, whose main representatives, Stendhal and Thackeray, unexpectedly returned to the freedom of picaresque novels and the snide skepticism of the eighteenth century. Scrupulously respecting the norms of historic and descriptive realism, these authors gave equal weight to historical determinism and to the study of the human heart, which they saw as constant in all times and places. In their view, the differences in customs among regions and epochs were not the most important factors influencing human life, however striking they might seem. Such differences may limit our range of action and choice of careers, but they do not control the individual energy that drives human beings and shapes their destiny.

While the school of irony was particularly strong on plot, the school of empathy concentrated on characters' self-awareness and mutual understanding. Like Fielding, Jane Austen distrusted the subjective perspective, but hesitated to intervene in her own name to debunk its fallacies. Instead, she used free indirect discourse, a stylistic device that vividly suggests the fallibility of the subjective perspective. The interiorization of plot as well as the careful notation of characters' opinions about themselves and those who surround them came to dominate late-nineteenth-century psychological novels, especially those of Henry James, whose work achieved a complete separation between moral skepticism and the comic tradition in which it had been rooted. This period injected a new moral seriousness into concerns that had hitherto tended to provoke laughter or irony, thereby continuing a more general tendency in the history of the novel. Thanks to this transformation, the school of empathy bequeathed to the twentieth-century novel its rich understanding of the infinitesimal fluctuations of the human psyche.

Under the influence of radical anti-idealist authors like Gustave Flaubert, Émile Zola, and the Goncourt brothers, the critique of idealism veered sharply toward pessimism. By allowing readers to become immersed in the minds and senses of the characters, the technique of empathy sought to reinforce the readers' repulsion at characters' flagrant moral deficiency. Living intimately with Emma Bovary, Germinie Lacerteux, or Gervaise, the protagonist of Zola's *Drunkard (L'assommoir)*, is a perpetual lesson in the sadness and depravity of the human condition. In the premodern novel, this repugnant spectacle was the exclusive specialty of the picaresque subgenre and was limited to characters on the fringes of society. In a remarkable reversal, Flaubert, Zola, and the Goncourts claimed that moral depravity is an inescapable truth of the human condition. The enchantment of interiority had ultimately engendered its opposite, and the universality of virtue, proclaimed by modern idealism, had given way to an equally universal sense of moral failure.

Syntheses: Tolstoy, Dostoevsky, Fontane, Galdós

In the second half of the nineteenth century, the majority of genuinely influential novels were written and published in France and England. Yet, with a single exception, the most interesting syntheses between idealism and anti-idealism came from other countries, whose relative marginality encouraged the development of original positions. The exception was George Eliot, whose *Middlemarch* relates the life of a strong woman who achieves happiness after the failure of her first marriage. As self-controlled and flawlessly honest as the heroines of ancient Greek novels, the protagonist is nevertheless fallible, but has the ability to recognize and correct her errors. Her story encompasses all the themes of modern interiorization of the ideal: the moral equivalence between public heroism and private, anonymous, greatness; the moral beauty of humble beings; and the vocation of the modern novel to honor those quiet souls who secretly keep idealism alive.

Tolstoy, by contrast, was deeply distrustful of everything that resembled modern idealism. He disliked the apotheosis of the individual, the cult of individual consciences making their own laws, and the idea that duty is indelibly inscribed in human hearts. He did not see social roles as a direct cause of personality but rather as invitations to change our ways of perceiving and acting on the world. Such change does not happen automatically, however. Tolstoy's best protagonists refuse ready-made norms in order to fight, naively and awkwardly, the burdens imposed by society, as well as the contradictions of their own moral instincts. Olenin in *The Cossacks*, Pierre Bezukhov in *War and Peace*, and Levin in *Anna Karenina* are all examples of beautiful souls who do not proudly exhibit virtue to the eyes of the world (since for Tolstoy, lack of modesty is one of the chief symptoms of moral failure) but stubbornly seek the rules of the good life. These characters ultimately embrace the splendor of the moral norm in their own hearts, but not in the form of evident truths that can be grasped by mere observation. What Tolstoy's beautiful souls discover by listening to themselves and to the world are inner illuminations or intimations and personal states of joy, uncertainty, or dissatisfaction, rather than explicitly formulated rules and prohibitions, as was the case for the protagonists of Richardson, Rousseau, Balzac, and Dickens. Striving to overcome their blindness and achieve self-understanding, Tolstoy's characters, deprived of the peremptory language of morality, remind us of the scrupulous innocence of pastoral heroes for whom, as for Bezuhkov, Levin, and Olenin, the world is a benevolent shelter that protects sincere hearts as they search for virtue.

In the work of Adalbert Stifter and Theodor Fontane, idealism penetrates into the heart of the real world even more deeply than in the novels of their predecessors and contemporaries. Yet, at the same time, the power of this idealism diminishes to the point of being barely perceptible. In Stifter's stories, the poetry of the heart can usually be found in human beings who lack physical beauty or sentimental success—beings, in short, who have not been elected by fate. These seemingly banal individuals, ostensibly battered by life, are nevertheless overflowing with energy and goodness. They are exemplary beings, and their exemplarity is all the more striking given the bland, unglamorous lives they live. Fontane, continuing in this vein, does his utmost to discover the poetry hidden within the most ordinary souls, an Effi Briest, an Innstetten, a Cecile, a St. Arnaud, prosaic beings who passively submit to the demands of their surroundings, even as they suffer from the conflict between moral duty and their desire to live in a kind, generous world. Their best-intentioned efforts to abide by social norms cannot fulfill their secret aspiration to give themselves wholeheartedly, to trust unconditionally, to love passionately. Even the happiest individuals, the ones whose worldly success seems perfect, are visited homeopathically by dreams reminiscent of Goethe's Werther. However minute the dose, it is sometimes sufficient to kill the dreamer.

Fyodor Dostoevsky defended a position radically opposed to Fontane's moderation and Eliot's optimism. He rejected idealist novels on the grounds that they exalt human grandeur and autonomy. At the same time, he refused anti-idealism because it derives a bitter amusement from human imperfection. In opposing the ancient idealist tradition, Dostoevsky sought to prove that the magnanimity and constancy of early heroes were utterly unreal. To refute modern idealism, which exalted the capacity of exceptional beings to create their own moral laws, he proposed the example of Raskolnikov, the student who, in the name of autonomy, takes the liberty of killing an innocent person. *The Devils* returns to this critique and, through the portrait of Stavrogin, shows that a superman who dreams of imposing laws on his peers can only be a predator. Unlike the anti-idealists for whom human imperfection was the undeniable truth of our condition, Dostoevsky nevertheless believed in the possibility of perfection, which he equated, in the Orthodox Christian manner, with contemplative holiness, self-immolation for the good of others, and, above all, abandonment into the hands of God. Reacting against those writers whose characters are beautiful souls in perfect control of their thoughts and actions, Dostoevsky depicted his ideal characters as awkward human beings, deeply humble, as if they realized that their efforts had scarcely earned them any merit and were asking pardon of their fellow human beings for having been chosen by God, despite their flaws. In a deeply corrupt world, the only beauty is that of these rare, naive, impulsive misfits. Dostoevsky thus distanced himself equally from idealism and anti-idealism, without creating a genuine synthesis between them. Instead, he established a novelistic formula based on the contrast between the most ethereal holiness and the most repugnant forms of human abjection.

Late-nineteenth-century Spanish writers brought yet another vision to the novel. Their characters are irrevocably flawed by pride and even by a grain of folly. While their nobility is enhanced by immense reserves of vital energy, they also suffer from a striking psychic imbalance, as evidenced by Fortunata's obstinacy and Maximiliano's angelic love in Benito Pérez Galdós's *Fortunata and Jacinta* and by the protagonist's holiness in his *Nazarin*. A similar current is evident in the tortured femininity of Ana Ozores in Leopoldo Alas's *La regenta*. The influence of Cervantes is surely responsible for this alliance of folly and idealism. Conversely, these novelists revive and modernize *Don Quixote*.

Another element deeply rooted in the Spanish prose tradition is the chasm separating characters touched by folly and the society around them. Like the picaros who are always persecuted by bad luck, Maximiliano Rubín marries the beautiful Fortunata, but she remains forever inaccessible; Fortunata is reunited with her beloved Juanito Santa Cruz only to endure even more suffering on his account; Ana Ozores ultimately finds carnal love but not happiness. To the extent that these characters comprehend their inevitable alienation from the world, they willingly accept their precarious condition. Indeed, thanks to a psychological reversal fostered by the stability of traditional societies, they often feel at home in an atmosphere wholly unfavorable to their aspirations. Their unhappiness, which is akin to tragedy, is thus laced with a kind of comic complicity between those who have been excluded and the world that tortures them. At once sublime and ridiculous, the characters of Spanish novels aspire to the chimera of autonomy. Their passionate quest commands respect, yet no one is surprised by their failure. In these novels, the shattering of the noblest dreams is perceived as the inescapable law of human existence, since everyone assumes that dreams cannot be achieved. Protagonists thus preserve all the grandeur of their ambitions in the very ridiculousness of their fall.

The Twentieth Century and the Return of Formal Multiplicity

In the last third of the nineteenth century novels displayed an array of options—idealism, anti-idealism, and the synthesis of both—yet they conformed to strikingly similar forms. Writers like Henry James who charted their own courses did so at their peril, and rare swatches of originality scarcely ruffled the massive monotony of the genre. At the level of plot, characters always demonstrate a mixture of imperfection and moral aspiration; they are almost always rooted in their surroundings, departing from them only rarely and, even then, almost imperceptibly. On the level of style, authors paid scrupulous attention to social and historic details, taking care to create realistic dialogues and to ensure the reader's sensory and affective immersion in the characters' world. These traits prevailed for a long time, as though the success of a formula discovered after so much effort discouraged any attempts at renewal.

Does this mean that the debate begun by the ancient novel and pursued by its modern descendants was over? That the progress of knowledge had finally reduced the fundamental axiological question to its true historical, sociological, and psychological dimensions? That the question of whether the world is our true home had been definitively and positively answered?

Not at all. The equilibrium reached by the novel in the second half of the nineteenth century may have given most writers and readers the impression that these perennial problems had been solved. Soon enough, however, a new generation of writers vigorously questioned the novel's apparently solid anchors in historical, sociological, and psychological reflection.

The history of the novel across the twentieth century is shaped by this questioning. The new era began with an aestheticist wave that was already present in J. K. Huysmans's *Against the Grain (A rebours)* (1884) and reached maturity by the time of André Gide's *Immoralist* (1902). This aestheticist current felt only contempt for the social condition and the moral aspiration of human beings and claimed, instead, that since we have the right to invent our own destinies according to aesthetic rather than moral criteria, we must take advantage of the world as we see fit. In ancient novels, moral laws were transcendent; subsequent writers situated ethical norms within the human heart; in a later avatar, these norms came to be rooted in sociohistorical contexts. Aestheticism is the first trend entirely to dismiss moral concerns, seeking instead freedom from society and norms.

Marcel Proust was both more moderate than Huysmans and Gide in his aestheticism and more radical in his rejection of the world. His masterpiece, *Remembrance of Things Past*, took advantage of all the subtleties of moral and social realism to show that the real world is decidedly not our true home and that art offers our only access to the plenitude of life. This new rupture between human beings and the world contrasts sharply with nineteenth-century depictions of individuals' dependence on society. It denies the appeal of the moral norm, whether external or internal, and affirms the radical irreducibility of human beings to their surroundings.

A kindred though even more somber spirit animates James Joyce's *Ulysses*. As in Proust's masterpiece, the protagonists of *Ulysses* remain strangers to their world. Even more than in Proust, their capacity for action atrophies. In hypernaturalist fashion, Joyce evokes the multiplicity of competing details that solicit our attention. *Ulysses* pushes the discoveries of the empathetic school to their logical limits by reproducing the most minute images, impressions, and fragments of thought that are assumed to form our stream of consciousness. Joyce's unquenchable stylistic verve and the abundant details, which might appear useless at first glance, suggest that the human mind, although overflowing with images and bizarre juxtapositions of ideas, sorely lacks rationality and the energy to act. While Proust saw art as a way to liberate human beings from their sad condition, Joyce used art to illuminate, but not overcome, this condition. In their own ways, Virginia Woolf and William Faulkner both pursued this *undigested form of writing* in which whole segments of the narration are presented without a prior elaboration that might help readers figure out the stakes of the story. After World War II, Nathalie Sarraute and other representatives of the so-called French New Novel continued to explore this vein.

Another fictional form that omits elaborate narratives is the essayistic novel as developed by Thomas Mann and Robert Musil. Here philosophical discourse is incorporated into the fabric of fiction. Abundant theoretical reflections in Mann and Musil ultimately produce the same effect as the sensory data of Joyce and Faulkner. In both options, readers have the impression of attending a brilliant performance during which very little actually happens. All these authors unwittingly return, along their own routes, to the ancient practice of Greek, medieval, or episodic picaresque novels. Like those early works, the texts of Joyce, Faulkner, and Musil present generalized relationships between the self and the world rather than specific cases of conflict between individuals and moral norms, as novellas traditionally did.

Franz Kafka, by contrast, uses the techniques of *elaborated narration* involving plausible characters, a clearly defined setting, a well-delineated subject, dialogues subordinated to the needs of the plot, and an easy-to-follow style. Describing the world from a seemingly objective point of view, Kafka emphasizes the gravity of the new rupture between humans and their milieu as well as the resulting strangeness of the world. His readers discover that the ties between the character and the world have for all practical purposes been severed, but not, as in Joyce and Musil, because of the idiosyncrasies of the protagonist, who, in Kafka's novels is always perfectly common, but because the world, behind its thin film of normality, is actually a half-terrifying, half-comic nightmare. This new rupture is so profound that love can no longer be considered capable of reconciling individuals and the world. In the twentieth century, for the first time in the history of the genre, love and the couple are no longer central to the novel.

Given his narrative simplicity at the formal level, Kafka renewed even more resolutely than Joyce, Faulkner, and Musil the premodern practice of multiple episodes that endlessly reiterate a general, abstract, relationship between self and world. Joseph K., the protagonist of *The Trial*, who is subjected to an exceptional and incomprehensible legal procedure, as well as K., the surveyor of *The Castle*, who tries in vain to gain acceptance from the local administration, can trace their ancestry to the characters of premodern idealist novels, who face incomprehensible danger at every step. The difference is that in Kafka's world there is no benevolent providence to protect and ultimately save the characters.

The deeply disturbing layer of reality discovered by the author of *The Trial* has become the canonical topic of many subsequent novels, just as the stream of consciousness worked out by Joyce, Woolf, and Faulkner exerted considerable influence on the novelistic depiction of individuals throughout twentieth-century narratives. In the so-called postmodern novel, the characters are prisoners of the perceptual and linguistic chaos of their consciousness and confront a world that is devoid of substance and riddled with illogical, incredible, or mythical elements. Prefigured in the ethnic surrealism of Jean Giono, Mircea Eliade, and Ismaïl Kadare, as well as in Alfred Doblin's late novels, the postmodern strand is illustrated in many different ways by Gabriel García Márquez, Georges Perec, Michel Tournier, Thomas Pynchon, Toni Morrison, Salman Rushdie, Umberto Eco, Mario Vargas Llosa, Don DeLillo, and others.

Clearly, these three major options—aestheticism, intellectualism, and depiction of the disoriented psyche and of the strangeness of the world—do not exhaust the immense novelistic production of the century. Dostoevsky's successors, François Mauriac, Georges Bernanos, Julien Green, Heinrich Böll, and Walker Percy, as well as existentialists Jean-Paul Sartre and Albert Camus, continued to reflect on moral imperfection. The heirs to social realism, Roger Martin du Gard, John Galsworthy, Doris Lessing, Hans Fallada, Saul Bellow, Tom Wolfe and, in Russia, where socialist realism carefully nurtured this method, Boris Pasternak, Aleksandr Solzhenitsyn, and Vassilii Grossman, remained faithful to the grand style perfected by nineteenth-century novelists. Neoromantics like Marguerite Yourcenar, Thornton Wilder, Julien Gracq, and Ernst Jünger sought to capture the destiny of exceptional beings in their historical context, while the heirs to the ironic and skeptic tradition, John Dos Passos, Louis-Ferdinand Céline, Jaroslav Hasek, Milan Kundera, Josef Skvorecki, John Barth, and Philip Roth, brought indefatigable verve to their portraits of human imperfection in a hostile, absurd world.

All these approaches remain alive in an age when the novel reaffirms its international vocation. The most ancient literary traditions as well as newly emerging ones choose the novel as a means of affirming their modernity. Over the past fifty years, recipients of Nobel Prizes in literature have come from diverse national backgrounds but almost all have been novelists. The disorientation of the self in a world that we have come almost serenely to accept as incomprehensible appears to be one of the most frequent themes of new novels written around the globe. It recalls the ancient chasm that separated the virtuous heroes of Greek novels from the precarious, sublunar world.

Translated by Carol Rigolot

MASSIMO FUSILLO

Epic, Novel

The Obsession with Origins

> But it is quite different with the *novel*, the modern
> *bourgeois* epic. Here we have completely before us
> again the wealth and many-sidedness of interests,
> situations, characters, relations involved in life, the wide
> background of a whole world, as well as the epic
> portrayal [*Darstellung*] of life. But what is missing is the
> *primitive* poetic general situation out of which the epic
> proper proceeds. A novel in the modern sense
> presupposes a world already prosaically ordered, then,
> on this grounds and within its own circle and with
> regard to both the liveliness of the events and the own
> sphere whether in connection with the liveliness of
> events or with individuals and their fate, it regains for
> poetry the right it had lost, so far as this is possible in
> view of that presupposition.
> —G.W.F. HEGEL, *Aesthetics: Lectures on Fine Art*[1]

The complex system of the arts outlined in the last part of Hegel's *Aesthetics*
dedicates a long section to the epic that ends with a short page on the novel,
from which the epigraph to this section is taken. Here we find his famous definition of the novel as the "modern bourgeois epic," which draws on common
themes of German aesthetic thinking.[2] Since the novel was not a primeval or
poetic form, Hegel did not dedicate more space to it within his grand architectural scheme. His "bourgeois epic" formulation, however, took on a life of
its own: it established the critical myth (in obvious need of reconsideration
today) of the epic as the primeval form *par excellence*, the genre that inaugurated literature and established national identity through its choral, impersonal, and totalizing poetry; and of the novel, instead, as the preeminent

---

[1] Trans. T. M. Knox (Oxford: Clarendon Press, 1975), 2:1,092. [Translator's note: The Knox
translation curiously renders the two key terms *Roman* and *bürgerliche* as "romance" and
"common," which I have emended in the citation and subsequent references.]

[2] See especially F. von Blanckenburg, *Versuch über den Roman*, ed. Eberhard Lämmer (1774;
facsimile, Stuttgart: J. B. Metzlersche, 1965); on the genealogy of Hegel's theory, see Hans Hiebel,
Individualität und Totalität (Bonn: Bouvier, 1974).

secondary form, a fragment longing for a lost totality. The young Lukács further developed this critical myth, as is well known, primarily in his *Theory of the Novel*, which opens with a lyric passage that captures the essence of romantic nostalgia for ancient Greece as a happy era unhampered by dissonance between self and the world: "Happy are those ages when the starry sky is the map of all possible paths—ages whose paths are illuminated by the light of the stars."[3] His canonical definition of the novel is that it is a form dominated by yearning for the epic: "The novel is the epic of an age in which the extensive totality of life is no longer directly given, in which the immanence of meaning in life has become a problem, yet which still thinks in terms of totality" (56).

   The Theory of the Novel is an appealing work—despite its convoluted style and at times overly schematic teleology—that influenced a variety of writers (Mann, Musil, Döblin, and others).[4] Lukács added Fichtian touches to his neo-Hegelian definition of the novel, calling it the appropriate form for a world abandoned by the gods and inhabited by demons. He concluded his essay abruptly with an apology for Dostoevsky, whom he considered the ideal model for a modern rebirth of the epic. He deemed Tolstoy's undeniably epic qualities, by contrast, to be a partial failure: precisely because of its fragmentary, heterogeneous form, he felt that the novel should be surpassed by new forms that corresponded more closely to the longing for palingenesis and utopia.

   Originally meant to be the second part of *Theory of the Novel*, all that remains of the essay on Dostoevsky are a few intriguing notes dripping with nihilism.[5] When he entered his Marxist phase, Lukács came to consider Tolstoy the true epic model for socialist realism. However, he held on to the basic idea of the epic as the authentic heir to the primeval form. His essay on the historical novel, for example, repeatedly emphasized the "epic genius" of the founding father, Walter Scott, whose stylistic power was said to reside entirely in the "immediate sociality" and "spontaneous popular character" of the life represented.[6]

----

   [3] György Lukács, *The Theory of the Novel: A Historico-Philosophical Essay on the Forms of Great Epic Literature*, trans. Anna Bostock (Cambridge, Mass: MIT Press, 1971), 29. Fredric Jameson made perceptive comments about Lukács's theories in *Marxism and Form: Twentieth-Century Dialectical Theories of Literature* (Princeton, N.J.: Princeton University Press, 1972).
   [4] Jürgen Schramke, *Zur Theorie des modernen Romans* (Munich: Beck, 1974), particularly concerning Musil's notion of the novel as the civic form of the epic (43).
   [5] Lukács, *Dostojewski: Notizen und Entwürfe*, ed. J. C. Nyíri (Budapest: Akadémiai Kiadó, 1985). See also Giuseppe Di Giacomo, *Estetica e letteratura: Il grande romanzo tra ottocento e novecento* (Bari: Laterza, 1999), pt. 1, chaps. 2 and 4.
   [6] Lukács, *The Historical Novel*, trans. Hannah and Stanley Mitchell (London: Merlin Press, 1962), 30–63. He compares the same features in Scott and Manzoni.

From a completely different angle, the same tendency to mythologize the two terms can be found in a theoretician who is the specular opposite of Lukács: Mikhail Bakhtin (Vittorio Strada rightly notes that parallel lives could be written about the two men).[7] For Bakhtin the epic is the negative pole associated with the monolithic, the monologue, immobility, absolute closure in the past, and crystallization in the canon. He sees the novel, instead, as the positive pole associated with the plurivocal, the dialogic, and the dynamic; he treats the novel almost as a metaphor for an antihierarchical, antiauthoritarian spirit belonging to a carnivalesque and Dionysian cultural lineage. Bakhtin's metahistoricist perspective delineates a new genealogy of the novel. Unlike Hegel and Lukács, he does not see the novel as a form that is tied to bourgeois culture (and hence to a social class whose "birth" has been so variously dated that it almost constitutes a transcultural category) but rather as one that is open to various marginal, underground forms of ancient and medieval narrative.[8]

I used the term *critical myth* earlier not to deny its heuristic value but because Hegel and Lukács represent the epic as a kind of Paradise Lost characterized by a perfect communion between poet and audience—a view later symbolically reversed by Bakhtin. Typical of Western thinking and its obsession with the problem of origins, this view posits a primeval unity from which the secondary forms—marked by disgregation and fragmentation—descend in an inevitably derivative evolutionary line (this model lends itself almost too easily to psychoanalytic interpretation because of its allusions to symbiosis with the maternal body). The opposition between the epic and the novel thus evokes the great dualities on which Western identity is constructed—and that contemporary culture has begun to challenge—whose first term of reference is always the original and hence superior term: nature/culture; public/private, collective/individual, orality/writing, tragedy/comedy, masculine/feminine. Such a system treats the epic as a spontaneous and auroral genre, centered on lofty and typically masculine themes such as war and heroic action, in which an entire people sees itself. The novel, by contrast, is considered the preeminent secondary genre; it was born when writing was already widespread (or even, according to some theories, in an age dominated by the printing press). It is related to the rise of a new private, sentimental dimension—a kind of metahistoric bourgeois dimension—and

---

[7] Vittorio Strada, introduction to *Tolstoj* by Mikhail Bakhtin (Bologna: Il Mulino, 1986), 21.

[8] See especially Mikhail Bakhtin, *The Dialogic Imagination: Four Essays*, trans. Caryl Emerson and Michael Holquist (Austin: University of Texas Press, 1981).

was therefore targeted for a predominantly female audience. This same orientation has been imposed on the ancient world retroactively, to the extent that some critics have ventured that the Greek novels were actually written by female writers hiding behind male pseudonyms.[9] (Samuel Butler advanced the same hypothesis for the *Odyssey*.)[10]

Comparison of the epic and the novel is, in any event, a delicate operation. They are two modes of literary representation that are subdivided into various genres and subgenres that still belong to the same great expressive typology, the narrative regime—as distinct from the dramatic and lyric regimes—in a triad that has been extremely fortunate. Within the narrative regime both the epic and the novel are long works with an ample system of characters (being written in prose or verse is not always a valid distinction). Although net distinctions cannot be made at the abstract level of expressive technique (some theorists, especially in German circles, use the term *epic* to encompass both forms), the two modes are quite distinct within the hierarchical statute: the epic is more codified and canonical, while the novel is more fluid and open. These qualities are all very favorable to hybridization: especially if we historicize this opposition and study its varied reception (which I will attempt later).

Let us begin with an immediate datum: the late birth of the novel and the precocious death of the epic. The epic was the first genre to rise. Indeed, it is the genre that inaugurated the literary system and the one whose decline would so quickly be lamented. In the European tradition, Milton's *Paradise Lost* is generally considered the last true epic poem, but the process of extinction was long and slow: the genre has survived mainly in the twisted and parodistic form of the mock-heroic epic, except for unexpected later appearances (such as Derek Walcott's recent postcolonial *Omeros*).[11] Things change, however, if one heeds Hegel's distinction between the original epic and the "artificially composed" (*künstliche gemachte*) epic, variously reformulated as literary epic or sentimental revival of the epic.[12] If we must

---

[9] Tomas Hägg, *The Novel in Antiquity* (Berkeley: University of California Press, 1983), 95–96.

[10] Samuel Butler, *The Authoress of the Odyssey* (Chicago: University of Chicago Press, 1967).

[11] Clotilde Bertoni, *Percorsi europei dell'eroicomico* (Pisa: Nistri-Lischi, 1997); Joseph Farrell, "Walcott's *Omeros*: The Classical Epic in a Postmodern World," in *Epic Traditions in the Contemporary World: The Poetics of Community*, ed. Margaret Beissinger, Jane Tylus, and Susanne Wofford (Berkeley: University of California Press, 1999), 270–96.

[12] Hegel, *Aesthetics*, 3:1,201; on what Northrop Frye calls the "sentimental" revival of the literary epic, see John Bryan Hainsworth, *The Idea of Epic* (Berkeley: University of California Press, 1991), 9.

exclude the second (to which Virgil belongs) from the true epic spirit, as an inauthentic product, then the death of epic truly becomes precocious: the only works that would ultimately be defined as epics are Homer's poems and similar works from other cultures, such as the *Epic of Gilgamesh*, the *Ramayana*, or the *Mahabharata*.

The late birth of the novel, by contrast, is an undeniable fact that is also partly to blame for the marginal and semiofficial status it has held for centuries. The actual moment of its birth is a matter of greater fluctuation, and tends to be assigned earlier and earlier dates. The prototype was long identified as *Pamela* or *Tom Jones*: the Anglo-Saxon distinction between *novel* and *romance* was taken for granted, treating the former, in the wake of Ian Watt's famous study, as the offspring of the Industrial Revolution and of the new larger publishing market.[13] Today there is a growing tendency to question this sociological framework and dispute the novelty of the *novel*: a critical operation performed most trenchantly in Margaret Doody's *The True Story of the Novel*, which attacks Watt's thesis as British chauvinism.[14] Often the role of the prototype is assigned to *Don Quixote*, especially because of the dissonance between hero and world that inflects the narrative as a whole, and because of the new epistemological models it establishes, at least with regard to the novel as a container that embraces several ranges of reality. The *Princess of Clèves* is usually considered the prototype for the psychological novel. Going even further back, there has been greater recognition of the founding role of the ancient novel in recent years. Although the term "novel" did not exist in the classical languages, the genre certainly did. It boasted clear though uncodified topoi and conventions. While the genre contained elements that were characteristic of *romance*, it was closer to the *novel* in concept, if for no other reason than the absence of fantastic elements and the presence of an everyday dimension. In this instance the prototype for the novel would have to be Chariton's *Chaereas and Callirhoe*, from the first century B.C. (although the papyrus fragments of lost texts suggest even older origins). Scholars have noted many distinctive features in the Greek novel that the Hegelian-Lukáscian vision considered typical of the modern novel as a bourgeois form (which speaks volumes about transcultural constants): secularization, individualism, the hero's isolation, the private and

---

[13] Ian Watt, *The Rise of the Novel: Studies in Defoe, Richardson, and Fielding* (Berkeley: University of California Press, 1957).

[14] Margaret Anne Doody, *The True Story of the Novel* (New Brunswick, N.J.: Rutgers University Press, 1996). This work deals extensively with the ancient novel and its ethnic and cultural "impurities."

sentimental dimension, and cultural syncretism.[15] These elements are already present, in part, in Menander's comedy—from the Hellenistic period, a "bourgeois" and individualistic age—and even earlier in Euripides' last atypical, exotic, and adventurous tragedies, which have not coincidentally been called "novelistic."[16] The antedating of the novel, however, does not end here: many of the peculiarities of Homer's second poem, which are probably related to the different period in which it was composed, have been interpreted as prototypical of the novel. In *Palimpsests*, a work summarizing all the forms of literature in the second degree, Gérard Genette has this to say:

> *Iliad/Odyssey*: the strongest argument in favor of the unity of the author is perhaps precisely the fact that the second work is not a mere mimicry of the first, which it would quite naturally have been had it been penned by a follower or a competitor. Only the author himself could have the energy and the good taste to avoid such self-imitation, being more tempted by an entirely different work, and one whose relation to the preceding work can be seen to be rather oblique: ten years later, the secondary character has become the hero; the theme of the action has changed (from exploit to adventure), as has the narrative attitude, which has become all of a sudden almost entirely focused upon the hero alone—and to a lesser degree upon his son, in the Telemachia—and completely breaks with the Olympian objectivity ("an external procession," says Hegel) of the epic mode. It is almost a change of the genre, since Homer here covers more than half the distance separating the epic from romance, with the shift from the war theme to the theme of individual adventure, the shrinking of the multiple cast to one central hero, the focalization of the narrative upon that hero, and finally the introduction—so alien to the narrative mode of the *Iliad* (and later also of medieval epics)—of the beginning *in medias res*, balanced by an autodiegetic first-person narrative in books 9 through 12.[17]

---

[15] See especially Bryan Reardon, *The Form of Greek Romance* (Princeton, N.J.: Princeton University Press, 1991). Reardon continues to prefer the term *romance*, unlike most contemporary British and American scholars.

[16] Massimo Fusillo, "Was ist eine romanhafte Tragödie? Überlegungen zu Euripides' Experimentalismus," *Poetica* 24 (1992): 270–99.

[17] Gérard Genette, *Palimpsests: Literature in the Second Degree*, trans. Channa Newman and Claude Dobinsky (Lincoln: University of Nebraska Press, 1997), 179. See also Uvo Hölscher, *Die Odyssee: Epos zwischen Märchen und Roman* (Munich: Beck, 2000). It is curious to note that precisely because of its elements of fable, believed to be of folkloric origin, some thinkers have claimed that the *Odyssey* predated the *Iliad*, or at least stemmed from an earlier era (see Hainsworth, *The Idea of Epic*, 33–35).

"More than half the distance separating the epic from romance": with splendid nonchalance the narratologist settles the Homeric question in a few lines, attributing the change to a single author. The *Odyssey*, the pre-eminent second and secondary epic poem (and thus also the prototype for intertextuality)—which the anonymous author of the *Sublime* considered a work of Homer's old age (chapter 9) and a model more suited to comedy—thus becomes the ideal prototype for the novel: from the *Satyricon* of Petronius and the *Aethiopika* of Heliodorus in antiquity to the sixteenth- and seventeenth-century theorists, and even as late as Melville and Joyce. The Homeric poem offered both thematic material—the journey, adventure, exoticism, private affections, and in general less sublime and indisputable values (shrewdness, deceit, pretense, which are not wholly extraneous to the Homeric poem), which Adorno clearly associated with bourgeois culture—and formal aspects: a narrative structure centered on a single hero, more closed and compact than the *Iliad*.[18]

The latter point deserves further attention. In *Theory of the Novel*, Lukács wrote that, "In the story of the *Iliad*, which has no beginning and no end, a rounded universe blossoms into all-embracing life" (55). He later reformulates this observation in general terms, calling the epic "homogeneously organic and stable," and the novel "heterogeneously contingent and discrete." The epic is thus portrayed as a flow of events that is intrinsically organic, from which all the poet has to do èxtract the narrative segment: the beginning and the end remain arbitrary and open. The novel, on the other hand, should channel its nonorganic, contingent matter through a more rigorous compositional architecture. At this point one has to deduce that the opposition between epic and novel, already foreshadowed in the contrast between the *Iliad* and the *Odyssey*, is represented as an open/closed opposition in terms of narrative structure. Many seventeenth- and eighteenth-century examples confirm this analysis (to which we shall return in the discussion of *War and Peace*). In the first centuries of the history of narrative, however, the relationship appears to be the reverse (a sign that the opposition between the two genres should always be placed in historical context): during sixteenth-century literary disputes, in particular, the epic provided a closed, organic and unified model by comparison with the novel (associated with chivalric romance at the time), which was seen as the realm

---

[18] Theodor W. Adorno, "Interpretazione dell'Odissea" (Rome: Manifestolibri, 2000), the first version of the essay he later included in *Dialectic of Enlightenment* (New York: Continuum, 1972).

of plurality and multiformity.[19] In truth the epic was being reread through Aristotle, who applied the rules of dramatic concentration and selection to the epic, thereby slightly distorting its features.

Let us return to our semiparadoxical itinerary of the birth of the novel and the death of the epic. By now we have the impression that the epic in its purest form is represented solely by the *Iliad* (or by medieval works close to the oral tradition, such as the *Chanson de Roland*): many critics support this view. Recent interpretations of Homer's first poem, however, encourage a more multifaceted perspective, emphasizing its plurality of viewpoints, expressive polyphony, and antiwar and antiauthoritarian sentiments.[20] Even the protagonist, Achilles (a presence that radiates from his absence, as Hölderin remarked), can hardly be said to embody a collective spirit, since he lives his emotional experience in opposition to the codes of the surrounding world.[21] Similar criticism has been made of the intertextual dynamic of other medieval epics, such as *Beowulf.* A neopragmatist might conclude at this point that the interpretive community is creating the text, and in this case, the novelistic *Iliad*. It would suffice to say that, while it may be operating under the pressure of the modern novel, contemporary criticism has brought to a focus the complexity of Homer's poetry, disputing long-dominant ideas such as objectivity, impersonality, and immobility. It is a poetry that appears at the end of complex cultural processes and is thus far from any primitive purity. Nor is it immune to contamination from the East.[22] The Western obsession with origins is what led to descriptions of the epic as an organic monolith, unattainable in its absoluteness: for that matter, one of the ways that modernity legitimizes itself is by emphasizing discontinuity and creating myths of an absolute past.[23] The same obsession has driven efforts to establish a mechanical equivalence between the epic and

---

[19] Patricia A. Parker, *Inescapable Romance: Studies in the Poetics of a Mode* (Princeton, N.J.: Princeton University Press, 1979); Sergio Zatti, *Il modo epico* (Rome: Laterza, 2000), 101–5.

[20] Irene J. F. de Jong, *Narrators and Focalizers: The Presentation of the Story in the "Iliad"* (Amsterdam: Grüner, 1987); Robert J. Rabel, *Plot and Point of View in the "Iliad"* (Ann Arbor: University of Michigan Press, 1997).

[21] Guido Paduano, "Le scelte di Achille," introduction to the Italian edition of *Iliade* (Turin: Einaudi, 1997).

[22] Walter Burkert, *The Orientalizing Revolution: Near Eastern Influence on Greek Culture in the Early Archaic Age* (Cambridge, Mass.: Harvard University Press, 1992), chap. 1.

[23] Hans Blumenberg, *The Legitimacy of the Modern Age,* trans. Robert M. Wallace (Cambridge, Mass.: MIT Press, 1983).

orality in "primitive" cultures, an equivalence that has been rejected or downplayed in the latest anthropological studies.[24]

If we abandon the distinction between authentic and literary epic, we can notice a gradual novelistic "contamination" that takes place under the sign of eros, a theme that is foreign to the epic's rigid masculine code.[25] While the eroticism in the warrior universe of the *Iliad* is implicit or collateral (for example, the relationship between Achilles and Patroclus or between Hector and Andromache), and takes on significant but circumscribed forms in the *Odyssey* (Calypso, Nausica, Penelope), it is instead central to the *Argonauts* of Apollonius of Rhodes, written at the peak of the Hellenistic Age and shortly before the birth of the novel. Apollonius's poem has also been considered a prototype of the novel because of its Odyssean blend of eros, travel, and adventure and its marked antiheroism, which actually thematicizes the loss of the epic code.[26] A similar process can be seen in Bretton romance (Chrétien de Troyes); in the chivalric poem (Ariosto)—where epic and novel intersect more closely and synchronically; and as late as Torquato Tasso, with his precarious and fascinating balance between epos and novel, eros and heroic feat[27] (this picture of romance epic does not include poems with more slippery canons that are deliberately open and unorganic, and thus anti-epic, such as Ovid's *Metamorphosis*, Nonno's *Dionisiache*, and Marino's *Adone*).

So what remains of the opposition between epic and novel? Many of the previous observations could lead to skeptical conclusions; some scholars, in fact, argue that in critical practice the two genres are self-deconstructing.[28] I do not think such negative conclusions are warranted. Epic and novel should not be thought of as two fixed, immutable entities but rather as two bundles of transcultural constants that can be more or less active from period to period and work to work, or even transformed altogether. In a highly codified genre such as the epic, it is obviously easier to identify constants

---

[24] See Jack Goody's "From Oral to Written" in volume 1 of this work.

[25] Barbara Pavlock, *Eros, Imitation, and the Epic Tradition* (Ithaca, N.Y.: Cornell University Press, 1990).

[26] Charles Rowan Beye, *Epic and Romance in the Argonautica of Apollonius* (Carbondale: Southern Illinois University Press, 1982); the controversial thesis that Jason was an antihero was introduced by G. Lawall, "Apollonius' *Argonautica*: Jason as Anti-Hero," *Yale Classical Studies*, 19 (1966): 119–26.

[27] Sergio Zatti, *L'uniforme cristiano e il multiforme pagano: Saggio sulla "Gerusalemme Liberata"* (Milan: Saggiatore, 1983); and *L'ombra del Tasso: Epica e romanzo nel cinquecento* (Milan: Mondadori, 1996).

[28] M. A. Sherman, "Problems of Bakhtin's Epic," in *Bakhtin and Medieval Voices*, ed. Thomas J. Farrell (Gainesville: University Press of Florida, 1995), 194.

(the narrating of a community's founding heroic, mythical or historic deeds; elevated, sublime language; encyclopedism); topoi; and expressive techniques (the formula, the catalog, similes, the descent into the underworld). It is much harder but not impossible to do so for a marginal and semiofficial genre such as the novel (the private, sentimental dimension; open form; pathological identification). Yet the intersection and interference between these two aggregates over the centuries has characterized the universe of narrative fiction, a universe with ambiguous rules that has often been the object of distrust and censure.

This censure has taken aim primarily at the novel because the epic has always been enveloped in a sacred aura, stemming from its anthropological function and only secondarily from its literary function. This aura has been conserved even after its original function has grown blurred, even when the epic has come to take on freer and more experimental or clearly novelistic forms, whereas for centuries the novel has undergone real and metaphoric trials related to its perceived social and moral threat, stemming mainly from its implausibility and the public's overidentification with its heroes (a phenomenon foreign to the sublime heights of the epic, which always implies a certain degree of hauteur).[29]

Leaving aside the abstract level of theoretical definition, I will outline, in diachronic order, a series of models of the relationship that the novel has instituted with the epic (using a few telling samples, with no pretense to giving every possible type or example). The novel has sought to transcend its marginal status and respond to attacks through this relationship, laying claim to the more canonical genre whose narrative rules and broad dimensions it shares. At first it did so simply for the sake of self-elevation or thematicizing its diversity; later, when the problem of marginalization had been largely overcome, it did so to expand and achieve new and increasingly totalizing forms.

The Epic as Ennobling Form

To our knowledge, the Greek novel flourished briefly but intensely. Originating around the first century B.C., by the third (or at the latest, the fourth) century A.D. it had disappeared, to reappear many centuries later in the Byzantine area. Yet in these few short centuries it experienced wide circulation (as the papyri attest) and remarkable development, divided into a preliminary,

---

[29] Walter Siti traces a long history in "The Novel on Trial," volume 1 of this work.

more paraliterary, folkloristic stage and a second stage of refinement of this sentimental, entertaining narrative. The last extant Greek novel, Heliodorus's *Aethiopika*, is also the most complex and influential in modern literature. Much of its complexity and fortune derive from its hybridization with the epic, particularly its adoption and amplification of the narrative structure of the *Odyssey*, the primary archetype for the novel. *Aethiopika* thus represents an early model of the epic recycled in order to ennoble a still hybrid genre.

Before Heliodorus, all Greek novels had a very linear structure—from beginning to end without long digressions—but one that narrated an invariably circular story: the enamorment (or marriage) of the two protagonists in their hometown, their separation followed by a series of adventures that were parallel in space and time, and their reunification in the city where the story began. In *Aethiopika* the reverse seems to be the case: the story is linear, narrating a gradual journey from Delphi to Ethiopia, during which the protagonist, Chariclea, regains her lost homeland. The plot, however, is circular: it begins *in medias res*, with one of the many conventional abductions of the couple, and then relates the events leading up to this moment in a long story within a story that ends exactly halfway through the novel. Both innovations are borrowed directly from the *Odyssey*: the journey's domestic destination, punctuated by theatrical recognition scenes, and the complex narrative structure, fully deploying the ancient technique of metadiegesis.[30] As is often the case with second-degree texts, it expands on its model significantly. The ending is not just a return home but the recovery of an identity and a utopian space. The beginning *in medias res* also becomes a means for creating suspense, and the embedding of stories within stories multiplies to the fourth metadiegetic level.

This amplification of the epic is closely tied to another operation that Heliodorus performs on the novel: philosophical rewriting. The initial mystery and the long journey before being able to reach the end are characteristic of a neoplatonic vision, which opens up space for the gradual deciphering of divine omens in parallel to the hermeneutic activity assigned to the reader.[31] It is thus no accident that the role of secondary narrator—which the *Odyssey* confers on its protagonist—should be assigned in the *Aethiopika* to the Egyptian prophet Calasiris, who is a treasure trove of neoplatonic and syncretic culture. A character with strong metaliterary features and completely

---

[30] [Translator's note: The term *metadiegetic*, referring to a story within a story, is borrowed from the narratological vocabulary developed by Gérard Genette in *Narrative Discourse: An Essay in Method*, trans. Jane E. Lewin (Ithaca, N.Y.: Cornell University Press, 1980), 229.]

[31] J. J. Winkler, "The Mendacity of Kalasiris and the Narrative Strategy of Heliodorus' *Aithiopika*," *Yale Classical Studies* 27 (1982): 93–158.

new to the Greek novel, Calasiris narrates a life of Homer depicting the poet as an exiled Egyptian prophet and thus as a kind of alter ego for himself (3.14–15). He often deploys typically Odyssean expedients, such as a beggar's disguise and a false tale. More interesting, however, in terms of the connection between the novel and its female public, is that the same Odyssean features are assigned to the female protagonist, the resourceful Chariclea, the first great heroine in a novel.[32] The male protagonist, Theagenes, is instead reluctant to practice deception, preferring a brand of martial heroism reminiscent of the *Iliad*. From a distance, the two halves of the couple seem to reflect the contrast between the two epic protagonists, Achilles (from whom Theagenes claims to be descended) and Odysseus, signaling the clear triumph of the latter, with his different axiological horizon (a triumph that will endure throughout the modern tradition).[33]

Heliodorus's rewriting of the Greek novel in an epic, philosophical key—and in dense, elaborate writing—should not make us forget that we are dealing with an uncodified marginal genre that developed in the Eastern provinces of the Roman Empire and that situates its plots in an everyday "bourgeois" reality—however theatrical that reality might be. In the *Aethiopika* one of the most characteristic topoi of the epic, the descent into the underworld—a test of the hero found in various epic rewritings of the novel—is transformed into a necromantic scene: the resurrection of a dead man is witnessed surreptitiously by the two Odyssean characters, Calasiris and Chariclea, allowing them to overhear the prophecy of the conventional happy ending (6.15). Odysseus himself appears to Calasiris in a dream, providing another anticipation of the ending and a conspicuous example of secularized myth and bourgeois epic (phenomena that would give life to the two Latin novels on the Trojan War by Dictys Cretensis and Dares Phrygius):[34]

---

[32] Brigitte Egger, "Zu den Frauenfolle in griechischen Roman: Die Frau als Heldin und Leserin," *Groningen Colloquia on the Novel* 1 (1988): 33–66. The bibliography on women in the ancient novel has doubled in recent years.

[33] See the considerable material in William Bedell Stanford, *The Ulysses Theme: A Study in the Adaptability of a Traditional Hero*, 2nd ed. (Ann Arbor: University of Michigan Press, 1968); for a more problematic approach, see Piero Boitani, *The Shadow of Ulysses: Figures of a Myth* (Oxford: Clarendon Press, 1994), trans. Anita Weston. The Achilles figure has not enjoyed similar fortunes in modern criticism.

[34] *Ephemeris belli Troiani*, by Dictys Cretensis, dates back to the second century A.D.; it narrates in ten books the siege and destruction of the city, and the return of the heroes, thereby combining the *Iliad* and the *Odyssey*. *Historia de excidio Troiae*, by Dares Phrygius, belongs to the following century (or even as late as the sixth century A.D.); it narrates the Homeric events from the Trojan point of view. The two novels are escapist works (possibly based on Greek models) that were popular in the Middle Ages, when they were the only source of information on the Trojan War.

Then in a dream an old man appeared to me whose form was withered away, except that where his doublet was trussed up he showed in his thigh muscles some relics of the robustness of his prime. On his head he wore a leathern cap; he looked about him with glances at once sagacious and wily; and he dragged a limping leg, as though he had been wounded. He drew near to me and said with a cunning kind of smile: "Reverend sir, you alone have treated us as persons of no account. From all who have voyaged past the island of the Cephallenians, and who have taken note of my house and made it their concern to acquaint themselves with my renown, you alone have distinguished yourself by such disdain that you did not show me even the courtesy of an ordinary greeting, although I was dwelling in the neighborhood. Consequently it will not be long before you pay the penalty of this behaviour. You will meet with sufferings similar to mine, at the hands of enemies on both sea and land. Give this message from my wife to the girl who accompanies you: she blesses her for prizing chastity above all things, and assures her that all will end happily for her."[35]

The rich modern reception of the *Aethiopika* took place almost exclusively between the sixteenth and seventeenth centuries, a period of intense theoretical debate on the epic and the novel. Heliodorus's use of epic conventions led to his being read as a prototype for the closed, compact narration that was basically faithful to Aristotle's dictates and thus opposed to the novel's endless digressiveness. *Aethiopika* was emulated and discussed by the key Italian figure in this great narratological and theoretical debate, Torquato Tasso.[36] Convinced that the novel was simply an anomalous variant of the epic, Tasso was obsessed throughout his life by the idea of unified, organic epic form that would rationalize the centrifugal forces of Ariosto's novelistic poem *Orlando furioso*, which was grounded in wandering and multiplicity (forces that persisted in the *Jerusalem Delivered*, but more as a latent temptation). In expansionistic, counterreformation Europe the epic

---

[35] Heliodorus, *Ethiopian Story*, trans. Sir Walter Lamb (London: J. M. Dent; Rutland, Vt.: Dutton, 1997), 5.22.122–23.

[36] Walter Stephens, "Tasso's Heliodorus and the World of Romance," in *The Search for the Ancient Novel* ed. James Tatum (Baltimore: Johns Hopkins University Press, 1994), 67–87. Another figure from the Italian baroque, Giambattista Basile, set the entire *Aethiopika* to verse, turning it into an epic poem entitled *Teagene*, a transformation that highlights the tension between the epic and the novel. See Clotilde Bertoni and Massimo Fusillo, "Heliodorus Parthenopaeus: The *Aithiopika* in Baroque Naples," in *Studies in Heliodorus*, ed. Richard Hunter (Cambridge: Cambridge Philological Society, 1998), 157–81.

genre generally assumed heavy political implications, placing itself in net opposition to the alterity of heresies and peoples to be subjugated. This is
when the epic/novel polarity came to incorporate a series of other polarities,
such as unity/variety, order/disorder, East/West, reason/insanity, and, once
again, masculine/feminine.[37] Filtered through Aristotle and modeled on
Virgil rather than Homer, the epic represented a repressive, centralized institution that sought to channel the dangerous deviancy of the novel (three
centuries later the opposite was more often the case).

Even amid the abundance of baroque novels, *Aethiopika* still served as a
model of classical rules. In the *Philosophía antigua poética* (1596), the essayist Alonso López Pinciano, who also influenced Cervantes, considered
Heliodorus to be the third-greatest ancient epic poet after Homer and Virgil. In the *Traité sur l'origine des romans* (1670), Pierre-Daniel Huet, an
early theorist of the novel, underlined the consistency of Heliodorus's
composition. One of the most important baroque novelists, Georges de
Scudéry, had already made similar comments in his preface to *Ibrahim*
(1641), a novel by his sister Madeleine.[38] By comparison with the magmatic
character of baroque narration, the heroic-gallant novel—also called Heliodoric because of its emulation of *Aethiopika* (and of Achilles Tatius's
Clitophon and Leucippe and Longus the Sophist's *Daphnis and Chloe*)—
stands out for its tighter compositional architecture: here, too, epic equals
closed form.

The Heliodoric lineage of the epic novel also reverberates in one of the
key figures in the birth of the eighteenth-century realist novel: Henry Fielding. Filling in a category that Aristotle left out in his partitioning of literary
genres into four types, in his preface to *Joseph Andrews* Fielding defines the
novel as a comic epic in prose, thereby underlining both its affiliation with
the canonical classical genre and its lower stylistic register (but the *Odyssey*,
as we have seen, was already considered more inclined to the comic).[39] Ian
Watt rightly maintains that this reference to the epic implies a strong desire
for enoblement; this does not exclude a direct borrowing of epic novel topoi

---

[37] David Quint, *Epic and Empire: Politics and Generic Form from Virgil to Milton* (Princeton,
N.J.: Princeton University Press, 1993).

[38] Alban K. Forcione, *Cervantes, Aristotle, and the Persiles* (Princeton, N.J.: Princeton
University Press, 1970), 55–87; Huet's treatise was translated into English only two years after its
publication in French: *A Treatise of Romances and Their Original* (London: Printed by R. Battersby,
for S. Heyrick, 1672).

[39] Gérard Genette, *The Architext: An Introduction*, trans. Jane E. Lewin (Berkeley: University
of California Press, 1992), 13; Federico Bertoni, *Romanzo* (Florence: La Nuova Italia, 1998), 18–20.

from Heliodorus (especially in *Tom Jones*), in addition to a peculiar Virgilian rewriting of *Amelia*.[40]

An echo of this vision of the epic as synonymous with rigid formalization can still be detected in a famous letter of Flaubert in 1852 in which he expresses the wish to write a book about nothing: "Form, as it is mastered, becomes attenuated: it becomes disassociated from any liturgy, rule, yardstick; *the epic is discarded in favor of the novel*, verse in favor of prose."[41]

The Lost Epic and the Experimental Novel

Two centuries before Heliodorus, Greek sentimental narrative had already been subject to a refined intertextual operation of a completely opposite tendency—parodistic abasement rather that epic elevation—in an extraordinary work that has unfortunately been lost. I am referring, of course, to the *Satyricon* of Petronius. The fragmentary state of the text makes even the literary genre difficult to define, although it has been correctly labeled as a novel, by contrast with the successful but slippery category of Menippean satire. The surviving parts are sufficient, however, to recognize the prototype for a new relationship between the novel and the great epic codex, based on nostalgia for a forever lost sublimity. The entire narrative structure of the *Satyricon* seems to transpose the *Odyssey* archetype to a grotesque key: a god, in this case the phallic god Priapus, punishes the protagonist by forcing him to embark on an endless voyage. Petronius's rich polyphony also contains many other echoes and borrowings, including long insertions in verse (*The Fall of Ilium*, a sample of epic poetry) attributed to a poet character with a suggestive name, Eumolpus. Gian Biagio Conte has recently reinterpreted this dense palimpsest in terms of two basic notions: the mythomaniac narrator and the hidden author.[42] The first is the narrative I, Encolpius,

---

[40] Ian P. Watt, *The Rise of the Novel: Studies in Defoe, Richardson, and Fielding* (London: Chatto and Windus, 1957), 230–45; James J. Lynch, *Henry Fielding and the Heliodoran Novel: Romance, Epic, and Fielding's New Province of Writing* (Rutherford, N.J.: Fairleigh Dickinson University Press, 1986); Nancy A. Mace, *Henry Fielding's Novels and the Classical Tradition* (Newark: University of Delaware Press, 1996).

[41] Letter to Louise Colet, January 16, 1852, in *The Selected Letters of Gustave Flaubert*, trans. Francis Steegmuller (New York: Farrar, Straus and Cudahy, 1953), 128; Pierre Chartier, *Introduction aux grandes théories du roman* (Paris: Bordas, 1990), 152.

[42] Gian Biagio Conte, *The Hidden Author: An Interpretation of Petronius' "Satyricon,"* trans. Elaine Fantham (Berkeley: University of California Press, 1996). The classic essay on the subject is R. Heinze, "Petronio e il romanzo greco" (1899), ed. L. Galli, in *Kleos* 2 (1997): 77–98.

a *scholasticus* filled with artificial learning and rhetorical artifice who is unable to distinguish between reality and literary fantasy, and always obsessively searches for situations out of the literature of the sublime, and thus mainly from the epic tradition. The hidden author elaborates a (sneaky) expressive strategy behind his back, continuously entrapping him in trivial scenarios from Greek novels. Unlike the satirists, Petronius never takes positions: he does not impose his own ideology, like a camp writer *avant le lettre*. But it is through this divarication between the now improbable epic sublime and the polyhedric voyage into the languages of the everyday and the corporeal that a new narrative form was born that we could call *realism*, despite the vagueness of the term.

The idea of a character who cannot distinguish between literary fantasy and reality clearly foreshadows one of one of modernity's great myths, *Don Quixote*, which is conventionally identified with the birth of the modern novel. As we have seen in Petronius, the development of a comic-realistic narrative often coincides with intertextual operations of parodistic degradation and metalinguistic reflection. This same phenomenon recurs during in the late-eighteenth-century English novel, particularly in Fielding's *Joseph Andrews* and Sterne's metanovel. The long-dominant formula applied to Cervantes, "parody of the chivalric romance," fails to take into account the complexity of the text. *Don Quixote*'s basic mechanism is quite different from parody or pastiche: placing at the center of a fictitious work a character who believes himself to be a hero is, in fact, a much more subtle operation. In *Palimpsests*, Genette gave it a separate classification, as an anti-novel, tracing its influence all the way up to Woody Allen's splendid performance in *Play It Again, Sam*.[43] The folly of a pathological reading releases a new dimension to the novel and gives the work a different polysemous depth. Hence is born a rich critical reception, from the romantic myth of Don Quixote as the defender of the idea against prosaic reality, to reading the novel in the relativistic perspective of differing visions of the world.

Don Quixote is, in fact, one of the most glaring cases of a gap between an author's theories and his creative practice. Cervantes was undoubtedly an Aristotelian, as is demonstrated by the various critical reflections attributed to the character of the canon of Toledo, a mouthpiece for the author. In a famous passage from the first part (chapter 47), he laments the lack of a

---

[43] Genette, *Palimpsests*, 170–84; on the complex relationship between *Don Quixote* and chivalric romance, see Edwin Williamson, *The Half-Way House of Fiction: Don Quixote and Arthurian Romance* (Oxford: Clarendon Press; New York: Oxford University Press, 1984).

plausible beginning, middle, and end in chivalric romances, which are thus considered hybrid monsters. Cervantes was also an admirer of Heliodorus, as he shows in his last novel, *Los trabajos de Persiles y Sigismunda*, a homage to *Aethiopika* that the author had hoped would be his greatest work. But the narrative structure of *Don Quixote* lacks the dramatic concentration that Aristotle had recommended for the epic or the compact, plausible architecture of the Heliodoric novel: it is built, instead, on variety, digression, and the free association of polyhedric material.[44] Cervantes recognizes this freedom of expression through the words of the canon, at the end of the theoretical chapter just mentioned, as the true positive feature of the novel. This discovery leads him into an open contradiction, listing a long series of themes, encyclopedic learning, and character types that the novel can include, showing itself to be "epic, lyric, tragic, or comic, and all the moods the sweet and winning arts of poetry and oratory are capable of, for the epic may be written in prose just as well as in verse."[45]

Within this organic polyphony the epic dimension comes to be identified with the ideal of selfhood that the protagonist so tenaciously and tragically pursues throughout the novel. Hence the heroic, sublime grandeur of the chivalric world, whose irrevocable loss provokes the dissonance between the self and the world, the incessant searching, the positing of melancholy as a figure for modernity. The narrative as a whole is structured around this omnipresent theme. However, there are also direct quotations of canonical epic topoi that are always attributed to Don Quixote (the creative reader par excellance) and his inexhaustible mythopoeic capacity. At the beginning of the journey, Don Quixote imagines a written account of his adventures in pseudo-epic style from which he quotes textually:

> Who knows . . . whether in time to come, when the veracious history of my famous deeds is made known, the sage who writes it, when he has to set forth my first sally in the early morning, may not do it after this fashion?
> "Scarce had the rubicund Apollo spread o'er the face of the broad spacious earth the golden threads of his bright hair, scarce had the little birds of painted plumage attuned their notes to hail with dulcet and mellifluous harmony the coming of the rosy Dawn, that, deserting the soft couch of her

---

[44] For a theoretical overview of Cervantes criticism, see E. C. Riley, *Cervantes's Theory of the Novel* (Oxford: Clarendon Press, 1962).

[45] Miguel de Cervantes, *Don Quixote: The Ormsby Translation, Revised Background and Sources Criticism*, ed. Joseph R. Jones and Kenneth Douglas (New York: Norton, 1981), 375. Subsequent citations of page numbers appear parenthetically in the text.

jealous spouse, was appearing to mortals at the gates and balconies of the Manchegan horizon, when the renowned knight Don Quixote of La Mancha, quitting the lazy down, mounted his celebrated steed Rocinante and began to traverse the ancient and famous Fields of Montiel." (30)

One of the most significant quotations is the topos of the descent into hell at the grotto of Montesinos, where Don Quixote has an extraordinary oneiric vision of his chivalric heroes (Part II, chapters 22-23). This episode has been interpreted recently as a grotesque purgatory, drawing the protagonist toward healing and wisdom, a function also performed by other less digressive episodes in the second part (for example, the cruel prank played by the Duchess).[46]

The episode that best illustrates how deeply rooted the epic paradigm is in Don Quixote's imagination and his distorted perception of reality is his confusion of two flocks of sheep and rams for battling armies. From the shapeless clouds of dust, he conjures up an epic catalog, a required topos of every epic poem from the *Iliad* onward:

> That knight you see over yonder in yellow armour, who bears upon his shield a lion crowned crouching at the feet of a damsel, is the valiant Laurcalco, lord of the Silver Bridge. The knight in armour with flowers of gold, who bears on his shield three silver crowns on an azure field, is the dreaded Micocolembo, grand duke of Quirocia. That other of gigantic frame, on his right hand, is the ever dauntless Brandabarbaran of Boliche, lord of the three Arabias, who for armour wears that serpent skin, and has for shield a gate which, according to tradition, is one of those of the temple that Samson brought to the ground when by his death he revenged himself upon his enemies. But turn your eyes to the other side, and you shall see in front and in the van of this other army the ever victorious and never vanquished Timonel of Carcajona, prince of New Biscay, who comes in armour with arms quartered azure, green, white, and yellow, and bears on his shield a cat on a field tawny with a motto which says *Miau*, which is the beginning of the name of his lady, who according to report is the peerless Miaulina, daughter of the duke Alfeñiquén of the Algarve. (120)

The grotesque abasement of epic conventions—the high-sounding names, the provenances, the precious historic weapons—is the mark of the

---

[46] Henry W. Sullivan, *Grotesque Purgatory: A Study of Cervantes's "Don Quixote," Part II* (University Park: Pennsylvania State University Press, 1996), a reading greatly indebted to Lacanian analysis.

mock-heroic, from the pseudo-Homeric *Batracomicomachia* to the *Gattomachia* of Lope de Vega, a contemporary of *Don Quixote*, and beyond. The mock-heroic is a genre with a tangential relationship to the novel. What obviously distinguishes Cervantes' particular branch is that the rewriting of the epic is triggered entirely by Don Quixote's overwrought and pathological reading of reality through literature. Therefore it springs from that form of triangular desire through the external mediation described by René Girard, which, turning more and more inward, will become the nucleus of novelistic "truth."[47]

While in the first model of the relationship between the epic and the novel the epic plays a large role in the structuring of the story, setting its aims high, in this second model the absence of epic is thematized, laying the groundwork for the free play of novelistic plot weaving.

The Epic as Encyclopedic Temptation

The era that unshackled *Don Quixote* from being read as pure parody or pure entertainment, early German romanticism (particularly the Schlegel brothers, Schelling, Tieck, and Jean Paul),[48] was also a time of unprecedented theorizing on literary genres, particularly the epic and the novel. At the beginnings of modernity—after the total historical break constituted by the Industrial Revolution and the great bourgeois revolutions—relations between the two literary genres were almost completely reversed. The novel became the hegemonic, canonical genre of the modern nation-states, thus shedding its marginality and polyphonic openness. The epic, instead, after the last unique experiment with it by Milton, seemed on its way to becoming a dead genre, destined to survive in the distortions of the mock heroic or to take on unexpected forms. The most radical change, however, was the idea of the epic, which was no longer seen in terms of Aristotle's organic unities, modeled on tragedy and converted to teleology through the Renaissance's imperialistic rereading, but rather as an endless, primigenial flow of autonomous episodes. Numerous lengthy historic and cultural processes that completely transformed the literary establishment are behind this change, but a single event stands out: the 1795 publication of Friedrich Wolf's

---

[47] René Girard, *Deceit, Desire, and the Novel: Self and Other in Literary Structure*, trans. Yvonne Freccero (Baltimore: Johns Hopkins University Press, 1965).

[48] Anthony J. Close, *The Romantic Approach to* Don Quixote: *A Critical History of the Romantic Tradition in Quixote Criticism* (Cambridge: Cambridge University Press, 1977).

Prolegomena. This work had a disruptive effect, postulating that the *Iliad* and the *Odyssey* were casual aggregates of works by two different poets. All the key figures of contemporary culture reacted to the work in different ways: the Schlegel brothers, who accepted its conclusions, completely renounced the idea of artistic unity in the epic, highlighting its basic openness and infinity. In 1796—around the time he was elaborating a theory of the novel as an eclectic, chaotic form—Friedrich claimed that the Homeric poems have no beginning and no end: they simply break off.[49] Goethe, like Hegel, would always remain convinced of the indivisibility of the Homeric poems, but he, too, was forced to rethink the nature of the epic genre and its different form of unity.[50] On the creative level, after having produced an idyllic epic in 1797, *Hermann und Dorothea*—the only possible epic in the modern world, according to Hegel—Goethe wrote the *Achilleis*, a singular attempt at recovering Homeric epic. Choosing a tragic theme that was not in the *Iliad*, the death of Achilles, he developed it in a subjective, sentimental key, remote from Homeric impassiveness. It comes as no surprise that the *Achilleis* remained unfinished, despite the author's wish to engrave *ewige Endlichkeit* upon it. Nor is it surprising that in an entry to his 1807 *Tagebuch*, Goethe wrote that he was planning to turn the work into a novel ("a psychological novel," according to Thomas Mann's later definition). As Sotera Fornaro has remarked, this entry contains *in nuce* Hegel's theory of the novel as bourgeois epic.[51]

Goethe had always dwelt on the boundaries between literary genres, starting with chapter 5 of *Wilhelm Meister*, which is dedicated to relations between drama and the novel, or his essay "On Epic and Dramatic Poetry." He often deprecated the excessive confusion of contemporary literature. Yet his own work would prove impossible to classify by traditional genres: the

---

[49] Friedrich Schlegel, "Über die homerische Poesie," in *Studien des klassischen Altertums*, ed. E. Behler Paderborn, 1979 (*Kritische Friedrich Schlegel Ausgabe* 1): 124–26, esp. 124: "In its essence the purely poetic narrative has neither beginning nor end." Schlegel saw the novel as a form that contained the three modes: epic, lyric, and dramatic. *Frammenti critici e poetici*, ed. M Cometa (Turin: Einaudi, 1998), 174–75, 267–76, 346–51; see also Cometa's introduction to the volume, xv–xxii.

[50] *Goethes Briefe an Friederich August Wolf*, ed. Michael Bernays (Berlin: Reimer, 1868), especially Bernays's introduction, which outlines the relationship between Goethe and Homer.

[51] Sotera Fornaro, introduction to *Achilleide* by Johann Wolfgang Goethe (Rome: Salerno Editrice, 1998), 41; the expression "das unendlich Endliche" comes from Goethe's letter to Schiller of March 9, 1799, in *Das Briefwechsel zwischen Schiller und Goethe* (Munich: Beck, 1984), 2:202. See also Elke Dreisbach, *Goethes "Achilleis," Beiträge zur neueren Literaturgeschichte* (Heidelberg: Winter, 1994).

totalizing anxiety of his hero, *Faust*—especially in the second part, where it is stretched to an extreme—is marked by a polyphony of forms, styles, themes, and periods represented. While the Homeric epic may therefore seem unrecoverable, its modern equivalent should still be sought in this liminal text and in similar ones: monumental texts bordering on the illegible that Franco Moretti has called *"opere mondo"* because of their aspiration to condense in the text the fragmentary totality of the modern universe.[52] To us the ancient epic looks encyclopedic because it contains a collective wisdom, an entire cosmos, through the functioning of a broad anthropological literature associated with systems of strong values (an "encyclopedia of morality," as Hainsworth so effectively puts it).[53] The modern epic is forced to aspire to totality through often failed attempts to create new sacred texts.

This striving for the encyclopedic also affected the novel, which adopted a new epic dimension far different from the closure and compactness that had lasted from Heliodorus to the baroque, and remote from the thematization of the loss of epic in Petronius and Cervantes.[54] Epic came to signify polyphonic openness: hence the inclusion of a broad variety of polyhedric material that unravels the structure of the novel, a genre that is no longer marginal but instead is invested with its own classicism. It is a totalizing tendency that also corresponds, at the thematic level, to the Promethean (and Faustian) gesture of heroic individuality. Where the eighteenth-century novel underwent its greatest developments—remembering that its uneven geographic distribution was focused in the great centralized homogeneous nation-states, the fulcra of modernity, like France and England—there was no such epic hybridization.[55] Instead it is found, unsurprisingly, in more marginal areas with a more ambivalent relationship to the European and epic traditions. Such was the case with the United States and Melville's masterpiece.

---

[52] Franco Moretti, *The Modern Epic: The World-System from Goethe to García Márquez*, trans. Quintin Hoare (London: Verso, 1996).

[53] Hainsworth, *The Idea of Epic*, 17. The Indian epic *Mahabharata* is even more encyclopedic. On the encyclopedic form, see Northrop Frye, *Anatomy of Criticism: Four Essays* (New York: Atheneum, 1968), 315–26. See also Louise Cowans, "The Epic as Cosmopoesis," in *The Epic Cosmos*, ed. Larry Allums (Dallas: Dallas Institute of Humanities and Culture, 1992), 1–26.

[54] Nevertheless, there is an encyclopedic strain in the Greek novel that derives from the influence of paradoxography and other neosophist rhetorical genres: this tendency toward digression is more contained in Heliodorus than in the works of his predecessor, Achilles Tatius. See Massimo Fusillo, *Il romanzo greco: Polifonia ed eros* (Venice, 1989), 68–77.

[55] Franco Moretti, *Atlas of the European Novel, 1800–1900* (London: Verso, 1998).

Ever since its rediscovery in the 1920s, *Moby-Dick* has been read as a great epic work associated with the distinctiveness of American identity. Lawrence, for example, saw the *Pequod* as a symbol of the United States and the melting pot.[56] Upon closer examination, Melville's project aimed to combine two different epic traditions: the more archaic tradition of the heroic enterprise, voyage and conquest, from Homer's two poems to *Beowulf*; and the religious epic of seeking a transcendental order, from the *Divine Comedy* to *Paradise Lost*.[57] The first vector gravitates toward the protagonist Ahab and his titanic struggle with the sea monster; the second, instead, toward the narrator bearing witness, Ishmael, and his interior experience. The two components are not simply juxtaposed but rather strictly subordinated to each other. Thanks to his distance from the story he is telling, Ishmael assumes even more mysterious and elusive features that are periodically reinterpreted through his complex narrative strategy.

The encyclopedic scope of *Moby-Dick* owes its peculiarities, in fact, to the extraordinary narrator, who fully exploits the instruments of allegory through two basic procedures. The first consists of associating the whale hunt, the primary theme, with a broad range of phenomena, weaving scientific, religious, historical, mythological, and anthropological digressions into the main story line. Ishmael presents himself as a common man and repeatedly underlines the supposedly base quality of his subject (by using, for example, a mock-heroic tone in the preface to chapter 86: "Other poets have warbled the praises of the soft eye of the antelope, and the lovely plumage of the bird that never alights; less celestial, I celebrate a tail").[58] But through these digressions he tends to elevate his theme: for example, a series of noble mythical ancestors—from Perseus and St. George to the Hindu god Vishnu—are assigned to the whaler, making him the direct heir of any hero who has ever fought with a monster (chapter 82). The same chapter ends on a similar note, with an ancient epic topos taken from the second book of the *Iliad*: the ineffability of the theme to be sung and the poet's powerlessness to capture its full disturbing breadth. This topos is further developed in chapter 104, "The Fossil Whale," in which the whale's mighty bulk visually represents the all-inclusiveness of the theme, overwhelming the narrator and

---

[56] Louise Cowan, "America between Two Myths: *Moby Dick* as Epic," in *The Epic Cosmos*, 232–33.

[57] Christopher Sten, *The Weaver-God, He Weaves: Melville and the Poetics of the Novel* (Kent, Ohio: Kent State University Press, 1996), 135–37.

[58] Herman Melville, *Moby-Dick; or, the Whale* (New York: W. W. Norton, 1976), 370. Subsequent quotations are referenced parenthetically in the text.

leaving him shaking: "I am horror-struck at this antemosaic, unsourced existence of the unspeakable terrors of the whale, which, having been before all time, must needs exist after all humane ages are over" (449).

While the diagram of this first procedure can be formulated as "from the whole toward the whale," the second moves in the opposite direction, "from the whale toward the whole." Every moment in the novel refers us to another moment, universalizing the primary theme in a moral key: the sea thus becomes a figure of the unconscious and the dark forces that surround the soul, while the whale assumes more metaphysical connotations, condensing "all the subtle demonism of life and thought" (184). Despite its sweet and sublime connotations, white is a color that instills absolute terror because of its vagueness and elusiveness, symbolizing emptiness and death.[59]

Melville's encyclopedism thrives on an inexhaustible chain of associations that restrain the novel's various centrifugal thrusts. This model of epic-encyclopedic novel underwent a radical polyphonic deflagration in the following century: especially in its most radical example, whose title already sends an explicit epic signal. Joyce and others have often defined *Ulysees* as an epic of language, of the body and of the metropolis, using the term "epic" to signify an aspiration to totality through the endless flow of the story—a fragmentary and frenetic totality that recognizes no hierarchies, thereby creating ample space for the banal insignificance of everyday life. The Homeric structure should give order to the chaos of the novel's constant alternating and intersecting of standardized languages and multiple perceptions, which deprive the subject of individuality. Rather, the structure is hidden from the reader, confined to paratextual forms such as Cliff Notes and introductory explanations. What does emerge, instead, is a jumbled flow of events, completely rejecting Aristotelian structure—a plausible beginning, middle, and end—in favor of a willfully arbitrary style.

The word "flow" necessarily suggests the most characteristic technique of the modernist novel, stream of consciousness, which takes to an extreme the desire for live action and dramatic narration in real time, for the sake of replicating the way thoughts and perceptions are formed. The same technique is used in less experimental novels, such as Faulkner's *The Sound and the Fury* (1929) and John Dos Passos's trilogy *U.S.A.* (1930–36), where it is inserted between long chapters of naturalistic prose and dialogue and excerpts of "real" newspaper material. This method of contamination also

---

[59] For the thematic connotations of the color white, which was cherished in romantic imagery, see Alberto Castoldi, *Bianco* (Florence: La Nuova Italia, 1998).

seeks to produce a totalizing fresco, albeit one more classical and organic than Joycean fragmentation.

The Epic Regained: War and Peace

"Without false modesty, [*War and Peace*] is like the *Iliad.*" This is how Tolstoy expressed himself—bluntly and peremptorily—according to Gorky's memoirs.[60] This was only the final statement in Tolstoy's series of denials of the rules of the novel dating back to 1865—when he wrote to the editor of a magazine that had published the first installments, demanding that it not be called a novel. It would continue three years later when he stated that *War and Peace* was neither a novel, epic poem, or historical chronicle.[61] Tolstoy's denials could initially be read as yet another instance of the self-censorship that has characterized the entire history of the novel as a noncanonical and ever assailable genre. Given the context, however, these statements should be considered a way of distancing himself from the European bourgeois domestic novel. *War and Peace* obviously has much in common with such novels, but to him they seemed too sentimental, private, and formal. In *Novel Epics*, a study whose title already suggests multiple levels of reading, Frederick Griffiths and Stanley Rabinowitz have illustrated the almost prophetic status of Russian novelists in the nineteenth century.[62] Following Napoleon's defeat in 1812, the national identity was constructed through an ambivalent relationship with the European tradition: the novel, the modern European form par excellence, was projected in terms of vast monumental architecture, unprecedented combinations, and primary values. It strove to become "the epic of our time," in the words of the celebrated literary critic Vissarion Belinsky.

The epic scope of *War and Peace* was immediately noted by contemporary critics and has often been cited by later critics as well (especially the

---

[60] Maksim Gorky, *Reminiscences of Leo Nikolaevich Tolstoy,* trans. S. S. Koteliansky and Leonard Wolf (New York: B. W. Huebsch, 1920), 53.

[61] Tolstoy's attitude toward the unclassifiable literary genre of *War and Peace* has been reconstructed in Reginald Frank Christian, *Tolstoy's* War and Peace*: A Study* (Oxford: Clarendon Press, 1962), 112–14. Christian is very skeptical about labeling *War and Peace* as an epic. Tolstoy's letter to Katkov, his editor, is dated January 3, 1865. See also Rimvydas Silbajoris, *"War and Peace": Tolstoy's Mirror of the World* (New York: Twayne, 1995), 108–23.

[62] Frederick T. Griffiths and Stanley J. Rabinowitz, *Novel Epics: Gogol, Dostoevsky, and National Narrative* (Evanston, Ill.: Northwestern University Press, 1990), 1–4.

formalists). Although the reader generally has this same first impression, it is not so easy to explain why. The primary, more obvious reason is the central theme of war, and thus the celebration of the victory over Napoleon as a victory of the Russian people and its authentic Christian and peasant values. This is certainly an impressive element, although there is nothing celebratory about Tolstoy's novel (or the great epics, in many cases), notwithstanding the propagandistic reinterpretation of the novel in the Soviet era (including Bondarchuk's 1967 film version). Tolstoy ultimately chose a historical subject that was more remote from the present than his initial project, increasing the novel's foundational and therefore epic character. From this perspective the true heroes of the warring parties—in a novel filled with antiheros—are the troops of soldiers whose self-sacrifice is mythicized and whose speech and thoughts are often represented anonymously and chorally, using a technique found throughout the *Iliad*.[63] From the same perspective, the single most epic character (the one embodying the collective spirit) is a nonprotagonist destined to play an important role in the ending: Nikolai Rostov, who wholeheartedly identifies with the simplest, poorest Hussar footsoldier and abounds with youthful enthusiasm. He even falls in love with the emperor, whom he describes, symptomatically, through topoi borrowed from Sapho ("What could I say to him now, when my heart fails me and my mouth feels dry at the mere sight of him?" 334). Following a trend toward polarization that animates the complex system of characters, Rostov is forever compared with his former childhood friend, Boris Drubetskoy, who prefers Petersburg to Moscow and is obsessed by social advancement and military hierarchies—everything that Tolstoy represents as artificial, inauthentic, and empty formalism (III, II, VI).

When we move from the chorus of collective characters to individual solo voices, we encounter another type of epic resonance. *War and Peace* is a multiform, stratified work that is deliberately nonunified. Its very title sets up two opposite poles. This can be seen in the protagonist, a function that is split between two characters, Andrei and Pierre, whose close friendship is based on their specular relationship (as Natasha states explicitly in the novel's final pages, 1,327) and, in a peculiar form of triangular desire, on their shared love object. Griffiths and Rabinowitz associate this pair of opposites, upon which

---

[63] Leo N. Tolstoy, *War and Peace*, trans. Rosemary Edmonds (Middlesex, Eng.: Penguin Books, 1982). See bk. 1, pt. 2, chaps. 15 and 21; bk. 4, pt. 4, chap. 8. Subsequent page references are noted parenthetically in the text.

the novel is structured, with the polarity of the two preeminent epic heroes, Achilles and Odysseus.[64] One is solipsistic, in constant profound dissonance with the surrounding world—the misanthrope, the "thinking hero," a thematic model that ranges from Hamlet to Alceste—and is destined to die tragically. The other embarks on a long journey of searching—entailing disguises and changes of identity—that culminates in the triumph of the family. These two models of heroism are the lifeblood of the epic tradition, starting with their fusion in Virgil's Aeneas, in which the Odyssean model gradually comes to dominate (as we have seen in Heliodorus).

Despite these considerations on theme and character, I believe that the fundamental epic quality of *War and Peace* lies elsewhere: in the shape of the narrative, which brings into play Tolstoy's complete vision of the world and history. To grasp this aspect, we must shift our focus back to a crucial character: Kutuzov, the Russian counterpart of Napoleon, who in the tormented genesis of the novel comes to assume a more positive profile.[65] His positive connotations stem from the antiheroic awareness of two negatives: it is not the individual who makes history, and the true task of a leader is to second the flow of events. Through the eyes of Prince Andrei, the narrator explains that Kutuzov despises intelligence, learning, and even patriotic sentiments: "[His] intellect (which co-ordinates events and draws conclusions) had resolved itself into the single faculty for *quietly contemplating the progress of events*" (886; my italics). For his part, the narrator often claims that the history of our era cannot follow the models of ancient poems, which are centered on single heros (III, II, XIX). Kutuzov's attitude captures the realistic skepticism in which the narrator embeds his philosophical digressions on history: the idea that historiographic interpretation is always an *a posteriori* imposition, based on an arbitrary perspective on events that instead have their own relentless flow.[66] A person living history from within this flow cannot grasp its meaning but only act under the force of interwoven casual and unconscious motivations ("The interdiction against tasting the fruit of the

---

[64] Griffiths and Rabinowitz, "Tolstoy and Homer," in *Comparative Literature* 35 (1983): 101–14; see also George Steiner, *Tolstoy or Dostoevsky: An Essay in the Old Criticism* (New York: Alfred A. Knopf, 1959).

[65] Alfonso Berardinelli, *L'eroe che pensa: Disaventure dell'impegno* (Turin: Einaudi, 1997).

[66] Isaiah Berlin, *The Hedgehog and the Fox: An Essay on Tolstoy's View of History.* (New York: New American Library, 1957), a beautiful analysis that illustrates the tragic tension between multiplicity and the aspiration to singular unity, as well as many cultural correspondences (e.g., Stendhal, De Maistre).

tree of knowledge come out more conspicuously in historical events than anywhere. It is only subconscious activity that bears fruit, and a man who plays a part in an historic event never understands its import. As soon as he tries to realize its significance his actions become sterile," 1,116). This idea also corresponds to the novel's image of the true Russian sentiment. A passage describing the ways that different populations feel self-assured—what we might call an "imagology" today—affirms that "A Russian is conceited because he knows nothing and does not want to know anything, since he does not believe that it is possible to know anything completely" (757–58). At the same time, as a motivation for Pierre's insane idea that he has been predestined to kill Napoleon, Tolstoy evokes "that vague and typically Russian contempt for everything conventional, artificial and accepted—for everything the majority of mankind regards as the highest good in the world" (1,067). This nihilistic, anticonventional sentiment stands in contrast, especially, to the rationalistic abstraction of German culture and its strategies. Tolstoy's anti-intellectual distrust covers every form of science, including medicine, whose foundations the narrator demolishes in an excursus on Natasha's illness (III, I, XVI).

This vision is directly reflected in the forms of the story. The rejection of categorization and segmentation as too abstract also implies a rejection of organic Aristotelian structure with a plausible beginning, middle, and end.[67] This is what Tolstoy meant when he said that he did not consider *War and Peace* a novel: he was rejecting the European form of a narrative centered on conclusive events, such as marriage and death, as well as the European idea of the hero embodied by Napoleon. *War and Peace* was, in fact, described as a "large, loose baggy monster" by Henry James, a key figure in the domestic psychological novel, who propounded a more Aristotelian narrative theory based on concentration and dramatic concision (not unlike Turgenev, the most European of Russian writers).[68]

Like Kutuzov, Tolstoy's narrator only wants "calmly to contemplate the course of events" without pegging them to hierarchies of meaning. This choice seeks to revive Homer's celebrated impassiveness: the infinite joy in

---

[67] On the anti-Aristotelianism of *War and Peace*, see Gary Saul Morson, *Hidden in Plain View: Narrative and Creative Potentials in War and Peace* (Stanford, Calif.: Stanford University Press, 1987), 144–46.

[68] Preface to Henry James, *The Tragic Muse*, available in Henry James, *The Art of the Novel: Critical Prefaces* (1934; reprint, New York: Charles Scribners' Sons, 1962), 84. James makes the same critique of Thackeray, Dumas père, and Tintoretto, while acknowledging how full of life their huge arbitrary works were.

storytelling that impassioned both Goethe and Schiller, the calm vastness that fascinated Hegel, the primigenial flow that Lukács defined as "organic-homogeneous continuum." It might seem paradoxical to invoke Homeric narration—which is notoriously impersonal and free of authorial intervention—with regard to a novel in which the narrator becomes more and more intrusive, and his ideology more explicit through the insertion of short essays (although this element, too, has epic antecedents, such as the Hesiodic subgenre of didactic poetry). But the narrator's intrusiveness in *War and Peace* is quite peculiar, because it consists mainly of renouncing all systematic forms of theory by contrast to the program of selecting "an infinitesimally small unit for observation—a differential of history" (975).

As I mentioned earlier, Friedrich Schlegel held that the epic has no beginning and no end; it simply breaks off. This idea is corroborated by the fact that an epic poem always belongs to a broader cycle of which it represents only one segment.[69] The narrator of *War and Peace*, in one of his theoretical incipits, rails against the very notion of a beginning as a hackneyed convention of historiography: "It is impossible for the human intellect to grasp the idea of absolute continuity of motion . . . the march of humanity, springing as it does from an infinite multitude of individual wills, is continuous. . . . The first proceeding of the historian is to select at random a series of successive events and examine them apart from others, though there is and can be no *beginning* to any event, for one event always flows without any break in continuity to another" (974–75). He goes further: "A commander-in-chief never finds himself at the *beginning* of any event—the position from which we always contemplate it. The commander-in-chief is always in the midst of a series of shifting events and so he can never at any point deliberate on the whole import of what is going on" (979).

Tolstoy remains consistent to this basic principle when he shifts from theory to narrative practice, at least in the *ex abrupto* beginning of the novel: readers enter in the midst of a conversation in Anna Pavlovna's salon, as if they were suddenly being thrown into the current of a river.[70] The ending is more complicated. It is common knowledge that *War and Peace* actually has three endings. The first, following the fourth book, has the same characteristics as the incipit. In a brusquely interrupted conversation, Natasha asks

---

[69] From this perspective the great novel cycles of Balzac and Zola disclose an epic aspiration for totality that is attenuated, however, by the autonomy of the single parts.

[70] Naturalistic and the Jamesian novels use the same technique but with a different configuration and function. James's use of it signifies a rejection of narrative voice but not of organic structure.

herself an unsettling question and then reassures herself ("Well, well, it is best so. . . . Eh, Marie? It is best so." 1,335). This perspective clearly recalls the open ending of the *Iliad*—in which openness does not signify incompletion and does not preclude a satisfying feeling of wholeness.[71] Tolstoy's genuinely epic ending is then supplemented by a double epilogue. The first epilogue is narrative: the story jumps ahead by seven years to depict the two marriages that were already splendidly implicit in Natasha's conversation. Conjugal life is praised. The only potential opening lies in the figure of young Nikolai, Andrei's son. The second epilogue is essayistic, recapitulating the main theses of philosophy of history. In this very controversial ending, ideology seems to have won out over poetics, and the monologic Tolstoy has gotten the better of his dialogic self.[72]

Through the epic flow that evades a rigid structure of cause and effect, Tolstoy's narrative seeks to recover a present that has not yet been caged into the logic of beginning and end: events in their concrete, corporeal immediacy, before interpretation has frozen them into an abstract, sterile form. This is the key to some of the techniques and topoi of *War and Peace*, such as the estrangement mechanism highlighted by Shklovsky, which aims to reproduce a pure, unmanipulated vision (Natasha's first visit to the opera, various episodes involving wounds, the death of Petya).[73] Other such examples are the many moments in which a character loses his or her rational grip on reality and falls into an oblivious dream state: genuine epiphanies that are almost always associated with the theme of the infinity of nature (the sky contemplated by Nikolai or Andrei, the comet seen by Pierre).[74] One particular case stands out: in Andrei's impaired thoughts, the image of Natasha appears, trying to tell him a story, describing everything "without connection" and complaining that she does not know how to tell a story. Yet it is this same disorderly narrative exuberance that best conveys to Andrei the "spiritual purity" of his beloved: "her soul that was almost bound to her body" (912–13). True communication thus occurs more frequently above and beyond traditional patterns.

---

[71] This analysis of the ending of the *Iliad* and of epic endings in general is obviously problematic: see Sheila Murnaghan, "Equal Honor and Future Glory: The Plan of Zeus in the *Iliad*" in *Classical Closure: Reading the End in Greek and Latin Literature*, ed. Deborah H. Roberts, Francis M. Dunn, and Don Fowler (Princeton, N.J.: Princeton University Press, 1997), chap. 2; and Don Fowler, "Second Thoughts on Closure," in the same volume, chap. 1.

[72] Lukács, for example, gave a very negative judgment in *Theory of the Novel*, 143, which he reconsidered in the preface to the 1962 edition, 14.

[73] Viktor Borisovich Shklovsky, "Art as Technique," in *Russian Formalist Criticism: Four Essays*, ed. Lee T. Lemon and Marion J. Reis (Lincoln: University of Nebraska Press, 1965), 3–24.

[74] John Kevin Newman, *The Classical Epic Tradition* (Madison: University of Wisconsin Press, 1986), 256–57. The parallel he draws with Alexandrian epic is, in my opinion, misleading.

While in the Renaissance the epic represented order, the norm, the repressive instance, and the novel, by contrast, represented disorder, transgression, and repression, now the terms were reversed. For Tolstoy, the European bourgeois domestic novel constituted a closed and artificial model, while the epic form allowed him to adhere more closely to the continuous rhythm of nature and history. This immediacy is obviously a myth, a calculated effect of the text. In this fluid, stratified form, increasingly contaminated by forays into historical commentary, there is also room to directly replicate epic features, such as repetition or extended similes, which are used in key moments such as the beginning of the battle of Austerlitz (I, III, XI) and the abandonment of Moscow upon the arrival of Napoleon (III, III, XX).[75] The latter example represents a glaring infraction of the conventions of the realistic novel and its fundamental referentiality. For two whole pages Tolstoy develops and symbolically eviscerates the image of the bee taken from Virgil's epic (1. 430–36), completely interrupting the direct narrative.[76] It is hard to imagine a more blatantly and aptly Homeric passage in another nineteenth-century novel: a glaring sign of Tolstoy's profound identification with the endless storytelling of Homer and epic poetry.

Postmodern Frescoes

After Joyce's great modernist epic a new type of epic novel did not appear for many years. The twentieth century questioned the entire system of genres and literary forms, making it difficult to hazard any type of generalization. The European novel explored subjectivity and then metalinguistic nihilism, culminating in the experimental *nouveau roman*. "Pure" fiction was delegated to "other" areas (Latin America, India), while epic devices reappeared in a downgraded form in televised fiction.[77] Critics still use the term *epic*, especially to describe war novels (such as Beppe Fenoglio's *Johnny the Partisan*, which gives the Italian resistance the epic treatment through an absolute,

---

[75] Natasha Sankovitch, *Creating and Recovering Experience: Repetition in Tolstoy* (Stanford, Calif.: Stanford University Press, 1998).

[76] I am not entirely convinced by Griffiths and Rabinowitz's argument (*Tolstoy and Homer*, 114–15) that Tolstoy initially parodied epic simile by applying it to mechanical phenomena (the clock, the flight of the bees), thereby rejecting its use for abstractions; only later did he rethink the figure, for example in his use of the ants' simile to illustrate the rebirth of Moscow. See J. M. Curtis, "The Function of Imagery in *War and Peace*," *Slavic Review* 29 (1970): 460–80, esp. 468–69.

[77] The inevitable reference is Florence Dupont, *Homère et "Dallas"* (Paris: Hachette, 1991). Although much of her argument is questionable, her comparisons are sometimes effective (e.g., regarding the infinite flow of the story).

distancing language). It is often used to describe the twentieth-century's most important art form, cinema (Eisenstein, Griffith, Ford). But it would take the historic caesura represented by the Second World War before a new form of the epic novel could be found: the controversial category of the postmodern.

However difficult it may be to outline a thematic map of postmodernism, such a chart should obviously include the fragmentation of the subject, time, and history, which are perceived differently than they were during the utopian season of modernism (a given, almost a playful cliché).[78] Taking this theme as their starting point, some recent novels—often labeled epic—have sought to produce a totalizing fresco (a "hypernovel") consisting of an assemblage of intersecting stories and characters, taking a disjointed approach to time, and constantly mixing fictional and real characters (such as *U.S.A.* by John Dos Passos). The sense of totality is born, paradoxically, by elevating the fragment to the level of a system, like the cinematic masterpiece of the 1990s, Robert Altman's *Short Cuts*. Some other examples are Philip Roth's *American Pastoral* (1997), Michael Chabon's *Amazing Adventures of Kavalier and Clay* (2000), and especially Don DeLillo's *Underworld* (1997).

The paratext of DeLillo's novel already contains a sign of the epic: the title alludes to the topos of the descent into the underworld. However, the underworld has multiple associations. It refers first to a primary theme of the novel, trash, an obsession of hypertechnological society and at the same time a widespread literary theme by virtue of its antifunctionalism.[79] The protagonist, Nick Shay, is the manager of a recycling plant, which creates the opportunity for long metaphysical descriptions of huge dumps that are virtually underground cities. However, the novel also features artists who reelaborate discarded objects and FBI agents who inspect the trash of criminal suspects, giving it to sociologists for analysis and allowing it to be used also for artistic performances. Like the whale in *Moby-Dick*, the theme of waste is repeatedly subjected to allegorical readings.[80]

> We built pyramids of waste above and below the earth. The more hazardous
> the waste, the deeper we tried to sink it. The word plutonium comes from
> Pluto, god of the dead and ruler of the underworld. They took him out to
> the marsher and wasted him as we say today, or used to say until it got
> changed to something else (106). *Weltanschauung.* I use this grave and

---

[78] Remo Ceserani, *Raccontare il postmoderno* (Turin: Bollati Boringhieri, 1997), 140–45.

[79] Francesco Orlando, *Gli oggetti desueti nelle immagini della letteratura: Rovine, reliquie, rarità, robaccia, luoghi inabitati e tesori nascosti* (Turin: Einaudi, 1993).

[80] Don DeLillo, *Underworld* (New York: Scribner, 1997), 111–12.

layered word because somewhere in its depths there is a whisper of mystical contemplation that seems totally appropriate to the subject of waste (282). Waste is the devil twin. Because waste is the secret history, the underhistory. The way archaeologists dig out the history of early cultures, every sort of bone heap and broken tool, literally from under the ground (791).

Underworld is also the title of film by Eisenstein that was lost and rediscovered (*Unterwelt*), which is screened in a crucial scene of the novel (423–45). The novel as a whole exploits the interference between typically postmodern codes, describing amateur videos that are more authentic than "derealized" contemporary reality or attributing to J. Edgar Hoover a morbid passion for Brueghel's painting *The Triumph of Death*.[81] Finally, the title alludes to the clichéd metaphor of the metropolitan inferno and to DeLillo's native Bronx, which one episode describes by using epic-sounding anaphora of the verb "they saw" and other verbs of perception (237–51).

In the dizzying alternation of historic periods (from the 1950s to today), emphasized by an organizational scheme that highlights the novel's breakdown into parts and chapters, one recurring element becomes the catalyst of the story: a baseball from a 1951 game, a mythic event in the American sports imagination. The search for this baseball is called "a wandering epic" (175). It becomes an obsession that has "its own epic character" (305). By the same token, a baseball player, Ralph Branca, has a name that recalls "a figure out of an old epic" (97). At one point the novel's protagonist appears to his wife in the dead of night with the baseball in his hand (the occasion for a long lyrical description). This image is compared first to Hamlet holding the skull of Yorick and then, better yet, to Aristotle with the bust of Homer. The narrator concludes with a pun: "Rembrandt's Homer and Thomson's homer. We smiled at that" (132).

From Calasiris to Heliodorus, who recounts the life of Homer and sees Odysseus in his dreams, to the waste recycler with baseball in hand, compared to the image of Homer, it has been a long road to show how the obsession with the epic as the original form of storytelling continues to leave its mark on the history of the novel.

Translated by Michael F. Moore

---

[81] On DeLillo's treatment of this theme in his works prior to *Underworld*, see Eugene Goodheart, "Some Speculation on Don DeLillo and the Cinematic Real," in *Introducing Don DeLillo*, ed. Frank Lentricchia (Durham, N.C.: Duke University Press, 1991), 117–30.

SYLVIE THOREL-CAILLETEAU

The Poetry of Mediocrity

The mystery of the novel derives from at least one lacuna: Aristotle did not define it; no great *poetic art* was consecrated to the novel. But how can we imagine a free genre without seeing a contradiction inherent in these very terms? We have to imagine then that the novel obeys secret rules. Most reflections on the novel are rooted in this assumption and explore this ambiguity. We may review several observations, all legitimate and yet problematic in some degree: the novel is a genre that develops late and that borrows its motifs from all the others—it is narrative like the epic, its accidents can multiply as in comedy, it is written in prose like history, and it is consecrated to the passions like tragedy.[1] The absence of clear rules might derive from the original particularity that all the other genres assemble within it and, with them, their discrete canons. We might observe also that the novel, making its appearance belatedly, is not fully recognized as high art until much later still. It is a *minor*, albeit pervasive genre, and generally despised—the romantics still seek glory in theatrical writing; the novel seemed even to them only a lesser evil.

The following aspects of the novel converge: the absence of poetic art, the haphazard assembling of diverse forms, and a value close to nil. The novel amuses; it is a product for consumption, often pernicious and implicated in corrupting moral purity—Rousseau recalls on the threshold of *La nouvelle Héloïse* that a proper young lady never reads novels, and the observation is commonplace.[2] All this seems to be confirmed in light of the material reality of the novel. From the seventeenth century onward, the novel is published in a small format, modestly bound, and carried in one's pocket in order to be read in solitude, far from the world. Novels are good commerce, and reading

---

[1] Cf. Pierre Grimal's introduction to *Romans grecs et latins* (Paris: Gallimard, Pléiade, 1958).

[2] "Never did a chaste maiden read Novels; and I have affixed to this one a sufficiently clear title so that upon opening it anyone would know what to expect. She who, despite this title, dares to read a single page of it, is a maiden undone: but let her not attribute her undoing to this book; the harm was already done" (Jean-Jacques Rousseau, *Julie, or the New Heloise, Letters of Two Lovers Who Live in a Small Town at the Foot of the Alps*, in *The Collected Writings of Rousseau*, translated and annotated by Philip Stewart and Jean Vaché [Hanover, N.H.: University Press of New England, 1997], 6:3–4). Cf. Jean-Jacques Rousseau, *La nouvelle Héloïse*, preface by Marc-Michel Rey, 1791 (Paris: Gallimard, Pléiade, 1964), 6.

a novel commits the individual who indulges in the practice to no communal forum.[3] The price attached to the novel depends inversely on commercial and social value. Reading the novel is delectable because it is intimate, private, and perhaps even shameful. Thus, Walter Benjamin would write in "The Narrator" that the novel emanates from a solitary individual addressing other solitary individuals and that its appearance is linked to the impossibility of giving or receiving counsel.[4] How then conceive of the novel as constrained by rules?

Even if it did not evoke a poetics, the novel was the object of numerous descriptions and characterizations that took the form of historical studies: In 1670, M. Huet, future bishop of Avranches, addressed to M. Segrais a precious letter devoted to the origin of novels. We find on the first page of this epistle: "those works which are properly called Novels are *false Stories of amorous adventures, written in prose with art, for the pleasure and instruction of the readers.*[5] This may seem a very modest definition and a surprising one to today's reader, little accustomed to identifying the novel with the narrative of "amorous adventures." Yet the idea that novels recount love stories was a very common one: Lenglet-Dufresnoy, who saw himself as Huet's heir, would contend as seriously as his predecessor that the novel is devoted to this sort of story and that one need only enter into marriage to exit the novel.[6] Father Bougeant, the author of a delectable utopia, *Voyage dans la Romancie*, would have it said to one of his characters that one enters the land of Romancie through love.[7] Several years later Hegel, whose intention

---

[3] Roger Callois observes "a relationship between two phenomena as distinct as the diffusion of the novel and the decadence of great architecture," in "Puissances du roman" ["Powers of the Novel"], in *Approches de l'imaginaire* (Paris: Gallimard, 1974), 211.

[4] Walter Benjamin, "Der Erzäler," *Orient und Okzident* (October 1936); cf. "Le Narrateur," trans. Benjamin (Paris: Mercure de France, 1952) and "Le Conteur," trans. Maurice de Gandillac, in *Oeuvres III* (Paris: Gallimard, Folio, 2000), 121: "The novelist has isolated himself. The birthplace of the novel is the solitary individual, who is no longer able to express himself by giving examples of his most important concerns, is himself uncounseled, and cannot counsel others" ("The Storyteller, Reflections on the Works of Nikolai Leskov," in *Illuminations: Essays and Reflections*, ed. and intro. Hannah Arendt, trans. Harry Zohn [New York: Harcourt Brace Jovanovich, Schocken Books, 1968, 1969], 87).

[5] Letter from Monsieur Huet to Monsieur de Segrais, in *De l'origine des romans* (1670), 2nd ed. (Paris: Sébastien Mabre Cramoisy, 1678), 2.

[6] Nicolas Lenglet-Dufresnoy, *De l'usage des romans* (Amsterdam: Chez la veuve De Poilras, 1734), 2 vols.

[7] Père Hyacinthe Bougeant, *Voyage merveilleux du Prince Fan-Férédin dans la Romancie* (1735), ed. Jean Sgard and Geraldine Sheridan (Presses Universitaires de Saint-Etienne, 1992), 65 : "I have finally, happily, arrived after many years in Romancie without being able to say how; and all that I have been able to learn in the time that I have lived in this country is that one enters here, they say, through the door of love, and that one leaves through that of marriage."

in *Aesthetics* is manifestly more serious, would develop ironically the theme of the incompatibility of the marriage contract with romantic (novelistic) values, which are amorous and individual. When novelists, finally, imagine a work that conjoins the novel and its parody, as do Cervantes, Diderot, or Flaubert, they reprise in effect the question of love: the story of Amadis de Gaule engages Don Quixote in the pursuit of his adventures in order to seduce a marvelous woman; *Jacques le Fataliste* derives its effect by devoting itself to the impediment of the pursuit of a narrative of amorous adventures; and Emma Bovary attempts to realize romantic wonders (defined by the novel) through adultery. It is banal and even trivial to identify the novel with amorous narratives, so we no longer do it, or even if we find amorous adventures romantic today, it is only in order to separate the romantic from the novel (*roman*) or novelistic. Huet specified that these stories were false or fictional, written in artistic prose, and that they aimed to please and instruct. He formally characterized the genre, taking as point of departure a thematic observation. I would like to examine that procedure and appreciate its richness.

———

Huet bases his definition on an observation: during the classical epoch everyone identifies a model of the genre in Heliodorus's *Aethiopica* (or *An Aethiopian historie*[8]). Huet insists on this model and even declares that the adventures of Theagenes and Chariclia are as necessary and capital a reference for the novel as the *Iliad* and the *Odyssey*.[9] It is true that the work's vogue was prodigious: the chivalric romance manifests traces of it, as do pastoral romances and Cervantes, even if the writing of *Don Quixote,* in the view of some modern scholars, guards against similar blunders. In fact, Cervantes ended his novelistic work in this direction, with a rewriting of the old

———

[8] The English translations include *An Aethiopian historie written in Greeke by Heliodorus: very vvittie and pleasaunt, Englished by Thomas Vnderdoune. With the argumente of euery booke, sette before the whole vvoorke* (London: Henrie VVykes, 1569); or *An Aethiopian historie written in greeke by Heliodorus and englished by Thomas Vnderdowne,* ed. Robert Hellenga (1969), 2 vols.; and *Aethiopica. The adventures of Theagenes and Chariclia: a romance, being the rise, progress, tryals and happy success of the heroic loves of those two illustrious persons . . .* (London: W. Taylor, 1717), 2 vols. The edition cited here is the French translation, *Les Ethiopiques,* in *Romans grecs et latins,* cited above in note 1.

[9] Huet, *De l'origine des romans,* 53: "It served as a model to all writers of Novels that followed, and one may say as truthfully that they all draw from this source as it is said that all poets draw from that of Homer."

Greek romance (*Trabajos de Persiles y Sigismunda*, 1617). Such a reading reaches as far as Voltaire, who offers a parodic version in *Candide*.

Two beings of equal beauty and purity, Theagenes and Chariclia are called to love each other, and numerous obstacles stand in their way: shipwrecks, pirate attacks, abductions, and dishonest attempts at seduction. Their perfect triumph over all and their union is sealed at the same time that their common ascendance, divine and, more precisely, solar, is discovered. The novel is devoted to the interlacing of two desires, that of recognizing one's origins and that of being united to the beloved, which converge through the concept of *coincidence*: Theagenes and Chariclia love each other because they share a same marvelous origin; their reunion here below consecrates their recognition in the beyond.

This happy story is doubled by perpetual commentary, by an explicit meditation on the promises that it suggests, since the *Aethiopica* is organized as an ensemble of framed narratives, artfully recounted. The anecdotes that multiply within the work are addressed to characters who solicit and respond to them with direct or indirect expressions of their curiosity and pleasure. Cnémon is the most present of these benevolent auditors. His situation is one of suffering. He loves listening to these stories and revels especially, despite or because of his grief, in those concerning the joys and sufferings of Theagenes and Chariclia. Heliodorus reflects on the source of this pleasure: Cnémon suffers because he is accidentally distanced from his own origins and because he does not know the happiness of love. Hence he hears the tale of Theagenes and Chariclia's adventures from a singular position: the sufferings of others move him, because he recognizes in them something of his own, and their ordering into a tale nurtures his hope (it is the property of the narrative to tend toward an end, rather than to suggest continuity). Heliodorus's romance is woven throughout with consoling stories in which virtue is rewarded, despite or through tribulations; we find in the work the disarray of virtue, but Heliodorus presents also a resolution, insofar as accidents succeed each other in such a way as to allow one to discern a purpose in them. Love, in these stories, opens up the possibility for a reunion of the individual with origins that surpass those of ordinary humanity; and the power of love is doubled by the presence of a mysterious entity, the *demon* of each character. Theagenes and Chariclia are not far from doubling each other; they bear, if only marginally, signs of their origin; they are conscious, and it is this that gives them their contour. This demon guarantees their virtue.

Love for another leads, thus, to the love of the beautiful and to the love of the most divine. The path pursued by Theagenes and Chariclia is platonic.

It seems indicated by the discourse of Diotima in *The Banquet*. This is what profoundly structures the *Aethiopica*, and this structuring principle is not a haphazard one, since it can be found in many other instances. The story of *Amour and Psyche* follows a similar line: Psyche has been delivered to a base beast when Amour disrobes her before everyone's eyes, and she raises herself little by little, further and further from the beast, to become that soul, disengaged from the chains of the body, promised by her name. Zola, very much later, will vary this story in writing *The Dream*, the one of his novels that he most apparently wanted to distance from naturalism, or the most romantic (related to the origins of the *roman*). It is remarkable that the story of Apuleius borrows from the myth of Perseus, so strongly present in the *Aethiopica*, as if the first novels had to devote themselves par excellence to the recognition of the divine in man (we can play on the proximity of this romantic or novelistic term, *recognition*, to the platonic idea of reminiscence) and to eluding the figure of the Medusa. We read in Heliodorus's work that long hair is the attribute of both terrifying warrior and delicious lover, which indicates a reversal of the image associated with the Gorgon. Theagenes, when he first appears to Chariclia, bears the aegis of Athena in the form of a broach; finally, Chariclia is imagined amidst frescoes recounting the adventures of Perseus, and she resembles Andromeda. This brings us to the conclusion that love, in these two nearly inaugural novels, is represented as fundamentally civilizing: it makes the next beast retreat and allows one to accede to divinity. The body becomes opalescent like a lamp, and the lover perceives through the radiant envelope of the beloved, as if transparent, the divine part that illumines him or her. We might also think of a note in *La nouvelle Héloïse*, which declares Plato *the philosopher of lovers*.[10] If we extend Huet's definition, Plato then also becomes the philosopher of novelists.

Thus, the first novels explore the human in its mediocre or intermediary dimensions, drawn between the animal and the divine, and this is confirmed in more formal aspects of the genre.[11] We might have paused above in our consideration of all that the novel borrows from earlier recognized genres and remarked on the correspondences between the novel, epic, and tragedy, in particular, or the novel and myth. But it is clearly distinguishable from

---

[10] "The genuine philosophy of Lovers is Plato's; while its spell lasts they never have any other. A man who is prey to emotion cannot do without this philosopher; a cold reader cannot abide him" (Rousseau, *Julie, or the New Heloise*, footnote p. 183). Cf. *La nouvelle Héloïse*, Pléiade edition, 223.

[11] This idea of mediocrity is essential in the platonic view of love, son of Wealth and Poverty, relegated to the status of demon, or of intermediary between man and divinity. Huet recalls this at the end of his letter to Segrais.

these neighboring and potentially seminal genres, by dint of a trait that it shares with comedy. There is certainly a question of religion, insofar as its exists in the novel as it is exercised in ordinary life; but if ancient novels or romances recount rituals and offer multiple references to the gods, they do not devote themselves to this end: their heroes, such as Heliodorus's characters, are in some sense anonymous, and if their excellence raises them above ordinary humanity, it does not extract them from the human fold. To the contrary, the ancient novel/romance values humanity in its most marvelous aspects, capable of surmounting accidental fortunes. We may pause at a beautiful passage in the *Aethiopica*, at the moment when Chariclia is first sighted by the brigands: "a young lady sitting on a rock, and of an unspeakable beauty, that could allow her to be taken for a divinity."[12] The young lady rises, seems even more divine to the terrified brigands, and advances toward her gravely wounded companion, whom she grievingly embraces, "seeing which, the Egyptians change their minds, saying: 'How could a goddess embrace a corpse with so much passion?' and they encourage each other to approach her in order to apprehend what she might really be."[13] *Amour and Psyche*, similarly, opens with the mention of the divine beauty of a mortal, and the entire story is determined by the fact that the young lady is merely human.

That the novel does not take the divine order as its object is expressed also by a characteristic trait of the novel underlined by Huet: the novel is presented in a volume in which the entire story has already unfolded; it is retrospective by definition. A novel is always determined by its end, and motivated by the indications that lead to that end. While the epic or tragedy, devoted to the divine, unfold in the present of the word, consecrate themselves to myths, and indicate, even if only though an address to the Muse or the god, how much fate governs everything on earth, novels evoke beings who negotiate with fortune. The novel, written in the past tense, does not determine humankind's fate according to destiny but rather confronts us with capricious fortune and manifests in its prosaic form the degree to which its object is human existence. The narrative gives all of this its sense. That the novel's stories are "written in prose with art" explains also the absence in the novel of any invocation of the Muse, a further distancing from the divine presence such as it manifests itself in epic or tragedy. The measure of verse is the trace (Muse, always) of music, whose original function in

---

[12] *Les Ethiopiques*, 1.2, in *Romans grecs et latins*, 522.
[13] Ibid., 253.

Greek literature is to evoke the presence of the divine on earth, to give to the word all of its magical power. Thus, the novel at least doubly distinguishes itself from the great genres codified by Aristotle: as plotted narrative, it devotes itself to a past that it is not a matter of rendering present; as prose, it evades the archaic function of poetry, which is to make the gods descend to where we are.[14]

This does not mean that myth is absent, but rather that it has undergone a profound transformation, in which Aristotle's *Poetics* plays a part: it is no longer called myth, or the magical word, by the time ancient novels are written, but rather argument, the subject of tragedy. And this allows us to sense the importance of yet another formal aspect of the novel, namely, that it is written and contains no traces of orality save the play of framed narratives that often constitute it. Not only are the heroes of the novel merely human, even when they represent the most divine qualities; not only does the novelist never assign himself the task of tying together the plot with a magical word capable of illumining the sublunar world through the intervention of the divine in its humble affairs; but his project seems, very distant from that, one of evading myth properly speaking, of distancing his fiction from the sacred—that is, of aligning himself with the fallen figures of myth. These figures are human, at once bodies promised to decay and death and souls promised to immortality.

A legend recalled by Pliny, in book 35 of his *Natural History*, allows us to understand what this is about. A young lady in Corinth learns of the imminent departure of her lover for a war from which he is certain he will not return; in order to preserve something of the luminous presence of her beloved, she traces the contour of the shadow projected by his profile and everyone admires its extraordinary resemblance. Then the father of the young woman, whose profession is that of working the earth in order to give it form, intervenes. The potter (who in Latin is called *figulus*, because it is a matter of *fingere* in order to realize *figurae*) fills in with earth the imprint limned by his daughter, bakes it, and thus realizes the first statue, thereafter conserved in a temple. The father thus realizes a very exact figure. The precision of the modeling guarantees the presence of a soul; the statue reflects a form or an idea (imprinted first in the heart of his daughter, before she traces its profile on the wall); it makes tangible that which is not tangible.

---

[14] On this matter, see Gregory Nagy, *Poetry as Performance: Homer and Beyond* (Cambridge: Cambridge University Press, 1996) or *Poésie en acte: Homère et autres chants*, trans. J. Bouffartigue (Paris: Belin, 2000).

This anecdote, which Pliny offers as an account of the origins of drawing, contains the germ of the idea that animates him in writing his book: painting becomes a liberal art from the moment that it aims to render visible that which by definition escapes vision, or the spiritual inherent in the material. The figure is material illuminated by grace or love, confounded here in the term *venustas*, with which Pliny translates *charis* (grace, but first radiance); it has as its function to please, and we know that for Quintilian (12.10.59) the aim of pleasing is that of the middle style (which is moved by the noble and instructed by the simple), whose attribute is tenderness and that which we still call *fleuri* (*antheros* or *floridas*). We can posit here that this is the aim of the novel: to discern that which is properly human, to devote itself to simple figures rather than to myths, and to charm.

This somewhat *lay* dimension of the novel expresses itself through the term that designates it in French, a term that Huet glosses at length. Novels (*romans*) are so called because they are written in *Roman*, that is, a language that is neither vernacular nor Latin:

> The Roman language was that which the Romans introduced among the Gauls after having conquered them and which, having been corrupted over time by the mix of the language of the Gauls that had preceded it with that of the Franks or the Tudesque language that followed it, was neither Latin, nor Gaul, nor Frank, but something mixed, in which Roman nevertheless took the upper part, and which for that reason was always called Roman. . . . Roman comprising thus the most polite, learned, and universally understood language, the Chroniclers of Provence, that is, the authors of prose, and the poets of the same country, who were called Trouvères . . . used it to write their Tales and Poems, which were thus called *romans* [novels].[15]

Romaniser thus means to express oneself in a language that is *mixed* and learned at the same time, incontestably refined but as incontestably profane. Taking into consideration their *Roman* language, together with the fact that these are written texts, that they take the form of narratives, and that they are conducted in prose, reinforces the idea that the novel devotes itself to the human condition as such.

Huet, based on his conception of the *Aethiopica* as a model, is not far from defining the novelistic genre in Aristotelian terms. Love appears not as a sentiment, but as the revealing agent of both the spiritual and material

---

[15] Huet, *De l'origine des romans*, 125–26.

aspects of man. Huet evokes, beyond that, the discourse of Diotima in *The Banquet*, in order to insist conjointly on the *middle* dimension of the loving demon and the middle dimension of the novel. In this way, Huet places the category of mediocrity at the center of his definition of the novel.

By insisting, on the other hand, on the conjunction of fiction and prose in these stories, Huet bases his argument on a passage glossed by Quintilian, in which Aristotle declares that it is not verse that makes poetry, but *mimesis* (he translates this as *fiction*).[16] He relies further on a great number of references to works, in particular Italian works, in which the novel is envisaged as a form of poetry in prose, and so Huet anticipates one of the most important debates of the eighteenth century, relative to the problems posed by the translation of Homer into prose, which concerns the question of whether one can conceive of a poetry that is not measured, a form of poetry that would not contain any trace of the ancient pretension of the word convoking the divine on earth. The writing of *La vie de Marianne* will inscribe itself in this context.

By employing the precise formula of fictive or "false stories," Huet distinguishes the novel from true stories and draws on the idea of verisimilitude. He distinguishes the novel from two neighboring genres, the fable and history. The novel is distinct from the first, in that it is still of Christian rather than pagan inspiration: the enchantments within the novel must be credible and not too numerous; novels can contain the marvelous, but the fiction serves an incontestable truth (whence the possibility of instructing as well as distracting). Nevertheless, novels are not true, and they demand a particular manner of reading; they suppose of the reader something already akin to a sense of the fiction. Why are they not true? Because they must console, and reality is not consoling, as the good does not always triumph in reality— Lenglet-Dufresnoy will develop this thesis at length. Thus, the novel does not reflect reality in its always singular diversity; rather it idealizes reality and makes it endearing. It is in this respect that it belongs to the order of *mimesis*, which substitutes for monsters and cadavers their representation; it weaves a veil of beauty over the world in which we are captive.[17]

---

[16] "It is evident from the above that the poet must be more the poet of his plots than of his verses, inasmuch as he is a poet by virtue of the imitative element in his work, and it is actions that he imitates" (Aristotle, *Poetics* 1451b27, *The Complete Works of Aristotle*, ed. and trans. Jonathan Barnes [Princeton, N.J.: Princeton University Press, 1984], 2323). Cf. Aristotle, *Poétique*, trans. Roselyne Dupont-Roc and Jean Lallot (Paris: Seuil, 1980), 67.

[17] "Though the objects themselves may be painful to see, we delight to view the most realistic representations of them in art, the forms for example of the lowest animals and of dead bodies" (Ibid., 1448b9, 2318).

History may certainly provide the framework or plot for the novel, and often does: already in the *Aethiopica* Heliodorus evokes with greater verisimilitude than one would expect the tempests and attacks by pirates that make up the everyday experience of peoples of the sea, and he translates, in a more indirect manner, the sense of disorder that may animate the men of his day. However, these do not constitute his subject: because it is a matter of verisimilitude rather than truth, but also because it is a matter of verisimilitude rather than falsehood. Classical verisimilitude, as Huet represents the concept by drawing, after so many others, on Aristotle, is a verisimilar moral, linked to the idealizing dimension of mimetic synthesis.[18] Since historical events and characters rarely furnish the novelist with material likely to give pleasure and instruction (particularly to give pleasure, or to instruct on a moral plane), it is not suitable for the novelist to borrow his characters from the ranks of military heroes or lords who govern the world: the falsity of the narrative would be patent. If the novelist can sometimes recount the interior life of real men and women (and we can see this, for example, in the narratives devoted to the actual personage of Don Carlos), it is more convenient to concentrate the action of the novel in characters who have made no name for themselves and whose adventures would thus not be contestable. Thus, not only does the novel not develop the story of mythological beings, a fact that constitutes a first constraint, but its privileged object is interior existence—whether the point of view adopted vis à vis the great is psychological and moral, or the subjects under consideration are more common characters who are not illumined by history and, consequently, who find themselves attributed an existence that is essentially intimate.

More than a century after Huet, in his preface to *Crimes de l'amour* [*Crimes of Love*], Sade will return in one way to the distinction between the novel and history:

> The novel being, if it is possible to express oneself thus, *the tableau of secular mores*, is as essential as history to the philosopher who wants to understand man; for the chisel of history depicts man only when he makes himself seen; and then he is no more himself; ambition, pride cover his face with a mask that no longer shows us anything but those two passions, and not the man; the paintbrush of the novel, to the contrary, captures him from within [*dans*

---

[18] The story of Zeuxis and the virgins of Croton, which Batteux will also take up, perfectly illustrates this conception. On the question of mimesis envisaged as idealizing synthesis, see Catherine Perret, *Les porteurs d'ombre: Mimèsis et modernité* (Paris: Belin, 2001).

son intérieur] . . . captures him when he abandons this mask, and achieves a far more interesting, and at the same time a far more true, sketch—this is the usefulness of novels.[19]

While history has as its object events as they appear and people as they allow themselves to be seen, the novel has as its task, alongside the representation of a factual and verifiable truth, the elaboration of an *interior* truth, or making human motivations transparent. That Sade employs the expression "tableau of secular mores" to designate the novel, even if he does so with some precaution, indicates at once that we are neither in the domain of the sacred, nor in that of exceptional appearances, of excessively sumptuous exploits or manifestations; rather, we find ourselves squarely in a *mediocre* register. Or, if we reprise the analogy of painting: the novel is the equivalent to genre painting, deemed unworthy relative to historical painting.

———

So it seems that, even if the novel is not assigned precise rules at the dawn of a poetics, nevertheless, these rules are defined over the course of centuries, in correlation to the imitation of the *Aethiopica*, an imitation that constitutes an obligatory exercise for so long. Further, the contours of the genre are less fluid than one often thinks: a novel is a profane narrative, written in prose to articulate episodes tending toward an end; this narrative is fictive but verisimilar, which is to say as distanced from fable as from history; it takes as its object the interiority of humans in their earthly existence, and it gives rise to a poetics of *mediocrity* itself linked to the idea of prose. But it is necessary to refine this term: novelists devotes themselves to mediocre characters or characters envisaged in their *médiocritas* (whether that involves, in the seventeenth century, their dignity or honesty, the reference is simply to the public[20]), to

———

[19] Marquis de Sade, *Les crimes de l'amour*, "Idée sur le roman" (1800), in *Oeuvres complètes* (Paris: Pauvert, 1988), 10:75. For a partial translation of Sade, see *Crimes of Love*, trans. and intro. Margaret Crosland (London: P. Owen, 1996), including "Faxelange or The Wrongs of Ambition," "Dorgeville or The Criminal through Virtue," "Rodrigo or The Enchanted Tower: An Allegorical Tale," "Lorenza and Antonio: An Italian Story," and "The Comtesse de Sancerre or Her Daughter's Rival: Anecdote from the Court of Burgundy."

[20] On this question, see Eric Auerbach's study, "La cour et la ville" in *Vier Untersuchungen zur Geschichte der französichen Bildung* (Berne: Francke, 1951), trans. in *Scenes from the Drama of European Literature* (Minneapolis: University of Minnesota Press, 1984), 133–79, notes 239–45, and in *Le culte des passions: Essais sur le XVIIe siècle français* (Paris: Macula, 1998), 115–79.

characters mediocre in that they do not shine on the outside (whose adventures are rather those of interior, individual experience), and this in a style that is itself mediocre, neither too elaborate, nor charged with references.

The contemporary reader may be surprised and tempted to invoke the great baroque novels of Mademoiselle de Scudéry, for example, to demonstrate the inanity of such a claim; however, the preface to *Ibrahim* develops in the most rigorous fashion the traits that have just been delineated and binds them together with a rather systematic precision:

> But amidst all the rules that one must observe in the composition of these works, that of verisimilitude is, without doubt, the most necessary. . . .
>
> It is not that I propose to banish shipwrecks from my novels; I approve of them in the works of others, and I make use of them in mine. I even admit that the sea is the theater most apt for making great changes, and that some have named it the theater of inconstancy. But as all excess is a vice, I have made but moderate use of it, in order to maintain verisimilitude. Now the same aim has made it also necessary that my hero not be overwhelmed by that prodigious quantity of accidents that are visited on others, since, according to my definition, this is far from verisimilitude; since no man's life has ever occasioned such a degree of accident, it is better, in my opinion, to separate the adventures and make diverse stories of them, and to make many people act, in order to seem fecund and judicious together, and to remain always within the domain of verisimilitude if necessary. . . .
>
> After having described an adventure, a bold scene, or some surprising incident, capable of generating the most beautiful sentiments in the world, certain authors are contented by assuring us that such a hero thinks very lovely things, without telling us what those things are, and that is all that I would want to know. For what do I know whether or not in these events fortune has played as much a part as he? whether his valor is no more than a brutal valor? whether he suffered as an honest man the misfortunes that came his way? It is not at all by outward things, it is not at all by the caprices of fate that I want to judge him; it is by the movements of his soul, and by the things that he says. . . . But before I finish, it is necessary that I turn from things to the way in which they are said, and that I beg you also not to forget that the narrative style of the work should not be too inflated, no more than that of ordinary conversations; that the more easy it is, the more lovely; that it ought to flow like streams and not bound like torrents; and that the less constrained it is, the more perfect. I have thus aimed to observe an exact mediocrity, between the a vicious elevation and rampant baseness; I have held myself back in narration, and let myself go in harangues and passions: and

without speaking like the most extravagant or like the common people, I
have tried to speak like honest folk.[21]

Thus, Mademoiselle de Scudéry sets out to recount the life of a historical
personage, Ibrahim, and confronts an initial difficulty, insofar as this man
has achieved so many exploits and experienced so many astonishing adventures that his case surpasses the verisimilitude required in novelistic tales.
The novel demands a first operation, which, without renouncing thereby
the ancient charm of shipwrecks, consists in dissociating the material from
this existence, diffracting and dividing it among other characters, whereby
Ibrahim emerges more human, to be sure, but necessarily less marvelous. A
second operation, corollary to the first, consists in the narrative's closing in
on the feelings and thoughts of this character: "It is not at all by outward
things, not at all by the caprices of destiny that I want to judge him; it is by
the movements of his soul, and by the things that he says"; these *outward
things* certainly stand in opposition to the interior life that Sade will evoke,
after the majority of novelists of the eighteenth century, an interior life that
forms the center of everything. The life of Ibrahim becomes novelistic to the
degree that the reader can find in it an order according to which it evolves
autonomously: an order that does not belong to the fabulous, but to the distinctly human, because the novelist opens up the mysteries of its interior. It
is on the condition of finding himself provided with an interiority that the
historical personage enters into the novel and becomes, in the sense discussed above, a *figure*, the tangible manifestation of a spiritual enigma. For
that which is hidden in the great feats of Abraham and that which the novel
must make manifest is the value or the honesty of a man superior to fate.
Mademoiselle de Scudéry recalls Theagenes and Chariclia: human characters who are greater than the fate that threatens to overwhelm them, capable
of resisting all sort of temptation, characterized finally by an inflexible
virtue. Beyond his acts and beyond appearances, the character retains, at the
core, a space that we might call sacred, a *temple* that we call *virtue*. His self-
consciousness and reflections concerning his future constitute a precious interiority, allow us to speak of the *interior* of the character. Finally, Mademoiselle de Scudéry attaches a price to the fact that the writing of the novel not
be overwhelmed with images, and she invokes a model that promises an

---

[21] Madeleine de Scudéry, *Ibrahim ou l'illustre Bassa* (Paris: A. de Sommaville, 1641), preface.
For an early English translation, cf. *Ibrahim, or, The illustrious bassa: an excellent new romance, the
whole work in four parts, written in French by M. de Scudéry and now Englished by Henry Cogan,
Gent.* (London, 1652 and 1674).

extraordinary fate (in the work of Marivaux, for instance)—that of conversation. This conversation naturally must be worthy of the novelist and of her public, which is to say honest: herein, too, it seems that the object of the novel does not go beyond the most human aim.

The novel has as its object the secrets of the individual and the elaboration of his or her individuality, alike to none other although comparable to all (without which there is no possible consolation), an individuality that is absolutely loveable in the eyes of any who can see it and in itself so highly estimable that it can survive death (whence the debate over suicide, which so profoundly occupies eighteenth-century writers: does something in us survive life itself? can virtue preserve itself at the cost of existence?). This is why the history of the genre is related to that of contracting space: while Theagenes and Chariclia travel the world and undergo adventures that put their virtue to the test as they multiply in an extraordinary manner, Daphnis and Chloé will never leave their village, and their tests will be less determined by exterior events than by their own maturation. Later the shepherds of *L'Astrée* will spend days in the Forez, and Julie will never leave her beloved Valois. Accidents will become increasingly rare, less spectacular, and more narrowly connected to human rather than cosmic nature. Correspondingly, novelistic space will tend to become (and we know how Balzac will play on this, as in *Le lys dans la vallée*) the echo chamber of that interiority in which everything will eventually be concentrated, a real space and at the same time a utopia.

The idea of mediocrity can be developed thus in numerous directions and permits us to recover the concept of grace, which we associated above with that of the figure and which we understand from a platonic perspective. When Jean-Pierre Camus makes his *praise of devout stories*, it is by proposing a sort of definition of the human that can be seen from the perspective that we have tried to trace: "Man is not only a body, or he would be a beast; he is not simply a soul, or he would be an angel; instead it is a body infused with a soul that makes up this animal that we can call rational; it is a spirit enclosed in a portable prison, who sees nothing except through the windows that are the senses, who understands nothing except through this fabric."[22] The thinking here is that the human, hence the novel, finds itself caught in an intermediary place. The mediocre style associated with the conversational model and soon with the letter is exactly that "prose written with

---

[22] Jean-Pierre Camus, *Agathonphile ou les martyrs siciliens*, in *Eloge des histoires dévotes* (Paris: Cl. Chappelet, 1621).

art" recommended by Huet. The letter to Segrais develops a parallel between the manner of recounting in verse and in prose, accentuating thematic differences: not only "novels are simpler, less elevated, and less figurative in their invention and expression,"[23] but, while "poems have as their subject a military or political action and only occasionally concern love, novels, to the contrary, have love as their principal subject, and treat war and politics only incidentally."[24] The poetics of novelistic prose does not hold to the production of remarkable effects but to the weaving of modest and sometimes barely apparent signs. We need not rehearse all the novels that will exhibit throughout the eighteenth century a mediocrity in both subject and style, linking this to giving voice to an individual who publishes his or her desires and thoughts. But this is announced earlier, from the moment that the point of view of characters begins to govern the organization of the novel.

This modern definition of the novel, founded on Aristotelian categories of *mimesis*, verisimilitude, and mediocrity, takes as point of departure the remarkable reduction of the novel, of which even the preface of that heavy volume *Ibrahim* gives some idea: that reduction concerns space, characters, events, and style. It is certainly *La Princesse de Clèves* [*The Princess of Cleves*] that accomplishes in the most exemplary fashion that which resembles a purge.

The novel presents itself as a historical novel and mentions several actual events such as the death of Henry II, the matrimonial contrariety of Don Carlos, and the death of Mary Stuart. However, the dauphine is not considered exactly in terms of that which distinguishes her from other members of the court, but in terms of that which brings her close to the reader, namely the refinement of her manners, her curiosity, her coquetry—she perfectly realizes the qualities proper to her rank and to the milieu in which she evolves. The duke of Guise, in the same manner, is primarily treated as one of the pretenders to the heroine, in the same way as the Prince of Clèves and, later, as the duke of Nemours. The great events with which the duke of Guise might have been associated and in which he establishes his worth are only marginally evoked; they allow the author to weave a background, and this great soldier, this great politician appears only as an ousted and jealous suitor. The protagonists of the novel, receptacles for the highest classical virtues, are themselves fictive, and often furnished with lesser ranks than the historical figures. But that which makes Monsieur de Clèves a rare being is

---

[23] Huet, *De l'origine des romans*, 5.
[24] Ibid., 6.

the admirable love that he devotes to the princess, and he recalls Céladon; the duke of Nemours is exceptional by dint of the beauty of his figure and his seduction; finally the princess distinguishes herself from any other by her grace and unfortunate loyalty to her spouse. In each of these it is the *interior* person, such as his or her face sometimes allows us to see, that is remarkable. The narrative is recounted with simplicity of style and composition appropriate to the evocation of these characters who radiate so discreet a brilliance, and it is devoted to exclusively interior events: Mademoiselle de Chartres has married a man whom she esteems; she falls for another man who pursues her with captivating charm; she is tormented by this love, descries it to her husband who dies of jealousy, and withdraws from the world. The action of the novel is extremely tenuous; it haunts only Paris and Coulommiers, where nothing is produced except through exchanged glances and a few words. Madame de La Fayette conducts with an astonishing subtlety a nearly nonexistent intrigue and manifests in relief nearly imperceptible traits: Nemours silently surprised by the princess whose portrait he disrobes, the princess perceived by Nemours while contemplating the painting in which he figures, Clèves scrutinizing his spouse while he recites the names of his possible rivals in order to discern any traces of disturbance. Each never ceases to spy on the others and to seek to penetrate the secrets of that interior existence that comprises that sole subject of the novel—tears, blushes, sudden pallor. A reading of Saint-Réal's *Dom Carlos* [*Don Carlos, or, An historical relation of the unfortunate life, and tragical death of that Princet of Spain son to Philip II*] would lead to comparable observations: there we find the same gathering of historical personages envisaged in intimate terms rather than in terms of their actions, the choice of *mediocre* heroes, in the sense of honest characters perfectly likely to achieve the virtues proper to their rank, and the principle of a continual examination of the most refined expressions.

Thus, it would seem that this genre, to which we ordinarily attach all the prestige of the marvelous, was worked over very early on by the temptation that Flaubert will call, in a manner that seemed extraordinarily modern, that of writing "a book about nothing"—in which intrigue is extenuated, in which it is a matter of paying attention to silences and to the slimmest of signs. Without doubt, Heliodorus's novel contained drama and astonishing acts; but their role was that of putting virtue and love to the test, permitting the author to weave together the characters' interior stories. A rift between interior and exterior begins to emerge, a gap that would widen definitively in the Christian vision of the world. When divine grandeur manifests itself in the throes of passion, when the facades of the cathedral are covered by monsters that guard its inner temple, then the conviction grows that the unity of the figure is not inherent, but rather the object of a quest. Appearances can dissimulate shameful secrets and be themselves fallacious. Two things becomes essential in the eyes of that modern individual shaped by Christianity and progressively exiled from an earthly existence: *intimate sentiment* (a rubric from Diderot and Alembert's *Encyclopédie*), which permits one to surpass any form of contingency; and the Christian idea of conscience powerfully relayed by the Cartesian notion of *fiction*, which is rooted in the formula of the *cogito*. Mademoiselle de Scudéry's or Jean-Pierre Camus's rereading of Heliodorus makes sense from this perspective: the marvelous is eliminated in the name of religion, which primarily determines the focus on the prestige of an interiority that exercises itself very little in the outside world.

A strange phenomena follows from this, manifest in eighteenth-century literature. The majority of novels will be permeated by references to the *romantic*, understood in at least two different senses: the *romantic* related to events, marvelous in some manner, and the psychological *romantic*, or the thought of the invincible charms of virtue. In many cases, the refusal of the former variant of the *romantic* will serve as the basis for the latter, linked to the prestige of interiority; but the form of the novel (*roman*) will tend to disintegrate (beginning in the final years of the eighteenth century) with the accusations leveled at the second variant of the *romantic*, which is constitutive of the genre from its very beginning and is not simply a category of the imagination. It is necessary to point this out in order to appreciate the degree to which the appeal to *nothing* is active throughout the history of the novel.

The notion of mediocrity cannot remain stable but undergoes flux, and soon the idea itself is degraded. Classical mediocrity was the guarantee of the suitability of the work to its public: in some sense it revealed polite mores and resulted from just scales. But the fate of the picaresque novel, which held to established values in reverse and introduced the ignoble in the place of the mediocre, which hatched the mediocre only in secret, discreetly transformed the genre. A suspect form, that of autobiography, would bear witness to this generalization. We know that the *picaro* takes over in his own voice in order to recount his life because he is unworthy of being evoked by another, and his prose contains traces of his infamous origins.[25] This form spreads over the course of the eighteenth century. The most ordinary procedure consists

---

[25] Cf. Maurice Molho, "Introduction à la pensée picaresque," in *Romans picaresques espagnols* (Paris: Gallimard, Pléiade, 1968); Thomas Pavel, *La pensée du roman* (Paris: Gallimard, 2003).

in loaning one's quill to one or several characters, authors of letters or memoirs, which, purportedly, are not destined for publication—a procedure that patently introduces imperfection into the work. Marivaux, Prévost, Diderot, Rousseau, Laclos, and later, Senancour or Benjamin Constant will all pass (though not without equivocation, to be sure) for simple editors of collections incidentally fallen into their hands. The majority will insist on the formal defects (reflections of the defaults of another order) attached to the fictive authors and will thus defend, in an oblique manner, a singular view of the value of the novel: the imperfection of the writing and of the characters themselves becomes a guarantee of the moral verity of the book, and ought to give rise to a new, paradoxical beauty. It is along these lines that Marianne repeats to the destined reader of her long letters that she does not know how to write; the purported editor underlines, at the beginning of the second part

> This is not written in the ordinary form of the novel, or of stories written simply to amuse. But neither did Marianne ever dream of writing a novel. Her friend asks her for the story of her life, and she writes it in her own way. Marianne has no formal model in mind. She is not an author at all; she is a woman who thinks, who has passed through various states, who has seen a lot; finally, whose life is a tapestry of events that have given her a certain knowledge of the heart and character of men and who, in telling her adventures, imagines herself with her friend, speaking to her, engaging her, answering her; and in that spirit, she mixes indiscriminately the events that she recounts with her reflections on these events; here is the tone with which Marianne undertakes her work. It is neither, if you wish, the tone of the novel, nor that of history, but her own; do not ask for any other. Imagine that she is not writing at all, but that she is speaking; it may be that by placing yourself at this vantage point, her manner of recounting will not seem so disagreeable to you.[26]

We find this preoccupation signaled by Madame de Scudéry concerning the style of the novel, which should be of an honest mediocrity based on a conversational model; but this preoccupation becomes all the more vivid here, as Marivaux needles his reader by proposing a novel that is not a novel, which is a clever way of making the reader feel its full verisimilitude. The character of Marianne takes up this part by insisting on the absence of style

---

[26] Pierre Marivaux, *La vie de Marianne* (1731–41), trans. R. Arienta (Milan, 1951), 2:508.

in her writing and by underlining the error inherent in reading her narrative as a novel, given the paucity of events recounted within it and the faults of certain personages, in particular Valville, who derives too much from Hylas rather than Céladon (but must we underline that the imperfect lover Hylas is also a character from a novel, and that La Fontaine viewed him as the pivotal figure of the story?). Marivaux thus contends that he does not cultivate in *La vie de Marianne* a great genre, but that he elaborates a philosophy of sentiment or feeling,[27] founded on the consideration of the most human. He will push this ambiguous path further when he invents that character of Jacob. A little later he adds:

> Further, many readers may not like the quarrel between the coachman and Mme Dutour. There are folk who find it beneath them to direct a glance at that which opinion has treated as ignoble; but those who are a little more philosophical, who are a little less dupes of the distinctions that pride has placed on the things of this world, those folk will not be annoyed to see what man is within a coachman, and what woman is in a mere shop girl. . . . [28]
>
> There are folk whose vanity mixes with all that they do, even their reading. Give them the history of the human heart in great conditions, that will become an important object to them; but do not speak to them of mediocre states, they do not want to see the acts of any but lords, princes, kings, or at least people who have cut a grand figure. Nothing but this exists for their noble tastes.[29]

These observations permit us to appreciate the quasi-*theoretical* value of the subject of *La vie de Marianne*. Because we do not know Marianne's social origins, she belongs to a no-man's-land; internally experiencing her election, Marianne seeks to adjust her situation accordingly, and the subtitle of the novel reveals that she succeeds. But the ignominy of the picaresque is never far from the honorable nobility that the character ascribes to him or herself, and the proximity of the two may comprise a new manifestation of ancient *mediocrity*. To adjust one's condition according to the idea one has of oneself might be called virtue; but the tribulations of the hero in such stories of social ascension come close to making him kin to the *picaro*. The story of Marianne's social ascension (the title of which reveals that she becomes a

---

[27] On this question, see the preface by Jean Dagen to *La vie de Marianne* (Paris: Gallimard, Folio, 1997).

[28] Marivaux, *La vie de Marianne*, 2:508.

[29] Ibid., 1:48.

countess) thus permits Marivaux to write in praise of *mediocrity* and of the novel as it is had been understood from the seventeenth century.

In a comparable manner, though far more ambiguously, in the second preface to *La nouvelle Héloïse* that takes the form of a dialogue with a sullen and glum editor, Rousseau insists on the stylistic imperfections of a work that he does not want to offer either as a memoir or as a novel:

> N. In other words, weakness of language proves strength of feeling?
> R. Sometimes it at least reveals its truth. Read a love letter written by an Author in his study, by a wit trying to shine. If he has at least a little fire in his brain, his letter will, as we say, scorch the paper; the heat will go no farther. You will be charmed, even stirred perhaps; but with a stirring that is fleeting and arid, that will leave you nothing to remember but words. In contrast, a letter really dictated by love; a letter from a truly passionate Lover, will be desultory, diffuse, full of verbose, disconnected, repetitious passages. His heart, filled with an overflowing sentiment, ever repeats the same thing, and is never done, like a running spring that flows endlessly and never runs dry. Nothing salient, nothing remarkable; neither the words, nor the turns, nor the sentences are memorable; there is nothing in it to admire or to be struck by. And yet one feels the soul melt; one feels moved without knowing why. The strength of the sentiment may not strike us, but its truth affects us, and that is how one heart can speak to another.[30]

The notes reinforce this discourse throughout these letters whose penetrating clumsiness and charm Rousseau will often underline conjointly. We have seen that ancient grace reflected the human orientation toward the divine and expressed itself through a perfection of the unsurpassable form (thus, Chariclia's beauty); but modern grace, which continues to comprise the object of the novel, is linked to the whole gamut of tangible particularities of a being, which is to say, to the fragility of the mortal. The moment when imperfection begins to become the peak of humanity announces the decline of the *figure* in the sense in which, following Auerbach[31] and based on Pliny, it has been defined above: already Marianne, but also Saint-Preux and Julie are touching because they err. The demand for a mediocre style is paired

---

[30] Jean-Jacques Rousseau, *Julie, or the New Heloise*, 10; cf. *Julie ou La nouvelle Héloïse Pléiade* ed., 15.

[31] Erich Auerbach, *Figura* (1944), in *Scenes from the Drama of European Literature*, 11–76, notes 229–37.

thus with a group of other demands, here formulated by N., which permit the novelist to make explicit his radical departures: "As for the focus, it is everywhere at once, it is nil. Not a single evil deed; not a single wicked man to make us fear for the good ones. Events so natural, so simple that they are too much so; nothing unexpected; no dramatic surprises. Everything is foreseen well in advance; everything comes to pass as foreseen. Is it worth recording what anyone can see every day in his own home or in his neighbor's?"[32] This amounts to Rousseau's positing that, in *La nouvelle Héloïse*, there is no novel or romance in the sense of the term used to designate the fabulous, that the characters are common though good, that nothing happens. Or further, that there is no intrigue, and there are no heroes—only is a form of confinement and the faltering style that has been at issue. Rousseau expresses here, well before Zola, the thought that "the first man who passes is a sufficient hero."[33] The widening of a rupture with the exterior world accentuates the outcome of a tendency of the novel to fold back on itself, which here takes the form of a meditation on virtue.

A comparison elucidates Rousseau's thinking, which he will develop within the novel itself; it permits us to elucidate the idea of a poetics of prose that appeared earlier: "It is a long ballad [romance/novel in verse] the stanzas of which taken separately are not at all moving, but their succession has a cumulative effect."[34] Thus, a continuity develops, a new harmony evolves, founded on the agency of modest and practically imperceptible objects; or a new voice makes itself heard, resonating between words, perhaps in the intervals between exchanged letters—this is truly a melody, Italian style, far from the great machines of French opera. All this is also, as we have seen, that which is gathered in the idea of mediocrity, which adjoins that of grace.[35] Poetry of the heart, in *La nouvelle Héloïse*, does not seem separable from poetic prose, written in a middle style in which it is clear that beauty depends on a particular organization, on a framework comparable to that veil with which Claire wraps Julie's dead face. We approach the second term

---

[32] Rousseau, *Julie, or the New Heloise*, 8; cf *Julie ou La nouvelle Héloïse*, 13.

[33] Emile Zola, *Deux définitions du roman* (1866), in *Oeuvres complètes*, (Paris: Cercle du Livre Précieux, 1968), 10:281.

[34] Rousseau, *Julie, or the New Heloise*, 12; cf. *Julie ou La nouvelle Héloïse*, 18.

[35] Cf. Abbé Antoine de Cournand, *Les Styles, poëme en quatre chants* (Vve Duchesne, 1781): Cournand distinguishes four styles or shades: the simple, the gracious, the sublime, and the somber. To the first corresponds the bucolic genre, to the second the novel "represented by Arioste, to the third the ode and to the fourth poetry of the tombs." It is remarkable that the gracious style thus comes to designate what had earlier been called *mediocre* or *average* [*moyen*, belonging to the middle].

of Flaubert's dream of "a book about nothing . . . , which would be held together by the internal strength of its style": a learned and rhythmic prose, that tends to undo/abolish itself.[36]

The novel is thus defined—through its prefaces, forewords of fictive editors, notes, and even the remarks of this or that narrator—as a minor genre, characterized by a search for simplicity, the diminishing of intrigue, and the foregrounding of the most ordinary events (which we should not confuse, however, with the trivial or base—such are Julie's pleasures at Clarens, pleasures such as drinking coffee from time to time or taking walks in the gardens that she cultivates). At the same time, the novel elevates the most modest to a higher rung than it seems at the outset, by dint of that organization based on the major theme of testing virtue.

But virtue in the novel is singular, and it ought not to be confounded with Christian virtue, though it may approach this at times. We ought rather to think of the idea of grace in terms of its more subtle and somewhat confusing aspects. And in order to apprehend grace in this sense, we might return to Pliny's evocation of painting and more precisely the art of Apelle, which consists in making objects and above all the figures represented on a canvas shine with a particular radiance: Pliny's vision of art anticipates the novel's grace more than Plotin's and the neoplatonism following from the *Banquet* by supposing that one may see the body as a possible repository of the Idea and reach this idea by means of love. The character in the novel is a vulnerable being in whom something of the divine is manifest, according to the old view of grace; in a more modern version, virtue is the promise of good that compensates for the misfortune of original sin; it can allow one to find happiness on earth (Lenglet-Dufresnoy insists on this at length)—and the whole instructive force of the novel lies in this promise. Virtue is thus that which gives beauty its value by veiling the crudeness of nature itself. We can perceive it as a principle of radiation, and it is exactly so that it strikes Valmont in the house inhabited by the president of Tourvel, as before him it struck Saint-Preux whenever he was near Julie. Virtue has its attendants: a modest veil, delicate blushing, a sweet voice, reserved and charming movements, the radiance of the whole person, and it is principally on the face that virtue expresses itself, inscribing the movement of the passions on the physiognomy. This is also to say that virtue holds to the definition of the human itself, if we

---

[36] Gustave Flaubert to Louis Colet, January 16, 1852, in *Correspondance* (Paris: Gallimard, Pléiade, 1980), 2:31. *The Letters of Gustave Flaubert, 1830–1857*, selected, ed., and trans. Francis Steegmuller (Cambridge: Belknap Press, Harvard University Press, 1980), 154.

take as human something along the lines described by Father Yves André, one of the theoreticians of grace in the eighteenth century, who described the human figure as a lamp that radiated as much as a page covered in signs:

> Does not [man's] face alone seem formed to be the seat of all the graces? The serenity of his face, which announces an easy approach; the sweetness of his eyes, which promises you a favorable welcome; a living brow that lights up in your presence; the smile of his mouth, that precede his words to assure you of the pleasure he has in seeing you; the whole enclosed in a subtle and transparent envelope that reveals to you, as through a fine gauze, all the feelings of his soul. We do not see in that face, it is true, as many colors as in our flowerbeds or on the plumage of certain birds: white and red brushed on with art make up all the coloring. The reason for this is entirely natural; the multiplication of too many colors would have banished graces far more estimable. A dull or lightly colored palette is necessary, if I dare say, to register new shades at every moment, according to circumstance, and to render the most touching expressions.[37]

We may conceptualize from this the importance of portraits in all of *romanesque* literature, as in *La nouvelle Héloïse*, in which we have such a description even of the virtue of Julie. It is self-evident that these portraits become increasingly individualized; fidelity is the sovereign virtue, and Saint-Preux reproaches a painter for having neglected an imperfection on Julie's face, an imperfection in which lies all of her grace.[38]

Virtue is a means of preserving that portion of the divine, far from any totality, that each person bears within; it is not content properly speaking: rather it is the delineation within the individual of a space that would be that of self-consciousness but that can also find many other formulations. We may find a valuable clarification of this concept in the rather enigmatic follow-up that Lenglet-Dufresnoy links to Huet's letter: *De l'usage des romans* [*On the Usage of Novels*] is a very conservative work, undeniably moral in its aims, but in which morality is confounded with purely social conventions. We thus learn in this work that, in novels, young ladies return from the abductions or seductions to which they fall victim more virginal

---

[37] Père Yves André, *Essai sur le beau*, 7th discourse, "Sur les grâces," in *Oeuvres philosophiques de Père André*, ed. Victor Cousin (Paris, 1843), 150.

[38] "He has made the lower face exactly oval. He did [not] notice that slight inflection that, separating the chin from the cheeks, makes their contour less regular and more graceful" (Rousseau, *Julie, or the New Heloise*, 238; cf. *Julie, ou La nouvelle Héloïse*, 292).

than when they departed, and that Oriane's virtue is not such that it would bore Amadis. Lenglet-Dufresnoy holds to the term *virtue*, however, because this term designates honesty (as a social value), with the corresponding aesthetic constituted by mediocrity. Further, he avows that virtue, in the sense that it was evoked in the beginning of this essay under the name of marvelous humanity, does not cease to be subjected in the novel to attacks that will be fatal to it, and to the novel along with it. Thus the virtue of Madame de Clèves, as little as we think of it, is a very ambiguous one: assuredly, the princess seeks to preserve something, which is decisive; but nothing allows her, as much as she convokes diverse arguments, to identify the nature of this something. Is it a matter of conjugal purity, of posthumous fidelity to her spouse, of his resting in peace? Is she afraid of being loved by Monsieur de Nemours or of no longer being loved one day? Could not that which she is trying to preserve be love as well as her avowed and often alleged faith? Nothing in the reading of the novel allows us to answer these questions, except precisely that which allows us to doubt the purity of the character.

This ambivalence becomes all the more problematic in the eighteenth century, in large part due to Marivaux. We may recall the story of Marianne: while she was still a very young girl, the carriage in which she was riding turned over, many people died, and it was impossible to determine whether the child belonged to the masters or to the servants. However, Marianne has a compelling appearance, which endears her to several people, and she intends to recuperate that which she esteems her native condition. This takes her to Paris, drives her to gain the admiration of several handsome young men during Mass, and to pursue an extraordinary comedy in order to seduce the young Valville. The scene of the accident and of its consequences is very eloquent: Marianne allows the young man to see her foot, an unconventional but necessary (?) move for medical reasons, which places her in a very delicate casuistry, according to which we measure the propriety of her consciousness according to the care taken with her rather than according to the sacrifices made to him. Valville desires to know her better, which requires the admission of an embarrassing fact (that she lodges and works at the home of the laundress Dutour). Marianne finds it expedient to cry, and thus makes evident at once her sincerity and natural suffering as a person obliged because of the unfolding of terrible events to live an ignoble life. Marianne then invokes her virtue, which she admits with some pleasure, and this will be her essential recourse in ascension, that she is very useful to him. Does she question herself in advance about this precious aid? Only to observe with surprise that in the worst of situations she retains certain preoccupations that fortunately distract her from more serious chagrins. Does she attach herself to anyone? Immediately, worries about finery arise along with expressions intended to be moving. But it is never possible to postulate about her virtue: Marianne's consciousness of herself forms the entirety of that virtue. In contrast, Tervire, all of whose actions demonstrate that she is in effect *predestined*, denudes herself, and we may think that the novelist confronted, before the formula became both very radical and very official, *the fate of vice* and the *misfortunes of virtue*. But the elaboration of this character is so subtle that we do not know whether the conjoining of candor and science that characterizes Marianne, like Jacob, is not a new mode of mediocrity.

One doubt persists, and we are tempted to posit a relationship between that which Marianne calls her virtue and that which others call vanity, characterized also by an anxiety about pretense. Here a reading of Diderot and Alembert's *Encyclopédie* is of great interest insofar as we observe in it precisely this suspect proximity. Virtue is defined as the principle of a possible reparation, since humankind was forced to leave the terrestrial paradise; humanity is not good (for goodness is an attribute of God alone) but it tends toward the lost good—in a certain way, the inaugural episode of the overturned carriage might well be, in Marianne's life, the equivalent of this fault and of this misfortune. But vanity is defined in very similar terms: it is that which remains to humans, banished from an earthly paradise and condemned to find, alone, means of expressing an interiority, which they are not certain is not empty. The implied conclusion is that virtue and vanity are extremely close, even that they are doubles for each other—the one without proper content, the other decidedly and etymologically empty.

The novels of the eighteenth century develop this ambiguity at leisure: we see in them virtue suffering without remedy (thus, the virtue of the religious heroine of Diderot, who in some senses announces Justine), and the *figure*, in the sense in which we understand the term, becomes dislodged. The novel's promotion of a new character, the libertine, is the cause or effect of this. The libertine shares with the *picaro* both cynicism and lucidity with regard to social rules; but the character's engagement is more metaphysical than moral, insofar as by taking the position of identifying virtue strictly with vanity, it denies that any radiance illumines humanity other than material itself, and it defies God. The libertine is thus a great lord or lady whose physiognomy announces the greatest virtues—it matters that appearance announces the best; but what drives the intrigue is that the expression of the character is also a grimace, and the face a mask. Even this is not always so certain, and doubt thus underpins the novelistic/*romanesque* in the work.

Is Manon then loose? Her figure promises sublime virtues that she does not possess, and her death is worthy of a pure lover. Is des Grieux a rogue? His figure announces the honest man. He may be virtuous, and Tiburce gives voice to the virtuous postulation that characterizes him, but he also plays on his good appearance to steal and murder. Des Grieux calls himself a Jansenist: grace does not command him, and he has been moved only by Manon. In the same way, in Laclos's novel, Valmont oscillates: he is truly taken and truly concerned with giving an extraordinary spin to his enterprise. The two planes of love and libertinage are superimposed and confounded—his letters to the Marquise de Merteuil representing the libertine version of love and the letters to Madame de Tourvel, the sentimental version of libertinage. He seduces his lover by invoking grace, through the intervention of a good father; he abandons her out of vanity; he dies because he loves her. Abbé Prévost and Laclos, following suit after Marivaux whose ambiguity we ought to take stock of, devote themselves to human complexity; they are not content to recount "the agony of virtue"[39] (according to Valmont's formula) but proceed to its autopsy.[40] The nature of mediocrity has changed; the term no longer recalls an intermediary position of humanity, midway between the material and the spiritual or the animal and the divine, but indicates our duality (or duplicity): rather than being neither angel nor beast, we are at once angel and beast, conjoining the noble and ignoble. Both these and those characters, in effect, invoke virtue: they also make evident its inverse, which is vanity. The inverse operation is possible and the work, ironically composed, may never find a point of resolution. In musical terms, the harmony is decidedly destroyed; the novel devotes itself to isolated, fragile voices, enchanted and deceiving—to melodies—which profoundly transforms its orientation.[41]

We have observed that the history of the novel is first that of an emptying out, of a diminishment of what is conventionally called the *romanesque* and

---

[39] Choderlos de Laclos, *Les liasons dangereuses* (Durand, 1782), pt. 2, letter 70, and pt. 3, letter 99; cf. *Oeuvres complètes* (Paris: Gallimard, Pléiade, 1979), 138, 220: "My plan, on the contrary, is to make her perfectly aware of the value and extent of each one of the sacrifices she makes me; not to proceed so fast with her that remorse is unable to catch up; it is to show her virtue breathing its last in long-protracted agonies" (*Les liaisons dangereuses*, trans. P.W.K. Stone [New York: Penguin, 1961], 150); "I assisted this eveing at the death-agony of virtue" (230).

[40] Diderot, in his reading of Shaftesbury, proposed in a note to undertake "the autopsy of virtue." Cf. "Principes de la philosophie morale, ou Essai sur le mérite et la vertu, avec des réflexions, d'après Anthony Cooper, lord Ashley, 3ᵉ comte de Shaftesbury," in *Oeuvres philosophiques et dramatiques de M. Diderot*, 6 vols. (Amsterdam, 1772), vol. 1.

[41] On this subject, see the thesis of Claude Jamin, *L'imaginaire de la musique au siècle des lumières* (University of Tours, 1996; C-D Dietwork verlag Aachen, 2001).

that attaches itself at the outset to the multiplication of events inclined to favor finally a recognition through the blossoming of love and virtue. This initial development lead to the denunciation of the *romanesque,* understood as the organization of a narrative around the virtue of characters exposed to the seductions of the world but preserved in their integrity by the power of love: it is not immaterial that the Marquise de Merteuil, railing against Valmont's love for the President and against her nascent virtue, accuses him precisely of being *romanesque,* and that Valmont, in turn, abandons the President in order to escape this insult.[42] The narrative's concentration on the interior core of characters understood in terms of their individuality rather than exemplarity, which especially allowed the appearance of the picaro and of the libertine in literature, results in a reorientation of the genre that is not only of a moral nature. We may observe a tendency to construct the novel as a long monologue—as is the case in novels written in the first person, such as Senancour's *Obermann,* Constant's *Adolphe,* or Chateaubriand's *René,* whether an epistolary novel in a single voice, a form of confession, or taking another form. Here we find a figure (is this still a figure?) drawn with fluid contours, who feels the void of virtue, the impossibility of loving, the distancing of nature (herein lies the whole question of the modern sublime), and the porous nature of any human being relative to the world. Each tries at first to test virtue, but virtue does not resist temptation, and the plot depends on a perduring failure. Concomitantly, a formal prowess seems also to have become the object of the work: characters are rarified, and nothing happens other than the elevation of a funereal chant—Constant and Senancour are proud exemplars. Adolphe is not far from the type of the libertine of good appearance, and his story plays with the possibilities to the point that one can never rule strictly on his conduct, which is, nevertheless, all that is at issue. Simultaneously, continuity is lost, as if the irregularity of breath and the precariousness of existence itself were becoming perceptible. We might be tempted to see in *René* the inaugural text of a new era, so clearly is the sole formula the "wave of passions" that serves as measure of the degree to which virtue, no longer envisioned as the precious temple we spoke of earlier, has revealed its reflexive or tautological dimension—or, in the end, its emptiness. *Obermann* permits us to appreciate forcefully the reach of this reversal, insofar as Senancour also uses, in several instances, the term

---

[42] *Les liaisons dangereuses,* pt. 4, letter 144; cf. *Oeuvres complètes,* 33: "Let the stern critics who accuse me of a romantic and unhappy love show me then what they can do; let them affect more prompt, more brilliant ruptures."

romanesque, which he associates with the thought of this defunct virtue in which he no longer believes. That which Obermann substitutes for virtue is sensibility, a painful opening to the world, which indicates, at the least, that the subject is no longer inexorable and that we can no longer, for any reason, identify the human being with "a vase in which spirituality would be enclosed."[43] To designate this new age, which is no longer *romanesque,* Senancour employs a new term, with a flexible content, which is that of *romanticism.*

Madame de Staël came close to pursuing in *Corinne* a theoretical reflection on this transformation: wounded by the unhappy love of that austere Christian, Lord Nevil, the inspired poetess, Corinne, no longer finds access to representation, loses the capacity to detect her own virtue, and no longer hears anything but the mortal voice that rises from within her. Thus, the sight of antique statues, such as *Niobé,* or suffering becomes equal to beauty, because the human is perceived in its tension toward the divine, and these evoke a long, fragmentary poem, which itself seems the image of her rent heart. Corinne's new grace is that of dying from having singled herself out, of no longer being the radiant sibyl that she had been, but a flower touched by death.

The entire nineteenth century would pursue this long task of an "anatomy of virtue," and we should understand this term *anatomy* in a fairly literal sense, noting well that it is a matter of opening and cutting out in order to learn and that at the end of the operation there may be nothing left. The novelists of the time will continue to place at the center of their interest the relationship between the inside and the outside—for example, the idea of the influence of a milieu corresponds to this concern. But no *virtue,* in the sense that we have discussed it from the first pages of this study, any longer resists this milieu, and the term itself seems obsolete, whether Rastignac is being corrupted or Eugénie Grandet is weakening. The matter is aggravated, as we know well, in *Madame Bovary,* and Zola, several years later, will make his case in terms of social determinism. The main object of the novel that we call *realist* seems to be to take the measure of that crushing weight suffered by humankind and to consider *interiors* rather than *interiority* or *insideness,* without passing thereby through the subtle hermeneutic system put in place a little earlier (during the era of discreet tears and delicate blushes). Novelists will make room for the most revolting flows and tears.

---

[43] Marcel Proust uses this formula in *Sodom and Gomorrhe* (1921–22) in *À la recherche du temps perdu* (Paris: Gallimard, Pléiade, 1988), 3:153–54.

All of them identify themselves as doctors and even surgeons: Balzac, still close, however, to eighteenth-century thought (we can be persuaded easily of this by reading *Les secrets de la Princesse de Cadignan* or *Massimila Doni*) sustained/supported/underpinned *La comédie humaine* with a biological metaphor, having Madame de Mortsauf die of a repugnant stomach malady. Saint-Beuve would gravely reproach Flaubert for having written "with a scalpel," and Zola compared himself, in the preface to *Thérèse Raquin*, to a surgeon forgetting himself in an amphitheater.

These were not simply metaphors; rather they actually produced something that is most pertinently expressed in Zola's phrase: "our analysis always remains cruel."[44] The question is precisely one of cruelty, to the degree in which the preservation of the figurative system rests on the envelope, because now it is the invisible that illumines tangible appearances. Appearances henceforth can no longer suffice, nor can expressions sufficiently elucidate the mysteries of interiority: Flaubert, the Goncourts, and Zola go beyond the play of light on the surface that still characterizes the novels of Marivaux or Rousseau (to a lesser degree). They penetrate their characters' consciousness and reveal the work of death in that domain. In a corollary move, they devote themselves to the existence of the body in its most concrete dimensions. At the same time, the novelist abandons the *mediocre* regime that had still maintained itself in the preceding century, despite the assaults of libertinage—or rather, the novelist decisively seeks to conjoin the base and noble. Thus, we read in Flaubert's letters, during the time he was writing *Madame Bovary*, that "the *hideousness* in bourgeois subjects ought to replace the tragic, which is incompatible with them."[45] The Goncourts then conceive of a modern form of tragedy in *Germinie Lacerteux*,[46] and Zola presents adaptations of *Phaedrus* and *King Lear* in *La curée* and *La terre de hideuses*.

Certainly Flaubert is still classical—we have demonstrated that his orientation toward "a book about nothing" is a defining trait of the novel and

---

[44] Émile Zola, *Le roman expérimental* (Charpentier, 1880) in *Oeuvres complètes*, 1,321: "our analysis always remains cruel, because our analysis cuts to the core of the human cadavre." Cf. *The Experimental Novel and Other Essays*, trans. Belle M. Sherman (New York: Haskell House, 1964).

[45] Gustave Flaubert to Louis Colet, November 29, 1853, in *Correspondance*, 2:469. This letter is not included in Steegmuller's two-volume edition of Flaubert's correspondence.

[46] "We were curious to know whether Tragedy, that conventional form of a forgotten literature and a vanished society, was really dead; whether, in a land without caste or legal aristocracy, the miseries of the humble and poor would mean as much to interest, to emotion, to pity as those of the great and rich; whether, in a word, the tears shed below could touch as deeply as those shed above" (Edmond and Jules de Goncourt, *Germinie Lacerteux*, trans. with intro. Leonard Tancock [Harmondsworth: Penguin Books, 1984], 15).

that his invention of a poetic prose, which was still wholly prosaic, had been long in the making. Further, Flaubert maintains the theoretical framework of ancient virtue: Emma is beautiful, superior to the fate allotted to her, and conscious of this; she conceives of love as the exclusive condition of recognition—and it is precisely this sense of grandeur that Baudelaire would underline in his reading of the novel. But as we know, Emma's virtue soon reveals its vanity, to the degree that it may seem crazy to some readers to point out the shadow inherent in *bovarisme*. Emma does not find love, rather she seeks love; she does not deceive her husband with one lover, as Yseult would, but rather with two lovers, which makes her a prostitute. And as she seeks love, she attempts to fabricate various envelopes, to compose a wondrous appearance, purchasing the dresses that will soon be her ruin. Whether we find her in the midst of the countryside or warming herself in a corner by the fire, her figure is not described, but rather we apprehend the sensations she feels, as if she were nothing but a body fashioned according to impressions of the outside—this would seriously scandalize Brunetière. Her thoughts are recounted in indirect free discourse, in a long novel that allows the duration of the imperfect tense to unfurl to such an extent that readers can believe they have entered the character's mind. Finally, she vomits ink with a hiccup at the moment of her death—this is not a death inspired by love—as if the very material Flaubert had used was her poison. Nevertheless, Emma's vision of the world enchants it no less than earlier visions, as Félicité's soon would also enchant the world; and the text gives rise to a form of beauty that is still one projected by a character, as mired as that character might be in a sordid reality. The Goncourts will pursue this direction, developing in *Germinie Lacerteux* the horrifying story of a servant enraptured with the *romanesque* and who allows us to see finally, in the final pages of the novel, that head of the Medusa from which novelists had been trying to distance themselves from the very origins of the genre.

———

This is the end. The novel had inscribed itself in the Aristotelian system that seemed to exclude it; it determined to make horror itself loveable, and that determined its tranquil and consoling course.[47] It seems that its ancient and

———

[47] This image of a tranquil navigation underpins Maurice Blanchot's study of the novel and narrative in "Le chant des Sirènes," in *Le livre à venir* (Paris: Gallimard, 1959); *The Book To Come*, trans. Charlotte Mandell (Stanford, Calif.: Stanford University Press, 2003).

very singular vocation of depicting the human in a strictly human framework led it to an irrevocable reversal of appearances. It was able to preserve a certain nostalgia for lost aspects, which can be discerned even in the darkest novels of Jean Genet or Céline, but evinced a new face: a poetic form, in effect, rooted in the depths of the body and in the fragility of that other material, the word, that seeks grace by revoking the figure and that we ordinarily call the narrative or plot. We understand, thus, that the novel in effect respected rules; and the first of these was to put its hope in love.

Translated by Sharon Lubkemann Allen

FREDRIC JAMESON

The Experiments of Time: Providence and Realism

Phenomenology of the Happy Ending

Happy endings are not as easy to bring off as you might think: at least in literature; but they are in any case a literary category and not an existential one. It is much easier to have your protagonist end badly; but perhaps here the perils of an arbitrary authorial decision are even more evident, and the outcome has to be more openly justified by some larger ideological concept—either the aesthetics of tragedy or that metaphysics of failure that dominated the naturalist novel and still very much governs our imagination of poverty and underdevelopment. Nor is the happy ending quite the same as the "living happily ever after" with which youthful adventures so often terminate. Comedy, on Northrop Frye's account the phallic triumph of the younger generation over the older one,[1] is a theatrical subset of that plot-type; but its novelistic equivalents already tend in a different direction, the providential one, which is my topic here.

Not only does the *Aethiopica* add a reconciliation with the father to the reunion of the lovers, it also (paradigmatically) separates them by way of a multitude of plots that must all be resolved in their individual stroke of good luck:

> "The child you regarded as your daughter, the child I committed to your keeping all those years ago, is safe," he exclaimed, "though in truth she is, and has been discovered to be, the child of parents whose identity you know!"
>
> Now Charikleia came running from the pavilion and, oblivious of the modesty incumbent on her sex and years, raced like a maenad in her madness towards Charikles and fell at his feet.
>
> "Father," she said, "to you I owe as much reverence as to those who gave me birth. I am a wicked parricide; punish me as you please; ignore any attempts to excuse my misdeeds by ascribing them to the will of the gods, to their governance of human life!"
>
> A few feet away, Persinna held Hydaspes in her arms. "It is all true, my husband," she said. "You need have no doubts. Understand now that young

[1] Northrop Frye, *Anatomy of Criticism* (Princeton, N.J.: Princeton University Press, 1957), 163ff.

Greek is truly to be our daughter's husband. She has just confessed as much to me, though it cost her much pain."

The populace cheered and danced for joy where they stood, and there was no discordant voice as young and old, rich and poor, united in jubilation.[2]

The greatest modern version of this narrative cunningly marshals its two immense trajectories (the plights of each lover) to map the geographical and the class levels of a whole historical society: at the same time, *I promessi sposi* now, at the end of the Christian era, includes the reflexive and philosophical questions about the providential and the salvational as its very content. At that price, the reunion of the young lovers turns out to include a temporal perspective far vaster than the triumph of youth over age.[3]

The point to be made is that the salvational is not a religious but a philosophical category. We must not grasp the tradition I want to propose as the mere secularization of a theological drama: indeed, Blumenberg has famously taught us that this concept is a paralogism, designed either to discredit the religious presuppositions of alleged secularizations (such as Marxism), or to assert the unconscious persistence of religion throughout the seemingly modern and modernized world.[4] In reality, we have here to do with empty forms, which, inherited, are reappropriated for wholly new meanings and uses, which have nothing to do with the historical origins of their borrowed articulations. Thus the very theme of resurrection itself— theologically the most glorious of all salvational representations—is scarcely to be understood in any religious sense: from its figural deployment in Proust ("l'adoration perpétuelle") to its literal celebration in Stanley Spenser's paintings (let alone in *The Winter's Tale*), resurrection expresses the euphoria of a secular salvation otherwise inexpressible in material or social terms, religious language here offering the means of rendering a material possibility rather than the other way round.

It is this possibility that the providential work embodies, and if I claim that it does so philosophically, I mean by that to imply that (unlike the long-existing theological concept) no philosophical concept for the matter exists independently and that therefore it is only by way of aesthetic representation that this reality can be grasped. But I also mean the word *philosophical* to imply that the local representation (the story of individuals, the empirical

---

    [2] B. P. Reardon, *Collected Ancient Greek Novels* (Berkeley: University of California Press, 1989), 586–87.

    [3] See also "Magical Narratives," in my *The Political Unconscious: Narrative as a Socially Symbolic Act* (Ithaca, N.Y.: Cornell University Press, 1981).

    [4] Hans Blumenberg, *The Legitimacy of the Modern Age* (Cambridge, Mass.: MIT Press, 1985).

reality) must always in this form be shadowed by a more transcendental philosophical idea—just as I have asserted that the naturalist rendering of bad luck and inevitable degradation is presided over by a constellation of class and scientific ideologies (from entropy to the bourgeois terror of proletarianization, as well as that of the "decline of the West").

It will be appropriate to illustrate the process in the very different register of science fiction: indeed, at the heart of one of Philip K. Dick's grimmest novels, *Archaeologies of the Future*, we encounter a salvational episode of the most radiant beauty. Like so much paraliterature (the relationship between modern detective stories and specific cities is well known), it is often a literature of place and landscape, albeit imaginary ones: Dick's Mars is the prototype of his characteristic desert of misery, in which the most dismal features of a provincial 1950s America are unremittingly reproduced and perpetuated against a backdrop of ecological sterility and the intensive use of low-yield machinery. Cultural reminiscences of Australia waft off this unpromising colony, which still has remnants of its aboriginal population (here called Bleekmen) and nourishes Tasmanian fantasies of extermination. Dick's multiple alternating plots, whose virtuoso practice recalls Dickens or Altman and that typically include political corruption and dysfunctional families, mental illness and professional failure, would not be complete without the opening onto nightmare and hallucination, here incarnated in the autistic child Manfred, whose speech consists in the single word: "gubble." It expresses Manfred's view through the appearances of things to "the skull beneath the skin," the horrible amalgams of machinery and garbage that constitute the deeper reality of the outside world and its population. It is a glimpse theorized by Lacan in his notion of *das Ding*, the monstrous indeterminate and inexpressible Other that bides its time in the "outside world" of each of us.[5]

But in fact Manfred's situation is a time-traveling one: the real life of the mentally paralyzed child is "in reality" the aged, infirm, hospitalized old man he will in many years become, imprisoned in an early version of that "Black Iron Prison" ("the Empire never ended") that haunted Dick's later life and work.[6] But here a redemptive solution is still possible, owing to the temporal simultaneity of the Bleekmen (patterned on the aboriginal cosmos), who, fleeing their own imminent genocide, are able to save another

---

[5] Jacques Lacan, *L'ethique de la psychanalyse*, Le Séminaire Livre 7 (Paris: Seuil, 1986), 55–86.

[6] Philip K. Dick, *Valis* (New York: Vintage, 1991), 48. I am grateful to Kim Stanley Robinson for this reference; he adds that "The Building, in *A Maze of Death* (chapter 9) is certainly a nightmare of a building, in a nightmare of a book. Then in *A Scanner Darkly* the ending happens in a forbidding mental hospital, 'Samarkand House,' and in *Galactic Pot-Healer*, the final Jungian project is to bring up The Black Cathedral (à la Debussy)."

orphan by rescuing the aged Manfred from his terminal confinement and carry him off into the eternal Dreamtime:

> At the front door of the Steiner house one of the Steiner girls met them. "My brother—"
>
> She and Jack pushed past the child, and into the house. Silvia did not understand what she saw, but Jack seemed to; he took hold of her hand, stopped her from going any farther.
>
> The living room was filled with Bleekmen. And in their midst she saw part of a living creature, an old man only from the chest on up; the rest of him became a tangle of pumps and hoses and dials, machinery that clicked away, unceasingly active. It kept the old man alive; she realized that in an instant. The missing portion of him had been replaced by it. Oh, God, she thought. Who or what was it, sitting there with a smile on its withered face? Now it spoke to them.
>
> "Jack Bohlen," it rasped, and its voice issued from a mechanical speaker, out of the machinery: not from its mouth. "I am here to say goodbye to my mother." It paused, and she heard the machinery speed up, as if it were laboring. "Now I can thank you," the old man said.
>
> Jack, standing by her, holding her hand, said. "For what? I didn't do anything for you."
>
> "Yes, I think so." The thing seated there nodded to the Bleekmen, and they pushed it and its machinery closer to Jack and straightened it so that it faced him directly. "In my opinion . . ." It lapsed into silence and then it resumed, more loudly, now. "You tried to communicate with me, many years ago. I appreciate that."[7]

It is a deliverance into which one can no doubt read Dick's later religious mysticism; yet the theme of modes of production (the modern and the archaic) also reminds us to reverse this direction and to sense a social and historical redemption at work behind the individual one.

Predestination and Collective Histories

And this is in fact the other axis that complicates our philosophical framework and that runs, not from success to failure and back, but from the individual to

---

[7] Philip K. Dick, *Archaeologies of the Future* (London: Verso, 2005), 218–19. And for more on the relationship of this episode to Dick's world generally, see my essay "History and Salvation in Philip K. Dick," (forthcoming).

the collective. Far more than providence and the providential, the notion of predestination can illustrate our point here: for even in the realm of theology itself, this notion has been a "hard saying" that often and traditionally "sticks in the craw." For predestination illustrates Kant's two levels of the empirical and the transcendent almost better than any other attempt at a concept, for it claims to solve this dilemma (which it merely names), namely that of the distinction between the realm of freedom and that of necessity, that of the noumenon and that of the phenomenon, that of the transcendental and that of the empirical, paradoxically locating the latter in the power of divine, and the former in that of human subjectivity. What the concept of predestination asserts, in other words, is that an iron necessity governs my empirical acts and my personal destiny—this iron necessity is that of God's providence and of his determination of that destiny from all eternity, and before time itself.[8] I am, in empirical reality, one of the elect or one of the damned, and I can exercise no freedom in influencing these outcomes; no individual act of mine exerts any kind of causality in their predetermined course. However, on the level of my individual consciousness or soul (Kant's noumenal realm of freedom), things stand utterly differently, and I can have no subjective sense of my election or my damnation: here I am left alone with my existential freedom and must necessarily choose my acts and make my decisions as though I were completely free.

Kant's philosophy in general and his ethics in particular—very much contemporaneous with the novelistic tradition we are here constructing—are mere secularized descendents of the official solution to the problem, which is not particularly interesting for our purposes, even though it does involve a dialectic of the sign or even of the symptom, which is very contemporary indeed. It is resumed in the famous phrase, "the outward and visible signs of inward election": and this rather casuistical cutting of the Gordian knot can be summarized as follows. Nothing we do can ensure our election (rather than our damnation): but if in fact we happen to be one of the elect (chosen from all eternity), our behavior on earth will reflect this condition and will therefore constitute an empirical sign of our noumenal and unknowable salvation in the transcendental realm. Hypocrisy is the tribute vice pays to virtue, someone famously said: and thus, even though it can have no causal effect, no genuine effectivity, we would do well to behave virtuously on the off chance our fate will be harmonious with this conduct. Only the more logical negative conclusion here—that if election is from all eternity, then it does not matter how I behave—has offered truly remarkable novelistic

---

[8] For at least the modern revival of Augustine's doctrine, see Bernard M. G. Reardon, *Religious Thought in the Reformation* (London: Longman, 1981).

possibilities, in James Hogg's *Private Memoirs and Confessions of a Justified Sinner*. But the dilemma gets more productively restaged on the political and historical level.

Here we move from the individual destiny to the collective one, and the salvation of the soul is replaced by that of the human race itself, or in other words by Utopia and socialist revolution. But the well-known alternative within the Marxist tradition between voluntarism and fatalism absolutely coincides with the theological antinomy, which can thus be said to anticipate it and to "prefigure" its more secular problematic in a distorted, still figurative and theological, and essentially individual way. The Mensheviks and the Bolsheviks are themselves mere personifications of this primordial opposition, in which a conviction as to the objective movement of history is opposed by a militant sense of the power of human beings to make history. Clearly, nothing is more debilitating than an opposition of this kind, which tends to sort itself out into a passive/active one in which neither alternative is satisfactory. For to oppose a placid, Second International confidence in the "inevitable" movement of history toward a socialist state is not necessarily only to show faith in the shaping powers of human beings; it is also to encourage the most mindless forms of suicidal attempts to "force" history, to break through its logic prematurely, to encourage young people to die in what are causes lost in advance owing to the fact that "the situation is not yet ripe, not yet a revolutionary one." As with predestination, however, there is nothing to guide us in this choice and no empirical signs are available to allow us to have any certainty of "election," that is to say, of the possibility of revolution as the one supreme salvational or providential event.

But in this secular and collective version, in fact there is a kind of solution, and one not unrelated to the unconvincing theological one in such a way as to demonstrate that the latter was only really a distorted anticipation of the former. For here what is taken as voluntarism—that is, the collective will to force history—is itself seen, not as a subjective choice, but as an objective symptom, in that sense very precisely an objective component of that history itself. Thus, an infantile leftism or anarchist voluntarism now becomes that "external sign" that revolution is not yet on the agenda and that the situation has not yet politically "matured." What was not solvable on the level of Hogg's theological hero here becomes a piece of historical evidence, a historical sign fully as significant as all others. It is in the old theological spirit that one may also say that the passive "inevitabilism" of the Second International was itself a sign of immaturity and of an insufficiently developed political situation. This new interpenetration of the subjective and the objective thus now suddenly signals a transcendence of the old antinomy, and a moment in which the providential and empiricism overcome as specific historical ratios. It thus also designates a new kind of social content for the novel as form and the possibility of new kinds of narration.

It is to these that we must now turn, with the help of such findings: the latter in effect signal the fundamental difference in possibility between the individual and the collective and suggest that we reinterrogate the novelistic form for just such consequences. The debate between revolutionaries about voluntarism and fatalism, to be sure, becomes a limited kind of specialized content for some officially political novel—what I have elsewhere called a sort of Third International literary dialectic in which this specific dilemma, most fully exacerbated by the peculiar position of Stalinist revolution in one country, gets played out.[9] (Sartre's works are some of the most interesting versions of these tragic paradoxes, which tend to be invisible in an anticommunist focus.) But as with the theological material, it is not this specific content, but rather the larger form in general that interests us here.

"Tendencies" of the Bildungsroman

I now therefore want to return to the mainstream realist novel in order to make a few further remarks about the form-generating and form-producing value of the providential within realism itself. For the moment what is crucial for us is the distinction between the individual perspective and the collective one, when it comes to providence or happy endings. This turns out to be an evolutionary matter, for as in the purely theological realm, there is a decided historical movement from the individual destiny to the collective one (or from issues of individual salvation to those of political and revolutionary transformations, as in our preceding discussion).

But there are intermediate steps, and as it were external operators, that move us from the individual narrative to the collective one. To be sure, the first theological transfers take place naturally enough in the framework of an individual destiny, and it has been universally recognized that the very prototype of a truly individualized and isolated individual destiny, *Robinson Crusoe*, is saturated with providential lore of various kinds.[10] The novel

---

[9] See my Introduction to Peter Weiss, *Aesthetics of Resistance* (Durham, N.C.: Duke University Press, forthcoming).

[10] The classic discussions are those of G. A. Starr, *Defoe and Spiritual Autobiography* (Princeton, N.J.: Princeton University Press, 1965) and J. Paul Hunter, *The Reluctant Pilgrim* (Baltimore: Johns Hopkins University Press, 1966).

uniquely enables the interiorization of the various external adventures and episodes that had hitherto formed the space in which the happy or the tragic ending was played out—the realm of accidents, the contingent, chance of a meaningful kind, and so forth. Later on, these will be simply omens and not causes, as when Julien Sorel finds a scrap of newspaper in a church early in *The Red and the Black*. The interiorization of chance now means that contingency can offer the opportunity for an inward experience or development. But I think that the debate as to whether Defoe himself was a Christian is misplaced: we have here rather the template for the organization of experiences in a new way, in which religious influence is itself a mere external and enabling condition. Such developments need to be seen synchronically, in obedience to Blumenberg's warning about the pseudo-concept of "secularization." To be sure, it is not wrong to say that the bildungsroman is then a secularization of this earlier, already secular "spiritual autobiography" of Defoe; but neither stage retains the meaning of the preceding one, but only the form. Thus it would be wrong to say that the bildungsroman is still religious in its (now secular) concern for the state of the individual soul: no, what is deployed now is a mere form that organizes its new social material in an analogous way.

For our topic, it may be said that *Wilhelm Meister* is the decisive turning point, and as it were, the true beginning of the nineteenth-century novel, the end of something as well as the beginning of something else, which is however its mutation and its adaptation to the new postrevolutionary society (a society that did not, of course, yet exist in Germany and scarcely elsewhere at that). This is a peculiarly central evaluation for such an odd and garbled book, immensely influential and yet a kind of literary white elephant, boring and fascinating all at once, and a perpetual question mark for the French and British traditions in which, as a text, it has played so small a role, yet which are incomprehensible without it, as we shall see.

The novel of formation, the novel of education?[11] It would be better to translate the term *bildungsroman* as the novel of a calling or vocation, a *Beruf*, to use that word which Max Weber charged with its most intense Lutheran accents in order to make his point about the new innerworldliness of Protestant behavior and virtue. Not that Wilhelm is at all secure in his ultimate vocation: the critics are at least sure that the latter is no longer the

---

[11] The perspective adopted here does not allow me to endorse Franco Moretti's ideological analysis of the form, in *The Way of the World* (London: Verso, 1987), which remains the most stimulating and comprehensive discussion of this novelistic subgenre. It will be apparent below that mine is rather an ideological indictment of what I call ontological realism as such.

artistic calling or the surrender to genius that had been projected in the first draft (the *Theatralische Sendung*). Yet the rhetoric of the ending—so glorious and so determinate for several generations of bildungsroman if not of providential narrative—is strangely at odds with the actual situation (Wilhelm is about to set off on a trip to Italy, just like Goethe himself):

> To my mind thou resemblest Saul the son of Kish, who
> went out to seek his father's asses, and found a kingdom.[12]

Indeed, the principal role of "providence" here would seem to be a negative one: "Flee, youth, flee!" Above all, he is not to become a mere actor, and his onetime success in the role of Hamlet is owing, as Boyle rightly insists, to the preestablished harmony between his own personality and that of the Prince.[13] But for the greater part of the play, the Prince is also tormented by the question of what to do, and what the superego—the father's Ghost (which also plays a significant part in *Meister*)—commands. Wilhelm's real father, however, proposes a life of commerce and trade, which, along with theatricals, is the one vocation quite decisively repudiated.[14] I will suggest in passing that at the end of the novel, the authority of the Father has been displaced by that of the brothers, but I do not want to overemphasize this theme of the Big Other, which does not seem particularly important for Goethe here or elsewhere.

That "providence" is a fundamental theme of the novel, however, can be judged from recurrent discussions, which seem to propose a philosophical alternative between destiny and chance: "I easily content myself, [says Wilhelm] and honor destiny, which knows how to bring about what is best for me, and what is best for everyone." To which the first of his mysterious acquaintances replies:

> It gives me pain to hear this word destiny in the mouth of a young person. . . .
> Woe to him who, from his youth, has used himself to search in necessity for
> something of arbitrary will; to ascribe chance a sort of reason, which it is a
> matter of religion to obey. Is conduct like this aught else than to renounce
> one's understanding, and give unrestricted scope to one's inclinations? We

---

[12] References are to Thomas Carlyle's translation of the novel (New York: Heritage, 1959), bk. 8, chap. 10, p. 657; and in the German, to *Wilhelm Meisters Lehrjahre* (Frankfurt: Insel, 1982), 626.

[13] Nicholas Boyle, *Goethe: The Poet and the Age* (Oxford: Oxford University Press, 2000), 2:336.

[14] Ibid., 239–40; see also Giuliano Baioni, "Gli anni di apprendistato," in *Il romanzo*, ed. Franco Moretti (Turin: Einaudi, 2002), 2:127–33.

think it is a kind of piety to move along without consideration; to let accidents that please us determine our conduct; and, finally, to bestow on the result of such a vacillating life the name of providential guidance.[15]

That this is not merely the expression of a standard Enlightenment denunciation of superstition and religion, and an appeal to secular reason, may be externally deduced by the obedience to one's daimon so dear to this author—as well as from texts like *Urworte Ophisch*. Here, however, it is enough to point out that the warning of this stranger inserts itself into the very web of chance and coincidence that make up the novel's stream of events: it is therefore itself drawn inside the theme and interrogated for its own function as that predestined chance we call providence.

We thus arrive at the work's well-known secret: innumerable characters (although mostly divided socially between the wandering theater people, whose triviality estranged Goethe's first intellectual readership, and the aristocracy of this Germany of the principalities in which Goethe was to make himself so eminent a place); a veritable orgy of interpolated stories and gothic destinies, full of rather random recognition scenes and rediscovered kinships of various sorts; love affairs meanwhile, of the tentative sort riddled with flights and avoidances with which Goethe's biography and psychology have familiarized us—these materials scarcely seem to add up to any very consistent focus of representation or stylization, nor are any of them particularly powerful or commanding in their own right. But abruptly, at the center of the text, there takes place a long dream, in which characters from a host of different plot strands come together:

> Strange dreams arose upon him towards morning. He was in a garden, which in boyhood he had often visited: he looked with pleasure at the well-known alleys, hedges, flower-beds. Mariana met him: he spoke to her with love and tenderness, recollecting nothing of any by-gone grievance. Erelong his father joined them, in his weekday dress; with a look of frankness that was rare in him, he bade his son fetch two seats from the garden-house; then took Mariana by the hand, and led her into the grove.
>
> Wilhelm hastened to the garden-house, but found it altogether empty: only at a window in the farther side he saw Aurelia standing. He went forward, and addressed her, but she turned not round; and, though he placed himself beside her, he could never see her face. He looked out from the

---

[15] Bk. 1, chap. 17: Carlyle, 63–64; Insel, 71.

window: in an unknown garden, there were several people, some of whom he recognized. Frau Melina, seated under a tree, was playing with a rose which she had in her hand: Laertes stood beside her, counting money from the one hand to the other. Mignon and Felix were lying on the grass, the former on her back, the latter on his face. Philina followed; but he screamed in terror when he saw the harper coming after him with large, slow steps. Felix ran directly to a pond. Wilhelm hastened after him: too late; the child was lying in the water! Wilhelm stood as if rooted to the spot. The fair Amazon appeared on the other side of the pond: she stretched her right hand towards the child, and walked along the shore. The child came through the water, by the course her finger pointed to; he followed her as she went round; at last she reached her hand to him, and pulled him out. Wilhelm had come nearer: the child was all in flames; fiery drops were falling from his body. Wilhelm's agony was greater than ever; but instantly the Amazon took a white veil from her head, and covered up the child with it. The fire was at once quenched. But, when she lifted up the veil, two boys sprang out from under it, and frolicsomely sported to and fro; while Wilhelm and the Amazon proceeded hand in hand across the garden, and noticed in the distance Mariana and his father walking in an alley, which was formed of lofty trees, and seemed to go quite round the garden. He turned his steps to them, and, with his beautiful attendant, was moving through the garden, when suddenly the fair-haired Friedrich came across their path, and kept them back with loud laughter and a thousand tricks. Still, however, they insisted on proceeding; and Friedrich hastened off, running towards Mariana and the father. These seemed to flee before him; he pursued the faster, till Wilhelm saw them hovering down the alley almost as on wings. Nature and inclination called on him to go and help them, but the hand of the Amazon detained him. How gladly did he let himself be held! With this mingled feeling he awoke, and found his chamber shining with the morning beams.[16]

Here suddenly we glimpse a principle of a wholly different formal nature at work: all these various characters are to be united in a central phantasmagoria just as musical themes are intertwined, in the contemporaneous emergence of the sonata form; just as the dumbshow passed in review the actors to come. The demonstration of a deeper unity now no longer has to be made in any logical or Enlightenment or even causal way, but by the very logic of the dream as formal moment, the moment of the reprise. Here is a form of

---

[16] Bk. 7, chap. 1: Carlyle, 402–3; Insel, 440–41.

closure utterly distinct from plot, but that demands its own verisimilitude: do we not now finally believe that all this holds together in some new principle of coherence? It is enough to think of Joyce's prodigious reassemblage of all his daytime motifs in the Nighttown scene in *Ulysses* (beyond which everything is anticlimax), or in cinema, that remarkable final hour of Fassbinder's *Alexanderplatz* in which everything that has happened in thought or deed returns oneirically in a new unity, to grasp what is formally original in this extraordinary moment of *Wilhelm Meister*.

But in Goethe, the oneiric superstructure is doubled by a very different infrastructural unity as well, and this is what sets *Wilhelm Meister* apart from all the generic norms and justifies its unique position as a synthesis of "world" and "soul" in Lukács's *Theory of the Novel*. Nor would I want to characterize this alternative unification—although certainly redolent of the eighteenth century, of Freemasonry and of the *The Magic Flute* of 1790—as narrowly Enlightenment: its basis is not Reason as a faculty but the collective as such.

For it famously transpires that the various chance events and contingencies that have marked Wilhelm's youthful career so far are all planned out in advance, as necessary errors (shades of the Hegelian dialectic!), and are the doing of a shadowy group of conspirators known as the Society of the Tower, whose principal figures he will come to know at the end of the book, and whose existence—with a certain Masonic hocus-pocus ("all you saw in the tower was but the relics of a youthful undertaking")—will be revealed to him.[17] The plot is thus turned inside out: from a series of chance happenings it is suddenly revealed as a plan and as a deliberately providential design. And the Enlightenment emphasis on reasoned persuasion and pedagogy here reaches a kind of bizarre climax in which life itself becomes the "lecon d'objets," the theoretically calculated pattern of test and error that the old theological concept ("justify the ways of God to man") only dimly rendered in distorted fashion. The Society of the Tower is a better pedagogue than God, and far more self-conscious and theoretical about its teaching method.

But it is important not to let all this slip (in the content) into a vapid kind of humanism and celebration of eighteenth-century virtue (there is very little of Blutarch and Rousseau here), although there is another kind of slippage, a purely formal one, which we will want to take more seriously. Yet it is significant that the Lukács of *Theory of the Novel*, only a year or so before his commitment to politics and to communism, should not have glimpsed the

---

[17] Bk. 8, chap. 5: Carlyle, 512; Insel, 564.

political significance of this "white conspiracy,"[18] which very obviously anticipates the structure of the Party itself, and the dialectic of a collective leadership, which both reflects the social order and works back upon its already present tendencies to develop them. Lothario and his friends have just returned from the New World, and the revolution of the colonists against the tyranny of the ancien régime: their political party is not only out to transform the old social world by the modernization of agriculture ("Here or nowhere is America!"),[19] it carries within itself the explosive spark of that element of the American Revolution that would expand into the French one, and become an international movement for the transition from feudalism to the republic—a movement then further elaborated in *Wilhelm Meisters Wanderjahre*, with Goethe's customary restraint (as befits that member of the late feudal bureaucracy he later also was). This is the collective task into which Wilhelm is to be initiated, exchanging that microcosm of the social that is the theater—Faust's "kleine Welt"—for the "great world" of the sociopolitical. It is a unique solution to the formal problem of the political novel, which, a kind of *hapax legomenon*, can never be repeated, nor can it serve as a model, and which is flawed in its very exemplarity, as though designating itself not as the concrete solution but rather merely the intent to find one. But this calls for a larger theoretical speculation about novelistic form, one that is no doubt deeply indebted to Lukács but seeks to replace the notion of the unified subject or soul in his text with a less "humanistic" thematics.

Even before that, however, we need to bid farewell to that whole novelistic development of providential interiority that led from Defoe to *Wilhelm Meister* in the first place. The future of this formal path will no longer be subjective but objective, no longer individualistic but rather collective. But it is important to see that Goethe himself liquidates this earlier tradition within his novel, in what has always struck readers of whatever period and generation as the most peculiar of his extrapolations, namely book 6, or the "Confessions of a Beautiful Soul," which from Hegel's famous discussion onward has often been taken as a pathology of introspection.[20] The form itself imitates, precisely by way of this self-sufficient extrapolation, the solipsism of interiority and of the subjectivity that seeks to enact its own virtue, even when issuing from a collective (the *Herrenhüter*), which still includes

---

[18] George Lukács, *Theorie des Romans* (Neuwied: Luchterhand, 1963), pt. 2, chap. 3. But see also the later *Goethe und seine Zeit*.

[19] Bk. 7, chap. 3: Carlyle, 407; Insel, 446.

[20] See *The Phenomenology of Spirit*, chap. 6, sec. C, sub-sec. c.

the ancient almost extinguished vibrations of the great religious revivals and revolutions. Goethe has as it were sealed this noxious individualism away in a kind of cyst or crypt,[21] in which the subjectivity can be separated out of the plot of his novel and formally excised (even though the book's author is as tightly knit by kinship into its cast of characters as all the other chance story-tellers of the novel). The thus sealed-off confessions then mark the grave of the "spiritual autobiography" and of any reading of providence as an inward or psychologico-theological phenomenon.

Transcendence and Immanence in Realism

But, as Lukács so usefully warns us, the "novel" as a form is never a success-ful solution to any of its problems, they merely change their terms when an older problematic individualism has been removed. The new terms in which I wish to codify the possibilities in a kind of structural permutation scheme will be the more Kantian ones (contemporaneous with Goethe himself) of transcendence and immanence. But perhaps it is better to start with the more familiar older Hegelian terminology that passed into New Criticism without taking any of its dialectical baggage with it: namely the so-called concrete universal, or alternatively the thoroughgoing fusion of form and content such that you cannot tell one from the other any longer.[22] This aes-thetic was probably a neoclassical inspiration, produced by the return to an-tiquity popular in Goethe's circles, which Hegel frequented when he worked in Jena and sympathized with ever after (not many novels ever find mention in Hegel, who died just as the first great wave of modern fiction, with Balzac in the forefront, was about to hit land; Goethe of course fa-mously mentions Stendhal).[23] Anyway, the unity of form and content thus far simply means that nothing stands out, there are no excesses either way wherever you inspect the artifact: no extra stylistic frills, no "extrinsic" or extraneous content poking out of the pillowcase. All this very much in the spirit of epic; and of course the ambiguity of the German word *episch*, also used for the novel and for narrative in general, means that the novel gets no special treatment.

---

[21] See Jacques Derrida, "Fors," in *Cryptonymie: Le verbier de l'homme aux loups*, ed. Nicholas Abraham and Maria Torok (Paris: Aubier Flammarion, 1976).

[22] See W. K. Wimsatt, "The Structure of the Concrete Universal in Literature," *PMLA* 62 (1947).

[23] *Conversations with Eckermann*, January 17, 1831.

So this aesthetic of fusion can very conveniently be adapted to the language of immanence. *Episch* is immanent, in the sense that meaning is inherent in all its objects and details, all its facts, all its events. They are meaningful in and of themselves, and require no outside commentary or explanation, as might be the case when you introduce modern technology of some sort, or events like financial crises, which are not self-explanatory and whose very nature as "events" in the first place is not secured in advance, which have to be explained in order to come into visible existence as things or phenomena. Yet when this miraculously happens—not in older modes of production, but in our own—we call it realism and have an interest in accounting for such texts, which we understand as being unusual and few in number. They are better explained, however, if we add the word transcendence to our repertoire in order to identify what is no longer present in them.

Or, we could try another alternative, the one suggested by Barthes's famous offhand remark that there is an incompatibility between meaning and existence in modern literature.[24] Transcendence is meaning, the immanent is existence itself, and so it is also best to enrich this layer of terms with an ontological significance. What is, whether in the text or in the real world, is not always meaningful (it is often therefore what we call contingent); what is meaningful is not always there as an existent, in the world, as is the case in with Utopia or nonalienated relationships. What we many now perhaps call ontological realism is found where these two coincide to the point at which we cannot tell them apart any longer or worry about the distinction.

What would be the opposite of all this? What would be a truly transcendent kind of text? Myths, religious texts or all sorts? But after all, we are here working within the framework of the already secular novel, and have ruled those texts out in advance; we have thus presupposed a certain immanence in the novelistic form to begin with.

Within this frame then, we can assume that what we call ontological realism is to be characterized as a truly immanent kind of immanence. In that case, and for purposes of differentiation, what would be a transcendental immanence? I think we can make a beginning by imagining this to be a kind of ethical literature or narrative: a narrative in which the categories of ethics—vice, virtue, evil, kindness, and sympathy, and on into anger, melancholy, and the like—are just at a slight distance from the narrated emotions

---

[24] Roland Barthes, "L'effet de réel," in *Oeuvres complètes* (Paris: Seuil, 1994), 2:485: "La 'représentation' pure et simple du 'réel,' la relation nue de 'ce qui est' (ou a été) apparaît ainsi comme une résistance au sens; cette résistance confirme la grande opposition mythique du vécu (du vivant) et de l'intelligible."

and feelings of the characters or from their characterological properties. In this situation of a barely perceptible gap between the characters' existence and what they seem to mean, the old dualism of the immanent and the transcendent reinscribes itself, however faintly. The "ethical" characters are not yet mere examples or illustrations, nor have they gone all the way toward those allegories in which nameless figures bear their ethical designations on their backs in the form of signs (I am Envy, I am Complacency), but we are close, and the mere glimpse of such a possibility is enough to cast an unsettling doubt over the assurances of a hitherto ontological realism. No sensible secular and historical person can any longer believe that the ethical categories are "in nature," are in any way inscribed in being or in human reality; and for the most part an ethical literature has come to reflect the closure of class—whether it is that of Jamesian aristocrats or Bunyan's tinkers. Ethical maxims and categories only work within a situation of homogeneous class belonging; when operative from one class to another, they absorb the signals of class struggle and tension itself and begin to function in a very different, sociopolitical way. At any rate, for the corpus of novels we are here considering, the novel that deploys ethical categories will be characterizable as betraying something like a transcendental status of social elements—the ethical categories and judgments—which looked like intrinsic and even banal elements of the social situation itself, until closer inspection revealed their operation to be somehow and barely perceptibly transsocial, metasocial.

In that case, would it make any sense to propose a parallel category of transcendental transcendence? I think so, provided we understand once again that we are operating within a secular corpus from which all genuine transcendence has been eliminated. We no longer have to do with religious or sacred texts, with texts bearing within them anything having to do with the divine or the angelic or even the supernatural (although at some point very early in our historical segment—the history of the novel—the ghost story reappears, with Defoe's Mrs. Veal, or Schiller's *Geisterseher*). So the transcendence we are evoking will be a transcendence bound and limited by secular immanence, a transcendence within our own "realistic" and empirical world: what form can it possibly take, and what would possibly be above this realistic world and yet still of a piece with it and flesh of its flesh?

I think that such transcendence could only be detected in one possible place, namely in the space of an otherness from what is, a dimension freed from the weight of being and the inertia of the present social order. It seems possible to me that this transcendence could conceivably operate in the past, by way of the historical reconstruction of societies that no longer exist: yet

insofar as, no longer existing, they nonetheless have been, the law of an ontological realism would presumably still be binding on them, and there is a
way in which *Salammbô* or Walter Scott's novels or *Romola* or *The Tale of
Two Cities*, is no less realistic than its contemporary counterparts. At any
rate, there here opens up the very interesting problem of the historical novel
as such, which we can no longer pursue.

But when we have to do with the future, with what does not yet and may
never exist, it is a different story, and we are confronted with politics itself.
Here we face the knotty problem of the political novel and political literature in general, and their very possibility of existence. Is it conceivable,
within the world of immanence, for this or that existent, this or that already
existing element, to breathe "the air of other planets," to give off even the
slightest hint of a radically different future? That the realistic novel absolutely resists and repudiates this possibility can be judged from its conventional treatment of political characters, of figures whose passion is political,
who live for the possibilities of change and entertain only the flimsiest relationship with the solid ontology of what exists right now. We need only pass
in review a few of the most famous representations of such figures to be convinced, and I will adduce three exhibits here.

There is Dickens's treatment of the "missions": all the crazed philanthropists who crowd the pages of *Bleak House* around the central character of
Mrs. Jellabee with her African mission and who wreak damage on all the
people close to them. Mrs. Jellabee's husband literally pounds his head
against the wall, her children are filthy and neglected, her oldest daughter
escapes into a marriage of whose drawbacks she is scarcely cognizant, and
her own daily life is a shambles—she is ill-dressed, living only for the
African correspondence and the African cause. When it is remembered that
in any case, politics for Dickens, in his supremely "liberalist" and free-
market society can only be embodied in philanthropy (but better the personal, "ethical" type represented by Mr. Jarndyce, than this wholesale collective type), then it will be understood not only that these are figures of the
political, but also that they represent the intellectual as well: the political intellectual, to whom these twin bugbears of abstraction and nonliving, of the
loss of ontological life and human reality to pure thought and idle speculation on the not-yet-existent must be conjoined.[25]

---

[25] Miss Wisk offers the generalized philosophy of the "mission" itself, being intent on showing
"the world that woman's mission was man's mission; and that the only genuine mission, of both
man and woman, was to be always moving declaratory resolutions about things in general at public
meetings" (*Bleak House* [London: Penguin, 1996], 482).

Once we learn to read these figures of the political, and to detect them throughout realism and in other places than the officially political—the parliamentary novels of Trollope, for example, where the political as such is a perfectly proper and respectable specialized dimension of life and being as such—we find that the satire of the antiontological is everywhere in ontological realism and indeed goes hand in hand with the very structure of the form and is inseparable from it.

Thus Henry James's feminists (in *The Bostonians*) are supremely emblematic of the political intellectual, and a far nastier and more malicious repudiation of politics than anything in the experiment of the *Princess Cassimissima*, or indeed in the contemporary treatment of anarchism generally (although Conrad's *Secret Agent* certainly comes close behind).

Finally, the whole animus spills over in Flaubert and is very far from being a mere personal ideology or idiosyncrasy. Whoever has read the extensive representations of the great political meetings in *L'education sentimentale*— imitations in 1848 of the Jacobin clubs of the great revolution and far too long to quote here in the savorous detail they merit—knows how much bile was destined for the political intellectuals by Flaubert, who sees them as obsessives and maniacs necessarily plural in their nature, repetitions of each other and groups rather than individuals. Whatever the psychoanalytic interpretations of Flaubert's unique passion and loathing, such scenes must also be taken as empty forms, which are reproduced throughout his work, most notably in *St. Anthony* but also in the comices agricoles in *Mme Bovary*, in court scenes in *Herodias*, and at various key points in *Bouvard and Péchuchet*. As such, Flaubert has solved the formal problem of how to represent the unrepresentable in the present context: in other words, how to lend ontological weight to the representation of figures and elements defined virtually in advance as lacking being, as having little ontological weight in their own right, either as characters or as meanings. The empty form of the obsessive exchange and multiplication of the maniacs and their words (rather than thoughts) thus allows a representation to be set in the place of the ontologically thin (and indeed, in this respect, Flaubert's solution folds back over Dickens's, which equally relies on the multiplication and proliferation of such maniacs to fill in his canvas and give it the requisite density).

I mention all of this, not merely to document the fragility of the new category of transcendental transcendence in the history of the novel, but also make the usual point about the structural and inherent conservatism and antipoliticality of the realist novel as such. An ontological realism, absolutely committed to the density and solidity of what is—whether in the realm of psychology and feelings, institutions, objects, or space—cannot but be threatened in the very nature of the form by any suggestion that these things are changeable and not ontologically immutable: the very choice of the form itself is a professional endorsement of the status quo, a loyalty oath in the very apprenticeship to this aesthetic. But since politics does exist in the real world, it must be dealt with, and satiric hostility is the time-honored mode of dealing novelistically with political troublemakers. Only Stendhal and Galdós offer mild exceptions to this rule, the one on the basis of the youthful inexperience of his characters (and also Stendhal's internationalism and relative abhorrence of narrower French "realities"), and the other no doubt in part as a result of the extraordinary political changeablity of Spain. But neither one loosens the lines that hold his work firmly to the ground of being, however much the narrative balloon surges and eddies in the winds of history. Were such lines cut, however, we would no doubt be confronted with truly Utopian forms, such as Chernyshevsky's *What Is to Be Done?*, which would slowly drift out of the province of realism altogether.

Perhaps these two transcendental categories—the transcendental immanence of ethics and allegory, and the transcendental transcendence of the political temptation—also open up a new space in which that normal and discursive phenomenon untheorizable in terms of realism might be grasped: I mean modernism, whose novels are, as I have insisted elsewhere, not at all to be understood as some opposite number of realism but in a very different and incommensurable aesthetic and formal fashion. Thus there are modernisms that can also be perfectly well interrogated with the categories and within the limits of realism as such—one thinks of *Ulysses* for example, certainly a prime example of a stubborn and hard-fought attempt to hold on to the absolute being of the place and day, the untranscendable reality of a specifically limited secular experience. But such categories may no longer be the best ones to convey everything that is unique about such modernist works.

Yet there remains a fourth category in our scheme that has not so far been specified. We have positioned "great realism" in the space of immanent immanence, a kind of miraculous unity of form and content, a unique ontological possibility, on which we will waste no more effusions. We have then identified two slight yet menacing and perilous deviations from this formal plenitude, the first one in a kind of transcendental immanence, in which certain of the categories of being—the ethical ones primarily—separate themselves out from reality and hover above it as a kind of organizing device that threatens to turn the events and narrative actions into so many examples and illustrations. And we have glimpsed a further possible deviation, the political one—transcendental transcendence—according to which the whole existing fabric of being is threatened by revolutionary and systemic overhaul and transformation.

But we have not yet taken into consideration the possibility that there could be something we might call immanent transcendence, in which a transformation of being would be somehow implicit in being itself, like a strange kind of wave running through matter, or a kind of pulsation of energy throbbing in the things themselves, without necessarily altering them or depriving them of their ontological status. The reader will have guessed that it is toward this final category that we have been working and that the immanent transcendence we have in mind is nothing less that the providential as such, its production what we have sporadically been calling the providential novel. Here truly we find what Lukács imagined himself to be describing when he evoked a realism of tendencies, which he understood as a representation of ontological change.[26] The examples were very precisely the passage of history throughout the regime changes of the early nineteenth century, as in *La cousine Bette*, which ranges from Napoleon to the first Algerian expeditions in the late 1820s; yet no one ever suggested that ontological realism could not handle history or the passage of time. It is systemic change that we have tended to rule out, yet Lukács's description of the "tendency" seems far better to describe the providential drifts at work in the novels we have been describing than anything else.

Conspiracies Black and White

We now return to those, and in the light of this "ontological typology" and also mindful of the unique structural properties of the *Wilhelm Meister* experiment, we need to offer some conjectures as to the historical development of these possibilities, that is to say, their concrete evolutionary realizations in those historically determined "evolutionary niches" (Moretti)[27] that the secular societies uniquely offered, in their various contingent ways.

The replacement of Providence by uniquely human energies was always a temptation for Balzac: the very character of Vautrin himself, as he desperately races to release Lucien (at the end of *Splendeurs et misères des courtisans*), just as he has magisterially pulled strings to secure the latter's good

---

[26] See especially *Writer and Critic* and the *Essays on Realism*. I believe that the theory of realism promoted in these essays is best grasped in terms of the way plot is able to represent historical tendencies, rather than as any static notion of "typical" social individuals.

[27] See his *Atlas of the European Novel, 1800–1900* (London: Verso, 1998).

fortune in the early moments of this novelistic series—this image of supreme
know-how and savoir-faire mesmerized the author of *La comédie humaine*
throughout his life, offering an image of action to be narrated as well as a
subject-position for the novelist himself. In this sense, we must accustom
ourselves to rethinking the pallid category of the "omniscient narrator" in
terms of sheer passion, as an obsession to know everything and all the social
levels—from the secret conversations of the great all the way to the "mystères de Paris" and the "bas fonds." Balzac was supremely what the Germans call a *besserwisser*, a know-it-all at every moment anxious to show off
his inside expertise (which he was unfortunately less able to put into practice). But surely Dickens had the virus as well, who was so proud of knowing
all the streets in London; and we many safely attribute an analogous concupiscence of knowledge to all the other great encyclopedic fabulators, from
Trollope to Joyce.

What interests us more for the moment is the way this conception of absolute knowledge spills over into the intrigue itself. Vautrin's status as the
superman is sealed by his ultimate failure (with its human reward in his
eventual promotion to chief of police—like the real-life Vidocq): but this
failure simply marks the sterility of the dialectic of the One and the Many.
What if the task of knowing the Many were rather assigned to the Many
themselves, in the form of a Meister-like Society of the Tower?

This is precisely what happens in Balzac, beginning with the *Histoire des
treize* (1833):

> In Paris under the Empire thirteen men came together. They were all struck
> with the same idea and all endowed with sufficient energy to remain faithful
> to a single purpose. They were all honest enough to be loyal to one another
> even when their interests were opposed, and sufficiently versed in guile to
> conceal the inviolable bonds which united them. They were strong enough to
> put themselves above all law, bold enough to flinch at no undertaking; lucky
> enough to have almost always succeeded in their designs, having run the
> greatest hazards, but remaining silent about their defeats; impervious to fear;
> and never having trembled before public authority, the public hangman or
> even innocence itself. They had all accepted one another, such as they were,
> without regard to social prejudice: they were undoubtedly criminals, but un-
> deniably remarkable for certain qualities which go to the making of great
> men, and they recruited their members only from among men of outstanding
> quality. Lastly—we must leave out no element of the sombre and mysterious
> poetry of this story—the names of these thirteen men were never divulged, al-
> though they were the very incarnations of ideas suggested to the imagination

by the fantastic powers attributed in fiction to the Manfreds, Fausts and Melmoths of literature. Today this association is broken up, or at least dispersed. Its members have peaceably submitted to the yoke of civil law, just as Morgan, that Achilles among pirates, gave up buccaneering, became a colonist and, basking in the warmth of his domestic fireside, made profitable use, without any qualms of conscience, of the millions he had amassed in bloody conflict under the ruddy glare of burning ships and townships.[28]

Here, this promising conspiracy results in little more than episodes (although they are among the most remarkable episodes in all of Balzac). Elsewhere, however, a rather different dialectic sets in motion, which suggests that the providential conspiracy is transethical—is beyond good and evil, to the degree to which it can serve feudal or individualistic passions (as in the *Histoire des treize*) or philanthropic ones indifferently. So it is that Balzac will fantasize a white conspiracy with equal enthusiasm, this one however nourished by the more conservative traces of the religious orders, rather than the sulphurous fumes of the carbonari and the other great political confraternities of Balzac's youth. Charity also needs its Machiavellis; as the organizational figure in *L'envers de l'histoire contemporaine* (1842–1947) observes: "Is it not our task to undermine the permanent conspiracy of evil? to apprehend it beneath forms so mutable as to seem infinite? Charity, in Paris, must be as cunning as the thief. Each of us must be at one and the same time innocent and mistrustful; we must have powers of judgment that are as reliable and as swift as a glance."[29] But if the "frères de la Consolation" are less exciting than the Thirteen, this has less to do with the moralism of the former than it does of the increasing "transcendence" of the providential conspiracy, which little by little comes externally to intervene in a situation to which it has a merely contemplative relationship of pity and moral judgment. Here then, we can observe the slippage of more purely immanent plots into their transcendental opposite numbers. Whether this movement can be reversed and develop into some more original novelistic structure is a question better addressed to Dickens.

Our Mutual Friend—for many readers the darkest, most exciting, and Wilkie Collins–like of Dickens's completed novels, and also the one in

---

[28] Honoré de Balzac, *History of the Thirteen*, trans. Herbert J. Hunt (Middlesex: Penguin, 1974), 21.

[29] Honoré de Balzac, *La comédie humaine* (Paris: Pléiade, 1977), 8:323 (*L'envers de l'histoire contemporaine*, first episode). My translation.

which the salvational note is most satisfyingly sounded, and sentimentalism lifted into a truly providential realm of being—this late novel testifies to the temptation of conspiracy in Dickens as well, and to the "master-strokes of secret arrangement"[30] whereby the great feuilletonist attempts to hold together plot strands so numerous as to defy memory itself. But here conspiracy reveals its structure by promoting itself to a heightened power. The systematic promotion of illusion fostered by the symbolically eponymous protagonist ("mutual" also means a participation in several plots at once)[31] when he decides to take on a second existence after his alleged and public death—something that cannot be called a conspiracy exactly—in turn promotes a deception on the part of Mr. Boffin, the Golden Dustman (or junk collector) and ostensible heir of the miser's fortune. Here, then, we enter the realm of genuine conspiracy, not diminished by its moral uses as test and lesson: it will no doubt promote the fortunes of the good and the discomfiture of the wicked, who do indeed recognize this human agency for Providence as such: such is indeed the last glimpse of meaning perceived by the obsessed Bradley Headstone, one of the darkest characters in Dickens, as he comes to understand his failure to dislodge his rival for Lizzie (the "separation" referred to in the following):

> For then he saw that through his desperate attempt to separate those two for ever, he had been made the means of uniting them. That he had dipped his hands in blood, to mark himself a miserable fool and tool. That Eugene Wrayburn, for his wife's sake, set him aside and left him to crawl along his blasted course. He thought of Fate, or Providence, or be the directing Power what it might, as having put a fraud upon him—overreached him—and in his impotent mad rage bit, and tore, and had his fit.[32]

Yet however glorious the apotheosis of the Golden Dustman in this salvational denouement, which Dickens, evidently uncertain of himself, then redoubles in his postscript (in which Mr. and Mrs. Boffin miraculously survive a destructive railway accident), it cannot for most readers match the outcome of *Bleak House* itself, which will therefore have some lessons as to the providential slippages of the later work.

---

[30] Charles Dickens, *Our Mutual Friend*, ed. Edgar Johnson (New York: Modern Library, 1960), 794.

[31] " 'I may call him Our Mutual Friend,' said Mr. Boffin" (116).

[32] Ibid., 816.

Dustbins, to be sure, they have in common, and old Krook—he of the spontaneous combustion, as in Zola—is no doubt a match for Mr. Boffin;[33] but we will understand nothing of the providential if we imagine it has only to do with the conventional happy ending and the marriage of Esther to her true beloved. On the contrary, the supremely providential moment, the truly sublime note of salvationality, lies elsewhere: it is an Event, in the most august sense of the term, and one that people feel approaching in the street: "an unusual crowd . . . something droll . . . something interesting . . . everyone pushing and striving to get nearer . . . and presently great bundles too large to be got into any bags, immense masses of papers of all shapes and no shapes, which the bearers staggered under, and threw down for the time being, anyhow, on the Hall pavement, while they went back to bring out more."[34]

Laughter, universal glee, is the sign of this event, in which a whole old world is swallowed up and a new one born: and no reader who has worked through the thousand pages and nineteen installments of this extraordinary novel will fail to be electrified by the outcome: "Even these clerks were laughing. We glanced at the papers, and seeing Jarndyce and Jarndyce everywhere, asked an official-looking person who was standing in the midst of them, whether the cause was over. 'Yes,' he said; 'it was all up with it at last!' and burst out laughing too."[35] And this in an ante-penultimate chapter entitled "Beginning the World"!

These passages return us to the euphoria of our initial quotations, with a few additional findings. For one thing, it has become clear that the jubilation will necessarily be a collective one; it will tell the climax of the story of the Many rather than the One. In that sense, it bears a strong relationship to Kant's idea of enthusiasm, which he associated with the French Revolution and whose jubilation at least partly underscores its kinship with the Sublime, a parallel we cannot further explore here, save to recall the profound ambivalence of the Sublime, for Kant, which must awaken monstrous feelings of terror and revulsion fully as much as those of the expansion of joy.[36]

---

[33] Edgar Johnson compiles an impressive list of items, among them "soot, cinders, broken glass, bottles, crockery, worn-out pots and pans, old paper and rags, bones, garbage, human feces and dead cats" (ibid, xi, note 6).

[34] Dickens, *Bleak House*, 973–74.

[35] Ibid., 974.

[36] See Immanuel Kant, "General Comment on the Exposition of Aesthetic Reflective Judgements" (it follows paragraph 29), in *Critique of Judgment* (Indianapolis: Hackett, 1987), 126–40; and also J. F. Lyotard's interesting commentary in *Le différend* (Paris: Minuit, 1983), 238–40.

The Web of Totality

But we must also recall the fundamental shift in the evolution of this kind of novel from the question of individual salvation to the interweaving of many plots and many destinies. George Eliot is subversively outspoken on the matter of point of view, democratically insisting on everyone's right to this narrative centrality and reminding us, in the middle of a chapter gravitating to Dorothea as naturally as water finding its own level, that her unattractive spouse, Mr. Casaubon, also "had an intense consciousness within him, and was spiritually a-hungered like the rest of us."[37] Such reminders are virtually a social Bill of Rights (or Droits de l'Homme) for the novel as a form and will be programmatically enacted by later novelists like Joyce or Dos Passos.

What this implies most immediately, however, is the shift from the diachronic to the synchronic: now not the fateful destiny of this or that privileged or at least narratively favored protagonist, but rather the immense interweaving of a host of such lots or fates will involve a prodigious shifting of the axes of the novel and usher in the serials of Dickens we have been examining, no less than the late work of George Eliot herself, virtually our central exhibit in this discussion.

For not only the fact that the very word *providence* is dropped fatefully in the course of virtually every chapter of *Middlemarch* (sometimes by the characters, sometimes by the author herself), but the deeper sense of this recurrence—the drawing into the light of this omnipresent ideology of providence and destiny, of the providential character of good and bad fortune—makes of this great work a reflexive practice of providential realism as such. This is to say, using a term that is more meaningful when sparingly appealed to, that *Middlemarch* can be seen as an immense *deconstruction* of the ideology of providence as such, a tracking down of its religious overtones and undertones, and an almost surgical exploration of its results and effectivities. I insist on the term *ideology*, for other ideas of interrelationship and inextricability would have been possible in this period of the Paris Commune and the unification of Germany: Darwinian visions, nationalist programs, the bitter experience of class antagonisms—all of these, along with later ethnic or gender forms, might well have presided over the narrative of collective necessity, and in fact sometimes did. But Eliot's peculiar identification of this essentially social experience uniquely reflects the survival and ideological function of religion in the English class compromise, and allowed her to

---

[37] George Eliot, *Middlemarch* (London: Penguin, 1994), 278.

double a remarkable narrative synchronicity with a secondary investigation of the concepts through which the participants thought their experiences. (The term *deconstruction* was chosen to underscore the nonpartisan nature of the investigation, which does not overtly denounce these religious survivals, as outright ideological analysis would surely have wanted to do).

But her word *spiritual* is also misleading, to the degree that it suggests otherworldliness. To be sure, there is here a remarkable emphasis on intellectual labor. Earlier novelists were willing to tolerate glorified images of various artists, reunited under the general romantic rubric of "genius": Balzac even indulged in alchemical inventors of genius (*La recherche de l'absolu*), and thinkers of genius (*Louis Lambert*) but can scarcely be said to have had the sympathy for what would later in the century develop into scientific research as Eliot follows it, with technical curiosity, in the story of Lydgate. *Idealistic* in Hegel's usage, we may recall, simply means "theoretical," and Eliot brings a passionate curiosity to her depiction of all kinds of productive activity (including Garth's engineering).[38]

But what is certainly central in *Middlemarch*, and nontheoretical fully as much as nonspiritual, is the "cash nexus" and the synchronic role of money in the play of these individual destinies (which bear the name of a collectivity). The novel is a historical one, no doubt (1830), and the intensifying grip of a money economy over the provinces is one ostensible theme the book shares with Balzac (in the France of an earlier period). But the financial essence of "providence" is the key to this particular unmasking or deconstruction, and it is worth comparing it with Dickens's version, only a generation earlier.

For *Bleak House* shares a character with *Middlemarch*, and Fred Vincy's "great expectations" is a virtual replay, in a wholly different register, of the fate of poor Richard Carstone, that equally amiable young man famous for being able to spend the numerical sum he has economized in previous purchases without necessarily having it. But Dickens has concentrated the thematics of money in one place—the famous trial—thus allowing him to denounce the psychological corruption of expectation as such ("there's a dreadful attraction in the place," says Miss Flyte; "there's a cruel attraction in the place. You *can't* leave it. And you *must* expect")[39] rather than in the money economy as such. But in *Middlemarch* there is no destiny that is not in one way or another touched by money. Dickens's "web" is thus occasional: "There, too, [at Jo's sickbed] is Mr. Jarndyce many a time, and Allan

---

[38] Ibid., 250–51.
[39] Dickens, *Bleak House*, 566.

Woodcourt almost always; both thinking, much, how strangely Fate has en-tangled this rough outcast in the web of different lives."[40] But George Eliot's web is constitutive, as the multiplicity of her figures, as the various webs, threads, lines, scratches (on a burning glass), and interweavings suggest. I leave it to the Casaubons of the English Departments to make an inventory of these recurrent figures (it being understood that no one with any interest in allegory and interpretation can afford utterly to despise Mr. Casaubon's labors, however ill-fated).

We need to dispel two persistent errors about this narrative "fabric" and the meaning to be assigned to it. The first, despite what we have said about money and the material basis of this alleged attention to "spirituality," is the religious connotation of a novel that begins with St. Teresa and ends with a memorable celebration of Dorothea's goodness: ". . . for the growing good of the world is partly dependent on unhistoric acts; and that things are not so ill with you and and me as they might have been, is half owing to the number who live faithfully a hidden life, and rest in unvisited tombs."[41] Surely, despite the strength of all the arguments against the concept of secu-larization that have been referred to above, such words, and the portrait of Dorothea that precedes and justifies them, testify to an unmistakable intent to secularize on George Eliot's part: the will to invent a figure of saintliness for a worldly and commercial society, and to reinvent a demonstration of the well-nigh material power of the kindness that radiates from Dorothea, grip-ping those around her with an almost physical force. It is clear enough that Eliot wishes to celebrate modernity (Lydgate's scientific passion, Garth's sat-isfaction in sheer productivity) without sacrificing the components of an older communal and religious culture virtually extinguished by it. But the ideological intent of the author never constitutes the "meaning" of the book, but rather, as Adorno pointed out, functions as a component of its raw ma-terials. It will be possible to reinterpret Dorothea's centrality in another and nonethical way, as we shall see in a moment.

The other fundamental misconception about the novels of this period (and of the later nineteenth century in general) is that, on the strength of their keen sensitivity to the movements of feeling and inner perception, they are somehow "introspective." But to range George Eliot (or Dostoevsky either, for that matter) among the novelists of introspection, from Benjamin Con-stant's *Adolphe* to Proust, is to obscure everything that is truly and formally original about her work. What we have here—as compared with Dickens, for

[40] Ibid., 732.
[41] Eliot, *Middlemarch*, 838.

example—is a significantly enhanced proximity to the relationships between individuals, a kind of intensified and virtually photographic enlargement of those barely perceptible adjustments to the Other, which Nathalie Sarraute, long after the fact, called "tropismes." What was wrongly identified as a self-consciousness or reflexivity of the individual self (now increasingly endowed with that private or personal reservoir entitled the Unconscious) can on closer inspection be seen to be a minute and microscopic negotiation with the shock and scandal of the Other, a reverberation of muffled reactions back and forth as with the dance of insects confronting one another and attempting to gauge degrees of danger or attraction, if not neutrality. If a new theory of modernity be wanted, then it might just as well be this one, the discovery, in philosophy and in artistic representation as well, of the existence of the Other as what Sartre called a fundamental alienation of my Being. Philosophy, before Hegel's Master/Slave dialectic, altogether ignored the existence of other people as a philosophical problem that changed the very nature of philosophizing; as for literature, as long as the "other person" or character is imagined to be a kind of self-sufficient substance in itself, which occasionally comes into momentary or violent contact with other objects like it but whose being is not fundamentally modified by the being of others, then it matters very little what kinds of psychological experiences are attributed to these independent tokens of narration. But when, as here, the other is seen to call me into question in my very being; when relationships take precedence over the beings in relationship and a registering apparatus is developed that can detect such perpetual changes; when connections are focused close-up in their intolerable proximity ("marriage is so unlike everything else," Dorothea reflects, "there is something even awful in the nearness it brings"),[42] then a new dimension, a new social continent, has been discovered, which is the microcosm corresponding to the new macrocosms of collectivity on the level of cities and social classes.

Only after this do the intricate molecular patterns of a Henry James or the violent spasms of cruelty and self-abasement of a Dostoevsky or the multiple subatomic languages of what we are pleased to call modernism itself emerge. We have already observed that the alternative modernism/realism does not correspond to a classification system, but rather to a methodological focus, in such a way that it can scarcely be paradoxical for a "great realist" like George Eliot also, and from another angle, to be identified as a nascent modernist.

---

[42] Ibid., 797.

What needs to be taken into account for this to become more plausible is the ostentatiously omniscient and relatively archaic character of the style itself: but the latter imitates proverbs and traditional collective wisdom instead of anything redolent of Proustian self-expression and thus disguises the innovative nature of its intersubjective raw material at the same time that it seeks to incorporate the latter into a quintessentially social knowledge rather than documenting the discoveries of some "new science" such as psychology or psychoanalysis.

This "web" of interrelationships is now on the one hand to be grasped as an immense and mobile concatenation of events—encounters, looks, demands, self-defenses—rather than a static table of equivalences; and at this point its synchronic nature also necessarily becomes visible, in the form of interconnections that fan out well beyond the reader's field of vision and are yet modified by the most minute adjustments in the "lives" thereby brushing against each other.[43] What we must observe about Dorothea's saintliness is that it not only prolongs and perpetuates its effects across a multiplicity of neighboring connections but that pain and suffering do so as well, and the various Dickensian wills—Mr. Casaubon's and Mr. Featherstone's, along with the deployment of money in his various projects by Bulstrode—are here transmuted into vehicles for the transmission of bad vibrations across the same immense capillary system. But what has been lost in the shift in the replacement of a diachronic providentiality—an attention to the salvation of the individual—by this synchronic vision is simply the ethical itself, or better still, any sense of evil as such. There is, in George Eliot, goodness, but its opposite is simply unhappiness; and we are forbidden to judge either Casaubon or Bulstrode as evil, even through their contemporaries may well do so.

The point is that, reinscribed in the web of interrelationships, what is painful or unhappy for one subjectivity in this immense network can, as it is transmitted over the links of a whole series, be transformed into something positive for others; just as the reverse can happen too.[44] But this possibility of the transformation of negative into positive, of suffering into happiness and back, clearly lifts these categories up into another suprapersonal dimension

---

[43] Ibid., 795.

[44] Mr. Skimpole's Panglossianism (in *Bleak House*) may be said to anticipate this transcendence of good and evil in a comic and aestheticizing (or contemplative) register: " 'Enterprise and effort,' he would say to us (on his back), 'are delightful to me. . . . Mercenary creatures ask, "What is the use of a man's going to the North Pole? What good does it do?" I can't say; but for anything I *can* say, he may go for the purpose—though he don't know it—of employing my thoughts as I lie here' " (Dickens, *Bleak House*, 294–95).

and tends to efface older ethical or eudaimonic meanings. (It also forfeits the great game of the ominiscient narrator, which is to know secrets that none of the characters involved will ever learn, ironically taking their un-happy ignorance to their graves. Here, "essence must appear," as Hegel says, and the secrets, already appearing under the guise of their effects, must necessarily be revealed.)

But is not their misery—so vividly registered here in ways unequalled in the other novels of the time—a proof of George Eliot's supreme insight into psychology? In fact, in both Casaubon and Bulstrode, what we confront are masterful diagnoses of what Sartre will later on call *mauvaise foi*, the bad faith of self-deception and agonizing and impossible attempts at self-justification. But these moments already contain otherness within them, in the form of judgment, in which the suffering subject interiorizes the gaze of the other and seeks to master and reorient it in his or her own favor. Indeed, as these tropismes become magnified by way of the novelistic or narrative medium, we glimpse a parallel magnification in the social itself, which is none other than the dimension of gossip itself, which enlarges the facts of in-terrelationship and transmits them onward to a circulation through the col-lectivity. It is the other face of my alienation by the other, and extends on into the vision of history itself as "a huge whispering-gallery" in which we are ultimately privy to "the secret of usurpations and other scandals gos-siped about long empires ago."[45]

Yet now providentiality returns, in an extraordinary and unexpected guise, at the moment when its actions and effectivities seemed all but unde-cideable. Casaubon and Bulstrode end unhappily; Lydgate's scientific ambi-tions are dashed, and his marriage loses all its enchantment; yet contrary to all expectations, Dorothea's ends well, and the renunciation (*Entsagung*) for which the German tradition, from Goethe to Fontane, had prepared us—let alone the terrible and emblematic solitude of spinster and widow from Balzac to Maupassant—is here dispelled by an utterly unexpected happy ending, for which we did not even dare to have "hope against hope" (and which, in hindsight, renders somewhat exaggerated the elegiac last lines about her which I have quoted above).

But the truly providential in *Middlemarch* lies elsewhere, and to appreci-ate it, we must note another significant feature of the providential-synchronic that we have hitherto omitted. We have learned, to be sure, that the synchronic and the diachronic are not to each other as space is to time,

---

[45] Eliot, *Middlemarch*, 412.

nor even as the ahistorical is to the historical, let alone the nonnarrative to the narrative; yet we would be justified in expecting time, history, and narrativity to undergo some fundamental modifications as they pass under a synchronic regime. When, as here, we have to do with the synchronic as a simultaneity of destinies and a coexistence of a host of different narratives, what happens to temporality is this: the simultaneous time lines become, as in Einsteinian relativity, difficult to reckon off against each other. It is simultaneity itself that becomes spatial, and in this new spatiality the various distinct temporalities can be adjusted against each other only with some difficulty, as in the voluminous historical concordances we might expect to find in Mr. Casaubon's papers. Indeed the two series of events run side by side like Einstein's trains: who can tell what time it is outside, let alone inside; there are many train tracks, parallel and infinite; they keep passing each other in some ideal present; their own times overlap, cancel, outleap each other, overtake, fall behind. But every so often they overtake, not the other's, but their own past; they speed ahead of themselves and run through the line a second time.

Here, then, occasionally, something miraculous happens; and it is just such a miraculous happening that we are able to witness in the destiny of Fred Vincy, whose hopes of an inheritance and the estate called Stone Court are properly dashed at an early crisis in the novel, in which "realism" demands that the unrealistic hope and expectation be brought to an expected unhappy end. This play with expectation constitutes a kind of novelistic "reality principle," which we find historically realized twice over in the classic Balzacian "hope against hope," and then in the gloomy fatalities of naturalism.

Here, on the contrary, it is the reality principle that must be joyously discredited; yet it is the test and the obligation of the form of providential realism to outwit sheer wish-fulfillment and daydream, to overtrump both fairytale endings and naturalist certainties with a new form of necessity. Fred Vincy will administer the estate after all (even if he does not technically inherit it), and this loop in time, in which the lost chance comes again against all odds, and the old hope is fulfilled after its definitive disappointment, is the concrete narrative embodiment of that religious iconography of resurrection with which we began, and the recuperation, by Eliot's voluminous realism, of the coming alive of the statue in *Pericles*: it is the salvational temporality of Ernst Bloch's privileged fable of the *Unverhofftes Wiedersehen* (a story by Hebel later rewritten and recapitulated by Hoffman), in which in extreme old age the widow of a dead miner is able to glimpse her long-lost husband one last time again as youthful as on the day he disappeared. What interests us here, however, is the way in which these stirring images find their own unexpected resurrection in the most seemingly unpropitious of forms, the nineteenth-century novel itself. It is an ecstatic ending that previous novels could only achieve by the glimpse of the ghosts of Heathcliff and Catherine wandering together over the moor.

Postmodern Providentialities

Now we must rapidly conclude, with only the briefest of glances at the descendency of this form in contemporary culture, and in particular in contemporary film. For both Quentin Tarantino's *Pulp Fiction* (1994) and Goran Paskaljevic's *Cabaret Balkan* (1998, also known as *The Powder Keg*), if not, indeed, Milcho Manchevski's 1994 *Before the Rain*, seem to testify to a revival of effects structurally dependent on the apparent simultaneity of narrative time lines. Despite the bloodiness and violence of all these films, each conceals a salvational note underscored by the conversion of a professional killer, in the first-named of these works, to the old-time religion.

But it is to their prototype, in Robert Altman's *Short Cuts* (1993), that we must turn for some more fundamental structural insight into this new and old form, which seems to reflect an intensifying feeling for the interrelatedness of the social totality. In much of Altman's work (*A Wedding*, 1975; *Nashville*, 1978; *Pret-à-porter*, 1994; *Cookie's Fortune*, 1999; *Dr. T and the Women*, 2000), the multiplicity of plot lines and characters frequently leads to providential sparks and fires; and these are also, as we have seen with George Eliot, beyond good and evil, which is to say that the providential outcome can absorb either a happy or an unhappy ending indifferently, from what is a kind of Spinozan elevation.

But *Short Cuts* is the most revealing of these works, insofar as it embodies the very gesture of totalization itself. The film is based, indeed, on a compilation of stories by Raymond Carver, which for the most part offer unrelieved glimpses of failure and private misery: the one exception, "A Small, Good Thing," in which a fatal accident is unexpectedly transfigured by a symbolic wake, is then itself amplified, in its providential content, by Altman's combination of all these separate stories into a web of episodes or multiple plots. Speaking of one of Balzac's shorter stories, Lukács once observed: "To treat this theme in a novel instead of a short story would require entirely different subject matter and an entirely different plot. In a novel the writer would have to expose and develop in breadth the entire process arising out of the social conditions of modern life and leading to these . . . problems."[46] Altman's unification, however, achieves this miraculous transformation without any modification of the subject matter or plots of the stories, simply by prodigious enlargement of their frame and context and a virtual creation, ex nihilo, of the totality they now come to express and represent. It is a passage from the private to the collective, from the static-ontological to the dynamic and the historically actual—the whole concatenation of episodes ominously overflown by the notorious med-fly fumigations of 1981 and shaken climactically by the long-awaited "major earthquake to come"—which reinvents the providential narrative anew for late capitalism.

---

[46] George Lukács, "Art and Objective Truth," in *Writer and Critic* (New York: Grosset and Dunlap, 1971), 54.

READINGS

Prototypes

MASSIMO FUSILLO

Aethiopika
(Heliodorus, Third or Fourth Century)

> The cheerful smile of day was just appearing, as the rays
> of the sun began to light up the mountain tops, when
> some men armed like brigands peered over the ridge
> that stretches alongside the outlets of the Nile and that
> mouth of the river which is named after Hercules. They
> halted there for a little while, scanning with their eyes
> the sea that lay below them; and when they had cast
> their first glances over the ocean and found no craft
> upon it and no promise there of pirates' plunder, they
> bent their gaze down upon the shore near by. And what
> it showed was this: a merchant ship was moored there
> by her stern cables, bereft of her ship's company, but
> full laden; so much could be inferred even at a distance,
> for her burthen brought the water as high as the third
> waling-piece of her timpers. The shore was thickly
> strewn with newly slain bodies, some quite lifeless, and
> others half dead whose limbs were aquiver, thus
> indicating that the conflict has only just ceased.
>
> —HELIODORUS, *Ethiopian Story*[1]

The Jamesian, cinematic incipit of Heliodorus's *Aethiopika* is a complete anomaly in the panorama of ancient narrative. The ancient Greek novels begin at the beginning, introducing the place where the action takes place and the two protagonists. Heliodorus, by contrast, adopts the strict point of view of a gang of brigands contemplating an incomprehensible scene that rightfully belongs to the middle of the plot (the topos of the hero and heroine being kidnapped by a group of pirates). The narrow point of view (or, as Genette would call it, the internal focalization) is a technique that would not be codified until Henry James, but this was not its first appearance in a Greek novel. Achilles Tatius had already used this device to create suspense in *Leucippe and Clitophon*, his ironic recycling of the novel's conventions (particularly the most spectacular: apparent death).[2] But the central role that it plays in the *Aethiopika* is unprecedented. Here the point of view is an integral part

---

[1] Trans. Sir Walter Lamb (London: J. M. Dent; Rutland, Vt.: Charles E. Tuttle, 1997), 1.1.3. Lamb's spelling of Greek names has been altered to reflect contemporary scholarly usage.

[2] See especially the episode in 3.15. B. Effe, "Entstehung und Funktion 'personaler' Erzählweisen in der Erzählliteratur der Antike," *Poetika* 7 (1975): 150–51.

of a complex semantic system built around the gradual circumstantial deciphering of the divine by both the characters inside the story and the readers outside of it.

The whole first book plays with the reader's horizon of expectation: the scene witnessed from the brigand's point of view culminates in a long description of the two protagonists, although their names and their role as main characters are not revealed until much later. Following the model of the *Odyssey*, the events leading up to the *in medias res* opening scene are related through a long story within the story, which is told not by the protagonist, as in Homer's poem, but by a key character, the Egyptian prophet Kalasiris. Kalasiris is the perfect embodiment of Heliodorus's innovative approach to the novel as a genre, which proceeds along two parallel axes: epic ennoblement and philosophical rewriting. The other Greek novels have a system of characters clearly subdivided into lovers and rivals (and thus into positive and negative elements). Kalasiris, instead, represents a thoroughly new element, completely escaping this binary logic. An aide to the protagonists (like Manzoni's Don Cristoforo) as well as the director and narrator of the story, he acquires a remarkably autonomous density (his adventures form a subplot of their own). Moreover, since he is described as having a broad syncretistic, neoplatonic, and neopythagorian formation, his figure reflects the author, creating the effect of a *mise en abîme*.

In this framework the relationship between Kalasiris and his implied reader, the young Athenian Knemon, is very important. Heliodorus greatly amplified the Homeric device of *metadiegesis* (story-within-a story): in addition to containing other narratives at one, two, and even three removes from the main story, the story-within-a story is frequently interrupted, not only to lend more focus to the span of time but also to comment, in a metaliterary way, on the pivotal points. Knemon represents the standard reader of the Greek sentimental novel: he does not distinguish between fiction and reality; he is curious and loves digression and spectacle; above all, he is singularly obsessed with the love theme. His monomania does not mean that his viewpoint is false: when he states that it would take a heart of stone not to be moved by the love story of Theagenes and Charikleia (4.4), he clearly reflects the author's hopes for the novel's success. It is, however, only partial: the *Aethiopika* is *also* a sentimental novel, but one that has been profoundly reinvented.[3] We read, for example, how Kalasiris reformulates in neoplatonic

---

[3] This is a controversial point in Heliodoran studies: Using a formula borrowed from Apuleius, John J. Winkler calls Knemon a "lector non scrupolosus," in "The Mendacity of Kalasiris and the Narrative Strategy of Heliodorus' *Aithiopika*," *Yale Classical Studies* 27 (1982): 93–158; John

terms the topos of love at first sight, which would prove to be so durable in the history of the novel (as well as melodrama and film), especially the mystic variant of the moment of recognition:[4]

> Then, my dear Knemon, we were convinced by what occurred of the divinity of the soul and its kinship with the powers on high. For at the moment of meeting the young pair looked and loved, as though the soul of each at the first encounter recognized its fellow and leapt toward that which deserved to belong to it. At first they stopped short, in consternation; then, with a lingering motion, she proffered and he received the torch, with eyes intently fixed on each other, as if they had had some previous knowledge or sight which they were recalling to memory. Next, they smiled slightly and furtively, a smile traceable only by the light shed forth by their eyes. Then, as though ashamed of what they did, they blushed; and again, their passion, I conceive, having seized hold also of their hearts, they turned pale and, in short, a thousand changes of expression in that brief moment spread over the features of them both, as every variation of hue and look declared the agitation of their souls. (3.5.70)

According to the standard plot of the Greek novel, two adolescents of the opposite sex fall in love at the beginning of the story, are separated, and live through a series of parallel adventures, often falling into the traps of malicious rivals, and are finally reunited in the unfailing happy ending. This schema tends to praise reciprocal, happy love, which materializes in the form of a tale of the desire for symmetry typical of unconscious logic.[5] Heliodorus's two lovers are represented as two faces of the same coin: both are adolescents (the mythical age of classical Greece), possess divine beauty (a secular vestige of the myth), and are of elevated social rank (belonging to the best families of the same city). This parallelism is an innovation over the canonical love relations of classical Greece (both marriage and pederasty,

---

Robert Morgan reverses the terms, arguing that Knemon mirrors in the text the public response that Heliodorus was hoping for, in "Reader and Audiences in the *Aethiopika* of Heliodoros," *Gronigen Colloquia on the Novel* 4 (1991): 85–103.

[4] Jean Rousset, *Leurs yeux se rencontrèrent: La scène de première vue dans le roman* (Paris: José Corti, 1981). This is a broad typological study, from Heliodorus to Roland Barthes, which also covers the anamnesis variant that found its way to Wagner.

[5] See Massimo Fusillo, *Il romanzo greco: Polifonia ed eros* (Venice: Marsilio, 1989), chap. 3; the concept of symmetrical logic is explained in Ignacio Matte Blanco, *The Unconscious as Infinite Sets: An Essay in Bi-Logic* (London: Duckworth, 1975). See also David Konstan, *Sexual Symmetry: Love in the Ancient Novel and Related Genres* (Princeton, N.J.: Princeton University Press, 1994).

the latter being more eroticized), which were always based on a sharp imbalance in terms of age and power. The couple's amorous investment remains intact until the end, when they triumph over having been divided by time and space. In *Candide*, Voltaire served up bitter irony on this novelistic convention, which had been passed down from the Greek novel to the baroque: by the end of the novel the protagonists are decrepit, unable to enjoy the marriage they had struggled so hard to achieve. Even one of the few theorists of the novel to deal with ancient narrative, Mikhail Bakhtin—who invented the category "adventurous chronotype" to describe it—argued that the Greek novel of love and adventure existed in an extratemporal hiatus between two moments in biographical time.[6]

In reality there are countless variations on this model: the only instance of it in a pure state is the *Ephesiaka* by Xenophon of Ephesus (second century A.D.), which some critics consider merely an abridged version of a longer work.[7] Even the first novel that we possess in its entirety, *Chaereas and Callirhoe* by Chariton (first century A.D.), has interesting variants and nuances. In general, however, we can distinguish between an earlier phase, of a more consoling or entertaining character (paraliterary, as it were), and a later more refined and more literary phase—the only one to have had great resonance in modern literature—that is neorhetorical and neosophist. During the later phase, an established, popular, and widely circulated genre is subjected to complex operations of rewriting. Such is the case of the ironic pastiche by Achilles Tatius, *Leucippe and Clitophon* (later half of the second century A.D.), or of *Daphnis and Chloe* by Longus the Sophist (third century A.D.), an erotic novel that is contaminated by the bucolic tradition, thus forgoing the topos of the adventurous journey.

Coming at the end of this later phase, the *Aethiopika* of Heliodorus (which can be dated to the third or perhaps fourth century A.D.)[8] takes the transformation of the novel's conventions to its extreme consequences. This

---

[6] M. M. Bakhtin, *The Dialogic Imagination: Four Essays*, trans. Caryl Emerson and Michael Holquist (Austin: University of Texas Press, 1981).

[7] The whole question is examined in Tomas Hägg, "Die *Ephesiaka* des Xenophon Ephesios: Original oder Epitome?" *Classica et Mediaevalia* 27 (1966): 118–61, which supports the thesis of the original text.

[8] Rivers of ink have been spilled on the issue of dating: for the third-century hypothesis (which connects the novel to the neopythagorian circle of Julia Domna), see T. Szapessy, "La siege de Nisibe et la chronologie d'Héliodore," in *Acta Antiqua Hungarica* 24 (1975): 247–76; for the fourth-century hypothesis (on the basis of controversial historiographic and bibliographic sources), see Pierre Chuvin, "Les dates des *Ethiopiques* d'Héliodore," in *Chronique des derniers païens* (Paris: Les Belles Lettres, 1990), 321–23.

perspective explains why a neoplatonic prophet was enlisted as the narrator to relate the main topoi (enamorment, family conflict, the journey, kidnapping by pirates, traps set by rivals, and separation of the couple). The main difference between *Aethiopika* and other Greek novels—and not only the popular, sentimental novels of the earlier phase—lies in the narrative structure of the whole. The other novels take a linear approach, following the chronological order of the fiction from beginning to end, relating a circular story that begins and ends in the same city, the hometown of both hero and heroine. In Heliodorus the situation is completely reversed. The story is not linear; it begins in the middle to create suspense and slowly recuperates the preceding events through flashbacks. Following a calibrated internal division of the whole into books (probably made by the author himself), we reread the opening scene at the end of the fifth book, in the dead center of the novel. This time, however, the plot mechanisms have been made clear, and we hear the scene through the more emotionally involved voice of Kalasiris, rather than from the outside perspective given by the incipit. Although the narrative is thus patterned on a circle—a serpent biting its tale, according to the Byzantine philosopher and theologian Michael Psellos (1018–81)—the story itself follows a linear orientation, borrowed from that great prototype for the novel, the *Odyssey*. This is the story, in fact, of a rather peculiar journey of return to the homeland: having grown up at Delphi in Greece, initially unaware of her true identity, the protagonist Charikleia, an Ethiopian princess, reaches her true home in the end and is reunited with her parents, in a spectacular baroque finale led up to in a slow crescendo (while the male protagonist, the Greek Theagenes, abandons his home country forever at the end).

This innovation in the plot structure is related to one of the most interesting characteristics of *Aethiopika*, especially today: its cultural syncretism or, in a manner of speaking, its multiculturalism. When Bakhtin defined the adventurous chronotype of the Greek novel, he stressed how its frenetic rhythm never implies a valorization of single geographic places or time periods.[9] A reader of the *Ephesiaka* will immediately note the constant succession of all of the spaces in the then known world, which is always a theater of the same peripeteia, without any cultural differentiation. It is a way to mythicize and eroticize the hero as well as his triumph in space and time (in addition to paying clear tribute to the childish pleasure in repetition, which popular literature has always exploited).[10]

---

[9] Bakhtin, *The Dialogic Imagination*.
[10] Daniel Couégnas, *Introduction à la paralittérature* (Paris: Editions du Seuil, 1992).

But the *Aethiopika* is completely different: it outlines a complex system of cultures that corresponds, in part, to the polyphony of the narrating voices. The preeminent negative pole is represented by Persia, the place of unrestrained sensuality and oppressive despotism, the setting for the erotic intrigues of Arsake, sister of the Great King, a powerful and sublime symbol of eros as disease and eros as madness, the model for a host of evil rivals (up to and including Verdi's Amneris): the sadistic persecution of the protagonist produces a latent, unconscious identification in the reader. A very low rung is also assigned to the center of classical Greece, Athens, represented by Knemon, both implied reader and narrator of an erotic novella based on the myth of Phaedra. Slightly higher is the position of Delphi, the home of an ancient oracular wisdom represented by the voice of Charikles, the protagonist's adoptive father and himself the narrator of a segment of the main story. Yet this is a partial and unsuccessful behavioral model. The culture of Egypt is greatly valorized, since it stands at the intersection of Greek and Eastern culture that would produce Homer. Egypt is personified by the prophet Kalasiris, a central figure who is not, however, destined to accompany the protagonists to their final objective. His death in Persia after rediscovering and recognizing his children—a unique case of pathetic, sublime death in the Greek novel that is neither apparent nor redemptive—brings the secondary plot to a close by rewriting Euripides' *Phoenicians* in a positive, antitragic key. Naturally, the top rung of this hierarchy belongs to Ethiopia, an almost utopian place, home of the ancient wisdom of the gymnosophists. The final consecration of Theagenes and Charikleia to Helios and Selene (identified with Apollo and Artemis) concludes the novel's syncretism, which becomes more prominent than the topos of consolatory marriage.

At plot's end, the hero and heroine are not remotely equal to what they were at the beginning. In particular for Charikleia—by far the most important character, a new model of the pragmatic, Odyssean heroine—the journey through different cultures signifies a recovery of identity. Heliodorus is, in fact, the only ancient Greek novelist to allude to ethnicity (skin color and Charikleia's journey from Greece to Africa, from white to black, a feature that has been commented on by African-American studies since as early as the nineteenth century).[11] He is also the only novelist to stress every aspect of linguistic communication (the language in which the characters speak and how they speak, whether they use an interpreter, and so forth). Finally, he

---

[11] Daniel L. Selden, "*Aithiopika* and Ethiopianism," in *Studies in Heliodorus*, ed. Richard Hunter (Cambridge: Cambridge Philological Society, 1998), 182–214; the same volume contains Tim Whitmarsh, "The Birth of a Prodigy: Heliodorus and the Genealogy of Hellenism," 93–124.

deliberately signs his novel by calling himself a Phoenician from Emesa rather than a Hellenized Greek.

Heliodorus's preference for complex forms and hierarchies is reflected in his writing: dense, precious, and always composed of long, elaborate sentences. This high register completely formalizes its basic operation: to epicize and ennoble a hybrid literary form, born in the Eastern provinces of the Roman Empire (which is strangely never mentioned), that had never gained admission to the official system of codified genres. The modern reception of the work also reflects its ambiguous, shifting position. After being directly imitated by the Byzantine novels, Heliodorus reappears in the high Renaissance, when he was read *tout court* as an epic poet, ranked immediately below Homer and Virgil. The baroque and the seventeenth century on the whole exhibited a special predilection for the *Aethiopika* because of shared thematic nuclei (eros, the relationship between fiction and reality, theatricality). In addition to the genre of heroic romance, key figures composed imitations, dramatizations, and versifications of Heliodorus, such as Tasso, Shakespeare, Cervantes, Calderón, Racine, Hardy, and Basile. After the emergence of the realist novel, the genre underwent a rapid, irreversible decline that ended, in part, a few decades ago (though only in the academic environment), when narratology on the one hand and paraliterary studies on the other compelled scholars to critically rethink the ancient genre that had been born even before the term *novel* (in fact, previous eras hesitated to recognize ancient Greek narrative as "novels"). For Heliodorus today the danger is that the whole corpus of Greek novels will be homogenized. Too often treated they are automatically cataloged as equivalent to the *feuilleton* or the soap opera. The risk today, in short, is the direct opposite of what happened in the baroque: rather than subjecting these works to excessive praise, they are being made to seem too ordinary. Such an approach would fail to grasp the profound ambivalence of Heliodorus to his chosen genre, which is one of the most enticing motifs that the elaborate architecture of the *Aethiopika* has to offer.

Translated by Michael F. Moore

ABDELFATTAH KILITO

Maqāmāt
(Hamadhānī, Late Tenth Century)

Known by the name of Badīʿ al-Zamān, "the Prodigy of the Age," Hamadhānī (d. 1007) is the originator of a narrative genre that had enormous success in Arabic culture, namely the *maqāma*, which can be translated, approximately, into English as "assembly" or "session," and into French as "séance." The word *maqāma* literally means "the place where one stands," and, by extension, an assembly, a meeting where one listens to an orator. The word also refers to the speech delivered on this occasion, a sermon, for example. But from the tenth century onward, *maqāma* (pl. *maqāmāt*) has been the term for a short narrative that opens with the fixed formula: " ʿĪsā b. Hishām has related to us and said: . . ." Writers after Hamadhānī usually retained this formula, varying the name of the narrator of course. Generally speaking, the *maqāmāt* are characterized by a narrative structure that is relatively stable, organized around a speech in verse or prose that is delivered by a rhetor before a standing or seated audience: a mixed crowd in the public square, the assembled worshipers in a mosque, a small group of friends gathered in a room or a tavern, and sometimes a traveling companion.

The *maqāma* thus presents two main figures—the one who speaks and the one, or those, who listen—between whom there develops a relationship of master to pupil. In addition to his other attributes, the rhetor distinguishes himself above all by his literary knowledge and his virtuosity in the use of language. Viewed from this perspective, the rhetor's adventures can easily be reduced to two basic types: either he reveals his knowledge of his own accord, or he follows an order or submits to a test. In both cases, as soon as he ends his speech, his listeners give free rein to their admiration and generosity, since it is well understood that in the *maqāma*, knowledge pays.

Among the listeners there must always be one character who reappears in each narrative and who, in addition to the role he plays in the story, takes it upon himself to recount afterward what he has seen and heard. This is the narrator or, more precisely, to use the Arabic term, a *rāwī* or transmitter. While the public varies from one narrative to another, the transmitter always remains linked to the figure of the rhetor; they go their separate ways, of course, at the end of each *maqāma*, but always find each other again in the next. The rules of the genre require that the *rāwī* is always present, keeping the speeches of the rhetor in his memory so that he can make them known to others. In this way he fulfills, as already mentioned, a double function: he is both a participant in the plot and a reporter of the speeches he has heard and the circumstances in which they were delivered.

To review the characteristics discussed so far: the *maqāma* presupposes a speech of indisputable value and a transmitter who records it directly from the mouth of a rhetor. These features replicate exactly those that characterize the *ḥadīth*, or the words of the Prophet. In the *ḥadīth*, there is someone who knows (the Prophet) and someone else who desires to know (a member of the Muslim community). The latter communicates what he has learned from the Prophet to another individual who, in turn, transmits his knowledge to others, and so on until the *ḥadīth* becomes fixed in its written form in a collection. The *ḥadīth* is composed of two parts: the *matn*, or speech attributed to the Prophet, often accompanied by details about the context in which it was delivered, and the *sanad*, or enumeration of the chain of guarantors who have soundly transmitted the speech. If the *maqāma* was able to constitute itself as a genre, it was in large part by borrowing the "stylistic signs" of the *ḥadīth*. The *maqāma* too is provided, though in the fictive mode, with a *matn* and a *sanad*: that is, the rhetor's speech and its context (*matn*), and the means by which it was transmitted (*sanad*).

Like many other writers of Persian origin, Hamadhānī wrote in Arabic, although that did not prevent him, on occasion, from also writing in Persian. He liked to compose bilingual poems, writing lines of verse with one hemistich in Arabic and the other in Persian. Doubtless one can consider this image of a poem conceived in two languages to be a game on Hamadhānī's part, a rhetorical exercise, a display of verbal juggling. But such poems also suggest Hamadhānī's love of disguise and doubles, a preoccupation that recurs throughout his narratives.

Hamadhānī's characters come in pairs, just as, later on, do Don Quixote and Sancho, Jacques and his master, or Bouvard and Pécuchet. At first sight, they appear to be opposites: 'Īsā b. Hishām, the transmitter, is elegant, refined, delicate; Abū-l-Fatḥ of Alexandria, the rhetor, is a beggar, a wandering mendicant (*mukaddī*). When the two meet, the former does not often miss a chance to blame the latter and reproach him for leading a degrading life. But the contrast is not firmly drawn: thus 'Īsā b. Hishām sometimes behaves like a vagrant, and Abū-l-Fatḥ of Alexandria sometimes acts like a respectable man, even consorting with princes. Their world is one of instability, uncertainty, reversals of fortune, changes in appearance and situation. Vagrancy is the dominant theme of the *maqāma*, which offers a veritable repertoire of the tricks of beggars, rogues, and brigands. But the true guiding thread through these texts is the theme of metamorphosis.

Metamorphosis, or shifting identities: when 'Īsā b. Hishām meets up again with Abū-l-Fatḥ of Alexandria, he often does not recognize him immediately. Indeed, the protagonist does not always appear in the same guise— sometimes he is imam in a mosque; sometimes showman with his monkey; sometimes preacher, blindman, beggar, madman, or theologian. His physical aspect is sometimes that of a youth, sometimes that of an older man. Moreover, he is not attached to any one particular place; though he is very much a native of Alexandria, he never returns there. And anyway, which Alexandria would it be, since Alexander the Great founded several? The rhetor travels through space, moving from one country to another without rhyme or reason. "I am a native of every country and every place," he says. It is not even certain he is an Arab; one night he may be, but in the morning he can appear as a Nabatean. And his religion changes with the time of day: "In the morning I am a priest in a monastery, in the evening a pious man in the mosque."

This fragmentation into various identities is, for Hamadhānī's rhetor, a reflection of his "century," of the "age" (*zamān*), which is constantly changing and offering new aspects. The world of the *maqāma* is governed by an anonymous and capricious force, which exalts or humbles individuals for no apparent reason and, ruling with absolute arbitrariness, is responsible for the madness of the world. No one can trust in such a force; the hero recommends letting oneself be swept along by the current and submitting to the surrounding madness. From this perspective, the *maqāmāt* are an apologia for cynicism and nihilism. They establish the rule of the double, expressed in the oppositions of language and behavior, speaking and acting. In one *maqāma*, for example, Abū-l-Fatḥ of Alexandria is imam in a mosque; after leading the prayers, he turns violently on the wine drinkers. Yet once the prayers are over, he heads into a tavern to drink and enjoy himself! An imam in a tavern: this is a semantic scandal, an oxymoron. It is worth mentioning here the existence in Arabic of *aḍdād*, or ambivalent words, in which a single sound can mean both one thing and its opposite. Hamadhānī's characters can, in this sense, be considered to be *aḍdād-s*, creatures of ambivalence.

The doubling is also evident at the level of style. The *maqāma* is a hybrid genre that mingles prose and poetry. Poetry, it should be noted, far from being a simple decorative element in the text, is an integral part of the narration. Prose predominates, but it is a rhythmic prose where each syntagma rhymes with the next. Rhyme consists, obviously, of identical sounds at the end of different words, and it is precisely such a "similarity in contrast" that characterizes the protagonists of the *maqāma*. Phrases, syntagmas, come in pairs, just like 'Īsā b. Hishām and Abū-l-Fatḥ of Alexandria.

Thanks to the works of Hamadhānī, Arabic literature, which up until this period had largely been confined to the courts of princes and salons of the notable, discovered the street, the public square, the common people, and the world of the marginalized, madmen, and rogues. With the character of Abū-l-Fatḥ of Alexandria, Hamadhānī has enriched Arabic literature with a new figure: the literary beggar, the wandering rhetor who tries to earn his living through his eloquence. The originality of such a figure, who appears for the first time, it seems, from this pen, is even more stunning when one realizes that Abū-l-Fatḥ of Alexandria is a rhetor who lacks all grandeur. He is a *mukaddī*, a rogue devoid of scruples, adept at vagrancy. He sometimes manages to get himself admitted to the courts of princes, but most often he is in the street, on the road, hungry and destitute, thrown into wretched adventures. Without faith or law, hearth or home, there is nevertheless one stable element to which he attaches himself, the Arabic language. At no moment is there any question for him of speaking another language: Arabic is his genealogical principle, his home, and the very root of his existence. Deprived of all ties, he is forever attached to this language and to the world that recognizes and uses it, "the empire of Islam" (*mamlakat al-Islām*) as it was called; and what is more, he has no thought of ever traveling beyond the frontiers of this empire.

Critics have established parallels between the *maqāma*, the *Satyricon* of Petronius, and *The Golden Ass* of Apuleius; in their wake, one could also invoke Till Eulenspiegel and Panurge. But it is the Spanish picaresque novel that seems to have the most links with the work of Hamadhānī. The title of Quevedo's novel, *Life and Adventures of the Buscon: Model of Vagabonds and Mirror of Rogues (Historia de la vida del Buscón: Ejemplo de vagamundos y espejo de tacaños)*, could apply perfectly to the adventures of Abū-l-Fatḥ of Alexandria. Don Pablo, Lazarillo de Tormes, and Guzman d'Alfarache are reincarnations of the *maqāma*'s hero with whom they have numerous points in common: wandering, begging, scatology, fraud, and a pessimism tinged with humor. But the influence of Hamadhānī on the Spanish novel has not been established convincingly. The appearance of the picaresque in Arabic literature in the tenth century and in Spanish literature in the sixteenth remains a mystery.

Hamadhānī had numerous imitators in the Arab world among whom one could mention Ibn Nāqiyā (d. 1092), but it is al-Ḥarīrī (d. 1122) who is particularly worthy of attention. A century after Hamadhānī, he composed fifty *maqāmāt* that had tremendous success. He is an epigone, certainly, but as sometimes happens, he surpassed his model; in his case, imitation revealed itself to be superior to creation. As in the works of Hamadhānī, the *maqāmāt* of Ḥarīrī include a rhetor, Abū Zayd al-Sarūjī, and a transmitter, al-Ḥarīth b. Ḥammām, and we also find the same structure based on oppositions between being and seeming, disguise and recognition. There is, however, more consistency in the narratives of Ḥarīrī. To depict this schematically, one could describe each work as unfolding the same sequence of episodes: the transmitter arrives in a village where he notices the rhetor (disguised) in the midst of seducing a group of listeners with a speech full of lies; once the speech is over, he is generously rewarded by his audience; the transmitter suddenly recognizes the rhetor and, taking him aside, reproaches him for his double-dealing; the rhetor defends himself in a rather cavalier manner; and finally the two characters go their separate ways.

But in addition to the regularity with which this sequence is reproduced in each *maqāma*, Ḥarīrī's work reveals a coherence within the whole corpus. There is, indeed, between Hamadhānī and Ḥarīrī, an important difference that should be underscored: while the narratives of the former are grouped into a *collection*, those of Ḥarīrī constitute a *book*. Hamadhānī supposedly composed about four hundred *maqāmāt*, though only about fifty of them have been preserved. He probably did not collect them together himself; in any event, the manuscripts and the published editions differ in placement, order, and even in number of narrative units. Their arrangement seems a result of chance rather than of any purpose or precise plan. None of them, chronologically, comes first and none of them last. The hero, moreover, does not appear in all of them. The resulting impression is one of a splintered, anomalous collection of undefined shape. Ḥarīrī, on the other hand, watched over the composition of his book, which could almost be described as a "closed" corpus, with a preface and conclusion. His *maqāmāt* are arranged in a rigorous order, even if this is not immediately apparent. Each *maqāma* is given not only a title (as in Hamadhānī's work), but also a number that positions it within the whole. The adventures of the two protagonists have, moreover, a beginning and an end: they become acquainted in the first *maqāma* and finally separate in the last.

The wanderings of Abū Zayd al-Sarūjī end, in fact, with the fiftieth *maqāma*. While Hamadhānī's hero never returns to his native Alexandria—and does not really wish to—Ḥarīrī's hero finally does return to his village of Sarūj. He moves from country to country as a vagrant, because the Crusaders have occupied Sarūj, a town that is accorded a precise place on the map, whereas the placement of Abū-l-Fatḥ's Alexandria remains uncertain. The loss of his place of origin leaves Abū Zayd with a sense of nostalgia. But that does not mean he feels exiled, or at least not irrevocably so, because from one sequence to the next, he moves within a space where the same cultural references hold true. But at the end, when the Crusaders have been chased out of Sarūj, he returns and renounces the life of a tramp, while Abū-l-Fath of Alexandria remains an eternal wanderer. The return of Sarūj to the world of Islam corresponds to a change in the personality of the hero. Abū Zayd repents, and abandoning his vagrancy, renouncing even literature (of which he retains only one form, the exhortation, or *parenesis*), he dedicates himself to prayer and orations. The *mukaddī*, the rogue, suddenly transforms himself into a *walī*, a saint, though who can tell if this is just another of his countless disguises?

While the *maqāmāt* of Harīrī are self-enclosed, there still exist among them numerous thematic links, besides the reappearance of the protagonists. There is also a skillful balancing of poetry and prose, the serious and the comic, throughout. The works are, moreover, divided into five series of ten: the first *maqāma* in each series is hortatory [*parenetic*], the fifth and the tenth are comic, the sixth is literary. By "literary" I mean that the *maqāma* is based on a verbal game, most notably the palindrome. This could be, for example, a poem in which the lines, when read from beginning to end or from end to beginning, retain the same letters and have, thus, the same meaning; or it may be an epistle that could be read both forward and backward but each with a different meaning, thus resulting in two distinct epistles. A single epistle with two aspects: this is not unlike the hero who always appears in disguise before revealing his true identity. The exploration of the possibilities of language pervades the work of Harīrī; each *maqāma* becomes the stage for a particular verbal game that distinguishes it from the others. In this respect the table of contents is most significant: the brief description it gives of each *maqāma* refers either to an element of plot or to a figure of speech.

The unity of the whole collection of narratives, however, rests on their geographical mooring. The *maqāma* is essentially an urban genre, but while each of Harīrī's narratives takes place in a different town as the titles in fact announce, the general space of the action is "the empire of Islam." This was already the case in Hamadhānī's works, but in Harīrī's writings the space is even greater, encompassing the totality of the Islamic world. Indeed, this author was studied in countries across the world, to such an extent that his book was said to be the Arabic work most frequently read after the Qur'ān. As Ernest Renan commented: "Few works have exerted such an extensive literary influence as the *Assemblies* of Harīrī. From the Volga to the Niger, from the Ganges to the straits of Gibraltar, they have been the model of elegant wit and style for all those peoples who have adopted, with the religion of Islam, the language of Mohammad." He evokes an immense space where Arabic is, ideally, the only language, where no other idiom hinders communication, at least among the learned. The latter, it should be noted, did not imitate Hamadhānī but rather Ḥarīrī; and they would imitate him not only in Arabic, of course, but also in Persian, Syriac, and Hebrew. The most successful imitation seems to be that of Ḥarīzī (whose name, curiously, scarcely differs from that of his model). Living in Spain at the beginning of the thirteenth century, Ḥarīzī first translated Ḥarīrī into Hebrew before composing in his turn fifty *maqāmāt*, which he entitled *Sefer Taḥkemōni* (*The Book of Taḥkemoni*).

The *maqāma* was cultivated, with varying results, for nearly ten centuries. The last great representative of the genre is probably Nāṣif al-Yāzijī (d. 1871), author of *Majmaʿ al-baḥrayn* (*Confluence of the Two Seas*), the two seas being those of prose and poetry. In 1907, Muwaylihī published a work whose title contained an allusion to Hamadhānī's "transmitter," *Ḥadīth ʿĪsā b. Hishām* (*ʿĪsā b. Hishām's Tale*). But with this author, the *maqāma* was quietly making its way toward the novel.

The death knell finally rang for the *maqāma* when the Arabs discovered European literature. A new literary model had appeared on the horizon, imposing new codes, new genres, a new style. There was a profound change in literary taste and in the reception of older texts, accompanied by a certain confusion and sense of bitterness, regret. The adoption of European writing by the Arabs has indeed brought with it the neglect of a whole swath of classical literature, most notably the *maqāma*, which, as it became obsolete, quietly disappeared. Neither Hamadhānī nor Ḥarīrī are read today as they were in the past; the rhymed and rhythmic prose of their narratives is no longer understood, and their didacticism, archaisms, verbal acrobatics, and "rhetorical artifices" are disdained. To a certain extent, Hamadhānī has been spared. He was, after all, the creator of a genre and, in truth, he did not overly exaggerate its elements of linguistic play. He is also admired for his skill in animating scenes of daily life in a "realistic" and "lively" way. Ḥarīrī, the writer who was once the most admired, is now scorned by almost everyone: did he not "sacrifice content for form"? But in truth, what he is not forgiven for, though it is never said openly, is that he never bound his fifty *maqāmāt* together in chronological order; in other words, what is held against him is that he did not write a novel. Needless to say, that was the last thing on his mind.

Translated by Mary Harper

Bibliography

Blachère, Régis, and Pierre Masnou. *Al-Hamadhānī, choix de maqāmāt*. Paris: Klincksieck, 1957.

Kilito, Abdelfattah. *Les séances: Récits et codes culturels chez Hamadhānī et Harīrī*. Paris: Sindbad, 1983.

Monroe, James T. *The Art of Badīʿ az-Zamān al-Hamadhānī as Picaresque Narrative*. Beirut: American University of Beirut, 1983.

Pellat, Charles. "Makāma," 6:107–15. In *Encyclopedia of Islam*. New ed. Leiden: Brill, 1986.

Renan, Ernest. "Les séances de Harīrī." In *Oeuvres complètes de Ernest Renan*, edited by H. Psichari, 2:205. Paris: Calmann-Lévy, 1948.

Lazarillo de Tormes
("Lázaro de Tormes," circa 1553)

If readers want to restore *Lazarillo de Tormes* to the flow of history, the first thing they must bear in mind is that around 1554, the year of the work's oldest preserved editions, it was not a novel; it was not presented as a work of fiction. In Italian, French, and Spanish, we group a heterogeneous assortment of prose narratives written in the most diverse periods, places, and languages under the label of *romanzo, roman,* and *novela.* We consider *Daphnis and Chloe* and *The Golden Ass, Erec and Enide* and *Petit Jean de Saintré, Arcadia* and *Don Quixote, Moll Flanders* and *Pamela, The Red and the Black* and *Anna Karenina,* and *Ulysses, The Radetzky March,* and *One Hundred Years of Solitude* to be novels. We are free to do so, as long as we are aware that we are applying a modern label, because in the old days, the category of *novela, roman,* and *romanzo* did not have the breadth we endow it with now.

The foregoing list, like so many others that are neither more nor less disputable, mingles stories of a perennial lineage—the fable constructed according to an ideal image of man and the world guided by an imagination hindered only by whim—with others of a sort severely restricted in time, which nonetheless constitute the most revolutionary and influential novelty in the history of European literature: fiction governed by the criteria of probability, experience, and common sense, by the same criteria of veracity that are generally used in daily life, and told in language that is in turn substantially in keeping with that of the everyday.

Only specimens of the first variety have a regular place in the literary practice and theory of the old regime. Examples of the second variety are not as plentiful, nor do they receive full valuation as works of art, but rather exist throughout the nineteenth century in the shadows of giants like Balzac, Dickens, Tolstoy, Eça de Queirós, Verga, and Pérez Galdós. The great nineteenth-century novel, the realist novel par excellence, responds to its own particular social and intellectual stimuli and a maturation process that is unequaled in other periods. But the goals of the *classic* realist novel, with different premises and starting points, had been attained by a few singular works that were, on the other hand, though not determinant, quite intensely felt during the maturation process in question.

The point I wish to make, then, is that those precursors of the canonical realist novel, the ground-laying books of the Spanish picaresque and, in succession, its most immediate heirs and closest relatives, did not emerge from an internal evolution of the fable of perfections and endless fantasies (the *romance* of Anglo-Saxon criticism), but rather on the fringes of it and far from what was once called "poetry" and what is now known as "literature." They appeared rather as supposed emulations of nonliterary types of writing (accounts of events, private letters, and stories about delinquents) more or less ambiguously postulating the same truthfulness as these modes. In short, the place of the realist novel par excellence could be none other: a place ultimately acknowledged as fictitious but to which the rules of the most familiar reality are nonetheless applied.

Everything begins with *Lazarillo*.[1] The first edition of the book, printed in 1552 or 1553, appeared with the title *La vida de Lazarillo de Tormes, y de sus fortunas y adversidades* (*The Life of Lazarillo de Tormes, and of His Fortunes and Adversities*) and was divided into a prologue and seven "tracts," each headed by an epigraph. The title, division, and epigraphs, each more boring and inappropriate, betray the author's wishes by all accounts, but they did not manage to hide from the readers of the period the genre of discourse the work adhered to: that of the epistle. Neither the content nor the form allowed for any doubts in that respect.

Lázaro de Tormes is a town crier from Toledo who recounts, in the first person, in an even style and good-humored tone, how he came by the "royal trade" (an administrative position, as we would call it today) and the circumstances of his family at the time of his writing. He was born in a mill on the banks of the Tormes River, a stone's throw from Salamanca. His mother, widowed and needy, placed him in the service of a blind man whose cunning and deception paradoxically opened his eyes to life. Later he served in the

---

[1] The interpretation sketched out here is extensively argued and illustrated in my books, *La novela picaresca y el punto de vista* (1970), 6th ed. (Barcelona: Seix Barral, 2000); Italian translation: *Il romanzo picaresco e il punto di vista*, A. Gargano, ed. (Milan: Bruno Mondadori, 2001); English translation: *The Picaresque Novel and the Point of View* (Cambridge: Cambridge University Press, 1984); and *Problemas del "Lazarillo"* (Madrid: Cátedra, 1988). See also "La invención de la novela" ("The Invention of the Novel") in my *Breve biblioteca de autores españoles* (Barcelona: Seix Barral, 1990), 109–19; Italian translation: *Biblioteca spangnola* (Turin: Einaudi, 1994), 105–15, and also as prologue to *Lazarillo de Tormes*, trans. V. Bodini, ed. O. Macrí (Turin: Einaudi, 1992), v–xv. For all other questions having to do with the text of *Lazarillo* and problems of dating, authorship, sources, etc., I refer to my edition of 1987 (Madrid: Cátedra) reprinted several times without corrections and, in particular, to my new critical edition that will appear shortly as volume 32 of *Biblioteca clásica* (Barcelona: Editorial Crítica).

house of an infinitely miserly clergyman with whom he had to fight a battle that was as tenacious as it was ingenious (and ultimately bloody) in order to keep from starving to death. His third master was a conceited, ruined squire of whom Lázaro nonetheless became very fond, to the point that he turned to begging in order to maintain him. Later, a swindling vendor of presumably false papal bulls taught him to keep quiet and not meddle in matters that did not concern him very directly. After a period as a sheriff in a risky and thankless job, Lázaro finally was employed as the town crier, thanks to the protection of the archpriest of San Salvador. Moreover, he has married the archpriest's housekeeper and lives happily with her.

It is at this point that Lázaro de Tormes decides to record a full account of his past "fortunes, dangers and adversities" to answer the question posed by an anonymous correspondent (whom he addresses as "Your Worship") about a certain episode that remains unclear In the first paragraphs. "Your Worship asks for a letter with a very detailed explanation of the case . . ." But in the last pages, the reader discovers that the episode in question is the idle gossip running through Toledo about whether the town crier's wife is or is not the archpriest's concubine: "to this day no one has heard us about *the case.*" Only then does one notice, in retrospect, that the autobiographical images that Lázaro has been offering to His Worship throughout the epistle are in large part intended to explain his behavior or the behavior that the citizens of Toledo attribute to him in relation to said "case": that of tolerating the situation and not opening his mouth in order to preserve the modest prosperity and relative well-being that he has finally achieved.

Lazarillo, then, appeared as a letter, and nobody was surprised that a private letter should be sent to the printer. "At that time we still did not have daily papers that printed rumors and news . . . so that we learned of such things through letters from merchants and others who corresponded with foreign countries" and other cities. Daniel Defoe's testimony about the London of 1665 is equally true for Spain or Italy a century earlier: news of a strange or important event was often spread because a bookseller decided to give the printer a private letter, labeling it, for instance, *Relación de un caso nuevamente acaecido* (*Account of a Recent Case*) that happened in such and such a place and under such circumstances.

On the other hand, the publication of the first volume of *De le lettere di M. Pietro Aretino* early in 1538 gave the public a panorama they would have sought in vain in other books: the story of an individual told through the anecdotes and shifting moods of his epistle with refreshing attention to the minutia and incidents of daily life. The success of that volume and the ones that Aretino himself kept adding caused the editors to collect the *carte messagiere* (personal letters) of other more or less well-known people in manageable small pocket volumes. When authentic letters were not available, the editors did not hesitate to offer *novelle*, jokes, and paradoxes, fabricated ad hoc. Thus, real missives gave way to false and humorous ones attributed to entirely invented subjects: the Venetian fishermen in Andrea Calmo (1547–52); the "valorose donne" (brave women) whose reputation was defended from slander in Ortensio Lando (1548); and in Cesare Rao (1562) the "mal maritato" (badly married man) who would apprise his comrades of the annoyances of being "mostrato a dito" (pointed at) and addressed with the title of "conte di Cornevacchia" (Count of the Cow's Horn).

So, *Lazarillo* emerged as a *carta messaggiera* at the exact moment when the development of the genre facilitated the author's plan: the town crier's letter posed as authentic and was in fact fictitious, with the same twist as in the "lettere volgari" (vulgar letters). More decisive and above all more articulated than in these, the starting point for Lázaro was a sustained assumption of truthfulness: in principle, the book was not to appear as the fruit of the imagination, but rather as a rigorously authentic history. (This is the reason that it does not occur to the author to reveal his name to us, which he persists in hiding, though probably he could not do otherwise: strictly speaking, *Lazarillo* is not an anonymous work by an unknown pen but rather apocryphal, attributed to a false author, Lázaro de Tormes.) The hero's adventures, then, the places he mentions, his language and his thoughts, what he tells or leaves out, could not contain anything to challenge that supposition with which the reading had to be tackled, nothing to suggest that it dealt with people, situations, and things born from the inventiveness of the fabulist. (Here again, early publishers of the work tended to betray the original intent, though not by very strident means.) The reader was not being offered a simply credible tale, but a true one. Not realistic: real.

It was a tall tale, to be sure. A nuanced tall tale, ironic and well intended, but a tall tale nonetheless. For one cannot play at fiction without a previous pact, without agreeing on a set of rules ahead of time. In the game's preliminaries, our novelist was a swindler who cheated when he dealt the cards without having his advantage exposed. He resorted to the neutral medium of prose: he gave Lázaro the genre or vehicle common to ordinary communication in everyday life, and he dispensed with the specific characteristics of literature. He could not expect his book, in and of itself, to be received as fictitious (because it had no equivalent in the prose of the imagination of the period), forcing the signs of historicity. In short: the author was not divulging a fiction, but rather a forgery.

Nevertheless, the tall tale has its limits, because the novelist also required that the imposture be discovered—yet with one condition: not completely, incontrovertibly discovered, not without leaving the smallest room for doubt. It is comprehensible. A joke looses its value if, for its very perfection, it is not ultimately recognized as such and the victim does not realize that his leg is being pulled. Had it not been possible to realize that *Lazarillo* was apocryphal, a falsification, the author would have composed a good book, but also a book that was less new. To accept Lázaro's letter as real would reward the reader with a lively plot and witty anecdotes, but to discover it to be not real, but plausible, was to participate in a fascinating game and consciously engage in a category of artistic perception hitherto unknown: the exploration of everyday reality through fiction with unprecedented tools and of unprecedented dimensions.

This twofold impulse, to pass for truth and be identified as a fable, inspires all of *Lazarillo*. The first goal is fundamentally achieved with a perspicacious and nuanced characterization of the hero and an exceptional sensitivity toward the materiality and details of his existence. A character of Lázaro's low standing had perhaps never before received such comprehensive, thorough, and respectful attention to the view that a town crier in his circumstances could have had of himself and of the world image, relativist and full of humanity, that had thereby taken shape. But in addition, the story's hero and extras are deployed with a magical precision in the details, circumstances, things, and places that determine or direct their behavior (from the stone bull of Salamanca to the squire's famous toothpick), and they do not need to be extensively described, but simply named with exactitude in order to become infinitely suggestive.

To achieve the second objective, the author played his wildest trump card with regard to the hero's family background. In fact, at the beginning of his letter, Lázaro recounted his mother's cohabitation with a black slave. He did so with delicacy and affection, but he did not conceal it. And who in the sixteenth century would have dared to write it almost outright? That piece of information could not but give rise to serious doubts (what if the whole thing was a tall tale?), and from that moment on readers would have had to scrutinize the text carefully, determined to find out if the assumption of truthfulness with which they had begun to read was infringed on elsewhere. But from that point on and up to the last page, Lázaro does not allow a single line to slip by that could be dismissed as implausible or unacceptable. (Only one characteristic could give away the game, and only to the shrewdest: the marvelous, humorous assemblage of materials that make one think of a literary construction rather than of a faithful reflection of a life. But it was certainly not this that put the author's plans at risk of being spoiled.)

The doubt is dispelled in the last two folios, when the town crier reveals another parallel episode still more embarrassing than that of his mother's loves: "the case" announced at the start, the relations between his wife and the archpriest. But up until the ending, the "case" that ties up all the loose ends, Lázaro does not mention anything that could not be excused as youthful mischief, nothing that could permit anything regarding the hero to be branded as implausible. The reader would feel obliged to continue reading the letter to His Worship with the suspicion that the whole of it could be a lie, but discovering, step by step, that nothing appeared to be out of keeping with the truth.

The objective of Lázaro's creator was to keep readers in suspense, unsure of whether they were dealing with a reality or a tall tale, sampling for the first time in Europe the art of a new kind of fiction, exposed to a story where everything could be authentic but nothing was. Thus, by teaching readers to look at fiction and reality with the same eyes; putting the fable in history's place; governing the imagination with the reins of experience shared by everyone; making *as if* the main key to *Lazarillo* and at the same time showing delight in rediscovering daily life as artifice; contrasting plausibility and historicity; shunning traditional models; and shedding unprecedented light on the plot of the everyday, the unknown marked out a place for fiction that had been denied to it up to that point and that with time would become, by choice, the place of the novel.

Translated by Linda Phillips

THOMAS DIPIERO

Le Grand Cyrus
(Madeleine de Scudéry, 1649–1653)

Published in ten volumes between 1649 and 1653, Madeleine de Scudéry's *Artamène, ou le Grand Cyrus* is one of the best-known examples of heroic fiction, a genre popularized in the 1630s that remained in demand well into the 1660s. Faithful to the conventions of the genre, *Le Grand Cyrus* recounts the title character's superhuman valor and indomitable will in his genuine odyssey to defeat his enemies, recapture his thrice-abducted paramour, and find himself "plus couvert de gloire, que jamais nul autre Prince n'en avoit esté couvert" ("more bathed in glory than any prince ever before").[1] Like virtually all heroic novels, *Le Grand Cyrus* found its reading public among an aristocratic audience who to all accounts took enormous pleasure in considering these works thinly disguised allegories of their own pasts and ways of life: Mlle. de Scudéry's contemporary, Charles Sorel, relates that readers eagerly anticipated the publication of each successive volume when he reports that *Le Grand Cyrus* "a esté tellement estimé, que ses dix tomes ayant esté donnez les uns après les autres, ils ont causé beaucoup d'impatience, jusques à ce qu'on en ait veu la conclusion" ("was so highly esteemed that the ten volumes following one after another caused great impatience up until people saw the conclusion").[2] Mlle. de Scudéry's work offers up in the guise of real historical figures verbal portraits of some of the most notable figures of her day, and she nostalgically casts an economically and politically troubled aristocracy in the form of a privileged hereditary elite whose skill at arms and constancy in love make them the representatives of an entire nation's fate. *Le Grand Cyrus* chronicles the events in the life of Cyrus, grandson of the king of Persia, recounting the wondrous and bellicose adventures in which he engages in the services of his friends and allies. What motivates him most in his travels throughout the ancient world is his pursuit of Mandane, daughter of the king of Media, with whom he is passionately but chastely in love. Cyrus's story begins as follows: Because of a prophecy that his birth will bring mayhem to all of Asia, Cyrus is hidden from his grandfather Astyage, the king. No amount of hiding can conceal his natural valor

---

[1] Madeleine de Scudéry, *Artamène ou le Grand Cyrus*, 10 vols. (Paris: Augustin Courbé, 1656), 10:850. Subsequent references appear parenthetically in the text. All translations are my own.

[2] Charles Sorel, *La bibliothèque françoise* (Paris: Compagnie des Libraires de Paris, 1667), 185.

and nobility of soul, however, and along with a coterie of friends he flees his native land and travels under the name Artamène. During a violent storm Cyrus lands in Cappadoce, where he first catches sight of Mandane. Cyrus strives to be worthy of the beautiful princess through service to her father the king, and one of his missions involves serving as emissary to Thomiris, queen of the Messagètes, to ask her hand in marriage for King Ciaxare. To Cyrus's greater misfortune, however, the queen falls in love with him and holds him prisoner. Cyrus escapes, but not before the first in a series of ab-ductions of Mandane, on this occasion by Aryande, one of Ciaxare's ene-mies. Cyrus joins forces with one of his principal rivals, Labinet, after the two agree to settle once and for all by means of a duel who will marry Man-dane after all of their military exploits have been accomplished. Along the way Cyrus joins forces with one Anaxaris, who later falls in love with Man-dane also; Anaxaris reveals to Mandane that Cyrus and Labinet are to duel over her, and then it comes to light that Anaxaris is really Aryante, brother of Thomiris, who begrudges his sister's usurpation of power after the death of their father. Mandane is abducted once again, and taken to Thomiris's realm, where all decisive battles now turn and where Cyrus emerges victori-ous and marries Mandane.

That impossibily abbreviated summary of *Le Grand Cyrus* necessarily omits the myriad subplots, cases of mistaken identity, digressive narratives, and secondary love stories that make up far and away the bulk of the work. Furthermore, it is because of these features that fall outside the novel's prin-cipal diegetic line that most modern commentators label *Le Grand Cyrus* and the vast majority of heroic fiction unreadable for today's readers. These works' typically labyrinthine, lifeless plots and two-dimensional characters are thought not to engage readers seeking a more or less linear narrative in which causal structures build to a single, motivated climax. Virtually all heroic fiction spans multiple tomes (*Le Grand Cyrus* consists of ten volumes and some seven thousand pages) and features courageous warriors and con-stant lovers who battle imposing armies and endure grueling separations yet nevertheless remain faithful to one another and to the image of their own *gloire* and *générosité*—the justly deserved reputation for magnanimity one achieves by facing adversity and remaining true to noble ideals. Heroic fic-tion typically consists of a framing narrative, generally not more complex than the delayed reunion of separated lovers, punctuated by series of en-counters with other characters who in turn tell their stories, stories that sometimes relate to the main plot but often do not, and often extend for hundreds of pages. Marin Le Roy de Gomberville's *Polexandre* (1629–37), Gautier de Coste de la Calprenède's *Pharamond* (1661–70), and Mlle. de

Scudéry's *Clélie, histoire romaine* (1654–60) were among the most popular heroic romances that exploited the proven formulas. If heroic novels seem unreadable today, it is generally assumed that is because we do not belong to the coterie for which they were intended and hence have no access to the cultural capital necessary to decode their often arcane references. Furthermore, we ostensibly lack as well the patience to wade through a narrative that, barely deserving that designation, strings together events not so much in causal fashion, but simply in order to celebrate specific individuals who remain unidentifiable to modern readers.

That is why critical attention focused on *Le Grand Cyrus* has generally centered on the portraits and the novel's ostensible key revealing the real identities behind characters' facades. Victor Cousin reports having discovered such a key in 1857, but today no trace seems to remain. Like many who succeeded him, Cousin notes that without the key the novel lacks any genuine literary interest, and he speculates that even Mlle. de Scudéry's contemporaries would have balked at plodding through it.[3] Among the portraits of Mlle. de Scudéry's contemporaries that have interested literary historians most are those of Condé (Cyrus), a Bourbon who earned fame and notoriety in military victories and in the events of the Fronde—the civil wars in France between 1648 and 1653 that arose when attempts were made to limit the king's power—in which he worked against the crown; the duchesse de Longueville (Mandane, Cyrus's paramour), Condé's sister who also conspired in the Fronde; and Mlle. de Scudéry herself (Sapho), described in detail in book 10. We should remember, however, when considering heroic fiction's ostensible unreadability, that simple linear narratives were far and away the exception before the last quarter of the seventeenth century. Readers sought not so much a satisfying resolution to narrative tension, but an aestheticized—and consequently politicized—chronicle of their lives in the guise of ancient history.[4] Mlle. de Scudéry registers her particular synthesis of the belletrist and the social domains in her preface to *Le Grand Cyrus*, where she explains her use of historical sources and traditional epic convention in a work of invention. In that preface she stipulates that her tale does not consist of mere flights of fancy, but rather finds its origins in the great historians of antiquity, among them Xenophon and Herodotus. Simultaneously acquiescing to the somewhat disparaged status of the *faiseur de roman* and defending

---

[3] Victor Cousin, *La société française au XVII siècle*, 2 vols. (Paris: Didier, 1873), 1:16.

[4] For a detailed reading of the political engagement of aristocratic authors focusing on heroic fiction, including *Le Grand Cyrus*, see Marlies Mueller's *Idées politiques dans le roman héroïque de 1630 à 1670* (Cambridge, Mass.: Harvard University Press, 1984).

her craft as a composer of narratives, she writes of her relationship to her historical sources: "quelquefois suivant leur exemple, j'ay dit ce qu'ils n'ont dit ny l'un ni l'autre: car apres tout, c'est une Fable que je compose, & non pas une Histoire que j'écris" ("sometimes following their example, I said what none of them said, for after all, I am writing a story, and not a history") (1:4A).

Mlle. de Scudéry makes a clear distinction between composing and transcribing, and in so doing she opposes fable to history, an opposition rigidly upheld in the popular and critical writing of the day. Although the political and aesthetic complexities inhering in that differentiation troubled philosophers and commentators well into the eighteenth centuy, in *Le Grand Cyrus* we might simply note that what is at stake is a fairly refined notion of the truth-value—*vraisemblance*—of historical and fictional narratives. Broadly speaking, the issue concerns whether the Cyrus we read about is realistic from a historical point of view, from a moral point of view, or from a political point of view, and to what extent drawing from ancient sources provides consistent and reliable information. Mlle. de Scudéry articulates the problem as follows: "Vous pourrez, dis-je, voir qu'encore qu'une Fable ne soit une Histoire, & qu'il suffise à celuy qui la compose de s'attacher au vray-semblable, sans s'attacher toujours au vray: neantmoins dans les choses que j'ay inventées, je ne suis pas si esloigné de tous ces Autheurs, qu'ils le sont tous l'un de l'autre" ("You will see, I say, that although a story is not a history, and that it is enough for its author to adhere to the verisimilar without always adhering to the truth, nevertheless in the things that I have invented, I am not so far removed from these authors than they are from each other") (1:3A). What constituted the *vray-semblable* for Mlle. de Scudéry and for readers of *Le Grand Cyrus* comprehended not so much veracity or plausibility in the modern sense of what *could* happen in a given situation, but rather a form of obligation, or what *should* happen, a concept of verisimilitude that obviously implies a determinate political position. The distinction between what could happen and what ought to occur is crucial in seventeenth-century heroic fiction, because it was precisely in works such as *Le Grand Cyrus* that one of the most compelling questions about narrative truth emerged: does *vraisemblance* concern *manner* or *mode* of representation, or both? Are moral truths preferable to an accurate equivalence of image and referent in literary imitation? In the words of Desmaretz de Saint-Sorlin, one of Mlle. de Scudéry's contemporaries, "La fiction ne doit pas être considerée comme un mensonge, mais comme le plus grand effort de l'esprit; & bien que la Verité semble luy estre opposée, toutefois elles s'accordent merveilleusement ensemble. Ce sont deux lumieres qui au lieu de s'effacer l'une l'autre & de se nuire, brillent par l'esclat l'une de l'autre" ("Fiction must not be considered a lie, but as the mind's greatest effort; and although truth seems opposed to it, the two never-theless get along marvelously. They are two lights that, rather than canceling each other out, shine by each other's brilliance").[5]

Attention to the manner and means by which literary imitation operated prevailed over intricacies of causal narration in heroic fiction—and, it must be noted, in historiography as well. Seventeenth-century audiences consid-ered the moral and social allegorical relationships between fiction's heroes and their own self-images, and because they possessed an iconographic repertory comprising generations' worth of visual and verbal images, they could savor the particular manner in which specific aristocratic forms and ideas were conveyed. Since the particular form of verisimilitude common to heroic fiction in the guise of *vraisemblance* explicitly encoded a specific world view, *Le Grand Cyrus* and most other heroic novels naturalized that ideology by constructing their narratives and their heroes as both real-world icons and moral emblems.[6] That is, Mlle. de Scudéry's Cyrus has a genuine historical referent, but the principal truth-values of that character focus on those of his traits that best highlight the aristocracy's gilded image of itself, an image becoming increasingly distanced from reality in troubled economic times and in a period of growing monarchic absolutism. Military prowess, ancient lineage, brilliant reputation, and social preeminence in the form of chivalric constancy and civility distinguished the novel's heroes. In many re-spects, Cyrus resembles the heroes of the ancient epics: he appears as a uni-vocal representative of the beliefs and destinies of an entire group. He is a sort of emblem linking an abstracted form of the past to ideologically based conceptions of what the present ought to be. One of the early portraits of Cyrus describes him thus: "En tout ce qu'il faisoit; & en tout ce qu'il disoit; il y avoit quelque chose de si grand; de si agreable; & de si plein d'esprit; qu'il estoit impossible de le voir sans l'aimer. Il estoit admirablement beau: & quoy que l'on vist encore en quelques unes de ses actions, cette naïveté charmante, & inseparable de l'enfance; il y avoit pourtant tousjours en luy, je ne sçay quoy qui faisoit voir, que son esprit estoit plus avancé que son corps" ("In everything he did and in everything he said there was something so great, so pleasing, and so intelligent that it was impossible to see him with-out loving him. He was admirably handsome; and although one could still see in some of his actions that charming naïveté inseparable from childhood,

[5] Jean de Desmaretz de Saint-Sorlin, *Rosane* (Paris: H. Le Gras, 1639), unpaginated preface.

[6] For excellent treatment of the iconographic aspect of heroic fiction's heroes, as well as of the tensions between fiction and history inhering in the genre, see Mark Bannister, *Privileged Mortals: The French Heroic Novel, 1630–1660* (Oxford: Oxford University Press, 1983).

one could nevertheless see in him that indescribable sign that his intellect was more developed than his body") (1:129). Cyrus's physiognomy harmonizes perfectly with his actions. A synchronicity of mind, body, will, and deed characterize the heroic ideal such that his corporality expresses his soul—or rather, that it might be difficult to separate the two: "Cyrus avait ce jour là dans les yeux, je ne sçay quelle noble fierté, qui sembloit estre d'un heureux presage: & à dire vray, il eust esté difficile de s'imaginer en le voyant: qu'il eust pû estre vaincu, tant sa phisionomie estoit Grande & heureuse" ("Cyrus had in his eyes that day an indescribable noble pride, which seemed to be a favorable sing. And, to tell the truth, it would have been difficult to imagine upon seeing him that he could be vanquished, such was his appearance great and confident") (3:344).

That is in striking contradistinction to Cyrus's enemies who attempt to thwart him in his righteous quest to reign over all of Asia and marry the woman destined for him. One such enemy is Artane, against whom Cyrus fights toward an uncertain victory. At the end of their military ordeal Cyrus and Artane must declaim to the crowds, each making his case for why he should be declared victor. At the end of Artane's speech "il s'esleva dans tout l'Assemblée un bruit confus sans acclamation" ("there arose throughout the assembly a muddled noise without acclamation") (1:282). When Cyrus finishes, however, "il se fit un bruit extrémement grand, dans toute cette Assemblée: mais avec cette difference, entre le premier qui s'estoit eslevé à la fin du discours d'Artane & ce dernier; qu'en celuy-là, l'on n'avoit entendu que des murmures & des doutes: & qu'en celuy ci l'on n'entendit que des exclamations & des loüanges, qui sembloient demander aux Dieux, aux Rois, & aux Juges, la Victoire pour Artamène" ("a tremendous noise was heard throughout the assembly, one that differed from the one that was heard at the end of Artane's speech; in the latter all that was heard were murmurs and doubts, but in this one, all that was heard were exclamations and praise, which seemed to ask the gods, kings, and judges for Artamène's victory") (1:288). Whereas contradiction and confusion greet the words of Cyrus's opponent, a striking univocality follows Cyrus in all that he does. In battle, in fact, "l'on eust dit qu'il estoit seul chargé de l'evenement de ce combat" ("you would have said that he alone was responsible for the outcome of the battle") (1:259), and thirty thousand of his men behaved "comme si ce grand Corps n'eust esté animé que d'un mesme esprit" ("as if this great body had been animated by a single mind")—that of Cyrus, "celuy qu'ils regardent comme un Dieu" ("he whom they consider a god") (3:9).

The univocality that surrounds Cyrus and his troops and in many respects defines the heroic novel's principal character also operates in the intercalated narratives that are ostensibly responsible not only for dragging heroic fiction out to impossible lengths, but for making it unreadable as well. Secondary characters' stories explain complex interrelations among the work's characters, often serving to elucidate how particular states of affairs, including military and amorous alliances, came to be. Rather than needlessly extending an otherwise fairly straightforward narrative, these intercalated narratives figure the form and function of *vray-semblance* in its mediation between factual and moral or social accuracy. That is, the long stories that characters tell, whether they provide the historical background to a principal character's situation or illustrate the intricate and sometimes convoluted manners in which illustrious figures live and love, perform a function far more complex than simply providing local color: just as the character of Cyrus links the domains of verifiable fact to an idealized view of the present, the intercalated narratives build meaning as a complex network of interrelated domains impossible to disarticulate. They link the historical to the present, and the economic to the social. Furthermore, in the sheer repetitive force of stories of steadfast and noble lovers they legitimize the absolute fusion of the personal and the political that characterized the heroic ideal in both art and the contemporary culture at large. Thus, the largest part of Mlle. de Scudéry's reading audience quite likely would have responded not with exasperation at the onset of yet another secondary tale, but more in the spirit of Mandane herself as she prepared to listen to the story of the king of Assyria: "La seule grace que je vous demande . . . est que vous ne fassiez pas comme ceux qui en faisant une narration, n'ont autre dessein que de dire beaucoup de choses en peu de paroles" ("The only favor that I ask of you is not to do as those who, when telling a story, have no other object than to tell many things in few words") (8:52).

No one would accuse Melle de Scudéry of mincing words, of course, but length and sinuosity in *Le Grand Cyrus*—or of any other heroic novel, for that matter—fail to characterize the novel's particular economy. That economy is based not on volume or narrative convolution, but rather on synthesizing a profound ideological unity from among a host of disparate cultural threads. The workings and movements of Cyrus's army in many ways figure the move to consolidate and articulate a unified class image from among a mass of otherwise disconnected elements. Thus, in the war on Cresus: "Jamais on n'a rien veû de si magnifique, que l'estoit cette grande Armée: car non seulement Cyrus, le Roy d'Assirie, Mazare, & tous les autres Princes estoient superbement armez; mais encore tous les Capitaines: & il n'y avoit pas mesme un simple Soldat, qui du moins n'eust rendu ses Armes claires & luisantes, s'il ne les avoit pû avoir belles & riches: de sorte que le Soleil estant ce jour là sans aucun nuage, fit voir en la marche de cette Armée, le plus bel objet qui soit jamais tombé sous les yeux" ("Never had anyone seen anything so magnificent as this great army was, for not only were Cyrus, the king of Assyria, and all the other princes superbly armed, but so too were all the captains. There was not even a simple soldier who had not at least made his arms shiny and bright if they were not already beautiful and rich such that the sun shining that day without a single cloud illuminated in that army's movement the most beautiful object that eyes ever beheld") (5: 740). Moving down the ranks from king and princes through captain and on down to the simplest foot soldier, we see not simply a military unit dedicated to a single purpose, but one that, under the benevolent rays of the brillian sun, synthesizes a host of separate and distinct individuals into a unified expression of idealized noble valor.

The intercalated narratives that so often seem to discourage modern readers from wading through *Le Grand Cyrus* thus provide that novel with what may well have been its most important literary and social function: that of articulating—both in the sense of enunciating and of joining together—divergent cultural phenomena as idealized aristocratic virtues. Like the sun in the passage cited above that caused the various and sundry soldiers in Cyrus's army to appear as a single and unified object, the secondary stories recounted by the book's various characters perform the epistemological work of explaining how different cultural forces work together in the service of particular class ideals. Everything fits together in Cyrus's world as part of a grand scheme of meaning. Love and valor correlate *gloire*, wealth, and prestige, and stories that characters tell not only construct a convenient historical precedent to justify current ideological configurations; they provide the epistemological links required to allow that world to make sense. Belonging to the privileged group thus entails in part understanding how all the pieces coincide. Mandane's interlocutor Orcame expresses the issue succinctly when he explains why he cannot omit certain unpleasant details from the tale he has to tell: "Je ne sçay si je dois continuer mon recit, & si vous trouverez bon que je vous parle si particulierement de l'amouor d'un Prince, qui a causé tous les malheurs de vostre vie: cependant les sentimens du Roy d'Assirie sont si meslez à la fin de l'Histoire d'Intapherne, d'Atergatis, d'Istrine, & de la Princesse de Bithinie, que je ne puis vous la dire sans vous parler autant de luy que de tous les autres" ("I do not know whether I should continue my tale, or that you will deem it right that I speak to you so candidly of the love of a prince who caused all the unhappiness in your life. However, the king of Assyria's feelings are so caught up in the end of the story of Intapherne, Atergatis, Istrine, and the princess of Bithnia, that

I could not relate it to you without speaking as much of him as of all the others") (8:271).

The densely encoded aristocratic iconography characterizing *Le Grand Cyrus* extends into the formal structure of the heroic novel itself, as secondary narratives help claim for that iconography elements not conventionally associated with that social group. Heroic fiction in general concerned itself less with narrative closure, and more with purveying resolutions to contemporary cultural contradictions in the form of aesthetic objects. *Le Grand Cyrus* attires ancient Egyptian characters in seventeenth-century aristocratic garb, not only providing a historical antecedent for contemporary cultural ideals, but also establishing allegorical parameters authorizing a specific class-based reading of the narrative it contains.

PERRY ANDERSON

Persian Letters
(Montesquieu, 1721)

Montesquieu thought that his novel founded a genre ("My Persian Letters taught people to write epistolary novels"),[1] while historians have seen it as the opening shot of an age, inaugurating the Enlightenment. It is doubtful whether any other work of European fiction could make such a double claim. Neither, certainly, can be accepted without qualification, and the validity of the first may look less clear-cut than the second. The origins of the epistolary novel are famously remote and heteroclite: straggling from Ovid's *Heroides* or Cicero's correspondence to Abelard and Heloise to Renaissance manuals of etiquette to romances of the *précieux*. Real and fictional letters were long contiguous as forms, with moralism, sentiment, and satire overlapping as successive impulses. The first pure epistolary fiction, whose title speaks for itself, Juan de Segura's *Proceso de cartas de amores que entre dos amantes passaron* (1548), had a real-life sequel in Alvise Pasqualigo's *Lettere amorose* (1563). Satirical uses of the form, again pioneered first in Spain and then in Italy, came later with Quevedo's *Cartas del caballero de la tenaza* (1627) and Ferrante Pallavicino's *Corriero svaligiato* (1641). Employed as a subsidiary device within narratives, the number of letters steadily increased in novels of French gallantry over the same period. The first two European best sellers, widely translated and repeatedly reprinted, were Pierre de Guilleragues's *Lettres portugaises* (1669) and Giovanni Marana's *L'esploratore turco* (1684), both unsigned texts purporting to have been composed from the social and geographical margins of the continent by a Portuguese nun and an Ottoman spy—setting new standards in turn for confessional intensity and satirical ambition.

So Montesquieu's novel by no means came out of the blue. Much in its formula had already been tried out: an anonymous finder or presenter of missives from another language—Greek (*Proceso*), Portuguese, Arabic, now Farsi; an ironic gaze at Europe from Asia; a mixture of registers, assorting the quotidian with the exotic, the affective with the philosophical. Montesquieu drew directly on Marana, even borrowing occasional details from the "Turkish spy." But he was not wrong in thinking *Lettres persanes* represented something new, something that would give birth to a genre. His novel appeared in 1721. Narrowly construed, simply as the device of a

---

[1] *Persian Letters*, translated by C. J. Betts (London: Penguin Books, 1973), 283; henceforward *PL*.

regard éloigné, it engendered a tidal wave of imitators—Russian (1735), Jewish (1736), Chinese (1739–40), Peruvian (1747), Siamese (1751), Iroquois (1752), Moroccan (1768), Indian (1769), Polish (1770), African (1771), Tahitian (1784) letters. Among those who tried their hand at these exercises in reverse Eurocentrism were Goldsmith, Voltaire, and Marat. But more broadly considered, *Lettres persanes* initiated the generic hegemony of the epistolary novel across the century, which counts among its landmarks *Pamela* (1731) and *Clarissa* (1748); *La vie de Marianne* (1731–41) and *Lettres de la Marquise de M*** au Comte de R**** (1732); *La nouvelle Héloïse* (1761) and *Die Leiden des jungen Werther* (1774); *Humphrey Clinker* (1771) and *Le paysan perverti* (1775); *Les liaisons dangereuses* (1782) and *Hyperion* (1797); ending perhaps with *Le ultime lettere di Jacopo Ortis* (1799) and *Delphine* (1802). Fielding and Prévost might complain of the artifice of the form, but even with Defoe, Voltaire, and Sterne at their side, they were no match at the higher end of prose fiction for the combined forces of Richardson, Marivaux, Crébillon, Rousseau, Goethe, Smollett, Restif, Laclos, Hölderlin, Foscolo, and de Staël.

What made *Lettres persanes* a turning point in this development? In the first place, a technical innovation. Structurally, epistolary fiction permits of five sender-to-receiver variations, although one of these has always remained a null class. Novels composed of letters may contain the following: a single correspondent and/or a single recipient; two reciprocal correspondents; a single correspondent and multiple recipients; multiple correspondents and multiple recipients; and multiple correspondents and a single recipient (of which there seems to be no example). *Processo de cartas* established the second. The *Lettres portugaises* consecrated the first. *L'esploratore turco* exemplified the third. It was Montesquieu who introduced the fourth, with a polyphonic correspondence of twenty signatures exchanging 161 letters. The possibilities of this more complex form were not to be fully explored until Laclos. In *Lettres persanes*, it remains highly asymmetrical, in keeping with the narrative structure itself. Two Persian nobles, Usbek and Rica, travel by stages from Ispahan to Paris, where they reside for eight years, reporting their observations of French life and customs to compatriots in Venice and Smyrna, or each other, with occasional messages between Usbek and his wives or eunuchs at home. The great bulk of the letters, both in number and length, are descriptions or reflections from Paris to correspondents in the Adriatic or Aegean, without interlocution: their recipients may write in their turn, but do not reply to them. True exchanges occur only between Paris and Persia, and these alone detonate actions. The "performative" potential of the letter—in other words, its most dynamic function—remains underdeveloped: the traditional "constative" register still has the upper hand. Dissociated from conduct, most of the correspondence moves on the plane of reflection: social comment or intellectual speculation without specific narrative force. In this mode, characterization—deprived of incident—inevitably remains weak. Rica is younger and supposedly more adaptable than Uzbek, but there is little sustained difference between what they write to each other, while Rhedi and Ibben are simply names. We are a long way from the personalities of a later novelistic world.

The fictional structure of *Lettres persanes*, however, is more than a flimsy vehicle for philosophical disquisitions. Montesquieu's narrative framework is far from perfunctory. He took great pains with its temporal and spatial coordinates, using a composite of the Muslim solar and lunar years, and calculating traveling times between cities with precision, for greater verisimilitude. Moreover, he deliberately used the imbalance between performative and constative elements of the correspondence for heightened dramatic effect, by placing the stationary central mass of political and philosophical reflections between two sequences of precipitating passion—Usbek's initial departure from Persia, prompted by curiosity and fear of court intrigue, and the final revolt by his wives against the oppression of the seraglio. The sudden outbreak of violent turbulence at the end of the story is all the more arresting for the ostensibly placid tenor of what precedes it. The generic discontinuities of the epistolary form were, of course, well suited to administer this kind of shock. But here their effect is intensified by the peculiar rhythms of Montesquieu's own style, whose principle he defined for himself: "il faut sauter les idées intermédiaires." Conjunctions all but banished, the signature of his laconic sentence construction is the semicolon—typically marking an abrupt swerve or ellipsis of thought, bringing a train of it to some crisp, unexpected conclusion. The staccato elegance of such gestures not only ensures the discursive side of *Lettres persanes* against longueurs. They give a powerful kick to its narrative denouement.

Over 150 years, the various strands of epistolary fiction—sentimental, didactic, satirical—had developed at different tempos and combined in any number of unstable mixtures, without real synthesis. The ingenious design of Montesquieu's novel permitted for the first time a kind of fusion. The key to it lay in a substitution: the displacement of the sentimental by the erotic as means of intellectual seduction. The brief opening of the Regency—France's moral equivalent of the English Restoration—allowed a freedom of sexual expression in polite culture that made *Lettres persanes* possible. Montesquieu was in his twenties when he embarked on it, and the atmosphere of the work is best described as gracefully libertine. Its audacities, of suggestion and situation rather than literal description, are not trailers for the porno-graphic writing that proliferated as the century wore on. But they were pi-quant enough to inflame readers of either sex: lyrical representations of fe-male desire, a tranquil defense of incestuous love, uncensorious allusions to sapphic embraces, glowing dreams of troilism. The literary strategy of *Let-tres persanes* depends on this calculated eroticism. Montesquieu went out of his way to underline it: the stories of Apheridon and Astarte, sibling lovers, and of Anaïs, basking in a polyandrous paradise, are inserted *hors-série* in the correspondence, tales within the tale that offer reveries of license be-yond even the first-order narrative itself.

The pretext for such erotica was furnished by Orientalism. French fasci-nation with Ottoman institutions went back two centuries by the time Mon-tesquieu was writing. The seraglio had always been a focal point of it, fan-tasies of polygamy irresistible to a monogamous society. For a long time, the military slavery and administrative efficiency of the Porte attracted awed fear and curiosity too. Marana's novel appeared at the high point of Turkish pressure on Christendom, as Ottoman armies were at the gates of Vienna. But by the time of the Regency, Turkish power was visibly decaying and in retreat. Within another few years China would become the new lodestar for Orientalist projection. Bayle had already singled it out for attention, and Leibniz looked forward to a description of the oddities of Europe by mis-sionaries from the Heavenly Kingdom; by midcentury Chinese allusions or fixations saturated the culture of the Enlightenment. Montesquieu's novel was written in the interval between the capture of the European imaginary by these two great empires. Persia could play the role of an intriguing, more indistinct third—close enough in culture to Turkey to retain the motif of the seraglio, distant enough to represent no threat to Europe, unfamiliar enough to offer no alternative model as sharp and definite as the mandarinate in China. Two Huguenot travelers, Chardin and Tavernier, had described the country in 1676 and 1686; a Persian envoy had visited Paris in 1715; the Safavid dynasty was nearing its end, at the hands of Nadir Shah in 1730. All this was enough to arouse curiosity about the land of Cyrus and Shah Ab-bas, without imposing any too determinate image of it. Persia was an ideal template for Montesquieu's exercise.

The Orientalism of *Lettres persanes* is, of course, first and foremost a de-vice of estrangement. Shklovsky's *ostranenie* has had many claimants to first use. If we set aside antiquity, La Bruyère's famous description of the misery of the French peasantry, perceived as an all but subterranean race of ani-mals, is a plausible candidate. Significantly, it was he too who wondered how the French would see it if the Siamese attempted to convert them to

Buddhism, and to build pagodas in France. In fact, the idea of the inverted gaze from afar was in the air by the end of the seventeenth century—Leibniz suggesting in all seriousness what La Bruyère had ridiculed. Without resort to the East, Swift would eventually go much further. Historically, however, it was Montesquieu who first systematically and self-consciously set the procedure to work. The term he used to describe the effect of his Persians' vision of Europe was stronger than *strangeness*. "The Persians," he wrote, "suddenly found themselves transplanted to Europe, that is, to another universe." In consequence, "their first thoughts were bound to be odd [*singulières*]": they in turn "sometimes find our dogmas odd [*singuliers*]," a source of "feelings of surprise and astonishment." Here, Montesquieu insisted, lay the charm of his book. "The whole effect was due to the perpetual contrast between the reality of things and the odd, naive or bizarre [*singulière, neuve ou bizarre*] way in which they were perceived."[2] Singularity is the keynote. What is strange may be common to a set. What is singular is more disconcerting: without antecedent, bizarre. The force of Montesquieu's travesty of Western conventions lies in his trio of adjectives—"the reality of things" is no more than a defense clause to parry clerical indignation.

The mask of Orientalism not only operated as the first sustained device of defamiliarization in fiction. It also unified the novel, because its substitution of the erotic for the sentimental allowed a natural movement to the political, within a single framework, that no previous epistolary novel had achieved. Sentimental fiction could, of course, offer tacit social criticism; but its range was limited, since appeal to the sentiments was inevitably to existing moral codes, however flouted in practice or secondary in standing— witness Richardson. Its earnestness, moreover, excluded the comic register of satire, indeed, even provoked it: *Shamela*. Combinations of the two within single works, not unknown, were inevitably disjointed. The door to moral conformism, on the other hand, was barred to erotic fiction, which by definition mocked earnest and hypocritical norms alike. Sexual liberties and satirical impulses were always more likely allies. Didactic intentions were, of course, another matter—they cohabited with tales of sentiment quite naturally, proving perfectly capable of supporting even the enormous edifice of *Clarissa* without strain. But the range of instruction was narrow. It could not extend to fundamental questioning of the established order without contradicting its own good intentions. Obviously, erotic fiction labored under no such inhibitions—already in defiance of ethical taboos, it could corrode political pieties much more readily.

---

[2] *PL*, 284. Translation modified.

This generic potential took a highly specific and focused form in Montesquieu's case, where the sexual and political were directly linked through his theory of *despotism*, a term that he invented. The tyranny of the seraglio, imprisoning women for the dwindling pleasures of one man, was the domestic image of the dominion of the sultanate, monopolizing wealth and power in the hands of a single ruler and reducing society around him to a desert in which his subjects were as passive and prostrate as women. Slavery at home and slavery in the state were one. The natural habitat of this despotism was the Orient, whose torrid climates enervated rulers and ruled alike. Such is the developed doctrine of *L'esprit des lois*, at which Montesquieu arrived a decade later. *Lettres persanes* is usually, and understandably, seen as the direct precursor of *L'esprit des lois*—an early fictional draft for the later theoretical masterpiece. But the fit between the two is not so complete. For an image of the Orient as the natural terrain of despotism, from which Europe is climatically delivered, does not square with an intention to use the Orient as an estranging device to criticize Europe. Leibniz and Bayle had wanted a vision of Europe from China, as a civilization in many ways superior to it. Persia possesses no such advantage in Montesquieu's novel. But nor, on the other hand, does it figure as a political bugbear either. The Safavid state is absent, and the cause of Uzbek's exile is a mere court intrigue of vaguely European stamp. It is despotism of the household, not of the palace, that sets the narrative scene.

For all its anticipations, the tenor of *Lettres persanes* thus differs significantly from *L'esprit des lois*. It is more radical. The first manifesto of the Enlightenment still remains the freshest, in the range of its reflections on leading themes of age, and the mordancy of its conclusions. Absent as yet the full theory of Oriental despotism, Montesquieu's political taxonomy acquires a sharper edge in Europe. The three fundamental types of government of *L'esprit des lois*—despotism, monarchy, and republic—are already present, together with the contrast between the limited power of European monarchs and the unlimited tyranny of Eastern rulers. But here Montesquieu ascribes a fundamental instability to monarchy alone, which always tends to reduce it to one of the other two. As Uzbek remarks: "Monarchy is a state of tension, which always degenerates into despotism or republicanism; power can never be divided equally between prince and people; it is too difficult to keep the balance. The power must necessarily decrease on one side and increase on the other; but the ruler is usually at an advantage, being in control of the armed forces."[3] A monarchy, in other words, is always closer to a despotism than to a republic. In his survey of the ancient world,

---

[3] *PL*, 187, letter 102.

Montesquieu could take "love of freedom and hatred of kings" as virtually indistinguishable.[4] Expressions of republican sentiment are much stronger in the novel than in the treatise. In the fable of the Troglodytes—another "gratuitous" insertion in the sequence of the letters—the elder asked by his fellows to become their king weeps for them: "You bring me the crown, and if you insist on it absolutely I shall certainly have to take it. But be sure that I shall die of grief, having seen when I was born the Troglodytes in freedom, and seeing them subjects [*assujettis*] today."[5]

If the Orient figures politically only in the novel's discursive register, without incidence on the action, in the domain of religion it serves a narrative as well as analytic function. Islam generates the seraglio, and the drama that follows from it, as structural elements of the work. Otherwise, rather than representing a more rational Eastern alternative to Christianity, as Confucianism was to do for Leibniz or Wolff, it offers instead a disturbing mirror image of Western superstition and irrationality—beliefs summed up by Uzbek: "I see Islam everywhere, though I cannot find Mohammad."[6] Montesquieu's scathing comments on the Trinity, transubstantiation, the papacy, bishops, monks, and confessors, are put in the mouths of Muslims, no kinder to the inanities of their own faith. "In our Koran, you often find the language of God and the ideas of men, as if, by a remarkable act of caprice, God had dictated the words, while mankind provided the thoughts."[7] Montesquieu's own convictions are calmly outlined: the evils of intolerance, the legitimacy of suicide, the impossibility of divine omniscience, the insignificance of the earth in the cosmos. Religion is allocated a purely civic function, as a cement of social cohesion—the path to Durkheim.

Laws, formally the great theme of the later work, are handled in similar spirit. Most are the product of arbitrary whims and prejudices; some of them are detestable; all are changeable. None can be compared to the dignity and immutability of the other kind of laws, that scientists discover in nature. The worst sort—not for the last time Montesquieu strikes a pointedly contemporary note—is international law. "In its present state, this branch of law is a science which explains to kings how far they can violate justice without damaging their own interests."[8] But, just as even superstition can serve as a social bond, even bad laws may be better than disobedience to them.

---

[4] *PL*, 233, letter 131.
[5] *PL*, 60, letter 14.
[6] *PL*, 89, letter 35.
[7] *PL*, 182, letter 97.
[8] *PL*, 176, letter 94.

If this conclusion anticipates the quietist note in *L'esprit des lois*, it is striking that the novel exposes to full view the deepest contradiction in Montesquieu's later work, which haunts his mature theory without ever being brought to the surface. Is justice purely conventional, contingent on particular periods and settings, or does it answer to universal and immutable principles? The whole of *L'esprit des lois* equivocates: if title and treatment appear to speak of facticity and diversity, declarative assertions insist on necessity and uniformity. In his youth Montesquieu was franker and less guarded. "Even if there were no God, we should nonetheless still love justice," writes Uzbek. "Even if we were to be free of the constraints of religion, we ought not to be free of those imposed by equity. It is this, Rhedi, which has led me to think that justice is eternal and does not depend on human conventions; and if it were to depend on them, this would be a terrible truth, which we should have to conceal from ourselves."[9] The semicolon is, as so often, a signal of the blow to come—a confession in advance of the operation *L'esprit des lois* would perform.

Politics, religion, law, justice. *Lettres persanes* has much to say about all of them. But organizing and dominating its caravan of ideas as a whole is the question that releases the narrative: relations between the sexes. The very first observation of the first letter sent back by the travelers from Europe, when they reach Livorno, gives the keynote: "The women here enjoy great freedom."[10] The second, when they get to Paris, speaks of Louis XIV, of the pope, and of the Gallican uproar against the bull *Unigenitus*, only to add: "The instigators of this revolt are women"—forbidden by the bull to read the Bible, "indignant at this insult to their sex, they have started a whole movement against the Bull; they have put the men, who in this case do not want to be privileged, on their side."[11] Not long after, male domination at large is mocked with arguments that have no counterpart until the final episodes of the Enlightenment, if then.

> It is a different problem to decide whether women are subject to men by the law of nature. "No," a very chivalrous philosopher said to me the other day, "nature laid down no such law. Our authority over women is absolutely tyrannical; they have allowed us to impose it because they are more gentle than we are, and consequently more humane and reasonable. . . . Why then should we be privileged? Because we are stronger? But that is completely unjust. We

---

[9] *PL*, 162, letter 83. Translation modified.
[10] *PL*, 71, letter 23.
[11] *PL*, 73, letter 24. Translation modified.

use all sorts of methods to reduce their courage. If our upbringing were similar, our strength would be also. Test them on the kinds of ability that their upbringing has not impaired, and we shall soon see if we are so superior."[12]

The tone is distinctively Regency—a long way from the *sérieux* of Condorcet or Wollstonecraft: gallantry rather than fervor or solicitude as the password to equality. But the logic is what would become theirs.

What then of marriage? As practiced, it is an object of raillery: "Frenchmen hardly ever talk about their wives; they are afraid to do so in front of people who may know them better than they," or, "here a husband who loves his wife is a man who has not enough merit to make another woman love him; who abuses the obligations imposed by law to compensate for his own lack of attraction."[13] But if the intellectual centerpiece of the novel opens with caustic or playful reflections on the life of the sentiments and the senses—sexual relations subjectively considered—it ends with historical considerations on their objective structures that form the most sustained of all arguments in the book. In a block of eleven successive letters (nos. 112–22) that breaks completely with the normal rhythm of the correspondence, Montesquieu contemplates a demographic enigma—what he took to be the decline of the world's population since antiquity. His error is more interesting than would have been its opposite, in illustrating at its very origins the extent of the misconception that the Enlightenment can generally be characterized as an optimistic doctrine of progress. Comparing Greece, Italy, Egypt, Turkey, and North Africa with classical times, Rica terms the depopulation of the earth "the most terrible catastrophe that has ever happened to the world; but it has scarcely been noticed, because it has occurred gradually, in the course of a great many centuries."[14]

Usbek's extended reply lays out Montesquieu's explanation of the decline, which turns essentially on the institutions regulating relations between the sexes. The Romans flourished because they banned polygamy but allowed divorce; whereas Christians banned divorce and Muslims permitted polygamy. Christian prohibition of divorce took all the pleasure out of marriage, incapacitating both partners for reproduction. "On an act so freely undertaken, in which emotion should play so large a part, were imposed constraint, necessity, and the inevitability of fate itself. . . . People were coupled together irrevocably and hopelessly, a mutual burden, almost always

---

[12] *PL*, 92–93, letter 38.
[13] *PL*, 118–19, letter 55.
[14] *PL*, 204, letter 112.

ill assorted; it was like those tyrants who had living men tied to dead bodies."[15] Conversely, the Muslim sanction of polygamy exhausted its practitioners: "It seems to me a Muslim is like an athlete doomed to compete without respite, who is soon weakened and overcome by his initial efforts, and languishes on the very field of victory, lying buried, so to speak, beneath his own triumphs."[16] Monks in the one culture, eunuchs in the other, were so many further deductions of vitality. Colonies were yet more subtractions, without compensating gains: the slave trade had laid waste Africa without filling the Americas. In China alone was there major population growth, because ancestor-worship made the lineage essential in this world and the next. The comparative cast of the argument makes this sequence of *Lettres persanes* closest to the procedures of *L'esprit des lois*, though there, as one might expect, the problem is prudently skirted.

In Europe at any rate, Montesquieu's demographic pessimism, for which commentators have profusely apologized, no longer looks like such an anachronism, as negative rates of reproduction in some of his lands of choice—Italy, Spain—haunt public debate today. More striking still, as a direct premonition of the future and token of reserve toward any confidence in technological progress, is an earlier letter from Rhedi: "You wrote at some length about the developments of the arts and sciences in the West. You will think me a barbarian, but I do not know whether the utility we derive from them compensates mankind for the abuse that is constantly made of them. . . . I am always afraid that they will eventually succeed in discovering some secret which will provide a quicker way of making men die, and exterminate whole countries and nations."[17] Usbek's reply, in its weak reassurance, has an even more contemporary ring: "No: if such a fateful invention came to be discovered, it would soon be banned by international law, and by the unanimous consent of every country would be buried."[18]

Placed toward the end of the philosophical correspondence in Europe, these reflections signal a shift in tone that prepares the descent toward narrative ruin. The final letters, exchanges between Usbek, his wives, and eunuchs from and to Persia, are grouped together out of temporal sequence. Though they spell misfortune for all concerned, their tenor could not be more affirmative. Montesquieu spoke of the secret chain of his construction, and the juxtaposition of the last letter about France, denouncing Law's system, with

---

[15] *PL*, 210, letter 116.
[16] *PL*, 207, letter 114.
[17] *PL*, 192, letter 105.
[18] *PL*, 194, letter 106.

the first news of the wives' revolt in Persia, has often been noted—and sometimes taken as a displacement of political to sexual rebellion, a remote household revolt acting as surrogate for an impossible overthrow of the local state. There is little doubt Montesquieu intended a parallel between the disorders of the budget and of the bedchamber, but this reading mistakes the priority of the novel. The sexual may mirror the political, but in this fiction also commands it. The ending of the tale is in place, affording Montesquieu the logical envoi.

For the revolt of the seraglio is a liberation in more than one sense. In the grieving words of one of the eunuchs: "there is a new atmosphere of gaiety everywhere here, which in my view is a sure sign of some new-found contentment; in the most trivial matters I notice liberties being taken which were formerly unknown." The link—gaiety-contentment-freedom—might be called the real secret chain of the novel. Sexual passion is a source, not of servitude, but of moral independence. (For Zelis, early on, adolescence was expressly "that critical moment when the passions begin to show themselves and encourage us to be independent").[19] Roxane's farewell to life makes the same connexion. "I have managed to turn your terrible seraglio into a place of delightful pleasures," she tells Usbek. "I may have lived in servitude, but I have always been free. I have amended your laws according to the laws of nature, and my mind has always remained independent."[20] Pleasure-nature-independence: the Enlightenment would ring many changes on these terms, but they are all echoes of this first, terse cry of emancipation. The closing lines of the novel are aware of what it has said: "Such language, no doubt, is new to you . . ."

Reflecting on *Lettres persanes* thirty years later, Montesquieu wrote that it differed from ordinary novels—where "serious discussion has to be excluded, since none of the characters having been introduced for purposes of discussion, it would be contrary to the nature and intention of the work"—in what he called its "digressions."[21] The epistolary form, however, freely permitted these, allowing him "the advantage of being able to include philosophy, politics and moral discourse in the novel, and to connect everything together with a secret chain which remains, as it were, invisible."[22] By later standards the chain is too loose: thoughts and deeds essentially inhabit separate planes. One way of closing the gap was the *conte philosophique*, in

---

[19] PL, 128, letter 62.
[20] *PL*, 280, letter 161.
[21] *PL*, 283. Translation modified.
[22] *PL*, 283. Translation modified.

which a single motivating doctrine generates a parable that illustrates it: *Robinson Crusoe, Candide, Rasselas*. Montesquieu's novel is one ancestor of this form, not an example of it. A better term of comparison is the modern novel of ideas, in which characters both articulate and embody different standpoints, whose conflicts detonate the action—Dostoevsky, Musil, Malraux, Sartre. Their narrative superiority is enormous, to the point where we are tempted to deny the term *novel* to any work, like *Lettres persanes*, which falls so far short of it. But a price came with the gain. The range and originality of the ideas that animate these works is less—had to be less, to shape a compelling plot—than those that the president of the Bordeaux Parlement offered so disarmingly to the public three centuries ago.

IAN DUNCAN

Waverley
(Walter Scott, 1814)

"The first historical novel." If Lukács exaggerated the claim, making Scott an author ex nihilo, recent critics have drawn attention to thriving prior traditions of historical fiction, gothic romance, and national tale that flowed into *Waverley*. It remains the case that Scott transformed these precursors into something new: nothing less than the novel of the nineteenth century, a genre that realizes its modernity in a discursive reckoning with history, from which it seizes—to make its own—the narrative of modernization. *Waverley* signals that renewal by telling, through its narrative of public and private histories, the tale of its own formation as the genre of modern life.

In *Waverley; or, 'Tis Sixty Years Since*, Scott established the historical novel as national genre. The title epigraph, from *2 Henry IV*, alludes to the precedent of Shakespeare's History plays: "Under which King, Bezonian? speak, or die!" Scott follows Shakespeare to make civil war the classical setting of historical fiction: it is the fiery, bloody rift in the fabric of common life through which history and national character become visible. *Waverley* makes its topic the 1745 Jacobite rising, the last civil conflict on British soil, and the last attempt of an elder dynasty to regain its forfeited historical sway—confirming only its belatedness, its exclusion from history, and the irreversible, inexorable drive of modernization:

> There is no European nation which, within the course of half a century, or little more, has undergone so complete a change as this kingdom of Scotland. The effects of the insurrection of 1745,—the destruction of the patriarchal power of the Highland chiefs,—the abolition of the jurisdictions of the Lowland nobility and barons,—the total eradication of the Jacobite party, which, averse to mingle with the English, or adopt their customs, long continued to pride themselves upon maintaining ancient Scottish manners and customs, commenced this innovation. The gradual influx of wealth, and extension of commerce, have since united to render the present people of Scotland a class of beings as different from their grandfathers as the existing English are from those of Queen Elizabeth's time. (340)

The publication of *Waverley* coincided with Bonaparte's defeat: a final settlement (or so it seemed) of the political form of modernity. At such a juncture, the novel assumes not just national but world-historical status.

Scott invested fiction with the imperial logic of Scottish Enlightenment philosophical history, which binds all human societies to a universal scheme of development, from hunting tribes through nomadic herders and farmers to a commercial modernity. The inner spring of history becomes visible, not in the difference between rival empires, dynasties, or parties, but in the difference between social and economic systems that marks the transition between developmental stages—in other words, in the difference between cultures, ways of life. Scott's hero travels north from an English estate through Lowland Scotland, with its local remnants of feudalism, up into the Highlands, the haunt of patriarchal clans. Scott installs the narrative drive of historical fiction: a movement across territories that charts a movement between cultures and epochs. And he develops, with unmatched subtlety, the main topos of this narrative, the *border*: the location of history as the site of cultural difference and transition, where identities and languages collide, mix, and exchange properties, as they define, transform, absorb, or dissolve one another.

Waverley claims for the novel the historical geography of uneven development, which represents the journey from the imperial core as a journey back in time. We learn that the journey itself—through the presence of the modern traveler, who carries our reading eye—is the act that converts a cultural difference into historical anteriority, as it rehearses the imperial penetration of the hinterland. We are able to see, since we are not Waverley but are reading him, the operation of an eye at first innocent, merely curious, not knowing itself to be the bearer of a politics. Young Edward Waverley, an English officer, leaves his regiment to tour the Highlands on the eve of the 1745 rising, which will end in the destruction of the clans by his own army and government legislation. Until it is too late Waverley fails to grasp the historical character of the Highlanders as Jacobite insurgents, already committed to a futile resistance to the regime whose arms he bears—a failure of interpretation that follows his inability to understand his own historical agency. Scott's narrative renders clearly the imperial logic that rewrites the other world as "archaic," already superseded, doomed to pass, in its very glamour and fascination for the modern reader. Waverley's Highland friends are executed for treason, but he survives and prospers. His survival changes the meaning of the experience he has been through. Once Jacobitism has been eradicated as a political movement, and the Highland clans dissolved as a social system, their values can be reclaimed in the form of cultural capital; empire renews itself ideologically through the absorption of primitive virtues of courage and loyalty.

A painting of Waverley's Highland adventure is unveiled in Scott's final scene. The novel shows us, framed within its own representation, the modern production of the past that historians have called "the invention of tradition":

> It was a large and spirited painting, representing Fergus Mac-Ivor and Waverley in their Highland dress, the scene a wild, rocky, and mountainous pass, down which the clan were descending in the background. It was taken from a spirited sketch, drawn while they were in Edinburgh by a man of high genius, and had been painted on a full length scale by an eminent London artist. Raeburn himself, (whose Highland Chiefs do all but walk out of the canvas) could not have done more justice to the subject; and the ardent, fiery, and impetuous character of the unfortunate Chief of Glennaquoich was finely contrasted with the contemplative, fanciful, and enthusiastic expression of his happier friend. Beside this painting hung the arms which Waverley had borne in the unfortunate civil war. The whole piece was generally admired. (338)

Scott exposes the imperial production of this work of art, across the metropolitan sites of Edinburgh and London. "The whole piece" comprises Waverley's rebel arms, converted from the evidence of treason to trophies or souvenirs, whose function now is to authenticate the hero's mythic sojourn among an organic brotherhood. The reader should recall that no such scene ever took place in the novel. The painting offers a sentimental purification of Waverley's confused motives during the Jacobite campaign, as well as his uneasy relationship with Fergus Mac-Ivor, at odds with Scott's persistently ironical narration. The *ecphrasis*, occupying the narrative's last page, mirrors the representation we have been reading—published in Edinburgh and London—but also invites us to think critically about that representation and its historical conditions, including the conditions of our reading. Only if we are reading badly, forgetting (like Waverley himself) what we have read before, can we acquiesce in its nostalgia, or mistake it for the narrative that frames it.

———

The historical novel secures the effect of history, as an overdetermined logic of "progress" or modernization, by synchronizing different levels of narration into a complex, unified, dialectical structure. The key homology, locking in the set, identifies a collective process of social change with an individual process of psychological, sentimental, and moral development: national history and bildungsroman mediate one other. The raw and uncertain modernity of the United Kingdom consolidates itself upon a final conflict with the social and political forces it designates as premodern, while Waverley attains rational adulthood through a cathartic indulgence in adolescent fantasy.

Two things are notable about the protagonist of this national and historical bildungsroman. One is the effect observed by all commentators, from the first reviewers to late-twentieth-century critics: the mediocrity or blankness of Scott's hero, as he occupies a passive relation to the crisis—historical, psychosexual—that whirls around him. Lukács reads the hero's blankness as the anonymous screen of a new, middle-class historical agency; Alexander Welsh reads it as the subjective correlative of property—itself inert, exerting gravitational force—in the symbolic order of commercial society. Scott's narrative sustains a dissociation, often drastic, between Waverley's intention and his experience: a divorce of consciousness from historical process that (acquitting him from free assent to treason) will eventually guarantee his survival. With this dissociation of narrative agency, Scott defines the protagonist of the modern novel, from the proper, anxious bourgeois gentleman of Victorian fiction to his more chronically alienated peers in the Continental empires: the superfluous man, the man without qualities.

The other crux of this subjectivity is its dialectical formation through a quixotic indulgence and disciplinary refinement of the aesthetic faculty. *Waverley* narrates the triumph of the aesthetic, threatened by the trauma of a repressed historical knowledge but then absorbing it, in the production of a critical consciousness for modern life. At the beginning of the novel Waverley inhabits a "feminine," narcissistic sensibility that secures itself by investing the world with romantic tropes and images. As the narrative unfolds, Waverley's narcissism enjoys a rich and complex expansion, however much ironized against his ignorance of the political realities that subtend events. His imagination, not limited to the projection of romantic associations, is also acutely sensitive to certain vibrations within a local scene, because it filters out the noise of historical, political meaning.

The most rapturous of Waverley's romantic encounters comes in his audience with Flora Mac-Ivor, the clan chieftain's beautiful and accomplished sister, in a wild Highland glen. Surrounded by appropriate scenery, Flora offers Waverley her "imperfect translation" of a Gaelic song: "To speak in the poetical language of my country, the seat of the Celtic Muse is in the mist of the secret and solitary hill, and her voice in the murmur of the mountain stream. He who woos her must love the barren rock more than the fertile valley, and the solitude of the desert better than the festivity of the hall" (106–7). Flora's "poetical language," troping the historical geography of her country, encodes an invitation to join the rebel cause—her song is a Jacobite call to arms. But the appeal to metaphor amplifies the historical irony that will negate her cause, and render her world—in every way—a barren desert. Waverley misconstrues the appeal. His aesthetic attunement to Flora's charms and to the picturesque landscape—to the tropes themselves—obliterates politics: "Indeed the wild feeling of romantic delight, with which he heard the first few notes she drew from her instrument, amounted almost to a sense of pain. He would not for worlds have quitted his place by her side; yet he almost longed for solitude, that he might decypher and examine at leisure the complication of emotions which now agitated his bosom" (107).

Waverley almost longs for solitude, but in the form of an interior space of aesthetic withdrawal and contemplation. This is, explicitly, a space of reading: presently occupied by ourselves. In fact, Waverley's "wild feeling of romantic delight" accurately predicts his destiny. As Flora later acknowledges, he belongs, not to the battlefield or the senate, but to "the quiet circle of domestic happiness" and "lettered indolence," where his chief occupation will be to "refit the old library in the most exquisite Gothic taste" (250). This invocation of the reader as teleological figure of Waverley's history—occupying the privileged horizon of a domesticity beyond "history," that is, social and political struggle—should disconcert us, as readers now, as much as it might have reassured Scott's original readers in the aftermath of the French wars.

The failure of the rising brings Waverley to a disciplinary reflection upon his experience: "[It] was in many a winter walk by the shores of Ulswater, that he acquired a more complete mastery of a spirit tamed by adversity, than his former experience had given him; and that he felt himself entitled to say firmly, though perhaps with a sigh, that the romance of his life was ended, and that its real history had now commenced" (283). Scott's novel, however, does not trace a progressive trajectory from "romance" to "real history." The narrative goes on to reward the chastened hero with his domestic haven; its chief ornament, the painting of Waverley's Highland adventure, commemorates the romance of his life rather than its real history. The difference falls in the melancholy recognition of defeat and loss that has intervened between the experience and its representation. That elegiac knowledge, which the reader shares, now makes the aesthetic sense fit for the inhabitation of history: in the medium of romance, through which we may imagine our relation to past and present conditions.

Scott's contribution to the history of the novel can be read in the key word *romance*, which he (more than anyone) fixed in its modern, double usage: a subjective state of the imagination, the narrative form of premodern cultures. In *Waverley*, for the first time, the novel narrates the history of its own formation as a genre—a historicization that touches not just literary form but the function and status of fiction as an institution, a set of material forms and social practices, including our act of reading.

The romance of his life was ended; its real history had now commenced. The early chapters of *Waverley* rehearse the convention of quixotism with which the early English novel had defended its fitness to represent modern life, opposing itself to a decadent, inauthentic kind of fiction called "romance." Young Waverley, secluded from the world, his education neglected, reads old romances. His reading forms his self-image and conditions his response to outward scenes: "He had now time to give himself up to the full romance of his situation" (78). Waverley's involvement in the Jacobite campaign is figured as enthrallment in an Italian courtly romance by Boiardo or Ariosto, in other words, an absolutist and Catholic genre—an enthrallment demystified, for the reader, by the narrator's running allusions to Protestant British authors. Spenserian allegory and Miltonic epic point up the historical character of the rebellion as a diabolical error, since these are the literary forms of decisive earlier stages of national history, the Reformation and Revolution. Belonging to the past, these genres are no longer historically sufficient, and *Waverley*, above all, reflects on the eighteenth-century "rise of the novel" as the national genre of modernity, secured at the very moment of the tale's action: Fielding's *Tom Jones*, echoed in Scott's opening chapters, also addresses 1745 as its own historical context. We are to understand that this kind of novel, too, now represents a superseded historical stage. The anti-Scottish bigotry professed by the spokesman of Fieldingesque English values in *Waverley*, Colonel Talbot, measures the more generous range of national sympathy encompassed by the novel in which he appears. The national novel was an Irish and Scottish achievement (Scott pays homage to Maria Edgeworth) rather than an English one. Indeed, Scott himself would go on to invent a national historical romance for England, in *Ivanhoe* (1820).

That generous sympathetic range extends to a diversity of literary and linguistic forms. *Waverley* marks its advance over the eighteenth-century novel in its character as a historical romance, comprising within its discourse the historical archive of a national culture, assembled in the antiquarian projects of the late-Enlightenment romance and ballad revivals. In addition to the courtly and polite genres of literary history, Scott's novel presents an anthology of vernacular materials: ballads, popular rhymes, and songs; "folklore," proverbs, and regional and social dialects; and legal and professional documents. With this innovative miscellany of sources and discourses, *Waverley* and its successors establish the nineteenth-century project of representing a complex, dynamic social world, extending in time as well as space. The representation includes an amplified, referentially saturated realism, but working alongside other mimetic styles, within the global category of "romance": designating the modes of interpretation, thought-experiment, and fantasy encoded in historically variable narrative forms. With Scott, for the first time, the British novel claims fiction as its motive principle—rather than some other discourse of truth of which it is the didactic vessel. The historical novel subsumes history to a cognitive work peculiar to fiction, and for which philosophical authority can be found in the empiricism of David Hume. The reader of Scott's novels is brought to recognize the imaginary, aesthetically and socially constructed character of historical reality, in the present as well as in the past. Although their author may well have wanted the recognition to bind us more closely to that reality, the novels themselves do not guarantee a particular ideological outcome, as their reception history shows us.

Works Cited and Further Reading

Buzard, James. "Translation and Tourism: Scott's *Waverley* and the Rendering of Culture." *Yale Journal of Criticism*, 8:2 (1995):31–59.

Chandler, James. *England in 1819: The Politics of Literary Culture and the Case of Romantic Historicism*. Chicago, 1998.

Christensen, Jerome. *Romanticism at the End of History*. Baltimore, 2000.

Craig, Cairns. *Out of History: Narrative Paradigms in Scottish and English Culture*. Edinburgh, 1996.

Crawford, Robert. *Devolving English Literature*. Oxford, 1992.

Duncan, Ian. *Modern Romance and Transformations of the Novel: The Gothic, Scott, Dickens*. Cambridge, 1992.

Ferris, Ina. *The Achievement of Literary Authority: Gender, History and the Waverley Novels*. Ithaca, N.Y., 1981.

Hamilton, Paul. *Metaromanticism: Aesthetics, Literature, Theory*. Chicago, 2003.

Lee, Yoon Sun. *Romanticism and Irony: Burke, Scott, Carlyle*. New York, 2004.

Lukács, Georg. *The Historical Novel* (1937). Translated by Hannah Mitchell and Stanley Mitchell. Lincoln, Neb., 1983.

Makdisi, Saree. *Romantic Imperialism: Universal Empire and the Culture of Modernity*. Cambridge, 1998.

Maxwell, Richard. "Inundations of Time: A Definition of Scott's Originality." *ELH* 68 (2001): 419–68.

McCracken-Flesher, Caroline. *Possible Scotlands: Walter Scott and the Story of Tomorrow.* New York, 2005.

McMaster, Graham. *Scott and Society.* Cambridge, 1981.

Millgate, Jane. *Walter Scott: The Making of the Novelist.* Edinburgh, 1984.

Moretti, Franco. *Atlas of the European Novel 1800–1900.* London, 1998.

———. *The Way of the World: The Bildungsroman in European Culture.* London, 1987.

Robertson, Fiona. *Legitimate Histories: Scott, Gothic and the Authorities of Fiction.* Oxford, 1994.

Scott, Walter. *Waverley* (1814). Edited by Claire Lamont. Oxford, 1986.

Trumpener, Katie. *Bardic Nationalism: The Romantic Novel and the British Empire.* Princeton, N.J., 1997.

Villari, Enrica. "Romance and History in *Waverley.*" In *Athena's Shuttle: Myth, Religion, Ideology from Romanticism to Modernism*, ed. F. Marucci and E. Sdegno, 93–111. Milan, 2000.

Welsh, Alexander. *The Hero of the Waverley Novels: With New Essays on Scott.* Princeton, N.J., 1992.

Wilt, Judith. *Secret Leaves: The Novels of Walter Scott.* Chicago, 1985.

PAOLO TORTONESE

The Mysteries of Paris
(Eugène Sue, 1842–1843)

"But when will you stop torturing us," protests a listener, losing patience
with the endless dragging out of a story that has gone on for too long. The
setting is a prison. The listener is a hardened criminal called "le Squelette,"
the skeleton. He is sitting amid a group of convicts forming a tight circle
around an equally criminal but less dangerous narrator, Pique-Vinaigre.
Both men have nonliterary motivations: one is in a hurry; the other is killing
time. At issue is whether to prevent or produce the conditions for a murder.
But the listeners ignore these motivations and hang innocently on the words
of a narrator who with lavish cruelty rivets them to a pleasure made all the
greater the more ruthlessly he defers it. A pleasure that is fed by postpone-
ments, swollen by deprivation, gratified by torment. The longer you await
pleasure, the more you enjoy it. Yet true pleasure does not arrive at the end
of the wait, when the obstacle is cleared and the end revealed: it lies instead
in the hurdles and deceptions themselves, the sadistic teasing constituted by
postponement, the torture of seeing the prey get away. Pique-Vinaigre, in his
way, is a professional storyteller. He even makes his fellow prisoners pay and
boasts of the powers of the story he is about to tell, strong enough to "break
one's hearts and make your hair stand on end." Who wouldn't shell out five
cents to "have his heart broken and his hair stand on end?" (8.8.1,029).[1]

This is how the two key elements of the *roman-feuilleton*, or serial novel,
are deployed within the genre's inaugural work: in the passage from the
Mysteries of Paris just quoted, the novel attracts interest through emotional
implications and narrative rhythm, each of which is indispensable: the
reader has to suffer twice, both as an empathetic participant in the character's suffering and as the victim of delaying tactics. It would seem that the

---

[1] Eugène Sue, *The Mysteries of Paris* (Chicago: M. A. Donohue Co., 1900). The name of
the translator of this oft-reproduced volume (in facsimile and on the Internet) is not given.
[Translator's note: The division of the English translation into parts and chapters does not
correspond to French text: the French is divided into ten parts and 159 chapters, plus epilogue; the
English is divided into three parts and 108 chapters, plus epilogue. Therefore, in the citations the
part and chapter numbers of the original French have been maintained, while the page numbers
refer to the English translation. Where the French *roman* was translated as "romance," it has been
emended to "novel." No page numbers are given for passages that were apparently not included in
the published translation.]

more passionate one's identification with the characters, the more painful (and pleasurable) the procrastination.

The phenomenon whereby another person's suffering becomes pleasurable when it is told in the form of a story is also deployed in another chapter of the novel. The abject misery of the Morel family is a source of entertainment for the doorman, Pipelet, who enjoys the spectacle through a hole in the wall of the adjacent garret. Pipelet calls this spot "his *box at the play*" (4.1.448), whence he can contemplate at his leisure the "sad scenes" of a working-class family slowly starving to death. The gratuitous catharsis of this improvised theater places the doorman in the same situation as the readers: curious, moved, indignant, satisfied. But while he can follow the Morel family novel at will (all he has to do is climb a few flights of stairs), the reader instead is forced to bear the tempos imposed by the writer, who organizes the narrative according to a rigorous economy of deferment. This holds true for a reader with a multivolume edition, but it was even more so for the first readers, who came upon *The Mysteries of Paris* in the pages of the *Journal del Débats* between June 19, 1842, and October 15, 1843.

The serial novel is, in fact, a rather particular literary genre tied to a publication style that seems to magnify its characteristics and, at first glance, to lay its foundations. Even away from the pages of a newspaper, however, this type of novel maintains its functioning and effectiveness. It is the product of a marriage between literature and journalism: there can be no doubt that the rhythm of the daily press was the key to an original style of administering narrative tempos. But it is likewise true that delaying tactics had already existed in the practice of writing novels outside the realm of periodicals. So if indeed it was a marriage, the dowry was provided by both families.

The fateful date of their courtship was 1836, the year when Emile de Girardin launched *La Presse*, the new newspaper that proposed to make money through advertising, which would thus cut the cost to subscribers in half. Girardin was the first great advocate of collaboration between newspapers and literature. He published Balzac's *The Old Maid* in October–November 1836 and Dumas's novella "Pascal Bruno" the following January, not only creating the conditions for his own success and that of his novelists but also for an accentuation of narrative methods aimed at keeping the reader's interest, an interest that became more precious than ever when newspaper subscriptions came to depend on the passions enflamed by the novel.

Between 1836 and 1841, *La Presse* published four more novels by Balzac and five by Eugène Sue (*Arthur, Arabian Godolphin, Kardiki, Aventures d'Hercule Hardi,* and *Mathilde*) in which he honed his narrative technique.

All of these works appeared either in newspaper columns or (starting in May 1839) in feuilleton, on the bottom of the first and second pages. This famous location is not essential per se, but it quickly became emblematic of the new winning alliance between literature and journalism. The feuilleton had already existed as a typographic space since 1800, but it had never before hosted novels. In fact it would continue to be occupied frequently by theater, literary, and artistic criticism, as well as society pieces. Prior to 1836, starting in 1829 to be specific, some magazines (*Revue des Deux Mondes* and *Revue de Paris*) had already begun to publish narrative works. Girardin took the decisive step, filling in the gap between magazine and newspaper and transforming the *rez-de-chaussée* into a meeting point for the press, the novel, and the public.

As is often the case, the relationship between cause and effect was not a one-way street. Although the novel benefited enormously from the feuilleton, journalism, for its part, clearly gained from the popularity of a form of the novel that was solidly rooted and destined to become even more so through the sustained increase in literacy rates. The trend would continue throughout the century. The roman-feuilleton would prosper alongside other genres, with which it came to share the now consecrated medium: almost all novels, even if they were not serial novels, came to be printed in feuilleton before becoming books. Later the medium and the genre would separate, when the press and literature would divorce in the late nineteenth century, allowing both the serial novel and other novel genres to address the public directly from the pages of a book.

The rise and fall of the serial novel thus took place between 1836 and the early years of the twentieth century. From the era when Balzac tried to wrest the laurels of popularity from Sue, Soulié, and Dumas, until the era of the serial detective novel masters, Gaston Leroux (Rouletabille), Maurice Leblanc (Arsenio Lupin), and Marcel Allain and Pierre Souvestre (Fantômas), the river of narrative and suspense flowed, fed by Paul Féval, Ponson du Terrail, Xavier de Montépin, Jules Mary, Émile Richebourg, Pierre Decourcelle, Georges Ohnet, Charles Mérouvel, and many other even more forgotten authors. Less forgotten are the masterpieces of the genre, especially of the historic and crime novel variety: *The Count of Monte Cristo* (1844–45) and the *Rocambole* series (1857–71).[2]

---

[2] On the birth and development of the serial novel, see René Guise, *Le roman-feuilleton, 1830–1848: La naissance d'un genre* ([Lille]: University of Lille III, 1985); Lise Queffélec, *Le roman feuilleton français au XIXe siècle* (Paris: Presses Universitaires de France, 1989); and Claude Witkowski, *Autour des feuilletons* (Saint-Cloud, 1990).

From this enormous mass of printed pages it is hard to extract absolute constants or methods that are followed everywhere, without exception. Nevertheless, it is not absurd to maintain that *The Mysteries of Paris* provided some long-term paradigms. The delaying strategy is not related exclusively to the daily deadlines; it is more deeply related to the narrative *métier* and its organization. It has been said that the *Mysteries of Paris* responds to a triple rule, antithetical to the canon of classicism: the rule of the "three multiplicities."[3] There is not one place, time, and action: there are many. They allow the game of deferments because the narrative regularly shifts from one place to another, one time to another, one action to another. Sue himself refers to a "récit multiple" (3.14). We are dealing not with a fragmentary or scattered structure: there is not a multiplication *ad infinitum*, a centrifugal proliferation; we are not in the universe of the *Manuscript Found in Saragossa*. We are in a world where it is easy to get your bearings. Places, times, and especially actions are plural but not excessively numerous: parallel stories converge at certain points, and the basic unity is preserved. Sue limits himself to making us zigzag between five or six plot lines, alternating chapters with each other, taking care to suspend the story at the best part and defer the moment in which the secret threads will appear that tie everything together.

Suspense is thus produced not so much by the wait for the next installment (which applied only to the 1842–43 readers) as by the alternating of parallel stories that constitute a comprehensive story. Sue's work is centered less on the main action than on a certain number of characters, around each of whom a story is spun and chapters are organized, ably redistributed in the novel as a whole. This character/chapter structure allows for alternation and deferment, and it poses the problem of synthesis, namely, of how to reconnect the individual adventures into the story as a whole. Suspense is produced in part by the wait for the moment in which the hidden connections between apparently unrelated characters and actions are revealed. The management of these connections is the supreme task of the author of the roman-feuilleton, who has different instruments at his disposal: the first is chance, which in this genre of the novel becomes an ordering and synthesizing principle. A reassuring French proverb assures us that "le hasard fait bien les choses" (chance does things well): in the roman-feuilleton, chance is intertwined and combined with consummate skill. The chance encounter,

---

[3] The expression was coined by S. Silvestre de Sacy in his introduction to H. de Balzac, *Splendeurs et misères des courtisanes* (Paris: Garnier Frères, 1958), and adopted by Jean Louis Bory, "Premiers éléments pour une esthétique du roman-feuilleton," in Bory, *Tout feu, tout flame* (Paris: Union Générale d'Éditions, 1979). Bory also published a biography, *Eugène Sue* (Paris: Hachette, 1962).

the providential error, and the fatal coincidence make it possible to weave together an otherwise impossible plot.

But chance has its tricks: to connect the unconnectable it employs special places that seem predisposed to encounters between strangers, places that serve as crossroads and enable coincidences: in the *Mysteries of Paris* they are the house on rue du Temple (in which four different stories cohabitate in the various apartments), the notary's study (filed through by five different characters who don't know each other, in quick succession, in five successive chapters), the prison, and the hospital. The encounter becomes almost plausible, the intertwining of the plot more possible.

When the topography of the novel does not suffice, one character becomes responsible for spinning the plot: the hero, Rodolphe, who thanks to his audacity, wealth, and power can move around, disguise himself, slip into the most varied environments, overcome all obstacles, or act from a distance and through other people. His exceptional geographic and social mobility allows the novelist to tighten the strings of the overall story. Sue does not, for that matter, seem overly concerned with the intelligibility of all the connections, and he issues a torrent of foreshadowings, harbingers, reminders, and recapitulations. With phrases like "You will recall that . . . ," or "in a future chapter we will relate . . . ," he takes readers by the hand and helps them not to get lost in the forest of connections.

The pleasure of the tale is related to the possibility of understanding it. The obstacles that the novelist places before the reader's gaze make sense only if they presuppose a final transparency that is guaranteed a priori. Passion and identification also demand this guarantee of intelligibility: if I suffer with the sufferer, I want to know why he is suffering.

The prisoners sitting in a circle around Pique-Vinaigre express a curious moral phenomenon. Criminal and violent, insensitive to the pain of their victims, they are paradoxically attracted by stories of "heroic recital where weakness, after a thousand crosses, finishes by triumphing over its persecutors" (8.1.961). While they themselves are oppressors in life, in fiction they side with the weak and enjoy seeing bullies punished: a moral paradox that seems consoling to Sue because it is the symptom of the hidden presence of good in places where only evil is manifested. The responses of the criminals are shared in general by all people. Sue recalls how in the boulevard theaters where melodramas were performed, the audience welcomed with "frenzied applause . . . the deliverance of the victim" and hurled impassioned curses at each successive villain (8.9.1,032).

In Sue's world, the plot is deeply related to the moral dimension and acts as a revealer of good. Even the philanthropy preached by the *Mysteries of Paris* is not without narrative implications. When Rodolphe seeks to convince Clémence d'Harville to perform charitable work, he does not speak of the divine reward that it will gain her but of a more earthly pleasure, straight from the pages of a novel: to perform charitable deeds for the poor is to "play the part of an inferior *Providence*," and "*good deeds* sometimes have all the piquancy of a novel" (3.17.411). In short, good can be no less "entertaining" than evil. After performing her first philanthropic deed, Clémence wonders, "What novel could give me such touching emotions, excite to this point my curiosity!" (5.6.617).

If literary pleasure can be so intimately connected to the moral dimension, it is because the reality represented by the novel is fundamentally driven by the opposition between good and evil. In this sense, emotional identification does not oppose but rather fosters an understanding of the world. Here the "melodramatic imagination," as formulated by Peter Brooks, acts with all its force: the novel reveals (with more schematic ingenuity in Sue than in Balzac or James) the presence of an organizing structure underlying the phenomena, a moral structure.[4] Both the morality of the novel and the emotional participation of the reader are based on the morality of reality.[5] At first glance, the novel's moral universe consists of the sharp contrast between scrupulously good and shockingly bad characters. One can rightly speak of Manicheanism in the roman-feuilleton and melodrama, but the word can be deceptive, suggesting an immobility of the two fields, an unimpeachable distinction, while Sue's world is actually characterized by the ease with which the bad become good and the good proves to be bad.

During his moments of rage, even Rodolphe, the standard-bearer of good, seems to be overcome by evil feelings, but more than anyone else the criminals prove to be driven by positive leanings. There are numerous examples, from the Slasher, who redeems himself and places himself at the service of Rodolphe; to Tortillard, who feels "the need to be loved" by a maternal figure, "an exception that disproves the notion of unity in vice" (3.5); to Louve (the she-wolf), another converted criminal, who is introduced immediately as "rather vicious than thoroughly bad" (5.7.609); to the Schoolmaster, who is gradually overcome by remorse. All of these characters pay witness to human contradiction and definitely not to the steadfastness of moral character: good and bad people wage war on each other ruthlessly, but good and evil carry on an even more pitched war within each character. While the moral dimension always triumphs, and the distinction between good and

---

[4] Peter Brooks, *The Melodramatic Imagination: Balzac, Henry James, Melodrama and the Mode of Excess* (New Haven, Conn.: Yale University Press, 1976).

[5] This wish is made explicit in 5.6.606.

evil is apparently the dimension that matters the most, there is still no reason for the wicked to remain unchanged. By the end of the novel, in fact, everyone has given in to opposite motivations: especially Rodolphe, who seeks to expiate an old error through good deeds. Rodolphe the guilty and good is Sue's most moral character, and only a surprising superficiality has allowed some critics to mistake him for a close relative of Nietzsche's superman.

None of this is at all incompatible with the logic of melodrama, which Peter Brooks called "the logic of the excluded middle" (35). The characters in the *Mysteries of Paris* are moral because they are good and bad at the same time. Their inner contradictions, however, produce not a balanced compromise but rather a piercing conflict and often a sudden reversal. This is how the rule of the excluded middle is maintained, never straying toward the objective pursued by naturalism in its opposition to the melodramatic imagination: mediocrity. The conversions of many of the bad characters in the *Mysteries of Paris* are reminiscent of Ivan's conversion in *La fille de l'exilé* by Guilbert de Pixérécourt, an 1819 melodrama that Brooks considers paradigmatic. The persecutor's repentance shows the moral mobility of the characters, who go from one extreme to another without knowing middle ways: "The characters that represent the extremes . . . have to face extreme situations, passing from the sublime to the object, or vice versa, almost instantaneously" (Brooks, 58).

Remorse and the prospect of redemption permeate the novel. If certain implacable villains are left untouched, such as Ferrand the notary and the perverse Cecily (the two most completely evil characters, who end up clashing, to such an extent that she becomes an unwilling instrument of good), the purest of all the good characters, the angelic Fleur-de-Marie, suffers torments so atrocious that she renounces the world and life itself, all in the quest for an impossible expiation.

Fleur-de-Marie also struggles with another contradiction, that of a crime committed (prostitution) and protestations of her innocence, since the evil was forced on her. This points to another aspect of the ideological organization of the *Mysteries of Paris*, an aspect that is surprisingly contrary to the absolute morality of Sue's world. When Fleur-de-Marie, rescued from the corruption into which she had fallen, is first introduced to a venerable priest, he is moved by her angelic demeanor and says, "You will soon merit absolution from those grave faults of which you have been the victim rather than the criminal" (1.14.97). This sentence is of capital importance: if you can be considered the victim of your sin, your guilt vanishes.

In the novel, the case of Fleur-de-Marie is isolated. No other sinner sees his or her responsibility so diminished. The author frequently interrupts the narrative with essayistic interventions that insist on the causes of evil, indicate the reasons for criminality, and even suggest remedies. With the exception of Cecily, to whom Sue attributes a "natural perversity" (2.7.182), and the evil burgher, Ferrand, all the other characters are subjected to the baleful influence of the environment, the devastations of a trauma (abandonment by parents, violence, and so on), or the curse of poverty.

Sue's determinism is staunch: the relationship between suffering and crime is strongly emphasized. Poverty in particular is seen as the cause of corruption in every sense: associated with ignorance and the bad example set by the ruling class, it fuels evil inclinations and comprises good ones. Moral evil is thus produced by an unjust, myopic society. Sue preaches charitable reforms that are supposed to help a degenerate people recover "the health of the soul" (7.15.949), and not just of the body. He rails against the "selfishness and neglect of the rulers," predicting a day when society will understand "that evil is an accidental, not organic malady" (ibid.).

The Schoolmaster, wracked by the pains of remorse, exclaims, "Man is not born evil." Sue adds that, "Generally one does not become wicked except through misfortune" (8.9.1,032), and seems unaware of the conflict that is opened up between this deterministic vision and the moral organization of his novel. Since responsibility is mixed with sociological causality, it ultimately deprives guilt of its fundamental premise: the free will without which neither sin, remorse, nor redemption makes any sense. *The Mysteries of Paris* thus seems to be a book that combines two opposing visions, both of which contribute to its success: what Brooks calls the "polarization of good and evil" (28) as real forces that operate in the world, and sociological determinism, which tends to extinguish the same polarization.

The limits that the novel encounters in the second instance, and that illuminate its difficulties in imposing itself on the first, are emblematized by the case of Fleur-de-Marie. The girl whose conscience should be completely cleansed by sociological explanation—since she is a sinner wholly against her will—is unable to find her place in the world from which she was violently excluded and dies of remorse. This may be because prostitution stains more deeply than murder, even multiple murders, but this innocent girl who condemns herself while everyone else absolves her clearly represents the resistance of moral tragedy to the offensive of social comedy.

Translated by Michael F. Moore

GEOFFREY WINTHROP-YOUNG

The War of the Worlds
(H. G. Wells, 1898)

> No one would have believed in the last years of the
> nineteenth century that this world was being watched
> keenly and closely by intelligences greater than man's
> and yet as mortal as his own. . . . Yet across the gulf of
> space, minds that are to our minds as ours are to those
> of the beasts that perish, intellects vast and cool and
> unsympathetic, regarded this earth with envious eyes,
> and slowly and surely drew their plans against us. And
> early in the twentieth century came the great
> disillusionment.
> —H. G. WELLS, *The War of the Worlds*[1]

They saw, came, conquered. Not since Homer invoked the muses to sing of the wrath of Achilles has a piece of invasion literature been introduced with such bardic fanfare—and with good reason. *The War of the Worlds* is one of world literature's most successful generic prototypes: never out of print since its first appearance, it has spawned countless literary imitations, several movies, and even its own television show, not to mention history's most famous radio broadcast. Together with *The Time Machine* it established H. G. Wells as one of the founders of what later came to be known as science fiction. Yet underneath its apocalyptic grandeur this famous opening paragraph reveals many of the clever uncertainties and ambiguities so characteristic of the voracious genre it helped create.

The War of the Worlds was not the first story about Martians, let alone extraterrestrials, but it introduced the fertile theme of the invasion of earth by hostile aliens. The story itself is a hybrid: it combined the now-forgotten nineteenth-century interplanetary romances with the widely read "future war" stories, popularized by George Tomkyns Chesney's *Battle of Dorking* (1871), in which England succumbed to continental invaders. The advance of the Martians—from Surrey northeast into London—duplicated the route taken by more terrestrial German or French invasion forces, yet despite its otherworldly combatants, Wells's interplanetary clash appeared to be more in touch with the technological momentum of its day than the

---

[1] In *The Works of H. G. Wells* (London: T. Fisher Unwin, 1924), 3:213. All further references are to this edition and follow the quotations in parentheses.

pseudo-documentary narratives it descended from. Critics have marveled at the story's uncanny anticipation of the military realities of the First World War, from the use of gas and the importance of heavy artillery to the plight of the civilian population and the ecological impact of modern war. The story's unflinching brutality captured the increasingly aggressive political climate within Europe, just as the narrator's insistence that the fate of the enslaved humans is akin to that of Tasmanians, who "were entirely swept out of existence in a war of extermination waged by Europeans" (216), reflected Europe's aggressive expansion abroad. Wells's story of blood-sucking imperialist Martians first appeared in serialized form in 1897, in the same year as Bram Stoker's account of the invasion by the blood-sucking Count Dracula, and both texts speak of the fear of reverse colonization. The Western homelands, and England in particular, stand to suffer what they have done onto others.

But as is so often the case with Wells, questions of social and political division are transformed into the biological realm, a change of register that is already apparent in the narrator's initial emphasis that humans are to the "vast and cool and unsympathetic" intellect of the Martians as germs are to self-aggrandizing humans. The constant recourse to analogies and comparisons makes of *The War of the Worlds* a structuralist's dream: a carefully plotted extravaganza of binaries, correspondences, and ratios that aim to explain the unknown in terms of the known just as they serve to estrange the familiar by referring it to a different framework. The story assumes the status of an evolutionary parable that depicts the invasion and subsequent defeat of the Martians as controlled by a Darwinian jockeying for positions. The Martians, whose attack is caused by the environmental pressure of their increasingly inhospitable home planet, push humans down the food chain into the animal reign, but animals from dogs to microbes appear at its top and vanquish the intruders. Ultimately, the battle over interplanetary real estate is subject to the iron laws of evolutionary chauvinism: "By the toll of a billion deaths man has bought his birthright of the earth, and it is his against all comers" (437). Thus, the Martians' journey across the Pascalian void separating them from Earth corresponds to the travel along the time axis in *The Time Machine*. The evolutionary differentiation of *The Time Machine* transforms the social antagonism between the oppressed working and the parasitical ruling class into biological speciation in the shape of the Morlock and Eloi, respectively, while *The War of the Worlds* presents a differentiated evolution by turning Mars into a planet similar to Earth but ahead of it in biological terms. *The Time Machine* depicts a trip forward into the future of humanity; *The War of the Worlds* describes that future coming back to haunt the present. With their sexless, atrophied bodies, Martians are humans that have evolved into walking heads, leaving behind the heart and other organs. But if Europeans in 1900 are already behaving like Martians, the future human race may well turn out to be worse than the worst Martians. With Freudian gusto Wells delivered yet another attack on human, and in particular Western, self-satisfaction.

The War of the Worlds, The Time Machine, and *The Island of Doctor Moreau* have secured Wells's reputation as the foremost manufacturer of Darwinian fables. It would no doubt be foolish to deny the influence of Charles Darwin or of Thomas Henry Huxley, whose 1884 lectures Wells later recalled as the most educational experience of his life, but Wells was as little Huxley's mouthpiece as Huxley himself was Darwin's clone. Beyond a couple of vague assurances concerning the future perfection of our mental endowments, Darwin avoided elaborating on the future ethical and sociopolitical implications of his theories. Huxley and Wells, however, did not, but while Huxley advocated that ethical progress should oppose the bloody slaughter of natural selection, Wells championed a politics more in line with the dictates of evolution. Darwin had given us an understanding of evolution, Huxley came to argue, so that we may rise above it; Wells responded by reiterating that our understanding will better enable us to live with it. The Martian invasion, then, was a fancy illustration of the savagery humans would inflict upon each other if they failed to understand the evolutionary pressures that controlled their actions. Ultimately, this transformation of politics into applied natural history established Wells as the foremost pornographer of evolution: he stripped it down to what he perceived to be its merciless and occasionally repulsive basic mechanics while insisting that we accept and try to make the best of them. From the point of view of literary evolution, however, it does not matter whether the Darwinian details are correct, it does not even matter whether the science itself is correct; what matters is that Wells introduced a new relationship between scientific theory and literary conjecture.

To use an example by J.R.R. Tolkien, anybody can invent a world with a green sun; the trick is to create a world in which a green sun makes sense. In the case of Wells, such internal coherence—so important for the suspension of disbelief—came to depend on a new and necessary degree of scientific plausibility in three related areas: the construction of the *novum*, the creation of narrative coherence, and the continuity linking the fictitious secondary world to the reader's empirical primary world. First, one does not simply create a green sun if such an object is in flagrant violation of accepted laws, hence Wells's preference for symbolically laden, but thermodynamically more credible entropic red suns (which also make an appearance in *The War of the Worlds*). Second, the maintenance of internal cohesion was subjected to scientific conceptualizations; in other words, the question how a green sun makes sense becomes a matter of speculating within the confines of a scientific framework how a changed natural environment (or the introduction of a powerful new technology) will affect, and subsequently co-evolve with, the social and psychological lifeworld. Third, broadening the gap that was opening up between more science-oriented conjectures and fantasy literature, it was assumed that while the alternative worlds could be very different, they still shared certain basic laws with the empirical world of the reader; hence there exists a clearly discernible continuity between the two that served to make the utopian or dystopian content of the narrative all the more socially relevant. Obviously, Wells did not always stick to these precepts, especially not to the first. Jules Verne, for one, criticized him for inventing impossibilities; and this point of contention between Verne and Wells is still apparent in the distinction between so-called hard science fiction, which restricts itself to established or carefully extrapolated science, and the speculations by scientifically less informed science fiction practitioners. Neither did Wells treat science as a holy cow; texts such as *The Island of Doctor Moreau* point ahead to the fundamental criticism of science in the new wave of the 1960s and feminist science fiction. The overall effect, however, was to raise the thresholds of acceptance and thus provide criteria for what is acceptable and what is not by infusing his narratives with dictates of scientific plausibility. The end result was a blueprint for future textual production that was as flexible as it was marketable. A couple of years before his death, Wells suggested for himself the epitaph: "God damn you all—I told you so." No, he did not, at least not in the way he thought he had. Wells was never as clairvoyant in his predictions as he or his disciples assumed; he did not tell us more about our future than other self-appointed prophets, but more than any other writer he told us how to tell stories about our future.

At this point we are already in the middle of trying to assess Wells's contribution to the evolution of science fiction. Unfortunately, it is great deal easier to look at Darwin through Wells than to look at Wells through Darwin, as it were. How and to what degree did he contribute to the morphological features of the genre? But then, does it make sense to talk about science fiction in 1900, thirty years before the term was institutionalized? Analyses of this kind tacitly presuppose what in fact has become increasingly uncertain: that there is a *literary* genre called science fiction and that we know what it is. More than with any other genre, the evolution of science fiction is caught up in intermedial dynamics that are increasingly governed by a cross-relationship with different media formats ranging from movies and video games to magazines, fan clubs, and conventions. The tendency to treat it as a purely literary phenomenon (and not also as a publishing category, a mindset, or a cultural matrix) tends to result in prescriptive definitions that claim to pinpoint what science fiction should be. These normative assessments are conspicuously at odds with more descriptive definitions that restrict themselves to summarizing what science fiction is and does in the marketplace. Attempts at definition appear to have become a Verdun of theory: definitions are no longer advanced to occupy new territory or regain lost grounds; they primarily serve to exhaust the participants by adding to the general fatigue. Increasingly, critics are caught between the capitulation to market forces (science fiction is all that is sold as such), the escape into subjective whim (science fiction is what I or any other critic label as such), and more sophisticated attempts to defy generic categorization altogether (because science fiction is fundamentally about transgression, it has to constantly question, erode, and transgress its own genre boundaries).

Nonetheless, it is possible to pinpoint certain elements that have made Wells a nodal point in the evolution of science fiction. In April 1926, in the first issue of *Amazing Stories*, Hugo Gernsback characterized "scientific-tion" as "the Jules Verne, H. G. Wells and Edgar Allan Poe type of story," a "charming romance intermingled with scientific fact and prophetic vision" that makes for "instructive" as well as "tremendously interesting" reading. To be sure, Poe was not very charming, Verne certainly was not romantic, and Wells was neither; but what united them was that unmistakable element of *prodesse et delectare* inherent in the combination of fact and vision that still underlies the more academic or sophisticated definitions of science fiction. Increasingly, however, definitions came to highlight the literary strategies of scientific plausibility outlined above rather than the genre's edifying potential. Thus, neither Wells nor Verne created science fiction, but they prepared its literary institutionalization by performing, each in his own way, a new, tighter and more self-aware relationship between fiction and science.

All genres are in search of an ancestry, but science fiction chroniclers have approached that task with particular verve; the unyielding possessiveness with which some of them turn everything from the *Gilgamesh* epic and the *Odyssey* to *The Divine Comedy, The Tempest*, and Goethe's *Faust* into antecedents of the genre makes the Martian invasion appear almost benign. The indisputable importance of Wells and Verne lies in their combinatory skills. *The War of the Worlds* is a hybrid of the interplanetary romance, the future-war story, and the adventure story (complete murder, mayhem, and cannibalism), all served with a noticeable dosage of Dickensian satire. *The*

Time Machine, in turn, borrows elements from Edison-type tales featuring the young male inventor-hero with the new awareness of time as a player—rather than a mere playground—in evolution, and scientific concepts of Darwinian and thermodynamic regression. Thus Wells and Verne combined plots and props from other writers, genres, and discursive practices in such a way that with the self-conscious institutionalization of this particular type of narrative during the so-called golden age of science fiction between the late 1930s and the early 1950s their names—rather than the many others that were forgotten—came to be used as shorthand representations of the essence of science fiction. This institutionalization was based on an ongoing close interaction between writers, readers, and a group of highly committed hands-on editors and publishers that soon resulted in the establishment of a set of protocols governing the production and reception of texts. The more these protocols were locked in, that is, the more this magazine-based synergy resulted in the emergence of the consciousness of the conventions appropriate to the genre, the more authors such as Wells, Verne, and Poe retroactively came to be seen as the prophetic initiators of the form. This evolutionary process underlying the institutionalized emergence of gene-specific rules is by no means unique to science fiction, but what makes it so remarkable is the speed and the laboratory-like clarity with which the splendid isolation of the golden age managed to bring about generic solidification. Maybe the disdain with which so many academic critics have treated science fiction is not only linked to its alleged intellectual poverty or technofetishist conservatism, or to the assumed adolescent mindset of its fans and practitioners, but to the fact that the history of the genre reveals in such lucidity the very mundane processes that govern the mysteries of literary evolution.

All genres are hybrid, but some are more hybrid than others. The trouble scholars have with science fiction is its peculiar acquisitiveness: following its experimental, polymorphic infancy and its secluded puberty during its golden age, science fiction appears to have reactivated the exuberance of its early stage. It is almost as if it embodied more than other genre the acquisitive features that characterize the novel; and it is precisely this capacity to borrow, mimic, assimilate, transgress, and proliferate that precludes its successful definition. But this is also where, once again, the importance of Wells emerges, not as futurist writer but as a novelist of Dickensian persuasion. Like Dickens, Wells took to satirically dissecting the details and delicacies of everyday rituals, particularly those of his home island. After all, what makes the attack of the Martians so truly memorable is not so much their genocidal ambition to conquer a planet but their unforgivable rudeness in intruding on English country life in all its stodginess. And, once again as in Dickens, an occasionally pungent streak of moralism emerges—fueled, no doubt, by a productive resentment that only a petty bourgeois English childhood constantly threatened by the descent into the working class could generate. Like Verne, Wells was at times unable to resist the temptations of didacticism, but while Verne only wrote like a schoolmaster, Wells actually turned into one. On the other hand, the artistically more talented Wells was able to move his messages from long-winded sermons into the narrative structure. Consider, for instance, the way in which *The War of the Worlds* is shot through with communication breakdowns, including the narrator's inconclusive debates with the curate and the artilleryman about the real meaning of the invasion and humanity's prospects. Underneath the drama and gore, Wells refers the interplanetary war back to human communication difficulties. *The War of the Worlds* is not only looking ahead to the sprawling or rambunctious space epics of Olaf Stapledon or Robert Heinlein, but also to more critical texts such as Stanislaw Lem's *Solaris* or the Strugatsky brothers' *Roadside Picnic*, which argue that if we cannot communicate with each other, if we cannot extract information from noise in a satisfactory manner, we will never be able to communicate with any alien civilization, either on earth or beyond—and maybe we should not even try.

But that is where the Dickensian heritage—if not the heritage of the novel itself—asserts itself most clearly. For the novel is a double-edged tool; it confirms and debunks, supports and erodes, creates and queries, tries to understand what is not yet understood, yet it also calls into question what is understood too well. Look at the contrast between the Homeric opening paragraph and the narrator's final realization of how strange "it is to hold my wife's hand again, and to think that I have counted her, and that she has counted me, among the dead" (451). If the opening paragraph insists that hitherto fantastic visions of interplanetary war have become harsh reality, the final lines render the most quotidian reality ever more fragile, contingent, and improbable—and both moves, assurance as well as estrangement, make up the "great disillusionment" (213) announced at the outset. This is the crucial chiasmus at the heart of science fiction: the more familiar the improbable, the more improbable the familiar. Any credible attempt to describe what could be will entail the realization that what is could have been very different. The war of the worlds is not only waged between Mars and Earth but also between Earth before and Earth after the invasion, that is, between a secure, untroubled past ignorant of its future and a troubled present that has experienced a terrifying glimpse of what is to come.

AMBROSIO FORNET

The Kingdom of This World
(Alejo Carpentier, 1949)

The process of colonization of the New World initiated at the beginning of
the sixteenth century transformed the America that we refer to today as
Latin America into the unusual setting of extensive and deep cross-breeding
that was as much ethnic as it was cultural. For this reason, the Latin American intelligentsia's yearning for legitimacy and autochthony has often taken
the dramatic form of an identity crisis. The notion of magic realism, expounded by Carpentier in a 1948 text that would serve as the prologue to
The Kingdom of This World the following year,[1] is part of an arsenal of metaphors with which the continent's intellectuals tried for years to ward off the
confusion of their hybrid nature, the trauma of their colonial origins.[2] But
here the metaphor, biting its tail, returned the reflection to the origins, since
the marvelous is at the very heart of the Spanish American historiographical
discourse. If the historical accounts were mere verbal artifacts, without links
to their possible referents, one could assert that certain passages of the
Crónicas de Índias (*Chronicles of the West Indies*) are the founding texts of
Spanish American fantastic literature.

Carpentier was well aware of that original link between autochthonous reality and literary fiction—in fact, in his famous prologue he alludes to certain
utopias that could turn into obsessions no sooner had the gullible and greedy

---

[1] "Lo real-maravilloso de America" appeared in the daily *El Nacional of Caracas* and was
reprinted without a title as a prologue to the first edition of the novel (which the author subtitled
"relato" (story). See Alejo Carpentier, *El reino de este mundo* (Mexico City, 1949), 7–17. See also
note 3, below. The concept of "real-maravilloso" is not to be confused, though it often is, with that
of "realismo mágico."

[2] On the poetics of the "real-maravilloso" and about Carpentier's work in general, see also
Irlemar Chiampi, *O realismo maravilhoso: Forma e ideologia no romance hispano-americano* (São
Paulo, 1980); Alexis Marquez Rodríguez, *Lo barroco y lo real-maravilloso en la obra de Alejo
Carpentier* (Mexico City, 1982); Roberto Gonzalez Echevarria, *Alejo Carpentier: El peregrino en su
patria* (Mexico City, 1993) (enlarged edition of *Alejo Carpentier: The Pilgrim at Home* [Ithaca, N.Y.,
1977]); Leonardo Padura Fuentes, *Un camino de medio siglo: Carpentier y la narrativa de lo real-
maravilloso* (Havana, 1994). Some of the most representative essays and criticism published to date
may be found in Salvador Arias, ed., *Recopilación de textos sobre Alejo Carpentier* (Havana, 1977).
Biobibliografía de Alejo Carpentier (Havana, 1984), by Araceli García-Carranza, with its nearly five
thousand entries, is the most complete of its kind; its only notable precedent is *Alejo Carpentier:
Estudio biográfico-crítico* (New York, 1972), by Claus Müller-Bergh.

Spanish adventurers set foot on American soil—but he only makes it explicit in two texts, one of which was published in Cuba, the other in Mexico. One of these, virtually unknown to critics, seems to be a paraphrasing of the other, which is included in his volume of essays, *Tientos y diferencias*. In it he makes the defiant, categorical statement that the *Verdadera historia de la conquista de la Nueva España* (*True History of the Conquest of New Spain*) by Bernal Díaz del Castillo is "the only true and reliable book of chivalry that has been written." Recalling the adventures of Hernán Cortés and his courageous followers in the conquest of Mexico—that world of wizards, fantastical cities, river dragons, and strange, snow-capped mountains belching smoke—the chronicler, without intending to, had narrated feats superior to those of the most illustrious characters in the novels of knight errantry.³ The other text, unsigned by the author, served as the prologue to the Cuban edition of *Verdadera historia*, one of the first works Carpentier published when he took the helm as the director of the Editorial Nacional de Cuba (National Publishing Company of Cuba) in 1962. It bore an epigraph by the North American hispanist, Washington Irving: "The extraordinary actions and adventures of those men who emulated the heroic deeds from books of chivalry have, *in addition*, the interest of veracity." That "in addition" (my emphasis) seems extracted from an essay about the theory of reception; one could say that for Irving the testimonial value of the *Crónicas* is secondary: it is above all its novelistic character that makes it interesting. Carpentier's reading of Bernal gives exactly the same impression. He says that in the old days, enthusiasts of books of chivalry, giving their imaginations free rein, dreamed about adventures in fabulous regions. Here, suddenly, the unexpected occurred: in extraordinary cities like Tenochtitlan, in unknown kingdoms like Tlaxcala, among magicians and wizards (the so-called *teules*), among smoking mountains (volcanoes) and aquatic dragons (crocodiles), Cortés and his companions experienced "their own Book of Chivalry," more fascinating than that whose hero is Amadis of Gaul himself. "Here the wonder was tangible, the enchantment was real, the wizards spoke in dialects never before heard." The marvelous had now become, "for the first time, magic realism."⁴

We are clearly confronting a quest for a personal lineage, that uncoercible urge that made Borges say that each writer ultimately creates his own

---

³ Carpentier, "De lo real maravillosamente americano" [*sic*], in *Tientos y diferencias* (Mexico City, 1964), 115–35. (The correct title, changed through an error of the publisher, is "De lo real-maravilloso americano.") It is in fact a new essay with the novel's prologue appended.

⁴ Carpentier, Prologue, in Bernal Díaz del Castillo, *Historia verdadera de la conquista de la Nueva España* (Havana, 1963), 11.

precursors. But we are also witnessing a daring intention to legitimate, on the strength of the prestige of the deeds, the ontological vision that allowed Carpentier to conclude the prologue to *The Kingdom of This World* with this outrageous question: "But what is the history of all of America if not a chronicle of the wondrous reality?" Thus, contradicting Hegel's theory, the New World ceased to be pure geography and inscribed itself in universal history with its own identity. One of the story's best qualities, in the author's opinion, is its irreducible autochthony: it was "a story that could not be set in Europe." But at the same time, I would add, it is inseparable from European history because Europe was the Other in whose patriarchal visage America could recognize itself as something different and outline—as it did throughout the nineteenth century—the distinctive features of its incipient personality. In fact, what Carpentier discovers in Haiti on his amazing trip in 1943 is not only the presence of the marvelous but also the viability of a method, of a hermeneutics of the [Latin] American space. He became aware of this before the ruins that bore witness to the odd presence of Pauline Bonaparte in Cap Francais. Here was a method that allowed for the demonstration, through subtle parallelisms, of the phenomenon of temporal simultaneity characteristic of a history, such as the colonial one, in which different modes of material and spiritual production, or better yet, different periods and cultures, tend to coexist. More than a discovery, this meant "a revelation" for the traveler. "I saw—he would say years later—the possibility of establishing certain possible, American, recurrent synchronies beyond time, relating one thing to another, the past to the present. I saw the possibility of bringing certain European truths to our latitudes."[5]

Europe also contributed the backdrop, the reflexive space that made it possible to show the specifics of the [Latin] American marvelous by contrast. The prologue to *The Kingdom of This World*, with Breton's usual declarations as a subtext, can be considered a real antimanifesto of the surrealist movement. The marvelous "presupposes a faith"; skepticism converts false miracle workers into bureaucrats of the wondrous, fit only to invent ridiculous tall tales like that of the casual encounter between an umbrella and a sewing machine in the operating room. That love of the prefabricated marvel—or, as Carpentier says, of the marvelous mustered at any cost—has no meaning on a continent that "is very far from having exhausted its supply of mythologies" and where, as a consequence, positivist rationalism has few opportunities to put down roots. Quoting France Vernier, the Colombian

---

[5] Carpentier, *Tientos y diferencias*, 129.

essayist Carlos Rincón has pointed out the often-forgotten fact that the marvelous is a historical concept that varies with the ages: it meant different things "in the Middle Ages, in the Romantic period and in the 1920's in France." Rincón insists on emphasizing the nuances that distinguish Giambattista Marino's *meraviglia* from the *meraviglioso* of Tasso, the *extraordinaire et merveilleux* of Boileau and the *Wunderbare* of Wieland and German romanticism. He maintains that the notion of the marvelous contributed to the forging of "a new aesthetic system" in Latin America. Nonetheless, it must be admitted that the metaphor's own field of signification is rather ambiguous because, in effect, if the marvelous "presupposes a faith," the doubt arises as to whether the marvel resides in things or in our way of perceiving them. Does the concept refer to ontology or to phenomenology? To doubt is to succumb once again to the pitfall of rationalism, this time on the opposite shore. Incredulity must be placed between parentheses: we are before a discursive strategy that aspires to recount natural and cultural realities of proportions unknown in Europe and not yet categorized by the European ratio. In other words, this is the poetic reason for a world where magic preserves its transforming quality and the strange inscribes itself in the everyday as part of a constant process of the contrasting and mixing of cultures. The method includes the [Latin] American writer's or artist's capacity for detecting the flaws in European discourse and settling in its faults and interstices, occupying the empty spaces—in the first place, those of the language itself. We are still far from the historical irony implicit in Caliban's capacity for cursing his master in his own language. When I talk about empty spaces, I am referring literally to the linguistic deficiencies that prevent the foreigner from carrying out a symbolic appropriation of an exotic realm, which could mean that the sounds characteristic of [Latin] America should be articulated in the European silences. Carpentier used to refer to Cortés' disconcertion when, in one of his letters to the king of Spain, he lamented that he lacked the vocabulary necessary to describe the world he was conquering for him. He did not have the words to domesticate that unprecedented reality. Carpentier's mission was clearly to find those words and give voice to those silences. In [Latin] American history he had found the only theme which, according to the Cuban critic Roberto Gonzalez Echevarria, could be placed alongside Homeric and biblical myths. Now he had only to develop the methods of representation that would allow him to approach it from a different perspective.

According to the North American critic, Seymour Menton, the literary movement that he himself termed the new historical Latin American novel began in 1949 with *The Kingdom of This World* and produced dozens works over the next forty years, some of them by Carpentier himself. One need only compare the inventiveness that emerges from *The Kingdom*, from its very title to its astounding and apocalyptic denouement, to grasp the novelty of his aesthetic proposal. But the fact that the historiographical framework barely stands out does not mean that it is absent. Referring to his visit to Paulina Bonaparte's house and the fortress of La Ferrière in Haiti, Carpentier asked himself with feigned candor, "What more does a novelist need to write a book?" Some of his critics replied without hesitation: an enormous bibliography in several languages. Emma Susana Speratti-Piñero, who tackled the arduous task of uncovering those sources twenty years ago, remarked that *The Kingdom of This World*, despite being a very imaginative book, "is eminently bookish." The author would probably have shrugged his shoulders at such a statement; in the novel's prologue he saw fit to record that his story was based on "extremely rigorous documentation" and "a meticulous comparison of dates and chronologies." Of course he was exaggerating. Upon finishing the novel, we believe we know who Henri Christophe was—the delirious and pathetic monarch who had the gall to betray his people and his people's gods. But "the only absolutely sure and irrefutable thing" that we know about the real Christophe—if we are to believe Speratti-Piñero—"is that he was born and he died." It is therefore not strange that Carpentier admired the way in which Valle-Inclan, novelizing the Carlist Wars, had taken on history without succumbing to it, or that the Czech critic Emil Volek should speak of the "arbitrary respect" Carpentier had for historical reality. It is what the author himself defined as the need to "go beyond the document."

What matters is not a greater or lesser adherence to the facts, but rather a historical consciousness itself, fueled in this case by the defiant conviction that the Caribbean islands had been the setting for one of the great epics of modern times (this certainty also underlies the discursive strategy of another masterpiece, *El siglo de las luces* [*Explosion in a Cathedral*]). In both novels, the Antilles cease to be on the periphery, history's garbage dump, to become the center of the universe, the great theater of the world in which all passions and all ideas—the very notions of humanity and universality—could be tested and tried. González Echevarría has pointed out that it was in the Caribbean that the enigma of the Latin American identity began to take shape and where, for the first time in the New World, phenomena like "colonialism, slavery, the mixing of and fighting among races, and consequently, the revolutionary and independence movements" appeared. The Brazilian critic, Irlemar Chiampi, pointed out this historical prominence when she described the Caribbean as "the meeting place of Columbus with the natives, the axis of expansion in the Spanish conquest of the New World, the irradiating center of the political, racial and anthropological problems that the conquest of America signified for Western History." And it is precisely there, in the French colony of Saint-Domingue (which would assume the aboriginal name of Haiti upon gaining its independence), that the action of *The Kingdom of This World* develops in a period of approximately eighty years between 1750 and 1830.

After the North American revolution, the revolution of Saint-Domingue was the first anticolonialist revolution in history. It was born in the heat of the French Revolution but—as the poet from Martinique, Aimé Césaire observes in his biography of Toussaint L'Ouverture—it had its very own qualities and shared only its rhythm with the French Revolution, that is to say, its cycles. As in a relay race, the different parts involved—in France the constitutionals, the Girondists, and the Jacobins—replaced each other in power successively. No sooner did one party accomplish its mission and demonstrate itself incapable of carrying the revolution further than another would eliminate it and take its place until its turn to be displaced arrived. Each one, as Césaire says, embodied a "moment" of the revolutionary process. It was what—*mutatis mutandis*—took place in Haiti with whites, mulattos, and blacks, who, in this context, either were or acted as masters and slaves. In the novel, the rebellion against the white colonialists gives way to Christophe's reign, and the rebellion against him gives way to a government by mulatto republicans who impose a forced work regime in rural areas. These are historical facts. But a mere glance at the text is enough to convince us that we are not dealing with the classic formula of the historical novel like the one written by Lukács in 1955. Here, the event, the historical magma is just a point of departure for a reflection on the meaning of history and therefore—as the Venezuelan critic, Alexis Márquez rightly observes— about the political problem of collective freedom and the ethical problem of individual liberty. In the classic historical novel, time affects not only the plane of the action—of the diegesis—but also that of the construction of the character, which changes under the pressure of the circumstances. In *The Kingdom*—appropriate to its episodic nature—the characters stay the same or change outside the narration, without our knowing how or why, subject to the logic of an extradiegetic time, to the secret will of the "old mole." Ti Noel, the connecting thread of the story, is a youth in the first chapter and an old man in the last, but he is basically the same person at both ends. Christophe, on the other hand, is a cook at the beginning of the second part of the story, an artilleryman shortly thereafter, and finally a powerful monarch, but we are told nothing of the process that led to that change and his incredible metamorphosis, as if to underline that the marvelous does not require an explanation because it does not answer to the laws of cause and effect. And this brings us back to the essential component of the new vision of [Latin] American reality and its forms of discursive representation.

It is about the role of myth, or more precisely, a mythic consciousness over the course of historical events and in the behavior of the characters. We are dealing with a system of beliefs and of magic rituals—voodoo—that enables slaves to see their leader escape being burned at the stake and fly over the heads of his executioners, causing them to cry, "Mackandal sauve!" at the very instant that the body is consumed by the flames. There is a simultaneity of visions here that, incidentally, Carpentier resolves masterfully on the discursive plane by alternating the third-person narration with the free indirect style. It was these beliefs that persuaded the blacks that victory over the whites was inevitable because the rebel leaders had made a pact with their ancestral gods, the great Loas of Africa. It was they who led the aged Ti Noel, in one of his few moments of lucidity, to the defiant conclusion that magic had in fact a liberating function, but only when projected toward the earthly as part of an ethic that demanded that man "set himself Tasks" to "improve what he is." So, induced by the author, at the end of his life Ti Noel accomplished a secret ideological mission: that of refuting Carpentier's detractors in advance, detractors who would accuse him of historical pessimism based on his supposed adhesion to Giambatista Vico's doctrine of *corsi e ricorsi*. Carpentier has never been a greater realist than when he concocted these iterations, first of all because the French and Haitian revolutions, as observed by Césaire, responded politically to a cyclical dynamic, and second because, in a more general sense, all societies subsequent to primitive communities—be they enslaved, feudal, or bourgeois—have shared the trait of reproducing a similar formula for domination. Over the centuries, mythological and everyday popular consciousness has perceived this phenomenon and has formulated it in different ways: through myths, like that of Sisyphus (whom Ti Noel literally embodies in a dramatic passage of the text), or through images and symbols like the cross that each human being must bear in order to reach his or her destiny in this Valley of Tears. But if man's mission consists of "setting himself Tasks" in order to "improve what he is," the time might come when the inexorable dynamic of the cycles will rupture once and for all.

If the thesis of magic realism had not been accepted as narrative material in the practice of writing, the prologue and body of *The Kingdom of This World* would not have gone down in the history of Latin American literature as an indivisible unit. Here, theory and practice, ground laying and narration are interwoven to establish an impressive reciprocal dialogue. Perhaps this coherence is the author's supreme success, which is also visible in a style that is wisely aged, giving the fable the flavor of a chronicle, and in the ironic, almost surreptitious way in which he draws us, time and again, into his subject: here, a reference to the idyllic passages of Bernardin de Saint-Pierre, there, a reflection on the moment at which Paulina Bonaparte heeds the call of her Corsican blood, and, further on, nearly at the novel's end, a description of Ti Noel's improvised shelter among the ruins of what had been his master's estate. Strangely, the shelter has become a replica of Lautremont's operating room; by a twist of fate an embalmed fish, a glass cylinder, a music box, and several volumes of the *Gran Enciclopedia* all wind up in that minute space. We must assume that the volumes are indeed voluminous, because Ti Noel likes to sit on them to eat pieces of sugar cane.

Translated by Linda Phillips

Writing Prose

FRANCESCO ORLANDO

Forms of the Supernatural in Narrative

An Unlimited Belief

While Don Quixote is sleeping, right after he has returned, badly beaten, from his first sally, the curate and the barber burn his books of chivalry, and they wall off the room where he had stored them. "Perhaps removing the cause will remove the effect." On the contrary, nothing will contribute as much to render unshakable his madness as the pretense they give him for the disappearance of the library. It was the act of an enchanter who arrived riding a snake and left flying from the roof: Quixote accepts the story as perfectly consistent with his chivalric imagination, so much so that he appropriates and enriches it. In the next chapter, during the first adventure of his second sally, the combined force of Sancho's arguments and reality would have prevailed had it not been for this very convenient explanation for his violent fall to the ground: "Moreover, I am convinced, and that is the truth, that the magician Freston, the one who robbed me of my study and books, has changed those giants into windmills to deprive me of the glory of victory; such is the enmity he bears against me" (1.8.99).[1]

Within ten chapters, it will be much harder for him, without the same trump card, to resist drawing "sane" conclusions from the stoning that has left him with shattered ribs, fingers, and teeth. That scoundrel, his enemy enchanter, whose kind can easily "make us see what they want us to see," has changed the ranks of his enemies into a herd of sheep out of envy for Quixote's glory. Does Sancho doubt it? Let him follow them for a while, and he will see them change back from rams into men (1.18.174). Sancho ends up learning the lesson so well that the knight will later have it administered to him by his squire, the roles having been reversed. When Quixote sees no more than an ugly peasant woman and her companions riding three donkeys, Sancho reassures him that she is in fact Dulcinea along with two damsels riding on their steeds. Quixote will be the first to declare, while he speaks to her thus transformed, that an enchanter has placed "clouds and cataracts over his eyes" (2.10.594).

---

[1] Miguel de Cervantes Saavedra, *Don Quixote of La Mancha*, trans. Walter Starkie, 3rd ed. (New York: New American Library, 1979). Subsequent references to this edition are cited parenthetically in the text.

Later on he will complain: "Enchanters have persecuted me in the past, they persecute me now, and they will persecute me forever" (2.32.760). It is not the case, however, that all the enchanters in chivalric tales are malevolent. Indeed, when he is surprised that Sancho has gone to Toboso and returned so quickly, as though he had the power of flight, he figures out who has mysteriously propelled Sancho through the air: "The wise magician who takes care of my affairs and is my friend, for he necessarily must, and does, exist, or I wouldn't be a good knight-errant" must have helped him in his journey. The annihilation of distances is an example of benevolent magic: a knight can be taken while "sleeping in his bed, and without his knowing how, he awakes the next day more than a thousand leagues from the place where he fell asleep." Similarly, while a knight is in danger of being overcome by dragons or monsters in the Armenian mountains, another knight in England can come to his rescue riding a cloud or a chariot of fire, and then return to England the very same night (1.31.313).

In the episode of the river mills, Quixote expects that he will be transported in the same way when he sees an empty boat. In order to reconcile the apparently promising beginning with the usual disastrous ending, at the end of the episode he goes so far as to postulate a double, simultaneous intervention: "In this adventure two powerful enchanters must have been at loggerheads, the one thwarting the other in his designs. So, when one furnished me with a boat, the other capsized me" (2.29.737). This is the only time that he resorts to a hypothesis endowed with such an unlimited and infallible power of explanation (even the hypothesis of one benevolent wizard in action remained merely an ex post facto conclusion in the passage above). But this is only because for him everything always goes badly. His theory of knowledge, rooted in magic, generates one of the most comic and sympathetic traits of Quixote's character—his imperturbability. In theory, his trust in the supernatural could even extend more broadly than is necessary to account for his actual misfortunes.

It is hard to say whether everything is accounted for because nothing is explained, or, on the other hand, whether nothing is accounted for because everything is explained. Does Sancho strive to undermine the belief that the barber's bowl is actually Mambrino's helmet? In Quixote's mind this only displays his "shallow understanding": "Is it possible that in the time you have been with me you have not yet found out that all the adventures of a knight-errant appear to be illusion, follies, dreams, and turn out to be the reverse? Not because things are really so, but because in our midst there is a host of enchanters, forever changing, disguising, and transforming our affairs as they please, according to whether they wish to favor or destroy us.

So, what you call a barber's basin is to me Mambrino's helmet, and to another person it will appear to be something else" (1.25.243).

While they are disputing about the same object at the inn, Quixote lets slips out that "not all the things in the castle are governed by enchantment," which is to say, something untouched by magic would be an exception. A little later, he does not hazard a positive affirmation about the alleged castle because he imagines that "everything here works by enchantment" (1.45.457). As we have seen, Sancho never misses a chance to take advantage of such a circumspect openness to possibilities. He obtains from his master the briefest of concessions, which would be meaningless were we not to take them literally for what they are: namely, the greatest degree of accomodating credulity. Perhaps, at the bottom of the cave of Montesinos, enchantment makes one hour the equivalent of three days and three nights? Don Quixote's reply: "That must be so" (2.23.692). Of course, what is dripping onto Sancho's face from the helmet is not ricotta that had been hidden there; is it then proof that he is persecuted by enchanters as well? Don Quixote's answer: "Anything is possible" (2.27.639).

Anything is possible; all things are turned into their opposite. Just a bit less dizzying than the first proposition, the second one today recalls one of Freud's postulates of the language of the unconscious, namely, "representation through the opposite." It is damned near impossible to foresee when this phenomenon is in effect and when it is not: "The dream . . . prefers to draw opposites together into a unity or to represent them as one. Indeed, it also takes the liberty of representing some random element by its wished-for opposite [*Wunschgegensatz*], so that at first one cannot tell which of the possible poles is meant positively or negatively in the dream-thoughts."[2] Is it not after all because of this irritating principle that the pre scientific validity of psychoanalysis has so often been contested? And, even before a scientific mentality became accustomed to evade the so-called irrational, did not absolute rationality already become unsettled when confronted with absolute irrationality? Midway between Cervantes and Freud, I mean, did we not have the Englightenment?

Voltaire never ceased to mock the logic that resists establishing a sharp boundary between contraries—a logic he found above all in biblical symbolism. For the sake of brevity, it is enough to mention, from his *The Princess of Babylon*, the oracle consulted out of devotion whose pronouncements are

---

[2] S. Freud, *The Interpretaton of Dreams*, trans. Joyce Crick (Oxford: Oxford University Press, 1999), 243.

notoriously obscure, and hence inconsequential: "A mixture of everything: life and death, infidelity and constancy, loss and gain, calamities and good fortune."[3] Surely Cervantes derived a similar logic, in great part, from the chivalric romances that he in turn intended to satirize. Still, I doubt whether in these romances and poems (from the sixteenth century back to the great twelfth century in France, the time when the subject matter of Brittany was absorbed and transformed into literature) the supernatural had ever enjoyed the great freedom it does in Quixote's mind. If he is presented to us as a madman, this freedom is not the ultimate reason. Among the many rules he knows by heart, he can find those of the supernatural in his books; there is no need, however, to apply them so broadly—so broadly that they over-shadow any victory of reality over the illusions that make him such a sympa-thetic and comic figure.

The Necessary Limits of the Credible

The rules of the supernatural: we all remember some from a fairy tale, and we know that they are sometimes explicit and precise. Let us return to the twelfth century. In the *Yvan* of Chrétien de Troyes, a knight of King Arthur in search of adventures happens upon a fountain under a tree whose water is at once hot and cold. If one pours this water with a basin hanging from the tree onto a boulder, a frightful storm is unleashed on the forest. Differ-ent characters follow these instructions on four different occasions; what-ever their meaning or origins in Celtic folklore, which are for us beside the point, these instructions set in motion and complete the poem's plot.[4] The point is that the rules of the supernatural are not at all limited to a case as clear as instructions.

In the most beautiful lay of Marie de France, *Guigemar*, the handsome and brave Breton prince who flees from love has shot and wounded a doe. The arrow ricochets, wounding the prince, and the animal speaks, proph-esying to him that only a woman who suffers for love as much as he does will be able to heal his wound.[5] Prophecies still have something to do with a

---

[3] Voltaire, *The Princess of Babylon*, trans. Tobias Smollett and revised by James Thornton (London: Heron Books, 1969), 303.

[4] Chrétien de Troyes, *Le chevalier au lion (Yvain)* (second half of twelfth century) (Paris: Champion, 1982), ll. 380–450; 800–10; 2,174–75; 2,220–24; 6,508–16; 6,523–32).

[5] Marie de France, *Guigemar* (second half of the twelfth century), in *Les lais* (Paris: Champion, 1981), ll. 37–68 and 89–121.

ritualistic prescription. This is not true, however, for what follows in the story: Guigemar finds a port where he had not known there to be one, boards an unmanned ship, and as soon as he lies down, the ship is already on the high seas. He then falls asleep (ll. 145–230). The old king of the land he will reach is jealous of his young wife and has her watched over in a room enclosed by an insurmountable wall and the sea. When the ship reaches the shore, the queen, along with her lady-in-waiting, wakes up the young prince, heals his wound, and hides him (ll. 209–378). Their subsequent affair lasts one and a half years before they are discovered by the king. The rival, brought by the sea, is returned to the sea with bad wishes, but the magic ship returns him to his country (ll. 527–42 and 577–632). The queen is imprisoned, but one day she finds the door unlocked and the ship ready to sail (ll. 655–90); the lovers will reunite in Bretonnia, facing few further vicissitudes.

This is a version of the supernatural untouched by Christianity and hospitable to natural love. It remedies a strange initial fact—the reluctance of the protagonist to engage with women. Just as strange and dreamlike is the tone of the poem that gets lost in a summary of its plot. Solitude precedes and follows the episode of the speaking doe, characterizes the magic voyages of the unmanned ship, and tacitly places the entrapment of the queen and the happiness of her liaison with the prince outside the bounds of this world. In theory, this is what interests us: if the supernatural merely had the function of expediting the narrative by circumventing obstacles, it could pass through ramparts and escape surveillance in the most varied but more predictable ways. Indeed, the supernatural is not merely thematically oriented in that it helps only the two lovers. In this case, it is, crucially, localized in space.

With the exception of the doe in the forest, the supernatural always appears in relation to the sea: that is to say, in relation to a distance or a journey. A distance separates the starting points of the lovers, just as a distance separates each of them from love. The journey brings them face to face and reveals the mysterious complementarity of their "situations"—in both a thematic and a spatial sense, as love arrives from the side where there is only the sea to imprison her, and the sea is nature unwalled and unwatched. We are very far from allegory, however. Rather, we are very close to understanding something that other texts of all genres will confirm for us, and that was veiled by the mad liberty of Quixote's logic.

In its literary articulations, which is all that I am concerned with, the supernatural can only be configured, sketched out, and delimited by rules—to the point that it consists in such rules. Their motivation may even remain obscure and latent (I picked a text like *Guigemar* for a reason); in some cases, their presence itself is sufficient motivation. Rules impose themselves on a field that is imaginary not only because it is literary fiction. Inside the fiction the supernatural is the supposition of beings, relations, and events that contradict the laws of reality perceived as natural or normal in a given historical situation—unless they are suspended by the conventions of a literary genre. In Aesop's fables, there is nothing supernatural about animals who speak; in lyric poetry, it is not supernatural for the metaphoric fantasy to connect everything with everything. I am aware that the definition of the supernatural that I have proposed is broader than the current ones. Nevertheless, to pursue it will allow us to articulate a greater number of connections and distinctions.

Inside this doubly imaginary field, the rules must counteract the boundlessness of fantasy, the formlessness of nonbeing, and the plasticity of the primal void: limiting by determining them, and determining by limiting them. Age after age, text after text, the rules are either invented on the spot or inherited from preexisting codes—codes that are either cultural or already literary. If an inquiry into the mytholgical-religious codes can shed light on why that precise form of the supernatural appears in precisely that work, an inquiry into the literary codes opens a vicious circle. Using the code to explain the works—or better yet, their success—means forgetting that the code itself is explained by the success of the works. At any rate, there is no supernatural that, through the imagination, subverts the entire order of reality but only one that modifies it in part—even when it is in great part. A truly radical alternative is inconceivable, even if it consisted in the pure, anarchic representation of one chaos.

In Another World, or in a World That Is Other

We have spoken of laws that are natural or normal for reality: what if literary fiction exempts itself from these laws and situates itself fully elsewhere? What if, whether borrowing from cultural codes or not, with its sovereign powers fiction were to create another reality? This is the case in nothing less than Dante's *Commedia*, in which theology and fantasy collaborate. With only one living character, it is a poem that starts by allegorizing the departure from the world of the living and ends at the very moment of reentering it. Dante's is a radical solution to the need of localizing the supernatural.

The journey through the land of the dead evokes, by charting it, a physical no less than moral topography. The spatial order leaves so little room for chance that it appears to manifest the admirable and infallible rationality of God—as if it were not in fact invented by the author:

> O supreme Wisdom, what great art you show
> in Heaven, on earth, and in the evil world,
> and what true justice does your power dispense! (*Inferno*, 19.10–12)[6]

Here localization is a complicated system of localizations—a motivated, grandiose, and totalizing one. It is the opposite of another world that is revealed by occasional and partial visions. An overwhelming fear of the void prohibits us from imagining it differently than according to the continuity of sensory, earthly experience. This localization may produce detailed similes that, moving backward from another world, always return us to our own—a world that, incidentally, is not always subordinated to the hyperbolic superiority of the supernatural. The true opposition of the two worlds is the eternal moral reversal: the order of divine justice presupposes the disorder of the sinful world when it replaces it by punishing or rewarding souls.

Here as nowhere else, the supernatural consists of rules. We can even have a rule related to the psychology of the beyond that speeds up the enforcement of the rules of distributive justice: for the despairing souls on the threshhold of punishment, "their very fear is turned to longing" (*Inferno*, 3.126). Far from being arbitrary, these rules, I believe, are tantamount to divine rationality; the topography is tantamount to these rules; and the journey is tantamount to topography itself: literally, we *move* from rule to rule. In the *Inferno*, where the itinerary is more physically plausible and has not been preordained only for the living Dante or for Virgil the parolee, their movements—whether hindered, ingenious, or exhausting—bring to light a second degree of the supernatural. In *Purgatorio*, the difficulty and suffering of the ascent along the ledges of the mountain, while retaining their physicality, have both an expiatory and an allegorical-moral meaning. In *Paradiso*, which is marked by sudden crossings—unfelt or felt as a kind of rapture— the fact that the blessed appear, only for the sake of the pilgrim, in a place where they do not reside, does not detract from their visionary character.

Croce's blasphemous criticism of Dante on the grounds that structure is unpoetic was also reinforced by his rejection of the supernatural, of this very tangible supernatural of late medieval rationalism—"the representation of the other world, of Hell, Purgatory, and Paradise, was not the intrinsic

---

[6] Dante, *The Inferno*, trans. Robert Hollander and Jean Hollander (New York: Anchor Books), 2000.

subject of his poem."[7] His case helps us to observe indirectly, among some visible figures of secular culture, how deeply the centuries-old looming presence of the Catholic Church has dulled the receptivity to the supersensible under the Italian sky. Regrettably, Contini was to revive in his own way Croce's thesis when he said "and hence there goes the journey" ("e dunque, addio viaggio").[8] The best, most concise refutation of this thesis comes in Dante's own lines: in the last canto, it is the sublime poetry of the retrospective gaze from above embracing the immensity of his journey and the progression of his steps:

> This man who, from within the deepest pit
> the universe contains up to these heights
> has seen the disembodied spirits, one by one. (*Paradiso*, 33.22–24)

What happens in the case when a reality that is totally other is created without building on preexisting codes, only with the sovereign powers of literary fiction? Is there an example of this? Jumping through the centuries, we find one in Borges' short story, *The Library of Babel*. As in Dante, and as always, the total substitution is only apparent. And yet, in the first sentence of the story it is imposed on the reader with the force of an iron fist: "The universe (which others call the library) is composed of an indefinite and perhaps infinite number of hexagonal galleries."[9] The library, which will endure after humanity's extinction, is a form of nature; as such, it is the perpetually elusive object of questions and investigations. Let us set aside, as we did for the short poem of Marie de France, any temptation to interpret: not because this task of all tasks is out of fashion, or because Borges makes interpretation itself the theme of an agnostic, mystical, bookish, and yet terrifying story. The ambition of this essay, much more modestly, is to contribute to theory.

We receive more information about the universe-as-library: the ventilation shafts between the hexagons, the shelves that cover four out of six walls, the narrow corridors that open onto other identical galleries. On the left and on the right, however, there are two very small closests: "In the

---

[7] Benedetto Croce, *The Poetry of Dante*, trans. Douglas Ainslie (New York: Holt, 1922), 73.

[8] Gianfranco Contini, "Un'interpretazione di Dante," in *Varianti e altra linguistica* (Turin: Einaudi, 1970), 369–70.

[9] J. L. Borges, *Labyrinths: Selected Stories and Other Writings*, ed. D. A. Yates and J. E. Irby (New York: New Directions, 1964), 51.

first, one may sleep standing up; in the other, satisfy one's fecal necessities" (51). These are residues of our universe whose incorporation into this other world that one cannot predict: there will be mention of suicides, respiratory illnesses, epidemics; there will be no mention of eating, or, say, making love. Nor is there even any mention of women; and all the men, it seems, are librarians. How can we understand concretely that their wanderings sometimes devolve into banditry? Corpses are buried, and dissolve, when they are cast through the shafts for eternity. The permanence in this universe of everything that comes from ours demands estranging modifications.

The first residue is the library itself, with all its parts and qualities. When the speaker of the story tells us "I have travelled in my youth," it means that he has left "my sweet native hexagon" (55) for other hexagons. The actual pieces of information we receive are fewer than the conjectures, opinions, demonstrations, and discoveries that, in their sheer number and instability, struggle unsuccessfully to understand the universe. For each hexagon, we know the number of shelves, books, pages, lines, and characters it contains; but "the formless and chaotic nature of almost all the books" estranges the library and makes the substitution of the universe contradictory. If we are to judge a book to be abnormal that contains three letters "perversely repeated from the first line to the last" or "a mere labyrinth of letters," or to speak of "senseless cacophony, verbal nonsense, and incoherency," we need to have some notion of a *normal* book. But where could this notion come from, if here, in the whole mass of books, we find at most "a sensible line or straightforward statement?" (53).

These examples incline toward that anarchy mentioned above, the only alternative to the irreplaceability of reality as a whole. "Only the impossible is excluded. For example: no book can be a ladder" (57, n. 1). The residues of our world intermix with one another to produce a humorous surrealism, disregarding geography and the distribution of languages on a continental scale; it will be learned in the end that "nearly two pages of homogenous lines," believed to be Portugese by "a wandering decoder," and Yiddish by others, are in fact "a Samoyedic-Lithuanian dialect of Guarani, with classical Arabian inflections" (54). With solemn trepidation it is said that the letters *"dhcmrlchtdj"* must have, in some secret language of the library, a terrible meaning; and that one cannot articulate a syllable without it being, in some language, the "powerful name of a god" (57). Everything is meaningless, or everything is meaningful, but even here we do not pass beyond all rules unless it is through an ideal hypothesis.

One Status among Many, the Only One Studied

The realistic dimension of daily life is deformed by Quixote's madness, removed by the subject matter of Brittany, transcended in Dante, and abolished in Borges. And yet, in the past two centuries, it is into the frame of daily life that we are most accustomed, and are most moved, to see the supernatural intrude. When it was first published in 1837, *Venus of Ille*, a short story by Merimée, was set in contemporary France, in Roussillon, and was narrated by a Parisian.[10] He is, sure enough, skeptical of what the terrified young provincial groom confides to him. Wanting to play lawn tennis, the young man slips his wedding-ring onto the finger of the recently excavated statue of Venus; when he returns to retrieve it, the statue grabs his finger. She is his wife, he concludes, since he has given her his ring. The superstitious conclusion, which for a moment makes the listener shudder, would not be enough to explain the inexplicable if it could not, like a rule, have further consequences. And indeed soon there will be grounds for us to fear that it will be tragically confirmed.

The short story is among the purest examples of a "fantastic fiction," defined by Todorov as a hesitation in the face of the supernatural.[11] His book has inaugurated a new generation of studies and has revived the concept of the fantastic. All reservations aside, I owe a double debt to this book. Its definition of the fantastic, and the related historico-literary periodization, will require only some adjustments to be used in the following argument. Second, and more important, the book demonstrates that it is possible to define in a convincing way *one* literary status of the supernatural and to document it in *one* determined stretch of time and in *one* set of genres. I have been asking myself for quite a long time why should not that which has been possible for one not be possible for *other* statuses, in *other* periods and genres—virtually for all?

In what follows I propose an experimental method of proceeding through a few examples. It has always seemed to me accidental that Todorov's potentially groundbreaking insight revolved around a status of the supernatural that one might define as central or symmetrical. That is to say, on *the* status that, while associating the supernatural with doubt, leaves it in an unstable balance between acknowledgment and refusal of its ontological substance.

---

[10] P. Merimée, *La Vénus d'Ille*, in *Théâtre de Clara Gazul: Romans et nouvelles* (Paris: Gallimard, 1978).

[11] T. Todorov, *The Fantastic: A Structural Approach to a Literary Genre*, trans. Richard Howard (Ithaca, N.Y.: Cornell University Press), 1975.

Looking back on the previous examples, who would not agree that in Chrétien or in Marie de France, in Dante, or even in Borges, the supernatural is
more substantial than what Merimée's hesitation allows; and that it is less
substantial in Cervantes, where humor and folly defuse it? Let us tackle the
problem from the opposite perspective and answer the following questions:
When the substance of the supernatural is greater, or even when it is greatest, is it always also total, that is, free from limitations and fissures? When it
is smaller, and even when it is minimal, is it always also deficient, that is,
lacking any allure or enticement?

I have already tried to show that it is impossible to answer such questions
in the affirmative—questions, that is, that put in terms of all or nothing the
faith that different kinds of literature elicit from the reader to benefit the supernatural. We laugh at Quixote's credulity when it comes to enchanters, just
as we do at all his other eccentricities; but, in a parallel way, we sympathize
and identify with him, for the one as much as for the others. This is certainly
not the only example that acts on us in this fashion. We board Guigemar's
ship, journey with Dante through the otherworld, and settle into the library
of Babel; but "that momentary suspension of disbelief in which the poetic
faith consists" (the famous words of Coleridge are more fitting than ever) is
not unconditional.[12] That it is not so depends on the very first concept I introduced, and to which I have given the largest scope: that of rules.

Trust, Critique, and Compromise-Formation

It is not a matter of all or nothing, it is, rather, a question of proportions. A
proportion between what two things? Asking this question does not help us
so much to see more clearly the forces we have already glimpsed in the oscillation between the strong and weak substance of the supernatural, as it does
to choose the names by which we can identify them. Is it legitimate to speak
of trust and critique? Of a trust, of course, that we extend to the supernatural so that it may exist; and of a critique leveled against the supernatural because it does not exist? The problems are particularly evident in the second
question. Those who use the word *critique*—or even worse, those who use
the word *supernatural*—are in danger of inviting upon themselves the same
critique they apply to the supernatural.

I refer to a lucid passage in Durkheim, written in a time free from the
suspicion of facile relativism. The idea of the supernatural presupposes the

---

[12] S. T. Coleridge, *Biographia Literaria* (London: Dent, Everyman's Library, 1967), 2:6.

notion of a natural order, of incontrovertible laws that bind all phenomena together; this kind of universal determinism arrives well after antiquity, when the most astonishing events were not perceived as "miraculous" in the modern sense.[13] Should we therefore wait for Bacon, Galilieo, and Descartes if we wish to speak of the supernatural and of critique? All three were born within fifty years of Cervantes—Cervantes, whose name takes us to the other side of our dilemma. Perhaps we should not speak of trust in the case of *Don Quixote*, which ends by stressing the desire "to arouse men's scorn for the false and absurd stories of knight-errantry" (1,050)—not to mention the problems raised by Voltaire's novels. Perhaps if it was wise of Todorov and others to restrict themselves only to the fantastic, it was because the balance between trust and critique could not waver too much in either direction.

Let us try not to yield to a historicism that we should not consider as the only or the best one: a historicism that, suffering from vertigo when confronted with long durations, closes its eyes to them and blinds itself to theory. Theory is born, instead, from the need to juxtapose any existing phenomenon with any other, however remote—and sometimes with phenomena that do *not* exist, in a purely hypothetical fashion. Of course, either of our terms—*trust* and *critique*—on whose precarious balance the nineteenth-century fantastic thrives, might in other eras be anachronistic, as if they were displacing one another. I suppose there might be medieval hagiographies that never exercise, as a limit on trust, that minimal set of rules that I have argued to be indispensable. And even a minimal limitation has less to do with the force of critique than with the simplest, most empirical prerogatives of a sense of reality.

On the other hand, I know from experience that there are Enlightenment texts in which an antireligious critique does not allow any unconscious yielding, any fascination with miracles, legends, or dogmas. This is all the more true the more ideological the text in question. However, even in the most narrative or literary texts, there may be the slightest level of trust in the supernatural. In the extreme cases, both terms sound improper, either an absolute faith in the supernatural or its violent demystification: the term critique hardly fits the positive pole of a barely regulated belief, and the term trust hardly fits the negative pole of militant incredulity. Both, however, are appropriate in the case where the opposing force seems to disappear, perhaps dipping below consciousness. Is this not enough, in theory, for both terms to be appropriate in all the intervening cases? I believe so, on one condition: that

---

[13] Émile Durkheim, *Elementary Forms of Religious Life*, trans. Carol Cosman (Oxford: Oxford University Press, 2001).

the series of cases can be charted on a graduated scale, connecting both extremes.

Those who are not convinced by this argument may have a reservation, if they continue to read—a reservation that is nonetheless innocuous, since it is beside the point for the examples which I will touch on. They may suspect that this writer, a modernist, is projecting onto the Middle Ages and antiquity paradigms that will be valid only after the rupture created by the growth of the modern critical spirit, between the Reformation and the Enlightenment. They may suspect me, that is, of projecting paradigms drawn from my familiarity with the nineteenth and twentieth centuries onto the eighteenth, seventeenth, and sixteenth centuries. I do not deny it: the bias by which I am compelled to retain the terms *trust* and *critique* has a Freudian origin. And it is tied to opinions that are difficult to summarize, let alone defend, in such a brief space.

My terminology is tied to the idea that after Freud it makes little sense to speak of irrationality pitted against rationality; rather, we should speak of diverse rationalities, more or less permissive or strict. It is connected as well to the idea that the true core of Freud's discovery—what he unfortunately called subconscious—is a logical, or better yet, antilogical structure: namely, the idea of the "compromise-formation."[14] This notion proves itself to be fruitful, to the point of being indispensable, for the theory and analysis of literature. Freud is as rigorous in his use of concepts as he is reluctant in providing definitions; therefore I will provide my own. I define the compromise-formation as a semiotic manifestation—linguistic in the larger sense—that by itself makes room simultaneously for two opposing psychological forces that have become contrasting signifiers.[15]

This notion underlies the following passage from Freud on the psychogenesis of the joke. It is a passage, it seems to me, that has broad applications, like other theoretical insights from that great book, to literature in general. It concerns the pleasure we take in the absurd and infantile playing with words:

> Whatever the motive may have been which led the child to begin these
> games, I believe that in his later development he gives himself up to them
> with the consciousness that they are nonsensical, and that he finds enjoyment

---

[14] See I. Matte Blanco, *The Unconscious as Infinite Sets: An Essay in Bi-logic* (London: Duckworth, 1975).

[15] Cf. F. Orlando, *Toward a Freudian Theory of Literature*, trans. by Charmaine Lee (Baltimore: Johns Hopkins University Press, 1978), 191–99.

in the attraction of what is forbidden by reason. He now uses games in order
to withdraw from the pressure of critical reason. But there is far more po-
tency in the restrictions which must establish themselves in the course of a
child's education in logical thinking and in distinguishing between what is
true and false in reality; and for this reason the rebellion against the compulsion of logic and reality is deep-going and long-lasting. *Even the phenomena
of imaginative activity must be included in this rebellious category.*[16]

Historicizing these extraordinary lines is more difficult than it seems. Of
course, *critical reason* and *logical thinking* are above all—or only—those that
Freud was able to imagine in 1905, at the end of the positivist period. And
yet the *education* he speaks of is not only *thinking correctly*, but also *distinguishing* the *true* from the *false*; the *compulsion*, in addition to stemming
from logic, stems *from reality* as well. Were there ever any historical periods
in which this last compulsion was not imposed at all? Or in which it did not
constitute a compulsion at all, and could not elicit any form of *rebellion*, neither superficial nor intermittent? At any rate, what interests us here is the
last brief statement that I have italicized. It establishes the same pleasure as
the origin of both literature in general (in my hypothesis, the analogue of the
joke) and of the literature containing elements of the supernatural. The
same pleasure grounds the primary imaginary field and the field that I have
called "doubly imaginary." Any kind of literature requires the simultaneous
presence of opposing forces, and it is therefore in itself a compromise-
formation: between the real and the unreal. Any themes of the supernatural,
whether the highest or the lowest, require a somewhat more sustained suspension of disbelief and introduce a second compromise-formation to complicate the first—as if they were producing literature of the second degree.

I know all too well that these themes, stretching from verse to prose and
to the most diverse literary genres, can be studied from many points of view.
These are not mutually exclusive; on the contrary, they can be combined and
can answer as many questions as there are variables worthy of attention. For
example, *where does the supernatural come from?* When it is not invented
from scratch, one finds the variables of national-historical traditions: Greek
and Latin, Judeo-Christian, Celtic, Germanic-Scandinavian, Orientalist,
world folkloric. Or even, what *does the supernatural consist of?* Whether invented, reinvented, or inherited, it offers many variables of subject matter, in
the themes, plots, and protagonists: magic and ghosts, metamorphoses and

---

[16] S. Freud, *Jokes and Their Relation to the Unconscious*, trans. and ed. James Strachey (New
York: Norton, 1963), 125–26.

animism, gods and the personifications of nature, prophets and saints, fairies and the devil, Medea, Moses, Jesus, Lancelot, Siegfried, Armida, Faust. *What does the supernatural mean?* Allowing for all the accidents of interpretation, the supernatural exists in variants both of the allegorical-moral kind—such as the eternal conflict between good and evil, the modern denunciation of the cost of progress—and of the symbolic-psychoanalytic kind, from the trauma of birth to every refiguration of eroticism. *What effect does the supernatural produce?* We encounter certain variables—let us call them tonal and affective, with all their nuances and contaminations: the smile of pleasure, the laugh of mockery, the enchantment of marvels, and the shudder of the sacred, the uneasiness of the sinister, the paralysis of terror. *What ages does the supernatural stretch through?* The historical-chronological variants are fundamental, but it is impossible to tackle them without having first distinguished among the many forms assumed by the theme. These variables return us to all the other variables as their necessary precondition.

Now, the methodological question is as follows: When the historical-chronological, historical-national, mythical or strictly thematic, allegorical or symbolic, tonal or affective are the same, there still remains another variable and another question. Namely, in what proportion does the supernatural allow, simultaneously and relatively, trust and critique? Put another way, but from the same point of view, the ultimate question is: *inside which formations of compromise does the supernatural take shape?* The comparison of texts diverse in time, language, subject matter, meaning conveyed, and emotions aroused can be illuminating when it is based on the basic similarity of the status of the supernatural in them. Texts can be brought together in one category based on the way in which two rationalities coexist in them—as always, one more permissive, and one more strict. We have to keep in mind all the aforementioned variables, but none of them seems to me compelling to study. My working hypothesis is that, from text to text, the trope of the supernatural in literature needs to be studied as a series of formations of compromise.

From the Homeric Fables to Voltaire's Mockery

In the beginning there were the rules—for the only good reason that, before the begninning, there is only chaos. The primary rule of the supernatural is localization, which limits and determines it by imagining its presence to be precisely *there* and not elsewhere. Ideally, we set off from the Homeric poem richest in monsters and marvels, *The Odyssey*. Throughout Ulysses' narrative to Alcinous, the landings of the hero become localizations of the supernatural in a fantastic geography: the lands, or better yet, the islands, of the Lotus-eaters, of the Cyclops, of Aeolus, of the Laestrygonians, of Circes, of the Cimmerians, of the Sirens, of the Sun, of Calypso; also the descent into Hades and the straits of Scylla and Charybdis (books 9–12). At a later date, the islands of the Nordic sea will be the portentous stepping-stones of a similar voyage of the living toward the island of the blessed. *The Navigation of Saint Brendan*, written by an unknown Irish author in early medieval Latin prose, enjoyed such great success for three or four centuries that it even reached Dante.

For thousands of years, until the seventeenth and eighteenth centuries, with the last epic-religious poems, the trust accorded to the supernatural could be total. We know that the full trust in the supernatural can still not dispense with rules; rather, it reduces them to a limiting force for which the term *critique* is hardly appropriate. Moreover, localization is not the only possible rule, nor are those in space the only possible forms of localization (transitional space, otherworldly space, remote space). There are also localizations in time. To skip over what precedes the advent of the modern novel, I list only those whose clarity allows me to dispense with quotations: the cyclical time of the night, and indeed the hour of midnight, the remote and irrepeatable time of the mythical past. Irrepeatable here means unverifiable: both features originally conferred nothing but majesty on such a time. And yet, if you will, it is a short step from the unverifiable to the incredible. The first to take the trouble of noticing their intimacy were the Latin and Greek writers.

In the first book of the *Metamorphoses*, Ovid tells the story of the flood and the only survivors, Deucalion and Pyrrha, and of the oracle who tells them to cast stones behind their backs to repeople the earth. When he comes to the metamorphosis of the stones into men, he interjects for half a line: "If those of old / did not attest the tale I tell you now, / who could accept its truth?" (1.400).[17] It is a question whose malice overturns the hierarchy it establishes: the authority of time does not verify the incredible, and one is lucky if the incredible does not undermine the authority of time. This time to speak of critique is not out of place. In that line, and throughout the poem, does a critique inversely proportional to trust have the same force as it will have in Cervantes? Answering "no" means being able to glimpse another one of the intervening cases and their gradual disposition on a scale.

---

[17] *The Metamorphoses of Ovid*, trans. Allen Mandelbaum (San Diego: Harvest Books, 1993).

If we want a case in ancient literature based on the highest degree of criticism with the minimal degree of trust, we must turn to Lucian instead. In his *Zeus the Tragic Actor*, the gods look from above on the public debate between a stoic and an epicurean; the latter, who denies their existence, gets the better of the former, who affirms it. Unlike *Zeus the Tragic Actor*, Lucian's *True Story* comes closer to the resevoir of sympathy aroused by Don Quixote, that is to say, to a latent trust. The most deliberately improbable of the tales in the *True Story* satirizes other novels. "The creator and master of such nonsense" was indeed Odysseus in his narrative to Alcinous. Here the narrator is, on the contrary, truthful when he portrays himself as a liar: "I am writing about things entirely outside my own experience or anyone else's, things that have no reality whatever and never could have."[18]

———

This is, perhaps, the right time to adopt some terminology. I will call the strongest literary supernatural a supernatural *of tradition*: accorded the greatest degree of trust, validated by the enduring crystallizations of the collective imagination, and limited solely by its own rules. Even though each text recreates it in a new form, the subject matter is transmitted through the centuries more or less faithfully. At the other extreme, I will call the weakest literary supernatural a supernatural of *mockery*: subjected to the greatest degree of critique, always derivative, always made historically possible by the progression beyond an inferior rationality. I would further distinguish from this, however closely related, a supernatural of *indulgence*—the smile in the place of laughter. In psychological terms, though, the distinctions would be more blurred, and the boundaries would be more porous than in the well-defined categories to which, after all, literary theory aspires.

The best way to define the difference between these last two kinds of supernatural is to say that, while both spring from the same implicit incredulity, the third kind reveals an indulgence in the return to a past credulity, in a regression to the irrational. The question of truth or falsehood is pushed aside by the allure of pleasure—a pleasure that is not gratuitous, but rather, in Freud's words, consists "in the attraction of what is prohibited by reason." In antiquity, the supernatural of tradition was dominant. Lucian and Ovid, however, would suffice to show that the supernatural of mockery came next to undermine it; in turn, the supernatural of indulgence arrived to soften it.

———

[18] Lucian, *True History*, trans. Paul Turner (Bloomington: Indiana University Press, 1974), 4.

I believe that the Middle Ages never came close to these last two stages of the supernatural—and if it did, it was only superficially, infrequently, or late. Out of prudence I decline to choose either of the two categories when confronted with the ambiguity of the cases of Brother Alberto and most of all Brother Cipolla, in Boccaccio's *Decameron* (respectively, *Decameron* 4.2 and 6.10).

At any rate, the true rediscovery of the supernatural of indulgence occurred during the Italian Renaissance. In Boiardo, the subject matter of Brittany is teeming with rules and fantastical localizations; but these do not shelter it from a pervasive irony that charges the archbishop Turpino, as the personification of the whole chivalric tradition, with being the "source" of all these pleasurable impossibilities. If Orilo, split in two by a sword, is to have the half of his body still on the horse reattached to the half on the ground (Don Quixote would love to be able to do this, 1.10.113), this is something that "I myself am ashamed of telling / although Turpino compels me to do so."[19] Ariosto, we know, eclipsed his predecessor, particularly when it came to irony. If the griffin in the sky is "so marvellous a wonder in the air / . . . that few will credit it" (4.4), to this and other phenomena we can apply two lines originally referring to something that is not supernatural, namely, the virginity of the adventurous Angelica: "it may be true, but no man in his sense / would ever credit it" (1.56).[20] Rabelais, on the other hand, insists that we should believe in the birth of Gargantua from his mother's left ear: "I am not sure you're going to believe this strange birth. If you don't, I don't give a hoot—but any decent man, any sensible man, always believes what he's told and what he finds written down"; all the more so since, first, in the sacred scriptures there is nothing to contradict it; second, nothing is impossible for the omnipotent deity; and third, precedents of abnormal births can be found in authorities ranging from mythology to the scientific writing of the Elder Pliny (1.6).[21]

The rise of Protestantism in France influenced what was censured in passages like this in one or the other editions of Rabelais's work. I would say, in general and over long periods of time, that the Reformation and the Counter-Reformation affected both the supernatural of tradition and the supernatural of indulgence. Better yet, they affected the system of alternatives that tradition and indulgence had combined to form. It was now as if the

---

[19] M. M. Boiardo, *Olando innamorato*, 3.2.54.

[20] Ludovico Ariosto, *Orlando furioso (The Frenzy of Orlando)*, trans. Barbara Reynolds (London: Penguin Books), 1975.

[21] François Rabelais, *Gargantua and Pantagruel* (1534), trans. Burton Raffel (New York: W. W. Norton, 1990), 21.

supernatural of tradition, in order to take part in the profoundity of a new masterpiece, needed to be burdened with some mixture of theological and moral problems. The best examples are hell, the devil, and demons, along with their pawns, enchanters, and enchantresses. Insofar as they are all ideologically condemned, they are allowed to catch the reader's fancy in the great epic-religious poems: from the Catholic Tasso to the Protestants Milton and Klopstock. The Fall, free will, sin, damnation, redemption, and resurrection stimulate poetic invention in proportion to the growing urgency of the controversies surrounding them. In theater, Shakespeare hides the horror of a crime against nature behind the ghost of Hamlet's father; Racine hides the frightful Jansenist predestination behind the monsters to which Phaedra is blood-related; in Calderón, the human will resists the magic portents of the devil who can move mountains.

At the same time, the new critical spirit, not at all foreign to this religious renewal, facilitated the shift from a supernatural of indulgence to one of mockery. In the early seventeenth century, while the subject matter of Brittany came under ingenious attack from Cervantes, in Italy and France the Greco-Roman mythology suffered more modest offensives from comic-heroic poems à la Tassoni, and burlesques à la Scarron. The battle between the ancients and moderns exploded in France only at the end of the century, but its premises were also in place before and elsewhere: smoldering in that modernist aspect of the baroque that made it Janus-faced and predestined it to violent rejections. It was Perrault, the trailblazer of the French moderns, who first drew from folklore an innocuous supernatural: one different from the discredited Breton, the worn-out classical, and the compromising Christian supernaturals. Consider these lines from the beginning of *The Donkey's Hide*:

Pourquoi faut-il s'émerveiller
Que la raison la mieux sensée,
Lasse souvent de trop veiller,
Par des contes d'ogre et de fée
Ingénieusement bercée,
Prenne plaisir à sommeiller?[22]

In the late eighteenth century in Germany, Wieland, at the beginning of his neomedieval *Oberon*, still addresses his muse about his audience: "behold thy hearers open mouthed and eyed / prepared to take the fond

---

[22] C. Perrault, *Contes* (Paris: Garnier, 1967), 57.

deception well, / if thou, on thy part canst deceive with grace" (1.8).[23] These lines could serve as epigraphs for the supernatural of indulgence; one that, more than any other, is entrusted not so much to the subject matter of the stories as it is to the delicate ironies of the writing. This is the only status of the supernatural that I am not able to locate in the novel, at least in the novel written for adults. In 1697, with Perrault's fairy tales, it entered into literature destined to be read by children, where it was to endure until the nineteenth century, in Andersen's fairy tales, Collodi's *Adventures of Pinocchio*, and Carroll's *Alice in Wonderland*—just as the supernatural of tradition, for its part, endured up through the genuinely archaic tales of the Brothers Grimm.

In 1704, with the translation of the *Thousand and One Nights* from Arabic, Galland endowed French prose with a "fabulous" previously unheard of for two reasons. First, it was drawn from without, from an exotic literature, rather than from within, from the folkloric tradition; and second, it was more open to an indulgent and even a mocking redeployment. His work contributed to late Enlightenment narrative's predilection for orientalist themes, from the *Persian Letters* to Zadig. In the exchange of letters that makes up Montesquieu's novel, to be Persian is to have an estranged and critical perspective on the West, on Paris, on Catholicism and its dogmas. And yet the East is and remains the most ancient homeland for many of the things that come under scrutiny: myth, metaphor, poetry, revealed religion, and the faulty logic underlying them—and all of it is deposited in sacred books. I refer the reader to the analysis I have made of letters 16–18, where the Koran, apparently placed on the same level as the *Thousand and One Nights*, is really a stand-in for the Bible.[24] And Montesquieu relates to both sacred books as Lucian or Cervantes related to their novels—as, in general, authors just as irreverent relate to some other serious texts. The supernatural of mockery triumphs when good logic and faulty logic engage in an impossible dialogue: impossible in the double sense that myth is outrageously wrong when confronting philosophy, but that there is also a secret pleasure in allowing its regressive rhetoric to speak.

The first of the philosophical tales of Voltaire is perhaps even less generous. The debate is set in Babylon: either the griffin does not exist, in which case we should not be prohibited from eating it; or, since there is a prohibition, we must conclude that the griffin exists. The nonexistent becomes the victim of Zadig's conciliatory wisdom, which turns its absolute inconsequentiality into

---

[23] *Oberon, A Poetical Romance in Twelve Books* (1780), trans. John Quincy Adams (New York: F. S. Crofts, 1940).

[24] F. Orlando, *Illuminismo, barocco e retorica freudiana* (Turin, Einaudi, 1997), 29–64.

a respectful gradation: "If there are any griffins, then let's not eat them; if there aren't any, we will eat even less of them" (chap. 4). Zadig runs the risk of becoming the victim of his own wisdom when he is challenged by the learned author of thirteen volumes about griffins. The nonexistent is verbose and persecutorial.[25] *The Princess of Bablyon* lets the smile of indulgence periodically reappear; still, we laugh unwillingly about the biblical patriarchs when we learn, for example, the age of Amazan's mother: "she was a lady of about three hundred, but something of her beauty remained with her, and one could well imagine that from about two hundred thirty to forty she had been lovely" (chap. 4). Less read than his masterpieces, *The White Bull* is the result of a propaganda that has become acerbic in Voltaire's old age. The literary quality of his dozens of antireligious pamphlets has made it a commonplace that in Voltaire, as never before, mockery has the last word. The supernatural barely retains the echo of an appeal as it is systematically reduced to silence.

The Thematization of Doubt

Under what conditions, after the Enlightenment, was a strong supernatural once more able have its say? This is the historical question to which studies of the fantastic actually respond, for the most part unknowingly. When Todorov defined the concept as founded in hesitation, his valid intuition attracted various reservations. Like many others, I am interested in challenging the excessive emphasis he placed on narrative resolutions: the fantastic would be that which, in the end, is neither rationalized as "strange" nor confirmed as the "marvelous." His thesis excludes the masterpieces of the English gothic. For instance, Radcliffe's *The Mysteries of Udolpho*, where the supernatural ends up rationalized, or Lewis's *The Monk*, where it is soon confirmed. For now, in the gothic tradition of Walpole's *The Castle of Otranto* (1764), up until Marturin's *Melmuth the Wanderer* (1820), I would like to consider primarily the meaning that the series of spatial and temporal localizations acquires.

In time, from novel to novel and through intermediate ages, we move from the eleventh-century of Walpole to the contemporaneity of Marturin's 1816. Why in space, instead, starting from a southern oriental extremity like Otranto, do we always remain in southern Italy and in Spain, never reaching farther north than central France? Because, I believe, such a space is also

---

[25] Voltaire, *Candide and Other Stories* (1747), trans. Roger Pearson (Oxford: Oxford University Press, 1990), 134.

itself a kind of time: the writers and readers alike of the most advanced European country project onto the Catholic, superstitious, feudal, turbulent, and passionate South their own superseded past. The negative localization implies a postive one, by which the borders of true civilization are made to coincide with the borders of England. For proof we need only turn to Austen's novel that, standing in relation to Radcliffe as *Don Quixote* stood in relation to the chivalric romances, comes deliciously close to the edge of the supernatural of mockery. The young Catherine has recovered her senses and is disillusioned after having believed that she could reenact Udolfo in the modernized *Northanger Abbey*, which sheltered her. But horrors like those, to be sure, could not remain hidden, here where "roads and newspapers lay everything open"[26]—surely not in the center of the country, if we don't want to vouch for the marginal regions.

At the beginning of *The Mysteries of Udolpho*, we find ourselves in 1584 between Gascony and Languedoc. But the poetics of the historical novel will come much later: the protagonist, Emily, just like her father, openly cultivates eighteenth-century, bourgeois, Protestant—in a word, English—values. This superior rationality, which will suffer severe scrutiny leading to hesitation, agrees with an individualistic intimacy, familiar and sentimental.[27] A solid realistic plane establishes itself through the clash between these values and the countervalues embodied by her worldly and ambitious relatives; a product worthy of other genres of the novel is the petulant character of her aunt, Madame Montoni née Cheron. Having lost her father, and fallen under the power of her terrifying second Italian husband, Emily is brought to Udolpho in the Apennines. She had already contemplated from the Pyrenees the awe-inspiring sublimity of the mountain—the core of the preromantic rediscovery of nature—which now becomes for her the other face of the sublime: that which Burke associated with terror.[28]

This is a terror of a social, in addition to a natural and prior to a supernatural, kind: traveling "through regions of profound solitude," the savage and secluded gorge seems to Emily "a spot exactly suited for the retreat of banditti."[29] The true object of what she initially feared in Montoni—even while admiring his sinister beauty and courage—turns out to be a will ready

---

[26] J. Austen, *Northanger Abbey* (1818), in *Northanger Abbey, Lady Susan, The Watsons, and Sanditon* (Oxford: Oxford University Press, 1990), 2:159. See also 2:160–61.

[27] A. Radcliffe, *The Mysteries of Udolpho* (1794) (Oxford: Oxford University Press, 1966), 1:1–26, 56–73, 82–98, and 4:580 and 595.

[28] Ibid., 1:1, 2:224–26, 241–42, and 3:467–68.

[29] Ibid., 3:402.

to disregard all laws, not to take responsibility for committed atrocities, to take the law into his own hands.[30] The anti-Catholic bias remains virtual, save for some brief passages directed against the convents (the author will more than compensate for this shortage in *The Italian*).[31] Of the two grand archetypal buildings taken as symbols of the ancien régime in that revolutionary close of the century—the convent and the castle—it is the castle that is called on to host the presumed supernatural. The supernatural's localization is the localization of the superseded past. Once the estranged gaze of a social class that is accustomed to much more intimate dwellings has populated the castle with phantoms, the dwelling of former lords is well qualified to serve as a sinister background: the emptied immensity of proud proportions, long since become useless;[32] the labyrinthine irrationality of the hallways, the twists and turns of the passageways, and the secret rooms;[33] and the impending decadence that will bring towers, roofs, walls, chapels, and entire wings to ruin.[34]

Immensity, irrationality, and decadence isolate and disorient us—and in that space we breathe death. One castle is not enough, and when she has escaped from Udolpho, Emily's vicissitudes will continue and be resolved at the Château-le-Blanc in Languedoc. She had traveled near it together with her dying father: their brief exchanges with the peasants are exemplary of the new kind of thrill, which, more than the strange things seen and heard, dissuaded them from spending the night there, with disquieting silences rather than with deterring reports.[35] The Italian castle, however, is what will put the courage and reason of the heroine to such a test that she will become intertwined with the place. The building sets the stage for a doubt that she must resist: "As she passed along the wide and lonely galleries, dusky and silent, she felt forlorn and apprehensive of—she scarcely knew what."[36]

This "apprehension of the unknown that goes back to the absolute quality of childhood terror"[37] makes her frequent faintings more palatable for the reader, and we still sense the originality of the novel, however faded it may now seem. It makes the moanings behind one of the innumerable

---

[30] Ibid., 1:122, 3:361. See also 2:224–25, 240, 329, and 3:367, 384, 435.

[31] Ibid., 3:475–76 and 489. See also 4:639–40.

[32] Ibid., 2:226–28 and 244–45.

[33] Ibid., 2:230–32, 257–58, 317–18, 320–21, 322, and 3:429–33 and 457–60.

[34] Ibid., 2:229–30 and 232, 3:344–46 and 376–77.

[35] Ibid., 1:62–64.

[36] Ibid., 2:308.

[37] F. Orlando, *Gli oggetti desueti nelle immagini della letteratura*, 2nd ed. (Turin: Einaudi, 1994), 175.

doors,[38] the silences or the sounds heard from a distance,[39] the tortuous chases,[40] the voices emerging from the walls,[41] the indistinct figures in the darkness,[42] the decomposed corpses (either real or made of wax),[43] and finally the mysterious music of midnight[44] unforgettable as an illusory, for the most part nocturnal, supernatural. The ever-present rationalizations do not defuse the atmosphere, precisely because they are unpredictably distributed in small or large doses, from the equivocations explained in a few lines or paragraphs, to the enigmas that sustain the entire plot through hundreds of pages.

Hesitation is a necessary but insufficient concept if, beneath the most linear and ephemeral time, the possible resolutions of such hesitation become almost inconsequential. How could we rename this redefined notion? Keeping in mind that fear is rooted in a depth where the breath of the supernatural is indelible, we should only attend to the thematization of the doubt: it is of little consequence how long it is protracted and how it may be resolved. In defining darkness as necessary for terror and "our igorance of things" as the cause of its powers, Burke allows us to speak of a supernatural of *ignorance* rather, and better than, one of uncertainty.[45] Theoretically, our typology could be structured around the symmetry of the three possible answers to the question of the ontologic substance of the supernatural: we would have a yes and a no at the extremes, with the attenuating circumstances we have seen; in the center, we would have a perhaps. This is, however, an unstable center, which tends imperceptibly to tip in the direction of a yes.

In Radcliffe, the pessimism of reason is part of her Enlightenment heritage: when, at the Château-le-Blanc, the discussion turns to whether spirits can return to earth, the gentleman who denies it has better arguments but fewer supporters.[46] The maid Annette, on the other hand, is the source of hearsay accepted with such an illogical faith that the cannon close to which "something" had appeared is for her proof of the apparition itself.[47] But

---

[38] Radcliffe, *Mysteries*, 2:258, 309, and 321.

[39] Ibid., 2:253 and 318.

[40] Ibid., 3:430–32.

[41] Ibid., 2:289, 291, and 394–95. See also 3:459–60.

[42] Ibid., 3:355–57, 367–68, and 373–74.

[43] Ibid., 3:347–48. See also 3:365, 2:233–34, 248–49, and 4:662–63.

[44] Ibid., 1:68–69, 3:525–26, 4:541–42, 550–51, 661, 2:330–31, and 3:386–88, 437–40, and 459.

[45] E. Burke, *A Philosophical Enquiry into the Origin of Our Ideas of the Sublime and Beautiful* (Oxford: Oxford University Press, 1990), 54 and 57.

[46] Radcliffe, *Mysteries*, 4:549–50.

[47] Ibid., 2:233, 236–39, and 254–55.

Emily is not only exposed to the ignorant loquacity of Annette. She herself hosts a doubt, and she constructs brief formations of compromise in many recurring thoughts, in which her vocabulary tends to critique what the content avers. We soon have an example: "Emily, though she smiled at the mention of this ridiculous superstition, could not, in the present tone of her spirits, wholly resist its contagion."[48] And the thematization of doubt would be inconceivable in the absence of the other and greater innovation brought about by the supernatural of ignorance in order to justify itself. For the first time, although the story is told in the third person, the supernatural appears throughout from the perspective of the character rather than from the perspective of the author: filtered through one subjectivity, considered from one point of view.

I will consider, then, a supernatural of ignorance in another case where the reasons for not speaking of the fantastic are precisely the opposite from those I have given for the gothic. There, the supernatural, which was plausible in a remote space and time, was disproved; here the supernatural, implausible because located in the here and now, is, at the end of the day, proved. In 1809, with his *Ritter Gluck*, Hoffmann had begun setting the supernatural in contemporary and daily life, almost renouncing localization: "The Golden Pot" (1813) is subtitled "Fable of the New Age."

The student Anselmus might easily have become a personal secretary or even a privy-counselor in Dresden had it not been for a series of unfortunate clumsy accidents like the one that opens the story. He takes shelter, disheartened, under an elder-tree, and when he starts to hear whispers and tinklings, seeing three green-golden snakes shining through the branches, he says to himself: "this is only the wind of the evening, which today speaks in words; and it is the sun that makes the foliage sparkle like emeralds."[49] We are familiar with this fork in the road: are they giants or windmills, is it a helmet or a basin? This is, however, a romantic Quixote turned upside down. The student—handsome but dressed unfashionably, as if his tailor had only heard about a modern tail-coat—will be right in indulging his hallucinations and bringing upon himself the suspicion of madness. The archivist Lindhorst is in fact his benevolent enchanter, and the witch who persecutes him under different guises is also real; Sancho's sense of reality, embodied by the wise functionaries, such as the codirector Paulmann and the chancellor Heerbrand, is wrong.

---

[48] Ibid., 1:68.

[49] E.T.A. Hoffmann, "The Golden Pot" (1814–15), in *The Golden Pot and Other Tales*, trans. Ritchie Robertson (Oxford: Oxford University Press, 1992).

Yet as we have seen, the oscillation is before anything else internalized by the protagonist. He embraces the elder-tree; invokes the vanished snakes; loses the memory of these wonders and evokes the pity of passers-by; recovers his memory in a boat, when he sees the fireworks reflected in the river Elba; is about to jump into the water, is again pitied, and suffers a terrible crisis; hears voices whispering "believe in us"; and sees again the three sparkling stripes, no, they are the reflections of bright windows (2.186–89). I have summarized three or four pages out of about one hundred. They all contain just as many transitions from uncertainty to either belief or disbelief in the occurrence of the supernatural. Sometimes they are wonderful, if a hazy perspective replaces the unquestionable localizations familiar to us from earlier forms of the supernatural, as when, at dusk, a tall, thin man "suddenly appear[s] in front of him," or after an exchange in which the identity of the archivist Lindhorst is compromised by the inverisimilitude, by the uncertainty of whether in the twilight it is a man or a kite that is taking flight, whether it is the wind that is moving the flaps of a coat or the big wings of a bird in flight (4.253–58).

Writing in the third person, Hoffmann, like Radcliffe, anticipates the perspectival use of the first person that will prove to be suitable for the supernatural of ignorance.[50] The constant thematization of doubt, the relapses— whether into trust or critique—position themselves in a mirror-formation under the opposite signs. With the same intermittence, Anselmus remains faithful to the apparitions even when he is in inside the bourgeois world of Veronika, the daughter of Paulmann. He sins again by exercising his skeptical common sense even as he approaches the feminine personification of Serpentina, the daughter of Lindhorst. Lindhorst, in turn, as well as being an archivist, is an enchanter and a salamander.

The "old house in a remote part of town" where Anselmus goes to copy manuscripts, and where the library moonlights as an enchanted greenhouse, is a certain localization of the supernatural—thus intensifying it to the highest degree, given that Hoffmann is at his best when he is the most concise. Metamorphoses and freely multiplied transfigurations may seem to border on *kitsch*, but we should remember that in Hoffmann the supernatural of ignorance is still emerging from the supernatural of indulgence, not from that of tradition. The same thing happens even more so in the fantastic tale that Lindhorst tells at the café, a fable that elicits two gales of laughter. To Heerbrand

---

[50] See T. Todorov, *La letteratura fantastica*, trans. Klersy Imberciadori (Milan: Garzanti, 1977), 86–90.

it seems "oriental bombast," even though Lindhorst considers it a "true story"; the narrative is not lacking in graceful ironies ("a devil of a fellow, who has just moved into a summer residence in Lapland" [3.244–48]).

In the parallel tale that Serpentina tells to Anselmus, the present appears as "that unhappy time in which the degenerate race of men will no longer understand the language of nature," unless it has a "child-like poetic spirit" (8.290–91). In an address to the reader, the supernatural is the object of a nostalgia "that the spirit, like a shy child who has been rigidly educated, does not dare to express" (4.250–52). In the end, it is Heerbrand who becomes counselor, and Veronika marries him once she has overcome the temptation of the black supernatural magic of the witch. In the meantime, Anselmus has joined Serpentina. Where? In Atlantis. The narrator's embarrassment in closing the story is resolved when he receives a letter and a potion from the archivist-salamander (13.315–21). The thematic doubt is dispelled by this imaginary of the second-power, which is literature par excellence; but the great future of the supernatural of ignorance was not to follow this regressive path.

The Remotivation of Mystery

The studies of the fantastic almost have us believe that the supernatural of ignorance was the only status operative between the end of the eighteenth and the end of the nineteenth centuries. I grant that it is difficult to forget the existence and the European success of Goethe's *Faust* and Wagner's *Ring of the Nibelungs*; but do we not have the omnivorous category of the marvelous to incorporate them? The starting point of my research has been the skepticism about this lazy, antihistorical retrospective assimilation. Soon after came a conviction: namely, that in the last decades of the eighteenth century, not one, but two post-Enlightenment statuses of the supernatural were born. *Faust* is not narrative. Still, I have to return at least in passing to the original model of the other status of the supernatural, which bore fruit, also for narrative, in the same time span. In the sources of *Faust*—the popular book of 1587 and the puppet show of the late 1600s—the one with whom the doctor signs a pact could well take the name of Mephistopheles, answer questions concerning hell, and have individual features. Nonetheless, he was still only a tautological redeployment of the supernatural of tradition. The devil is the devil. In Goethe things are not so simple.

The identity of the devil has already been the topic of discussion between teacher and student, leading to the same alternatives we found in *Don*

Quixote: was it a ghost dog or an innocuous poodle?[51] Faust has later witnessed more than one metamorphosis before he cuts to the chase: "Enough, who are you then?" The answer sounds unexpected, nor could it be immediately clear: "Part of that force which would / do evil evermore, and yet creates the good." The doctor has to insist: "What is it that this puzzle indicates?" (1.1,335–37). The new response is only slightly less unexpected and obscure; it is unnecessary to reproduce it here. In this case, even more than others, I am permitted to gloss over what a theoretical essayist is fortunately exempt from—that is to say, interpretation.

Let us only ask about the effect of Mephistopheles' reply on cultivated readers who do not have a commentary available in front of them or in their memory. There is a *force* that *seeks to do evil* and *does only good*, that *always* does this, and of which the devil *is a part*. What kind of talk is this? It does not bring to mind passages from the scriptures; it does not echo any one theology. Despite its coming from the devil's mouth, it may well not refer at all to a supernatural sphere. Are we in the field of metaphysics or of secular ethics? Is this what Voltaire had begun to call a philosophy of history? One thing is certain: here the devil defines himself, and the self-definition is so peculiar that it becomes a *re*definition.

In order for a strong literary supernatural to become once more acceptable in a desacralized world, it could take a path only apparently less modern than the one marked by doubt and perspective, by daily life and the contemporary. One could go back, as though nothing had happened, to tradition: resorting to its localizations, its legendary or remote settings, its full-fledged presences. The supernatural that I am about to define often dwells with that of tradition, and alternates with it through unseen transitions. What matters is that at important junctures, the old motivations, weakened or lost, were replaced with powerful remotivations. The untimely becomes, then, all the more timely insofar as its timeliness is supremely problematic—for the following reason.

Starting from the historical turning point that accelerated as never before the rhythm of progress, the present started to have features felt not only as traumatic, but also as enigmatic. Transposing them into the supernatural, in order to signify them, meant resorting to what is mysterious par excellence: and that is, from the start, mysterious, since it is also, par excellence, something anterior. Thus the supernatural rediscovers and recovers ontological substance. It borrows it from the reference it makes, peremptory even if

---

[51] Goethe, *Faust*, trans. Walter Kaufmann (New York: Anchor Books, 1963), 145–49 ("Outside the City Gates," ll. 1,145–77).

latent, to the objective data of reality. This is a kind of reference I might call allegoric-referential in order to distinguish it from the old or new allegory. Such objects, the points where reality is more vulnerable and resistant to interpretation, find an adequate enigmatic expression in the supernatural. They are the sole referents endowed with sufficient meaning to remotivate the supernatural; conversely, the supernatural is the only form with enough mystery to express them.

Let us call this the supernatural of *transposition*, which, rather than being veiled or seen through a veil, is presented as knowable when it is allowed to speak. Its voice is not an unknowing one that comes to report the little it can understand from the outside, but is rather an authentic voice that reveals what it wants from the inside. While I am refraining from deciding what Mephistopheles' self-definition hinted at in Goethe, in return I assure you he will not remain the only devil to remotivate himself in the nineteenth century. In doing so, several of his literary offspring will presumably relate themselves to the rationality of progress—albeit in negative terms, as only befits their kind. It is a pity that Baudelaire's *The Generous Gambler* is a prose-poem, and that I cannot read Dostoeevsky's *The Brothers Karamazov* in the original. In order to stay close to the genesis of the supernatural of transposition, as I did with that of ignorance, I will consider a text dating between 1781 and 1787: *Vathek, an Arabian Tale*, written in French by the Englishman William Beckford when he was little more than twenty.

It is influenced by more than one narrative genre: the orientalist fable, the philosophical tale, and the early gothic—for us, three distinct statuses. The supernatural of mockery à la Voltaire is so amusing, in the uninhibited impertinence of nine-tenths of the text, that we can say the terrible ending is unexpected, without doing an injustice to the unity of the whole. And yet, who is Giaurro, the foreigner who immediately plays the part of Vathek's monstrous double, exaggerated in his physical appetites as he is in his thirst for knowledge? As for the former, Giaurro surpasses him; as for the latter, he presents a mysterious goal. He speaks little and ambiguously about himself, but nevertheless he speaks. And what does this "extraordinary" and "impossible" merchandise he exhibits as soon as he appears mean? "Slippers, which, by spontaneous springs, enabled the feet to walk; knives, that cut without motion of the hand, sabres, that dealt the blow at the person they were wished to strike."[52]

When Vathek descends never-ending stairs and passes a portal, we understand that the place he has reached and the Giaurro who greets him

---

[52] W. Beckford, *Vathek*, in *Four Gothic Novels* (Oxford: Oxford University Press, 1994), 87.

serve as an Islamic version of hell and the devil. The tradition to be remotivated establishes itself as oriental; yet nothing is more Western than its remotivation. The immensity of the place, the height of the vaults, the distance from which a twilight brilliance shines, are phantasmagoric. But in the crowd of those who pass by, pale as corpses, with eyes of a necrotic phosphorescence and one hand on a burning heart, all are silent. Whether absorbed or frenzied, they avoid one another, wandering as though each one were alone. A true display of riches, food, and enticements is laid out on every side—material goods, in short: as colossal as those that, according to Marx, will characterize capitalistic society. Free to pass through at their leisure, without any doors to shut them out, they all pay no attention to the display or regard it with indifference.

If this is hell, where one descends a stairway without being aware of having died, perhaps we were already there when we were alive? The implicit equation with the contemporary world makes us look for the country that no one has heard of and to enter the uncharted region where Giaurro came from, not knowing what place we seek and what place we enter. Profusion and waste, satiety and an artificial lack of appetite prophetically reveal themselves from behind the powerful appetites of the heroic-bourgeois era in which Beckford lived (the origins of his enormous family fortune were niether commercial nor industrial, but colonial and bound up with the slave trade).

Borges claims that it is the first truly atrocius hell in literature.[53] He felt its modernity, even while reading it only in a metaphysical key. And without such an additional key, we cannot pass through the horrifying portal. Let us be clear: the supernatural of transposition is fully empowered as supernatural, stronger than that of ignorace, and just slightly weaker than that of tradition. Its allegorical-referential connection does not become an allegory of referents; rather, it transmits their transfiguration. As a proof, it is not necessary for the reader, or even the author, to become conscious of this connection or referents. It is enough to perceive something known and familiar in it, even if it is not recognized (a bit as in the Freudian definition of the uncanny, without the effect of the texts always having to be uncanny).

Since it is from this status that our inquiry departed, I venture to call myself as a witness: and I touch here upon Wagner—theater, and to make it worse, musical theater—even more briefly than I did on Goethe. I have become convinced over time that it is impossible to watch and listen to the

---

[53] J. L. Borges, "Sobre el 'Vathek' de William Beckford," in *Otras inquisiciones* (from *Obras completas,* 1952–72) (Barcelona, 1996), 108–9.

third scene of *Das Rheingold* without seeing behind the mythical magic a nightmarish nineteenth-century capitalist workshop. It is similarly impossible not to see behind the magic helmet, in that scene just as at the end of the first act of the *Twilight of the Gods*, the threatening omnipotence of modern technology. And yet, I have not forgotten my past naïveté in listening: those metallic, crushing presences of oppressive machinery, those horns played *in pianissimo*—sounding gray, insidious, and equivocal—already transmitted to me a surplus of uneasiness less fablelike than science-fictional. To have understood that they translate antinature into the supernatural, on the other hand, does not at all prevent them from making me tremble.

We can consider Flaubert's *Temptation of Saint Anthony* as narrative, despite its theatrical form (for a century not performed on stage)—the stylistic intensity of the copious stage directions is sufficient reason for our doing so. I confess having had a different experience with this text. Even in the definitive and less prolix version, for a long time I had thought of it as an exercise in artistic prose and decadent erudition—two of the most boring things to read that I know of. In the very moment when I first caught a glimpse of the alleogrical-referential connection, I discovered the work's beauty: its eventful coherence, its fascinated and obsessive monotony. In Saint Athanasius's fourth-century *Life of Anthony*, a pure supernatural of tradition, devils, and temptations was represented in the plural. Flaubert takes this plurality and makes it his essential theme.

A thousand-year plurality of civilizations and beliefs, stretching across continents, hardly still contained in the political unity of the late Roman Empire, and already constrained in the religious unity of a triumphant Christianity: this is what the tempter marshals against the saint. He moves to assail the exclusive foundations of a faith armed with the precariousness, relativity, and interchangeability of any cultural heritage, of every ideological elaboration. If, on the one hand, the connection is with the boundless plurality of the cultures of the whole globe, hardly unified by modern imperialism, on the other hand, it unsettles the self-confidence of nineteenth-century ethnocentrism. The supernatural of transposition is often prophetic; today, all of this sounds like eclectic, postmodern dissolution (minus the indulgence).

The visions, whether in themselves supernatural or not—and if so, imaginary in the third degree—serve as temptations in two opposite ways. The prevailing one is a centrifugal force, which tries to disperse the unity of Christianity into the heterogeneity of everything else. Rarer but more troubling is the centripetal attack: unexpected resemblances besiege that unity from many different sides. It is difficult to list the innumerable pluralities evoked. Formally, the list itself is the rhetorical figure of choice, together with a luxuriant onomastic exuberance; materially, the exotic, the periph-eral, the hyperbolic, and the fabulous are the objects of choice. Stage direc-tions, monologues, and dialogues intertwine with the voice of the author and the voices of Anthony, of his disciple Ilarione, and of the devil who has taken the shape of the latter; but most of all we hear the voices of beings of all kinds who present themselves, and most of the time define themselves, in succession.

We are confronted by a plurality of peoples, foods, and currencies:[54] Of heretics ("all of them accosting you to argue and convince" [63]), and their assertions, narrations, and exclamations that rage there. Of regions, cities, distances traveled ("how big the earth is!" thinks Anthony [149]); certain merchants "require forty-three interpreters on their journey" (86). Of gods, those of each people unknown to others, whose procession ("how many there are! what do they want?" [166]) ranges from talismans and idols to eastern and Olympian gods, all the way to Jehovah. Of animals that will en-ter, or at least could enter, Borges' manual of fantastic zoology. How many and how varied are the direct objects—for example, in the offerings of the queen of Sheba ("Here . . ." "Would you like . . . I have . . ." [84–89]) or of Apollonius of Tiana ("I will make you . . ." "You will understand . . ." "I will explain to you . . ." [158–59]).

But it gets worse, as I was saying. The reappearance of Apollonius, pre-sumed dead, makes the saint cry out: "Like Him!" (155). Among the divini-ties in the procession, the most bloodthirsty of them gives the false disciple the pretext to allude to the sacrifices demanded by the Hebraic-Christian God; a three-faced God is the pretext for enunciating the dogma of the trin-ity. The life of Buddha recalls in more than one place the Gospels; Venus weeping on the dead Adonis recalls the mother of Jesus. Aside from resem-blance or lineage, there is always a succession linking the false religions to the true one. If Anthony, an Egyptian, calls Isis shameless, the reply is: "Re-spect her! It was the religion of your forbears! You wore her amulets in your cradle" (183). The Greek gods still have worshipers, the beauty of their cult deserves to be idealized, and the patriarchal regret for the household gods sounds affectionate.

Further east there were monstrous gods, and yet "You have just wit-nessed the belief of several hundred million men" (171). After the Old Tes-tament God at the end of the row, Ilarion says: "All but I!" But he cannot reveal himself as the devil without immediately redefining himself: "I am

---

[54] The edition used here is G. Flaubert, *La tentation de Saint Antoine* (1874) (Paris: Garnier, 1954). Page numbers are cited parenthetically in the text.

called Science" (203). And in Ilarion's dialogue in flight, while he is carrying Anthony among the stars, the visions only suggest rational objects of modern beliefs: astronomy and pantheism. Jupiter and Saturn survive as names of the planets. One stage direction makes mention of "all the planets and stars which man will later discover" (208), the only words in which the supernatural flight makes direct and explicit reference to a contact between modernity and antiquity: between, that is, modernity, whose attraction is always masked by the allegorical-referential connection in the rest of the text, and antiquity, whose suggestiveness the connection exploits.

It was unlikely that the two juxtaposed statuses we have considered might live together for more than one century, without cross-breeding and mixing their characteristics. The staging in legend characterizing one of them is rarely compatible with the prospective presentation typical of the other. This is, however, the case in *Ondina* by de La Motte-Fouqué (1811), at least in the first seven chapters: after that, the elemental creature will start explaining her own nature. When it is located in contemporary and daily life, the question stemming from ignorance frequently remains thematic, without affecting principally, or after having ceased to affect, the issue of substantiality. In other words, we do not question so much, or no longer, *if* the supernatural exists; rather, we do not know what it is, and why it is, and what it means. Judging from the answers emerging from the texts of this kind, when we compare them with the allegorical-referential connection I have treated so far, the greatest missing element seems to be historicity: in what degree is it fundamental?

When we shift our emphasis from whether the supernatural exists to *what* it is, we reduce, in various ways and measures, the distance between the supernatural of ignorance and that of transposition. This change of emphasis works also, by the way, as an antidote to the widespread temptation to deny the existence of the supernatural of ignorance in texts written in the first person: we deprive doubt of any terror and interest, we apply at any cost the category of the "unreliable narrator," and we reduce everything to hallucination, psychology, and subjectivity. Prized victims are Henry James's *The Turn of the Screw*, and more anachronistically Hogg's astonishing *Memories and Private Confessions of a Redeemed Sinner* (1824). In the key not of *if* but of *what*, Cazzote's *The Devil in Love* (1772) is better suited to occupy the position of forerunner that Todorov attributed to it. I am reduced to naming random texts in chronological order: Chamisso's *The Wonderful Story of Peter Schlemihl*, Mary Shelley's *Frankenstein*, Stevenson's *The Strange Case of Dr. Jekyll and Mr. Hyde*, and Bram Stoker's *Dracula*.

The Tyranny of the Arbitrary

Kafka's *The Metamorphosis* (1916) asserts its own escape from the real in just three lines, with the same iron fist we spoke of for *The Library of Babel*. For the status that these two texts share, I would like to speak of a supernatural of *compulsion*. "As Gregor Samsa awoke one morning from uneasy dreams he found himself transformed in his bed into a giant insect."[55] The abrupt beginnings are, however, mirror opposites. In Borges, were it not for the indispensable residues, the displacement of the ordinary universe would be total. In Kafka, the departure from the unaltered totality of our world is absolutely singular. If the status in question was widespread in the twentieth century, we must compare it with both of its antecedent statuses, not merely with the fantastic.

Both the supernatural of ignorance and the supernatural of compulsion alike conquer daily life. But all the formal mediations, such as perspective and first-person narration, which would suit an ontological substance in doubt, become superfluous when such substance is imposed instantaneously. One can say anything to the reader, show anything to the characters, and do so all at once—like Gregor's metamorphosis in just one line. Compared with the the supernatural of transposition, the supernatural of compulsion is not only more absolute and aggressive. It also changes the sanction of the allegorical-referential connection that it still requires: we can no longer pin down singular, determinate, or, still less, historical referents, just as we no longer encounter entities that define themselves for us.

Let us be cautious, however, that in the absence of precise referents, we do not fall into nonsense or into whatever sense we choose. There is something in between: in our case, between understanding the metamorphosis as a deadly illness or oedipal punishment or anti-Semitic discrimination, and claiming that the meaning is indecipherable, leaving its tremedous effect unaccounted for. In between the all or nothing of interpretation, there are smaller and larger meanings available to us—large and narrow enough to force this reader to lose his breath, clamped within the text: the sudden, the irreversible, the inability to communicate, marginalization, degradation, reconaissance, progression, adaptation, resignation, elimination, and many others.

No less strange than the initial imposition is the readiness with which the characters accept it. It is eminently unrealistic that it poses no problem, or at

---

[55] Franz Kafka, *Collected Stories*, ed. Gabriel Josipovici (New York: Everyman's Library, 1993), 75. Subsequent quotations are cited parenthetically in the text by page number.

least not as big a one as would be the case if the absurd hypothesis were to explode in reality; once we have moved beyond that imperturbability, nothing is more realistic than the rest of the text. These are things that have repeatedly been observed. But if they are true, we can rethink them as a compromise-formation: once again, the rules by which the supernatural is shaped, and the degree of trust that it hoards, implicate one another. The supernatural of compulsion assumes its full power just as does the supernatual of transposition, but in totally different ways (more powerful than that of ignorance, just slightly less so than that of tradition).

The befuddling impropriety of the character's first thoughts set the tone. An ordinary anxiety about train schedules and the likely medical-bureaucratic consequences, the almost humorous displacements of emotional reactions: "Gregor's eyes turned next to the window, and the overcast sky—one could hear raindrops beating on the window gutter—made him quite melancholy" (75). The reactions of all the others—his sister, his parents, the accountant, the first and the second maid, the three boarders—will always lack problematic specificity, however horrified or disgusted they might be. What has befallen the family is just a "disgrace," even if it is the greatest disgrace to have befallen their circle of family and friends (113). The immediate, indignant disappointment of the boarders differs very little from what could happen had they witnessed the dirty spectacle of a real cockroach or mouse (121).

The problems of the initial imposition posed to Gregor and the others as mere imposition do not hinder the normalization of the supernatural as such. As for Gregor, he immediately begins to explore his own body—or, better yet, the relationship between his body and the world: a body and a relationship that have suddenly become mysterious. The road from the first shocking perceptions (his underbelly and legs flailing in the air, itch and shivers, his squeaking voice) through his reassuring or demoralizing discoveries (his shell is bendable, his legs are sticky, his teeth have been replaced by strong jaws, he is able to adhere perfectly to the ground, but going backward is disorienting), to his final free, animalistic happiness (crawling along the walls, hanging from the ceiling) is a long one. If there is a progression of knowledge, it occurs in the field of knowing, not in the field of understanding. It does not take as its object the metamorphosis, that is to say, the supernatural; it directs a myopic gaze within it, which leaves its arbitrariness untouched.

A moral rediscovery, even more excruciating, follows this physical exploration. It consists in Gregor's adaptation to his own adaptation, in his resignation to his resignation. In the meantime, the others slowly grow accustomed to him, in a way both complementary and divergent. Less and less in the sense that they accept him with empathy, and more and more in the sense that they treat him with irritated indifference; all the way to their deadly rejection of him and the removal of the carcass. Through a prolonged figure of reticence or litotes, the imposition of the supernatural refers to a vague but indisputable core of pathos, which is inexpressible in natural terms. Gregor is never understood even as he continues to understand; the others are confident that he cannot understand. To spare his sister the sight of him it is not enough to hide himself under the couch; rather, it is necessary to drape a sheet over it, and "it cost him four hours' labor" (101). Only when the agonizing character is a cockroach do sentences like the last one, reflecting his interiority, become moving: "He thought of his family with tenderness and love" (124). Then the third-person narrative can close over him, fluidly shifting its gaze onto the relief—more frank than ashamed—of the others.

What will happen, in the next fifty years, to the use of the word *surrealism*? Will it be used, as happened with *romanticism*, in a wider literary-historical sense than the strict designation of a school or an avant-garde? Insofar as it is a systematic vindication, in the twentieth century, of—among other things—the supernatural, surrealism would deserve to claim a Kafka or a Borges as its own. The long-standing relationship between French literature and the supernatural, is, when we think about it, curious. It was the literature that had shaped the Arthurian myths in the twelfth-century, bestowing on Europe an inexhaustible subject matter from the thirteenth to the sixteenth centuries. At the same time, starting from the age of scholastic, not Cartesian, reason, it is as if French literature had been deprived of the strongest statuses of the supernatural—comparatively speaking, of course. France never had, not even in the nineteenth century, its Goethe or its Wagner; nor (*pace* Gautier, Maupassant, and others) its Hoffmann or Poe, its Stevenson or James.

In the most celebrated surrealistic narrative, Breton's *Nadja*, his commitment to autobiographical, anagraphical, and photographical truthfulness, precludes resorting to invention. The presumption that the marvelous is widespread in the ordinary naturalizes the pursuit of the marvelous. Thanks to an effect of veto and counterveto, the supernatural, in the end, remains at large. It is necessary to return to the great precursors whom Breton claimed—if not to the distant Swift, then to the truculent, unflinching, and excessive Lautreamont. In his *Songs of Maldoror*, mockery had been turned against the ascendant postivism. Or we have to leave surrealism in the strict sense and look outside of France, and, sooner or later outside, of Europe itself.

The texts I regret I could not make room for here are part of Western literature, but belong to traditions that developed far away from the old center. In closing, I would like to mention the crowning achievement of the most recent of the supernatural statuses I have treated in chronological order (tradition, mockery, indulgence, transposition, and compulsion). If we move the first of these five to the end, and if we treat the last two as equivalent, we can see a gradual proportion of increasing trust and decreasing critique, or the other way around.

I am thinking of Bulgakov's *Master and Margarita*—if I knew Russian I would have discussed it here—for its light, ferocious, bloodthirsty, satanic, sumptuous, awesome tautological supernatural: a punitive denial of its materialistic and bureaucratic deniers. Also, I am thinking of Cortázar and his short story "Letters of a Mother", where the collapse of a defensive insincerity, together with the non-impunity from guilt, produce in the end something like an annulment of death, which in itself fails to impress all that much. And finally, I allude to García Márquez's *One Hundred Years of Solitude*, in which equatorial nature overheats reality so much that the first to endorse the surreal are the obsessions with science and technology of an incurable and progressive Don Quixote.

Translated by Simone Marchesi and Daniel Seidel

MICHAL PELED GINSBURG
LORRI G. NANDREA

The Prose of the World

> This is the prose of the world, as it appears to the
> consciousness both of the individual himself and of
> others—a world of finitude and mutability, of
> entanglement in the relative, of the pressure of necessity
> from which the individual is in no position to withdraw.
> —G.W.F. HEGEL, *Aesthetics*

"The prose of the world": for Hegel, this phrase indicts all the external factors that limit an individual's freedom and independence, hindering "the
higher aims of spirit."[1] Circumstances, accidents, illness, natural needs, social systems and conventions, everyday obstacles; the aims and demands of
others, which reduce one to a means; the need to use others as means to
achieve one's own ends—all this is "prose." This "world of prose and everyday" is one of contingency, wherein the individual is rendered relative, tied
to context, "intelligible not from himself, but from something else" (149).
As that which prevents individuals from teleologically realizing an implicit
internal totality, "prose" impedes transcendence. In contrast to "the look of
independence and total life and freedom that lies at the root of the essence
of beauty" (149), moreover, "prose" is a kind of ugliness. Its deficiencies
produce a need for the beauty of art, "through which the poverty of nature
and prose no longer peeps" (152). Art lifts truth "out of its temporal setting;
out of its straying away into a series of finites" (152), leaving prose behind.

But why use the word *prose* to describe this state of affairs? And conversely, what does this expression reveal about prose, or "prosaic" texts such
as the novel? Though Hegel's formulation articulates a line of thought specific to his philosophy, the expression "the prose of the world" carries wider
resonance, suggesting that by the late eighteenth century a certain notion of
the everyday and of prose as a particular kind of discourse may have become
interdependent, and at the same time opposed to terms that carry higher
value (the spiritual, the transcendent, the poetic). Common usage bears this
out: the *Oxford English Dictionary* defines prose as "the ordinary form of

---

[1] G.W.F. Hegel, *Aesthetics: Lectures on Fine Art*, trans. T. M. Knox (1835; Oxford: Clarendon,
1975), 149. The passage quoted in the epigraph is on 150. All further quotes from Hegel are to this
edition and will be given within the text.

written or spoken language, without metrical structure . . . opposed to *poetry*, *verse*, *rime*, or *metre*." Used figuratively, the word means "plain, simple, matter-of-fact, (and hence) dull or commonplace expression, quality, spirit, etc." Likewise, *prosaic*: "lacking poetic beauty, feeling, or imagination; . . . unpoetic, unromantic; commonplace, dull, tame ('Do you get impatient with the prosaic life around you—the dullness, and the earthliness and the brutishness of men?'; 'Marriage settlements are very prosaic things')."

The figurative use of *prose* to describe the dull or commonplace is rather paradoxical, since one of the attributes of prose is its "straightforwardness" (the word is derived from the Latin *prorsus*, "straightforward, straight, direct"), hence, its lack of the "turns" (tropes) or figuration associated instead with verse. The use of the supposedly straightforward as a trope suggests the inevitable entanglement of prose and verse. Indeed, the notion that prose as common, everyday language dispenses with figures of speech (considered an artistic add-on) and that writing prose means "simply" reproducing the "normal" language common people use in everyday life is clearly untenable; no language can totally dispense with figuration, and the impression of "plainness" is merely an effect of a particular use of figuration (for example, the privileging of metonymy over metaphor). Equally untenable is the notion that prose is free of "turns" in the sense of disruptions to forward movement. True, poetry highlights "turns" in the form of line breaks, as well as rhyme and meter, whose effect depends on what came before (turning back), in contrast to prose whose sense depends on what lies ahead (the end of a sentence; the next event in the plot of a novel). But various forms of "linking forward" occur in verse (cf. enjambement), and pauses in which one rests and reflects back regularly occur in prose (paragraph and chapter breaks, as well as the final rupture of forward movement that constitutes the end).

In their study of the history of prose in France, Jeffrey Kittay and Wlad Godzich trace the manner in which prose and poetry get constructed as opposites of each other during the modern "emergence of prose" in the fourteenth century.[2] This emergence of prose is related to a change in structures of authority. Whereas the authority of verse was invested in the person of the performer, prose, in the Middle Ages, established its authority mainly by making a claim to referential truth (Kittay and Godzich, 153). This is also the manner in which the novel established its authority in its youth, especially in England. In both cases the emergence of a "new" form—prose, the novel—is anchored in class-based struggles not only for

---

[2] *The Emergence of Prose: An Essay in Prosaics* (Minneapolis: University of Minnesota Press, 1987), 145–47, 153–55, 187–95. Further references will be given within the text.

epistemological authority but also for social power and political legitimacy. We can get a sense of the extent to which prose has succeeded in establishing its authority from the surprising fact that at a certain historical moment it required a particular effort *not* to write verse (Kittay and Godzich, 28–39). Prose has come to appear "natural": what we all, like Molière's M. Jourdain, speak without even knowing it and write without needing a special talent or art.

As a noun, *prose* carries potentially positive connotations: the accessible, honest, unadorned telling of things as they truly are—"the frank prose of undissembling noon" (*OED*). Yet if prose can claim moral and epistemological superiority (as opposed especially to "verse," which is, etymologically at least, linked to "fraud or imposition" [*OED*]), the "prosaic" world is defined by a lack: lack of beauty and art, imagination, feeling, and spirit. The world of prose is one where poetry is lacking; the world of poetry is inhibited, destroyed, or produced as a fantasmatic other by the world of prose. This widespread negative valorization of the prosaic, in which Hegel clearly participates, directs our attention to a paradox that we can see in different forms in many literary texts: Though as a culture we embrace the values with which prose is associated (the straightforward, the common, the egalitarian) we still cannot think of *prosaic* but as a pejorative term; though prose is considered to have the moral high ground, the "real" superiority is felt to be all on the side of its supposed opposite, poetry. The presence of such an "inferiority complex" in texts dating from the rise of the novel might be explained by the hegemony of poetic, heroic values in the world where the new form of prose writing struggled to achieve acceptance and authority. But the notion that the prosaic is inherently negative, defined by lack and loss, lingers long after aristocracy has been dismantled and the novel has become a dominant literary form. Prose achieves hegemony—indeed, becomes Hegel's figure for the prevailing state of affairs—but "the poetic" continues to name that which has greater sway over our imagination and desires. Literary texts in which the contest between poetry and prose is in some way staged suggest that this may be the case because, on the one hand, prose can never make good its claim to truth and thus never achieves full legitimacy, and on the other hand, wealth, associated with beauty, romance, imagination, and creativity, creates a new version of the "poetic" in the world of capital.

Though one cannot equate prose with novels, it can be argued that Hegel's notion of the "prose of the world" is particularly pertinent to the study of the novel because some elements (or versions) of this concept became common thematic concerns. But though the prosaic world of the everyday, of the common man, of the home and its cares, is what the "truthful" language of prose was called on to valorize by making it an object of serious representation, it is also true that novels perpetuate the notion that the real is "prosaic" in the negative sense of the term. Indeed, novels often do so even at their own expense, claiming, somewhat self-contradictorily, that "poetry" and "romance" exist only in . . . novels. Thus, for example, the most prosaic—indeed, prosy—of novelists, Trollope: "Romance is very pretty in novels, but the romance of a life is always a melancholy matter."[3] Trollope here practices a sleight of hand typical to realism: the text distances itself from art that would overcome the perceived deficiencies of the real, but does so by attributing such artfulness to the novel as a genre while disavowing its own status as one of that genre. While the status of novels as true representations of the world is here both implied and denied, one thing is unambiguously asserted: the world is prosaic—infelicitous, dreary, constraining. Within novels, books and reading often appear to represent an elsewhere to this prosaic reality, as does the idea of a noble, heroic, "poetic" past. The world of the past and the world of books, as two alternatives to a dystopic present, are sometimes directly linked (the books represent a past, or are artifacts of a past) but more often resemble each other only in being above and apart from "the prose of world" (represented in novels and presumed to exist outside them) whose deficiencies they may thus seem to highlight.

There is, however, another line of thought (to be found in both novels and critical discourses) that sees prose as "new" in the sense of unpredictable, free, and infinitely open and takes its "messiness," heterogeneity, and unpredictability as positive values. Such an understanding of prose and the novel can be gleaned from the (suitably unsystematic) writings of Bakhtin,[4] but it is significant that despite his popularity, Bakhtin's radical view of prose and the novel has not become the dominant one. Similarly, ideals of unsystematicity, irreducible heterogeneity, freedom, and creativity appear in the writing of various novelists at different historical moments, but they often cannot be fully embraced (by the novelist, narrator, or characters). Ironically, it is even possible that particular characteristics of prose as a medium compromise novelists' attempts to represent the world of relations and contingency from this angle and thus celebrate, rather than denigrate, truth's "straying away into a series of finites" (Hegel, 152).

---

[3] *He Knew He Was Right* (1869; New York: Dover, 1983), 1:272.

[4] For a discussion of Bakhtin's notion of prose, see Gary Saul Morson and Caryl Emerson, *Mikhail Bakhtin: Creation of a Prosaics* (Stanford, Calif.: Stanford University Press, 1990), esp. 15–40.

Writing Prose: Middlemarch, The Waves

George Eliot's *Middlemarch* can be seen as a perfect illustration of Hegel's notion of the "prose of the world." Just as in Hegel's account "the higher aims of spirit" are hindered by external determinations, so Dorothea's and Lydgate's noble aspirations are hampered by the middling, meddling medium of Middlemarch. Dorothea's predicament is specifically attributed to her belatedness: a Saint Theresa in the nineteenth century, she is compared at the very beginning of the novel to "a fine quotation from the Bible, or from one of our older poets" that, unfortunately, finds itself inserted "in a paragraph of to-day's newspaper."[5] Thus, implicitly, it is the world that has become as prosaic as today's newspaper, leaving no room for, indeed actively hindering, poetic souls.

But the difference between Dorothea's lot and that of her impossible model is not, really, that the latter could carry out her noble goals unhindered whereas the former finds in the world only limitation and constraints: after all, Saint Theresa too has seen her quest for martyrdom thwarted by "domestic reality . . . in the shape of uncles" (3). The difference lies, rather, in the way the struggle between individual aspirations and restrictive reality becomes—or does not become—endowed with meaning. If Saint Theresa's life could achieve epic grandeur in spite of "domestic reality in the shape of uncles" it is because, unlike Dorothea, she found in the world around her shared structures of intelligibility within which her ardent aspirations could become meaningful: "She found her epos in the reform of a religious order" (3). If Dorothea's life, on the other hand, appears as "a life of mistakes," "blundering," and "no epic life," it is at least in part because she was "helped by no coherent social faith and order which could perform the function of knowledge for [her] ardently willing soul" (3). For a life to achieve intelligibility, let alone grandeur, the self, like the poet, has to confront limits and constraints within which its aspirations would appear meaningful. The problem with the "prose of the world," then, is not—or not so much—that it poses obstacles to the aspirations of the soul but that it is formless. The prose of the world is then the product of the loss of enabling, meaning-producing, forms—social, epistemological, and literary.

Eliot does not ignore the capacity of domestic reality and the mediocrity of environment ("hindrances," "meanness of opportunity") to crush the aspirations of the individual, as the story of Lydgate amply demonstrates. But

---

[5] *Middlemarch* (1874; Boston: Houghton Mifflin, Riverside Edition, 1968), 5. All references to *Middlemarch* are to this edition and will be given within the text.

she also ironizes, especially through the example of Rosamund, the conceit of a "stupendous self" who sees "the universe as a trap of dullness in which [its] great soul has fallen by mistake" (473). The stupendous self is just a selfish one, and the dullness of the world is just the fact that there are in it "disagreeable people" (Rosamund's expression for Lydgate's creditors) who have their own desires. It may therefore be enough to espouse the point of view of others (through sympathy, identification, and imagination) and take a closer look at the behavior of others—as through a microscope (43–44)—for the relation between self and world to lose much of its binary, antagonistic neatness and start appearing as a complex and not entirely predictable interplay of innumerable forces. Alienation and ennui, according to that view, are merely errors of interpretation, caused by narrow vision. The old "forms" now reveal their other side: enabling and productive of meaning as they were, they functioned through the exclusion of many points of view owing to an interested privileging of a few. Thus Eliot gestures toward a notion of prose far different from that formulated by Hegel.

This view of the prose of the world as an extension of vision that overcomes the limits produced by our (personal and collective) self-centeredness, is not unproblematic in Eliot. The decentered vision may be less "coarse," but can end up being "diffused"; it may be more detailed, but the accumulation of details, all at least potentially meaningful (meaningful from some point of view), may create a crisis of meaning. The narrator points out the problem explicitly: "If we had a keen vision and feeling of all ordinary human life, it would be like hearing the grass grow and the squirrel's heart beat, and we should die of that roar which lies on the other side of silence." Hence our need to be "wadded with stupidity" (144). This stupidity is a certain blindness and deafness that excludes things from our field of perception (and hence also from representation). The limits and constraints that were first seen as the condition of possibility for the creation of the "poetic" and meaningful, then as forms (of knowledge, of social interaction, of representation) imposed by a self motivated by personal or class interests, reappear now as the necessary limit for prose, for the infinite, decentered, unhierarchized world it tries to capture. The notion of the novel as a "slice of life," as well as the investment in "closure" can be understood as historically specific solutions to the problem of limitless prose articulated by Eliot.

Eliot suggests that the prose of the world, when seen as unhierarchized, decentered, multiperspectival, is not only "diffusive" (as opposed to poetry which is "dense," as in *"Dichtung"*) but also unpredictable. The metaphor of the "web" she uses in order to describe social relations can be understood as an image for the overdetermination of social relations: the individual (every individual) is not engaged in a dual relation with another individual whereby each responds to and prompts the action of the other; rather, every action participates in multiple chains of events, involving many independent agents and intersecting in an unforeseen manner. We can find such a view of social relations in the novels of Balzac where the rise and fall of the hero comes through the convergence of unrelated and quite trivial acts of different agents; that the hero of one novel can reappear as a secondary character in another novel suggests that we can see the same story from different points of view or see different parts of the story: what was a point of convergence in one tale is a negligible event in another. But whereas Balzac sees this complexity of the world as exciting (since it generates endless plots), Eliot often views the weblike nature of the world negatively, as when she speaks of the "hampering threadlike pressure of small social conditions and their frustrating complexity" (133–34). In addition, *Middlemarch* (especially its subplot) can be seen as adhering to another view of the web of relations, one we see, for example, in Dickens, where interrelations are determined and events are produced by one original act—indeed, an original sin.

Eliot's wavering between different views of the prose of the world is evident throughout the novel. Just as Dorothea, a belated Saint Theresa, could not find an "epic" life, so Eliot, a belated historian, cannot write the epic novel that was possible for Fielding. In the end, Dorothea seems reconciled to the fact that "the effect of her being" will remain "incalculably diffusive," and the narrator seems to agree that this is not such a sad state of affairs (while continuing to ascribe it to the self's being "determined by what lies outside it"). But Eliot has certainly not produced a novel that is the proper medium for that experience. Though judged to be formless (Henry James's famous "baggy monster"), the novel is a willed effort at concentration. Contrasting her novel with that of Fielding, Eliot explicitly justifies limiting her scope to "this particular web," "concentrating" her "light" rather than "dispersing" it (105). Though Eliot proposes, implicitly at least, to "reform" the novel through an extension of the franchise (recall that the Reform Bill is the main political event in the novel), and though the novel insists on not being centered on one self and on seeing things from different points of view, it is clearly hierarchized: the struggles of Dorothea are a worthy topic for serious drama, whereas the travails of the truly prosaic Garths are treated as comedy. Similarly, though she gestures toward an affirmative embracing of the prose of the world as productive of the new, the incalculable, and the nonsystemic, though she advocates a humanistic, democratic prose that grants "unhistoric acts," "not widely visible" issues, and "hidden" lives (613) their due, she does not give up entirely the negative notion of the prose of the world (the world as hindering the self, prose as inconsistency resulting from the loss of forms).

Like other modern novelists (Stein, Joyce, Proust), Virginia Woolf attempts to revalue this "incalculably diffusive" world of prose. In *The Waves*, diffusion of spirit is not the result of failure or blockage, the consolation prize when an individual cannot achieve transcendental aspirations. The ongoing process of becoming oneself takes place altogether within a milieu of relations and connections (to nature, bodies, objects, books, other people, and social machinery), a milieu that is quintessentially "prosaic" in that nothing is independent, nothing is unique or absolute, everything is in relation to other things equally dependent. Events, encounters, and accidental perceptions have the power to send ripples through the fabric of the narrative without regard to their objective magnitude; indeed, there is no standard by which one might calculate the magnitude of an event. Everything is charged with potential significance, a fact of which Bernard, in particular, is keenly aware:

> To speak, about wine even to the waiter, is to bring about an explosion. . . .
> The entirely unexpected nature of this explosion—that is the joy of intercourse. I, mixed with an unknown Italian waiter—what am I? There is no stability in this world. Who is to say what meaning there is in anything? Who is to foretell the flight of a word? It is a balloon that sails over tree-tops. To speak of knowledge is futile. All is experiment and adventure. We are forever mixing ourselves with unknown quantities.[6]

Yet while the novel explores and often celebrates the aesthetic and subjective potential of this common realm of everyday happenstance, it also highlights the difficulties involved in representing such "prose." Bernard records his perceptions in an alphabetized notebook of "phrases to be used when I have found the true story, the one story to which all these phrases refer" (187). Despite his delight in the promiscuous potential of the self to alter through minor relations and encounters, this search for story in a dehierarchized world gives rise, as in Eliot, to a problem of selection: "Look now from this terrace at the swarming population beneath. . . . I could break off any detail in all that prospect—say the mule cart—and describe it with the

---

[6] *The Waves* (1931; New York: HBJ, 1978), 117–18. All references to *The Waves* are to this edition and will be given within the text.

greatest ease. But why describe a man in trouble with his mule? . . . Why stress this and shape that and twist up little figures like the toys men sell in trays in the street? Why select this, out of all that,—one detail?" (187–88). Rather than resolving this problem, Bernard simply moves on, and as he moves, the problem disappears:

> But observe how dots and dashes are beginning, as I walk, to run themselves into continuous lines, how things are losing the bald, the separate identity that they had as I walked up those steps. . . . I am moving too, am becoming involved in the general sequence when one thing follows another and it seems inevitable that the tree should come, then the telegraph-pole, then the break in the hedge. And as I move, surrounded, included and taking part, the usual phrases begin to bubble up. . . . (188)

Walking forward provides the physical equivalent of syntax, creating sequence and continuity, lending itself to phrasing. This movement—a mode of combination—erases the problem of selection because Bernard is no longer the chooser. He is "involved in the general sequence," more like a reader than a writer, one for whom the sequence seems inevitable because it has already been chosen.

In the novel as a whole, the act of choosing is the apparent activity of an abstract narrator whose presence is indicated by the signal phrases ("Bernard said") and the italicized descriptions of sun and sea that section the book into intervals. Unlike Bernard's walking prose, the novel's own movement is not entirely straightforward: its continuity is based on rotation—rhythmic, cyclical, repetitive movements (the sun, the waves, Bernard said . . . said Rhoda). Moreover, each monologue (except Bernard's closing monologue) is spoken in the same verb tense—the pure present, without progressives, producing time itself as a uniform field that is folded over by the simple past tense of the narrator's signal phrases. This present and this past are never situated in relation to each other. The monologues, the relations and perceptions they record, are thus "unhistoric" in a somewhat different sense than Eliot intended when she used the word to describe Dorothea's acts. Instead of a chronology, we are confronted with a series of present moments, all of which are past, each of which becomes multiple as it is registered from different perspectives, all on the same temporal plane. Prose here unfolds the complexity of particular moments, spreading each moment out horizontally rather than creating a straightforward time line.

Yet the narrator must choose who speaks first, who speaks second, and so on, constructing a sequence that will be read in/as time. In this sense, the novel remains bound by the linear, forward movement of prose. If the novel cannot escape this current, however, one character does. In contrast to Bernard, who is unable to select, Rhoda is unable to combine: "One moment does not lead to another. . . . I cannot make one moment merge in the next. To me they are all violent, all separate" (130). She lacks the perceptual syntax that would coordinate moments in a forward flow. Her predicament suggests that without a principle of syntactic continuity to link individual moments (or individual consciousnesses), one is left with the "violence" of discrete perception. Though novelist and characters seem to reach for a third alternative—a form for the simultaneous, the multiple, the diffusive—such an alternative is excluded by the linear nature of prose: the novel can only relate multiple, concurrent, mutually inflected consciousnesses by sequentially presenting a series of individual perspectives. Thus, while Woolf's virtually plotless novel succeeds in eradicating certain social and literary hierarchies, hierarchies of being and significance that Eliot retained, it reveals another tension in the idea of prose. Syntax—the ability to combine things horizontally, "articulate," add, and extend—suggests the relational, the dependent, and the joined. But because it is a linear medium, prose lacks the capacity to articulate simultaneously, and thus pulls irresistibly back toward the individual, the separate, the unifocal. Syntax is thus proposed as both what can "involve" one in this world of prose (world of relations) and as what occludes relations, retaining the discreteness of that which is joined while channeling for the reader a single central course.

In his closing monologue, Bernard confronts these problems. By now, he has become aware of the artificiality of sequences as they appear in stories, and also of discrete forms, but he is unable to narrate without them: "Let us again pretend that life is a solid substance, shaped like a globe. . . . Let us pretend that we can make out a plain and logical story" (251). Uncomfortably aware that "Life is not suceptible perhaps to the treatment we give it when we try to tell it" (267), he believes that all orders and designs falsify the surge of ordinary life, "a rushing stream of broken dreams, nursery rhymes, street cries, half-finished sentences and sights—elm trees, willow trees, gardeners sweeping, women writing—that rise and sink even as we hand a lady down to dinner" (255). Wishing to represent this stream, Bernard grows frustrated with the linear pace of prose: "there should be music . . . a painful, guttural, visceral, also soaring, lark-like, pealing song to replace these flagging, foolish transcripts—how much too deliberate! How much too reasonable! . . . What is the use of painfully elaborating these consecutive sentences when what one needs is nothing consecutive but a bark, a groan?" (250–51). He begins to desire a language that would be closer to things, more sensory, less formal: "I need a little language such as lovers use, words of one syllable such as children speak when they come into the room and find their mother sewing. . . . I need a howl; a cry. . . . None of these resonances and lovely echoes that break and chime from nerve to nerve in our breasts making wild music, false phrases. I have done with phrases" (295).

In describing what for him is the failure of prose, Bernard's lines incorporate a sensory and emotional density traditionally associated with poetry. As a whole, the novel incorporates poetic elements, using lyric language, rhythm, and repetition, tampering with the boundary between prose and verse, demonstrating that this boundary may not lie between texts. Poetry, the poetic, and the spiritual are not proposed as something that would be external to prose, an elsewhere to the ordinary. Because prose does not here oppose or exclude verse, in his dissatisfaction with his medium Bernard reaches beneath both, under language in general, for something like a pure signal. The other of prose here is not a poem, but a howl or a cry.

In *Middlemarch*, Eliot ambivalently critiques the perception that the web of everyday relations hampers the aspirations of the individual and prevents greatness, miring one in the mundane. But she suggests that the alternative to this perception—the notion that the realm of tiny everyday interactions might carry its own "incalculably diffusive" significance—is both risky to the individual (one must be "well wadded") and impossible for the novelist to trace. In *The Waves*, Woolf has constructed a novel that would trace such "fine issues" (Eliot, 613), not just those of a single individual (Dorothea's "channels"), but the mutual inflections of a group ("waves"). Yet Woolf's attempt to represent "the prose of the world" as a full, interesting, and often beautiful milieu in which one's being is altogether invested—formed rather than impeded by ordinary events, perceptions, and connections—is to some extent limited by the very medium that was for Hegel this world's metaphor. Together, these novels suggest that the nature of prose itself, as well as certain conventions of the genre, can become obstacles to the representation of the nonlinear diffusion of significance and the innumerable unsequenced horizontal relations that characterize this everyday world.

Prose in Time: Don Quixote, Jude the Obscure, Madame Bovary

In tracing the history of the prose of the world, *Don Quixote* functions as a mythical starting point. Michel Foucault positions the novel on the border between two discontinuous epistemes.[7] In the first, governed by principles of resemblance, similitude, analogy, and correspondence, words are things just as things are signs, grounded by the "absolutely initial" word of God.[8] In the second, governed by principles of identity and difference, "resemblances and signs have dissolved their former alliance; . . . [things] are no longer anything but what they are; words wander off on their own, without context, without resemblance to fill their emptiness; they are no longer the marks of things" (47–48). Don Quixote himself belongs to the first episteme: "He is the hero of the Same. He never manages to escape from the familiar plain stretching out on all sides of the Analogue . . . he travels endlessly over that plain, without ever crossing the clearly defined frontiers of difference, or reaching the heart of identity" (46). Taking the romances of Amadis de Gaule as a script for his own adventures, he attempts to find in reality the confirmation and proof that his books "really are the language of the world" (47). But Don Quixote's endeavor is triply doomed. Not only does his own prosaic present fail to match the world of romance; the books of romance were never intended to represent reality: "those extravagant romances are, quite literally, unparalleled: no one in the world ever did resemble them" (47). The network of correspondences in which the romance had a place, moreover, is no longer operative. Don Quixote does not understand the nature of his failure and attributes it to sorcery; the prosaic world becomes for him the world of romance distorted by a terrible spell. But in the second part of the novel, Cervantes' narrative begins to play the role that the romances of Amadis played in the first. Don Quixote, "the real man," has "become a book that contains his truth—that records exactly all that he has done and said" (48). Don Quixote's truth, however, "is not in the relation of the words to the world but in that slender and constant relations woven between themselves by verbal signs. . . . *Don Quixote* is the first modern work of literature, because in it we see the cruel reason of identities and differences make endless sport of signs and similitudes" (49).

---

[7] Michel Foucault, *The Order of Things: An Archaeology of the Human Sciences*, English trans. of *Les mots et les choses* (1966; New York: Vintage, 1994), 46–50. Further references will be given within the text.

[8] For this reason, Foucault uses the phrase "the prose of the world" to characterize this preseventeenth-century episteme. In this context the phrase carries a meaning very different from Hegel's, referring to the manner in which the world is seen as a text authored by God, a text writing strives to replicate.

Whereas for Hegel "the prose of the world" is lacking in relation to a future that will transcend it, Don Quixote, in Foucault's reading, views his own "prosaic" world as lacking in relation to a superior past. In fact, Foucault's own language betrays a sense of loss ("resemblances and signs have *dissolved* their former alliance; . . . [things] are *no longer* anything but what they are; words wander off on their own, *without* context . . ."), reinforcing the idea that this particular past—the world in which a discourse of correspondences was operative—had a cachet that is missing from later eras. However, if we take into account the reading of the novel *Don Quixote* by subsequent generations of readers, we can see yet a third articulation of the relations between time and the prosaic: the present world is seen as lacking in relation to a past, but this perception depends on the relation between an ever-changing present and the past it generates in its wake (rather than on the intrinsic value of different time periods). Borges, for example, argues that if for Cervantes "the dusty roads and sordid wayside inns of Castille" were prosaic, for the contemporary reader, acquainted with "filling stations," they appear poetic. Cervantes, according to Borges, "did not suspect . . . that La Mancha and Montiel and the knight's lean figure would be, for posterity, no less poetic than the episodes of Sinbad or the vast geographies of Ariosto."[9]

Whereas Foucault's reading sees the meaning of the text as determined by the context of its production, indeed as a sort of parable of its original historical context, Borges sees the text as always open to a future of reading. Thus, in "Pierre Menard, Author of the *Quixote*" Borges suggests that in reading from the perspective of the always changing present (but refusing to "modernize" the past, to erase the difference between it and the present), the Menard-like reader transforms the novel without changing anything in its text. Menard's text is "more subtle than Cervantes'. The latter, in a clumsy fashion opposes to the fictions of chivalry the tawdry provincial reality of his country; Menard selects as his 'reality' the land of Carmen during the century of Lepanto and Lope de Vega."[10] The "reality" of the *Quixote* is no longer prosaic; indeed, it is no longer reality but a text whose meaning has changed and will continue to change in time.

If we follow Borges' lead, we may argue that the prosiness of the world (and of the book) is not a timeless quality (what was prosaic for Cervantes is poetic for a later reader), nor does it inhere in certain features of the world

---

[9] "Parable of Cervantes and the *Quixote*," in *Labyrinths*, ed. Donald A. Yates and James E. Irby (New York: New Directions, 1964), 242. See also "Partial Magic in the *Quixote*," in *Labyrinths*, 193.

[10] *Labyrinths*, 42.

(dusty inns) or in a certain style of writing. The prose of today may become the poetry of tomorrow, opposed to a new prose, a new reality; the two terms are purely relational.

———

The Quixotic predicament does not necessarily involve nostalgia—the pitting of a sordid present against a beautiful and noble past. Rather, it involves, more generally, a particular consciousness of time or historical consciousness that we can associate with prose. On the one hand, what passes is lost forever and is irrevocable; there is no "return." On the other hand, time moves only forward, it is not cyclical, and we always move toward the new and the unknown. Thus in *Jude the Obscure* Hardy describes a "tragic Don Quixote" who, like the Don, longs for the world of books and is often impeded by prosaic needs, "the mean bread-and-cheese question."[11] Jude, according to the narrator, is wrong to long for the world of the past and of books (represented by Christminster), but his misfortunes and Sue's do not come from this error but rather have to do with their being ahead of their time.

Like other characters who feel imprisoned in "the world of prose," Jude's "dreams were as gigantic as his surroundings were small" (26); his yearnings are "for some place which he could call admirable" (29). He sees Christminster, the site of learning and knowledge, as a "heavenly Jerusalem" (24); there, people live "in their minds" just as other, regular folk, live "in their body" (29). Accordingly, Jude's desire to get there is arrested by the temptations of the flesh—Arabella, who is repeatedly associated with pigs. But Jude's difficulties in achieving knowledge are attributed, in the first place, not to the call of the flesh but to the fact that the books he can lay his hands on are old, behind their time, whereas his own notions of the relations among languages "were further advanced than those of his grammarian" (35). Jude's confinement to the "world of prose" has therefore less to do with sexuality than with temporality. And indeed Arabella leaves Jude fairly early on and is replaced as an object of desire by the almost bodyless Sue (she is often called "aerial" [215] or "ethereal" [217]). At the same time, Jude reaches Christminster and discovers that the city of books is also a material city—a city of stones, indeed, of crumbling stones. Not only is it not as beautiful as he thought when he saw it from far away or at night but it is also, unlike the heavenly Jerusalem, subject to time: "What at night had

---

[11] *Jude the Obscure* (1895; New York: Signet, 1961), 203, 86. All references to the novel are to this edition and will be given within the text.

been perfect and ideal was by day the more or less defective real. Cruelties, insults, had, he perceived, been inflicted on the aged erections. The condition of several moved him as he would have been moved by maimed sentient beings. They were wounded, broken, sloughing off their outer shape in a deadly struggle against years, weather, and man" (86). The buildings of Christminster are like bodies, and the damage they suffer is like that inflicted by one human being on another. The spiritual becomes material, and the material becomes social. What hinders Jude's access to the world of the spirit and of books is not his body but a wall, and this wall is a social one—the wall of privilege and class structure (88, 115). Moreover, Jude reaches the conclusion that "the prose of the world" is superior to learning as defined by Christminster: "He began to see that the town life was a book of humanity infinitely more palpitating, varied, and compendious than the gown life" (120). Jude's disenchantment leads him to temporarily denounce his own thirst for knowledge and see his own desire to reach "the heavenly Jerusalem" as but a desire for "social success," a "mundane ambition" (128, 129), part of the world of prose.

The deconstruction of the ideal world of books and knowledge is accompanied by a keen awareness of time. This takes various forms. The narrator's critique of the institution of marriage has to do with the marriage vows' denial of change brought by time; it is an attempt to arrest time and ignore change. As the narrator ironically says: "And so, standing before the aforesaid officiator, the two swore that at every other time of their lives till death took them, they would assuredly believe, feel, and desire precisely as they had believed, felt, and desired during the few preceding weeks" (61–62). The symbolic value attributed to the sexual act strengthens the false notion of permanence, and Jude begins "to inquire what he had done, or she [Arabella] lost, for that matter, that he deserved to be caught in a gin which would cripple him, if not her also, for the rest of a lifetime" (66). If human beings—minds and bodies—change all the time, then the change we see around us is not simply of decay and decline (the nostalgic view). Jude discovers the difference of the present from the past when he visits the stonemason yard. The new carved stones are "the ideas in modern prose which the lichened colleges presented in old poetry. Even some of these antiques might have been called prose when they were new. They had done nothing but wait, and had become poetical. How easy to the smallest building; how impossible to most men" (87). Prose is the new but the truly new is, by definition, transgressive, and by the time it is accepted, consecrated, turned into poetry, it is too late for the particular individual. Prose as newness creates a tragic consciousness of time because of the obduracy of social institutions and their inherently conservative nature. The life of Jude and Sue after their divorces from their first spouses shows this in a hyperbolic fashion. "The grind of stern reality" which has "spoilt" Jude's thirst for knowledge (387) is not so much the need to earn a living or the demands of the flesh as the weight of social conventions and their resistance to change.

It is as champions of prose—of the new—that Jude and Sue not only question conventions per se but also define a radical principle of equality that does not acknowledge the right of any form of exclusivity: "The excessive regard of parents for their own children and their dislike of other people's, is, like class-feeling, patriotism, save-your-own soul-ism, and other virtues, a mean exclusiveness at bottom" (270–71). Thus the novel gestures toward a totally unhierarchical, decentered, free and open world (a world of prose in the positive sense of the term). But it is not at all clear that this world lies in the future: the doctor who attends them after the children's deaths suggests that Father Time's actions signal "the beginning of the coming universal wish not to live" (331). Nor is it certain that were it to come into being it would be more hospitable to the likes of Jude and Sue. At the same time, Jude (and arguably Hardy himself) does not give up entirely the world of Christminster—the world of noble pursuits, of books and learning, but also of outdated modes of thinking, of stifling tradition, and of exclusivity. More significant in this respect than Jude's return to the city is his change of profession: from a stonemason who repairs and renews, he turns into a baker who represents in his pastries the buildings of the city that remained closed to him. This improbable representation in dough indicates how little Jude freed himself of his desire to belong to a world he elsewhere condemns; it also shows a rather naive attempt to overcome the prose of the world through "art."

———

The hatred of the nineteenth century as the century of prose—bourgeois, materialist, philistine, unheroic, with no spirit or beauty—is a topos in French literature of that era and receives explicit thematic treatment in the novels of Stendhal and Flaubert. Probably no other novel has granted more "objective reality" to the world of prose than Flaubert's *Madame Bovary*. The world of Yonville, with Homais and Bournisien, not to mention Charles, Léon, and Rodolphe, is truly mediocre, narrow, and dull. But no other novel perhaps has as clearly argued that the "poetic" or "romantic" aspirations of the self caught in this prosaic reality are fundamentally part of that world. Not only are Emma's desires mediated by a whole array of social discourses (chief among them, novels) but they are also predicated on a mistaken belief (that of a society of commodities, of consumerism) in the quasimagical capacity of objects to transform the world. If Emma's striving to find "felicité," or "passion" is thwarted, the reason is not only the narrowness and meanness of opportunity offered by the provinces; it is also because with all her dreaming she cannot even imagine a truly other world and mistakes difference in setting and props for otherness. For Emma there is no true alternative to the "prose of the world," no temporal or spatial "elsewhere" that is substantially different. For Flaubert himself the only alternative to the hated prosaic world is the oasis of art. But the opposition between art and the "prose of the world" takes on here a special meaning, since Flaubert's art is the art of prose. The aesthetic of prose Flaubert develops in order to create an alternative to the "real" is an aesthetic not of beauty but of difficulty. His ironic definition of prose in the *Dictionaire des idées reçues*—"Prose: Plus facile à faire que le vers" ["Prose: Easier to compose than verse"]—indicates his own contrary belief that prose is as difficult to write and hence, on these grounds, as artistic as verse. His aesthetic is not of poetry, of the inspired, elected bard but of prose, of value gained through labor.

Prose and Verse: Caleb Williams

In his infamous autobiography, Tristram Shandy ponders the discursive entanglements of the seemingly antinomial principles of forward and backward, progress and digress: "Could a historiographer drive on his history, as a muleteer drives on his mule,—straight forward; . . . without ever once turning his head aside either to the right hand or to the left,—he might venture to foretell you to an hour when he should get to his journey's end;- - - - but the thing is, morally speaking, impossible: For, if he is a man of the least spirit, he will have fifty deviations from a straight line to make with this or that party as he goes along. . . . There are archives at every stage to be look'd into . . . which justice ever and anon calls him back to stay the reading of:- - - -In short, there is no end of it. . . ."[12] Yet if it is impossible to go *straight* forward, Tristram discovers that turning (turning aside, turning back, returning) carries one forward in prose in a way that it does not do in space. Hence he can claim that "the machinery of my work is of a species

---

[12] Laurence Sterne, *Tristram Shandy*, (1759–67; Oxford: Oxford University Press, 1983), 32–33.

by itself; two contrary motions are introduced into it, and reconciled, which were thought to be at variance with each other. In a word, my work is digressive, and it is progressive too,—and at the same time" (58). In the process of unwittingly deconstructing-in-advance many conventions of the novel, Tristram here exposes the generically illicit involvement of *prorsus* and *vers*.

But while the blending of these two orientations is possible—indeed, inevitable—on a rhetorical or formal level, it is also true that prose and verse are routinely associated with competing values and ideals that are less easily reconciled. The world of prose is often the democratic world, the world of social mobility (subtended by the modern view of a universe governed by cause and effect), as opposed to the old "poetic," epic world of privilege and social hierarchy (which a belief in correspondences helped to render natural). Yet novels that articulate class-based struggles for legitimacy and authority in terms of a conflict between the principles of prose and those of verse also show that in moving forward prose does not quite leave verse behind. A case in point is William Godwin's *Caleb Williams*.

A particular passage from this novel can serve as a preliminary illustration of the difference between the old interpretive principles of verse and the new ones of prose. The persecuted Caleb is caught in a storm and loses his way. He reflects: "There was no strict connection between these casual inconveniencies [the storm and its effects], and the persecution under which I laboured. But my distempered thoughts confounded them together."[13] In momentarily associating this chance obstacle with the motivated persecution of his enemy, Falkland, Caleb invokes a "poetic" reading of the storm as part of a universal order of correspondences, one element in a larger design, a symbolic manifestation of an overarching idea (persecution, negative providence) with meaningful connections to other manifestations of the same idea. But this reading is included as the cancelled, a product of "distemper." Caleb knows that the storm is not part of a system designed for his destruction—but this does not mean either that it lacks significance or that it becomes significant "in itself." In the profoundly anthropological world of the novel, the storm becomes significant in the "prosaic" terms of cause and effect, as a link in the chain of events that constitutes the plot of Caleb's story. In this instance, the storm causes what turns out to be a fortunate delay. But still it remains a "fortuitous" event, in the new sense of an unplanned, uncontrolled happenstance whose effects are unpredictable, in no

---

[13] William Godwin, *Caleb Williams* (1794; New York: Norton, 1977), 251–52. All references to the novel are to this edition and will be given within the text.

way linked with will, fate, or just desserts. In self-consciously pitting these two readings of the storm against each other, however, Caleb's lines imply that the poetic universe continues to haunt this world of prose like a fevered dream.

The central conflict in *Caleb Williams* takes place between two characters who can be read as representatives of the worlds of verse and prose. The aristocratic Falkland, who has "imbibed the love of chivalry and romance" from "the heroic poets of Italy" (10), is consistently associated with verse (which he reads, writes, analyzes, and imitates), the heroic code of honor, and a dated discourse of correspondences: "I smile at his malice, and resolve to spare him, as the generous lord of the forest spares the insect that would disturb his repose" (175). Caleb, on the other hand, is consistently associated with prose: "I delighted to read of feats of activity. . . . [Curiosity] produced in me an invincible attachment to books of narrative and romance. . . . I read, I devoured compositions of this sort. They took possession of my soul" (4). In contrast to Falkland's elaborate figures, Caleb's speech is "artless and untaught . . . having an air of innocence, frankness and courage" (108). Caleb values the individual above the general, character above reputation, the private above the public, and rational, empirical truth above appearances or symbols—values that directly oppose Falkland's (e.g., 110–11). Where Falkland seems to embody certain dynamics of verse, particularly return, limit, and speedy resolution, Caleb embodies the dynamics of prose: going forward, being straightforward, and "tracing the variety of effects which might be produced from given causes" (4). Thus, even the physical action of the novel has a rhetorical component (Falkland, for example, repeatedly forces Caleb to turn back where he would go forward). But this action is punctuated by a series of overtly rhetorical contests, in which Caleb's story is pitted against Falkland's powerful personal word. In this light, the novel traces a contest between signifying practices, addressing the question, as Kittay and Godzich put it, of what would allow prose to "command assent" (xix); what would make it believable, what would give it a claim to truth.

Falkland's word, of course, is guaranteed by the enormous social and political power of its author. Caleb has to make his story hold in the absence of such a guarantee, independently of the social position or reputation of the writer; it has to convince readers or listeners through its own internal qualities. "Virtue rising superior to every calumny, defeating by a plain, unvarnished tale all the stratagems of vice, and throwing back upon her adversary the confusion with which he had hope to overwhelm her, was one of the favorite subjects of my youthful reveries" (160), Caleb writes. But Virtue's story must be plausible: "If . . . you trust your vindication to the plausibility of your tale, you must take care to render it consistent and complete" (170). Thus, the novel proposes a certain set of values for prose—plain, unadorned, unvarnished, consistent, and complete—terms that suggest distance from the poetic and that align prose with the true. Yet consistency and completeness can make false stories believable, too. In a "very awful moment" (173), Caleb finds that a false story can indeed be made more plausible than the truth; his attempts to counter misapprehension with an "honest explanation" repeatedly fail (297), and by the end of the novel the connection between prose and truth has been thoroughly riddled. Caleb is thus forced to qualify his claims for the narrative he is writing: "My story will at least appear to have that consistency, which is seldom attendant but upon truth" (3).

What is on trial in the final court scene is, first, whether the "truth" of prose can compete with the Word of verse (and the sheer social power to which it is attached); and second, whether prose can succeed in establishing its own authority. In Godwin's original manuscript ending, prose loses both contests. The impersonal truth of fact and reason is overruled by the avatar of verse: exploiting the visual power and pathos of his own person, Falkland simply vetoes Caleb's story. Having failed, prose starts to represent its own dwindling: "I should like to recollect something—it would make an addition to my history—but it is all a BLANK!—sometimes it is day, and sometimes it is night—but nobody does any thing, and nobody says any thing—It would be an odd kind of history!" (appendix 1, 333). As this conclusion goes on, Caleb's prose is reduced to pure sequence, empty structure, content-free narrative: "I have dreams—they are strange dreams . . . they are about nothing at all—and yet there is one thing first, and then another thing, and there is so much of them, and it is all nothing" (334). In this version, prose finally falls still: "If I could once again be thoroughly myself, I should tell such tales! . . . [But] it is wisest to be quiet, it seems. . . . I do nothing—am a stone—a GRAVE-STONE!—an obelisk" (334). This discarded ending paradoxically figures the death of prose. As an obelisk, whether monument or printer's sign (†), prose would become a standing mark of its own cessation, an empty frozen pointing.

In the published ending, prose achieves an ambivalent victory: Caleb defeats the "godlike" Falkland. But the victory takes place only because verse gives its word to prose: "I stand now completely detected. My name will be consecrated to infamy, while your heroism, your patience and your virtues will be for ever admired" (324). In addition to giving his word on the level of diegesis (affirming the truth of Caleb's tale), Falkland gives his word to prose on the level of style. During the contest, Caleb uses repetition, rhythm, and balance to gain acoustic power: "I have reverenced him; he was worthy of reverence: I have loved him; he was endowed with qualities that partook of the divine" (321). The penultimate paragraph, an apostrophe to the fallen Falkland, is written in archaic, poetic language markedly different from the earlier prose: "Falkland! thou enteredst upon thy carreer [*sic*] with the purest and most laudable intentions. But thou imbibedst the poison of chivalry . . ." (326). Prose seems to have sublated verse, declaring victory over the other principle by mastering and incorporating it, but incorporating it as the lost, the sacrificed.

These final pages express profound ambivalence about this victory. Caleb's initial motive for writing was to achieve justice by revealing the truth (via complete and consistent prose). His objective mirrors Godwin's own: the novel is intended to reveal "things as they are"—"things passing in the moral world" (1)—in a convincing and readable form. But in the end, telling the truth makes Caleb guilty: "I have been his murderer. . . . Alas! I am the same Caleb Williams that, so short a time ago, boasted, that, however great were the calamities I endured, I was still innocent" (325). Consistency and completeness, the highest claims of prose, are no longer aligned with innocence, or with justice—and these have lost their clear connections to truth. Injustice, like ambiguity, like prose itself, turns out to be uncontainable. Verse leaves to prose a legacy of guilt; prose transforms the story of its victory into a story of loss.

Caleb's failure to install prose as superior and assert the worth of his own enterprise allows us to see the peculiar predicament of prose (and of the novel). Though it "wins out" over verse and becomes the hegemonic form, it never achieves full legitimacy, since the principle on which its legitimacy is predicated—the abstract and "pure" principle of full and faithful telling the truth about the world—is not a principle that can be fully realized. In this respect, prose and the novel are analogous to the world of democratic values they often represent; those values too achieve hegemony and yet are always in a crisis of legitimacy because the reality in which they are enacted never fully conforms to them.

America, Land of Prose: The American, The Great Gatsby

The association of verse with an old world of class privilege and prose with the modern world of class mobility can have geographic as well as diachronic or historical resonance. In novels, America is very often coded as a region of informal democratic prose vis-à-vis the formal traditions of Europe; this opposition has also been reinscribed within America, where the middle is coded as the prosaic plain vis-à-vis the sophisticated urban coasts. In these contexts, the two terms are not primarily engaged in a direct contest or struggle for authority. Rather, the opposition demonstrates the continuing sway of the poetic in a world that takes prose to be the norm.

Close to the climax of James's *The American*, Valentin de Bellegarde, the young son of an ancient, aristocratic French family, tells his American friend, the ex-business man Newman, that he is about to fight a duel. When Newman shows astonishment and dismay, Valentin justifies himself by saying: "It is our only resource at given moments, and I hold it a good thing. Quite apart from the merit of the cause in which a meeting may take place, it strikes a romantic note that seems to me in this age of vile prose greatly to recommend it. It's a remnant of a higher-tempered time; one ought to cling to it."[14] Newman counters by, first, dismissing the very idea of clinging to the customs of the past. Whereas the Bellegardes' social life is regulated by a set of inherited obligations, Newman creates social ties "freely." His "nature," we are told, includes an "irregularly sociable side . . . which had always expressed itself in a relish for ungrammatical conversation and which often . . . had made him sit on rail fences in the twilight of young Western towns and gossip scarce less than fraternally with humorous loafers and obscure fortune-seekers" (67). He then adds: "If a man has a bad intention on you it's his own affair till it takes effect; but when it does, give him one in the eye. If you don't know how to do that—straight—you're not fit to go round alone. . . . If anyone ever hurts you again . . . come straight to me about it. I'll go for him" (360). Newman, the American, is characterized by acting in a manner that is both "straight" and indiscriminate, irregular, whereas the European, aristocratic Valentin clings to the "twists and turns" that are "forms and ceremonies" (46) as an antidote to the world of prose.

The choice of the duel to represent forms that are not "straight," are not "vile prose," suggests that part of the function of "forms and ceremonies," or manners, is to formalize social relations and thus contain aggression and hostility. The duel then will be the opposite of the jungle of the business world, which Newman is supposed to represent, where the struggle to achieve material goods in a "free" economy pits everybody against everybody

---

[14] *The American* (1877; Boston: Houghton Mifflin, 1943), 359. All references to this novel are to this edition and will be given within the text.

else. But Newman, we know, does not belong—or does not belong any longer—to that world. Though for many years he experienced "the heat of battle, the high competitive rage" (101), he had, one day, a change of heart that turned him away from his intention of showing "the weight of [his] hand" to a business rival who "had once played off on [him] one of the clever meannesses the feeling of which works in a man like strong poison" (30). As a result of this "turn," Christopher Newman feels "a new man under [his] old skin" and "long[s] for a new world" that is, paradoxically but appropriately, not America but Europe. And yet because Newman, as he puts it, has "the instincts . . . if [not] the forms of a high old civilisation" (45) he can befriend Valentin and love Claire de Cintré but ultimately cannot understand them. As he says at the very end of his experience, "he had learnt his lesson—not indeed that he the least understood it—and could put away the book" (534).

What may the book in question be? At Valentin's bedside Newman finds Laclos's *Dangerous Liaisons*, which he fails to (that is, cannot) read. By placing this novel at the dying man's bedside, James suggests that we read Valentin as an avatar of Laclos's hero, Valmont. As their names suggest, they both represent "valor"—"intrinsic worth or merit" (*OED*), an aristocratic or "poetic" virtue, quite different from Newman's equivalent, courage—which, as a physically defined trait ("A stout heart . . . and a firm front," 125), aligns with the material and the prosaic. Both Valmont and Valentin are killed at a duel and before they die reveal a secret and ask for, or suggest the possibility of, revenge. But whereas Valmont's revenge is carried out by his rival/double/heir, Danceney, who by revealing the treachery of Mme. de Merteuil causes her expulsion and thus brings the world of manners back into its normal order, Newman finally renounces the revenge proposed to him by Valentin's revelations and burns the letter that proves the Bellegardes' crime. And the narrator explains: "Newman's last thought was that of course he will let the Bellegardes go. . . . He was ashamed of having wanted to hurt them. He quite failed, of a sudden, to recognize the fact of his having cultivated any such link with them. It was a link for themselves, perhaps, their having so hurt him; but that side of it was not his affair" (534). Short of hurting the Bellegardes by taking revenge (just as he thought of hurting his former business rival by taking revenge), all Newman can do is deny the existence of the social link: he cannot come up, finally, with a substitute for the duel. Ultimately he proves Valentin's words true: "You can't invent anything that will take the place of satisfaction for an insult. To demand it and to give it are equally excellent arrangements" (360).

Though Newman leaves for Europe because he became conscious of the insufficiency of the "free" social life he has led in America, at the end of his experience he has failed to adopt, or even understand, European "forms and ceremonies," nor has he discovered a better way (than his old way, than the Bellegardes' way) of dealing with antagonism and hurt. The novel thus suggests that the transition from the old heroic code (figured as European) to a new world of democratic "prose" (figured as American) has been both incomplete (the duel persists as a remnant) and unsatisfactory (there is no substitute for the duel; prose is "vile").

––––––––

If banished aristocratic values show a certain staying power in the novel, held under the sign of guilt or loss, it may be in part because these values serve, not the new politics (democracy and republicanism), but the new economics (capitalism). Whereas the prose of a democratic culture, as Franco Moretti has argued, values equality above all, and thus features the " 'common' hero," "capitalism (which is not the same as democracy) offers [great individualities] a new and immense field of application."[15] More broadly, F. Scott Fitzgerald's novel *The Great Gatsby* suggests that capitalism offers a new field of application for poetic principles earlier associated with the old European aristocracy. Part of what Gatsby symbolizes for readers, and Daisy for Gatsby, is the poetic side of capital—the connection of wealth to beauty, imagination, romance, and creativity. Thus the enigmatic power of Daisy's voice is linked, finally, to money: "that was the inexhaustible charm that rose and fell in it, the jingle of it, the cymbals' song of it. . . . High in a white palace the king's daughter, the golden girl."[16] Gatsby, who is characterized by his "elaborate formality of speech" (53) and the "luminosity of his pink suit under the moon" (150), "sprang from his Platonic conception of himself. He was a son of God—a phrase which if it means anything, means just that" (104). Freed of historical and genealogical determinations, he has created himself through the power of his own word. His fictional autobiography lacks verisimilitude: "the very phrases were worn so threadbare that they evoked no image except that of a turbaned 'character' leaking sawdust at every pore" (70), but like Falkland, Gatsby carries an ontological authority that transcends the particulars of his story.

––––––––

[15] Franco Moretti, *The Way of the World: The Bildungsroman in European Culture*, trans. Albert Sbragia, (1987; London: Verso, 2000), 191–92.

[16] F. Scott Fitzgerald, *The Great Gatsby* (1925; New York: Collier, 1992), 127. All references to the novel are to this edition and will be given within the text.

The underside of Gatsby's world is the underworld of crime—another dimension of "verse" ("to impose upon: to cozen, cheat, defraud," *OED*). The sources of Gatsby's fortune clearly indicate that you do not get from nowhere to West Egg in a straightforward manner. Gatsby's crookedness stands in sharp contrast to the ethical behavior of Nick Carraway, who shares many of Caleb's prosaic traits. An "honest, straightforward person" (186) from the prosy Midwest, Nick has "an unaffected scorn" (6) for all that Gatsby represents: showiness, spectacle, extravagant expenditure, elaborate deceitfulness. But the task of prose in this wildly irrational world of poetic money is not to vie against it, nor to reconcile the values of this world with its own. Rather, prose sets out to tell the story of verse as false but strangely admirable, while retaining the moral high ground. Instead of pitting the two characters (and dynamics) against each other, the novel divides what the reader trusts and respects (Nick) from what the reader finds fascinating (Gatsby), leaving intact a famously problematic gap between the ethical (prosaic Midwestern democracy) and the interesting (poetic coastal capital).

Standing at a distance from the action, Nick is Gatsby's chronicler from beginning to end; his own story merely provides a normative matrix that can order the events he witnesses. Consistent with his character, Nick is concerned to provide a true and accurate version of the story, to set the record straight. Competing but salacious and unreliable versions exist—the rumors about Gatsby's past spread by partygoers; the stories told by the taxi driver (188), "some garrulous man" (163), and the journalists, in particular, whose reports "were a nightmare—grotesque, circumstantial, eager and untrue" (171). Nick's approach is defined against these others; his writing is not gossip and not journalism; at the same time, it is not lyric. Refusing to be seduced by east or west, old or new manners, romance or despair, Nick presents his "rather literary" (8) prose as the language of the mean, the middle way, reason and right vision.

As Nick tells it, the story is generally linear. When Nick violates chronology, he informs us of his reasons for doing so: "He told me all this very much later, but I've put it down here with the idea of exploding those first wild rumors about his antecedents, which weren't even faintly true" (107). Thus, Nick straightens out the story, giving sequential form to something that in itself would not be sequential but spectacular, episodic, legendary, fabulous, and self-contradictory: something that could not, in other words, tell its own story. Likewise, Nick scrupulously records the names of the partygoers in the empty spaces of an "old time-table . . . disintegrating at its folds and headed 'This schedule in effect July 5th, 1922' " (65). But the names themselves are unreal, purely figural, clearly conjured from imagination—Leeches, Snells, Endive, Orchid, Faustina O'Brien, Claudia Hip; they don't belong on the timetable. They cannot be true, they are not part of the world of prose (trains and schedules), and they do not even masquerade as history, though Nick himself is clearly unaware that they have been fabricated. We do not suspect him of making them up; we suspect, rather, that the matrix of the timetable is fundamentally incompatible with Gatsby's poetic world. Nevertheless, Nick's prose carries forward these heterogeneous, unstraightforward terms without argument. In fact, Nick is so successful in presenting himself as a trustworthy chronicler that despite its patent fictionality the book has inflected history, shaping many readers' image of this place and time. That this is so despite Fitzgerald's own notorious ineptitude as a chronicler (the book is rife with factual errors)[17] suggests the manner in which prose almost effortlessly "commands assent" in the twentieth century (Kittay and Godzich, 205–9). It has established its authority as the language of the real to such an extreme degree that postmodern novelists will have to go to great lengths to *disrupt* the misguided assumption of modern readers that realistic prose reflects the real, and also the more insidious idea that the real was always a lot like prose.

The dynamics of prose, which suggest that one can neither return to a past moment nor escape its present consequences, relegate Gatsby's goal to a region of the impossible. Believing in the immediacy and power of voice, of the poetic Word, Gatsby disbelieves in chronology. " 'You can't repeat the past,' " Nick says; " 'Can't repeat the past?' [Gatsby cries] incredulously, 'Why of course you can!' " (116). A great avatar of *versus*, Gatsby believes that one might simply return to the spot where things went awry and play it all out differently. Consistent with this disregard for the effects of time, Gatsby is not a character who "develops": his self-conception is static, without room for growth, or movement toward wisdom. Nick is the only character who gains knowledge, wisdom, or understanding through experience, and in the end, Nick's rules—the rules of the timetable, the rules of prose— turn out to be the rules of the real. There is cause and effect; the past affords no return. Nick speculates that before Gatsby's death he must have renounced his dream: "he must have looked up at an unfamiliar sky through frightening leaves and shivered as he found what a grotesque thing a rose is and how raw the sunlight was upon the scarcely created grass. A new world, material without being real, where poor ghosts, breathing dreams like air,

---

[17] See Matthew J. Bruccoli, "The Text of *The Great Gatsby*," in *The Great Gatsby*, by F. Scott Fitzgerald (1925; New York: Collier, 1992), 191–94.

drifted fortuitously about" (169). This passage describes a punctured poetic, in which what is left is not Nick's straightforward prose but antipoetry, the Valley of Ashes, desiccated pastoral under a billboard god. Here, what opposes or negates poetry is not the prosaic. Prose remains at a distance from both sets of "distortions," both the dream and the nightmare: Nick can return in space, though not in time, to an unsoiled, unspectacular middle west.

Yet the novel's closing paragraphs introduce questions about what it means to go back, how straightforward a chronicle can be, and whether clocks really only run in one direction. First, Nick reflects that Gatsby must have believed his dream was "so close that he could hardly fail to grasp it. He did not know that it was already behind him, somewhere back in that vast obscurity beyond the city, where the dark fields of the republic rolled on under the night" (189). In the process of debunking Gatsby's delusion, chronology here collides with geography: the passage positions the dream in space, as though one might go there after all, a question of terrain and not of time. Next, Nick asserts that Gatsby believed in a future that will never become present: "the orgastic future that year by year recedes before us" (189). The "us" here institutes a shift in perspective, and the closing line presents a general moral truth from no one's point of view: "so we beat on, boats against the current, borne back ceaselessly into the past" (189). In suggesting that the current of time runs backward, this line paradoxically grants Gatsby's wish. In this sense, the lyrical, alliterative line indicates a certain captation of prose by the self-conscious romance of Gatsby's poetic ideal, as if the prose has been tripped up by verse. Countering Nick's earlier assertion that you cannot repeat the past, the figure implies that you can only repeat the past. Not only is it possible to go back, it is impossible not to, and there is no pure going forward. Forward-oriented discourse, ceaselessly borne back, cannot be other than the language of memory and lost worlds. Yet in departing from Nick's voice and Nick's perspective, the closing figure remains a borrowed trope, imported from elsewhere. The manner in which it artificially chokes off an otherwise almost seamless narrative strongly suggests that Nick's language, the language of the middle, cannot be the language of the end.

Prose and Closure

From the point of view of prose, one of the more salient questions to ask about the novel is how and why it ends; how it creates a limit beyond which there is no more prose to be read. Clearly, prose, as *prorsus*, has no internal principle of ending. Minimalist writing like that of Samuel Beckett demonstrates that paring down the sentence (leaving out articles, transitions) does not change the fact that prose is immeasurably extendable; one cannot run it out. Because prose can always just continue forward, the end of a novel must come from elsewhere, from foreign dynamics of verse, perhaps, or formal principles of the genre rather than its medium.

What does a novel look like when its prose approaches the asymptotic point of pure forwardness? We can use as an example a recent Israeli novel, Ya'akov Shabtai's *Past Continuous* (in Hebrew, *Zichron Devarim*, literally, "memorandum"). The reader of the Hebrew original encounters a 275-page text that is not broken into paragraphs, let alone chapters. These 275 pages are written in a particular prose style: very long sentences (in the Hebrew original, about two sentences per page with many sentences being longer than a page) whose length is not the result of subordination—the creation of a hierarchical structure that distinguishes between principal and subordinate clauses—but rather of coordination, the piling on of details that are all of equal importance.[18] Shabtai's text is continuous and nonhierarchical, and its anomalous status (as well as the serious changes effected by its translation into English) suggests to what extent we have come to rely in our reading of prose on "natural" stopping points that allow us to "turn back," rest and reflect, sift out the unimportant from the important, and formulate provisional meanings. To this piling—or stringing—of equally important (or equally unimportant) detail we can add the large number of characters who populate this text (eight of them are mentioned on the first two pages alone), and who are not so much introduced as mentioned by the way—though we always find, eventually, who they are and what they do, think, and feel. The large number of characters and the offhanded way in which they are inserted in the text strengthen the impression created by the syntax of a crowded but flat world where all things are linked and are equally (un)important. But this is far from a static, dull, or boring world. Though a reader may find it difficult to emotionally engage with the particular destinies of the characters (the way they drop in and out of the text makes this almost impossible) the reader does feel all the time carried forward by a movement, which is, precisely, the movement of the syntax. Here is part of a sentence taken from the beginning of the novel:

> Israel sat down on the edge of the couch and asked whether they couldn't possibly skip the funeral and make do with a condolence call at Goldman's

---

[18] Moshe Ron, "Past Continuous: The Sentence" (in Hebrew), *Siman Kri-ah* 16–17 (April 1983): 272–78.

house instead—especially since both of them were well aware of the nature of Goldman's relations with his father, as well as the fact that Goldman set no store by, and even detested, religious ceremonies, and would have been only too happy to stay away from his own father's funeral if he possibly could, never mind the funeral of one of his friends' fathers, but Caesar, who liked all kinds of gatherings and celebrations and calamities and dramatic events, insisted that it was their duty to attend the funeral, since the nature of Goldman's relations with his father was irrelevant, especially now that his father was already dead, and despite Goldman's negative attitude toward religious ceremonies and his rationalism he, Caesar, had no doubt at all that in his heart of hearts he would never forgive them if they stayed away and left him alone with his mother at his father's funeral, and in this connection he also remarked that there were limits to the reason and logic of the most logical person in the world, and that life often forced us to things that were not only illogical but also unpleasant, and in the end he said that at any rate he was going to the funeral no matter what, alone if need be, and urged Israel to get up and go with him, and Israel got up and went poker faced to the bathroom to wash, cursing Caesar and himself and Goldman's father, whose death had caused him no sorrow. . . . [19]

After reading for a while the reader gets the feeling that not only can the text go on for ever (every end will be contingent and arbitrary) but, more radically, that this movement is not semantically but syntactically determined. The foregrounding of the syntactical structure creates the impression that though the semantic content (the characters, the accidents that befall them, the time and place in which they are located) is vehicled by syntax, the syntax is in some sense "indifferent" to it, that it would have been the same if the characters and the events were totally different. The syntax does not exist in order to convey a particular meaning, and it is because it is not subordinated to the formulation of particular meanings that it can go on and on.

Shabtai's novel is unusual in that it abstracts the movement forward of its content (without, however, ceasing to be a realistic novel about the demise of a certain form of life in a particular time and place). In most novels the readers' eagerness to move forward results from their investment in the characters and their fate and resides in the pleasurable expectation that with every turn of the page some new event will unfold. This investment in

---

[19] *Past Continuous*, trans. Dalya Bilu (1977; New York: Jewish Publication Society of America, 1985), 7–8. Translation modified.

forward movement—in prose qua *prorsus*—has often been equated with the reader's desire for the end, an investment in closure. The two, however, should be kept separate, as they are, in fact, one the opposite of the other. Closure adds to the movement forward its opposite—a return back to the beginning that allows one to consider the narrative as a delimited totality and thus give it meaning. Closure therefore goes against the notion of prose not only as unlimited, but also as moving forward without turns and returns. Critics' tendency to collapse movement forward and desire for the end shows the extent to which the novel has succeeded in making closure appear the natural product of prose. And in so doing, the novel paradoxically makes it difficult for us to fully imagine and embrace the world of prose. By making closure appear as an organic part of the movement forward, the novel becomes delimited and centered, with all its meanings referring back to a specific point of origin; it thus excludes prose as the infinitely open, de-centered, and incalculable. At the same time, the humdrum routine of every-day life, of labor and of the domestic, remains at the margins or background of the novel. Until it becomes a clue to a psychological, existential, social, or criminal puzzle, the everyday cannot be the locus of meaning. Thus, while the investment in closure, in totalized meaning, signals a resistance to the euphoric notion of prose, it also keeps the traditional novel at an arm's length from the dysphoria of the prosaic everyday.

UMBERTO ECO

Excess and History in Hugo's *Ninety-three*

In 1902, a small review, *L'Hermitage*, asked two hundred French writers who their favorite poet was. André Gide replied, "Hugo, hélas!" Gide would have to go to great lengths in the years to come to explain his statement.[1] In the present essay I am not particularly interested in this episode, since Gide was speaking of Hugo the poet, but his cry (of pain? disappointment? begrudging admiration?) weighs heavily on the shoulders of anyone who has ever been invited to judge Hugo the novelist—or even the author of a single novel. Such is the case with this revisitation of *Ninety-three*.

Alas (*hélas!*), however many shortcomings in the novel one can list and analyze, starting with its oratorical incontinence, the same defects appear splendid when we begin to delve into the wound with our scalpel. Like a worshiper of Bach and his disembodied, almost mental architecture, who discovers that Beethoven has achieved mightier tones than many more temperate harpsichords ever could—why fight the urge to surrender? Who could be immune to the power of the Fifth or Ninth Symphony?

Was Hugo the greatest French novelist of his century? With good reason you might prefer Stendhal, Balzac, or Flaubert. Reread *Ninety-three*, however, and you become enthralled by the power of excess. It is this attraction that we shall explore, in a book that, like Hugo's other novels, turns excess into a golden mean and thrills us through sheer excess. You could avoid entering a Pantagruelian feast, but once you are in the game, it makes no sense to recall your dietician's advice or to yearn for the delicate flavors of *nouvelle cuisine*. If you have the stomach to join in an orgy, the experience will be memorable. Otherwise it is better to leave immediately and fall asleep reading the aphorisms of an eighteenth-century gentleman. Hugo is not for the faint of heart. While the battle of the Hernani may be a belated form of *Sturm und Drang*, the shadow of that storm and stress was still illuminating the last romantic in 1874, the date of the novel's publication, though not of its gestation.

I am well aware that I love Hugo because of his sublime excessiveness, which I have celebrated elsewhere: Excess can transform even bad writing and banality into Wagnerian tempests. To explain the allure of a film like

---

[1] For the story of this reply and the ensuing justifications, see André Gide, *Hugo, hélas*, ed. Claude Martin (Paris: Editions Fata Morgana, 2002).

Casablanca, I have argued that while a single cliché produces kitsch; a hundred clichés, scattered around shamelessly, become epic. I once remarked that while the *Count of Monte Cristo* may be badly written (unlike other novels by Dumas, such as the *Three Musketeers*), redundant, and verbose, it is precisely because of these bad qualities, pushed beyond reasonable limits, that it borders on the sublime dynamic of Kantian memory and justifies its grip on the attention of millions of readers.[2]

Going back to *Ninety-three*, let us try to understand what is meant by excess. Before doing so, let me summarize the story that, at its heart, is elementary, sufficiently melodramatic, and, in the hands of an Italian librettist, could have produced the equivalent of, say, *Tosca* or *Il Trovatore* (but without the musical commentary that allows us to take the verses seriously).

It is the *annus horribilis* of the revolution. The Vendée has risen in revolt. An elderly aristocrat, a skilled warrior, the marquis of Lantenac, has come ashore to take command of the peasant masses, who are emerging from mysterious forests like demons, firing their weapons while saying the rosary. The revolution, which is expressed through the Convention, has sent its men against him. First comes Gauvain (Lantenac's nephew), a young aristocrat turned republican, of a feminine beauty, blazing with war yet also an angelic utopian who still hopes that the conflict can be settled through mercy and respect for one's enemy. Next is Cimourdain, whom we would call a police commissioner today: a priest as ruthless in his way as Lantenac, he is convinced that the only way to achieve social and political regeneration is through a bloodbath, and that today's pardoned hero is tomorrow's murderous enemy. Cimourdain, in yet another coincidence (melodrama has its demands), was once the tutor of the young Gauvain and loves him like a son. Hugo never conjures up a passion that is anything other than the total identification of a man—chaste because of his faith and later because of his revolutionary fervor—with spiritual fatherhood. But who knows? Cimourdain's passion is fierce, total, and carnally mystic.

In this struggle between revolution and reaction, Lantenac and Gavuain attempt to kill each other, clashing and fleeing in a spiral of nameless massacres. Yet this story of multiple horrors opens with a battalion of republican soldiers coming upon a starving widow and her three children. They decide to adopt the little ones on a radiant day in May. The children

---

[2] Umberto Eco, "*Casablanca*, o la rinascita degli dei," in *Dalla periferia all'impero* (Milan: Bompiani, 1977), 138–46; and "Elogio del *Montecristo*," in *Sugli specchi e altri saggi* (Milan: Bompiani, 1985), 147–58.

will later be captured by Lantenac, who shoots the mother and takes the little republican mascots hostage. The mother survives the execution and wanders about desperately looking for her children. The republicans fight to free the three innocent prisoners, who are locked in the gloomy medieval tower where Lantenac will later be attacked by Gauvain. Lantenac manages to escape through a secret passageway, but his followers set fire to the tower. With the children's lives hanging in the balance, the distraught mother reappears, and Lantenac (who undergoes a transfiguration from Satan into Lucifer, the guardian angel) reenters the tower, rescues the children, and brings them to safety, allowing himself to be captured by his enemies.

Cimourdain arranges for a trial right then and there, bringing in a guillotine for the occasion. In the meantime Gauvain wonders whether it is right to execute a man who has already paid for his errors through an act of generosity. He enters the prisoner's cell, where Lantenac reaffirms the rights of the throne and of the altar in a long monologue. In the end Gauvain allows him to escape and takes his place in the cell. When Cimourdain learns of this gesture, he has no choice but to put Gauvain on trial and cast the deciding vote for the death of the only person he has ever loved.

The recurrent motif of the three children accompanies the tormented adventures of Gauvain, who in the name of kindness and mercy submits to the punishment he has brought on himself. Both motifs cast a ray of hope on a future that can only be ushered in through human sacrifice. The entire army raises its voice, demanding grace for its commander, but to no avail. Although he is deeply moved, Cimourdain is a man who has dedicated his life to duty and law. He is the guardian of the revolutionary purity that has come to be identified with terror, or rather, with the Terror. Yet at the moment that Gauvain's head rolls into the basket, Cimourdain takes his own life with a pistol: "And those two souls, tragic sisters, took flight together, the shadow of the one blending with the light of the other."[3]

———

Is that it? Hugo only wanted to make us weep? Not at all. My first observation has to be made in narratological rather than political terms. Today the repertory of every scholar of narrative structures (I promise to avoid erudite references to secondary theoretical variants) includes the idea that while there are indeed actors in a story, they are embodiments of "actants," narrative roles

---

[3] Victor Hugo, *Ninety-three*, trans. Frank Lee Benedict (1874; New York: Carroll and Graff, 1998). Subsequent quotations will be referenced parenthetically in the text.

through which the actor goes, perhaps changing his function in the plot structure.[4] For example, in a novel like *The Betrothed*, the forces of evil or human weakness can act against the forces of providence, which controls everyone's destinies, and an actor like the Unnamed One can suddenly change from being an Opponent to being a Helper. Hence, by comparison to actors tethered to an immutable actantial role, such as Don Rodrigo, on the one hand, and Fra Cristofero, on the other, the ambiguity of Don Abbondio makes sense: an earthenware crock in the midst of iron pots, he constantly drifts from one role to the other, ultimately making him seem worthy of our forgiveness.

By the time the elderly Hugo finally started to write the novel he had long contemplated (he had mentioned it some years earlier in the preface to the *Man Who Laughs*), his youthful political and ideological positions had undergone a profound change. As a young man he had expressed legitimist ideas and sympathized for the Vendée, seeing 1793 as a dark spot in the blue sky of 1789. He later shifted toward liberal and then socialist principles. After the coup d'état of Louis Napoleon, he gravitated toward socialist, democratic, and republican positions. In his 1841 admission speech to the French Academy, he paid homage to the Convention, "which broke the throne and saved the country . . . which committed acts and outrages that we might detest and condemn, but which we must still admire." While he could not understand the Paris Commune, after the Restoration he fought for amnesty for the communards. The gestation and publication of *Ninety-three* coincide with his completed evolution toward more radical positions. To understand the Commune, he also had to justify the Terror. A long-standing opponent of the death penalty, he was mindful, nevertheless, of the reactionary lesson of an author he knew well, Joseph de Maistre: he knew that redemption and purification also come about through the horrors of human sacrifice.

Hugo's mentions de Maistre in book 1, chapter 4 of *Les miserables*, in the scene where Monsignor Myriel contemplates the guillotine:

> He who sees it quakes with the most mysterious of tremblings. . . . The scaffold is a vision. . . . It seems a sort of being which had some sombre origin of which we can have no idea; one would say that this frame sees, that this

---

[4] [Translator's note: The term *actant* was coined by the French structuralist Algirdas Julien Greimas to describe a form of agency in the text distinct from that of the "actor," since several characters in a narrative may embody a single actant. His fundamental work on the subject is *On Meaning: Selected Writings in Semiotic Theory*, trans. Paul J. Perron and Frank H. Collins (Minneapolis: University of Minnesota Press, 1976).]

machine understands, that this mechanism comprehends; that this wood, this iron, and these ropes have a will. . . . The scaffold becomes the accomplice of the executioner; it devours, it eats flesh, and it drinks blood . . . a spectre which seems to live with a kind of unspeakable life, drawn from all the death which it has wrought.[5]

But in *Ninety-three* the guillotine, which will claim the life of the revolution's purest hero, passes from the side of death to the side of life. A symbol of the future in contrast to the gloomiest symbols of the past, it is erected in front of the Tourge, the stronghold where Lantenac is under siege. The tower condenses fifteen hundred years of feudal sins, a tough knot to untangle. Before it stands the guillotine, as pure as the blade that slices the knot. The guillotine was not born ex nihilo: it was fertilized by blood spilt for fifteen centuries on that same land. It arises from the depths of the earth, an unknown vindicator, and says to the tower, "I am your daughter." And the tower senses that the end is near. This was not a new analogy for Hugo. It recalls *The Hunchback of Notre Dame*, when Frollo compares the printed book to the cathedral's towers and gargoyles: "Ceci tuera cela." While the guillotine is always and still a monster, in *Ninety-three* it takes the side of the future.

What do you call a ferocious, death-sowing monster that promises a better life? An oxymoron. Victor Brombert has commented on the many oxymora that populate the novel: rapacious angel, intimate disagreement, colossal sweetness, odiously helpful, terrible peacefulness, venerable innocents, tremendous misery, hell in full daybreak, and Lantenac himself, who at one point shifts from being an infernal Satan to being a celestial Lucifer.[6] The oxymoron is "a rhetorical microcosm that affirms the substantially antithetical nature of the world," although Brombert emphasizes that the antitheses are ultimately resolved into a higher order. *Ninety-three* relates the story of a virtuous crime, a healing act of violence whose deep purposes must be understood for its episodes to be justified. *Ninety-three* aims to be not the story of what some men did but rather the story of what history forced those men to do, independently of their will, which is often fraught with contradictions. And the idea of those purposes justifies even the force ostensibly opposed to such purposes, the Vendée.

---

[5] Victor Hugo, *Les miserables*, trans. Charles E. Wilbour (New York: Modern Library, 1992), 16. Subsequent quotations will be referenced parenthetically in the text.

[6] Victor Brombert, *Victor Hugo and the Visionary Novel* (Cambridge, Mass.: Harvard University Press, 1984), 203–29.

This leads us back to the relationship between small actors and actants in the novel. Each individual and object, from Marat to the guillotine, represents not so much itself as the great forces that are the true protagonists of the work. Cocteau once claimed that "Victor Hugo was a madman who believed he was Victor Hugo."[7] He was exaggerating. Victor Hugo merely believed that he was God, or at least God's official interpreter, and every story he told tries to justify itself from God's perspective.

On every page *Novantatré* repeats that the true actants appearing on the stage of his novel are the people, the revolution. Behind the scenes, implacable, is God.

Whatever Hugo's God may be, it is always present in his narrative to explain the blood-drenched enigmas of history. He might never have written that everything real is rational, but he would have agreed that everything ideal is rational. Hugo always adopts a Hegelian tone, recognizing that history marches toward its own purposes, above and beyond the heads of actors who are condemned to personify its intents. Take, for example, the symphonic description of the battle of Waterloo in *Les misérables*. Unlike Stendhal, who describes the battle through the eyes of Fabrizio, a youth in the thick of it unable to comprehend what is happening, Hugo describes the battle through the eyes of God, who sees it from above. He knows that if Napoleon had known that beyond the ridge of the Mont-Saint-Jean plateau there was a cliff (which his scout failed to mention), Milhaud's cuirassiers would not have been defeated by the English Army; that if the shepherd boy who had guided Bülow had suggested a different route, the Prussian Army would not have arrived in time to decide the fate of the battle. But who cares? Once Hugo has described Waterloo as a first-rate battle won by a second-rate captain, who cares about the miscalculations of Napoleon (actor), the ignorance of Grouchy (actor)—who could have returned but did not—or the tricks, if any, of the actor Wellington?

> This madness, this terror, this falling to ruins of the highest bravery which ever astonished history, can that be without cause? No. The shadow of an enormous right hand rests on Waterloo. It is the day of Destiny. A power above man controlled that day. . . . This disappearance of the great man was necessary for the advent of the great century. One, to whom there is no reply, took it in charge. The panic of heroes is explained. In the battle of Waterloo, there is more than a cloud, there is a meteor. God passed over it. (296)

---

[7] Jean Cocteau, *Le mystère laïc*, in *Oeuvres complètes* (Lausanne: Maguerat, 1946), 10:21.

God also passes through the Vendée and the Convention, gradually taking on the actorial guise of fierce Bushman peasants or aristocrats converted to *égalité*, shadowy nocturnal heroes like Cimourdain or solar ones like Gauvain. At the rational level, Hugo saw the Vendée as a mistake, but since it was a deliberate mistake held in check by a providential (or fatal) plan, he was fascinated by it and made it into an epic. He is skeptical, sarcastic, and petty about the small men that populated the Convention, but as a group he saw them as giants. At the very least, he gives us a giant image of the Convention.

This is why Hugo did not care that his actors were psychologically one-dimensional and hindered by their destiny. He did not care that the cold furor of Lantenac, the harshness of Cimourdain, and the hot passionate sweetness of the Homeric Gauvain (Achilles? Hector?) were implausible. Through them he wanted us to perceive the great forces that were in play. Hugo wanted to tell us a story about excesses, about excesses that were so inexplicable that they could only be described through oxymora. What style could he adopt to tell of one, of many excesses? An excessive style. Straight from his stylistic repertory.

The dizzying reversals of perspective and dramatic scenes are one of the first manifestations of excess. This technique, of which Hugo is the master, is hard to explain. He knows that the rules of tragedy demand what the French call a *coup de théâtre*. One such scene is usually more than enough in classical tragedy. Oedipus discovers that he has killed his father and slept with his mother: what more could you ask for? End of the tragic action and catharsis—if you want it in bite-sized pieces.

But one scene was not enough for Hugo (who believed, after all, that he was Victor Hugo). Let us take an example of reversal in *The Laughing Man*. Gwynplaine is horrendously mutilated by *comprachicos* who turn his face into a carnival mask. He is suddenly recognized as an English peer, Lord Clancharlie, the heir to an immense fortune. Before he even knows what has happened to him, he is introduced, in splendid aristocratic vestments, into an enchanted palace. The series of marvels that he discovers (alone in that shining desert) in the suite of rooms and chambers is mind-boggling for both him and the reader. The chapter, incidentally, is entitled "The Resemblance of a Forest and a Palace," and the description of this particular Louvre or Hermitage fills five pages. From this point on I shall measure excess in pages, since what matters in such cases is quantity.[8] So Gwynplaine wanders from room to room until he reaches an alcove where sitting on the bed, next to a tub of water drawn for a virgin bath, he sees a naked woman.

Not literally naked, Hugo mischievously tells us. She is clothed. But in a long chemise so fine as to appear wet. Seven more pages follow on what a naked woman looks like, and how she looks to the laughing man, whose only love till that point had been his chaste adoration of a blind girl. No description of a naked woman could ever surpass the erotic mischief of these pages. She appears to him like a Venus sleeping in the immensity of the soap bubbles. Stirring in her sleep she creates and then undoes seductive curves through vague movements of the watery vapor, shaping billowy clouds against the blue of the sky. It is hard to imagine pages of equal sensuality. Yet Hugo always has a sententious comment to add to an excess of representation. He tells us that "a naked woman is an armed woman."

Seven ecstatic pages of the woman sleeping and Gwynplaine trembling, dying to run away yet hypnotized by the vision, realizing that the woman is the same Lady Josiana, sister to the queen, who had tried to approach him once before, excited by his monstrous appearance. Josiana awakes, sees Gwynplaine, and initiates a furious seduction (ten pages) that the unhappy man cannot resist, except the woman leads him to the brink of desire but still does not give herself over to him. Instead she erupts into a series of fantasies, more eroticizing than her own nudity, in which she reveals herself to be both virgin (still) and prostitute, anxious to enjoy not only the pleasures of teratology promised by Gwynplaine but also the thrill of defying the world and the court, a prospect that intoxicates her, a Venus awaiting the double orgasm of private possession and public exhibition of her Vulcan.

When Gwynplaine is just about to give in, a message arrives from the queen telling her sister that the Laughing Man has been recognized as the rightful Lord Clancharlie and that a marriage between them has been arranged. Josiana comments, "So be it." She stands up, holds out her hand (shifting from the familiar to the formal), and tells the man with whom she has so ferociously wanted to mate, "Leave," adding, "since you are my

---

[8] My calculations are based on current Italian editions, but I also checked the French editions and, depending on the typesetting, there might be very slight variations. In my estimate the pages I have calculated always have between 2,200 and 2,500 characters, so if I speak of fifteen pages one could imagine between sixteen and eighteen pages of two thousand characters each. But, as you can see, the differences are minimal. To describe the movement from one room to another, five or six pages is, at any rate, a considerable quantity.

husband, leave . . . you have no right to be here. This place belongs to my lover."

Excess abounds: Gwynplaine in his deformity, Josiana in her initial sado-masochism and in her reaction to the letter. The situation, which had already been reversed through a normal recognition device (you are not a monster but a lord) and enriched by a double change of fortune (you were a wretch, now you are a lord, a lord coveted by the loveliest woman in the kingdom whom you now covet with every inch of your flustered, quaking soul—and this would suffice if not for the sake of tragedy than at least for that of comedy) is reversed again. Not into tragedy (at least for the moment: Gwynplaine will kill himself only at the end) but into grotesque farce. Readers are exhausted: in one fell swoop they have grasped both the threads of Fate and the fabric of the eighteenth-century's gallant society. Fear not, we are only two-thirds of the way through the novel. There's more to come. Hugo is shameless. Josiana, by comparison, is as modest as a saint.

Now back to the initial reversal in *Ninety-three*. The sloop-of-war *Claymore* is trying to infiltrate the republican naval blockade off the coast of Brittany in order to bring to shore Lantenac, the future head of the Vendée revolt. From the outside the ship looks like a freighter, but it is armed with thirty pieces of artillery. The drama unfolds—Hugo, fearing that we have underestimated its moment, announces that "something tremendous has happened." A twenty-four-gauge cannon breaks loose. In a ship that is tossing and turning at the mercy of choppy seas, a cannon rolling from one side of the ship to the other is worse than an enemy salvo. It hurtles from right to left like a cannonball, crashing through walls, making leaks—no one can stop it. They are headed for a shipwreck. It is a supernatural beast, Hugo exclaims. Concerned that we might not grasp the import and seeking to prevent any misunderstanding, he describes the catastrophic event for five pages. Until one brave gunner, playing with the iron beast like a matador with a bull, faces it down, throws himself in front of it, risking his life, dodges it, provokes it, attacks it again, and is about to be crushed by it when Lantenac throws a bale of counterfeit banknotes between the wheels, halting its run for an instant, allowing the sailor to stick an iron bar between the spokes of the back wheels, lift up the monster, turn it upside down, and restore it to mineral immobility. The crew rejoices. The sailor thanks Lantenac for saving his life. Lantenac praises his courage before the entire crew and takes the St. Louis Cross from one officer and pins it on his chest.

Then he orders him to be shot.

He was brave, but he was also responsible for the cannon and should have made sure that it did not break loose. The man, with the decoration on his chest, offers himself up to the firing squad.

Is this reversal enough? No. Because the ship has been compromised, Lantenac has to make the rest of his journey on a dingy rowed by a sailor. Halfway there the sailor reveals that he is the brother of the executed man and announces that he will kill Lantenac. Lantenac rises before the avenger and delivers a five-page speech. He explains the meaning of duty, reminds him that their common task is to save France and to save God, convinces him that he, Lantenac, has acted in the interest of justice while if the sailor succumbs to the desire for revenge he will be committing the greatest injustice ("You steal my life from the king and deliver your own eternity to the devil!"). The sailor, overcome, asks him for forgiveness. Lantenac grants it, and from that moment forth, Halmalo, the failed avenger, becomes the servant of his brother's executioner, in the name of the Vendée.

Enough about the excess of endless reversals. Now let us move on to the other, primary engine of excess, the endless list. Having described the leader, the author has to convey some idea of his attending army. Hugo seeks to depict the full breadth of the promonarchy insurrection, village by village, castle by castle, region by region. He could have flatly reproduced a map of the townships, marking the centers of the revolt with a cross. But he would have reduced what he saw as a cosmic event to regional dimensions. So with prodigious narrative invention, he conjures up an omen from the memoirs of a certain Pico della Mirandola. Halmalo doesn't know how to read, which does not bother Lantenac: a man who can read might get in the way. All he needs to be able to do is remember. Lantenac delivers his instructions, which I will only excerpt, as the list goes on for eight pages:

> "That will do. Listen, Halmalo. You must take to the right and I to the left. I shall go in the direction of Fougères, you toward Bazouges. Keep your bag; it gives you the look of a peasant. Conceal your weapons. Cut yourself a stick in the thickets. Creep among the fields of rye, which are high. . . . Leave passers-by at a distance. Avoid the roads and the bridges. Do not enter Pontorson. . . . You know the woods?"
>
> "All of them."
>
> "Of the whole district?"
>
> "From Noirmoutier to Laval."
>
> "Do you know their names too?"

"I know the woods; I know their names; I know about everything."

"You will forget nothing?"

"Nothing."

"Good! At present, attention. How many leagues can you make in a day?"

"Ten fifteen—twenty, if necessary."

"It will be. Do not lose a word of what I am about to say. You will go to the wood of Saint-Aubin."

"Near Lamballe?"

"Yes. On the edge of the ravine between Saint-Reuil and Plédiac there is a large chestnut-tree. You will stop there. You will see no one." . . .

"You will give the call. Do you know how to give the call?" . . .

He held out the bow of green silk to Halmalo.

"This is my badge of command. Take it. It is important that no one should as yet know my name; but this knot will be sufficient. The *fleur-de-lis* was embroidered by Madame Royale in the Temple prison." . . .

"Listen well to this. This is the order: Up! Revolt! No quarter! On the edge of this wood of Saint-Aubin you will give the call. You will repeat it thrice. The third time you will see a man spring out of the ground." . . .

"This man will be Planchenault, who is also called the King's Heart. You will show him this knot. He will understand. Then, by routes you must find out, you will go to the wood of Astillé; there you will find a cripple, who is surnamed Mousqueton, and who shows pity to none. You will tell him that I love him, and that he is to set the parishes in motion. From there you will go to the wood of Couesbon, which is a league from Ploërmel, who has belonged to what is called the Constituent Assembly, but on the good side. You will tell him to arm the castle to Couesbon, which belongs to the Marquis de Guer, a refugee. . . . Thence you will go to Saint-Guen-les-Toits, and you will talk with Jean Chouan, who is, in my mind, the real chief. From thence you will go to the wood of Ville-Anglose, where you will see Guitter, whom they call Saint Martin; you will bid him have his eye on a certain Courmesnil, who is the son-in-law of old Goupil de Préfeln, and who leads the Jacobnery of Argentan. Recollect all this. I write nothing, because nothing should be written. . . . Then you will go to the wood of Rougefeu, where is Miélette, who leaps the ravine on a long pole." (59–61)

I skip three whole pages:

"You will go to Saint-Mhervé; there you will see Gaulier, called Great Peter. You will go to the cantonment of Parné, where the men blacken their

faces. . . . You will go to the camp of Vache Noire, which is on a height; to
the middle of the wood of La Charnie, then to the camp of the Fourmis.
Then you will go to Grand Bordage, which is also called the Haut de Pré,
and is inhabited by a widow whose daughter married Treton, nicknamed the
Englishman. Grand Bordage is in the parish of Quelaines. You will visit
Epineux-le-Chevreuil, Sillé-le-Guillaume, Parannes, and all the men in all of
the woods." (64)

And so on, until their parting words:

> "Forget nothing."
> "Be tranquil."
> "Now go. May God guide you! Go."
> "I will do all that you have bidden me. I will go. I will speak. I will obey.
> I will command." (66)

Of course it is impossible for Halmalo to remember everything. Even the
reader quickly realizes with each succeeding line that he has already forgotten the names in the previous line. The list is boring, but it has to be read
and reread, like music. It is pure sound. It could be the index of names at
the back of an atlas, but this catalogical fury makes the Vendée seem infinite.

The list is an ancient technique. When something appears so immense
and confusing that a definition or description could not capture its complexity, a catalog is used to create the sense of a space and all that it contains.
The list or catalog does not fill a space—which would be neutral per se—
with significant appearances, associations, clues, or eye-catching details, but
rather aligns the names of things, persons, or places. It is an example of hypotyposis that *shows* by deploying an excess of *flatus vocis*, as if the ear had
assigned to the eye the difficult task of memorizing everything that it hears,
or as if the imagination were striving to construct a place to accommodate
all of the named things. The list is a Braille hypotyposis.

In canto 2 of the *Iliad* the list of armies gives an example of a multiplicity
of events that evoke the space they invade by filling it:

> As ravening five rips through big stands of timber
> high on a mountain ridge and the blaze flares miles away,
> so from the marching troops and the blaze of bronze armor,
> splendid and superhuman, flared across the earth,
> flashing into the air to hit the skies
> > Armies gathering now

as the huge flocks on flocks of winging birds, geese or cranes,
or swans with their long lancing necks—circling Asian marshes
round the Cayster outflow, wheeling in all directions,
glorying in their wings—keep on landing, advancing,
wave on shrieking wave and the tidal flats reserve.
So tribe on tribe, pouring out of the ships and shelters
marched across the Scamander plain and the earth shook,
tremendous thunder from under trampling men and horses
drawing into position down the Scamander river flats
breaking into flower—men by the thousands, numberless
as the leaves and spears that flower forth in spring.

The Iliad. Book 2, ll.539–59.[9]

Despite a series of other similes, the poet still seems to feel that he has not made clear the immense plain of armies that he wishes to represent. Thus he employs the list. Homer appeals to the muses to show through the sounds of fame that which we cannot see, and immediately admits that he will not be able to name all the men, only their leaders, and will therefore list, by synecdoche, the captains and the ships. Schedeius and Epistrophus appear, leading the Phoceans. Ajax commands the Locrians, the Abantes of Euboea, the men of Styra commanded by Elephenor, Diomed and Sthenelus leading the men of Argos and Tiryns, and Agamemnon the men of Mycenae, and so on for four hundred verses.

At times the list is not meant to tell us that it would be impossible to describe a space otherwise but rather as a sign of descriptive weakness, as happens in Sidonius Apollinaris's presentation of the city of Narbonne in poem 23:

Hail, Narbo, surpassing in thy healthiness, gladdening the eye with thy town and thy countryside alike, with thy walls, citizens, circuit, shops, gates, porticoes, forum, theatre, shrines, capitol, mint, baths, arches, granaries, markets, meadows, fountains, islands, salt-mines, ponds, river, merchandise, bridge and brine; thou who hast the best title of all to worship as thy gods Bacchus, Ceres, Pale and Minerva in virtue of thy corn, thy vines, thy pastures, and thine olive-mills![10]

---

[9] Homer, *The Iliad,* trans. Robert Fagles (New York: Viking, 1990), 114–15.

[10] Sidonius Apollinaris, *Poems and Letters*, trans. W. B. Anderson (Cambridge, Mass.: Harvard University Press, 1936–65), 1:284–87.

At other times the list aims to capture not only the space but the movement and excitement that animate it, as in the description of a battle in *Gargantua and Pantagruel*:

To some others he spoiled the frame of their kidneys, marred their backs, broke their thigh-bones, bashed in their noses, poached out their eyes, cleft their mandibles, tore their jaws, dug their teeth into their throat, shook asunder their omoplates or shoulder-blades, sphacelated their shins, mortified their shanks, inflamed their ankles, heaved off of the hinges their ishies, their sciatica or hip-gout, dislocated the joints of their knees, squattered into pieces the boughts or pestles of their thighs, and so thumped, mauled and belaboured them everywhere, that never was corn so thick and threefold threshed upon by ploughmen's flails as were the pitifully disjointed members of their mangled bodies under the merciless baton of the cross.

If any offered to hide himself amongst the thickest of the vines, he laid him squat as a flounder, bruised the ridge of his back, and dashed his reins like a dog.

If any thought by flight to escape, he made his head to fly in pieces by the lamboidal commissure, which is a seam in the hinder part of the skull. If anyone did scramble up into a tree, thinking there to be safe, he rent up his perinee, and impaled him in at the fundament. . . . Others, again, he so quashed and bebumped, that, with a sound bounce under the hollow of their short ribs, he overturned their stomachs so that they died immediately. To some, with a smart souse on the epigaster, he would make their midriff swag, then, redoubling the blow, gave them such a homepush on the navel that he made their puddings to gush out. To others through their ballocks he pierced their bumgut, and left not bowel, tripe, nor entrail in their body that had not felt the impetuosity, fierceness, and fury of his violence. Believe, that it was the most horrible spectacle that ever one saw. . . . Some died without speaking, others spoke without dying; some died in speaking, others spoke in dying.[11]

At times (once again in *Gargantua and Pantagruel* 2:26 and 28), as in the priceless list of "pairs of little sacring bells," the list has a purely musical function, acting almost as a metalist that bares the essence of its technique. In other places, however, the list, in the vastness of irrelevant objects that it catalogs, tries to create the sense of an accumulation of nonessential items. Such is the catalog of objects in Leopold Bloom's kitchen in the penultimate

---

[11] François Rabelais, *Gargantua and Pantagruel*, trans. Thomas Urquhart and Peter Anthony Motteux (Chicago: Encyclopedia Brittanica, 1955), 1:27.

chapter of James Joyce's *Ulysses*. This single passage on a drawer's contents should suffice (the list goes on for seventy pages in the Shakespeare and Company edition!):

> A Vere Foster's handwriting copybook, property of Milly (Millicent) Bloom, certain pages of which bore diagram drawings, marked *Papli,* which showed a large globular head with 5 hairs erect, 2 eyes in profile, the trunk full front with 3 large buttons, 1 triangular foot: 2 fading photographs of queen Alexandra of England and of Maud Branscombe, actress and professional beauty: a Yuletide card, bearing on it a pictorial representation of a parasitic plant, the legend *Mizpah,* the date Xmas 1892, the name of the senders: from Mr & Mrs M. Comerford, the versicle: *May this Yuletide bring to thee, Joy and peace and welcome glee:* a butt of red partly liquefied sealing wax, obtained from the stores department of Messrs Hely's, Ltd., 89, 90, and 91 Dame street: a box containing the remainder of a gross of gilt "J" pennibs, obtained from same department of same firm: an old sandglass which rolled containing sand which rolled: a sealed prophecy (never unsealed) written by Leopold Bloom in 1886 concerning the consequences of the passing into law of William Ewart Gladstone's Home Rule bill of 1886 (never passed into law): a bazaar ticket, no 2004, of S. Kevin's Charity Fair, price 6d, 100 prizes.[12]

Hugo is more on the side of Homer, and not far from that of Rabelais. Nothing about the list that Halmalo is pretending (I hope) to remember is nonessential: the ensemble and amplitude of the counterrevolution, its rootedness in the land, hedges, villages, forests, and parishes. Hugo knows the ins and outs of lists, including the conviction (which Homer may have shared) that readers would never read the whole list (or that the *aedo*'s audience would have listened to it the way one listens to the rosary, surrendering to its enchanting mystique). I have no doubt Hugo knew that his readers would skip these pages, as Manzoni himself must have when, in violation of every narrative rule, he leaves us hanging at the moment when Don Abbondio faces the bravos, and proceeds to give us four pages of proclamations (actually, four in the 1840 edition but almost six in the 1827 edition). Readers skip these pages (perhaps they might dwell a little longer during a second or third reading) but they cannot ignore the fact that the list is right before their eyes, forcing them to skip it because it is unbearable, gaining

---

[12] James Joyce, *Ulysses* (New York: Random House, 1934), 230.

strength from its very unbearability. Going back to Hugo, the insurrection is so widespread that in reading about it, we could not remember all the protagonists or even just the leaders if we tried. Our remorse over this deferred reading is what makes us feel the sublimity of the Vendée.

Sublime is the legitimist revolt, as must be the image of the Convention, the quintessence of the revolt. We come to book 3, entitled "To the Convention." The first three chapters describe the hall. The descriptive abundance of the writing in the first seven pages already leaves the reader dazed and without any sense of space. But then it continues, and for another fifteen pages, with the list of the members of the Convention, along the following general lines:

> To the right, the Gironde,—a legion of thinkers; to the left, the Mountain,— a group of athletes. On one side Brissot, who had received the keys of the Bastille; Barbaroux, whom the Marseillas obeyed; Kervélégan, who had under his hand the battalion of Brest, garrisoned in the Faubourg Saint Marceau; Gensonné, who had established the supremacy of the Representatives over the generals . . . Sillery, the cripple of the Right, as Couthon was the paralytic of the Left. Lause-Duperret, who, having been called a scoundrel by a journalist, invited him to dinner, saying, "I know that by scoundrel you simply mean a man who does not think like yourself." Rabaut Saint-Etienne, who commenced his almanac for 1790 with this saying: "The Revolution is ended." . . . Vigée, who called himself a grenadier in the second battalion of Mayenne and Loire, and who, when menaced by the public tribunals, cried, "I demand that at the first murmur of the tribunals we all withdraw and march on Versailles, sabre in hand!" Buzot, reserved for death by famine; Valazé, destined to die by his own dagger; Condorcet, who was to perish at Bourg-la-Reine (become Bourg-Egalité), betrayed by the Horace which he had in his pocket; Pétion, whose destiny was to be adored by the crowd in 1792 and devoured by wolves in 1794: twenty others still,— Pontecoulant, Marboz, Lidon, Saint-Martin, Dussaulx, the translator of Juvenal, who had been in the Hanover campaign; Boileau, Bertrand, Lesterp-Beauvais, Lesage, Gomaire, Gardien, Mainvelle, Duplentier, Lacaze, Antiboul, and at their head a Barnave, who was styled Verginaud. (150–52)

And so on, for fifteen pages, like the litany for a Black Mass, Antonie-Louis-Léon Florelle de Saint-Just, Merlin de Thionville, Merkin de Douai, Billaud-Varenne, Fabre d'Englantine, Fréron-Thersite, Osselin, Garan-Coulon, Javogues, Camboulas, Collot, d'Herbois, Goupilleau, Laurent Lecointre, Léonard Bourdoin, Bourbotte, Levasseur de la Sarthe, Reverchon, Bernard de Saintres, Charles Richard, Châteauneuf-Randon, Lavicomterie,

Le Peletier de Saint-Fourgeau, as if Hugo were fully aware that in this mad catalog the reader would lose sight of the individual actors for the titanic dimensions of the single actant that he intended to put on stage: the revolution in all its glory and misery.

Yet Hugo seems (out of weakness, shyness, excess of excess?) to fear that the reader (who is nevertheless expected to skip this part) cannot truly grasp the dimensions of the monster that he wishes to represent and behold. In a new technique in the history of the list, different in every way from the description of the Vendée, the author's voice intervenes at the beginning, at the end, in the middle of the list, to continuously draw its moral:

> It's the Convention. . . .
> At the sight of this summit, one is dumbstruck
> Nothing higher had ever appeared on the human horizon.
> There are the Himalayas and there is the Convention. . . .
> The Convention is the first avatar of the people. . . .
> Taken as a whole it was violent, barbaric, normal. Respectability in ferocity: it was a little like the entire revolution. . . .
> Nothing more chaotic and more sublime. A crowd of heroes; a mob of cowards. Fallow deer on a mountain; reptiles in a marsh. . . .
> A convocation of Titans. . . .
> Tragedies knotted by giants and untied by dwarfs. . . .
> Spirits which were a prey of the wind. But this was a miracle-working wind. . . .
> Such was the unmeasured and immeasurable Convention,—a camp cut off from the human race, attacked by all the powers of darkness at once; the night-fires of the besieged army of Ideas; a vast bivouac of minds upon the edge of a precipice. There is nothing in history comparable to this group, at the same time senate and populace, conclave and street-crossing, Arcopagus and public square, tribunal and the accused.
> The Convention always bent to the wind; but that wind came from the mouth of the people, and was the breath of God. . . .
> It would be impossible not to remain thoughtfully attentive before this grand procession of shadows. (150–68)

Unbearable? Unbearable. Magniloquent? Even worse. Sublime? Sublime. You can see that I am captivated by my author and have even begun to speak like him: but when the magniloquence overflows and breaks down the wall of sound of excessive excess, one begins to suspect the presence of poetry. *Hélas!*

An author (unless he or she is writing only for money, without hope of immortality, from a readership of seamstresses, salesmen, or pornophiles known for their tastes in one specific moment in one specific country) never writes for an empirical reader but rather tries to construct a model reader; in other words, a reader who, having accepted the textual rules proposed from the outset, will become the book's ideal reader, even a thousand years later. What model reader did Hugo have in mind? I believe he was thinking of two. The first was someone reading in 1874, eighty years after the fatal Ninety-three—someone who still recognized many of the names of the Convention: as if an Italian today were reading a book about the 1920s, and was not completely unprepared for the appearance of figures such as Mussolini, D'Annunzio, Marinetti, Facta, Corridoni, Matteotti, Papini, Boccioni, Carrà, Italo Balbo, or Turati. The second reader is the future reader (or even the foreign reader of Hugo's time), who—with the exception of a few names, such as Robespierre, Danton, and Marat—would be bewildered by such a medley of names. At the same time, however, this person would have the impression of overhearing an unstoppable gossip speaking of a village that the reader is visiting for the first time and where he or she is slowly learning to unravel a multitude of contradictory figures, sniff out the atmosphere, and gradually get used to moving through the crowded arena where every unknown face may be imagined as the mask of a story drenched in blood and, ultimately, one of the many masks of history.

As I have said, Hugo is not interested in the psychology of his wooden or stone characters. He is interested in the antonomasia to which we defer or, if you prefer, to their symbolic value. The same attitude applies to things: the forest of the Vendée or the Torgue, the immense "Tour Gauvain" where Lantenac is besieged by Gauvain—two men connected to the ancestral residence that both are seeking to destroy, the assailant from outside and the besieged from within, threatening a final holocaust. Much ink has been spilled on the symbolic value of the tower, also because another innocent symbolic gesture is consummated inside it, the destruction of a book by three children.

Hostages of Lantenac, who has threatened to blow them up if the republicans attempt to free them, locked in the library of the besieged tower, the children can do little more than destroy things, so they turn a precious book on St. Bartholomew into a flurry of torn paper. Their gesture has been universally interpreted as a negative imitation of the night of St. Bartholomew, the shame of the former monarchy, and therefore, perhaps, a historic revenge, a childish antistrophe of the annihilation in the past whose work would be concluded by the guillotine. For that matter, the chapter that narrates this story within the story is entitled "The Massacre of St. Bartholomew," because Hugo was always concerned that his readers were not trembling enough.

This gesture, too, takes on symbolic hues thanks to excess. The childish games are related in minute detail for fifteen pages. Through this excessiveness Hugo notifies us that here, too, we are dealing not with an individual story but with the tragedy of an actant who may not have been redemptive but was at least benevolent: Innocence. He could obviously have resolved everything through a fulminating epiphany. That he was capable of doing so can be seen in the last lines of book 3, chapter 6: little Georgette gathers by the handful the parts of the book assigned to the sacral *sparagmos*, throws them out the window, sees them soaring on the wind and says "papillons." So the ingenuous massacre segues into butterflies vanishing into the sky. But Hugo could not fit this brief epiphany into a plot with so many other excesses, at the risk of its seeming imperceptible. If excess has reason to exist, even the most dazzling apparitions of the numinous (contrary to all mystic traditions) have to last for long periods. In *Ninety-three*, even grace has to appear in the form of murkiness, a bubbling of white-hot lava, waters overflowing, inundations of affects and effects. What is the use of asking Wagner to squeeze his entire tetrology into the measures of a Chopin scherzo?

To shake lose of our author's grasp, let us jump ahead, critically, to the ending. After a truly epic battle (Hugo would have been a great screenwriter!), Gauvain finally captures Lantenac. The duel is over. Cimourdain has no hesitations, and, even before the trial, gives orders to erect the guillotine. Killing Lantenac would be tantamount to killing the Vendée, and killing the Vendée would be tantamount to saving France.

But Lantenac, as I said at the beginning, gives himself up voluntarily to save the three children, who have risked being burned to death in the library to which he alone has the key. In the face of this humane gesture, Gauvain does not have the heart to send him to his death, so he rescues him. Hugo consumes other oratorical resources to compare the two worlds, first in the dialogue between Lantenac and Gauvain, and then in the dialogue between Cimourdain and Gauvain, who at that point is awaiting his death. In Lantenac's first invective against Gauvain (before realizing that the latter means to save him), he deploys the full arrogance of the *ci-devant* before the representative who had guillotined the king. In the confrontation between Cimourdain and Gauvain an abyss emerges between the high priest of vengeance and the apostle of hope. I want the man of Euclid, Cimourdain says. Gauvain replies that he wants the man of Homer. The whole novel tells us (in stylistic terms) that Hugo would take Homer's part, which is why he fails to make us loathe his Homeric Vendée, but in ideological terms this particular Homer tried to tell us that to build the future we have to pass through the straight line of the guillotine.

———

This is the story that the book tells us, the story of Hugo's stylistic choices, the story of a reading (my own—and others are possible). What can we say? That the historians have identified many anachronisms and unacceptable liberties in the book? What does it matter? Hugo was not trying to write history. He wanted us to feel the panting breath, the often stinking roar of history. To deceive us like Marx, who claimed that Hugo was more interested in the individual's moral conflicts than in understanding the class struggle?[13] If anything it was the opposite. Hugo carves out his psychology with a hatchet to make us feel the forces in conflict. While he may not have been thinking of the class struggle, he was certainly contemplating the ideals, as Lukács realized, of a "revolutionary democracy that indicates the way of the future." Lukács later tempered his judgment with the severe admonition that "the real human and historical collisions of the aristocrat and the priest, who have aligned themselves with the Revolution, are turned into ingenious conflicts of duty based on this abstract humanism."[14] For crying out loud, it has even been said that Hugo was not interested in the social classes but rather in the people and God. Typical of Lukács's mental inflexibility in his last works was the inability to understand that Hugo could not be Lenin (if anything, Lenin was a Cimourdain who did not kill himself) and that indeed the tragic and romantic magic of *Ninety-three* lies in bringing together on the same playing field the reasons of history and the reasons of various single morals, to measure the constant fracture between politics and utopia.

Nevertheless, to understand the deep movements both of the revolution and of its enemy, the Vendée—which is still today's ideology for the many people who are nostalgic for *la France profonde*—I believe there can be no better reading. To tell the story of two excesses, Hugo's only choice (faithful to his poetics) was the technique of excess taken to excess. It is only by accepting this convention that one can understand the Convention, and

[13] Karl Marx, *The Eighteenth Brumaire of Louis Bonaparte*, trans. Eden Paul and Cedar Paul (New York: International Publishers, 1926).

[14] Georg Lukács, *The Historical Novel*, trans. Hannah and Stanley Mitchell (London: Merlin Press, 1962), 257.

thereby become the model reader for whom Hugo yearned—constructed not with a wiry armature but rather with an *opus incertum* of barely blocked-out rock. If you enter into the spirit that animates this novel, however, you might come out dry-eyed but with your mind in tumult. *Hélas*!

Translated by Michael F. Moore

ALEX WOLOCH

Minor Characters

> Character is arguably the most important single
> component of the novel. Other narrative forms, such as
> epic, and other media, such as film, can tell a story as
> well, but nothing can equal the great tradition of the
> European novel in the richness, variety and
> psychological depth of its portrayal of human nature.
> —DAVID LODGE, *The Art of Fiction*

> Character is the major aspect of the novel to which
> structuralism has paid least attention and has been least
> successful in treating.
> —JONATHAN CULLER, *Structuralist Poetics*

Theorizing Character-Space

The history of the novel is littered with a panoply of characters, a multitudinous, almost countless, array of human possibilities, splintered and partial images of ourselves.[1] But if characterization is "the most important single component of the novel," a retreat from characterization seems almost equally central to the twentieth-century theory of the novel. The dismissal of the literary character originates, as we will see, in a heightened attention to narrative form. But it has actually clouded a great formal question—and problematic—of the novel: the interaction among and competition between a multitude of characters who are coimplicated within a single narrative structure. Turning our attention to this competition—a competition that only takes place within, and in relation to, literary form—elucidates a process that is crucial to the history of the novel as genre. The problem of social competition—so central a theme and concern of the novel—is also manifested in the formal logic of novelistic characterization itself. Each implied person in a novel, whether hero or subordinated character, gets configured and developed as a character within a larger narrative form, jostling for space and attention among a crowded field of other characters. To put this programmatically: every character has two destinies in a novel. The novel

---

[1] Portions of this essay, particularly the section "Theorizing Character-Space," are revised or excerpted from Woloch, *The One vs. the Many.*

simultaneously unfolds his or her fate as an implied person within the plot or story-world itself and his or her fate as a potential narrative site of attention with a precarious, contingent, and always dynamically developing space in the narrative discourse. In some cases either one of these destinies might lead nowhere—or nowhere of significance. But the novel, perhaps more than any other genre, often develops each of these destinies in complicated interaction with the other: narrative fate (within the discourse) and social fortune (within the story) are intertwined, synthesized or, just as fruitfully, placed in mortal combat.

Consider these two passages from Trollope and Dostoevsky, both of which self-consciously allude to the pressures of inscribing the implied person into a delimited form. First, from *The Idiot*:

> Let us not forget that the motives behind human actions are usually infinitely more complicated and various than we assume them to be . . . do as we will, we are now under the absolute necessity of devoting to this secondary character in our story rather more space and attention than we originally had intended. (502)

And, from *Barchester Towers*, at the very end of chapter 3:

> Mr. Slope, however, on his first introduction must not be brought before the public at the tail of a chapter. (21)

Both of these passages explicitly render the novel's own awareness of the amount of narrative space allocated to a particular character. Squeezing a character into the end of a chapter creates a tension between our sense of the character as an actual human placed within an imagined world and the space of the character within the narrative structure. Trollope's example (a character who is too important to get pushed into the end of a chapter) is expanded into a general principle by Dostoevsky: all characters are potentially over-delimited within the fictional world—and might disrupt the narrative if we pay them the attention that they deserve. Trollope's comment about Mr. Slope and the tail of a chapter is so suggestive because it relies both on our ability to imagine a character as though he were a real person, who exists outside of the parameters of the novel, and on our awareness of such a highly formal aspect of the narrative structure as chapter divisions. The character-space marks the intersection of an implied human personality—that is, as Dostoevsky says, "infinitely" complex—with the definitively circumscribed form of a narrative. It is the point where Mr. Slope can meet the "tail of a chapter." In this sense, the implied person is never directly reflected in the literary text but only partially inflected; each individual portrait has a radically contingent position within the story as a whole.

This essay will consider how the idea of character-space bears on the history and theory of the novel—and how it might recast the dilemma that characterization has posed for narrative theory. The stark contrast between the two epigraphs by Lodge and Culler—which frame the character as, respectively, the "most" important and "least" attended aspect of the novel— is not incidental. We can find echoes of Culler's admonition in any number of narrative theorists who have tried unsuccessfully to elaborate a rigorous or conceptual account of characterization within the novel. The problem of the literary character is, in fact, connected to the grounding premises of narrative theory. For much twentieth-century theory, identifying with or investing in the literary character might be the engine of the novel's popularity as a literary genre, but it is also the most glaring sign of readerly naïveté. Twentieth-century formalisms continually get derived against the literary character: the naive "recognition" of characters ensures a misrecognition of the constructed novel itself, an elision of the formal technique and narrative structuration that underlies and motivates our fictional investments. The formal mode of interpretation does not merely posit itself in opposition to a general reader's unmediated response to novels but also in opposition to a long-standing and antithetical tradition of criticism, which revolves precisely around extracting an implied person from the literary text in order to contemplate his or her ethical, cultural, or existential import and bearing.

In *The Craft of Fiction*, Percy Lubbock frames this ethico-humanist approach to character in perhaps its most familiar guise, describing the experience of reading Samuel Richardson's *Clarissa*: "It is so easy to construct the idea of the exquisite creature, that she seems to step from the pages of her own accord; I, as I read, am aware of nothing but that a new acquaintance is gradually becoming better and better known to me. . . . And so, too, with the lesser people in the book, and their surroundings." (8)

It is precisely this transformation of the literary character into an implied person outside the parameters of the narrative text that underlies the attack on characterization by twentieth-century literary theory. The Russian formalists, for example, seek to eviscerate the trope of a character who "step[s] from the pages" precisely to remind us that we can never forget about these "pages"—or the actual, material and linguistic structure that underlies narrative signification and literary form. In a polemical version of this, Boris Tomachevski argues that the protagonist in a literary work has no significance other than holding the pages of the narrative together. For Tomachevski the hero should not be understood as the central person whose story the literary text elaborates but rather a central device that acts as glue for the text itself, "a sort of living support for the text's different motifs." Tomachevski continues: "The hero is hardly necessary to the story. The story, as a system of motifs, can entirely bypass the hero and his characteristic traits. The hero . . . represents . . . a means to tie together the motifs. . . . [He] is necessary so that one can tie together anecdotes around him" (293–98). Tomachevski's transformation of person into motivating device encapsulates the way that many theories have sought to bind the literary character to the narrative text. We can think here of Propp's morphological typology; Greimas's subsequent absorption of characters into fixed "syntactic" positions (all characters are variations of six actants with specific narrative roles); Bakhtin's reduction of the character to "an image of a language"; or Barthes's dissolution of the character into the dispersed thematic field that surrounds him.[2] All of these theorists halt the critical movement from character to person. Characters function in this critical perspective; they point us not to an imagined person whom we might identify with, evaluate, or reconstruct but rather to the hidden narrative processes that underlie this identification in the first place. A specific critical drama is repeatedly enacted with Propp, Greimas, Barthes, Bakhtin, and numerous other twentieth-century theorists. Narrativity becomes visible only through the effacement of the characters' referential bearing; the decoupling of literary characters from their implied humanness becomes the price of entry into a theoretical perspective on characterization.[3] And interpretation of character—whether in cutting-edge scholarship or an introductory literature course—comes to rest above all on that well-known shibboleth: don't treat the character like a person.

Such a process has inevitably generated a critical reaction, a countergesture that seeks to rehabilitate the referential plentitude that seems elided by a purely narratological, structural, or ideological configuration of the character. Analysis of character tends to devolve into polemical argument, with both sides ironically depending on the very viewpoint that they are dismissing. Consider two passages from L. C. Knights's famous 1933 attack on

---

[2] See Vladimir Propp, *Morphology of the Folktale;* A. J. Greimas, *Sémantique structurale,* 172–92; M. M. Bakhtin, *The Dialogic Imagination;* and Roland Barthes, "Introduction to the Structural Analysis of Narratives," and *S/Z.*

[3] As Propp already writes in 1928, "The functions of a folktale's dramatis personae must be considered as its basic components; and we must first of all extract them as such. In order to extract them we must, of necessity, define them. . . . First of all, definition should, in no case, stem from the dramatis persona—the 'bearer' of a function" (19).

Shakespearean character-criticism and Irving Howe's more recent broadside against the poststructural elision of character.

> To examine the historical development of that kind of criticism which is mainly concerned with "character" is to strengthen the case against it. . . . Wherever we look we find the same reluctance to master the words of the play, the same readiness to abstract a character and treat him (because he is more manageable that way) as a human being. . . . The habit of regarding Shakespeare's persons as "friends for life" or, maybe, "deceased acquaintances," is responsible for most of the vagaries that serve as Shakespeare criticism. (11, 27–28)

> The sophisticated if just barely readable French theorist Hélène Cixous writes that a novel with mimetic characters turns into "a machine of repression" . . . since it presents a historical given as if it were everlasting and thereby thwarts all hope for transcendence. . . . There is something bizarre in the notion that fictional characterization is an agency of repression; . . . this is to confuse narrative conventions with social categories. Where, in any case, have our strongest visions of possibility, as also our most telling social criticisms, come from if not the great novelists—it is they who have given imaginative substance to what the young Marx called "the human essence," and far better and more fully than any social theorists. . . . The great fictional characters, from Robinson Crusoe to Flem Snopes, from Tess to Molly Bloom, cannot quite be "fitted" into or regarded solely as functions of narrative. Why should we want to? What but the delusions of system and total grasp do we gain thereby? Such characters are too interesting, too splendidly mysterious for mere functional placement. (38, 42)

These two starkly contrasting—but perhaps equally convincing—perspectives are typical of theoretical positions about characters: both Howe and Knights are urging the reader to choose. Each reading is generated in large part through the opposed position, which it configures into an extreme in order to reverse. But in this opposition, we can begin to see a single process that structures and gives form to two seemingly irreconcilable points of view. Characterization has been such a divisive question in twentieth-century literary theory—creating recurrent disputes between humanist and structural (or mimetic and formal) positions—because the literary character is itself divided, always emerging at the juncture between structure and reference. A literary dialectic that operates dynamically within the narrative text gets transformed into a theoretical contradiction, presenting us with an unpalatable choice: language or reference, structure or individuality.

The character-space opens up a mode of analysis to comprehend this dialectical process. In Lubbock's grounding image of referentiality, for example, we can already see the working of form: the "lesser people" whom we extract together with "the exquisite" protagonist are not actually lesser as "people" but are, precisely, subordinate in terms of narrative structure. Conversely, we might consider the ubiquity of "functionality," which is so often the fulcrum of structuralist and formalist models of characterization. Structuralism demonstrates how it is impossible to read characters outside of their continual absorption into the thematic, symbolic, and structural economies of the text. In one of the most incisive elaborations of this, Roland Barthes describes the "level-jumping" that is involved in reading any narrative: the vertical "integration" that takes place, necessarily, alongside of any horizontal progression (through the world of the story itself). Even as we are reading details that unfold in relation to the implied individual, each detail is absorbed into numerous, and consequential, narrative levels that are directed away from this specific character. This is one of structuralism's great insights into narrative fiction. But rather than simply extracting the thematic "yield" from a character, we need to pay attention to an often dramatic, and dynamically elaborated, conflict between the implied person who underlies this significance, and the abstracted value of the significance itself. In his essay on vertical integration, Barthes is thus drawn to offer another abbreviated version of the double bind that bedevils theories of characterization.

> The problems raised by a classification of the characters of narrative are not as yet satisfactorily resolved. Certainly there is ready agreement on the fact that the innumerable characters of narrative can be brought under rules of substitution and that, even within the one work, a single figure can absorb different characters. . . . A difficulty, however, is that when the matrix has a high classificational power (as in the case of Greimas's actants) it fails adequately to account for the multiplicity of participations as soon as these are analyzed in terms of perspectives and that when these perspectives are respected (as in Bremond's description) the system of characters remains too fragmented. ("Structural Analysis," 107–8)

In somewhat technical language, Barthes here broaches the same dilemma we have been discussing. Either the distinct "perspectives" of individual characters are effaced or attention to, and "respect" for, these multifarious perspectives "fragments" the comprehension of structure. By "perspective," Barthes is gesturing at the implied point of view of a discretely configured character. His rhetoric of "respect" implicitly underlies this point: what else, if not the implied personhood of these characters (understood referentially) would motivate such a verb? Barthes himself does not suggest a new answer to this double bind but rather is prompted to raise a number of questions, questions that correspond surprisingly well to our elaboration of character-space: "The real difficulty posed by the classification of characters is the place (and hence the existence) of the *subject* in any actantial matrix, whatever its formulation. *Who* is the subject (the hero) of a narrative? Is there—or not—a privileged class of actors?" (108, Barthes's emphases). Why does Barthes underline this "who" [*qui*]? His emphasis works to accentuate the necessarily referential implication of a question that is produced by a structural problem. Here is a salutary example of the way that the referential dimension of character can loom over efforts to conceptualize or discuss narrative in strictly formal terms. In another twist, however, Barthes's second question, which seems to follow logically from the first, quickly recasts this problem of identity back into structure: the problem of the "who" is only worked out through an axis of distribution that is constructed in relation to the closed narrative form. The inextricability of the "whoness" and the "whereness" of characters (their implied identity and their location—and configuration— within the form) becomes apparent in a third subtle turn of the screw: the "privilege" of character, like Barthes's earlier "respect," emanates out of the referential ground, even if the term functions overtly to describe a simple structural hinge (one class of actor appears more frequently within the structure, one class of actors less frequently).

Barthes's idea of the "privileged class" of characters leads us somewhere else as well, with its overtone of social or economic class emerging out of the structural matrix (but also, implicitly, in relation to the referential bases of character). As I've suggested, this overtone relies on—and thus again demonstrates—the implicit interplay between the "who" and the "where" of character. The distributive configuration that underlies privilege cannot be located outside of the areferential arrangement of characters within the narrative discourse, but this configuration cannot be translated into or understood as privilege without reference to the imputed value or merit of the characters as implied human beings. The character cannot be understood as merely a structural element (as in Knights's description) nor an implied person (as in Howe's): rather, every character arises only in the charged interaction between the implied person and the narrative structure.

The "privileged class" of characters illustrates the most fundamental way that the distributive grid both takes form and signifies: through arranging attention among a series of simultaneously configured character-spaces. Each figure is trapped differentially in the form. It is precisely in this way that the fate of any character—as implied individual—cannot be detached from his or her fate in the narrative discourse. There is, however, never a purely isolated conflict between one character and the form—as in the image of Mr. Slope clashing against the edge of a chapter. Characters do not exist inside an empty structure, like Robinson Crusoe on his deserted island.[4] Rather the space of a particular character only emerges vis-à-vis the other characters who crowd her out or potentially revolve around her. This interaction between character-spaces—within a character-system—is qualitatively distinct from (even if often related to) any social interactions that we might derive or extrapolate outside of the form, in the referenced conflicts and relations between implied persons within the world of the story itself. For the character-system offers not simply many interacting individuals but many intersecting character-spaces, each of which encompasses an embedded interaction between the discretely implied person and the dynamically elaborated narrative form. While characters themselves might or might not gain a relationship, character-spaces inevitably do. To put this differently, any character-spaces ultimately point us toward the character-system, since the emplacement (and final "destiny") of a character within the narrative form is largely comprised by his or her relative position vis-à-vis other characters. If the character-space frames the dynamic interaction between a discretely implied individual and the overall narrative form, the character-system comprehends the mutually constituting interactions between all the character-spaces as they are (simultaneously) developed within a specific narrative.

Pursuing this further, I want to juxtapose Barthes's comments on the "privileged class" of characters with these remarks by Raymond Williams in *Marxism and Literature*:

> In modern class societies the selection of characters almost always indicates an assumed or conscious class position. The conventions of selection are more intricate when hierarchy is less formal. Without formal ratification, all other persons may be conventionally presented as instrumental (servants, drivers, waiters), as merely environmental (other people in the street) or indeed as essentially absent (not seen, not relevant). . . . The social hierarchy or social norms that are assumed or invoked are substantial terms of relationship which the conventions are intended (often, in the confidence of a form,

---

[4] This example is meant ironically: the great novelistic representation of solitude is notable for the number of characters who flood into the narrative, and onto the island, by the end of Crusoe's captivity. There is, in fact, much to be said about the character-system in Defoe's novel.

not consciously) to carry. They are no less terms of social relationship when the hierarchy or selection is not manifestly social but is based on the assignment of different orders of significant being to the selected few and the irrelevant many. (175)

Williams's comment, beginning from an extraliterary perspective, crosses paths with Barthes's formal observations. Williams stresses that actual contexts of social relation underlie the formal organization of characters within a narrative structure. At first glance, this might seem to draw a too direct, unmediated relationship between the literary and extraliterary: there is a "modern class society" that squeezes persons into class roles; characters in the novel are also squeezed into roles; the servant in the novel, reduced to his instrumental labor, directly reflects the class society that motivates this arrangement. But the servant's work is, in fact, only instrumentalized through that very functionality which takes place in relation to the narrative discourse (understood, at least momentarily, as a closed, areferential semantic field). In this respect, we need to tease out the formal implication of one of Williams's comments, which strikingly complements Barthes's oddly referential invocation of "respect" and "privilege." By "different orders of significant being," Williams wants to suggest the ontological status dependent on the referential dimension of the character (a being is significant), but this bleeds into the thematic status of the character (a being has significance). Having significance, or playing a functional role within the construction of a narrative's signifying structure, often drains a character of "significant being": their significance makes them useful or functional in relation to something else, not in and of themselves.

As we have seen, this instrumentality or functionality rests close to the heart of the structuralist account of character. Characters are always being put to use, and such usefulness travels quickly from discourse to story. In fact, narratology has had trouble distinguishing between two kinds of instrumentality: a secondary character can become significant in so far as he is "absorbed in an atemporal matrix structure" (Barthes, 98), or in more specific relationship to another (more central) character. The most convincing of Greimas's six actantial categories (which have survived as a bolster for the entire structuralist account of character) are certainly the "adjuvant" and the "opposant"—the helper and the opposer, whom we can immediately recognize within almost any novel. A helper, at the simplest level, is a character who aids in the construction of the plot, or, in other words, helps the progress of another character. It is hard to dissociate the helper's signifying role from a character-structure that, as Williams suggests, assigns "different orders of significant being to the selected few and the irrelevant many." The organization of the signifying structure itself, in other words, can comprehend a complicated social world—a world that is elaborated in part through the tension between a minor character's status as a discrete, significant being and his or her abstraction into the role of a functionalized, signifying discursive element.

The "selected few" and the "irrelevant many": the novelistic character-system turns, above all, on the dynamic orchestration of, and relationship between, dominant and subordinate elements within the narrative construct. Who is the focus of the story and how is attention apportioned? Many genres rely on some version of the protagonist and, at the same time, have needs—both formal and mimetic—to incorporate numerous other individuals into the narrative structure. This conflict can take many forms. In some genres, the subordinated characters who flood into a protagonist's world might go relatively undistorted: they have smaller character-spaces, but the configuration and texture of the character-space strongly resembles the space of the protagonist himself. In other cases, as often with highly allegorical texts, the ideology of the protagonist tamps down the dynamic potential of the subordinated character-space: the right kind of form, like the wrong kind of government, can simply make people fall into place. The novel is perhaps uniquely animated by these conflicts, because of its investment in the democratization of the hero. The novel has always been praised for two contradictory generic achievements: depth psychology and social expansiveness, depicting the interior life of a singular consciousness and casting a wide narrative gaze over a complex social universe. In the paradigmatic character-structure of the realist novel, any character can be a protagonist, but only one character is. In fact, the commitment to everyday life both intensifies and threatens to obviate the drive toward a privileged (or central) character. The extension of psychological depth to ordinary persons creates a fundamental conflict, built into the very logic of the novel's development, between revitalizing and deploying the vehicle of a (now socially typical) protagonist and abolishing the centrality of the protagonist altogether.

This is a creative choice with deep social consequences: a choice (or series of choices) that any particular novel faces but also one that is intertwined with the historicity of the genre as a whole. In one way, certainly, the strong protagonist is a crucial vehicle of democratization in the history of the novel. By insisting that a servant, an orphan, the child of a peasant or a worker can function as hero, novels like *Pamela, La vie de Marianne, Tom Jones, Le rouge et le noir, Jane Eyre*, or *Germinal* dramatize the "infinite" depth of ordinary persons. These novels do not merely deploy but actively depend on the ideology of the hero, which we can define as the imputation of psychological or ethical value (or at least, with the antihero, significance) through narrative centrality. The technologies of the protagonist are crucial to the way these novels widen the social framework of worthiness. But this very extension of psychological depth to common persons simultaneously creates a problem for the array of newly configured heroes, unsettling the subordination of the various characters who still constitute the socionarrative world of the protagonist. The novel provokes its own unreliability, its own instability: using strong protagonists to dramatize the interior plenitude of common persons, it suggests that the very device of the protagonist might inherently compress, and distort, the experience of all the other persons in the novel. (The prevalence of the antihero in the history of the novel could then be explained as a curious compromise formation between these two tendencies).[5]

Beginning with the consolidation of omniscient narrative in the nineteenth century, almost every novel is informed by the problematic of character-space: both in terms of the contingent elaboration of a particular "hero" or central protagonist and in the inflection of inevitable (and often numerous) minor characters. The dominant model of characterization in the nineteenth-century third-person novel is an asymmetric one: a strong, central protagonist is foregrounded, whereas many minor characters are integrated into the story while becoming subordinated as individuals. The rise of the third-person (and increasingly omniscient or pseudo-omniscient) voice in the nineteenth-century novel loosens the intrinsic motivation of centrality that we often find in many earlier novels: distribution of narrative attention becomes much more unstable and contingent when the narrative as a whole does not emanate from a character who is inscribed within the story. Often the most significant protagonists of the nineteenth-century novel emerge into centrality, while their destinies (in both story and discourse) unfold in relation to numerous other figures who do not share the attention of the detached narrator and thus are emplaced in more compressed, and frequently

---

[5] We might say that the antihero arises when these two modes of democratizing the hero intersect—as though the social-formal problem of privileged centrality is introjected *into* the character or personality of the central protagonist himself. More than in other genres, the novelistic antihero is burdened by the problem of *unearned centrality*. Consider the way that Stendhal and Austen reconfigure centrality in shifting from the meritocratic protagonist (Julien Sorel, Elizabeth Bennet) to the overprivileged or underqualified protagonist (Fabrice and Emma in the former case, Fanny Price in the latter).

distorted, positions within the narrative. If a first-person narrative immediately consigns centrality to a specific figure, the main character in a third-person novel can get developed as a protagonist: in fact, his or her centrality is refracted over the course of the entire narrative.

A key example of this, treated at length in my study *The One vs. the Many*, is the belated emergence of Elizabeth Bennet in *Pride and Prejudice*—whose discursive centrality is subtly developed over the course of the narrative, even as the character "develops" or grows within the story itself. In fact, these two forms of "growth" are often conjoined in the nineteenth-century bildungsroman—the development of the protagonist (as central character in the narrative discourse) intertwined with the protagonist's development (as youthful character in the story itself). Austen's novel stunningly embeds the very development of the central protagonist's interiority (as it takes place across story and discourse) within a larger asymmetric field organized around the social—and narrative—competition resulting from the looming threat of disinheritance (a threat, we remember, that underlies this novel's marriage-plot). Beginning with the differentiation of the five Bennet sisters (all of whom share a single social predicament), the novel rigorously establishes a relationship between its achieved representation of the protagonist and the flattening and distortion of a manifold group of minor characters. Asymmetry in *Pride and Prejudice* is manifested most clearly in the relentless transformation of characters into characteristics: flat characters are reduced to single qualities (think of Mary, Collins, or Lydia) that function to define, by way of contrast, the central protagonist's depth. Think of Charlotte Lucas: she suffers not just a different—more unfortunate—fate in the story but a radically different elaboration in the narrative discourse. Moreover, Charlotte's delimited development is leveraged to enhance the fullness of Elizabeth: as numerous critics have argued, the protagonist grows in the comparison with her more practical or less principled friend. Indeed this process is systematic in *Pride and Prejudice*—every minor character, becoming subordinated, is absorbed into the protagonist's constructed depth.

In the nineteenth-century novel, more generally, the flatness and functionality of characters develops together—and both ultimately emerge out of the underlying asymmetric structure itself. Forced to circumscribe the interior lives of many characters in the elaboration of a singular, central consciousness, the asymmetric character-system has to radically delimit, and thus distort, the discursive actualization of subordinate characters' "infinite complexity." The descriptive conventions that arise around minorness depict the symptoms of such disjunction, which takes two dominant forms: the engulfing of an interior personality by the delimited signs that express it and the explosion of the suffocated interior being into an unrepresentable, fragmentary, symptomatic form. These two existential states lie behind the two major extremes of minorness within the nineteenth-century novel: the worker and the eccentric, the flat character who is reduced to a single functional use within the narrative (if not explicitly in the plot or story), and the fragmentary character who plays a disruptive or oppositional role. In *Pride and Prejudice*, for example, we could think of Lydia and Mary (one forced to stay monotonously at home; one in a perpetual state of displacement); or, in *Jane Eyre*, we might consider the way that one of the most famous eccentrics, Bertha Mason (with the "continued outbreaks of her violent and unreasonable temper" [291]) is first confused with the much more taciturn servant Grace Poole (a "person of few words" "hard-featured and staid, she had no point to which interest could attach" [101]). These two kinds of characters (with their distinct narrative function and existential bearing) form two sides of a single coin. In one case, the character is smoothly absorbed as a gear within the narrative machine, at the cost of his or her own free interiority; in the other case, the minor character grates against his or her position and is usually, as a consequence, wounded, exiled, expelled, ejected, imprisoned, or killed (within the discourse, if not the story).

The "worker" and the "eccentric" suggest modalities through which we can begin to organize the varied ways that characters can get positioned in a narrative—functionalized, compressed, exiled, contained, distorted, abstracted. The character-space opens up, in fact, a wide spectrum of artistic choice. A minor character might be squeezed into one free-standing episode or (more frequently) be rendered sporadically in a series of episodes, so that we need to reconstitute the implied person across the seams of his or her truncated or iterated inflection. Novels might split between two dueling co-protagonists; delay the elaboration of or actively submerge the central character; catapult a minor character into the central position (think of Hurstwood's sudden rise to centrality in *Sister Carrie*); or even suggest that the real protagonist has been hidden all along as a minor character (perhaps exemplified in Melville's stunning novella *Benito Cereno*). In all of these cases, we cannot consider the social, psychological, or thematic relationships between the characters, as implied persons, without comprehending the formal relationships between the characters as emplaced and dynamically positioned elements within the narrative structure.

Reading Character-Space

In the rest of this essay, I want to offer readings of three specific minor characters. Yet it is a little misleading to present my analysis as a "reading" of character. Characters have been subjected to numerous kinds of interpretations, used to facilitate dazzling psychological, aesthetic, thematic, and ideological interpretations of different novels. But unlike all these kinds of character-criticism, analysis of character-space does not merely seek to accrue interpretive significance through the character but also, simultaneously, to elucidate the extraction of significance from a character, an extraction that is intertwined with the delimited (and specific) emplacement of the implied human being within a form. Conceptualizing character-space allows us to examine a social, and formal, drama that always potentially underlies interpretation, hinging on the encounter between the implied person and a contingent—often heavily functionalized—position within an "integrated" narrative structure.

In this view, Lodge's "great tradition of the European novel" does not merely offer us the richest gallery of imaginary characters but rather constructs and manipulates a particularly wide-ranging spectrum of strategies for inflecting characters within the textual world. Given the limited space of this essay, it would be a mistake to rush too quickly through the interpretation of particular characters toward a larger character-system. But I do not want to frame the theoretical question of character-space only in the abstract, precisely as we are looking at how the abstraction of persons (into theme, function, meaning, structure) is such an important part of literary characterization. The rest of this essay will focus instead on three particular character-spaces that suggest distinct ways in which the specific qualities of a minor character (that is, his or her referentially grounded "character" or characteristics) are indissociable from his or her subordinated narrative position. These character analyses are case studies, then, in how a discussion of reference and a discussion of form might be not just intertwined but mutually constitutive. While many characteristics can be configured in this way, I have chosen actions—working, departing, lingering—that are implicated in the very nature of minorness itself. In fact, these three qualities suggest a new kind of typology that we might compare with the (usually instrumental) categories that narratology has used to theorize character. All minor characters, we could argue, "work" (as they are functionally integrated into the narrative totality), "disappear" (as they are, necessarily, overshadowed by a more central character), and "linger" (insofar as they are in a narrative—that ultimately does not concern them—at all).

Working: Chaucer's Yeoman in the General Prologue

Chaucer's "General Prologue" to *The Canterbury Tales* suggests a stark horizon of distributed attention: person, after person, after person. "A KNYGHT
there was . . . With hym ther was his sone, a yong SQUIER . . . A YEMAN hadde he
and servantz namo . . . There was also a Nonne, a PRIORESSE . . . Another NONNE
with hire hadde she . . . A MONK there was, a fair for the maistrie . . ." The prologue ends, but the essential mechanism of narration could go on indefinitely.
The paratactic structure of the prologue is motivated by the compelling pull
of each person on the narrator's attention. In fact, Chaucer's prologue presents one of the great paradigms of character-space: each individual portrait
(and they vary greatly in both tone and extent) only emerges in its radical juxtaposition with many others. Because the extent and tone of every portrait is
distinct, we need to conceive a relationship between every implied person and
the specific modalities of representation they elicit. Each character-space weds
a specific strategy of representation with a discrete object of representation.

As with most such efforts to comprehend, the prologue dramatizes the
radical potentiality within the omniscient view even while registering the
(social) pathos of delimited form. One tempting way to close off Chaucer's
catalog of persons is to read them as a sort of extended dramatis personae: a
list that is motivated by, and serves to encapsulate, the organized aesthetic
structure that will follow. Rather than an incomplete inflection of persons
from a world that precedes it, the prologue would then function as a complete reflection of the text that follows it. But the catalog of persons in
Chaucer's prologue is not a precise encapsulation of the narratives to come.
Chaucer prevents the prologue from collapsing into the tales: several characters are introduced and ramified who will not be given a tale later on. In this
way the prologue includes the excluded, describing persons who will have
no voice, creating a kind of shadow between prologue and tales: the shadow
of social extensiveness itself.

At first, however, the chain of portraits that constitute the prologue is
motivated by a singular individual. The first three figures in the prologue
(Knight, Squire, Yeoman) make it clear that we are not just concatenating
different characters but rather confronting radically differentiated
character-spaces. One powerful character, the Knight, leads, asymmetrically,
into two others: "with hym ther was his sone . . . A yeman hadde he and servantz namo." Already the modification—"and no more servants"—suggests
the basic site of pressure. The last character to have a purely motivated inclusion in the prologue (in relation to another character), the Yeoman is also
the first character to appear who will not narrate his own tale later on. The

Yeoman has an oddly privileged place as the first distinctly minor character in Chaucer—he follows the Knight; serves the Knight; has a much more limited portrait than the Knight; and, unlike the Knight or the Squire, will not become a narrator in the actual tales.

Below I quote only the end of the Knight's portrait, which has unfolded over fifty lines, and the Yeoman's entire portrait:

> But for to tellen yow of his array,
> His hors were goode, but he was nat gay.
> Of fustian he wered a gypon
> Al bismotered with his habergeon,
> For he was late ycome from his viage,
> And wente for to doon his pilgrymage. (ll. 73–78)

> A YEMAN hadde he and servantz namo
> At that tyme, for hym liste ride so,
> And he was clad in cote and hood of grene.
> A sheef of pecok arwes, bright and kene,
> Under his belt he bar ful thriftily
> (Wel koude he dresse his takel yemanly;
> His arwes drouped noght with fetheres lowe)
> And in his hand he baar a myghty bowe.
> Of wodecraft wel koude he al the usage.
> Upon his arm he baar a gay bracer,
> And by his syde a swerd and a bokeler,
> And on that oother syde a gay daggere
> Harneised wel and sharp as point of spere;
> A Cristopher on his brest of silver sheene.
> An horn he bar, the bawdryk was of grene;
> A forster was he, soothly, as I gesse. (ll. 101–17)

The juxtaposition of the Knight's lengthy depiction and this compressed one makes us aware that the Yeoman—as implied person—is getting squeezed into this narrative space. By including the brief portrait of the Yeoman, Chaucer forcefully underlines this dimension of literary characterization: the Yeoman makes us aware that all characters emerge only in-and-through their delimited space within a narrative. In this sense it is quite appropriate that the Yeoman does not get a tale of his own later on (just as the Knight's status, already actualized by the way he motivates attention to the Squire and Yeoman, is further elaborated when he gains the first tale).

The Yeoman partially resembles the Knight himself (they are both characters who motivate a description, a narrative pause) and partially resembles the property of the Knight ("a Yeoman hadde he"), functioning like the articles of clothing that fill the end of the Knight's description. It is important that the Knight's clothing comes at the end of his description; in the subtly dismissive transition toward his garb ("But for to tellen yow of his array") the narrator suggests a divide between the Knight's essential moral character and his physical trappings. The narrator thus refuses to present this character in terms of external signs or physical details. The description of the Knight's clothes is only the outermost (and least valuable) layer of his portrait; just as the clothes themselves are only the outermost layer of the Knight. This division suggests one basic choice informing any configured character-space: should it be organized around the implied person's interiority (the way he reflects on or looks at the world) or exteriority (the way he appears, acts, or gets positioned in the world)? The Yeoman's portrait contains nothing but a description of his clothing—any sense of the Yeoman's personality, or personhood, must emerge only through this description. The very shift to the external plane itself registers the consequences of form: there is a significant relationship between the compression of narrative attention and the deflection of the description toward the surface, the sartorial. (Is the description of the Yeoman itself merely a form of "clothing" for the Knight?)

The stark compression of this character-space, however, does not merely serve to efface or distort the implied person. On the contrary, a specific kind of referential configuration is realized through the Yeoman's very flattening. It is Chaucer's ability to realize the fullness of the Yeoman in-and-against his very compression that makes this character-space such a suggestive point of contrast for the modern novel. The Yeoman is depicted as an individual who labors under an extremely compressed social—and narrative—role and, at the same time, as a "full," and harmoniously realized, person. The tension between the Yeoman's socionarrative subordination and his humanity is dramatized in the dynamic unfolding of his character-space. Unlike the Knight, the Yeoman's interior characteristics are not directly presented. Instead, the reader needs to work backward: looking carefully at this exterior description we can discover interior character traits of the Yeoman. We must pay attention here to the adjectives that are scattered through the portrait, mostly attached to objects, which can be used to reconstruct the Yeoman's personality: "careful," "useful," "gay," "sharp." The Yeoman is partially buried underneath the description, just as he is covered by his clothes (and social position). Rather than simply decoding these signs we need to realize how it is the very nature of the encoding itself (linked, of course, to the subordinate character-space) that gives us our sense of the Yeoman—as a person who successfully and fully manifests himself in his delimited social (and narrative) role. Thus the first significant characteristic that we tease out of the description is appropriately "thrift" or proper care—an interior quality that depends precisely on how the Yeoman treats exterior objects: "A sheef of pecok arwes, bright and kene, / Under his belt he bar ful thriftily." The syntax of the Yeoman's thrift is only formed in relation to the object (the arrows under the belt), as an adverb modifying an action that is itself contingent on the object. This adverb then itself gains a modifier, as "thriftily" is, crucially, elaborated by "ful." The Yeoman's implied fullness—which, I would argue, is the key term of the entire portrait—emerges only as it is ironically buried under the weight of a complicated associative chain ("ful" modifies an adverb, "thriftily," which describes an action, "bar," that takes place in relation to an object: the arrows that the Yeoman bears underneath his belt). In this remarkable description, then, the Yeoman only emerges belatedly—partially and potentially—out of the objects that define him; and yet he emerges precisely with some achieved degree of "fullness."

I dwell on these details of adverb and adjective for two reasons. First, the depiction of the Yeoman illustrates the way that the pressures of the character-space, ultimately structured by the narrative totality, can often devolve down to this linguistic and syntactic level. The character-system, encompassing the dynamic interaction between competing character-spaces, frequently generates this kind of drama and significance out of a subordinate clause, a superfluous adjective, an extra or an elided phrase. These details illustrate the radical hermeneutic consequence of the character-space, which, as I have suggested, transforms what it means to read a character: to analyze the character-space is not merely to gain or accrue meaning (interpretive significance) through the character but also, simultaneously, to gain a hold of the dramatic extraction of significance from a character, an extraction that is intertwined with the delimited emplacement of the implied human being within a form.

Second, the taut balance between the Yeoman's implied "fullness" and discursive compression should remind us of E. M. Forster's distinction between "flat" and "round," the most influential of all of criticism's tropes for comprehending the literary character. The Yeoman's flatness is both social and discursive, manifested in his markedly subordinate role as the Knight's helper and in the stark compression, and exteriority, of his portrait. Both kinds of flatness take place in relation to the social and narrative power of the Knight. The service of the Yeoman meets at the juncture of story and discourse, content and form—his service, in other words, is implicated into the very structure of the character-space as such. In this sense, the Yeoman's portrait both confirms and extends William's comments on the social conventions that underlie characterization. The emergence of any specific individual takes place, almost necessarily, within a larger socionarrative context. The Yeoman's loss and gain, his freedom and constraint: all of this gives palpable social meaning to the very condition of the literary character. And in this way many character-spaces are imbued with social and historical charge, facilitating not merely the achieved representation of specific fictional persons but also the comprehension of the competition, specialization, exploitation, functionality, and distribution (of power, freedom, and wealth) that constitutes so much of the social world.

Expulsion: Mrs. Guppy's Departure from *Bleak House*

Near the end of *Bleak House*, right before the chapter in which the Chancery suit finishes and Richard Carstone dies, Dickens presents the return of Mr. Guppy, Esther Summerson's comical suitor. This chapter will mark the last appearance of Mr. Guppy and as such belongs to a larger process that attains in *Bleak House* as well as in many other novels: a narrative that introduces an extensive, multifarious cast of characters also needs to call an end to each character's appearance in the narrative. In *Bleak House* (or *Anna Karenina*, or *Germinal*) this task is considerable. With so many characters occupying narrative attention there are several challenges that face the narrative. How can characters drop out of the novel and not begin to dramatically level off the scope and range of the narrative at its end? Often we sense a deflation, a sudden narrowing: the novel has depicted many lives but must end by only paying attention to several, or to one. How can the novel integrate the end of each character's story into the narrative as a whole—without either falsely emphasizing her role or suggesting that she was not fundamentally necessary to the novel in the first place?

Sixty pages before the end of the narrative, for instance, Esther casually writes—"As it so happened that I never saw Mr. Skimpole again, I may at once finish what I know of his history" (864)—and then proceeds to tell of events that occur well after most of the narrative that will follow. If a character such as Skimpole can leave the novel before the final scenes have unfolded, how important could he be, finally, to the narrative as a whole—and how unified is the narrative itself as a whole? *Bleak House*, in this sense, has numerous and interlinked endings: one for each character who enters into the novel. The final ending—Esther's last self-regarding words about her own life—is prefaced by a summary of many of the remaining characters: "Caddy Jellyby passed her very last holidays with us. . . . As if I were never to have done with Caddy, I am reminded here of Peepy and old Mr. Turveydrop" (912). But before this final chapter there have been many other departures. The most extreme and obvious examples of this are the many deaths that famously litter the novel. As important characters like Krook, Jo, Tulkinghorn, Lady Dedlock, and Richard die, there is a close, sometimes exact, alignment of story and discourse: they exit the narrative at the precise moment that they cease to exist in the story-world itself. But this alignment begs the question. There are two kinds of potential death in *Bleak House* or in any narrative: the disappearance of a character from the story-world itself and the equally portentous disappearance of a character from the narrative. Which departure is more radical or final: Caesar in *Julius Caesar* or the Fool in *King Lear*? Dickens manipulates this convergence by cunningly varying the alignment of story and discourse in the death scenes: whereas Richard, Jo, and Gridley expire in the discourse, Dedlock, Tulkinghorn, and Krook are all discovered belatedly, creating a noticeable gap between the event and its representation.

As with Skimpole, the novel calls attention to the final appearance of Esther's first hapless suitor, Mr. Guppy. Guppy arrives at *Bleak House* intent on asking for Esther's hand again, and this time he is accompanied by his mother, Mrs. Guppy. It is his mother who carries the comic weight of the scene, outraged at her son's rejection:

> "Oh!" said Mr. Guppy, with a blank look. "Is that tantamount, sir, to acceptance, or rejection, or consideration?"
>
> "To decided rejection, if you please," returned my guardian.
>
> "Indeed?" said he. "Then, Jobling, if you was the friend you represent yourself, I should think you might hand my mother out of the gangway, instead of allowing her to remain where she ain't wanted."
>
> But Mrs. Guppy positively refused to come out of the gangway. She wouldn't hear of it. "Why, get along with you," said she to my guardian, "what do you mean? Ain't my son good enough for you? You ought to be ashamed of yourself. Get out with you!"
>
> "My good lady," returned my guardian, "it is hardly reasonable to ask me to get out of my own room."
>
> "I don't care for that," said Mrs. Guppy. "Get out with you. If we ain't good enough for you, go and procure somebody that is good enough. Go along and find 'em."

I was quite unprepared for the rapid manner in which Mrs. Guppy's power of jocularity merged into a power of taking the profoundest offence. (897)

Mrs. Guppy's anger has a kind of uncanny logic, as she continues to repeat insistently that Mr. Jarndyce should "get out" of his own house. The import of the Guppys' expulsion from the apartment only gains significance as it is embedded in, and comes to stand for, their expulsion from the novel. It is as crazy ("hardly reasonable") for Mrs. Guppy, as the mother of the rejected suitor, to demand that Mr. Jarndyce get out of Bleak House (the house) as it is for Mrs. Guppy, a distinctly minor character in the novel, to demand that Mr. Jarndyce get out of *Bleak House* (the novel). And the "offence" that Mrs. Guppy feels might stand in for the offence of narrative minorness itself, even as Mr. Jarndyce's bemused reaction resembles Wayne Booth's exasperation with critics who make just such an unreasonable narrative interpretation: "A given work will be 'about' a character or set of characters. It cannot possibly give equal emphasis to all, regardless of what its author believes about the desirability of fairness. . . . In centering our interest, sympathy, or affection on one character, [the novelist] inevitably excludes from our interest, sympathy, or affection some other character" (78–79).

This conflation of story and discourse continues as the scene develops: Mrs. Guppy is literally expelled from Bleak House and *Bleak House* at the same instant, which also brings the chapter to a close.

"Mother," interposed her son, always getting before her, and pushing her back with one shoulder, as she sidled at my guardian, "*will* you hold your tongue?"

"No, William," she returned; "I won't! Not unless he gets out, I won't!"

However, Mr. Guppy and Mr. Jobling together closed on Mr. Guppy's mother (who began to be quite abusive), and took her, very much against her will, down-stairs; her voice rising a stair higher every time her figure got a stair lower, and insisting that we should immediately go and find somebody who was good enough for us, and above all things that we should get out. (897)

The end of the chapter marvelously conflates Mrs. Guppy's irate suggestion that Jarndyce and Esther should be removed from their own house with the actual expulsion of Mrs. Guppy *herself* from the narrative. This inversion, in fact, structures the rich comic effect in this scene, as Mrs. Guppy's strangely compelling unreasonableness actually points to and hyperbolically enacts the real processes of exclusion—and possession—that are going forward here. The comment by Guppy—"Mother, *will* you hold your tongue?"—adds another dimension to this process. The exclusion of a character is, in one sense, nothing other than a kind of verbal silencing, insofar as representation within prose narrative revolves around both the speech of a character and the larger linguistic discourse within which he or she is inscribed. Bakhtin even goes so far as to suggest that characters are nothing *but* their speech-images. "Characteristic for the novel as a genre is not the image of a man in his own right, but precisely *the image of a language*" (336, Bakhtin's emphasis). At the same time, even this comment by Mr. Guppy suggests that characters have a surplus beyond their realized discursive presence, as his use of an italicized *will* registers Mrs. Guppy's essential intentionality. This use of "will" is, in fact, an early and constant stylistic device of Dickens. In chapter 2 of *Sketches by Boz* he already italicizes the word to suggest intention, aggression, eccentricity, and narrative forwardness:

> A very different personage, but one who has rendered himself very conspicuous in our parish, is one of the old lady's next door neighbours. He is an old naval officer on half-pay, and his bluff and unceremonious behaviour disturbs the old lady's domestic economy, not a little. In the first place he *will* smoke cigars in the front court, and when he wants something to drink with them—which is by no means an uncommon circumstance—he lifts up the old lady's knocker with his walking stick, and demands to have a glass of table ale, handed over the rails. In addition to this cool proceeding, he is a bit of a Jack of all trades, or to use his own words, "a regular Robinson Crusoe"; and nothing delights him better, than to experimentalise on the old lady's property. . . . Then he took to breeding silk-worms, which he *would* bring in two or three times a day. (14–15)

The italicization of "will" (and "would") functions as a literal enactment of the character's will: characterization here is not merely a speech-image but also an image or representation of this intentionality itself. This is perfectly phrased in the narrator's comment that the neighbor had "rendered himself very conspicuous," and in this case, as in *Bleak House*, this self-rendering takes the form of trespass: trespass into the "domestic economy," certainly, but also narrative trespass, since this character is a literal addendum to the second chapter of *Sketches by Boz*, who attaches himself to Boz's sketch of the old woman even as he is continually "experimentalising" on the old woman's property itself. This word, *experimentalise*, probably emerges out of the character himself, as is more explicit in the Bakhtinian clash between the narrator's description "Jack of all trades" and the character's own phrase " 'a regular Robinson Crusoe.' "

"Us[ing] his own words" is clearly a linguistic equivalent to "render[ing] himself," but it would be a mistake to conflate these two processes. On the contrary, the passage from *Bleak House* dramatizes the disjunction between a character's intentionality and speech in the wonderfully economic description of Mrs. Guppy's "voice rising a stair higher every time her figure got a stair lower." Here character and voice split; she yells louder as she is removed from the house (and the novel) "very much against her will." This estrangement of the character's speech from herself, in the process of her exclusion, is furthered by a subtle discursive shift at the end of the chapter. Mrs. Guppy's final comments are not presented in her "own words," but on the contrary by Esther herself: "her voice rising a stair higher every time her figure got a stair lower, and insisting that we should immediately go and find somebody who was good enough for us, and above all things that we should get out." Ironically, Esther's indirect presentation of Mrs. Guppy's discourse precisely confuses the subject and object of the expulsion. This shift is crucial to the comic effect, which would be blunted if the chapter ended in direct discourse ("insisting that 'You should go and find somebody good enough for you and you should get out' "). The indirect presentation deflates, and indeed clashes with, Mrs. Guppy's irrational anger. But this discursive shift also narratively develops the exclusion that provokes this anger in the story: Mrs. Guppy's words are literally separated from her, even as her rising voice is separated from her descending figure. This takeover of Mrs. Guppy's speech ends by reversing, once again, the fault line of exclusion and inclusion, of who gets to stay in the house of fiction: filtered through the protagonist, but only through the protagonist, the final words of the departing minor character are nothing other than "we should get out."

Debt: Borrowing from Robert Cohn in *The Sun Also Rises*

Consider the openings of two quite different modernist novels, *Mrs. Dalloway* and *The Sun Also Rises*:

> Mrs. Dalloway said she would buy the flowers herself.
>
> For Lucy had her work cut out for her. The doors would be taken off their hinges; Rumpelmayer's men were coming. And then, thought Clarissa Dalloway, what a morning—fresh as if issued to children on a beach.
>
> What a lark! What a plunge! (3)

Robert Cohn was once middleweight boxing champion of Princeton. Do not think that I am very much impressed by that as a boxing title, but it meant a lot to Cohn. . . . He was Spider Kelly's star pupil. . . . He was so good that Spider promptly overmatched him and got his nose permanently flattened. This increased Cohn's distaste for boxing, but it gave him a certain satisfaction of some strange sort, and it certainly improved his nose. In his last year at Princeton he read too much and took to wearing spectacles. I never met any one of his class who remembered him. They did not even remember that he was middleweight boxing champion. (3–4)

Lucy and Cohn: these two characters are similarly abject within the structure of the narrative. But in both cases, the direct appearance of the protagonist is briefly delayed by the minor character. If Chaucer's Yeoman enters into the text only after the Knight whom he serves, the protagonists here emerge belatedly and in contingent relation to the secondary characters. Lucy is the implied audience of the protagonist's opening words; and it is her (still hidden) presence that underlies the protagonist's appearance as "Mrs. Dalloway" (rather than as "Clarissa") in the first two words. This depiction of the central character as she is seen (by Lucy) rather than as she sees herself is linked to the way a representation of Clarissa's speech narrowly precedes a representation of her thought ("What a lark! What a plunge!"). The opening speech, already a concession to the exterior is, moreover, rendered indirectly. (Under the pressure of Lucy's inscription, "I will buy the flowers myself" gets changed into "she would buy the flowers herself"). As the presence of Lucy converts a "myself" into a "herself" (even as Clarissa's comment seems to assert her will), so this opening passage, so starkly poised between servant and master, motivates the way that the novel as a whole hovers inside and outside of the protagonist. In this sense the dialectical structure of the novel—hinging on the double configuration of the protagonist's problematic identity ("Clarissa"/"Mrs. Dalloway")—is built out of this relationship not just between master and servant but also between protagonist and minor character.

The Sun Also Rises begins with an oddly similar socionarrative relationship. The appearance of the "I" in the second sentence is only the most evident way in which the protagonist, Jake Barnes, belatedly emerges out of a story that at first veers toward a different character—and emerges, first of all, in his very rendering of this other person. In fact, the arrival of every protagonist (and every minor character) within a novel is subject to artistic choice: Is the protagonist introduced immediately (the first sentence of *Emma*) or only after a delay (the second sentence in *The Sun Also Rises*, the second chapter of *Pride and Prejudice*, the third chapter of *Madame Bovary*)? Is he or she first depicted from the outside (which itself can vary: consider the different opening inflections of Raskolnikov in *Crime and Punishment* and Lily Bart in *The House of Mirth*) or the inside? In speech or in thought? And this crucial problem of introduction is merely the beginning of what I have suggested is a series of choices, which often become much more structural and consequential. *The Sun Also Rises* merely makes these questions more explicit by presenting exactly one sentence that seems to be a third-person narrative before revealing Jake as narrator (and protagonist) with: "Do not think that I am very much impressed by that as a boxing title, but it meant a lot to Cohn." The "I" is only manifested here in negative relation to Cohn, or, to put this on a different register, the central protagonist is initially manifested in negative relation to the minor character, who thus gets subordinated but also gains a strange priority. In one sense, Jake depends on Cohn the way that any first-person narrator depends on the other (minor) characters whom he or she observes and represents. The novel intensifies such dependence with this brief delay. The "I" must wait one sentence and then enters in only to reflect on the opening sentence—an opening whose enunciation only now appears to be in something other than the simple third-person.

Jake's narrative "feint" toward Robert Cohn—who we presume is being constructed as protagonist in the opening of *The Sun Also Rises*—resembles a number of false starts within third-person narrative that can serve to contextualize, and often ironize, a protagonist's achieved centrality. At the same time, Jake's narrative feint mirrors the kind of move that Cohn himself might have performed inside the ring at Princeton. This is a boxing match, indeed, on the level of narrative discourse—another illustration or figuration of the competition between characters (within discourse) as a form of battle or violent conflict. We might almost say that the quarrel between the minor character and the protagonist-narrator flattens Robert Cohn (in E. M. Forster's sense of this word) in much the same way as his nose gets "flattened" as a college boxer. And it is this conflict that seems to underlie the ethnic slurs, not unrelated to the flattened nose, that begin here and continue throughout the novel.

In other words, we can't dissociate the belittling of Cohn—which will prove to be quite important to the story—from both his and Jake's positions within the narrative structure. As with many minor characters, the novel actually owes much to Cohn: it depends on Cohn to provide the opening material from which the narrative will proceed. No matter how much the text is dismissive of Cohn, it is ultimately reliant on the catalyzing role he plays.

And like the narrative itself, interpretations of *The Sun Also Rises* are also often indebted to Cohn—who has proven extremely useful to critics of the novel, providing for any number of contrasts and juxtapositions that bring out the character of the protagonist and, indeed, the thematics or ideology of the novel as a whole.

This kind of debt, based on the extraction of interpretive value from a minor character, is common to the critical or interpretive histories of many novels. *The Sun Also Rises*, through its continual attention to borrowing and debt within the story itself, inscribes a social analogue for the way that the narrative—as well as the interpretations that it generates—depends on, or owes something to, its minor characters.

> I had been having Brett for a friend. I had not been thinking about her side of it. I had been getting something for nothing. That only delayed the presentation of the bill. The bill always came. That was one of the swell things you could count on. (148)

> The letters were from the States. One was a bank statement. It showed a balance of $2432.60. I got out my check-book and deducted four checks drawn since the first of the month, and discovered I had a balance of $1832.60. I wrote this on the back of the statement. (30)

> The waiter came and said the taxi was outside. Brett pressed my hand hard. I gave the waiter a franc and we went out. (24)

These three passages briefly suggest the (much more sustained) way that *The Sun Also Rises* insistently frames Jake's human relationships in terms of credit and debt. The novel's foregrounding of Cohn literalizes this debt, embedding a discursive process within the storied world. Not merely integrated into the web of social exchange, Cohn is also privileged as the character who kicks off the narrative economy. Cohn provides the opening material for the discourse in much the same way that we are soon told that, within the story-world itself, "he still had a little of the fifty thousand left, [and] in a short time he was backing a review of the Arts" (3).

The role of Cohn as a narrative "backer" or "lender" continues as his character-space gets elaborated after the opening scene: we could say that he never escapes from his fraught narrative position at the opening of the novel; or, conversely, that the novel can never pay off this debt. As though interest were accruing, Cohn continues to appear, and Hemingway manipulates one of the most typical attributes (or conditions) of minorness: separation across narrative extent renders a character as sporadic, unstable, and episodic. This structural position within a narrative often redounds on a minor character's personality, such as with the memorable and minor Mr. Raffles in *Middlemarch*, whose unpredictability (in story and discourse) is again tied into a complicated process of economic exchange. Like Raffles, and many other nineteenth-century minor characters, Cohn continually appears, and disappears, in an abrupt manner. And, as with Eliot's minor character, Hemingway connects this narrative condition to a psychological (and referential) one: Cohn's tendency to linger on, showing up after his role should have been played, to the continual annoyance of the protagonist and other characters.

> The Ledoux–Kid Francis fight was the night of the 20th of June. It was a good fight. The morning after the fight I had a letter from Robert Cohn. (81)

> There, standing with the hotel runners, was Robert Cohn. (89)

> Two hours later, Cohn appeared. (159)

> As we came out the door I saw Cohn walk out from under the arcade. (182)

> "Is Cohn gone?" Brett asked.
> "Yes," Bill said. "He hired a car." (206)

These sudden entrances and temporary exits function like an extracted kind of interest on the debt that Cohn is owed: if the narrator's "I" emerges only in distinction to Cohn in the opening lines, such dependence motivates Cohn's continual (and sporadic) appearances, which eventually become crucial to the plot. In what we could almost call narrative "usury," Cohn's disruptive and periodic "lingering" is thus connected to the ethnic deflation motivated by, and contributing to, his narrative flatness. The connection is made explicit at least once by one of the novel's own angry characters: "Brett's gone off with men. But they weren't ever Jews, and they didn't come and hang about afterward" (143). Here Cohn's belittled Jewishness is explicitly linked to the way he "hang[s] about" in the story, to that narrative lingering that, as with any minor character, is necessarily manifested in sporadic, fragmentary form.

In this way the memorable hostility of the novel's opening tone is absorbed into the asymmetric character-system, and the final motivation of the puzzling anti-Semitism that underlies the hostile tone is nothing other than this usury itself. Here is another striking connection of the "whoness" and "whereness" of character, illustrating once again the way that reference (the depiction of Cohn) emerges in relation to (rather than against) narrative form, and a character's very functional subordination. The opposition between nineteenth-century realism and twentieth-century modernism is perhaps the most entrenched partition in the history of the novel. The dynamics of character-space, however, runs resiliently through this divide. The abstraction and functionalization of secondary characters within a thematic structure; the elaboration of interiority in relation to narrative centrality; the novel's concern with the distortion that such centrality might elicit: these elements, so successfully formulated in the nineteenth-century novel, persist in numerous strands of twentieth-century fiction—realist and antirealist; modernist and minimalist; postmodern fiction and postcolonial fiction, alike. The break from a realist poetics in so many genres of twentieth-century fiction has not weakened the role that the referential dimension of the implied person still plays within the larger construction of character-space. In particular, Dickens's radical (and paradoxical) foregrounding of minor characters—and the implicit connection he draws between subordination, disruption, and eccentricity—saturates the poetics of the twentieth-century and the contemporary novel. (Thus even many novelists with much more commitment to psychological naturalism than Dickens still distribute eccentricity—if not actively comic distortion—out toward the peripheries of a character-system; while any number of antirealist and experimental writers—think of Beckett, Conrad, Kafka, or Rushdie—directly manipulate, and work within the ambit of, Dickensian asymmetry.) Perhaps this is because the social problems and dilemmas that underlie nineteenth-century character-space (problems of distribution, instrumentality, and stratification) are still at the heart of our shared social world and thus continue to constrain and catalyze the artistic organization of implied persons within narrative form.

Works Cited

Bakhtin, M. M. *The Dialogic Imagination*. Trans. Michael Holquist and Caryl Emerson. Austin: University of Texas Press, 1981.

Barthes, Roland. "Introduction to the Structural Analysis of Narratives." In *Image, Music, Text*, trans. Stephen Heath, 79–124. New York: Hill and Wang, 1977.

———. *S/Z*. Paris: Éditions du Seuil, 1970.

Booth, Wayne. *The Rhetoric of Fiction* (1961). Chicago: University of Chicago Press, 1983

Brontë, Charlotte. *Jane Eyre* (1848). New York: Bantam Books, 1981.

Chaucer, Geoffrey. *The Riverside Chaucer*. Ed. Larry D. Benson. 3rd ed. Boston: Houghton Mifflin, 1987.

Culler, Jonathan. *Structuralist Poetics: Structuralism, Linguistics and the Study of Literature*. London: Routledge, 1975.

Dickens, Charles. *Bleak House* (1853). Oxford: Oxford University Press, 1996.

———. *Sketches by Boz and Other Early Papers* (1836). Columbus: Ohio State University Press, 1994.

Dostoevsky, Fyodor. *The Idiot* (1869). Trans. Henry and Olga Carlisle. New York: New American Library, 1969.

Forster, E. M. *Aspects of the Novel* (1927). London: Edward Arnold Publishers, 1958.

Greimas, A. J. *Sémantique structurale: Recherche de méthode*. Paris: Librairie Larousse, 1966.

Hemingway, Ernest. *The Sun Also Rises* (1926). New York: Charles Scribner's Sons, 1954.

Howe, Irving. *A Critic's Notebook*. San Diego: Harcourt Brace, 1994.

Knights, L. C. *How Many Children Had Lady Macbeth?: An Essay in the Theory and Practice of Shakespeare Criticism*. Cambridge: Minority Press, 1933.

Lodge, David. *The Art of Fiction*. New York: Viking Press, 1992.

Lubbock, Percy. *The Craft of Fiction* (1921). New York: Viking Press, 1957.

Propp, Vladimir. *Morphology of the Folktale*. Trans. L. Scott. Austin: University of Texas Press, 1968.

Tomachevski, Boris. "Thematique" (1925). In *Théorie de la literature: Textes des formalists russes*. Ed. Tzvetan Todorov. Paris: Éditions du Seuil, 1966.

Trollope, Anthony. *Barchester Towers* (1857). London: Penguin Books, 1983.

Williams, Raymond. *Marxism and Literature*. Oxford: Oxford University Press, 1977.

Woloch, Alex. *The One vs. the Many: Minor Characters and the Space of the Protagonist in the Novel*. Princeton, N.J.: Princeton University Press, 2003.

Woolf, Virginia. *Mrs. Dalloway* (1925). San Diego: Harcourt Brace, 1981.

NATHALIE FERRAND

Toward a Database of Novelistic Topoi

Let us begin with a story. Straying on the open moor on a stormy night, a traveler takes refuge in the ruins of a manor house. At dawn, he wanders through the mansion and discovers, purely by chance, a packet of old letters left in the library. He begins to read them, and what he reads becomes the subject of the novel.

It is the story of a young English nobleman who embarks on a grand tour of Europe and spends some time in Paris. One day, he sets off for a walk through the Tuileries gardens and sits down for a moment on a bench. All of a sudden, he hears the murmur of two women, who are talking behind a bush. He cannot help but hear them and is especially attracted by the voice of the youngest, who tells her friend how, several days earlier, while looking out the window, she noticed a young man whom she had never seen before and who had just recently settled into her neighborhood. She is troubled by his presence, without knowing why.

In the same manner, without knowing why, the hero of the story—who is, of course, the very young man of whom the young woman has just spoken— feels interested in her and compelled by some inexplicable force to follow the women. He follows them into a church. During Mass, the unknown beauty lifts her eyes from her book, their eyes meet . . . and at that very moment they fall in love.

But several days later, the unknown beauty disappears, carried off by some pretender whom she had refused. Our hero succeeds, however, in following her traces across all of Europe. By chance, their misadventures lead them to Algiers, where he is sold as a slave and she is secluded within a harem. Finally, they find each other again. But at the very moment they are about to marry, their unfortunate fate demands their rude realization of the reason for their mutual affection: they are brother and sister. Despairing, she secludes herself in a convent, and he sets off for exotic isles where he falls ill and dies.

Those who read seventeenth- and eighteenth-century novels may have the impression that this is a familiar story, that they have already read it somewhere. But where? In fact, it was never written, or, rather, it was written dozens of times: a simple interweaving of novelistic topoi, it is a concentration of the narrative threads that make up many of the novels written under the ancien régime and constitute what an anachronistic look at that literature would classify as clichés.

To recapitulate, mentioning only the most visible topoi: a found manuscript, in this case, letters; a young man coming of age while traveling through foreign lands; a conversation involuntarily overheard; love at first sight; a kidnapping; a hero reduced to slavery and a heroine secluded in a harem; a scene in which real identities are finally recognized; a retreat to a convent and a death occasioned by despondent love. As the landscape of the novel unfolds, we find each of these topoi opening onto a long string of particular occurrences, drawn from a few works among many others that attest to the same topos. The examples that follow are drawn, with few exceptions, from seventeenth- and eighteenth-century French novels.

EXAMPLES OF LITERARY THEMES IN NARRATIVE FICTION

Topoi	Occurrences
Found manuscript[a]	• Terrasson, *Séthos* [*The Life of Sethos. Taken from private memoirs of the ancient Egyptians. Translated from a Greek manuscript into French . . .*], 1731
	• Lesage, *La valise trouvée* [*The Found Suitcase*], 1740
	• Laclos, *Les liaisons dangereuses* [*Dangerous Liaisons*], 1782
	• Potocki, *Manuscrit trouvé à Saragosse* [*The Manuscript Found in Saragossa*], 1805
Coming-of-age journey through foreign lands	• Crébillon, *Les heureux orphelins* [*The Happy Orphans*], 1754
	• Johnson, *Rasselas* [*History of Rasselas, Prince of Abissinia*], 1759
	• Rousseau, *La nouvelle Héloïse* [*The New Heloise*], 1761
	• Abbé Barthélémy, *Anacharsis* [*Travels of Anacharsis the Younger in Greece*], 1788
Conversation involuntarily overheard	• Mme de Lafayette, *La Princesse de Clèves*, 1678
	• Marivaux, *Lettre de M. de M.*** contenant une aventure* [*The Letter of Monsieur de M.*** Including an Adventure*], 1719–20
	• Crébillon, *Les egarements du coeur et de l'esprit* [*The Wayward Head and Heart*], 1736–38
Love at first sight[b]	• Heliodorus, *Adventures of Theagenes and Chariclea: a romance, being the rise, progress, tryals and happy success of the heroic loves of these two illustrious persons . . .* ,[c] fourth century A.D.
	• Mme de Lafayette, *La Princesse de Clèves*, 1678

(continued)

EXAMPLES OF LITERARY THEMES IN NARRATIVE FICTION (*continued*)

Topoi	Occurrences
	• Prévost, *Manon Lescaut* [*History of Manon Lescaut and of the Chevalier des Grieux*], 1731
Kidnapping of the beloved	• Scarron, *Roman comique* [*Comical Romance, or A facetious history of a company of stage-props interwoven with divers choice souls, rare adventures, and amorous intrigues*], 1651–57
	• Mme de Graffigny, *Lettres d'une Péruvienne* [*Peruvian Letters, including the letters of Aza*], 1747
	• Sade, *Aline et Valcour*, 1795
	• Révéroni Saint-Cyr, *Pauliska*, 1798
Hero reduced to slavery	• Fénelon, *Aventures de Télémaque* [*Adventures of Telemachus, the Son of Ulysses*], 1699
	• Marivaux, *Les effects surprenants de la sympathie* [*The Surprising Effects of Sympathy*], 1713–14
	• Prévost, *Mémoires et avantures d'un homme de qualité qui s'est retiré du monde* [*Memoirs and adventures of a man of quality who has retired from the world*], 1728–31
Beauty held captive in a harem	• Prévost, *Histoire d'une grecque moderne* [*The Story of a Modern Greek Woman*], 1740
	• Johnson, *Rasselas*, 1759
	• Sade, *Aline et Valcour*, 1795
Recognition of true identities	• Longus, *Daphnis and Chloe, a most sweet and pleasant pastoral romance . . .* , first century A.D.
	• Prévost, *Cleveland* [*The Life and entertaining adventures of Mr. Cleveland, natural son of Oliver Cromwell, written by himself, giving a particular account of his unhappiness in love, marriage, friendship, and of his great sufferings in Europe and America . . .*], 1731–39
	• Bricaire de la Dixmerie, *Toni et Clairette*, 1773
Retreat to a convent occasioned by despondent love	• Mme de Tencin, *Mémoire du comte de Comminge* [*Memoirs of the Count of Comminge*], 1735
	• Laclos, *Liaisons dangereuses*, 1782
	• Mme Mérard de Saint-Just, *Le château noir* [*The Black Mansion*], 1799

[a] According to the medievalist scholar E. Baumgartner, the topos of the found manuscript appears for the first time in the twelfth century in Benoît de Sainte-Maure's *Roman de Troie*, as far as the French novel is concerned. See "Du manuscrit trouvé au corps retrouvé," in *Le topos du manuscrit trouvé: Hommages à Christian Angelet*, ed. Jan Herman and Fernand Hallyn (Louvain: Editions Peeters, 1999), 3.

Given all of this, we still find ourselves apparently far from the database or full inventory of novelistic topoi that, after all, comprises the subject of these pages—but only apparently. In fact, we find here those narrative mechanisms that, strung together, produce stories and that have long put into motion that "machine of literature" noted by Calvino,[1] and whose essential cogs are exposed here, stripped naked.

––––––––

Now we may turn to a second story, a true story this time. Back in the 1980s, a group of literary historians, gathered together thanks to the efforts of Marc Fumaroli in the very solemn halls of the Collège de France, had the idea—a magnificent, but, we might note, rather mad idea—of engaging in systematic research to recover the topoi of French novels from the Middle Ages through the revolution and of generating an inventory in the form of a computerized database based on that research. Prior to setting off on such an adventure, the instigators of the project, including Henri Coulet,[2] a great specialist in the French novel through the revolutionary period, circulated a questionnaire among the international literary community and received

––––––––

[1] *La machine littérature* is the title of the collection of essays published by Italo Calvino in 1984. He gathers together in this collection articles that appeared in *Una pietra sopra: Discorsi di letteratura e società* (Turin: Einaudi, 1980), including "Cybernétique et fantasmes ou de la littérature comme processus combinatoire." These are published in English translation in *The Uses of Literature* (San Diego: Harcourt, Brace, Jovanovich, 1986).

[2] Henri Coulet is, notably, the author of *Le roman jusqu'à la révolution* (Paris: Armand Colin, 1975, subsequently republished in multiple revised editions).

––––––––

[b] Among these topoi, certain ones, such as love at first sight, transect the entire history of the novel, finding their origins in the Greek romance. Jean Rousset has devoted a magnificent essay to this constitutive scenario of the novel, *Leurs yeux se rencontrèrent: La scène de première vue dans le roman* (Paris: José Corti, 1981). For a more general work on the topoi of the Greek romance, see Françoise Létoublon, *Les lieux commun du roman: Stéréotypes grecs d'aventure et d'amour* (Leiden: E. J. Brill, 1993).

[c] The full title includes references to other of the novelistic topoi addressed here: *Adventures of Theagenes and Chariclia: a romance, being the rise, progress, tryals and happy success of the heroic loves of those two illustrious persons: wherein the following histories are intertwined, I. The treacherous slave, or, Cruel Stepmother, II. The wandering prelate, III. The fighting priest, IV. The royal adulteress, with several other curious events . . .* [translator's note].

three hundred affirmative answers from persons interested in and willing to collaborate in the realization of the inventory project.

This initiative thus responded to an actual imperative within the literary community. Consequently, an international scholarly society was formed, the Société d'Analyse de la Topique Romanesque [Society for the Analysis of Novelistic Topoi] (SATOR), bringing together European, North American, and other scholars, one hundred people representing fourteen different nations. Since 1986, this group of researchers has organized fifteen annual colloquia, published thirteen volumes of proceedings,[3] and elaborated two successive versions of its database that is now online in Canada under the name Satorbase.[4]

It is this adventure that is reconsidered here, a true work in progress that is not anywhere near completion and that, since 1986, espoused the eventful introduction of new technologies into practices of literary scholarship: the developing use of personal computers, e-mail, online discussion groups, textual and bibliographical databases increasingly available online, and the explosion of the Web.[5] This story is not offered as a model, but rather as a *case study*, which is of little interest unless one considers its innovative aspects

---

[3] Nicole Boursier and David Trott, eds., *La naissance du roman en France: Topique romanesque de "L'Astrée" à "Justine" (Toronto, 1988)* (Paris, 1990), bibliography, 17–54; Jean Macary, ed., *Colloque de SATOR à Fordham (1989)* (Paris, 1991), bibliography, 17–61; Pierre Rodriguez and Michèle Weil, eds., *Vers un thésaurus informatisé: Topique des ouvertures narratives avant 1800 (Montpellier, 1990)* (Montpellier: Service des Publications, 1991); Teresa Sousa de Almeida, João Amaral Frazão, and Ana Paiva Morais, eds., *Secret et topique romanesque du Moyen Âge au XVIIIe siècle (Lisbonne, 1991)* (1995); Michel L. Bareau and Santé A. Viselli, eds., *Utopie et fictions narratives (Winnepeg, 1992)* (*Parabasis* 7, Alberta: Alta Press, 1995); Colette Piau-Gillot, ed., *Topiques du dénouement romanesque du XIIe au XVIIIe siècles (Orsay, 1993)* (Paris: Apte, 1995); Jan Herman and Paul Pelckmans, eds., *L'Épreuve du lecteur: Livres et lectures dans le roman d'ancien régime (Louvain-Anvers, 1994)* (Louvain: Éditions Peeters, 1995); Martine Debaisieux and Gabrielle Verdier, eds., *Violence et fiction jusqu'à la révolution (Milwaukee-Madison, 1995)* (Tübingen: Gunter Narr Verlag, 1998); Denise Godwin, Thérèse Lassalle, and Michèle Weil, eds., *Actes du dixième colloque international de la SATOR: "Les objets d'art dans le roman" (Johannesburg, 1996)* (1999); Nathalie Ferrand and Michèle Weil, eds., *Homo narrativus: Recherches sur la topique romanesque dans les fictions de langue française avant 1800 (Montpellier, 1997)* (Montpellier, 2001); Arbi Dhifaoui, ed., *Espaces de la fuite dans la littérature narrative française avant 1800 (Kairouan, 1998)* (Publications of the Faculty of Letters and Human Sciences of Kairouan, 2002); Elzbieta Grodek, ed., *Écriture de la ruse (Toronto, 1999)* (Amsterdam: Rodopi, 2000); Suzan Van Dijk and Madeleine Van Strien-Chardonneau, eds., *Féminités et masculinités dans le texte narratif avant 1800: La question du gender (Amsterdam-Leyde, 2000)* (Louvain: Editions Peeters, 2002).

[4] http://www.satorbase.org.

[5] For an analysis of this project in relation to other computerized efforts concerned with the novel, see N. Ferrand, *Banques de données et hypertextes pour l'étude du roman* (Paris: PUF, 1997).

alongside its impasses, vicissitudes, and the thrilling, but also difficult reality introduced by a new, collective, and cumulative instrument for research in the humanities.[6]

But let us return for a moment to the *literary project* of this society: What exactly does it mean to compile an encyclopedia or thesaurus of novelistic topoi? And of what use would it be? First, we might define more precisely the particular sense here given to the term *topos*, an ancient and complex concept, at the core of numerous debates, and reinvested by twentieth-century literary theory, most notably through the work of Ernst Robert Curtius.[7] To be sure, the choice of christening the object of this research *topos*—a choice made in the context of a *revival* of rhetorical studies and a choice that suggests the reevaluation of the novel as an argumentative form—promises long theoretical and terminological debates, to which the proceedings of this society abundantly attest and that constitute one of the achievements of this research.[8] In short, we may specify that the word *topos* here does not recall the original significations of the term, derived from Aristotle's or Quintilian's rhetoric, that is, abstract structures of argumentation or repertories of places associated with discrete forms of discourse. In this project, the concept of topos serves rather a historical and narratological analysis of the novel and is defined as a recurrent narrative sequence.[9]

---

[6] On the rhythms of appropriation of these new tools available for literary research, see the results of the recent questionnaire developed by the sociologist Jean-Marc Ramos, "Étude sociologique des pratiques émergentes d'une communauté savante face aux nouvelles instrumentations numériques: Le cas de la Société Internationale d'Analyse de la Topique Romanesque 1986–2001" (January 2002), in N. Ferrand, *Locus in fabula: La topique de l'espace dans les fictions françaises d'ancien régime* (Louvain: Editions Peeters, 2004).

[7] Besides the classical text by Curtius, *Europäische Literatur und lateinischus Mittelalter* (1948) [*European Literature and the Latin Middle Ages*, trans. Willard R. Trask, with a new epilogue by Peter Godman (Princeton, N.J.: Princeton University Press, Bollingen Series, 1990)], a whole section of which (5) is devoted to "historical topoi," several recent works have reactivated the concept of topos, particularly in current writing on argumentative rhetoric, where the term has an acceptation close to its Aristotelian sense of logical-discursive stereotype. Cf. Christian Plantin, ed., *Lieux communs, topoï, stéréotypes, clichés* (Paris: Klimé, 1993) and Jean-Claude Anscombre, ed., *Théorie des topoï* (Paris: Klimé, 1995).

[8] See, most notably, Aron Kidébi Varga, "Les lieux de la rhétorique classique" and Gerald Prince, "Remarques sur le topos et le dénarré," in *La naissance du roman en France*, 101–12 and 113–22; Jan Herman, preface to *L'Épreuve du lecteur*, 5–11; and Madeleine Jeay, "A la recherche d'unités discrètes de narration," and François Rastier, "Les unités topiques et leur interprétation," in *Homo narrativus*, 33–45 and 83–105.

[9] "Recurrent configuration of narrative information," says the definition for narrative topos adopted by SATOR. See Michèle Weil, "Un logiciel pour l'histoire littéraire," *Revue d'Histoire Littéraire de la France* 6 (1994): 1,038–55.

It is like a scenario that transects the long history of the genre, taking many different forms, a scenario that is reinterpreted and varied within the novel, but that is also required by the novel in certain moments: the scene of the storm, the discovery of a sleeping beauty, or the amorous rivalry of two friends. Succeeding in documenting the history of these scenarios—ideally, discovering their date and place of birth, their original and banal reprisals, their slow exhaustion, their parodies, their eclipse—is the primary aim of this enterprise. That the project has already aroused the interest of novelists, particularly those of the Ouvroir de la Littérature Pontentielle [Workshop for Potential Literature], in its capacity as a potential repository of forms available for the elaboration of the novel is in no way surprising.[10]

The French novel from the Middle Ages to the revolution—this immense mesh of thousands of texts that leads medievalists to work with specialists of other periods—is framed by totally opposed uses of literary topoi, which are omnipresent and almost ritually invoked in medieval romance,[11] but suspect and progressively depreciated toward the end of the ancient régime. Thus, the chosen term for this study also has a historical sense, insofar as nineteenth-century romanticism, with its valorization of personal expression and originality, disqualifies topos, degrading it as cliché, and later as stereotype.[12] Topos is transformed from material ready for use and which one can freely reuse into an object of shame, to be banished or hidden,[13] and against which the most modern of novelists declare war, as does Martin Amis in his recent essay on the literature of the end of the twentieth century, *The War against Cliché*: "All writing is a campaign against cliché. Not just clichés of the pen but clichés of the mind and clichés of the heart. When I dispraise, I am usually quoting clichés. When

---

[10] Here we should specify that topoi thus defined should not be confused with Proppian functions, the fixed number and sequence of which reveal, according to Propp, a specific genre, that of the fairy tale, whose true nature they are supposed to reveal. Propp presents greater correlations between these functions and narrative unities that folklorists such as Antti Aarne tried to inventory, giving Propp a basis for his reflections on the syntax of tales. Nevertheless, it is clear that his notion derives as much from the lessons of formalism and from research on the logic of narrative: an element of a novelistic vocabulary worth noting, narrative topos also invites reflection on the syntax through which it is inserted into narrative.

[11] Danielle Régnier-Bohler, "Le topos et les mutations du sens: A propos de quelques narrations médiévales," in *L'Épreuve du lecteur*, 18–27.

[12] Ruth Amossy and Anne Herschberg Pierrot, *Stéréotypes et clichés: Langue, discours, société* (Paris: Nathan, 1997).

[13] Might it be possible to find these clichés en masse in the drafts and scenarios filed away by novelists? We leave that question to genetic literary historians and critics.

I praise, I am usually quoting the opposed qualities of freshness, energy, and reverberation of voice."[14]

Let us return to the question, "how might such a survey be put to use?" To speak of the final results of such an inventory whose end is not in view is, obviously, to offer only hypotheses and hopes, since it is self-evident that such a thesaurus cannot achieve its aims except after a certain amount of enrichment. As long as a critical mass of topoi and occurrences has not been achieved, consultation of the thesaurus cannot offer significant results for any statistical or comparative study. It is also probable that results other than those projected at the project's inception will manifest themselves in the future. But we can already sketch out a few objectives of such a survey and say that such an instrument can allow us

- to engage in statistical studies of topological usage within the works of a given author, period, novelistic genre, or subgenre;
- to understand better the agency of stories by analyzing the combinations of topoi in comparable works and by analyzing the topicality of a given work, period, or genre;
- to engage in transversal and serial readings of the novel throughout its long history and to interrogate the relationship between a given community and its representations from a historical standpoint, by studying the subtle dialectic between fixity and change manifest in any topos. This brings us back to an essential question: "If a topos is maintained, is this due to conformity or mimesis on the part of writers, or is it rather a symptom of a persistent interrogation in society? In other

---

[14] Martin Amis, *The War against Cliché, Essays and Reviews 1971–2000* (London: Vintage, 2001), xv. Amis contends that we are witnessing in contemporary literature a reevaluation of cliché as a reusable serial product, on the condition that this reuse is rendered explicit. Cf. the literary manifesto written by Pierre Alferi and Olivier Cadiot, "La mécanique lyrique," published in the first issue of the *Revue de Littérature Générale* (1995): "What is it that distinguishes a commonplace transformed into Object from a simple cliché? A virtual stereotype from an exhausted stereotype? A ready-made object from its material content? . . . As the method of the ready-made consists in making a singular object out of a serial product . . . while conjuring up the phantom of the original, the method of the cut-up consists in giving an object a second life precisely in displacing the parts of a text already subject to necrosis. The great difference between the depressing use of literary stereotypes and the free use of stereotypes lies in literalness—that goes without saying. One may think one has discovered unidentified Objects and reformulate implicit clichés: one thus falls into representations belonging to a past that has already been surpassed. On the contrary, one may make use of clichés as such and treat them as literal sign sequences: [so that they become] free Objects" (11).

words, is it literary history that lends itself to a reading through topicality
or is it rather the history of mentalities?";[15] and

- to study, in combination with a similar critical historical survey in the
theater, poetry, or cinema, topological migrations from one art to
another—which Curtius sketched out in *European Literature and the
Latin Middle Ages*, showing, for example, how the topos of the
"invocation of nature" is transferred at one point from Greek poetry to
the Greek romance. The survey might, thus, be expanded to include the
European novel, to study the circulation of topoi from one literary form to
another, and to consider the eventual existence of national topicalities.

But if all that is yet to come, after fifteen years of collective study and
reflection, after an initial collection of topoi and the progressive construction
of a database, this project has already produced a result that we might qualify
as hermeneutic or methodological. In reading the volumes of proceedings
published by the society, we note already a marked concern with setting up a
certain number of a priori methodological conditions in order that literary
interpretation may truly gain rather than lose out from the application of a
research instrument of this sort. For what will be left for the research scholar
to do once the machine is capable of aligning comparable instances? Once it
can hand-deliver the keys to files of ready-made readings, to a canvas of articles or information that can be skimmed at scant cost in the footnotes of a
critical edition in the making? Further, is there not a risk of promoting a
false view of what constitutes a work of literature by reducing it to a sum of
its elements? And an equal risk of erasing a historical view of literary evolution by compressing the temporal duration of several centuries of rewriting
through the speedy compilation of computerized data files? Among the
comments often expressed by scholars who have worked on the project, we
find counsel for hermeneutic prudence with respect to results that may save
the survey from these dangers, as well as a desire to define more precisely the
principles underlying the project's results.

First, this project does not seek to dissect works in order to reduce literature to a vast compendium and textuality to an intertext. To be sure, this thesaurus will demonstrate the degree to which literature is based on the technique of borrowing. But that which we study is the manner in which the
novelistic text recycles a part of its material—and invents the rest—and how
mutations of meaning come about through this process of recycling. What

---

[15] Dominique Garand, "Rabelais au risque de la topique," in *Violence et fiction jusqu'à la
révolution*, 122.

comes into view is the great cohesive force of the novelistic genre, a genre that is often described as lacking poetic art, but which is at least endowed with a rich repertoire of forms.

Furthermore, there is a recurrent insistence on the fact that the analysis should associate any perception of invariables—the constituents of the topography that give the work its fundamental architecture—with a view of the "variant" that contextualizes and reinterprets the topographical web.[16] If the topos is necessarily decontextualized in order to be inserted within the thesaurus, it is necessary at the moment of interpretation of the series of occurrences to work out the successive recontextualizations undergone by the topos. And this is how the historical mutations of meaning can make themselves manifest.

Finally, insofar as the topos is an element that plays on the expectations of readers and on their capacity to recognize a genre or an author, one cannot economize at the moment of interpretation on the cultural horizon that determines the genesis of works, on the horizon of intelligibility that permits reading and eventual recognition of the work. In a certain sense, the database indicates the mental encyclopedia of readers of the novels in the centuries under consideration.

Computers and Topoi

The emergence of the computer was a necessity for this project, a precondition that made it viable. It was essential, first, in order to facilitate communication among this international community of scholars distributed essentially across Europe and North America, which, beginning in 1989, converted to e-mail, electronically exchanging numerous literary texts—a chapter of Scarron's *Roman comique* for a collective experiment in topical indexing—as well as brief messages.[17] At a time when the use of e-mail was nearly nonexistent among the literary community, this was truly pioneering work.[18] A little later, at the beginning of the 1990s, when the Internet was becoming

---

[16] "At the same time that the core of a larger organism is characterized by the embedding, transplantation, or fusion of that which we may call motifs, procedures of signification develop. The hermeneutic usefulness of the concept of *topos* is clearly apparent here: the web that remains unaltered underpins the signs that inform the mutation of meaning," writes Danielle Bohler in *L'Épreuve du lecteur*, 24.

[17] David Trott, *Colloque de la SATOR à Fordham*, 12.

[18] And the underlying cause in the French case was that France was not fully linked to the Internet until 1988. Cf. Christian Huitema, *Et Dieu créa l'Internet . . .* (Paris: Eyrolles, 1995), 8.

more widespread, a discussion list (sator-l) was created as a forum for debating theoretical or practical concerns of the society. But, above all, the computer would provide the tool toward which all efforts were converging, the database that would assemble all the pieces of the puzzle cut out of the novels by somewhat special readers. This would take some time.

The development of this machine in effect required the establishment of a dialogue between literary scholars and computer programmers, demanding that they learn to speak a common language and that they define together an object of research and the desired functions for a database. There was nothing self-evident in all this, either for the programmers who found themselves facing a fluid object, the topos, or for the literary scholars obliged not only to conform to a formalized descriptive procedure, but also to rethink their practices and their kind of contribution to research. The basic unit of our work is normally the article, not microcontributions to a cumulative project whose true results are temporally deferred and that—far more problematically!—are most likely destined to be formulated by others. The realization of this project thus raised multiple problems.

And so, what sort of database would this project generate? The word *toward* in the title of this article assumes its full meaning here, as it suggests the time and effort necessary to produce this interdisciplinary object comprised by a database destined for literary analysis. In the course of the past fifteen years, the project has, in fact, generated not one but two successive databases, with very distinct spirits and aims, which shared most notably their use of the Web. The first database belongs to a very experimental phase of collective work in which reflection on the object of inquiry and on the machine as a means of research are constantly mixed and in which they constantly lead to each other; the second belongs to a period of stabilization of theoretical concerns and reflects the choice of a simplified interface for common work, seeking to facilitate access to the data as well as a quantitative acceleration in the collection of data.

The first database, realized with Fourth Dimension by a team of French academics, was called Toposator and was used for a decade (1989–99).[19] The essential question driving the conception of the database at that point was the following: is the topos possible to formalize? Conscious of having to deal with a peculiarly literary object, the computer programmer sought to invent a system that would be capable not only of containing descriptive

---

[19] The database was conceived and programmed by the engineer Eric-Olivier Lochard, with the assistance of Daniel Savey, Pierre Rodriguez, and Michèle Weil.

FIGURE 1

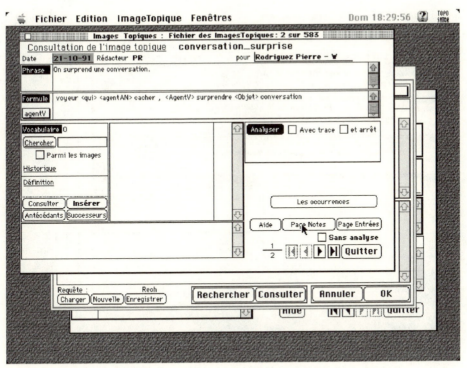

files but also function as an original and powerful analytical tool to critically examine the data.

Let us take up again one of the topoi that served our little liminal story, in order to consider its double computation: "the overheard conversation" (fig. 1). When entered into the database, each topical file needed to respond to the following rubrics: *denomination*, that is, the name attributed to the topos ("overheard conversation"); *phrase*, a description in ordinary language of the action ("one overhears a conversation"); and *formula*, the group of syntactically structured key terms that would allow sophisticated searches or research dealing with the entire sequence and not only one of its semantic elements.[20] At another level that we might qualify as philological,

---

[20] This electronic gestation of the elements of a topos comprised the computing innovation of this database; cf. Pierre Rodriguez, "Des souris et des craintes," in *Secret et topique romanesque*, 370. But this innovation came at a cost: the necessity of having an expert programmer initially encode each topos.

FIGURE 2

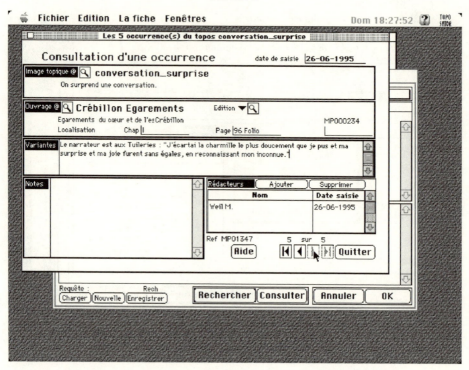

the file presented *instantiations* of the topos and comprised for each—here, an example drawn from Crébillon's *Wayward Heart and Head*—mention of the title, of the author, of the date of composition or publication, the citation of the passage, and a space left open for commentary (fig. 2).

Each semantic element constitutive to the formula, called a *toposeme*, was itself linked to a dictionary and to a group of related terms (selected and judged relevant by the research scholar at the moment of entering the topos in the database), so that a user consulting the thesaurus in order to find there, for example, the topical uses of objects of art in the novel could find the novelistic topos of the "unmasked portrait"—the toposeme "portrait" having been already associated with the word "art" in a lexical ramification that constituted one of the foundations of the program. Besides this, the program was conceived to permit chronological searches or searches by author or work, as well as to answer to questions such as: which are the topoi used by Mme de Lafayette? Between 1670 and 1730, which novels make use of the topos of the masked beauty? Or also, which topoi are used in *La nouvelle Héloïse*?

Thanks to the computer workshops held at the beginning of the annual colloquia, the members of the society set to work with enthusiasm and with the sensation of being engaged in a new enterprise. Those who so desired received a version of the database that they could install on their personal computers and could regularly submit their data to the team responsible for maintaining the database in order to then receive an updated version. In 1996, Toposator contained 610 topoi, 1,660 instantiations, and 220 indexed works.

This is not bad, particularly if we consider the difficulties inherent in this work. The first difficulty resided in the program itself, which certainly performed well for expert users seeking to pursue sophisticated searches, but which was not especially suited to the neophyte literary scholar seeking to use the data for the first time. As for the formula, it incontestably constituted an added difficulty. In demanding that the researcher bend to that discipline of formalization, the machine multiplied its demands. Certain members of the group voiced their resistance or, rather, their strong, principled opposition to the idea that literary objects as subtle and polysemic as novelistic fragments could be subjected to the encoding inherent in any linguistic formalization destined to automatized manipulations. What would become of literary signification? That which seemed to some to promise fecund heuristic discoveries, seemed to others like the reduction of literature to an equation, marked by every possible deviation. Whether problematic distrust or justified fears, in any case, all this led back to a dilemma very familiar to linguists, concerning all encoding and normalization of literary texts, which inevitably effaces part of the novel's meaning in the course of the operation.[21]

In a certain way, this first version of the thesaurus reversed priorities with relation to the necessities of collective work. Although during its initial phase, the society needed the simplest possible program capable of collecting data, the actual program was conceived by its future users rather than by those who at that time, through their work, would give the thesaurus its wealth of data and permit it to produce its first results. In pragmatic terms, the community was thus oriented toward a paradoxical mode of functioning, in which the discussion list and e-mail played a primordial role facilitating the exchange of files, not to mention the paper that remained an important vector in the communication of data. These exchanged files were then

---

[21] On the problem of coding, see Rastier, "Les unités topiques et leur interprétation," in *Homo narrtivus*, 93.

to be integrated in the command center by the technical team. This produced a situation that proved fairly inconvenient for all involved, but it would find its resolution in the use of the Web.

Whence SatorBase, a new online version of the thesaurus, belonging to the generation of databases specifically designed for the Web (fig. 3). This program inherited the data incorporated in Toposator and, while preserving its presentation—each file follows more or less the same rubrics—also proposed new management. This version was conceived and realized in 2000–2001 by a Canadian team of SATOR scholars, situated in Toronto and Kingston.

SatorBase's central concern is to make the data maximally available and simple to manipulate, as well as to ensure a significant increase in the pace of

FIGURE 3

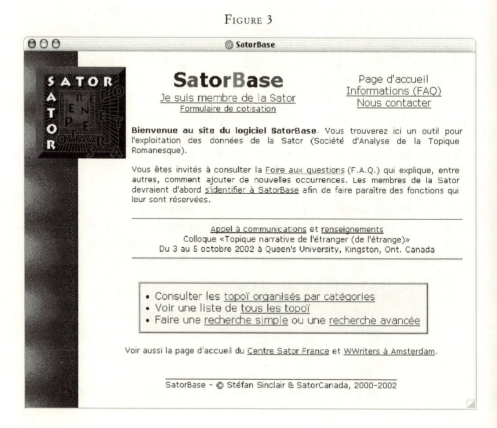

contributions to, and consultations of, the thesaurus. As far as content, it included 1,025 topoi and 2,866 instantiations drawn from 404 works as of March 2002. The objective is to bring together for the members of the society and for Web users the entire body of published contributions, even the most recent ones. As soon as a proposal is submitted, it is immediately visible—even if it receives provisional status while waiting for accreditation.

What has become of the topos of the "overheard conversation" in Sator-Base? First, its name was changed, defined more specifically as "to overhear-conversation-garden," the setting for the action having been judged sufficiently discrete to define a new topos, while the syntax of the topos also evolved, demanding the use of an infinitive that marks the priority given to the action in progress. The denomination, phrase, and numbered occurrences, along with the identity of contributors to the thesaurus, as well as the date of the contribution now appear on the same screen (fig. 4). While

FIGURE 4

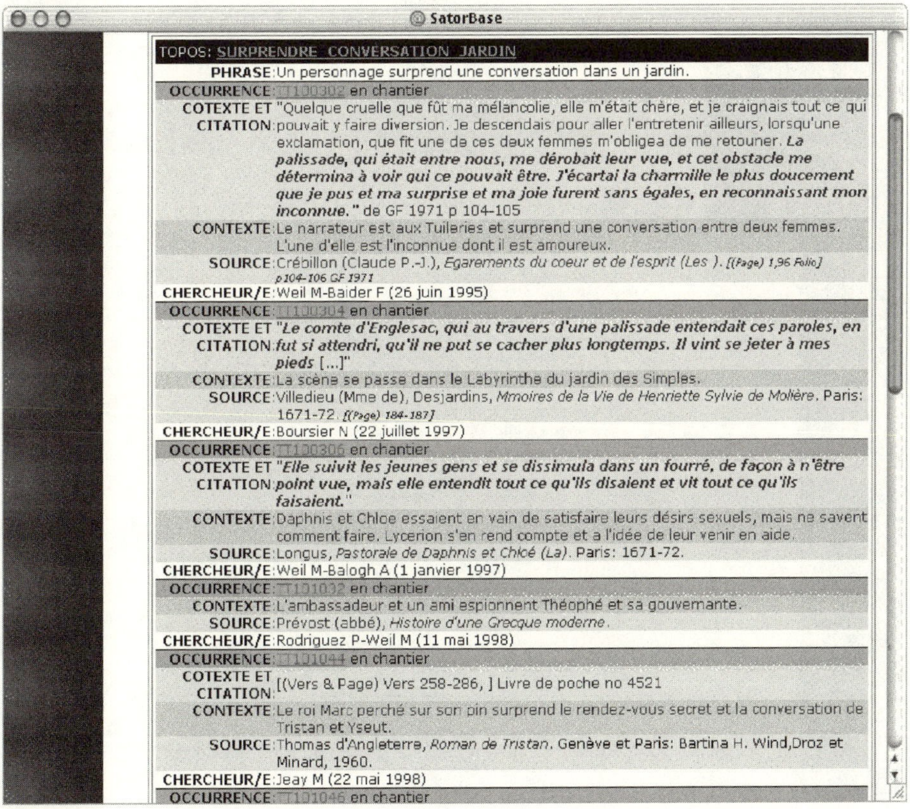

becoming more specific, the topos also saw its number of occurrences double—from five, they grew to eleven—drawn from different novels, from the sixteenth-century French translation of *Daphnis et Chloé* to the works of Marivaux, the Abbé Prévost, and Crébillon. We might note that the programming formula has disappeared from the screen in this version, since, for now, SatorBase emphasizes the ergonomics and accessibility of data more than the sophistication of inquiries, even if a whole range of research is made possible by use of the key terms (fig. 5).

This online thesaurus is a living and evolving instrument, whose content will be changing in perpetuity thanks to the active participation of research scholars and to the work of those responsible for regulating data entry. For the moment, roles and functions of terms have been defined and distributed to guarantee the homogeneity of contributions, most notably through the

FIGURE 5

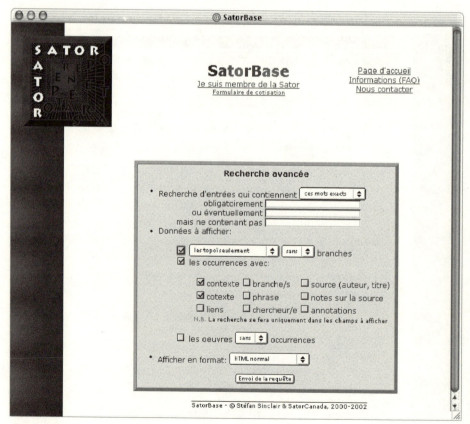

work of the accreditation committee that validates or invalidates proposals submitted directly online and that attributes a particular status to each submission. For example, for the topos of the woman who withdraws from the world, a *topos* typically found in the denouement of the novel written under the ancien régime and mobilized as such for our history, appears under three different qualifications: "accredited," "under construction," and "provisional" (fig. 6). The first is, thus, accepted, while the other two need further review and revision. The thesaurus also admits data categorized as "proposed," for instance, an entry that has just been submitted. This ramification of data allows for more rapid processing by the accreditation committee.

FIGURE 6

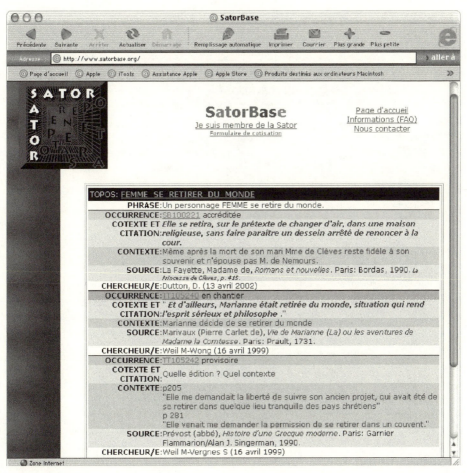

This mechanism concerns current data. For older data, inserted into the database over the course of preceding years during which there was little actual organized control and which one often finds qualified as a topos or linked site "under construction," a vast retrospective evaluation was initiated by the French team in 2000, with the aid of an online module aimed at diagnosing the problems that might be inherent in each data file, homogenizing the content of the files, eliminating irrelevant topoi, rendering formulations less ambiguous, verifying the correspondence between the topos and its instantiations, signaling doubles or useless approximations, and effecting new associations between topoi in order to correct the numerical correspondence between a given topos and its attestations in literary works (fig. 7).

FIGURE 7

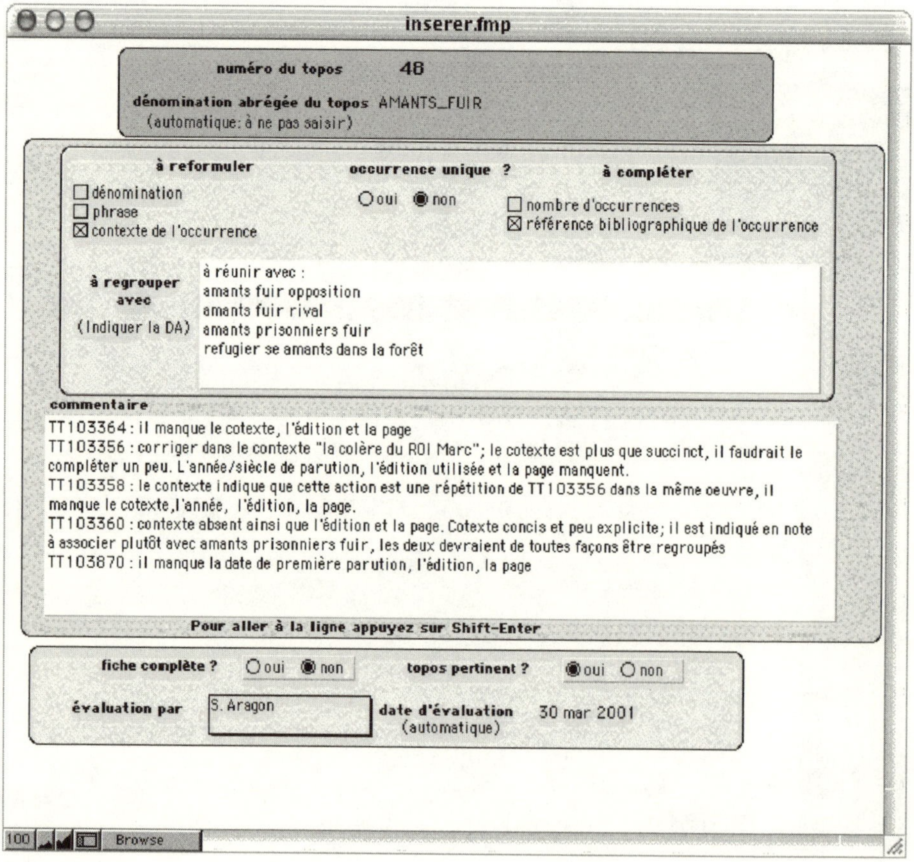

Articles, Topoi, and Occurrences: The Unit of Measurement
in Scientific Research

Thus, in the wings of a lovely and unreasonably ambitious literary and scholarly project, launched at the end of the 1980s by literary historians unaware of what lay ahead, not only did there gradually develop a computerized thesaurus facilitating analysis of the novel, whose constitutive principles, cogs, and incompletion I have just described; but there was also the autonomous invention of a whole structured system of organizing and administrating collaborative research within a community of specialists, taking as its point of departure a panoply of new tools made available by new technologies.[22] The experimental character of this project was thus played out on two levels—on the one hand, intellectual and theoretical, and, on the other, technological, involving the invention of modes of functioning appropriate to the new tools and of internal procedures for scientific regulation and evaluation. We may show a certain understanding then, with so many simultaneously open fronts, if certain battles were not won and certain ambitions left unfulfilled (the program, the dictionary of toposemes). At least, these problems were faced and identified. In openly playing the card of the Web, constituting an open site conceived in the spirit of the Web as open source and capable, moreover, of communicating with other online databases, the thesaurus can now become a truly reticulated instrument, open to being exploited by neighboring projects—as it is, for example, by the online database Women-Writers (www.database.womenwriters.nl) constructed in Holland by Suzan van Dijk (fig. 8), who created links to SatarBase for her analysis of novels written by women and of their reception history, SatorBase's topoi serving as one of the indexes of narrative content in these feminine novels (fig. 9).

We may also sketch out prospects for the thesaurus's development, which, thanks to Canadian institutions, now benefits from a certain perennial support. In the immediate future, SATOR should continue to reflect on theoretical questions concerning topos. It may be that the subject is nebulous and inexhaustible, but its reason for being and its originality reside in the term. And the most appropriate time and place for such reflection are the annual colloquia that rhythmically sound out the society's lifespan and

---

[22] An autonomous invention with respect to the editorial circuit that, until its current disengagement, was one of the great initiators of any great project involving cumulative collaborative erudition, or even with respect to the institution of the university that did not intervene to fix rules of collaboration—rules that it did not even know itself yet. The counterpart of this autonomy was the lack of any public or private funding for the first ten years of the project.

FIGURE 8

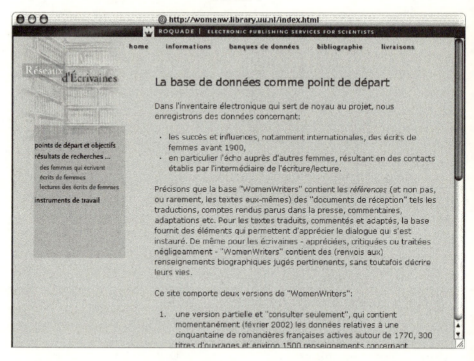

give it human cohesion, far more than any computerized instruments, even given their great capacity for ubiquity. Subsequently, in order to develop the thesaurus, SATOR should probably return, as it did already in the initial phase of its activities, to the study of modalities of computerized research of the great corpus of electronic literary texts that now offer far better performance than fifteen years ago, both in terms of the quantity of texts available and in terms of the quality of requests to which these texts can be subjected, facilitating and speeding up the location of topoi within texts likely to contain them.[23] Finally, and in a more general manner, in order that such a system develop and an authentic cumulative process be set up to make use of this sort of instrument in the humanities, it is necessary that academic systems begin to take into account—as is already the case in the natural sciences—the micro-contributions constituted by the discovery or development of a topos or

---

[23] See the reflections of the lexicographer Jean-Michel Messian on the preliminary construction of this type of program for computerized research within great corpuses of texts, in "Violence et son réseau lexical (1600–1800): Prémisses sémasiologique," in *Violence et fiction*, 33–41.

FIGURE 9

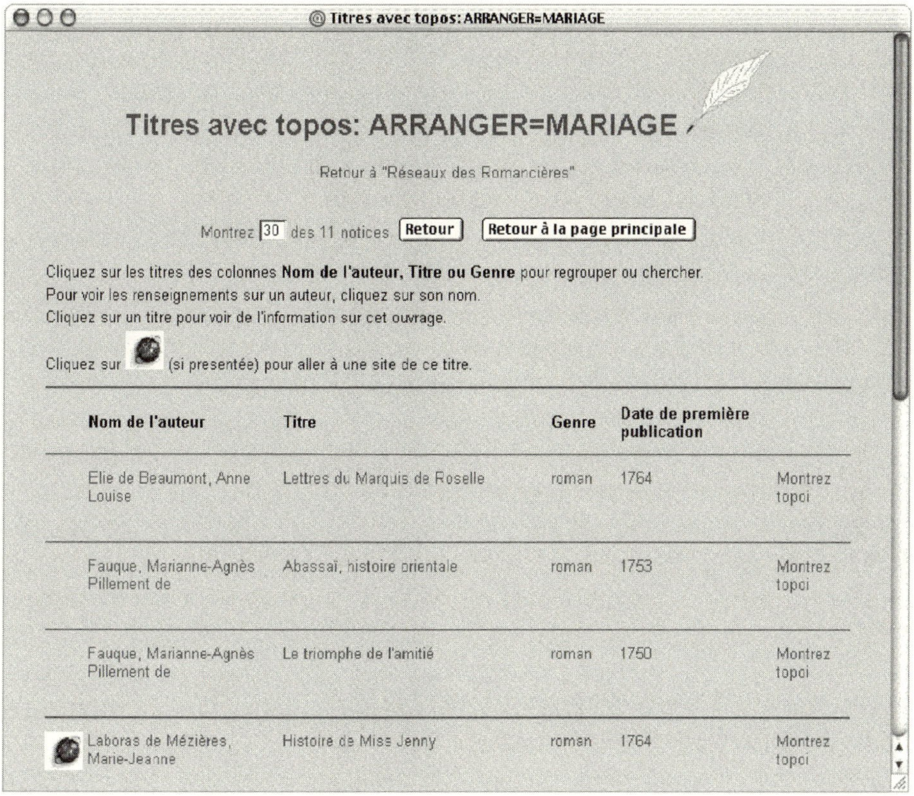

Titres avec topos: ARRANGER=MARIAGE

occurrence within the SatorBase. Otherwise, researchers will not truly engage this sort of tool. It is not by chance that the richest thesaurus produced up to now by SATOR comprises its thirteen volumes of proceedings. Given that the unit of scientific production constituted by the article is recognized in the research world, it comes as no surprise that research scholars should devote to it their best work.

———————

Translated by Sharon Lubkemann Allen

Themes, Figures

NANCY ARMSTRONG

The Fiction of Bourgeois Morality and the Paradox of Individualism

Edward Waverley is a misfit. In this respect, he harks back to Robinson Crusoe and anticipates any number of later protagonists who cannot inhabit the social position into which they have been born. What else allows Elizabeth Bennet, Pip, Jane Eyre, Maggie Tulliver, Michael Henchard, Dorian Gray, and Stephen Dedalus to represent the claims of unacknowledged individuality in general, if not the fact that they are first and foremost something more than the consequently obsolete place assigned them? Literary history has indeed smiled on fiction that sets a protagonist in opposition to the prevailing field of social possibilities in a relationship that achieves synthesis when two conditions are met: (1) the protagonist acquires a position commensurate with his or her worth, and (2) the entire field of possible human identities changes to provide such a place for that individual. To be a novel, the sheer preponderance of examples suggest, a narrative must strive to produce this outcome, no matter how difficult that may turn out to be. As a result, we tend to recognize a narrative as a novel when it evaluates both a protagonist and the field of possibilities in which he or she acquires a social identity on the basis of whether they further or frustrate such a synthesis. This standard and its disciplinary rhetoric are what we generally mean by the term *bourgeois morality*.

Contrary to prevailing critical opinion, bourgeois morality is not a value in and of itself so much as a way of reading, assessing, and revising existing categories of identity and whatever cultural apparatus may authorize them—often the novel itself. From this perspective, bourgeois morality cannot possibly draw its tremendous and enduring authority from institutional religion, the Bible, or even Judeo-Christian ethics in the most general sense. Bourgeois morality appears to emanate from the very core of an individual, as that individual confronts established systems of value and finds them lacking. Often suspicious of pleasure, unconcerned with profit, and heedless of life's little necessities, bourgeois morality appears to be the assertion of pure individuality.[1] In fact, however, bourgeois morality adds something to

---

[1] Leonard Tennenhouse and I argue this point in "A Mind for Passion: Locke and Hutcheson on Desire," in *Politics and the Passions, 1500–1850*, ed. Daniela Coli, Victoria Kahn, and Neil Saccamano (forthcoming, Princeton University Press). In his chapter "Of Power," in *An Essay*

that individual which entitles him or her to a social position affording gratification superior to mere economic rank. In the process, bourgeois morality
also authorizes as humane and good any social order that affords individuals
their rightful places. I cannot call this supplement *material* in any familiar
sense of the term. But I will nevertheless insist that bourgeois morality inflects the material wealth of a modern nation and its ruling elite just as powerfully as the elements of birth and rank inflected the early-modern nation
and an old aristocracy. We can consequently think of bourgeois morality as
our own distinctive brand of magical thinking and the novel as the most effective means of disseminating it. Let me explain why.

Whenever we refer to a society of individuals, we unwittingly pose a contradiction in terms. As the inheritors of liberal Western culture, how else do
we define someone's individuality if not by virtue of his or her deviation from
some social role, norm, or stereotype? How else, on the other hand, does civil
society ensure the right of any one individual to express that individuality
if not by limiting all individuals' right to self-expression? The premise is
that one individual cannot fully realize his or her individuality except by
encroaching on another's ability to do so. To cherish individuality is consequently to agree that certain constraints be placed on it. This paradox translates rather easily into the situation confronting the protagonists of our most
enduring works of English fiction. In order to be good members of society,
those protagonists must fit in; they must observe the same rules observed by
their fellow citizens. At the same time, in order to represent the claims of un-
expressed individualism, those protagonists must give expression to asocial
desires, which they can do only by bending the rules that define their given
places in society. They are clearly misfits. The novel takes it upon itself to
solve this contradiction by creating fantastic situations in which one can become a good member of society precisely by risking exclusion from it.

The novel resolves the inherent conflict between individual interests and
those of the collective in one of two ways. The social order might expand,
grow more flexible, and acquire heterogeneity, as it incorporates excluded

---

Concerning Human Understanding, Locke contends that from our sensations of pleasure and pain
arise our notions of good and evil, and reason prompts us to prefer the good. But Lockean reason,
as Frances Hutcheson observed, does not explain why men subordinate their immediate desires to
the greater good. To behave in this way, he argues, humans must have a internal moral sense. Even
before reason goes to work ordering our sensations, Hutcheson declares, our desires "are fixed for
us by the Author of our Nature, subservient to the interest of the system; so that each individual is
made, previously to his own choice, a member of a *great Body*, and affected with the fortunes of the
whole" (*An Inquiry into the Original of Our Ideas of Beauty and Virtue* [London, 1734; reprint,
Charlottesville, Va., 1986], 65).

elements of the individual. Alternatively, the protagonist might grow deeper, more complex, and internally conflicted, as he or she incorporates the norms of the culture and subordinates his or her antisocial impulses to them.[2] In the first instance, society becomes more flexible and inclusive as it incorporates and sublates the excesses of individualism. In the second instance, the novel produces an antithetical effect; we end up with a morally constraining social order and with individuals who have sublimated, exhausted, or otherwise personally come to terms with their own worst desires in ways that make them seem mature and more interesting individuals. Such individuals have incorporated the contradiction between a morally authorized individualism and a morally authorized normalcy. Many a novel demonstrates the formal compatibility of these ideologically incompatible resolutions. Jane Austen's heroines especially do so; they not only come to regret acts of irreverence toward the finely gradated social hierarchy in which they live but also marry into higher positions than their money and upbringing warrant. This essay will examine the formal strategies of British fiction that sought to reproduce the social contract out of the most unlikely materials. I will be especially attentive to changes in the dialectical operations of the social contract that allowed both individualism and the British fiction that reproduced it to endure from the eighteenth century to the present day.

Franco Moretti has argued that the literary market did not distribute novels to readerships according to nation: "between 1750 and 1850 the consequence of centralization is that in most European countries the majority of novels are, quite simply, *foreign books.* Hungarian, Italian, French and English novels become *models to be imitated.*"[3] During the nineteenth century,

---

[2] Etienne Balibar, *Subjection and Subjectivation,* in *Supposing the Subject,* ed. Joan Copjec (London, 1994). Balibar offers perhaps the most concise description of the problematic in terms of which I will be reading British fiction and abstracting the cultural logic that we call "bourgeois morality." This logic begins and always returns to the double meaning of *subject.* As *subject* in the "neutral, impersonal notion of a *subjectum*" the term refers to "an individual substance or substratum for properties, but we also translate as *subject* the personal notion of a *subjectus*: a political and juridical term, which refers to *subjection* or *submission,* i.e., the fact that . . . a human person is *subjected to* the more or less absolute, more or less legitimate authority of a superior power" (8). At some point roughly coinciding with the wars of national independence, in Balibar's account, these two meanings came into contradiction: "the humanity of man is identified not with a *given* or an essence, but with a *practice* and a task: the task of self-emancipation from every domination and subjection" through some kind of collective effort or reform. This political redefinition of the individual had an ethical corollary: "the value of human agency arises from the fact that no one can be liberated or emancipated *by others,* although no one can liberate himself *without others*" (12); emphasis in original.

[3] Franco Moretti, *Atlas of the European Novel, 1800–1900* (London, 1998), 187; emphasis in original.

Moretti observes, the English book market could be distinguished from that of every other nation, as English publishers continued to distribute English novels internationally. With domestic sales, however, these same English booksellers grew increasingly Anglocentric. As a result, the English novel offers a privileged field in which to observe how, over the span of three centuries, individual resistance to birth and wealth regenerates the moral authority of the modern middle class. I am especially interested in identifying the formal strategies by which that class continued to authorize itself in this manner once industrial capitalism had displaced an agrarian economy. Indeed, by 1851 we find Queen Victoria herself not only opening the Crystal Palace Exhibition in London to celebrate new developments in science, industry, and trade, but also publicly observing many of the same practices that characterized households well beneath hers in station. Finally, I will explore the basis on which modernism and contemporary fiction drew authority from their opposition to a morality that they accused of stifling artistic originality and debasing alternative cultural practices.

Morality and Social Resistance

To embark on a genealogy of bourgeois morality as it informs and is produced by the novel, let me start with a well-known example of the cultural logic I will be tracking. Perhaps no other passage from British fiction reveals just how social resistance generates moral authority and succeeds in turning the tables on established wealth and position better than this scene from Charlotte Brontë's *Jane Eyre*. Here the young Jane contests the authority of her aunt to subordinate her in the traditional family hierarchy:

> "Go out of the room: return to the nursery," was her [Aunt Reed's] mandate. My look or something else must have struck her as offensive, for she spoke with extreme, though suppressed, irritation. I got up, I went to the door; I came back again: I walked to the window, across the room, then close up to her.
>
> *Speak* I must: I had been trodden on severely and *must* turn: but how? What strength had I to dart retaliation at my antagonist? I gathered my energies and launched them in this blunt sentence: —
>
> "I am not deceitful: if I were, I should say I loved *you*; but I declare I do not love you: I dislike you the worst of anybody in the world. . . .
>
> . . . Shaking from head to foot, thrilled with ungovernable excitement, I continued: —

"I am glad you are no relation of mind: I will never call you aunt again as long as I live. I will never come to see you when I am grown up; and if any one asks me how I like you, and how you treated me, I will say the very thought of you makes me sick, and that you treated me with miserable cruelty."

"How dare you affirm that, Jane Eyre?"

"How dare I, Mrs. Reed? How dare I? Because it is the *truth*. . . ."

Ere I had finished this reply, my soul began to expand, to exult, with the strangest sense of freedom, of triumph, I ever felt. It seemed as if an invisible bond had burst, and that I had struggled out into unhoped-for liberty. Not without cause was this sentiment: Mrs. Reed looked frightened: her work had slipped from her knee; she was lifting up her hands, rocking herself to and fro, and even twisting her face as if she would cry."[4]

Why on earth would a hapless orphan risk the relative comfort of a country estate by this outrageous display of ingratitude toward her benefactor? More to the point, why would a middle-class readership allow her to condemn that benefactor as a tyrant, given that the novel offers absolutely no one there on the spot who can identify Jane as the voice of moral authority?

To answer these questions, we must read this episode as a model of the dialectical redefinition of social positioning carried out by the novel as a whole. Let us assume that a fictional individual who speaks on behalf of all those who have been unfairly held back or kept down by an unjust social order mobilizes a distinctively modern form of authority. Brontë makes such authority appear to come from within her heroine alone and manifest itself in her verbal aggression. "*Speak* I must" simultaneously performs a speech act and endows such an act with a power capable of overthrowing her adversary. Mrs. Reed has made a classificatory mistake so basic to Jane's identity that Jane would cease to be herself were she not to defy that misclassification. Mrs. Reed has placed Jane outside the family and in opposition to it. Jane begins to return to her place in the nursery, a gesture that would have confirmed that she is not a full-fledged member of the household, but something prevents her from doing so. She "turns" to claim a place as a speaker on the same level as her aunt and surrogate parent, whom she defines as her "antagonist." Performing, we might say, as the figure of antithesis itself, Jane poses the question, "What strength had I to dart retaliation at my antagonist?" She promptly answers thus: "I gathered my energies and launched them in this *blunt sentence*" (italics mine). This answer to the question

---

[4] Charlotte Brontë, *Jane Eyre* (1847; Oxford, 1998), 37–38. Subsequent references are to this edition and have been included in the text.

"What strength had I?" overtly transforms the conflict between antagonists from the dynamic interaction of hereditary owner and dependent into a war of words. In the linguistic battle, Jane's very position as outsider gives her the daunting power of interrogation, the power, that is, to question traditional forms of domination and pass "sentence" on them.

Jane responds to her aunt's traditional imperative with an explosion of what appears to be self-expression. I stress the fact that the power of resistance only "appears" to come from Jane herself, because a deus ex machina is as much at work in this narrative as in those of premodern cultures. Modern readers tend to forget that Jane is the putative author as well as the outspoken protagonist of the narrative, and that she performs her act of self-assertion in protest of her cousin's having deprived her of the coveted book, *Bewick's History of British Birds*. If the act of turning against her benefactor subtly asserts the power of words over property, then the novel's representation of that act still more subtly asserts the power of the written word over the speech of this rebellious girl. Conspicuously lacking in natural charms and feminine accomplishments though she may be, Jane is sublimely literate. It is in this capacity alone that she can serve as the measure of measures against which the values maintaining class position are themselves evaluated. On Jane's ability to read those who occupy positions above and below her for the discrepancies between their outward and social behavior and their inward and individual qualities of mind depends her ability to occupy the social position from which she can convincingly author her own history. At the same time, her ability to rewrite social distinctions with a righteousness that strikes fear in the heart of her social superior is what momentarily levels the playing field on which they do battle, creating an opportunity for Jane to move forward historically. The same aunt who unjustly banishes Jane to the nursery at the beginning of the passage consequently cowers before her by the end, and Jane is packed off to Lowood School in the aftermath of this *auf hebung* at the microlevel of the narrative. Through repeated instances of this move, the novel simultaneously moralizes the practices of everyday life and grants material force to the verbal outbursts that tailor those practices to the individual's needs.

To the degree that a specific brand of literacy gives Jane the authority to tell the story of herself as a self-generated individual, the declaration, "*Speak I must,*" cannot of course be said to come from Jane herself. Indeed, the product of this speech act is another self independent of the very institutions responsible for nurturing and educating her. As Jane declares, "ere I had finished this reply, my soul began to expand, to exult, with the strangest sense of freedom, of triumph, I ever felt" (38). In that speaking out indicates how much there is that cannot be contained by the role Jane is supposed to play, the novel is, as Gayatri Spivak contends, a soul-making apparatus capable of endowing whole categories of individuals with sensibilities that make them into unique companions for the reader.[5] Assuming that Jane Eyre's verbal behavior is one and the same as that of the novel, then the novel also acquires its moral authority as it pits the force of writing against what it considers the more substantial and enduring authority of family and class. By 1848, the economic and social practices of the novel's readership had succeeded in displacing those of a landed aristocracy. In view of the fact that their culture was the dominant culture, under what conditions, one must ask, could middle-class readers approve of Brontë's obstreperous heroine? Bourgeois morality had apparently become so firmly affixed to political resistance that the bond did not come unglued even after the modern middle-class came into power. To understand how resistance could garner moral authority and yet affirm rather than threaten the status quo, we must understand how morality and political resistance came to be read as interchangeable in the first place.

Contractual Morality

If Daniel Defoe can be called the first novelist and exponent of possessive individualism, it is chiefly because *Robinson Crusoe* inadvertently defined resistance as the necessary expression of certain qualities of mind, especially the tendency to be no less critical of oneself than of others, qualities worthy of written expression. I will not dwell on the self-criticism Crusoe turns on himself when he disobeys his father, comes to doubt the traditional Christian God, and so reasons his way into complete self-sufficiency. For purposes of this essay, I am far more interested in a form of authority that emerges when Crusoe discovers other men on his island. To coexist with other people, he must hold them to the same code of conduct that he brings to bear on himself, one that increasingly acknowledges its philosophical debt and narrative logic to theories of the social contract. According to John Locke's *Second Treatise of Government*, an individual does not step into his father's position but earns his citizenship as he comes to understand the law.[6] To understand

---

[5] Gayatri Chakravorty Spivak, "Three Women's Texts and a Critique of Imperialism," in *"Race," Writing, and Difference,* ed. Henry Louis Gates Jr. (Chicago, 1985), 262–80.

[6] John Locke, *Two Treatises of Government,* ed. Peter Laslett (Cambridge, 1988). When the son's "understanding be fit to take the Government of his Will," according to Locke, father and son "are equally Subjects of the same Law together, without any Dominion left in the Father over the Life, Liberty, or Estate of his Son" (2.59.26–30).

the law is to obey it and thus to fulfill the precondition for governing others. According to the political model on which that state was founded and still justifies itself, citizenship depends entirely on one's ability to harness the very aggression by means of which that individual expresses his or her own individuality, much as we have seen Jane Eyre do. In this respect, the modern state can be understood as a defensive formation, a collective dedicated to protecting not only its citizens but also their dependents, indeed all those unfit to be citizens, from any form of aggression that would encroach on their rights to property and personal autonomy. The modern state is justified, in other words, by the need to defend individualism against forms of aggression that often bear uncanny resemblance to expressions of that very same individualism. Bourgeois morality distinguishes, first, self-expression that springs straight from the heart from what the culture and circumstance may dictate. Paradoxically, however, bourgeois morality also distinguishes those passions and drives that we harness for the general good from those that disrupt the social order. Thus we consider Jane virtuous for momentarily overpowering her caretaker, while Bertha Mason is clearly a menace to those around her for doing much the same thing.

The first half of Crusoe's story reads as a striking example of the paradox of individualism. His compulsion to classify and map the natural landscape of his island exceeds the limits of his position as a stranger there and spills out onto the surrounding landscape. As he lends order to this information, he also acquires control over the unstable elements of nature, which—as he learns from a bout with tainted turtle soup—include his own body and mind. As the island subjects him to its natural order, he in turn subjects the island to rational control. It becomes his in the process. Defoe's purpose in this part of the novel is rather self-evident, and generations of commentators, including Rousseau and Marx, have provided a rich legacy of readings that testify to this fact. Less interesting to readers is the process by which Crusoe becomes governor of a peaceful cosmopolitan nation, for in so doing he no longer represents the individual's individuality so much as an aggregated citizenry that exacts a sacrifice of individuality in return for the protection of one's private property. From the perspective of such a government, an individual's willingness to stay in place makes him or her a good citizen, and those who resist the status quo act in defiance of the general good rather than the corrupt institutions of early-modern culture. We can regard the curious process by which Crusoe assumes the role of "governor" over the variegated population that happens to wash up on his island as an early product of this paradox.

The paradox of individualism, as I construe it, is one and the same as the logic of the social contract. This contract demands that the individual willingly restrain his individuality, in the form of desire, in exchange for the state's protection of that individuality, in the form of property, against the desire of other individuals. To constrain his fellow individuals, Crusoe must not only place similar constraints on his own desire, but also remain in a defensive position. That Crusoe has never been characterized as a desiring man is owing to the fact that Defoe represents his protagonist's insatiable desire for independent prosperity, not as desire, but as the fear of losing exclusive ownership of his property. Moreover, Crusoe's rise to leadership comes to us as a series of conflicts in which he rescues other individuals from forms of first native, and then European, savagery implicitly connected to an international aristocracy and the superstitious practices that authorize its violent ways. Against overwhelming physical strength, Defoe pits Crusoe's literacy, which includes his ability to count, map, measure, classify, and disseminate fictitious accounts of the island and its inhabitants to those who lack such intellectual mastery. In the process, Crusoe distinguishes his own brand of resistance from those of prisoners and mutineers. That he considers violence both necessary to and incompatible with his new social identity becomes especially clear when Crusoe asks Friday to help out by blowing the heads off a few of their adversaries. Only by disavowing his own violence can Crusoe put reason itself on the defense against the physical superiority of the invaders. His indirect use of violence nevertheless implies that the contractual state must back up individual consent with force.

Although Crusoe is himself a latecomer to the island, his unique ability to mix his labor with the land makes that land an extension of his mind and body that it is the governor's sole purpose to defend. Although the manual labor that he eventually delegates entirely to Friday makes it possible for Crusoe to inhabit the island, his intellectual labor allows him to dominate that territory strategically. The whole purpose of the manual labor is to create the property that he proceeds to defend by means of his intellectual labor alone. At the same time, once there is neither father, nor abusive sea captains and plantation owners, nor female cats, cannibals, and mutineers against whom to defend himself, the moral energy seems to drain out of the story, despite Defoe's elaborate efforts to maintain his hero's minority status and defensive posture. Indeed, in assuming the role of the governor, Crusoe becomes the virtually invisible figure of a self-suppressed rather than a self-expressive self. However "middle-class" we might consider this ability to claim as his the labor of those whom he supervises, and no matter how English we might assume his methods of supervision to be, Crusoe proves curiously incapable of reproducing his successful rise to power upon returning to the country of his origins. Having left his assigned position within the middling ranks, he cannot feel at home in England. Such are the wages of his success, that Crusoe ceases to be an admirably resistant hero.

Sexual Morality

In becoming a self-governing subject, Crusoe gains control over a self endangered by external forces, which he conquers, along with his fear, by means of observation, information gathering, and classification, precisely the faculties associated with Enlightenment rationality. Moll Flanders and Roxana work as industriously as Crusoe. Rather than rely on the products of labor whose steady flow can be ensured by reason, Crusoe's female counterparts trade in sexual labor. Yet they become who they are by a process instructively analogous to Crusoe's. When they gain control of their labor, they also gain control over their sexuality and, with it, the power to trade up to social positions of respectability. Where early-modern cultures would have it be their fathers', brothers', guardians', or owners' prerogative to trade them, Moll and Roxana trade themselves to men. In so doing, they not only acquire the autonomy of a modern individual but also put a name and a face on the irrationality that drives Crusoe to leave his father and a succession of employers. That is to say, in becoming mistress of her sexuality, the female picaro acquires modern sexuality, which is the specific form of irrationality that cannot be governed by reason. Only morality can govern sexual desire and make it serve the logic of the social contract. In entering the social contract, the individual agrees to exchange some disruptive form of sexual desire for what might be called reproductive desire, the will to reproduce him- or herself as a nuclear family. In other words, the protagonist must violate the prevailing rules of kinship that gives the father sole right to exchange his daughter in order that the daughter might establish new rules of kinship. According to these new rules, each and every individual finds the only individual capable of transforming desire into bourgeois love, the one expression of sexual desire compatible with bourgeois morality.

In this respect, *Moll Flanders* and *Roxana* make a special contribution to the cultural logic that I am calling bourgeois morality. Robinson Crusoe's story suggests that before he can constitute something approximating the ideal society, the citizen-subject must be reconstituted from the ground up. He must be able to express himself through the acquisition of property, but he must also curtail that same acquisitive impulse and share his island with other acquisitive individuals. In assuming the position of governor, Crusoe appears to have done exactly that. Similarly, we might say, Moll and Roxana assume positions within respectable society from which they survey and evaluate their former behavior, positions therefore indicative of their capacity for self-government. Judging by the critical response to these novels, however, one has to ask if Defoe did in fact allow his female protagonists to become full-fledged individuals whose stories consequently helped to imagine a new ruling class. Too many readers conclude that, to the contrary, his female protagonists succeed in a way that simply serves to expose the predatory nature of prevailing social relations. Rather than encourage his readers to condemn female protagonists who fornicate their way into respectable circles, Defoe made very sure that any moral disapproval we might direct at them would redound to the greater discredit of their social superiors.

The man who coerces sexual favors from a woman without agreeing to assume her father's role is flying in the face of the contract between the householder and his dependents, which had long served as a metaphor for the ideal contractual state. In place of anything resembling a Christian soul, Locke, for example, substituted the rational ethic of the social contract. In partnership with his wife, each householder ideally reproduced his own understanding of and respect for the law in each of his offspring.[7] The individual reared in such a household would respect other households, just as they respected each and every member of their own, because such reverence for the autonomy of others was necessary to the preservation and prosperity of each. To coerce sexual favors either from a commoner like Moll or from one who has fallen in social position, as has Roxana, would be to invert this principle. Indeed, we find the corruption of the old society increasing incrementally as Defoe's heroines ascend the ladder of power and expose those on top who routinely corrupt those economically beneath them. But even those who can excuse Moll and Roxana on grounds that their seducers were the ones to overturn the social contract find it difficult to accept Moll's lack of remorse for inadvertently marrying her own brother and all but impossible to forgive Roxana for conspiring to murder her daughter. That *Roxana* in particular affords special access to the history of bourgeois morality is clear from the very start.

Despite her final words of repentance, this heroine repeatedly crosses the line distinguishing the exploited dependent from the licentious parent

---

[7] John Locke, *Second Treatise of Government*. To dispute any God-given right over one's children, Locke contends that "the *Power*, then, *that Parents have* over their Children, arises from that Duty which is incumbent on them, to take care of their Off-spring, during the imperfect state of Childhood. To inform the Mind, and govern the Actions of their yet ignorant Nonage, till Reason shall take its place" (2.58.105).

to become no different from those who have corrupted her. She reproduces her own licentious qualities in her maid-servant Amy, thereby reproducing the corruption of the class into which she was born. To trade up is, in that case, to exchange the self-possession required of the moral individual for a self that can be exploited by other such individuals. "Here," Roxana concludes her account, "after some few Years of flourishing, and outwardly happy Circumstances, I fell into a dreadful Course of Calamities, and *Amy* also: the very Reverse of our former Good Days; the Blast of Heaven seem'd to follow the Injury done to the poor Girl [Roxana's daughter], by us both; and I was brought so low again, that my Repentance seem'd to be only the consequence of my Misery, as my Misery was of my Crime."[8]

Defoe died in 1731. In 1745, a version of the novel appeared, revised by a printer, in which the disturbed, shifting, and yet tenacious relationship between Roxana, her servant Amy, and the daughter who threatened their position in the prevailing system of exchange appears to have troubled the novel's reception. The revised edition included a second volume that expanded the heroine's reversal of fortune to include a protracted account of her repentance and budding parental concern. Yet another revised edition published in 1775 proved to be equally popular with late-eighteenth- and nineteenth-century readers. In this edition, according to a modern editor, "the narrator's very vocabulary becomes more respectable, and her actions, while still to be repented, are considerably less criminal. In particular, that strangest and most disturbing part of the plot, the relentless pursuit of the narrator by her discarded daughter, is entirely omitted. Instead, in lengthy additions to Defoe's text, "Roxana" discovers the joys of being a good wife and mother."[9]

Do these revisions by later hands indicate that Roxana was originally crafted to be morally reprehensible in a way that Crusoe, though demonstrating a similar lack of parental concern, was not? I would say no. The novel is written as if Defoe and his readers were more concerned with the economic consequences of being female than with her capacity for maternal feelings. If social status trumped gender in determining an individual's identity, then her material circumstances rather than her emotional inclinations would have determined a heroine's morality in the period prior to Samuel Richardson's *Pamela*. There is indeed little evidence to suggest that

---

[8] Daniel Defoe, *Roxana, or The Fortunate Mistress* (1724; Oxford, 1996), 329–30.

[9] John Mullan, "Appendix: The Textual History of *Roxana*," in *Roxana, or The Fortunate Mistress* (Oxford, 1996), 338.

the social contract would have asked more of Roxana as a parent than to pay a reliable couple to give her children a relatively wholesome upbringing. If there is any truth to my claim, then we must regard later revisions of the novel as efforts to bring Roxana's behavior in line with the morality of a later historical moment. Despite these attempts, as Homer Brown observes, *Roxana* occupied only a tenuous relationship to the tradition of British fiction until the period when modernists began to write in opposition to bourgeois morality.[10]

The contract that *Roxana* strikes up with the reader is another matter. By representing itself as the memoirs of a woman of pleasure who has little choice of profession, Defoe's female picaresque did for writing what *Jane Eyre* would do for speech. The novel defined writing as an act of resistance. It is true that both Moll and Roxana write from a position of hard-won respectability that signifies a life of unrestrained desire rather than one of contractual obligations met and exacted from others. In this respect, neither achieves the physical autonomy that embodies modern individuality. Not so, however, for their writing. Their stories are as consistently and sharply critical of the sexual practices of the old regime as any that Samuel Richardson produced. As a result, their lack of sexual self-possession is contradicted by self-possession at the level of the text, which looks ahead to the standard of personal integrity that he endorsed. In writing first *Pamela* and then *Clarissa*, Richardson indeed exploited the advantages of both the male and the female picaresque, a fact that critics seldom acknowledge. Let us but imagine Crusoe in a petticoat and using personal letter writing to fend off nearly constant sexual assaults, and we have Pamela, whose body is nothing if not her property. Further, let us imagine Moll and Roxana resisting the blandishments of their masters with the same compulsion that drives Crusoe to resist his father, God, nature, and foreigners. Then strip those women of their anonymity, and have them tell readers capable of similar indignation how they were forced to receive unwanted sexual advances on pain of losing all economic support. In thus transforming Moll along the lines of Crusoe, we end up with an a discursively aggressive protagonist rather like Clarissa. By acknowledging Richardson's debt to salacious novels often attributed to the French, we can arrive at a more accurate sense of the distance between the new morality and earlier definitions of human virtue.

---

[10] Homer Brown, *Institutions of the English Novel: From Defoe to Scott* (Philadelphia, 1997), 171–202. Brown provides a detailed account of the centuries-long process by which various texts came to be attributed to Defoe and classified as novels.

A New Class Ethos

If there is any truth to my claim that bourgeois morality comes from and attaches itself to the logic of the social contract as the individual resists all other bases for social relationships, then the question we must ask of Richardson is why he chose to focus on the father-daughter relationship. Locke, in contrast, thought exclusively in terms of the father-son and even the parent-son relationship, when he formulated his version of the social contract and tried to figure out how it might reorganize social relations. As the novel began to imagine the logic of the social contract reproducing itself, much as Locke had suggested, at the microlevel, household by household, the daughter began to emerge as the appropriate vehicle of cultural reproduction. Long before Defoe, the dissenting tradition had argued for a government that begins at home and functions as a moral obligation. During the early eighteenth century, the novel gave the old formula a new and decisive twist. If the wayward daughter reflects poorly on her father to the point of threatening his position in the community of men, then the coercive father would reflect badly on that entire community by implying that it is unfit to care for a population of dependent individuals. The only way around this double bind, as Richardson apparently saw it, was to authorize the daughter to choose a husband for herself, a man of her class or better who valued her more for her qualities of mind and heart than for her physical charms and social position. Pamela manages to engineer this kind of marriage by means of letter writing, and she elevates her entire family in the process. But still more compelling than Richardson's first attempt at fiction was the international best seller, *Clarissa*, which put its stamp on all subsequent fiction of the European nations. Bourgeois morality, as we now know it, emerged along with modern culture by means of narratives designed to harness sexual desire for specific biocultural ends, a desire that could only be so harnessed and redirected by certain forms of writing.

Between the prolix epistolary novels of Richardson and Jane Austen's precisely wrought fiction the novel took a quantum leap, without which it is difficult to imagine Charlotte Brontë's heroine facing down her guardian. Henry Fielding's claim that Richardson's heroines used self-restraint to entrap wealthy suitors implied that the fiction that offered so many scenes of seduction and professed so many scruples was nothing more than a tease as well. Austen leaves no room for readers to imagine that her heroine's reluctance to enter into relationships with men is anything less than genuine, when her narrator follows her heroine's words and gestures back to their sources within that heroine to feelings of which she herself is unaware. The voice of truth, in this case, describes neither the heroine's thinking nor that of the author so much as the voice of a culture telling us how heroine, author, and reader ought to think. Indeed, were it not for the fact that truth issues from a minority position in Austen's fiction, we might equate the narrator who gently and yet axiomatically declares that "a single man in possession of good fortune, must be in want of a wife" with the aggregate of good citizens who provide a model of how to read and evaluate human character.[11]

Austen's narrator endorses only small acts of resistance to the elaborate rules governing sexual relations among an extremely narrow slice of English society, acts of rebellion performed strictly in words, yet acts that constitute sublime moments of individuality in the terms of the author's world and time. Her heroines tend to say no to offers of marriage that would mean a definitive move up the social ladder and secure their economic comfort for life. Their refusals erupt in minor scandals. Indeed, so incredible is Elizabeth Bennet's resistance to marriage with Mr. Collins—to whom the Bennet's country residence has been entailed—that Collins himself dismisses her blunt refusal as "usual with young ladies [who] reject the addresses of the man whom they secretly mean to accept, when he first applies for their favour" (72). To do away with any resemblance between her own motivations and those of a Richardsonian heroine, Elizabeth wastes no time in assuring him, "I am not one of those young ladies (if such young ladies there are) who are so daring as to risk their happiness on the chance of being asked a second time. I am perfectly serious in my refusal.—You could not make *me* happy, and I am convinced that I am the last woman in the world who could make *you* so" (72).

This signature move on the part of the Austen heroine marks the perfect realization of the paradox I am pursuing. By refusing to consent to marriage in the terms it has been proposed, she becomes a rule-breaker in the only way that can be considered truly good. Heedless of the economic security she stands to lose, she holds out for a contract based on a certain quality of feeling. This feeling arises directly from Elizabeth Bennet's resistance to the hauteur of Mr. Darcy, his class-coded displays of superiority, and the disproportionate luxury of his friends and family when compared with her family's precarious circumstances. This is resistance that can neither be overcome in a wink nor softened with money. Indeed, so intense is the antagonism between her moral values and the material values she attributes to people of his rank that her father, who would ordinarily be delighted to marry off a

---

[11] Jane Austen, *Pride and Prejudice* (1813; New York, 1996), 3. Subsequent references are to this edition and included in the text.

daughter to a man of Darcy's position, feels compelled to ask, "what are you doing? Are you out of your senses, to be accepting this man? Have you not always hated him?" Upon hearing her recant those feelings, Mr. Bennet continues, "He is rich, to be sure, and you may have more fine clothes and fine carriages than [your sister] Jane. But will they make you happy?" (242). To ensure that readers would answer with a resounding no, Austen has already offered them the example of Charlotte Lucas, who consents to marry the odious Mr. Collins simply because he will provide her with a comfortable home. Elizabeth "had always felt that Charlotte's opinion of matrimony was not exactly like her own," the narrator informs us, "but she could not have supposed it possible that . . . she would have sacrificed every better feeling to worldly advantage. Charlotte the wife of Mr. Collins, was a most humiliating picture!" (84). In speaking Lizzie's unspoken thoughts, the novel and the very culture implicitly share her moral indignation.

If Charlotte Lucas's marriage is clearly not an example to follow, are we then to assume that *Pride and Prejudice* advocates a marriage contracted in defiance of those principles? Would the novel have us find Lizzie's marriage superior to those of her sisters simply because there was little or no resistance for them to overcome? Austen puts these questions to rest as her heroine conquers Mr. Bennet's incredulity "by repeated assurances that Mr. Darcy was really the object of her choice, by explaining the gradual change which her estimation of him had undergone, relating her absolute certainty that his affection was not the work of a day, but had stood the test of many months suspense" (242). The episode where Elizabeth stands before Darcy's portrait at Pemberley as his housekeeper sings her master's praises is the episode scholars most often identify as the moment when the heroine falls in love. Lizzie rereads the signs of the class above hers as anchored, in Darcy's case, to qualities within the man that allow her to recalculate his worth in terms of bourgeois morality. Indeed, of this encounter the narrator inquires, "What praise is more valuable than the praise of an intelligent servant? As a brother, a landlord, a master, she considered how many people's happiness were in his guardianship! . . . How much good or evil must be done by him! Every idea that had been brought forward by the housekeeper was favorable to his character, and as she stood before the canvas, on which he was represented, . . . she thought of his regard with a deeper sentiment of gratitude than it had ever raised before" (159–60).

Were this novel's purpose only to resubordinate the upstart heroine by convincing her of Darcy's superiority in her terms as well as his, *Pride and Prejudice* would never be considered the exemplary novel that it is. While it is true that Elizabeth is won over as the signs of Darcy's rank come to represent the virtues of the responsible head of household, Austen assigns him the task of further enlightening the heroine: "As a child I was taught what was *right*, but not taught to correct my temper. I was given good principles, but left to follow them in pride and conceit. . . . Unfortunately an only son, I was spoilt by my parents, who though good in themselves . . . , allowed, encouraged, almost taught me to be selfish and overbearing, to care for none beyond my own family circle, to think meanly of all the rest of the world, to *wish* at least to think meanly of their sense and worth compared with my own" (237). With this statement Darcy reinscribes the signs of rank that spoke so eloquently to Elizabeth at Pemberly within the tradition of meaning that maintained such status distinctions.

With the next statement, however, Darcy lends new moral value to traditional rank by means of an economic explanation that makes Elizabeth the source of value added: "Such I was, from eight to eight and twenty; and such I might still have been but for you, dearest, loveliest Elizabeth!" First, according to his explanation, she strips away the value of his rank: "By you, I was properly humbled. I came to you without a doubt of my reception." Then she demonstrates that this value, in and of itself, has little value: "You shewed me how insufficient were all my pretensions to please a woman worthy of being pleased." In this way, finally, she made it possible for him to acquire value of a superior kind: "What do I not owe you! You taught me a lesson, hard indeed at first, but most advantageous" (237). Thus out of the mutual antagonism of the codes they respectively embody—he to her family and rank, she to his conviction that his family and superiority of rank mean moral superiority—a subtle synthesis emerges: a new "truth" that attaches traditional signs of class to the logic of the social contract. The novel itself affords access to this truth. For it simultaneously revises the basis of class superiority and teaches the reader, much as Darcy claims Elizabeth taught him, to transform the signs of mere rank into those unselfish social principles that the novel associates with the constraint of sexual desire and thus with bourgeois morality.

Morality as Discipline

As envisioned by the eighteenth century, the social contract exacted from individuals a promise to curb their inviduality. Enlightenment intellectuals—and I would include Austen under this umbrella—saw this curb on selfishness as the first and best guarantee of full citizenship. To their way of thinking, such self-restraint entailed no loss of individuality but, quite the contrary, indicated an accretion to the self of individual rights. The Enlightenment individual was a rights-bearing subject, even if she were a woman whose only claim to such rights rested on the largesse of the man whom she married. During the decades following the French Revolution, however, English fiction launched a critique of the very individualism that earlier fiction had brought to life and disseminated in popular narrative form. Those novels for which we remember the first three decades of the nineteenth century began to question what Defoe and Richardson represented as the wholly positive exchange of aggression toward persons and property for individual rights and the sanctity of private property. Nineteenth-century intellectuals infused the irrational animosity of the savage with new value as they identified that animosity, on the one hand, with the tribal loyalty and honor code of the old aristocracy and, on the other, with the aggression that Darwin identified as the trace of our natural origin.

Victorian fiction transformed modern humankind's lack of this savage element into a loss of the primal individuality that connected individuals both to a heroic past and to their own competitive nature. Under these conditions, to enter into the contractual relationship that gained them membership in a modern social order, individuals had to renounce what was most essential to their individuality. This is no less true of Anne Elliot's quiet refusal of Captain Wentworth in Austen's *Persuasion* and Waverley's involuntary renunciation of Flora Mac-Ivor in Sir Walter Scott's *Waverley*, than it is of Jane Eyre's empassioned rejection of a bigamous marriage to Rochester. In all three cases, moreover, the kinship rules that nineteenth-century protagonists must obey at the peril of their very existence always collides with an alternative morality based on fidelity to one's own desire. By no coincidence, this turn against individualism on the part of bourgeois morality during the thirty-year period between Austen and Brontë coincides with the rise to hegemony of the novel and of the class whose interests that genre consistently served.

One can observe the unsteady shift from emergent to dominant in novels that hyperbolically extend individuality in order to mark the limits past which one cannot expand and still remain a member of the community. Thus, for all their differences in gender, ideology, national affiliation, and preferred fictional genre, both Walter Scott and Mary Shelley objectified Enlightenment individualism in ways that simultaneously gave it heroic form and drained away the desire with which earlier literature had infused it. That both Scott and Shelley had a serious problem representing individualism—its lack and its excess, respectively—stems from the fact that the medium in which they worked had given popular form to an earlier belief that the nation should be the vehicle for individualism and vice versa. The eighteenth-century novel was simply not made to reverse the culturewide ideological gears that morally compelled any and all individuals to achieve what fulfillment they could within the limits of the prevailing social order. Such fiction can be credited for giving palpable form to vast territories within the individual that could not exist within the given social categories. By the same token, we have to blame nineteenth-century fiction for turning those exclusions into spectacular excesses of individuality that stood in the way of a stable and internally coherent community. In order to turn this important literary corner, romantic-era novelists came up with protagonists who embrace a large-scale cultural contradiction (as demonstrated by the English and Scottish sides of Waverley, for example, or by Frankenstein's attempt to be both scientist and family man). Together, authors so different as Scott and Shelley set a future course for British fiction that turned the novel itself against the very expressions of individualism likely to bring about a more inclusive social order. Both authors focused on the revolutionary energy that had infused morality into the community capable of opening to include new forms of individualism. Both, however, focused on such larger-than-life figures as Fergus and the monster with something like affection, only to denounce these figures for seeking self-fulfillment at the expense of the entire community.

Scott and Shelley had very different readerships in mind when they set their respective protagonists on the road to excess and potential exclusion. Scott has Waverley carry his English identity into the Scottish Lowlands in order to formulate an imaginary Britishness that could include both England and Scotland, but Scott also lets us know that such sleight of hand can work only if Highland culture is eliminated. Shelley, on the other hand, has her protagonist set out to exceed the limits of the human itself, allowing the reader to imagine a transnational republic capable of representing virtually any individual. In the resolution to *Waverley* we encounter a community that simultaneously expands to embrace modern Britishness and contracts to exclude what were the prevailing Scottish kinship systems. In apparent contrast, Shelley's novel transforms a pan-European community from an organically integrated whole to one made of many hostile parts that can be made to cohere only by some extraordinary act of violence. Both authors initially seem to push the individual beyond the limits of collective identity in order to expand the social contract beyond the limits of a nation, class, or race and include members of an outside group selected to challenge those boundaries. *Waverley* and *Frankenstein* open the floodgates of inclusion, however, only to establish irreducible differences between cultural material that can be contained within the collective identity and that which would nullify any such identity. To the degree that both authors use figures of romance and epic hostile to the novel for purposes of marking this limit, Scott's Highlanders perform the same function as Shelley's "devilish race" of monsters. They set certain elements of individuality in vivid contradiction to the social role that modern individuals must assume in order to be regarded as moral. By the end of both novels, the full weight of bourgeois morality comes down on the side of the community and at the cost of an older individualism.

Scott, by his own admission, uses the Highlanders to express ageless desires that modern men and women feel but can no longer express in action.[12] In order to form a single nation, these men and women have to turn this element of their own humanity to a common purpose. Scott differs historically from Austen in that he identified the component of the individual that resisted socialization as the protagonist's most individual part. (Beginning with Catherine Moreland of *Northanger Abbey*, virtually all Austen's heroines relinquish a notion of the class above them acquired either from too much novel reading or from the gossip of resentful friends and relatives.) Shelley in turn seems to think and certainly has her double protagonist speak in philosophical abstractions, as if the limits of universal humanity were her whole concern, as if, moreover, virtually anything human belonged to a single category and could be expressed in the same language. The quasi-philosophical dialogue that makes up so much of her fiction is just that, however—speech and largely hearsay, which Frankenstein subsequently narrates for the sea-faring narrator, Walton, who in turn writes it up as a letter for his sister back in England. The reader consequently finds that the inward telescoping structure of Shelley's successively embedded plots ultimately encloses the cosmopolitan and universal character of her imagined community within a purely English envelope. Like Scott, she stretches English toleration for other people a good bit farther than it could actually have gone, thereby establishing a limit beyond which nothing can be considered compatible with Britishness. Beyond this point the novel cannot push individualism and still remain a novel.

---

[12] Sir Walter Scott, *Waverley; or, 'Tis Sixty Years Since* (1814; Oxford, 1986). In his opening chapter, Scott explains what he hopes to demonstrate by his venture into the past: "The wrath of our ancestors . . . was coloured *gules*; it broke forth in acts of open and sanguinary violence against the objects of its fury: our malignant feelings, which must seek gratification through more indirect channels, and undermine the obstacles they cannot openly bear down, may be rather said to be tinctured *sable*" (5).

Thus, I would suggest, Shelley shares with Scott an ambivalence toward the limitations of the very medium in which they were both working. To be sure, the monstrous potential of unleashed individuality in Shelley's novel offers us a striking contrast to the overly domesticated interior to which Scott relocates the modern individual in *Waverley*. At the same time, the two authors provide equally eloquent testimony to the aesthetic loss entailed in abandoning the heroic genres of an earlier tradition for the mundane categories of modern realism. Given that the limits of the genre are one and the same as the form of the novel's ideological imperative, fiction must develop ways of defending middle-class sexual practices against forms of desire that would endanger the reproduction of those practices. Thanks in large part to the novel, I believe, certain forms of sexual desire not only became expressions of one's individuality, but were also the means of exposing the limitations of an earlier society. Given its original mission, we should not be surprised to find the novel's relationship to bourgeois morality growing progressively vexed as Victorian novelists sought to outlaw the very forms of desire that it had once been fiction's stock and trade to promote.

During the romantic era, fiction took local cultural economies, on the one hand, and the practices of a cosmopolitan leisure class, on the other, and synthetically produced a culture at once national and novelistic. To accomplish this feat, however, the novel itself underwent a major change in narrative form and ideological mission. The novel abandoned the task of imagining an increasingly democratic nation and began to represent the nation as one that required of its citizens progressively greater feats of sublimation. Bourgeois morality was simultaneously transformed in the manner forecast when Robinson Crusoe achieved hegemonic authority over the island. Bourgeois morality was for Victorians, as for readers of the previous century, something that appeared to come from within the protagonist as he or she resisted the limits placed on individuality by one's position in society; morality had to be one's own rather than someone else's. At the same time, in the early decades of the nineteenth century, the novel grew suspicious of individualism, much as Crusoe did, and sought a means of harnessing its energy for collective purposes. Indeed, to push the analogy between the nineteenth-century novel and the closing chapters of Crusoe's story one step farther, we might say that fiction began to think of itself as the means of discipline rather than resistance. Thus Crusoe imagines a fictional "governor" and assumes that role for the mutineers who populate his island. It is crucial, as Michel Foucault has explained at some length, that this governor remain only a fiction.[13] As Crusoe takes on this role, we find it increasingly difficult to value him for the plucky individualism that compelled him to resist father, owner, or God, for he begins to exercise the very authority that he himself resisted in all three.

Moving to the end of the eighteenth century, the same problem disappears into the narrowing gap between the plucky heroine and the narrator whose collective wisdom she must embrace in order to become mistress of Pemberley. The narrator might be characterized as Elizabeth Bennet's best self, hovering just outside of her consciousness until the highly individuated protagonist develops her own powers of surveillance and partakes of that purely cultural form of authority. Victorian fiction transforms bourgeois morality into something on the order of Defoe's governor and Austen's narrator. Neither a function of individual desire nor a form of social authority, bourgeois morality comes to constitute a category that is separate from both and mediates between them. In his reading of Rousseau's *Contrat sociale*, Louis Althusser calls attention to the discrepancy at the heart of contractual rhetoric on which its persuasive power depended. The contract represents itself—and this, I would argue, holds true of the English version as well—as a voluntary act on the part of the presocial individual. That individual does not lose individual agency by submitting to the laws of the state, because that act of submission, like Friday's gesture of placing of his head beneath Crusoe's foot, is an act of his or her own volition. In submitting to a collective composed of individuals who have themselves similarly submitted, moreover, the presocial individual gains freedom, because she or he has submitted to no one else but her- or himself. The presupposition is that any and all individuals will not only submit but, in so doing, come to understand themselves and their interests in much the same way.

This fantasy can never be realized, as Althusser points out, without a third party to ensure that the exchange between individual and collective is in fact an exchange between an individual and an aggregate of more or less similar individuals.[14] For the ideology of exchange to become both psychological

---

[13] Michel Foucault, *Discipline and Punish* (1975), trans. Alan Sheridan (New York, 1979). In his well-known description of *panopticism*, Foucault lays out the spatial strategies of modern institutional power as a periphery of compartments that makes their inmates highly visible and a central tower, where "one sees without ever being seen. It is an important mechanism, for it automatizes and disindividualizes power. Power has its principle not so much in a person as in an arrangment whose internal mechanisms produce the relation in which individuals are caught up" (202).

[14] Louis Althusser, *Montesquieu, Rousseau, Marx: Politics and History* (1959), trans. Ben Brewster (London, 1982), 113–60.

and sociopolitical reality, he insists, there has to be a cultural apparatus to determine that many different individuals imagine their relation to the real in approximately the same way. In the modern state, he observes, only education can supply this third, or mediating, component of the social contract. In theory at least, education does not impose the general will on individuals but rather shapes individuals' wills to regulate their own desires. Here, I would contend, the novel was paramount. In contrast with both domestic culture and the official institutions of education, the nineteenth-century novel provided a form of mediation that appeared to be only mediation, as it declared itself fiction rather than truth. Like Defoe's figure of the governor or Austen's narrator, however, that fiction had a peculiar power to constitute the two parties it presumed only to mediate. In speaking for the collective, Defoe's governor and Austen's narrator reshaped in some irreversible way the authors who created them, much as Rousseau's presocial individual was remade as a citizen in the act of agreeing to submit to the state. So too is the second party or aggregate of citizens changed each time another individual agrees to submit. Crusoe is not all that happy as successive waves of immigration change the character of his collective identity, which soon after his departure becomes unstable, prone to factionalism, and manifests individual differences through violence rather than words.

No other medium then available could have reconstituted the imagined relation between individual reader and national readership quite so well as the novel. By means of the reading contract that novels established with readers, the novel not only revised the way those readers imagined both parties of the social contract but also put a moral stamp of approval on the exchange that guaranteed the normalcy if not the homogeneity of its readership. To authorize a culture that depended, as Crusoe did, on an imagined authority, bourgeois morality changed horses in midstream and began to authorize resistance, not to one's assigned role, but to desires that compelled one to occupy someone else's. According to the fiction of the Brontës, Dickens, Thackeray, Gaskell, Hardy, and Trollope, the forms of desire that had to be resisted could take any number of forms—adultery, business fraud, false identity—as long as the protagonist's act of resistance placed him or her momentarily and wrongfully in someone else's shoes. To earn the moral approval of novel readers, these protagonists had to become demonstrably more capable of governing themselves. Moreover, they had at the same time to defend the community against the leveling effects of a consumer-driven mass culture, a growing demand for full citizenship on the part of women and the working classes, and forms of violence endemic to indigenous cultures. As if to prepare its readership for an age of increasing imperial expansion, the novel put bourgeois morality on the defense against the very forces it would attempt to contain and regulate on a multinational scale.

The Moral Core

I concede Georg Lukács's point that the early-nineteenth-century novel understood its mission as representing a progressively more inclusive political system.[15] I agree as well with Jürgen Habermas's explanation of the kind of culture that ideally accompanied increasing democratization and why it failed to materialize.[16] But I part company with their respective arguments when they claim that the novel's betrayal of its mission and dissociation from the political publicity it had originally encouraged did not occur until the midnineteenth century. In Scott, the novelist whom Lukács portrays as the staunch defender of the novel's progressive tendency, one can already observe a structural resemblance to Shelley's gothic masterpiece. *Waverley*, like *Frankenstein*, is shaped by a reflux whereby political resistance no longer serves the good of the community so much as the will to dominate in a manner ascribed to the old aristocracy. Resistance so reconceptualized no longer creates a reproductive unit, as it did in Austen. On the contrary, such resistance ruptures the family in ways that cancel out that unit's ability to reproduce itself both biologically and socially. The novel, we must conclude, was just not made to turn against the class whose emergence it recorded and moralized, despite the criticism that fiction levels at the practices of that very class during the ages of realism and modernism.

---

[15] Georg Lukács, The Historical Novel (1962), trans. Hannah Mitchell and Stanley Mitchell (Lincoln, Neb., 1983). Lukács describes Sir Walter Scott as "giving perfect artistic expression to the basic progressive tendency of [his] period" (63). The threat posed by an armed and organized proletariat in 1848 inspired the bourgeoisie to turn its back upon its earlier aims and ideals, a change that "affects all spheres of bourgeois ideology," including the novel (171). In Flaubert, Lukács notes, there is consequently "no such connection between the outside world and the psychology of the principal characters" as one finds in Scott (189), and "history becomes a large, imposing scene for purely private, intimate and subjective happenings" (199).

[16] Jürgen Habermas, *The Structural Transformation of the Bourgeois Public Sphere: An Inquiry into a Category of Bourgeois Society* (1962), trans. Thomas Burger (Cambridge, Mass., 1992). The idea of a public sphere, as formulated in eighteenth-century England, was to subject all government policies, procedures, and decisions to the scrutiny and criticism of public opinion. At around the same time that Lukács pinpoints the novel's betrayal of its cultural mission, Habermas identifies the erosion of the very principle of the public sphere: "The *principle* of the public sphere, that is, critical publicity, seemed to lose its strength in the measure that it expanded as a *sphere* and even undermined the private realm" (140).

Here I want to consider the novel's irreversible contraction of the imagined community in relation to the entrenchment of the modern middle class and Great Britain's geographical expansion around the globe. Only in this context, omnipresent in Victorian fiction, can the exclusions characterizing the culture of commodity capitalism find their moral justification. In discussing the fiction of Daniel Defoe, I sought to show that he found it rather easy to justify the enterprises of a social underdog. Defoe's fiction becomes morally confused, at least by nineteenth-century standards, once such a protagonist actually succeeds in occupying a position of power. As Defoe would seem to forecast, the old oppositional politics was no longer possible once the middle classes came into power, and novelists had to figure out ways around the dilemma of how to be political dominant and morally superior at once. In order for the dialectical engagement of an unacknowledged individual with the field of permissible social positions to yield the necessary synthesis, novelists had to revise the terms of the social contract. To the imperative to resolve the problem created by the cultural presuppositions of the genre itself, I am suggesting, we may attribute the most important formal innovations of later nineteenth- and early-twentieth-century fiction.

First, let us consider how Victorian fiction modifies the protagonist who had operated within an earlier agrarian society as the figure of antithesis itself. We are only one chapter past the paradigmatic encounter between Jane Eyre and her guardian aunt, when Charlotte Brontë begins to formulate alternative forms of resistance that must be cancelled out before Jane can achieve a place in the social body where she can indeed exemplify all its members. After Sandra Gilbert and Susan Guber's argument that Rochester's mad creole wife personifies the author's own proto-feminist anger at the constraints of a masculinist genre, it is no wonder that recent criticism has dwelled obsessively on Bertha Mason.[17] There is, moreover, good reason to seize upon this same character to confirm both Edward Said's claim that the colonies are omnipresent in canonical British fiction and Gayatri Spivak's contention that the soul-making project of British fiction excludes those who

---

[17] Sandra M. Gilbert and Susan Gubar, *The Madwoman in the Attic: The Woman Writer and the Nineteenth-Century Literary Imagination* (New Haven, Conn., 1979). Gilbert and Gubar famously argue that in lashing out at patriarchal authority, Bertha Mason becomes Jane Eyre's antithesis in that Bertha enacts the anger that the author could not allow her heroine to express. Brontë had to rein Jane in, according to Gilbert and Gubar, because the heroine's submission to her future husband was one and the same as the novelist's submission to the masculine genre in which she herself wrote.

resist colonization.[18] What we tend to overlook in the process of appropriating Bertha for contemporary purposes is that she is not the first recalcitrant female to be offered up by the novel and then eliminated as an unacceptable expression of individualism. Like so many of Dickens's characters, Helen Burns, Jane's mortally ill classmate at the Lowood school for girls, displays a spiritual capacity to transcend her place in society, a capacity that qualifies as morality but not as resistance. *Jane Eyre* clearly refuses to throw its moral weight behind the acts of Christian sacrifice that send both Helen Burns and St. John Rivers to untimely graves. In the novel, conventional spirituality can do little if anything to transform the spectacle of punishment practiced at Lowood into the more modern practices of discipline organizing Jeremy Bentham's model prison. In Bentham's ideal world, an individual acquires moral value on the basis of how well that individual harnesses his or her desire to the demands of a social position. As George Eliot regretfully says of Dorothea Brook, the heroine of *Middlemarch*, "Her full nature, like that river of which Cyrus broke the strength, spent itself in channels which had no great name on earth. But that effect of her being on those around her was incalculably diffusive . . . and that things are not so ill with you and me as they might have been, is half owing to the number who lived faithfully a hidden life, and rest in unvisited tombs."[19] This passage exemplifies Eliot's lyricism, as it simultaneously memorializes and minoritizes the "far sadder sacrifices" that novels and their readers were, in the narrator's view, actively preparing for Dorotheas yet to come.[20] From this perspective, Bertha Mason would be more accurately construed not as the other side of Jane but of Helen Burns in that, for opposing reasons, both Bertha and Helen fail to meet the minimal requirements for consenting to the social contract. If the one is all spirituality, then the other is all resistance. By depriving both Helen and Bertha of the inner conflict essential to the making of self-governing citizens, the novel finds each deficient in terms of bourgeois morality. Their exclusion from the good society is especially important in Helen's case, because Brontë uses the heroine's girlhood companion to represent the consummate Christian soul.

---

[18] In *Culture and Imperalism* (New York, 1993), Edward Said makes the claim that "nearly everywhere in nineteenth- and early-twentieth-century British and French culture we find allusions to the facts of empire, but perhaps nowhere with more regularity and frequency than in the British novel" (62). In "Three Women's Texts," Gayatri Chakavorty Spivak argues that "Bertha's function in *Jane Eyre* is to render indeterminate the boundary between human and animal and thereby to weaken her entitlement [to a soul] under the spirit if not the letter of Law" (268).

[19] George Eliot, *Middlemarch* (1871–72; New York, 1977), 578.

[20] Ibid.

Like Moll's memoirs and Clarissa's letters, Jane's claim to such morality rests entirely on the fact that her rise to a position of respectability offers a sustained critique of the very people on whom she depends for economic survival. Eighteenth-century protagonists from Moll to Clarissa tend to launch that critique from outside the dominant culture, where they are exposed to all the exclusions and oppressions which that culture unleashes on those who most depend on it. By way of contrast, the imperiled heroine of Victorian fiction speaks from a critical position that deprives the true outsider of her righteousness. By representing Bertha as culturally unfit to occupy a position within Thornfield Hall, Jane can assume Bertha's position as the one wrongfully excluded from domestic comforts and companionship. She can be a Victorian heroine and speak as an outsider only so long as she refuses to cross the moral line that would make her a true outsider; she can never gratify her sexual desire for Rochester. Nineteenth-century fiction characteristically situates one of its own, someone highly articulate, in the outsider's position, making it clear, by exquisitely testing her morality, that she is out of place in that position. By taking the ungrateful Jane to its bosom, that fiction opens up within the dominant culture positions for legitimate opposition and critique. Indeed, we might regard *Jane Eyre* as a historical record of the process by which this criticism from inside receives the benediction of bourgeois morality. Jane's claim that "this social order is bad, because it excludes me" proves perfectly compatible with the claim that "this social order is good insofar as it includes me." Where the first claim launches a critique, the second limits that critique to a demand that updates the status quo and lends it a sense of adequacy.

Bertha's purpose in relation to Jane is much the same as Orlick's relation to Pip in *Great Expectations*, Jo's relation to Esther in *Bleak House*, or Bradley Headstone's relation to Eugene Wrayburn in *Our Mutual Friend*, as well as the many ingenious examples of the so-called divided self that mark the literature of this epoch. By means of such wholly indigestible lumps of cultural traits, Victorian fiction could simultaneously embrace and exclude precisely what that fiction designated as most hostile to middle-class culture. This move becomes abundantly clear once we compare *Jane Eyre* with Brontë's later novel *Villette*. This novel relocates Lowood, the unreformed educational institution, in Belgium, a terrain where Protestant England can confront Catholic France and appear to soften its disciplinary edge. Institutional culture so-conceived promises to offer the notably repressed heroine both the possibility of marriage with the flamboyant M. Paul and the authority to educate self-governing girls. Having offered this promise and set its realization in motion, however, *Villette* will have none of it. M. Paul, charming and utterly socialized though he may seem within the Belgian context, ultimately fulfills the same purpose as Bertha Mason. Accordingly, he dies an equally contrived death on the voyage back from overseeing his investments in the colonies. The novel's ending (". . . leave sunny imaginations hope. Let it be theirs to conceive the delight of joy born again fresh out of great terror, the rapture of escape from peril, the wondrous reprieve from dread, the fruition of return. Let them picture union and a happy succeeding life.")[21] demonstrates that M. Paul must be exorcised from the classroom before Lucy can assume a place of authority within it.

To understand what Victorian culture did to bourgeois morality, then, it is necessary to dissociate that culture from simple-minded prudery and read these figures symptomatically. The appearance of the outsider who must be kept out in order for the protagonist to assume a place within the social order marks a major historical shift from a culture where individual identity is based on similarity (that is, "I am me, because I am like you in some essential way") to one in which identity is based on difference (that is, "I am like you to the extent that neither of us is that other thing"). This shift amounts to a shift from positive to negative identity. Where eighteenth-century protagonists become who they truly are by virtue of their difference from some assigned social position, not so with nineteenth-century protagonists. They become who they are by conquering difference and filling a rather ordinary but utterly respectable position. To do so, all those Janes and Pips must make very sure to resist their most individual impulses and drives, which are invariably criminal rather than progressive or regenerative. Yet individualistic desire is every bit as much the central player in these high Victorian dramas of contractual affiliation as it is in the work of Defoe and Richardson. From Fagin and Bertha to Dracula and Dorian, Victorian fiction is known for its criminals, madmen, prostitutes, profligate spenders, predacious children, and sexual perverts—and for good reason. These figures are as central to the later nineteenth century as Mr. Darcy was to Austen's moment, because it is in relation to them that all other behavioral options in the novel earn their respective degrees of moral value. Not only of similar magnitude to Darcy but also in polar opposition to him, these figures personify what an individual cannot become and still belong to the community of readers. On the emergence, consolidation, and excorporation of traits composing the negative category of being, or symptom, in Victorian fiction depends a decisively negative redefinition of bourgeois morality as well.

---

[21] Charlotte Brontë, *Villette* (1853; New York, 1979), 596.

I have used *Jane Eyre* to demonstrate how such fiction gives its protagonists the critical stance of the outsider so that they might claim the moral
center by virtue of their difference from people whose nature confines them
to the periphery. But what happens to the other side of the contractual
model, or imagined community, when it incorporates individuals on the basis of their negative identity? William Booth's *In Darkest England and the
Way Out* enjoins the viewer to follow sinners as they ascend from the hell of
poverty and crime through redemptive labor to a relatively blessed life as
citizens who can enjoy the fruits of their hard-won prosperity.[22] What is
most significant about this modern version of medieval iconography, however, is that it does not depict the progress of a soul from one station to another but a flow of population. As Booth routes it, moreover, this flow does
not in fact ascend from a lower to a more elevated moral station. He locates
the center of his chart in the center of the metropolis, where—heedless of
natural geography—there stands a stately lighthouse radiating beams of
light and surrounded by a corona of cumulus clouds representing various
institutions of social reform. Here members of the poor and criminal population linger until they acquire the twin faculties of work and self-
government. Representing members of Booth's Salvation Army, figures in
red coats direct the flow of indigent humanity up from the slough of depravity and out to the sea coast, where they are shipped off to the colonies.
Rather than have them scale the ladder of Christian salvation, in other
words, Booth transforms that hierarchical structure into a map that, in a
manner more like Bentham's prison, redistributes the population of England into a normative metropolitan core and deviant colonial periphery.

In offering this map, Booth simply repeats in bold outline the fantasy of
imperial nationhood implicit in every novel, journalistic account of Great
Britain's colonial exploits, popular photograph, and government policy published over a period of some fifty years. This, for example, is how *Jane Eyre*
represents the transformation of Rochester's estate, once a haven for the
mad, profligate, illegitimate, and racially tainted, into the moral core of a regenerated middle-class England: "My Edward and I, then, are happy: and
the more so, because those we love are happy likewise. Diana and Mary
Rivers are both married: alternately, once every year, they come to see us,
and we go to see them. Diana's husband is a captain in the navy: a gallant
officer, and a good man. Mary's is a clergyman: a college friend of her
brother's; and, from his attainments and principles, worthy of the connexion. Both Captain Fitzjames and Mr. Wharton love their wives, and are

---

[22] William Booth, *In Darkest England and the Way Out* (1890; Montclair, N.J., 1975).

loved by them" (476). By a process resembling the circulation of bodies depicted on Booth's map, the novel enjoins us to imagine the imperial nation as a moral core constantly replenished when and wherever there is sufficient discipline to produce self-governing individuals. As in that map, the total of such regenerated souls is notably low, and the number of those who either remain in cultural limbo or perish is disproportionately high. As indicated by the dull-witted schoolchildren whom Jane teaches while living with her cousins at Moore House, or Adèle, her charge at Thornfield, most individuals lack the critical awareness necessary for their own reform. Their lack of the raw material for soul-making locates them permanently at the culture's moral periphery, along with poor and indigenous peoples, despite the dominant culture's best efforts to reform them.

Booth's map makes it clear that belonging to the moral core has more to do with what one does than where one is located geographically. Inclusion within a homogeneous household where identity based on sameness can prevail signals that moral redemption in Dickens on many occasions when the novel shifts the center of English society from such focal points of traditional wealth as Dedlock Hall or Miss Havisham's residence to the fragile nests of domesticity characterized by affectionate bonding—for example, Mr. Brownlow's, the second Bleak House, Biddy and Joe's, and so forth. Only in such pockets of identification, Dickens seems to be saying, can the kind of affection survive that flourishes when individuals renounce the very differences that make them individuals according to Victorian culture. Fostered neither by traditional wealth nor by new money, but mysteriously supported by either and often both, the moral core provides sanctuary for individuals capable of identifying themselves as no more nor less than a member of that group. In that most individuals are incapable of adhering to the terms of the social contract as the Victorians understood it, the moral core is always a community on the defense against predatory individualism.

What is nineteenth-century realism, from this perspective, if not a fictional encounter of a protagonist with an unaccommodating social order, in which each party reshapes the other so as to produce a new and limited means of individual gratification while leaving that order perfectly intact? The Victorian novel does not transform the way we imagine the real, in other words. What it offers more often than not is a recuperated middle-class man who has abandoned the quest to fulfill some individual desire and receives cultural compensation for so doing. Following in the tradition of Pip and Rochester is a brilliant succession of indelibly tainted men that includes Dickens's Mr. Dombey and Eugene Wrayburn, Eliot's Stephen Guest and Silas Marner, and any number of masculine characters in the novels of Thomas Hardy and Anthony Trollope. Fiction's effort to master what Victorians had evidently come to see as inherently antisocial about individualism itself gives rise to a new category—call it culture with a capital "C." This category, in contrast to the individualism of old, behaves more like a complement, or simple addition to the social whole, than as a supplement requiring some pervasive reorganization of that whole. The issue of whether that category can and should be dominated by bourgeois morality divides literary modernism from its Victorian predecessors.

The Return of the Repressed

Together with a highly individuated style, a novel's sustained critique of the bourgeois morality at work in the popular fiction of the Victorian age classifies that novel as a work of literary modernism. Victorian novelists sought to mediate between individuals and a social body that was increasing in size, geographical expanse, and demographic heterogeneity. In contrast, their modernist counterparts set art, in the form of a carefully crafted style, against the highly legible surface that popular culture had inserted between self-enclosed individuals and the social world they had to negotiate. When it went to work in the novel, that style made the two parties of contractual exchange engage one another, much as Leopold Bloom does Dublin society, as the starkly incompatible entities that they are. To make this point, Virginia Woolf offers this memorable account of the horrors of war that the veteran, Septimus Smith, relives as he sits on a park bench in London anticipating a visit to his psychiatrist:

> He sang. Evans answered from behind the tree. The dead were in Thessaly, Evans sang, among the orchids. There they waited till the war was over, and now the dead, now Evans himself . . .
>
> "For God's sake don't come!" Septimus cried out. For he could not look upon the dead.
>
> But the branches parted. A man in grey was actually walking towards them. It was Evans! But no mud was on him; no wounds; he was not changed. I must tell the whole world, Septimus cried, raising his hand (as the dead man in the grey suit came nearer), raising his hand like some colossal figure who has lamented the fate of man for ages in the desert alone with his hands pressed to his forehead, furrows of despair on his cheeks, and now

sees light on the desert's edge which broadens and strikes the iron-black
figure . . . , and with legions of men prostrate behind him he, the giant
mourner, receives for one moment on his face the whole.[23]

This passage produces an unbridgeable discrepancy between the individual's true desires and fears and the socially permissible forms of self-
expression. The difference between the world that Septimus sees (his dead
comrade in arms, Evans) and the world that observes him (Woolf identifies
Peter Walsh as the man in the gray suit) is only an extreme instance, the
novel insists, of a more general discrepancy between individuals and the social positions they must occupy, whether soldier, psychiatrist, socialite, wife,
daughter, or parliamentarian.

D. H. Lawrence identifies bourgeois morality as the force that keeps such
individuals in line. To free the reader from what he regards as a harmfully repressive brand of morality, Lawrence offers sexually explicit love scenes.
This passage from *Lady Chatterley's Lover* strives to undo the sexual contract authorized by *Jane Eyre*, as Lawrence has his adulterous lovers translate a potentially pornographic engagement into a sophisticated parody of
high romance:

> "It suddenly came to me. You are the Knight of the Burning Pestle."
>
> "Ay! And you? Are you the Lady of the Red-Hot Mortar?"
>
> "Yes!" she said. "Yes! You're Sir Pestle and I'm Lady Mortar."
>
> "All right, then I'm knighted. John Thomas is Sir John, to your Lady
> Jane."
>
> "Yes! John Thomas is knighted! I'm my-lady-maidenhair, and you must
> have flowers too. Yes!"
>
> "She threaded two pink campions in the bush of red-gold hair above his
> penis.
>
> "There!" she said. "Charming! Charming! Sir John!"[24]

Neither pornography nor romance, this passage synthesizes the two by means
of language that simultaneously locates Victorian romance in the sexual
organs and places potentially obscene material within a category reserved
strictly for art.

---

[23] Virginia Woolf, *Mrs. Dalloway* (1925; New York, 1953), 105–6. Subsequent references are to
this edition and have been included in the text.

[24] D. H. Lawrence, *Lady Chatterley's Lover* (1932; New York, 1959), 172. Subsequent
references are to this edition and have been included in the text.

In both novels, a desirous woman serves as the figure of sexuality itself and the rallying point for the modernist recuperation of those elements of humanity sacrificed in the effort to chain men and women to labor and property, respectively. This figure returns in the modernist novel to exert an uncanny power—familiar but utterly other—that harks back to Roxana's daughter.[25] Indeed, the case of the daughter who would not go away, despite every attempt to elude, cajole, bribe, threaten, and even murder her, anticipates the form of repression that fiction itself had to undergo in order to become "the novel" and vehicle of bourgeois morality. Not since Richardson's Clarissa made readers prefer a woman's death to her sexual dishonor did the British novel allow its illustrious string of protagonists to accept a sexual invitation without suffering punishment greatly in excess to the crime. The spectacular deaths of Clarissa, Catherine Earnshaw, Lady Dedlock, Maggie Tulliver, Tess, and Lucy Westenra are just a few examples of the discursive behavior that turned the desirous woman into the symptom of bourgeois morality. By repeating this move, novelists ensured that bourgeois morality achieved ideological coherence and continuity in relation to her. The individual became a member of respectable society in terms of this negative standard by harnessing her sexual desire to the single-minded purpose of reproducing the nuclear family so that it might ensure the gendered division of labor and social relations under capitalism. When, however, this figure emerges in modernist fiction, she is hardly the same. This is especially true of *Mrs. Dalloway*, where the fact of desire only shows itself in radically displaced forms. The reanimated specters of her unfulfilled relationships with Peter Walsh and Sally Seaton haunt Clarissa's party and influence the dynamic of the evening more powerfully than the individuals themselves.

Molly Bloom and Clarissa Dalloway appear to come from different social universes and live according to contrary moral standards, but fiction empowers them to reorganize modern urban life in curiously similar ways. Each serves as the center of an interpersonal flow, where submerged currents of desire meet and discharge their energy in various forms of intercourse—at once sexual and verbal—to revitalize a society enervated by

---

[25] In *The Political Unconscious: Narrative as a Socially Symbolic Act* (Ithaca, N.Y., 1981), Fredric Jameson urges criticism to abandon "a purely individual, or merely psychological, project of salvation" so that we might "explore the multiple paths that lead to the unmasking of cultural objects as socially symbolic acts" (20). My borrowing of the "return of the repressed" from Freudian vocabulary engages Jameson's notion of the political unconscious and, specifically, the strategies by which the novel entered into a mutually authorizing relationship with bourgeois morality that compelled many different novelists over a considerable period of time first to degrade, debase, and abject and then to resurrect and idealize a figure of female desire.

mass communication. To become the repository of authentic human nature in a world given over to the frenzied production, reproduction, and exchange of mere signs, the deidealized figure of female sexuality undergoes a curious transformation. Molly Bloom, Clarissa Dalloway, Ursula Brangwen, and many others recombine certain features of Bertha Mason, the woman whom Charlotte Brontë reduced to a beast in *Jane Eyre*, with those of Helen Burns, Bertha's disembodied spiritual counterpart. The cultural logic compelling this synthesis becomes especially apparent in Jean Rhys's revision of Brontë's narrative.

In *Wide Sargasso Sea*, we encounter Bertha as Antoinette, the daughter of creole plantation owners traded to Rochester in a purely economic exchange. By giving Antoinette the name of her mother, Bertha, Rochester transformed her yearning for him into the debased sexuality of a racially tainted woman. In Rhys's account, this act of classification says more about the Englishman than the woman whom he degraded. His gesture dramatizes European fear of the island's natural beauty and this creole woman's strange affinity with it. "I hated the sunsets of whatever colour," he confesses, "I hated its beauty and its magic and the secret I would never know. I hated its indifference and the cruelty which was part of its loveliness. Above all, I hated her. For she belonged to the magic and the loveliness."[26] As she reveals what Rochester repressed in renaming his creole wife, Rhys endows Bertha with the fullness of being that Brontë had reserved for Jane alone. That fullness identifies the limits of Rochester's classification system and demonstrates the lethal consequences of subjecting sexual desire to bourgeois morality. It is in these terms that the servant Christophine accuses Rochester of destroying her mistress: "She is Creole girl, and she have the sun in her. Tell the truth now. She don't come to your house in this place England they tell me about, she don't come to your beautiful house to beg you to marry her. No, it's you come all the long way to her house—it's you beg her to marry. And she love you and she give you all she have. Now you say you don't love her and your break her up. What you do with her money, eh?" (158).

Brontë endeavors to show that a man like Rochester would in fact prefer the plain but constrained English girl over far more sensual women. Rhys demonstrates that desire for the likes of Jane served as his means of disavowing a far more authentic desire for the natural beauty and unrestrained

---

[26] Jean Rhys, *Wide Sargasso Sea* (1966; New York, 1982), 172. Subsequent references are to this edition and have been included in the text.

sexuality associated with the colonies: "She had left me thirsty and all my life would be thirst and longing for what I had lost before I found it." Terrified of going native, Rhys's Rochester has to debase the object of his desire: "I saw the hate go out of her eyes. I forced it out. And with the hate her beauty. She was only a ghost. A ghost in the grey daylight" (170). Rochester rejects Bertha as subhuman, because he believes nothing so beautiful can be moral. Is this act of aggression an act in defense of individualism? Modernism says no.

Modernism accedes to the Victorian opposition between aesthetics and morality in order to come down decisively on the side of art and argue for those elements of humanity that Victorian fiction had sacrificed on the altar of bourgeois morality. In accepting the opposition of aesthetics and morality, however, modernism also detaches art from politics. Let morality amass and regulate various elements of society as it must, modernism seems to say; we men of imagination, misfits all, will suggest alternative ways of organizing that world and deriving pleasure from it. The desirous woman, like the madman, pervert, and child, affords us the means of doing so. As a result, there is, for modernism, no final synthesis of the kind that readers came to expect in such novels as *Jane Eyre* and *Middlemarch*. Instead, modernist novels accompany every gesture toward the mutual infusion of self and society with some discursive sign of an essential lack. The conclusion of *Mrs. Dalloway* might offer the reader a sense of plentitude and wholeness achieved— "What is it that fills me with extraordinary excitement? It is Clarissa, he said. For there she was" (296)—had such presence not already been defined as a lack of presence. Clarissa was never really there, as we learn early in the novel: "She began to go slowly upstairs, with her hand on the bannisters, as if she had left a party, where now this friend now that had flashed back her face, her voice . . . There was an emptiness about the heart of life; an attic room" (45). The ending of *Lady Chatterley's Lover* is perhaps too heavy-handed in making the point that social existence requires repeated acts of self-annihilation. A continent apart, the lovers await Constance's divorce, and Mellors writes: "In the end he [Sir Clifford Chatterley] will want to spew you out as the abominable thing . . . a great deal of us is together, and we can abide by it and steer our courses to meet soon. John Thomas says good-night to lady Jane, a little droopingly, but with a hopeful heart" (283). For all its criticism of the shallow materialism endorsed by Victorian realism, the modernist novel never opens up a category for the fully realized and integrated individual within the existing social order.

Indeed, modernism consigns the potentially synthesizing desires of Molly, Constance, Ursula, or Antoinette to a domain outside and apart from the material world. Given this remove from social history, any reimagining of the social order can never amount to more than just that—imaginings that would have to be received as dream, hallucination, or art. To blur the distinctions between the psychic and the real so that desire overrides the reality principle indicates that we are under the spell of either primitive thinking or some long-repressed, infantile wish. Fiction, according to Freud, is especially good at producing uncanny effects.[27] What makes the unmistakable difference between Victorian depictions of the so-called buried life and modernist versions of the same phenomenon is not the fact that the repressed inevitably returns so much as the form it takes when it does so. During the eighteenth century, the desirous woman exposed the threat of excessive individualism to a nation imagined as an aggregate of self-governing individuals; she was intrepid, witty, honest, and insincerely repentant. The Victorians turned bourgeois morality to the task of debasing and abjecting her; she grew inarticulate, disgusting, often mortally ill, and always repentant. The examples I have offered from modernist novels tell us that the paradox of individualism intensified after the modern middle classes came into power. But with the advent of modernism, lo and behold, precisely what had been debased and cast out emerged in all innocence, exotic, fresh, archaic, familiar, strange, and able to work her invigorating magic within a tightly limited domain.

The Class That Is Not One

It is difficult to imagine a definition of the English middle class that does not include a reference to a morality that reproduced the nuclear family and preserved social relations under capitalism. This morality was a sexual morality. It decreed that each and every individual was inhabited by his or her own worst enemy in the form of desires that did not lead straight to monogamously heterosexual love. Individualism would certainly energize the community, provided those expressions of individualism respected the

---

[27] Sigmund Freud, "The 'Uncanny' " (1919) in *Studies in Parapsychology* (New York, 1963), 19–62. A contemporary of Woolf, Lawrence, and Joyce, Freud obviously thinks of the uncanny in terms of the modernist aesthetic: "In the main we adopt an unvarying passive attitude towards experience and are acted upon by our physical environment. But the story-teller has a peculiarly directive influence over us; by means of the states of mind into which he can put us and the expectations he can rouse in us, he is able to guide the current of our emotions, dam it up in one direction and make it flow in another" (58).

person and property of others. But individualism would just as surely destroy the community, if individual desire ran roughshod over the social contract. Nothing threatened the formation of the nuclear family more than a desirous woman, who was therefore such an act of violence waiting to happen. Always on the lookout for precisely this threat, bourgeois morality provided the means of subduing wayward desires and turning them to the appropriate reproductive ends. In this respect, ironically, nothing ensures the reproduction of the nuclear family more than a desirous woman. Modernism constituted its antagonist as a monolithic and exclusively empowered majority—an extension of the tyrannical majority that made John Stuart Mill flee from the public sphere of political debate into autobiographical writing and poetry. To do so, novelists imagined society from the viewpoint of those excluded from the moral core—women, children, homosexuals, the Irish, or working-class people. In order to write art-quality novels, these novelists not only introduced libidinal disruptions often verging on pornography into the linear narrative of Victorian fiction but also lived bohemian lives that broke the most important rules of heterosexual monogamy. By fashioning lives in opposition to bourgeois morality, however, those intellectuals and artists who took their example from the early-twentieth-century avant-garde did not challenge the norms of Victorian fiction so much as give those norms a social tangibility that they may otherwise have lacked for twentieth-century readers.

I have allowed the term *bourgeois* to wind through this essay with very little interrogation. For this very reason, I want to conclude by asking if there ever were in fact a class of people with an ethos so unified, so focused on controlling female sexuality, as three centuries of British fiction has made the modern middle class out to be. The novels I have discussed indeed indicate that by virtue of its negative definition, bourgeois morality achieved durability over the span of time and despite changing national cultures. That is to say, these novels proliferated examples of what the Lawrentian protagonist Mellors called "the abominable thing," a woman inhabited by masculine desire. The prevalence of such a negative definition should be an indication, I would propose, that we are not being offered the kind of self-definition that comes from within the group in question and circulates among its members. If canonical fiction did in fact represent middle-class life, practices, values, limitations, desires, and hopes for the future from within and for that group, then that fiction would, I believe, be far less concerned with relaxing the boundaries around that group and making its internal categories seem capable of accommodating diverse individuals. As I have already suggested at several points in this essay, the modernist critique of bourgeois morality does not so much overthrow as perpetuate the cultural logic played out in the fiction of Defoe. To authorize themselves as novelists and spokespeople for heretofore excluded aspects of the individual, these novelists set themselves outside and at odds with a ruling class at once lax and rigid and ever in need of supplementation from those just below or peripheral to that class in social position. From this perspective, modernist authenticity, originality, and redemptive desire can be regarded as appropriations of the function of bourgeois morality itself.

Rita Felski helps this argument by debunking the literary historical tendency to conceptualize modern social history as an opposition between, on one hand, a Bakhtinian working class that was ribald, licentious, given over to the body, and extremely irreverent of boundaries, and on the other, a ruling class that was contrastingly puritanical, industrious, and frugal.[28] The modern middle class indeed included and still includes more than one class position, all of which are extremely fluid and lack sharp cultural definition. According to this way of thinking, someone in Samuel Richardson's position would have to be particularly concerned with respectability precisely because his toehold on that virtue was not particularly secure. As a member of the petit bourgeoisie, he probably saw the attribution of compulsive morality to his social superiors as a way of denying his inferior rank. Such overly vigorous moralizing was an expression of shame specific to a class unique for lacking a positive self-definition. If authors and readers not quite so solidly in the middle class were responsible for attributing bourgeois morality to those just above them, then those novelists who turned against bourgeois morality during the nineteenth and twentieth century were probably more middle class than they would have us believe. In keeping with the tradition inaugurated by the very group it denigrated, modernist fiction represented bourgeois morality from a peripheral position in relation to those who exemplified that class ethos. Modernism, according to Pierre Bourdieu,

---

[28] Rita Felski, "Nothing to Declare: Identity, Shame, and the Lower Middle Class," *PMLA* 115.1 (2000): 33–45. British fiction in turn supports Felski's claim that "opposing a repressed and repressive bourgeoisie to an unruly, pleasure-driven working class leaves little room for exploring the various class fractions that fall outside this opposition. The lower middle class is one such amalgam of symbolic practices, structures of feeling, and forms of life." She characterizes this class as feeling "itself to be culturally superior to the working class . . . , while lacking the cultural capital and the earning power of the professional-managerial class" (35). Felski suggests, in other words, that the peculiar status of the petit bourgeoisie prompted them to constitute the middle class in terms with which they could, as marginal members, identify themselves.

characteristically seized, not on the upper middle class, but on the petit bourgeoisie as the object of its critique.[29]

The point in thus stressing the negative definition of the modern middle class is twofold. First, to put it simply, the neither-nor character of the novel's definition of the class whose interests it serves strongly suggests that that class is largely held together by fiction and is, in all probability, largely a fiction itself, in much the same way that so-called normal individuals are. Anyone who must insist on his or her normalcy probably is not normal, I would contend, while those of us who would never claim to be so probably are. Second, in rethinking the British novel as a delivery system for bourgeois morality, one cannot help but notice how faithful British fiction remains to the cultural logic that first brought this kind of narrative into being and proclaimed it "the novel." So long as it thinks of whom it represents in relation to bourgeois morality, the novel remains true to its original mission, which was to open a space within the field of social positions for previously unacknowledged forms of individualism. This principle holds true from Defoe to Brontë, from Dickens to Woolf, and from James Joyce to Angela Carter and Salman Rushdie. Furthermore, the rhetoric of progressive inclusion proves a miraculously effective strategy for ensuring that things remain exactly the same. Indeed, the novel invariably marks the contours of any new social classification system as science fiction or gothic romance and usually a nightmare at that. As successive waves of immigration entered Great Britain and tried to fit in, the novel acknowledged the presence of various subcultures as a subterranean flow of ethnic practices that appealed to the reader's well-honed touristic sensibility. Indeed, one could easily rewrite the novel's relationship to bourgeois morality as the history of the "impurities" that fiction either assimilated to bourgeois morality or else cast out of its imagined community.

It would appear that those on the periphery of the class they themselves defined as united around an obsession with the sexual purity of its women have paid consistent lip service to bourgeois morality. But those in a peripheral relationship to the imaginary middle class were hardly a stable group in themselves. This group is perhaps more fluid than any other. While the

---

[29] In "Nothing to Declare," Felski draws on Pierre Bourdieu's notion of "distinction" (*Distinction: A Social Critique of the Judgement of Taste* [Cambridge, 1984], 327) to contend that the "division between the lower middle classes and the intelligensia arises from a difference of styles rather than of objects of consumption. . . . But the fundamental distinctions between these class groupings," she continues, "irony versus earnestness, cultural knowledge versus cultural ignorance—remain constant" (41).

novel envisioned no thoroughgoing structural transformation once the middle-class hegemony was in place, a combination of ethnic infusions into the petit bourgeoisie, on the one hand, and into the intellectual avant-garde on the other, radically transformed the demographic content of both. As that content changed, so too changed the ways in which those who occupied those social categories could express individualities that eluded the gate-keeper of bourgeois morality. Although the British novel remained ever true to the cultural logic that brought it into being, we are left with the fact that it, perhaps more than any other genre, remains ever responsive to historical change.

A. S. BYATT

The Death of Lucien de Rubempré

"One of the greatest tragedies of my life," wrote Oscar Wilde, "is the death of Lucien de Rubempré. It is a grief from which I have never been able completely to rid myself. It haunts me in my moments of pleasure. I remember it when I laugh."[1] The last phrase might suggest ambivalence. Proust in *Contre Sainte-Beuve* is interested in the way Wilde's "attendrissement" in the days of his brilliance prefigured his own imprisonment and fall. Proust assumed that "he felt moved by Lucien's death, like all readers, by seeing it from Vautrin's point of view, which is Balzac's own."[2]

I was surprised when I first read the scene to find tears rising in my eyes, partly at least because until that moment I had intensely disliked Lucien, in a way I dislike few fictional characters. Indeed, as Lucien writes his self-satisfied farewell messages, he remains small-minded, self-regarding, and distasteful. What is moving is the one moment of selflessness he experiences as he prepares to hang himself and sees from his window the unexpected revelation of the "primitive beauty" of the medieval architecture of the Palais de Justice. "Making his preparations for death, he asked himself how this marvel could exist, unknown, in Paris." He sees the colonnade, "slender, young, fresh." They are unexpected adjectives for architecture, adjectives that would serve just as well to describe a beautiful woman. Seeing the "demeure de St. Louis" with its Babylonian proportions and its oriental fantasies, Lucien becomes two Luciens—"one Lucien, a poet walking about under the arches and the turrets of St. Louis, and one Lucien preparing his suicide."[3] He moves into the eternal present of art and history; this is the last we see of him or his consciousness.

---

[1] Oscar Wilde, "Intentions," in *The Artist as Critic*, ed. Richard Ellmann (Chicago: University of Chicago Press, 1982), 299. N.B. Wilde used this sentence in several contexts. I have cited the one I had at hand.

[2] "il s'attendrissait sur elle [la mort de Lucien] comme tous les lecteurs, en se plaçant au point de vue de Vautrin, qui est le point de vue de Balzac. . . ." Marcel Proust, "Sainte-Beuve et Balzac," in *Contre Sainte-Beuve* (Paris: Pléiade, 1971), 273n. Throughout, all translations of French quotations are my own.

[3] "En prenant ses mesures pour mourir, il se demandait comment cette merveille existait inconnue dans Paris." "svelte, jeune, fraîche." "un Lucien poète en promenade dans le Moyen Age, sous les arcades et les tourelles de St Louis, et un Lucien apprêtant son suicide." *Splendeurs et misères des courtisanes* (Paris: Bibliothèque de la Pléiade, 1977), 794. All subsequent references to this text are from this edition.

What moves and startles me about this vision in the end is the courage—even foolhardiness—of the writer, of Balzac. The simplicity of Lucien's vision is preceded by a contentious "scientific" paragraph about the nature of hallucination; the effects of opium, hashish, and nitrous oxide; and the idea of thought itself as a vital physical force, injecting blood into the brain, summoning up unreal things as though they were solid. There is even—one sentence before the exquisite description of the primitive beauty of the Palais—a reference to another balzacian text. "Voyez," he tells us in parenthesis, in midsentence, "*Louis Lambert,* ETUDES PHILOSOPHIQUES." His insistence on the physiological effects of thought is part of the solid, hallucinatory intensity of his own art—he "saw" his scenes and people like Coleridge's "vivid spectra" that made up Kubla Khan. And it is an essential part of the nature of his text that it constantly stitches together all the parts of the fabric of the *Comédie humaine*—character, social analysis, history, myth, science, cross-referencing all. The death of Lucien de Rubempré is not tragically moving, partly because Lucien does not have the central importance of a tragic hero—his life and death are part of all the lives and deaths that make up this book and all the others. But it is one of the points where Balzac the artist knotted all his threads tightly together, and the wildness of the prose of that paragraph is part of the knotting.

When I marked master's theses on realism in the 1980s, it had become a habitual remark among British students that Balzac thought reality was solid and simple—like bricks in a wall, they all said, quoting some source I never found. It isn't so, of course—he can create a hallucinatory phantasmagoria because he sees the solid shot through with the visionary and the spiritual, the temporal shot through with the eternal. The *Human Comedy* is haunted by the forms and order of the *Divine Comedy*, not least because Balzac himself believed in the Christian story and order.

"There has only ever been one single religion since the beginning of the world. Christianity created modern nations and will preserve them. Whence, without doubt, the necessity of the monarchic principle. . . . I write by the light of two eternal Truths: Religion and Monarchy."[4]

The references to divine beings, angels, and demons are both ornamental and more than ornamental.[5] Lucien, whose name recalls Lucifer the

---

[4] ". . . il n'y a jamais eu qu'une même religion depuis l'origine du monde. Le Christianisme a créé les peuples modernes, il les conservera. De là sans doute la nécessité du principe monarchique. . . . J'écris à la lueur de deux Vérités éternelles: la Religion, la Monarchie." Avant-propos to the *Comédie humaine* (Paris: Pléiade, 1951), 8–9.

[5] I am writing mainly about the long text constituted by *Les illusions perdues* and *Splendeurs et misères des courtisanes.* The existence elsewhere in the *Comédie*—most especially in *Séraphita*—of real angels and demons adds a shimmer and glitter to the use of this vocabulary in this text.

Lightbearer, inhabits a web of descriptions of him as a minor angel. He is blond and shining and floral. His hair, when he goes to see his editor, "streamed in shining curls," his "feminine hands were well-groomed, their almond-shaped nails were pink and manicured. On his black satin collar the rounded white curves of his chin were gleaming. Never did a lovelier young man step down the hill of the Latin Quarter."[6] The mountain is contemporary Paris; the words *montagne* and *latin* inhabit the world of Dante. The shining hair is angelic; the sparkling of the white chins gently absurd. He is also a "Greek god," and the actress Coralie sees his divinity in Swedenborgian terms—he has a "superhuman beauty," and she hopes to make one soul with him in heaven, having been two bodies on earth. She feels "sanctified" by making love to him. At the beginning of *Splendeurs et misères* he appears at a masked ball with Esther, the second courtesan to love him, and Balzac remarks that the two masked figures "brought to mind those angels involved with flowers or birds, which the brush of Gianni Bellini painted beneath the images of the Virgin-mother; Lucien and this woman belonged to Fantasy which is above Art, as the cause is above the effect."[7]

Here is a real suggestion that Lucien and Esther's "childlike" and innocent love is natural and its beauty the beauty of the imagined world—indeed, it is the creative imagination itself. But that world is of course already corrupt through its association with Vautrin/Herrera/Collin, who is the devil with whom Lucien has made his fatal pact.[8] Vautrin shows Rastignac the glories of Paris, like Satan tempting Christ on the pinnacle of the Temple. Rastignac resists. Lucien succumbs. Vautrin takes "Lucien et la pauvre courtisane" out of "la maison de garde" into a place from which they too see the glories of the world, that is, of Paris. Balzac's use of the word *désert* is enough to recall the temptation in the wilderness. "He took Lucien and the poor courtesan to the edge of a deserted path, to a place from which they could see Paris, and where nobody could hear them. All three sat as the sun rose, on a felled poplar trunk, in front of this landscape, one of the most magnificent in the world, which takes in the course of the Seine, Montmartre, Paris, St. Denis."[9]

---

[6] "ruisselaient en boucles brillants" "mains de femme furent soignées, leurs ongles en amande devinrent nets et rosés. Sur son col de satin noir, les blanches rondeurs de son menton étincelèrent. Jamais un plus joli jeune homme ne descendit le montagne du pays latin." *Illusions perdues* (Paris: Pléiade, 1977), 349. All subsequent references to this text are from this edition.

[7] "rappelaient ces anges occupés de fleurs ou d'oiseaux, et que le pinceau de Gian-Bellini a mis sous les images de la Virginité-mère; Lucien et cette femme appartenaient à la Fantaisie qui est au-dessus de l'Art comme la cause est au-dessus de l'effet." *Splendeurs et misères*, 445.

[8] Though Lucien is corrupt long before he meets Vautrin.

[9] ". . . il amena Lucien et la pauvre courtisane au bord d'un chemin désert, à un endroit d'où l'on voyait Paris, et où personne ne pourrait les entendre. Tous trois ils s'assirent au soleil levant sur

Vautrin saves Lucien from suicide at the end of *Illusions perdues*, and offers him riches and fame in exchange for becoming his creature, "sa chose." Lucien's vulnerability to temptation is noticed long before he meets his supreme tempter. D'Arthez, the archangel of the gathered "angelic intelligences" of the Cénacle, criticizes him in a letter to his sister Eve. He is a poetry person, not a poet, says d'Arthez. He dreams and doesn't think; he agitates himself and creates nothing. He is "an effeminate being who likes to show off, the great vice of the French."[10] He would "happily sign a pact with the devil [le démon] in exchange for a few years of brilliance and luxury." D'Arthez knows that Lucien will succumb to the temptations of journalism—which Lousteau, the tempter, describes to him as Mephistopheles describes hell to Faust. "I see myself in you as I was, and I am sure that you will be, in one or two years, as I am now." Lousteau speaks counsel "dictated by the despair of the damned who can no longer get out of Hell."[11] The Duc de Rhétoré understands that he himself has opened the political horizon to Lucien, this greedy but wayward creature, as the journalists had showed him—"from the pinnacle of the Temple, as the Devil showed Jesus, the literary world and its riches."[12] It is perhaps on the allegorical level of shining beauty and corruptible human weakness—and only on this level—that Lucien arouses sympathy.

Vautrin is seen as a Faustian demon and also—as he himself points out—as Milton's fallen Satan, the rebellious true hero of *Paradise Lost*. In his long, brilliant, and terrible speech of temptation to Lucien at the end of *Les illusions perdues*, he claims that his own motivation is like Satan's need for companions. He imagines a Prologue to *Paradise Lost* (perhaps on the analogy of the Prologue to *Faust*) in which this need might be dramatized—and characterizes *Paradise Lost*, as Blake did, as simply "the apologetics of rebellion."[13] Vautrin has the grandeur of Milton's Satan and also his motivation. His passion for Lucien, like Coralie's, makes two bodies into one soul—Balzac writes of "the alliance of these two, which had to join in a single being." He penetrates the body and soul of the weakling poet and subjects him. "Evil, which in its poetic form takes the name of the Devil, deployed its

---

un tronçon de peuplier abattu devant ce paysage, un des plus magnifiques du monde, et qui embrasse le cours de la Seine, Montmartre, Paris, St Denis." *Splendeurs et misères*, 569.

[10] "une femmelette qui aime a paraître, le vice principal du Français." *Illusions perdues*, 578.

[11] "Je me vois en vous comme j'étais, et je suis sûr que vous serez, dans un ou deux ans, comme je suis." *Illusions perdues*, 347.

[12] "du haut du Temple, ainsi que le démon à Jésus, le monde littéraire et ses richesses." *Illusions perdues*, 465.

[13] "l'apologie de la Révolte." *Illusions perdues*, 708.

most seductive advances toward this man who was half a woman, and at first asked little from him, whilst giving him a great deal."[14]

Balzac's description of the devil as the "poetic configuration" of simple Evil, tells us something about the various forms of thought and meaning that go to make up the *Comédie humaine*. One configuration of Vautrin is the devil. Both as a devil and as a ferocious ex-convict, he lives in and through his creature, "sa chose." "This figure, base and great, obscure and famous, devoured above all by a fever of life" loves Lucien because "more than a son, more than a beloved woman, more than a family, more than his life, he was his revenge."[15] This is both satanic and romantic.

If, like the *Divine Comedy*, the *Comédie humaine* represented human and superhuman beings in a hierarchical structure, it was equally aware of itself as a natural history, classifying and exhibiting humans and animals in all the forms of their organization. The "Avant-propos" to the *Comédie* ascribes the original idea for the work to a comparison between Humanity and Animality. In a phrase that by justifiable sleight of hand Balzac makes equally applicable to his own work and to the researches of Cuvier and Geoffroy Saint-Hilaire, he writes of the "unity of composition." In the case of the great quarrel between Cuvier and Geoffroy, the dispute was about whether animal structures were determined by the function of the structure (Cuvier) or were derived from a "common plan of organization" (Geoffroy) that gave rise to all forms of life. Balzac believed that on this point Geoffroy had triumphed. "There is only one animal. The creator made use of a single, identical pattern for all organized beings. An animal is a principle that assumes its exterior form, or, to speak more exactly, the particular differences of its form, in the surroundings in which it is required to develop."[16]

What Balzac finds most interesting about human animals is that they make things. And he describes the things they make—artifacts, arts, and sciences—as *representations* of customs, thought, and life. The scientific

---

[14] "l'alliance de ces deux êtres, qui n'en devaient faire qu'un seul." "Le Mal, dont la configuration poétie s'appelle le Diable, usa envers cet homme a moitié femme de ses plus attachantes séductions, et lui demanda peu d'abord en lui donnant beaucoup." Splendeurs et misères, 504.

[15] "Ce personnage ignoble et grand, obscur et célèbre, dévoré surtout d'un fièvre de vie . . ." "plus qu'un fils, plus qu'une femme aimée, plus qu'une famille, plus que sa vie, il était sa vengeance." *Splendeurs et misères*, 502.

[16] "Il n'y a qu'un animal. Le créateur ne s'est servi que d'un seul et même patron pour tous les êtres organisés. L'animal est un principe qui prend sa forme extérieure, ou, pour parler plus exactement, les différences de sa forme, dans les milieux où il est appelé à se développer." *Comédie humaine* (Paris: Pléiade, 1976), 1:8.

"law" that led to this development of *homo faber*, Balzac says, is yet to be researched. But its existence has meant that the form of his novel, the representation of the human aspect of unity of composition, should have a triple form—"men, women and things, that is to say, people and the material representation they give to their thought; that is, man and life."[17]

I shall leave the fascinating consideration of material representations of thought until later. For the moment I want to consider the idea of the effect on the shape of the novel of Balzac's belief that there is only one animal. Metaphoric comparisons of humans to animals in medieval allegories are very different from the sense Balzac's descriptions give us of nineteenth-century Paris as a human jungle, in which predators stalk their squeaking prey. Lucien in this context is steadily diminished by the animals with which he is compared—usually with a touch of the Aesopian fable. When he travels to Paris with Madame de Bargeton, he fails to understand the effect on her self-esteem of his "nice behavior of a young rat come out of its hole." But mostly he is a lapdog, a spaniel. The animal world mingles comically and tragically in the suicide letter of Esther, who uses diminutive domestic animals as terms of affection—she is "your poor faithful dog," he and she are both "fawns," and he is "my cat." She has made sure that the poison she is about to take is sudden and not disfiguring by trying it out on her graceful white—and affectionate—greyhound, Romeo, whose name, she says (ignoring his companion Juliette), destines him to die in this way. Lucien the romantic thinks of Shakespeare's Romeo in deciding for suicide. After his death, the idea of canine fidelity takes another metaphorical turn, as Balzac turns his attention—in another initially apparently clumsy authorial address—to the grief of Vautrin. He asks his reader whether Vautrin is not monstrously beautiful in his "his devotion, worthy of the canine species, to the man he makes his friend." And he ends on a fabulous note. Once "the little spaniel is dead, we wonder whether his terrible companion, the lion, will live."[18]

In the preface to the first edition of *Les illusions perdues*, Balzac claims that society adapts men to its needs and "deforms" them so successfully that they cease to resemble each other—society has "created as many species as

---

[17] "les hommes, les femmes, et les choses, c'est-à-dire les personnes et la représentation matérielle qu'ils donnent de leur pensée; enfin l'homme et la vie." Avant-propos, 5.

[18] "gentillesses de jeune rat sorti de son trou." *Illusions perdues*, 256. "ton pauvre chien fidèle," "biches" "mon chat." *Splendeurs et misères*, 760. "attachement digne de la race canine envers celui dont il fait son ami." "Le petit épagneul mort, on se demande si son terrible compagnon, si le lion, vivra!" *Splendeurs et misères*, 812.

there are professions" and "indeed social Humanity displays as many varieties as Zoology."[19] He claims also, in the "Avant-propos," that unlike Buffon's male and female lions, men and women can often be different kinds of animal, requiring different kinds of attention from novelists and classifiers.

A further example I cannot resist quoting, in this context, is Balzac's extraordinary characterization of Esther's female sexuality in animal terms. It is a wonderful cross-breeding, so to speak, of biblical symbols and scientific observation. There is a melodramatic scene where the false priest, Carlos de Herrera, drives the repentant courtesan into reciting the Ave Maria and the Pater Noster, after which she is assumed, so to speak, into the divinely comic aspects of the story. "This was no longer a courtesan, but an angel rising after a fall." Balzac comments portentously on her "oriental" (Jewish) voluptuousness—she is "a creature in whom sensuality took the place of thought," and after only a few more days of dissolution she would "have arrived at embonpoint."[20] Herrera sends her to a convent, where the poor woman is tormented by her sensual memories.

Here Balzac introduces a scientific observation drawn from sheep. Instincts are "living facts" of which the cause is "a necessity undergone."[21] Animal varieties, he tells his readers, are the result of the exercise of these instincts. English and Spanish sheep, it has been observed, feed in close flocks on plains of plentiful grass and are solitary in mountains where food is scarce. Move them, however, to Switzerland or France, and they will keep to their instilled instincts, which persist for generations. Esther is a Scottish sheep (preserving a throwback inclination to oriental *volupté*), keeping herself to herself in a convent of innocent French young ladies. But her behavior is an innocent parody of the biblical—described in terms of modern physiology. Both body and mind have memories—nostalgia is a "sickness of physical memory"—and Esther's body is nostalgic for its old ways. So, as she runs in the magnificent gardens of the convent, "coquetting" with the trees—"she gave way to the demon,"[22] Balzac tells us, judging her. She is driven to run along the inside of the garden walls, in the evening, her shoulders naked and

---

[19] "l'état social adapte tellement les hommes à ses besoins et les déforme si bien que nulle part les hommes n'y sont semblables à eux-mêmes, et qu'elle a créé autant *d'espèces* que de *professions* . . ." "enfin l'Humanité sociale présente autant de variétés que la Zoologie." *Illusions perdues*, preface to the 1st ed. (1837) (in the 1977 Pléiade ed.), 110–11.

[20] "Ce n'était plus une courtisane, mais un ange qui se relevait d'une chute." "une créature à qui la volupté tenait lieu de la pensée" *Splendeurs et misères*, 464ff.

[21] "Les instincts sont des faits vivants, don't la cause gît dans une nécessssité subie." *Splendeurs et misères*, 465.

[22] "elle succombait au démon," *Splendeurs et misères*, 469.

uncovered by a shawl—"comme une couleuvre"—like a snake indeed, but a grass snake, and not venomous. Balzac's mixture of modern sententiousness and ancient poetry is very much his own.

The form of his picture of society in *Les illusions perdues* and *Splendeurs et misères* is a contrast between the provinces and Paris; between the printing and binding of books, and literature and journalism; and between high society and the demimonde, the criminal world. He described Lucien's story in a letter as "the journey from the poetic world to the real world, in other words the unsealing of the eyes of a young man from the provinces."[23] Lucien's disillusion in the Vanity Fair of Paris is the classic tale of the country innocent corrupted by urban greed. Its symbolic setting is the wonderful Galeries de Bois, then situated just opposite the Bourse, in the courtyard of the Palais Royal, where financiers and literary men mingled with the "filles de joie" who hunted there. Balzac describes this place as stinking, filthy, animated, and brightly colored. "It was horrible and gay."[24] Everything he picks out in his appallingly energetic description is man-made. The temptations are mechanical, things human animals have made in representation of themselves. "Out of all the little doors issued the same voices, which sang the praises of Cosmoramas, views of Constantinople, puppet-shows, automatons that played chess, dogs who could pick out the loveliest lady in society."[25] Even—and this is important—the flowers you think you see are nothing of the kind. "Discarded rags of fashion choked the vegetation: you found a knot of ribbons on a tuft of greenery and you were disappointed in your idea of the flower you had just admired when you saw a twist of satin that imitated a dahlia."[26]

Here Lucien observes at firsthand the spectacle of "an eminent poet prostituting his muse to a journalist, humiliating his Art as Woman was humiliated, prostituted below these ignoble galleries." He has heard a voice that cried, "Intelligence is the lever with which to move the world." And he has heard another that also cried out that the "lever handle" of intelligence

---

[23] "le passage du monde poétique au monde réel, en d'autres termes le dessillement des yeux d'un jeune provincial." *Illusions perdues*, Introduction, 5.

[24] "C'était horrible et gai." *Illusions perdues*, 360.

[25] "De toutes les petites portes partaient des voix semblables qui vous vantaient des Cosmoramas, des vues de Constantinople, des spectacles de marionettes, des automates qui jouaient aux échecs, des chiens qui distinguaient la plus belle femme de la société." *Illusions perdues*, 359.

[26] "Les débris de modes étouffaient la végétation: vous trouviez un noeud de rubans sur une touffe de verdure et vous étiez déçu dans vos idées sur la fleur que vous veniez admirer en apercevant un coque de satin qui figurait un dahlia." *Illusions perdues*, 356.

was money. After the visit to the Galeries, Lucien is lost in an abyss of thought, flying above "the world as it is." (The metaphor combining height and depth is part of a recurring pattern in the novels.) He has seen the strings that operate the world of bookselling, the kitchen of fame, the wings of the theater, and this leads to a vision of "the reverse side of consciences, the play of the cogs and wheels of Paris life, the mechanism of all things."[27]

Within this artificial, temporary structure of mechanisms turning on money (the most pervasive human artifact, representing life) a mocking booth invites the gullible to come in and see what God himself has never seen. The curious are admitted two by two and find themselves confronted with a large mirror—to see, a Hoffmannesque voice informs them, their "semblable. Dieu n'a pas son semblable."[28] Men in a mechanical society repeat and reflect themselves. God is not there. In this world Esther's beauty is seen as "capital" for Vautrin's schemes to make money by selling the image of nothing—false debts she is mendaciously said to have incurred. But unlike the prostitution of Lucien's talent, the prostitution of both Esther and other women is seen as a natural phenomenon, created by the "deforming" aspects of society. The Galeries de Bois are constructed round the natural soil of Paris, augmented by the artificial soil—the city dirt—brought in on boots and shoes. The women are, in Balzac's eyes, still natural beings. He says in the preface to the first edition of *Splendeurs et misères* that society has destroyed both energy and nuances of character in human behavior. Only in those outside society—whores, thieves, and convicts—do "comic and clearcut" habits persist. The reverse of this observation is his odd comparison of prostitutes' ideas of men, and critics' ideas of works of art—both are so jaded by overexposure to variety that they become indifferent and cease to discriminate. Prostitution and theft, Balzac says *in propria persona,* are the two live human protests, male and female, against the social state.

If Lucien's vision of the machinery of Paris was Balzac's final vision, the students who see Balzac as a stolid materialist would be right. But "le mécanisme de toute chose," though a truth, is not all the truth. His people and his world exist in history and eternity, as well as in the Paris of the 1820s. Balzac's buildings, like his novels, are representations of history and thought. The Galeries are temporary, a "hangar impudique," which lasted from the revolution of 1789 to the revolution of 1830. They stand, partly at

---

[27] "point d'appui" "l'envers des consciences, le jeu des rouages de la vie parisienne, le mécanisme de toute chose." *Illusions perdues*, 385.

[28] This phrase is untranslatable. It means literally that God is the only being who has no exactly similar being, nothing that resembles him.

least, against the building in which Lucien dies: St. Louis's Palais de Justice become the Conciergerie, looking out onto the river that still flows past it.

Balzac spends pages on his varied descriptions of this dreadful place. He tells the history of how the palace of St. Louis—of which the Sainte Chapelle still remains—was converted into the Conciergerie. He describes the Tour d'Argent, where medieval silver money was minted, and the elegant fantasy of the "oriental" carvings. "The Palace of Justice is a confused mass of constructions, superposed one on the other, some of them full of majesty, others mean, all damaging each other through a lack of unified order. The hall of Lost-Steps is the largest of the generally known rooms, but its bareness is appalling, and discourages onlookers. This vast cathedral of chicanery crushes the royal court. And finally the gallery of shops leads to two sewers."[29]

Within this structure, both grandly designed and cobbled together, the offices of justice are found in dark, narrow, nasty corridors down winding stairs that Balzac describes as the shame of architecture—both that of the city of Paris and of France. "Our principal department of justice surpasses the prisons in the hideous aspect of its interior spaces." More than once he describes these interiors as a "dédale" (labyrinth). He describes the modern black shroud of soot and makes his readers shudder at the thought of the horrible cells and last toilettes of Marie Antoinette and Madame Elisabeth— "The prisons were one of the crimes of the revolution of 1789."[30] He points out also that improvements have been made since the restoration. As a result of these, Lucien finds himself, in his cell—in a furnished room that takes him back to his first days in a garret in the Hotel Cluny in Paris—a cell that has a bed, and the necessary privacy, to facilitate his suicide.

Balzac's descriptions of prisons and the criminal world are related to the contemporary works of Victor Hugo and Eugène Sue, as well as to the real criminal-turned-policeman, Vidocq, part-original of Vautrin. After Lucien's death, the descriptions of the Palais de Justice and the activities in it become frenetic as Vautrin Trompe-la-Mort sets about to save his condemned protégé, also blond and beautiful, with the assistance of Asie, his aunt Jacqueline

---

[29] "le Palais de justice est un amas confus de constructions superposés les unes aux autres, les unes pleines de grandeur, les autres mesquines, et qui se nuisent entre elles par un défaut d'ensemble. La salle des Pas-Perdus est la plus grande des salles connues; mais sa nudité fait horreur et décourage les yeux. Cette vaste cathédrale de la chicane écrase la cour royale. Enfin la galerie marchande mène à deux cloaques." *Splendeurs et misères*, 778.

[30] "Dans ses intérieurs, la première de nos justices souveraines surpasse les prisons dans ce qu'elles ont de hideux." "Les prisons ont été l'un des crimes de la révolution de 1789." *Splendeurs et misères*, 778.

Collin. Balzac's interest in criminal argot was related to Sue's, but his descriptions of the space where the condemned men exist carry metaphorical hints and visions, cached in the language itself. Balzac writes of the "affreuse poésie" (horrible poetry) of the language of the criminal world and points out that the word *affreux* itself derives from a very ancient word *affe* meaning life—what is *affreux* is what troubles life. What is most *affreux* in this world is the machine invented by Guillotin in 1790, which has been given the name of "l'Abbaye-de-Monte-à-Regret." Its action is described by the verb *faucher* (to scythe, to reap).[31]

Balzac has a wonderful brief sentence about the *préau*, the exercise space for the prisoners in the Conciergerie. "We need to understand what the *préau* is for the two hundred prisoners of the Conciergerie; it is their garden, a garden without trees, earth, or flowers—a *préau*, precisely."[32] This treeless, flowerless space is what exists inside the historical and beautiful medieval palace suddenly glimpsed by Lucien de Rubempré, the poet of "Les Marguerites" and the Archer of Charles IX. Lucien's poems are floral, and the word *Rubempré* itself suggests a rosy meadow. His first attempt to kill himself—from which he is rescued by Vautrin—takes place in a pastoral setting, where he has found an equally flowerless, but beautiful depth in which (like Narcissus?) to plunge. It is "one of those round patches of water, which can be found in small watercourses, where the stillness of the surface indicates very great depth. The water is no longer green or blue, clear or yellow; it is like a mirror of polished steel. The rims of this bowl no longer held out gladioli, or blue flowers, or the large leaves of the water lily, the grass of the bank was cropped and dense, the willows wept round about, all arranged in a quite picturesque way. It was easy to imagine a precipice filled with water."[33]

This pool defined by negatives is part of the imagery of heights and depths that goes with Lucien (and Vautrin) as fallen angel. It is also part—even in its absences—of the pastoral and Edenic imagery that goes with the

---

[31] *Splendeurs et misères*, 824.

[32] "On doit maintenant comprendre ce qu'est le préau pour les deux cent prisonniers de la Conciergerie; c'est leur jardin, un jardin sans arbres, ni terre, ni fleurs, un préau enfin." *Splendeurs et misères*, 824. I take the word *préau* to be cognate with the countryside and lyrical word *pré* or meadow—but the *préau* in question is a covered exercise yard.

[33] "une de ces nappes rondes, comme il s'en trouve dans les petits cours d'eau, dont l'excessive profondeur est accusée par la tranquillité de la surface. L'eau n'est plus ni verte, ni bleue, ni claire, ni jaune; elle est comme un miroir d'acier poli. Les bords de cette coupe n'offraient plus ni glaïeuls, ni fleurs bleues, ni les larges feuilles du nénuphar, l'herbe de la berge était courte et pressée, les saules pleuraient autour, assez pittoresquement placés tous. On devinait facilement un précipice plein d'eau." *Illusions perdues*, 689.

early days of the earth, in Balzac's mind, and with the beauty of the allegorical meadows of the *Paradiso*, with medieval gardens, architecture, and order. The two aristocratic women courted by Lucien carry with them the connotations of the medieval. Mme. de Bargeton appears in a "new" fashion of a black velvet beret designed to recall the Middle Ages, and Balzac the materialist compares her society to old silver cutlery, blackened by tarnish, but weighty. But the pastoral image is moving in her case too, when she desires the "sublime, the extraordinary, the strange the divine, the marvellous"— with a thirst for "everything which was not the clear water of her life, hidden between the grasses."[34] And Clotilde de Grandlieu, if she is ugly, is ugly in an emphasized, flat-breasted way that recalls the "stiff, sharp design sought by medieval sculptors in those statues whose profiles are cut out of the cathedral niches they place them in."

A society carries and inhabits its history. So does a novel. So it is natural that Vautrin's speech of temptation to Lucien on the country road where they meet, as Lucien makes for his liquid precipice, should be a temptation made up of wicked reworkings and revisions of the history of France and of earlier things—back to the biblical story of Cain and Abel—whose blood, says the false priest, is mixed in himself; he is Cain for his enemies, and Abel for his friends.[35] His lessons are secrecy, discretion, and using all men as instruments of ambition. His examples are Napoleon, Richelieu, and the Medicis, who were worth the whole of their societies, who used and named their times. He is contemptuous of the virtues of Joan of Arc and the bourgeois Jacques Coeur, a faithful servant of a king who accuses him falsely and exiles him. Without Joan of Arc, he cynically observes, the British Isles would simply be Angevin provinces, alongside what is now France, one country. An atheist and immoral history diverts Lucien from one suicide and leads him to a later one, in a building that embodies history, in its beauty and terror.

Proust criticizes Lucien's suicide note, addressed to the Abbé Carlos de Herrera, and containing comparisons of great men—Attila, Charlemagne, Mahomet, Napoleon, with lesser instruments like Fouché and Louvel—for sounding too like Balzac. Lucien at that point, he says, ceases to be "a real person, different from all others."[36] But Lucien sounds like Balzac because

---

[34] "tout ce qui n'était pas l'eau claire de sa vie, cachée entre les herbes." *Illusions perdues*, 157–58.

[35] Cain is a recurring romantic symbol of revolt and alienation.

[36] "une personne réelle, différente de toutes les autres." *Contre Sainte-Beuve*, 293 (Notes complémentaires).

Balzac sounds like Vautrin, and Lucien is Vautrin's echo—he has by now no voice of his own—and is using Vautrin's own language to hurt him. Proust comments also, without elaborating, on the way in which Balzac's people are both individuals and types. He could have observed, and does not, although the balzacian paragraph he is criticizing implies the idea, that in Balzac all individuals run in and out of being types, like different flowers in a tapestry with repeating patterns.

One of the odder parts of Vautrin's temptation by narrative is a digressive tale of a beautiful young man, the secretary of a certain Baron de Goertz, who developed a curious habit of chewing and devouring paper, and was finally condemned to death for eating a treaty between Russia and Sweden, about Finland. The moral of this story appears to be that Vautrin has lost one secretary and needs another—the connection is tenuous. The fact that Vautrin's secretary is dead and the paper-eater has been executed casts a sinister shadow, which deepens retrospectively when we meet Vautrin's previous favorite in the condemned cell in the Conciergerie. The connection to the larger shape of the *Comédie humaine*, and to these two novels in particular, nevertheless gives Balzac's readers a clue to the way in which he constructed the huge looping and then knotting patterns of his narratives. For the idea of Lucien as a successor to a paper-eater does relate to the brother-in-law he has just betrayed, David Séchard, who has invented a new cheap way of paper-making, and is in solitary confinement for debt, owing to Lucien's earlier use of his forged signature and later stupid betrayal of his whereabouts.

A passage everyone remembers, and mocks, in *Les illusions perdues* is David Séchard's proposal to Eve, Lucien's beautiful, devoted, and virtuous sister. It consists of a history of papermaking, from the earliest days to the present. It is, and Balzac knows it is, absurd and unromantic. It starts in Asia Minor with cotton paper in A.D. 750. It proceeds through the histories of printing ("when the immortals, Faust, Coster and Gutenberg had invented THE BOOK")[37] and describes the varieties of early paper: "le Jésus, le Colombier, le papier Pot, l'Ecu, le Coquille, le Couronne," names of marks as far as the Grand Eagle of Napoleon—an innocent figure in David's narrative, as he is not in the feverish imaginings of Lucien, or the cynical ones of Vautrin. On and on David talks—a love-speech less improbable than a romance-reader may think, since he is offering Eve his essential self, his understanding of the world and his place in it. Rag paper may be succeeded by vegetable paper. The world of manufacture is like the world itself: "This

---

[37] "lorsque les immortels Faust, Coster et Gutenberg eurent inventé LE LIVRE." *Illusions perdues*, 218ff.

quick survey demonstrates invincibly that all great gains achieved by industry and intelligence were made extremely slowly, by imperceptible accumulations, exactly in the way Nature itself works. In order to reach perfection, writing—maybe even language—went through the same tentative experiments as typography and papermaking."[38]

Balzac prefaces this dense historical summary with another authorial address to the reader—rather like his intrusive admonition at the moment of Lucien's death and here also (not, I think, by accident) about the connections between the material and the spiritual world. Lucien sees a vision of the pure world of poetry and form, but it has a material cause and nature, the *solidity* and force of thought as in its effect on the brain, in causing hallucinations. David's history of papermaking—even if it is only a résumé, its real author insists—is the material aspect of a spiritual object: the book we are reading. "David gave her information about papermaking that is in no way out of place in a work whose material being is owed at least as much to paper as to the press."[39]

When David comes to make his great scientific discovery, he makes paper of weeds—nettles and *chardons*, or thistles, those field weeds after which Lucien's paternal family are named. It was Lucien's Chardon father who rescued his noble de Rubempré mother from the "fauche" (scythe) of the guillotine, and it was from a process partly discovered by M. Chardon the chemist that David derived his idea for his invention. David is a papermaker, as Lucien is a paper-eater, a destroyer, a consumer. David's speech is interrupted by Lucien, whose self-love has been wounded by humiliation at Mme. de Bargeton's.

———

I have been arguing that Balzac proceeds typically, and particularly at his most intense, by a kind of manic inclusiveness of many levels and styles of discourse, by a need to see an event, an object, or a person as a part of a whole, of which his text—a particular novel, the whole *Comédie*—is itself a representation. This is not to say that Balzac did not have the conventional

---

[38] "Ce rapide aperçu démontre invinciblement que toutes les grandes acquisitions de l'industrie et de l'intelligence se sont faites avec une excessive lenteur et par des agrégations inaperçues, absolument comme procède la Nature. Pour arriver à leur perfection, l'écriture, le langage peut-être! . . . ont eu les mêmes tâtonnements que la typographie et la papeterie." *Illusions perdues*, 218ff.

[39] "David lui donna sur la papeterie des renseignements qui ne seront point déplacés dans une oeuvre dont l'existence matérielle est due autant au papier qu'à la presse." *Illusions perdues*, 218ff.

and fundamental skills of a storyteller and a dramatist. Oscar Wilde said his characters have "a kind of fervent fiery-coloured existence" that "reduces our living friends to shadows and our acquaintances to the shadows of shades."[40] His characters are both powerful and intricate. As I have suggested, if we consider only those passages in which Lucien acts or is seen in relation to other human beings—he is one of the most unpleasant characters in literature.

Balzac argues in his "Avant-propos" that he wishes to show the loss of illusions working in families. Families, he claims, are the primary unit of his unity of social organization. It is the illusions of Lucien's womenfolk that lead to his spoiling as a charming child and a presumed genius. But he has no virtues, and when he writes pathetically in his first suicide note that he is dangerous and "fatal" to everything he touches, he is telling no more than the truth. He cannot do David and Eve the ordinary courtesy of waiting for their wedding before eloping; he betrays d'Arthez himself by writing a destructive critique of his masterpiece which that ironically virtuous man helps him to construct; he feeds off Coralie and can only return to the provinces after her death on the proceeds of a brief foray into prostitution by her faithful maid. He is prepared to sacrifice Esther; he vacillates about Mme. de Bargeton. He is not only weak and narcissistic. He is fatally stupid. There is a terrible and unforgivable moment in his last conversation with Esther, when he catches sight of her intention to commit suicide and can only blurt out—as a hopeful sign—that he has managed to see Clotilde, marriage with whom will fulfill his ambitions. (And will do nothing at all for Esther.) Esther cries out "with a note of concentrated fury, 'Toujours Clotilde!' " and the hopeless Lucien mumbles on, that he will be able to talk to Clotilde on the road to Fontainebleau.[41] Balzac allows his readers to sympathize with Lucien only when he is humiliated—when the Grandlieus decide not to receive him, for instance.

And Balzac distinguishes between suicides whose self-esteem is injured and those whose honor is at stake.[42] Lucien dies because he is mortified at having, in his prison interrogation, betrayed Vautrin and their joint dealings, when Vautrin himself has kept the curious magistrate at bay, by claiming that Lucien is his natural son. "At the moment when Jacques Collin had saved everything through his audacity, Lucien, the clever man, had ruined everything through his lack of intelligence, and his failure to think things

---

[40] Oscar Wilde, "The Decay of Lying," in Ellmann, ed., *The Artist as Critic*, 299.

[41] *Splendeurs et misères*, 689.

[42] *Illusions perdues*, 688.

out."[43] He kills himself because he cannot live with his own stupidity—the animal analogy Balzac uses is that of a baffled ox in a slaughterhouse that has been missed by the mallet.

I do not think Balzac is weeping for Lucien with Vautrin, as Proust suggests. He is partly perhaps weeping for Vautrin, who has lost the object both of his affection and of his surrogate ambition. Balzac has surrounded his tinsel angel—his "half-criminal"—with configurations of high suicide. When he first appears, he discusses André Chénier's "Elegy on a Suicide" and is associated with the dead genius Chatterton, and beyond him, with Werther. But this is merely a force-field of associations that pulls him along. Esther's suicide—however febrile—is both generous and genuinely a matter of honor. She has sold her body after redeeming it. She cannot go on. Lucien is a realist portrait of a pretty, mean-spirited charmer.

So why do the tears rise to my eyes? Because of *lacrimae rerum*, because of all the things that make up the history of the Ste-Chapelle and the Conciergerie, and because one stupid man, in the midst of all this death and fear, lost his sense of self at the moment of his own death enough to admire a svelte colonnade. And because of Balzac and his dreadful courage as a writer, taking on a world.

———

Vautrin in his temptation of Lucien spends some time quizzing him about the operations of the games of chance, at which he has lost the money he has subsequently had to steal from David and Eve. Meditations on the nature of chance, fate, destiny, determinism, and control of events make up a considerable part of the thought both of Vautrin and of his creator. All novelists have to think about the relations of accident and causation in the stories they tell—and in this sense the novelist is God, or at least a demiurge, setting in train the events of the history of the microcosm he is representing. Reading Lucien's history one can feel his creator—as well as his evil genius—ratcheting up the machinery of his downfall, stacking the cards against him, annihilating the possibilities of good luck, or a fortunate fall out of the tragic careering curve he is embarked on.

"Character is destiny" is a truth that does not take us very far in Balzac's world. For character is formed by causes that can be observed and

---

[43] "Là où Jacques Collin avait tout sauvé par son audace, Lucien, l'homme d'esprit, avait tout perdu par son inintelligence et par son défaut de réflexion." *Splendeurs et misères*, 773.

analyzed—physiological, historical, intellectual. And fates are formed by accidents that seem destined, not least the chance meeting on the road with the false priest of no God. The nineteenth-century novel lives in both the providential world of the Bible and in protestant Christianity, in the judged world of catholic eschatology, and in the modern scientific world of anatomical, geological, political, and historical structures—all these made up by accidental processes that produce determined forms. Esther is a Scotch sheep, a repentant Magdalen, an instinctual female rebel, or an exploited and betrayed woman, depending on which threads of thought and description we are following.

Balzac tells us in the "Avant-propos" that "chance is the greatest novelist in the world; to be a productive writer one has only to study it."[44] Lighthearted Lucien, arriving in Paris and cheered by his new clothes, reflects that Paris is the capital of "le hasard" and for a moment he believes in "le hasard." He turns this idea in the very next sentence into an idea of destiny. "Did he not have, in manuscript, a volume of poems and a splendid novel, *The Archer of Charles IX*? He believed in his destiny."[45]

Balzac remarks drily a few pages later that in Paris there is only a chance for the well-connected and the big battalions. Vautrin, on the other hand, has his criminal's sense of fatality and opportunism combined. He is a fatalist like Napoleon, Mahomet, "and many great politicians." "It is odd that almost all men of action tend to believe in Fate, whereas most men of thought incline toward Providence."[46]

Vautrin expatiates on chance and providence in his dialogue with M. de Grandville at the end of the novel, when the two have become allegorical representations of "La Justice" and "l'Arbitraire."[47] Critics have disapproved of these last scenes, in which Balzac's need to reduce his vision of the world to a schematic form is, they say, too insistent. But in a layered Human Comedy, allegory has its place, as it does in the Divine Comedy. Justice, Balzac has already told his readers, three hundred pages back, is "a being of reason, represented by a collection of individuals, continually renewed, whose good intentions, and whose memories are, like themselves, continually shifting

---

[44] "Le hasard est le plus grand romancier du monde: pour être fécond il n'y a qu'à l'étudier."

[45] "N'avait-il pas un volume de poésies et un magnifique roman, *L'archer de Charles IX* en manuscrit? Il espéra dans sa destinée." *Illusions perdues*, 289.

[46] "Chose étrange, presque tous les hommes d'action inclinent à la Fatalité, de même que la plupart des penseurs inclinent à la Providence." *Splendeurs et misères*, 112.

[47] *Splendeurs et misères*, 887.

places. Prosecutors and tribunals have no capacity to provide against crimes, they are constructed to accept them as they happen."[48]

Justice as a "being of reason" is a real part of human thought. Vautrin as the incarnation of the Arbitrary represents the "Bagne" that is a symbol of the "daring that suppresses calculation and reflection" to which all means are equally good. *Justice* and *arbitration* are of course almost synonyms. Balzac says that the confrontation of the two is a question of "the conjunction of the social and the natural state, poured [*vidée*] into the narrowest possible space." And in that space Vautrin tells Grandville that Lucien's death—to be precise, sitting through the night holding the frozen hand of the dead young man—has caused him to renounce his twenty-year senseless struggle against society as a whole. "For twenty years I've seen the underside of the world, from its cellars, and I have recognized that there is an active power in the way things happen, which you call *Providence*, which I used to call *chance*, and which my companions called *luck*. Every bad act is met by some sort of vengeance, however fast it is hidden away."[49]

In this scene, the representative of personified Justice (who is responsible, among other things, for the operation of the guillotine, which is a human form of deciding the end of a life story) comes to terms with Trompe-la-Mort, the criminal who through luck and cleverness has so far evaded human justice and has now decided to work on its side—partly at least in order to pursue his personal vendetta against the detectives and spies who were responsible for the failure of his plotting, and indirectly for Lucien's death. It is allegorized, yes, but it does demonstrate something of the complexity of human thinking about chance, fate, vengeance, and judgment.

———

Balzac's world is not an easy one to hold in the head as a whole, partly because of its magnificent scope and extravagant proliferation of plots and persons, living and dead. Proust makes a brilliant and illuminating comparison with the Monet who made fifty cathedrals or forty water lilies. He says

---

[48] "un être de raison représenté par une collection d'individus sans cesse renouvelés, dont les bons intentions et les souvenirs sont, comme eux, excessivement ambulatoires. Les parquets, les tribunaux ne peuvent rien prévenir en fait des crimes, ils sont inventés pour les accepter tout faits." *Splendeurs et misères*, 587.

[49] "Eh bien! J'ai vu, depuis vingt ans, le monde par ses envers, dans ses caves, et j'ai reconnu qu'il y a dans la marche des choses une force que vous nommez la Providence, que j'appelais le hasard, que mes compagnons appellent la chance. Toute mauvaise action est rattrapée par une vengeance quelconque, avec quelque rapidité qu'elle s'y dérobe." *Splendeurs et misères*, 922.

rightly that Balzac's novels originated in good ideas, not simply in good observations—and we find ourselves tracking the ideas through the texture of the shifting prose, with its disquisitions and its lurid melodramas, with its flaming characters and its repeating types. One of the clues to his work, perhaps, is his relation to his great predecessor Walter Scott, who also had the idea of a series of long novels that together would make up a world in history, public and private. Scott, Balzac says, raised the novel to the philosophical value of history. "He put into it the spirit of past times, he brought together drama, dialogue, portraits, landscape, description, he introduced the marvellous and the real, those elements of epic, he mixed up poetry with the familiarity of humble common speech."[50]

D'Arthez gives Lucien an excellent lecture on how to improve on Scott, how to toughen and improve *The Archer of Charles IX*. He suggests avoiding long dialogues—*not dramatizing*. It is interesting that Henry James in his essay on Balzac, "The Lesson of the Master," praises Balzac precisely for his sparing use of dialogue. Balzac was the master who created the textured prose that could do everything at once—the variety of which, and the success of which, have not been admired as much as they should have been, partly because the French mind is interested in "good style" that can be taught and assessed by rigorous rules and partly because his transitions and juxtapositions make his readers uneasy. They feel, as Proust also did, that Balzac writes down whatever comes into his head. This is true, but as I have hoped to show—with flowers and weeds and meadows, or with paper and books and minds and lovers—he connected everything to everything, sometimes at considerable distances in the texts. His heir in this regard is the George Eliot of *Middlemarch* who used the metaphor of Bichat's idea of "primitive tissue," spiderwebs, and the nature of optics to bind all her text together—science and mythology, love and death, little England and larger Europe.

There is a curious passage in *Le Cousin Pons* that perhaps provides an image for Balzac's way of seeing his world and holding it together. It is about "visions," as the death of Lucien centers on a vision. In this case the visions are those of a clairvoyant, who like the novelist, interrogates the world of men, women, things, and artifacts, and observes their hidden connections. It is a wonderful piece of balzacian inclusiveness. For that reason the quotation needs to be expansive.

---

[50] "Il y mettait l'esprit des anciens temps, il y réunissait à la fois le drame, le dialogue, le portrait, le paysage, la description, il y faisait entrer le merveilleux et le vrai, ces éléments de l'épopée, il y faisait coudoyer la poésie par la familiarité des plus humbles langages." Avant-propos, 6.

As to the means employed to induce *visions*, this is the easiest wonder to explain, from the moment when the hand of the enquirer lays out the objects that are to represent the chances [*hasards*] of his life. In fact, everything is connected, in the real world. Every movement corresponds to a cause, every cause is an element of the whole, and consequently the whole is represented in the least of movements. Rabelais, the greatest spirit of modern humanity, the man who contains Pythagoras, Hippocrates, Aristophanes and Dante, said, three centuries ago now: man is a microcosm. Three centuries later, Swedenborg, the great Swedish prophet, said that the earth was a man. The prophet and the forerunner of unbelief meet here in the greatest of conceptions. Everything is fated in human life, as it is in the life of our planet. The least accidents, the most futile, are all part of it. Therefore the great matters, the great designs, the great thoughts, are necessarily reflected in the smallest actions, and this so faithfully, that if some conspirator shuffles and cuts a pack of cards, he will write out the secret of his conspiracy for the seer who is called a gipsy, a fortune teller, a charlatan etc. From the moment one admits fatality, that is, the linked sequence of causes, judicial astrology exists, and becomes what it once was, a huge science, for it includes the deductive capability that made Cuvier so great, but it is spontaneous, not, as it was in the case of this fine genius, something put to work in the long nights in the study.[51]

---

[51] "Quant aux moyens employés pour arriver aux visions, c'est là le merveilleux le plus explicable, dès que la main du consultant dispose les objets à l'aide desquels on lui fait représenter les hasards de sa vie. En effet, tout s'enchaîne dans le monde réel. Tout mouvement y correspond à une cause, toute cause se rattache à l'ensemble; et conséquemment, l'ensemble se représente dans le moindre mouvement. Rabelais, le plus grand esprit de l'humanité moderne, cet home qui résume Pythagore, Hippocrate, Aristophane et Dante, a dit, il y a maintenant trois siècles: l'homme est un microcosme. Trois siècles après. Swedenborg, le grand prophète Suédois, disait que la terre était un homme. Le prophète et le précurseur de l'incrédulité se rencontraient ainsi dans la plus grande des formules. Tout est fatal dans la vie humaine, comme dans la vie de notre planète. Les moindres accidents, les plus futiles, y sont subordonnés. Donc les grandes choses, les grands desseins, les grandes pensées s'y reflètent nécessairement dans les plus petites actions, et avec tant de fidélité, que si quelque conspirateur mêle et coupe un jeu de cartes, il y écrira le secret de sa conspiration pour le voyant appelé bohème, diseur de bonne aventure, charlatan etc. Dès qu'on admet la fatalité, c'est-à-dire l'enchaînement des causes, l'astrologie judiciaire existe et devient ce qu'elle était jadis, une science immense, car elle comprend la faculté de déduction qui fit Cuvier si grand, mais spontanée, au lieu d'être, comme chez ce beau génie, exercée dans les nuits studieuses du cabinet." *Le Cousin Pons* (Paris: Pléiade, 1977), 7:587.

BRUCE ROBBINS

A Portrait of the Artist as a Social Climber:
Upward Mobility in the Novel

Künstlerroman

H. G. Wells's novel *Kipps: The Story of a Simple Soul* (1905) describes a lowly draper's assistant (Wells's own occupation at the same age) who receives an unexpected inheritance and suddenly finds himself rich. As a result, he becomes engaged to the upper-class woman he has long adored from afar. However, his efforts to adapt to the conventions of the genteel world soon begin to weary and oppress him, and he goes back to his childhood sweetheart, who has meanwhile found work as a servant. He then loses most of the inheritance, swindled by the former fiancée's brother. He and his sweetheart live happily ever after.

The apparent moral of this story is that happiness depends neither on acquiring a lot of money nor on climbing the social ladder. Late in the novel, after Kipps has renounced his fiancée but before he loses his riches, this moral is articulated for him by a character with the Nietzschean name of Masterman, a figure of the working-class intellectual apparently modeled on George Gissing. " 'You were starting to climb,' [Masterman] said at dinner. 'That doesn't lead anywhere. You would have clambered from one refinement of vulgarity to another, and never got to any satisfactory top. There isn't a top. It's a squirrel's cage. Things are out of joint. . . . You'd have hung on, a disconsolate, dismal little figure, somewhere on the ladder, far below even the motor-car class, while your wife larked about, or fretted because she wasn't a bit higher than she was. . . . I found it all out long ago. I've seen women of that sort. And I don't climb any more' " (242–43).[1]

Aside from its somewhat dated misogyny, this little speech might have been pronounced by a novelist today, explaining (one wonders to whom) why the theme of social climbing no longer holds much appeal. Who believes that there *is* a "top"? Who would suggest that even the fate of a "simple soul," if there is such a thing, can be accounted for by the crude social topography of "up" and "down"? There is no doubt that upward mobility persists as a habit and even an annoying obsession of our storytelling, both

---

[1] H. G. Wells, *Kipps: The Story of a Simple Soul*, ed. Peter Vansittart (1905; London: J. M. Dent, 1993). Subsequent quotes are from this edition and are referenced in the text.

public and private, but there is considerable doubt that such stories have much to do with observable social reality. This point is elegantly expounded in Monty Python's "Four Yorkshiremen" skit, a series of reminiscences about childhood poverty around a bottle of expensive wine at a Hawaiian resort:

> Eric Idle: . . . I was happier then and I had *nothin'*. We used to live in this tiiiny old house, with greaaaaat big holes in the roof.
>
> Graham Chapman: House? You were lucky to have a *house!* We used to live in one room, all hundred and twenty-six of us, no furniture. Half the floor was missing; we were all huddled together in one corner for fear of *falling*!
>
> Terry Gilliam: You were lucky to have a *room*! *We* used to have to live in a corridor!
>
> Michael Palin: Ohhhh we used to *dream* of livin' in a corridor! Woulda' been a palace to us. We used to live in an old water tank on a rubbish tip. We got woken up every morning by having a load of rotting fish dumped all over us! House!? Hmph.
>
> EI: Well when I say "house" it was only a hole in the ground covered by a piece of tarpaulin, but it was a house to *us*.
>
> GC: We were evicted from *our* hole in the ground; we had to go and live in a lake!
>
> TG: You were lucky to have a *lake*! There were a hundred and sixty of us living in a small shoebox in the middle of the road.
>
> MP: Cardboard box?[2]

Readers are of course prepared to acknowledge that dramatic disparities of wealth and income exist and that they are deeply scandalous for a society that would like to think of itself as civilized. We know that every once in a while an unrepresentative upstart makes the passage from rags to riches. Whether we see such ascents as figuring an absolute economic improvement, and thus a matter for rejoicing, or a relative gain in status that allows one to exult over others, hence deserving a cooler welcome, or as something else entirely, most of us would not conclude that sophisticated fiction should be or has ever been centrally "about" anything so coarse and so uncommon. Fairy tales and satire, yes; the realist novel, no. Suspicious of ladders and of stories

---

[2] Monty Python's Flying Circus, "Four Yorkshiremen" sketch, from *Live at City Centre* (1976; New York: Arista Records, 1997).

that involve climbing them, educated common sense today tends to prefer categories that overlap with upward mobility but put the emphasis elsewhere. The young person's "coming-of-age" story and the immigrant's "coming-to-America" story, for example, are also concerned, if only inadvertently, with attaining greater access to economic goods and services. But they seem to leave themselves more space for the exercise of literary imagination by focusing respectively on the individual life cycle and personal development, on national belonging and cultural assimilation. Even the *Künstlerroman*, or portrait of the youthful artist, which might look like a rather more specialized category, probably resonates with more actual experiences of novel-reading than does a neologistic phrase like "the novel of upward mobility."[3]

And this makes intuitive sense, given how much of what is called upward mobility in fact takes place in more or less autobiographical first novels (sometimes the author's only novel) whose real subject is the novelist's struggle to overcome various obstacles, achieve a certain distance from his or her society of origin, and thus become a novelist. In addition to James Joyce's *A Portrait of the Artist as a Young Man*, the prototype, one thinks for example of D. H. Lawrence's *Sons and Lovers*, Ralph Ellison's *Invisible Man*, V. S. Naipaul's *The Mystic Masseur*, Tayeb Salih's *Season of Migration to the North*, Tsitsi Dangarembga's *Nervous Conditions*, and Zadie Smith's *White Teeth* (to the extent that it is Irie's story). *Kipps* was not Wells's first novel, but one might argue that the real subject of Masterman's speech is his own and Wells's situation as writer and intellectual. In cases like this social distance (up or down the ladder) seems indistinguishable from intellectual or critical distance. The endpoint of social climbing becomes conflated with getting an education, discovering a sense of artistic vocation, producing the book one is holding in one's hands.

And yet one cannot escape this conflation by expressing a preference for one theme (the literary) at the expense of the other (the social). The argument swings both ways: if the real kernel of the upward mobility story is often the emergence of the writer, even the novel's most reflexive or inward-looking treatments of the writer's emergence are often (though not always) also treatments of upward mobility. Indeed, I will be suggesting that they may well turn out to be among the most intriguing discussions of upward mobility we have—intriguing because the career path of the writer is by no means all they represent.

---

[3] On the *Künstlerroman*, see Herbert Marcuse, *Der Deutsche Künstlerroman* (Frankfurt: Suhrkamp, 1978).

Bohemia

Wells's case against social climbing is not as open-and-shut as it might appear. Its reference to "women of that sort" leaves an obvious and gaping loophole. It offers the possibility that social climbing fails to make men happy only because women, or the women men want as the reward of their striving, *are* of "that sort"—because women are more intent than men on an endless, insatiable accumulation of the signs of higher and higher status. A not very convincing gender stereotype is imported into the scenario in order to rescue men from recognizing that they themselves are ambivalent about, and cannot simply repudiate, social climbing.[4] As might be expected, however, this effort to conceal the positive attractions of social climbing does indeed fail to convince. In suggesting that marriages founder when the female partner cannot rest content with what she has and stop striving for more, Wells's mininarrative hints that though more is bad, *some* of the same unnamed ingredient may be good and even necessary. It hints, in other words, that social climbing may after all mean acquiring something of value.

This hint is confirmed by the very terms in which Masterman repudiates social climbing. Society is not a ladder, he says, but a squirrel's cage. When you think you are climbing, you are in fact staying in place while one "refinement of vulgarity" after another whirls around you. There is no "top," or no "satisfactory" top—not quite the same thing—that would make the climb worth undertaking. And yet we know that Masterman himself *has* done some climbing in the past, for he tells us that he doesn't climb "any more." Was the former episode of climbing alluded to here simply an embarrassing mistake? It appears not. His story goes as follows: "I found myself at thirteen being forced into a factory like a rabbit into a chloroformed box. Thirteen! . . . But even a child of that age could see what it meant, that hell of a factory! Monotony and toil and contempt and dishonour! And then death. So I fought—at thirteen! . . . I got out at last—somehow. . . . Some of us get out by luck, some by cunning, and crawl on to the grass, exhausted and crippled, to die. That's a poor man's success, Kipps" (210–11).

Masterman himself clearly expects an imminent and premature death. On the other hand, this expectation is described at one point as a "pose" he can "abandon" (207). But whether or not his resignation is a pose, one must risk a certain callousness by declaring that his is indeed the story of a

---

[4] It is by no means sure that Masterman's speech reflects Wells's own misogyny. Wells may be caricaturing one of Gissing's well-known and eccentric positions.

"success." Against all expectation, he has managed to educate himself. Despite his exhaustion, he is no longer doing exhausting work. Now he has access to such authoritative judgments as "Things are out of joint." "All the old tradition goes or has gone," he opines, "and there's no one to make a new tradition. Where are your nobles now? Where are your gentlemen?" (206). In order to know that there once existed an "old tradition" of nobles and gentlemen that is now going or gone, one must command a view of the whole, historically speaking—but also socially speaking. That is, one must have knowledge of the top as well as the bottom of the social ladder. Such a view is not available, at least on Masterman's telling, from the floor of a factory, where all is "monotony and toil." There has to have been something very much *like* social climbing, if not social climbing itself, in order for him to see enough of the world so as to judge whether it is indeed a ladder or a squirrel cage or something else entirely. Moreover, these ambitiously comprehensive opinions are imbued with a palpable nostalgia for the bygone era when gentility had not yet disappeared. In what he reveals of his values, Masterman aligns himself with the real gentility that has been lost: "there's no place or level of honour or fine living left in the world, so what's the good of climbing?" (208). Once upon a time, he implies, there *was* a place or level of honor, there was such a thing as "fine living." At that time these values were authentic and deserving of respect, and thus social climbing made sense. As it still would, one infers, if only these genteel values had not been kidnapped and perverted by the newly moneyed classes. The one who knows this is the one who carries those values forward into the present. The torch of authentic gentility has passed from the people at the top of the ladder to the educated person without money. If the rise of uneducated people with money is a perversion—Kipps himself would seem to furnish a convenient model—there is no suggestion here that Masterman would object to the upward mobility of those like himself. His story almost cries out for that alternative resolution.

Both Masterman's decline narrative and its accompanying self-flattery should sound familiar to academic readers, for they reproduce a founding myth of literary criticism in the academy. That is, they explain both to the general public and to upwardly mobile academics themselves why society benefits from offering them a discipline to inhabit along with its attendant career opportunities. Like *The Waste Land* as read by F. R. Leavis and the *Scrutiny* group, the sad conviction that "the world is out of joint" becomes a source of pleasing self-legitimation to those who can claim to know through literature when the world was not yet out of joint and who thus can sell the memories they have preserved (in other words, knowledge of the canon) to a society now convinced of how much it has lost.[5] In other words, the case *against* social climbing that Masterman makes to Kipps disguises a case *for* the social ascent of critics like Masterman himself, or like those later intellectuals and academics whose monastic self-image of dead-to-the-world disinterestedness gives collective institutional form to Masterman's sickly asceticism.

Unlike Kipps's inheritance, which comes to him randomly by no logic other than kinship, the upward mobility here might be described as "earned." A figure seeking to rise adopts an intellectual posture or position that those above him have reasons of their own to reward. I will come back to this contrast between earned and unearned mobility. On it rests the possibility of a redemptive reading of the genre. For the moment let us note that neither the logic by which mobility is attained nor even the fact that it *is* attained appears to register in Masterman's consciousness, highly sensitive though that consciousness is. Denial that one occupies any place on a social ladder, or even that such a thing as a social ladder exists, is of course not restricted to the guild of writers. But the writerly version of this general ideological formation is pervasive. As Masterman insists that he has climbed out, not up, so his prototype Gissing often has his heroes declare that they are social aliens, at home nowhere. The protagonist of *Born in Exile* believes he is an exile both from his own former class and from the class system in general: "I myself belong to no class whatever" (296).[6] As in *Kipps*, however, the novel tends not to accept statements like this at face value. For better or worse, the genre's commitment to densely textured social determinations leads it to underline the many ways in which such characters are in fact determined by the social locations they claim to have escaped. Even a novelist who believes that one can belong to "no class whatever" is likely to be betrayed into presenting the character who affirms this as unintentionally comic and, more to the point, misguided.

Consider for example an autobiographical first novel, roughly contemporary with *Kipps*, by the young Australian novelist Miles Franklin.[7] The teenage heroine of *My Brilliant Career* (1901), raised "up country" in a family beset by drought and squalid privation, wants only to be permitted to read and write, for in books she finds "the unspeakable comfort and heart-rest of congenial companionship" (61) that her actual companions cannot provide.

[5] See Francis Mulhern, *The Moment of "Scrutiny"* (London: New Left Books/Verso, 1979).

[6] George Gissing, *Born in Exile*, ed. David Grylls (1892; London: J. M. Dent, 1993).

[7] Miles Franklin, *My Brilliant Career* (1901; Sydney: A&R Classics/HarperCollins, 1973).

She accepts a marriage proposal from a wealthy suitor only after he loses everything, telling him, "Do you think I am that sort, that cares for a person only because he has a little money? Why! that is the very sort of thing I am always preaching against" (173). And yet the truth is that she knows she cannot attain "the dream-life with writers, artists, and musicians" (21) she longs for without moving away from a life ruled by necessity and toward a life among the leisured and educated, which is to say moving up the social ladder: "I was always desirous of enjoying the company of society people who were well bred and lived according to etiquette, and possessed of leisure and culture sufficient to fill their minds with something more than the price of farm produce and a hard struggle for existence" (74). If other people will perhaps value these same amenities for other, less disinterested reasons, that is their affair. This is an irony that Wells applies laconically to his would-be superman. " 'I don't climb,' said Masterman, and accepted Kipps' silent offer of another cigarette" (206). One must not appear to be arranging to have cigarettes provided, yet it is convenient that a listener who possesses both an inquiring mind and a sizable inheritance is there to provide them.

Cultural history has a well-known name for this partial disavowal of social situatedness, a simultaneous impulse to veil the mystery of how artists and writers manage to get themselves provided for and to offer that mystery as a sort of tourist attraction. Since the early nineteenth century, the mysterious location of art on the social scale or in the social landscape—the choice of metaphor cannot be innocent—has been assigned the floating place name of Bohemia. An urban underworld, a miraculously self-sustaining counter-cultural neighborhood, both glamorous and impoverished, where avant-garde art is produced and, or rather because, the usual social rules are suspended, Bohemia has often been described as a myth.[8] If so, it is a myth that was useful both to artists and to bourgeois society. It was useful to artists because it permitted them to believe they could sustain themselves without compromising themselves. It was useful to bourgeois society because it encouraged values of radical individualism, transgression, novelty, and experimentation that were necessary to an emergent consumerism but conflicted with traditional social codes. And this double usefulness helps explain the interesting and little-noticed fact that, from Balzac's *Illusions perdues* and Flaubert's *L'éducation sentimentale* to Hanif Kureishi's *The Buddha of Suburbia* and Jamaica Kincaid's *Lucy*, the protagonists of upward mobility stories so often spend a significant portion of their time in a Bohemian setting.

---

[8] See, for example, Elizabeth Wilson, *Bohemians: The Glamorous Outcasts* (New Brunswick, N.J.: Rutgers University Press, 2000).

The affinity between the upward mobility story and Bohemia brings out a provocatively value-laden twist or bias of the genre (if it is a genre) that might otherwise be eclipsed both by its indulgence of wish-fulfilment fantasy and by its comforting, predictable satire of the parvenu. Almost hidden between these two central tendencies, one finds something one might not have expected to find: the paradox or utopia of rising *without* rising, of success that would somehow evade the ethical self-betrayal of assimilation into the ruling order. According to Pierre Bourdieu, Bohemia is the place where commercial failure signifies artistic success and commercial success signifies artistic failure. Like a latter-day Masterman, Bourdieu asserts confidently that art and thought can be true to themselves—that is, to their oppositional role—only by failing to be recognized by a society whose values are conventional and mercenary. But there are two problems with this argument. First, it cannot explain what the novel most wants to know: how the residents of Bohemia in fact keep body and soul together. That is why, like Wells's era of genuine gentility, Bohemia's "golden age of authenticity . . . untainted by commercialism and tourists" (9) is always seen as already gone or at the point of disappearing.[9] And it is why Bourdieu must concede that Bohemia's secret, the only way in which the paradox can be sustained, is the artist's offstage possession of an independent income. "The artist cannot triumph on the symbolic terrain except by losing on the economic terrain (at least in the short run)," Bourdieu writes, "and vice versa (at least in the long run). It is this paradoxical economy that gives inherited economic properties all their weight—also in a very paradoxical manner—and in particular a private income, the condition of survival in the absence of a market. . . . As in *Sentimental Education*, 'inheritors' hold a decisive advantage when it comes to pure art: inherited economic capital, which removes the constraints and demands of immediate needs (those of journalism, for example, which overcame a Théophile Gautier) and makes it possible to 'hold on' in the absence of a market, is one of the most important factors in the differential success of avant-garde enterprises, with their doomed or else very long-term investments" (83–84). This helps explain the novel's persistent and embarrassing inability to do without the seemingly anachronistic convention of the inheritance.

The second problem with Bourdieu's formulation is that, again like Masterman's, it precludes any socially recognized success that would not involve artistic and political self-betrayal. Even while acknowledging the bohemian's likely dependence on "a private income," Bourdieu leaves no room for any

---

[9] Pierre Bourdieu, *The Rules of Art: Genesis and Structure of the Literary Field*, trans. Susan Emanuel (Stanford, Calif.: Stanford University Press, 1995).

accomplishment on "the economic terrain," any means of coming into a state of provisional economic sufficiency or independence that he would not describe as "artistic failure" or selling out. Yet surely the whole point of Bohemia, from the perspective of the novel as much as that of the artist, was to permit a certain experimentation with social possibilities that could not be imagined elsewhere, unprecedented selves to be fashioned and roles to be rehearsed that were not merely imaginary escapes but called out for some form of generalized social embodiment. If art could signify both a radical opposition to the status quo and an almost magical means of raising oneself out of poverty, then Bohemia, as the site where it oscillated between these meanings, became associated with the hypothesis that they might somehow be united—with the hypothesis, in short, that there might be something resembling a socially radical or responsible version of upward mobility.

One of the few novels Miles Franklin mentions by name is George Du Maurier's *Trilby* (1894), which contributed enormously to the already popular image of the artistic life of Paris's Quartier Latin.[10] At the center of *Trilby* is the unconsummated love between Little Billee, one of three British artists sharing a Parisian loft, and Trilby, an enchanting and impoverished English girl who delivers milk, chatters away in French slang, poses for painters in the nude, and lives in gay bohemian innocence without the benefits of respectability. When she comes to the attention of the Englishman's highly respectable family, they suspect her of scheming to catch a rich husband (a well-established plot convention, since for centuries this was the only way a woman might imagine achieving upward mobility) and arrive in Paris to head off the *mésalliance*. Trilby nobly renounces all claims and disappears without a word. Five years later, however, she reappears. She who could not sing a note is now the greatest singer in Europe thanks to her musical mentor Svengali, the talented but sinister Jew who once lived in the same bohemian poverty but now rides the wave of her, or rather their, artistic accomplishment.

This upward mobility story is easily missed, distracted as the reader is by the picturesque delights of bohemian love and by a tour guide voice that is solidly and complacently aligned with the three respectable Britons. Upward mobility is not on their agenda. In Paris they are merely slumming, absenting themselves for a time from gentility. Once they have returned to England and their habitual levels of comfort—"well groomed, frock-coated, shirt-collared within an inch of their lives" (175)—they will look back on Bohemia as a stage of life whose loss, though painful, was no less inevitable

---

[10] George Du Maurier, *Trilby* (1894; Harmondsworth: Penguin, 1994).

than the passage from youth to maturity. In spite of them and almost in spite of itself, however, the novel obliges us to imagine Bohemia as something that persists and indeed follows after them, and in so doing gives to social relations not just an alternative style but an alternative content. This is accomplished by the bohemian upward mobility story of Trilby and Svengali. The revulsion the three friends come to feel for their fellow bohemian, Svengali, when he shows up in London seems only partly racial. It also includes the establishment's disgust for the Uriah Heep–like figure of the parvenu. But Svengali lacks the gentlemanly dignity of the British artists precisely because he is a true bohemian. He both fawns and mocks, thereby embodying Bohemia's two-faced relation to the rest of society. And society must accept this, for it is Svengali to whom the novel gives genius. It is his artistic talent, detached from his own racially stigmatized body and relocated via mesmerism in his surrogate, that makes possible the conjoined social rise— makes it possible, that is, as something more than a simple abomination in respectable eyes.

The pairing of Trilby and Svengali strikes the British artists as incomprehensible. But if Trilby is not, as she appears to Little Billee's family, the designing villain of a classic female upward mobility plot, hence just as sinister as Svengali, she does bring along with her a social disturbance that transcends her own personal innocence. By acting as Svengali's surrogate, it is as if Trilby forces a general acceptance and even celebration of his rudely upthrusting talent, and does so in spite of everything else society feels about him. And though she pays a high price for her surrogacy—via mesmerism she is merged in her male counterpart with almost supernatural thoroughness, more so than she would have been in a conventional marriage—she is strangely unable to let anyone forget the blow she has struck against society or to let them forget the countersociety she and Svengali together embody. Even after Svengali's cruelty has been exposed to her true friends and Trilby is on the point of death, the fact that Svengali and not Little Billee has carried her off resonates with a truth that cannot, it seems, be taken back. It is Svengali's name that Trilby murmurs as she dies. "That ruffian's name on her lips!" (264), as Little Billee exclaims, expresses the intensity of the author's own apparent sense of violation. One thinks of the ending of *Jane Eyre*, in which the novel's last words are given to St John Rivers, another mentor figure whom neither the reader nor the heroine prefers in marriage, and yet who presides over her social self-fashioning in ways that a mere husband seemingly cannot.

Thus the mention of *Trilby* in *My Brilliant Career* is unexpectedly pertinent. For though that novel is never set in any actual Bohemia, its resolution offers a sort of bohemian surprise. The heroine suddenly refuses to wed the same highly desirable man, his wealth now restored by a timely inheritance; she announces instead that she has chosen a life of writing. However abrupt and awkward, this decision to become a writer rather than to marry can be said to *work*, I think, and the reason is that here, as in *Trilby*, art becomes a figure for a social relation. To be precise, *My Brilliant Career* turns success as a writer into a defiant identification with the lives of Australia's ordinary working people: "I am proud that I am an Australian, a daughter of the Southern Cross, a child of the mighty bush. I am thankful I am a peasant, a part of the bone and muscle of my nation, and earn my bread by the sweat of my brow, as man was meant to do. I rejoice I was not born a parasite, one of the blood-suckers who loll on velvet and satin, crushed from the proceeds of human sweat and blood and souls" (257). The implicit term of contrast is the proposed marriage, though she seems to forget that her suitor is hardly a lolling bloodsucker. More important and more surprising, however, is the implicit continuity with her own childhood, which she had once seemed so eager to leave behind. Once writing seemed to require, and to take its value from, total separation from that laborious childhood. Now, on the contrary, it is presented as reaching back to include that childhood, indeed as an ideal synthesis between the contradictory values of labor and leisure, of her (lower) social origin and her (higher) social destination. What she wants out of writing, if not necessarily what it is guaranteed to provide, is an answer to the implied charge that success will mean self-betrayal: a plausible means of remaining loyal to her society of origin while also leaving it.

There are no such visions at the end of Wells's *Kipps*, yet the ending again differs slightly and interestingly from a mere renunciation of upward mobility. Kipps ends the novel as the proprietor of a bookshop, thus fulfilling a slowly developing dream that has been nurtured by his acquaintance with Masterman. This cultural self-employment is made financially possible because, as I said, Kipps does not lose all the money he has inherited. We discover well after the fact that in his brief period of prosperity he had given money to one Chitterlow, an aspiring playwright who had knocked him down with his bicycle while he was still poor and then befriended him. The gift was presented under the fiction of investing in a quarter-share of the latter's as yet unproduced play. Chitterlow must be described as a bohemian. He both does and does not belong to the society into which Kipps is ascending. He is an educated man, but it is clear that when Kipps attains full and fearsome gentility, Chitterlow will be discovered to be unpresentable. When he "loom[s] up" suddenly in Kipps's "new world" (166) and is explained as "a Nacter chap" who "writes plays" (167), the genteel fiancée quickly insinuates that he does not "compel her complete confidence" (168). Once again, the bohemian is at the margins of social respectability. And once again, much more strangely, he is also somehow a source of funds. Kipps was completely disinterested when he invested in Chitterlow's play. Yet in a variant of the last-minute inheritance motif, the long-forgotten play turns out in the end to be an enormous success, and the philanthropic pseudo-investment, which Chitterlow respects as real, turns out to be a gold mine. The only part of his inheritance that Kipps retains is the part that he had freely given away.

There is a reasonably close parallel here to that aspect of the ending of *Great Expectations* that most readers probably find least memorable. Pip, who has never taken money for himself from Miss Havisham and has forfeited the money he took from Magwitch, finds himself provided for (as a clerk—something less than a gentleman, but more suitable to what he has now become than a return to manual labor at the forge would be) only because of the money he once gave, and persuaded Miss Havisham to give, to his impecunious friend Herbert. Following the money trail leads again to a semibohemian relationship between men, set apart from marriage, functioning as the paradigm of a society that is almost but not quite self-sustaining. In each case, there must be patronage from outside. But in each case the internal recirculation of outside funds allows the original project of ambitious status seeking (the great expectations) to be succeeded by a chastened, subdued version of upward mobility, a climbing of the social ladder that paradoxically happens under the sign of democracy, reciprocity, and responsibility.

The same principle can of course coexist with a heterosexual love story, though perhaps not with the love story's most passionately orthodox forms. In Jamaica Kincaid's *Lucy*, a Caribbean au pair eventually leaves her employers behind (having watched their marriage disintegrate and caught its disintegration on camera) and embarks on a life among artists in which she can work with photography, something she enjoys more than caring for children.[11] Lucy is not interested in status or material wealth; she probably has more access to luxuries as an au pair than in her independence afterward. Yet this certainly deserves to be called an upward mobility story. And its symbolic center, picking up and carrying on her identification with Gauguin, is the bohemian world of her lover Paul—not Paul himself, whom she coolly treats as expendable, nor the mere fact of her having a lover who is also something of a mentor, but rather the social milieu into which their relationship introduces her, a milieu of irresponsible artists, "people who stand apart" (98). Bohemia here does just what it did in *Trilby*: it launders Lucy's upward mobility, refiguring it both as the taking of an acceptable distance

---

[11] Jamaica Kincaid, *Lucy* (New York: Farrar Straus Giroux, 1990).

from her (lower) society of origin and at the same time as a means of remaining true to that society, taking responsibility for it. Lucy's photographs offer a thinly disguised parallel to Kincaid's own career of writing about the Caribbean, and her departure from it, to a largely North American audience. They both carry the protagonist into a higher society and yet also prevent what might be called her social climbing from counting as an instance of incontrovertible treason to her origin.

Picaro, Parvenu, Pariah

A stubbornly hostile viewer could of course question whether Lucy's sudden attraction to the loft-living Paul might not result from a channeling of erotic energy to self-interested ends. Is Lucy seeking a new self, or is she self-seeking? The skeptical view of the upwardly mobile heroine's motives goes back well before Fielding's hostile makeover of Pamela into Shamela. Before the novel existed, theatrical comedy was already getting easy laughs by mocking braggarts, imposters, and clowns who pretend to be or try to become what they are not. From its origins on, the novel abounds in stories that are told from the point of view of what we can call, with studied vagueness, the upper classes, and that look down with mild ridicule or moralistic contempt at someone who is trying to escape from his or her natural, predestined social place. It is tempting therefore to narrate the history of fiction about upward mobility, following Erich Auerbach on the representation of reality in general, as a move away from the standard of comic disapproval and toward a perspective closer to that of the parvenu himself, a more sympathetic, less judgmental treatment.[12] This is the story Peter Brooks tells about the emergence of French and English realism from Spanish picaresque: "By the nineteenth century, the *pícaro*'s scheming to stay alive has typically taken a more elaborated and socially defined form: it has become ambition. It may in fact be a defining characteristic of the modern novel (as of bourgeois society) that it takes aspiration, getting ahead, seriously, rather than simply as an object of satire (which was the case in much earlier, more aristocratically determined literature), and thus makes ambition the vehicle and emblem of Eros, that which totalizes the world as possession and progress" (39).[13]

---

[12] Erich Auerbach, *Mimesis: The Representation of Reality in Western Literature*, trans. Willard R. Trask (Princeton, N.J.: Princeton University Press, 1953).

[13] Peter Brooks, *Reading for the Plot: Design and Intention in Narrative* (New York: Vintage, 1984).

This large and valuable hypothesis enables us to pose some further questions. What about the ambitions of those below or to the left of bourgeois society? Are there no upward mobility stories of the working class or of those (often within it) who for better or worse prefer to see their state of initial disadvantage in ethnic, racial, or gender terms? And is there not a tension between Eros and ambition over which is to be the vehicle and emblem of which? How much of the novel's Eros belongs to Eros itself—that is, to the linked histories of gender and sexuality, histories whose claims to priority are at least arguably comparable to the claims of class? Vautrin tells Rastignac in *Père Goriot* that what women really want in a man is ambition. This is a convenient premise for the novel of upward mobility, but its convenience is also cause for misgiving. What about the equal and opposite sexiness of the young man's *refusal* of ambition, as for example in Fabrice of Stendhal's *La chartreuse de Parme* or Kiyoaki in Mishima's *Spring Snow*?[14] One can only begin to indicate the many ways in which the linearity of the Auerbachian history might need to be inflected by such factors. If the Pamela/Shamela ambiguity clearly results in part from a difference in class perspective—looking up from below one sees the virtuous Pamela, and looking down from above one sees the designing Shamela—that ambiguity is also gendered. The spotless absoluteness of Pamela's virtue, with its irresistible invitation to mudslinging, is produced in part by the patriarchal injunction that makes it difficult if not impossible for a woman to be conscious of her own social ambition without being universally perceived as a monster. Moll Flanders and Roxana and their descendant Becky Sharp can do without this cultivated unconsciousness only at the cost of being identified as criminals.

The historical hypothesis of a growing respect for ambition is also vulnerable to contestation in its own terms. The novel's early "conservative" tellings, to use Michael McKeon's word, are balanced from very early on by "progressive" versions that allow themselves more sympathy for the pretender or parvenu.[15] If the novel is not, pace Marthe Robert, on the parvenu's side, "a commoner made good who will always stand out as something of an upstart, even a bit of a swindler, among the established genres"

---

[14] D. A. Miller speaks, for example, of "Fabrice's inability to cathect the plot of worldly ambition that Gina and Mosca seek to promote for him" in "Body Bildung and Textual Liberation," in Denis Hollier, ed., *A New History of French Literature* (Cambridge, Mass.: Harvard University Press, 1989), 684.

[15] Michael McKeon, *The Origins of the English Novel 1600–1740* (Baltimore: Johns Hopkins University Press, 1987).

(3), neither must it await the rise of realism in order to be something other than generically snobbish, committed to satirize or criminalize all upstarts.[16] McKeon suggests that aside from an alternation between conservative and progressive tellings, there is no historical regularity in the upward mobility story at all. This blurred irregularity is especially noticeable at the other, far end of the Auerbachian history, during and after the flood tide of realism. This is when the story of ambition must be supposed to have come into its own. Has it?[17]

Consider the linkage of ambition and Eros in Gissing's *Born in Exile*. The novel possesses no Bohemia, and this lack is presented at least half seriously as the reason why the protagonist's hopes of upward mobility are thwarted. Godwin Peak claims that only genteel women, who look down on him and his unconventional beliefs, are sexual, while women who share his skepticism are not: "The truly emancipated woman . . . is almost always asexual" (202). The ideal synthesis of sexuality and emancipation is explicitly associated with Bohemia, but he denies there is such a thing: "'An ideal!' exclaimed Peak. 'An ideal akin to Murger's and Musset's grisettes, who never existed'" (114). His eventual benefactor, Marcella, feels the same disappointment when she seeks out an author who sounds like a kindred spirit and discovers not a free-thinking salonnière but a proper lady in her parlor (237). What is crucial here is not that an English Bohemia does not exist—its verifiable existence has never been its strong point even on the Continent—but rather that even the *idea* of it does not turn Gissing's protagonist on. Peak finds no emancipated women who are sexual not because there are none, but because the women he *does* sexualize are their opposites: ladies swathed in respectability and the hierarchy for which they stand. He has invested his desire in that code of gentility in terms to which he does not measure up. Hence Peak's erotic choices (though not those of his author) can come only from those above him.[18]

This conservative vector of erotic choice might be correlated with a pattern of sociocultural development, often seen as characteristically English, in which the aristocracy continues to wield what looks like a disproportionate

---

[16] Marthe Robert, *Origins of the Novel* (1972; Bloomington: Indiana University Press, 1980).

[17] On this period, see Franco Moretti, "'A Useless Longing for Myself': The Crisis of the European Bildungsroman, 1898–1914," in Ralph Cohen, ed., *Studies in Historical Change* (Charlottesville: University Press of Virginia, 1992), 43–59.

[18] The lower-middle-class Gissing himself was repeatedly entangled with working-class women. This is not the only sense in which his own life—that of the successful but principled author of *New Grub Street* rather than either of the writers it represents, one successful and the other principled—cannot be figured within his fiction.

amount of cultural influence long after a supposed bourgeois revolution was to have generalized the middle-class values of Weber's Protestant ethic.[19] The failure of the middle class to supplant its aristocratic predecessors in the domain of culture helps explain, in other words, why a text like *Born in Exile* is still sexualizing the genteel world of the leisured, a world supported by independent income emanating from undeclared sources, so long into the period of realism when hard-working self-reliance was to have become the norm. Or why Wells, whose protagonist does escape from his sexual enthrallment to his superiors, rewrites Dickens forty years later from a perspective that is not less but more blandly patronizing toward the "dismal little figure" of its protagonist than Dickens was to Pip.

This may not make us like the upward mobility story more, but it has at least one benefit. In the larger landscape of world literature, the stubborn cultural power of a seemingly outmoded aristocracy makes the English case not exceptional but representative. Even a quick survey of other national traditions reveals that much of the novel's treatment of upward mobility continues to come from the perspective of the aristocracy—often a declining aristocracy, but an aristocracy nonetheless. The great Italian realist Giovanni Verga, whose *Mastro don Gesualdo* (1888) was translated by D. H. Lawrence, features a protagonist who "started as a navvy, with stones on his shoulder," yet as a character correctly prophesies, "in a very little while you'll be able to say that Mastro-don Gesualdo is the boss of the place!" (42). How is this ascent seen? "Nowadays there's no respect for anybody. Nowadays it's whoever has got the money is in the right. . . . Today there's no other God. You can be a gentleman—or a girl born of a good family! But if you've got no fortune!—Whereas one who has sprung from nothing—like Mastro-don Gesualdo, for example—!" (24).[20] Though Verga is not uncritical of the people of "good family" who make statements like this and might insinuate that by its bad behavior the falling nobility has forfeited its right to judge, there is no class perspective in the novel to which he is closer.

Writing in Hungary in 1942, Sándor Márai centers his novel *Embers* in an aristocrat's view of his best friend's upward mobility. The friend, Konrad, has disappeared mysteriously. The disappearance comes after a hunting incident in which the aristocrat, Henrik, thinks that Konrad has wanted and perhaps even planned to kill him. Later he visits Konrad's apartment and decides that this is because Konrad has been having an affair with his, Henrik's,

---

[19] See Perry Anderson, *English Questions* (London: Verso, 1992).

[20] Giovanni Verga, *Mastro Don Gesualdo*, trans. D. H. Lawrence (1888; Sawtry: Dedalus, 1984).

wife.[21] If there is an erotic entanglement between friend and wife, as seems likely, is it the work of Eros or ambition? Nothing other than ambition is allowed onstage to explain it. The one active ingredient in the men's friendship, the only instability pointing toward a possible passage from absolute loyalty to suspicions of the desire to murder, is the much-stressed fact that, though both are from well-born families, Konrad is poor and Henrik rich. But this action-oriented and even melodramatic account gives precisely the wrong idea of the novel. The friendship between Konrad and Henrik is presented largely in retrospect, and from Henrik's point of view. At the time of the retrospective narration, forty-one years after the action takes place, both men are seventy-five years old, and Konrad too has acquired—via inheritance, then years of work in Southeast Asian colonies—all the material possessions he requires. There is an upward mobility story here, indeed one that is central to the plot. But this story is almost totally concealed by the facts of Konrad's high ancestry and by the narrative viewpoint of Henrik, who is born with everything a human being could desire and thus has no need to rise. Upward mobility disappears into their shared old age and into the articulation of a matching philosophy: an old man's philosophy of disinterestedness or generosity so profound as to become almost indifference, indeed almost deathlike. It is as if the novel equated an old man's wisdom with an old world aristocrat's wisdom: the passive wisdom of the futility of striving, coupled with active contempt for a new world in which material striving has become all-pervasive. Extraneous to the plot but central to the exposition of this philosophy is the figure of Henrik's ninety-one-year-old servant, Nini. Nini embodies a happy, self-forgetful subservience. She lives, indeed has always lived since she arrived at the age of sixteen, only in order to offer perfect service to her employer. Omniscient, she is also perpetually unmoved, thus echoing Henrik's willingness to pardon and even find value in Konrad's passion from a position of utter withdrawal from all passions, including the passion for revenge.

Writing her *Rahel Varnhagen: The Life of a Jewess* in roughly the same period, Hannah Arendt used the word *parvenu* to sum up Rahel's eager efforts to assimilate into aristocratic German society, culminating in her baptism. Arendt's preference and self-description is the pariah. Judith Shklar

---

[21] Sándor Márai, *Embers*, trans. Carol Brown Janeway (1942; New York: Knopf, 2001). It is perhaps worth noting the similar use of colonial exoticism in *Effi Briest*, including the "Chinaman" buried in Kessin (73), the trade-related cosmopolitanism that ought to have turned the town into more fun, and Instetten's late reflection that a meaningful life would have required going to the colonies.

comments: "The choice of the word parvenu to describe this humiliating be-havior is not insignificant. It is *the* classic snob word, which is thrown at the *bourgeois gentilhomme* by the aristocrats whom he tries to join, and at the 'new rich' by those who have inherited their money. The parvenu is a univer-sal figure of ridicule and contempt. That she should have used this word for assimilated Jews tells us a good deal about Arendt. The pariah is so sure of her superiority that she no longer wishes to make efforts to join the larger so-ciety. She has, in fact, absorbed the attitudes of its upper class so completely that there is no impulse for her to rise from her actual condition" (363).[22]

To see these three texts side by side is to feel the power that an aristo-cratic perspective continues to exert on various national traditions well into the twentieth century. And to add Arendt to the other two is to feel how strongly this force works on those who, like Gissing, are not aristocrats but self-described pariahs, literary outsiders who somehow fall into the ideolog-ical orbit of the aristocracy in the course of becoming writers and intellectu-als. The viewpoint of the aristocracy rhymes handily with the viewpoint of literature itself. This is precisely the transfer we observe in Wells's Master-man: the writer or intellectual identifying himself with the declining gentry or aristocracy (intimations of mortality included) at the expense of the new money, which is to say at the expense of those with whom his own location among the aspiring have-not's would seem to ally him.

Master, Man, Mentor

If identifications like this are a large and representative fact about the social placement of the writer, then it is clear why there can be no simple linear history of the upward mobility story. One never arrives at that hypothetical point where the narrative perspective shifts from a predominantly negative to a predominantly positive view of the aspiring protagonist—unless per-haps when the story is recast as tragedy, as in *Jude the Obscure*. Much can no doubt be inferred from upward mobility stories about changes in who runs society, but the result of this inference would have to be a complicated figure in which Raymond Williams's useful categories of dominant, residual, and

---

[22] Hannah Arendt, *Rahel Varnhagen: The Life of a Jewess*, ed. Liliane Weissberg, trans. Richard Winston and Clara Winston (1957; Baltimore: Johns Hopkins University Press, 1997); Judith N. Shklar, "Hannah Arendt as Pariah," in Stanley Hoffmann, ed., *Political Thought and Political Thinkers* (Chicago: University of Chicago Press, 1998), 362–75. Thanks to Ross Posnock for the reference.

emergent would be hard to distinguish from one another. This is in part because, as I noted above, Masterman's aristocratic critique of social climbing is also a disguised means of social climbing—intended, by definition, for nonaristocrats. So the writer's aristocratic identification does not entail a simple rejection of upward mobility, nor a simple embrace, even a wishful one, of everything the aristocracy stands for. But this blurring of class identifications also reveals the genre's best or most salvageable side.

The class-blurring role that Masterman plays in *Kipps* is that of a mentor or mediator. Among the most distinctive formal characteristics of the fiction of social climbing, the mentor personifies much of what Bohemia spatializes. Hence they often overlap, as in the character of Masterman. Upwardly mobile himself in spite of his admonition against it, Masterman is located, structurally speaking, midway between the upper-class fiancée, on the one hand, and the lower-class sweetheart, on the other—another woman who must reject upward mobility absolutely in order to be classified as virtuous. Masterman shares with the fiancée his pride in his education, and he shares with the sweetheart his rejection of upward mobility. The convention by which marriage indicates a definitive choice of values would omit this mediation between the two sets of values. But it is precisely the mediation, rather than one set or the other, that the novel comes closest to choosing. In this sense we would have to understand Masterman's name as neither announcing a Nietzschean *Übermensch* nor taking the part of the masters against the men, but rather as suggesting that Masterman is both master *and* man, or something that is not quite the one nor quite the other. The same might be said of Balzac's considerably more satanic Vautrin. Vautrin makes the case for rather than against the protagonist's unscrupulous upward mobility. But he too is distinguishable from his advice. For that advice—about treating society as a jungle of competing self-interests—is contradicted by the at least partly altruistic bond of friendship he himself seeks to establish with Rastignac. Just as Masterman's refusal of upward mobility involves entering into a relationship that entails upward mobility of a certain chastened sort, so Vautrin's endorsement of upward mobility involves entering into a social relationship that transcends the social climber's pure self-interest. Mediation commits him to a counterintuitive and even inexplicable benevolence to the protagonist as well as an evasion of good/bad binaries. Both bestow on the mentor, whatever his other traits, a touch of the sinister. As sites of power's vulnerability, transit points where some degree of power can change hands, these figures embody the great novelistic principle that the Rolling Stones named "sympathy for the devil." Hence the structural devilishness that Masterman and Lucy's innocuous lover share with the more obviously diabolical

company of Vautrin, Svengali, and—to take a more recent example—
Hannibal Lecter.

The mentor might be said to descend from Cinderella's fairy godmother,
or more generally from those "helping" figures whom Vladimir Propp
called, in his essay on the folktale, "donors." In a commentary on Propp,
Fredric Jameson suggests that the donor embodies the very essence of the
story, for better than anything else in the narrative this figure "explains" the
all-important transition from have-not to have, from initial lack to final triumph.[23] The suggestion is so useful not because it applies everywhere but
because it reveals both similarities and significant differences. Consider for
example one subgenre of female gothic, or upward-mobility-via-marriage as
told from a woman's point of view. Here the crucial fact, based in the actual
subordination of women, is that in effect the fairy godmother and Prince
Charming are the same figure, the two combining to form a beast or ogre
who is perhaps susceptible of redemption. When she wrote *Rebecca*, an offspring of *Jane Eyre* and a classic of the genre, Daphne Du Maurier was
much more charmed by her own version of her grandfather's Svengali, an
older and (here) richer man who is asked to play the parts of conventional
husband and sinister mentor at the same time. And she wrote more into her
lowly heroine's magical ascension than a simple acquiescence in or enjoyment of a place at the top of the social hierarchy. After the events of the
novel are past, the heroine sees an allegory of them in a dream about Manderley, the house that she won by her efforts but that then burned down: "I
saw that the garden had obeyed the jungle law, even as the woods had done.
The rhododendrons stood fifty feet high, twisted and entwined with
bracken, and they had entered into alien marriage with a host of nameless
shrubs, poor, bastard things that clung with about their roots as though conscious of their spurious origin. A lilac had mated with a copper beech."
(2).[24] The "alien marriage" among the flora is of course her own. The devastation she sees is the democratic result, seemingly unwilled by her, of the mat-
ing between Manderley and her own "spurious origin." Even when the mentor does not, like Masterman or Vautrin, disappear from the plot in the
middle, but persists into the ending in the form of a husband, the sinister

---

[23] Fredric Jameson, *The Prison-House of Language: A Critical Account of Structuralism and
Russian Formalism* (Princeton, N.J.: Princeton University Press, 1972), 67.

[24] Daphne Du Maurier, *Rebecca* (1938; New York: Avon, 1971). The passage goes on: "Nettles
were everywhere, the vanguard of the army. They choked the terrace, they sprawled about the paths,
they leant, vulgar and lanky, against the very windows of the house" (3). This reminds us of the
complicity between the heroine and Rebecca herself, who has loosed her vulgar lover on the place.

note does not necessarily disappear, and the final outcome is not necessarily an affirmation of the status quo.

The persistence of motifs like the fairy godmother into more or less sophisticated fiction might tempt us to set a positive, fairy-tale view of upward mobility, expressing the desires of the disadvantaged in somewhat crude form, against a largely negative and often aristocratic view, expressing itself in the refined mode of narrative irony. It is true of course that the *Pamela* formula approaches the pole of pure propaganda, as in the Sunday School–like fictions of Horatio Alger and Samuel Smiles, intended to inspire children and other supposedly impressionable souls to feel that virtue (of a certain sort) will indeed be rewarded. And it is true that the contrary formula by which great expectations are chastised or chastened, as in Dickens and Wells, is on the other hand readily identified as "literary" by virtue of the severe disciplining it administers to simple wish-fulfilment. And yet the subtlest effects of literary distancing pervade those examples of the genre that come up most bluntly from below.[25] Consider how Naipaul's *The Mystic Masseur* (1957), Tayeb Salih's *Season of Migration to the North* (1966), and Tsitsi Dangarembga's *Nervous Conditions* (1988) all deploy the same estranging device: a primary protagonist, who is upwardly mobile in a dramatic and threatening way, is observed from a distance by a secondary character, who is also upwardly mobile but in a less dramatic, perhaps more cowardly or more scrupulous way. It is this secondary character who serves as the narrator, thus weaving a web of potential irony around the central story.[26] Arguably this ironic self-consciousness reflects a certain belatedness vis-à-vis the European novel, which was in a sense looking over these authors' shoulders when they treated themes of social aspiration and personal development. This was also Joyce's case. Thus his *Portrait of the Artist as a Young Man* comes to seem a more paradigmatic instance.

"At long range," Harry Levin once remarked, *Wuthering Heights* looks like "a variant of the demon-lover motif," and *Good Soldier Schweik* is "one

---

[25] Abraham Cahan's classic first-person novel, *The Rise of David Levinsky* (1917), is an elegant trap for unwary identifications. Like many would-be heroes of nonfiction, the protagonist of Junot Diaz's *Drown* (1996) rewrites the American Dream as the fragile day-to-day success of a New York drug dealer. That is the endpoint of his immigrant family's saga, but he breaks up the chronological sequence to end the book with his father's story rather than his own, thus restoring heroic freshness to a faded tale. Abraham Cahan, *The Rise of David Levinsky* (Harmondsworth: Penguin, 1993); Junot Diaz, *Drown* (New York: Riverhead, 1996).

[26] V. S. Naipaul, *The Mystic Masseur* (New York: Vintage, 1957); Tayeb Salih, *Season of Migration to the North*, trans. Denys Johnson-Davies (1966; London: Heinemann, 1969); Tsitsi Dangarembga, *Nervous Conditions* (Seattle: Seal Press, 1989).

of many folk-tales about shrewd simpletons."[27] By noting how often such tales are embedded within realism and inform its interest in social mobility, Levin urges us to ask whether, at least from long range, we can perceive the novel's folkloric borrowings as expressions of the wishes of the poor. The answer seems to be mixed even within the folktale itself. The folktale has its own means of distancing and control; it can as easily frustrate as fulfill those wishes. The Danish fairy tale writer Hans Christian Andersen had no peer in the cravenness with which he licked the boots of the wealthy. In tales like "The Little Mermaid" and "She Was No Good," the poor are indeed "good": they struggle to be content with their assigned place and willingly die rather than upset the social order that keeps them down.[28] When Andersen does portray successful mobility, for example in the male Cinderella story "Clod Hans," he does it (as Auerbach might say) without seriousness. Even "The Ugly Duckling," probably his most famous upward mobility story, is difficult not to read as flattering an aristocratic preference for birth as opposed to merit: going from ugly to beautiful means realizing you were born not to be a duck but to be a swan. Blood will tell. The joke—unless it's another sign of the ugly duckling's disguised natural superiority—is that no other animal acknowledges the superiority of swans, which the duckling feels instinctively the first time he sees them. While allowing the duckling to climb the social ladder, in other words, the story also gives the ladder metaphor a gentle shake, asking us to experiment with the alternative notion of distinct cultural species, arranged side by side, each deluded into thinking itself superior.

Taking sides with nature, even a nonhierarchical nature, would seem to mean taking sides with an aristocratic ideology. When Charlotte Brontë rewrites "The Ugly Duckling" in *Jane Eyre*, she takes the opposite side: her "plain Jane" stands for middle-class merit, merit that reveals itself in competition with an array of women who are born beautiful and whose beauty stands for a social order based on birth. Yet the countermetaphor of diverse natural species can also produce a similar argument in favor of upward mobility, or in favor of a mobility that chooses not to see itself as pointing upward: the liberal individualist argument that translates mobility into self-expression (of one's nature) rather than into the gaining of an advantage over others. Should we prefer the ladder, with its muted suggestion

---

[27] Harry Levin, *The Gates of Horn: A Study of Five French Realists* (New York: Oxford University Press, 1966), 64.

[28] Hans Christian Andersen, *The Complete Fairy Tales and Stories*, trans. Erik Christian Haugaard (New York: Random House, 1974).

(a seesaw would be more emphatic) of a zero-sum relation between your success and my failure? Or is there a third option?

When it takes folktale motifs as its raw material, the novel likes to remind us both of its omniverous universality and of its ironic distance from the vulgarity of popular plotting. In Yukio Mishima's *Spring Snow*, the Japanese protagonists, listening to a royal visitor from Thailand talk about the stories told him by his nurse, are "surprised to find that many of the fairy tales that had been told to them were very similar to the prince's story" (230).[29] But the beautiful maiden who is about to marry a prince instead chooses suddenly to hide herself away in a nunnery. Theodor Fontane's *Effi Briest*, in which a young girl does marry a high official, is full of early references to Cinderella.[30] The point is ironic: her prince will not turn out to be nearly charming enough. Like *Trilby*, each of these novels invokes folktale motifs while looking down at upward mobility from a point higher on the social ladder. In so doing, each also offers evidence of the specificity of its national context. In *Effi Briest*, the Cinderella-like heroine belongs by birth to the same (aristocratic) stratum of society as her much-older husband. Nor is there (as in so many English novels) a significant difference of wealth between bride and groom. Yet there is enough difference to animate the theme of careerism and upward mobility, the difference being the status conferred on the husband by virtue of his position as a high official of Bismarck's government. The hero of *Spring Snow*, son of what the translator calls a "Marquis," is raised so very high in the world that he has nothing left to desire. His rebellion, expressed as lethargy and transgressive eroticism, represents his identification, over the head of his immensely wealthy, powerful, and aristocratic father, with the samurai values of a provincial aristocracy that had not yet been subordinated to the centralized and modernized state.[31]

Here, as in *Effi Briest*, upward mobility is identified with the state, and the renunciation of upward mobility is given no outlet other than death—much the same conclusion that Andersen offered in "The Little Mermaid." Or is it? Like *Kipps* and *Great Expectations*, "The Little Mermaid" ends not

---

[29] Yukio Mishima, *Spring Snow*, trans. Michael Gallagher (1968; New York: Vintage, 1972).

[30] Theodor Fontane, *Effi Briest*, trans. High Rorrison and Helen Chambers (1895; Harmondsworth: Penguin, 1995). More interested in playing tag with her friends than in meeting her grown-up visitor, Effi has been late getting dressed, and reassures her mother: "in five minutes Cinderella will be transformed into a princess" (12). An hour later she has become engaged.

[31] Rebuking the father's upward mobility, the novel also lends some intriguing impulses of sympathy to members of the servant class, like the hero's tutor and the heroine's maid, who must make their own way in the world and in so doing express devious, ambivalent hostility to their masters.

with the failure of the upward mobility project but with a sort of compensatory sequel or afterword. After the heroine's death, she is informed by "the daughters of the air" that she still has something to aspire to. Three hundred years of good deeds will win her an immortal soul. All she has to do is fly invisibly through "the homes of human beings" and smile upon the good children when she finds them. "In three hundred years," she says, "I shall rise like this into God's kingdom" (76). A more modest upward mobility (no marriage with a king's son this time) achieved via zealous surveillance of private citizens on behalf of a higher power: the allegory of the career civil servant is clear, which is not so different from the state-centered life that the protagonists of *Effi Briest* and *Spring Snow* reject. But by its turn back to some version of the general welfare (however sinister), it is different both from natural individualist self-expression and from a ladder-climbing identification with the aristocracy.

The state, which marks a point of national diversity among upward mobility stories, also allows us to attempt some fresh generalizations. The French historian of sociology Charles-Henry Cuin remarks that for many years, while upward mobility was one of the most energetic research fields for American sociology, no French work was done in the field at all—indeed, in France there *was* no field. For French sociologists, this set of problems was dealt with under an entirely different heading: the institutions of education, which are of course state institutions.[32] From this perspective, we might reconsider one of the classic moments in the French fiction of upward mobility: Rastignac's "à nous deux maintenant," addressed as a challenge to the Paris he looks down on from the hill where he has just buried Goriot. Rastignac's story thus far has been an effort to join together Paris with the provinces, where he was born into genteel poverty. If the problem of the upward mobility story is whether one can remain connected to the origins left behind (here represented by Goriot) once one makes one's way upward in the capital, and if so how, then the novel offers two hesitant alternatives to a simple "no." The first is the mentor, Vautrin. The death of fatherhood in Goriot's sense, located in the private home, is the birth of Vautrin's mentorship, which injects self-interest into the absolute personal ties of the family but also refashions the public space of the *pension* into a sort of incipient civil society. As such, it points toward the second answer, the state, conceived as a hypothetical unity that would include both the capital and the provinces, individual aspiration and the good of the social

---

[32] Charles-Henry Cuin, *Les sociologues et la mobilité sociale* (Paris: Presses Universitaires de France, 1993), 27.

whole. For better or worse, this is where Vautrin himself is headed, though not within the covers of *Père Goriot*. Just as Masterman's version of upward mobility leads, via Bohemia, to the modern university, so Vautrin's leads from poetic, beauty-loving criminality to a position as chief of police— another arm of the modern state.

Neither example is very convincing in itself, but the pattern is at least intriguing. For what the state seems to stand for here, if only obliquely, is another version of that bending backward toward the origin and the general welfare that we find in the endings of *My Brilliant Career* and *Lucy*, but that is associated there with a career in art.[33] The idea that the state, like art, can aim stories of upward mobility toward the general welfare is of course somewhat counterintuitive. But if one is willing to accept fragments and variants, this idea is surprisingly pervasive. Pat Barker's *Border Crossing* (2001), which looks through the eyes of a English social worker at his relationship with a troubled and violent adolescent, might be described as the latter's upward mobility story. One would simply add the proviso that the outsider's view from above, which once would have belonged to the genteel, has now been relocated in the helping professions, here not especially prosperous and working as a functionary of the state.[34] The implication is that the social worker's own small privileges are earned by what he does for others not entirely different from himself.

As we have seen, art too is a site of arguments that upward mobility can be earned. Like the state's, which try to resolve some of the same general contradictions, its arguments should always be greeted with a certain skepticism. But they cannot be rejected out of hand in favor of easier, instinctive, caricatural judgments. For the upward mobility story is very much alive, and what is most alive in it, literarily speaking, is often its intricate and ongoing debate over the individual's rise and the general welfare.

Like Naipaul's *The Mystic Masseur* (1957), another first novel, Hanif Kureishi's *The Buddha of Suburbia* (1990) is a portrait of the artist as a young man of South Asian blood. But its title, again like Naipaul's, designates not the artist, but a public charlatan. Why lead into a *Künstlerroman* by means of a suburban guru (the father of Kureishi's protagonist) and an uncredentialed, dangerously ignorant healer (Naipaul's protagonist when he is not

---

[33] Kincaid seems more troubled than Franklin by the question of who might remain excluded from such a synthesis. Aboriginal claims to the land do not arise in *My Brilliant Career*. But I would argue that both there is no version of the general welfare that can escape being so troubled and that the troubling does not discredit the project.

[34] Pat Barker, *Border Crossing* (New York: Farrar, Straus and Giroux, 2001).

writing)? In both novels there is considerable irony directed at these figures, but the irony is undercut by the fact that they are versions of the writer and artist. As such they act out the mystery of how writers and artists sell their wares to an even more ignorant public. It is often hard to tell whether these texts are more ironic at the expense of the artist/charlatan or at the expense of the public to which the artist is appealing. Sometimes it is the one, sometimes the other, and the oscillation between them creates a reasonably neutral space in which upward mobility can occur. Or rather can occur—this is a bit of a shock—without becoming an object of instant and unambiguous satire.

What is still more shocking, however, is the slow realization that, in spite of all the justified ridicule, both artist and charlatan may indeed be rising in the world by doing their public some good. This is clear for example when Naipaul's mystic masseur performs a somewhat impromptu but highly theatrical cure on a boy who is under a cloud (117–25). The cure makes his fortune and does so because it is both good therapy and good literature. Equally decisive in the career of Kureishi's Karim Amir is his wickedly funny theatrical impersonation of a family member, a recent arrival from India, who is physically and socially crippled. He has been warned that public use of his relative's troubled life will constitute a betrayal. He has promised not to betray. Yet he sets to work on "the invention of Changez/Tariq, . . . concentrating for the first time since childhood on something that absorbed me. . . . This was worth doing, this had meaning" (217).[35] Head-on collision seems inevitable between his family's sensibilities and his own sudden conversion to the gospel of hard-working self-reliance. Must one betray one's society of origin in order to make it into the society of destination? The performance is wildly successful, and yet there is no collision, no indignant moral. The object of the impersonation, watching from the audience, has not noticed any resemblance to himself. Another joke on the ignorance of the public—but a decisive one, for it offers the suggestion (while underlining its fragility) that upward mobility need not mean betrayal of the society of origin.

And indeed, as it turns out, such upward movement may serve that society. The final success in the uneven curve of Karim's theatrical career involves "a part in a soap opera which would tangle with the latest contemporary issues: they meant abortions and racist attacks, the stuff that people lived through but that never got on TV. If I accepted the offer I'd play the rebellious son of an Indian shopkeeper" (259). A militant friend has called

---

[35] Hanif Kureishi, *The Buddha of Suburbia* (London: Faber and Faber, 1990).

Karim "you little parvenu!" (166). But what we see here is that there is no hard-and-fast line between the parvenu and the pariah. If his rebellious, critical distance from his Indian family is part of what he sells to the entertainment industry, so is his desire to do and say something about "the stuff" that his family goes through but that never gets on TV, including racist attacks. The parvenu is and remains a pariah. This is why the portrait of the artist on the make makes so successful an image of success—success imagined not as a simple sell-out to the powers that be, but as a negotiation between those powers and the interests of all those who have not risen.

FREDRIC JAMESON

A Businessman in Love

When I ask myself why this extraordinary novel—*Lalka* (*The Doll*, 1890) by
Bolesław Prus, nom de plume of Aleksander Głowacki—is so little known,
so little read in the West, the first answer that inevitably arises has to do with
the so-called small-power languages.[1] Never mind the fact that Polish is the
oldest Slavic literary language, with a rich Renaissance literature dating from
a period in which Poland was the largest country in Europe—a language
that also boasts the greatest romantic poet in any language (he will figure
significantly in *The Doll*). Never mind the heroic stereotype of the Poles as
the Irish of the East, in their gallant doomed revolts against the powerful imperial neighbor and overlord (it will also be a question here of the greatest of
those failed revolutions, the Warsaw uprising of 1863, in which the author
also fought). Never mind the central significance of Poland for European
Jewry—they also play a profoundly historical role here, nor its peculiar class
system—a numerous petty and impoverished nobility and small bourgeoisie,
only slowly emerging in the towns—so alien from the Western experience of
snobbery that the readers of Proust or of English literature in general would
find its social content incomprehensible. *Mais quoy, ils ne portent point de
haut de chausses!*

But perhaps they are remote from us, and too exotic, after all: a businessman in love! Such is the subject of this long masterpiece of postnaturalism,
and to put it this way is for the Western reader to evoke comedy and caricature. Here we do not have the hungry young arriviste of Zola's diptych (*Pot-
bouille/Au bonheur des dames*) or of Maupassant's *Bel ami*: indeed the radical difference of Paris as the very capital of Western modernity will furnish a
stunning bravura excursion at the center of *The Doll*:

> Wokulski walked on and looked attentively at the buildings. What splendid
> shops! Even the most paltry looked better than his, although it was the
> finest in Warsaw. Stone houses: almost each floor had great balconies and
> balustrades along the entire façade. "This Paris looks as though all the
> inhabitants must feel the need of constant communication, either in the cafes

---

[1] The English translation by David Welsh (New York: Twayne, 1972) is not altogether complete
(but its pages are referenced here in the text). UNESCO has published a complete translation into
French in three volumes (*La poupée*). For more on Prus, see Czesław Miłosz, *History of Polish
Literature* (New York: Macmillan, 1969).

or on their balconies," Wokulski thought. The roofs were impressive too, high, loaded with chimney-stacks, prickly with chimney-pots and spires. A tree or lamp or kiosk or column mounted with a globe rose every few paces along the streets. Life was effervescent here, so powerfully that it was unable to use up its energies in the never-ending traffic, in the swift rush of people, in the erection of five-story houses, so it had also burst out of walls in the forms of statues or bas-reliefs, and out of the streets in the shape of innumerable kiosks.

Wokulski felt he had been extricated from stagnant water and suddenly plunged into boiling water which "storms and roars and foams." He, a grown man, energetic in his own climate, felt like a sensitive child here, impressed by everything and everyone. Meanwhile, all around him, the city "seethed and boiled and roared and foamed." Unable to see any end to the crowds, carriages, trees or dazzling store windows, or even of the street itself, Wokulski was gradually overcome with stupefaction. He stopped hearing the passers-by chattering, then grew deaf to the cries of the street traders, finally to the rattle of the wheels. (373)

It's a marvelous city, isn't it?" she exclaimed, suddenly looking into his eyes. "Let people say what they choose, but Paris—even conquered—is still the center of the world. Did it give you that impression?"

"It was very impressive. After a few weeks there I seemed to gain strength and energy. Not until I went to Paris did I really learn to be proud of the fact that I work for a living."

"Pray explain . . ."

"It's very simple. Here, human labor produces poor results: we're a poor and neglected country. But there, work illuminates like the sun. The buildings, covered from roof to side-walk in ornaments like valuable caskets. . . . And those forests of pictures and statues, whole regions of machinery, and that chaos of factory and craftsmen's products! In Paris I realized that man only seems to be a frail, weak being. In reality, man is a creature of genius and an immortal giant, who can erect cliffs with as much ease as he creates from them something more delicate than lace." (449–50)

The Doll is no bedroom farce, nor is it to be ranged under the category of that novel of adultery that is virtually the central genre of Western European nineteenth-century literature and the most profound expression of its critical negativity.[2] But this Polish novel is also not to be assimilated to the Russian

---

[2] Herbert Marcuse, *Eros and Civilization*; or T. W. Adorno, *Minima Moralia*.

tradition: Catholicism, urban life, logical positivism, and coloniality, along with the literary traditions I have mentioned, beside which a late-developing Russian literary language is little more than an upstart, combine to produce a very different novelistic discourse, in which the city/country opposition is insignificant, compared with the Russian great estates; the nationalism is oppositional and political; and the mystical and transcendental overtones of Dostoevsky (or in a different way, of Tolstoy) are wholly absent.

Perhaps I should have said that their place is taken by a rather different kind of mysticism: the secular one of romantic love, whose high priest was Mickiewicz, and which is here diagnosed as that fatal sickness recognized in a tradition that runs from the Greeks to Proust. But rarely has this disease been visited on so interesting a character as the protagonist of *The Doll*. I choose my terms carefully and prefer this specification to the conventional laudatory terms of "complicated" or "complex" precisely because we never really get to know Stanislas Wokulski or to find out how "complex" he is, despite chapters of third-person point-of-view narrative in which his feelings are generously exposed and his own thoughts about them faithfully recounted.

Here, indeed, we touch on one of the formal peculiarities of *The Doll*, an external or structural design, which, although no innovation, has far deeper consequences for the content of this only seemingly conventional work. This is the alternation of two modes of narrative: Wokulski's third-person chapters, which sometimes wander, in highly un-Jamesian carelessness, over onto other figures; and a recurrent set of first-person narrative chapters told in the voice of Wokulski's faithful clerk—to be sure an interesting person in his own right, particularly in his own intersection with History, but probably for most readers a "flat" rather than a "round" character, and one in any case wholly given over (in that, not unlike the Serenus Zeitblom narrator of *Doktor Faustus*) to devotion to his master. These are not yet the "pseudo-couples" of Beckett,[3] but it is time to admit that we have here yet another version of *Don Quixote*, the one that might have emerged had Sancho written his memoirs and shared his anxious concerns about the knight's obsessions with his readers.

But it is precisely those obsessions that make Wokulski enigmatic, and even—I do not hesitate to use this theoretical term anachronistically, for nineteenth-century realism—undecideable. More is at stake than some mere alternation between inside and outside, between Wokulski's consciousness

---

[3] See the discussion of this figure in my *Wyndham Lewis: The Modernist as Fascist* (Berkeley: University of California Press, 1979), 58–61.

and the judgments other people draw from his behavior. There is an unde-cideability posited by his consciousness itself, which has a family likeness with Proust's "intermittences du coeur" but includes more brutal disconti-nuities across a void no Proustian narrative voice is there to conceal.

This void is social and historical, as well as existential: such is the first of the many originalities of this wonderful novel. It is an open wound left by Poland's subalternity; by the underdevelopment of a commercial bour-geoisie; by the utter absence as well of Wokulski's childhood (he seems to ap-pear full-grown, and out of nowhere); and finally by the signal event I have already alluded to, the abortive revolution of 1863, in which the youthful protagonist fights, spending an equally unmemorialized decade in Siberia for his pains. We will return to this encounter with History later on, which I will not enlist in any characterization of *The Doll* as a national allegory (al-though I believe it to be one), contenting myself with observing that the lit-erature of small or non-first-world power is necessarily more political than that of the hegemonic countries because politics is for their citizens un-avoidable and History necessarily intersects existential experience in them, whereas the mark of first-world affiliation is our individual capability of avoiding history altogether and of retreating into private lives in which, in general and for most of the time, we are protected from it.[4]

As for Wokulski's youth—we first meet him retroactively in this novel as a mysterious, darkened, looming "bearded figure in a sealskin overcoat" on his return from Siberia—it is itself already a juxtaposition of unrelated di-mensions. He has a passion for science and invention, which is to say, for Western modernity, but utterly impoverished, he has to earn his living as a waiter. Nevertheless, he is also a rich businessman—in fact he marries for money, not the most endearing trait for a romantic hero-to-be, and he has as uncle a romantic nobleman, now deceased, but still fondly remembered. Yet he himself surely counts as one of the foremost representatives of the rising bourgeoisie and is indeed made to wear the stigma of a mere businessman, even though he is also an adventurous entrepreneur, capable of taking dra-matic risks and throwing himself into dangerous wartime expeditions. He uses his wealth and power brutally:

> Thus thought Wokulski as he coolly eyed Maruszewicz. But the decayed
> young man, who was moreover very nervous, wilted under the gaze like a
> dove eyed by a spotted snake. First he turned a little pale, then sought to rest

---

[4] See my "Third World Literature in the Era of Multinational Capitalism," *Social Text* 15 (Fall 1986): 65–88.

his weary eyes on some indifferent object, which he looked for in vain on the walls and ceiling of the room, until finally, drenched in a cold sweat, he knew his wandering gaze could not escape Wokulski's influence. It seemed to him that the sombre merchant had caught hold of his soul with grappling-irons, and there was no resisting him. So he shifted his head a few times more, then finally sank with complete surrender into Wokulski's gaze. (212)

Yet he frequently indulges in Dostoevskian acts of charity, without the salvational aura, in sordid scenes and surroundings that enable a properly naturalist glimpse of the new urban and industrial miseries, in a novel mainly confined to the privileged classes.

"A horse?" Wokulski whispered, and somehow his heart ached. Once, last March, as he had been crossing the Jerusalem Way, he had seen a crowd of people, a black coal-wagon standing across the street by a gate, and an un-harnessed horse a few feet away. "What's happened?" "Horse broke its leg," one of the passers-by replied cheerfully; he had a violet scarf on, and kept his hands in his pockets.

Wokulski looked at the culprit as he passed. It was a lean nag with its ribs showing, and kept lifting its back leg. Tied to a small tree, it stood quietly, looked with its rolling eye at Wokulski and gnawed in its pain at a branch covered with hoar-frost.

"Why should I be reminded of that horse just now?" Wokulski thought. "Why do I feel this pity?"

He walked thoughtfully up Obozna and felt that, in the course of the few hours spent by the river, a change had come upon him. Formerly—ten years ago, a year ago, even yesterday—while walking about in the streets he never met anything unusual. People passed by, droshkies drove along, shops opened their doors hospitably for customers. But now a new kind of idea had come to him. Each ragged man looked as if he were shouting for help, the more loudly because he said nothing but only cast a fearful glance, just as that horse with the broken leg had done. Each poor woman looked like a washerwoman, supporting her family on the brink of poverty and decline with her worn hands. Each pitiful child seemed condemned to premature death or to spending days and nights on the garbage heap in Dobra Street.

It was not only people who concerned him. He shared the weariness of horses pulling heavy carts along, and the sores where their horse-collars had drawn blood. He shared the fright of a lost dog barking in the street for his master and the despair of a starving bitch as she ran from one gutter to the next, seeking food for herself and her puppies. And on top of these sufferings

he was even pained by the trees with their bark cut, the pavements like broken teeth, dampness on broken pieces of furniture and ragged garments. It
seemed to him that every object like this was sick or wounded, complaining:
"See how I suffer . . . ," and that he alone heard and understood their
laments. And this peculiar capacity for feeling the pain of others had been
born in him only today, an hour ago. (82–83)

I want to celebrate, as a narrative and novelistic achievement the consequence of this heterogeneity, namely, that these multiple traits and features
are not unified into an organic totality, a psychologically coherent if protean
figure; but rather all remain at a distance from each other, in an addictive or
external way, which leaves its central subject as an absence. Wokulski—
vehicle as we shall see of a grand passion if there ever was one—is a cipher. I
do not know any other nineteenth-century novelistic protagonist of whom
this can be said, but I also wish to underscore the undramatic, un-
Dostoevskian quality of this enigma, so different from the interminable
monologues and confessions through which the Russian characters seek to
express, if not already to construct, their mysteries. It should also be added
that Prus's dialogue has nothing in common with these great Russian con-
frontations but rather crackles with the dry wit we find everywhere at the
end of the century from Gissing to Galdós and Fontane (and even going
back as far as George Eliot, but leaving the French naturalists out of it).

What is this void at the center of Wokulski's being? The thing called passion, certainly, about which we need to report that his first glimpse of Isabella
Lenska in a theater is the pretext for an all-absorbing lifelong obsession,
which leads him to make a fortune in business (risking his own life in the
Balkan wars) and then secretly to support her father, an impoverished nobleman incapable of believing in his own bad luck and pennilessness or of
living according to his means. Indeed, almost everything Wokulski does is in
one way or another dependent on winning the esteem of this extraordinarily
beautiful but still unmarried young woman, about whom one cannot tell
whether she is empty-headed and frivolous or cold and unapproachable,
whether she is afraid of Stanislas's plebeian energy or simply contemptuous
of his social standing (a tradesman!).[5] Isabella is thus also enigmatic, after
her fashion, and it is important that we not blame her for Wokulski's fate.

---

[5] Yes, of course Isabella is in some sense the eponymous doll, in all her beauty and uselessness.
But the title actually springs from a later interpolated episode in which a little girl is falsely accused
of having stolen a doll she admires in the apartment of a miserly and quite peculiar neighbor (in
fact, it is Wokulski who has given her the doll from his own emporium).

This is not the belle dame sans merci: we are given to witness her astonishment at this force of nature that her limited social circle has not hitherto allowed her to observe.

> On meeting Wokulski, she had for the first time made the acquaintance, not only of a new personality, but also of an unexpected phenomenon. It was impossible to define him in a single word, or even in several hundred words. He was unlike everyone else, and if it was at all possible to compare him to anything, then perhaps it was to a place through which one travels all day, and where valleys and mountains, woods and lakes, water and desert, villages and towns are to be found. And where too, beyond the mists of the horizon, some vague landscapes appear, unlike anything known before. She was amazed and wondered whether this was the play of an excited imagination—or was he really a supernatural being, or at least a super-drawing-room one. (219)[6]

Nor are the casual flirtations that drive Wokulski to the edge of madness anything more than her social being—indeed, we are able to observe her gradual but not unwilling reconciliation to the idea of marrying this remarkable, but also very wealthy, commoner.[7] It is Wokulski who makes a final decision in the matter, and we may conjecture that perhaps in that like all great passions this one is not only doomed to failure but in some more obscure fashion wedded to it. The grand passion cannot be "successful" without abolishing itself; the very word *success* is vulgar in relationship to it, as in the very first modern novel (after the obvious predecessor), *La Princesse de Clèves*, the only way to preserve a grand passion and to keep faith with it is to avoid its consummation. Not that Wokulski takes that path either, exactly.

But now we have to look more closely at the thing itself, about which it would be wrong to think that it is something psychological, or even an emotion or feeling of some sort: it is rather a metaphysical experience, an

---

[6] This entire chapter (14) documents Wokulski's enigmatic personality by way of an enumeration of Isabella's changing impressions and opinions of him.

[7] Wokulski's great mood swings, as T. S. Eliot noted about Hamlet, are insufficiently motivated by his frequent suspicions and attacks of jealousy. The world changes abruptly, from one moment to the other: "He became pessimistic. The women looked ugly, their colorful dresses barbarous, their flirtations hateful. The men were stupid, the crowd vulgar, the band out of tune. Entering the stand, he sneered at its squeaking steps and old walls, stained with rain leaks" (199). This metonymic *Stimmung* is, however, also capable of shifting to the metaphoric: "Unutterable rage was fuming within his heart. His hands were becoming like iron bars, his body taking on such strange rigidity that surely any bullet would rebound from it. The word 'Death' crossed his mind and for a moment he smiled. He knew Death does not attack the bold; it merely confronts them like a mad dog, and glares with green eyes, waiting for a muscle to twitch" (206).

experience of the Absolute, that "mystic point where all his memories, long-ings and hopes coincided, a hearth without which his life would have neither sense nor meaning" (75). I believe that bourgeois or individualistic psychol-ogy is poorly placed to grasp such a phenomenon, which only the absent cen-ter of a properly unspeakable event (unspeakable because prohibited by Russian censorship), namely the failed revolution of 1863 can explain. Only a philosophy of the "event" (such as Alain Badiou is currently developing)[8] can convey the unity of form and content (or theory and practice) inherent in this supreme moment, in which History touches its Absolute, and whose loss can be redeemed only by the analogous absolute of Wokulski's love-passion. But I do not even want to claim, as Lukács will in various places,[9] that the love-passion is the substitute for a political passion that was not fulfilled: that love is the second-best after the historical defeat, that it is something like the cul-ture of the world-historical experience of defeat. *Defeat* is no doubt a nobler word than *success*, but I am inclined to see these two Absolutes—revolution and Wokulski's passion—as somehow profoundly interrelated, by way of subterranean "vases communicants." What we take to be the inhuman center of Wokulski's subjectivity and the impersonal nature of his obsession, the pri-mal void around which the more seemingly human and psychological traits of this personality seek inconsistently to reunite themselves, is rather that deeper interrelationship of the absolutes, that unconscious or even metaphys-ical unity of individual and collective that makes Wokulski over into a vehicle for these unidentifiable and indeed untheorizable drives. *The Doll* is thus, all appearances to the contrary, a great political novel, a narrative whose absent center is a primordial political impulse that is never mentioned and that is everywhere present in its absence.

It is a reading confirmed by the more *gemütlich* subplot, the story of the faithful clerk Rzecki, whose one great adventure turns out to have been the Revolution of 1848 and his enlistment in the Hungarian revolutionary army, his subsequent picaresque wanderings across a henceforth counterrevolution-ary Europe, his nostalgia for Napoleon, and his lifelong memory of the fallen comrade Katz (significantly, foreshadowing Wokulski's own fate, the latter seems to have committed suicide). All the warm sympathies of the novel, the affective, melancholy, and elegiac pleasures, take refuge in this subplot, as though in flight from the icy inhumanities of the principal one.

Still, let's not exaggerate: we have already seen Wokulski's charities, which are often moving indeed. We should also talk about his passion for science

---

[8] See, for example, *L'être et l'événement* (Paris: Seuil, 1988), sec. 4.

[9] See, for example, his discussion (*Essays on Realism*) of Hulot's passions in *La cousine Bette*.

and invention, which is truly childlike and full of an infectious enthusiasm. For Paris and its modernities are in fact personified for Wokulski by an anomalous figure, Geist (even the name is no doubt significant), something of an eremitical if not alchemical scientist, in pursuit of unique chemical combinations and substances, which in ancient times would have been identified as the philosopher's stone, or at the very least that gold into which the magicians transformed lead, but which today would merely make lots of money. Geist's laboratory is a perpetual temptation for Wokulski and the old man—"a Moses leading an unborn generation into the Promised Land" (404)—and it constitutes Isabella's opposite number in the struggle for the hero's soul.

How are we to understand this vision of science, whose experimental puttering reminds us less of the Curies than of the monumental and absurd, tragic father figure of Céline's *Mort à crédit*, less of the laboratory than of the home workshop, from *La recherche de l'absolu* onward? The word to be pronounced is *positivism*, and we need to set ourselves back into a late-nineteenth-century intellectual climate in which the ideals of Auguste Comte have triumphantly made the tour of the world, leaving their slogans embedded in the Brazilian flag and their spirit faithfully venerated everywhere that "development" is sought after. Poland has its own folk periodization for this matter, which it is instructive to distinguish from the Russian-style (revolutionary/anarchist) chronologies of the "man of the fifties, man of the sixties, man of the seventies," and so forth. Here in Poland Wokulski's destiny is itself a figure for this particular historical periodization: one of the wiser characters, a Jewish doctor close to him, puts it this way: "two men are merged in him; a romantic of the pre-1863 kind, and a positivist of the '70s" (153) (here Faust's "two souls in one breast" receiving social and historical specification).

With this, everything is said, at least on the ideological level. The great Mickiewicz, epic and lyric poet alike, and poet of revolution as well (his play *Dziady* [*Forefathers*] sparked another kind of revolution in Warsaw a century later, in 1968), is also a central player in this drama, which, just as much as *Don Quixote* or *Madame Bovary*, is also about the corruptions of literature. "I know, now," murmurs Stanislas, "by whom I am bewitched. . . . All you poets have wasted my life. . . . You have poisoned two generations. . . . These are the results of sentimental views of love." (406). Thus the novel as a form turns back on itself in autoreferentiality and designates that literary genre and language that is to be uprooted, canceled, negated, and utterly refused, if it is itself to come into being.

But it is not only positivism (and Monsieur Homais) that trivializes romanticism and transforms it into mere bovarism: the former is also trivialized unless we see it as a working ideology of industrial modernization itself. Early in the novel (and to be sure, in France, the very heartland of Western modernity for these Slavic tourists), Isabella, glimpsing an iron foundry, has a remarkable vision of the emergence of a whole new world, and the end of the old aristocratic one in which alone her privileged life has meaning:

> While traveling down from the mountains into a region of woods and fields under a sapphire sky, she saw an abyss of black smoke and white steam, and heard the dull rattling, creak and hiss of machinery. Then she saw the foundries, like the towers of medieval castles breathing flame, powerful wheels that revolved like lightening, great scaffolds that moved on rails, streams of molten iron glowing white, and half-naked laborers like bronze statues with sombre expressions. Over it all was a blood-red glow, the sound of rumbling wheels, bellows panting, the thundering of hammers and impatient breathing of furnaces, and underfoot the terrified earth trembled.
>
> Then it seemed to Isabella that she had descended from the heights of Olympus into the hopeless chasms of Vulcan, where the Cyclops were forging thunderbolts that might shatter Olympus itself. She recalled legends of rebellious giants, of the end of this splendid world of hers, and for the first time she the goddess, before whom senators and marshals bowed their heads, was afraid. (40–41)

It is of these terrifying energies that Wokulski himself is for her allegorical; indeed, it is this future that he emblematizes for her whole class. "I congratulate you on a complete triumph," remarks a knowledgeable lawyer on the occasion of the proposition of a business consortium Wokulski makes to a selected group of aristocrats; "the Prince is quite taken with you, both the Counts and the Baron too. . . . They are all somewhat scatter-brained, as you will have noticed, but they're men of good will. . . . They want to do something, they're intelligent and educated—but they lack energy. A sickness of the will, my dear sir: their whole class is affected by it." (169). This is then the ultimate diagnosis of the specifically Polish misery, recorded with comical precision in the satiric pages of this tale of passion: but it is not in the light of some supreme value of passion (as, for example, in Stendhal) that the hilarious and cruel social panorama is staged. Rather it is the failure of a whole class to undertake its historic mission that is indicted here, and it is in the space of that failure that the Jews of this novel find their opportunity.

"I have noticed over the last year or two," observes Rzecki, "that dislike of the Hebrews is increasing; even people who, a few years ago, called them

Poles of the Mosaic persuasion, now call them Jews. And those who recently admired their hard work, their persistence and their talents, today only see their exploitation and deceit.

When I hear such things, I sometimes think a spiritual twilight is falling on mankind, like night." (145)

In the absence of a bourgeoisie, and in the debility of this aristocracy, the Jews have become the entrepreneurs by the end of the time span of the novel; and Wokulski's contempt for anti-Semitism (and the author's own) cannot save them from the malice and envy of their impotent competitors, nor indeed from a gamut of characterological traits that range from revolutionary enthusiasm to outright greed and avarice. It is an interesting document on the historic role of Jews in Poland's economy (and in a country so central to Jewish history and experience in general) and makes a fascinating juxtaposition to the picture of a glittering and cultured Jewish high society in Copenhagen in Pontoppidan's *Lykke-Per* (*Hans im Glück*, 1904).

The latter was also, the reader will recall, one of the works enumerated in Lukács's *Theory of the Novel* as examples of his first typological category, the so-called novel of abstract idealism, which centered on *Don Quixote*, and which was opposed to the ironies of "romantic disillusionment" (epitomized by *L'éducation sentimentale*). *The Doll* is also a novel of lost illusions but finally continues to keep faith with those illusions no less absolutely than *Don Quixote*. "All the same, Don Quixote was happier than I," thinks Wokulski toward the end. "He didn't begin to awaken from his illusions until the brink of the grave. But I?" (623). Perhaps Prus's novel is that rare form that combines both of Lukács's types into one. At any rate, by the time Wokulski thinks this, he is also on the brink of the grave, of his own choosing. Offstage, like the hero of *Pierrot le fou*, he binds dynamite around himself, in a mountainous place associated with the less unhappy passion of his uncle, memorialized on stone by equally immortal verses of Mickiewicz. Fittingly, however, our last thoughts are for Rzecki: indeed, what can Sancho possibly find to do with himself after the disappearance of his master?

Narrating Politics

BENEDICT ANDERSON

Max Havelaar
(Multatuli, 1860)

These were truly four anni mirabiles. In 1818 were born Ivan Turgenev and Emily Brontë, in 1819, Herman Melville and George Eliot; and in 1821, Fyodor Dostoevsky and Gustave Flaubert. Right in the middle, in 1820, came Eduard Douwes Dekker, better known by his nom de plume, Multatuli. His novel *Max Havelaar*, which over the past 140 years has been translated into more than forty languages and has given him a certain international reputation, appeared in 1860. It was thus sandwiched between, on the one side, *On the Eve* (1860), *The Mill on the Floss* (1860), George Sand's *Le marquis de Villemer* (1860), *Great Expectations* (1860–61) *Adam Bede*, *The Confidence Man*, *Madame Bovary*, and *Oblomov* (all in 1857); and on the other, *Silas Marner* (1861), *Fathers and Sons, Salammbo*, and *Les misérables* (1862), *War and Peace* (starting in 1865), and *Crime and Punishment* (1866). This was the generation in which Casanova's "world republic of letters," subdivision the novel, hitherto dominated by French and British males, was first profoundly challenged from its margins: by formidable women in the Channel-linked cores and by extraordinary figures from beyond the Atlantic and across the steppe. Douwes Dekker, who emerged startlingly from one literary terra incognita, the tiny kingdom of The Netherlands (*ons kleine land*, as the Dutch still like to say), newly cooked up by the Holy Alliance, and wrote about another on the remote southeast fringes of Asia—the vast royal colony in the Indies—was another remarkable contributor to the ranks of these "I will be heard" novelists.

Douwes Dekker's father, a Calvinist sea captain of simple means but with extensive experience in Europe as a smuggler undermining Napoleon's Continental System and in Asia as a long-distance transporter of tropical products, arranged in 1839 for his half-schooled, highly intelligent, romantic, and egotistical nineteen-year-old boy to sail to the East Indies to seek a career and a fortune in the colonial administrative service.[1] In 1857, having achieved neither, the embittered, indebted son resigned and returned to

---

[1] Dik van der Meulen's *Multatuli: Leven en Werken* (*Multatuli: Life and Works*) (Nijmegen: Sun, 2002), almost nine hundred pages long, is now the overweight standard work on Douwes Dekker's life, if not his work. The most acute literary study of *Max Havelaar* is Marcel Janssens, *Max Havelaar, de held van Lebak* (*Max Havelaar, the Hero of Lebak*). (Utrecht: Standard, 1970).

Europe. Three years later, his life until then almost exactly divided between The Netherlands and the Indies, he had become the most talked-of man in his home country. With *Max Havelaar* reasonably soon translated into English (1868), French (1876), and, exceptionally badly, German (1875), he started to be esteemed as the first European novelist to unmask in detail the exploitation and oppression inflicted by colonialism on Asia. Frans Rademaker's visually splendid 1976 adaptation of the novel for the screen perpetuates exactly this "Harriet Beecher Stowe of the East" reputation.

But D. H. Lawrence shrewdly understood Douwes Dekker as above all a satirist and ironist. He wrote that for the novelist pity for the oppressed natives in the Indies was merely a "chick" hatched by the "bird of hate." "The great dynamic force in Multatuli is as it was, really, in Jean Paul and in Swift and Gogol, and in Mark Twain, hate, a passionate, honourable hate."[2] The strange narrative structure of *Max Havelaar* amply confirms this estimation and shows the reader how hatred creates a narrative bridge across two continents.

The Netherlands in which the author grew up was a shadow of the dominant world power of Rembrandt's midseventeenth-century Golden Age, when Dutch fleets burned their way up the Thames and dominated the huge maritime arc between the Cape of Good Hope and Kyushu. Overrun by France's revolutionary armies, given its first brief monarch by the Corsican Emperor, annexed into France, beggared by war and the Continental System, and subjected by London and Berlin to Orange absolutism, it had

---

[2] See his striking, but hasty and slovenly introduction to the second, worse English translation by William Siebenhaar, and published in New York by Knopf in 1927 (ix). He thought that compositionally the book was "the greatest mess possible," completely missing its intricate, sophisticated structure. Dutch literary historians, with some irritation, note that Lawrence has been the only "world-class" writer to have devoted some real published attention to Douwes Dekker. But it was a curious business. Siebenhaar was a Dutchman who emigrated to western Australia as a young man and served as a local civil servant from 1895 to 1916, when he was dismissed on charges of subversion and anarchism. He was an admirer of *The White Peacock* and *The Rainbow*, and attached himself clamlike to Lawrence and his wife on their visit to Perth in 1922. When he showed Lawrence a long essay he had written on Dekker, the famous man was sufficiently interested ("it's a queer work—real genius") to urge Siebenhaar to do a modern translation of *Max Havelaar*, promising to help find a publisher for it. Knopf, Lawrence's American publisher, finally did agree to print the translation, but only on condition that Lawrence write an introduction that could be prominently advertised. By this time, Lawrence had decided that the translator was "a bore" and resented being stuck with his commitment. These circumstances help explain the odd character of what Lawrence produced. This amusing history is described well in Oskar Wellens, " 'A queer work': De toestandkoming van de Tweede Engelse *Max Havelaar* (1927)" (" 'A Queer Work': How the Second (1927) English Translation of *Max Havelaar* Came into Existence"), *Over Multatuli* 48 (2002): 36–40.

become a backwater consoled only by pietism, gradgrindery, *and* hope from the exploitation of the Indies, the last significant residue of the once hegemonic intercontinental imperium.[3]

In the seventeenth and even part of the eighteenth centuries, the United East India Company, headquartered in Amsterdam, was the largest and most transnational corporation in the world, dominating the Indian Ocean by control of the Cape of Good Hope, Ceylon, and the Malacca Straits, as well as the South China and Java seas as far as the shores of Japan. Its executives and personnel were recruited from all over Protestant Europe (except rival England), as well as from many parts of Asia and Africa. Collaboration with subordinated native elites ensured an abundant, coerced supply of profitable agricultural products, while maritime supremacy guaranteed a high-markup monopoly on their delivery to European and Asian destinations. Increasingly corrupt, inbred, and incompetent, The Company finally went bankrupt in 1799, and the beginning of a modern state-controlled colonialism was undertaken. But twelve years later, just after Napoleon had liquidated The Netherlands as a political entity, the English had seized all the former Company possessions. The Netherlands eventually got back the East Indies only by ceding the Cape and Ceylon to London. Thus the Indies to which Douwes Dekker came at the end of the 1830s was not at all a conventionally exotic, unexplored nineteenth-century new colony, but a terrain so long familiar that *Max Havelaar* scarcely needed to locate its toponyms or to explain to readers its casual borrowings from Malay and Javanese. They had been seeping into Dutch for two centuries.

But it was also, in his time, a shrunken inheritor of the past. Now the property of bourgeois-absolutist Willem I of Orange, the colony was closed not merely to foreigners, but even to most Dutchmen. The Cultivation System, installed three years before Douwes Dekker's arrival, and lasting until 1870, pitilessly systematized the traditional practices of the Company, while vastly expanding the range of coerced crops (tea, coffee, sugar, indigo, quinine, and so forth). Meantime, the royally controlled Dutch Trading Company monopolized the export of all these commodities. The colossal profits of this racket made possible The Netherlands' economic stabilization and its late passage to industrialism.[4] Lacking serious military power and dependent

---

[3] Napoleon put his brother Louis on the newly created Dutch throne in 1806, but kicked him out in 1810 because of what the emperor described as his *manie d'humanité*, and then decreed the annexation.

[4] Over the four decades of its life, the Cultivation System paid off the company's standing debt of 35.5 million guilders and provided The Netherlands with an additional, staggering 664.5 million.

ultimately on London for their security, the colony's rulers more than ever relied on the cooptation of native aristocrats whose enthusiasm for the Cultivation System was ensured by a substantial share of its profits. There was nothing adventurous or new here. Colony and metropole have rarely been so intermeshed: as the old saw went, *Indië verloren, rampspoed geboren* (the Indies lost, instant calamity). Such was the terrain in which Douwes Dekker, self-imagined child of *Emile*, *Kenilworth*, and *Don Quixote* spent almost two decades.

He was convinced that his more-or-less forced resignation from colonial service was the consequence of his efforts to protect the peasant population that he supervised in the district of Lebak (on the western tip of Java) from a huge array of abuses—illegal corvée labor, expropriation of land, theft of property, torture, and murder—practiced by the local native aristocrats with the connivance of the colonial bureaucracy to which he belonged. On his return to The Netherlands, armed with hundreds of copied documents and letters, he tried—fruitlessly—to get himself reinstated and promoted. *Max Havelaar* was composed by a man who felt he had very little to lose.[5] But he had also become acutely aware of the paradox that a "true story" (like his own) entered society only as what Walter Benjamin contemptuously described as "information," but that the same society could be gripped by a

---

Of the latter, 236 million went to reduce the public debt, 115 to cover a reduction on the taxes Dutchmen paid, 115 to create the state railway system, and 146 to the useless, but employment-creating, improvement of the country's fortifications. George McT. Kahin, *Nationalism and Revolution in Indonesia* (Ithaca, N.Y.: Cornell University Press, 1952), 11.

[5] With some tergiversations. At one brief point, he actually offered to withdraw the manuscript from publication if he were rehabilitated, promoted, given a lucrative new post in Java's sugar belt, and awarded a royal decoration. There is some evidence that he decided to use a nom de plume partly not to jeopardize the chance of rehabilitation. Probably more important, he wanted to bury the failure of "Douwes Dekker" under the éclat of a new historical figure: "Multatuli." As for the choice of this odd Latin pen name, one can take one's pick. It may have been drawn from lines 413–24 of Horace's *Ars Poetica*: *Multa tulit fecitque puer, sudavit et alsit, Abstinuit venere et vino* (As a youth [he] endured much, and much achieved, he sweated and shivered, and abstained from sex and wine). In his article "Nomen est omen," (*Over Multatuli* 24 [1990]: 63–70), G. Koops-Van Bruggen makes a good case for this interpretation on the basis of Douwes Dekker's attendance at a Latin school when a boy, and the fondness for Horace he exhibited in his published writing and private letters. The author goes on to say that the meaning of the name is that Douwes Dekker has "paid his dues" as an artist by his experience, training, and achievement. On the other hand, the popular interpretation is "I have suffered much," and if this is right, a possible source is Paul's Second Epistle to the Corinthians, verse 5: "For as the sufferings of Christ abound in us, so our consolation also aboundeth by Christ." By 1860, Douwes Dekker was certainly a free-thinker, if not yet an atheist, but his writing is full of biblical references and quotations. It may have amused him to melt Horace into Jesus.

"fiction." He had before his eyes Harriet Beecher Stowe's capture of millions of readers for her fictional *Uncle Tom's Cabin* (1852) and probably also the market failure of her follow-up, *A Key to Uncle Tom's Cabin*, an impressive five-hundred-page dossier of the documents on which the novel had been based.[6] But he also—because after all his own case was involved—wanted the "truth of documents" to speak. One could say that his motto should have been: Besides, it's true.

Max Havelaar's ironical subtitle reads *The Coffee Sales of the Netherlands Trading Company*. The reader will eventually discover that no coffee grows, or can be grown, in Lebak, and that no one in the Indies portion of the narrative even speaks about coffee. The subtitle turns out to be the title intended by the narrator of the early chapters of the book, and of bits and pieces later on. This "I" immediately identifies himself as Batavus Droogstoppel, a successful Amsterdam coffee broker, whose wealth depends on the Indies, then the most famous producer of coffee (we used to call it "java") for a large, addicted Western public. Batavus Droogstoppel is a brilliant figure, quasi-Linnaean as an animal genus, but also linked to the colonial capital, Batavia, the ancient Batavi, usually reliable sepoys for the ancient Romans (a.k.a. the modern English), and the French revolutionary Batavian Republic of 1795–1806. But it is the surname Droogstoppel (Drystubble) that has become an indelible negative national trope for a prevalent type of Dutch middle-aged bourgeois male—hypocritical, grasping, pompous, puritanical, and utterly provincial.[7]

Droogstoppel confides to the reader that he recently ran into an old

---

[6] He had mixed feelings about the novel. In chapter 17 of *Max Havelaar* the momentary "I" says: "Can its main point be denied to Uncle Tom's Cabin, just because there never existed an Evangeline? Shall people say to the author of that immortal plea—immortal not by art or talent, but by purpose and intensity—shall they say to her, 'You have lied; the slaves are not ill-treated; for there is untruth in your book—it is a novel.' " (My translation, from the critical edition of G. Stuiveling, *Max Havelaar* [Amsterdam: G. A. van Oorschot, 1950], 204. All subsequent quotations are my translations from this edition. Any italic is in the original.) From other writings of his, it is pretty clear that he thought his "campaign" for the Javanese paralleled hers for the American slaves, but he had all the genius that she lacked.

[7] Although Dekker never acknowledged this, it is generally accepted today that the coffee broker is an ingenious mixed borrowing from Walter Scott, whose novels were hugely popular in eighteenth-century Holland, as elsewhere. The name comes from Dr. Dryasdust, the antiquarian Scott uses to introduce or frame *Peveril of the Peak*, *The Adventures of Nigel*, *Redgauntlet*, etc. The transition proceeds thus: literal translation of *Droog-als-stof*, to Droogstoffel, and finally to Droogstoppel. The coffee broker's manner and style comes partly from the business-obsessed elder Osbaldstone in *Rob Roy*. See Jan Paul Hinrichs's well-argued case in his "Rob Roy en Max Havelaar," in *Over Multatuli* 34 (2000): 39–51.

schoolmate, who once saved him from a beating. Fallen on hard times, this personage wraps himself in an old shawl against the winter cold— Droogstoppel Irishly calls him Shawlie (that is, Sjaalman). The poor wretch begs the coffeebroker's help in publishing a manuscript and a dossier of documents concerning coffee cultivation in the Indies. It turns out that Shawlie is a former colonial civil servant who now earns a pittance helping a successful book dealer whose name translates as Talentsucker. Droogstoppel is gradually lured into accepting Shawlie's bundle of papers by the idea of publishing under his own name Something Important on Coffee. He turns over the dossier to a German boy invited to board with the Droogstoppel family. ("Young Stern" is the son of a wealthy coffee merchant on the Hamburg Exchange, whom Batavus thereby hopes to keep as a customer.) Ordered to work up the material into "something that resembles a novel," the German lad, in alliance with Droogstoppel's increasingly "insolent" son Frits, produces chapters to be read aloud at weekly intervals to friends and family. These readings increasingly delight the boys and the daughters of Droogstoppel's friends, while horrifying and boring most of their elders, including the now proverbial Parson Wawelaar (Twaddler), a biting caricature of the kind of stupid Calvinist preacher who justified the colonial project *in nomine Eius*.[8]

The effect of these early chapters, in which Douwes Dekker's perfect ear for different kinds of bourgeois cant is displayed, is not to make the absurdity of the framing device plausible, but to engage the reader's laughter and complicity, and seduce him or her to keep on reading as the setting moves from Europe to Asia. Most of the novel's remaining chapters purport to be Young Stern's transformation of Shawlie's documents into a "novel," but in the narrative few traces of a young German just beginning to learn Dutch are visible.[9] The "I" not only knows a great deal that no young German could possibly know, even from a dossier, but is the obvious doppelgänger of the ostensible hero, rebellious colonial civil servant Max Havelaar. In a marvelous tactical move, Douwes Dekker split himself into a young idealist fictional hero and an older, sardonic narrator,[10] a mix too of the non-Dutch

---

[8] After Drystubble, Talentsucker, and Twaddler, one might expect that the name Havelaar would also be coded. There is no such word in Dutch, but *haveloos* (ragged, in rags) is a close neighbor.

[9] Douwes Dekker was great admirer of Schiller and Goethe, and knew much of Heine by heart. Droogstoppel observes scornfully that Young Stern "like Germans in general, has a smattering of literature." He also, says the coffee broker, is a dreamer (*hy schwärmt*).

[10] Many critics have suggested that the figure of Havelaar is modeled partly on the altruistic aristocrat in Eugène Sue's 1842–43 *Les mystères de Paris* and also partly on *Don Quixote*. In the

Stern and the fallen Shawlie. There is only minimal concealment of the artifice of this split, which also limns Douwes Dekker's own transformation
from young administrator to mature satirist. The reader is to be intrigued
by the equivocation and gradually swept into the "true" story of Douwes
Dekker's career now masked to "resemble a novel." Yet not entirely. There
are frequent Droogstoppel interventions, commenting on the fictionality
("lies") of Stern's "draft-novel," as well as amusing digressions—in the vein
of Tristram Shandy's creator, who delighted Douwes Dekker—on everything from the ludicrousness of para-Gothic architecture to the symbolic
meaning of dysentery for the arc of official careers in the colony.

The narrator takes the reader straight to the scene of the sensational
denouement, the fatal few months of Havelaar's Indies bureaucratic
service, now in, of course, Douwes Dekker's Lebak. But the earlier career of
Havelaar/Douwes Dekker is recapitulated in Havelaar's sharp and funny
dinnertime monologues about his years on the west coast of Sumatra, the
north of tip of Celebes, and Amboina. In these chapters the reader is probably bemused by Multatuli's narrating Stern's narration of Shawlie's narration
of Havelaar's story. But the layering is carried off by the brio of Douwes
Dekker's style and his frequent written winks. It is Havelaar, not Shawlie or
Douwes Dekker, who regularly insists that he has the documents to prove
that what he is narrating really happened. This is the way in which the political truth of Java is tied to the social-moral truth of midcentury Holland.

The core "story" describes how Havelaar and his family arrive in Lebak
with every intention of ending the abuse of the native population by the local native chiefs. It is characteristic of Douwes Dekker's account that the
"feudal" abuses practiced by these chiefs are described as basically age-old
features of Oriental despotism and in this sense are part of native culture.
Havelaar rather likes his main adversary, an elderly aristocrat trying to live
out the lifestyle traditional to his class within the constrictive carapace of
Dutch colonial monopoly-capitalism. His fury is directed overwhelmingly at
the corruption, cowardice, and racism of Dutch officialdom. Frustrated by
his subordinates and threatened by his immediate superiors, he demands that
the key native chiefs be arrested and indicted, only to discover that the highest authority, the royally appointed governor-general—who understands no

letters he wrote to woo his first wife, Dekker often spoke admiringly of Rodolphe and Sue's novel
(his fiancée hated both), and he is said always to have had a copy of Cervantes' masterwork about
him. See, for example, Janssens's *Max Havelaar*, 16–17; and Paul Vincent, "Multatuli en Rizal
Nader Bekeken" ("Further Reflections on Multatuli and José Rizal"), *Over Multatuli* 5 (1980):
58–67.

native language—has little intention of upsetting any applecarts.[11] Influential and loyal chiefs are scarce commodities, whereas young, troublesome Dutch officials are easily replaced.

Toward the end of the novel there is another abrupt narrative break for a chapter devoted to the melodramatic and sentimental story of two poor village sweethearts, Saidjah and Adinda—the only part of *Max Havelaar* widely known and loved in contemporary Indonesia. Saidjah's father is robbed of his livelihood by the chiefs, leaves Lebak to find work elsewhere, is mercilessly flogged for traveling without papers, and eventually dies. Saidjah goes to work in Batavia, expecting to return after three years with money enough to marry Adinda and settle down peacefully. But on his return he finds her family house razed and her father and his children fled across the Sunda Strait to join rebels fighting near the southern tip of Sumatra. He follows them only to find they have been killed by Dutch troops, Adinda mutilated into the bargain, and ends his own life with a desperate solo attack on his oppressors.

Droogstoppel is dismayed that the young ones around him adore this "fiction" above all else in "Stern's novel." (It is also the core episode in Frans Rademaker's film.) Strikingly, the "authors" partly concur. A narrative "I"—who seems more and more plainly to be Douwes Dekker/Multatuli himself, announces a confession: "Yes, a confession, reader! I do not know whether Saidjah loved Adinda. Nor whether he went to Batavia, Nor whether he was murdered in the Lampongs with Dutch bayonets. I do not know whether his father succumbed as a consequence of the rattan-scourging he received for having left Badoor [home] without a travel-pass. . . . All this I do not know! But I know *more* than this. I know *and I can prove* that there were *many* Adindas and *many* Saidjahs, and that *what is fiction in a particular case is truth in general* (204).[12]

The novel ends with an extraordinary collapse of the entire layered framework. "Enough, my good Stern! I, Multatuli, take up the pen. You

---

[11] Although full Orange absolutism came to an end in the magic year 1848 with the drawing up a constitution, the Indies continued to be personally controlled by the Dutch monarchy—largely beyond the purview of the newly constituted parliament. This situation did not change politically until 1870, nor socially, until the opening of the Suez Canal and the abolition of passports for Dutch people who wanted to enter the Indies.

[12] It is interesting that exactly this idea underlies the Cuban Gertrudis Gómez de Avellaneda's visionary nationalist-abolitionist novel *Sab*, published in 1847 (of course, in Spain, not Cuba), five years before *Uncle Tom's Cabin*. She also wrote of her eponymous slave hero (before Flaubert's cross-gendered identification with Emma Bovary): "*Sab, c'est moi.*' See the fine account in Doris Sommer, *Foundational Fictions* (Berkeley: University of California Press, 1991), chap. 4.

were not called upon to write Havelaar's history! I called you into being. I made you come from Hamburg. . . . I taught you to write pretty good Dutch, in a very short time. . . . It is enough, stern, you may go. . . . Halt! Miserable product of dirty moneygrubbing and blasphemous hypocrisy! I have created you. . . . You grew into a monster under my pen. . . . I am nauseated by my own creation: choke on coffee and vanish!" (236). In the concluding peroration we are warned that "*I will be read!*" (237). Should nothing be done radically to improve the condition of the Javanese: "[I would] translate my book into the few languages that I know and into the many languages that I can still learn, so to ask from Europe what I would have sought in vain in the Netherlands. And in all the capitals songs would be sung with refrains like this: *a pirate state lies on the sea between* the Scheldt *and Eastern* Friesland! And if even this did not avail? Then I would translate my book into Malay, Javanese, Sundanese, Alfurese, Buginese, Batak . . . and I should hurl *kléwang*-wielding [a native machete, but he does not need to explain this] warsongs into the hearts of the martyrs to whom I have promised help, I, Multatuli . . ." (238) This is a call, not for an antifeudal insurrection of natives against their abusive chiefs, but rather for the overthrow of colonialism itself, aided long-distance by a former colonial ruler. This stance one will not find, even half a century later, in Forster's *A Passage to India*, or Farrère's *Les civilisés*, or still later in Orwell's *Burmese Days* Perhaps one has to wait till Genet's play *Les paravents*.

In The Netherlands, Douwes Dekker is almost universally regarded as the father of modern Dutch prose based firmly on the vernacular and in the street. In *Max Havelaar*, he invented the "novel that resembles a novel." From a certain angle, the book can also be seen as an olio of pitch-perfect parodies of existing genres—colonial bureaucratese, Calvinist sermons, sentimental romances, bad poetry, antibourgeois boutades, policymaker puffery, romantic self-aggrandizement and self-abasement, gothic intrigues, dilettante-journalistic social criticism, and so on. Since parody is necessarily parasitic, its peculiar stylistic pleasures are, alas, largely untranslatable, let alone in their zigzag juxtaposition. But no one can miss the aptness of Lawrence's final English point: "When there are no more Drystubbles, no more Governor-Generals or Slijmerings, then *Max Havelaar* will be out of date. The book is a pill rather than a comfit. The jam of pity was put on to get the pill down. Our fathers and grandfathers licked the jam off. We can still go on taking the pill, for the social constipation is as bad as ever" (ix).

Max Havelaar strikes one today as very remote from its untricky coevals, *On the Eve*, *The Mill on the Floss*, and *Madame Bovary*, which seem firmly, if nervously, embedded in national or quasi-national societies. But one can feel certain affinities with the relentless ironizing, angry laughter, and reader-toying of the man who had seen his *Moby Dick* plummet into public oblivion. It is quite possible to read *The Confidence Man* as located in something boundless and transcontinental, with Memphis and Boston as far from, and near to, each other as Batavia and Amsterdam. From this point of view, Douwes Dekker's novel, like Melville's, serves as a portent of the world we endure today.

It remains to consider the absorbing history of *Max Havelaar*'s entry into the world-republic of letters as that institution expanded its dominion and experienced internal transformations. As has been noted, Douwes Dekker's visibility should have been substantial in that he was translated into the key languages of English, French, and German in his own lifetime. The German version, however, excising half the original and full of errors, sank without a trace. The clumsy French version was briefly and mostly favorably noticed but also seems to have had little impact. The English version, nicely accompanied by a detailed map of Java and executed by an Anglophile Dutchman, Baron Alphonse Nahuys, was well received and is still very readable. But against Douwes Dekker's hopes it led to no political movement of solidarity, despite the Great Sepoy Mutiny of 1857 and the liquidation of the English version of the United East India Company. Probably, the contemporary hegemon was too certain that it always did things better, including colonialism, than the people across the Channel. It was almost certainly this version that so excited José Rizal, then researching Philippine history in the British Museum, that he wrote to his friend, the Austrian ethnologist Ferdinand Blumentritt on December 6, 1888: "Multatuli's book, which I will send you as soon as I can obtain a copy [in Dutch], is extraordinarily exciting.[13] Without a doubt, it is of a much higher quality than my own. [His great *Noli Me Tangere* was published in Berlin in 1887, about the time that Douwes Dekker died.] Still, because the author is himself a Dutchman, his broadsides [*Angriffe*] are not as powerful as mine. Yet the book is much more artistic, far more elegant than my own, although it exposes only one aspect of Dutch life on Java."[14]

---

[13] The correspondence indicates that Rizal thought the German-speaking Blumentritt would find the Dutch original easier going.

[14] I have translated the original German as cited in Vincent, "Multatuli en Rizal," 61. Vincent takes the opportunity to point to the odd parallels between the two novels. Both have Latin on their title pages, though Rizal's came from John 20:17, not from either Horace or Paul. Both have idealistic young heroes who are destroyed by the machinations of the colonials. But Vincent notes that both descended independently from Sue's Rodolphe. He observes, however, that there are traces of Dekker's narrative strategy and rhetorical style in *El filibusterismo* (*The Subversive*), the sequel to *Noli Me Tangere*, published in 1891 in Ghent.

Although Douwes Dekker's death was respectfully recorded in French, English, and German newspapers, it was only as a consequence of Wilhelm Spohr's new German version of *Max Havelaar* in 1900 that a wider readership and admiration can be observed.[15] It was followed by translations into Danish in 1901, Swedish in 1902, Polish in 1903, and Russian in 1908. All these versions were translations of Spohr's German.[16] The renewed interest in *Max Havelaar* in Germany and in the "German-language" sphere was certainly connected to the rise of large and powerful socialist parties in many of these countries, German's role as the core language of Marxist thinking, and also wider intra-European critique of imperialism and colonialism. Berlin had also been the site of the spectacularly cynical imperialist carve-up of Africa little more than two decades earlier.

Between the two world wars, Europe's attention was focused inwardly on its own alarming problems—the rise of various fascisms as well as the Depression. Douwes Dekker almost disappeared from sight, with the exception of Siebenhaar's translation in the United States. However, a new Russian version appeared in 1936, as a portent of the next wave of Douwes Dekker enthusiasm. In the initial revolutionary era, and most likely long after, the key figure was the much-loved southern Cossack writer Konstanin Paustovsky (1892–1968), who had been a sailor in his youth and had thus spent time in Dutch ports. As early as 1923, he had published the article "Mnogostradal'ni Mul'tatuli" ("Much-suffering Multatuli") in a newspaper wonderfully titled *Gudok Zakavkaz'ia* (*Trumpet of the Transcaucasus*); he followed this up in 1926 with the short tale "Golandskaya koroleva" ("The King of Holland") in the Odessa newspaper *Moryak* (*The Sailor*) in which Douwes Dekker was praised for his selfless dedication to the suffering

---

[15] Spohr moved in anarchist circles, like his successor, William Siebenhaar, and French contemporary, Alexandre Cohen, who in 1893 started publishing fragments of *Max Havelaar* (first in an obscure anarchist "rag," later in the *Mercure de France*. One can see why Douwes Dekker would have appealed to anarchists.

[16] See J. J. Oversteegen's excellent "Multatuli in het buitenland" ("Multatuli Abroad"), in Pierre H. Dubois et al., eds. *100 Jaar Max Havelaar: Essays over Multatuli* (Rotterdam: Ad. Donker, 1962), 134–48. It will be recalled that as a consequence of the late-eighteenth-century partition of Poland between Vienna, Berlin, and St. Petersburg, turn-of-the-century Hohenzollern Germany included many bilingual Polish intellectuals and literary people. It is not impossible that the Russian translation relied on the Polish version, though Spohr's is more likely. See also Jerzy Koch, "De invloed van de Duitse Multatuli-receptie op de Poolse" ("The Influence of the German Reception of Multatuli on the Polish"), *Over Multatuli* 28 (1992): 13–28. This article includes a valuable graph of the number of Douwes Dekker texts translated into German and Polish for each five-year period between 1860 and 1985. Up to World War I, the movement of the two languages runs parallel, but not thereafter.

Javanese. Paustovsky's interest in Douwes Dekker never faded; in his 1956 book *The Golden Rose*, he included a detailed sketch of Douwes Dekker's life and work.[17]

As Stalin's Soviet Union consolidated its control over Eastern Europe in the decade after Hitler's downfall, *Max Havelaar* underwent a third boom, this time based probably on the 1936 Russian translation, rather than that of Spohr. Slovenian versions were published in 1946 and 1947; East German in 1948, 1953, and 1959; Polish in 1949 and 1956; Hungarian in 1950 and 1955; Slovak in 1954; Armenian in 1956; as well as two more Russian editions in 1956 and 1957.[18] Paustovsky, Order of Lenin awardee, was surely behind at least some of this explosion. Douwes Dekker had become a martyr to imperialism and a stalwart friend of the colonized. That he was also a skirt-chaser, a gambler as compulsive and disastrous as Dostoevsky, and once in a while fantasized himself as the future king of Java was unspoken, perhaps indeed unknown.

The most recent wave of translations largely came out of the consolidation of the European Community and the concern of its members to institutionalize "mutual recognition" of each other's cultural value. One could say that Douwes Dekker finally had all Europe on his side. An Italian version was published in 1965, and an Estonian in 1973.[19] In 1975 the first Spanish translation appeared—in Catalan Barcelona.[20] In an ironic move that Douwes Dekker would have appreciated, the Dutch government bought up a thousand copies to be distributed through its embassies in South America. Translations into Urdu (1983) and Korean (1994) were done by young nationals of Pakistan and Korea who had lived and studied in The Netherlands.[21] In London, Penguin published in 1987 a new translation in its Classics series—Douwes Dekker was probably there to represent European Community member The Netherlands.

And what about the Indies, which, at the end of 1949, after a bloody four-year armed struggle against the Dutch, following three and a half years

---

[17] Information drawn from Jan Paul Hinrichs, "Paustovskij en Multatuli," *Over Multatuli* 34 (1995): 3–5. A Dutch translation of "The King of Holland" appears on 6–9.

[18] This information is from Oversteegen, "Multatuli in het buitenland."

[19] On the latter, see Külli Prosa, "Multatuli in Estland" ("Multatuli in Estonia"), *Over Multatuli* 32 (1994): 58–64.

[20] See the text by translator Francisco Carrasquer, "De Ontvangst van de *Max Havelaar* in het spans" ("The Reception of the Spanish *Max Havelaar*"), *Over Multatuli* 8 (1981): 34–35.

[21] See Dik van der Meulen and Olf Praamstra, "Droogstoppel en Slijmering in het Urdu," *Over Multatuli* 30 (1993): 40–43; and Myong-suk Chi, "Multatuli in Korea," *Over Multatuli* 37 (1996): 68–72. Chi is quite explicit about Amsterdam's financial support.

of occupation by the Japanese, had "joined the family of free nations" as Indonesia? The first and only translation into Indonesian appeared twenty-three years later: in 1972, just nosing out Estonia, and 112 years after its original's incendiary publication. Until Hirohito's armies wrapped up Dutch military resistance in two weeks of March 1942, Douwes Dekker was still regarded as a dangerous firebrand in the colony, and no edition of his work was ever permitted to be issued there. But the Dutch-educated nationalist elite—born between about 1896 and 1916—was familiar with him and his reputation, and it was not difficult, privately, to obtain copies of *Max Havelaar*. He was the "good Dutchman" who had spoken out against Dutch oppression four decades before the first self-recognizing "Indonesians" could do so.

In any case, after the suffering of 1945–49, the new Indonesian state, which had bad relations with a still-resentful, ex-imperial Netherlands, was determined to abolish the teaching of Dutch to its young citizens. The nationalist elite continued to use Dutch among themselves—offstage (it was still for them a closeted status symbol)—but emphatically denounced what President Sukarno called, unself-conscious of the irony, *Hollands-denkers* (Dutch for Dutch-minded people). This stance was only strengthened when the Dutch refused to negotiate the "return" of West Papua to Jakarta, and in retaliation the Indonesian government nationalized all Dutch enterprises in 1957, leading to an almost total emigration of Dutch and Eurasians from the archipelago.

Only with the installation of the brutal right-wing dictatorship of General Suharto in 1966 did the stance change. In desperate need of political and above all financial support, the new regime opened its doors widely to "Western" (and Japanese) capital, as well "state-to-state aid." The Dutch then returned, if in diminished force, as businessmen and cultural missionaries who now knew their postcolonial place. The empire gone, and the prosperous European Community in place, Douwes Dekker could be positioned as The Netherlands' ex post facto Nobel candidate and great friend of the Javanese (a.k.a. Indonesians). Since General Suharto knew little Dutch, and in any case never read novels, the time for an Indonesian translation had finally arrived—"in cooperation" with Dutch scholarly specialists, of course. The necessary Indonesian translator was Hans Baguë Jassin, an elderly, conservative literary critic, with a Calvinist religion and a Dutch Christian name, who had been persecuted as a *Hollands-denker* in the left-wing newspapers of the late Sukarno era: perfect for the regimes in both The Netherlands and Indonesia. The correct assumption on both sides was that only a handful of young people would actually read the book. But the outcome was quite different when a distinguished Dutch film director Frans Rademaker just a few years later proposed to make a film of *Max Havelaar*, again in" full co-operation" with the Indonesian state and the Indonesian filmworld. Such coooperation meant the virtual elimination of Douwes Dekker's ironical multiple framing; what survived was a beautifully acted and shot tropical melodrama. For Saidjah and Adinda—Multatuli's fictions described them with the sparsest physical detail—Rademaker found two stunningly beautiful young actors who even had talent. But quarrels among the film's makers started quickly—mainly from the side of the Indonesian "cooperators," who increasingly disliked the idea of a rare Cannes-candidate film about Indonesia in which the hero was a Dutchman. But the real reason why Suharto banned the film from circulating in Indonesia until he fell from power in 1998 was much simpler. Douwes Dekker would have savored it. With the Dutch almost completely removed from the screen, except for the Havelaar family, the villainous "native chiefs" could too easily be read by viewers as the lineal ancestors of their own oppressors. At close to the same time, and for the same reason, Hollywood buff Ferdinand Marcos banned the screening of *The Godfather* in the Philippines.

LUISA VILLA

The Tiger of Malaysia
(Emilio Salgari, 1883–1884)

La tigre della Malesia—the original version of the *Tigri di Mompracem*
(1900) published in an appendix to the *Nuova Arena* in Verona from October 16, 1883, to March 13, 1884—certainly is not the book by Salgari we
remember having read as children, even if the plot is more or less the same,
featuring Sandokan's risky expedition to Labuan, attracted by the fame of
Perla; his being wounded and his sojourn, in disguise, in the house of Lord
Guillonk; his falling in love; and the escape, the return, and the abduction of
the lover with all the subsequent vicissitudes of sea and land. Written by
a twenty-one-year-old intellectual who still did not think of himself as a
children's author, but was directing himself—with a certain *scapigliato*
[bohemian] taste for the provocative—to the adult audience of a provincial
daily paper, it was collected and edited only in recent years by the publisher
Viglongo, with an eye toward the desires of devoted Salgari-philes rather
than the tastes of the common reader. It is not, therefore, the most representative of the novels with colonial settings, much less the finest or most carefully written. It is, however, the text that baptized the pirate Sandokan, that
sketched his profile and the motives of his vengeful theft, and tells the story
of his love for Marianna, with the attendant loss of ferocity that will predis-
pose him to become the hero of the successful novels for young people in
which he will be the protagonist.

The first work in a cycle that—insofar as it is a cycle—would commence
only eight years later, as much as it prefigures with cunning foresight the
destinies and the deeds related in those popular serials, *La tigre della Malesia*
precedes and exceeds the other stories of Sandokan and represents a
still unformed and volatile phase of the Salgarian narrative—a stage that already contains all the essential ingredients of his happy formula.[1] Primary,
of course, is the exotic setting, here represented by the Malaysia of the
midnineteenth century, with conflict between the continually more invasive

---

[1] *I pirati della Malesia*, the novel that inaugurated the series recounting the adventures of
Sandokan and Yanez, intertwined with those of Tremal-Naik and Kammamuri (protagonists of
Misteri della junglia nera), was published, in its first version in parts, in an appendix to the *Gazzetta
di Treviso*, between October 1891 and January 1892. The last novel of the series, *La rivincita di
Yanez*, was published posthumously in 1913.

English colonizers and the pirates of Borneo. It was a time and place in history up until then ignored in European literature, and it fell to Salgari to invent it with great imagination, its small islands whipped by waves and wind, its nighttime sea illuminated by mysterious "phosphorescence," its forests and "bushy clearings," the entangled plants with strange names (the *arecche*, the *arenga*, the *artocarpo* with their fruits of "improbable size," the *betel*, the *sagú*, the *cavoli palmisti*),[2] and its tropical fauna—not only the obvious tigers, serpents, and dogfish (including the feared *zigaene*) but also "monkeys with black skin and long tails, commonly called in Malaysia *bigit*," "baboons," "flying lizards," and "colossal ostriches capable of eating at least two men."[3] These are just fragments of that enormously rich repertoire of eccentricity that Salgari would collect in his journals for his entire life and would later use in his novels—not only to make the reader more erudite, or to create an atmosphere, but actually for that irrepressible attraction to deformity that would declare him, before everything else, a decadent devotee (or a late-positivist) of individuality in a time when it infringed on what was considered normal. And just because individuality is the exception, the privileged place for his epiphany must be "elsewhere"; not, that is to say, in the tedium of daily life in which the realist or domestic novels unfolds, but rather on the stage of adventure, situated beyond the confines of prosaic and normalized modernity according to the standard version of exotic evasion.[4]

The decided inclination of the Salgarian narrative to join with the cause of resistance against the great "imperial" powers seems to arise from this dominant passion for the individual's infringement and eccentric excess. Starting with this first novel, modern England, that "thief of lands," will be confirmed the supreme antagonist in the entire pirate cycle of Malaysia, just as Spain will be in the other famous cycle set in a more remote historical past, that of the Corsairs of the Great Gulf. Lacking true political motivations, if not the inevitable antipathy toward the British colonial superpower in a "small Italy" where the memory of Risorgimeno ardor was still alive and well, Salgari tends inevitably to take the part of the small versus the great, of the weak *prahos* against the English ships "that cruise those seas not their own" (49). These steamships symbolize progress and a civilized *Aufklärung*

---

[2] Translator's note: Salgari invents strange names for exotic plants.

[3] E. Salgari, *La tigre della Malesia* (1883–84), preface by R. Fioraso (Turin, 1991), 213 and 58, hereafter cited directly in the text by page number in parentheses.

[4] Cf. C. Bongie, *Exotic Memories: Literature, Colonialism and the Fin de Siècle* (Stanford, Calif., 1991). Certainly Salgari's "instinct" for that which contains "a morfologic infraction, a stepping over the norm" is discussed as well by Emanuele Trevi in his introduction to E. Salgari, *Il Corsaro nero* (Turin, 2000), viii.

in those "disgraced" regions, but they also represent the hateful arrogance toward a "simple" people, incapable of defending "the native land" (cf. 24–25). It is not a coherently antiimperialist stance: in fact, *La tigre della Malesia* celebrates retrospectively the imperial expansion of the young Sandokan who, having risen to the throne of Maldu at only twenty years of age, "in a brief time collected around him all the neighboring peoples, having won them over" (248), thereby arousing the envy of the rival powers that would plot his fall. What is at stake is, rather, the contrast between an archaic and indomitable natural royalty, with which this "extraordinary" man is endowed, and that bureaucratic and military regime, poor in individuality but rich in means and technology (a regime that obscures and dilutes its own will to dominate under the pretext of an economic and disciplined administration of a portion of the world that does not pertain to it).

This is why antagonists with a distinct personality are missing in this novel (James Brooke is merely mentioned, the Baron William is a half-figure, and Lord Guillonk—only slightly more rounded—is not much to speak of either) and the "tiger" dominates undisputed with its regal ferocity, the symbol of an uninhibited access to the excessive passions housed in the jungle of the human heart, which civilization dresses up, controls, and represses. It should be noted that the tiger is not only associated with the indomitable Sandokan; equally savage and really "tigerlike" are the Europeans who enter into contact with the protagonist and who are shaken by the emotional hurricane he unchains—the tender Marianna (whom Yanez sees get herself up "with the movement of a wounded tiger"), the self-controlled Lord Guillonk ("The lord let out a true roar"), and finally the ironic Yanez ("Look, I feel myself being invaded by inebriation in the blood, I would be capable of becoming a tiger myself," 247). In addition, everyone—with the help of a writing style that melodramatically underscores the pathos of the scenes—exhibits the connections between corporeality and the affections of the spirit: their faces shine with "flames" more or less sinister, the rage makes them "grind their teeth," their faces make them "red with anger," the blood "swells up in the veins." All this resonates with the character of the protagonist, underlining the proximity to the animal world, the impulsiveness that tends to connect (destructively, of course, but with such an immediate sense of liberation!) feeling and action. These are characteristics that perhaps constitute the source of vitality that remains in Sandokan even in the final and mildest pages of the cycle, the reason why his character has held such fascination for generations of bourgeois children repressed in their daily life (within the family, at school, at catechism) and set free, therefore, by the story of the "Tiger" into the very serious space of fantasy and game.

But such archaic dimensions of existence, that these scenes of adventure still bring to us, are destined to disappear under the pressure of the imperatives of good breeding, of adult self-control, and of progress, which in the final reckoning are precisely what the heroes of the Salgarian cycle resist. They belong to the lineage of ex-dominators (like Yanez de Gomera, "a descendent of the ancient adventurers of Portugal," 5), of the dethroned "on the counterattack," of implacable vengeance-seekers on the model of that incomparable popular justice that was the Count of Monte Cristo, and of pirates—in short, all those who in these novels are bloodthirsty and violent but at the same time generous and cavalier, "capable of anything" but in fact reduced to living and dying in the margins, the last standard-bearers of a mythic fullness of experience in the world that is hostile to them and that in the end, in La tigre della Malesia, will have the better of them: "Yes, my love, we were beaten. . . . The strong have won smashing the brave. Fatality was inexorable" (304).

Of this contradictory mixture of exaltation and failure, Sandokan of La tigre della Malesia appears as a sublime precipitate, whose demonic traits will become domesticated enough so as to permit him to live inside of a narrative cycle for children. Yet here he is, in fact, "the most terrible and most capricious of the pirates of Malaysia, a man that was more than once seen to drink human blood, and, horrible to say, to suck the brains of the expiring" (2). From the first pages of the novel he inhabits a world that in its most private recesses is marked by vice and violence, and surrounded by death.[5] Beautiful and cursed, in short; equipped with superhuman energies and perceptions; ascetically dedicated to his cause ("I that ignored always what it would be to drink from the cup of love for to drink from the full, calm cup of human blood," 100); often caught cultivating the fury of a narcissistic delirium of greatness ("I am invulnerable!" 9) and of destruction

---

[5] The baroque disorder is seen in the "den" of the Tiger: "In an angle, a Turkish sofa, no less rich for golden decorations and sculptures, with ripped fringes, and textiles mud-covered and often bloody; in another angle an *armonium* encrusted with gold, with ivory keys, that brought here and there certain signs to believe that they were made by the blows of scimitar, lanced by the pirate in his moment of delirium, and everywhere mountains of disorder, rich costumes, paintings on canvases, perhaps from the brushes of famous painters, rolled up rugs . . . and shields, scimitars, shutters, adzes and knives, covered with blood and the remains of brains!" (1). Consider also the cemetery-like "labyrinth of trenches" without end that surrounds his inaccessible dwelling "among ramparts keeping the shadows of themselves, of ancient, broken arms and fragments of every sort, in the middle of which lugubrious skeletons with empty eyes and mounds of bones peep out. While passing by, the pirate put his feet on a human skull, that broke, cracking" (3).

("I will make you see Labuan lit up by the fire's ashes, I will make you see rivulets of human blood run through the woods, and I will make you see a mountain of skeletons!" 39); he is also a gentleman when in the company of women, magnanimous toward valiant enemies, and, even though triumphant on the seas, uneasy, melancholic, and divided among discordant passions that from time to time attract him with mad transport, leading him to defeat.

In particular, there is another central (even fundamental) component to the structure that delineates the protagonist's difference and creates the conflict that makes the plot dynamic: the often observed conflict between the heterosexual *eros* and the masculine world of adventure. The schema is that of a division between, on the one side, an austere and exclusive passion for oneself and, on the other, the desire of the female-object, a desire that opens a fissure in the hypermasculine identity of the hero, exposing him to a dangerous, inebriating drift toward the "other," with the consequent mimetic "weakening" that this brings with it. Pulled to Labuan only by the evil name of Perla, Sandokan is first wounded in a bloody "fight," then maddened by love, then constrained to leave his island, then held prisoner, and in the end is reduced to "sobbing" "in the arms of his adored Marianna"—deprived of his reign, of a great number of his men, and even of his glorious and terrifying "notoriety" ("God! God! The Tiger of Malaysia is dead forever," 364). It is in some ways the most conventional aspect of the novel (one knows it is unseemly to mix pleasure and duty, or—if one is given to virile adventure— to bring a woman aboard ship or on an island)—an aspect that the text nevertheless resists, refusing to construct Marianna according to the model of the *femme fatale* that inhabits Sandokan's mind. While for him Perla is a "enchantress with golden eyes," a "siren" that "seduces," "fascinates," "witches," "tames," and "wins," this girl concedes her own love with alacrity and escapes with her man, showing herself to be courageous, resolute, and well-disposed to embrace for her love the destiny of a "bandit." "I am ready for everything" [361], she declares, and in fact she kills an enemy on the first opportunity: she seems, in short, capable of resolving in fact that aporia of imagination (or adventure or of love) that instead afflicts the protagonist without relief.

It should be noted, to conclude, that as much as the paroxysmal and ruined emotional opposition, as well as the dauntless resolution of one character, situate themselves under the sign of excess that dominates *La tigre della Malesia*, these qualities will become, as I have hinted, somewhat moderated in the subsequent novels. The mature Salgari will often write of decisive women of action (female pirates, adventurers, even bloodthirsty headhunters); but in the other stories of Sandokan, as there will not be space for the frantic cannibalism of the hero, for smashed craniums and cerebral material thrown about, so also will the feats of the "tiger" Marianna be missing. She dies of cholera offstage and is therefore present only as a sweet memory and bitter regret by the second episode in the series.

Translated by M. F. Rusnak

EDOARDA MASI

Ah Q
(Lu Hsün, 1921–1922)

Ah Q has become an emblematic character, the most famous protagonist in all of twentieth-century Chinese fiction.[1] Yet to this day who he is and what he represents, according to the author's intentions or otherwise, are still uncertain. In fact, Lu Hsün himself seems undecided about his character's makeup. In his introduction to the Russian edition of the novel (1925),[2] he claims not to know how to write about the soul of the Chinese people, because what divides them is a high wall erected by the saints of antiquity—a wall of multiple hierarchies—that prevents individuals from becoming acquainted with others and perceiving their evils. And there is still another wall, that of the difficult Chinese script which, given that it must be learned word for word, remains comprehensible only to a limited minority. As such, what is heard and circulated is only some idea or reason transmitted through the heirs of the saints (the literate) in a great circle of self-reference. The people themselves are "born quiet, grow pale and die desiccated, like grass that has been pressed beneath a stone for four thousand years." To speak of the soul of this silent populace is therefore extremely difficult; communication is not reciprocated, to the point that each individual's "hands do not understand his own feet." For those who are on the other side of the wall, few make any attempt to get out, to understand. Says Lu Hsün: "Therefore all I have left is to count on the strength of my own perceptions, to write in solitude about what passes before my eyes and appears to be the life of the Chinese people." He then adds that he has been called comical, satirical, cold, and ironic, "to the point where I ask myself if I might be hiding a piece of ice in my heart."

---

[1] *A Q zheng zhuan* (*Ah Q*), by Lu Hsün, was first published in weekly excerpts in the newspaper *Chen bao* from December 1921 to February 1922, then later included by the author in a collection entitled *Nahan*. The story had a number of successive editions and is included in various editions of the complete works of Lu Hsün (*Lu Xun quanji*), in particular the Beijing editions of 1956–58 and 1973. The English version can be found in *Ah Q and Others: Selected Stories of Lusin*, translated by Wang Chi-chen (Westport, Conn.: Greenwood Press, 1971). Citations in this essay are translated from Masi's Italian versions of the text, which were translated directly from Lu Hsün's Chinese.

[2] Published in Chinese in the magazine *Yu si* (*Argument Threads*), no. 31 (1925).

In another article from 1926, Lu Hsün recalls how, owing to the polemical atmosphere at the time, readers tried to identify some sort of real personality in the character Ah Q and came up with the most absurd interpretations of the story, with the result that both the story and the character became bogged down with exaggerated, weighty meanings. The author repudiates this, refusing to be cataloged and assuring his public that he has no specific thesis to sustain, just an impatient disposition and an irresistible impulse to unleash cries of alarm and incitement, leaving those who hear them to do with them as they please. Lu Hsün is not a Kang Youwei nor a Liang Qichao (two great reformers from the end of the nineteenth century); his recognition is of a different sort, as he feels constrained to hide himself within himself. He wrote *Ah Q* in excerpts for the literary supplement *Chen bao*, and with every passing due date, his weekly assignment became a sort of obligatory exam, an obsession. When certain critics concluded that, in the final pages of *Ah Q*, the character was no longer consistent with his earlier form, Lu Hsün defended himself accordingly.

Given this author's extremely controlled and always self-ironic composure, it is hard to understand whether what he says should be taken at face value or not. Nonetheless, it is senseless to interpret *Ah Q* as an essentially satirical account of the Revolution of 1911, or even worse, to see in the protagonist Ah Q the spirit of the Chinese people. *Ah Q* is at once far less and something more.

———

Ah Q is probably a name or a nickname. But "Q" is neither a name nor part of a name and is written in Latin characters, a simple *Q*. In 1921—the date of the text—the use of such a letter was already enough to indicate the political and cultural stance of the author. Lu Hsün unravels his argument in the introductory chapter, in which he amuses himself by furnishing an ordered list of the four difficulties he met in narrating the story: first, what title to give it; second, finding a real last name for Ah Q; third, how to write the name "Ah Q"; and fourth, determining his character's place of origin. Lu Hsün plays a bit of a game with the canons of historiographical tradition, toying around with the idea of inserting a measure of quotidianity into the written form of the Chinese language itself. With the canons and writing system such as they are, how does one title a story? Or how does one trace the last name of some poor little guy (especially if he shares the last name with a town gentleman) or imagine how to write a name in which the only thing recognizable is the sound (*quayee*, basically)? Or how should one arrive at determinations of time and place? The satirical nature of these concerns would probably be nearly incomprehensible, or at least somewhat diluted, for a Chinese individual of today whose culture is a bit lacking, so for a European reader, only greater miscomprehension should be expected. Even worse, many of the story's discussions refer back to these name-related details, and the strength of the arguments is often based on subtle expressions or linguistic games. Without falling into a specific context concerning certain details about time, place, and script, I should point out that not only is the universal meaning of this introductory riddle rather evasive but so is the entire story. The up-front and continuous confrontation between a theoretical (and languishing) map of high society and the desperate, miserable reality of the present is where the story's profundity lies.

The work consists of nine chapters, introduction included. In the second chapter, a chronicled account of Ah Q's "victories," the contours of the protagonist are drawn out. We encounter him in the village of Wiezhuang (in Zhejiang, the province where Lu Hsün was born), but his origins are unknown. Ah Q has no fixed job, no family, and no home; he is simply a guest in a guardian's temple like any other wanderer or homeless person. He gets by doing odd jobs for the other villagers, but for the most part he is simply ignored—even though at one point an old man says, "That Ah Q, he's a great worker." He does not even have a last name. While drunk he claims that his last name is Zhao, then winds up getting insulted and slapped around by the father of the winner of the competition in the state exams, whose last name is also Zhao. Thereafter, everyone (including Ah Q himself) disregards the idea of giving him a last name. Ah Q is the laughing-stock of the village but retains nonetheless a "high opinion of himself." He hardly even shows much respect for the more affluent villagers who put their children through school, believing that if he had kids, they "could do so much better." After having been to the city, he begins to give himself still greater airs, but even the city's residents feel the brunt of his disdain. When they tease him for the patches of scabies he has on his head, he squares up to whomever insults him and, if it is someone apparently weaker than he, beats him up. But as it turns out, Ah Q is usually the one who gets the worst of the situation by getting his hair pulled or his head smacked up against a wall, and he almost seems to play along in the game of his own demise. Nevertheless, he always finds a way to console himself after such misfortunes. As such, when he is extremely humiliated and forced to call himself "a worm," he leaves the scene "satisfied to have won the match and believing to be 'his own greatest scorner,' a title which, by leaving out 'his own scorner,' simply means that he is 'the greatest.'"

The third chapter carries on the theme of Ah Q's "victories." Here, Ah Q manages to profit personally from the slapping around he received from Mr. Zhao, whose prestige as a bully gets cast onto Ah Q the victim and endows him with a certain degree of local fame that lasts for years. Until, that is, he suffers two even greater humiliations. The first one comes as a result of his jealousy toward Wang the Mangy Vagrant thanks to his ability to crush lice between his teeth. For this Ah Q insults him—calling him a "hairy worm" and thereby prompting Wang, the most downtrodden and disgraced of everyone, to pull Ah Q by the ponytail—despite his ardently Confucian protests that "a real man moves his tongue, not his hands!" and to bang his head several times against a wall and push and throw him staggering to the ground. "Maybe . . . it was true: given that the emperor had abolished the state exams and thereby caused the Zhao family to lose prestige, perhaps Ah Q had to lose prestige too?"

The second great humiliation comes from the "fake foreign devil," Mr. Qian, whom Ah Q detests for the false ponytail he wears ever since returning from Japan, where he had been studying, with his real one cut off. (At the time, wearing a ponytail was obligatory in China as a sign of subjection to the Manchu Dynasty.) Once again, Ah Q is unable to hold back his insults—"baldy, ass!"—earning himself a swift beating on the head. Coming to his aid, however, is his hereditary gift of "knowing how to forget." Afterward, perturbed by a group of jeering men at a restaurant, Ah Q turns to a little nun (she, too, is bald) who happens to be passing through and pinches her on the cheek. "It was as if he had vindicated himself of all the misfortune that had befallen him that day. . . . He felt better, lighter, on the brink of flying away. . . . He doubled over with laughter. . . . Even the people in the restaurant were laughing."

After pinching the nun, Ah Q still feels on his hand the sensation of her smooth skin, awakening a certain desire within him. This is the theme of the fourth chapter, "The Tragedy of Love," an irresistibly amusing satire on the sexual repression and conventional moral principles inherent in the stupidity of village conformism—a stupidity, of course, shared by Ah Q himself (including a disdain for women), even if it conflicts somewhat with his instinctive simplicity. "He continued to live in an exalted state." Thoughts of women do not abandon him—"I should get married," he thinks. Then, when going to work for the Zhao family, Ah Q is overwhelmed by his obsession and winds up throwing himself at the feet of a widowed servant and tactlessly begging her for affection—"Let's go to bed together!"—it is all over. The servant runs away crying and threatens to kill herself, Ah Q is beaten and berated in Mandarin by the younger Mr. Zhao, then escapes shirtless and winds up having to pay a double fine, in addition to being heavily indebted to the Zhao family. But Ah Q has no money, and the only way he is able to pay off his debts is by selling the last few articles of clothing he has left.

Following this episode, Ah Q must deal with "The Problem of Survival," the theme of the fifth chapter. Everyone avoids him, women duck away and hide when he passes by, and even the guardian of the temple threatens to chase him away. But the real problem is that he is no longer able to find a job. And as if that were not enough, he finds out that he has been replaced at work by Little D. (a bum even more miserable than Wang the Mangy Vagrant), with whom he then ends up getting into an epic street fight. He has nothing more to sell for food, and all he has left are the pants he wears. By the end of the chapter, in yet another scene of terrible farce, he is reduced to stealing turnips from a garden kept by nuns.

Ah Q finally decides to go back to town, where "Rebirth and Ruin" (chapter 6) await him. At his first visit back to the restaurant, he is better dressed and even has some money in his pocket. He tells of having worked in the home of the winner of the state exams, a job that granted him great prestige even if, for some reason, he ended up having to leave the home. Though they are a bit doubtful of his stories, Ah Q's fellow townsmen seem to have forgotten his past troublemaking. They seek him out and even display a certain degree of fear when around him. Women no longer run away from him; instead they compete with one another to buy the articles of clothing and fabric he has brought back with him. But misfortune gets the best of him again when he cannot make good on Mrs. Zhao's request for a fur coat. For this, the Zhao family starts to circulate rumors throughout the town, until Ah Q gets bold and takes it on himself to recount to a group of lazy bums everything that had happened. In short, he tells them that he had played lookout for some thieves, then got scared and ran off and for this reason came back to the village. From this point on, his fellow townsmen no longer fear him. Instead, they just consider him despicable.

In the meantime, news arrives about the outbreak of the revolution (that of 1911), which serves as a backdrop for the final three chapters: "Revolution," "Excluded from the Revolution," and "Happy Ending." Alongside other events that make Ah Q curious, the younger Mr. Zhao, winner of the state exams, sends his father some cases of precious goods from the city to have them safely hidden. "Ah Q had heard people talking about the revolutionaries for quite a while, and in that same year he had even seen some of them decapitated." (On his return from the city, he had spoken of the beheadings as if they were great spectacles.) "He thought the revolutionaries were simply rebels and that a rebellion would have made life difficult for him. . . . For that reason he had always despised them. . . . But who would have ever thought that they could scare someone as famous as the winner of the state exams? For this, Ah Q was crazy with joy, and the terror of the other residents in the village only gave him even greater satisfaction."

Believing himself to be one of the revolutionaries, Ah Q gets drunk and goes around yelling, "Rebellion! Rebellion! Rebellion!" and singing, "I'll beat you with a steel club!" He is then looked on with renewed fear, even by Mr. Zhao, Mr. Zhao's son, and the guardian of the temple. At night he fantasizes about the arrival of the revolutionaries: "They'll come to the temple yelling: 'Ah Q, come with us, come!' . . . And when they all . . . drop to their knees before me and beg: 'Ah Q, spare our lives!' then I'll have fun. Who will be there to hear them! The first to die will be Little D. and Mr. Zhao, then his son and the fake foreign devil. . . . Once I might have considered saving Wang the Vagrant, but now I don't even want him."

Before long Ah Q will come to find out that the younger Mr. Zhao has rolled up his ponytail and has passed through the revolutionaries with the fake foreign devil, and that the revolutionaries' arrival in the city has not brought about great changes. Some reform has come, though: everyone, even Little D., rolls his ponytail up on his head, and the younger Mr. Zhao buys his way into the liberty party (which the townspeople call "the persimmon oil party"). But when Ah Q tries to get into contact with the revolutionaries through the fake foreign devil—who on this occasion is called instead "Mr. Foreigner"—he is chased off forthwith. That same night, the cases of goods won by the younger Mr. Zhao are stolen from the Zhao residence, along with various other valuable objects. Four days later, Ah Q is accused of the crime and dragged into the city by a group of soldiers.

The final chapter, "Happy Ending," is the story of Ah Q's trial, death sentencing, and execution—"to make an example of him." The absurdity of the entire process is too much for Ah Q to bear and he proves himself unable to counter it, even at the very end when, riding in a cart full of prisoners who have been sentenced to death, he attempts to play his part in the tradition of singing an opera piece along with his condemned peers. But despite his hopes of making a courageous, arrogant display, he fails pathetically. Then, terrified, he dies—and hardly even realizes it.

———

The story of Ah Q is absolutely unrealistic. It must read as if it were the estranged recitation of a Chinese theatrical piece—a comical, terrible theatrical piece entirely devoid of catharsis. Ah Q himself is imaginary, a projection of the author, an allegory. He defies definition, he is a no one, a voluntary participant in a social context that excludes him and eludes his comprehension. Ah Q is the embodiment of a man who represents nothing, not even his own misfortunes—he is a nonexistence whose nonpresence is bolstered by his so-called moral victories, his bad luck, and his lack of conscience and his flaccid comportment after his arrest, during his trial, and on his way to death.

Like most learned Chinese of his century, Lu Hsün is dominated by his people's feelings of humiliation when compared with Europeans and by an obsession with modernity. According to the author's intentions and desires, Ah Q is just a typical Chinese individual: backward and miserable to the point of objectively negating himself, hidden behind the ridiculous, expired mask of a great tradition. Despite his ironic reserves, Lu Hsün is aware of the universal import his work carries in terms of literary and artistic truth, but he perhaps overlooks how far the quality of his work extends beyond limits of time and space. Because it deals with extreme deprivation, his work forgoes specificity with regard to historical time and definite place. For this reason Ah Q can take a seat next to some of the greatest protagonists of nineteenth-century European literature—such as Woyzeck or Violetta—representing a state of ultimate alienation from all time and place. For Lu Hsün, to paint Ah Q's portrait as a tragedy would be impossible; as always in Chinese literature, the author's presentation has its roots in satire, and the portrait's form might be considered that of a farce. Nonetheless, at the story's end, in the nearly intolerable coldness of the last chapter—in a suffocated cry of human compassion—the image of Lu Hsün as an author with a "piece of ice" in his heart simply melts away.

———

Translated by Paul D'Agostino

THOMAS LAHUSEN

Cement
(Fedor Gladkov, 1925)

"*Cement*—one of the first novels about the working class, about the birth of new interpersonal relations—is proof, if proof were needed, that the work of a great artist is immune to the ravages of time."[1] These words, which figure on the back cover of the last (1981) Soviet edition of Fedor Gladkov's novel in English translation, could not contradict more blatantly the history of the production and publishing of this book. No Soviet novel was less immune to the ravages of time than *Cement*. After its first serialized publication in the journal *Krasnaia Nov'* in 1925,[2] the novel underwent thirty-six different editions until Gladkov's death (1958) and has earned, thanks to the relentless labor of its author, the reputation of Soviet self-censorship incorporate. However, representing, to some extent, the history of Soviet literature in one single work, the many fragments of this endlessly rewritten novel embody also—and better than any other narrative of the Soviet time—the contradictions between utopian impulse and state building, or, in other words, between the quest for the "transcendental home" (in Lukács's terms) and the history of "real existing socialism."

History is indeed one of the three narrative strands that organize the novel. Separate episodes, developed in chapters or subchapters, narrate the main events of the country's life at the level of one region, from the end of War Communism to the implementation of the New Economic Policy (NEP). The reader learns about the last revolutionary measures, such as the grain requisitions, the pacification of the peasant rebellion, and the expropriation of the bourgeois, followed by the new political climate after the civil war and the life of the Party after the Tenth Party Congress in 1921 (which proclaimed the NEP but also made important decisions against fractionalism). We witness the start of new private enterprise, as well as reactions against it by romantics of the revolution who have contracted the "leftist disease." They will be purged during a dramatic session of Party cleansing, a chapter that became, as we shall see, the object of much rewriting. The same goes for another episode, showing the return of repentant white officers, which alludes to the "Changing Landmarks" (*smena vekh*) movement, initiated by an appeal launched in

---

[1] F. Gladkov, *Cement*, trans. Liv Tadge (Moscow: Progress, 1985). All other translations are mine, unless indicated otherwise.

[2] F. Gladkov, "Tsement," *Krasnaia Nov'*, 1–6 (January–August 1925).

Prague in July 1921, urging émigrés to accept and collaborate with the Soviet state, seen now as the heir of the Russian Empire.

The life of the factory, from sterile idleness to victorious production (of cement) is the second narrative strand of the novel. It forms a chronotope of its own against a background of industrial and administrative landscape. *Cement* was indeed one of the first models of the "production novel" that flourished in subsequent years in Soviet literature. The two strands are tightly interwoven: production alternates or interacts with "historical moments." It is endangered and slowed down by attacks of the open enemy (the counterrevolutionary bandits) or by the sabotage of the internal class enemy. Part of the intelligentsia, however, in the persona of the foreign specialist Kleist, can be won over to the revolution. Production triumphs over all of its obstacles thanks to those "eyes that never sleep" of Chibis (the head of the local Cheka, or State Security); the courage of the workers; and the dedication of the Party organizers, who are able to discern in their local groups what is healthy from what is not, and to find a remedy against bureaucratese or leftist disease. The two strands—history and the life of the factory—are related on the symbolic level: the cement produced by the factory serves to build the Workers' Republic. But the construction of a better world is described as a "road of torments":[3] "In the whole Republic there was not a road, not a footpath, which had not been stained with human blood."[4] And so are the personal lives of the novel's heroes, which form the third narrative strand of *Cement*. Niurka, the daughter of the two main Communists of the novel—Gleb and Dasha Chumalov—dies in an orphanage, and Sergei, the intellectual Party member, must sever his ties with his biological family: his parents are expropriated and forced to take the road of emigration, while his brother is arrested and shot for sabotage.

What distinguishes this strand from the two others is that it has no resolution. Unlike the production—literally and symbolically—of cement, love, or, to use the formula of the already quoted line from the last English edition of the novel, the "birth of new interpersonal relations" has no denouement. There are signs of "free love" and of the "withering away" of the family, but both remain episodic and inconclusive. Gleb Chumalov, a hero and veteran of the civil war, returns to the factory to continue the struggle on the production front. But when he meets his wife, Dasha, after long years of separation, she is not the same any more. Also "reborn" by the fire and blood of the civil war, she has become a new woman, a Party member, who cannot accept the

---

[3] Title of a novel by Aleksei Tolstoi, published between 1921 and 1929.

[4] F. V. Gladkov, *Cement*, trans. A. S. Arthur and C. Ashleigh (London: Martin Lawrence, 1929), 2–3. This translation is based on one of the early 1926–28 variants of the Russian text.

patriarchal outpourings of her husband: "Now the nest was empty; and his wife Dasha, who had clung to him so desperately at the time of their parting, had not welcomed him as should a wife, but had passed on by him, like some cold and hostile ghost in a dream."[5] Much of the novel is devoted to Gleb's attempts to understand and to "reeducate himself." Scenes of jealousy and attempts of "love comradeship" à la Alexandra Kollontai alternate, but the burden of tradition is too heavy to allow for a happy end.[6] Instead, Dasha uses her freedom to sleep with the virile and forceful secretary of the executive committee: "Dasha had never seen Badin as he was that evening. . . . He did not leave her for a minute all the evening, tender and shrewd. And in the guest room of the Executive Committee, Dasha (how it came about she never knew) spent the night with him in one bed, and for the first time during the past years his stormy blood brought her in the night hours the unforgettable passion of a woman."[7] In an edition of a few years later, this scene is entirely rewritten: "Intent, full of affection and concern, meek, subdued and gentle, he never left her side until they parted to go to bed. And for some reason Dasha found it funny: she felt that Badin had drained, that his strength had poured into her—she would only have to give the word and he would meekly fulfill her every demand."[8]

By draining the secretary of the executive committee of his "stormy blood" and by frustrating Dasha's "passion," the author attempted to increase the chances for the happy end, but at a price: the draining of what made *Cement* testify and participate in the history of its time, the literal bloodletting at all levels of the novel, from mimesis to poesis. It took the author "years of self-abnegation and titanic work."[9]

Censorship was present from the very beginning of *Cement*'s publication history. In the first serialized version in *Krasnaia Nov'*, whose chief editor

---

[5] Gladkov, *Cement*, trans. Arthur and Ashleigh, 6.

[6] Alexandra Kollontai (1872–1952), Russian revolutionary, diplomat, and writer. Her fame comes from her leading role in the "woman's question" during the early twenties and her advocacy, among other things, of "free love." Kollontai also led the "Workers' Opposition" that called for more democracy within the Party and more political freedom for the trade unions. The Workers' Opposition was dissolved at the Tenth Party Congress in 1921 after Lenin passed a resolution condemning "fractionalism" within the Party.

[7] Gladkov, *Cement*, trans. Arthur and Ashleigh, 134.

[8] Gladkov, *Cement*, trans. Liv Tadge, 190.

[9] L. N. Smirnova, "Kommentarii k romanu *Tsement*" ("Comments on the Novel *Cement*"), in Fedor Gladkov, *Sobranie sochinenii v 5-ti tomakh* (*Collected Works in Five Volumes*) (Moscow:

was Aleksandr Voronskii, an ally of Lev Trotsky, many passages were left out, including chapter 14, which related the return of the repentant white officers. Was the theme of "changing landmarks," which entailed a compromise with the forces of reaction, contrary to the ideology of the "permanent revolution"? In a letter to Gladkov from his Sorrento exile (August 23, 1925), Gorky congratulated Gladkov for his novel. But together with praise, Gorky criticized the author for his "stylistic flourishes," his "lack of modesty and seriousness." Despite the fact that the dialogues were "original" and "truthful," the many regionalisms and dialectisms made the novel difficult to understand. "Like many other contemporary authors, you artificially curtail the sphere of influence of your book, of your creation. The showing off with local jargon and expressions is specially unpleasant at the present time, when Russia is all reared up and needs to listen to and understand itself."[10] When the first separate book edition appeared in 1926 under the publication logo of Zemlia i Fabrika (Land and Factory), the author had already started to comply.[11] Between 1926 and 1928, the novel was republished ten times, and each time, the author revised his text. What attracted considerable attention was the scene of the Party cleansing, and with time, criticism would become more threatening. The writer represented the scene "one-sidedly," and he "would have to account for the distortion of political facts of the utmost importance" wrote one critic in 1931.[12] Concerning the language and style of the novel, opinions were divided into two camps. A majority saw in *Cement* the birth of a new literary style; others blamed the author for the "naturalism" of his dialogues.

Khudozhestvennaia literatura, 1983), 1:534–54. For the history of rewriting of *Cement*, see also Maurice Friedberg, "New Editions of Soviet Belles-Lettres: A Study in Politics and Palimpsests," *American Slavic and East European Review* 13 (1954): 72–88; L. N. Smirnova, "Kak sozdavalsia *Tsement*" ("How *Cement* Was Produced"), in *Tekstologiia proizvedenii sovetskoi literatury: Voprosy tekstologii*, ed. V. S. Nechaeva and A. G. Dement'ev (Moscow: Nauka, 1967), 4:140–227; and Robert L. Busch, "Gladkov's *Cement*: The Making of a Soviet Classic," *Slavic and East European Journal* 22 (1978): 348–61. For an analysis emphasizing the implications of rewriting on the theme of gender and sexuality, as well as the poetic system of the novel, see Leonid Heller and Thomas Lahusen, "Palimpsexes: Les métamorphoses de la thématique sexuelle dans le roman de F. Gladkov *Le Ciment*; Notes pour une approche analytico-interprétative de la littérature soviétique," *Wiener Slawistischer Almanach* 15 (1985): 211–54. The present essay reiterates some of the arguments of this publication.

[10] M. Gor'kii, *Sobranie sochinenii v 30-ti tomakh* (*Collected Works in Thirty Volumes*) (Moscow: Gosudarstvennoe izdatel'stvo Khudozhestvennoi literatury, 1949–55), 29:438–40.

[11] F. Gladkov, *Sobranie sochinenii*, t. 3. *Tsement* (*Collected Works*, vol. 3. *Cement*) (Moscow: Zemlia i Fabrika, 1926).

[12] I. Astakhov, "O tvorchestve F. Gladkova" ("On the Work of F. Gladkov") *Literatura i iskusstvo* 11–12 (1931): 65.

In 1928, a new Zemlia i Fabrika edition of *Cement* appeared, again revised by its author. It is generally considered as concluding his work on the novel during the 1920s. Most of the changes concern the characters Gleb and Dasha, "whose interactions are now better motivated psychologically and therefore, better explained."[13] The author smoothed Gleb's language to temper its "partisan roughness." In the first ten editions, Gleb threatens that anyone who does not share his convictions will be "shot" or "put against the wall."[14] In the 1928 rewrite, these threats disappear. Gleb's discourse becomes less crude, less emotional, more argumentative, calm, and rational. But in the process, the novel loses some of its "edge." L. N. Smirnova writes: "There is a tendency to flatten, to smooth out the contradictions between workers and Party organizers, which overall is an important aspect of the novel." Also, she argues, the cleansing of dialectisms, vulgarisms, spoken language, and "stylistic flourishes" lowers the expressivity of the text, in which clichés have become more abundant.[15] Gladkov commented himself on the result of his five years' labor on the novel in a 1931 article, entitled "My Work on *Cement*": "I wanted my novel to sound, in its whole entity, like a harmonious, energetic symphony. It was important for me that every character spoke with his own language, acted and felt according to his *nature*, so that the depiction of nature would coincide organically with the "inside" of people, like some kind of lyrical variation of their psychology, so that no single word would be uttered in vain, but would express a maximum of thoughts and emotions, and would fit together with all others, side by side, like a parquet floor."[16]

What is stunning in this statement is the acknowledgment, by the writer, of both the poetic system and the time his novel was initially part of, and of its increasing demise—the flattening, the smoothing out of contradictions. What characterizes the novel in its early variants is indeed a "harmonious, energetic symphony," a poetics of *integration* typical of the 1920s. *Cement* is, in its first versions, part and parcel of the poetics of the Proletkult,[17] where gender, sexuality, politics, and production are interconnected by a system of metaphors, the well-known "ornamental" prose of the early twenties. When Gleb comes back from the civil war, the factory is empty, like Motia

---

[13] Smirnova, "Kommentarii k romanu *Tsement*," 545.

[14] Ibid.

[15] Ibid.

[16] F. Gladkov, "Moia rabota nad *Tsementom*," *Literaturnaia ucheba* 9 (1931): 104.

[17] On this movement, see Lynn Mally, *Culture of the Future: The Proletkult Movement in Revolutionary Russia* (Berkeley: University of California Press, 1990).

Savchuk's womb: "From the huge dark belly of the factory there breathed the stench of mildew."[18] Motia, a young worker, yearns for children, for "chicks," "like a hen." And when the factory starts to produce cement, Motia is pregnant. Many passages of the "original" *Cement* remind us of the "Electropoems" of a Mikhail Gerasimov, or of the "Dawns of the Future" or "The Iron Messiah" of a Vladimir Kirillov, with their mix of industrial religiosity ("god building"), cosmic dreams, and the cult of the machine: "[The] severe and youthful music of metal, amid the warm smell of oil and petrol, strengthened and soothed Gleb's being. . . . Only here could one find that which was essential, vital, significant—amid the gentle ringing, and the singing of these black altars standing so firmly in compact squares. From behind the safety-barrier, he would gaze long at the gigantic fly-wheels, at the broad red belts, running as on wings, and palpitating as if alive. . . . Fascinated, he would lose all consciousness of time, his mind absorbed in this iron flight."[19]

A new wave of editorial changes starts after the severe critique, in an article of 1933, by Maxim Gorky of the language of Gladkov's new novel (and sequel of *Cement*), *Energy*.[20] From then on, *Cement* (together with *Energy*) undergoes continuous rewriting. The status of the text seems to be so "unstable" during the otherwise troubled 1930s (the time of the great purges) that no edition was acknowledged as "canonical" by its author. It is only between 1939 and 1940 that Gladkov submitted his text to a new fundamental revision. The novel was practically rewritten and shortened by about sixty pages. Gleb's language was again polished, and so was the language of other protagonists. The relations between Gleb and Dasha improved quite a bit. Where previously Dasha was accused "of not having slept a single night at home," the incriminating absence has now been reduced to a couple of days, and words of tenderness have started to appear on her lips. Dasha's previous sexual relations with partisans during the war are no longer mentioned, and, as we have already seen, she does *not* sleep with secretary of the executive committee, Badin. Likewise, an act of rape, committed by the same Badin against Polia (Dasha's somewhat hysterical leftist friend) is "weakened" to the point of nonrecognition, and so is a nascent "love triangle" among Gleb, Dasha, and the same Polia. But what suffers most is the integration of the various thematic and stylistic levels of the text, which have lost their links and motivations.

---

[18] Gladkov, *Cement*, trans. Arthur and Ashleigh, 15.

[19] Ibid., 286.

[20] M. Gor'kii, "O proze" ("On Prose"), in *Sobranie sochinenii v 30-ti tomakh*, 26:527–28.

These changes may be summed up formulaically: reproduction, which was previously integrated by the same process of production—that of cement, sexuality, and text—has been replaced by cloning. Motia still gets pregnant at the end of the story, but the "belly" of the factory is missing; some remnants of "cosmism" can still be found, but they pop up suddenly, unmotivated, and so do many metaphors and other tropes, lacking part of the bow that tied them together and integrated them into the same textual production. The overall result is a standardization of language, where the idiomatic roughness and flowery expressions characterizing the "Workers' Republic" have been transformed into "socialism" and enthusiastic quotes of Lenin. Finally, one of the most dramatic changes is in the time frame of the narrative, which from the present now shifts predominantly to the past.

Cement has become the "truthful, historically concrete depiction of reality in its revolutionary development," as states the 1934 definition of "socialist realism." Did the rewriting of *Cement* bring its heroes, and readers, closer to the new transcendental home of classless society? Probably not. Toward the end of *Energy*, the novel that continued the story of Gleb and Dasha, and that underwent analogous processes of rewriting, we see the tranquil and contemplative Party worker Tsezar' writing in his notebook, entitled "Voice toward the Future": "Before going to bed Tsezar' was sitting over his notebook and writing down his thoughts and impressions. This was not a diary, not a story of his life and deeds, and not a chronicle of daily life on the construction site. These were simply fragments of an unknown entity—scraps of thoughts, conclusions, characterizations of people, aphorisms, written down hastily, as though the author was afraid that if he did not fix them on paper, they would melt, die down, disappear irretrievably."[21] Tsezar' is of course Gladkov's double. And in his notebook are the fragments of *Cement*, of *Energy*, and other novels that became part of the now-forgotten pantheon of socialist realism. As to the "unknown entity," it is, no doubt, the unachieved history of socialism itself.

---

[21] Fedor Gladkov, *Energiia: Roman* (*Energy: A Novel*) (Moscow: OGIZ, 1947), 187.

PIERGIORGIO BELLOCCHIO

A Private Matter
(Beppe Fenoglio, 1963)

A study of Beppe Fenoglio could be entitled *Fenoglio: Resistance*, and not only because the partisan war is the dominant, privileged, and almost exclusive theme of his narrative, a focus unparalleled by any other writer. In the vast body of literature on resistance (fiction, chronicles, and testimony) so rich in first-rate works, Fenoglio's writings stand apart because of their engagement in the sphere of history and collective morality that transcends their artistic value.

Fenoglio's character Johnny baptizes himself the "eternal partisan."[1] Even though this formulation intentionally recalls religious ordination, Fenoglio is loyal not to a doctrine or a cult but to the decisive experience of his existence. His combination of ideas and feelings, passions and rigor, undoubtedly evokes the concept of religion, but not as a commonplace. In fact he rejects Catholicism as well as the confessional and sectarian character of communism, which we can see, for example, in Johnny's clash with Cocito in chapter 2 of *Partigiano Johnny* (*Johnny the Partisan*).

Fenoglio's "religion" is one of duty, engagement, and loyalty until death, and "his" Resistance—which seeks to refound Italy on the values of truth, liberty, and justice—has strong ethical, rather than political, connotations. He would have liked "writer and partisan" to be written on his tombstone. He gave Italo Calvino his comrade Dario (Tarzan) Scaglione's last message to be included in the *Lettere dei condannati a morte della Resistenza italiana*

---

[1] Fenoglio was almost immediately recognized as a "great writer" after the publication of *Partigiano Johnny* (*Johnny the Partisan*) in 1968, five years after his death. The debate regarding the date of composition of the novel began among critics and philologists, making Fenoglio a writer for university professors. If, paradoxically, *Johnny the Partisan* had been Fenoglio's only work, it would have still guaranteed him an important place in Italian literary history, albeit a less important place than his actual one. We cannot know if *Johnny the Partisan* would have been the great novel it has the potential to be had Fenoglio lived longer to continue working on it. But, since this is not the case, I do not agree with those critics who are seduced by the excesses of linguistic experimentation and who therefore consider *Johnny the Partisan* to be Fenoglio's most expressive and mature work. The novel lacks emotional and stylistic focus as well as the narrative measure of the stories of *Una questione privata* (*A Private Matter*). To give just one example, the story recounted in eighteen pages in *I ventitre giorni della città di Alba* (*Twenty-three Days of the City of Alba*) is expanded to four chapters (a total of sixty-six pages) in *Johnny the Partisan*. The condensed version is by no means incomplete and actually has clear advantages over the novel.

(*Letters from Italian Resistance Fighters Sentenced to Death*), a book he considered sacred.[2]

The great fresco of the Resistance painted by his stories never indulges in celebration, apology, or mythicization. *I ventitre giorni della città di Alba* (*Twenty-three Days of the City of Alba*) (1952) received little praise from the communist press and even bitter criticism—an understandable reaction given the climate of restoration in a time when the Resistance was ignored, denigrated, and criminalized. Fenoglio did not care and was almost unaware of the negative reviews, as Anna Banti recalled: "I was amazed by the exceptional naïveté of a youngster who had not even thought of keeping track of the destiny of his first work."[3] The naive Fenoglio could see much farther than his myopic and slightly bigoted censors. Rather than being "an evil act" against the Resistance, as Carlo Salinari wrote in the Roman edition of *L'Unità* on September 3, 1952, *Twenty-three Days of the City of Alba* contributed to the construction of an epic of the Resistance, all the more authentic because of its "political correctness." The case of Babel's masterpiece *L'armata a cavallo* (*Red Cavalry*) is somewhat similar. Badly received by communist critics and suspected of being "counterrevolutionary," it is in fact one of the greatest testimonies in favor of the Russian Revolution.

Fenoglio's relationship to the communist hegemony over leftist culture is characterized by a fundamental estrangement that has social and almost biological roots. Fenoglio began his partisan activity in a communist brigade but would feel at ease, in his element, only after switching to an autonomous unit (the "blues" or *badogliani*, as they were pejoratively called by the "reds").[4] The problem is one of blood and culture, which for Fenoglio are complimentary—as reflected in the dream/nightmare of being captured in *Inizi del partigiano Raoul* (*The Early Days of Partisan Raoul*). A recruit who by chance joined a Garibaldine unit pleads to be executed "alone," "to die by himself": "It disgusts me to share the wall with *them*! I don't know them!" Fenoglio respects and admires the great qualities of the communists and honestly acknowledges the high price of sacrifice and risk that they pay: Anglo-American provisions of weapons, clothes, food, and cigarettes (the *lanci*) are all for the "blues," and if a blue is captured by the fascists, he might have a remote chance of surviving, whereas a red has no chance at all

---

[2] Beppe Fenoglio, *Lettere 1940–1962* (Turin: Einaudi, 2002), 53.

[3] Ibid., 60, cf. footnote.

[4] Translators' note: The term *badogliani* refers to Italian soldiers who joined the Resistance after the armistice between Italy and the Allies was signed.

(see *Un altro muro* [*Another Wall*]). In *Una questione privata* (*A Private Matter*), Milton's hope of saving Giorgio is based on his belonging to autonomous units, as well as to an upper-middle-class family.

But all this is not enough for Fenoglio to overcome the distance that separates him from the communists. He refuses to compromise by making choices and endorsing behavior that he does not fully approve of, both in wartime and in civil life. It is helpful to remember some facts in order to understand the character of the man and that of his work, which rarely coincide as much as in Fenoglio's case. His mother reproached him for refusing to continue attending college in 1946, and he told her that his university degree would be the first book he published. (Nowadays it is difficult to understand what a university degree meant to the lower middle class anxious for the security associated with social ascent). It goes without saying that as a war veteran he could have finished his studies with little difficulty, but this may in fact be one of the reasons why he did not. Fenoglio had little interest in things he did not deeply know, from which he felt estranged ("I don't know them!"). In 1960 he married—there was only a civil ceremony, at the time a rather scandalous choice in his milieu. And on his deathbed he requested the simplest nonreligious funeral ("A nonreligious funeral on Sunday morning, without flowers or speeches"). On the other hand, his vote in favor of monarchy in 1946 is striking. In 1953, he voted for the Social Democrats, that is, in favor of the government coalition and of the so-called *legge truffa*, despite the fact that the opposition front also included moderate forces.[5] This was a choice against his cultural background and his publishers. "Of course it was painful not to vote for Parri and Calamandrei," he wrote to Vittorini on June 9, 1953.[6] Rather than acting without conviction, Fenoglio preferred inaction. However, in a country like Italy—a country of fickle enthusiasms, conversions, and movements—Fenoglio's reluctance is a rare example of independence and nonconformity.

Fenoglio's other major theme is peasant culture, a topic that can be studied independently, since he devotes several short stories to it. It is nonetheless frequently connected to the theme of the partisan war. The link is organic because the Langhe countryside, rather than being scenery or background, is itself a protagonist of the war in which the peasants are inevitably involved through active participation, aid to the partisans, and the

---

[5] Translators' note: *Legge truffa*, literally a "scam law," refers to the electoral reform of 1953 designed to ensure a stable majority of seats for the Christian Democrats in the Italian parliament.

[6] Ibid., 62.

known risk of retaliation, as well as the misery they shared with the fighters. The partisan war was characteristically "pro aris et focis," that is, fought at home, in defense of hearth, family, and property.

The peasant world is one governed by the harsh law of need and labor, in which nature always appears ungrateful and menacing (snow, rain, wind, fog, mud). It is a stoic and violent world of bitter passions (frequent homicides and suicides)—reflective of the fierce guerrilla warfare prevalent between 1943 and 1945—yet also a world of humanity and fraternity. A moment in which extreme desperation and extreme humanity converge with an almost intolerable tension occurs in chapter 8 of *A Private Matter*: "In the darkness he found the house by groping his way around, despite knowing it by heart. It was low and misshapen as though it had never fully recovered from a tremendous slap on the roof. It was of the same gray as the tuff of the narrow valley with small windows whose tattered frames were almost completely masked by weather-rotted boards, with an equally rotted wooden porch patched with bits of oil cans. A wing was in ruins and debris was piling up around a wild cherry tree."[7]

In the squalor of this house—quintessential of the Italian countryside until just a few decades ago—Milton waits for several hours to return to the "hunt" in the company of the only inhabitant, an old, "dry, greasy, toothless, stinky" woman, "whose hands were reduced to a bundle of small bones" (Milton tried "desperately to imagine the young girl she had been"). The woman is a widow, and her two sons died of typhus in 1932 when they were respectively twenty and twenty-one years old ("To the point that I became desperate and went crazy, and they wanted to have me admitted. . . . But now I'm happy . . . and so tranquil. Oh!, my two poor sons are just fine, just fine buried in the ground, safe from men"). She almost no longer sleeps: "I just lay there, eyes wide open, thinking of nothing, or about death" (1,084–85). Desperation has infected even the animals. Milton is alarmed by the growling of the dogs, but the old woman reassures him: "He does that not because there is danger, but because he is angry at himself. He is a dog who cannot stand himself. He never could. I wouldn't be surprised if I went out one morning into the farmyard and found that he had hanged himself with his own paws" (1,086). She treats Milton like a son, feeds him ("an egg!"), chats with him, willingly agrees to keep his weapons hidden away,

---

[7] Beppe Fenoglio, *Una questione privata* (*A Private Matter*), in *Romanzi e racconti*, ed. D. Isella (Turin: Einaudi, 2001), 1,082. Hereafter the page number of the reference will be cited in parentheses in the text.

and offers him a place to sleep. She begs him to spare the prisoners (on the other hand, the old peasant man says, "All of them!, you must kill them all!," 1,098) and bids him farewell, screaming into the night, "And think more often about your mother!" (1,091).

In *A Private Matter*, the two interlaced themes of guerrilla warfare and peasant life are joined by a third: the "romantic" love between Milton and Fulvia. The narration is fueled by Milton's feverish struggle against time to save Giorgio (a prisoner of the fascist execution platoon), possible only if he captures a fascist soldier to exchange for his friend. Milton has another reason besides friendship to save Giorgio: Giorgio was probably Fulvia's lover, and perhaps she is in love with him. The friend must be saved so that he can confirm or deny this, and for Fulvia's choice to be meaningful, it must be between two living men. It is a "private matter" for which Milton will need to act completely alone, without involving others. The plan is partially successful: Milton captures the fascist, but despite his reassurance, the hostage does not trust him, and in a panic he tries to escape. Milton must kill him. And the matter is no longer "private": two very young partisans will pay for that death, two virtually innocent boys who are prisoners of the fascists (in the penultimate chapter, the only one in which Milton is not present).

The inclusion of the "private" motive does not diminish or blur the fundamental themes, the Resistance and the peasant world, which on the contrary are further highlighted and given an unprecedented expressive force. In his insightful monograph, Gabriele Pedullà writes: "The political theme intersects, blends and ultimately fuses with the sentimental one" and yet, as in Foscolo's *Ortis*, "the preeminent focus is political passion."[8] And shortly thereafter, Pedullà continues:

> Even if the first impression points in the opposite direction (beginning with the titles themselves) the influx of great History in the plot of *A Private Matter* is actually more incisive than in *Spring of Beauty* or in *Johnny the Partisan*. In the latter two, after all, the events of the civil war are relegated to the background, without actually affecting the protagonist's life. It is as though the stubbornness with which Johnny remains unaffected by adversity and resistant to change keeps him distant and almost separate from the outside world. This is exactly the opposite of what happens in *A Private Matter*, in which individual and collective destiny intersect and clash on every page,

---

[8] Gabriele Pedullà, *La strada più lunga: Sulle tracce di Beppe Fenoglio* (Rome: Donzelli, 2001), 60.

finally flowing together in a common—and not at all consoling—image of existence.[9]

The truth that Milton seeks and demands goes far beyond the "private matter": what truly matters is knowing the truth in order to live—and die—in the truth.

Translated by Alberto Bianchi and Esther Marion

_____

[9] Ibid., 60–61.

SIMON GIKANDI

Arrow of God
(Chinua Achebe, 1964)

Chinua Achebe's third novel, *Arrow of God*, is one of the most powerful
fictional texts in the history of modern African literature. In both its concern
with the question of colonialism in Africa and its appropriation of the dominant conventions of European fiction, it can be read as an example of the
ambition of the novel in the period of decolonization and an enigmatic text
within the field of postcolonial theory as it has emerged since the early
1980s.[1] To describe *Arrow of God* as both an exemplary and enigmatic text
is another way of calling attention to three sets of problems that have come
to haunt the history of the novel in the so-called third world. The first problem concerns the relation between texts and generic conventions. Like most
classical texts of colonialism and decolonization, *Arrow of God* foregrounds
the issues that arise when the conventions of the metropolitan European
novel are transferred to the (post)colonial world. Although first published in
1964, Achebe's novel seems to reflect all the conventions of the realist tradition of the novel dominant in Europe in the nineteenth century. Indeed, part
of the authority of this novel within the canon of African literature depends
on its use of forms of representation whose goal is nothing less than the presentation of a knowable system, an intelligible world defined by symbols and
cultural norms that can be used to counter the blankness of Africa as it is inscribed in powerful colonial texts such as Joseph Conrad's *Heart of Darkness.*[2] If this concern with reality and realism is what makes Achebe's novel
attractive to African readers, it could be argued that it is also the source of
alienation not so much from readers unfamiliar with this world (since it
could be said that the novel already inscribes a world that, because it is set in
the past, is alien to all readers), but from institutions of interpretation that
are impatient with what Frederic Jameson has called "traditional realism."[3]

A second problem, which is directly connected to the first one, regards the
tenuous and asymmetrical relation between a third-world text and theoretical

---

[1] Chinua Achebe, *Arrow of God* (1964; New York: Doubleday, 1989). Further references to this
edition will be made in parentheses in the text.

[2] See Simon Gikandi, *Reading Chinua Achebe* (London: James Currey, 1991).

[3] Frederic Jameson, "Third World Literature in the Era of Multinational Capitalism," *Social
Text* 15 (Fall 1988): 82.

models developed primarily in regard to modes of artistic production in the West. What appears to be the dominant mode of representation in *Arrow of God*—realism or the mimetic contact—is at odds with almost all the models that have been developed to explain the nature of the novel in the postcolonial world. Indeed, it could be said that the central problem in texts such as *Arrow of God*, works that are intended to imagine national communities and to recover repressed historical experiences, is their historical belatedness. These works appear to be always behind intellectual and technical trends in the development of their genre. Confronted by this belatedness, critics of postcolonial literature have tended to either pretend that these texts did not exist, or to bemoan the fact that their concern with realism, subjectivity, historicism, and totality runs counter the poststructuralist desire for hybridity and difference. Alternatively, some critics try to force these texts to fit into the dominant theoretical infrastructure without considering the fact that what appeared to be old-fashioned realism is generated by the imperative to respond both to the dilemmas of the past (the period in which the novel is set) and the contingent needs of the moment of decolonization in which it is written.

The third problem, then, concerns the identity of the novel itself: in both its thematic and temporal concerns, *Arrow of God* is a fictional work enmeshed in the world of colonialism and the process of colonization. At the same time, however, it is a novel of the postcolonial period. It is written after the end of colonialism and within the crisis of decolonization, or what Frantz Fanon aptly described as the pitfalls of national consciousness.[4] In the circumstances, what ultimately determines what John Frow would call the "constructional elements" of the novel are anxieties not simply about its manifest thematic concerns but its time and site of reception—postcolonial Nigeria or Africa—and the crisis of decolonization.[5]

———

Let us start with the question of realism in the novel. On the surface, there is no doubt that *Arrow of God* adopts familiar traditions of realism, displays its mimetic codes proudly, and thrives on its didactic intentions. Against Conrad's image of Africa as a blank darkness, Achebe recuperates a community defined by its totalized cultural signs, its sense of its own past, and most

---

[4] Frantz Fanon, *The Wretched of the Earth* (1963; New York: Grove Press, 1968), 148–205.

[5] John Frow, *Marxism and Literary History* (Cambridge, Mass.: Harvard University Press, 1986), 104.

significantly, the sets of contradictions that are inherent in the idea of culture itself. On an ideological level, *Arrow of God* might appear to be a novel about the destruction of traditional, precolonial society by the forces of European imperialism. But on closer examination, the logic that drives it, on both the level of content and form, consists of some of the central doctrines of modernity, including historicism, a unified subject, and rationality. All these concerns are echoed in those moments in the novel when, even in the face of the social strife that seeks to tear it apart, the imagined community of Achebe's novel falls back on the symbols and narratives of everyday life to affirm its essential unity. When it comes to representing African society in the novel, nothing is as important to Achebe than the representation of the quotidian and the everyday as the very measure of a polity. Central to the structure, language, and logic of the novel is the preponderance of the everyday—what Peter Osborne calls, in a different context, "the medium of cultural form."[6] In *Arrow of God*, rituals of the everyday are enacted on both the collective and individual level in scenes, such as the following, in which the myth of the intelligible community is put on display:

> The market place was filling up steadily with men and women from every quarter. Because it was specially their day, the women wore their finest cloths and ornaments of ivory and beads according to the wealth of their husbands or, in a few exceptional cases, the strength of their own arms. Most of the men brought palm wine in pots carried on the head or gourds dangling by the side from a loop of rope. The first people to arrive took up positions under the shade of trees and began to drink with their friends, their relations and their in-laws. Those who came after sat in the open which was not hot yet. (67)

In contrast, the African world appears, from the colonizer's perspective, as one of mere figures, refracted through the hermeneutical delirium made famous by Conrad in *Heart of Darkness*:

> Captain T. K. Winterbottom stood at the veranda of his bungalow on Government Hill to watch the riot of the year's first rain. For the past month or two the heat had been building up to an unbearable pitch. The grass had long been burnt out, and the leaves of the more hardy trees had taken on the red and brown earth colour of the country. There was only two hours' respite in the morning before the country turned into a furnace and perspiration

---

[6] Peter Osborne, *The Politics of Time* (London: Verso, 1995), 197.

came down in little streams from the head and neck. The most exasperating was the little stream that always coursed down behind the ear like a fly, walking. There was another moment of temporary relief at sundown when a cool wind blew. But this treacherous beguiling wind was the great danger of Africa. The unwary European who bared himself to it received that death-kiss. (30–31)

One of the devastating criticisms made against the mimetic contract in postcolonial theory is that it assumes that the experiences represented in the texts of colonialism are unmediated and transparent.[7] There might be some powerful reasons to argue against the very notion of unmediated reality, but still it is important to acknowledge that Achebe premises his work on his ability to represent the African world as both mediated (hence the prevalence of calculated rituals in his novels) and unmediated (hence the significance of scenes of the everyday such as the market). Still, the evocation of a world that appears as unmediated is important because it simultaneously counters the colonial image of the African world as irrational and modernism's embrace of this world as one of pure figures.

There are also critics, most notably Frederic Jameson, who argue that traditional realism makes novels such as *Arrow of God* less effective than "the satirical fable."[8] But less effective in what context and to what community of readers? This kind of criticism fails to recognize the affinity between the mimetic contract and the mandate of decolonization, to realize that traditional realism was appealing because of its inherent pedagogical function. Achebe has expressed this pedagogical imperative in two famous statements made at the beginning of his career: The first one was the claim that he saw his role as a novelist in the age of decolonization as essentially that of a teacher: "to help my society regain belief in itself and put away the complexes of the years of denigration and self-abasement."[9] For Achebe, the pedagogical function of the novel is connected to historicism, or rather the idea of an African culture as the production of a temporal process.

We may have now come to be suspicious of historicism as part of the white mythology that underwrites Eurocentrism, but for Achebe, it is hard

---

[7] See Homi Bhabha, "Representation and the Colonial Text: A Critical Exploration of Some Forms of Mimeticism," in Frank Gloversmith (ed.), *The Theory of Reading* (Sussex: Harvester Press, 1984).

[8] Jameson, "Third World Literature in the Era of Multinational Capitalism," 82.

[9] Chinua Achebe, "The Novelist as a Teacher," in G. D. Killam (ed.), *African Writers on African Writing* (London: Heinemann, 1973), 3.

to conceive of an African culture outside the orbit of the historical: "I would be quite satisfied if my novels (especially the ones I set in the past) did no more than teach my readers that their past—with all its imperfections—was not one long nightmare of savagery from which the first Europeans acting on God's behalf delivered them."[10] The desire for historicism is not merely the expression of an authorial craving that is extraneous to the text. On the contrary, the scenes of everyday life and ritual that dominate the novel, the sense of temporality and especially teleology, are what make *Arrow of God* an authoritative work in its tradition.

On a structural level the novel is itself organized around two competing narratives: the African one that insists on the unity of its essential symbols, its history and dynamism, and the colonial narrative that insists on the emptiness of the very culture whose integrity Achebe wants to recover. Ironically, the colonial narrative in the novel depends on a certain mimicry of Conradian modernism, with its impressionism, its deployment of fetishistic figures, and its dependence on the irrational. As the following example illustrates, the world of the colonizer is one of interiorization:

> "But this is funny," he told himself. Why should he feel so nervous because Winterbottom was coming to dinner? Was he afraid of the man? Certainly not! Why all the excitement then? Why should he get so worked up about meeting Winterbottom simply because Wright had told him a few background stories which were in any case common knowledge? From this point Clarke speculated briefly on the nature of knowledge. Did knowledge of one's friends and colleagues impose a handicap on one? Perhaps it did. If so it showed how false was the common assumption that the more facts you could get about others the greater your power over them. Perhaps facts put you at a great disadvantage; perhaps they made you feel sorry and even responsible. Clarke rose to his feet and walked up and down, rather self-consciously. (106)

The use of interior monologue and free indirect discourse in passages in which the European colonizer reflects on Africa stand out in contrast to the direct representation of village scenes. Now, some of the devices Achebe uses to represent speech are not themselves antithetical to realistic representation. Indeed, some of them, most prominently free indirect discourse, function in the nineteenth-century European novel to complicate the process of realism.

---

[10] Ibid., 4.

Still, Achebe constructs his novel around a basic opposition: this is between externalized representation, which is designed to represent the precolonial world as it was imagined to be and thus to recuperate and exhibit the world colonialism has repressed, and a more interiorized language, which the colonizer uses to empty Africa of its subjects and its cultural logic. Even after the violent eruption of colonialism in the novel, an event represented by Ezeulu's exile, Achebe still strives to maintain the authority and continuity of the culture of the everyday against the contingency of the grand narrative of empire:

> The people of Umuaro had a saying that the noise even of the loudest events must begin to die down by the second market week. It was so with Ezeulu's exile and return. For a while people talked about nothing else; but gradually it became just another story in the life of the six villages, or so they imagined.
>
> Even in Ezeulu's compound the daily rounds established themselves again. Obika's new wife had become pregnant; Ugoye and Matefi carried on like any two jealous wives; Edogo went back to his carving which he had put aside at the height of the planting season; Oduche made more progress in his new faith and in his reading and writing; Obika, after a short break, returned to palm wine in full force. His temporary restraint had been largely due to the knowledge that too much palm wine was harmful to a man going in to his wife—it made him pant on top of her like a lizard fallen from an iroko tree—and reduced him in her esteem. But now that Okuata had become pregnant he no longer went in to her. (193)

From another perspective, however, the enigma of *Arrow of God* lies in the modernism that it seeks to undermine but cannot do without. This is a surprising claim in itself because the preponderance of the codes of realism in the novel is such that many readers would be hard-pressed to recognize any modernist signs except in those instances when the language of modernism is subjected to *la bêtise*. Significantly, the most innovative aspects of the novel are to be found in those moments in which the narrative seeks to secure the authority, intelligibility, and reliability of realism only to discover that it can do so only by incorporating the indeterminacy of modernism into its own schema. This is most apparent in the deployment of Ezeulu, the central subject in the novel.

The whole question of a unique and unified subject is important to

Achebe's novelistic project because, as he noted early in his career, a fundamental theme of his works is the restoration of the African character to subjecthood as it were. Colonialism, Achebe argued, had deprived the African people of their dignity, and this lack was one of "the worst things that can happen to people." The role of the writer, then, was to help the people regain their dignity "by showing them in human terms what happened to them, what they lost."[11] As we have already seen, it is in realism that the novel performs its act of restoration and restitution, and central to this act is the production of a self-conscious and rational subject. Ezeulu is such a subject. He is represented as the self-conscious figure of modernity, located at the center of his culture as an intellectual and ethical subject, proud of his role as "the only witness to truth" (6).

But Achebe also wants to produce a narrative of crisis, of the collapse of traditional modes of cultural explanation under the weight of the colonial encounter, and he can only do so by transforming Ezeulu into a split subject, a familiar figure in modernism. Indeed *Arrow of God* can be read as the story of how Ezeulu becomes displaced from the center of his culture and becomes a double exile—displaced from the institutions of colonial governmentality and his own people. This displacement is now represented using the very language of modernism that Achebe had mocked in the discourse of the colonizer in the first part of his novel. In fact, readers come to realize that Ezeulu has become alienated from the collective narrative that he was supposed to embody when the novel falls back on the familiar tropes and languages of modernism: the schizophrenic subject, the displaced temporality, and the interiorized experience. Above all, there is the narrative's focus on Ezeulu as the internal and eternal exile: "Ezeulu wanted to hear what Umuaro was saying but nobody offered to tell and he would not make anyone think he was curious. So with every passing day Umuaro became more and more an alien silence—the kind of silence which burnt a man's inside like the blue, quiet, razor edge flame of burning palmnut shells. Ezeulu writhed in the pain which grew and grew until he wanted to get outside his compound or even into the Nkwo market place and shout at Umuaro" (219).

Arrow of God opens by endorsing Ezeulu's claim to be the embodiment of his culture, its values, and its sense of history; it begins by endorsing the mimetic contract because it enables us to recuperate the repressed; and it starts with a parody of the language of modernism, which it associates with

---

[11] Chinua Achebe, "The Role of the Writer in the New Nation," in *African Writers on African Writing*, 8.

the colonial project of misrepresenting Africa. But the novel ends by indict-
ing Ezeulu for holding on to old values in the face of the changes triggered
by colonialism, for insisting on the unchanging nature of truth and the
authority of history. In order to perform these two tasks, Achebe must use
both realism and modernism. In this sense *Arrow of God* is both exemplary
of many texts produced in the age of decolonization but an enigma within
the schema promoted by postcolonial theory in which realism no longer
seems to be connected to emancipatory projects.

JOSÉ MIGUEL OVIEDO

Conversation in the Cathedral
(Mario Vargas Llosa, 1969)

Along with *La casa verde* (1965) [*The Green House*] and *La guerra del fin del mundo* (1981) [*The War of the End of the World*], this novel, the author's third, is one of Mario Vargas Llosa's most complex, all-encompassing, and ambitious works of fiction. It also signals the start of his interest in political subjects that would increasingly become one of his main concerns as a novelist. Published in Barcelona in 1969, it was considered one of the high points of the novelistic language, profoundly renewing the genre in Spanish America during that decade, a true literary dawning known as "the Boom," for lack of a better name. The book confirmed Vargas Llosa, born in Arequipa in southern Peru in 1936, as the youngest member of the greatest triad of the period, alongside the Colombian Gabriel García Márquez and the Mexican Carlos Fuentes.

It is important to emphasize that the vast portrait of Peru during the political period known as "el ochenio" (1948–52) under the military regime of General Manuel A. Odría is part of the author's personal experience as a young man. While studying at the University of San Marcos, he began to write and publish his first stories. (In a later novel, *La tía Julia y el escribidor* [1977] [*Aunt Julia and the Scriptwriter*], he self-satirizes these early stories.) The University of San Marcos is one of the novel's central themes as the center of the political activism of the period and opposition to the regime. In short, the novel is closely linked with the author's intellectual and political education in the midst of great hardship, which explains the pathos and feeling of failure that pervade it. The first lines of the story are justly famous: "From the doorway of *La Crónica* Santiago looks at the Avenida Tacna without love: cars, uneven and faded buildings, the gaudy skeletons of posters floating in the mist, the gray midday. At what precise moment had Peru fucked itself up?"[1]

This initial chord establishes the climate of decadence, tedium, and moral decomposition with which Vargas Llosa portrays a country under a dictatorship. In this sense, this is a political novel that resembles so many others (those of Miguel Ángel Asturias, Alejo Carpentier, Augusto Roa Bastos,

---

[1] Mario Vargas Llosa, *Conversation in the Cathedral* (Barcelona: Seix Barral, 1981), 13. My translation from the Spanish edition. Subsequent quotations from this work are cited in the text.

García Márquez, and others) that have converted the so-called novel of the dictatorship into a tradition in Spanish American literature. But one would have to make at least a few distinctions. *Conversation in the Cathedral* presents the rare instance of a political novel because the emphasis is not on the ideological aspect of denunciation or much less on expressing a militant sense of "commitment" but rather on the moral questioning of Peruvian society as a whole, without taking sides with any particular group. A second feature, related to the first, is that the figure of the dictator himself is almost completely absent (he appears only in one line of book 2: "Finally the balcony doors of the Palace opened and the President came out")(249). The story does not focus on him personally but rather on his system of intimidation and seduction maintained by an obscure army of henchmen and marginal characters. The narrator's attention is focused on the vast web of debasement and corruption spreading from the high circles of power to the bottom. The narrative model for this novel then is diametrically opposed to the author's most recent political novel: *La fiesta del chivo* (2000) [*The Feast of the Goat*], whose great character is the Dominican dictator, Rafael Leónidas Trujillo.

Starting with the question in the cited initial passage, the novel unfolds as an inquiry extending to all strata, surroundings, and confines of the country to demonstrate that nothing escapes the pernicious reaches of power. Even those in various ways opposed to the regime are steeped in its intrigues or paralyzed by a foreboding sense of defeat. Everyone is part of a strict hierarchy within a pyramidal structure of the society. The novel is at once a thorough study of the personal troubles of certain characters and a mural or frieze of collective behavior under the pressures of the dictatorship.

The plurality of the heroes, historical facts, and narrative spaces and times, spun into a plot that tends to proliferate constantly, all correspond to a type of literary composition that aims for a kind of total representation common in Vargas Llosa's epic style. The novel includes the large and the small, the private and the public (as announced in the work's Balzacian epigraph), the violent and the sentimental, the tragic and the melodramatic, mixed like the many threads of an enormous tapestry. We can appreciate the details from a short distance away, but we have to see it from a distance to grasp the overall design. There is a variegation and a sharp contrast between the scope and the social density of certain episodes, the anguished introspective tone, and the kitsch flavor of the decor and atmosphere of the underworld. All of this assures the novel that quality the author often seeks for his creations: that of being the fictional double of the real world, not to be confused with the idea of a passive representation of the objective world.

The work follows a rigorous order, a design that, in the end, bestows a precise and revealing meaning on each fragment. For the way in which he blends a subject of great breadth and complexity with extreme technical virtuosity, this novel is perhaps the paradigm of the author's aesthetic. Because of its extraordinary complexity, it is not easy to summarize the story (or stories) it contains without disfiguring it, especially for those who have not read it in its entirety. In large measure it is the text's very density that guarantees its indelible impact on the reader. As in *The Green House*, each major narrative line has stylistic qualities that lend it its particular identity, but at the same time, there is a constant play of interrelations, layering, and furtive contacts between them that affects the general design. (The difference is that the structure of *Conversation* lacks the almost obsessive tendency in *The Green House* toward symmetry among its five main stories.) *Conversation* is not the mere sum of its parts, nor do these lose their identity beneath the weight of the whole.

It is nonetheless worth discussing the four key figures whose makeup and actions dynamize the principal channels through which the story flows. Since each of these main characters acts within different social levels—in a way similar to the protagonists of *La ciudad y los perros* (The Time of the Hero) (1964)—their respective personal stories provide valuable insights about the historical behavior of those classes, their interests, their connections, and their differences. The most captivating and conflictive is Santiago Zavala, "Zavalita" as he is called by his colleagues at the newspaper, *La Crónica*, where he works. The sharp sensation of mediocrity that the environment and his work within it cause in him, his frustrating introduction to political activity at the university, and his early marriage, which the family regards rather unsympathetically (these experiences reflect the author's own), have immersed him in an abyss of "bad conscience" in the existential sense of the expression. He does not recognize himself in what he does but is unable to do anything different because he lacks the conviction necessary to make the big, definitive leap. He is a rebel whose hesitations and moral scruples ("the little worm" that is gnawing away at him, filling him with doubts) have led to a kind of spiritual paralysis. In the novel, Zavalita appears as the paradigm of the young, nonconformist middle-class man, half-estranged from the values of his class, facing the void of society under a dictatorship. The disillusionment, apathy, and insidious ugliness he perceives in everything propel him into a permanent state of introspection, questioning, and auscultation in search of reasons that prevented him from acting. The agonizing, heartbreaking tone of the novel derives mainly from Zavalita's deep malaise.

The other three figures are Ambrosio, Cayo Bermúdez, and Fermín Zavalo. They are so closely linked that it is best to examine them as a group. Ambrosio is a modest man whose life is marked by racial (he is black), social, and sexual humiliation. After having been a chauffeur for Santiago Zavala's father's household, he survived all manner of menial jobs until he became the chauffeur of Cayo Bermúdez, an important figure within the power ring of the dictatorship. While Cayo is a man who has managed to escape his lowly social origins (he met Ambrosio at some point in his poor hometown) thanks to his ambition and his skill at manipulation and intrigue in the hallways of political power, Ambrosio is a passive character, resigned to his fate, blindly faithful to the master he serves, no matter who that may be. This servile attitude makes him very useful in Cayo's schemes, especially when Ambosio's homosexual affair with Fermín is revealed. (Fermín is Santiago's father and a typical middle-class man trying to make the best of the political situation.) Fermín is then blackmailed by Cayo, and the final crisis occurs in his relationship with his son, who as a good journalist has done his own research into the matter and made his own discoveries.

As we can see, the lives of these characters cannot be more different from one another, but at the same time, they have the most unexpected contacts and overlaps. Although the class system creates rifts between them, an intense play of chance, interests, and purposes spins them all into the same web and makes them face difficult dilemmas. The resolution of these conflicts will determine the destiny of the others. The best example of this is the casual encounter of Ambrosio and Zavalita years after the events, in a sleazy bar called "La Catedral," near the municipal dog pound where Zavalita has just rescued his lost dog and where Ambrosio works beating unclaimed animals to death. The conversation lasts a few hours and turns into a vast retrospective examination of the political period that both experienced and its arduous consequences that affected both their lives in such different ways.

One of the most characteristic aspects of the novel has to do primarily with the way in which power and its mechanisms of intimidation and seduction are portrayed. The novel carries us from the highest political circles to the lowest levels of society, although it focuses on individuals and classes that are destitute and on the fringes of everything: the base of the pyramid. The "popular" point of view predominates, not as the incarnation of the heroic role of resistance against the regime (with the exception of the episode of the worker, Trinidad López) but rather like a melodramatic element of human sordidness, well known in the author's oeuvre. The book is inhabited by a pathetic parade of people who have been humiliated and trampled on by those above them but who defy complete obliteration nonetheless and struggle for a small space that will allow them to survive in a society ruled by the law of supremacy. They are servants, prostitutes, informers, bodyguards, thugs, nightclub dancers, night owls, and second-rate journalists. Poor and miserable, they all hang on to the flickering hope of surviving from one day to the next. The novel makes us feel how the dictatorship works in the midst of these dark masses seething at the bottom of the pyramid looking for favors from the influential and yearning for some scraps of power. They are the submissive clientele used and abused by the regime to achieve its ends almost without anyone's noticing its grip on the last reaches of society.

On one hand, this perspective sharpens the work's radical pessimism and the gloomy, grimy, and melancholic atmosphere that pervades everything. On the other hand, these low-life characters exude an incurable sentimentality and garish bad taste that the author uses to distinguish between the sincere but aesthetically questionable taste of the masses and the kind of decorum the upper classes tried to exhibit and maintain during the dictatorship. Popular music, the melodramas on the radio, trite family conflicts, and the sentimental formulas of Mexican movies tend to serve as models for the fate and actions of characters like the maid Amalia, the prostitute Queta, and even Zavalita's own life as a journalist and Ana's husband. There is a continuous process of degradation that runs from Ambrosio's complete moral inertia in submitting to sexual subjugation with Fermín to the vaguely literary ideas of Zavalita, buried under the mediocrity of his trade. It is not surprising that the editorials he writes on banal topics are a kind of intellectual abdication or abandonment of literature. Just like the cadet, Alberto, in *The Time of the Hero*, who writes pornographic "novelettes" on commission from his peers. Zavalita is an "escribidor" (not a real "escritor," or writer), a parody of the writer who is an important element in the work of Vargas Llosa. This recalls, for instance, Pedro Camacho's radio soap operas in *Aunt Julia and the Scriptwriter*. Scatological imagery abounds: Zavalita's articles for *La Crónica* are referred to as "cacografías" (shitographs); "a shit-colored adobe wall" makes him think that that is "the color of Lima . . . the color of Peru" (166); Cayo's nickname is "Shit Cayo," and so on.

Structurally, the novel is written as a very long series of dialogical circles that are superposed and shift like waves. Their rippling reverberations and displacements subtly alter the whole. The movement is concentric but occupies different planes of time and space. The main axis of the entire construction is the four-hour conversation between Ambrosio and Zavalita in "La Catedral," because it comprises and triggers, in a real or virtual way, all the vast effort of evocation, reflection, and retrospective analysis that the other dialogues and actions set in motion. All the backward and forward movements that are unfurled in the novel ebb and flow from this axis, configuring a complex system of dialogues. In the maze of voices, the reader recognizes the center thanks to unmistakable rhetorical clues: the present tense ("says") identifying the speaker and the vocative "niño" (boy), referring to a master's son, which Ambrosio uses in deference to Zavalita, something he maintains despite the fact that present circumstances are different. Another key dialogue among those that emerge from this one is that between Fermín and Ambrosio, which takes place somewhere in the middle of the time period evoked at the bar. Through this conversation we learn of their homosexual affair, the crime Ambrosio commits in an attempt to save his master, and his [Ambrosio's] subsequent flight into the jungle. We recognize him, even though the speakers are not identified, by the formulaic "don" that Ambrosio uses to address his master. This dialogue tends to appear like a flashback between the interstices of the others, triggered by a mechanism of association or contrast.

This novel actually offers a complete catalog of the repertoire of technical resources that characterize the author's fictions. Parallel or interwoven stories, interior monologue used as a constant psychic refraction of the objective facts, and the transformation of conventional elements of narrative dialogue such as "he said," "she said" into dramatic devices to intensify the action are just a few of these. But the most remarkable and versatile technique is the "telescopic" structure of the dialogues that allows Vargas Llosa to incorporate absent speakers who answer, from the past, questions that others ask in the present, masterfully creating a kind of oral "bridge" spanning time and space.

It is difficult to find novels that match the scope and richness of this one, the poignant depth of its vision, and the technical virtuosity it exhibits. The project's ambitious proportions and its precise execution indicate a very high point in the effort to renew language and the concept of the novel in the whole area of the Spanish language.

Translated by Linda Phillips

KLAUS R. SCHERPE

The Aesthetics of Resistance
(Peter Weiss, 1975–1981)

At the close of the twentieth century, most critics, at least in Europe, agree that the "grands récits," or "master narratives," or "große Erzählungen" of our knowledge, history, and culture have come to an end. All we have left are quotations, imitations, and variations: copies of an original that is lost forever, if it ever existed at all. If that is the case, then Peter Weiss's monumental historical narrative, *The Aesthetics of Resistance*—which the influential German critic Walter Jens considers an epic equal in stature to Joyce's *Ulysses*—is a work of memory about the originality of class struggle and about the authenticity of art, a memento of the cultural revolution and of the avant-garde, an expression of faith in the explosive force of the authentic in the social realm.[1]

Weiss's three-volume essay-novel represents one further attempt to contain in a single work the totality of lived experience, political history, and aesthetic reflection. We can read it as the effort of memory to overcome the desire to forget, as an artistic striving to defy the indifference that in postmodernity has become transfigured into something enchanting and that determines aesthetic values. Thus we would identify its artistic character as an incessant struggle with history, even when, from the point of view of historical consciousness, history takes the form of the ahistorical.

Yet Weiss knew very well that an *aesthetics* of resistance does not revolve around historical narrative, and that it may not revolve around the demonstration of power offered by historical images, and certainly not by the image of authoritarian rationality. In *The Aesthetics of Resistance*, Weiss often writes of dreams as a symbol of the sphere of art, a sphere that is always disconnected from the pragmatic process of history. By this he never means an unreal, antihistorical positioning of art, but always a deeper penetration of historical reality, an act of rebellion through the possibilities of art against the reality enforced by the ruling class. Weiss believes in the surrealists' vision of "making the unrecognizable knowable," embodying history, and combining aesthetic experience with political action—of arriving at a *conception* of one's own capacity to act.

---

[1] Volume 1 appeared in 1975, volume 2 in 1978, volume 3 in 1981 (Frankfurt on Main: Suhrkamp). References to volume and page numbers appear parenthetically in the text.

What awaits the reader in *The Aesthetics of Resistance*? Weiss develops a collective narrative about the antifascist resistance and the history of the workers' movement in Germany. The settings are Berlin as the imperial capital up to 1937, then Spain during the Civil War to 1938, followed (after the defeat of the Republic) by exile in Paris and Stockhom until the German capitulation in 1945. The action follows both the political history of the resistance and, in parts, the stages of the author's own emigration. The novel's political settings are expanded through a history of art and culture from the point of view of the oppressed and defeated, such as Brecht wanted to give voice to in his poem "Questions of a Reading Worker." In Weiss's novel, the principal characters are young workers and resistance fighters who, by visiting the Pergamon Museum in Berlin, reading Kafka's *The Castle* and Dante's *Divine Comedy*, and looking at Géricault's *Raft of the Medusa* or Picasso's *Guernica*, extract from those works of art the meaning that connects to their lives and actions. This aesthetic experience stands in contrast to the ruling culture, which *takes possession of* the paintings and their meanings and excludes the underprivileged from artistic pleasure and from aesthetic experience.

The Aesthetics of Resistance documents historical reality. The young resistance fighters—Hans Coppi, the son of workers, and Horst Heilmann, the intellectual from the Hölderlinstraße—were actual members of the Schulze-Boysen/Harnack resistance group (the so-called Rote Kapelle [Red Orchestra]) and were executed by the Nazis in Berlin-Pötzensee in December 1942. Weiss depicts this scene in horrifying detail in the third volume. Lenin, Herbert Wehner (the communist and later Social Democrat), Willi Münzenberg (the leader of the Communist Youth Association who later turned against the party), and the socialist playwright Bertolt Brecht all appear as characters and as witnesses to history—to *their* history in the broader historical context. And the female characters who are especially important to the narrative are also based on documentary material: Rosalinde, whose father Karl von Ossietzky died in a concentration camp; Karin Boye, the Swedish writer who committed suicide; and Lotte Bischoff, the resistance fighter who was smuggled from Sweden into Germany by the illegal KPD (German Communist Party). All these figures are positioned in a network of relationships within a collective historical fiction. Through their stories, history itself is retold, but also constructed anew. As a whole, that history is reported by a first-person narrator. But even that narrator is more than an individual person. He was born in 1917, the year of the Russian Revolution and—significantly—he is a *nameless* character, in search of an artistic and political identity. If I am not mistaken, Weiss has in an exemplary manner captured in the literary form of his novel the historical and aesthetic impossibility of the nineteenth-century German bildungsroman. The "means of individuation" that he brings out in the three stages of the whole work does not simply serve to establish the linear progress of the active individual but is also taken up in that individual's reflection, in an attitude of registering and commenting on the historical material. In the narrative pattern of the novel, the narrating "I" is always operating on the verge of identity-loss, constantly politically endangered, but also in conflict with those who share his views and with himself. The motif of searching for one's identity is carried over into various figures: the novel's key mythological hero Hercules; the poets Rimbaud and Hölderlin; and Hodann, the Berlin doctor and a despairing comrade. All of them are pieces in a "rebus," as Weiss says, a pictorial puzzle in which individual self-assertion and capacity for action are to be brought together and tested out in the fiction of a *collective action*.

On reading the opening volume, one is first of all struck by the tremendous effort being made to accomplish something impossible, namely to create a synthesis out of the contradictions on which novel writing is based, to reestablish the "totality of the novel." Art and politics, the literary revolution of the dadaists, and the political revolution are united in a surprising way in Zurich's Spiegelgasse, where Lenin lived in 1916. Moral confession is built into the aesthetic structure: nothing may be hushed up, neither the horrific consequences for the communist movement of the Moscow trials and the Hitler-Stalin pact nor the reign of terror in the movement's own ranks; also not the rhetorical optimism with which socialists and communists dismissed their historic defeats. This is exactly what art is capable of doing: expressing what cannot easily be clarified, identifying and characterizing those forces that run counter to political reason—the unconscious, the instinctive, and the violent. Collectively, all of that can function just as effectively as organized rationality, and mostly with destructive results. It is striking that the politically committed author surrenders unconditionally to this "inferno" (as he puts it with reference to Dante's *Divine Comedy*)—that he knows no "deviation anxiety." Only through this admission and through consciousness of one's own instinctive nature can one, in Weiss's view, arrive at anything like subjective political capacity for action. That is the prerequisite for his thematization of historical time, of political power that appears irrational, and of the circumscription of the field of action for those who put up resistance. And under these conditions, Weiss assigns expressly to art the task of *not* excluding the shapeless and the irrational, but rather of stating it more precisely through language, like the surrealists, making the repellent and the ungraspable imaginable. Art's purpose is not—as the conflict with socialist realism shows—to illustrate supposed political truths, relativize individual suffering, and programmatically negotiate antagonistic contradictions.

Weiss's obsessive opposition of reason and sensuality develops into a nightmare vision of history. Death and horror are indifferent to the political violence that produces them. The scene featuring the execution of the antifascist resistance fighters has the same awful intensity as the imagined depiction of Trotzky's face (with blood-soaked bandage, like Marat) and the evocation of Willi Münzenberg's murder in the Caugnet woods. The passionate coldness of the literary description stems from the artist's sensitivity to pain and his ability, proven in his painting, to draw the body with relentless precision and to make it present. The physical liquidation of the comrade by Stalin's henchman is not a teaching-play à la Brecht; Weiss connects it with a depiction of the effects of illness on Lenin's body. Sentences relating to a political argument are altogether absent, as are any that might elucidate the historical context. And this point warrants consideration: Weiss always presents the most impressive and politically most eventful images in *The Aesthetics of Resistance* when the story that the novel is telling as a historical process stops for a moment, is brought to a halt: "In thinking about the hanging in the woods . . . I tried to imagine the second in which the rope pulled tight around Münzenberg's neck" (3:23). Readers wishing to grasp what Weiss meant by an *aesthetics* of resistance need to focus all their attention on this detailed statement of perception and on the *construction* of the political in these sentences—on what Weiss called his "rebus," his enigmatic textual pattern.

How those sentences are historically and politically "mediated" was suggested in the 1930s by Walter Benjamin—who is extremely important to understanding *The Aesthetics of Resistance*—in connection with his Arcades project. In a December 9, 1938, letter to Adorno, Benjamin makes note of something that Weiss arguably then wrote out in full: "in the final analysis this involved not . . . mere loyalty to dialectical materialism but also solidarity with the experiences we all have had in the last fifteen years [that is, since 1923]. . . . An antagonism exists and I could not dream of wishing to be relieved of it. The problem posed by this work consists in overcoming this antagonism and has to do with the work's construction. What I mean is that speculation will enter upon its necessarily bold flight with some prospect of success only if it seeks its source of strength purely in construction instead of donning the waxen wings of esotericism."[2] In his dialogue with Adorno, Benjamin simultaneously resists a simple dialectic of knowledge and experience, and a negation that might put on the 'waxen wings of esotericism.' He

---

[2] Walter Benjamin, *The Correspondence of Walter Benjamin 1910–1940*, ed. Gershom Scholem and Theodor W. Adorno, trans. Manfred R. Jacobson and Evelyn M. Jacobson (Chicago: University of Chicago Press, 1994).

insists on the antagonism that is constructed as a chiasmus: the more intimate word *loyalty* is assigned to dialectical materialism, the political and public word *solidarity* to one's own experiences.

Peter Weiss feels solidarity with the experiences of the degraded and the politically persecuted. He remains loyal to those at whose side he did not fight during the 1930s—out of conviction, combined with guilt over having not fought in the Spanish Civil War. Hamburger, called Marcauer, the German woman comrade from an upper-middle-class Jewish family, dies in Spain. In the episode set in a Spanish medical camp where the comrades are faced with the superiority of Franco's murderers, they discuss Stalin's Terror—the Moscow trials. The usual arguments are presented: the victims' deaths are justified by the perpetrators' position, by threatened Soviet power. The historical materialism that has taken political power calls upon and then violates the loyalty of its soldiers. "Loyalty" is now nothing more than the annihilation of one's own historical experiences. All "logic" and "continuity" must be subordinated to Stalin's Soviet power, all "order" and "consistency," "obedience" and "discipline." Marcauer contradicts the Moscow teaching-play about the subjugation of renegade comrades to the Stalinist common good. Where the male comrades only discuss the question of political power, the female anarchist feels the physical violence of annihilation, at whose mercy she finds herself also: "only torture, which is part of the enforceable power of your world, can alienate a human being to the point where she accepts her annihilation with gratitude" (1:294). As an observer remarks, Marcauer speaks only for nature and not for the society that demands this sacrifice. Weiss carries his discourse right into the abyss of this antagonism. No link is forged here, nor is there any socialist teaching as there is in Brecht. Weiss must decide, and he decides in favor of the suffering creature, sensitivity, the female voice that contradicts the "patriarchical world," since there is no justification for it, not even a political one in extreme circumstances: "And before long the early morning hour when she was taken away by the military police became blurred, and all that persisted was the impression of her describing the sand downstairs in the hall of the Villa Candida, lit up in pale yellow by the dimmed lantern, the whites of her wide-open eyes, the backs of the firing squad lined up right next to each other" (1:313–14).

Like Benjamin's Arcades project, Peter Weiss's *The Aesthetics of Resistance* is a "construction" made brittle by historical experience. Weiss practices a kind of archeology of control and oppression and, as concerns the descriptions of art, a history of the signification and interpretation of images and texts. In the process, the novel's political and enlightening conception repeatedly strays into the "dangerous realm" of the unconscious, of what threatens the rational, and into the reality of a social activity that does not agree with the party's rationality. Weiss's "construction" of history is an aesthetic construction that departs from "real" history yet without thereby becoming unhistorical. It has been demonstrated that Weiss designed *The Aesthetics of Resistance* according to the pattern of Dante's *Divine Comedy.* Thus the first volume contains the magic number of thirty-three narrative sections, plus the introductory Pergamon "song." One finds in the smallest detail traces of Dantean animal allegory and associations with the Beatrice story. More important is what one might term the "morphological" support provided by Dante's work: Weiss took the pattern of the *Comedy*—inferno-purgatory-paradise—as the basic shape of his three-volume work. "Inferno" stands for the world of self-assured power and for brutal oppression, "Purgatorio" for the zone of doubt, of resistance, and of efforts to bring about change. "Paradiso" does not stand for a next world of salvation but (in this secularization of the Dantean work) for the void following destruction. The third volume narrates the death throes of the antifascists, the traces of hope in the midst of defeat and the void.

How does Peter Weiss imagine a liberating engagement with art, one that would strengthen the capacity for action and for resistance—how is an *aesthetics* of resistance to be practiced, in the novel and in a reading of the novel? The proletarians and resistance fighters whom the author calls "real" historical figures and yet invents are artistic figures. To some extent they serve as a model for the *possibility* (the *prevented possibility*) of engaging with art even though one is excluded, for the possibility of winning a culture for oneself. Preoccupation with a culture that is not one's own is thus not understood as a fleeing, not as adaptation, nor even simply as the appropriation of a humanistic inheritance, but rather as a rebellion, as "preparation for a conquest" (1:53). This is a battle in a double sense: fighting one's own way free of the quotidian depletion of the labor force and fighting to free cultural wealth from interpretations that identify it as art for the rulers.

Here too, political experiences do not allow for simple identification. In the dimmed light in front of the Pergamon frieze in Berlin, the young workers see the "defeated and perishing" in the tumult of battle but also the collective power that hints at violent change as an "inevitable consequence" (1:11). To them, Hercules is an "advocate of action," a friend of the poor, but also a traitor because his productive strength first serves the rulers' interests. They recognize in works of bourgeois realism the contradiction "that what emanated from the people was only given shape on a higher level," namely where it was "no longer reliable as authentic expression"

(1:63). Thus labor only takes on cultural meaning *in the work of art.* The workers standing *in front of* the frieze search for ways to win that meaning back for themselves. In doing so they distance themselves from the apparently familiar and look for the traces of an already prevented authenticity precisely in an alien realm—a realm that often remains alien even for the rulers.

They understand Picasso's painting *Guernica* as their own, without reservation. They treat its strangeness as a challenge, its apparent ambiguity as an incitement to extend their capacity for perception. Precisely because "the outer level of reality had been lifted up," it seems to them that the "oppression and violence, class consciousness and bias, mortal terror and heroic courage" have been combined into a "new whole" (1:334–35). In the midst of the disunity, this novel calls for epic integration and assures totality. Thus Weiss consciously calls for that which in modern literature is impossible.

The proletarian view of "classical" works of art from the past and of "modern" works from the present is not the evil eye that fixes or destroys its object. Nor do these works alter their owners through being looked at differently. Weiss keeps the bourgeois conception of art, its institutionalization, in the background. There is no need to fight for access to the museum. Nor does the perspective of *The Aesthetics of Resistance* encompass the concept of a cultural revolution in which art must prove itself "directly" and "operatively" as praxis. The aesthetic experience that Weiss's proletarian heroes wring out of the hostile reality is in its *form* still the bourgeois one: a cerebral effort to enter the work of art through consciousness and empathy. In its *content*, however, it conflicts irreconcilably with the bourgeois privilege of artistic enjoyment (polemically conceived as the self-indulgent esotericism of the true, the good, and the beautiful) and contrasts with intellectual melancholy, including "leftist melancholy" (Walter Benjamin).

And that is why the world of disillusion in Franz Kafka's novels and stories does not depress these proletarian figures in the least. The experience of annihilation of human beings and of violence in modernist literature feels much closer to them than classical literature's utopian assurance of a humanistic inheritance. For them, Kafka's *The Castle* is a "proletarian novel" because it gives expression to people's dependence on an anonymous system of power, a dependence that becomes so thoroughly internalized that it appears natural to the dependents themselves: "What I read in Kafka's book did not plunge me into despair; it made me feel ashamed" (1:177).

On a bench near the Hedwigskirche in Berlin, the workers read and study Dante's *Divine Comedy*, the work that Weiss's novel all but reproduces in the form of a proletarian world poem. And these working-class characters equate their lives and experiences with what Dante created, with the labor of his *writing* as it can still be discerned in the religious epic:

> We were able to compare the beginning of his journey with drowsiness, we knew about the sudden loss of what you possess, the onset of dreaming, the moments when the hook on the crane's chain could hit you in the skull or when the drive belt of the machine could tear your arm off, or in the night, early in the morning, when it was not possible to tell whether the room we found ourselves in was part of a dream or the dream was descending on your room, and in this in-between state, enveloped in severe exhaustion, and yet still capable of seeing, of hearing, searching for thoughts to give shape to what is appearing, what can be sensed, that is when he [Dante] began to put letters on the page. (1:80–81)

Weiss establishes a simple correspondence, an analogy between Dante's writing work and industrial work (the hook), and by implication between productive force and productive reading. Yet that equation only functions through the acceptance of a very particular third party that is characteristic in both instances: *danger*, and above all the straying of reality into the sphere of fatigue, dozing, and dreaming, the *traumatic* saturation of reality. Weiss's aesthetic key word is *anaesthesia*. Unlike the discoveries of science or the activity of politics, aesthetic experience must dive down into the abyss of the unconscious and grasp reality in all its depth in order to overcome it. In one of the last letters he wrote before his death in 1982, Weiss described *The Aesthetics of Resistance* as the expression of a dream: "And while *Aesthetics of Resistance* may well look like an ambitious novel about a historical period, with a consciously executed line of psychological and political development, for me it's much more the expression of a method that has its basis not in the contradictions and collisions of external reality, but in that element—so difficult to capture—of dreaming."

Weiss's novel ends by going back to its beginning. We are returned to the Pergamon frieze in Berlin with its emblematic representation of domination and oppression in the battle of the giants, of bodies and weapons. On the altar, which has only been preserved in fragments, Hercules' lion's skin is missing. One sees only the remains of a lion's paw, that is, in the symbolic interpretation of the novel, oppressed people's historically completed act of liberation. The final sentence can only be in the conditional, not in the historical indicative: "and one spot in the melee would be free, the lion's paw would hang there, available to anyone, and as long as those down below did not abandon each other, they would not see the paw of the lion's skin, and no recognizable person would come along to fill the empty space, they would themselves have to seize this single handhold for the far-reaching swinging movement through which they would eventually be able to sweep away the awful pressure weighing them down" (3:267–68).

Peter Weiss's *The Aesthetics of Resistance* wishes to function as a memento, a symbol for a process of liberation that has not—for Hegelian/Marxian philosophy has *not yet*—become history. The empty space in the frieze at the spot where Hercules' lion's paw ought to be clearly visible precisely marks an absence, something not realized. Literature cannot and should not fill in that empty space and compensate for it; rather it should identify that emptiness with as much precision as possible. "No recognizable person would come along"—thus also not a writer who has control of language—to liberate the oppressed from their speechlessness and namelessness. The writer is no representative. *The Aesthetics of Resistance* imagines in the historical conditional, in the language of literature, the struggle against namelessness. But as the former German Democratic Republic writer Volker Braun said on reading *The Aesthetics of Resistance*, quoting Karl Marx, in the end the oppressed must find their own names: "if we do not free ourselves, then it will have no consequences for us."

Translated by Neil Blackadder

The Sacrifice of the Heroine

APRIL ALLISTON

Aloisa and Melliora
(*Love in Excess*, Eliza Haywood, 1719–1720)

"It is one of the more appalling and therefore interesting facts of literary history that the three most popular works of fiction before *Pamela* were *Gulliver's Travels*, *Robinson Crusoe*, and Mrs. Haywood's first novel, *Love in Excess; or, the Fatal Enquiry*. In the decade that followed she was to establish herself as the most important producer of popular fiction before *Pamela*."[1] The problem has not usually been to explain why *Love in Excess* (1719–20) was forgotten after such a warm reception but rather to explain the "appalling" fact of its initially having challenged the supremacy of now canonical works by Swift and Defoe. It is time to get beyond this traditional critical embarrassment and ask, not how *Love in Excess* could ever have been so much read, but why it was largely forgotten for the better part of two centuries, after having been "widely and continually read during the first four decades of the eighteenth century."[2] What did it have in common with *Gulliver* and *Crusoe*, in the eyes of contemporary readers? The way to some answers lies hidden in the most obvious place: the title. Why *Love "in Excess"*? What is *The Fatal Enquiry*, and how is it linked to excessive passion? And what did it really mean to call a book "A Novel" when its title page announced that generic marker in 1719?

The Power of Love and the Plot of Excess

"Every thing happened according to their desire."[3]

Utterly unlike *Gulliver* and *Crusoe*, *Love in Excess* is about—well, "love"—but not love simply or tamely. It is about love *in excess*, a desire that causes characters to stray—not, like Gulliver and Crusoe, beyond the boundaries of "civilized" Europe, but frequently beyond the bounds of European

---

[1] John J. Richetti, *Popular Fiction before Richardson: Narrative Patterns, 1700–1739* (1969; Oxford: Oxford University Press, 1992), 179.

[2] Ibid., 120.

[3] Eliza Haywood, *Love in Excess; or, The Fatal Enquiry*, ed. David Oakleaf (Peterborough, Canada: Broadview, 1994), 249. All further references to page numbers in this edition will be made parenthetically.

civility. It is about transgressive desire. The energy that drives this novel's plot is, then, like that of so many other works of literature, the tension between desire and prohibition; but here the specific battleground for these two forces is a certain conventional femininity—what we nowadays call "gender"—or, as it was generally called in the eighteenth century "female character." In 1719, conventions of female character still included the idea that, despite the crucial social importance of female chastity, women were special prey to fierce and uncontrollable sexual desires, too weak mentally, morally, and physically to control them as well as men could: "But when he considered how much he had struggled, and how far he had been from being able to repell desire, he began to wonder that it could ever enter into his thoughts that there was even a possibility for *woman*, so much stronger in fancy, and weaker in her judgment, to suppress the influence of that powerful passion; against which, no laws, no rules, no force of reason, or philosophy, are sufficient guards" (177). Twenty years later, Samuel Richardson would help make this early-modern concept of femininity obsolete by replacing it with the still familiar one of the modest woman lacking in strong sexual desires, whose best social function is to domesticate the unruly passions of men.[4] At the beginning of her career, however, Haywood was still working with older conventions of womanhood.

Note that in Haywood's mythology of gender and desire, men too can and do "love in excess"; even their superior "force of reason" is not a sufficient guard against the passion of love. "That passion is . . . absolutely *controller* of the *will*. . . . When love once becomes in our power, it ceases to be worthy of that name; no man really possest with it, *can* be master of his actions; and whatever effects it may enforce are no more to be condemned, than poverty, sickness, deformity, or any other misfortune incident to humane nature" (191; emphasis Haywood's). Haywood's definition of "love," which she inherited from the seventeenth-century French tradition of female innovators in prose fiction, is a form of heterosexual desire that can be combatted more or less successfully (although only with great violence to the self) but remains ultimately beyond the individual's control, and indeed controls the body (in blushes, swoons, and all the other involuntary signals that would later in the century be called symptoms of "sensibility") as well as the unconscious mind (in dreams, fevers, and other subconscious states). In this sense "love" is a precursor to Freud's concept of the unconscious libidinal drives, which must be repressed but always return. It is in this sense

---

[4] See, for example, Nancy Armstrong, *Desire and Domestic Fiction: A Political History of the Novel* (New York: Oxford University Press, 1987).

as well that desire is "fatal," in both of the meanings current in the eighteenth century: deadly, but also operating with the force of fate, directing the actions of the characters and determining their destinies.

In a novel where both sexes are subject to this heterosexual destiny "female character" becomes the prime battleground for love's conflicts because of women's supposedly greater susceptibility—an effect not simply weakness, but also of the greater strength of their imagination ("stronger in fancy")—set against the immeasurably greater social prohibitions placed on the expression of their desires. The story begins with the desire of Aloisa, an heiress in the exceptionally independent position of having no father or brothers to control her conduct or fortune, for D'Elmont, and with her expression of it in several letters that increasingly violate "that custom which forbids women to make a declaration of their thoughts" (41). These letters are highly dramatic because in them Aloisa, although a wealthy heiress, does what no eighteenth-century woman of the literate classes could do and hope to retain a good "character" in the then-current sense of "reputation," meaning one that would allow her to receive marriage proposals and be invited by other women to social events—in other words, to function as a member of her class. Aloisa (named after Héloïse, who continued to declare her passion in letters to her former lover long after he had been castrated, had entered a monastery—as she had—and had claimed to have renounced all earthly love) vividly embodies this fatal conflict between female desire and the social prohibition of its expression. She "languishes, and almost dies for an opportunity of confessing (without too great a breach of modesty)" her desire—but there's the rub, for to confess it *as her own,* to identify her self with her desire, constitutes an unthinkable, and certainly unsurvivable, breach of feminine modesty. Driven by her desire to "confess," she composes a letter in which she does indeed make a "full . . . discovery of her heart," and is "about to sign her name to it," but stops herself before the signature: "No—let me rather die! . . . then [*sic*] be guilty of a meanness which would render me unworthy of life" (49–50). She "almost dies" of the social blockage to the expression of her desire, yet to express and own it would mean a social death that would make her wish for a physical one. The unsolicited expression of female desire breaks the cardinal rule of respectable society for women, and thus it is the definition, for this novel and for its original audience, of love *in excess.*

In Haywood's world, then, female sexual desire is fundamentally inexpressible, and the paradox she faces as a woman author attempting to write about it shapes her plot, her characters, and her rhetorical style. In order to write about unspeakable female desire, Haywood reverses the gender roles found in Greek romance; Count D'Elmont is the male equivalent of a Hellenistic heroine like Kallirhoe, who is so irresistible that wherever she wanders, everyone, from the boy next door to the king of Persia, immediately falls in love with her and will go to any lengths to obtain her. The plot of Greek romance is driven by Eros, at once the personified god and a kind of generalized male desire, which is everywhere cathected onto the female whom the god has made perfectly and inevitably desirable. Haywood similarly makes D'Elmont a bland, perfect object of generalized heterosexual desire and has "the little god" set the force of this desire in motion, beginning with the heart of Aloisa (41–43). Thus the force of destiny here is still Eros, but Eros in the form of generalized female desire for a male object. Yet this reversal of ancient gender codes conjures up another, quintessentially Enlightenment fatal force very unlike the Eros that orders the plots of Greek romance. Aloisa dares to express her love in the hope of inspiring a similar passion in D'Elmont, imagining that "that god had touched his heart, which so powerfully had influenced hers" (42). Instead of inspiring love, however, Aloisa's letters inspire a closely related yet very different passion: curiosity. Curiosity in this novel is, like love, a fateful passion to which both sexes are subject. Both passions involve a desire for "knowledge" (in every sense, including the biblical) of another person. But for Haywood, curiosity, unlike Eros, always misses its mark. Although Aloisa is herself initially moved by a "Curiosity" about D'Elmont—as Barbara Benedict has observed—Eros quickly fixes that wayward passion as an unwavering love for him alone. Like that of letters ("I am sensible of the accidents that happen to letters"; 65), curiosity's characteristic trajectory is miscarriage. If Eros plays the role of fate in Greek romance, guiding characters toward a divinely ordained destination, then in Haywood's work curiosity plays the role of chance, so characteristic a force in the modern novel as opposed to the older romances.

The Fatality of Enquiry: the Passion of Curiosity

"Enquiry will discover all," wrote Edward Young in the same year that *Love in Excess* first appeared—and this tendency to "discover all" is exactly what makes enquiry "fatal" in Haywood's novel. The other two quotations chosen in the *Oxford English Dictionary* to exemplify the eighteenth-century usage of "enquiry" relate particularly, as does Haywood's own, to the search for a concealed truth of character: some clue to a person's true but secret identity or nature.[5] The "fatal enquiry" of *Love in Excess* is, in the most direct sense, the curiosity aroused in Count D'Elmont in response to Aloisa's anonymous letters and his consequent attempt to discover the true identity of their author. This enquiry proves "fatal" in both the senses mentioned above in the discussion of the power of love. It is deadly: the novel's beginning, middle, and end are dominated by three different female characters who must each die once their identities are revealed as the subjects of their expressed desire for the ineluctably desirable Count, for such avowal breaks their society's laws of gendered character. They must die because their desire must be silenced. Indeed, Aloisa's physical death is described simply as a silencing: the only indication of her passing is the sentence, "Alovysa spoke no more" (163).

In the other sense of the word "fatal" (no longer in use today), the Count's enquiry into the secret identity of his first anonymous correspondent actually mirrors love as a force like fate. A power as irresistible as love, the passion of curiosity is the one that sets the plot of *Love in Excess* in motion. The Count's desire to know who the woman is who would thus boldly write her passion eventually leads to Aloisa's identification and death, but not before it repeatedly misses its intended mark, becoming displaced onto one woman after another. It first leads to the ruin of another woman (Amena—"delightful") whom he initially though mistakenly identifies as his mysterious correspondent. Although his enquiry results in the marriage desired by the letter-writer once she is correctly identified and Amena disposed of to a convent, it is "a hymen, where love (the noblest guest) was wanting" (94). His destiny is not yet fixed because the Count is not driven by love, but only by curiosity (and ambition, another powerful passion that Barbara Benedict has identified with curiosity in this period; this motivates him to wed the wealthy heiress despite his lack of love for her).[6] This marriage concludes the first volume, but there are two more to follow, and it very soon proves a false resolution that becomes an obstacle to the fulfillment of the Count's own desire for yet a third woman. Melliora ("superior") is the true heroine of the novel and the true object of the Count's desire because she is the only one of the novel's throng of lovelorn women who never consciously or openly expresses her desire for him before marriage. Although it is made clear that Melliora desires the

---

[5] From Fielding's novel, *Tom Jones* (1749), *OED* cites the phrase, "to enquire the character of a servant" (that is, to request a reference from a former employer), alongside Steele's line from *Tatler* no. 120 (1709), "Upon Enquiry, I was informed that her name was Jealousy."

[6] Barbara Benedict, *Curiosity: A Cultural History of Early Modern Inquiry* (Chicago: University of Chicago Press, 2001).

Count every bit as much as her rivals do, she wins him in the end by struggling to repress her desire, by tergiversation, and finally by setting up a ruse whereby her own sexual desire can masquerade as passive obedience to the command of her male guardians—one of whom turns out to be the Count himself (267–68). Thus the plot is shaped and extended through Melliora's refusal to short-circuit it by merely satisfying the Count's curiosity, by putting off owning her desire until her guardians—lover and brother—have destined her for the husband she has herself chosen. Only thus can she merit both continuance of life and the gratification of her own, disowned desire.

The Count's curiosity about Aloisa initiates his "fatal enquiry," but his is not the only curiosity, nor perhaps the most "fatal," in the book. Like love, curiosity is an overpowering passion to which both sexes are subject, but again women, as weaker in reason and self-control, are more fatally subject to it than men are. The Count's curiosity about his anonymous admirer is extremely powerful: "D'elmont . . . would have given good part of his estate to satsifie his curiosity" (50–51). He is able to restrain himself, however, in consideration of the unknown lady's reputation. Women in this novel are less able to control any of their passions, and curiosity is the one that most characterizes "the sex." Aloisa's crime is not only that of being so possessed by the power of Eros as to be unable to stifle the expression of her desire; even more damning is her continued possession by "that devil curiosity, which too much haunts the minds of women" even as she loves D'Elmont alone (161). This passion is what makes her enquire into the identity of her husband's mistress (143, 163). "What will some women venture to satisfy a jealous curiosity?"—in Aloisa's case, much more than a part of her estate (152, 154). The miscarriage of her elaborate plot to discover the identity of this mistress (Melliora) causes the accident in which she is literally penetrated to death by her husband's sword. Thus the most "fatal enquiry" is Aloisa's own, and the most fatal passion, that of curiosity.[7]

Curiosity and Character

The passion of curiosity so resembles love as a fatal force driving characters to action through a desire for knowledge of another that the one significant

---

[7] Cf. Benedict's similar reading of the same passages (ibid., 140–41). I differ mainly in arguing that curiosity in *Love in Excess* (as in many other works of the period) is primarily directed toward the discovery of another person's character, whereas Benedict claims that this novel "defines inquiry strictly as the quest for sexual knowledge" (139).

difference between them stands out in the contrast. The crucial difference between love and curiosity is that love *fixes character*, whereas curiosity involves endless change or displacement from one character to another. This is true in a double sense: true love permanently cathects a subject's libidinal desires onto a single object, and in so doing also renders the desiring character unchanging. Contrasting this "devotion of souls" to "that passion which aims chiefly at enjoyment," Haywood's narrator explains: "love *there* is a divinity indeed, because he is immortal and unchangeable, and if our earthy part partake the bliss, and craving nature is in all obeyed, possession thus desired, and thus obtained, is far from satiating" (230–31). Only this divine, unchanging Eros renders the desiring subject similarly divine: "I know thou art all sincerity!—all godlike truth, and can'st not change—" (205). Such a desiring subject does not change because the knowledge that sates mere curiosity cannot satisfy the desire of true love: "Yes, my lord, the soft, the trembling fair, dissolved in love; yielded without reserve, and met my transports with an equal ardor; and I truely protest to your lordship, that what in others, palls desire, added fresh force to mine; *the more I knew, the more I was inflamed*" (203; emphasis mine). The figure of Ciamara, who doubles for Aloisa in the second and third volumes as the woman who must be denied, silenced, and killed off because her love for the Count is "proferred" rather than "granted," exists to show that the Count, having been introduced as a universal object of female desire immune to love himself, has now been converted from feeling only the passion of curiosity to feeling true love at last (256). "Dead, even to curiosity!" she shrieks, when he fails to respond as expected to the naked body she has just revealed to him (172). He is far from dead, we are carefully informed, but love for Melliora has fixed and transformed him: "The Count could not forbear gazing on [Ciamara] with admiration, and perhaps, was, for a moment, pretty near receding from that insensibility she had reproached him with; but the image of Melliora, yet unenjoyed, all ravishingly kind and tender, rose presently in his soul, filled all his faculties, and left no passage free for rival charms" (176). By contrast, D'Elmont's earlier "love" for Amena had proven merely "fancied" when he "could not forbear kissing and embracing [Amena's maid] with such raptures as might not have been very pleasing to Amena, had she been witness of 'em" (57). If the passion of curiosity sets the plot in motion by starting a potentially limitless series of displacements of desire from one object to another, only the passion of love can bring it to rest.

Nevertheless, it is made clear that just as women are especially prone to "jealous curiosity," the desire to know the identity of a rival, so men, even men who love, are always susceptible to sexual curiosity when the knowledge that would gratify it is sufficiently pressed upon them: "in fine, tho' he realy was . . . the most excellent of his kind, yet, he was still a *man*! and, 'tis not to be thought strange, if to the force of such united temptations, nature and modesty a little yielded; warmed with her fires, and, perhaps, more moved by curiosity, her behaviour having extinguished all his respect, he gave his hands and eyes a full enjoyment of those charms" (231–32; emphasis Haywood's). Curiosity being soon sated, however, D'Elmont remains faithful to Melliora forever after. The passion of curiosity is not replaced by that of love, but rather subsumed in it. Not only is D'Elmont still susceptible to curiosity in the presence of Ciamara even after having experienced true love for Melliora, but his reunion with Melliora at the end of the novel is also a scene of narration in bed, in which she begins to satisfy the double aspects of his desire for knowledge about her, both the sexual one and his narrative curiosity, by telling him the story of what has happened to her in his absence, and revealing her body to him at the same time: "this kind digression made the Count give truce to his *curiosity*, that he might indulge the raptures of his *love*" (259; emphasis Haywood's). Complete gratification of sexual desire is of course deferred until marriage, and the triple wedding that ends the book several delays later would also seem to put an end to narrative desire, the curiosity that demands new knowledge in the form of narrative. Yet by this time Haywood has already established that love paradoxically allows for narrative closure precisely because, unlike curiosity, it can *never* be sated by its unique object. That is why it leads to narrative closure rather than to any further displacements of desire.

Sympathy: A Passion for Reading

"From my observations of human nature, I found that curiosity had more or less a share in every breast; and my business, therefore, was to hit this reigning humor in such a manner as that the gratification it should receive from being made acquainted with other people's affairs should at the same time teach every one to regulate their own."[8] Here Haywood identifies readers' "reigning humor" as curiosity about other people and insists that its gratification through fiction has to be justified by instruction. The lesson of *Love in Excess* is that a woman's desire, when "proffered" rather than "granted," only arouses curiosity, and since curiosity is free-floating by definition, such freely expressed love will always be disappointed (256). Yet this cautionary

---

[8] Eliza Haywood, *The Female Spectator*, 1, no. 1 (April 1744).

instruction is not allowed to impede the reader's delight in the gratification of curiosity: for many pages are devoted to conveying the exact words in which female characters express their desire and the precise actions with which they both proffer and grant their bodies. And the point driven home in the many passages about the irresistible nature of love's power has the opposite tendency from that of leading readers to pass a moral judgment on those who love in excess, instead urging them to sympathize with the "woes of love" (230). In the passage quoted near the beginning of this essay, we are told that we should no more blame those who suffer from love than those who suffer from disease or misfortune (191). Curiosity sets the plot in motion, but love brings it to closure without extinguishing desire; similarly, curiosity brings readers to the novel, but the real work of the text is emphatically not to lead them by it to judge others and themselves in the process, but rather the opposite: to convert curiosity into sympathy, a passion that, like love in Haywood's book, refuses to objectify or commodify the other.

The work of commuting readers' curiosity into sympathy is accomplished stylistically through the narrator's persistent refusal to represent the characters' feelings, demanding instead that readers draw on their own feelings and experience to supply a vivid sense of others'. Representation distances and objectifies; this text insists instead on the most literal sympathizing—actually feeling with the characters—on the readers' part. The novel is full of gestures towards the trope of inexpressibility, the suggestion that feelings cannot be described, but only sympathized with by those who have felt them too. The passage below encapsulates so much that is essential to understanding this novel's rhetoric that it is worth quoting at length:

> There is nothing more certain than that love, tho' it fills the mind with a thousand ideas, which those untouched by that passion, are not capable of conceiving, yet it entirely takes away the power of utterance. . . . and only fancy! a lovers fancy! can reach the exalted soaring of a lover's meaning! But, if so impossible to be described, if of so vast, so wonderful a nature as nothing but it's self can comprehend, how much more impossible must it be entirely to conceal it! What strength of boasted reason? What force of resolution? What modest fears, or cunning artifice can correct the fierceness of it's fiery flashes in the eyes, keep down the strugling sighs, command the pulse, and bid the trembling, cease? Honour, and virtue may distance bodies, but there is no power in either of those names, to stop the spring that with a rapid whirl transports us from our selves, and darts our souls into the bosom of the darling object. This may seem strange to many, even of those who call, and perhaps believe that they are lovers, but the few who have delicacy enough to feel

> what I but imperfectly attempt to speak, will acknowledge it for truth, and
> pity the distress of Melliora. (127; see also, for example, 47, 68, 197, 201, 257)

Elsewhere, true love deprives characters of their powers of expression: "indeed there is not greater proof of a vast and elegant passion, than the being uncapable of expressing it" (106).[9] In the passage above, love seems to have the same stifling effect on the narrator as on the characters, even though the former is addressing an unknown reader, not a beloved. It is clear that what affects the narrator is not exactly love, but sympathy, in which the reader is challenged to join as one of the select "few who have delicacy enough" to sympathize with, rather than judge, either the heroine racked with desire or the narrator who "speaks imperfectly."

That sympathy should produce the same effects as love is not surprising in the context of the rest of the novel, where the two passions are frequently conflated. The very first sign that D'Elmont is at last touched by love is sympathy: "he sympathized in all her sorrows, and was ready to joyn his tears with hers, but when her eyes met his, the god of love seemed there to have united all his lightnings for one effectual blaze" (90–91). Later, Ciamara mistakes his sympathy for love (210). Sympathy as a basis for same-sex friendship is born, as in Haywood's other novels, of the shared experience of the sufferings of heterosexual love (216).[10] Like curiosity, then, sympathy is love's double, and like it can substitute or be mistaken for love. By a transitive property or syllogism of the passions, curiosity and sympathy stand in the same relation to one another as each does to love, producing such similar narrative effects as to seem interchangeable. Several of the scenes of narration in *Love in Excess* represent narrative as a response either to sympathetic desire or to curious desire. D'Elmont's sympathy for his brother is what allows him to perceive a change in the latter's "character," raising "an impatient desire in the Count to know the reason of it"; this sympathetic desire introduces the brother's intercalated story, and thus prolongs the Count's own (73). Conversely, narrative can spark a curiosity that leads to love, as when the brother reports that "the wonders [a friend] told me of this young ladies wit, and beauty, inclined me to a desire of seeing her" (74).

If the gratification of readers' curiosity requires the justification of instruction, the sign of successful instruction is sympathy. "The woes of love

---

[9] Thus even a man's desire, despite "the natural confidence of his sex," becomes inexpressible in words, as female desire always is, when it is motivated by the passion of love rather than curiosity (106).

[10] Haywood's *The British Recluse* (London, 1722) is an especially good example of this.

are only worthy commiseration, according to their causes"—to inspire sympathy, that is, the cause of suffering must be love rather than any other passion, such as curiosity, jealousy, or ambition; we are also carefully reminded that "honour, and virtue may distance bodies" even in the midst of all the pains of true love. Rather than instructing the reader to retreat from the passions, however, Haywood's novel offers love and sympathy as means of regulating curiosity, and thus of avoiding the judgment, objectification, and commodification that distinguishes the knowledge about others' character aimed at by the passion of curiosity from that sought by love or sympathy. Just as D'Elmont is transformed from a character untouched by love, motivated only by curiosity and ambition, into a true lover, so the curious reader must be transformed by the narrative process into one who sympathizes with, takes pleasure in, and forgives the woes of love.

Canonical Amnesia

Why then would a novel that gratifies so many of its readers' passions—and clearly did so successfully for decades after its publication—have been so long abandoned? What made the appeal of *Love in Excess* similiar to that of *Crusoe* and *Gulliver* for its early readers but so different for later audiences? For the taste of later ages, particularly the later eighteenth through the nineteenth centuries, *Love in Excess* may have been at once too regulated and too risqué; it may have both gratified and chastened readers' curiosity too much, or in the wrong ways. The problem, in other words, was both the love and the excess.

The "novel" in the early eighteenth century was an unfamiliar commodity; calling itself "the new," it embodied its own promise—to gratify readers' curious desire for the "new and strange."[11] Defoe and Swift provide just that. Their best sellers of the early eighteenth century, which we all still read today, are about curiosity *to the exclusion of love*. Heterosexual love is absent from

---

[11] Aphra Behn writes pointedly in *Oroonoko* (1688): "I shall omit, for brevity's sake, a thousand little accidents of his life, which, however pleasant to us, where history was scarce, and adventures very rare; yet might prove tedious and heavy to my reader, in a world where he finds diversions for every minute, new and strange." Aphra Behn, *Oroonoko, The Rover and Other Works* (Harmondsworth, England: Penguin Books, 1992), 75. See also the discussions of the logic of "strange, therefore true" in the early English novel by Michael McKeon, *The Origins of the English Novel, 1600–1740* (Baltimore: Johns Hopkins University Press, 1987); and J. Paul Hunter, *Before Novels: The Cultural Contexts of Eighteenth-Century English Fiction* (New York: W. W. Norton, 1990).

Robinson Crusoe and is reviled, to the extent that it can be said to be present at all, in *Gulliver's Travels*. These novels are designed rather to satisfy the quintessentially Enlightenment passion of curiosity—that curiosity about other people's affairs, and about the new and strange, that seeks knowledge through travel, exploration, and access to the private reflections of an exploring, experiencing, *enquiring* mind. Barbara Benedict's analysis of *Robinson Crusoe* and *Gulliver's Travels* in terms of the passion of curiosity is very useful in developing one answer to the question of why those two best sellers of 1719–20 have outlived Haywood's. Benedict writes that these two novels "dramatize the contemporary opposition between curiosity as an ambition that is heroic and curiosity as an ambition that is monstrous," Defoe promoting "the ideology valuing the new," that is, the "cultural ambition" to discover, consume, and create new things, ideas, and worlds, while Swift "doggedly repeats the term 'curious' so that it becomes the degraded litany of modernity." The third best seller of the same year, as we have seen, is also all about curiosity. Haywood, like Swift, dwells more than Defoe does on the negative aspects of this driving passion of the age. Unlike either of these contemporaries, however, she advocates the disciplining of curiosity through love and sympathy, passions that refuse the commodification or objectification of the other implied by curiosity—or of the self by the same token, and of the female self in particular, which Benedict describes rightly as particularly commodifiable in these terms. If Benedict is right in claiming that in the eighteenth century "the appetite for information proves the entrée to modernity," then clearly Haywood's take on curiosity, derived from and informing as it does a transnational feminine tradition in fiction, declined in popularity during the intervening centuries.[12]

Another notable and related distinction setting *Love in Excess* apart from both *Robinson Crusoe* and *Gulliver's Travels* is that it does not take the form of travelogue. Travel was actually a most ancient mainstay of the romance tradition on which *Love in Excess* draws, the inevitable peregrinations around the Mediterranean in the Greek romances having their origins in the folk material that informs *The Odyssey*. In that epic there is repetitious horror at the barbarity of each group encountered, but in the romances there is not even this sense of the otherness of foreign cultures.[13] *Love in Excess* is

---

[12] See Benedict, *Curiosity*, 115–17.

[13] See Mikhail Bakhtin: "All adventures in the Greek romance are thus governed by an interchangeability of space; what happens in Babylon could just as well happen in Egypt or Byzantium and vice versa." Quoted from *Forms of Time* by Franco Moretti, *Atlas of the European Novel 1800–1900* (London: Verso, 1998), 70.

also set in foreign lands: the characters journey from France to Italy. France serves simply as a gesture toward French romances, however, and Italy as the place identified by the French writers as the land of unbridled passion.[14] Aphra Behn's *Oroonoko* provides a good illustration of the difference between the uses of travel in romance and novel. That work includes settings in both Africa and Surinam. Africa (itself a stock element of Greek romance, as are the slavery and piracy Behn depicts there) is represented in purely romance terms, in that its characters, with whom the reader is led to sympathize, are entirely recognizable within European cultural codes. Her Surinam Caribs, on the other hand, are utterly new and strange, and they are approached by the narrator in a very different spirit of exploratory curiosity. Because of this contrast, *Oroonoko* has often struck modern readers as a monstrous hybrid of romance and novel. The fact that travel is featured both in romance and in the narratives of Defoe and Swift points up the relevant distinction all the more clearly: in romance (and in *Love in Excess*) voyages represent the repetitive stations of desire and the universality of love's power, rather than the drive of Enlightenment curiosity toward knowledge of the new and strange. Like Defoe and Swift, Haywood too recognized curiosity as the predominant passion to which novels should be addressed. Her disciplining of curiosity by insisting on its conversion to love and sympathy, however, and her moral privileging of these latter passions over it, aligns her work with the older tradition of romance—a narrative genre that came increasingly to be set in opposition to "the novel"—and specifically with a modern romance tradition that was French, feminine, and on both counts doomed, the more the English novelistic tradition became legitimized and nationalized.[15]

In 1719–20, the novelty sometimes called "novel" was still viewed in England as a French commodity, and Haywood was heavily engaged in this

---

[14] For example, in Marie-Madeleine de Lafayette's *La Comtesse de Tende* (1718), the Comtesse de Tende, who was spirited and of Italian descent, became jealous. She allowed herself no rest; she gave none to her husband" until she has an affair and perishes of the effects of her own unchecked passion. Mme. de Lafayette, *The Princesse de Clèves, The Princesse de Montpensier, The Comtesse de Tende*, trans. Terence Cave (Oxford: Oxford University Press, 1992), 191.

[15] John J. Richetti and Ros Ballaster agree, although their arguments are very different, that Haywood aligns her fiction with romance rather than with what eventually came to look like "novels." Richetti argues that Haywood's fictional world privileges ideal, religious values over those of an emerging secular realism, while Ballaster is closer to my argument in observing that Haywood derived the idea of love as an overwhelming force that could either give women a high degree of power or be utterly ruinous for them from the French female fiction writers of the seventeenth century. See Richetti, *Popular Fiction*, and Ros Ballaster, *Seductive Forms: Women's Amatory Fiction from 1684–1740* (Oxford: Oxford University Press, 1992).

import trade as a translator. In *Love in Excess* she mentions Mme D'Aulnoy (a novelist) and Mme. Dacier (a translator; 196). It is intriguing that *Love in Excess* bears the generic marker, "A Novel," on its title page, given that when the work was first published, there was very little agreement about what "a novel" was. In critical discussions from the late seventeenth through the eighteenth century, it was often set in opposition to romance, as the genre of probability or verisimilitude. One of the earliest sources of this opposition is a French essay by the Sieur Du Plaisir appended as a preface to Marie de Lafayette's *La Princesse de Clèves* (1679), which was later translated and appended as a preface to Delarivier Manley's *The History of Queen Zarah, and the Zarazians* (1705)—and long incorrectly assumed by critics of English literature to be her original work. Du Plaisir does indeed distinguish the *nouvelles historiques* as more probable than the older Scudéry romances, but they are closer to the French and Italian novella tradition than to the English tradition of news, travelogue, and spiritual autobiography. Haywood's novel is a French *nouvelle*, while Defoe's and Swift's are English news.

As the eighteenth and nineteenth centuries progressed, there was increasing reaction against the international and feminocentric tradition with which Haywood had aligned herself. As the novel became more legitimized as a genre in England, it also became more nationalistic and literally insular; Franco Moretti has discussed "how narrative England becomes an island, repudiating its eighteenth-century familiarity with French books for Victorian autarky."[16] Even in this twentieth century, a prominent critic dismissed Haywood as having been "largely influenced by French fiction," as if such infidelity to the pure lineage of English literature in itself explained and justified the neglect into which her work had fallen.[17] And as the English novel became more nationalistic, it also grew more "masculine" in its associations, to the extent that nineteenth-century women novelists had to take masculine pseudonyms in order to publish, whereas in Haywood's time a large proportion, if not most, novels were published under feminine signatures, some of which even belonged to men.

Within the French feminocentric tradition, however, Haywood's lineage from the *nouvelle historique* as opposed to the *roman* is far from pure. *Love in Excess* has all the general features of romance, some of which have been discussed above—extraordinary characters loved by all who set eyes on

---

[16] Moretti, *Atlas of the European Novel*, 156–58.

[17] Bonamy Dobrée, *English Literature in the Early Eighteenth Century* (Oxford: Oxford University Press, 1959), 409–10; quoted in Richetti, *Popular Fiction*, 119.

them; an Eros as tyrannical and powerful as Fate; travels, flights, and abductions traversing national boundaries; disguises and cross-dressing; scenes of astonishing recognition; and highly improbable coincidence. It shares these not only with ancient romances but with the Renaissance novella tradition (for instance, many of the tales in Boccaccio's *Decameron*). It also bears the specific marks of seventeenth-century French female-authored romance. The romances of Madeleine de Scudéry were Haywood's models for her precise anatomies of love (for example, 170) and for love's capacity to invest enormous power in women—as well as to bring about their utter ruin, an emphasis that, as Ros Ballaster has argued, is more characteristic of the *nouvelle*.[18] Either way, her French settings and associations are not simply marks of Haywood's homage to her literary precursors; invoking the French *nouvelles* and *romans* both points to a strong transnational tradition of female authorship and lends a certain generic verisimilitude to her representations of the "excess" of female desire—which itself was another obstacle, ultimately, to her literary survival.

The predominant critical truism about Eliza Haywood is that she had not one but two careers as a novelist; the first in the bawdier years before the Richardsonian turn toward feminine virtue and sympathy as the mainstays of morality, and the second after 1740, when she adapted to the times and drastically changed her moral tone to reemerge after a silence as a more "conservative" novelist. This change is attributed variously to the chastening effect of satirical treatments of her by Pope, Fielding, and Savage; the moralizing influence of Richardson on popular taste; and the marked change in gender conventions around the middle of the eighteenth century already discussed at the outset of this essay, which I like to call the "great gender shift."[19] Mary Anne Schofield sums up the effect of the change on Haywood's fiction: "The majority of her novels of her first period (1720s and 1730s) depict the troubled situation of the divided heroine who is unable to

---

[18] "From the romance's presentation of love as a form of elaborate artifice, we have moved to the depiction of love as an uncontrollable and entropic effect of nature." Ballaster, *Seductive Forms*, 54.

[19] For interesting discussions of Haywood's relation to Pope and Fielding respectively, and her response to their satirical accounts of her, which complicate the traditional critical line that they "silenced" her for a time before she reemerged as a more conservative writer, see John R. Elwood, "Henry Fielding and Eliza Haywood: A Twenty Year War," *Albion* 5, no. 3 (Fall 1973): 184–92; Christine Blouch, "Eliza Haywood and the Romance of Obscurity," *Studies in English Literature, 1500–1900* 31, no. 3 (Summer 1991): 535–52; and Sarah Prescott, "The Debt to Pleasure: Eliza Haywood's *Love in Excess* and Women's Fiction of the 1720s," *Women's Writing* 7, no. 3 (2000). On Savage's attack in *An Author to Be Lett*, see Ros Ballaster, "Preparatives to Love: Seduction as Fiction in the Works of Eliza Haywood," in *Living by the Pen: Early British Women Writers*, ed. Dale Spender (New York: Teachers College Press, 1992), 53.

reconcile diverse elements within herself and accept her position in society; she ends her struggle in exile or death. The novels of her later period (1740s and 1750s) offer a more conservative portrait of the virtuous heroine who is tested throughout the novel but remains true to her virtue and her womanly position and is happily rewarded with marital bliss at the conclusion."[20]

Indeed the shortest and easiest answer to the question of why *Love in Excess* was forgotten would be to say that its model of female character and desire was rejected during Haywood's lifetime, and all evidence for the lustful early-modern woman had to be not merely covered with opprobrium, as it generally had been all along, but buried now in oblivion. This answer would be true, albeit partial. We might nuance it by observing that Haywood's very first novel already includes both of the models Schofield outlines above, for Melliora perfectly fits her description of Haywood's *later* heroines, even as the whole series of heroine's foils—Aloisa, Amena, Ciamara, and more—are accurately described by the early model. Haywood's own statement, quoted above, about the necessity for justifying the novel's gratification of readers' curiosity by supplying moral instruction, dates from her later period, yet applies perfectly to her first work. Thus, as others have observed, it would be more accurate to say that Richardson was influenced by Haywood than vice versa.[21] The maxim of *Love in Excess*, that a woman must not speak her desire until she is spoken to (and spoken for) is the very same one that Richardson hammered home in *Clarissa* twenty years later. Richardson follows Haywood in much more than this moral. The plot of *Love in Excess*, its theme of the inexpressibility of female desire, and the privileging of the

---

[20] Mary Anne Schofield, "Exposé of the Popular Heroine: The Female Protagonists of Eliza Haywood," *Studies in Eighteenth-Century Culture* 12 (1983): 94.

[21] See also Jerry C. Beasley: "Yet the actual originals of the fictional character types repeated in the portraits of Pamela Andrews, Clarissa Harlowe, Sophia Western, and Smollett's Narcissa appear in dozens of earlier narratives by gifted and prolific ladies. If all this be acknowledged, then the old conventional wisdom that women storytellers regularly imitated the men in hope of gaining favor and success seems both doubtful and facile. There is a certain riskiness in the observation, but something like the reverse may be closer to the truth. In other words one might say—and with more than a smattering of real justice—that male novelists, even innovative geniuses like Defoe, Richardson, Fielding, and Smollett, felt obliged to write with at least some resemblances to the work of their female counterparts, who had already won the attention of the reading audience by appealing insistently to its deepest and most abiding preoccupations." "Politics and Moral Idealism: The Achievement of Some Early Women Novelists," in *Fetter'd or Free? British Women Novelists, 1670–1815*, ed. Mary Anne Schofield and Cecilia Macheski (Athens: Ohio University Press, 1986), 221. See also Margaret Anne Doody's detailed discussion of Richardson's debts to Haywood specifically in *A Natural Passion: A Study of the Novels of Samuel Richardson* (Oxford: Oxford University Press, 1974), 138–50, 333.

particular conventions of sympathy described above all prefigure Richardson's oeuvre. Melliora is put on trial much like Clarissa and Pamela are—like them abducted and then "courted" in captivity, she proves her virtue impervious even to violence. Like Pamela, she is rewarded for a feminine virtue that appears passive in relation to sexual desire. The difference between Haywood's earlier fiction and Richardson's, then, might seem to be one of representation rather than of moral maxims asserted: in early novels like *Love in Excess*, Haywood offers the reader quite a bit of the very pleasures she officially condemns. But this is really just another trick Richardson learned from Haywood, Defoe, and other predecessors: *Pamela* and *Clarissa* too are notoriously full of prurient episodes, despite all their moralizing.

The real difference between Haywood's work and that of her canonical male contemporaries, finally, is not so much one of the representation of sex as of the expression of female sexual desire. Such dangerous expression, supposedly to be avoided even at the cost of life, makes its way onto page after page despite incessant denials of its expressibility. This expression of the inexpressible is the real "excess" of the title—and it overflows on nearly every page. This "excess" is just what Haywood derived from her French sources and is what her English successors and male contemporaries eschewed.[22] Although female characters are the eponymous heroines of the novels of Richardson and Defoe and supply their primary first-person voices, they do not openly speak sexual desire as so many of the female figures in *Love in Excess* do. Even Defoe's Moll Flanders and Roxana, who are unabashedly salacious and improper (yet are considerably more excused by their author than any of Haywood's heroines), are driven primarily by ambition, a desire to "speed"—to survive, profit, and live in material comfort and social respectability—rather than by love or sexual desire, which serve mainly as means to these more bourgeois ends. Like Robinson Crusoe, they are driven by curious ambition to the exclusion of love and sympathy. Reduced to a commodity or a means of making a living (whether through marriage or prostitution), the sex in which Defoe's heroines so frequently engage is not presented as an expression of female desire so much as a response to male desire enforced by economic necessity. And sex in Swift is of course reduced even further, to the level of the scatological. Gulliver's

---

[22] Ballaster, *Seductive Forms*: "the *histoire galante* or *nouvelle* maintained a feminocentric tradition in prose narrative but introduced a reversal in many romance conventions. The feminocentric world of love remains the structural centre and motivating force of history, but *the female libido substitutes for the desireless heroinism of the romance as the dynamic force in historical process*" (56; emphasis mine).

rare encounters with the female body and female desire are grotesque, inspiring only repugnance in him and his reader. Richardson's heroines are fantastically passive and unconscious of their own desires. Clarissa admits at most, when pressed, to "a conditional kind of liking" for Lovelace, and indeed one of the main preoccupations of that novel is the impossibility of knowing even one's own heart. Even this Richardson derived from Haywood; for while most of the female characters in *Love in Excess* die of the expression of their desire, the virtuous Melliora is not granted so much consciousness: "How little did she know the true state of her own heart?" (135).

Ros Ballaster makes a compelling argument that the once-famed and rather bawdy "fair Triumvirate of Wit" (Aphra Behn, Delarivier Manley, and Eliza Haywood) was rejected later in the eighteenth century not because of disapproval by male writers, but by the large numbers of women novelists who by then had to disassociate themselves and their fiction from anything of moral questionability in order to publish at all.[23] There is surely a great deal of truth in this idea, and yet Haywood had an enormous influence on these subsequent generations of women. Melliora's strategy of allowing the expression of her own sexual desire to appear as obedience to the commands of her male guardians is one that reappears frequently in novels authored by women through the end of the century, as does the related one of allowing the virtuous heroine to express her desire only in a state of dream or delirium (121ff.).[24] More significant, virtually all the women novelists of the later eighteenth century (as well as Richardson) followed Haywood's textual strategy of privileging sympathy and love over curiosity (a strategy that had signally distinguished *Love in Excess* from its contemporary best sellers), while censoring the excesses of expressed female desire.

Toward the end of the eighteenth century one of these disguised daughters of Haywood was still trying to argue that the novel should not be thought of as opposed to romance but rather that it *was* romance. Clara Reeve's 1785 *The Progress of Romance*, however, was one of the last gasps of the feminocentric and transnational tradition in which Haywood had begun her career, for by then the decriers of romances as "female quixotism" were gaining the day. The topos of female quixotism was in itself a tribute to the continued resonance of feminocentric romance through the eighteenth century, as a whole

---

[23] Ballaster, *Seductive Forms*, 3, 196–211.

[24] Many examples could be adduced, but *The Recess; or, A Tale of Other Times* (1783–85) by Sophia Lee, ed. April Alliston (Lexington: University Press of Kentucky, 2000) is a good example of the former strategy, and *The Delicate Distress* (1769) by Elizabeth Griffith, ed. Cynthia Booth Ricciardi and Susan Staves (Lexington: University Press of Kentucky, 1997), of the latter.

literature was generated to ridicule its fantasies of female power as just that—mere quixotic fantasies.[25] The ambivalence with which women writing toward the end of the century, including Charlotte Lennox and Jane Austen, joined in this attack on feminocentric romance is played out in their antiromances, where Lennox lampoons what she nevertheless portrays as a sustaining maternal inheritance for her heroine (the library of French romances her dead mother leaves her), while Austen shows equal respect for the gothic romances that she similarly takes to task for lack of realism. As in the original *Quixote*, it is rather the literal-minded reading of romances than the works themselves that ridiculed. Still, these novels served to distance their authors from the tradition even as they evoked it. The European world really did leave even less room than before for female power and the expression of female desire by the end of the eighteenth century. Later women novelists may have defined themselves against the "fair Triumvirate" in order to be heard—but even in the process of doing so, they kept invoking their romance tradition and built on Haywood's most important innovations. Even though the modern West has increasingly valorized a commodifying curiosity over loving sympathy with others since the eighteenth century, as more novels by women throughout the period are being published and read again, we are able to rediscover the continuities of her legacy.

---

[25] Charlotte Lennox's *The Female Quixote*, Jane Austen's *Northanger Abbey*, James Fenimore Cooper's *Tales for Fifteen*, another American work entitled *Female Quixotism*, and Flaubert's *Madame Bovary* are just a few of the entire works devoted to the widespread topos of female quixotism.

JULIET MITCHELL

Natasha and Hélène
(*War and Peace*, Leo Tolstoy, 1863–1869)

Natasha Rostov, heroine of *War and Peace* and Tolstoy's portrait of "a good woman," and Hélène Kuragin, his portrait of a bad woman, marry (at different times) the same man—the novel's hero, Pierre Bezuhov. They have also both been seduced by the same rake: Anatole Kuragin. (Hélène and her brother Anatole, identically good-looking, are thought to have had an incestuous affair.) Yet in this novel in which everybody encounters everybody in a wide range of places and times, Natasha and Hélène meet each other only briefly, and that meeting is in the context of Anatole's seduction of Natasha, which Hélène assists. Rather than meeting as two people, Natasha and Hélène are implicitly linked through sexuality and fertility (or its absence) with the same men.

After the elopement of Anatole and Natasha has been prevented (the seduction is not consummated), Pierre "could not reconcile the agreeable impression he had of Natasha, whom he had known since her childhood, with this new picture of baseness, folly and cruelty. He thought of his wife [Hélène]. 'They are all alike,' he said to himself, reflecting that he was not the only man whose unhappy fate it was to be tied to a worthless woman."[1] This comment, coming almost exactly halfway through the novel, acts as a switchpoint; Natasha, like Russia, has her faults that make her succumb to an enemy (Anatole or France), but, like her homeland, she can survive this. Though it would be a mistake to push the parallel too far, Hélène, admired and adulated like Napoleon, triumphs for a hollow and deathly victory. Whereas Natasha, who has consistent qualities but also laughs and sobs, develops, and changes; Hélène is static—a fixed image, a stunning statue with a poised, irrelevant smile. Put crudely, Natasha is "life" and Hélène is "death."

If men can live in peace by surviving the irredeemable but life-related horrors of war, women can do so by surviving the unspeakable but necessary dangers of sexuality and come through to maternity. Non-procreative sexuality and war are death; peace and fertility are life. This reductive scheme

---

[1] Leo Tolstoy, *War and Peace* (1863–69), trans. Rosemary Edmonds (Harmondsworth: Penguin Books, 1982) 700. All subsequent quotes are from this edition and are cited in the text within parentheses, by page number.

indicates how the basic structure of the novel is gendered both between women and men, and between women—the good and the bad. Though the novel exceeds this conventional gendering, we can see how its insistence shows through in the relative flatness of the conclusion—a philosophico-political treatise on the one hand and an idyll of multiple fertile marriages on the other. In the latter, as long as Pierre puts his wife Natasha and the family first, he can have his business and intellectual pursuits. She will be his "slave" and make him see himself only in the mirror of her exclusive emphasis on his goodness. Neither treatise nor idyll are simple, the weakness is that they are blueprints rather than creative fiction. That they are so seems to me to be a consequence, at least in a large part, of the fact that Tolstoy, because of his concern with psychology, is trying both to work out gender relations in a radical way and, like Pierre, falling back onto conventional and unwise wisdoms.

The novel does far exceed its gendered structure. The parallel of Natasha and Hélène is residual—one has to search it out. Yet this parallel does inform the novel's iconography and its values. The fact that, the conclusion aside, this conventional gendering does not detract from these visual images and ethical values, nor these from the novel as a whole, must of course be put down to Tolstoy's "genius." However, more worryingly, it may also owe something to the persistence of such gendering in all our understanding of human relationships. What is at stake in this possibility is the relationship of creativity to ideology.

The extraordinarily wide tableau of *War and Peace*, the sense we have that we are witnessing and involved in "la condition humaine" depends in part of the ratio of particular creative insight to general ideologies. We get "the world" at war and at peace through eighteen principal characters—all Russian aristocrats—and eight "others" among whom are the tsar and Napoleon. Even the "others" do not include the peasants, serfs, house servants, or companions although a number of these are highly individually characterized and play catalytic roles. This selection of characters reflects the hegemony of the feudal aristocracy of midnineteenth-century Russia—seen from the top, a class structure in which even if some servants are individually important, they are part of the background, and a small intermarrying social group are the foreground—and this is "the world." It is the same with sexuality, fertility, and gender. The novel reflects hegemonies: sexuality is dangerous, fertility is good, and the genders must be utterly different. Yet here too we have "the world." In fact is it not precisely because of this creative presentation and extraordinary understanding of our deepest ideologies of social class and gender differences that the novel can claim universality?

But if the novel reflects ideologies, it also exceeds them. Although Tolstoy is frightened, like Pierre, that all women are worthless and the same, he shows that they are not. Nor is his portraiture only or even dominantly in terms of the good and the bad. Even more interesting, Tolstoy does not confirm the usual perception in which the only "gender" is the woman. Gender here also exceeds its category of psychobiological sex and is presented as a relationship not only between women and men but between men and men and between women and women. "From that day one of those tender and passionate friendships such as exist only between women was established between Princess Maria and Natasha. They were constantly kissing and saying tender things to one another, and spent most of their time together. If one went out the other became restless and hastened to join her. They felt more at peace together than when alone. A tie stronger than friendship sprang up between them: a singular feeling of life being possible only in each other's company" (1,280). Once again this love exceeds the gendered convention—Maria and Natasha come together in their overwhelming grief for one man—Maria's brother, Natasha's betrothed, Prince Andrei.

Crucially, Tolstoy avoids a gender ideology in his portrait of men. Again we touch on ideology, so that where Pierre's bumbling intelligence goes against the grain of masculinity in his social strata, it nevertheless conforms to the gender stereotype by being juxtaposed to Natasha's feminine intuition. Yet again the novel exceeds this simple formulation; the men are no more nor less interesting than the women. Above all, the ideology is surpassed in that men are gendered instead of being assumed to be "the human," while women are "the sex" (as in Pierre's remark about "all women"). The portrait of men is of beings as dependent on their gender and gendering as are women.

Tolstoy's use and transcendence of gender ideology informs the novel at all points. In focusing on Natasha and Hélène we can see, I believe, the vital reference point of this interaction between convention and creativity on which the assumption (or portraiture) of universality rests. Tolstoy is explicitly writing a "psychological" novel. The psychology is both of individuals and of their relationships, of singletons and of groups. What is remarkable, is that Tolstoy shows that whatever he has made his characters to "be," they also always feel, think, and act *in contexts*. To discuss them here as isolates is bound to betray this contextuality.

However, Hélène is one of the least contextual and Natasha, the most contextual of the characters—this fact conforms to stereotypes of evil and good, yet even here it is exceeded. Hélène is described from, so to speak, the outside, but it is a layered "outside." Tolstoy depicts Pierre as knowing that his first wife is "worthless" and being puzzled that she is glamorous not only because of her beauty but because her stupidity is perceived as high intelligence. (Natasha's intelligence appears as simplicity.) This is a disquisition on the inappropriateness of intellectual women, but it is also an observation on individual psychology to show that mimesis works—to a degree. Hélène can imitate brilliance: her character is an imitation so brilliant that no one notices this.

Hélène first copies the model of a hostess, then having become one, *acts herself*. We are not *told* this; it becomes apparent through the bizarreness of her final triumphs. Having conquered all of St. Petersburg and Moscow high society, married, divorced, and gained Pierre's wealth, she cannot decide which of two suitors to choose—she wants them both. Natasha too cannot choose between her betrothed Prince Andrei and Anatole—she loves them both. Where Natasha's is a dilemma of a self-divided adolescent who is differently attracted by two very different men, Hélène's is a madness that comes from the indeterminacy of her mimetic being. Her character is worthless, not only in the moral sense, but it is worth nothing—there is nothing there—and when the show has nothing more to gain, the hollowness is conveyed by the pointlessness of her not being able to distinguish between those who court her. Her narcissism being based on nothing except a body that she admires in exactly the same way others admire it, is empty and hence destructive. (Natasha inhabits and enjoys her also admired body.)

Hélène refuses pregnancy, aids and abets Anatole's seduction of Natasha, abandons the spiritual implications of her homeland (she becomes a Jesuitically influenced Roman Catholic), trusts to foreign quacks, and kills herself. Self-sufficient narcissism is very appealing. (Freud writes of the charm of narcissistic toddlers, women, and cats!) But if there can never be any love for others, it can only end in self-destruction. In gender ideology, women, unlike men, need adoration; they do have a propensity to narcissism. Natasha too is adored—but she *thrives* on this adoration. It makes her yet more alive and able to love; it gives her the self-esteem necessary to value others. Again the contrast between the two women is that while both share a characteristic, it leads in opposite directions—to life or to death. The implication of adoration is bound up with the question of seduction.

At the center of this contrast between Natasha and Hélène, between a life force and a deathly stasis (proleptic of Freud's Life and Death drives), is the part played by, and the meaning of, seduction. Anatole's seduction of Natasha comes at the midpoint of the novel. It is the occasion of the only meetings between the two women. Natasha, in Moscow without her mother, goes to the opera.

To Natasha, fresh from the country, and in her present serious mood, all this seemed grotesque and extraordinary. She could not follow the opera, could not even listen to the music; she saw only painted cardboard and oddly-dressed men and women who moved, spoke and sang strangely in a patch of blazing light. She knew what it was all meant to represent, but it was so grotesquely artificial and unnatural that she felt alternately ashamed and amused at the actors. She kept looking . . . at the half-naked women in the boxes, especially at Hélène in the next box, who, quite uncovered, sat with a quiet, serene smile, not taking her eyes off the stage and basking in the bright light that flooded the theatre and the warm air heated by the crowd. Natasha little by little began to pass into a state of intoxication she had not experienced for a long time. She lost all sense of who and where she was, and of what was going on before her . . . Natasha, following the direction of [Helene's] eyes, saw an extraordinarily handsome adjutant approaching their box, with self-assured yet courteous bearing. This was Anatole Kuragin whom she had seen and noticed long ago at the ball in Petersburg. He moved with a discreet swagger, which would have been ridiculous if he had not been so good-looking and his comely features had not expressed such good-natured complacency and high spirits. . . . "Charming, charming!" said he, evidently referring to Natasha, who did not exactly hear the words but divined them from the movement of his lips. (663–64)

In this state of trance, Natasha finds herself admired by Anatole, Hélène's brother, whom she has never met. Anatole and Hélène are look-alikes; in her turn, Natasha starts to smile meaninglessly in the manner of the "half-naked Hélène." The opera set is a cemetery. Anatole and Natasha gaze into each other's eyes; then he is looking at her bare shoulders. "Looking into his eyes she was frightened, realizing that between her and him there was not the barrier of decorum she had always been conscious of between herself and other men" (668). "She felt with horror that no barriers lay between him and her" (669).

This lack of a barrier is the equivalent of sexual intercourse. When she is away from the opera, Natasha is appalled at what has happened, but at the time "there in the protecting shadow of that ["nearly naked"] Hélène, it had all seemed simple and natural" (670). But later still, "again under Hélène's influence what had struck her before as terrible now seemed simple and natural." Nakedness of body and soul combines with the absence of barriers, and beneath this, the motif of incest—not only Anatole's and Hélène's, but that described by the old, fat actress who declaims in French at Hélène's salon a soliloquy describing her guilty love for her son (to a chorus of

"Adorable!—Divin! Délicieux") and where Natasha is borne into a frighteningly exciting world where there was "no knowing what was good and what was bad" (677). Seduction takes place in an economy of doing what one wants. If one enters that economy, it is remarkably simple, a place of enjoyment without good and evil or any implications for other people, a place of quasi—or actual—incest, that icon of boundlessness and of nakedness.

Pierre became trapped into marrying Hélène the moment he stopped looking at her beauty from a distance and became instead, engulfed by her nakedness. Yet, this absence of decorum and of boundaries in seduction is perilously close to an ideal of identifying with others in love. But it is close also to killing. In fact one could say that seduction which prevents the other from being known to be other is flanked on each side by two passions—the passion of love and the passion of murder. Tolstoy presents this at both an individual and a general level. Having been seduced by Hélène, Pierre, implicated through this in her depravity, the meaningless way she refers to who may or may not be her lover, starts to kill her. "He felt the transports and fascination of frenzy, shouting 'Go' in a voice so terrible that the whole house heard it with horror" (374).

On the other side, is his and Natasha's love. When their passions are sublimated, once ("as her mother has always known") Natasha had a husband and children, her "waywardness" would vanish. For Hélène, barren and empty, seduction is all there is to life and a living death. Natasha is nature, Russia, fertility, a woman. Hélène is artificiality, "French," childless—in other words, like a man. "Hélène, like a truly great man who can do anything he pleases, at once put herself in the right, as she really believed, and placed the blame on everyone else" (989). For Hélène, the descent into seduction's possible evil is a way of life. Unlike Hélène, Natasha does not stop long in seduction's economy of doing anything one pleases; she and Pierre realize that a person is somehow, somewhere inevitably guilty or at fault. It is part of the human condition, one has to know it and suffer if one is to live life to the full.

Gender difference is one way out of the pitfalls of seduction's boundlessness; it produces the frontiers and hence the decorum that allows women and men to be humanly the same while falling fully in love. "When he now and again looked into [Natasha's] eyes Pierre felt that he was vanishing away, that neither he nor she existed any more, that nothing existed but happiness" (1,331). Pierre thinks of this period of loss of distinction between himself and Natasha as a "period of blissful insanity" (1,333). But something of the identification of each with the other will persist into the sanity of marriage and family with its clear-cut gender roles.

Moving from the individual to the general level, the boundarylessness of seduction can be taken up into the sublime interdependence and alikeness of all human beings and beyond into nature in a cosmic pantheism. However, it can equally well provide the conditions, the frenzy, and the fascination that allow for the murderousness of war. Natasha and Hélène stand at this apex of seduction. Seduction thus can be psychologically and emotionally the same while being structurally different, leading to love and life for one and amoral sexuality and death for the other. It is seduction that is essential for Tolstoy's exploration of goodness and depravity. Its exponents are the two women who act as each other's foil—Natasha Rostov and Hélène Kuragin, the two wives of Pierre Bezuhov, who himself has often been considered a version of his author, as indeed doubtless are the two "heroines."

SYLVIE THOREL-CAILLETEAU

Nana
(*Nana*, Émile Zola, 1880)

In 1880, Émile Zola was at the crux of the battle that would impose his aesthetic mode: *The Experimental Novel* appeared, shortly followed by that violent, antipatriotic heptameron, *Les soirées de Médan*, and then by what may be the most audacious in the Rougon-Macquart series, *Nana*. Like Nana, in that terrible episode in which she floats and swoons with pleasure at the spectacle of her beautiful body, composing herself as a work of art, Zola's naturalism is reflected and deploys its full force in the novel. *Nana* resonates with the disquietingly infantile name of its heroine, who makes men babble like newborn babes; *Nana* shines, with the brilliance of that idol that radiates everywhere and rises, mute, in its illumined grotto in the final display of *Mélusine*.

Nana is the daughter of Gervaise: when she recounts her story, it is *L'assommoir* that comes to the reader's mind; when she reads a realist novel, the reader recalls yet again the story of her parents and earliest youth; when she evokes her dream of a tender love in a clean corner, we think we hear her mother. Her aunt, Mme. Lerat, evokes the neighborhood of the Goutte-d'Or, as does Satin. One scandalous novel echoes another scandalous novel; Zola is intoxicated by his *formula*. In chapter 7, Fauchery writes about Nana in the form of an allegory: *The Golden Fly*, which escapes the charnel house, and ends up corrupting everything in turn. This segment summarizes the novel, while the novel in its turn completes the chronicle. Later on, Doctor Pascal will take it up again, during his reading to Chlotilde.

Nana's date of birth is 1851, the year of the coup d'état. Nana's death coincides with the declaration of war, an empire in its final agonies. Nana is empire; she is also *Les Rougon-Macquart*, whose framework is defined by the course of her existence. Nana speaks: men are pigs, and pigs all the more as they show off their black suits amidst the gilded paneling of elegant salons. "The beast lies deep within," and Nana reveals the beast—like the quill of the naturalist novelist. Naturalism incessantly folds back on itself, demonstrates its necessity, consolidates its foundations, and reflects itself; this is one of its most remarkable traits.

———

Like all the novels conceived by Zola, *Nana* can be read on several levels. It is the story of a girl who gives an account of prostitution at the time of

Napoleon III and who condemns the mores of the late Second Empire. It is also the song of all-powerful sex; now Nana is not simply a girl, but absolute woman, strange and fatal bearer of truth. Muffat is also grand chamberlain, and he stands for all men. Thus, dying empire and decaying flesh are conjoined: death is unchained through Nana, and we follow a fragmented fissure along a line that is not only hereditary, but also modern. As always, Zola takes up the cause of naturalism, and he devotes himself to disaster.

The force of the fiction and of its interwoven reflection can be understood as rooted in the reference to Venus, a figure that determines the story itself and points the novel as a genre in new directions. For if the novel is a supple and ductile form, it still obeys rules in the nineteenth century. As Huet wrote to Segrais in 1670, "those works which are properly called Novels are *false Stories of amorous adventures, written in prose with art, for the pleasure and instruction of the readers.*"[1] It is certainly true that in *Nana* amorous adventures are not absent. But even the most distracted observer of the history of the Western novel, from the *Aethiopica* onward, notes that the movement of these love stories is Platonic in its orientation, in the sense that everything that touches on the body is subject to spiritual considerations; thus, the beauty of Julie d'Estanges or Madame de Mortsauf is indicative of the elevation of their souls, and the love that Saint-Preux and Félix de Vandenesse have for these women retraces the trajectory of a quest—so much is the love of a beautiful body propaedeutic to a disinterested consideration of the beautiful. In contrast, love for Nana abases rather than elevates; far from reflecting a lovely soul, her beauty envelopes a charnel house. Thus, the condition of classical representation itself is violently reversed, through an unsettling of the figure of Venus.

At the beginning of the novel, Nana plays the part of Venus at the theater ("Call it my knocking shop, will you?"[2] insists the well-named Bordenave[3]), in an operetta visibly inspired by Offenbach's *La belle Hélène*. We recall that in *La curée*, in which neoclassical decors proliferate, Renée seeks to live out *Phèdre* and finds herself, despite her efforts, engaged in a parody

---

[1] Letter from Monsieur Huet to Monsieur de Segrais, *De l'origine des romans* (1670), 2nd ed. (Paris: Sébastien Mabre Cramoisy, 1678), 2.

[2] Emile Zola, *Nana* (Paris: Charpentier, 1880), in *Oeuvres complètes* (Paris: Cercle du Livre Précieux, 1967), 4:23; *Nana* (New York: Penguin), 3. All English translations are from this edition unless otherwise noted. In this case, a more literal translation would be, "Call it rather my brothel, will you?"

[3] *Bordenave* meaning to board a ship or vessel.

of the ancient tragedy, doubled by a spectacle also inspired by Offenbach—Hippolyte eating jam tartines.[4] To be sure, Zola multiplies the signs: "This carnival of the gods, in which Olympus was dragged through the mud and the poetry and religion of an entire civilization were made fun of, was seen as a delicious treat,"[5] with Nana, "her hand on her hip, . . . her Venus in the gutter and all set to walk the streets."[6] Cupid [*Amour*], rather than conjugating the verb to love [*aimer*], generates loose women [*cocottes*]. This pitiable spectacle is that of the empire itself, mired in the material, having retired the gods, ignorant of anything except gold or flesh (we return to *La Curée*, the masked ball of the gods). We have entered into an era of disaster; earth is henceforth abandoned by heaven.

The audience mocks the spectacle. Nana does not know how to behave on stage, and she sings in a falsetto. We might say then that she acts badly, if it were not for something far more disquieting. Nana does not act well because she does not act; her own persona is implicated in the failure of the act insofar as she herself *is* "the blond Venus" and does not *represent* anything other than herself. She is simply, intensely, present:

> As she was reaching the end of her song, her voice gave out completely, and realizing she'd never be able to finish it, she gave a sideways flick of her hip, so that the curve of her buttock showed under the thin tunic and, leaning back, she held out both arms, thrusting her breasts out towards the audience. People started applauding, whereupon she quickly swung around and moved upstage; from the back, her blonde hair looked like the tawny mane of a wild animal. The applause became furious.[7]

Zola can thus designate Nana herself, rather than her role, with the name Venus: "It was Venus begin born out of the waves, hidden only by her hair. And when Nana lifted her arms, in the glare of the footlights you could glimpse the golden hair in her armpits."[8] Here then is the Second Empire

---

[4] "That joke sent a chill up the young woman's spine. Everything came unhinged in her head. La Ristori was no more than a big puppet, hitching up the flounce of his blouse and sticking out his tongue at the audience like Blanche Muller in the third act of *The Belle Hélène*; Théramène was dancing the cancan and Hippolyte ate jam tartines while sticking his fingers up his nose." *La curée* (Paris: Charpentier, 1872), in *Oeuvres complètes*, 11:469.

[5] *Nana*, 18; *Oeuvres complètes*, 4:35.

[6] *Nana*, 18; *Oeuvres complètes*, 4:36.

[7] *Nana*, 14–15; *Oeuvres complètes*, 4:32.

[8] *Nana*, 40–41; *Oeuvres complètes*, 4:25.

version of Aphrodite Anadyomene, of a celestial Aphrodite whose representation according to the classical system generated the possibility of all representation because her natural unblemished beauty indicated the blossoming of a perfect figure, rising out of the churned-up foam cresting the waves. In contrast, Nana's nudity is that of *undress*—she is not divine, not celestial, but bestial; her hair is not a veil, but a mane, a sexual attribute. We find ourselves at the greatest possible distance from Botticellian grace when the physiological existence of the *obscene* actress, incapable of the least bit of acting or, more precisely, of any bit of representation, imposes herself so crudely. This is the equivalent of Coriolis's canvas, in which the portrait of the model, Manette Saloman, becomes a substitute for the figure of Venus, which it should indicate. Aphrodite *ourania* is transformed into Aphrodite *pandemos*—as signaled by the golden down that shines in Nana's armpits. Nana evinces every vulgar trait: stupidity, satisfaction, pusillanimity, a taste for the grossest objects, and prostitution that delivers her to everyone. We are very far from the statues dear to Winckelmann, which were all the more precious because they pointed only toward the divine, constituting the negation of any merely psychological existence.

Zola is assuredly not neoclassical. He cultivates rather those "corrupting seeds" that Baudelaire discerned in the works of Girodet and Guérin and that, according to Baudelaire, announced romanticism, which is to say decadence.[9] Without a doubt, satire of the Second Empire involves, for Zola, the upsetting of mythological references, such as we already find in *La curée* and *Son Excellence Eugène Rougon*; but this is not all that is at stake in this text. The confusion of the two Venuses signifies, on an aesthetic level, that representation is no longer possible, that the veil of mimesis is torn. Instead, all that is possible from this moment on, is the present (a present-tense presentation) of an exhibition.

Henceforth, the character can be no more than a figure of death, rather than of beauty, an inverted figure. Zola's parody is akin to Daumier's in the series *L'histoire antique* in which Baudelaire saw the denuding or flaying of modern man.[10] Nana's presence is literally infernal, or, more precisely, *poisonous*. This is apparent from the first chapter, with the mention of the red-headed

---

[9] Cf. Charles Baudelaire, "Ingres," *Le Portefeuille*, August 12, 1855; reprinted in *Curiosités esthétiques* (Michel Lévy frères, 1868), in *Oeuvres complètes* (Paris: Gallimard, Pléiade, 1976), 2:584: "As for Guérin and Girodet, it would not be difficult to find in them—who were in any case very preoccupied, like the prophet, with the spirit of melodrama—a few corrupting seeds, a few sinister and amusing symptoms of future Romanticism."

[10] Charles Baudelaire, "Quelques caricaturistes français," in *Le Présent*, October 1, 1857; reprinted in *Curiosités esthétiques*, in *Oeuvres complètes*, 2:554: "All that it includes of horrifying,

beast that is already that of the Apocalypse, and it is orchestrated throughout the fiction, Nana's infernal qualities resounding ever more loudly and power-fully. We need think only of the young woman's moment on stage, of the dressing rooms where she unsettles Muffat to the point of his gradually losing hold of reason: a red cat passes, the heat is unbearable, as if a fire were burn-ing nearby—the wings are hell itself, and Muffat, overtaken by a great night-mare, damned, will never be able to reach any other than satanic ecstasy. Everything around Nana goes up in flames—the fortunes of her lovers and Vandeuvres's stables (involving the most memorable of suicides, the lover among his horses)—and the spark is carried in Nana's hair. She is herself a flame from Hell. "Her grand residence was like some glowing furnace where desire was constantly at white heat and her slightest breath could turn gold into fine ash, to be swept away by the wind."[11] This is clearly the devil's forge. In the final pages of the book, we find an abominable apotheosis: "Like those dreaded monsters of old whose lairs were littered with bones, she was walk-ing on skulls while the fiery red of her pubic hair [or sex] glowed tri-umphantly over its victims stretched out at her feet, like a rising sun shining in triumph over a bloody battlefield."[12] Nana's final apparition as Melusina, in the fiery grotto where she remains silent, will be precisely that of this idol. We find ourselves thinking of Wagner, of his Venusberg (we must understand the term in its physiological sense also), which becomes a mountain of corpses where the goddess herself reigns, triumphant and carnivorous.

One very secondary character in the novel makes an incidental remark to another marginal character: " 'Monsieur de Vandeuvres,' called Madame Chantereau in a loud voice. 'Didn't they boo Wagner last Sunday?' "[13] They had booed Wagner and, more precisely, booed *Tannhaüser*, which is the op-posite or perhaps the inverse of the operetta with which the novel opens. The Wagnerian Venus reigns over Venusberg, omnipotent and fatal, and Venusberg is one of the mouths of Hell. Or, in Baudelairean terms:

> The radiant ancient Venus, Aphrodite born of the white foam, has not tra-versed the horrific shadows of the Middle Ages with impunity. She no longer inhabits Olympus or the banks of a perfumed archipelago. She has withdrawn

---

grotesque, sinister, and mocking treasures, Daumier knows. The living, but starving corpse, the fat, well-fed corpse, the ridiculous miseries of the home, all the stupidities, pride, ambitions, despair of the bourgeois—none of these is lacking."

[11] *Nana*, 367; *Oeuvres complètes*, 4:303.
[12] *Nana*, 489; *Oeuvres complètes*, 4:335.
[13] *Nana*, 69; *Oeuvres complètes*, 4:76.

to a magnificent cavern, it is true, but one illumined by fires that are not those of the benevolent Phoebus. In descending underground, Venus has drawn close to Hell, and she will go, without doubt and with certain abominable solemnities, render homage to the Archdemon, prince of the flesh and of sin.[14]

These were capital lines, accounting for the greatest reversal in the history of representation, already underlined above: to paint Venus was to justify painting itself (as indicated by Boticelli's Anadyomene or Titian's *Profane Love, Sacred Love*), by positing that tangible forms are the reservoir of the intangible to they which grant access—this perspective was idealist, neoplatonic. From the moment that the celestial Aphrodite ceases to be naked in order to appear partly undressed, that she is reduced to the "shameful and so powerful nothing"[15] of organic reality (which renders her *vulgar, pandemos*), it is clear that the figure henceforth obfuscates the form that it ought to express and that the tangible no longer designates anything beyond the tangible, but only its own fate, which is decomposition. The body is no longer identifiable with "a vase in which a spirituality might be enclosed," illumined by grace. On the contrary, it has become the primary repository of death. No representation, no figuration can be envisaged; the veil of mimesis is torn. Herein lies the Baudelairean category of the "heroism of modern life," of which Zola makes himself the aède throughout the Rougon-Macquart novels. In other words: "Venus was decomposing."[16]

We can imagine that the novel that would thus dress Nana in the brilliance of her flesh might seem even more scandalous on an aesthetic than on a moral plane, such that it provoked this comment from Mallarmé: "Nana's flesh, which we have all caressed, all that painted in wondrous washes, is the result of a truly admirable organization! But literature manifests something far more intellectual than that: things exist, we do not have to create them, we have only to apprehend their relations; and it is the strands of these relations that form verses and orchestrations."[17] Certainly,

---

[14] Baudelaire, *Richard Wagner et* Tannhaüser *à Paris* (Dentu, 1861); reprinted in *L'art romantique* (Michel Lévy frères, 1868), in *Oeuvres complètes*, 2:450–51.

[15] *Nana, Oeuvres complètes*, 4:332.

[16] *Nana*, 348. This decomposition of Venus is compounded by that of another figure. Satin, Nana's lover, is always compared to the Virgin, whose pure face she has. Like Venus, this Virgin envelopes a charnel house.

[17] Stéphane Mallarmé, response to Jules Huret, *Enquête sur l'évolution littéraire*, in *L'Echo de Paris* (March 3–July 5, 1891) (Charpentier, 1891), in Mallarmé, *Oeuvres complètes*, ed. Mondor (Paris: Gallimard, 1945), 871.

the novel itself is obscene: scabrous scenes multiply within it (Nana's onanism before the mirror, Daguenet's loss of virginity, Muffat's masochism), along with stylistics that would be the equivalent of this form of exhibitionism. Aristotle writes that where there is no representation that allows us to appreciate the spectacle of the most odious aspects of reality (its monsters and cadavers), death itself becomes active. This is what Mallarmé's observation, admiring nevertheless, finally indicates about this writer who sought to open the way for "the intrinsic and dense forest of trees" and the stone of palaces into the book itself, on which "the pages would hardly close."[18]

There is a follow-up to this adventure in *Les Rougon-Macquart*: it is *L'oeuvre*. Claude Lantier, the painter fascinated by the brilliance of flesh, who has juxtaposed a nude and dressed figures on a single canvas, attempts a final masterpiece: a woman of radiant beauty, naked, posing on a boat in the midst of the Saint-Nicolas port. But this modern Venus Anadyomene eludes the painter; a reflecting and decaying idol has invaded the canvas. The painter can no longer paint anything but himself.

Translated by Sharon Lubkemann Allen

---

[18] Mallarmé, "Crise de vers," in *Divagations* (Fasquelle, 1897), in *Oeuvres complètes*, 367–68.

VALENTINE CUNNINGHAM

Tess
(*Tess of the d'Urbervilles*, Thomas Hardy, 1891)

Thomas Hardy's moral tone was more than usually insistent when *Tess of the d'Urbervilles*, his twelfth published novel, came out for the first time between hard covers (the usual Victorian three-volume, "three-decker," format) in December 1891, following its earlier serialization in the *Graphic* magazine and assorted papers in England, India, and Australia (July 4–December 26, 1891). At the last moment he had added the subtitle *A Pure Woman, Faithfully Presented*, and he provided an "Explanatory Note" as well, stressing the truth of the tale. Here was a story "sent out in all sincerity of purpose, as an attempt to give an artistic form to a true sequence of things." Hardy anticipated giving offence with his novel. The Nonconformist novel-syndicating publishers Tillotson's had been "taken aback" by the contents of his manuscript. Two national magazine editors had turned the story down because of its "immoral situations" and the sensuousness of its heroine. The wildly sexy village dance in chapter 11 and Tess's private baptism of her child in chapter 14 had each been required to appear separately in the the *National Observer* and the *Fortnightly Review*—periodicals more permissive than the *Graphic*. But anybody taking offence at the book's "opinions and sentiments," said the explanatory note, should "remember a well-worn sentence of St Jerome's: If an offence come out of the truth, better is it that the offence come than that the truth be concealed."[1]

The truths Hardy was so pugnaciously—as well as no doubt sincerely and faithfully—promoting in this novel were about sexuality, especially the sexuality of women. "Everybody nowadays thinks and feels" as the novel's author does, said the explanatory note (an exaggeration, of course), but what Hardy is doing is speaking these things out loud. The "catastrophe" that befalls Tess—having a child out of wedlock—was "well-known," as Hardy would put it in his preface to the novel's fifth edition of 1892. And indeed Victorian

---

[1] Unless otherwise indicated, all quotations from *Tess* are referenced parenthetically in the text by chapter number and are from the Clarendon Press edition, ed. Juliet Grindle and Simon Gatrell (Oxford, 1983), which is the text of the Oxford World's Classics edition (Oxford University Press, 1998). The novel's complex publishing history is nicely set out in the Clarendon edition's long "General Introduction," 1–54, as well as being most informatively analyzed in J. T. Laird, *The Shaping of "Tess of the D'Urbervilles"* (Oxford: Clarendon Press, 1975); and Simon Gatrell, *Hardy the Creator: A Textual Biography* (Oxford: Clarendon Press, 1988).

England, the Victorian city especially, was full of "illegitimate" children, many of them disowned, cast out, but visible on the street. And the Victorian novel was correspondingly well peopled with these embarrassing reminders of unoffical sexual desire and illegal bodily activity (think of George Eliot's *Adam Bede*, Dickens's *Bleak House*, Mrs. Gaskell's *Ruth*, Trollope's *The Vicar of Bullhampton*, and so on and on). But Hardy would go further than his fictional predecessors and contemporaries, believing, as the fifth edition's preface goes on, that "there was something more to be said in fiction than had been said about the shaded side" of the "well-known catastrophe." For his part, he would speak out very loudly about desire, and not just men's desire—the sexuality of the moneyed, moustache-twirling villain Alec, a melodramatically seducing type long familiar to fiction, and of Angel Clare, the genteel student-age son of a vicar who had his guilty few days' fling with a woman in London before he met Tess—but the desire of women, and young women especially.

Tess's work mates, the farm girls of chapter 12, jostle at the window for a mere glimpse of the desirable Angel. They would "marry him tomorrow." "And more," adds Izz Huett. She would sleep with him without benefit of clergy. So would "the more timid" Retty. When Angel carries the girls over the flooded lane on their way to church in their thin Sunday frocks and shoes (ch. 23), they flush, their hearts throb, their bodies shake, their lips are "dry with emotion." "Retty was a bunch of hysterics." Tess's cheeks burn. She "was embarassed to discover that excitement at the proximity of Mr Clare's breath and eyes, which she had contemned in her companions, was intensified in herself." Their shaking, throbbing bodies are made wonderfully palpable in the writing. Marian is a "dead weight of plumpness." Angel feels Tess, he says, "like an undulating billow warmed by the sun. And all this fluff of muslin about you is the froth."

Hardy never lets the reader forget the flesh beneath the frock. The body of the reaping Tess "seduces" even "casual attention" (ch. 14). Glimpsed bits of her body from beneath her workclothes mightily excite the narrative. "A bit of her naked arm is visible between the buff leather of her gauntlet and the sleeve of her gown." That is what Angel likes noticing. When he catches Tess unawares and yawning (ch. 27), her arm is "stretched . . . so high above her coiled-up cable of hair that he could see its satin delicacy above the sunburn"—the upper part of the arm normally concealed by clothing. In the next chapter the pair work at the curd-vats, she with her "sleeves rolled far above the elbow," and "bending lower he kissed the inside vein of her soft arm." Hardy grants access to parts of a woman's body the Victorian fiction of courtship and marriage normally curtained off.

On their aborted wedding-night (ch. 34) Angel has Tess put on the Clare family jewels and then pulls back her "bodice" at the neck, baring her arms and her breasts (big ones, the novel repeatedly implies), as if she were some society beauty at a "crush" or ball.

Angel, like other men in the novel, is maddened by Tess's body. Her eyes, but above all her lips, her mouth—her "mobile peony mouth" (ch. 2)—are especially alluring. In the yawning scene he "saw the red interior of her mouth as if it had been a snake's." No reader ever forgets the way Tess is turned thus into both the lovely Eve of Milton's *Paradise Lost* and also the devilish serpent who tempts her to fall. Tess is sex incarnate, in fact. "The brim-fulness of her nature breathed from her," as she yawned. "It was a moment when woman's soul is more incarnate than at any other time; when the most spiritual beauty bespeaks itself flesh; and sex takes the outside place in the presentaiton." *Incarnate*: the theological term was deliberately challenging. That Tess's glorious body—and here, as elsewhere in the novel she is offered as representing all womankind—should be granted such lovely overwhelming force not only reversed the convention, adhered to by most Victorian novels, that woman's spiritual beauty and power were superior to her merely physical attractions, but in granting it Christ-like status the novel was making the rights of the body absolutely central to the novel's large roster of heretical, even blasphemous, challenges to Christian orthodoxy.

The Pauline, Platonic orthodoxies of the Rev. Mr. Clare, Angel's father, so hotly disavowed by the son and by the novel, of course revered the soul above the body, the spirit above the flesh. According to St. Paul in his Second Letter to the Corinthians, the "earthly tabernacle" of the body would be happily swapped for a heavenly body at the resurrection. It is Hardy's Christianity-challenging insistence that this preference is the wrong way round. For him, the "soul," the essence of persons, is manifest most truly in their bodiliness, their fleshliness. When Alec in his Methodist preacher phase (ch. 45) tries to blame Tess's sexy body for luring him from the path of Pauline righteousness ("Don't look at me like that") she is made to feel, once more, "that inhabiting the fleshly tabernacle with which nature had endowed her was somehow doing wrong." It is clearly implied that she is wrong to feel this. It is the Christian denigrators of the fleshly tabernacle who are wrong—preacher Alec, Parson Clare (he wants a "pure and saintly woman" for his son's wife, ch. 26), and the conventional novel. In all this, Hardy's novel is standing to Victorian Christianity and Victorian fiction as the writings of the notorious sexologist Havelock Ellis stand to the Victorian discourse on sexuality at large.[2] It is no accident that the novel keeps quoting the verses of Browning and Swinburne, the arch exponents of what pious Victorian critics dismissed as "The Fleshly School" of Victorian Poetry.[3] This novel is nothing if not voyeuristic and fetishistic, as Hardy himself was. (In *The Life of Thomas Hardy*—compiled by himself—he reveals himself as often relishing the bared bodies of society women at crushes and parties; he thinks of undressing them and wonders how they would look in Tess's field-girl wrappers in a turnip field. He also tells of mingling with the "wily crew" of prostitutes around Picadilly Circus.)[4] Tess is a painstaking celebration, in fact, of what the editor of *Macmillan's Magazine*, Mowbray Morris, rejected as "too much succulence"—the tasty stimulations of Tess's body and "her capacity for stirring & . . . for gratifying" men's "purely sensuous admiration for her person."[5]

According to Mowbray Morris, Tess's succulent bodiliness made the story "entirely modern"—and thus unlikable. And Hardy was indeed being self-consiously modern in these bodily exhibitions. His pronounced didactic position was that it was time the novel registered what was not only thought and felt but also done "nowadays," in the 1890s, in the period when the old sexual restraints and certainties were faltering. Their dying, their decrepitude, is at the heart of what Hardy thinks of as the modern. The decay of the old rules does, though, make for vulnerability. Tess's extreme bodily vulnerability stands for, is central to, Hardy's larger case that, in one way or another, to be modern is precisely to be vulnerable, woundable, wounded.

Tess is terribly victimized, especially by men. She is the ready object of the predatory gaze of every passing male—rapist Alec, desirous Angel, nasty Farmer Groby. This is why, on the road (ch. 42), she disfigured herslf, "snipped" her eyebrows off ("nipped" them, in most versions), hiding her face in a handkerchief. To be noticed, fragile, soft, and delicate as she is

---

[2] Havelock Ellis and Hardy corresponded, and Ellis reviewed Hardy with some favor and even sent him his writings. See *The Collected Letters of Thomas Hardy*, ed. Richard Little Purdy and Michael Millgate (Oxford: Clarendon Press, 1978, 1988), 1:117f. and 7:113f.

[3] "Thomas Maitland" (Robert William Buchanan), "The Fleshly School of Poetry: Mr. D. G. Rossetti," *Contemporary Review* 18 (October 1871): 344–50.

[4] "Florence Emily Hardy," *The Life of Thomas Hardy, 1840–1928* (London: Macmillan, 1962), 224, 235. *The Personal Notebooks of Thomas Hardy*, ed. Richard H. Taylor (London: Macmillan, 1979), 233, indicates that "wily crew of harlots" in Hardy's typescript became merely "wily crew" in the *Life*.

[5] Quoted in the Clarendon *Tess*, 8–9.

(for all her toughness in the swede field and up on hayricks), is to be hurt. Readers, especially feminist ones, have worried over her apparent passivity and compliance. And she does seem oddly willing to go gadding about in Alec's seducer's spring-cart and to go off with him on horseback to her rape. She is constantly allowing herself to be carted, driven, or transported by men. But the point seems to be that women, and working-class women especially, are being produced, especially in modern times, for victimhood, culturally and economically as well as bodily. The most grueling occasion, perhaps, of Tess's being transported, is at her family's lowest point when they are evicted by an ethically aroused owner (ch. 52). In this novel, the woman cannot help it—but because of the cruel way of the world. "No, no!" Tess protests, as Alec tries to stick a strawberry into her mouth (ch. 5), but he will not take no for an answer, and the protest itself opens her lips to receive the unwanted fruit, so that she "took it in." Like it or not, she and her female, working-class kind are presented as having bodies and lives that exist to be invaded by men, to be violated by masters and pastors (and pastors' sons), and to be victimized by the entrenched social institutions and powers, the employer, the law, the church, the landlord.

The novel is about progress, in ideas, behavior, and technology, about modernism in its various modes—from the sense of cosmic "blight" (ch. 4) and the moral challenges consequent upon the decline of the Christian grand narrative, to the advent of steam power that makes agricultural work even harder and more intolerable than before. Modernism brings an "ache" all round (ch. 19), but the ache is felt most by those weakest in society according to class and gender. It is Tess who most feels the seriousness of what Angel calls "this hobble of being alive" (ch. 19). It is Tess, and by implication her kind, with whom the President of the Immortals sports, who is the hardest-pressed plaything of her times ("Time, the Arch-Satirist," as the *Graphic* version of the last chapter put it, "had had his joke out with Tess"). She is the one who is, in the novel's repeated harking back to one of *King Lear*'s most terrible pronouncements, like a fly to godlike wanton boys killing helpless creatures for their sport. It is, as the title of "Phase the Fifth" has it, "The Woman," and working-class woman at that, who "Pays," who is the tragic victim of the forces of modern culture, belief, economics, law, even nature itself. The police and the hangman get her in the end, as the well-off seducer got her in the beginning.

Tess of the d'Urbervilles is so deeply consternated at how modernity is constructed that it is small wonder that its narrative procedures should be so messy, that it is so overthrown by verbal dismay and incoherence, so repeatedly confused by the prospects of knowing and seeing, of being seen and known by others—and not least by narratives, novels, and novelists. The text itself aches under its awareness of the ache of modernism.

One large manifestation of that ache is the way Hardy never stopped worrying over what his novel would actually say. He tinkered with it endlessly—in the manuscript, for the magazine version, for the first hardback edition of 1891, for the second heavily revised one-volume edition of 1892, all the way along the publishing road through to the "Wessex Edition" of 1912, and on still after that in his own desk copy of the 1912 version. The need to bowdlerize and appease certain bourgeois Christian taste certainly drove some of what was changed for the *Graphic* (like his having Tess in that version deceived into thinking she had been properly married to Alec at a ceremony conducted by a chum posing as a Registrar, so she would not appear to be living in sin with him, or having the girls carried across the flooded path in a wheelbarrow in order to minimize the palpable fleshly contact), but bowdlerizing in order to get published does not explain all of the shifts from manuscript to magazine. It is clear that Hardy was perennially dissatisfied with key aspects of his plot and his people. How actually was Tess seduced? Was she tipsy? Did she make a noise of protest or not? How sincere is Alec as Methodist? What is Angel's moral problem? It is rather astounding to learn that a whole segment of chapter 11 that was in the *National Observer* simply got "mislaid" until 1912. Like a man only partly in the light, Hardy kept on fumbling and fiddling with the telling details. There are hundreds of verbal differences between the various versions of his novel—which makes the question of which *Tess* one is actually reading as tricky as the question, Which *Hamlet*?

Europe got to know *Tess* in translations of the 1890s versions. For some time after 1912, the Wessex Edition was standard in the anglophone world. But its standing is no longer secure. The new Penguin Classics edition (1998) chooses to reprint the 1891 text. As for the great Clarendon edition, which is also the Oxford World's Classics version, it is based on the manuscript versions; yet it reproduces more or less the 1912 version, and it can dodge about quite wilfully between all the versions, even incorporating changes made in Hardy's desk copy. Without textual footnotes to guide you, the World's Classics text is full of surprises! With its thousands of clashing footnote variants, the Clarendon edition's *Tess* is enough to warm any postmodernist heart, emerging from a tortured textual history as a truly postmodernist text, one thoroughly resistant to any allegedly dull and boring concept of the single-unified fictional text. Be that as it may, though, what the Clarendon text certainly does do is to bring home, formally and linguistically, the utter mess of this novel.

It dismayed Hardy's earliest readers that his style was so jarringly disso-
nant. What place "in Arcadia," complained the poet Richard Le Gallienne,
had words like *dolorifage, photosphere, heliolatries, arborescent*, and the
like?[6] Clash of register is an ongoing Hardy problem, but here it is on an
epic scale. Readers never know which linguistic class or group they will be in
from one sentence to the next. Voices, ideolects, registers, levels, and literary
kinds fluctuate with deeply unsettling speed, as does point of view. Some
critics find this disjunctiveness, as Le Gallienne did, a high barrier to reading. The modern tendency is to praise it as a glorious Bakhtinian heteroglossia.[7] But like it or not, it is difficult to keep your textual and generic bearings. Now we are outside Tess looking down at her like some wanton boy,
now we're inside her. Now we're in a tragedy, now a pastoral, now a satire.
Now the text is all gothic novel with moustache-twirling seducers, oaths extracted at ill-omened places with names like Cross-in-Hand, and a murder
victim's blood dripping through the ceiling; now it is a short story of
Zolaesque realism about swede-hacking or the advent of steam-threshing
machines and their effects on Dorset laborers; now it is a sequence of proleptic symbolisms and allegories with Tess asleep among dying pheasants
(ch. 41) and a piece of blood-stained butcher's paper blowing up and down
the road as she knocks in vain at the Clare parents' door (ch. 45).

There is, clearly, to be no settled narrating in an unsettled and unsettling
universe. Referring to the gothicity of the Cross-in-Hand spot, Hardy talks
of an aesthetic "so far removed from the charm which is sought by artists
and view-lovers as to reach a new kind of beauty, a negative beauty of tragic
tone" (ch. 45; "tragic blackness" in 1891). Elsewhere he says he seeks an art
of 'disproportioning . . . distorting, throwing out of proportion."[8] Modernist pressures are, evidently, forcing a sense of horrific alienation not only

---

[6] "Mr Hardy's New Novel," *Star*, December 23, 1891, 4: a discussion usefully collected with
many others from the whole history of *Tess* reaction in *Thomas Hardy, "Tess of the d'Urbervilles":
A Reader's Guide to Essential Criticism*, ed. Geoffrey Harvey (Duxford: Icon Books, 2000).

[7] David Lodge was classically disconcerted by Hardy's two voices in *The Language of Fiction*
(London: Routledge and Kegan Paul, 1966), 164–88. Ian Gregor rather relished the "calculated
ambivalence" in his *The Great Web: The Form of Hardy's Major Fiction* (London: Faber, 1974), as
do many more obviously postmodernist enthusers about heteroglossia—for example, Penny
Boumelha in her fine *Thomas Hardy and Women: Sexual Ideology and Narrative Form* (Brighton:
Harvester Press, 1982); or Peter Widdowson in his later writings on Hardy, as in " 'Moments of
Vision': Postmodernizing *Tess of the d'Urbervilles*; or, *Tess of the d'Urbervilles* Faithfully Presented
by Peter Widdowson (1994)," in his *On Thomas Hardy: Later Essays and Earlier* (Basingstoke:
Macmillan, 1998).

[8] *Life*, 229.

upon people but upon narrations, the narratives that seek to register the modern story. The plight of the modern is upsetting the whole business of doing fiction, of making persons, and of achieving what ancient rhetoricians called *prosopopoeia*, personification.

Hardy is an extravagant personifier. He is famous for his personalized, sentient topographies and the way he makes landscape repeat and mirror action and character. What John Ruskin dismissed as an irrational illusion, as the *pathetic fallacy*, is for Hardy a principle of knowing and seeing and writing. Out on the "lonely hills and dales," Tess is said to be "of a piece with the element she moved in." "At times her whimsical fancy would intensify natural processes around her till they seemed a part of her own story. Rather they became a part of it; for the world is only a psychological phenomenon and what they seemed they were" (ch. 13). But this most ancient of poetic notions and rhetorical means, which traditionally makes literary characters and things knowable, is for Hardy a mainly unpleasant affair of hurt and plight. "The midnight airs and gusts, moaning amongst the tightly-wrapped buds and bark of the winter twigs, were formulae of bitter reproach" (ch. 13). Who would know and be known like that?

Hardy's novel is a huge program of intense mutual looking, inspecting, and scrutinizing—comprising all at once an illustration and exemplification of Hardy's own fraught efforts to see and know amidst the modernist ache.[9] People inspect each other; natural phenomena exchange looks (like the "white face" of the sky looking down on the "brown face" of the earth in ch. 43); people exchange glances with animals and vegetables and minerals (Tess, ch. 19: "The trees have inquisitive eyes, haven't they? . . . And the river says, 'Why do ye trouble me with your looks?' "), and with machines (as at the station in chapter 30 where Tess is momentarily illuminated by the milk-train's electric light and looks "foreign to the gleaming cranks and wheels" that she is regarding with the "the suspended attitude of a friendly leopard at pause"). And these prosopopoeic relations are inevitably deeply troubled ones. In the *Life* Hardy glossed this way of seeing the world in relation to his people as an allegorizing of all "the forces opposed to the heroine." And tellingly he justified his controversial presencing of these antagonistic forces as "the President of the Immortals" by saying this was just one more act of old-fashioned prosopopoeia: the old rhetorical trope by which

---

[9] It is Widdowson's admirably made point in his " 'Moments of Vision' " piece. J. B. Bullen, *The Expressive Eye: Fiction and Perception in the Work of Thomas Hardy* (Oxford: Clarendon Press, 1986) is informatively strong on the visual interests in Hardy.

(and he quotes a rhetoric textbook) "life, perception, activity, design, passion, or any property of sentient beings, is attributed to things inanimate."[10] The oldest device in the book—for characterization, for knowing and seeing—bespeaks a violently troubled epistemology, a distressed ethic, sociology, and history, within an utterly distressed mode of narration.

A distress of saying and naming, of textuality, then, that is commanded by a distressing intertextuality. As Hardy pointed out in the *Life*, that final and ultimate prosopopoeia in which the President of the Immortals ends his sport with Tess is "a literal translation" of Aeschylus's *Prometheus*, line 169.[11] And in the novel, the whole of the Western canon lines up with its "President" to heap awesome models of character and selfhood around Tess. "Call me Tess," she urges Angel (ch. 20) when he loads her with the contradictory and "fanciful names" of Artemis and Demeter—the Greek goddesses of chastity and fertility. But the novel is rather on Angel's side in feeling the need for models, for analogues, from the tradition. And how they pile up—as irresolute a gathering of names as anything in this most textually unresolved of writings. Is Tess to be thought of as a modern Desdemona or Juliet, or Milton's Eve, or the Bible's pair of promiscuous sisters Aholah and Aholibah in the Book of Ezekiel (ch. 14), or the Queen of Sheba, or Bunyan's Pilgrim, or the little sister in Tennyson's *In Memoriam*, or the fallen Mary Magdalen or the Madonna, or the hermaphroditic Fragoletta from Swinburne's poem of that name? It is an irresoluteness without completeness or unity except in one regard: there is something terrible about most of these possible literary models. Reach for a literary model for Tess and it is like reaching in this novel for a prosopopoeia—something distressing and hurtful keeps emerging from the tradition. "Poor wounded name!" declares the novel's epigraph from *Two Gentlemen of Verona*. It might easily read "Poor wounded naming." What is available from the textual tradition is a pot of mainly malign resources for naming and knowing. "THY, DAMNATION, SLUMBERETH, NOT. 2 Pet. ii.3" (ch. 12). In glaring letters of red, the old biblical text emerges into the scene of the modern—brokenly, of course, the past writing arriving in the ruinous condition literary modernism is well acquainted with—but speaking above all damningly, with menace. "Call me Tess," she pleads. But the naming possibilities the novel has learned from all of literature, from the whole history

---

[10] *Life*, 244.
[11] Ibid., 243.

of writing women, will not sanction such simplicity of address, such inno-cence about namings.[12]

A whole literary history, from Aeschylus on, cumulates, then, in *Tess*, with venomous force. And of course, throughout the novel, writing, like the business of seeing and being seen, is recognized as a bad business. Hardy's own struggle with the words on the page has been clear to readers from the start. There is so much he could never bring himself to say satisfyingly, clearly, or straight. Too much is allowed to happen in the gaps between the novel's "Phases" or when Tess is woozy or sleepy or asleep. She is indeed, as feminist critics are wont to complain, too often denied a voice of her own.[13] She is indeed at her most powerfully eloquent when she is repeating Angel's skeptical words ventriloquially to Angel. And epistles, those key models of writing as such, do keep going terribly wrong—when Tess's confessional note to Angel gets stuck under the doormat, and she cannot finish her letter to him in chapter 44, and when her appeal from the depths of her distress about Alec's renewed pressures meanders to and from Brazil (chs. 48 and 53). And that bloodstained piece of butcher's paper speaks with unforget-table eloquence about the awful possibilities of paperwork.

But for all the irritating shakiness of Hardy's text, for all the disquieted hesitations and anxieties of it and its people about vision and speech and writing, about imagining and reading and making sense, especially in a work of the imagination so full of literary historicity and the prosopopoeic essences of the literary, we do after all have a *Tess* and a Tess. It is simply not true to say, as Peter Widdowson does in his confident postmodernist fash-ion, responding to all the formal hesitations and linguistic disquiets he cher-ishes, that "Tess *has no character at all.*"[14] Through the forest of textual per-plexities we do indeed see Tess, and know her; we are indeed enabled to call her Tess. Like the so often silent Tess, the stuttering text of *Tess* has, after all, its particular eloquence. With good reason *Tessimism* became a synonym for the novel's awesome pessimism. Hardy hated Andrew Lang for allegedly

---

[12] On the violence of the novel's language and style and of the intertextual heritage's linguisticity, see Jean Jacques Lecercle's powerful essay "The Violence of Style in *Tess of the d'Urbervilles*," in the useful *Alternative Hardy*, ed. Lance St John Butler (Basingstoke: Macmillan, 1989), excerpted in the even more useful *"Tess of the d'Urbervilles": Contemporary Critical Essays*, ed. Peter Widdowson (Basingstoke: Macmillan New Casebooks, 1993).

[13] See Kaja Silverman, "History, Figuration and Female Subjectivity in *Tess of the d'Urbervilles*," *Novel*, 18, 1 (1984); excerpted in the Widdowson New Casebooks collection, 1993.

[14] "Postmodernizing Tess," in Widdowson, *On Thomas Hardy*, 133. Italics in the original.

originating the gibing label.[15] But it circulated because readers recognized in it the knowable essence of a woman and her story. Hardy was gratified to receive numbers of letters from husbands telling him that their story was not unlike Angel's and even more from wives "with a past like that of Tess, but who had not told their husbands, and asking for his counsel under the burden of their concealment."[16] Under the aching burden of his novel's modernistic stutterings and shufflings, its tense anxieties about the writing-out of modern plights, *Tess* was manifestly managing to get its "truth" across. And, of course, it still does.

---

[15] See discussion at note 15 to Hardy's preface to the 5th ed., Penguin Classics ed. (1998), 467.
[16] *Life*, 244.

PETER MADSEN

Elsie
(*The Dangerous Age*, Karin Michaëlis, 1910)

On March 27, 1911, the readers of *Danziger Zeitung* would come across an announcement directed "To the Women of Danzig!" with the following content: "The advertised lecture by Karin Michaëlis on the dangerous age induces the subscribing associations to hereby point out that ladies and girls who adhere to female dignity should stay away from this lecture."[1] It was signed by all the women's organizations in Danzig. The next day the same newspaper could summarize a brochure by the author Therese Wallner-Thurm from Dresden in the form of an open letter to Karin Michaëlis provoked by her novel *The Dangerous Age*: ". . . if she had given the book the title 'Hysterical Women' or even more appropriately 'On Women Afflicted by Nymphomania' she would rather have hit the nail on the head and her book at least have had a certain raison d'être." Karin Michaëlis's lecture was scheduled for the following day. The protests had prompted the police authority to ask for the manuscript. After the person in charge had read it, however, according to *Danziger Zeitung*, he had not only given it clearance, but he had "as we have been informed also personally described it as 'highly interesting.'"

The Dangerous Age was published in Danish in 1910.[2] It consists (as the subtitle indicates) of *Letters and Diary Notes* by the protagonist, the

---

[1] The account of events and debates in Danzig and elsewhere is based on newspaper clippings in the Karin Michaëlis archive at the Royal Library in Copenhagen.

[2] (Copenhagen: Gyldendal). The latest (third) Danish edition is from 1987 (with an afterword by the author Dorrit Willumsen). Recent years have witnessed a renewed international interest in the novel and in Karin Michaëlis's quite remarkable life: *The Dangerous Age: Letters and Fragments from a Woman's Diary*, with a foreword by Phyllis Lassner (Evanston, Ill.: Northwestern University Press, 1991) uses the English translation from 1911. See also *L'età pericolosa*, with critical notes by Donatella Ziliotto, Giunti Barbéra (Florence, 1989) (a new translation); and *Das gefährliche Alter: Intime Tagebuchaufzeichnungen*, (Freiburg: Kore, 1998). Karin Michaëlis wrote her memoirs in Danish in two versions, the first in the 1920s in a fictional form, the second, less fictional, in the late 1940s. A shorter English version was published in the United States with the title *Little Troll* (New York, 1946); a German translation was published in 1998 with the title *Der kleine Kobold: Lebenserinnerungen von Karin Michaëlis* (Freiburg: Kore). All quotations from the novel are taken from the new American edition (1991) and are cited parenthetically in the text.

forty-two-year-old Elsie Lindtner. After twenty-two years of marriage in the higher bourgeoisie in Copenhagen, she has decided to leave her husband and live alone in a villa on an island: "I must live alone. . . . Call it hysteria— which perhaps it is" (29). The villa has been designed by a young friend who turns out to be her great love. She realizes her feelings for him and invites him for a visit, but their meeting is a disappointment. He leaves. She then turns to her former husband for reconciliation, but he has married a much younger woman: "That he should have dared to replace me by a mere chit of nineteen!" (207). She decides to travel around the world together with her housemaid. This simple story line is the frame for a variety of reflections on her own life and the life of other women whom she addresses or writes about to other correspondents. "Do men and women ever tell each other the truth? . . . Between the sexes reigns an ineradicable hostility" (60–61). "Women's doctors may be as clever and sly as they please, but they will never learn any of the things that women confide to each other" (66). Some of these secrets are, as it were, revealed in the book, although not all: "I sit here and write for myself alone. I know that no one else will ever read my words; and yet I am not quite sincere, even with myself" (71). Once again in the history of the novel the fictional paradox—intimate writings made public—is used as a vehicle for confessions, in this case of an intricate complex of sensuality and fear of aging, as well as a variety of feelings that are not compatible with public morality. "If I had more sensibility, and a little imagination . . . I think I should turn my attention to literature. Women like to wade through their memories like one wades through dry leaves in autumn. I believe I should be very clever in opening a series of whited sepulchres, and without betraying any personalities, I should collect my exhumed mummies under the general title of 'Women at the Dangerous Age,'" Elsie Lindtner writes in her diary (130). This is, in a sense, what Karin Michaëlis has done. Her method is interestingly similar to the procedure of contemporary psychiatrists: demonstration of a more general theme through a series of "cases."

In the lecture she presented during her tour in Germany and elsewhere[3] she stressed a distance from her protagonist: "A lot of what is written in the diary by this lady . . . is hysterical and overwrought tommyrot. But why is it so? Because Mrs. Elsie Lindtner is at an age at which most women really are at the mercy of their moods and whims." The lecture has in a sense the same structure as the novel: general statements are interspersed with examples

---

[3] The manuscript is in the Royal Library.

from her own life or from the lives of women she knows. In fact, the book itself is based on such examples, among them her own experiences.

———

The Dangerous Age was published in Germany at about the same time. It immediately became a huge success not only there, but also in France, the United States, and elsewhere. The first German printing was sold out in one day after a very positive review that occupied the entire front page of *Berliner Tageszeitung*. In July 1911, the *New York Times* introduced an article with this summary of the success: "When a novel goes through its hundredth German edition within six months, when Marcel Prévost goes to the exertion of putting a Danish work into French dress, when there are translations of that work into eleven different languages, the English and American public is perhaps justified in trying to find out something about the author."[4]

In his introduction to the French edition, Marcel Prévost, a then very famous writer of novels about women, remarked that "in all the countries of Central Europe, the most widely read novel at the present moment is *The Dangerous Age*."[5] To Prévost, Michaëlis's book was "one of those rare novels by a woman in which the writer has not troubled to think from a man's point of view." It was a "sure diagnosis of the vital conditions under which woman exists, and an acute observation of her complicated soul," the "most sincere and complete, the humblest and most moving of feminine confessions." The memories of the protagonist seems like "a revel in which the modern demons of Neurasthenia and Hysteria sport and sneer."[6] "The nearer she gets to the crisis, the more painfully and lucidly she perceives the antinomy between two feminine desires: the desire of moral dignity and the desire of physical enjoyment."

"Hysteria," then, seems to be at stake everywhere in the reception of *The Dangerous Age*. But was the protagonist, Elsie Lindtner, an extreme case, or was the depiction as realistic as Marcel Prévost perceived it to be? The influential Viennese writer Karl Kraus introduced his commentary on the debate

———

[4] July 30, 1911.

[5] *The Dangerous Age: Letters and Fragments from a Woman's Diary*, translated from the Danish of Karin Michaëlis with an introduction by Marcel Prévost (London: John Lane, Bodley Head; New York: John Lane, 1912), 8.

[6] In *Journal des Débat*'s "feuilleton," Maurice Muret agrees: "Ces mots ne sont pas trop énergiques," but in a more skeptical mood, October 6, 1911.

sparked by the novel in a characteristic fashion: "The decent society subsists on Elsie Lindtner's being an exceptional case. The furies of the pen and the masochists of the feuilleton soon answered the question if the dangerous age really is that dangerous affirmatively and insisted that women who were still driven by some sense of honor rather than sexuality should go to their grave in the end with the sunny memories of the measure of joie de vivre doled out by the marriage broker."[7] Kraus could not agree that "sensuality is a disease or immoral" and scorned "the ladies' doctors": "They support under all circumstances public decency and cannot but declare that Elsie Lindtner is a scum of humanity."

Karin Michaëlis *did* give her lecture in Danzig, where the protest had engendered a wide interest. An anonymous commentator in *Danziger Allgemeine Zeitung* found it beyond "our plain German notion" that she can bring herself to talk about "the most intimate sexual matters in women's lives" in front of a public that to a considerable extent consists of men. Her remarks about equal distribution of obligations in the home between wife and husband are judged horrendous: "We have, thank God, in general not yet gone that far in Germany, just as we do not allow women to give speeches in the parliament." The writer firmly underlines that "self-control works even better against hysteria than against nervosity. It is not accidental that the less firm husbands most often suffer from wives who are capricious and eccentric beyond endurance."

A few days later a presentation takes place in Leipzig. *Leipziger Tageblatt* finds the speaker "wise, appealing," but has no sympathy for her opinions, "Mrs. Michaëlis speaks and writes only about sickly, hysterical, *decadent* women and all her examples are still more stories of disease, yet she has no eye for the healthy. . . . Mrs. Michaëlis *over*estimates the corporeal and *under*estimates human life's moral imponderables." *Thüringer Morgenzeitung* reacts to a presentation two days later in Weimar in a positive manner: "The most interesting work . . . may become a warning sign, directing many toward cautiousness and moderation." *Neues Tageblatt* in Stuttgart was even more positive after her talk there a few days before the events in Danzig: "She has with a sorrowful heart realized that it is natural processes that the

[7] *Die Fackel*, no. 319/320, 31 (March 1911): 6.

woman cannot avoid, just as natural as the regularly returning disturbances in the female organism."

———

Are such feelings pathologic or "natural," that is, a common phenomenon under the reigning circumstances? The interaction between medical literature and fiction in nineteenth-century France has been stressed in recent research in the cultural history of hysteria: "In short, the doctrine of the hysterical character, as it emerged in French psychiatric thought during the 1860s, reads remarkably as a codification into diagnostic theory of the fictional character of Emma Bovary."[8] Flaubert himself was interested in medical literature. Seen in this light, the impact of *The Dangerous Age* takes on a larger signification, since hysteria once again was at stake. This time, however, the concept—or rather the subject matter it referred to—was so to speak taken out of the hands of the professionals and brought into *the public sphere of exchange of experience.* Karin Michaëlis's novel and lectures represented furthermore a *normalization* in the sense that some of the symptoms classified as hysterical were interpreted as reactions to a normal life experience at a certain age and thus not necessarily a matter for special institutions and professional knowledge, but rather a matter for husband and wife, perhaps with some help from the family doctor.

The predominant psychiatric approach to hysteria was that it was a matter for specialists and that separation from the family was an important precondition for treatment.[9] In these respects the approach the book and the ensuing debate helped to promote was different. One Danish critic neatly demonstrates this contrast: "The public outside Denmark was astonished to realize that Danish ladies' literature was concerned with phenomena that would rather belong in an institution for hysterical female diseases."[10] In the end, professional psychiatry welcomed the novel, however, and in the 1920s

———

[8] Mark S. Micale, *Approaching Hysteria: Disease and Its Interpretations* (Princeton, N.J.: Princeton University Press, 1995), 233.

[9] The most relevant example in Denmark was the prominent psychiatrist Knud Pontoppidan (the author Henrik Pontoppidan's brother). To summarize very briefly, he was a proponent of "a firm iron hand" that should be experienced as covered by "a deep and sincere empathy's soft glove" (quoted in Vagn Lyhne, *Eksperimentere som en gal: Psykiatriens sidste krise* [Århus: Modtryk, 1981], 67).

[10] Svend Leopold, *Tres Talenter* (Copenhagen: Gyldendal, 1918), 120.

Karin Michaëlis was even invited to give a lecture at an international medical congress.

This development assumes an even wider perspective, because it is a symptom of a change in the cultural construction of one of the central thematic clusters in interpretations of modern European culture. The late nineteenth and the early twentieth centuries was an age of sweeping "philosophies" concerning the "spirit of the age." Nietzsche was *en vogue*, and two of the most influential books were Max Nordau's *Entartung* (*Degeneration*) in 1892 and Otto Weininger's *Geschlecht und Charakter* (*Sex and Character*) in 1903. Both were about the characteristic features of the age. Nordau's diagnosis was formulated in terms that were close to psychiatric concepts; Weininger's diagnosis was based on the dichotomy between male and female traits of character.

————

Hysteria as a word did not have any stable relation to a clearly delineated and defined phenomenon in the real world, neither in the older tradition, nor during the period of the later nineteenth and early twentieth centuries when it became a central concept in psychiatric debate and research: "It was during the nineteenth century that hysteria moved center stage. . . . Hysteria came to be seen as the open sesame to impenetrable riddles of existence: religious experience, sexual deviation, and, above all, that mystery of mysteries, woman."[11] The word also functioned as a clue to the problems of the age: "We stand now in the midst of a severe mental epidemic; of a sort of black death of degeneration and hysteria," Nordau wrote.[12] Among the symptoms enumerated in his extremely influential book were "a brain incapable of normal working, thence feebleness of will, inattention, predominance of emotion, lack of knowledge, absence of sympathy or interest in the world and humanity, atrophy of the notion of duty and morality." It is easy to see how a similar characterization could be applied to ideas about the difference between male and female. This is even more plausible when Nordau's remedy is taken into consideration: "The hysteria of the present day will not last. People (die Völker) will recover from their present fatigue. The

————

[11] Roy Porter, "The Body and the Mind, the Doctor and the Patient: Negotiating Hysteria," in Sander L. Gilman, et al., eds., *Hysteria beyond Freud* (Berkeley: University of California Press, 1993), 227.

[12] Max Nordau, *Entartung*, 2 vols. (Berlin: Verlag von Carl Ducker, 1893), 2:523. *Degeneration* (Lincoln: University of Nebraska Press, 1993).

feeble, the degenerate, will perish. . . . Such is the treatment of the disease of the age that I hold to be efficacious: Characterization of the leading degenerates as mentally diseased; unmasking and stigmatization of their imitators as enemies to society; cautioning the public against the lies of these parasites."[13]

Otto Weininger's wild, yet no less influential *Geschlecht und Character* concentrated on the opposition between male and female, and took the female as destructive for contemporary culture.[14] Hysteria was the effect of the attempts to dominate the female character and impose male ideals: "One cannot artificially suppress and supplant one's real nature, the physical as well as the other side, without something happening. The hygienic penalty that must be paid for woman's denial of her real nature is hysteria" (357). The remedy, according to Weininger, is to realize that female nature is fundamentally determined by the obsession with *"Koitus"* (coitus) and *"Kuppelei"* (procuring). His diagnosis of hysteria is simultaneously a diagnosis of an age that is too influenced by the female principle and should stick to male principles.

————

Cultural disorder could thus be interpreted as a female disorder or a disorder brought about by too much influence of female characteristics. Hysteria was—at least in the popular mind—a quintessentially female disease. Any attempt to normalize what was interpreted as symptoms of hysteria—and *The Dangerous Age* was such an attempt—would thus by implication contribute to a reworking of both the idea of "the female" and the idea of the "spirit of the age."

The broader issue was mythical: it belonged to the realm of popular philosophies of the spirit of the age, yet it was simultaneously very concrete. It was the age of agitation for female voting rights as well as a period of increasing female participation in the working market. Two years *before* the publication of *The Dangerous Age* the National League for Opposing Woman Suffrage was founded in England, and two years *after*, the English example inspired the foundation of Deutsche Bund zur Bekämpfung der

————

[13] Similar formulations are among the roots of twentieth-century reactions against "degeneration"—*decadence* in the communist tradition and *Entartung* in the Nazi tradition; in Nordau's case the issue was reason, empathy, social consciousness, and the feeling of duty, cf. 561–62.

[14] *Geschlecht und Character: Eine prinzipielle Untersuchung* (Munich: Matthis and Seitz Verlag, 1997). *Sex and Character* (London: William Heinemann; New York: G. P. Putnam's Sons, 1906).

Frauenemanzipation (German League for Combating Women's Emancipation) in the aftermath of the Deutsche Frauenkongress (German Women's Congress) early in 1912. The manifesto of this organization provides a view of this mixture of crazy mythology and direct politics: "Even if all the European people (*Völker*) should decay by [the influence of] woman, the German people (*Volk*), the most masculine people of the Earth, whose essence yet will cure the World, must be protected against this destiny in the most holy interest of Humanity."[15]

Karin Michaëlis's novel and her lectures thus hit several nerves: first, a feminist propagandistic interest in a denial of the problems she stressed; second, the interest of the psychiatric establishment in keeping the issues as a matter of professional institutional treatment; third, the general debate about gender nature or character; and fourth, the broader "philosophies" concerning problems and diseases in contemporary society—the "spirit of the age."

———

These last issues, however, were not Karin Michaëlis's concern, although they were important parts of the background for the reactions and probably contributed quite considerably to the novel's extraordinary success. *Her* interest was women's real lives. Two retrospective evaluations formulated several decades later provide glimpses of the lasting importance of her work. In a review of her memoirs, *Little Troll,* the *New York Herald Tribune Weekly Book Review* wrote in 1947 about the impact of Karin Michaëlis's work: "It is plain that hundreds of women have escaped from convention into living and fighting for themselves and others, and have been willing to document their own experience that others might not feel singular or shameful, because of the Danish author. . . . Many of her books will be read in Europe at least for a long time yet, and the phrase, 'the dangerous age,' will be used a million times to explain twists and turnings of human behavior."

In a portrait of Karin Michaëlis from 1948 in a German monthly, *Sie und Er,* what the book had meant to its audience is summarized: "Women who had so far been passive and resigned or embittered and self-destructive endured their changed state; men who no longer understood their formerly 'normal' wives were aroused from their torpor. The wise and sensitive authoress showed women the way to get older with dignity; she opened the

———

[15] Quoted in Ursula Baumann, *Protestantismus und Frauenemanzipation in Deutschland 1850–1920* (Frankfurt: Campus Verlag, 1992), 206.

eyes of the men to their lack of instinct and their coldness; and she tried with tact and ingenuity to bridge the gulf between the sexes."

Finally, we should also compare Karin Michaëlis's version of making the private public with the renewed focus on female experience from the 1960s and onward—and the various responses to this cultural change.[16] In 1918, a Danish critic summarized a widespread negative reaction: "Mrs. Michaëlis revealed to the entire world in what direction taste and trends went in our country where erotic hysteria became still more widespread in our literature."[17] The young and already prominent critic Tom Kristensen may have had this or similar formulations in his mind when he wrote in 1925: "The resentment against private literature that has been dominating in our country since the turn of the century has first and foremost been directed against our female writers. . . . Under cover of this resentment a moralistic and narrow-minded reaction has tried to make them suspect. This has been a real danger for the freedom of Danish literature."[18]

The readers of *The Dangerous Age* in general seem to have been more grateful than the majority of the critics.

---

[16] Thus Phyllis Lassner in her introduction to the new American edition.

[17] Leopold, *Tres Talenter*, 120.

[18] *Politiken*, October 20, 1925, reprinted in *Mellem Krigene* (Copenhagen: Gyldendalske Boghandel, 1946), 59.

Space and Story

MIEKE BAL

Over-writing as Un-writing: Descriptions, World-Making, and Novelistic Time

Thoughts about particular states, objects, and individuals expressed in the subject-predicate form: such a definition makes it immediately obvious that *description* is a major activity of all writers, including those storytellers who produce the bulk of Western literature, in the form we call, more on the basis of intuition than of clear definitions, "the novel"—a form that represents actions and events ("doings") caused and undergone by characters ("beings"). Yet the theory and criticism of Western literature have traditionally treated description as, at best, a stepchild, albeit a fascinating one. Rhetorical and critical treatises generally have been judgmental, as have the older discussions of literature. But even modern theoretical texts show traces of the old positions. Whereas individual authors and their novels are often praised for their concrete, visionary, or visual imagination, narrative theory has traditionally cast description as a "boundary of narrative," a Derridean supplement both indispensable to yet lying outside of narrative "proper."[1]

As it tends to go in such cases, discourse on description is either critical or defensive. Description is accused of interrupting the flow of narrative, of stopping time in its tracks. In the first section of this article, "Robin," I will begin with a short framing of these debates by presenting description as generative of narrativity. In the remainder of the essay, I will avoid these attempts to evaluate description as a unit, discourse, or style in and of itself. Instead, I will take description as a "natural" discursive form in narrative and hence, in the novel—a form that is as much a part of novels as the representations of actions, which appear to be more "properly" narrative. Rather than endorsing these reasons or explaining them away, I will use the traditional grounds for rejection to reverse the perspective and derive from them a description-bound narratology of the novel. Thus I will advance the argument that far from being an alien element, description is at the core of the novelistic genre.

To make such a view of description plausible, in the second section of this article, "Albertine," I will reverse some of the oft-alleged reasons for

---

[1] On criticism of description, see Genette's famous article, "Frontières du récit" (1969); Hamon's classical studies (1981, 1991); and Adam (1993). For the logic of the supplement, Derrida (1967).

casting suspicion on description. The heterogeneity of descriptive discourse in relation to smooth narrative will serve to characterize novelistic narrative. This section is named after the character whose overwhelming importance to the novel in which she figures goes hand in hand with the refusal to make her a "real," that is, "dense," character: Proust's narrator's object of love, that is, of jealousy. Instead of a flesh-and-blood individual, I will argue, Albertine embodies metanarrative reflection on the status of characters in novels as *descriptively generated pictures*. This double-edged descriptive discourse suggests that Proust's novel is as close to postmodernism's metanarrative probings as it is to modernism's subjectivist explorations. As such, as "proto-postmodernist," it reframes historical precedents. Proust's descriptions demonstrate what novels are and do, and as such they have an *apodeictic* function.

In the third section, "Lucretia," I will go back in the history of descriptive discourse to the alleged roots of description—to attempts to isolate descriptions and probe their autonomy—to look at the time-honored tradition of considering "ekphrasis" the quintessential descriptive extension in the novel, rather like separate text pieces or *pièces montées* (French for tiered wedding cakes, such as Flaubert described and Proust recycled). The tension between the description of the objects or the individuals (the continuous elements of a *fabula*) and the narration of the actions or the events (the *fabula*'s dynamic elements) will also be seen as characterizing relatively autonomous descriptive pieces. Moreover, ekphrasis itself is as narrative as it is descriptive. Therefore I will argue that description, far from stopping the flow of time, slows it down, but only to better explore its fundamental heterogeneity. The *epideictic* quality of description complements its ekphrastic inner structure.

From that point on, I will develop a view of narrative as generated by a descriptive motor rather than the other way around. I will start doing so in the fourth section, "Nana," named after Zola's most famous female character, whose beauty is as much a motor of the narrative as is her horribly destroyed face on her deathbed, which cannot but close the novel. I propose that by reading from description to description, the reader complies with, falls for, and perhaps incidentally, resists, the novel's appeal to her to construct the imaginary but coherent-enough world in which the recounted events can happen. In most cases—in the fiction we tend to call "realist" simply because we get carried along by it—this reading naturalizes descriptions. In rare but significant cases, the descriptions' mismatch with the world they help shape teases the reader into an awareness of his inability to read. This might happen in postmodern literature, but it also happens in novels that are, for completely different reasons, a more or less "smooth read."

In the final section, "Emma," the argument for a descriptive narratology, or perhaps a "descriptology," will be completed, on the basis of the *deictic* function of descriptive discourse. This function encompasses the four functions already presented. Through an intranovelistic form of deixis, description's intricate network of references, which only work within the claustrophobic universe of the novel, ties other narrative units into the descriptive units, so that the latter come to stand out as the *cores*, foci, or centralizing sites of fictional worlds, rather than as the *sores* of the narrative pestilence that both traditional narrative theory and rhetoric have made of them. The final part of this essay, then, performs what it states, binding the five functions of description together, into a descriptology that defines the novel as everything that grows and pullulates out of the paradoxical meaning of the "de-" of description: "writing about" un-writes.

Robin (the Frame)

On the second landing of the hotel . . . a door was standing open, exposing a red carpeted floor, and at the further end two narrow windows overlooked the square.

On a bed, surrounded by a confusion of potted plants, exotic palms and cut flowers, faintly oversung by the notes of unseen birds, which seemed to have been forgotten—left without the usual silencing cover, which, like cloaks on funeral urns, are cast over their cages at night by good housewives—half flung off the support of the cushions from which, in a moment of threatened consciousness she had turned her head, lay the young woman, heavy and disheveled. Her legs, in white flannel trousers, were spread as in a dance, the thick lacquered pumps looking too lively for the arrested step. Her hands, long and beautiful, lay on either side of her face.

The perfume that her body exhaled was of the quality of that earth-flesh, fungi, which smells of captured dampness and yet is so dry, overcast with the odor of oil and amber, which is an inner malady of the sea, making her seem as if she had invaded a sleep incautious and entire. Her flesh was the texture of plant life, and beneath it one sensed a frame, broad, porous and sleep-worn, as if sleep were a decay fishing her beneath the visible surface. About her head there was an effulgence as of phosphorus glowing about the circumference of a body of water—as if her life lay through her in ungainly luminous deteriorations—the troubling structure of the born somnambule, who lives in two worlds—meet of child and desperado.

Like a painting by the *douanier* Rousseau, she seemed to lie in a jungle trapped in a drawing room (in the apprehension of which the walls have made their escape), thrown in among the carnivorous flowers as their ration; the set, the property of an unseen *dompteur*, half lord, half promoter, over which one expects to hear the strains of an orchestra of wood-wind render a serenade which will popularize the wilderness. (Barnes, 56)

Here Felix Volkbein meets Robin Vote. An aristocrat in search of a wife meets the most fugitive human being, and the story of *Nightwood* can begin. Form-wise, this piece presents itself as a classical novelistic description. It comprises an introductory frame, a clear subject-object split, and a detailing of the perception of the object and the elements constituting it. But it also turns away from description through its deployment of metaphor, its decentering evocation of endless other things—sea, forest, mushrooms, painting, circus ("unseen *dompteur*," a key ambiance for the man Felix, framer of this description), music—and through its narrativity. The reader is warned: "the thick lacquered pumps looking too lively for the arrested step" counter rational knowledge.

This passage ruptures linearity through its anticipatory foresight, turning from the metaphor-announcing "as if " to the referent, which escapes the focalizer and will continue to escape him forever: "the born somnambule," who cannot be a wife to him, nor a lover to anyone, "meet of child and desperado." Through a rhetoric ranging from expansion to ekphrasis, disorder to distraction, and deceleration to intensification of the moment, this description contains, in a nutshell, the history, the theory, and the criticism of description.

"On the second landing," "on a bed": these phrases literalize the realistic framing that is so characteristic of the modernist novel's predecessors. The former narrativizes the focalizer, Felix, whose vision of Robin is the narrative referent of the description. He goes up, then looks down. The focalization establishes the link of perception between subject and object. Ascending in body, the focalizer descends in vision. Presenting the future object of obsessive pursuit—and the subject of obsessive withdrawal—as lying on a bed, the passage presents itself not only as a view from above but also as a traditional painting. The frame comprises the paraphernalia of the late-nineteenth-century artist's studio—"potted plants, exotic palms and cut flowers"—and the subliminal orientalism inherent in it. The fake fairy atmosphere of that site of representation is further expanded by "faintly oversung by the notes of unseen birds," a clause that thickens the subjectivism with senses other than vision, with sound, for example (smell will soon be added), while enhancing the limited focalization. Recalling, also, Huysmans's bizarrely perverse novel *A rebours,* the description's polyphony inscribes episodes of cultural and literary history within a single frame.

The intensification of the focalizer's perception together with the narrative expansion of the moment, prepares the reader for a heightened sense of suspense, giving anticipatory importance to what will come. And here she is, the image of an obelisk in a Matisse painting: "half flung off the support of the cushions from which, in a moment of threatened consciousness she had turned her head, *lay the young woman*, heavy and disheveled." Half flung, she is a spectacle of arrested intimate movement, unsuitable for the public gaze, so that the man looking down on her is caught up in the inevitably voyeuristic position. Passive, with the door open, the young woman "asks for it." And, although the two people involved in this description are soon to marry and procreate, it seems predictable that in terms of *relationship,* their case is hopeless.

This description of Robin Vote, the central character of Djuna Barnes's *Nightwood,* foregrounds quite precisely what it is that has made description such a bone of contention, so subject to paradox, such an object of contempt. It also demonstrates subjectivity and chance as two critical responses to realism, whose traps these two states of mind constitute. Moreover, anticipating later sections of the present essay, it recalls the dual status of ekphrasis as interruptive and constitutive of narrativity. I allege this passage as a *mise en abyme* of the argument I wish to put forward. This convoluted and self-undermining love story begins when one of Robin's prospective lovers, Felix, chances upon her in a hotel room, where he goes because someone told him to. This description, therefore, is a beginning. It is also a prediction of an end. Thus it comprises the time of the novel, including the body of its *fabula,* which is none other than the repetition of the failure to relate that is staged here.

Is the comparison "like a painting by the *douanier* Rousseau," a decorative, expansive, or specifying metaphor that clarifies the vision so that it can become visible for the reading viewers? Earlier, the woman was already described as "earth-flesh, fungi, which smells of captured dampness," so that the painted jungles follow, logically and aesthetically, rather than flesh out what is there on stage. If this description is ekphrastic, does the ekphrasis produce the woman, or the woman the ekphrasis? While the reader goes along with Felix, adopting his perceptual apparatus, including sight, sound, and smell, our narrative goodwill is put to the test when the focalizer loses his power in favor of the awakening text, departing from the Sleeping Beauty to turn him into a generalized "one." The description neither presents nor explains the character for the narrative. Instead, it produces the former *as the latter*, seducing the realistic reader into getting lost in the modernist jungle. This is why modernist novels appear "difficult."

To the contemporary literary sensibility, the gap between a criticism that applauds description and a narrative theory that marginalizes it, appears to come from the "experience" of reading versus the logic of structure. I contend that it is more plausible to understand it as historiographical. The history of the novel has privileged a certain kind of literature—say, to use an overextended term, "realist"—whereas narratology took its initial lead from folktales. To break through this divide, I draw extensively on modernist novels. Like Cervantes, these novels both deploy and de-naturalize description. Whereas Cervantes' antihero is declared "mad" for seeing what is not there—for seeing an army in a cloud of dust produced by a herd of sheep—and Zola and company boasted the referential existence of their described objects, modernism, with its dual philosophy of subjectivity and chance, is well placed to demonstrate an altogether different status for description.[2]

To start with the obvious: among the many reasons that have generated negative views of description, the one least mentioned in the rhetorical handbooks so preoccupied with the issue yet the one most often alleged by readers is the one that says that long, descriptive passages are *boring*.[3] What does "boring" mean? To cite only one example of many, Shadi Bartsch begins her study of ancient Greek novels with the remark that they are considered unattractive because "the advance of the plot is frequently interrupted by discursions and descriptive passages that seem manifestly irrelevant to the 'real' business of the story" (3). In all its simplicity, this is a representative view. The boredom or, for Bartsch, the "strangeness" is due to both the lengthiness and the irrelevance to the *fabula*. The latter—supposedly distinguishable from the descriptions that interrupt it—is the real stuff of narrative literature. The implied assumption is that readers read "for the plot," as Peter Brooks has it, accepting a certain amount of delay as long as the relevance to the course of events flowing toward the ending remains convincing.

---

[2] Caserio (1999) foregrounds chance in the modernist novel in England. Banfield (2000) probes and complicates facile characterizations of the modernist novel as subjectivist.

[3] In *Souvenirs d'égotisme*, Stendhal complained that the boredom of writing descriptions distracted him from writing novels. Gide's narrator in *Les faux monnayeurs*, who indicts description for hindering the imagination, phrases the more common complaint. Although expressed by writers, both complaints point to readerly difficulties that I prefer to call "boredom."

This is a reception-oriented readerly judgment that is overwhelmingly frequent and the target of much literary experimentation.

Theoretically, unbound by narrative sequentiality, the enumeration of the elements of the object in description is fundamentally arbitrary. In contrast, the narration of events follows the chronology in which the events take place. If it does not, the deviations are indicated by a narrative rhetoric of flashback or flash-forward, or, to use Genette's consistent if somewhat stilted terminology, of analepsis, prolepsis, paralepsis (side steps), and the like. To remedy this problem, description tends to follow the order of the object as it is commonly perceived. But one can often argue that the gaze describes or follows description rather than being followed by it. This is a complex rather than a simple order, in which the elements refer not to the described object but to description. The cited passage from *Nightwood* makes the complexity abundantly clear. The introductory frame represents the difficulty of keeping that frame within its own bounds. In this way framing is put on the table. The passage posits itself as ostentatiously far from naturalizing the description through diegetic focalization. It is its *metadeictic* function to do so and thus "comment" on descriptive discourse. Binding— through internal deictic functions—each element to a larger whole, which is *not a woman* but a domain of sense-perception, a painter's studio, a painting, and an object that refuses to stay still, respectively, descriptive discourse comments on the "deicticity" within narrative as an altogether different kind of order.

This is quite unsettling for those used to realist narrative. In the case of a person, for example, the description would move from head to foot or from the eyes to the rest of the face. This is the order from top to bottom, combined with the move from center to periphery. For landscapes, the order might be from foreground to background, vague to clear, left to right. Alternately, the description could run through the different senses involved in the perception of the object. The famous opening of Balzac's *Le père Goriot* follows the long shot zooming into a close-up, a move that, as it turns out, follows the steps of the character. And, as Eugène enters the rooming house, the sense of sight is complemented with the sense of smell. This ordered and neatly hierarchicized expansion is parodied in Barnes's novel, where smell intervenes too early and practically takes over.

The device is so naturalizing that its rhetorical efficacy is hard to undermine. For example, the first description of Yonville that opens the second part of *Madame Bovary* follows the imagined itinerary of the stagecoach in which the Bovaries almost, but not quite, travel to their new home: toward the end of the description, the discourse is stitched to an anonymous "tourist," who follows the itinerary into town even when the couple has already stopped at a resting place. But no one notices this. Felix, ascending the stairs to reach the view of Robin, similarly but more radically gets lost in the jungle of perceptions and associations. As a result, the woman is being de-scribed, un-written.

If description means to write ("-scription") about ("de-")—suspending emphasis on the object—then it makes sense that the artificial ordering that stitches the description into the narration through the perceiving (focalizing) character, could easily pass unnoticed. Thus, the modernists felt, it is in need of de-naturalizing commentary. By following the order of perception of the hypothetical object, description has a soothing, illusionistic effect that is possibly but not inherently realistic. After all, the object does not exist; it is written into existence by the description that purportedly "renders" it. If the object is believed to exist, however, in principle independently of a perceiving agent, there is no inherent reason why the order of the description should follow any pattern at all. Yet to sustain that belief, a "natural" order is more strongly called for than ever, precisely because the arbitrariness must not start to itch the reader. Robin's description turns the convention inside out: it begins with the proper frame, but only to produce waves of associations that take away that order, and with it, the object-status of the object.

The only reason descriptions tend to have a relatively "reasonable" order is because of the implied assignation of the work of constructing coherence for the reader, the stand-in for the diegetic focalizer. But this work necessitates an objectification of the described object with which even a lifeless object cannot comply. Robin did not wake up, but "her" text did. Her description, written in the objectifying "third person," disempowered the hidden "first person" of the focalizer, then ran off with its own associative chains: jungle, smell, and sound; painting, orientalist model, child, desperado.[4] As we will see, Proust, writing "in the first person" and invested in examining subjectivity to the hilt, did not endorse the traditional solution either. But his descriptions stand at the opposite end of Barnes's. Whereas he does motivate description by stitching it to the perceiving "I," even almost obsessively so, he still manages to keep coherence at bay. He allows it only to hover, experimentally, over the tension between time-bound, incidental, collective, and singular appearances. Thus, he, too, in a different way and with a different vision than Barnes's, replies both to the traditional critique of

---

[4] I put these grammatical "persons" in quotation marks because of the logical problem of the notion of speaking "in the third person" (explained in Bal 1997a), and because of the ideological problems of the concept of "voice" for grammar, suggested by Paul de Man (1979).

descriptive disorderliness and to the realistically motivated defenses of it. As his novelistic practice "argues," this is where modernist hypersubjectivism *necessarily* rather than accidentally tips over into the ontological querying that characterizes postmodernism.[5]

Something similar and much easier to quote occurs in the oft-cited passage from a book of short "stories" significantly (and Proust-like) titled *Instantanées*. Here, Robbe-Grillet demonstrates the arbitrariness of description. But his target is only a small fragment of Barnes's and Proust's complex questioning. Robbe-Grillet's experiment probes the false melding of descriptive discourse to a hypothetical object. In this short text, called "Le mannequin," he describes a coffeepot whose ear is the occasion for an exercise in circularity: "L'anse a, si l'on veut, la forme d'une oreille, ou plutôt de l'ourlet extérieur d'une oreille; mais ce serait une oreille mal faite, trop arrondie et sans lobe, qui aurait ainsi la forme d'une 'anse de pot.' "[6]

Jean-Michel Adam advances this passage to sustain Robbe-Grillet's defense against accusations of antihumanist objectivism (60). He alleges the phrase "si l'on veut" (if you wish) as a trace of the describing subject as "human," and, one might add, rhetorical. The human agent of which it is a trace is the projected reader—which turns the trace into a Derridean one—rather than the de-scriptor. The reader, I contend, is addressed by the interjection in the second person, even if this is disguised by the impersonal form ("si l'on veut" means "si vous voulez"). This address inscribes the reader as the focalizer's beneficiary, the "focalizee." In the description of Robin, this deictic of address can be seen in the impersonal "one" that binds focalizer and reader into ambiguity. Making the reader's perception converge with the (diegetic) focalizer, to save the humanistic flavor of Robbe-Grillet's prose—a defense the author apparently supported—seems a return to a pre-Proustian descriptive facility, closer to Hardy than to the modernist fiction on which the *nouveau roman* experiment rests.

This figure, the addressee of the descriptive display, is more clearly delineated in the adjustment of the reality claim of the description, as is further fleshed out by "plutôt," the conditional verb form, the evaluative "trop," and the insistence on outward appearance in "forme." These textual markers of

---

[5] Brian McHale makes this claim about Faulkner's late novels, such as *Absalom, Absalom!* (1987). Since I wish to use the term *postmodern(ist)* in a specific sense, not as a pass-partout for things contemporary, I refer the reader to Ernst van Alphen's analysis of the term's current uses (1989).

[6] "The handle has, if you wish, the form of an ear or rather the exterior contour of an ear; but that would be a poorly made ear, too round and without earlobe, which would thus have the form of an "ear of a pitcher." Quoted in Adam (1993, 60; my translation).

visual address make the reader complicitous with the make-believe that underlies any description in fiction. In other words, instead of writing *about* (de-) an object, description *un*-writes (de-) the ear of the pot into an ear that looks like a bad ear but is rather *like*—not *being* but only *appearing* to be like—the ear of a coffeepot. From "about" to "un", the preposition *de-* is turned against itself as the rhetoric bites itself in the tail. Similarly, Barnes's figure, presented as a painting with shoes too mobile for it, ends up looking "like a painting."

In a far more ambitious experiment similarly based on the arbitrariness of the order of description when the object can no longer sustain it, Georges Perec's *La vie mode d'emploi* describes a building in seven hundred pages. The energy of the text is invested in experimenting with alternative orderings—mathematical, according to a checkerboard, all kinds of configurations being generated by some logic or other—invented after the demise of any "natural" order. The book may be important as a literary experiment, but it is not a particularly gripping read; not in the way Proust's much longer novel is to this day. Yet it usefully goes to show that order, or a lack of it, is not the aesthetic issue, for Perec's book as well as Robbe-Grillet's novels are meticulously ordered. More relevantly, these experimental texts sharpen our sense of the aesthetic by *eliminating* such facile criteria.

What such experiments afford, then, is a triple realization: they demonstrate that description is a form of *un*-writing the reality claim of fiction; they show the price that has to be paid as a result of the transgression of the limit defended by the ancient rhetorical treatises, the limit where fiction loses its narrativity; and, they lay bare the way descriptive discourse inevitably turns into a discourse *on* description—a sample of poetics. This is not a privilege of the period whose ambition was to overcome modernism. Instead, the triple realization folds back onto the past, on which it sheds a postmodern light. Thus, as Adam (44–45) points out, the description of the door of the Temple of Apollo in Virgil's *Aeneid* (6.13–39) turns out to similarly collapse the description of an ideal place into an exercise of ideal description.[7]

This last remark raises issues of historiography that this essay cannot undertake to address but that are at the heart of the series of books to which it contributes. I contend two incompatible things simultaneously: that Robbe-Grillet and Perec *continue* that one strand of Proust's more complex questioning of description that led the way out of modernism's remnant belief in the representability of reality, if only in terms of subjectivity; and that they continue Barnes's questioning of the tenability of the diegetical framing of

---

[7] Adam refers to Perrine Galand-Hallyn's study of Virgil (in Meyer and Lempereur 1990).

description. This represents a historical limitation to the validity of the theoretical skepticism proposed there. At the same time, I claim that Virgil already did this. This would appear to make the claim ahistorical and thus confirm theory's alleged—and criticized—ahistoricism. The reason this allegation is wrong is the one I have theorized elsewhere as a *pre-posterous* historical position (1999). To claim that a phenomenon that becomes apparent in modern or contemporary literature can retrospectively be noticed in older literature is not to claim universal validity for that phenomenon. On the contrary, the modern case makes visible something that *could not be known* before.

From the vantage point of the present—a historical moment that cannot be ignored in any truly historical analysis—it becomes possible to perceive something essential to the nature of description in narrative thanks to the continuity between Barnes, Proust, and later writers. This is the standard, forward-moving line of "historical development." We also notice the impoverishment that accompanies the "specialization" of Barnes and Proust with regard to the modernists' more tentative, and therefore richer and more complex search. This specialization, then, facilitates a retrospective look at the past in which the outcome of this so-called development already took place. What makes this double-edged historical perspective pre-posterous is the need for later texts to understand earlier ones, which consequently emerge as different from what they could ever have been before this later reflection took place.

If both the aesthetics of order and the logic of definition lead right into the problem of fictional representation, as I have suggested, a third complaint about description that Barnes's presentation of Robin tackles, appears to derive its meaning from Hardyan description. This complaint is based on the reverse perspective. Owing to the arbitrariness of its order and its vagueness compared to definition, description tends to reductionism. Thus it allegedly limits the presentation of the object to the commonplace view of its traits. This is parodied and reversed in the orientalist cliché within which Robin cannot be captured. Clichés, this description stipulates, are only lures.

Description's alleged ideological reductionism can be taken to lead back from the order of representation to the more general semiotic issue of the Peircean *interpretant*. This notion, to be seen in this context as an early American-behaviorist equivalent to the notion of *chain of signifiers,* points to several aspects of meaning production:

A sign, or *representamen*, is something which stands to somebody for something in some respect or capacity. It addresses somebody, that is, creates in the mind of that person an equivalent sign, or perhaps a more developed sign. That sign which it creates I call the *interpretant* of the first sign. The sign stands for something, its *object*. It stands for that object, not in all respects, but in reference to a sort of idea, which I have sometimes called the *ground* of the representamen. (Peirce 1984; emphasis added)[8]

First, the notion of the interpretant—the new sign that emerges "in the mind of " the receiver when he is presented with a sign—foregrounds the input of the receiving subject of a sign, who turns it into a *more specialized* sign that he or she can deal with in the new context of reception. Second, it points to the temporal shift that is necessarily involved. Between the initial proposal of the sign and the reworking of it by the recipient in charge of attributing meaning to it, a temporal logic of sequentiality must be inferred. Both these aspects make the notion of the interpretant eminently suitable as a generalization of description. I would phrase it as follows: a description is to the object produced in its wake what the sign is to the interpretant that is its follow-up. This places on the shoulders of the subject the responsibility for the ideological reduction, not of the description or the sign but of the production of the object, the new, more specialized meaning. In both cases, the subject of reduction is the receiver.

This problem is inherent not in the novel but in representation, and takes specific shape in narrative. The following example is taken from a genre that was almost the novel's counterpart in nineteenth-century America—the literary sketch. An underilluminated genre much practiced by women, the sketch is relevant here for its primarily descriptive nature and the incipient narrativity its descriptive discourse produces. It is ideologically fraught with the reduction of social "others" to the spectacle of sentimentalized poverty called *picturesque*. A second element of its ideological reductionism is its distancing take on modern city-life. This may be attributed to the visualization of description, but, obviously, it also holds a nostalgic overtone in its dystopic representation of the present.

"Hurry, drive and bustle; coaches, wheelbarrows, carts and omnibuses, dogs and children, ladies and shop-girls, apprentices and masters, each one at tip-top speed. . . . Everybody looking out for number one, and caring little who jostled past, if their rights were not infringed. . . . The overtasked sempstress, in her shabby little bonnet, looked on hopelessly at the moving

---

[8] Among those who complained about this feature of description is André Breton (in his first surrealist manifesto). But he was neither the first nor the last to do so (Adam 1993, 22).

panorama."[9] The first sentence of this description appears to be a picture of busy city-life that any writer under the shock of modernity (Benjamin) might have produced. Its primary feature is the dynamic mixture of people and material phenomena evolving through time with *speed*. The second sentence inserts an explicit value judgment that qualifies the picture as dystopic. The third sentence zooms in on a single individual. But the woman—as this description prefigures, soon to be swept away by the crowd, thus leaving her aging father to be hit and left dying in the more straightforwardly narrative discourse—is presented as "poor" not only by qualifiers such as "shabby" but, more insidiously, by the feminizing word "little" and by the suggested inability to cope signified by "overtasked" and "hopelessly." The latter word, derived from a verb that, moreover, implies temporal anticipation, generates the narrativity that produces the subsequent anecdote about the accident.

As this example confirms, any representation is shaped by the ideological vision that informs it. This is why it is important to be suspicious of the belief in the possibility of non- or zero-focalized description, defended by narratologists such as Genette (1980; reiterated with passion in 1983). Description only appears to stand out in this regard because of its elastic extensibility, owing to the arbitrariness discussed above. But whether plots evolve around weak or wicked women, or whether descriptions present these characters as such makes no difference to the ideological reductionism involved. If anything, the descriptive passages are more overtly focalized, hence, subjectively limited, than the more easily naturalized stock plots to which Roland Barthes, among others, alerted us in *S/Z*. In any case, it is fitting that the reader, in her guise of "focalizee," produces a specific object or meaning that incorporates the assessment of the ideological makeup of the object. This is why critical attention of the frame as solicited by its unboundedness in Barnes is so important.

Hence, the charge of ideological reductionism is obviously both true and wrongly attributed to this particular discourse. In the quoted passage, for example, the ideological reductions to dystopic fear, picturesque poverty, and feminized incapacity, respectively, are presented to the reader, who thus "sees" the scene, the focalizee, in a particular sequence. With each step of the sequence—each visual sign—the latter is activated to construe the spectacle that, without that work, simply does not exist. Both the visuality and

---

[9] Sara Payson Parton, "Leta: A Sketch from Life," in *Fern Leaves*, quoted and commented by Hamilton (1998, 145).

provisionality implied in the genre's name put these features forward as a way of putting in the reader's lap the burden of the production of an ideologically more complex and specific *interpretant*.

One particular variation of this charge deserves attention since it accompanies experiments conducted—in the wake of Proust—by Robbe-Grillet and Perec. Robbe-Grillet's critics have led him in particular to a certain defensiveness regarding the alleged de-humanizing effect of the rigorous limiting of narrativity to the juxtaposition of descriptions in his work. I have already mentioned that he answered this charge by defending the human subject "behind" the objectifying descriptions. The *nouveau roman* is exclusively interested in man and his place in the world. It seems disingenuous to try to produce novels with no interest in human subjects, for that would be to leave behind all standard conceptions of the genre itself. As J. Hillis Miller points out, personification is an indispensable element in narrative, and the novel has developed out of a fascination with this element in particular.[10] But, rather than defending his extreme experiments by claiming their humanistic bias, I would favor a defense of this experimental practice with reference to another feature of the novel. This, once again, leads us to Proust's Albertine.

Albertine (the Object)

"But I could not arrive at any certainty, for the face of these girls did not fill a constant space, did not present a constant form upon the beach, contracted, dilated, transformed as it was by my own expectancy, by the anxiousness of my desire, or by a sense of self-sufficient well-being, the different clothes they wore, the rapidity of their walk or their stillness" (Proust, 2:867).[11] Is this a description? According to the Russellian definition with which I began this essay—thoughts about particular states, objects, and individuals expressed in subject-predicate form—it is. And if, rather than a passive, reified object, literature is an interlocutor for the critic and theorist, as I submit it is, then it is in those novels in which generations of readers have been engrossed that we are most likely to find a theory of the novel that is neither simplistic nor beside the point. I see these late-modern novels as exemplary in this respect because they are both modern and a bit tired of modernity, disenchanted, and in search of ways out of it. Thus they stand at

---

[10] See Miller (1995).

[11] All citations are from the English translation.

a key moment of change, a situation that works its way into the novels in the form of a fundamental undecidability about narrative and reflection on it. At the center of this period's literature, we find texts like Marcel Proust's *A la recherche du temps perdu.*

Among the many things he did to militate against assumptions on what literature was, and with the realist novel as the primary target of his biting sarcasm, Proust, more overtly than Barnes, *de-naturalized* description. And, to drive the point home that description cannot be detached from narration, he did so by displaying the difficulty of describing all his major characters. In realist fiction—the most common and most commonly read kind— characters bind text to *fabula* because they are both "being" and "doing." They *are* (continuous beings) and *do* (perform) the actions that propel the *fabula* and make the novel suspenseful, pushing it to a satisfying denoue- ment. It is because characters are the (humanistic) hubs of so many novels that love and sexuality are such central themes. For this essay, then, charac- ters would be the best place to inquire into the place, function, and nature of description.[12]

For a theory of description in the novel, it seems relevant that love and the jealousy it generates are overwhelmingly and deceptively important in Proust's novel. Yet for Proust, characters are not *beings* at all. This has two consequences: his attempts to describe them necessarily fail, and the tradi- tional division of narrative into narration and description shipwrecks. The descriptions of the many characters populating the world of *La recherche* are not renderings in words of their static, or at least continuous, being; nor are they the creations of fictive entities contributing to the world in which the *fabula* takes place. Instead, the major players of *La recherche* are described along—and sometimes as representatives of—the two axes of the novelistic world: space and time. The descriptions of the main characters—or rather, the difficulties of describing them—are the "essence" of the novel. Fugitive and ungraspable, the novel they generate is essentially without essence. The frame that failed to capture Robin in *Nightwood* is in Proust the only re- maining object of description. This novel is a demonstration of thoughts about the novel. In this sense, Proustian description is *apo-deictic.*

This is clearest where the two primary love objects are concerned. Alber- tine, the overt one, and Robert, the closeted one, are systematically pre- sented in terms of the opposition of their outward appearance. This is

---

[12] The distinction between "being" and "doing" is part of the traditional narratological distinction between elements subject to description and elements subject to narration. See Rimmon-Kenan (1983).

already obvious in their coloring—Albertine is dark, Robert is blond—and, of course, their gender positions. One is female, the other male; both have straight relationships, while the fundamental unknowability of both turns around their uncertifiable homosexuality. But, more important than these two traits—the one utterly superficial, the other too "deep" to be knowable, and both predicated on binary opposition—is the *ground* of their *distinction*. This must be understood in the semiotic, Peircean sense. What, the descriptions of them appear to ask, *makes* them? What, if anything, *are* they, as individuals? Proust, we could say, pre-posterously, zooms in on Barnes's questioning of the frame.

The question has literary, philosophical, erotic, and epistemological relevance. Albertine and Robert stand out in the crowd of indistinctness so that they can *become* love objects, that is, the subject matter of a novel. "Love" here is a philosophical inquiry into the relationship between two distinct beings, based on impossible knowledge and the ontological uncertainty this entails—a relationship Barnes's description predicted to be impossible.

Both Albertine and Robert are first seen on the beach. Albertine is selected primarily for the way she detaches herself from the group of young girls on the *esplanade*, while Robert is chosen for his temporal distinction, the rapidity of his movements. The former is, literally, *seen*—perceived in her distinction—when she pushes her bicycle out of the group of young girls. Her distinctiveness is primarily spatial, but, like Robin's, designed as—necessarily—in movement. Both the difficulty of making the distinction and the precariousness of that distinction are of great concern to the narrator—of greater concern, in fact, than the reasons for which he finally selects her as a love object. Robert—as blond as the sand, his clothes as white as the light surrounding him—is distinct as a character eligible to be an object of fascination because the rapidity of his movements, combined with his lightness so similar to the surrounding sunny beach, makes him, precisely, hard to see.[13]

The description of Albertine is not simply an account of the narrator's perception of her. Others evoke her first as "the famous 'Albertine'" (1:552), then as "You've no idea how insolent she is, that child" (1:643). Both pre-descriptions, if I may call them that, occur while the narrator is still pining for Gilberte, his first love (*qua* color, a redhead, *qua* sexuality, overtly straight but covertly gay). The real "sighting" of Albertine—there is not yet a meeting—occurs in an extended descriptive-reflective passage lasting no fewer than ten pages, in "Place-Names: The Place" of *Within a Budding Grove*.

---

[13] On this production of characters and the *fabula* of love in Proust, see Bal (1997b), esp. part 3. For all narratological terms used in this paper, see Bal (1997a).

It begins with "In the midst of all these people..."(1:847), and ends when Marcel enters the hotel ("I went indoors," 1:856), at the end of his stroll, hence, in terms of the *fabula*, quite arbitrarily. This piece is an astonishing allegory of the difficulty of describing, owing to the impossibility of knowing other people. The problems of *distinction* and its eventual arbitrariness are at the heart of the event and highlight the fundamental artificiality of description. Let me just select—arbitrarily, artificially!—a few moments from this extended passage. And—in anticipation of my conclusion—the length of the passage is not an indication of the slowness of the description. On the contrary, it is motivated by a struggle to keep abreast of an accelerated temporality that rules the novel's combined temporalities of *fabula*, discourse, and reading.[14]

The phrase "*In the midst* of all these people... the girls *whom I had noticed...*" introduces a description of the girls' collective movement through space as they walk toward the narrator. The latter is diegetically walking toward, discursively "speaking" about, and allegorically reading the *spectacle* of the girls. When he sees them from closer proximity, the rationale for the collective description is rendered in a combined terminology of taxonomy and aesthetics: "Although each was *of a type* absolutely different from the others, they all had *beauty*;... I had yet not individualized any of them." The struggle for distinction is rendered in a synecdochic nightmare that resembles a parody of descriptive detailing, and is explained through the effect of time: "I saw a pallid oval, black eyes, green eyes, *emerge*, I did not know if these were the same that had already charmed me *a moment ago*, I could not relate them to any one girl whom I had set apart from the rest and identified" (1:847).

The narrator experiences the incapacity to distinguish as a lack ("want") but also as a source of beauty thus being placed outside of himself and his subjectivity as perceiving agent: "And this *want*, in my vision, of the demarcations which I *should presently* establish between them *permeated* the group with a sort of *shimmering* harmony, the *continuous transmutation* of a fluid, collective and *mobile* beauty" (1:847–48). The source of beauty is the negation of distinction, yet time lifts a prescriptive finger ("should presently"). Clashing with this routine temporality is the temporality that inheres in the group: "continuous transmutation," the mobility that is the site of beauty. Clearly, a stable character endowed with permanent beauty is not going to result from this descriptive dystopia.

---

[14] References are to the Scott-Moncrieff and Kilmartin translation (1981). Emphasis is added unless otherwise indicated.

The rhetorical makeup of this initial stage is reconfirmed throughout the passage (for example, "to the delight of the other girls, especially of a pair of green eyes in a doll-like face . . . ," 1:849). But even when distinction is achieved, the result is emphatically not closer to an individualizing and stabilizing character description. "By this time their charming features had ceased to be indistinct and jumbled" (1:850) confirms the narrator in an uncharacteristically short, summing-up sentence, but "I had dealt them *like cards* into so many heaps to compose . . . : the tall one who had just jumped over the old banker; the little one silhouetted against the horizon of sea with her plump and rosy cheeks and green eyes; the one with the straight nose and dark complexion who *stood out among the rest.*"

Curiously, the first act of distinction is hidden in a subclause ("who stood out"), whereas the actual description of the chosen one is couched in an emphatically parallel series ("the one with the straight nose"). The next step is based on the usual (deceptive) appearances and negativity: "a girl with brilliant, laughing eyes and plump, matte cheeks, a black polo-cap crammed on her head, who was pushing a bicycle" is cast as belonging to the popular classes, as being of light virtue, and rather vulgar. Ideological reduction appears, in effect, to result from description.

But distinction on the level of the *fabula*—the represented object—is not enough to facilitate successful description. Even after this crucial moment of election, the narrator continues his musings on the impossibility of individualizing descriptively. Again synecdoche is the figure that emblematizes that difficulty: "Though they were now separately identifiable, still the *interplay of their eyes*, animated with self-assurance . . . an invisible but harmonious bond, like a *single* warm shadow . . . making of them a whole as homogeneous in its parts as it was different from the crowd through which their procession gradually wound" (1:851).

The taxonomic principle, compared to the card game earlier on, does not, however, deny the object of description her subjectivity. On the contrary, it is because, ultimately, she cannot be objectified that Albertine cannot assume novelistic autonomy. Ultimately, the critical process Proust is engaged in here leads up to a fierce critique of realism precisely on the grounds of its seductively objectifying power. Gradually, the narrator merges his awareness of her unknowability with his decision to elect her.[15]

---

[15] In spite of his impassioned engagement with and emulation of visual representation, Proust's suspicion of description is often, as here, also continuous with Jewish cultural attitudes toward images, which suspect them of seducing the reader/viewer into an excess, the excess of realistic belief. The religious variant of this excessive belief is idolatry. See Meltzer (1987).

If she appears to be just a playing card here or a snapshot later, it is because she remains resistant to narrative integration. Descriptive discourse is the representation of that resistance. The resistance is mutual: not only can she never be known, he cannot "place" himself within her world either. "For an instant, as I passed the one with the plump cheeks who was wheeling her bicycle, I caught her smiling, sidelong glance, aimed from the center of that inhuman world which enclosed the life of this little tribe, an *inaccessible, unknown world* wherein the idea of what I was could certainly never penetrate or find a place."

As this last passage demonstrates, the stakes are high: description presupposes the existence of the object. But, since the other is not an object but a subject, her existence can never be *posited,* that is, fixed, assumed to *be* (as in *being*). Instead, the other holds power over his own being. As a result, the question not, or at least not only, of her but of *his* visibility creates an existential and, therefore, descriptive despair: "had she seen me . . . At the moment in which the dark ray emanating from her eyes had fallen on me? If she had seen me, what could I have represented to her? From the depth of what universe did she discern me?" (1:851), and sure enough, the metaphor of the telescope, never far away when Proust's narrator questions representability, shows up in the next sentence.

This is followed by a triple reflection on eyes and the ideas that cannot be read in them; on the lives of the girls and the narrator's happiness derived from them, a happiness curiously phrased as "that prolongation, that possible multiplication of oneself"; and on the fundamental *heterogeneity* between him and the girls as the surest motor of desire, in other words: as a motor of narrative. The passage does not lead to a resolution of the process of perceiving, noticing, or selecting the love object. Instead, it ends with a flourished metaphor of the commonplace kind, in which the girls, still collectively, are compared to fresh roses and butterflies, and the subject of selection to a botanist. It will take a long time before anything happens as a follow-up to this descriptive moment.

These initial presentations are not isolated cases. Both Albertine and Robert are consistently described in their existential fragility. Until the end of both the Albertine episode and the novel itself, the narrator, who sometimes appears so cruel toward both, is keenly aware of the impossibility of pinning them down, of describing them. This is clear, for example, with Albertine's first appearance—the word is appropriate—as the one who leaves the group and later returns in the middle of the romance, when the narrator is again realizing that his stare is, *by definition*, vaguely amorous. By analogy, Proust pronounces on the function of description in the novel. Love, like the novel, the genre of which it is the primary subject matter, is not so much an encounter with another subject existing in continuity as the search to see, and hence, distinguish, highlight, one being in the drab anonymity of "the world." And it is the search, not the result, that matters. It is the spatial, world-making equivalent of his search for lost time. Thus Proust theorizes representation: its (im)possibility, its ethics, and its necessity.

Later, when he is already firmly ensconced in his paranoid relationship with Albertine—paranoid, of course, because the descriptive exploration has demonstrated the impossibility of knowledge, hence, of assurance—the narrator describes in minute detail, for example, how at the beginning of the summer season, his searching eye seeks out the young girls who had so enraptured him before. Now he does not need to distinguish the girl with whom he so significantly but poignantly had said to have decided to "have his novel." Yet distinction is still the object of the search. In the following fragment, the gaze, distant at the beginning of the sentence, moves closer toward the end: "But I could not arrive at any certainty, for the face of these girls did not fill a constant space, did not present a constant form upon the beach, contracted, dilated, transformed as it was by my own expectancy, by the anxiousness of my desire, or by a sense of self-sufficient well-being, the different clothes they wore, the rapidity of their walk or their stillness." (2:867). The focalizing subject transforms the incorrect grammatical form of a singular noun (face) accompanied by a plural predicate (these girls) into a zoom effect.[16] The combination is maintained right to the end of the sentence. It is partially neutralized by the increasingly rapid succession of nouns (clothes—in the plural—rapidity, stillness). As I have argued elsewhere, the search here is primarily *photographic*. I would now add that photography is selected as the model for this search because it is ambiguously situated between producing and recording a vision. Hence, it poses the problem of, precisely, distinction. Specifically, distinction is not only a spatial issue. It is also a temporal one. If only the model would pose for him, he would be able to fix the lens at the right distance, that is, at the distance necessary to hold the image still.

Through photography, Proust challenges the humanistic assumptions inherent in realist literature. Indeed, photography challenges any simple idea of description as distinct from narration. With its glossy, shiny, flat surface, it is neither "profound"—it has no *depth*—nor stable; it resists any attempt to subordinate description to the service of the humanistic ideal of "dense"

---

[16] This creative deployment of grammar finds a reversed parallel in the unexpected plural of the title of this novel: *A l'ombre de jeunes filles en fleurs*.

characters, as advocated by Proust's younger contemporary, E. M. Forster (1927). More strikingly perhaps, in a revisionist appreciation of description, Proust challenges the notion that a connection between appearance and person is possible at all, both in terms of visual bonding and of the flatness and fragmentation that vision also entails. In *La prisonnière*, in a passage marked by negativity, Albertine, who has now lost the aspect she had in the photograph on the beach that set her apart, consists of nothing but a series of snapshots: "A person, scattered in space and time, is no longer a woman but a series of events on which we can throw no light, a series of insoluble problems" (3:99–100). This shattering of the object inflects spatial coherence, a requisite for description, into temporal fragmentation, thus further melding together description and narration.

This dissolution into a flat, visual series only gets worse, eventually becoming the base on which the images of jealousy fix themselves: "For I possessed in my memory only a series of Albertines, separate from one another, incomplete, a collection of profiles or snapshots, and so my jealousy was restricted to a discontinuous expression, at once fleeting and fixed" (3:145–46). The last words, "at once fleeting and fixed," define very precisely the nature of photography and, in particular, the nature of the series of snapshots, as well as of the jealous passion that uses such images as its *support*. They also define description in the novel. It is clear, then, why the snapshot's vocation is to become the *mise en abyme* of description and its limitations according to Proust, in the same way that Sleeping Robin is a *mise en abyme* for Barnes's questioning of description's frameability. These words explain the specific use Proust makes of the photographic mechanism. But they also underwrite his efforts to de-naturalize description, in a novel that makes such abundant use of that discursive form.

The quarrel implied, it seems to me, is with the assumptions that hold literature to standards of "nature," whereas literature's primary function is to be artifice. Against the humanistic ideology of naturalness, Proust promotes an awareness of artificiality. In a culture where "naturalism," "realism," and "illusionism"—not identical but affiliated notions—are near-impossible to discard, even today, this plea for an endorsement of the fundamental artificiality of art remains an embattled position. Proust, uniquely, realized this and worked through the numerous difficulties underlying that dispute.

For example, the narrator composes "an album of Albertines" not in the vain hope of fixing that inaccessible being, but precisely to demonstrate that he cannot. The "flatness" of the photograph, however, has an additional quality that frustrates such attempts: it invites pretence, masks, and play-acting. Thus it is the production and recording of artifice. It only fixes the external aspect, thereby hiding the "inner being" all the more effectively. But who is to say, in the case of Albertine, that such a being actually exists? While the series of snapshots gives the subject an epistemological way out, the photograph also affects the object. Consequently, the latter's existence, its "being," is denied: "And before she pulled herself together and spoke to me, there was an instant during which Albertine did not move, smiled into the empty air, with the same feigned spontaneity and secret pleasure as if she were posing for somebody to take her photograph, or even seeking to assume before the camera a more dashing pose" (3:146). In a realistic reading, the young woman would seem insufferably vain and artificial. Inside the experimental writing here, this description reveals something else: faced with the "collage" the narrator is desperately trying to create, Albertine takes her place in the "picture" as best she can. But the snapshots reveal all the more clearly and thus all the more painfully, the essential impossibility of "fixing" her down.

"Albertine," then, stands for the figuration of novelistic character as not-human, not-real, artifice. There is neither existential certainty nor continuity or contiguity between such flat, glossy paper products and other elements of the world in which they circulate. This represents one of the problems of description insofar as it undermines the notion that description presupposes a stable object. This view seems astonishingly contemporary; it embodies the "proto-postmodern" side of Proust's work. But there is a good reason why Proust was so invested in undermining the traditional use and view of description, and why he used, specifically, *character* as his ground for experimentation. That reason lies in the rhetorical tradition.[17]

The complaint of description's inability to offer an adequate "copy" of the world, the central complaint to which all others I have discussed in the previous section can be tied, is evidence of the most profoundly realistic bias in all of these debates. Representation is possible precisely because it *cannot* copy, and it is culturally relevant because it will not try. Proust's *petit pan de mur jaune* can do the work it is called upon to do, including killing the writer Bergotte because of his unfulfillable ambitions, not in spite of but *thanks to* the pictorial inadequacy of the description. The latter is ambiguous in the strong, logical sense, and consequently does not "exist," cannot

---

[17] Proust ridiculed more classical descriptions of entities more stable than characters, for example, of buildings or nature, as in his own boyhood description of the church of Combray. He also experimented with such descriptions more constructively (Genette 1972). I am interested, here, not in Proust's theoretical and critical views on descriptive literature, but in his novelistic solutions to the problems of description.

be pinpointed in Vermeer's painting. Moreover, the ambiguity concerns, precisely, the existence of the patch.

Like eyes, words can kill. The yellow patch does not exist, but it does kill a character. Killing a character: what better place than fiction—where no live subjects are endangered—to explore the dangers that cultural habits such as language, voyeurism, and ethnographic othering allow us to incur?

Lucretia (the Killing)

And from the towers of Troy there would appear
The very eyes of men through loop-holes thrust,
Gazing upon the Greeks with little lust:
Such sweet observance in this work was had,
That one might see those far-off eyes look sad.
In great commanders grace and majesty
You might behold, triumphing in their faces;
In youth quick bearing and dexterity;
And here and there the painter interlaces
Pale cowards, marching on with trembling paces;
Which heartless peasants did so well resemble,
That one would swear he saw them quake and tremble.[18]

Performativity, *pace* Austin, at the very heart of the constative utterance: illusionistic, narrative painting is its model. This is why description, of necessity, generates narrative. After two descriptions generative of love stories, it is now only fair to turn to murder. Together with love, murder is perhaps the most frequently deployed novelistic theme. Of the two, murder is the more clearly narrative. The themes are each other's systematic opposite, and hence, engaged with the same problem: the relation of self to other in the order of representation. Either the perceived other is easily objectified, which turns her or him into a dead thing and thus makes description epistemic murder; or the other is accepted, respected, indeed, welcomed, as irreducible, which turns her or him into an inaccessible subject, and makes description, then, impossible—and love kills *it*. The description of character is, therefore, the emblematic case of the paradox of description.

This is another reason why the rhetoricians' worry about the lack of "natural" order in description seems utterly beside the point. In the same way as

---

[18] Shakespeare, *The Rape of Lucrece*, lines, 1382–93.

word order is regulated by syntax and narrative order by chronology, so descriptive order is guided by the double agency of the focalizer and the narrative this agent's gaze generates. For, I will argue in this section, as in any act of showing, description is subject to the properties of *epi-deiknumai:* the one who shows, shows himself, and also argues, for praise or blame, moral or aesthetic. In such acts, the moral values of describing and of "seeing" subjects merge or clash. The order, thus, is rhetorical, but not only in the narrow, tropological sense.

Although interested in precisely that narrower rhetorical issue, of figuration, Hayden White makes a comparable point when he states, a propos of Proust's description, properly ekphrastic, of the Hubert Robert fountain, that the tropological structure of the description generates narrativity: "The relation between the scene of the encounter with the prince and that in which the fountain is described is only tropical, which is to say that it is unpredictable, unnecessary, undeducible, arbitrary, and so on, but at the same time functionally effective and *retro*dictable as a narrative unit once its tropical relationship to what comes before (and what comes after) it is discerned" (138; emphasis in text). In a move comparable to what I have proposed as pre-posterous history, White here posits a pre-posterous narrativity for description. In this sense, too, description, especially in its perfected state of ekphrasis, is a master-discourse of the novel.

The story of Lucretia has a description as its primary agent, as its murderer. From time immemorial, the name "Lucretia" has signified a narrative of triple victimization: the Roman heroine was raped; then she killed herself, unable to judge in favor of life once her subjectivity had been effectively destroyed; and finally, the tradition of rhetorical reading erased her story by interpreting it, ironically, as "just" an allegory of the victory of democracy over tyranny. This short story, which came to us through the Latin classical canon, from Livy and Ovid, has been recycled many times throughout the history of Western literature; church fathers, medieval allegories, Renaissance poetry and painting were all fond of it, for the opportunity it offered of fine-tuning juridical and theological questions of the right-to-life versus the right-to-choice. It made it into opera and theater. Numerous paintings exploited the opportunity it presented to whitewash the nude with moral righteousness. Strangely, dramatic as it is, and as rich in potential for psychological scrutiny, Lucretia's story has never, as far as I know, made it into a novel.

Of course, it is pointless to speculate on why this is so. But I can imagine that its plot—perfectly narrative, suspenseful, eventful—would make novelists of the realistic persuasion stumble. For, on a level quite different from

that of Albertine's entrance into the perceptual orbit of the Proustian narrator, the plot revolves around the primacy of description as the motor of narrativity. The ancient sources already suggest that it was the boasting description of her by her husband Collatine to his buddies in the army that set the
rapist Tarquin in motion. Shakespeare, who never wrote novels but who did
write two long narrative poems, came as close as he ever would to writing a
novel with his *Rape of Lucrece*. He did so by composing a story that revolves
on description. And, since the plot consists of two decisive events—rape
and suicide—he doubles the descriptive causations of these events. The initial description by Collatine is matched by the description of a (nonexistent)
painting of the Trojan War. The second description triggers the suicide.
And, if it can be said that rape is soul-murder, the second description, a typical ekphrasis, and parallel to the first one, triggers the second murder,
which inherently follows the first.

It is an extensive story, with an intricate plot, characters, settings, sex,
murder, and a gripping denouement: we may as well treat it as a novel. I propose to do so, provisionally, also for theoretical reasons. Responding, pre-
posterously, to Proust, Shakespeare underwrites the former's theory of description as both impossible and crucially generative of narrativity. By
assigning a double murderous effectivity to description—the first one generating both the first murder and the second murderous description—the
early baroque writer elaborates on the ethical consequences of Proust's radical epistemic doubt that tipped the latter's work over into the ontological
skepticism that heralds postmodernism. Between proto-postmodernism and
proto-baroque, a dialogic link is thus established about the narrative striking
force of description. And, as if to resume the age-old rhetorical discussion
within which Shakespeare was immersed (but Proust was not), the final battle is fought over the description of a nonexistent painting of the war that inaugurates narrative literature in the Western tradition, the Trojan War.

The Rape of Lucrece is, indeed, a war of images, and *as such*, an early
novel. This claim is based not only on the relationship to Proust's elaboration
of descriptive dystopia; it also has a more common historical framing. The
poem is an incipient novel to the extent that, negatively speaking, it is not a
play and, positively speaking, it generates narrative out of description. For
Shakespeare, who was so skilled at writing the kind of tragedy suitable for
mise en scène, avoided doing so in the case of Lucretia. This was not owing to
lack of material. His narrative poem of 1594 is at least the right length (1,855
verses), much longer than the play by the little-known baroque/classicist
French author Pierre de Ryer that was devoted to the subject some forty
years later, in 1638 (1,538 lines). Nor can it be because of lack of drama; his

poem uses as many characters as de Ryer's play, and its action is so condensed that in this respect it can almost be called classical. De Ryer's play goes to show that it is not impossible, or "indecent," to show suicide on stage. But—and this is relevant—representing rape is. Why, then, did Shakespeare turn the subject into a narrative when he normally wrote so many plays with so many murders and so few narratives? The speculative answer to this question further confirms the generative role description has played in the development of the novel as a "descriptologically" defined genre.

Is it through the question of visualizing or not visualizing catastrophe that tragedy is defined? I believe it is, but not in any direct way. Consider the rules of French classical tragedy and the idea that so much of Racine, tragedy's primary master, solved so many of its problems in such "baroque" ways—by deploying description. Obeying the rules by disobeying the genre that framed his work seemed a very clever way of enabling himself to do what, on all accounts, he could not. In accord with classical tradition, from antiquity onward the famous evocation in *Phèdre* of Hypolite's ghastly death is represented in a narrative rather than a dramatic mode. As a technical consequence of this decision, it is set in the past tense and offstage, so as to create enough aesthetic distance for it to be bearable. But it is common knowledge that, whereas the modality of its telling respects the rules, the representation itself, with its highly baroque imagery, labors to convey the extent of the horror. On the level of narrative representation, the "récit de Théramène," made famous by Leo Spitzer, links this classical drama to the baroque dramas discussed by Walter Benjamin to the extent that it raises the paradox of spectacle. Like these dramas, the narrative of catastrophe modifies the aesthetic, thus rupturing the totalizing harmony of classicism. The modality of representation involved in this process is, not coincidentally, visualization. But it is visualization of a narrative, not a dramatic, kind.[19]

On the one hand, the récit fragments classical harmony; on the other, that fragmentation reintegrates the visualization on which theatrical spectacle had cast a taboo. The double mission of the récit—to respect the modesty dictated by classical aesthetics and to bridge the gap between experience and witnessing that catastrophe itself necessitates—inevitably visualizes Hypolite's violent and horrible death. This is not just baroque exuberance—theater-over-life so to speak. For, it is in order to force the so-far indifferent womanizer Thésée, rival of his son, to *see, to bear witness to*, the consequence of his reversed Oedipal, murderous impulse, that the récit's spectacle, hence,

---

[19] These remarks are further developed in my article "Aestheticizing Catastrophe" (2005); Spitzer 1983; and Benjamin (1977).

its descriptive thrust, is necessary.[20] This is just one—rightly famous—instance of the internal conflict in Racine's aesthetic that led him to practice description in a way that exceeds the mode of classical drama and enters the domain that will come to generate the novel. But there are many more. Suicide is the prime example. The imperative of tightening the action into a single passion or obsession made it difficult to represent suicide on stage—not, of course, that it was impossible or offensive to *bienséance*, as De Ryer's rather successful *Lucrèce* demonstrates. But such a spectacle would inevitably arouse strong feelings and thus distract from the passions that *caused* the suicide. Thus, the importance of the emotional logic of causality overrules that of the *mise en scène* of catastrophe. And, in the case of Lucretia, that causality is located in description itself.

Ekphrasis: text "full of vivid description" (Wagner, 2). First occurring in Dionysius of Halicarnassus in the fifth century A.D., this term became limited to descriptions of works of art. In modern literary theory, it is used in this limited sense. But, as many have argued, this limitation points to a more general problem inherent in description as such: How to represent something that exists, or might exist, in an order different from that of the medium of representation?[21] Descriptions of visual artworks only sharpen that problem. But the de facto specialized use of this term is responsible for its being treated in conjunction with other terms that indicate phenomena displaying a "family resemblance" to this limited use.

Ekphrasis is a deployment of visibility within a linguistic discourse. The radical, ontological difference between visual and linguistic utterances is suspended in favor of an examination of the semiotic power of each and their relation to truthful representation. The age-old trust in the reliability of vision yields to the delicate balance of word and images in the production of *evidence*. The discursive genre of ekphrasis traditionally stands for this "intermedial" ambition, investing ekphrastic description with the mission to make present an object of visual art that does not even exist. This is only one way toward fictionalizing the desire to perfect epistemological grounding. A more general interpretation of the term implicates the act of showing, in the sense of showing *in detail*. The novelistic aftermath of the belief in the act of showing in detail is well known. And, without suggesting a continuity between Shakespeare and, say, Zola, I read, in this protonovel, a fictionalized

---

[20] In fact, this murderous rage is a *locus classicus* of the notion that the Oedipal complex is as much a problem of the father as it is of the son.

[21] Mitchell (1994, 157n19): "all ekphrasis is notional, and seeks to create a specific image that is to be found only in the text as its 'resident alien.'"

theorization of what makes description crucial to the fabrication of the novelistic world.

Description not only produces those exhilarating pieces (such as Flaubert's wedding cake) that suggest autonomy for description, albeit deceptively. It also inherently generates both the world in which events take place and subsequently the events themselves. On the basis of the descriptions examined so far, I would even venture to say that description is the novel's masterpiece. For, as a narrativity machine, description succeeds where narrative "proper" fails—because narrative is inadequate, inappropriate, or both. It succeeds in creating a world for the narrative—the events—and in questioning that world, simultaneously. It points epideictically to the elements it holds together, while at the same time demonstrating apodeictically how artificial that coherence is. Metadeictically, it argues for the need and dangers of such an internal coherence as cannot be contained. By failing to fix Robin, by shattering Albertine, and by murdering Lucrece, description, in the case of Zola's most beautiful character, kills not only the person but also the very beauty that sustains her existence. Writing—the novel—is unwriting; making is unmaking, says description, in the type of novel most famously built up by way of descriptions.

Nana (the Decomposition)

A thrill ran through the audience. Nana, who was very slightly clad, appeared in her semi-nudity with a calm audacity, confident in the all-powerfulness of her flesh. A slight gauze enveloped her; her round shoulders, her amazonian breasts, the rozy tips of which stood out straight and firm as lances, her broad hips swayed by the most voluptuous movements, in fact, her whole body could be divined, nay, seen, white as the foam, beneath the transparent covering. It was Venus rising from the waters, with no other veil than her locks. And when Nana raised her arms, the glare of the footlights displayed to every gaze the golden hairs of her arm-pits. (Zola, 26)

Nana was left alone, her face turned upwards in the candle-light. It was a charnel-house, a mass of humour and blood, a shovelful of putrid flesh, thrown there on a cushion. The pustules had invaded the entire face, one touching the other; and, faded, sunk in, and with the greyish aspect of mud, they already seemed like a mouldiness of the earth on that shapeless pulp, in which the features were no longer recognisable. One of the eyes, the left one . . . (Zola, 409)

I find it problematic to commit the act of collusion that completing this quotation would entail. For the description that in unison ends the novel, Nana's beauty, and her life is aggressively voyeuristic. Reading is affected by ethical judgment as is any other act. Dealing with description can thus be a matter of right or wrong. The text proposes, the reader disposes. Each has a job to do and a decision to make. In the case of *Nana*, for example, the two descriptions—of physical glory and of decomposition—propose their effects in different ways. The identification of the reader with the voyeuristic gaze that motivates the initial description of the main character—the first of many scattered throughout the novel—can be either endorsed or denied. Identification, it is useful to remember, may rhetorically be encouraged but it is not enforced. Moreover, the reader has a choice between reveling in the sexual arousal of the presumably male focalizer and rejoicing in the glory of the successful actress so skilled at making a living off her beauty.[22] Confronted with the choice, any choice, the reader is liberated from the confinement of the trappings realism entails and is instead asked to face what reading amounts to, and where that leaves the character. This is one thing descriptions can do. The closing description does not allow such freedom.

Voyeurism and description: do they hang together "naturally"? This question is raised by the combined descriptions of Zola's Nana; no answer is provided, but still, this is an issue no theory of description can ignore. The relation between the bringing into view and the obsessive myopism that the peephole or obscurity of the theater encourages, is so easily overtaken by erotic one-sidedness that pornography barely needs a story. There are, of course, various way to undermine this tendency, but only if it really is a tendency. Zola undermines it in the quoted description by foregrounding Nana's self-determination in her role as sex object, even though the life story does not sustain it. The fantastic provides additional ways of undermining it. From the mideighteenth century to the midnineteenth, roughly, the genre of the fantastic—the genre of the "catless grins"—in its most characteristic form, the life of detached body parts, puts these issues on the table without catering to the voyeuristic illusion. Instead, as Deborah Harter claims, "fantastic narrative brings to life the 'coming-into-view' as much as the view itself, resurrects the parts just as much as it resurrects the whole." She continues: "This literary form allows to remain unanchored those pieces that underlie every effort at totalization in narrative art. Its texts reveal the illusory wholeness of mimesis and its ironic dependence on a binding together

---

[22] The viewer is only presumably male; also among the spectators in the theater is the young woman Satin, Nana's future lover, who is equally fully described.

of shattered parts." (Harter, 15, 25). The double discourse of irony is eminently suited for this; and hence, also, for the novel.

It is, precisely, choice, the foregrounding of illusion itself, and fragmentation that are absent from the final description of Nana. Cruel and sadistic in its detailed (epideictic) representation of death in a woman who is still alive, it is more profoundly voyeuristic. In its position at the text's closure, it barely lends itself to nuanced and differentiated response. The description, informed by descriptive reveling, seems less designed to represent the agonizing woman than to represent her agony; less designed to represent Nana than to represent the vengeful hatred of the men who caused her horrendous death. And, whereas in the description of Nana's glorious entry on stage the theater is full of life-sustaining admirers, the final description pushes the devastation of its detailed object to utter isolation. The framing gaze moves away so that the reader alone remains, unable to offer comfort to the dying woman if he or she should wish to do so. Neither sustained by choice nor trapped in identification, the cathartic moment purges the reader of the fearful identification offered for contemplation, which would have been offered for contemplation if a diegetic focalizer had preceded his gaze. The dangerously contagious pus in Nana's boils that are taking over her entire face remains enclosed within her body.

Zola deploys the same strategy at the end of *Le ventre de Paris*. Here, the main character, male this time, is expelled from the community and from diegetic focalization simultaneously. But now, the reasons are political, not sexual. Clearly, description can be more than just an accompaniment to the closing scene or event; in these two cases, by withdrawing companionship it *constitutes* that ending. For a novelist who specialized in description, both practicing and preaching it, this rhetoric that conflates description and narration, has a programmatic thrust. It seems useful, therefore, to take a closer look at the kind of description found in the work of this utterly naturalistic and naturalizing novelist, to see what it was, precisely, against which Barnes and Proust militated, and for which Shakespeare offered a preposterous user's guide. Descriptive routine follows a fixed structure. If abstract, it seems innocent enough; if fleshed out, it tends to absorb a lot of narrative power.

Philippe Hamon, one of the most sophisticated theorists of description, also demonstrates, most persuasively, that a certain degree of structuralism is indispensable for adequate narrative analysis. Not coincidentally, Hamon is a Zola specialist. His view of description is contingent on a distinction between narration and description, and although he, more than anyone, is committed to validate the importance of descriptive discourse, that distinction remains in place too firmly for what I feel comfortable with at this point. It is my hope that, against the background of the later (and earlier) challenges to such a view, the categories and tools or grids offered there will be both more meaningful and more relative than they might otherwise appear to be.

At the end of his chapter on what he calls "a typology of description," Hamon spells out the factors that would sustain such a typology (1981, 174–75). These constitute the elements that can be found, hence analyzed to varying degrees, in the kind of classically realist descriptions that are so overwhelmingly "natural" yet deeply contradictory. Hamon's concept of description elaborates the Russellian one. The mode in which the predicates are attributed to the subject or theme is determined by a narrative regime of readability. The relation between the series of descriptive elements and this regime or *motivation* can vary—from diegetic focalizer to anonymous external focalizer (*not* to be considered zero-focalization in my view). For Hamon, descriptions vary formally according to the kind of relations that exist between the elements of the object mentioned and the predicates attributed to those elements. Such series, in turn, can be connected to each other in different ways.[23]

In the examples from *Nana*, these formal possibilities are in place. Both descriptions are readerly; they contribute to the naturalizing representation of the novelistic world. And, in this world, kindly remember, objects (Hamon's *themes*) are not simply represented as they purportedly *are*, as a supplement and clarification of what they *do*. Nor are all elements presented equally. In the early description of Zola's famous *courtisane*, men, rarely objects of description, are sitting before a spectacle that is therefore presented to the reader. In other words, the primary sense perception involved is the visual one, erotically colored. In the final description, the object has the same identity or *rigid designation* (the proper name "Nana"), but lacks any feature in common with the earlier object. And, as if to drive the point home through the form of narrative that feeds so parasitically on description as to be virtually nonexistent without it, the descriptive types, or modes, differ profoundly.

The first description is *motivated*, clearly, by means of diegetical focalization. Not only is the description focalized by the spectators, but, as if anticipating Barnes's and Proust's questioning of the frame as natural, the

---

[23] A propos of a discussion with Gérard Genette, I have argued against the epistemological leap involved in narratological typology (1991). Hamon looks especially to texts of readability, according to Barthes's conception of readerliness versus writerliness. Lodge (1977) offers a rhetorical typology that can usefully be integrated with Hamon's. In *Narratology*, I have attempted a synthesis of both (1997a, 36–43).

entire setting also enhances the theatricality, right up to the final spotlights that make the body hairs visible. This emphasis on setting constitutes the permeable boundary between the diegetic world in which this event supposedly happens, and the extradiegetic world within which the reader *makes* the spectacle. Under the realistic regime, diegetic motivation *naturalizes* description. Hence, the theatricality, here, is paradoxical, potentially ironic in that it foregrounds artificiality. The parallel series—from the compared object, Nana and her hair, to a comparant from the pictorial tradition, Venus and the waves—contributes to the production of enthusiasm in viewers and character alike. But this enthusiasm is emphatically constructed within the diegetic world as well as *qua* construction. The motivating frame, in other words, is not designed to fool anyone.

The vision itself is equally artificial. It is represented in its effect, and although this effect follows the appearance, its specification—the collective thrill of the personified theater—precedes the description of the appearance that caused it. Similarly, the character is not presented in a homogenous series constituting the nomenclature. She is qualified first—naked, self-confident, bold—then detailed, from top to bottom: shoulders, breasts, hips, thighs. Each element of this catalog of body parts is either further specified—after the breasts, the nipples—or qualified in some way. The breasts are amazon-like, the nipples rigid, predicates that are then metaphorically elaborated on as if in celebration, to enhance the collective euphoria: rigid like lances, rolling hips. The structure of the description is, in other words, neither logically nor rhetorically systematic. It appears, as a *mise en scène* of a mode of reading—of seeing "before the mind's eye"— particularly apt for anticipating the role of spectacle in the *fabula* about to unfold. Description, it appears here, is going to dominate the events.

"Nana restait seule": the closing description is the systematic opposite. First and most important, as mentioned above, it is not motivated by diegetic focalization. On the contrary, the withdrawal of the focalizing agent is the narrative-descriptive enactment of abandonment: descriptive more than narrative, since the verb's tense, the durative imperfect, insists that the description is definitive and thus, that this is the final image. Yet, strangely, the flame of the candle that makes the character visible accompanies the first descriptive mention of the theme. This would appear to be an unnecessary detail. If there is no witness, there is no spectacle. Yet the flame casts a particular—and particularly spooky—light on the object of description. The contrast with the floodlights, the oblique nature of the light, the relative obscurity of the room—all contribute to alert the reader to the kind of contrastive description that overrides the narration.

Instead of the reversed relationship between cause and effect, we are left with cause only. The spectacle is dystopic, to say the least, and the cause of that effect is posited first. There is nothing human in the description of the face, no enhancing comparisons and metaphors here. It is even hard to tell whether the elements of the nomenclature are metaphorical or not. The words "un tas d'humeur et de sang, une pelletée de chair corrompue" are not details but superposed descriptions of the same non-face of the "face en l'air." With the "shovel of corrupted flesh," the description anticipates the death to come, and the participle "jetée là" further thickens both the rejection and the anticipated funeral. The strange contradiction between the stated absence of a diegetic focalizer and the invitation to enter the room handed by the detail of the candlelight is here given as evidence that extradiegetic motivation is also a form of focalization. The verb form is passive; the corrupted flesh has been tossed by no one in particular, yet the action of tossing is mentioned.

There is no festive theatricality here, no foregrounding of artifice. Instead, the detail mentioned—the *pustules*, the festering sores—is, again, subject to superposed qualifications, this time more clearly metaphorical ones that undermine its stability. The sores are represented in the way that they expand beyond individual visibility. This is an image of anti-detailing: the small sores expand to become one. Again, with the word *déjà*, the funeral beyond death and beyond the novel's ending is announced. Thus the description merges yet another boundary, the one between text and after-text. From here on, the monstrosity of the sight is overtly hateful. The face has lost all of its coherence. To dust thou shalt return. Punishment, for the sins of the men, is visited on the woman. There can be no zero focalization.

The setting of the two descriptions is also opposed. From the upright body with its upright nipples, detailed from top to bottom, standing on a stage, hence, in public, we have moved to the deathbed attended by no one. In much narrative literature, characters are set in places. In medieval novels, the relationships between character and setting are fixed topoi in which particular events can take place. Descriptions of the latter precede descriptions of the former. In upbeat stories, the places are filled with euphoric beauty, to fill the characters with the enthusiasm that sets their adventures in motion. Then, narrative recuperates description. But it cannot forget its starting point. The description, explicit or not, elaborated or not, establishes the world within which the events unfold. "At nine o'clock, the theater of the Variétés was still empty," begins *Nana*. Time and place are marked. The spectacle can begin. No moment is mentioned at the end; only still description remains.

The closing description of Zola's *Nana* demonstrates that place and character are interdependent, inseparable. This is, ultimately, the meaning of the candle. Firmly entrenched within the world of the *fabula*, the reader, the only remaining witness after the cowardly withdrawal of the diegetic focalizers, can *see* the shadows on the walls of the sickroom that the wavering flame turns into a *locus horridus*. This is no gothic castle; there is no sound of rattling chains. But, reminiscent of the gothic yet distinct from it, the character herself has dissolved into horror. Thus the description that stages the withdrawal of the focalizer affirms the impossibility of zero-focalization. Where descriptions appear orphaned of diegetic focalization, it is best to look more keenly for traces of the repressed focalizer. In *Nana*, this trace is the horror of the sight itself; its motivation, the misogyny that permeates the novel.[24]

Emma (the End)

> . . . as she sewed she pricked her fingers, which she then put to her mouth to suck them. Charles was surprised by the whiteness of her nails. They were shiny, delicate at the tips, more polished than Dieppe ivories, and almond-shaped. Yet her hand was not beautiful, perhaps not white enough, and a little hard at the knuckles; besides, it was too long, with no soft inflections in the outlines. Her real beauty was in her eyes. Although brown, they seemed black because of the lashes, and her look came at you frankly, with a candid boldness.
>
> The bandaging over, the doctor was invited . . . (Flaubert, 28–29)

One remembers the scene where Emma and her would-be lover Rodolphe are sitting on a balcony to watch the annual parade-cum-agricultural fair, *les commices agricoles*. The moment is well chosen so that Rodolphe can initiate his Don Juan wiles to interrupt Emma's straight way of life, for heterogeneity reigns. While his lover's platitude-ridden discourse runs through the noisy and smelly air, other voices praise a maid for lifelong servitude rewarded by a paltry medal, cows suitable to be slaughtered, and the weather. Moreover, the totally incongruous combination of discourses imitates and parodies that of Zola's *Ventre de Paris*, where cheeses are cataloged as the voices of the market cry out in all directions. Romantic discourse, Flaubert's prime target, is properly framed—by vulgarity, hypocrisy, and banality.

---

[24] And, even more so, its reception. The fact that Nana is involved in a lesbian relationship is, unfortunately, not indifferent to some readers' responses. See my comments on this (1996, ch. 6).

On a more modest scale is the description in which Emma, still Mlle. Rouault, and watched by the mesmerized country doctor Charles, is literally detailed and judged. The heterogeneity, here, is double: narrative and description mingle and motivate each other, and the charmed lover's focalization is undercut by the ruthless "objectivity" of the faceless focalizer. Charles's surprise is an event; the whiteness of the nails is a state. White offset against red blood; the black hair that completes the portrait of Snow White that inserts the perversion of fairy tales, is understood by implication. Emma's sucking her finger and later inserting her tongue into the small glass to finish the last drop of *liqueur* point to the extent of Charles's erotic fantasy. Brilliant, cut in almond shape, ivory: we see idealization a mile away. But whose focalization is put forward in the "however" of "sa main, pourtant, n'était pas belle"? Are we supposed to think that this man, in love and endowed with mediocre intelligence and little subtlety, is detailing and weighing what is and is not pretty about Emma? But then, in retrospect, would he be sophisticated enough to characterize the kind of ivory of the metaphoric network put in place around the nail? Suddenly, it all falls apart. Not only is Emma epideictically detailed to death by incoherence; so is the discourse that describes her.

Whoever says heterogeneity thinks of Bakhtin. Indeed, the scene of the *commices agricoles* is a perfect emblem of this philosopher's view of language use in general and of novelistic discourse in particular. For Bakhtin, the point is that the novel mixes discourses originating from all social strata. For Flaubert, once discourses show their messiness, there is no stopping the heterogeneity machine, against which characters do not stand a chance. Emma can only die in the end, and even then there is the blind beggar's song that destroys the moment of sublime suffering. For the present inquiry into description in the novel, it matters that this heterogeneity comprises both history—in the always present parody that de-naturalizes the *fabula*—and discursive modes. Description is not only a narrative motor, as in Zola; it is also a narrativity machine run wild. Only narrative motivation can offer a semblance of containment, and it does so through the deployment of a multilayered form of deixis.

Look again at this relatively simple quotation. Charles "fut surpris," hence, the poor man is bound hand-and-foot to the spectacle that follows even if he cannot control it. The primary framing suggests, at first sight, that the narrative embeds the description: Charles watches, Emma sucks, the description of her nails follows. The detail of the nail asks for the larger detail of the hand, presented in the generic singular that frame-freezes it. But once both Charles and the external "focalizee," the seeing reader, have been sucked into the *fabula* by way of this stitching-together of the two discourses, the mastermind of the perverse negativity—*pourtant*—shows his hand and points out that the spectacle is staged for the deception of the male victim of fate. It is not pale enough; but by what standard? Too dry, too large. The devastating judgment "sans molles inflection de lignes sur les contours" braids into the lover's gaze a discourse from beauty parlors, variety shows, and ladies' magazines, against which Emma's mediocrity is offset. But once this devastation is achieved, we are confused yet again when the idealization reclaims the power to look. The beauty she did have—the description contradicts the critique—was in the eyes. There is no comfort even in heterogeneity.

The enumeration of elements to form, shape, and contrive a whole object, shipwrecks halfway and leaves the object in pieces. Instead of *its* wholeness, we have the fragile totality of Charles's paltry infatuation and a novelistic situation no more whole than poor Emma's body. Instead of the mechanism through which anchoring is possible so that the object described "exists" within the narrative world and the description is a recapitulation or a reformulation of an element assumed to have prior existence, we have elements tied to other elements "existing" on different ontological levels. Flaubert's postmodernism *avant-la-lettre* will inspire Proust's.

Through the triple contributions of aspectualization, modalization, and subjectivization, three levels of binding description and narrative make the former fundamentally deictic: even if we weep for Emma when she completes her gradual self-destruction, we are left with no figure except the one whose universe fails to sustain her. What we end up with, in Marc-Elie Blanchard's view, is a mixture of style, world/self, and desire. Deixis versus reference: the fragment on Emma's hands displays, like a user's guide, the functions of description in relation to the act of *reading the novel*. It is no coincidence, then, that the master novelist is also a master ironist. Flaubert offers irony as a semantic theory of the novel.[25] As a result, that emblem of readability that description appears to be solicits a decoding of hidden meaning, but it also leads to an awareness of an inability to read. One of description's functions in reading as a cultural activity is temporalization. Deceleration, but not stopping, makes acceleration possible. Without description there is no narrative, and, more important, no way to read narrative.

We can now contemplate what a "descriptology" for a history of the novel might comprise. Intuitively, the critics of description have known it all along:

---

[25] Blanchard uses this phrase (1980, 104–5).

description is dangerous and must therefore be fought against. Like education for slaves, it opens doors that no violence, no rules, can ever close again. Descriptions are endless, and they betoken the endlessness of the novel. The compulsion to naturalize descriptions through framing is symptomatic of descriptive fear. Descriptions must be contained because they are, by definition, boundless. The metadeictic function flaunts this paradox self-critically. Nor can the object be pinned down, as I have argued through Proust's elusive object of obsession. This apo-deictic aporia made the need to bind clearer at the same time that the impossibility to do so became obvious.

Description has always been a problem because its anarchy seemed violent. Ekphrasis, as constative killing through epi-deictic detailing, emblematizes the force of descriptive discourse. Epideixis works when the object is detailed. But that murderous decomposition also affects the novel itself *qua* discourse. For the novel falls apart into descriptive detail. This raises the question of mastery over time (slave narrative) as the paradigmatic stake of the novel. All five strands of my quest end in the same predicament: the impossibility to delimit that is inherent in the impossibility to disentangle. By binding, description unbinds. Look again at *Madame Bovary*.

Significantly and, in view of *Nana*'s disturbing end, unsettlingly, Emma's death is not the end of the novel. Both beginning and end are emphatically outside the frame of diegesis. The beginning, which still contains the trace of the narrator—the unforgettable description-narration duet of "nous étions à l'étude quand le proviseur entra"—precedes the novel, while the end, extending beyond itself, lies beyond the end. This is true for both the *fabula* and the discourse, which includes all manner of discourses within its voracious genre. It is within this tension between a text with a beginning and an end, aesthetically correct according to Aristotle, and an unlimited texture, whose deictic tightness obeys no laws of nature or reality, that the nature of the novel lies.

For a historical deployment of such an overly bold generalization, the analysis of description proposed by structuralist theory can be usefully reframed and recuperated. Recall David Lodge's historicizing typology based on the different deployments of tropes (1977). His analysis is limited to rhetorical figures, but it can be extended to the forms of deixis-run-wild that we have observed in Flaubert's piece. For these tropes stand as synecdoches for the heterogeneity of worlds, a heterogeneity that expands as each era denaturalizes what its predecessors have painstakingly bound together. A descriptological history of the novel thus becomes a history of binding. Description binds elements and aspects otherwise disconnected, whatever their ontological status. What needs binding, what appears disconnected, depends on the relation between the novel and the world (of the readership).

This turns description into a form of world-making that is distinct in yet another sense from the illusory sense of mimetic representation. There is nothing realistic about that. On the contrary: fiction makes worlds, hence, undoes (the self-evidence of) that form of world-making we think we know.

References

Adam, Jean-Michel. 1993. *La description*. Paris: Presses Universitaires de France.

Alphen, Ernst van. 1989. "The Heterotopian Space of the Discussions on Postmodernism." *Poetics Today* 10 (4): 819–38.

Bakhtin, Mikhail. 1968. *Rabelais and His World*. Trans. H. Iswolsky. Cambridge, Mass.: MIT Press.

———. 1970. *La poétique de Dostoievski*. Trans. Isabelle Kolitcheff, introduction by Julia Kristeva. Paris: Editions du Seuil.

———. 1981. *The Dialogic Imagination*. Ed. Michael Holquist, trans. Caryl Emerson and Michael Holquist. Austin: University of Texas Press.

Bal, Mieke. 1991. *On Story-Telling: Essays in Narratology*. Ed. David Jobling. Sonoma, Calif.: Polebridge Press.

———. 1996. *Double Exposures: The Subject of Cultural Analysis*. New York: Routledge.

———. 1997a. *Narratology: Introduction to the Theory of Narrative*. 2nd rev. ed. Toronto: University of Toronto Press.

———. 1997b. *The Mottled Screen: Reading Proust Visually*. Trans. Anna-Louise Milne. Stanford, Calif.: Stanford University Press.

———. 1999. *Quoting Caravaggio: Contemporary Art, Preposterous History*. Chicago: University of Chicago Press.

———. 2005. "Aestheticizing Catastrophe." In *Reading Charlotte Salomon*, ed. Monica Bohm-Duchen and Michael Steinberg, Ithaca, N.Y.: Cornell University Press.

Banfield, Ann. 2000. *The Phantom Table: Woolf, Fry, Russell and the Epistemology of Modernism*. Cambridge: Cambridge University Press.

Barnes, Djuna. 1936. *Nightwood*. With an introduction by T. S. Eliot. London: Faber and Faber.

Barthes, Roland. 1976. *S/Z*. Trans. Richard Miller. New York: Hill and Wang.

Bartsch, Shadi. 1989. *Decoding the Ancient Novel: The Reader and the Role of Description in Heliodorus and Achilles Tatius*. Princeton, N.J.: Princeton University Press.

Benjamin, Walter. 1977. *The Origin of German Drama*. Trans. John Osborne. London: New Left Books.

Blanchard, Marc Elie. 1980. *Description: Sign, Self, Desire: Critical Theory in the Wake of Semiotics*. The Hague: Mouton.

Brooks, Peter. 1984. *Reading for the Plot: Design and Intention in Narrative*. New York: Alfred A. Knopf.

Caserio, Robert. 1999. *The Novel in England 1900–1950: History and Theory*. New York: Twayne.

Derrida, Jacques. 1967. *De la grammatologie*. Paris: Editions de Minuit. (English: *Of Grammatology*. Trans. and with an introduction by Gayatri Chakravorty Spivak. Baltimore: Johns Hopkins University Press, 1976.)

Flaubert, Gustave. 1938 (1856). *Madame Bovary*. Trans. Eleanor Marx Aveling. Zurich: Limited Editions Club.

Forster, E. M. 1927. *Aspects of the Novel*. London: Edward Arnold.

Genette, Gérard. 1969. "Frontières du récit." In *Figures II*, 49–70. Paris: Editions du Seuil.

———. 1972. "Métonymie chez Proust." In *Figures III*, 41–66. Paris: Editions du Seuil. (Published in English as *Figures*. 3 vols. Trans. Alan Sheridan. New York: Columbia University Press, 1982.)

———. 1980. *Narrative Discourse: An Essay in Method*. Trans. Jane E. Lewin. Ithaca, N.Y.: Cornell University Press.

———. 1983. *Nouveau discours du récit*. Paris: Editions du Seuil.

Hamilton, Kristie. 1998. *America's Sketchbook: The Cultural Life of a Nineteenth-Century Literary Genre*. Athens: Ohio University Press.

Hamon, Philippe. 1981. *Introduction à l'analyse du descriptif*. Paris: Hachette.

———. 1991. *La description littéraire: Anthologie de textes théoriques et critiques*. Paris: Macula.

Harter, Deborah. 1996. *Bodies in Pieces: Fantastic Narrative and the Poetics of the Fragment*. Stanford, Calif.: Stanford University Press.

Lodge, David. 1977. "Types of Description." In *The Modes of Modern Writing*, 93–103. London: Edward Arnold.

Man, Paul de. 1979. "Semiology and Reading (Proust)." In *Allegories of Reading: Figural Language in Rousseau, Nietzsche, Rilke, and Proust*, 57–78. New Haven, Conn.: Yale University Press.

McHale, Brian. 1987. *Postmodernist Fiction*. London: Methuen.

Meltzer, Françoise. 1987. *Salome and the Dance of Writing*. Chicago: University of Chicago Press.

Meyer, M., and A. Lempereur, eds. 1990. *Figures et conflits rhétoriques*. Brussels: Editions de l'Université de Bruxelles.

Miller, J. Hillis. 1995. "Narrative." In *Critical Terms for Literary Study*, ed. Frank Lettrichia and Thomas McLaughlin, 66–79. Chicago: University of Chicago Press.

Mitchell, W.J.T. 1985. *Iconology: Image, Text, Ideology*. Chicago: University of Chicago Press.

———. 1994. *Picture Theory*. Chicago: University of Chicago Press.

Peirce, Charles Sanders. 1984. "Logic as Semiotic: The Theory of Signs." In *Semiotics: An Introductory Anthology*, ed. Robert E. Innis, 4–23. Bloomington: Indiana University Press.

Proust, Marcel. 1987–89. *A la recherche du temps perdu*. 4 vols. Ed. Jean-Yves Tadié. Paris: Gallimard, Bibliothèque de la Pléiade. Trans. C. K. Scott-Moncrieff and Terence Kilmartin as *Remembrance of Things Past*. 3 vols. London: Penguin Books, 1981.

Racine, Jean. 2002 (1677). *Phèdre*. Paris: Hatier.

Rimmon-Kenan, Shlomith. 1983. *Narrative Fiction: Contemporary Poetics*. London: Methuen.

Shakespeare, William. 1912 (1598). *The Rape of Lucrece*. Ed. Charlotte Porter. New York: Thomas Y. Cromwell.

Spitzer, Leo. 1983. *Essays on Seventeenth-Century French Literature*. Trans. and ed. David Bellos. Cambridge: Cambridge University Press.

Wagner, Peter, ed. 1996. *Icons—Texts—Iconotexts: Essays on Ekphrasis and Intermediality*. Berlin: Walter de Gruyter.

White, Hayden. 1999. "Narrative, Description, and Tropology in Proust." In *Figural Realism: Studies in the Mimesis Effect*, 126–46. Baltimore: Johns Hopkins University Press.

Zola, Emile. 1948 (1880). *Nana*. Trans. F. J. Vizetelly. New York: Limited Editions Club.

HANS ULRICH GUMBRECHT

The Roads of the Novel

One of the more canonical definitions of the novel compares the genre to a mirror that is moving along a road. It comes in the nineteenth chapter of the second book of Stendhal's *Le rouge et le noir* where the narrator, using a device that was still quite conventional around 1830, tries to draw attention to his characters by asking himself whether he should apologize for what the reader might find unpleasant or even scandalous in their description. This is the narrator's answer to his own question:

> Eh, monsieur, un roman est un miroir que se promène sur une grande route. Tantôt il reflète à vos yeux l'azur des cieux, tantôt la fange des bourbiers de la route. Et l'homme qui porte le miroir dans sa hotte sera par vous accusé d'être immoral! Son miroir montre la fange, et vous accusez le miroir! Accusez bien plutôt le grand chemin où est le bourbier, et plus encore l'inspecteur des routes qui laisse l'eau croupir et le bourbier se former.[1]

There are two aspects that make Stendhal's comparison plausible, independently of the larger rhetorical strategy that he is pursuing here. In the first place and quite obviously, the movement and the experience of somebody who walks along a road is similar to the founding structure of any narrative—which is the structure of lived experience.[2] The phenomenological tradition defines "lived experience" ("*Erlebnis*") as the sequence of those changing sensual perceptions on which our consciousness focuses during any given stretch of time, and it distinguishes "lived experience" from "experience" ("*Erfahrung*"), that is, from lived experience that has been transformed into elements of knowledge by acts of interpretation, synthesis, and structuring. That lived experience, different from experience, always has the form of a sequence, which is the reason for our belief that the world is temporal, follows necessarily from the temporal structure of human consciousness. Narratives typically produce the impression that their contents correspond to

---

This essay is dedicated to the memory of Undine Gruenter, *romancière*, and to Karl Heinz Bohrer.
[1] Stendhal, *Le rouge et le noir: Chronique du XIX siècle*, ed. Henri Martineau (Paris, 1960), 337.
[2] See my essay, "The Role of Narrative in Narrative Genres," in *Making Sense in Life and Literature* (Minneapolis, 1992), 41–53.

the flows of unstructured, lived experience, whereas descriptions—despite the linearity of the text as medium—evoke objects in a form that corresponds to the well-circumscribed elements of experience. This is the basis for the double association between the temporality of our consciousness and the world as we live it, and between the world as we live it and the spatial form of the road.

In the second place, that mirror which, in Stendhal's comparison, is attached to the body of a person walking along the road, also refers to the expectation that the novel will present, as what should appear as a random sequence, events and things that make up everyday reality, without too much of an attempt at literary stylization, embellishment, or interpretation. The apparent randomness in the sequence of its things and events is meant to be similar to the unpredictability of the encounters and observations that one makes along a road. Stendhal even goes so far to insinuate that, with the reflections in the mirror depending on what the road has to offer, the contents and effects of the novel escape the author's control and responsibility. And the history of the novel indeed gives us the impression that, over the centuries of its existence, the genre has not observed any consistent restraints in its contents.

But would it not be equally plausible to say that the novel resembles a street, or a path, or a way? It is true that the standard dictionaries of the English language indicate that the denotations and even the connotations of these words largely overlap with *road*. And yet *way* and *path* seem to emphasize, more than *road*, that they will lead to a goal or to any other kind of a predefined and therefore meaningful endpoint—which would suggest a teleological directedness that the genre of the novel does not imply. In comparison to *street*, which we tend to connect with the protectedness of a space within a town or a village, *road* brings out more clearly the always surprising and sometimes even dangerous character in the encounters and observations that can happen to a traveler. With all of its aspects seen together, Stendhal's complex metaphor points to a concept of the novel that is broad enough to be applied in a metahistorical (and if it were necessary for our purposes, also in a transcultural) fashion. Our search for roads in the novel, then, will not be limited to the centuries of the recent past, since early European modernity, as is, for example, the debate about the "rise of the novel." On the other hand, an interest in the roads of the novel obliges us to pay specific attention to the moments of surprise and eventfulness in its narratives. We think of the novel as a genre that, typically, directs the readers' curiosity to the unknown endpoint of a story—and not just to the ways through which a more or less predictable endpoint will be reached.[3] This emphasis often seems to go along with that strong impression of immediacy I mentioned before, meaning that the novel pretends to confront us with unaltered lived experience.

My choice of Stendhal's famous description of the genre as a starting point will then have far-reaching consequences for the limits and the premises under which we will discuss the roads of the novel. As it will be important to have these consequences in mind, I shall present them in a numbered sequence. First, as we have associated the concept of the road with the basic temporal structure of the novel (that is, the structure that underlies its varying narrative surface forms), the road can well play an important role in any individual novel without being explicitly thematized. This probably is the most surprising and the most interesting result of my search for the roads of the novel: that many of those novels whose plots unfold along a road—as, to for example, Cervantes' *Don Quijote*—hardly ever focus on the road itself as a topic. If this observation may be surprising because we seem to "remember" that we have "seen" all those roads, it only proves that our imagination is readily able to fill such textual voids (and that we can thus "see" roads for which we find no words in the texts).[4]

Second, even those nonthematized roads, in an almost paradoxical way, show us a broad variety of different structures. For although the reader will often not find any descriptions of the roads in play, her imagination about the roads will be inspired and directed by the patterns and principles in which the different events occurring along the road are connected. In this sense, an implicit road, for example, whose events and stations develop the narrative curve of a progression, will "look" different from a road "on" which anything can occur at any given moment. This notwithstanding, any implicit road will constantly produce encounters and events (or at least the expectations thereof).

Third, I have gained the impression that there is only one limited segment in the history of the Western novel during which the roads along which the protagonists move became more frequently and also more extensively

---

[3] See Clemens Lugowski, *Die Form der Individualität im Roman* (Frankfurt on Main, 1976), 40–42. According to Lugowski, the novel typically directs its readers' curiosity to the question of whether something will happen at all ("*Ob überhaupt Spannung*") and not only to the question how it will happen ("*Wie-Spannung*").

[4] This observation of course follows Wolfgang Iser's long canonical theorem about voids ("*Leerstellen*") in literary texts activating the readers' imagination. See, above all, *Der Akt des Lesens* (Munich, 1976), 301–15.

thematic. This segment spans just a few decades during the middle of the nineteenth century—after which time the topic of the road begins to recede again. We will have to ask which intrinsic and extrinsic conditions from the history of the novel can explain that interval.

Fourth, in general, we can regard both the different implicit structures of the roads in the novel as well as the different degrees of their explicit thematization to be indicative of different layers in the history of the social knowledge and of the *mentalités* that surround and accompany the history of the genre. In this sense it will be our central premise and our guiding hypothesis that the roads of the novel can help us understand how different cultures and different historical periods conceived in different ways of man's relation to space and time, and of the range and the limits of human agency within larger religious, cosmological, philosophical, and even scientific worldviews.

Overture: Roads of Crisis

Our historical narrative will begin with two famous literary roads from texts that, at least from a strictly formal point of view, do not belong to the history of the novel. These are the road between Thebes and Corinth, in Sophocles' tragedy *Oedipus Rex*, where Oedipus slays his father Laius; and to the road between Jerusalem and Damascus where the Acts of the Apostles stage the conversion of Saul, the Jewish persecutor of Christians, into Paul, the Apostle. In Sophocles' tragedy, the chorus and several protagonists repeatedly and quite insistently evoke the place of the crime as a crossroad:

Oedipus
> Where is this place, Jocasta
where was he murdered?
Jocasta
> Phocis is the country
And the road splits there, one of two roads from Delphi,
Another comes from Daulia.[5]

Trying to escape the oracle that has announced Oedipus will kill his father and sleep with his mother, he has left Corinth, which he believes to be the town of his parents, while Laius, the king of Thebes and his true father, is on

---

[5] *Oedipus Rex*, vv. 733–36, quoted from the English translation by David Grene, *Sophocles I*, 2nd ed. (Chicago, 1991), 42.

his way to the Delphic oracle. In the most extensive among several descriptions of their fatal encounter, Sophocles' tragedy gives us an impression of the fear and the intense psychic tension that the appearance of a stranger on the road must have produced in archaic societies. Speaking to Jocasta, his wife and mother, Oedipus remembers:

> And as I journeyed I came to the place
> Where, as you say, this king met with his death.
> Jocasta, I will tell you the whole truth.
> When I was near the branching of the crossroads,
> Going on foot, I was encountered by
> a herald and a carriage with a man in it,
> just as you tell me. He that led the way
> and the old man himself wanted to thrust me
> out of the road by force. I became angry
> and struck the coachman who was pushing me.
> When the old man saw this he watched his moment,
> And as I passed he struck me from his carriage,
> Full on the head with his two pointed goad.
> But he was paid in full and presently
> my stick had struck him backwards from the car
> and he rolled out of it. And then I killed them all. (vv. 800–813)

It is telling that Laius's family and his subjects at Thebes are under the impression that "highway robbers" (v. 842) have killed their king—for in the unprotected open space of the road each person was a potential threat, a potential robber or even murderer for those who met him.

But how can we explain that Oedipus's fate was fulfilled not just on the road but at the marked place of a crossroad? Classical scholarship does not seem to provide a standard answer to this question.[6] Of course crossroads can stand for the complexity of a decision with which a protagonist is confronted; of course they are the accumulated risk of two potential trajectories coming together, with a momentary narrowing of the total space available, rather than with an opening of it.[7] More important must have been the religious understanding of crossroads as places where humans owed the chtonic

---

[6] I thank my friend Andrea Nightingale for an enlightening conversation, over dinner, about the road between Corinth and Thebes.

[7] See, for the symbolic value of the crossroad in medieval literature, Wolfgang Harms, *Homo viator in bivio: Studien zur Bildlichkeit des Wegs* (Munich, 1970).

deities a sacrifice, that is, a sacrifice to Hecate, Persephone, and the Furies. There is at least one passage in the tragedy that seems to imply an awareness, on Oedipus's side, of the possibility to interpret his crime in the sense of such a religious overdetermination of space:

> Crossroads
> and hidden glade, oak and the narrow way
> at the crossroads, that you drank my father's blood
> offered you by my hands, do you remember
> still what I did as you looked on, and what
> I did when I came here? (vv. 1,398–1,402)

The motif of the crossroad in Sophocles' text and the episode of Saul's conversion in the Acts of the Apostles do not only share the status of being the connection between a dramatic turning event in the protagonist's life and the open space on a road between two cities. In addition, both texts associate this dramatic event with blindness. Oedipus blinds himself once the truth about his encounter on the road from Corinth to Thebes has become apparent and inevitable, whereas Saul is temporarily stricken with blindness after Jesus appears to him, as blazing light, on the road between Jerusalem and Damascus:[8]

> Now as he was going along and approaching Damascus, suddenly a light from heaven flashed around him. He fell to the ground and heard a voice saying to him, "Saul, Saul, why do you persecute me?" He asked, "Who are you, Lord?" The reply came, "I am Jesus, whom you are persecuting. But get up and enter the city, and you will be told what you are to do." The men who were traveling with him stood speechless because they had heard the voice but saw no one. Saul got up from the ground, and though his eyes were open, he could see nothing; so they led him by the hand and brought him into Damascus. For three days he was without sight, and neither ate nor drank.[9]

It is obvious what Oedipus's blindness and the blindness of Saul symbolize in these texts. The fate that they encounter on the road, under different circumstances and with very different consequences, is too large and too

---

[8] Acts 9.1ff. The passage about his conversion on the road refers to the Apostle exclusively as "Saulus." From 13.9 onward he becomes Paulus (probably because of the transition to a different fragment in the textual tradition).

[9] I am quoting from *The New Oxford Annotated Bible*, college ed. (Oxford, 1991), 173.

powerful for their immediate understanding—and there is not even a thought about changing it through human action. Human existence, in the ancient world, appeared to be as incapable of protecting itself against fate as a traveler was unable to absolutely protect his life in the open space of the roads. So current must this association between fate and the openness of the road have been in the times of Sophocles—and still in the times of the Apostles—that, rather than being talked about as landscape, the literary roads brought forth and indeed *were* this fate. They were roads of crisis and of catastrophe in the etymological sense. For they "turned around" lives—"undoing" and overwhelming all their previous stages.

Roads of Meaning

There is a quite plausible scholarly tradition that places the beginning of the history of the novel in the twelfth century, in the form of the medieval romance, as it has become related to the name of Chrétien de Troyes. Whoever follows this tradition makes the history of the novel, implicitly and quite literally, begin "on the road." As the recurrent central role in all of Chrétien's text, the courtly knight is under the obligation to seek adventures ("to seek," "to postulate" is the meaning of the word *queste*, an alternative name for the genre of the romance), and his "adventures" are nothing but the dangerous encounters constantly produced and provided by premodern roads—under the premise that, rather than trying to avoid their challenges, the heroes of the romance need and desire them. While the roads of medieval romance never turn into landscape, they awaken, from the first episodes onward, an active curiosity in the reader/listener about their possible end and about whether and how the knights will reach such an endpoint. Furthermore, in contrast to the travelers on the literary roads of antiquity, the protagonists of the romance do what they can to make their adventures become more dangerous and thus more rewarding. Erec, the young hero in what probably was Chrétien's earliest romance, does not only use the first opportunity that the roads offer to him—the insult by an unknown knight and of the dwarf who accompanies him—to set out for the adventures that will in the end give him status at the court of King Arthur. He also very harshly prohibits his wife Enide (who becomes his traveling companion at a later stage of the narrative) to ever warn him against dangers that she may have identified before him:

Departi sont a quelque poinne.
Erec s'en va, sa feme en moinne,

Ne set quel part, en aventiure.
"Alez, fait il, grant aleure,
Et gardez ne soiez tant ose,
Se voz veez aucune chose,
Que vos me diez ce ne qoi.
Gardez ne parlez ja a moi,
Se je ne vos aresne avant."[10]

It is as if Erec, the adventurous knight, wanted to impose the handicap of a deliberate deafness and blindness on himself just to make his life more difficult—whereas Saul, on the road from Jerusalem to Damascus, would certainly have preferred not to be stricken by blindness, as Oedipus would have wished to recognize his father at the crossroad between Corinth and Thebes. But while, by taking additional difficulties upon their shoulders (the motif will reach grotesque extremes by the fourteenth century), the adventurous knights of the romance intensify their merit and the admiration of their readers, the structure in which the texts present these adventures is not as random as it may appear at first glance. When subjected to a structural analysis,[11] the roads of the romance reveal a complex network charged with meaning, a network whose basic features are recurrent in most, if not in all of Chrétien's texts. The central protagonists (Erec, Yvain, Lancelot) set out twice from King Arthur's court to seek adventures, and they return twice. Only at the end of the second cycle of adventures, however, will they have proven what was not yet clear when they returned to the court for the first time: only by the time of their second return have they shown that they are capable of "living" an ideal balance between the knight's double obligation of being a warrior and of being a courtly lover. The specific progression of each protagonist's adventures is adapted to his specific weakness in this balance between *amor* and *militia*: Lancelot and Erec, who tend to neglect their military prowess for their erotic passion, have to survive the most amazing physical threats and dangers (and it is of course very fitting, form this perspective, that Erec cuts himself off from any communication with his wife). Yvain, on the other hand, who tends to forget his obligations toward the ladies because he so enjoys tournaments and warfare, has to prove that he is capable of returning into his lover's arms within a limited "leave" that she

---

[10] "Erec et Enide," vv. 2,661–71, quoted from Michel Zink, ed., *Chrétien de Troyes: Romans* (Paris, 1994), 148.

[11] See the pioneering essay, first written in 1948, by the German medievalist Hugo Kuhn, "Erec," in Kuhn, *Dichtung und Welt im Mittelalter* (Stuttgart, 1959), 133–50.

has given him. This is how, as specific sequences of adventures, the never visible roads that the knights are traveling shape their specific identities.

There is one eminent case where the protagonist's specific weakness becomes condensed in a symbol that itself is directly connected to the roads of the romance. So eager is Lancelot to find his lady Guinièvre, King Arthur's adulterous wife, that, having lost his horse in a battle, he decides to follow her on a cart, which is the ultimate shame for a courtly knight—and thereby public proof for Lancelot not taking seriously enough his obligations as a warrior. The inhabitants of a city at which he arrives do not trust their eyes when they see him on that cart—rather than on horseback:

> Del chevalier que cil aporte
> Sor la charette se mervoillent
> Les genz, mes nie nel consoillent,
> Einz le huient petit et grant
> Et li veillart et li anfant
> Parmi les rues a grant hui,
> S'ot molt le chevaliers de lui
> Vilenies et despit dire. (vv. 402–9)

Compared with the following stage in the history of the romance, we cannot only say for Chrétien's protagonists that they tend to achieve, in the end, a well balanced "courtly" identity. The roads on which they travel, too, display a balance between producing the excitement of dangerous, seemingly random encounters and an underlying order that gives joint meaning to these episodes.

From the thirteenth century onward, however, the roads of the romance begin to diverge, on the one hand, into an explicitly allegorical function and, on the other, into a function that ceases to imply an overarching meaning. Those prose versions of the courtly romance in which, centuries later, Don Quijote will specialize as a reader, multiply the sequence of knightly adventures to a degree where they lose any plausible connection to the final goal of the knight's journey and where their meanings no longer add up to shape the specific identity of each central protagonist. In addition to the familiar evil dwarfs, robbers, and giants that continue to pop up along the road, the prose romance offers its heroes all kinds of thresholds and borders, often guarded by strong enemies and, above all, a broad variety of so-called narrow passages where the road, quite literally, does not allow for two knights on horseback to pass each other without physical conflict. In the thirteenth-century German *Prosalancelot*, the always rushed Lancelot runs into such an obstacle whose explicit description as a space is strictly adapted to the function of motivating the narration of a potential adventure:

> Des morgens was er neben dem tage uff und wapent sich, und des wirtes
> sune waren beide bereit. Da nam Lancelot urlob zum wirt und zur wirtinne
> und reit sin strass, und die zwen gebrueder ritten mit im. Da sie wol sehs
> milen von der herberge geritten waren, sie qwamen zu einer passaien, von
> dem Steyn genant. Der weg war sere eistlich und ging zwuschen zweyn leyen
> hien, die gross und hoh waren, wol einer clafter breit die ein von der andern.
> Da vor hielt ein gewapent ritter uff eim ross.[12]

From our present-day perspective it is hard to imagine how the endless reiteration of such events in the knight's *queste* could so intensely fascinate readers throughout the late-medieval and early-modern centuries. It was as if the original structure of the romance had been degenerating and grown wild along those imaginary roads that were the lives of their protagonists— in order to offer a rich enough world for the development of the heroes' subjectivity in the literature of later ages.[13]

On the other side of the generic bifurcation that follows the time of Chrétien de Troyes, the motif of the road establishes itself as the standard metaphor for the life of the Christian, seen both from the angle of its challenges and from that of its final destiny. Nobody could miss the meaning of the three verses with which Dante opens the *Divina commedia*:

> Nel mezzo del cammin di nostra vita
> Mi ritrovai per una selva oscura,
> Che la diritta via era smarrita.

Life is thought of and stereotypically represented as a way (or a road) whose temporal progression can be measured and represented by distance in space, and in the "middle of that road" man necessarily finds himself lost in that dark forest that stands for existential guilt in the Christian sense.[14] Like

---

[12] *Lancelot und Ginover II*, in *Prosalancelot II*, ed. Hans-Hugo Steinhoff. Deutsche Klassiker Bibliothek. Bibliothek des Mittelalters (Frankfurt on Main, 1995), 15:370.

[13] This is the intuition of Karlheinz Stierle, "Die Verwilderung des Romans als Ursprung seiner Möglichkeit," in Hans Ulrich Gumbrecht, ed., *Literatur in der Gesellschaft des Spätmittelalters: Grundriss der romanischen Literaturen des Mittelalters* (Heidelberg, 1980), 1:253–314.

[14] I follow Robert Harrison's interpretation in *Forests: The Shadow of Civilization* (Chicago, 1992).

the heroes in the contemporary prose romance, Dante is soon confronted with one of those literary "narrow passages" when he discovers a wild leopard and a wolf that will not let him proceed any further (vv. 31–60). At this point precisely Virgil comes to his rescue helping him find "another path that [he] must take" (v. 91)—which of course is the *Commedia*'s cosmological itinerary through Hell, Purgatory, and Paradise, the three spaces of Christian transcendence.

Far from disappearing from the range of literary forms with the waning of medieval culture, the allegorical association between the Christian's life and the motif of the road as its allegory probably reached its greatest popularity in the pious texts of the early-modern centuries. As opposed to the "wild" complexification of the road-narrative in late-medieval prose romance, the allegorical use of the structure of the road and, with increasing enthusiasm, of the pilgrimage[15] as its concretization, allowed for the return to a sometimes obsessive and even tautological theological overdetermination of the narrative structure. In the *Pilgrim's Progress*, by John Bunyan, first published in London in 1678, the traveler whose name, unsurprisingly enough, is "Christian" arrives twice at the city of God, thus producing an identity for himself that, in its semantic structure, is similar to the knightly identity produced by the double circle of adventures in Chrétien's texts. The difference lies indeed in the degree of obsessiveness with which the pious literature of early-modern culture follows the principles of allegorization— and for which the frequently added interpretations and clarifications in parentheses are a clear symptom. However complicated the map of the Pilgrim's spiritual movements may grow, there is never a single movement, direction, or road to which the author would fail to attach a specific meaning. Mountains, for example, never appear as individually described parts of a landscape. Without any exception they function as particularly unambiguous objects of meaning projection:

> But when they saw that the Hill was steep and high, and that there was two other ways to go; and supposing also that these two ways might meet again, with that up which *Christian* went, on the other side of the Hill: Therefore they were resolved to go in those ways; (now the name of one of those ways was *Danger*, and the name of the other *Destruction*). So the one took the way

---

[15] See Friederike Haussauer, *Santiago. Schrift. Körper, Raum. Reise* (Munich, 1993), esp. 57–140.

which is called *Danger*, which led him into a great Wood; and the other took him directly up the way to *Destruction*, which led him into a wide field full of dark Mountains, where he stumbled and fell, and rose no more.[16]

Roads of Contingency

What we call *contingency* reflects the status of future events than can happen but will not necessarily happen. Both the roads in early-modern prose romance and the roads in the pious allegorical narrative are incommensurable with the dimension of contingency. For, in the prose romance, there is no identifiable limit, at any given moment of the narrative, as to what adventure might occur next—so that no distinction exists between what could happen and what cannot happen. While it is true that the genre had a highly standardized repertoire of typical challenges and mischievous characters (narrow passages and torrential rivers; evil dwarfs, brutal giants and hungry beasts), it never implied the logic of a specific type of probability that would have excluded any specific phenomena from appearing along the roads of the protagonists; nor did the prose romance have a narrative logic that could have made any specific sequence of episodes binding (and would thereby have precluded any specific types of episodes from following after a given previous type of episode). The pious allegorical narrative, in contrast, was incommensurable with the category of contingency because its intense theological overdetermination did not allow for any episodes whose content and whose structural position was not predictable and "necessary." For example: it is predictable and it appears necessary, from the perspective of the reader, that Bunyan's Pilgrim will have to walk the way of Danger (and not the way of Destruction), and it is predictable and necessary that his itinerary will end in the City of God.

In the very sense of *contingency* that, for opposite reasons, is incommensurable both with the prose romance and with the allegorical narrative, the road to Canterbury along which Chaucer has his pilgrims tell the *Canterbury Tales* is indeed a road of contingency. This is because the idea of weaving a number of narratives throughout and within the frame narrative of a journey is based on the elementary association of a linear movement in space—via the structural pattern of lived experience—with the flow of narrative. This

---

[16] John Bunyan, *The Pilgrim's Progress: From this World to That Which Is to Come*, ed. James Blanton Wharey (Oxford, 1960), 42.

becomes transparent in the Host's monologue, which initiates and structures the narrative sociability of the pilgrims on the road to Canterbury:

> And I don't doubt, before the journey's done
> You mean to wile the time in tales and fun.
> Indeed, there's little pleasure for your bones
> Riding along and all as dumb as stones.
> So let me then propose for your enjoyment,
> Just as I said a suitable employment.
>
> . . . .
>
> Each one of you shall help to make things slip
> By telling two stories on the outward trip
> To Canterbury, that's what I intend,
> And, on the homeward way to journey's end
> Another two.[17]

Within such an arrangement, both the sequence of the narrators and the order of their tales is contingent. For, on the one hand, the set of pilgrim-narrators who may tell a tale as the journey unfolds is not unlimited, given that they have all been introduced in Chaucer's Prologue. On the other hand—and for all the critical discussion about structuring principles in the sequence of the tales—there may well be a growing probability, in the transitions between tales, about what narrator and what tale will be next; but there never is a necessary sequence.

Probability indeed is the principle that occupies the logical range between absolute arbitrariness and absolute necessity, the two poles excluded by the concept of contingency. In other words: probability enables and describes all the anticipation and prediction possible in a sphere of contingency. And while, as roads of contingency, the roads of the early-modern novel continue to be roads that produce risks and adventures, the genre of the novel now develops its identity as it unfolds, between authors and readers, a sophisticated play of probabilities. The novel begins to become the testing ground for what readers find compatible with their own everyday experience. In its early-modern stages of development, the literary sphere of probability emerges both against the background of the principle of arbitrariness, from the prose romance, and against the principle of necessity, from the allegorical narrative. Miguel de Cervantes was the master of this double narrative play between arbitrariness and overdetermination, contingency and probability.

---

[17] *Canterbury Tales*, vv. 791ff. Quoted from the translation by Nevill Cogill (London, 1984), 40.

As if it had been written to mark and to monumentalize his place in the history of literature, the prologue to his novel *Los trabajos de Persiles y Sigismunda*, for all we know the last literary text that Cervantes wrote before his death, offers a scene that had only just then become possible—for an already famous author—within the play of probability. That scene, which a contemporary reader could indeed imagine from everyday experience, is a conversation that Cervantes says he had, a few days before his death, with an enthusiastic reader on the road from Toledo to Madrid. Once his reader, a student from Salamanca who rides a donkey, has encountered and identified Miguel de Cervantes, the young man declares, in the most glowing words, his eternal admiration and gratitude. Cervantes, however, tries to tone him down to a level of everyday rationality. Like the Host in the Prologue of the *Canterbury Tales*, he proposes that they "spend the little that was left of their journey in good conversation": "Yo, señor, soy Cervantes, pero no el regocijo de las Musas, ni ninguna de las más baratijas que ha dicho vuesa merced. Vuelva a cobrar su burra, y suba, y caminemos en buena conversación lo poco que nos falte de camino."[18] The roads of the novel have become a space for narrative and conversation and, as Cervantes suggests to the student from Salamanca with mild criticism, the tone of this conversation is a tone of probability and of reason.

In his conversations with Don Quijote along the roads of Castile, this precisely is the tone—and, we may add, the world picture—of the peasant Sancho Panza, whereas Don Quijote, the addicted reader of prose romance, continues to see the road as a sequence of hyperbolic adventures, as a sequence in which nothing is excluded by any principle of probability, as a sequence of events, finally, into which he obsessively projects the heaviest, the most literary, and the most lunatic meanings. Everything must be possible on the road *and* everything must be meaningful; these are the incompatible premises under which Don Quijote is traveling, while Sancho's road is a road of contingency, on which certain things cannot happen at all and some things are more likely to happen than others (it was indeed probable, during Cervantes' time, to meet merchants and beggars, criminals and policemen, actors, students, and poets on the road—and this exactly corresponds to Sancho's perception). Every single episode in the two parts of Cervantes' master novel illuminates the contrast between the two protagonists' views of the road and the multiple effects of style and meaning that the author produces through this duality.

---

[18] Quoted from Miguel de Cervantes Saavedra, *Obras completas*, ed. Angel Valbuena Prat (Madrid, 1967), 1,528.

Particularly impressive, even for present-day readers, is this effect at the end of chapter 22 in book 1. Thanks to a sequence of random happenings, Don Quijote has "liberated" a bunch of criminals who, heavily chained, handcuffed, and guarded by police troops, had been on their way to the galleys. As Don Quijote has convinced himself, against the advice of Sancho Panza's realism, that these criminals are all noble princes, he now expects them to be grateful enough to carry the tale and the glory of this adventure along the roads of Castile to Dulcinea de Toboso—which projection ends up becoming the reason why the potential galley slaves, before they finally escape, throw a "rain of stones" at Don Quijote and Sancho Panza. The chapter ends with a picture of misery—a picture of prosaic probability also—whose distance from the prose romance and from the allegorical narrative is marked by its focus on Don Quijote's horse and on Sancho's donkey, rather than on the protagonists:

> Solos quedaron jumento y *Rocinante*, Sancho y Don Quijote; el jumento, cabizbajo y pensativo, sacudiendo de cuando en cuando las orejas, pensando que aún no había cesado la borrasca de las piedras, que le perseguían los oídos; *Rocinante*, tendido junto a su amo, que también vino al suelo de otra pedrada; Sancho, en pelota, y temeroso de la Santa Hermandad; Don Quijote, mohinísimo de verse tan malparado por los mismos a quien tanto bien había hecho.[19]

Very sporadically, under these or similar circumstances, the space of the road can now become visible in the novel—when it helps to produce a prosaic view on the everyday world. For Don Quijote, this world continues to be a mere sequence of potential adventures—which presupposes that he does not see the space of the road. But while Don Quijote resembles the protagonists of the prose romance also inasmuch as he has only a vague sense of where his journey should lead and through which stations it must go (he certainly is a reactive, rather than a proactive traveler), the author Cervantes has carefully structured his novel according to the pattern of the "double cycle" of adventures, as we have seen it in the texts attributed to Chrétien de Troyes. Like Erec and Yvain, Don Quijote returns to his village (his "court") after a first series of adventures; as in the courtly romance, his final return marks the fulfillment of the hero's development. But different from the cases of Erec and Yvain, Don Quijote will of course not end up acquiring all the qualities of a perfect knight. Rather, we can say that Don

---

[19] Ibid., 1,117.

Quijote dies as soon as he has become aware of the complexity of his own subjecthood. For he dies as Alonso Quijano el Bueno, as a country squire under whose former foolishness everybody, including the former Don Quijote, now recognizes his good heart and a particular brand of wisdom. Therefore, the chamber where Alonso Quijano el Bueno dies is the endpoint of all the roads that Don Quijote has been traveling, and it becomes the space for a scene of unheroic—subjective—sobriety, a scene in which the hero finds a discourse of probability to finish his life: "Señores—dijo Don Quijote—, véamonos poco a poco, pues ya en los nidos de antaño no hay pájaros hogaño. Yo fuí loco. Y ya soy cuerdo: fuí Don Quijote de la Mancha, y soy ahora, como he dicho, Alonso Quijano el Bueno. Pueda con vuesas mercedes mi arrepentimiento y mi verdad volverme a la estimación que de mí se tenía."[20] Subjectivity—the now rising conception of human life of which Alonso Quijano becomes aware on his deathbed—is a state that cannot be described nor measured by any abstract or general values. It is the never-ending process of finding and developing a singular identity for oneself. For the novel, this process typically takes place on the road and in confrontation with the obstacles that the road brings forth.

Although we know for a biographical fact that Cervantes disliked the genre of the picaresque novel, many literary critics have misidentified Don Quijote as a *pícaro*. What Don Quijote and the literary *pícaros* do share is obvious to the point of being banal: they both are on the road all the time. But if the roads of the *pícaro*, like the roads in *Don Quijote*, become roads of contingency, the background against which this happens is not the background of the chivaleresque prose romance. Rather, the discursive point of reference for the picaresque novel's double play, a point of reference to which its first-person narrators allude with gestures of—more or less—open cynicism, are the roads from the allegorical narrative of the ideal Christian life. Published around 1555, *La vida de Lazarillo de Tormes y de sus fortunas y adversidades*, the earliest picaresque novel, sets the tone. It is written in the form of a confession that the hero, a servant of many masters, presents to a priest. This priest appears to be the friend of another priest who protects Lazarillo and to whom Lazarillo lends his wife as a concubine. There is not a single sentence in the original version of the novel, however, that makes explicit this exchange of services between Lararillo and his master. If we ask how a reader can know that the fictional protagonist is lying, the answer is in the discursive duplicity of Lazarillo's confession. Each of his adventures makes him more aware of the merciless hostility of the world around him,

---

[20] Ibid., 1,522.

although his frame narrative presents all these adventures as edifying steps toward an endpoint of Christian perfection. For example: as Lazarillo crosses the River Tormes to leave Salamanca, his hometown, with the blind man to whom his mother has given her son as a servant, the new master plays a brutal trick on him. This trick will "awaken Lazarillo to life" by teaching him forever that dissimulation and physical brutality, not honesty and mildness, will be the conditions for his survival:

> Salimos de Salamanca y, llegando a la puente, está a la entrada della vn animal de piedra que casi tiene forma de toro, y el ciego mandóme que llegase cerca del animal e, alli puesto, me dixo: "Lázaro, llega el oydo a este toro e oyrás gran ruydo dentro dél." Yo simplemente llegué, creyendo ser ansi. Y, como sintió que tenía la cabeça por la piedra, afirmó rezio la mano y diome vna gran calabaçada en el diablo del toro, que más de tres días me duró el dolor de la cornada y dixome: "Necio, aprende: que el moço del ciego vn punto ha de saber mas que el diablo." Y rió mucho la burla. Paresciome que en aquel instante desperté de la simpleza en que como niño dormido estaua. Dixe entre mi: "Verdad dize éste, que me cumple abiuar el ojo y auisar, pues solo soy, y pensar como me sepa valer." Conmençamos nuestro camino.[21]

Despite the edifying tone of his discourse, there can never be a doubt that the roads that Lazarillo is walking with the blind man are the roads of contingency and not the roads toward Christian perfection—for the anonymous author never allows the first-person narrator to completely maintain this ceremonious tone. Once Lazarillo has proven to himself how much he has learned from his first master by taking revenge and letting him jump against a stone pillar, he seeks a new master. His encounter with the next one—and with all of his following masters—is discursively staged in a strange contradiction between narrative necessity and complete randomness: "Otro día . . . fuyme a vn lugar, que llaman Maqueda, adonde me toparon mis peccados con vn clérigo."[22] If the episode that begins with these words is indeed seen as a punishment for his "sins," then it will appear as necessary that Lazarillo runs into the stingiest of all masters. But at the same time the text underlines the randomness of their encounter by saying that Lázaro just "hit upon" ("*toparse con*") this clergyman.

Different picaresque novels make ironic use of different religious maxims in order to provide a center of religiously motivated coherence for their

---

[21] *La vida de Lazarillo de Tormes*, ed. Julio Cejador y Frauca (Madrid, 1969), 77–78.
[22] Ibid., 109.

autobiographical narratives. Lazarillo, for example, insists that, following advice from his mother, "he always tries to lean on the good persons" (*"arrimarse a los buenos"*), which the reader will understand both as an allusion to and as a negation of the "deal" that he has cut with the priest who sleeps with his wife. In Francisco de Quevedo's *Vida del Buscón llamado Don Pablos*, written more than fifty years after *Lazarillo*, the equivalent "religious" leitmotif is the monastic quest for solitude. Whenever the protagonist is forced to hit the road because the police are on his heels, he speaks about his journey to the next place as if it were the result of a spiritual desire for solitude: "Determiné de salirme de la corte, y tomar mi camino para Toledo, donde ni conocía ni me conocía nadie."[23] Only the final paragraph of Quevedo's picaresque novel undercuts the claim that movements in space could ever have an impact on the protagonist's morals: "Determiné . . . de pasarme a Indias . . . a ver si, mudando mundo y tierra, mejoraría mi suerte. Y fueme peor, como v.m. vera en la segunda parte, pues nunca mejora su estado quien muda solamente de lugar, y no de vida y costumbres."[24] The announcement of a "second part of the novel" which, for all we know, Quevedo never had any serious intention to write, is part of a discourse that stages *El Buscón* as a parody of its own genre. Seen from this perspective, however, it becomes clear that crossing out one allegorical layer in the parody of a religious discourse will only lead to another religious discourse in which, once again, the narrator cannot possibly believe. The discursive duplicity of the picaresque novel thus transforms itself into a potentially infinite play of multiple levels between narrative and commentary, into a play of levels and perspectives that produces vertigo in the reader's imagination.

But Quevedo's text is only a particularly transparent case of what had become, by the end of the seventeenth century, a driving principle of the early-modern novel. Over and again, the novel transformed and complexified its structure by staging itself as anti-novel in relation to a previously established standard, and in doing so the genre progressively sharpened its implicit concepts of probability. One final example with which I want to illustrate this dynamic is Paul Scarron's *Roman comique* from 1651. It is a novel about a group of traveling actors, that is, about one of those professions whose existence was expected to be essentially an existence on the road. Now, the background against which Scarron makes the actors' world appear as a prosaic (and often pathetic) world of contingencies is the high-sounding tone of their theatrical discourse. Already in the first sentences of the *Roman*

---

[23] Quoted from the critical edition by Fernando Lázaro Carreter (Salamanca, 1965), 253.
[24] Ibid., 280.

comique, the author produces a grotesque effect by making the traditional allegorical discourse about the alternation of sunrise and sunset overlap with a description of the actors' cart and its horses. It is as if the "carriage of the sun" had inadvertently exited the mythological world and were now rolling along the roads of the French province:

> Le soleil avait achevé plus de la moitié de sa course et son char, ayant attrappé le penchant du monde, roulloit plus viste qu'il ne vouloit. Si ses chevaux eussent voulu profiter de la pente du chemin, ils eussent achevé ce qui restoit du jour en moins d'un demy-quart d'heure: Mais au lieu de tirer de toute leur force, ils ne s'amusoient qu'à faire des courbettes, respirant un air marin qui les faisoit hannir et les advertissoit que la mer estoit proche.[25]

The closer the actors come, at least in some chapters of the book, to a social sphere that corresponds to their ambitions and pretensions, the likelier their disillusionment seems to be. On the way to a castle, for example, where they are expected to perform at a wedding celebration, they have to pass through a forest. As soon as the actors sight another group of travelers on the road, they become as nervous and as excited as Don Quijote or as the knights of the prose romance in similar situations: "L'on ne trouva pas bon d'arrester, mais de se tenir chacun sur ses gardes." Soon the actors find out that they are facing, as so often before, a highway patrol whose lieutenant has long turned into their enemy. When the two groups finally meet, a situation of tension emerges that resembles the "narrow passage" scenes in late-medieval romance. It is this nervousness that will push Ragotin, one of the actors, into a situation of insuperable public embarrassment:

> Comme [le lieutenant] entretenoit la Compagnie, le cheval d'un de ses Archers, qui estoit fougueux, sauta sur le col du cheval de Ragotin auquel il fit si grand'peur, qu'il recula et enfonça dans une touffe d'arbres, dont il y en avoit quelques-uns dont les branches estoient seiches, l'une desquelles se trouva sur le pourpoint de Ragotin et qui luy piqua le dos, ensorte qu'il demeura pendu; car, voulant se degager de parmi ces arbres, il avoit donné des deux talons à son cheval, qui avoit passé et l'avoit laissé ainsi en l'air criant comme un petit fou qu'il estoit: je suis mort, l'on m'a donné un coup d'épée dans les reins![26]

---

[25] Quoted from the edition by Antoine Adam, *Romanciers du XVIIe siècle.* (Paris, 1968), 533.
[26] Ibid., 853–54.

The main principle about the roads of the novel that we have observed throughout the early-modern centuries remains unbroken in this scene. Whatever details about the road may be revealed, they can always be subsumed under the sole function of explaining the adventures and events that the road produces. But perhaps the roads of the seventeenth century, those roads that lieutenants and their archers had begun to patrol, were already too safe to be associated forever with the challenges of adventure. After all, not some aggressive enemy was responsible for Ragotin's embarrassment. It was his own—all too theatrical—excitement.

Roads Contracting

Between the twelfth and the seventeenth centuries, the roads of the novel had undergone a profound transformation. If the literary roads had been a sequential pattern along which normative concepts of identity (above all, the identity of the courtly knight) could be displayed, they were becoming, by 1650, a representation of those world-contingencies in confrontation with which the protagonists would be able to shape their subjectivity. If probability was now the dimension through which a world of contingent observations, encounters, and events came under the control of the subject, the impact of probability on the novel was still confined, with very few exceptions, to the selection of what might possibly happen along the road—whereas there was hardly yet any description of those roads themselves.

Many novels in the age of Enlightenment show a tendency to reduce even further—or to surround with the brackets of irony—the scarce and rather formulaic elements which until then had been the only explicit reference to the roads. When Jones and Partridge, on their way to London in Henry Fielding's *Tom Jones*, arrive "at the bottom of a very steep hill," they undo its spatial reality—and they ultimately manage to bypass it—thanks to a strange convergence between Jones's preromantic projections and Partridge's moral allegorization. This is what Tom Jones proposes to his friend:

> "Partridge, I wish I was at the top of this hill; it must certainly afford a most charming prospect, especially by this light; for the solemn gloom which the moon casts on all objects is beyond expression beautiful, especially to an imagination which is desirous of cultivating melancholic ideas." "Very probably," answered Partridge; "but if the top of the hill be properest to produce melancholy thoughts, I suppose the bottom is the likeliest to produce merry ones, and these I take to be much the better of the two. I protest you have

made my blood run cold with the very mentioning the top of that mountain; which seems to me to be one of the highest in the world. No, no, if we look for anything, let it be for a place underground, to screen ourselves from the frost."[27]

Later in the novel, but still on their way to London, a similar move of de-realization (within fictional reality) is applied to one of the typical literary road events—an attempt of robbery. "The poor fellow . . . was in strength by no means a match for Jones." He is easily overwhelmed, and on the road "much pleasant discourse passed between Jones and Partridge, on the subject of their last adventure. In which Jones expressed a great compassion for those highwaymen who are, by unavoidable distress, driven, as it were, to such illegal courses, as generally bring them to a shameful death."[28]

Denis Diderot's *Jacques le fataliste et son maître* develops this tendency of de-realizing the roads of the novel and their potential events into an ongoing play between the narrator and the readers' expectations. Before the two protagonists even begin their dialogue, a narrator explains to the reader, with strong gestures of intellectual condescendence, that all situational circumstances of their conversation, including the direction in which the are moving while they speak, are without any importance: "Comment s'étaient-ils rencontrés? Par hasard, comme tout el monde. Comment s'appelaient-ils? Que vous importe? D'où venaient-ils? Du lieu le plus prochain? Où allaient-ils? Est-ce que l'on sait où l'on va?"[29] The classic association between the movement on the road and the progress of the conversation is now reduced to a convergence between conversation without progress and movement without space, and even this convergence, observes the narrator, is not a necessary one. "Only a novelist," the narrator says following the historical logic of the anti-novel that drives the transformations of the novel toward a different concept of reality, "only a novelist would pay attention to such details":

Ils continuèrent leur route, allant toujours sans savoir où ils allaient, quoiqu'ils sussent à peu près où ils voulaient aller; trompant l'ennui et la fatigue par le silence et le bavardage, comme c'est l'usage de ceux qui marchent, et quelquefois de ceux qui sont assis. Il est bien évident que je ne fais pas un roman, puisque je néglige ce qu'un romancier ne manquerait pas

---

[27] Quoted from the edition by John Bender and Simon Stern (Oxford, 1996), 383.

[28] Ibid., 593–94.

[29] Quoted from the edition by Henri Bénac: Diderot, *Oeuvres romanesques* (Paris, 1962), 493.

d'employer. Celui qui prendrait ce que j'écris pour la vérité, serait peut-être moins dans l'erreur que celui qui le prendrait pour fable.[30]

Finally, when the travelers, after hundreds of pages filled with conversations, are approaching Paris, they learn that no exciting accidents on the road will further complicate their journey because, says the narrator, such accidents simply did not happen to them: "Lecteur, qui m'empêcherait de jeter ici le cocher, les chevaux, la voiture, les maîtres et les valets dans une fondrière? . . . Mais il n'y eut rien de tout cela. Le chevalier et le maître de Jacques arrivèrent à Paris."[31]

Compared with its status in the novels of early modernity, the emphasis and the narrative space given to the motif of the road becomes clearly reduced and contracted during the Enlightenment. In no other period is our thesis more pertinent that the roads of the novel function, above all, as a presupposition for the construction of narrative structures and as a semantic void to be filled by the readers' imagination, rather than as an object of detailed description. In addition, the passages from Fielding and Diderot seem to suggest that this contraction of the roads in the novel occurred with the authors' deliberate intention. One simple reason for this structural development may have been that the roads, in the more densely populated spaces of Europe, had by now become less uncanny and less dangerous—so that it would have violated the expectation of probablity had the authors continued to feature roads filled with adventures. At the same time, Diderot's text especially seems to indicate that the conversation (and any other type of communication—this was, after all, the century of the epistolary novel) had moved into the center of a widely shared conception of reality. "A novelist," we have read in *Jacques le fataliste*, would have "used" accidents and other road adventures. "Who takes what I am writing about"—that is an almost endless conversation—"for the truth is less confused than he who takes it for an invention." The core reality of the eighteenth century was indeed the life of the mind, the Cartesian dimension of human existence—and this also was the dimension that the new dominant form of the novel, the bildungsroman, would soon occupy. It was the novel about the education of mind and soul, a novel whose ideal, quite obviously, was a world that harmoniously fit under the control of the subject's agency, a novel, also, that had no more use for bumps in its roads.

---

[30] Ibid., 505.
[31] Ibid., 746.

Not even the texts of the Marquis de Sade make an exception from this historical rule of the mind dominating over the body. They mostly consist of detailed conversations about all kinds of improbable sexual practices and their moral legitimacy in the view of the *libertin*. And while de Sade's imagination was more productive on the varieties of claustrophobic space, he sometimes could not avoid the motif of the open roads in order to stage the drama of the—never successful—escape of the virtuous, naive, or simply dumb heroine from her relentless persecutors. In all the innocence of her heart, Justine has just walked to the river "to breathe fresh air," and is now "sitting down to think" for a while, when this highly predictable road accident happens:

> Cependant la nuit vint sans que je pensasse à me retirer, lorsque tout à coup je me sentis saisie par trois hommes. L'un me met la main sur la bouche, et les deux autres me jettent précipitamment dans une voiture, y montent avec moi, et nous fendons les airs pendant trois grandes heures. . . . La voiture arrive près d'une maison, des portes s'ouvrent pour la recevoir, et se referment aussitôt. Mes guides m'emportent, me font traverser ainsi plusieurs appartements très sombres, et me laissent enfin dans un, près duquel est une pièce où j'apperçois de la lumière.[32]

Madame Dubois, "that horrible monster" whose "appetites" Justine had tried to escape will immediately appear on the scene, with a candle in her hand and "full of the most burning desire for vengeance." And this is how most of the innocent protagonists' short road trips end in de Sade's novels.

While it is impossible to imagine a greater contrast in novelistic tone than that between de Sade's *Justine* and Goethe's *Wilhelm Meister*, the prototypical bildungsroman, there can be no doubt, on the other hand, that, in his own very specific self-understanding, de Sade would have subscribed to the "educational" function of the novel. This potential convergence explains why the fictional roads of the constantly traveling hero Wilhelm are as contracted as the roads of Justine. In a decisive letter to his brother-in-law that explains why Wilhelm has made up his mind not to return to his hometown and become part of the family business, he explicitly celebrates traveling; "seeing the world" is praised as the most important method of individual self-education: "Mich selbst, ganz wie ich da bin, auszubilden, das war dunkel von Jugend auf mein Wunsch und meine Absicht. Noch hege ich

---

[32] Quoted from Marquis de Sade, *Justine ou les malheurs de la vertu*, ed. Gilbert Lély (Paris, 1969), 278.

eben diese Gesinnungen, nur dass mir die Mittel, die es moeglich machen werden, etwas deutlicher sind. Ich habe mehr Welt gesehen, als Du glaubst, und sie besser benutzt, als Du denkst."[33]

Self-governing and self-education, which the eighteenth century so intensely associated with traveling, have now turned into principles of resistance against any world interpretation based on concepts like fate and randomness: "Wehe dem, der sich von Jugend auf gewoehnt, in dem Notwendigen etwas Willkuerliches finden zu wollen, der dem Zufaelligen eine Art von Vernunft zuschreiben moechte."[34] In this spirit, the roads of the novel can no longer be spaces where the protagonists are exposed—or willingly expose themselves—to unpredictable adventures. The roads of the bildungsroman reflect the hero's determination to educate himself, and they do it so intensely and with such consequences that, for the time being, the description of those roads as spaces or landscapes is still excluded. One of the very few actual traveling scenes of Goethe's slow-paced novel, quite symptomatically, comes in an episode where the coachman chooses a certain itinerary in order to confuse one of his passengers about the endpoint of the journey. Instead of representing a subject's intention, the road as landscape is here hiding what is going on in the coachman's mind: "Lydie bestand nun darauf, man solle umkehren; der Kutscher fuhr zu, als verstuende er es nicht. Endlich verlangte sie es mit groesster Heftigkeit; Wilhelm rief ihm zu und gab ihm das verabredete Zeichen. Der Kutscher erwiderte: 'Wir haben nicht noetig, denselben Weg zurueckzufahren; ich weiss einen naehern, de zugleich viel bequemer ist.' Er fuhr nun seitwegs durch einen Wald und ueber lange Triften weg."[35] But as long as the protagonists have agency over their movements in space, the evocation of that space will not turn into detailed description.

Written during the years before his death in 1778, Jean-Jacques Rousseau's *Rêveries d'un promeneur solitaire* marks an endpoint in that contraction of the literary roads that we have observed in the novels of the Enlightenment. The traditional conversation between two travelers has collapsed into the dialogue of the lonesome individual with himself. The author indeed explains, in the first *Promenade*, the choice of this form as a consequence of his definitive withdrawal from the social world.[36] It is supposed that he walks through the landscape while he is thinking—but under normal circumstances this

---

[33] *Wilhelm Meisters Lehrjahre*, in *Goethes Werke* (Hamburg, 1965), 7:290.

[34] Ibid., 71.

[35] Ibid., 441.

[36] *Rêveries d'un promeneur solitaire*, in J.-J. Rousseau, *Oeuvres complètes*, ed. Bernard Gagnebin and Marcel Raymond (Paris, 1969), 1:998.

condition of his thinking will not be mentioned. When, however, in the second *Promenade*, Rousseau mentions the road on which he walks for the first time, it is to describe an accident that he wants to be understood as ultimate proof of his irreversible solitude and victimization as an individual:

> J'étois sur les six heures à la descente de Menil-mon-tant presque vis-à-vis du galant jardinier, quand des personnes qui marchoient devant moi s'étant tout à coup brusquement écartées, je vis fondre sur moi un gros chien danois qui s'élançant à toutes jambes devant une carrosse n'eut pas même le temps de retenir sa course ou de se détourner quand il m'apperçut. Je jugeai que le seul moyen que j'avois d'éviter d'être jetté par terre étoit de faire un grand saut si juste que le chien passât sous moi tandis que je serois en l'air. Cette idée plus prompte que l'éclair et que je n'eus le temps de raisonner ni d'exécuter fut la dernière avant mon accident. Je sentis ni le coup, ni la chute, ni rien de ce qui s'ensuivit jusqu'au moment où je revins à moi.[37]

Roads as Landscape

As both the autobiographical and the historical Jean-Jacques Rousseau, the heroes of the great nineteenth-century novels are—and fervently want to be—individuals. This implies not only that they find themselves driven by the ambition of being unique. They also need moments of distance from society—and if it were only because many of them believe that such distance is a condition for their subsequent triumph over society. Such scenes of individual distance are often scenes on the road. Now, these literary roads of individual distance, finally, turn into more than implicit presuppositions for the imagination of varying narrative structures. Numerous nineteenth-century novelists indeed describe them as part of the landscape.

As a general rule, Balzac's *Comédie humaine* still participates in the almost exclusive concentration of Enlightenment literature on conversation and thought, on interaction and social environment.[38] But there is at least one scene where a famous literary conversation "on the road" is preceded by a description of the same road as landscape. Toward the end of *Illusions perdues*, Lucien de Rubempré, after what he believes to be the terminal economic and social collapse of his life, takes the road from Angoulême to Poitiers. His intention is not to reach Poitiers or to return to Paris. Lucien is

---

[37] Ibid., 1,004–5.

[38] I thank my friend, the eminent Balzac scholar Joachim Kuepper, for a conversation about this question.

looking for an appropriate place to commit suicide, and he thus finds himself at a maximum distance from society. Thinking about the perfect solution to make his body disappear, he arrives at a place where the road climbs a hill, steeply enough to oblige the passengers of the stagecoach to walk a short distance on foot:

> Il chemina donc vers Marsac, en proie à ses dernières et funèbres pensées, et dans la ferme intention de dérober ainsi le secret de sa mort, de ne pas être l'objet d'une enquête, de ne pas être enterré, de ne pas être vu dans l'horrible état où sont les noyés quand ils reviennent à fleur d'eau. Il parvint bientôt au pied d'une de ces côtes qui se rencontrent si fréquemment sur les routes de France, et surtout entre Angoulème et Poitiers. La diligence de Bordeaux à Paris venait avec rapidité, les voyageurs allaient sans doute en descendre pour monter cette longue côte à pied. Lucien, qui ne voulut pas se laisser voir, se jeta dans un petit chemin creux et se mit à cueillir des fleurs dans une vigne. Quand il reprit la grande route . . . il déboucha précisément derrière un voyageur vêtu tout en noir, les cheveux poudrés, chaussé de souliers en veau d'Orléans.[39]

The passenger behind whom Lucien finds himself is Vautrin, the dark eminence par excellence and the *deus ex machina* in several of Balzac's novels; it is Vautrin in the clothes and with the false identity of a Spanish *abbé*. Soon Vautrin and Lucien will engage in a conversation that shall become the beginning of Lucien's return to glory—a conversation that also seems to turn the narrator's attention away from any spatial details. But for the short moment of Lucien's extreme solitude the novel had provided details about the road on which the hero was walking.

Written and published several decades after Balzac's novel, the second version of Gottfried Keller's *Der gruene Heinrich* appears to be, on many levels, a bildungsroman much in the tradition of Goethe's *Wilhelm Meister*, which implies that it does not contain many detailed descriptions about movements in space. Even when the first-person narrator and protagonist travels from his native Zurich to Munich, where he wants to cultivate his talent as a painter, there are only some very short descriptions of the alpine landscape, followed by the obligatory historical reminiscences. It is then finally an odd object (perhaps I should say, an odd object that will become the emblem of Heinrich's individuality)—a skull that he wants to take on his journey, without exactly knowing why, that triggers a short border narrative:

---

[39] *Illusions perdues*, in Balzac, *La comédie humaine*, ed. Marcel Bouteron (Paris, 1973), 4:1,014.

Als ich mich aus dem Schlage bog, sah ich einen starken Strom unter mir da-
her ziehen, dessen an sich klargruenes Wasser, das junge Buchenlaub, das die
Uferhaenge bedeckte, sowie die tiefe Blaeue des Maihimmels vermischt
widerstrahlend, in einem so wunderbaren Blaugruen heraufleuchtete, dass
der Anblick mich wie ein Zauber befiel und erst, als die Erscheinung rasch
wieder verschwand und es hiess: "das war der Rhein!" mir das Herz mit
starken Schlaegen pochte. . . . Bei der ersten Wechselstelle der nachbarlichen
Post lag auch die Zollstaette mit dem fuerstlichen Kronwappen, und
waehrend das Gepaeck der uebrigen Reisenden kaum geoeffnet und le-
ichthin geprueft wurde, erregte mein unfoermlicher Koffer eine genauere
Aufmerksamkeit der Zollbeamten; was am gestrigen Abend sorglich
eingepackt worden, musste unbarmherzig herausgenommen und auseinan-
der gelegt werden bis auf die Buecher am Grunde, und diese wurden erst
recht abgedeckt. So kam der Schaedel des armen Zwiehan zu Tage und er er-
weckte wiederum eine Neugierde anderer Art.[40]

When Heinrich is finally allowed to close his suitcase, this skull will not fit
with his other baggage, so that he is obliged to carry the odd object in his
hands. This is how, just one page further, he arrives at Munich, without any
further words about the landscapes and towns through which he might have
traveled.

More intensely than Balzac's Lucien de Rubempré and than Heinrich,
Gottfried Keller's autobiographical protagonist and narrator, Julien Sorel,
the energetic hero of Stendhal's *Le rouge et le noir* relishes projecting his
feelings of individualism into the alpine landscape of Haute Savoie. As he
has left behind his first lover, Madame de Rênal, together with her family
and the narrowness of provincial town that the Rênals embody, Julien, for a
short moment, views both the social world and his own future from a heroic
distance that resembles the solemn distance of the mountains from all towns
and villages:

Enfin il atteignit le sommet de la grande montagne, près duquel il fallait
passer. . . . Caché comme un oiseau de proie, au milieu des rochers nues qui
couronnent la grande montagne, il pouvait apercevoir de bien loin tout
homme qui se serait approché de lui. Il découvrit une petite grotte au milieu
de la pente verticale d'un des rochers. Il prit la course, et bientôt fut établi
dans cette retraite. Ici, dit-il, avec des yeux brillants de joie, les hommes
ne sauraient me faire de mal. . . . Pourquoi ne passerais-je pas la nuit ici?

---

[40] *Der gruene Heinrich*, ed. Peter Villwock, 2nd ed. (Frankfurt on Main, 1996), 494.

Se dit-il, j'ai du pain, et je suis libre! Au son de ce grand mot son âme s'ex-
alta, son hypocrisie faisait qu'il n'était pas libre même chez [son ami]. Sans y
songer il vit s'éteindre, l'un après l'autre, tous les rayons du crépuscule. Au
milieu de cette obscurité immense, son âme s'égarait dans la contemplation
de ce qu'il s'imaginait recontrer un jour à Paris.[41]

There are two ambiguities that interfere in this somehow "romantic" description of nature, thus producing its remarkable narrative and semantic
complexity. One is the obvious ambiguity in Julien Sorel's relationship to the
social world: while the mountainous landscape gives him the dominant position and perspective of a "bird of prey," it also offers him, as a potential and
imagined victim, protection from all possible human attacks. But there is
also an ambiguity of the narrator vis-à-vis his hero, which oscillates between
a sympathy for Julien's Rousseau-like feelings of abandoment and an awareness that it is more Julien who wants himself in a potentially dominant position than society that pushes him into isolation. Through this double ambiguity, the very detailed description of the road on which Stendhal's hero
walks is both romantic and antiromantic. The road begins to become fascinating as a landscape as soon as the narrator ceases to trust the hero's expansive projections.

No other European novel, within the dialectic tradition of the genre that
seems to always progress via the negation of a previous standard, can probably compete with Gustave Flaubert's *Education sentimentale* in the merciless
critique and parody of the bildungsroman as a double legacy of Enlightenment and romanticism. If Stendhal casts an ambiguous light on Julien
Sorel's self-fashioning, Flaubert's hero Frédéric Moreau embodies and expresses, quite unambiguously, the unlimited shallowness of individualism as
a life form. Flaubert's parodic reference to the previous—and still well-
established—state of the novel certainly includes the motif of the hero's
travels. When it finally dawns on Frédéric that there has never been a horizon of fulfillment in his "love" for Madame Arnoux, he knows that it is time
to undertake all those voyages that had been part of his unremarkable adolescent dreams.[42] And if even the most serious bildungsroman concedes very

---

[41] Quoted from the edition by Henri Martineau (Paris, 1960), 72.

[42] See the conversations between Frédéric Moreau and his friend Charles Deslauries at the
beginning of the novel: "Ils parlaient de ce qu'ils feraient plus tard, quand ils seraient sortis du
collège. D'abord ils entreprendraient un grand voyage avec l'argent que Frédéric prelèverait sur sa
fortune à sa majorite." Quoted from *Education sentimentale: Histoire d'un jeune homme*, ed.
Edouard Maynial (Paris, 1964), 13.

little space to the hero's experience (rather than "adventures") on the road, Flaubert literally brings this motif to an insuperable degree of contraction:

> Il voyagea.
>
> Il connut la mélancholie des paquebots, les froids réveils sous la tente, l'é-tourdissement des paysages et des ruines, l'amertume des symapthie inter-rompues.
>
> Il revint.
>
> Il fréquenta le monde et il eut d'autres amours encore.[43]

There is nothing more conventional: thus the reader comes to believe more in the seemingly "impersonal" narrative discourse than in the risk-free adventures of traveling. But, as a rule, things are more complicated in Flaubert's novels than to allow for such an unambiguous—and somehow self-complacent—reaction. Indeed the novel features the very extensive description of an excursion from Paris to Fontainebleau (a "journey" by mid-nineteenth-century standards) that Frédéric undertakes with the charming Rosanette, whose favors he shares with Monsieur Arnoux and many other friends. Catered by the emerging tourist industry, Frédéric and Rosanette have every opportunity—and all the time of the world—to experience as an expansion of their inner selves the landscape through which they drive in a coach and the forests through which they walk on foot. But the ample descriptions of that landscape provided by the novel mostly remain, quite strangely, between the discourse of romantic projection and the scientific language of botany. Here is what Frédéric and Rosanette see (and cannot see) from their carriage:

> La diversité des arbres faisait un spectacle changeant. Les hêtres, à l'écorce blanche et lisse, entremêlaient leurs couronnes; des frênes courbaient molle-ment leurs glauques ramures; dans les cépées de charmes, des houx pareils à du bronze se hérissaient; puis venait une file de minces bouleaux, inclinés dans des attitudes élégiaques; et les pins, symétriques comme des tuyaux d'orgue, en se balançant, semblaient chanter.[44]

The grotesque (rather than subtle) ambiguity of such passages makes for the protagonists' awkward relationship to nature. They both know of the obligation for cultivated people to experience nature as an expansion of

---

[43] Ibid., 419.

[44] Ibid., 326.

their souls and as a refuge from society. But they also seem to be aware—and embarrassed to feel—that the moment of such saturated *correspondance* never arrives. Nervously they fill this void with any topic of conversation: "Et ils causaient de n'importe quoi, des choses qu'ils savaient parfaitement, de personnes qui ne les intéressaient pas, de mille niaiseries."[45] All of this culminates in an unbeatably stupid and desperately sad feeling: "Ils se croyaient presque au milieu d'un voyage en Italie"—which makes these most banal of all romanesque lovers appear, all of a sudden, as the victims of romanticism. Perhaps they would just have had sex on their *promenade* and quite happily—had it not been for those impossible (and therefore torturing) expectations that romantic poems and novels can produce.

Flaubert marks, I believe, the end of that short historical interval during which the novel—at least sometimes—describes as landscape the roads that its heroes are walking. From the angle of narrative economy, it is easy to explain how and why this happens. Describing the road as landscape was an effective—because implicit—way to emphasize that the road had ceased to be the space where all those adventures emerged that helped the protagonist to become a strong subject. Above all, however, it was a way to show that the road—as landscape—did not even offer a position of self-indulgent solitude and refuge to the individual anymore. The road as landscape was thus the topos for a double self-disillusionment—the self-disillusionment of the strong modern subject and the self-disillusionment of its ecstatic variation, the romantic individual.

But this is only one layer of the cultural history to be told in this context. Another layer is the discovery of nature as landscape in the late eighteenth and early nineteenth centuries, when—thanks to multiple technological, economic, and political innovations—nature no longer needed to be experienced as a threat and could therefore turn into an object of desire and projection.[46] Finally, if the appearance of the road as landscape indeed stands for the noncorrespondence, for the recently discovered incommensurability between nature—as matter—and the cosy projections of the human psyche, then a potential relationship needs to be taken into account between the appearance of the road as landscape in the novel and some of the most passionate philosophical debates of that time. Those were debates about the

---

[45] Ibid., 328.

[46] See, among many other publications on this topic, the brilliant essay by the philosopher Joachim Ritter, "Landschaft: Zur Funktion des Aesthetischen in der modernen Gesellschaft," in *Subjektivitaet: Sechs Aufsaetze* (Frankfurt on Main, 1974), 141–63.

compatibility or incompatibility between world-appropriation through concepts and world-appropriation through the human senses.[47]

Agent Roads

There are not many roads leading through the *Les Rougon-Macquart*, the sequence of twenty novels that Emile Zola dedicated to his obsessive experiment of explaining and exploring the determination of collective and individual agency by the double influence of genetic heritage and social environment. As each environment whose spatial articulation Zola describes needs to function, in his narrative design, as an agent that determines specific forms of human behavior, he has a preference for those patterns and topics that suggest a stable relationship between the milieu and his protagonists: this is why the coal mine and its workers, for example, the stock exchange and its brokers, the battlefield and its soldiers, or the tavern and its alcoholic proletarians, became some of his most famous motifs. In the few cases, however, where a novel within the Rougon-Macquart series features a road as environment, this road develops the narrative function of an agent road, that is, it becomes a road that does not only define the direction of the protagonists' movements but also—quite miraculously—inspires them with energy. The opening novel of Zola's cycle, *La fortune des Rougons*, narrates the reactions of a southern French town to the future Napoleon III's coup d'état in 1851. Encouraged by a tradition of revolutionary marches from the south to Paris that began in 1790, with the march of the citizens of Marseille to the capital (where they participated in the Fête de la Fédération), the proletarians and the republican intellectuals in Zola's novel join in such a march—which will be brutally repressed by the bourgeois supporters of the new government. But as long as this march of the poor and the powerless is alive, it is the road—the road as a political agent—that defines their enthusiasm and their collective movement:

Le grand chemin, formant chaussée du côté de la rivière, passe au milieu des rocs énormes, entre lesquels se montrent, à chaque pas, des bouts de la vallée. Rien n'est plus sauvage, plus étrangement grandiose, que cette route taillée

---

[47] See, for a detailed account of this historical situation (and for ample bibliographical references), the second chapter of my book *Production of Presence: On the Silent Side of Meaning* (Stanford, Calif., 2003).

dans le flanc même des collines. La nuit surtout, ces lieux ont une horreur
sacrée. . . . Cette nuit-là, la Viorne, au bas des rochers de la route, grondait
d'une voix rauque. Dans ce roulement continue du torrent, les insurgés distinguaient des lamentations aigres du tocsin. Les villages épars dans la plaine,
de l'autre côté de la rivière, se soulevaient, sonnant l'alarme, allumant des
feux. Jusqu'au matin, la colonne en marche, qu'un glas funèbre semblait
suivre dans la nuit d'un tintement obstiné, vit ainsi l'insurrection courir le
long de la vallée comme une trainée de poudre. . . . Ces hommes, qui mar-
chaient dans l'aveuglement de la fièvre que les événements de Paris avaient
mise au coeur des républicains, s'exaltaient au spectacle de cette longue
bande de terre toute secouée de révolte.[48]

Being determined by an environment, as the insurgents in this scene are determined by the road to Paris, always goes along, in Zola's novels, with a loss
of agency. The insurgents thus are marching "in the blindness of a fever"
which will soon explain why their movement will be so brutally repressed.

In the world of the late nineteenth century whose new technologies had
set free new sources and uses of energy, one of the most famous literary emblems for these energies and for the subsequent impression of a loss in human agency was the engine in the final scene of Zola's particularly successful
railroad novel *La bête humaine*. What is suggested to the reader of *La fortune des Rougon* through a complicated network of descriptions and metaphors, is caught in a single image here. After the two engineers have killed
each other in a fight on the running train, the energy of the locomotive is left
as the only power of "agency" that determines the fate of hundreds of passengers (they are mostly soldiers traveling to the battlefield of the Franco-
Prussian War). The novel ends with the terrifying vision of a train without
engineers rushing, faster and faster, through all the stations along its track—
into the night:

Il n'y avait plus de sifflet, à l'approche des signaux, au passage des gares. C'é-
tait le galop tout droit, la bête qui fonçait tête basse et muette, parmi les obstacles. Elle roulait, roulait sans fin, comme affollée de plus en plus par le
bruit strident de son haleine. . . . Qu'importaient les victimes que la machine
écrasait en chemin! N'allait-elle pas quand même à l'avenir, insoucieuse du
sang répandu? Sans conducteur, au milieu des ténèbres, en bête aveugle et

---

[48] Emile Zola, *La fortune des Rougon*, in *Les Rougon-Macquart: Histoire naturelle et sociale
d'une famille sous le second Empire*, ed. Armand Lanoux and Henri Mitterand (Paris, 1960),
1:162–63.

sourde, qu'on aurait lâcheé parmi la mort, elle roulait, elle roulait, chargée de cette chair à canon, de ces soldats, déjà hébétés de fatigue, et ivres, aui chantaient.[49]

Once again, the overpowering energy of the directed movement produces effects of blindness and intoxication. In an allegorical reading, the "future" into which the train without engineers is running, is the one future scenario that Zola feared the most (and was the most fascinated by at the same time): this was the future of a society perverted and destroyed by the effects of unbridled industrialization. Zola saw the war of 1870–71, for which the train in *La bête humaine* provides the cannon fodder, as the self-destruction of a culture fallen to the wildest forms of capitalism; a self-destruction from whose ashes he also hoped the phoenix of a new society would arise.

Only a few decades later, Franz Kafka who, like Emile Zola, was obsessed with the failures of and with our illusions about human agency, would have probably found too much meaning, critique, and political hope in the roads of Zola's novels. The road to the castle in Kafka's *Schloss* certainly is a road with agency—because it constantly both awakes and frustrates K.'s hope to reach the castle and to be received, perhaps, by the anonymous bureaucracy that he imagines to function there. Indeed, the road "takes" K. to the castle and then somehow—he cannot exactly explain how—derails him:

> Es zog ihn unwiderstehlich hin, neue Bekanntschaften zu suchen, aber jede neue Bekanntschaft verstaerkte die Muedigkeit. Wenn er sich in seinem heutigen Zustand zwang, seinen Spaziergang wenigstens bis zum Eingang des Schlosses auszudehnen, war uebergenug getan. So ging er wieder vorwaerts, aber es war ein langer Weg. Die Strasse naemlich, diese Hauptstrasse des Dorfes fuehrte nicht zum Schlossberg, sie fuehrte nur nahe heran, dann aber wie absichtlich bog sie ab und wenn sie sich auch vom Schloss nicht entfernte, so kam sie ihm doch auch nicht naeher. Immer erwartete K., dass nun endlich die Strasse zum Schloss einlenken muesse, und nur weil er es erwartete, ging er weiter.[50]

Decisive in this passage is the adverbial phrase that characterizes the movement of the road "as if it were intentional" ("*wie absichtlich*"). For it explicitly concedes its own, stubborn agency to the road ("*absichtlich*") and it brackets, at the same time, this interpretation by giving it the status of an "as

---

[49] *La bête humaine*, in *Les Rougon-Macquart* (Paris, 1966), 4:1,320–21.
[50] *Das Schloss: Roman*, ed. Malcom Pasley (Frankfurt on Main 1994), 19.

if" ("wie *absichtlich*"). The road in *Das Schloss*, thus, has agency but no meaning—which is a recurrent narrative mode pointing to a philosophical disposition in many European novels of the early twentieth century.

Most of Louis-Ferdinand Céline's books, for example, are travel narratives. But where the roads of Céline's novels will take his protagonists and, above all, with what these roads will confront the protagonists (perhaps I should rather say: "what they will throw at the protagonists") is not brought to a convergence, in any way, with the protagonists' intentions and plans. It is this lack of convergence between the agent roads and their protagonists that produces the impression of a world that is both subject to strong tensions and chaotic. The road that he walks indeed seems "to throw at" the first-person narrator in Céline's novel *Mort à crédit* the corpse of Pereire, the crazy inventor for whom he used to work. And the narrator will see, approach, and describe this person-turned-into-a-thing in all its gory detail, without ever getting derailed in his movement, whose direction remains unclear for the reader (and probably, if one could say so, also to the narrator himself):

> Après une grande traite en plat . . . à travers les molles cultures, c'était une raide escalade à flanc de la colline. . . . Arrivés là, tout là-haut, on découvrait bien par example. . . . pour ainsi dire tout le paysage! . . . De là, du sommet, après la descente et la Druve qui coulait en bas . . . le petit pont et puis le petit corchet de la route. . . . Là j'ai discerné alords en plein . . . au beau milieu de la chaussée une espèce de gros paquet. . . . Y avait pas d'erreur! . . . A peut-être trois kilomètres ça ressortait sur le gravier! . . . Ah! et puis à l'instant même . . . Au coup d'oeil. . . . j'ai su qui c'était. . . . On y est parvenus tout doucement. . . . Mais le sang alors a regiclé . . . recoulé en grand abondance. . . . Son gilet de flanelle c'était plus qu'une grosse gélatine, une bouille dans sa redingote.[51]

If most of the movements, reactions, and actions imposed on the protagonists of twentieth-century novels by these agent roads seem to imply a moment of intense pain, such pain is not always the beginning of an existential crisis. On the contrary, accepted and lived through with composure, such pain will give the suffering protagonist the aura of a true existential hero. This exactly occurs in the closing scene of *Don Segundo Sombra*, Ricardo Güiraldes' classic novel about the intense and quiet life of the Argentinian *gauchos*. Don Segundo Sombra, a gaucho who has become "like an adoptive

---

[51] *Mort à crédit*, in *Céline: Romans*, ed. Henri Godard (Paris, 1981), 1:1,040, 1,043.

father" to the narrator, after an unusually long stay of three years at one farm, gives in to an inner agitation telling him that it is finally time to move on to the next farm. But it will not be Sombra's decision that takes him away from the narrator. The novel lets the road on which they ride appear as the agent of their separation:

El caballo de Don Segundo dio el anca al mío y realicé, en aquella divergencia de dirección, todo lo que iba a separar nuestros destinos. . . . Por el camino, que fingía un arroyo de tierra, caballo y jinete repecharon la loma, difundidos en el cardal. Un momento la silueta doble se perfiló nítida sobre el cielo, sesgado por un verdoso rayo de atardecer. Aquello que se alejaba era más una idea que un hombre.[52]

It is quite banal—but quite inevitable at the end of my essay—to affirm that the emergence of these agent roads in the novels of the past hundred years, in all their variations, must be a symptom (and in many cases, a deliberate expression or even an allegory) of a widely shared loss of optimism about the powers of human agency. Unlike the roads in the novels of the early-modern centuries, the agent roads of our present hardly ever provide adventures that would allow the hero to grow and develop her subjecticity and agency. The events on the agent roads are rather encounters or departures that need to be survived.

But there is another philosophical story that needs to be told if we want to try to understand the most recent movements of the roads in the novel. This is a story about the return of concepts—and "feelings"—like "substance," "matter," and "space" to the stage of Western philosophy and the challenging of the hitherto dominant ways of thinking about human existence that had been centered on concepts like "mind," "time," and "language" since the mid nineteenth century. From the 1920s onward, most critics of the Western philosophy of consciousness have pointed to its tendency—and perhaps to the tendency of modernity at large—of bracketing the dimension of space, which necessarily entails a loss of the world of reference. To be in-the-world, to be in the world as a body, that is, to experience the world in the spatial dimension, has turned into an existential value for many of us. Therefore, agent roads in the novel are not only the literary form of a loss of agency. They also are the literary place where we can recuperate the space that allows us to be-in-the-world.

---

[52] Ricardo Guiraldes, *Don Segundo Sombra*, ed. Angla B. Dellepiane (Madrid, 1990), 382.

Riding in a truck through the southern United States with her newborn baby boy, Lena Grove, the heroine of William Faulkner's novel *Light in August*, feels good about "her body getting around." I am sure that Faulkner did not mean this to be simple-mindedness:

> . . . after a while I says, "Here comes Saulsbury" and she says,
> "What?" and I says,
> "Saulsbury, Tennessee" and I looked back and saw her face. And it was like it was already fixed and waiting to be surprised, and that she knew that when the surprise come, she was going to enjoy it. And it did come and it did suit her. Because she said,
> "My, my. A body does get around. Here we ain't been coming from Alabama but two months, and now it's already Tennessee."[53]

---

[53] *Light in August*, in *William Faulkner: Novels 1930–1935*, ed. Joseph Blotner and Noel Polk (New York, 1985), 774.

MARGARET COHEN

The Chronotopes of the Sea

Nautical and maritime spaces have figured prominently across the develop-ment of the novel, from the form's prehistory in antiquity, with the castaway Odysseus, to its modern genesis with adventurers like Robinson Crusoe, and to modernist works questioning the novel's basic conventions epitomized by Virginia Woolf's *The Waves*. As is the case for all spaces depicted in litera-ture, the seas, rivers, coasts, and islands found in novels are at once geogra-phies and topoi; their contours are shaped by historical reference, and they are rhetorical structures with poetic function and imaginative resonance. In prose fiction, their poetic function is narrative—to help advance the action—as well as to convey theme and content.

Mikhail Bakhtin proposed the notion of the chronotope to characterize the poetic dimension to the literary representation of space, and specifi-cally its poetic dimension within narrative forms. In coining the concept (*chronos* + *topos*), Bakhtin indicates his insight, particularly powerful for narrative, that the representation of space always entails the representation of time and that time and space are intrinsically connected, both as literary and conceptual structures. Reading between the lines of his analysis, it be-comes evident that by time he means at once the time represented in the novel and the time in which its events are narrated, and that the notion of the chronotope encompasses other patterns of narration, such as the charac-ters and plots associated with specific spaces, as well as the emotional re-sponses they solicit from the reader. In addition, Bakhtin suggests that the chronotope is a figure of thought, working at the level of the concept and ideology.

Thus, what Bakhtin calls the chronotope of the road is at once a plot line comprised of random and chance events and encounters linked together with little causal connection; a cast of characters including "the most varied people," who meet on this profoundly social space, and a thematics where encounters collapse hierarchical distances that usually separate people in other areas of society.[1] In writing of antique and medieval romance, Bakhtin isolates a distinct experience of time associated with the chance events of the road that affects both characters and the reader: an "empty" adventure time

---

[1] Mikhail Bakhtin, "Forms of Time and Chronotope in the Novel," in *The Dialogic Imagination*, trans. Caryl Emerson and Michael Holquist (Austin: University of Texas Press, 1981), 243.

that propels two unchanging lovers through an exotic, alien world, which he differentiates from the cumulative, transformative time of biography. Another example of the chronotope making evident its multilayered structure would be the provincial village so important to the nineteenth-century novel, which links everyday, ordinary characters and events with a plot moving in "narrow circles," "devoid of advancing historical development," and unfolding in "commonplace, philistine, cyclical everyday time."[2]

Waterways too take the form of chronotopes when they are represented in literature. Sea spaces have an intriguing affinity with Bakhtin's concept of the chronotope because of the multiple aspects of seafaring where space is experienced as movement, as a vector conjoining spatial and temporal coordinates. Robert Foulke explains:

> Space and time have always merged more obviously at sea than they do in much of human experience. The simple act of laying out a ship's track on a chart by using positions determined on successive days connects time and space visibly. The nautical mile, spatially equivalent to one minute of latitude, is also the basis of the knot, a measure of speed in elapsed time. Until late in the eighteenth century, European navigators calculated their position by deduced reckoning, measuring the number of miles they had sailed a particular course by combining time and speed. The invention of reliable chronometers made more precise celestial navigation possible by interlocking measurements of time and space in a more sophisticated way. Before the era of electronic global positioning systems, to find longitude one had to have a precise reading of the time at Greenwich, England. Then to get an accurate fix of the ship's position, one added a spatial measurement, by taking the altitude of the sun at noon or of a star at dawn or dusk.[3]

The sea thus has a particular affinity with narrative representations of space, which exist as movement as well, and which make evident space's dependence on temporal parameters, its intrinsic temporality. Hence, perhaps, the important role narrative forms have historically played in seafaring, including the tradition of pilot's manuals dating at least to the Middle Ages, which guide mariners on their voyages using a verbal narrative of visual landmarks and lengths of time to be expected; the ship's log, where the officer frames the events and course of a voyage as a daily journal; and the oral tradition of the "tale" and "yarn," that common sailors use to recount their travels.

---

[2] Ibid., 248.

[3] Robert Foulke, *The Sea Voyage Narrative* (New York: Twayne, 1997), 9–10.

There are six waterside chronotopes across the history of the English and French literary traditions that date back to the novel's prehistory in antique forms. These chronotopes are (1) *blue water*, the open sea; (2) *brown water*, the murky depths of the river; (3) *white water*, when bodies of water are riled up into extreme natural danger; (4) *the island*, land entirely surrounded by water; (5) *the shore*, a zone of contact between land and sea; and (6) *the ship*, an unstable piece of terra firma that propels humans across the sea's inhospitable territory. Bakhtin speculates that chronotopes have "relative typological stability" and may even be sufficiently distinct narrative patterns to provide the basis of a genre.[4] But the chronotopes of the sea prove to be remarkably constant across different subgenres of the novel, from adventure fiction to domestic and sentimental fiction, from the early-modern to the modernist novel. They are stable across each of these subgenre's historical transformations as well. The stability of maritime chronotopes extends beyond the novel to poetry and nonfictional travel writings. Such continuity suggests that they are structured by intrinsic aspects of the spaces they represent. It also points to the power of preexisting rhetorical patterns to organize the perception and representation of fact as well as fiction.

The chronotopes of the sea retain their characteristic traits across different geographies, though these geographies add symbolic and often historically located significance. Throughout the eighteenth century, for example, the Atlantic region is associated with the workaday world of early-modern capitalism. So powerful is this association that, when Defoe embodies the spirit of capitalism in Crusoe, he relocates his shipwrecked mariner from the Juan Fernando Island off the coast of Chile in the Pacific, where the historical prototype of Crusoe was abandoned, to an island off the mouth of the Orinoco River near Trinidad. Defoe further pinpoints the trade routes of the early-modern Atlantic at issue in his narrative with the name of his novel's protagonist that he substitutes for the Scottish sailor, Selkirk, on whom Crusoe is patterned. Crusoe evokes the Dutch island Curaçao, or Curasoe, as Defoe himself spelled the island in another novel of seafaring, *The Adventures of Captain Singleton*.

Bakhtin's essay makes clear that the scale of the chronotope is quite flexible. It can structure an entire novel, or it can structure a single episode. Like other rhetorical figures, chronotopes exist at the level of a literary field and tradition rather than a single work. Prose narratives pass through them and dwell in them with differing degrees of intensity. The chronotopes of the sea have such flexibility. While Defoe's *Robinson Crusoe* brings together brown

---

[4] Bakhtin, *Dialogic Imagination*, 85.

water, blue water, white water, the ship, the shore, and the island, and also contains the land-based space of the road, Melville's *Moby Dick* is almost entirely defined by the interaction of the ship with blue water and white water, and the shore structures only one episode within Austen's *Persuasion*. Yet there is continuity in the narrative dynamic and symbolic resonance of each of these chronotopes of the sea when it is invoked.

Given the range of works where chronotopes of the sea figure, the question arises how most effectively to illustrate their contours: by citing across the broad range of texts where they are found or by an in-depth analysis of one text where they appear in distilled form? I've chosen an intermediate strategy, which is to reference a limited corpus composed of some of the best-known examples of these chronotopes. I do so to give a sense that they extend beyond a single text, without, however, swamping the reader with distracting details. It should not be forgotten that the chronotopes of the sea appear in other texts besides those I mention, and that there is flexibility and play in their specific realization, rather than static conformity.

Blue Water

Blue water is the realm of the open ocean containing immense and violent powers of weather, terrain (currents, tide, water depth), monstrous animals, and aggressive warriors, as well as pirates and adventurers seeking gain in unpoliced zones beyond the control of sovereign and law. On blue water, individual characters test their agency by meeting these violent forces and struggling to survive the clash among them. In Hans Blumenberg's estimation, the fundamental imaginative significance of the sea is to form "a naturally given boundary of the realm of human activities," sometimes demonized as "the unreckonable and lawless, on which it is difficult to find one's bearings."[5] The lawless disorder of blue water takes shape in productive tension with the chronotope of the ship, which is a rigid, hierarchically regulated space, as discussed below.

The kinds of events that occur on blue water have affinities with the chance encounters that Bakhtin associates with the chronotope of the road. The depths of the sea reveal the unexpected, but while the random disorder of the road contains only the full scope of one's society, the scale of blue water increases exponentially to the level of the cosmos. We may grasp the

---

[5] Hans Blumenberg, *Shipwreck with Spectator*, trans. Steven Rendall (Cambridge, Mass.: MIT Press, 1997), 8.

specificity of blue water by examining the plausibility of events situated there. Plausibility is a narrative criterion that brings plot sequencing and the delineation of character together with reader expectation. In Bakhtin's chronotope of the road, events have the plausibility of actual social existence, but the unthinkable is the limit for the open sea. This is the case from antiquity to the twentieth century, whether the encounter is with the enchanted monsters of *The Odyssey* and the haphazard marauders of classical romance, or with natural monsters that cross the boundaries of species in the disenchanted world of the modern novel, like the vengeful white whale of *Moby Dick* endowed with almost human psychology, or the prototype of *l'informe*, the demonic octopus in Hugo's *Les travailleurs de la mer*. The unthinkable on blue water also includes terrifying weather and the monstrosities of second nature, like the destructive hulk randomly surging from the depths in Conrad's *Lord Jim*. Blumenberg points out that the sea's defiance of expectation and causality is the logical expression of its fundamental lawlessness. Blumenberg writes, "in the purest forms, odysseys are an expression of arbitrariness."[6]

Conrad made ample use of implausibility in his blue-water moments, and commented on this aspect of blue water as he invoked the convention. The occasion for *Typhoon* is a storm presaged by a barometer reading in which the mercury drops lower than the seasoned captain has ever seen it. As the storm starts to reveal its horrible power, the narrator comments about the first mate Jukes: "His distress was by no means alleviated by an inclination to disbelieve the reality of this experience. Though young, he had seen some bad weather, and had never doubted his ability to imagine the worst; but this was so much beyond his powers of fancy that it appeared incompatible with the existence of any ship whatever."[7] Jukes's reaction captures two aspects of the implausible events situated on blue water that might seem contradictory but in fact reinforce each other. Exceeding the powers of the imagination as well as conventional plausibility, the extravagance of blue-water happenings is not a mark of their fanciful status, as in some literary contexts. Rather it is testimony to their existence: blue-water events are strange *and therefore* true. Nowhere is this use of the strange to prove the true more fertile than in the importance of blue-water adventuring in Verne's invention of science fiction, epitomized by Captain Nemo's undersea world of marvelous technology in *Vingt mille lieues sous les mers*.

---

[6] Ibid., 8.

[7] Joseph Conrad, *Typhoon* in *Three Sea Stories,* ed. Keith Carabine (Hertfordshire: Wordsworth Classics, 1998), 36.

The high degree of implausibility—this quality of "strange and therefore true"—is one of the importance differences between the chronotope of blue water and novelistic depictions of life in land-based domestic and high society. From the beginnings of the modern novel, critics have invoked plausibility as the goal of psychological and sentimental fiction, notably. Debates about the merits of Lafayette's *La Princesse de Clèves* (1678) when the novel first appeared focused on whether its heroine could plausibly have made an effort to resist the seductions of her perfect lover, Nemours, by telling her husband of her adulterous passion. But the violations of expectation that are provocative in the salon or drawing room are the norm on the open sea. Rather then worthy of representation because they are plausible, blue-water events are "strange," "noteworthy," and "remarkable," qualities that *The Life and Strange, Surprizing Adventures of Robinson Crusoe* shares with nonfictional narratives of discovery and exploration, from *The Strange and Dangerous Voyage of Captain Thomas James, in his intended Discovery of the Northwest Passage into the South Sea. Wherein the Miseries indured both Going, Wintering, Returning; and the Rarities observed, both* Philosophical *and* Mathematicall, *are related* to the "Remarkable Occurrences on Board his Majesty's Bark Endeavor," the subtitle of Captain Cook's *First Voyage.* These remarkable events may transcend the distinction between history and romance, as is the case of Captain Johnson's "history full of surprising turns and adventures," of the cross-dressing female pirates, Anne Bonny and Mary Read, in his *General History of the Pirates,* whose "rambling lives," full of "odd incidents," "are such that some may be tempted to think the whole story no better than a novel or romance; but since it is supported by many thousand witnesses, I mean the people of Jamaica who were present at their trials . . . the truth of it can no[t] . . . be contested."[8]

One notable implausible aspect of blue water is that the unfathomable and ungovernable zone of the open sea is not altogether arbitrary. While beyond human laws, it is subject to natural laws that have their own predictability. When we see Ahab, "threading a maze of currents and eddies," the narrator remarks that "to any one not fully acquainted with the ways of leviathans, it might seem an absurdly hopeless task thus to seek one solitary creature in the unhooped oceans of this planet. But not so did it seem to Ahab, who knew the sets of all tides and currents; and thereby calculating

---

[8] Captain Charles Johnson, *General History of the Pirates* (London: Creation Books, 1999), 30. Whether Johnson was the pen name of Daniel Defoe has been the subject of debate throughout the twentieth century. Scholars generally now believe that Defoe authored at least substantial portions of the work, if not all of it.

the driftings of the sperm whale's food; and, also, calling to mind the regular, ascertained seasons for hunting him, in particular latitudes, could arrive at reasonable surmises, almost approaching to certainties, concerning the timeliest day to be upon this or that ground in search of his prey."[9] The characters who are able to decipher such natural laws can only do so with long experience. Their experience is gained from hands-on practice. It is not a knowledge found in books, and is often opposed to it. It yields itself only to those who are strong enough to engage the overwhelming powers of blue water and survive its dangers.

This survival skill is beyond conventional morality; indeed, seafaring narratives valued survival of the fittest long before Darwin set sail on *The Beagle*. It is a skill based in deeds and violence, though strength is not sufficient in an environment containing so many overwhelming powers. Protagonists who survive have luck, combined with cunning and resourcefulness. They are epitomized by Odysseus and Nemo, characters who, like Captain Johnson's pirates are "pistol proof," evincing the ability to live, in Johnson's words, "beyond the line." In Conrad, this skill has been tempered by professionalism and aesthetics to become "the fine art," "the craft," "the right stuff."

In an environment where heroism takes the form of action, language approaches as closely as possible to action as well. A captain's words to his crew are offered with performative intent, to direct them in executing maneuvers. Treatises on navigation written to guide pilots are set in the present and future tense of action in the process of unfolding, rather than couched as descriptions of what the writer has himself seen. The pressure to close the gap between words and deeds is also evident in the diction of blue-water narratives, whether fictional or nonfictional, which are characterized by dynamic sentences, full of verbs, and a zero-degree figuration. Centuries before the author of *The Old Man and the Sea* was calling for a language of action, critics who objected to the enduring vogue for sea voyage literature, like François Misson, parodied the "plain style" of blue-water adventuring: *"We cast Anchor: We made ready to Sail. The Wind took Courage. Robin is Dead. We said Mass. We Vomited."*[10]

Heroism in action is an attribute of adventure forms, and unfolds in what Bakhtin has characterized as a curiously "empty" "adventure" time. For Bakhtin, "adventure time" is empty because it changes nothing in the life of

---

[9] Herman Melville, *Moby Dick* (New York: Library of America, 1983), 1,004.

[10] Quoted in Michael McKeon, *The Origins of the English Novel* (Baltimore: Johns Hopkins University Press, 1987), 114.

its protagonists; it is a time outside the markers of biographical history and contrasts with the developmental time of bildungsroman forms. The natural correlate of this emptiness is the physical geography of blue water, which remains unmodified by human projects and constructions. Blumenberg writes of Goethe's interest in "the metaphor of ships' course across the sea that disappears without a trace," which Goethe used to express the Enlightenment's overvaluation of its accomplishments.[11] Goethe declares, "It was maintained that the path had been opened, forgetting that in earthly things a path can very rarely be spoken of . . . as the water that is dislodged by a ship instantly flows in again behind it."[12]

Though the emptiness of adventure time may seem impoverished to readers used to the progressive psychology common in realist fiction, Bakhtin points out that it serves a poetic function, which is to affirm protagonists' stability, their "identity, their durability and continuity."[13] In the episodes of testing so important to romance and adventure forms, the work of the narrative is to show characters' virtue as resistant to change, no matter what the situation. This affirmation of the character's virtue through testing is true for blue-water adventuring as well, though with the resourcefulness of Odysseus, Robinson Crusoe, or the Pilot, virtue takes on an ambiguous cast. It approaches the amoral strength of what Nietzsche calls the superman in his writings filled with references to seafaring. Gramsci was unknowingly responding to the protagonists of blue water, when he commented that Nietzsche's superman reaches back through Balzac to "le bas romantisme"—for in fact Balzac and Dumas both get their supermen from Byron's pirates, as mediated by the heroes of the newly minted genre of sea fiction, like the brooding John Paul Jones in Cooper's inaugural *The Pilot*, or the forthright *fils du people*, Paul, and the dark, mysterious Szaffie in Eugène Sue's tale of shipwreck and cannibalism, *Le salamandre*.[14] Though supermen usually are loners, they sometimes come together in elective communities joined by common temperament and aims. Members of this community share a radical equality that can suspend differences in status, wealth, blood, race, and even gender, as resourcefulness in the face of danger forges what Conrad terms "the bond of the sea."

---

[11] Blumenberg, *Shipwreck*, 58.

[12] Goethe, *Aus meinem Leben: Dichtung und Wahrheit*, 3, 15, cited in Blumenberg, *Shipwreck*, 58.

[13] Bakhtin, *Dialogic Imagination*, 107.

[14] Antonio Gramsci, *Quaderni del carcere* (Turin: Giulo Einaudi, 1975), quad. 14, sec. 4, pp. 1,657–58. A French version of Gramsci's comments is currently available online at http://www.marxists.org/francais/gramsci/intell/intell3.htm (accessed October 2005).

The nature of that resourcefulness ranges across ethical systems and cultures. On the "wine dark sea" of the enchanted Mediterranean, Odysseus employs mortal cunning against mythical forces. For Robinson Crusoe, the struggle on blue water entails the war of all against all in the pursuit of wealth. For the Pilot, as throughout the era of political liberalism (mideighteenth to midnineteenth centuries), blue water's lack of constraints makes it a zone where the individual can pursue his or her private and political freedom. Byron captures this aspect of the "dark blue sea" in the pirate's song that opens *The Corsair*:

> O'er the glad waters of the dark blue sea,
> Our thoughts as boundless, and our souls as free
> Far as the breeze can bear, the billows foam,
> Survey our empire, and behold our home!
> These are our realms, no limits to their sway—
> Our flag the sceptre all who meet obey.
> Ours the wild life in tumult still to range
> From toil to rest, and joy in every change.[15]

At the turn of the twentieth century, literary modernism makes the freedom of blue water artistic freedom in rebellion against stifling, ossified hierarchies, like the freedom from both colonial oppression and outmoded poetics sought by Joyce's Stephen Dedalus. Virginia Woolf associates blue-water freedom with textuality's ability to subvert the oppressive hierarchies of form. In *To the Lighthouse* and *The Waves*, the sea of language sweeps away the patterns of the novel of manners—biographical time, linear narrative, even the syntax of prose.

Brown Water

The tension between home and the wide world structures the genre of the novel from its prehistory. River water gives this tension elemental form as it derives its distinctive muddy aspect from the homebound earth found in the river banks and riverbed, mixed with the river's water that flows to the open oceans. The river also connects the earth of home and the great waters of the wide world in its linear flow. This connection is evident whether

---

[15] Byron, "The Corsair," in *Lord Byron: The Complete Poetical Works*, ed. Jerome McGann (New York: Oxford University Press, 1981), 150.

the protagonist follows the river to the ocean, the promise Stephen Guest offers Maggie Tulliver in his fluvial seduction in Eliot's *The Mill on the Floss*, or whether the protagonist fights against its current to find the way back to home, family, and origins, from Heliodorus's *Ethiopian Romance* to Conrad's *Heart of Darkness*.

The tidal reaches of the river flow in both directions, like the lower Thames, where Conrad sets the narration of *Heart of Darkness*, "crowded with memories of men and ships it has borne to the rest of home and the battles of the sea."[16] In the remainder of the novel, Marlowe will struggle upriver in a search for hidden origins, though in Kurtz's savagery, he uncovers the regressive secret not of an individual or family, but rather of the modern world system. This social inflection of brown water is, in fact, common in the nineteenth century, particularly when processes of modernization are at issue. Then the landed space of home and the wide world of blue-water adventuring, both contrasted and connected in the river's flow, become the opposition between an upriver retreat from a premodern lifestyle and a downriver space associated with various aspects of social modernity (technology, industrialization, urbanization).

The journey upriver against the current recalls the dynamics of the plot of suspense that, as Roland Barthes has explained, works through the tension between the reader's pushing forward in her desire to know the outcome of the story and the resistance of plot points that defer its resolution. It is thus fitting that the journey upriver often pushes toward uncovering a secret, even in plots otherwise utterly lacking in suspense, from the time that Heliodorus's Chariclea journeyed upriver to the source of the Nile in Ethiopia to discover the secret of her birth, after a picaresque career of adventuring around the Mediterranean basin (*Ethiopian Romance*). In the nineteenth century, this struggle upriver toward the mysteries of origin can also be flipped ninety degrees to become a vertical descent into the depths of the river's secrets, particularly in narratives of urban life. In a novel like Dickens's *Our Mutual Friend*, the traffic of the modern city streams around and on the river's surface, while the riverbed is a chthonic realm of death that harbors the mysteries of family secrets and regressive, primal passions.

White Water

In the flood at the end of Eliot's *Mill on the Floss*, humans encounter the deadly power of the violent and dangerous forces harbored by waterside

---

[16] Joseph Conrad, *Heart of Darkness* (New York, W. W. Norton, 1988), 8.

spaces fully unleashed. This is the chronotope of white water, a moment when the violence of maritime elements gets so excessive that it throws the narrative into a crisis threatening its breakdown, whether it is the power of the mythic creatures animating the whirlpool of Scylla and the storms of Poseidon, the power of nature in the storms that threaten sailors from Crusoe to Conrad's Captain Allistoun, or the human violence manifested in sea battles like the battle for Cartagena in Smollett's *Roderick Random*.

In the crisis situation of white water, the characters who seek to defy the overwhelming force massed against them by matching it strength for strength are headed for certain death, like Melville's Ahab. If they do survive, it will be by themselves going beyond the limit of what is human, like the sailors who resort to cannibalism on board Sue's *Le Salamandre*. The best chance in white water is to exercise what Blumenberg calls "Descartes's 'provisional morality' ": to stay the course, fusing cunning and determination with the flexibility to change tactics, and a large dose of humility before superior powers.[17] When Odysseus is caught in a ferocious storm in book 5, he successfully modulates his defiance of mythic forces and obeys a water nymph who bids him throw her girdle back into the water after she rescues him. At the other end of the tradition, Conrad's MacWirr altogether lacks imagination, but has the perseverance to make his voice heard, however imperfectly, above the gale, and to steer a steady course, once he has engaged his vessel in a typhoon it would have been prudent to avoid.

The whiteness of white water traverses natural states, from liquid, the white crests of waves and the white foam of the whirlpool's "sullen white surf" of Melville's vortex that swallows the *Pequod*;[18] to solid, white water frozen to the ice floes that trap Captain Nemo when Verne imagines him conquering the South Pole in 1869; to vapor, the "blind whiteness of the fog" that threatens the steamer going up the Congo in *Heart of Darkness*;[19] to organic matter, the whiteness of the corpse in the illnesses that devastate ships' crews epitomized by the nightmare allegory "Life in Death" in Coleridge's *Rime of the Ancient Mariner*. This natural white, both the origin of all the colors and their absence, is an alternative to the schematic use of white in Western moralities. In its natural state, white is beyond morality, just as it demands an ethos of action beyond a black-and-white notion of good and bad. The existence of a natural white that would be an amoral alternative to the use of whiteness in schematic moralities is of great interest to Melville. *Moby Dick* devotes an entire chapter to "The Whiteness of the

---

[17] Blumenberg, *Shipwreck*, 15.
[18] Melville, *Moby Dick*, 1,407.
[19] Conrad, *Heart of Darkness*, 43.

Whale," which offers a series of searching questions about moral relativism and the arbitrariness of meaning. In this chapter, white becomes "a colorless all-color" and a quintessence for resistance of all sorts.[20]

In keeping with its status on the edge, white water is not only a dangerous space but a dangerous time, a representation of time as crisis. In contrast to the empty time of blue-water adventuring, the time of white water is full, indeed almost to the point of overflowing the container of the narrative. It is a moment when time is experienced by the protagonists as in short supply, when timing is all, when a maneuver must be made under the impending threat of death. The phenomenology of this crisis time is complex, not just the sudden rupture of the storm, but also the stasis of being becalmed, immobilized in ice, or disoriented in a blinding fog.

The chronotope of white water further heightens the reader's sense of crisis time in its use of suspense, which draws attention to the urgency of time in the telling of the tale, on the level of *discours*. In the dangers of white water, the time of narration dilates, and the narrative's continued progress becomes a gamble, hanging on the outcome of a risky maneuver. Dramatizing the danger of time, suspense performs on the level of poetics the power of the forces with which the heroes struggle in white-water content. A good example of a white-water episode that uses suspense to connect *discours* and *récit* would be the section "Lack of Air," in Verne's *Vingt mille lieues sous les mers*, where Nemo must free his submarine from a cube of freezing ice. The substance of this episode is Nemo's race to find an escape route before the *Nautilus* is crushed by the impinging ice or the air within the vessel runs out. Its structure is the countdown, as the reader is teased with stratagem after stratagem punctuated by the ticking clock.

White water, of course, figures prominently in the Romantic conception of the sublime, and the related notion of the oceanic, where pleasure is derived from the prospect of terror, boundlessness, and obscurity. But within the narrative chronotope of white water, characters do not enjoy the contemplative distance necessary for the sublime. A character's removed and aesthetic stance toward the struggle to survive would be a road to certain death. Readers, of course, can savor the power of the elements unleashed in white water, but then the divide opens between the position of the reader and the danger of the representation. The most self-conscious poets of the sea have dwelt in this metamoment of white water, whether it is the whiteness of the blank page organizing the tension between tale and explanation

---

[20] Melville, *Moby Dick*, 1,001.

in Coleridge's *Rime of the Ancient Mariner* or the unbridgeable gap between words and deeds that Melville called "the deadly space between" in *Billy Budd*.

The Island

The island is a piece of land defined by its relation to water. From a land-based perspective, the island appears a prime "empty" space of orientalist discourse, a fresh, untouched realm that can be shaped as it serves the metropolis: to offer a utopian counterpart to its injustices and problems, and/or to be conquered and cultivated to further its aims. Located within the chronotopic network of the sea, what is salient about the island is its tempered vision of nature, contrasting with the unleashed violence of nature in blue and white water. On the island, nature appears a harmonious and pliable force; moderated in temperate zones by ocean currents like the Gulf Stream and cooled in the tropics by the trade winds. In such a temperate environment, the cunning and know-how that are survival skills on blue water can be directed toward the project of construction. When resourceful adventurers like Crusoe come to the island, they discover a laboratory for transforming nature into wealth and beauty.

There are islands that remain untransformed, and some islands translate to land the brutal version of nature as the struggle for survival found on blue water. But more often, the island's temperate environment provides the occasion to construct an ideal society dedicated to moderation. Such a society expands until it reaches an equilibrium of needs and their satisfaction, in keeping with the island's moderated climate. More's *Utopia* was located on an island, as was Crusoe's desolate prison that he turned into a fruitful bower. The social orders constructed on these islands are generally balanced and moderated as well. They erase oppressive social inequalities, though not difference and inequality per se. Rather, difference and inequality are represented as gentle and natural, in keeping with the environment. Crusoe initiates Friday into the benefits of European civilization and Bernardin de Saint-Pierre's Paul and Virginie treat their slaves as their family.

Island time resets the historical clock to zero, enabling protagonists to establish their ideal society working from this new origin. Yet the vision of that origin is as historical as the specific vision of island society, and both shift with social context. This context is often implicit; sometimes, it surfaces in one of the challenges of the island, which is to tame what might be called the *genius loci*, a character or characters who express the island's difference from the mainland society. These characters can be savages or supernatural creatures; they can also be outlaws from mainland society. Thus the ideology of a liberal era dominated by a contractual view of social obligations surfaces negatively when the island harbors outlaws who defy the social contract, adhering to a presocial view of life as ruled, in Rousseau's words, by "the right to what tempts . . . and one can take," like the pirates in Stevenson's *Treasure Island.* Long John Silver's buffoonish associates, however, offer a good example of how the moderation of the island environment extends to its dangers, which are toned down just enough to make them subduable, in this case by a boy hero. If the island has held an ongoing attraction for children's writers, it may well be because of the safety of its tempered environment, opening an ideal space for children's play.

Ticking away off the clock of world history, island time sees change and growth, but it has a repetitive quality; it is lacking in fullness and differentiation. This repetitive quality comes from the fact that work on a controlled environment has a certain predictability, despite its challenges.[21] The predictability is experienced by characters when they have achieved their equilibrium of needs and desires, and it is felt by the reader, when she realizes that the challenges will be surmounted and the character will survive. But it is already present in embryo form on islands that are self-contained natural settings, where nothing comes from outside. Crusoe indicates the tedium of this self-containment in the very shape he gives to the days when he realizes that he might "lose my Reckoning of Time for want of books and Pen and Ink, and even forget the Sabbath Days from the working Days; but to prevent this, I cut it with my Knife upon a large Post, in Capital Letters. . . . Upon this square Post I cut every Day a Notch with my Knife, and every seventh Month was as long again as the rest, and every first Day of the Month as long again as the long, and thus I kept my Kalander."[22] Time that can change everything would seem to have its own emptiness as island time flips around and reveals its affinity with the adventure time that changes nothing in the character of its protagonists. This repetitive time is represented both as alluring (land of the lotus eaters), and oppressive. Crusoe consistently experiences his island as at once a self-sufficient society, with harmony in its equilibrium, and a prison.

---

[21] Diana Loxley notes the homogeneous nature of island time when she writes that *Treasure Island* permitted "unconstrained scope for heroic action in a 'neutral' environment." In *Problematic Shores: The Literature of Islands* (New York: St. Martin's Press, 1990), 149.

[22] Daniel Defoe, *The Life and Strange, Surprizing Adventures of Robinson Crusoe of York, Mariner* (New York: Oxford University Press, 1999), 65–66.

On the level of *discours*, the problem is how to produce events that maintain the reader's interest. Once the island community matures, the novelist has no more story to tell, unless its harmony is disrupted. This disruption generally comes from across the water and appears on the island via the chronotope of the shore (see below), as is epitomized by the fateful turning point in Cruose's exile: "It happen'd one Day about Noon going towards my Boat, I was exceedingly surpriz'd with the Print of a Man's naked Foot on the shore. . . . I stood like one Thunder-struck, or as if I had seen an Apparition."[23] The shore can bring white water, or the hierarchical social order left behind on the mainland via the intermediary of the ship. In *Paul et Virginie*, it is hierarchies that come from France to reawaken the social chasm between the illegitimate Paul and the highly born Virginie.[24]

The Shore

The shore is an intensely social space that bears some resemblance to the chronotope of the road, which, according to Bakhtin, is characterized by the encounters of habitually separated groups, who inhabit the same world but that social stratification keeps apart. On the shore, the scope of that social world expands from one society or even several societies to include people from all over the globe, and, indeed, all who take human form, even if they have no place to call home, or traffic in the supernatural: pirates, renegades and castaways, demigods, and magicians. In promoting the contact between different members of the same social world, the shore offers a good example of what Pratt calls "a contact zone," a liminal space of meeting that has its own identity even as it is shaped by the distinctive cultures it brings together. As a liminal zone, the shore bears some relation to blue water, with its disorder and affinity for monsters that cross the boundary between species. On blue water, however, monstrous creatures like great white whales and cut-throat pirates flourish, while the shore is a place where the boundaries are tested, only to be reaffirmed rather than dissolved.

Shore encounters test boundaries by mixing danger and desire. Social difference produces fascination, whether the encounter is across culture and

---

[23] Ibid., 155.

[24] When Virginie and Paul get lost within their island paradise and discover slavery, they reveal how Bernardin has constructed a mise en abîme of his island, making it an island within an island. The larger Ile Maurice turns out to be a colony reproducing the oppressive social hierarchies found on the mainland rather than an escape from them.

race—think of Crusoe's attraction to Friday, or attraction across class—think of Roderick Random's meeting with a gentlewoman's daughter when he is shipwrecked and washed up on the beach. In *Persuasion*, Austen is invoking the chronotope of the shore when she has Captain Wentworth's misplaced flirtation with Lydia come to a head not only in a walk along the beach at Lime Regis, but in Lydia's jump from a wall, a structure where the boundary takes on architectural existence, and where the danger attending its transgression poses a physical threat to the body. Physical danger is underscored when the chronotope of the shore is absorbed into novels of urban anomie that thrive from the nineteenth century onward. From the Thames in Dickens's *Our Mutual Friend* to the port city of Brest where Genet's *Querelle* cruises in search of victims, the city's docklands and quays become the gateway to violent death in some way linked to boundary transgression.

The association of boundary transgression with bodily harm looms in the fear of cannibals that surfaces when ships approach non-European shores. As anthropologists have made clear, cannibalism challenges the ability to draw boundaries in a number of different ways. These ways range from the physical dismemberment of the human body—Crusoe speaks with Horror of "the Shore spread with Skulls, Hands, Feet and other Bones of humane bodies"—to the way in which cannibalism throws into question the authority of European culture's transcendent value system.[25] Montaigne made this point in his essay on cannibals, and Crusoe reiterates it with his realization that "the People were not Murtheres in the Sense that I had before condemned them, in my Thoughts; any more than those Christians were Murtheres who often put to Death the Prisoners taken in Battle."[26]

The danger of boundary dissolution is in keeping with the geology of littoral territories, whose unstable contours are affected by the tides and subject to erosion from the water and wind. In the chronotope of the shore, as in fact, these territories take multiple forms. The beach is the most common version, but in a text like *Les travailleurs de la mer,* Hugo dwells on the variety of specific geological formations that are the edge between land and sea, nuancing their symbolic resonances. The sea cliffs where little boys steal the eggs of wild birds and risk falling to their deaths is a moderated version of shoreline danger in comparison with the great reef on which Clubin mistakenly wrecks the steamboat, *Durande*. An expression of the hideous "informe" of blue water, the reef at the same time locates its "ruche d'hydres," opening

[25] Defoe, *Crusoe*, 166.
[26] Ibid., 172.

a circumscribed theater of action within blue-water flux, where its monsters can be challenged and dominated by the cunning fisherman, Gilliat.[27]

In Hugo's text, the dangers of boundary transgression prove, however, to be inescapable. Even though Gilliat succeeds in freeing the engine of the *Durande* from the reef, all his prudence and skill does not enable him to abolish class stratification and win the love of the steamboat owner's lovely daughter. Déruchette prefers instead a parson higher on the class ladder who corresponds to her bourgeois fantasies of romantic love, driving Gilliat to suicide. In keeping with the enchantment exercised by the young woman who is the occasion for his mortal encounter with the dangers of boundary transgression, Gilliat chooses to die on a shoreline site where these dangers take enchanting guise. He seats himself in La Chaise Gild-Holm-Ur, a rock on the sea coast where the viewer can savor the vast panorama of the open horizon, enjoy the wind, and feel conquered by "l'assoupissement de l'extase," until the rising tide swamps the rock and he drowns.[28]

The Ship

Melville distills the chronotope of the ship in *White Jacket* when he writes that "a ship is a bit of terra firm cut off from the main; it is a state in itself; and the captain is its king."[29] Like the island, the ship is "self-sufficient narrative ecosystem "and offers a microcosm of society.[30] While the island offers the utopian possibility to reinvent society from a tempered nature, the ship is organized according to a rigid hierarchy. Generally, this hierarchy works through force. Again, *White Jacket*: "it is no limited monarchy, where the sturdy Commons have a right to petition, and snarl if they please; but almost a despotism, like the Grand Turk's."[31]

The ship's repressive authority is justified as necessitated by the hostile environment of the sea, where everyone must sacrifice comfort, ego, personality, and even life for the welfare of all under the surveillance of a leader vested with supreme authority. This authority, however, can easily get out of hand, and the chronotope of the ship negotiates the line between the necessary exercise of force to get the job done in stringent working conditions and the

---

[27] Victor Hugo, *Les travailleurs de la mer* (Paris: Bibliothèque de la Pléiade, 1975), 760.

[28] Ibid., 651.

[29] Herman Melville, *White Jacket* (New York: Library of America, 1983), 371.

[30] Cesare Casarino, *Modernity at Sea* (Minneapolis: University of Minnesota Press, 2002), 28.

[31] Melville, *White Jacket*, 371.

sadistic application of brutality and violence. Like the chronotope of the island, the composition of shipboard society varies historically, depending on the land-based societies framing it as well on the historical specifics of shipboard life.

When a novel passes through the chronotope of the ship, its portrayal of the ship's hierarchical society is revealing of its politics. Austen's *Persuasion* offers the image of Mrs. Croft snug on a naval ship that epitomizes a harmonious domestic universe, where all are snug in their social place. When Staël's Corinne visits a vessel from the British navy at about the same historical moment, in the midst of a narrative concerned with gender inequality, Staël's feminist heroine views the ship as the microcosm of an authoritarian society where women are subjected to men.

In narratives where the ship is a central organizing chronotope, this hierarchical society becomes animated into a voyage, as the dangers of the repressive hierarchy on board ship interact with the dangers of other chronotopes of the sea that the protagonist must surmount. Foulke observes that "voyages . . . suggest larger patterns of orientation because they have built-in directionality and purpose, an innate teleology."[32] The narratives set on shipboard dwell on the in-between space of passage, rather than the goal. Nonetheless, they have the teleology of a character's passage in personality, a *rite de passage*, quite often from youth (Conrad's "Youth," "Kharein," and "The Secret Sharer") to maturity through the acquisition of cunning and know-how. Youths set sail beguiled by romance tales of shipboard life, which are debunked. However, this disillusionment is not purely bitter. It is accompanied by the acquisition of another more valued form of knowledge that has its own romance, the romance of practice.

The protagonist of the extensive shipboard narrative is thus generally the youth who passes to maturity. Shipboard life surrounds this youth with a moral panorama common to land-based overviews of the social macrocosm. The hypocrite, the socialite, and the unscrupulous adventurer have their maritime counterparts in "the stowaway and the jinx [who] serve as the intruder and the scapegoat in shipboard society, and the bully mate becomes the enforcer of rigid rules that encroach upon the crew's slender margin of freedom. Yet others, like the green hand or neophyte, become the central figures who grow to manhood at sea; they usually cross class barriers as soon as they set foot in the forecastle and need the help of the older seamen who become their mentors."[33]

---

[32] Foulke, *Sea Voyage Narrative*, 10.
[33] Ibid., 20–21.

In land-based narratives, characters generally maneuver to procure social advantage. On board ship, characters work, and indeed this chronotope, in interaction with other chronotopes of the sea, provides one of the most extended opportunities for the narrative dramatization of human labor. In work, humans seek to surmount the resistance of matter with their intelligence and their bodies, and the human body has long been used to figure the polis. When the body takes center stage in the chronotope of the ship, connections are made to the ship's importance as at once an economic, political, and social microcosm.

From the *Odyssey* onward, there are detailed representations of how characters use their bodies when they navigate and sail, explore, kill, and suffer. From such details, at once description and narration, we see the power of the body, its beauty, and also its vulnerability. One expression of the importance of the body to the ship is the undead sailor. The malingering James Wait in *The Nigger of the Narcissus* epitomizes this figure. In *Two Years before the Mast*, R. H. Dana links the ghostly life of the phantom sailor to the particularly unresolved and painful nature of death at sea. "At sea, the man is near you—at your side—you hear his voice, and in an instant he is gone, and nothing but a vacancy shows his loss. Then, too, at sea—to use a homely but expressive phrase—you miss a man so much. . . . It is like losing a limb. There are no new faces or new scenes to fill up the gap."[34]

Bakhtin observed that rigidly hierarchical societies have moments of release, a practice he terms the carnival. Shipboard societies have their carnivals as well, and as is the case in land-based societies, the carnival exalts the grotesque life of the body, allowing it unruly license to suspend and challenge the rigors of the workaday world. In keeping with the structure of the carnival on land, these moments of release on board ship are sometimes ritually ordained, sometimes occur by chance, and sometimes explode when the pressures of hierarchy become too great.

An example of the ritually ordained carnival on board ship would be the ceremony that accompanies the moment of crossing the Equator, or, as it was also called, crossing the line. On this occasion, as Cook explains, "the Ceremony . . . practiced by all Nations was not omitted: everyone that could not prove upon a Sea Chart that he had before crossed the Line, was either to pay a bottle of Rum or be ducked in the sea, which former case was the fate of by far the greatest part on board, and as several of the Men choose to be ducked, and the weather was favorable for that purpose, this ceremony was performed on about twenty or thirty to the no small diversion of the

---

[34] R. H. Dana, *Two Years before the Mast* (New York: Modern Library, 2001), 77.

rest."[35] An example of the chance eruption of carnival within the rigors of work would be the scene where sailors share the "sperm of human kindness" as they squeeze spermaceti in *Moby Dick*. Mutiny is the most dramatic example of carnival resulting from the explosion of pressure that finds no other outlet; going AWOL is its more comic version. A good example of temporary evasion would be the escapades of the gentleman's son, Jack, and the African cook, Mesty, when they take a Spanish boat in Captain Marryat's *Mr. Midshipman Easy*. Forming a superhuman team linked by bonds of cunning and skill, Jack and Mesty triumph not only through strength but also through their comic talents. In temporarily suspending the social differences between them stemming from class and race, their escapades exemplify the democratizing dimension of the carnival—the contrast between the egalitarian carnivalesque body politic and the ship's usual rigid hierarchy.

The pirate communities that shadow lawful ships are a kind of permanent carnival, where the ship's structures of authority are inverted and undone. The alternatives offered by pirate communities to the authoritarian societies on ship include an order founded on utopian aspirations of equality, a comic version of the medieval ship of fools concerned only with pleasure, and presocial communities where all are out for themselves dedicated to the sheer pursuit of gain. Another dark version of the carnival is the dance of death that levels social distance. In close shipboard quarters, disease is rampant, and while the contagion certainly spreads fastest in the crowded forecastle, it also exposes the division aft and before the mast as a psychological line that crumbles easily under pressure.

The ship navigates blue, brown, and white water; brown water empties into blue water; blue and brown water turn to white water in icy weather, fog, tempests, or when the waves crash against the leeward shore; the shore edges the island; and the island encounters the ways of the mainland via the ship. The chronotopes of the sea edge each other and help define each other's specificity. They exist as interlocking parts of a single narrative system. In their evident interrelation, they raise to the level of content a model of the cosmos as system. They are a poetic link in the genealogy of globalization.

---

[35] Captain Cook, *First Voyage* in *The Journals of Captain Cook* (New York: Penguin Books, 1999), 18.

PHILIP FISHER

Torn Space: James Joyce's *Ulysses*

The space of our common experience we sometimes think of as changing, but usually at the hands of philosophical or scientific speculation. So we speak of Copernican, Newtonian, Cartesian, or Einsteinian space as revolutionary even though we find it difficult to trace or test in a reliable way the exact consequences in everyday perception or self-location. The more modest claims that we might make about changes in space found in art (for example, our coming to see the world as landscape in the rather precise terms of Poussin) are often linked to our ability to work on the world that we perceive so as to make the experience self-confirming. By "improving" nature, creating and designating views and prospects, siting our houses and paths in certain ways, we build ourselves into the world at the right angle to discover, again and again, that it is a landscape and returns answers to our visual questions.

The city as a space, because it is completely man-made, involves the most complete conversation between experience and design, between how we see what we have and how we then build in a way that clarifies or shifts what we will next see or experience. The opacity and mystery of the stone and brick out of which the nineteenth-century city was built created a curiosity, a hunger to see into and behind walls that then, in the plate glass and then curtain walls of glass of the buildings of the next generations could be fed and perhaps even satisfied. The smoke-blackened stone of one time created the very aesthetic questions that the washable, shining glass surfaces of the next would answer. Similarly, the close, crowded texture of visual events in the city is answered with the reciprocal emptiness of highways and widely spaced suburban housing to which the children of the city dwellers move.

The vocabulary that we find ourselves requiring to describe changes in space and spatial experience is often already given to us in common experiences, but in those located at the edges, devalued or neglected episodes that, once moved to the center of what we take experience to be, design an order and comprehension around themselves. For example, our normal central understanding of looking is conveyed by the phrase "looking at x" or "at y," in which the object looked at explains and orders the experience. Whereas, if we replace this focused, attentive, concerned mode of looking with what we take to be the marginal, defective, and less interesting mode of what we call "looking around," we find ourselves with an entirely new, and in the case of the city, or a city novel like Joyce's *Ulysses*, more adequate hierarchy of experiences of looking. The difference between looking at and looking around, where first one and then the other is understood to be the norm, commits us to a very large psychological and even moral shift.

In what follows I will look at two of the many shifts in perception and design that accumulate between the midnineteenth and early twentieth centuries, shifts that accommodate the lived momentary experience of the city and its overall order, trace themselves in everyday life, and alter the narrative of that everyday life that we find in the modern novel, specifically in Joyce's *Ulysses*. The first is the shift from narration to tabulation as the destination of experience. We can say that the postromantic goal of experience is to end up as information, ordered information rather than memory.[1] Or, to reverse the terms: we can say, that to be complete, an account must include a far wider arc of events—the realm of facts and information—rather than the too narrow realm of the memorable and the experientially significant. The city itself is such a tabulation that records and stores in its physical appearance tens of thousands of separate decisions: alterations, facts of care and neglect, decisions to build and destroy, all in a retrievable form. The city and its small, temporary, hand-held image—the newspaper—satisfy the two goals of completeness and order, as I will try to show. A shift in value is intended by locating, as Joyce does, the newspaper and the city as models for the outline of experience.

Second, in the small common episodes of experience, I will try to describe an open or torn space: a multiple, distracted, interrupted spatial experience that is related to "looking around" and derives from our everyday, usually overlooked experiences in the city street. Moved indoors, domesticated, designed into structures much as landscape was into nature, this open or torn space becomes morally and psychologically central, and along with it, the multiplied and partial attention that we ordinarily dismiss as distraction. These ordinary episodes of brief experience are essential to what I would like to call a humanism of perception, a perceptual model for a modest but secure humanism that makes it possible for Bloom in the hour of his betrayal, 4:30 in the afternoon, to master the narrowness of what could be an obsessive and jealous day and hour by locating obsession and jealousy in a perceptual world more open than the mind or will. Such experiences make possible Bloom's final state as he crawls into the bed recently vacated by his wife's lover: the state of equanimity. Such equanimity and satisfaction are

---

[1] Walter Benjamin, "The Storyteller," in *Illuminations*, ed. Hannah Arendt, trans. Harry Zohn (New York: Shocken, 1969).

best described by one of the final phrases of Bloom's day. He and his wife are "at rest relatively to themselves and to each other."

One way of describing Joyce's *Ulysses* would be to say that it is not the description of Molly Bloom's day, a day spent in a closed domestic space, engaged with a single drama. A morning of predictions (fortune-telling cards and the letter that announces that her lover will come in the afternoon); followed by a day of preparation for and anticipation of the single event, lasting through the arrival of the presents that precede her lover, Blazes; then the climactic hour; followed by sleep, memory, and conclusion. This drama, centered around the self and its will and satisfactions, occurs in a closed world—that room that epitomizes the world of family life and its violations—with a small set of intimate figures sloping toward and then away from a single event. All other events take their meaning only as they forward or impede the sexual climax of Molly's day. In many ways this closed house with its single decisive entrance and departure (that of the lover); its bracketing departure and reentrance (that of the husband); and its single human act of satisfaction—its characters limited to the relevant small circle, its time made significant by anticipation, action, and memory is the spatial world of the traditional novel.

Bloom, on the other hand, is a man who could have spent the entire day anxiously or furiously waiting for the one moment when his wife would be joined by her lover. He could have been enclosed in this claustrophobia of self, like Othello. Instead, he invites the world to distract him, to interrupt him, and he is redeemed by this distraction. At times when he is near Blazes in the street the need to distract himself becomes urgent, even desperate: a need not to think at all. Experience in *Ulysses*, unlike the experiences that center in the will, is completed and ordered by what lies outside itself. Its enemy is the closed room, and, although fewer than half of the episodes of the novel take place in the streets, the qualities of multiple and interrupted space lend themselves to the public indoor world of restaurants, library, bar, and brothel and alter the indoor world fundamentally.

Once again the small-scale model of this experience is the newspaper, particularly its front page where we are encouraged to read by a set of glances and distractions from story to story, headline to headline: dip a little into this story, be interrupted by the picture next to the story, glance away, return and maintain a divided attention, alert to the swarm of disparate events on the total page, much as one does on a busy city street. The newspaper encourages a scanning and a leveling of reality. As Bloom glances at his newspaper in the cab stand he sees: "Great battle Tokyo. Lovemaking In Irish 200 damages. Gordon Bennett. Emigration swindle. Letter from His

Grace William. Ascot *Throwaway* recalls Derby of '92 when Captain Marshall's dark horse, *Sir Hugo*, captured the blue riband at long odds. New York disaster, thousand lives lost. Foot and Mouth. Funeral of the late Mr. Patrick Dignam."[2] Horse race and ship disaster do not ironize or explain one another. The comic and the tragic, the local funeral and the battle in Tokyo all coexist and invite momentary and partial attention. By means of a newspaper we look at the world at a distance that in earlier days was that of the gods. The newspaper is both a product of the city and a daily exercise in practicing the perceptual skills needed in the city itself.

Tabulation and Order

In his autobiographical fragment, which he called "A Berlin Chronicle" after the city in which his childhood had taken place, and which he wrote from afar in Spain to carry out an idea that had come to him in Paris, Walter Benjamin described how he had for years "played with the idea of setting out the sphere of life—bios—graphically on a map."[3] With this biograph he would update biography by discarding the elements of time and story, replacing them with the skeletal structure of the city itself.

On his map of the city center he would mark with one colored symbol the houses of friends, and with another the rooms of lovers; with yet other symbols and colors he designated the rooms where political debates had taken place, the key park benches where he had liked to sit, the tennis courts where he had played, the practice halls where he had been sent to the hated dancing lessons, and, of course, the graves he had stood by to see filled. Because every room in which he had slept with a lover would be marked with the same symbol, there would be no sign of earlier or later, important or casual affairs, nor even any way to see at a glance if it were a question of different lovers at different times in different rooms. Persons would disappear with events and places. Or, rather, the symbols would function like pronouns in language, capable of shifting from reference to reference and creating classes more essential than the members of classes. Molly Bloom's soliloquy with its use of "he," "him," and "his" shifting over a lifetime of lovers in

---

[2] James Joyce, *Ulysses* (New York: Random House, 1961), 647. All later quotations refer to this edition and will be followed by page numbers in parentheses.

[3] Walter Benjamin, *Reflections*, ed. Peter Demetz, trans. Edmund Jephcott (New York: Harcourt Brace Jovanovich, 1978), 5.

ways that we often cannot at first separate is like one element of Benjamin's map replaced into the traditional locus of individual memory.

For his imaginary biograph Benjamin thought that he would need a military map, the kind prepared by the general staff. In fact, the finished picture would seem to record his conquest of the city, the sectors that he had come to occupy in almost the military meaning of the word. Several years earlier, sitting in a café in Paris, Benjamin had had a visionary moment in which he had drawn another diagram of his life, a diagram that was like a set of family trees and in part like a labyrinth with many entrances.[4] Each entrance stood for a person whom he had met in some special way. Then, like the corridors of a labyrinth, he drew branching lines for persons met through the first group and so on. With cross-connections and meetings that led back after several steps to someone already known from another direction, Benjamin's second map records that fascination with contacts and connections that frequently seems to have a priority over relationships in the city. Contacts and connections give to the day-by-day experience of running into someone, or as we say, "bumping into someone," an unexpected weight and significance. Much of Bloom's day in *Ulysses*, in human terms, consists in running into someone or avoiding running into someone. Bloom's contacts are of the kind described by the sociologist Louis Wirth in his classic essay of the 1930s, "Urbanism as a Way of Life," where he wrote: "The city is characterized by secondary rather than primary contacts. The contacts of the city may indeed be face to face, but they are nevertheless impersonal, superficial, transitory and segmental."[5]

By the end of his day, Bloom has been with or in contact with M'Coy, Flynn, Simon Dedalus, Hynes, Richie Goulding, the blind boy, the Citizen, and a dozen or two others in just this secondary way. Insofar as his day has an interpersonal texture, it is made up of the brief connections with these acquaintances rather than with either intimate experiences or at the other extreme, encounters among strangers.

Unimportant as the acquaintance himself is in Bloom's life, banal as the words exchanged are, the encounter reasserts the deeper value of the web itself. Such a web of persons with the random and unexpected interconnections and encounters is a familiar element of the novel of the city, replacing what Henry James had called the circle of relations within which the economy

---

[4] Benjamin, *Reflections*, 30.

[5] Louis Wirth, *On Cities and Social Life: Selected Papers*, ed. Albert J. Reiss Jr. (Chicago: University of Chicago Press, 1964), 71.

of action can be described. Whether Dickens or Joyce, Balzac or Dostoevsky, the web of contacts is evidence less of the nature of events than of our
preferred mastery of the past by means of a spatialization that resolves
episodes and particles of experience into at least a pattern in the absence of
any continuous and significant story.

Walter Benjamin's two maps depend on the conversion of experience
into knowledge, or, if we wish to be more cautious, into information. As a
destination for experience, information is the opposite of memory and demands that experience be uprooted in order to gain form and order. In his
1906 book-length essay, *Abstraction and Empathy*, the art critic Wilhelm
Worringer called this process *abstraction* and linked it to what he referred to
as a "dread of space," a dread that linked primitive to highest civilizations
and, in the latter, resulted from, in Worringer's words, the final "resignation
of knowledge." Abstraction requires that the "object of the external world
be uprooted and purified of all dependence upon life so as to find in the
contemplation of it a point of tranquility."[6]

The final chapter of Bloom's day in *Ulysses*, composed as it is of questions and answers, suggests this picture of the final destination of the day's
experience—lists and tabulations, a sorting that pulverizes events into information. As information, every day can be sorted and congregated into
those experiences where money was spent or earned, into events that
Bloom does or does not tell his wife, papers and objects that happen to be
in a drawer, and so on. As information, the questions of what relation existed between Bloom's and Stephen's ages blossoms into a wealth of facts:
"16 years before in 1888 when Bloom was of Stephen's present age Stephen
was 6. 16 years after in 1920 when Stephen would be Bloom's present age
Bloom would be 54. In 1936 when Bloom would be 70 and Stephen 54
their ages initially in the ratio of 16 to 0 would be as 17½ to 13½ . . ." (679).
All of which is true and none of which exhausts the particular wholeness of
the idea of information itself. To turn on the faucet, as Bloom does, in the
world of information rather than that of experience, links him to the reservoir, the water pipes, the clouds, the construction of the water system and
so on. It links him to everything, an indiscriminate web very different, as I
will show later, from the open and yet limited links of the world of perception, which is, in its turn, very different from the traditional web of storytelling, the web of memory.[7]

---

[6] Wilhelm Worringer, *Abstraction and Empathy*, trans. Michael Bullock (Cleveland: World
Publishing Co./Meridian Books, 1967), 15–18.

[7] See Benjamin, "The Storyteller," in *Illuminations*.

The primary form in which information exists is either the tabulation or the series, each of which is shy of causality and experiential connections. With tabulation the arbitrary order of information is acknowledged. In the newspaper, Bloom glances several times at the obituaries, this one day's information about death. Bloom sees a list: Callan, Coleman, Dignam, Fawcett. In this list, Paddy Dignam occurs where he does only because his name begins with "D" rather than "A" or "R."

The ideal of accuracy in the world of information is provided by the word *complete*. It is an ideal of exhaustiveness. It has often been said that we know more about Leopold Bloom than about any other character in literature. We do know more information about him, more anecdotes and rapidly sketched in stories. We know that his collar size is 17; we know that it is ten years, five months and eighteen days since he and Molly last had complete sexual intercourse. We know what books he owns and what position he sleeps in and that he likes the inner organs of beasts and fowls. We know the story of his pointing out the stars on a carriage ride home and that once, having paid for a bowl of soup, he walked up and down the platform eating it when the train was ready to start. But we do not know him as characters are generally known: by how, in a few decisive moments of life, they came to make certain choices and in those moments marked themselves on and with their experience.

Toward the end of Bloom's day he reads about himself in the newspaper. The story says:

> This morning the remains of the late Mr. Patrick Dignam were removed
> from his residence, no. 9 Newbridge Avenue, Sandymount, for interment in
> Glasnevin. The deceased gentleman was a most popular and genial personal-
> ity in city life and his demise, after a brief illness, came as a great shock to cit-
> izens of all classes, by whom he is deeply regretted. The obsequies, at which
> many friends of the deceased were present, were carried out . . . by Messrs.
> H.J. O'Neill & Son, 164 North Strand road. The mourners included: Patk.
> Dignam (son), Bernard Corrigan (brother-in-law), John Henry Menton, solr.,
> Martin Cunningham, John Power, Thomas Kernan, Simon Dedalus, Stephen
> Dedalus, B.A., Edward J. Lambert, Cornelius Kelleher, Joseph M'C. Hynes,
> L. Boom, C.P.M'Coy, M'Intosh and several others. (647)

Here we have resolved into information—times, places, names, lists, even a hidden advertisement for the funeral establishment—what we have earlier experienced, when we read the sixth chapter, as the social ceremony of the funeral, and then, in a later chapter, as the private memories of the son. The young Dignam recalls his dead father: "His face got all grey instead of being red like it was and there was a fly walking over it up to his eye. The scrunch that was when they were screwing the screws into the coffin: and the bumps when they were bringing it downstairs. Pa was inside it and ma crying in the parlour and Uncle Barney telling the men how to get it round the bend" (251). The funeral at 11, along with the betrayal at 4 are the two focal events of Bloom's day, and to find himself, officially noted, if imperfectly, as the mourner L. Boom at the end of the list locates him just as longitude and latitude do, in the world of information.

Throughout the novel the newspaper that Bloom carries, works for, kneels on, writes and reads love letters behind, glances at, gives away, wraps his soap in and wipes himself with, articulates by matching both the structure of the novel and of the city by sorting and composing events. The newspaper is a quickly discarded, everyday-renewed sampling of the world. Bloom, looking at the obituaries, calls it "inked characters fast fading on the frayed breaking paper" (91). Like *Ulysses*, it is one day's worth of life. The paper is an installment, a miniature, total image of our psychic lives, as a day is, and given in direct quantity to our appetites.

What is it that explains the scale (the "coverage," as it is called) and the shape of content in a newspaper? Why is there just this much space devoted to food, to death, to sports, to money, to stories of disaster or stories of luck or salvation or reunion? Why in some cultures and times would the newspaper report in detail on the sermons preached in church while in other times and places baseball games would be represented in great detail? Why would stories of danger in the streets or trials of murderers be prominent in the newspapers of one culture while stories of remorse or religious miracles would be featured in another? The answer lies in the fact that a newspaper in its proportions and omissions is an accurate record of the psychic economy of a culture with money and love playing the parts that they do play, as well as sports or comedy, crime and wisdom. The newspaper is dietary in that it replenishes daily the existing system of needs.

In its use of sections—a financial section, a sports section, a section of obituaries and another of engagements, a food section—the newspaper orders experience, much as *Ulysses* does in the location of its chapters in given and functioning institutions (school, library, cemetery, restaurant, hospital, brothel) by accepting the concrete social form in which events and information occur. In this way it acts as a hand-held miniature version of the city itself.

The city expresses by means of congregation and concentration. All of the dead are concentrated in the cemetery, those who are eating are in restaurants, those who wish to pray congregate in churches, those who read, in libraries. By means of this congregation the city creates a shelter for a culture's common humanity, which it houses just as a home is the shelter for an individual's humanity and an expression of it. The city is an objectified humanism of an encyclopedic kind. That is, it has the structure, once again, of experience converted to knowledge or made available in the ordered form of knowledge. For any city or civilization there are precise balances between the representation in buildings and institutions of learning or bravery (libraries and schools, or bull-fighting arenas and coliseums). There are precise balances between piety and sensuality, the need for solitude or for conviviality, or the fear of solitude or conviviality. The shortest study of a city with its number of taverns per district or its number of churches per square mile, the numbers and care with which flowers or food are offered, the number of places to be alone or where conversation is discouraged or demanded would produce a common public biograph.

A city with a sports arena at its center is profoundly different from one where a cathedral occupies the prime location, or from one with majestic office buildings. This transparent human record of the cultural mind that can be seen in the shabbiness or the gaiety of the places where food is to be eaten; the poverty or the luxury of libraries or places of work; the grandeur or the bureaucratic anonymity of political buildings and locations, records and manifests the culture in a more telling way than even its experiential history. It is a frozen language or discourse about the balances and imbalances of a common shared humanity.

It is, of course, this city rather than the mysterious and oppressive nineteenth-century city that Joyce records in *Ulysses*. By basing his chapters on locations and institutions—school and cemetery, library and restaurant, hospital and brothel—all places that record and institutionalize, congregate and shelter one sector of experience in its socially given form, Joyce accepts the map as an accurate and proportional graph of the sphere of Dublin life in the year 1904. That real learning does or does not go on in the school or that in the brothel there is only talk and fantasy, but no sex, does not mean to ironize or challenge the way in which buildings or institutions articulate sectors of experience. The city is the large common home in which Bloom spends his day, a home that replaces the traditional private house in which the complementary, but unrecorded day of Molly Bloom takes place. The rigidity of this process of congregation—prayer in church, death in the cemetery, intellectual talk in the library, erotic fantasy in the brothel—has as its counter force what I will describe later as a refusal of concentration, a courting of multiple spaces that returns completeness by inviting a scattered attention of the mind moment by moment.

The city that Joyce has represented as a whole, sheltering and making visible the themes of a cultural humanity, represents a complete 180-degree turn from the common midnineteenth-century picture of an infernal, oppressive disorder that stifles and mystifies the individual's capacity to act or to locate his own image or place. This reversal is not a personal achievement of Joyce's but rather a profound indication of the growing mastery of and intellectual comprehension of the city by society at large. Between the time of the city of Dickens and that of Joyce a number of key intellectual and practical relations to the city had changed. In brief, the city changes from a monstrous, given adversary to an environment open to planning, control, and clarification. I will describe only a few details of this shift in the hope that these can stand for a much more widespread and coherent change.

In the midnineteenth century the sanitary reforms, which we associate with Dr. Chadwick, involved the capacity for society to perceive the city in a systematic way and then to act on it from centralized power. To control disease it was necessary to understand the interconnection between the system delivering water and that removing waste, and further, the links between the circulation of air, the size of rooms and their darkness or openness, and access to light and space for recreation and movement. Concern for public health demanded an integrated picture of the city as an environment made up of systems, many or most of which could be taken under government control and planned into the city itself. This demanded a violation of liberal political theory. The city would have to be seen systematically and as a set of factors subject to human control, and finally as an expression of society itself rather than as a confluence of private acts of will and calculation that just happened as an aggregate to have effects at a higher level.

At the same period in France, the redesign and rebuilding of Paris by Haussmann, in which the city was taken under central authority, articulated as a set of social meanings, and altered by massive destruction and rearrangement of the physical city itself, achieved the same humanization of the whole in a more radical way.[8] From Haussmann onward, through the work on Vienna and Amsterdam at the turn of the century, down to the central planning and rebuilding activities of the recent half-century after the end of the Second World War, the city came to be grasped as a work of art, controlled by shared visions and carried out by means of designs that clarify the moral, active, and human structures of city life.

---

[8] Leonardo Benevolo, *History of Modern Architecture* (Cambridge, Mass.: MIT Press, 1971), 1:61–96.

Even more than the reconstruction of given cities, the later nineteenth century saw the creation of thousands of new cities and settlements in the American West and in the colonial empires of England and France.[9] In America the many cities designed by the Mormons as they were forced west, to take only one example, represent a high point of the assumption of control within the possibilities of unified human and spiritual expression in the physical design of the city.[10] Utopian communities or plans, such as those of the followers of Fourier frequently have as one of their central images the map of a harmonized and ordered settlement or city. Numerous individual plans from the early Garden City movement in England to the Broad-acres plan of Frank Lloyd Wright or the Radiant City of Le Corbusier propose the more individualistic design of the city as a work of art.[11]

Torn Space

The large-scale features of the designed or at least perspicuous city have as their complement the episodes of small-scale experience that build in the open quality of action within the city. We do not have to agree with the absoluteness of André Breton's striking statement that the street is "the only valid field of experience"[12] to accept the fact that, as spatial frame, the street has a central value in city experience, its qualities of the accidental and the temporary, its invitation to a varied and multiple attention, its courting of adventure and interruption and its presentation of a number of partial events within the same field of vision so that anyone can, while carrying out his or her own action, watch or scan a variety of disconnected acts: all of these suggest that the open space of the street is the antithesis of the room—that classic space of drama and the novel—with its fixed and interrelated set of characters, its single unifying action, and its consecutiveness of development. From at least the time of the *flaneur*, the disorder and perceptual shock of the street were sought for their own sakes, developing in Baudelaire's prose poems a literary form suitable in its momentary qualities of action, mood, surprise, and mystery.

---

[9] See ibid., 190–218, as well as John Reps, *Cities of the American West: A History of Frontier Urban Planning* (Princeton, N.J.: Princeton University Press, 1979).

[10] Reps, *Cities of the American West*, 286–312.

[11] Giorgio Ciucci, Francesco dal Co, Mario Maniere-Elia, and *Manfredo Tafuri, The American City: From the Civil War to the New Deal* (Cambridge, Mass.: MIT Press, 1979).

[12] Quoted in Benjamin, *Reflections*, 131.

The architectural historian Benevolo, whose *History of Modern Architecture* is now the standard work, describes the aesthetics of this experience as it can be found for the first time in impressionist painting.

> Impressionism grasped the character of the urban scene more clearly than any of the critics or writers of the time: the continuity of its spaces, all interconnecting, each open to the next and never enclosed within a single self-enclosed frame of perspective, the fact that it was composed of recurrent identical elements, qualified in an ever-changing way and therefore dynamically in relation to the surroundings, the new relationship between the architectural frame, which was now indefinite and unbounded and the traffic of men and vehicles, the renewed unity between architecture and the street, and in general the sense of the landscape as a dense mass of objects all equally important but perpetually in a state of flux. . . . The greater or rather the total openness of these painters to every natural or man-made object restored the unity of the landscape which had been broken by the industrial town; nevertheless the intensity and emotional involvement typical of the realists was lacking and in its place was a sort of detachment and impassivity.[13]

What Benevolo calls detachment and impassivity is described from another point of view, that of the sociologist Georg Simmel, as "reserve" or the "blasé attitude," typical and psychologically necessary within the city as a survival device within the solicitations of attention and concern that are too various and demanding to be accommodated.[14] Simmel describes the response to this space as one in which the intellect, in order to protect the deeper layers of the personality, becomes the dominant faculty sent out to receive and sort the swarm of experiential episodes. Simmel's 1905 essay, "The Metropolis and Mental Life," had an extraordinarily wide effect on the sociological theories of the city that follow. The Chicago School of Park and Wirth begins out of direct study with Simmel.[15] Walter Benjamin's studies of Paris and Baudelaire are deeply indebted to Simmel and are in many places a restatement. Spengler's treatment of the city in his *Decline of the West* uses all of Simmel's primary categories. The more essential work of Weber implicitly follows the psychology of urban experience first described by Simmel.[16]

---

[13] Benevolo, *History of Modern Architecture*, 1:145–47.

[14] Georg Simmel, "The Metropolis and Mental Life," in The *Sociology of Georg Simmel*, ed. Kurt Wolff (Glencoe, Ill.: Free Press, 1950), 410–13.

[15] Ulf Hannerz, *Exploring the City* (New York: Columbia University Press, 1980).

[16] The classic studies are in effect a closely interwoven set of variations on the ideas of Simmel and Weber.

The detachment, passivity, and intellectuality that recur as elements of the city mind make of Bloom, that amateur scientist of the everyday, a representative, even a climactic figure. His reserve or detachment extends even to his own betrayal. When he sees Blazes near four o'clock still in the Ormond Hotel, he thinks, "Has he forgotten? Perhaps a trick. Not come: whet appetite, I couldn't do" (266). In other words, he reproaches Blazes for the cheap trick of making Molly wait so as to whet her appetite. The final state of Bloom's day, equanimity, is a form of resignation to the inevitable, a detachment from his own life as a drama that is the final goal of this reserve.

Although as a terrain of experience the street called up such specific forms of representation as the prose poem and the urban form of impressionist painting, far more important than the seeking out and collecting of street experiences is the architectural and technological attempt to make the characteristics of this experience available indoors or at home; that is, to give to our rooms and enclosed spaces many of the qualities of spatial experience for which we have developed a psychological attraction in the field of experience of the street. The great department stores of the late nineteenth century, particularly the Grands Magasins of Paris created the crowds, the possibilities of observing and connecting open-ended glimpses of action and drama, that resettled the world of the streets indoors in a glamorous and spatially exciting setting. Benevolo's description of the space of the street draws on his earlier description of the dramatic and novel indoor space of the London Crystal Palace Exposition.[17]

More important than these public and commercial spaces is the transformation of the psychology of domestic and familial experience brought about by the introduction of the open floor plan within modern architecture. The open floor plan of the modern house, which we usually associate with Frank Lloyd Wright and the set of houses that he designed in the Midwest between 1890 and 1910, soon became the standard for domestic space. Rudolf Arnheim has described these houses as creating an outside space inside.[18] What the open floor plan encourages is a variety of actions and tasks taking place within sight of one another. While one person cooks, another reads, the children play, and each person is aware of the others in an intermittent way. Each interrupts the others from time to time. Concentration on any one thing is segmented, and distraction is a natural and pleasing element. By eliminating the walls and doors behind which cooking or reading, conversation or

---

[17] Benevolo, *History of Modern Architecture*, 1:102.
[18] Rudolf Arnheim, *The Dynamics of Architectural Form* (Berkeley: University of California Press, 1977), 227.

play took place, the open floor plan lent itself to a psychology in which concentration or attention gave way to a moment-by-moment multiple focus. Corridors and transitional spaces are eliminated. The increasing use of glass, one of the most essential spatial facts about modern buildings, permits the felt presence of the outside to mix with the inner world.

The effects on experience of these architectural features are multiplied by the technological innovations that have directly to do with spatial experience and that become common in the period. The telephone, for example, permits anyone to interrupt or break into the space of another person at any moment. In a more controlled way the radio or television permits events in one space to occur within another. Such technology intensifies the openness of modern space, or rather, limits the self-contained quality of any experiential setting by including the outside, as a window does, as a possible element of the inside. If we picture for a moment a man sitting in his living room with his children playing on the floor and the sounds of cooking and occasional conversation coming from the kitchen area behind him, we already have someone within a complex space. We can imagine that he has the television on to watch a baseball game, an image carrying into his living room an actual event going on in a space hundreds of miles away. While watching the game, he glances from time to time at the children. The telephone rings, and because it is an important business call, he talks to his caller, while following the game and from time to time quieting the children. On the telephone, in the background he can hear the office sounds that carry that space along with the voice speaking to him into his room. At this moment of following many situations simultaneously the cast of characters with whom he is involved includes himself, his family, the man on third base and the ten or eleven other players who might affect his fate, and his business partner at the office. Many of these groups are not even aware of one another, and the entire group gains coherence, like Benjamin's map, only from the central ego within the world of perception. He exists in a varied and mutually interrupting spatial situation that both the architecture and the technology were designed to make possible.

This small scene that I have built up using anachronistic elements (when we consider 1904) represents a spatial outcome of many features and demands that have a constant and incremental effect in the city both before and after the turn of the century. Within closed space the patterns of street experience have their basis in interruption, the breaking of the flow of attention from many sides, an interruption that does not close off attention or redirect it, but rather segments it into a finer and finer grain, reducing it perhaps to a set of glances.

With this preparation, I would like to look briefly at one of the typical moments of Bloom's day in *Ulysses*, the meeting with M'Coy, an event that takes about three pages of Joyce's novel, and one without antecedents and having no later consequences of any importance. In the encounter in the street Bloom experiences that reserve that Simmel has said, in the end is not indifference but a "slight aversion, a mutual strangeness and repulsion."[19] This slight aversion is frequently just below the surface in Bloom's contacts. On meeting M'Coy he thinks at once: "Get rid of him quickly. Take me out of my way. Hate company when you" (73). M'Coy has interrupted him just as Bloom, returning from the post office, is secretly tearing open an envelope in his pocket to try to determine what might be attached to the letter he has received from Martha. Throughout the conversation the letter in his pocket, which he explores with his finger, attracts part of his attention from time to time. While talking to M'Coy, he keeps watching the scene across the street in front of the Grosvenor Hotel where a well-dressed woman will at any moment step up into a carriage. This is the third partial space in addition to the conversation itself and the letter being probed in his pocket. M'Coy begins to tell Bloom about the scene the night before in Conway's when he learned of Paddy Dignam's death. This adds a fourth space. All four scenes are followed simultaneously until M'Coy's anecdote ends just as the woman is about to step up and suddenly a tram passes interrupting Bloom's line of vision, creating a fifth partial event and depriving Bloom of his hoped-for glimpse of her leg. His dull sigh and phrase, "Yes, yes . . . Another gone," binds the two losses, Dignam's death in space four and the woman's unseen leg in space three.

Then, as the second half of the conversation begins with M'Coy's question about Bloom's wife, Bloom, as he answers, "O yes, Tiptop, thanks . . . ," unrolls his newspaper, and casually reads the advertisement for Plumtree's Potted Meat.

What is home without
Plumtree's Potted Meat?
Incomplete.
With it an abode of bliss. (75)

The newspaper in his hand, like the letter in his pocket, is a symbolic space from which further possibilities can be sought. That Bloom glances at the newspaper for no reason at this moment instead of giving M'Coy his

---

[19] Simmel, "Metropolis," 415.

undivided attention shows a search for complex space, restlessness in the face of the possibility of concentration. The newspaper has as one of its uses the possibility of dividing attention, multiplying the spatial resources at any moment when the situation impoverishes itself as it has in this case by the vanishing of the woman and the conclusion of the conversational scene in the bar the night before. The power of the interrupting, outside spatial fragments to break in and resolve events is one of the persistent spatial features of *Ulysses*. While Stephen Dedalus and his employer Mr. Deasy spar verbally inside the school office, the schoolboys struggle in a game in the field outside, and their search for goals and their shouts interrupt but at the same time resolve and define the debate about the goals of history inside.

The climactic example takes place at four o'clock, the hour of Bloom's betrayal, an event that he masters as he sits in the Ormond Hotel within the most complex and interwoven open space of the novel. In a room of mostly empty tables Bloom and Richie Goulding sit across from one another and, mostly without talking, eat. They are a little like Cézanne's card players: together, yet alone, each staring, not into a hand of cards, but into a plate of liver or a steak and kidney pie. At times they are physically separated by the newspaper that Bloom holds up so as to write in private his love letter to Martha. Across the next barrier, in the adjoining room, Simon Dedalus and Ben Dollard sing and talk with their friends. Across the next barrier, the wall, the progress of the blind piano tuner tapping along the street toward the bar and Blazes Boylan, progressing away from the bar toward Molly, can both be followed. The complex space absorbs and obliterates, distracts and interrupts Bloom from the drama of his private fate, a fate he can even duplicate or parody by simultaneously, but indirectly, betraying Molly by writing the love letter to Martha.

Both in Bloom's meeting with M'Coy and in the larger chapters such as the Ormond Hotel or the final beach scene, events not in the same space are unified by means of timing. To use the term *synchronicity* with its Jungian or mystical overtones is to distort this crucial effect and rob it of its connection as an aesthetic fact with the deeper social facts for which it is the partner term. The timing of events draws attention to the exact integration of lives and actions. Simmel, for one, has pointed out that punctuality, calculability, and exactness are essential in a new way to the functioning of life at the level of complexity and extension within the modern city.[20] Such life has at its center a ballet of appointments, meetings, schedules, anticipated encounters— that is, the timing of lives in a way that has no precedent—so as to permit

---

[20] Ibid., 413.

the maximum number of coordinated events to take place. Contemporary with Joyce's elevation of timing to a fundamental principle of order are wider social phenomena with equally strong roots in temporal integration. The opening quarter of the twentieth century has, in the world of work, its primary breakthrough in the time and motion studies of Frederick Winslow Taylor, the system of scientific management with its close analysis and integration of gestures in adjacent spaces.[21]

Timing, like interruption and distraction, plays a key part in the release of experience from its confines within the will and within the forms of perception appropriate to the will: concentration and attention. The active humanism of the nineteenth century was a humanism of the will. On the other hand, a humanism of perception, which both the large-scale order and the small-scale spatial experiences of the city encourage, is modest and skeptical of the will. The contents of perception are for the most part what is not the self. The small letter in Bloom's pocket as he speaks to M'Coy and the occasional reminders of his betrayal as he sits in the Ormond Hotel are the personal residues of the will suspended within the wider perceptual situation. The senses (unlike the will or thought or memory) include the self in the world in an extremely modest but secure way. Although I see my hand, most of what I see is not myself, and yet I always see myself within this wider field. Although I can hear my voice, most of what I hear I do not originate, and so for all the senses.

One of the great achievements of literary naturalism, of which Joyce's *Ulysses* is the final masterpiece, is to propose alternatives to the reigning humanism of the will. From Bentham to Carlyle to Nietzsche the will is the central human attribute in the nineteenth century. Zola and Hardy with their encompassing natural rhythms, and Joyce with his encompassing perceptual world, diminished, as did Lawrence from another direction, the factor of the will. By using the city, which is an objectified form of the general human will as the setting for perception, Joyce did not eliminate the will in an escapist way but located it outside the self in the community to which one both belongs and yet with which one is never completely identified. He created a humanism for which the city is at the same time the setting, the sponsor, and the monument.

---

[21] Siegfried Giedion, *Mechanization Takes Command* (New York: Oxford University Press, 1948), 96–129.

The New Metropolis

LEO OU-FAN LEE

Shanghai
(*Midnight*, Mao Dun, 1932)

Midnight (*Ziye*) is the first major long novel in the history of modern Chinese fiction. Written in 1931–32 and published in 1932, the five hundred-odd page novel had the original subtitle *A Romance of China, 1930*, which clearly indicates that the author, Mao Dun (pen name of Shen Yanbing, 1896–1981), had in mind a contemporaneous portrait of modern Chinese society. A "hedgehog" in fiction writing, Mao Dun always aspired to create a fictional panorama of Chinese society in "epic" proportions, and *Midnight* was his first attempt.[1] It is also a prime example of historical novel suffused with an acute consciousness of the immediate present. Time and narrative play a major role in all of Mao Dun's fictional works, for he fully subscribes to the view that the aim of fiction writing is to mirror the particular era and milieu in which the author lives. This conception may have had traditional roots, but Mao Dun clearly professed his allegiance to nineteenth-century Western fiction models.[2] In his original design, the novel constituted only the first part of a three-part novel that encompasses the entire Chinese society, both urban and rural. It was supposed to show, in light of his acquired faith in Marxism, the inevitable decline of the forces of Chinese feudalism and "native capitalism" at this particular juncture in time, when China was already caught under the massive weight of Western economic imperialism. However, he was not able to realize his own vision: only one chapter of this nineteen-chapter work deals with the devastation of the "agricultural

---

[1] The word *epic* as applied to Mao Dun's fiction, was first used by Jaroslav Prusek; see Leo Ou-fan Lee, ed., *The Lyrical and the Epic: Papers on Modern Chinese Literature by Jaroslav Prusek* (Bloomington: Indiana University Press, 1980). Prusek uses the term loosely in referring to the "objective' panoramic scope of Mao Dun's novels. A more relevant model may be drawn from Franco Moretti, *Modern Epic* (London: Verso, 1996). The fictional text of *Midnight* does indeed contain diverse elements, especially of urban material culture, and in certain passages much extraneous information is packed into the narrative. Still, Mao Dun conceived it as a novel that approximates a "romance." This term was again left unexplained, but it might contain both the conventional meaning of historical romance à la *Ivanhoe* (which was translated into Chinese in the early twentieth century) and the sense of a larger-than-life fictional canvas, as defined in *An Anatomy of Criticism*.

[2] For a perceptive analysis, see David Wang, *Fictional Realism in Twentieth-Century China* (New York: Columbia University Press, 1996), 27–35.

economy" of the Chinese countryside. Instead, the entire novel is focused on the urban metropolis of Shanghai, circa 1930.

In the narrative foreground is the novel's central protagonist, Wu Sunfu, a Chinese "native capitalist" whose grandiose ambition of building up his own industrial empire by amassing financial wealth through the stock market is eventually thwarted by his enemy, an artful "comprador" working for Western interests. However, this Marxist-inspired economic factor is eclipsed by the human melodrama involving a dozen characters mostly of the Shanghai bourgeoisie: aside from Wu himself, who occupies center stage, there are his underlings, other urban financiers, small entrepreneurs, socialites, and above all petit bourgeois intellectuals. This last category of people—both men and women—is especially close to Mao Dun's heart, as he had found himself defending this group's historical role in a previous debate with some of his more eagerly revolutionary critics.[3] This kind of "contradictory" (the Chinese meaning of Mao Dun's name) stance for which Mao Dun was repeatedly taken to task is derived from two sources. On the one hand, Mao Dun was a self-declared "realistic" writer from the May 4th movement (he became editor of the influential *Short Story* magazine in 1921, which overnight was transformed from a rather traditional popular magazine into a journal of New Literature). Thus he owed a loyalty to French realism, in particular Balzac, in the fictional design of the novel.[4] On the other hand, as a newly converted Marxist, he was groping toward a "master narrative" of historical stages and of the historical role of each social class in them. In his view, China at that time was entering the stage of capitalism, and a proletarian society was yet to emerge. Thus the petit bourgeoisie was destined, though doomed, to play out its historical role in the "present."

In so doing, however, Mao Dun found himself confronting yet another reality that was also somewhat at odds with his historical vision—that is, the urban culture of a rising Chinese modernity as manifested in Shanghai's material and commodity culture. In the very beginning of the novel we find the following famous passage:

> The sun had just sunk below the horizon and a gentle breeze caresses one's face. . . . Under a sunset-mottled sky, the towering framework of the Garden Bridge was mantled in a gathering mist. Whenever a tram passed over the

---

[3] See Mao Dun, "Cong Guling dao Dongjing" ("From Guling to Tokyo"), in *Mao Dun lun chuangzuo* (*Mao Dun on Creative Writing*) (Shanghai: Shanghai wenyi chubanshe, 1980), 28–43.

[4] See Mao Dun, "Ziye shi zenyang xiechengde" ("How Midnight Was Written"), in *Mao Dun lun chuangzuo*, 61.

bridge, the overhead cable suspended below the top of the steel frame threw off bright, greenish sparks. Looking east, one could see the warehouses of foreign firms on the waterfront of Pootung like huge monsters crouching in the gloom, their lights twinkling like countless tiny eyes. To the west, one saw with a shock of wonder on the roof of a building a gigantic Neon sign in flaming red and phosphorescent green: Light! Heat! Power![5]

Indeed it is the "shock of wonder"—at the dynamism of the dawn of urban modernity—that is vividly registered by Mao Dun's prose: the three key words *light*, *heat*, and *power* as well as the word *Neon* are written originally in English with exclamation marks attached. The passage seems to suggest that all this outburst of modernity was doomed to failure since it would not stand the encroaching economic onslaught of Western capitalism and the eventual rise of the proletariat. Hence the evocation of sunset and the obvious metaphor of "midnight." At the same time, however, the novel, especially the first few chapters, is suffused with emblems of Shanghai's material culture—cars, electric lights and fans, radios, Western-style dresses, mansions and furniture, guns, cigars, perfume, high-heeled shoes, and beauty parlors—that belie the intended messages of doom. This gallery of "materials" inevitably gives rise to a picture of cosmopolitan splendor, the like of which was seldom depicted in previous modern Chinese fiction. In this "sunset" world of urban modernity the characters throw themselves into a fervid pursuit of sensual pleasures. Indeed, their manifested stance of decadence—of repressed desires that find release in whirlwind of activities— is what really animates the narrative. The women characters, in particular the mystical socialite, Xu Manli, are described with a florid style bordering on purple prose that nevertheless imparts a surrealistic visual dimension: the scene in chapter 17, in which the socialite dances and cavorts with her male admirers in a drunken nocturnal orgy on a ship sailing along the Whampoa River, seems to be a fictional replica of Hollywood musicals. From a gendered point of view, one can even argue that the woman's body is a pronounced feature in a narrative structured entirely from the point of view of the male gaze. The sensuous sight of the various parts of the female

---

[5] Mao Dun, *Midnight*, trans. Sidney Shapiro, 2nd ed. (Beijing: Foreign Languages Press, 1979), 1. Also quoted in Leo Ou-fan Lee, *Shanghai Modern: The Flowering of a New Urban Culture in China, 1930–1945* (Cambridge, Mass.: Harvard University Press, 1999), 3. I have also given more extensive analysis of the material milieu of Shanghai's modern culture in chapter 1 of this book. For an analysis of Mao Dun's fiction in terms of revolutionary discourse, see Jianhua Chen, *Geming de xiandaixing: Zhonghuo geming huayu kaolun* (*Revolutionary Modernity: On the Discourses of Revolution in China*) (Shanghai: Shanghai guji chubanshe, 2000), 286–336.

body—particularly breasts and legs—is sufficient to cause the instant death of an old member of rural gentry (Wu Sunfu's father) who has just landed on Shanghai's foreign Bund (chapter 1). Near the end of the novel (in chapter 14), Wu Sunfu releases his pent-up sexual desire by raping his woman servant: this "naturalistic" scene reminiscent of Frank Norris's novel *Octopus* was presumably inserted at the suggestion of a friend, Qu Qiubai, another Marxist and onetime chairman of the underground Chinese Communist Party.

Side by side with the novel's decadent bourgeoisie is a collective portrait of the other social forces in Chinese society. Since the peasants and landlords in the countryside receive short shrift, mentioned only in chapter 4 early in the novel, the bulk of the novel's latter part is devoted to the urban workers' failed strike and the financial maneuvers in the city's stock exchange. The former is depicted in a rather twisted plot of evil and betrayal, whereas the latter is done with detached observation. Mao Dun claimed that he had done on-the-spot research of the Chinese stock market in order to give these scenes a sense of reality. But he was obviously a layman, as were most May 4th writers, with regard to the workers' world and their "ressentiment." The chapters (13–15) of the workers' strike invites comparison not only with Fritz Lang's cinematic evocation in *Metropolis* (which was shown in Shanghai) but also with another contemporary novel, *Shanghai*, written and published at roughly the same time (1929–31) by the Japanese "neosensualist" writer Yokomitsu Reiichi, in which the evocation of a workers' strike is depicted as a tidal wave of humanity in an imagistic prose style that fully conveys the terror evoked by the rising Chinese masses.[6] Yokomitsu's mostly foreign protagonists, like Mao Dun's native capitalists, find themselves both alienated and fascinated by this new force.

But Mao Dun seems to be at a loss in finding an appropriate style that can do full justice to the emergence of this new fictional character, the proletarian collective. Herein lies perhaps another "contradiction" between the author's intention and his fictional realization. One need not invoke Lukács to see the semblance of a fictional "totality" that is at odds with the writer's intention and ideological predilection. Whether or not Mao Dun's novel meets Lukács's criteria of realism—whether his novel's technique was mainly to "describe or to narrate"—is subject to interpretation.[7] Most

---

[6] See my analysis of the novel in *Shanghai Modern*, 316–20.

[7] Though he may or may not have read Lukács, Mao Dun is in fact quite aware of Balzac's "contradiction" between his political conservatism and his fictional grasp of historical totality. But Mao Dun attributes it to Balzac's technical "vision" (*yanguang*), a technique grounded in

Chinese scholars of the novel, however, simply invoke Mao Dun's own intention but fail to subject the text to any detailed scrutiny. Western scholars, on the other hand, choose to find fault with Mao Dun's descriptive prose (C. T. Hsia, for instance, considers it deficient when measured against the yardstick of good fictional writing),[8] or seek out the structures of the novel's allegorical or revolutionary meaning.[9] Mao Dun himself, however, was quite interested in the craft of fiction, as evidenced in his numerous articles on the subject. His inability to give a full and vivid account of the rising proletariat can be attributed to his lack of personal experience, as he himself once acknowledged. But more significantly, Mao Dun may have been caught in another form of historical "contradiction": because the full force of capitalism was yet to exert its impact on the Chinese writer's imagination, he was in a sense caught in a similar situation as that of the Italian futurists. "The Italy in which the Futurists first appeared was not a highly industrialized country. Although these Futurist poets, novelists, and painters had a subjective demand—to use a new technique in order to express the life atmosphere of a modern industrial metropolis—the situation of their own lives was not yet equipped with the objective conditions. As a result, their self-styled creative technique was rather comparable to that of kids painting tortoises on the wall."[10] Given such a negative comparison, we might say that Mao Dun's more realistic technique fared rather better.

That *Midnight* represents a masterful attempt at historical fiction is beyond doubt. For scholars in modern Chinese literature, the novel stands as a milestone that established not only Mao Dun's own reputation as a major writer whose official fame ranked him in second or third place (behind only Lu Xun and Ba Jin) but also the classic status of revolutionary fiction in the history of modern Chinese fiction. As such, it continues to hold some fascination for students in the field. For educated laymen, however, what makes

---

"typicality" and comprehensiveness. See Mao Dun, "Cong sixiang dao jiqiao" ("From Ideas to Technique"), written first in 1943 and included in *Mao Dun lun chuangzuo*, 513. Mao Dun himself acknowledged, however, that it is easier to learn technique from reading literary masterpieces than from life experience.

[8] See C. T. Hsia, *A History of Modern Chinese Fiction* (New Haven, Conn.: Yale University Press, 1960), chap. 6. Hsia's yardstick is derived from F. R. Leavis's "great tradition" of realism as moral critique.

[9] Wang, *Fictional Realism in Twentieth-Century China*, chaps. 2–3.

[10] Mao Dun, "Tan miaoxie de jiqiao" ("On the technique of Description"), in *Mao Dun lun chaungzuo*, 507. The only Western scholar who has given a full account of Mao Dun's literary theory and technique is Marian Galik. See his *Mao Dun and Modern Chinese Literary Criticism* (Wiesbaden: F. Steiner, 1969).

it still worth reading, even in English translation, lies in its portraiture of character and mood, its rich repository of material details, as well as its strange intimations of a historical era that was once so close to the author but is now passé. It is obvious to all that present-day Shanghai as a global metropolis on the rise has all but eclipsed its revolutionary past. What Mao Dun saw as its final twilight glow on the eve of the revolution turns out to be ironically prophetic, except that after a long revolution the "midnight" has somehow metamorphosed into a new dawn of global capitalism.

ERNESTO FRANCO

Buenos Aires
(*Adán Buenosayres*, Leopoldo Marechal, 1948)

Leopoldo Marechal's *Adán Buenosayres* is a work hiding behind a mask. Its earliest reviewer, Julio Cortázar (one of the few impassioned fans of the book's more than seven hundred pages) praised it for its "multiple excesses" comparing it to a masked ball—an exchange and mixing of hidden meanings and disguised characters.[1] These veiled elements include the author's autobiography; portraits of the leading figures of the Argentine literary avant-garde during the 1920s that gathered around the journals *Proa* and *Martín Fierro*; satirical profiles and anthropological sketches of countless society figures; and the "unbridled flood" of literary allusions and an entire encyclopedia of stylistic and compositional parodies.[2]

These thousand masks are part of an enduring fresco of Buenos Aires in the 1920s, the years that would define the city for the entire twentieth century and that would be transformed, updated, or merely remembered by its greatest authors, from Jorge Luis Borges to Osvaldo Soriano, from Julio Cortázar, to Manuel Puig. Even popular culture would come to know the Buenos Aires of this era through the words and music of the tango.

In *Adán Buenosayres*, the city is depicted with great realism—its streets, its neighborhoods, and even real addresses. But the city is there first and foremost as a place where cultural and psychological identity moves beyond circumstance and becomes—as is the author's explicit intention—a place of the soul, an "archipelago of island-men who have no connections to one another."[3]

The title of the book is the first indication of this internalized world: in one of his autobiographical notes, Leopoldo Marechal remembers that when he was a child, his playmates in the Maipú countryside did not know or did not care to know his name, and so they called him "Buenos Aires," a toponomastic stratagem shared by children all over the world. "This is the origin of the surname *Buenosayres* that I have given to the main character of

---

[1] J. Cortázar, "Leopoldo Marechal: *Adán Buenosayres*," in *Realidad* (Buenos Aires) 14 (March–April 1949). Cited in L. Marechal, *Adán Buenosayres*, Collección Archivos, ed. J. Lafforgue and F. Colla (Paris, 1997), 879–83.

[2] Ibid., 879.

[3] Marechal, *Adán Buenosayres*, ed. Lafforgue and Colla, 39.

my novel," wrote the author.[4] The name *Adán*, or Adam, makes perfect sense when the book is read (in accordance with the author's instructions) as an initiatory journey where Adam from Buenos Aires, a city flooded with many peoples and cultures, can never be the one to initiate experiences. He is rather someone who from the outset will be the recipient of previously completed experiences.

During the same period, other famous Argentine authors, essayists, and meditative moralists, attempted to portray the "national character" and the city, like Ezequiel Martínez Estrada in *La cabeza de Goliat, microscopía de Buenos Aires* (*Goliath's Head, a Microscopic View of Buenos Aires*, 1940) or Raúl Scalabrini Ortiz in *El hombre que está solo y espera* (*The Man Alone, Who Waits*, 1931). Contrarily, *Adán Buenosayres* is a much more complex national autobiography and a narrative map that can be used to plot a journey through the city's intersections and neighborhoods.

The long voyage of this novel moves through seven "books" preceded by an "Indispensable Prologue," in which the author (who also signs off as the narrator) briefly recounts the funeral of the main character, Adán Buenosayres. To free the reader of any lingering doubt, Marechal twice repeats that the coffin is so light that it appears to contain "not the surrendered flesh of a man defunct, but the slender material of a finished poem."[5] Just before dying, Adán left the author two manuscripts. The first is *Cuaderno de tapas azules* (which can be translated as the *Notebook with Blue Covers*); the second is *Viaje oscura ciudad de Cacodelphia* (or *Voyage to the Obscure City of Cacodelphia*). The author-editor decides immediately to publish these two extraordinary works, and, in order that they may be better understood, he decides to preface them with a portrait of Adán Buenosayres and his adventures in the twenty-four hours that preceded his death. The portrait occupies the space of the first five books, the *Cuaderno* the sixth, the *Viaje* the seventh.

Leopoldo Marechal was born a poet. He always considered himself to be a poet who wrote a novel about Adán Buenosayres because the genre momentarily suited the material in question. He worked on the book for many years, beginning in Paris in 1929 and continuing until its publication in 1948. He would return to it again and again at conferences and in essays on poetics in which he reconstructed "keys" for its interpretation and its genesis.

In "Autobiografía de un novelista," for example, he remembered how it all began with a discussion of the nature of the novel with Macedonio

---

[4] Cited by F. Colla, "Cronologia," in Marechal, *Adán Buenosayres*, 566.

[5] Marechal, "Prólogo indispensable," *Adán Buenosayres*, 5.

Fernández, an author not very well known today but much cited in the pages of *Adán Buenosayres* and a true guiding light in the circles of the Argentine historical avant-garde.[6] Macedonio believed that "the novel is the story of destiny fulfilled," while Marechal, a man of deep religious beliefs, added that "destiny" must be understood as a journey both historical and spiritual.[7] In other words, destiny is a metamorphosis of life and a ripening of the soul.

Marechal had a vague plan for his work, and he had a model: Cervantes and his *Quixote*. But he also continued to devour works on critical theory, until he finally concluded that "the novel is nothing more than a substitute for the epic poetry of antiquity," from which the gods, heroes, and prosody have vanished.[8] He then began to read Homer, the *Aeneid*, chivalric poetry, and in particular, the *Orlando furioso* and Dante's *Divine Comedy* and the *Vita nova*, for their spiritual content. Marechal borrowed not only inspiration from these works but also motifs, stylistic and compositional calques, and even narrative figures, which are appropriated directly, but lightly veiled. "My hero," said Marechal, "had to complete a journey that was both physical and metaphysical," adding that "I myself had to complete a voyage in the company of Argentine heroes, with Argentine ontologies, and Argentine geographies."[9]

The journey that unfolds in the first five books of *Adán Buenosayres* is divided into two movements:

[They] take place along Gurruchaga Street, which starts in my neighborhood, Villa Crespo, crosses Warnes [Avenue] and ends up in the Palermo Quarter. One of these movements is expansive, or rather, centrifugal. The character abandons his home and his center, and he loses himself in the sensation of centrifugal movement. He irremediably travels along the street of dispersion, multiplicity, and adventure. The movement that follows is complementary. It consists of centripetal concentration. In other words, the character begins to concentrate again and returns to his center along the very same street.[10]

---

[6] L. Marechal, "Autobiografía de un novelista," *Proa* 49 (September–October 2000): 61–71. Marechal had already espoused similar ideas in "Claves de *Adán Buenosayres*," which was included in his *Cuaderno de navegación*, published in Buenos Aires in 1966.

[7] Ibid., 62.

[8] Ibid., 63.

[9] Ibid., 64–65.

[10] Ibid., 66.

The first movement consists of a search for a woman, Solveig Amundsen, a very real girl who lives in the Saavedra Quarter. Someone is singing the first lines of a tango, and Adán slowly awakes, and with him, as if in a "parody of the Genesis," Buenos Aires begins to come to life, as do the neighborhood voices and the dockworkers. We are watching the world as it unfolds, but we are also watching the birth of 303 Monte Egemont Street (today's Tres Arroyos Street), Buenos Aires, Argentina. Then Adán, the first man, goes to wake up his friend the philosopher, Samuel Testler, whose robe is described as a parody of Achilles' shield. Adán begins to cross the city, and he is determined to present his beloved with the *Cuaderno de tapas azules*, in which the secret of his soul is preserved: "He knew that as soon as he reached Warnes Avenue, he would enter a universe of restless creatures: on the other side of the street, it was as if all the peoples of the earth were congregating. Their languages were being mixed in a terrific chord. They were battling one another with gestures and punches, and they were preparing the elementary scenery for their tragedies and farces in broad daylight. They transformed everything into sounds, longing, happiness, hate, and love."[11]

This novel is a sort of "Argentinopea" or Argentine epic. The mythical figures of ancient Greece have been costumed in metropolitan garb: Polyphemus is a blind beggar who notices everything; Circe is a waitress and aspiring actress; and then there are the sirens, the street battles, and the funerals. Adán finally arrives at the Amundsens' home and enters the bourgeois salon of his beloved, Solveig. Together with philosopher Samuel Testler, he meets some easily recognizable friends: Luís Pereda is Jorge Luis Borges; Bernini, the sociologist, is the above-mentioned Raúl Scalabrini Ortiz; Shultze, the astrologist, is Xul Solar, a painter and important intellectual figure of the Argentine avant-garde, who took to the streets with the Martinfierristas. At the Amundsen residence, these salon philosophers participate in a bizarre discussion where the question of Argentine identity is main topic of conversation. Marechal humorously portrays their endless bantering and the ceremonies of friendship—classic themes in Argentine literature. "What is your position as an Argentine?" Pereda-Borges asks Adán-Marechal. Confused by the question, he answers:

> I do not feel any solidarity with the reality that the country is currently living, and so I am alone and immovable: I am a hopeful Argentine—at least in regard to the country itself. In regard to myself, this is not always the case.

---

[11] Marechal, *Adán Buenosayres*, 1.48.

When my grandparents came to this country, they severed their ties to their traditions and they abandoned their value system. It is up to me to bind those ties once again and to reconstruct the values held by my race. That's where I am. I believe that when everyone does this, our country will find its spirituality.[12]

His beloved, Solveig, ignores the poor Adán, and in his disappointment, he leaves the Amundsen residence with his friends and sets out on what is called an "absurd evening," wandering around the Saavedra Quarter where the city and the desert battle one another. The reader can clearly hear the echoes of Joyce's *Ulysses*. Their conversation continues deep into the night, and the "spirit of the earth" reappears, degraded and derided, as a *guacho*, as a beggar, as the "voice of the river," or as the body of a dead horse—the richest symbolic figure of them all. This is as if to say that the fragile *guacho* tradition was fractured when it collided with metropolitan excess. The group happens upon a long funeral vigil. Marechal uses it as a stage on which the entire cast of linguistic and commonplace figures of the metropolitan tradition can move between satire, participation, and humor. A good indicator of this long and complex scene is what is said of one of the minor characters: "The words of a tango could contain your whole story."[13] The "absurd evening" continues along these lines, and the party finds itself visiting Italian Ciro Rossini's newsstand and then the depressing brothel run by Doña Venus. Then, back at home, Adán dreams of Philadelphia, the ideal city where all will be brothers.

The next day, Adán is "captious and sad." His amorous anguish is a projection of a greater anguish. "It is borne out of an existential crisis," noted Cortázar. It is "the same crisis that defines every Argentine on all mental, moral, and sentimental levels, and above all, it defines the *Porteño* [that is, an inhabitant of Buenos Aires] who is lashed about by irreconcilable winds."[14] The same evening, Adán returns home, and he finds a beggar on his doorstep. He invites him in, and then angels and demons fight over his soul. The beggar is the Christ and spiritual truth that has been discovered after having passed through the deceit of the world. This is the end of Marechal's second centripetal movement. The physical and metaphysical voyages have ended together with the first five books of the novel.

---

[12] Ibid., 2.123.
[13] Ibid., 3.195.
[14] Cortázar, "Leopoldo Marechal: *Adán Buenosayres*," 880.

All that remains is the *Cuaderno* and the *Viaje*. The former is an explicit calque of the *Vita nova*, in which Adán recounts his love as a spiritual journey and he depicts Solveig Amundsen as an angelic *Porteña* woman. The latter is a parody of Dante's *Inferno*, including circles, punishments, and *contrapasso*, and a Virgil who is dressed for the occasion as the astrologist Schultze. The Buenos Aires of the first five chapters passes once again before the reader's eyes with the addition of yet more historical figures like Silvina Ocampo. Again, emblematic characters appear, like the one who is called the Character, an archetypal figure drawn from administrative bureaucracy; or Don Ecumenical, a sad everyman who is transformed into an insect, as in Kafka; or Belona, a woman too beautiful to avoid a tragic fate, as in Poe.

The city is portrayed no longer in the phenomenology of daily life but rather in its moral essence. Marechal uses the *Viaje* as a platform for populist moralism—a symptom of the Perónist leanings that caused him to be ostracized him for many years. He considers these chapters, and especially the *Cuaderno*, as the center and the essence of *Adán Buenosayres*. They form the "metaphysical" part of the main character's journey, and they distanced the book from the *Ulysses* model that the critics often cited. Cortázar was right when he called them appendices to the book, or at the least, excess weight carried by an already complete novel.

Furio Jesi has interpreted this book as a trace "of a love that we fight but cannot suppress: the survival of mythical figures from whom we defend ourselves but who cannot be excluded from our psyche."[15] When read as a parody, it is also true that daily life in Buenos Aires is capable of fulfilling such an ambitious literary project. In the *Cuaderno* and the *Viaje*, myth—however metropolitan, modern, and commonplace—disappears, and its place is taken by an exercise in literary cultism that cannot be the apex or conclusion but only a single symptom of an entire universe previously traversed.

In his marginal notes to *Adán Buenosayres*, Ricardo Piglia remembers an episode taken from *Viajes en Europa, Africa y América* (*Travels in Europe, Africa, and America*) by Domingo Faustino Sarmiento, the most important political and literary figure of nineteenth-century Argentina, author of *Facundo*, a so-called national book of Argentine culture. Sarmiento recounted how he once saw Balzac from a distance at a ball in Paris. Sarmiento remained right there, at a distance, in a corner of the ballroom. Piglia wrote of this glimpse from afar that it could be the opening scene of the history of the

---

15 F. Jesi, *Letteratura e mito* (Turin, 1968), 189.

Argentine novel.[16] Marechal and his generation looked upon European culture in the very same way. Even this epic tale of the southern, metropolitan Adam shows that this gaze finds its power only when it passes through lenses purchased in a Buenos Aires eyeglass shop. Maybe the one at 303 Monte Egmont Street.

Translated by Jeremy Parzen

[16] R. Piglia, "Notas al margen de un ejemplar de *Adán Buenosayres*," in Marechal, *Adán Buenosayres*, xvii.

ERNEST EMENYONU

Lagos
(*People of the City*, Cyprian Ekwensi, 1954)

People of the City is the first West African novel in modern style to be published in the English language. Published in England by Andrew Dakers in
1954, it was not originally intended as a novel. It was rather a stringing together of thirteen different short stories, similar only in the fact that they all
had one city as their setting. In 1949, Cyprian Ekwensi, a pharmacist by profession (with a flair for broadcasting), was a teacher at the Lagos School of
Pharmacy in Nigeria. Lagos was then an emerging but fast-growing urban
metropolis that was also the capital city of Nigeria. Along with his teaching
assignments, Ekwensi wrote and published short stories in newspapers,
and also hosted a weekly radio program, "West African Voices," which was
broadcast by the Nigerian Broadcasting Service every Wednesday night. In
1951, Ekwensi won a government scholarship for further studies in pharmacy at the Chelsea School of Pharmacy, London University. It was in the
ship that took him to England that Ekwensi began stringing together thirteen stories he had broadcast on Radio Nigeria into one long story to be
titled *Lajide of Lagos*, after an obnoxious, capitalist-oriented real estate
entrepreneur, Lajide. At the end of the fourteen days aboard, however, it
was as *People of the City* and not *Lajide of Lagos* that the finished manuscript
emerged. As *Lajide of Lagos,* the focus of the story was to have been on a
new capitalist class in the developing West African urban centers. But as
People of the City, the author shifted focus to the city itself as a center of corruption and immorality.

The novel thus becomes a stinging indictment of the city, a new feature of
the post–World War II African environment. Ekwensi's redirected focus
was intended to warn Africans about the consequences of development as
well as to confront the city dwellers with the revolting social injustices and
outrageous immoralities that seem to have become part of their way of life.
Ekwensi contended that the role of the novelist was to hold a mirror up to
nature and describe the reflection truthfully, regardless of any oversensitivity
of his public to this truth. In this self-assigned role, Ekwensi has inimitably
made himself into a chronicler of city life in Africa and built for himself both
fame and notoriety as the African Daniel Defoe with an unusual preoccupation with the social meaningfulness of the novel as a work of art. But
Ekwensi brings to the African literary scene some positive attributes of

Daniel Defoe's literary models, including the depiction of scandalous sophisticated womanhood, incipient immoral and aberrant pageantry, and the choice of the city replete with its diverse iniquities, as a veritable setting of the novel as a work of art.

The first reviewers of *People of the City* were chiefly attracted by this phenomenon. South Africa's Peter Abrahams saw Ekwensi as becoming as important to the future literature of West Africa as was Kwame Nkrumah (the first African in British West Africa to become prime minister in a modern twentieth-century democratic fashion) to its politics. A reviewer in the *Times* of London saw *People of the City* as a vivid picture of life in a West African city. And yet another reviewer declared that *People of the City* told more about West Africa than fifty government reports. However, in Ireland, the novel was banned as pornographic and obscene.

Part 1 of *People of the City* is titled "how the city attracts all types and how the unwary must suffer from ignorance of its ways."[1] The key word is "attracts," because it implies that people are drawn and lured to the city by its glittering appearances, but upon contact, the city destroys the individuals with its corrupting influences. This is in alignment with Ekwensi's theory of the evolving midtwentieth-century new African cities: "The city is a terribly corrupting influence, a den for Ali Baba where forty thieves have stored all their gold, and anyone who has the magic words can go and help himself. And sometimes greed traps the *sesame* and the thieves come back and stab the intruder to death as they did to Ali Baba's brother."[2] The new city, therefore, becomes the *dream* of the emerging African middle class, but rather than crystallizing into glorious self-fulfillment, the dream becomes merely a mirage that constantly eludes and finally violates the dreamer.

Amusa Sango, the main character of the novel, is one such dreamer. He thinks he knows exactly why he is in the city—to live his own life and make a name for himself as a famous bandleader and powerful journalist. He is in the city to achieve success and become a celebrity. His goals are self-oriented. His search is a personal search. He wants his road toward this to be free from interference.

Ekwensi was writing at a time when nationalist movements and the struggle for political independence were gaining ground in Nigeria. Many people had started to anticipate the golden era of freedom and emancipation. The society was at a point of transition between the old order and the new.

---

[1] Cyprian Ekwensi, *People of the City* (London: Andrew Dakers, 1954; reprint, London: Heinemann, 1963), 1. All quotations are from the Heinemann edition.

[2] See Ernest Emenyonu, *Cyprian Ekwensi* (London: Evans Publisher, 1974), 29–46.

Emerging new urban centers became symbols of the new consciousness and of enticing material opulence. They were colorful and enchanting, but they were also crowded, multiracial, and full of aberrant new behavior that was corrupt and complex. The individuals of the new age and environments were soon torn apart by selfish aggrandizements. Despite all promptings to share in the development and challenges of their new nation, they clamored for empty self-sufficiency as they were caught up in ecstatic enjoyment, frivolity, and sensual excitement. Ekwensi chose the then Nigerian capital city of Lagos as the base for reflecting these confused priorities and emotions of his new Africans. The youth in rural locations surged to Lagos to be part of its landscape and transformation.

True to his setting, the characters in the novel are drawn between choosing the picturesque rural life of the village, which is tradition-bound, and the recently established city, which is devoid of personal and familial ties and any continuity of custom. In such a setting the maverick transient characters evolve and grow. They find themselves thrust into the anonymous, alien atmosphere—forlorn, alone, and rejected as their dreams crumble before their very eyes. Yet they remain in the city that has turned into a barren wasteland where businessmen are dishonest, politicians corrupt; where neighbors turn into enemies and friends are at best conniving manipulators. Still undeterred, they meet few people with whom they can genuinely commune or truly say they love. Rather, they are confronted daily by an environment no less depressing than its human inhabitants—filthy, decadent, hopeless, and elusive. The greedy, the violently ambitious, and the licentious surround and dictate the pace of the city. Internally they are empty carcasses, but outwardly they manifest a self-impressed sense of synthetic importance and plastic glory. Despite immediate superficial attractions, the hopes and dreams of the young newcomers to the city (for success and material wealth) remain unfulfilled until they perish or are swept into oblivion. This picture of the evolving new African environments on the eve of political independence became the consuming theme of Ekwensi's urban adult fiction. *People of the City* was his first serious expression of the theme, but in the enthusiasm to provide cautions and blueprints for living in the new urban centers, Ekwensi, in the views of some critics, unconsciously allowed art to be drowned by the pursuit of social realities. Emmanuel Obiechina has declared that in *People of the City*

> we are led from the beginning not to expect a deep and extensive exploration of character but the use of characters as puppets for furthering the writer's design, which is the exposure of the utter rottenness of city ways.

There are in fact no characters strictly speaking but "people" and there is no intense exploration of life but a description of incidents which condition life. The city with its squalid life is exposed through incidents and events in the lives of its men and women.

To carry out his declared purpose of tearing the veil off the city, and exposing its many corruptions, Ekwensi chooses for his main character, a young crime reporter of a Lagos newspaper who also leads a dance-band in his spare time. Now, this choice is crucial. From the vantage point of crime journalism, the hero, Amusa Sango, could ferret out and report the wicked happenings in the city just as from the equal vantage point of the night club he could observe the sordid night life of the city people. In other words, by making his chief character both a journalist and a dance-band leader, Ekwensi has provided himself with a character through whose eyes he sees the whole spectrum of the city's corruption.[3]

Indeed, the novel has an array of fleeting characters through whose fancies and fantasies the reader captures in cinematographic bubbles the ugly events in the city. But the characters show only passing glimpses of themselves and very little of their inner selves. Amusa Sango's "desire in this city was peace and the desire to forge ahead." But he is not seen vigorously striving to achieve this goal. The author declares, "No one would believe this, knowing the kind of life he led: that beneath his gay exterior lay a nature serious and determined to carve for itself a place of renown in this city of opportunities" (3). This authorial comment, rather than in-depth exploration of the inner dynamics of the character, is evident throughout the novel. The reader knows each character mainly by what the author says about him or her. Lajide, the landlord; Aina, the teenage prostitute; Beatrice I, the tantalizing female who seeks and dispenses sensual pleasures; Grunnings, the soon-to-vanish residual crust of colonial double standards and lechery; and Elina, Mama's distant choice for Sango, are all shadowy stereotyped figures created to meet certain preconceived ends of the author. Sango never actually comes to terms with his real self. Any idealized plans that the reader is informed he may have had are quickly smothered and swept off the stage. His expectations of becoming a bandleader are destroyed, and then he is abruptly relieved of his job as a crime reporter because he has let his personal feelings interfere with his reporting. Similarly, within a very short time, Bayo, Beatrice I, Lajide, De Perira, and Sango's mother all die. This

---

[3] See Emmanuel Obiechina, "Cyprian Ekwensi as Novelist: Reflections on *People of the City*," in Ernest Emenyonu, ed., *The Essential Ekwensi* (Ibadan: Heinemann, 1987), chap. 2.

obvious habit of killing off the characters for which he has no more use is an artistic defect, but it fulfills Ekwensi's virtual puritanic dictum that "the wages of sin is death."

These often generally orchestrated faults notwithstanding, *People of the City* occupies a major place of importance in the historical development of West African fiction in English in the twentieth century. Charles Nnolim, in his seminal study of Ekwensi's comic vision, points out that as a novelist Cyprian Ekwensi "is in the position of a pioneer in West African fiction." Elaborating further, Nnolim describes Ekwensi's pioneering literary role in comparative and lucid terms:

> He [Ekwensi] is historically important to us in the sense that John Bunyan, Jonathan Swift, and Henry Fielding are important in the history of the English novel. John Bunyan (in *The Pilgrim's Progress*), Jonathan Swift (in *Gulliver's Travels*) and Henry Fielding (in *Jonathan Wild*) were writers of what Arnold Kettle calls *The moral fable*. The above writers formed a buffer and provided a transition from the medieval allegory and the Bible to the eighteenth century novel. Their major concern was society which they satirized with their sharp pens. The origins of the moral fable were from the Bible, the morality plays of the middle ages, and the Sermons. And the moral fable generally illustrates some moral concept or attitude, although Kettle is quick to point out that the author of the moral fable is not necessarily more concerned with morals than other novelists; his only distinction is that in the moral fable, the central moral discovery seems to have been made by the author prior to the conception of the book. In other words, the author starts off with his moral truth (e.g., "Honesty is the best policy") and then blows life into it. Ekwensi starts with the moral vision "the wages of sin is death," and manages to blow life into it.[4]

Ekwensi, who was a pioneer of the pamphlet literature in West Africa, was also a pioneer in the transition of the African moral fable from its oral to the written form. His *Ikolo the Wrestler and Other Ibo Tales* (London: Nelson, 1947) was one of the earliest attempts to recreate African folktales into written forms in the English language. Similarly, his *When Love Whispers* (Onitsha: Tabansi Press, 1948) was the first title in the famous *Onitsha Market (Pamphlet) Literature*, which formed the historic bridge from journalistic

---

[4] See Charles Nnolim, "Cyprian Ekwensi: His Comic Vision," in Emenyonu, ed., *The Essential Ekwensi,* chap. 11.

to novel writing in West Africa. But with *People of the City*, Ekwensi established himself not only as a pioneer key figure in the historical development of modern West African writing in English, but truly the father of the twentieth-century Nigerian novel. Nnolim has succinctly articulated this legacy: "Ekwensi's historical importance in the Nigerian novel as a buffer between nothingness and a realistic written tradition may not have been sufficiently appreciated. Before Ekwensi, there may have been sermons and the Bible, but no Nigerian novel. That he wrote *When Love Whispers* (1948) and *People of the City* (1954) before Nigeria's first real novel *Things Fall Apart* (1958) with its strong roots in the oral tradition, puts him across clearly as the father of Nigerian fiction."[5]

What makes *People of the City* still a vital reading in the twenty-first century is the fact that it captured an era, which although passed, now provides a better understanding of the foundations of the lopsided values and sociopolitical disequilibriums that pervade present-day African cities, thereby making them legitimate concerns of the modern novel in Africa and of writers who focus on those concerns with integrity—the committed artists and sensitive consciences of their era.

---

[5] Ibid., 81.

ROGER ALLEN

Cairo
(*The Cairo Trilogy*, Naguib Mahfouz, 1956–1957)

When the Egyptian novelist, Najib Mahfuz (Naguib Mahfouz [1911–]) was announced as the 1988 Nobel Laureate in Literature, the committee's citation laid particular stress on one work, the trilogy of novels that Mahfouz had completed in 1952 (before the Egyptian revolution) and published during 1956 and 1957. They noted that "[T]he depiction of the individuals relates very closely to intellectual, social and political conditions," and that "through his writings Mahfuz has exerted considerable influence in his country." Named after three streets or quarters in the old city of Cairo, the novels are *Bayn al-Qasrayn* [*Palace Walk*], *Qasr al-Shawq* [*Palace of Desire*], and *Al-Sukkariyyah* [*Sugar Street*]. Previous to the Nobel award, Mahfouz had become famous as a writer of fiction throughout the Arab world, with many novels and short-story collections to his credit, but it was and is *The Cairo Trilogy* that has remained his most famous work, one that earned him the State Prize for Literature in Cairo in 1970.

Mahfouz has reported that his preparations for writing this enormous work took up five years of his life. It may be seen as the culmination of a novelistic project that he began in the 1940s. That was, of course, the time of the Second World War, when Cairo and its people found themselves playing unwilling hosts to the British Army, a situation that was the continuation of a process of occupation that had lasted, albeit under different terms of reference, since 1882. The general political unrest and social deprivation that such circumstances engendered were sufficiently powerful to cause Mahfouz to transfer his purview from ancient Egypt (he had published three novels set in that period) to contemporary Egypt and especially the life and aspirations of the poorer segments of society in the older quarters of the capital city.

The streets and alleys of those quarters serve as the backdrop for the three novels of the *Trilogy*. Each volume is named after a street where the members of different generations from a single family, that of 'Abd al-Jawwad (Gawwad, in Cairene dialect), live. The daily existences, the trials and tribulations, and the generational squabbles of the individuals who make up this family all become emblematic of an entire period of twentieth-century Egyptian life, spanning a period between about 1916 and 1944. At every conceivable level—the international and national, the public and private—this is a period of confrontation and profound change. The level of Mahfouz's interest in and research on this period is aptly reflected in the highly successful way in which he manages to capture historical moments, social trends, and intellectual movements within a broad canvas that his readers soon recognized as being totally authentic. In another remark he informs us that, in order to keep track of so many characters over such an extended time frame, he resorted to maintaining a file on each one—a small but telling reflection, no doubt, of the organizational methods of someone who spent his professional career working as a civil servant.

In the first volume, *Bayn al-Qasrayn* (1956), we are introduced to the rituals and tensions within the household of Sayyid 'Abd al-Jawwad, a complex personality who maintains a rigid discipline in his own house while indulging in all sorts of pleasures during his nocturnal excursions. His eldest son, Yasin, is just like his father in his continual pursuit of the good things in life (in fact, it emerges that they share the same girlfriend, Zannubah), but it is Fathi, the second son, who provides the first volume with its political focus in that he becomes one of the leaders of the student movement in opposition to British occupation and in the call for independence. One of the major events of the volume occurs when Aminah, 'Abd al-Jawwad's long-suffering wife, defies her husband by leaving the family home in order to visit the mosque of Al-Husayn to pray. On the way home she is knocked down and injured; when her husband finds out, he allows her to recover and then throws her out of the house, much to the dismay of her children and especially her daughters, Khadijah and 'A'ishah. The matter is eventually resolved, and family life returns to normal—until, that is, the first volume is brought to a conclusion with a description of the fateful day in 1919 when Fathi is killed during a huge demonstration.

With the tragic death of Fathi (and the confrontation between Yasin and his father) as continuing realities for the family, the focus in the second volume, *Qasr al-Shawq*, shifts to the younger son, Kamal. Many commentators (including Mahfouz himself) have linked the depiction of this young man who attends Teachers College and falls hopelessly in love with an aristocratic girl to the author himself. The great intellectual debates of the interwar period, and most especially the confrontation between religion and science, the theories of Darwin and traditional beliefs (as personified by Kamal's own father), these form the backdrop to the second volume, along with Kamal's friendship with the brother of his "beloved," 'A'idah.

The final volume of the three, *Al-Sukkariyyah,* focuses on the third generation of the family, the grandchildren. During the interim (even if it is in fact less than two decades) much has changed within the society. There is now a secular university where members of the younger generation may receive their higher education, and—a major revolution—it admits both male and female students (the consequences of which are not explored in detail in these novels, but are very much the focus of Mahfouz's later work, *Al-Maraya* (1972). The nationalist struggle continues, and yet the seeds of those problems that are to beset Egyptian society following its 1952 revolution are already evident. It is certainly a reflection of Mahfouz's own studies in philosophy and religion, as well as his astute observation of social patterns, that the two grandsons in the third novel, 'Abd al-Mun'im and Ahmad—the sons of Khadijah—are portrayed as living in the same household and yet adhering to totally different value systems: 'Abd al-Mun'im has joined the Muslim Brethren, while his brother is a Communist. Mahfouz thus brilliantly depicts the prerevolutionary situation in which disparate elements collaborated in the process of ousting the utterly corrupt ancien régime, only to find themselves shoved aside (and often imprisoned) after the revolution itself—a situation that is by no means confined to Egypt alone. Indeed, at the end of the third volume, Sayyid 'Abd al-Jawwad has died during an air raid; his two grandsons are in prison for their political activities; and Aminah, the figure who has tried valiantly to hold the family together against insuperable odds, is herself close to death. Much has changed in a span of three decades of political and social life, but clearly much still remains uncertain.

―――

These three novels appeared at a crucial moment in the modern history of Egypt and the Arab world. The primary goal of the Egyptian revolution of 1952 had been to get rid of the corrupt political system, with the king as its figurehead. By 1954, Colonel 'Abd al-Nasir (Nasser) had emerged as the primary figure among the Free Officers, but his participation in the Bandung Conference (1955) and the deft way in which he handled the Aswan Dam crisis, the Czech arms deal, and the Suez crisis of 1956 that followed these developments, all turned him into an instant hero, not merely for Egypt but for the entire Arab world. The long-awaited benefits of independence seemed to be at hand, and Mahfouz's great novelistic monument was published at this precise historical moment, providing a vivid and detailed fictional record of the period of struggle that had led up to this point in modern Arab history. Lukács's notions regarding the role of time as the great changer and organizer and its role in social-realist fiction were here illustrated in their clearest form, and critics across the Arab world immediately welcomed this work as confirmation of the novel genre's enormous importance as an advocate of change within all the emerging postindependence societies of the Arab world.

Like many of the world's great novel-sagas, Mahfouz's *Trilogy* thus became a major participant in the process of writing the narrative of Egypt's political and social history during a crucial period of the twentieth century. Beyond that significant and continuing role, however, the *Trilogy* is also a capstone in the process whereby the novel genre itself has become embedded within the different local cultures of the Arab region. The beginnings of this long, complex, and variegated development are to be found in the nineteenth century and form part of the process of change known in Arabic as the *nahdah* (renaissance), one with widely divergent forms and chronologies in the different subregions of the Arab world. In spite of such variations, however, the literary subset of the process involved two forces: first, the translation and adaptation of Western genres, and second (and often as a consequence of or reaction to the first) the search for indigenous forms that might serve as inspiration for a neoclassical revival. Here it has to be admitted that our knowledge of the Arabic narrative genres of the premodern period, and especially the more popular genres, such as the great sagas (*'Antar*, the *Bani Hilal*, and *Baybars*, for example, and, of course, *A Thousand and One Nights*), whose level of language has, until recently, excluded them from assessment as contributors to the literary tradition, is both randomized and incomplete. Thus any rigorous estimate of the relative role of indigenous elements in the development of modern Arabic fiction cannot as yet be undertaken. What is clear, though, is that the translation movement that began in the midnineteenth century in Egypt and that saw the rendering of European novels into Arabic (particularly those of historical romance—Dumas and Scott being two obvious examples) played a major role in the development of a reading public for novels. As was the case in the various European traditions of novel-writing, that public comprised a large percentage of female readers. In this context, the role of the Lebanese émigré author, Jurji Zaydan (d. 1914), cannot be overestimated. Other authors used older forms for contemporary purposes: Ahmad Faris al-Shidyaq (d. 1887), for example, uses a travel-narrative to Europe for astute observations on cultural and gender difference, all within the framework of an autobiography that relishes the stylistic complexities of earlier prose narratives (*Al-Saq 'ala al-Saq fi-ma huwa al-Faryaq*, 1855). The Egyptian Muhammad al-Muwaylihi (d. 1930) uses his renowned narrative, *Hadith 'Isa ibn Hisham* (1907), to paint a thoroughly critical and humorous portrait of the Egyptian capital in the throes of cultural confrontation, once again, however, reviving an older narrative genre and style and thus confining his readership to an educated elite.

By the first decade of the twentieth century, therefore, many examples of Arabic fictional narratives existed, most of which clearly demonstrate the early stages in a prolonged process of generic development. It is in this context that Muhammad Husayn Haykal's *Zaynab* (1913), a novel of frustrated love set in the Egyptian countryside, represents an important further stage on the road to Mahfouz's *Trilogy*, in that Egyptian characters are utilized to explore contemporary issues—and primarily the status of women in society. In the following decade there were a few isolated efforts at novel-writing, but litterateurs seem to have concentrated primarily on the short-story genre. It was not until the 1930s that a concentrated focus on the novel genre can be detected, and it is during that decade that Naguib Mahfouz begins the writing career that has had such an enormous impact on fiction writing in Arabic. During this period many prominent Egyptian literary figures tried their hand at writing in this relatively new "vogue." Tawfiq al-Hakim (d. 1987) with *'Awdat al-ruh* (1933) and *Yawmiyyat Na'ib fi al-Aryaf* (1937), 'Abbas Mahmud al-'Aqqad (d. 1964) with *Sarah* (1938), Taha Husayn (d. 1973) with *Adib* (1935), and Mahmud Tahir Lashin with *Hawwa' bi-la Adam* (1934)—these are just some of the many forays in novelistic writing during this decade. At this very same time Naguib Mahfouz, who had begun writing short stories while still a graduate student, turned his attention to the novel genre, but he did so in a typically methodical fashion. Wishing to understand clearly what were the narrative possibilities and generic characteristics of the novel, he consulted John Drinkwater's work, *The Outline of Literature*, and then proceeded to read a large cross-section of European novels, mostly in English or English translation. At the time he was working on a translation into Arabic of James Baikie's short history, *Ancient Egypt* (1912), which, as *Misr al-Qadimah*, was to be Mahfouz's first publication in book form. This survey of Egypt's earlier historical periods clearly had a major impact on Mahfouz, in that he planned an entire series of historical novels set in the ancient period; indeed, three such novels appeared between 1939 and 1944. However, it was the hardships and deprivations—not to mention the rampant opportunism and corruption—associated with conditions in Egypt during the Second World War that led Mahfouz to make his crucial decision to transfer his attention and developing novelistic craft to the present and the fate of his fellow countrymen. Beginning with *Al-Qahirah al-Jadidah* (1945), he penned a series of novels that place the lives of middle-class Egyptians into the authentically drawn neighborhoods and alleys of old Cairo (which give their names to several of the novels). It is this series of works that culminates in the three volumes of the *Trilogy*, an accomplished piece of social-realist fiction that serves to confirm and illustrate the complete incorporation of the novel genre into the tradition of modern Arabic literature. It may be said that it was this capstone achievement that is best reflected in the award of the Nobel Prize in Literature to Mahfouz in 1988.

Within the historical matrix of novelistic development that has just been outlined, that prize was, needless to say, a retrospective gesture (as is often the case with the Nobel awards), and it is one that raises interesting questions about the future, and more particularly, the direction of the Arabic novel that is based on the firm foundation of the generic framework furnished by Mahfouz in the *Trilogy*. However, it should be added that within such a framework, the designation of Mahfouz as the Dickens or the Balzac of Cairo, a view often expressed in the wake of the Nobel award and apparently intended as a positive assessment of the *Trilogy*'s literary merits, is not without implications; indeed, it may be viewed instead as the expression of an implicit cultural hegemony that needs at least to be called into question.

Within the history of the Arabic novel Mahfouz's *Trilogy* is an important monument, but it also represents a transitional stage in the context of his own career as a creative writer. In two of the most crucial elements of realist fiction, time and place, Mahfouz's set of three novels brings the Arabic novelist's craft to new levels of artistry. I have already noted above the masterly fashion in which the major events of Egyptian political history are interwoven with his depictions of the social fabric of Cairene society during the interwar period. However, what Egyptians, citizens of the Arab world, and—at a later date—Western readers came to appreciate about Mahfouz's carefully wrought craftsmanship was the incredible attention to detail that emerges, particularly from his scene-setting techniques at the beginning of each chapter in the long saga. Whether that scene involves a street, a houseboat, a rooftop, or a room, it is depicted with a subtlety, authenticity, and care that creates new artistic standards. The opening of the very first chapter of *Bayn al-Qasrayn*, with Aminah arousing herself to welcome home her carousing husband, is the reader's initial encounter with a facet of these novels that will continue throughout the work. Place names—quarters, streets, alleys—also contribute in major ways to the creation of a portrait of a city and a community that can serve as a microcosm within which issues of much larger scope can be explored.

It is also clear that Mahfouz makes use of the novels of the *Trilogy* to continue his own experiments with other features of novel-writing technique, and no more so that in the dramatic aspects of dialogue and its subsets. In this realm the *Trilogy* emerges as a genuinely transitional text, one in which the experiments of earlier novels of the 1940s are brought to new levels of accomplishment while certain new directions emerge less successfully. It is in the second volume in particular, *Qasr al-Shawq*, that the agonized musings of Kamal are reflected in both his conversations with his beloved's brother and in internal monologues; the juxtaposition of these two elements occasionally seems forced. Nevertheless, the set of novels that Mahfouz published in the following decade, most notably *Al-Liss wa-al-Kilab* (1961), *Thartharah Fawq al-Nil* (1966), and *Miramar* (1967), show not only a mastery of the subtleties of internal monologue and its uses but also a new allusive mode of writing that was a most effective reflection of the political and social realities of the period. Indeed, it seems reasonable to suggest that Mahfouz's most accomplished contributions to Arabic fiction are to be found among this latter set of works.

———

Mahfouz's *Trilogy* is thus a major monument in the development of modern Arabic fiction. Viewed in retrospect it is the one work that undeniably confirms the domestication of the novel genre within the societies of the Arab world, thus bringing to a high point a prolonged period of development and experiment. It also serves as the foundation upon which younger generations of writers have felt empowered to explore new directions in novel-writing. Like the process that began fiction's modern history in the Arab world during the nineteenth century, experiments in Arabic novel-writing now involve both an awareness of the latest trends in novel-writing in other world cultures (and especially the West) and an exploration of more particularizing tendencies that reflect a continuing search into the heritage of the past for useful narrative forebears.

Bibliography

Allen, Roger. *The Arabic Novel.* Syracuse, N.Y.: Syracuse University Press, 1995.

Beard, Michael, and Adnan Haydar, eds. *Naguib Mahfouz: From Regional Fame to Global Recognition.* Syracuse, N.Y.: Syracuse University Press, 1993.

El-Enany, Rasheed. *Naguib Mahfouz: The Pursuit of Meaning.* London: Routledge, 1993.

Enani, M. M., ed. *Naguib Mahfouz: Nobel 1988.* Cairo: General Egyptian Book Organization, 1989.

Le Gassick, Trevor, ed. *Critical Perspectives on Naguib Mahfouz.* Washington, D.C.: Three Continents Press, 1991.

Milson, Menahim. *Najib Mahfuz: The Novelist-Philosopher of Cairo.* New York: St. Martin's Press, 1998.

Moosa, Matti. *The Early Novels of Naguib Mahfouz: Images of Modern Egypt.* Gainesville: University of Florida Press, 1994.

Peled, Mattityahu. *Religion My Own:The Literary Works of Najib Mahfuz.* New Brunswick, N.J.: Transaction Books, 1984.

Somekh, Sasson. *The Changing Rhythm.* Leiden: E. J. Brill, 1973.

ARDIS L. NELSON

Havana
(*Three Trapped Tigers*, Guillermo Cabrera Infante, 1967)

When the Cabrera Infante family moved in 1941 from a small town in Cuba's Oriente Province to Havana, the young Guillermo was awestruck by the city's exciting lure. He soon immersed himself in the vibrant culture of Havana, a city that in the 1940s and 1950s was in many ways comparable to Paris in the 1920s. Havana was an international playground that attracted artists and glitterati like Frank Sinatra, Ava Gardner, Arthur Rubenstein, and Ernest Hemingway; the corporate elite; wealthy tourists; and, not surprisingly, the Italian Mafia. The city offered something for everyone.

Cabrera Infante had a love affair with Havana. This romance and the countless opportunities to explore the sensuous side of life are documented in his autobiographical novel *La Habana para un Infante difunto* (1979) [*Infante's Inferno* (1984)]. At age seventeen, he was inspired by a university professor to become an avid reader, and by age nineteen he was an editor for *Bohemia*, a leading Cuban publication. Shortly thereafter he co-founded the literary magazine *Nueva Generación*, started writing a weekly movie column, and co-created the film club *Cinemateca de Cuba*. Cabrera Infante's youthful idealism was deflated abruptly when his short story, "Balada de plomo y yerro," which contained profanities in English, was published in *Bohemia* in 1952 and landed him in jail. He was expelled from the School of Journalism, and his writing continued to be subject to censorship. This rude awakening led to his involvement in clandestine activity against the dictator Fulgencio Batista.

The undercurrents of oppression in *Tres tristes tigres* are just as much about what had become of the revolution by the mid-1960s as they are about the Havana of the 1950s. Both Batista and Castro subjected many Cubans to repressive tactics. *Tres tristes tigres* introduces the reader to this historic epoch in Havana. It is a tribute to the artists and writers who supported the revolution and wanted to help bring it to fruition. The urban landscape, the sounds, rhythms, locales, and characters that bring the city to life are a metaphor for the struggle to end tyranny by revolution and the ultimate failure of the revolution.

The original inspiration for *Tres tristes tigres* grew out of the censorship of the film *PM* (1961), an event that signified a dramatic shift in the revolution's cultural politics. This twenty-minute black-and-white film produced by Guillermo's brother Sabá Cabrera Infante and Orlando Jiménez Leal documents the pleasures of Havana nightlife in the bars along the waterfront. There is no dialogue—only dancing, drinking, and camaraderie. The sound track is the music of the clubs: guitars, a kettledrum, and bottles played with drumsticks. At the time, Cabrera Infante was director of the popular literary supplement *Lunes de Revolución*, which sponsored a TV program dedicated to international experimental cinema. When *PM* was aired on the *Lunes* TV program, the government's response was to confiscate *PM* and close down *Lunes*, leaving Cabrera Infante without a job.[1]

This was the first time in Fidel Castro's revolutionary Cuba that a work of art was banned for its form and content rather than for expressing explicit counterrevolutionary ideas. Censoring *PM* revealed the puritanical bias of the communist leadership that could not accept the visceral, life-affirming side of the city and the revolution. It was the beginning of a downward spiral for artists and intellectuals in Cuba, as well as the turning point for Cabrera Infante in the development of his career as a writer. There followed a chain of events culminating in Castro's infamous one-sided "Conversations with the Intellectuals" in which he proclaimed that "Dentro de la Revolución todo; fuera de la Revolución nada" ["Within the Revolution everything; outside the Revolution nothing"].

In 1962, after a year of internal exile, Cabrera Infante was given a diplomatic post in Belgium, the Latin equivalent of being sent to Siberia. It was there that he wrote a literary version of *PM*, featuring the fictional La Estrella as the uncompromising artist. She is a soulful black singer who insists on performing without accompaniment and whose tragic story provides a unifying element in *Tres tristes tigres*. In the prologue, a bilingual master of ceremonies at Havana's famous Club Tropicana regales the audience with showbiz hype to introduce that night's stage show. What follows is a loosely structured but highly charged collage of parodies, letters, phone calls, psychiatric sessions, dialogues, and dreams in which the characters, that is, the tigers and their friends, recount the intrigues, affairs, and events that take place over several nights in 1958, the eve of the revolution.

On the surface *Tres tristes tigres* is a celebration of the ebullient nightlife of pre-Castro Cuba, a gallery of voices, mostly of the late-night revelers who inhabited Havana's clubs and cruised its streets. Like the diverse mix of

---

[1] For more in-depth analysis of the social and cultural transitions of the Cuban Revolution, see William Luis, "*Lunes de Revolución*: Literature and Culture in the First Years of the Cuban Revolution," in *Guillermo Cabrera Infante: Assays, Essays, and Other Arts*, ed. Ardis L. Nelson (New York: Twayne, 1999), 16–38.

people in any great city, the characters speak in their unique dialects and colloquialisms. We do not get to know any of them in depth. Rather, they are like the performers on the Tropicana stage—colorful, enticing, and integral to the urban setting, yet ultimately anonymous, with impersonal names that speak of cameras, typewriters, the silver screen, or literary conventions. There is no omniscient narrator who tells us what is really going on or what anyone is thinking. We only know the inhabitants of the city through inference, by what they say, and we are just as likely to catch them telling a joke as a lie. We may find them in a state of confusion or paralyzed by paranoia.

Silvestre, a journalist and film buff, is the writer/assembler of *Tres tristes tigres*. He and his best friend Arsenio Cué, an actor and radio announcer, club hop around Havana picking up girls. Their escapades are recounted in the bacchanalian "Bachata," a lengthy section filled with the riotous jokes and wordplay characteristic of two adventurous fellows out on the town. Códac is a photojournalist who tells of La Estrella's rise from poverty to fame in "Ella cantaba boleros" ["She Sang Boleros"]. Eribó, a bongo player and unsuccessful commercial artist, fails to win the heart of Vivian Smith-Corona, a country-club *criolla* [Creole].

The deceased poet Bustrófedon is the center of attention in *Tres tristes tigres*, and his linguistic prowess is unequaled by any other Latin American fictional character. He is an intriguing example of the spirit of the *choteo*, a Cuban personality that is defined by a habitual irreverent and joking attitude. He takes nothing and no one seriously. Bustrófedon's wordplay, literary parody, and folkloric recitations are innovations that break away from the constraints of conventional language, both spoken and written, and especially the "sacred cows" of literary style. Bustrófedon exists only through memory, having already died during an operation for a cerebral aneurism before the action in *Tres tristes tigres* takes place. He is deified by his buddies, who make him a manifest presence in the book and a key player in the city. He is a master of parody and represents the spontaneous flow of spoken language—as found in folklore or conversation—which dies when analyzed.

Bustrófedon believed in the transcendence of graffiti and rap: "la única literatura posible estaba escrita en los muros . . . de los servicios públicos, lavatorios, retretes, inodoros o escusados y recitó trozos escogidos entre las heces" and "la otra literatura hay que escribirla en el aire, queriendo decir que había que hacerla hablando" ["the only possible literature was written on . . . the walls of public conveniences, men's or gents' bogs, W.C.s, johns, cans, loos, escusados, shit or pisshouses and he gave a recitation of his analectasy or selected pieces of Faecetiae" and "the other literature should be written on the air, in other words you make it simply by talking"].[2] Bustrófedon represents freedom of speech, and his philosophy suggests that literature can no longer be written in Cuba. Bustrófedon's "Algunas revelations" ["Some Revelations"], for example, are three blank pages. His death is symbolic of the eradication of memory and the repression of artistic freedom under Castro. It is impossible to "reveal" what is to come if memory is lost.

In the eyes of his fellow tigers, Bustrófedon's stinging parodies of seven Cuban writers are the pinnacle of his work. Códac says he thinks Bustrófedon invented the parodies called "La muerte de Trotsky referida por varios escritores cubanos, años después—o antes" ["The Death of Trotsky as Described by Various Cuban Writers, Several Years After the Event—or Before"] in order to show Silvestre and Cué that literature is no more important than conversation. As to why Cabrera Infante chose the topic of Trotsky's death for the parodies, some contend that he had Trotskyist leanings at the time and that he incorrectly thought that Trotsky's assassin was Cuban. But more to the point, the theme of Trotsky's death may have been Cabrera Infante's way of expressing the current reality in Cuba: writers now had to write on state-approved topics, specifically those considered to be "within the revolution." He also identified with Trotsky's idealism and feared a similar fate. Both were important revolutionary figures in their respective countries; both were forced into exile.

Trotsky's presence as a literary figure in *Tres tristes tigres* is suggestive of the unexpected shift to socialism in Cuba in 1961. Continual jumps from one verb tense to another reflect the disruptive moods the novel depicts, as past, present, and future swirl in a vortex of social upheaval. Although the novel is set in the late 1950s, its conception, writing, and rewriting span nearly six years, from 1961 to 1967. The essence of those years and Cabrera Infante's perception of what the revolution had become in the mid-1960s are telescoped into a few nights in the lives of five friends in Havana.

By the time Cabrera Infante began writing what eventually became *Tres tristes tigres*, the revolution had triumphed. Hence the characters in their 1958 milieu are infused with a heady sense that they will soon be freed from the tyrannical gangster-style Batista dictatorship. There is a restrained enthusiasm for new beginnings. Within a few years another form of repression had emerged under Castro. Anyone could be an informer. No one could be

---

[2] The quotes are from *Tres tristes tigres*, special ed. (Barcelona: Editorial Seix Barral, 1999), 285; and *Three Trapped Tigers*, trans. Donald Gardner and Suzanne Jill Levine (New York: Harper and Row, 1971), 277–78.

trusted, not even one's family or best friends. This lack of trust and communication among the friends, or tigers, as they navigate the territory between a dictatorship and the elusive freedom promised by the revolution prefigures the Kafkaesque situation Cabrera Infante encountered in 1965 when he returned to Havana for his mother's funeral.

The joyful, sensuous nightlife represented by the verbal creativity of Bustrófedon and his friends was anathema to the openly communist regime in Cuba. What Cabrera Infante found was closer in spirit to the city depicted in Jean Luc Godard's *Alphaville* (1965) than the Havana he knew and loved. In Godard's film the protagonist Lemmy Caution goes to Alphaville with the mission of finding the computer expert who has dehumanized most of the population through a technocratic authoritarianism. The inhabitants live only in the present, have no memory or goals, and are spied on by neighbors and police. Literature is forbidden, humor is programmed, and language is restricted to a state-approved vocabulary. Expression of emotion is punishable by public execution. At the whim of a mad scientist, Alphaville dies, forgetting its humanity, its poetry, and its language. The ubiquitous censorship in Alphaville finds its diametrical opposite in Bustrófedon, who reads dictionaries and invents his own language. The doctor—the system that wanted to find a logical explanation for Bustrófedon's verbal diarrhea—kills him on the operating table. This cautionary tale reminds the reader to hold on to the quicksilver of freedom, which can easily disappear as it did in Havana.

A secret agent and friend who lives in Alphaville gives Caution a forbidden book by Paul Eluard, *Capitale de la douleur* (1926) [*Capital of Pain*], from which Caution reads with Natasha as she rediscovers the meaning of love. While the characters in *Alphaville* struggle toward the light, the characters in *Tres tristes tigres* struggle to avoid overexposure to light. The tigers' frantic and hedonistic lifestyles belie any number of nightmarish possibilities ready to burst through the surface of their frivolous existence. These nightmares are the norm in Alphaville and became the reality for many in Havana: paranoia; cruelty; a lack of humor, trust, love, and creativity; a loss of memory and understanding; and a clandestine search for light, or escape. In *Tres tristes tigres* these symptoms of cultural malaise are disguised in a cloak of linguistic fun and games.

When Cué arrives in Havana from the countryside in a delusional state of near-starvation, he thinks he has been shot by the man who was supposed to help him. Later his jealousy over a woman prompts him to stomp on a young man's fingers at the country-club pool. He is known to memorize facts forward and backward without any genuine understanding; he cannot express his feelings, even to his best friends or to Laura, the woman he loves and later loses to Silvestre. Rather, he vents his frustration in escapist antics like racing around the city in a sports car and making jokes. His best buddy Silvestre is the writer who loves to remember and is searching for a meaningful human connection that he hopes to find in his upcoming marriage to Laura. He is unable to discuss his betrayal with anyone. By the end of the book he is at home, isolated by silence. Memory is a problem for Laura, who in her psychiatric sessions cannot remember if it was she or a friend who was molested as a child by a neighbor. Apocalyptic dreams confirm the turmoil in the city and the tigers' traumatization. Cué dreams of a tidal wave of searing light engulfing the city, and Laura dreams of burning dogs, rape, and abandoned worms.[3] Although not explicitly stated, censorship and exile have robbed Cué, Laura, and their friends of language, literature, and love, the lifeblood of Havana.

Prior to publication, *Tres tristes tigres* (submitted as a manuscript) won the 1964 Biblioteca Breve award in Spain. At the insistence of his publisher Cabrera Infante removed the political sections of the book, a series of vignettes depicting the sad and violent history of Cuba, one tyranny after another. This edited text later appeared as *Vista del amanecer en el trópico* (1974) [*View of Dawn in the Tropics* (1978)]. The revised *Tres tristes tigres* was published in Spain in 1967 and translated as *Three Trapped Tigers* in 1971. Because of its glorification of prerevolutionary hedonistic Havana nightlife, the book was the center of serious political debate in Cuba. It was banned there, and its defenders were labeled counterrevolutionary. Cabrera Infante was among the few of the revolutionary vanguard who as early as 1968 had the courage to publicly criticize Castro's betrayal of the promises made by the revolution's leaders.[4]

Tres tristes tigres is a eulogy for a great city that no longer exists. The epigraph: "And she tried to fancy what the flame of a candle looks like after the candle is blown out . . ." from Lewis Carroll's *Alice in Wonderland* expresses what Cabrera Infante tried to achieve in this novel: a remembrance of Havana as Cuba underwent the dramatic changes of the revolution.

Remembering the music, the freedom, and the voices of Havana in *Tres*

---

[3] "Worm" [*gusano*] is the label Castro gives to any Cuban who has left Cuba since the revolution.

[4] Guillermo Cabrera Infante, "La confundida lengua del poeta," *Primera Plana* (Buenos Aires) 7, 316 (January 14–20, 1969): 64–65.

tristes tigres is anathema to Castro's revolution, and all that can be heard now is the gibberish of the crazy lady in the park on the book's last page. The candle has been extinguished and yet, as Cabrera Infante writes in his book of essays on the city, "La Habana guarda una extraña belleza entre las ruinas" (*El libro de las ciudades*, 1999) [Havana exudes a strange beauty from its ruins].[5]

---

[5] This sentence is an allusion to the title of a made-for-TV film directed by George Cukor, *Love in the Ruins* (United Kingdom, 1975), starring Katherine Hepburn and Laurence Olivier.

Bombay
(*Midnight's Children*, Salman Rushdie, 1981)

I was not one of midnight's children. My belated birth, some years after the midnight hour in August 1947 that marked India's tryst with freedom, absented me from that epochal narrative. I was not there to witness the emergence of India and Pakistan, born together from a cleft womb, still as restless in relation to each other as the day they stepped into the harsh light of nationhood. But great events persist beyond their happening, leaving a sense of expectation in the air like the telling vacancy of weather, the empty, echoing silence that often follows a spectacular storm, never letting you forget that it happened. My childhood was filled with stories of India's struggle for independence, its complicated histories of subcontinental cultures caught in that deadly embrace of imperial power and national liberation that always produces an uncomfortable residue of enmity and amity, loathing and longing. My version of Salman Rushdie's Methwold Estate—the middle world of Saleem Sinai's 1,001 midnights—was an interrupted itinerary that stretched from our swiss chalet–style 1950s family home in Colaba (where the Koli fisherfolk smelled of dried bombay duck and pomfret guts) to the other end of the island, where my grandmother lived in a rip-off of Barchester Towers, just shy of the Parsi burial grounds, the Towers of Silence, where the sated vultures circled lazily around decomposing bodies, while the grandes dames of the Parsi parlors picked their living relatives to pieces.

Growing up in Bombay, as a member of the Parsi community, was to inhabit a kind of middle-class Indo-English demimonde. I was part of an urban bourgeois elite whose formal education and "high" culture colluded in emulating the canons of elite "English" taste (or what we knew of it) and conforming to its civilizational customs and comforts. My everyday life, however, provided quite a different inheritance. It was lived in that rich cultural mix of languages and lifestyles that most cosmopolitan Indian cities celebrate and perpetuate in their vernacular existence—"Bombay" Hindustani, "Parsi" Gujarati, mongrel Marathi, all held in a suspension of Welsh-missionary accented English peppered with an Anglo-Indian patois that was, at times, cast aside for American slang picked up from the movies or popular music. For me, the English language had, at times, the archaic feel of an antique carved cupboard that engulfed you in the faded smell of mothballs and beautiful brittle linens; at other times it had the mix-and-match quality of a moveable feast, like Bombay street food, spicy, cheap, available in all kinds of quantities and combinations, delicious as much for its flavors as its dangers.

There, in my cosy Parsi-Zoroastrian world that was both bravely cosmopolitan and intensely communitarian, I learned the history and the gossip of midnight's grumpy grown-ups by listening to my own relatives: "Mahatma Gandhi was *almost* admirable: why, just because he was not Parsi we should not appreciate . . . ? Look, nonviolence is a *good* thing, . . . who's doubting? And he was sincere, *nobody* will deny . . . *Sala* . . . he walked all the way to Dandi for some salt business—details are not important: *but why* he had to walk in hundred-degree heat, *sala we don't have trains and rickshahs*—okay, but, all I'm saying is, why not *dress* properly? Why all this *dhoti-bhoti* business? Who are we Indians? *Benchod* [Fuck it]! Are we bhangis and roadsweepers?" My great uncle raged against Gandhi's dress sense, praising Jinnah for his Saville Row suits, admiring Nehru for hanging out so assiduously with Lord and, particularly, Lady Mountbatten, the last viceriene of India and Jawarharlal's great lost love. My elderly great-aunt Shirin, she of the prodigious Parsi posterior of card-playing ladies who lunched far too much at the Willingdon Club, happily renounced her Irish linens and French chiffons for the cause of independence, so long as she was allowed a daily dab of Yardley's "lily of the valley" perfume from Old Bond Street, London, to liven her homespun khadar saree with pleasures of a different age. And so the Parsis, whom John Stuart Mill had rightly praised as a progressive liberal minority, tread a "fine balance" between castes, cultures, communities, and customs.

———

I was not one of midnight's children, but Saleem Sinai was my older brother. And Cyrus the Great who played St. Joan at Cathedral School was my next-door neighbor, and years later, married my first cousin. And I became a foot-fetishist—unlike the Brass Monkey who became a foot-arsonist, setting fire to shoes (171)—by ogling at Mr. Dubash's suede shoes and Lila Sabarmatti's stilleto heels and the stone hooves of Shivaji's great equestrian statue: shoes, feet, and hooves are not merely fashion accessories or body parts in this great novel of wanderlust and itinerant imaginings. Never forget that the last paragraph of the novel has Saleem Sinai being trampled underfoot. But before that happens there is so much traveling to do:

> Drive! On Chowpatty sands! Past the great houses on Malabar Hill, round
> Kemp's Corner, giddily along the sea to Scandal Point! And yes, why not, on

and on and on, down my very own Warden Road, right along the segregated
swimming pools at Breadh Candy, right up to the huge Mahalaxmi temple
and the old Willingdon Club. . . . Throughout my childhood, whenever bad
times came to Bombay, some insomniac night-walker would report that he
had seen Shivaji's statue moving; disasters in the city of my youth, danced to
the occult music of a horse's gray, stone hooves.[1]

Saleem has a nose for the energy of Bombay, just as it is Bombay's
energeia that brings the narrative to life. And what does this Aristotleian
rhetoric of *energeia* amount to when it translates imperfectly into the
English *energy*? The *Oxford English Dictionary* states: "With reference to
speech or writing: Force or vigour of expression. [This sense is originally derived from an imperfect understanding of Aristotle's use of *energeia* (Rhet.
III. xi. §2) for the species of metaphor, which calls up a mental picture of
something 'acting' or moving]." *Midnight's Children* survives because it lives
on, and off, this remarkable "energy" to move across the city, and the country, like an insomniac streetwalker—profligate and promiscuous, vulnerable
and venereal—hungrily in search of *language* in which to picture mental images of the *movement* of the city, and hungrily in search of *pictures* that roll
as the director calls "Action," and the narrative moves in a single page from
the coconuts of Juhu beach and Chowpatty Beach, to the ritual of rice eating
in the city, to the Ganesh Chaturti festival of the Elephant god at Chowpatty
Beach where both rice and coconuts are cast into the sea as ritual offerings
(103). A mere taxi ride reveals the itinerant taxonomy of the material culture
of this city where every detail registers both plenitude and plurality: "But
still, in the city, we are great rice-eaters: Patna rice, Basmati, Kashmiri
rice . . . [one could add Malbari rice]" (103). The narrative "energy" builds
up list by list, word by word, name by name, place by place, in that signature
style of layered descriptions of people and things. If Shivaji's nocturnal wanderings are omens of bad times (the Shiv-Sena are patrolling the streets in
his name if not his spirit), Saleem's olfactory explorations of the city also reveal an underlying anxiety, an ongoing awareness that independence comes
at the cost of partition, and the dream of pluralism may be threatened by the
nightmare of provincialism, regionalism, and communalism. The nightwalker
is kept awake by the sound of the hobbed-nail boots on the cobbles.

There is an anxiety in the midst of all this energy, driving it and threatening it at at the same time. And it is Saleem's Ganesh-like elephant snout, a

---

[1] Salman Rushdie, *Midnight's Children* (New York: Penguin Books, 1980), 102. All quotations
are from this edition and are hereafter referenced parenthetically in the text.

proboscis that serves as his perceptual apparatus and his authorial pen, that suggests that the excessive energy of the narrative—the desire to name, classify, fix, and label—is itself a kind of creative fetishism. A fetish is both a disavowal of difference and a desire to register its presence in a kind of displaced and distracted way. In *Midnight's Children* there is a brilliant creative transformation of the idea. The *fetish* of profuse and *desperate* description represents a desire to preserve in minute and persistent detail the elements of a larger pluralism associated with Bombay, *that feels itself under threat.* The larger idea of India was, regrettably, achieved only by disavowing and destroying the "constitutive" difference of the way of life of the subcontinent's majority populations, Hindus and Muslims, by cracking the country by partition and dividing its peoples. *Division is not the "independence" of difference; it is the disappearance of difference.* Bombay, itself, is the stage set for this conflictual double scene of prose and politics. It is signified by myriad images, incessant words, and perpetual pictures that drive the story, and the city, with an energy that somehow preserves an image of Bombay "as a whole" while the narrative continually renames and redefines the city in terms of its bits and pieces, its fragments, its lists, its items, its discontinuities, its fantasies, its errant and aberrant taxonomies—"the process of revision should be constant and endless; don't think I'm satisfied with what I've done!" Saleem insists (530). The doubling, even demonic *energeia* of narrative person (Saleem Sinai) and geomythical place (Bombay) turns the story's end into a kind of nuclear fission; a totemic terror that flies in the face of both citizenship and syntax: "fission of Saleem, I am the bomb in Bombay, watch me explode, bones splitting breaking beneath the awful pressure of the crowd, bag of bones falling down down down . . . only a broken creature spilling . . . into the street, because I have been so-many too-many persons, life unlike syntax allows one more than three, and at last somewhere the striking of a clock, twelve chimes, release" (533).

I was not one of midnight's children, but I also know that terror, history's error. The fission of syntax that blows up Bombay—the bomb in Bombay—is a wonderful image of this city of "too-many persons" and too many stories. But it is also a prophetic vision of the bombs that tore through Bombay in 1993, burning down at least five skyscrapers in a matter of as many hours. The world's media, busily searching for historical precedents after 9/11, did not spare a thought for that day in Bombay. *"Bones splitting breaking beneath the awful pressure of the crowd."* Attacks of terror and incidents of communal rioting have tragically left their mark on a city that seems, on the surface, to work busily against, and across, such ethnic and religious boundaries.

Rushdie most often takes the coastal road, along Marine Drive, as he makes his way from south to north. The North is the world of Bollywood with its left-leaning Muslim Communists, Qasim the Red, who hang out at the Pioneer Café with Amina Sinai. But if you turn away just before Chowpatty Beach, into the city's old interior, you enter a different world. You drive past Azad maidan, just the other side of Cathedral School, past the Goan-Roman Catholic communities around Girgaum, then around the Parsi settlements in Grant Road and toward the Muslim areas in Mohamedalli Road. If you made a sharp left before getting to the poorer Anglo-Indian communities of Byculla, you would enter the once-Jewish quarters of Nagpada with wraithlike women selling string-cheese and flat Iraqi-Jewish sesame breads. The teeming hinterland of the city is where the communal riots have left their most lasting memories. It is there that the stairwells of Muslim tenements were torched, leaving the inhabitants with no way to descend, there that the pavement dwellers were trampled underfoot. *"Bag of bones falling down down down . . . only a broken creature spilling pieces of itself into the street."*

I was not one of midnight's children, but I am a Bombayite too. "Note," says Saleem Sinai, "that despite my Muslim background, I'm enough of a Bombayite to be well up in Hindu stories, and actually I'm very fond of the image of a trunk-nosed, flap-eared Ganesh solemnly taking dictation! . . . But must I now become reconciled to the narrow one-dimensionality of a straight line?" (170).

A straight line does not exist in Bombay, certainly not in the world of its writers and poets and movie makers. The city, like its movies, has always lived "on both sides of the tracks," and you've got to read its tales *between the lines*. The Bombayite of Muslim background takes his dictation from Ganesh, and that marvelous fiction, that *halwa* of hybridity, midnight's children is born. Years later, you will remember, in a crucial scene at the center of *The Satanic Verses*, Salman the Persian scribe resists taking dictation and interpolates his own words into the sacred text . . . and the rest is history.

But this multistoried world of Bombay exists beyond the inspired *metier* of Methwold. It develops a very different voice in the interior landscape of Bombay's northwest suburbs, part of the hinterland I just sketched out for you. Here the old closed-down cloth mills decay, and the unemployed settle in slums around their former workplace as if to suck on a dried-out teat. There, in a poem titled "Under Dadar Bridge," named after a Bombay landmark, the Marathi Dalit (Untouchable) poet Prakash Jadhav tells a different Hindu-Muslim story:

Hey, Ma, tell me my religion. Who am I?
What am I?
You are not a Hindu or a Muslim!
You are an abandoned spark of the
World's lusty fires.
Religion? This is where I stuff religion!
Whores have only one religion, my son.
If you want a hole to fuck in, keep
Your cock in your pocket![2]

The totemic statue of Shivaji, the great Maratha warrior who cut off the southern progress of the Moghuls, presides over the Gateway of India, Bombay's embrace to the inland coast of the rest of India. A few miles into the university area there is a statue of the great legal scholar and Untouchable/Dalit leader Dr. Ambedkar, who was an alumnus of Columbia, a disciple of Dewey's, and went on to chair the committee that drafted the Indian constitution. If Shivaji lived by his sword, Ambedkar lived largely by the pen. And it is around the poet-politicians of the Dalit movments inspired by Ambedkar that some of the most innovative thinking about the future of the city has recently emerged. There are, for instance, discussions about the possibilities of "enfranchising" those who live in slums and shantytowns in the heart of the city and providing them with fuller services—water, electricity, and medical and educational provisions—that most of them have, at present, been denied. The spirit of Bombay, if I may quote Rushdie one last time, "is supported equally by twin deities, the wild god of memory and the lotus-goddess of the present" (170).

"Do you consider yourself a Bombayite today?" I was recently asked in an interview for the *Times of India*.

Yes, I anwered. To be a "Bombayite" is as much about a style of mind as it is about actually living in Bombay. I will always be a Bombayite in my love

---

[2] Prakash Jadhav, "Under Dadar Bridge," in *Poisoned Bread: Translations from Modern Marathi Dalit Literature*, ed. Arjun Dangle (London: Sangam, 1992), 56–57.

of the vibrancy and vitality of contrasts that are so much a part of Bombay's urban experience. Wherever I live in the world I shall always serve goa prawn curry, and biryani and bhel-puri and beef wellington and "sahs ni macchi" all at the same dinner party, and yes, that indulgence and excess and hospitality (with a touch of vulgarity perhaps) is what it means to be a Bombayite. And I will always listen to the taxidrivers lament or the dhobis' late-night bhajans across from my bedroom window in Colaba, because the Bombayite loves street-talk and street-sounds and the surprise of a good story. I will always protest against poverty, dirt, property prices, corruption and privilege because I am a Bombayite. I will never fail to jump the queue, demand special treatment, further corrupt an already corrupt bureaucracy because I am a Bombayite. I will condemn petty nationalisms, regionalisms, and ethnic and communal intolerance because as a Bombayite I know that the world is a place large enough for diverse identities, cultures and affiliations. As a Bombayite I admire the sheer spirit of survival, even as I complain that pavements are for walking not sleeping. Being a Bombayite is a frame of mind, and yes, I will always be a Bombayite.[3]

---

[3] E-mail correspondence with Shabnam Minwalla for an article on Bombay and Bombayites in the *Times of India*, November 8, 2002.

SIBEL IRZIK

Istanbul
(*The Black Book*, Orhan Pamuk, 1990)

One of the most memorable sections of *The Black Book* is an early one titled "The Day the Bosphorus Dries Up." This newspaper column written by Jelal could be read as his fantasy of a city that bares itself to the gaze of the author in a state of ultimate visibility and readability:

> On the last day when the waters suddenly recede, among the American transatlantics gone to ground and Ionic columns covered with seaweed, there will be Celtic and Ligurian skeletons open-mouthed in supplication to gods whose identities are no longer known. Amidst mussel-encrusted Byzantine treasures, forks and knives made of silver and tin, thousand-year-old barrels of wine, soda-pop bottles, carcasses of pointy-prowed galleys, I can image a civilization whose energy needs for their antiquated stoves and lights will be derived from a dilapidated Romanian tanker propelled into a mire-pit.[1]

Although clearly apocalyptic in its detailing of a mock civilization that will be established in the mire after the Bosphorus dries up, this fantastic vision is accompanied by a remarkable sense of aesthetic possession. Jelal and his pen are triumphant in the wasteland that emerges as the withdrawal of the water eliminates spatial and temporal depth.

The Black Book links the vision of "the lacuna once called 'The Bosphorus'" (15) with the threat of an end to writing, of a blank space where Jelal's column should be: "Every time Galip contemplated the possibility of a blank column on page two, he felt the anxiety of anticipating a catastrophe that was fast approaching. It was a catastrophe that reminded him of the day the Bosphorus dries up" (237). This anxiety is at least partially alleviated, however, by the fact that the dried up Bosphorus is also a scene of surprising reappropriations. Jelal imagines how new districts will be built in the mire and how a sunken British submarine will provide shelter to "our citizens now who are comfortable in their new home . . . , drinking their evening tea

---

[1] Orhan Pamuk, *The Black Book* (1990), trans. Güneli Gün (London: Faber and Faber, 1996), 15. Page numbers of further references are given in the body of the text.

out of China cups, sitting in the velvet officer's chairs once occupied by bleached English skeletons gulping for air" (17).

He himself is equally comfortable as he sneaks into this new hell in order to locate a black Cadillac, now guarded by Crusaders' skeletons, driven into the dark waters thirty years before by a "Beyoğu hood." Scraping off the moss on one of the windows with his pen, he reveals the embracing skeletons of the hood and his moll, their skulls welded together in an eternal kiss. What thus emerges is an image of Istanbul as the type of text that Jelal likes: "After all, the coincidence of details dating back years ago, centuries ago—like his imagining the Byzantine coins stamped with Olympus and the caps of Olympus soda-pop bottles in the mire of the Valley of Bosphorus—was the sort of observation which delighted Jelal and which he worked into his column every chance he got" (20).

This fantasy of a comprehensive view in which the past and the present are fused is related to the terms in which Pamuk declared himself a "novelist of Istanbul" in a special issue of the journal *Istanbul* dedicated to his writing: "Nobody until now has seen the entirety of Istanbul as I have, horizontally and perpendicularly, that is, in depth, in a manner which penetrates its history and its soul, and which comprehends its positioning, the way it settles on the seas, the way it extends. The view from my office has such a privilege that suits a novelist. Sometimes I think I deserve everything that I see from here."[2] What enables such a privilege in *The Black Book* is a series of panoramic perspectives and aesthetic appropriations through which the author is relocated at "the heart of the city." Having been banished from the Heart-of-the-City Apartments by his relatives, Jelal returns victoriously as a famous columnist to the place he was kicked out of, while the family is displaced to an unfashionable street. Later, Galip ("victorious") moves into Jelal's deserted apartment when he is ready to take over Jelal's column in the newspaper. He also begins to identify with Mehmet the Conqueror and to notice with astonishment that "Istanbul still remained a newly conquered city" (299).

Centuries after Mehmet, Istanbul remains newly conquered because it is a third-world metropolis, inevitably the gateway of the intrusion of the foreign. It is a city that conceals much from the view of its citizens, one that "has always been an underground city throughout its history" (165) because it is a repository of repudiated pasts and repressed identities. Its constantly shifting borders, illegal settlements, architectural incoherence, and the "provinces"

---

[2] Orhan Pamuk, "Bir Istanbul Romancısıyım" ("I Am a Novelist of Istanbul"), *Istanbul* 29 (1999): 69.

replicating themselves within its limits make it a city populated with citizens who have an uncertain, embattled relationship with urban space. The typically Turkish habit, described in one of Jelal's columns, of always looking down while walking in the city is only one manifestation of this uncertainty. In a recent article, Pamuk states that everyone is a stranger in Istanbul: the conquerors because they found an already formed city, the ruling Ottoman elites because they came from different countries, and 90 percent of the present population because they migrated into the city during the past fifty years. But the true reason for the strangeness is deeper: "The secret of Istanbul is that it has not been categorized and ordered, its knowledge has not been created, it has not been comprehended by its inhabitants. The lifestyle here consists of crowds that experience the richness of the city coming from its history, the civilizations stratified in it, without possessing them, only sensing them as strangers."[3]

Pamuk's claim to being a novelist of Istanbul rests on the ability of *The Black Book* to counter the timidity and incomprehension of the "citizens" with a "conquest" in the name of art and authorship. To this end, Pamuk initially employs romantic-realist techniques of intimating a design in what appears to be urban chaos, of investing the sights of the city with the promise of meaning. He mobilizes these techniques in the detective-story plot of Galip's search for his wife Rüya ("dream") after her sudden disappearance, which has been instigated by Jelal's appeal to the absent lover at the end of his article on the drying up of the Bosphorus. As this disappearance turns everything, especially discarded objects, into clues, Galip becomes engaged in the activity that Benjamin describes as common to the artist and the ragpicker in the city: "Ragpicker or poet—the refuse concerns both and both go about their business in solitude at times when the citizens indulge in sleeping."[4]

Thus, while he views the city at dawn from the minaret of the Mosque of Suleyman the Magnificent, prefiguring, as it were, Pamuk's image of himself looking out from his office window and taking in all of Istanbul, Galip recognizes the potential of an illumination that the city offers up to him and withholds from the sleeping citizens: "Just as on the surface of a planet that was still being formed, it felt as if the uneven pieces of the city buried under concrete, stone, wood, plexiglass, and domes might slowly part and the

---

[3] Orhan Pamuk, "Şehrin Ruhu" ("The Soul of the City"), *National Geographic Türkiye* 13 (2002): 46.

[4] Walter Benjamin, *Charles Baudelaire: A Lyric Poet in the Era of High Capitalism*, trans. Harry Zohn (London: NLB, 1985), 80.

flame-colored light of the mysterious underground seep through the darkness" (174). As he expands his search, his relationship to the city is further shaped by the notions of mystery and signs, giving him the strong impression that what he must unravel is a secret much older and more comprehensive than Rüya's disappearance, a mystery enveloping the city. This view of the city as the site and the product of a conspiracy holds the promise of textualizing and thus possessing it as a city of signs to be interpreted: "Not only were inscriptions, faces, pictures the pieces in the game played by the hidden hand, but so was everything. . . . Patient like someone nearing the end of a crossword puzzle, he felt that everything was about to fall into place" (189).

But if everything were to fall into place, the city as constituted by the mystery would become transparent and insignificant. To base the readability of the city on a "hidden hand," a conspiracy, is to risk not only the absurdities of paranoia, but also the end of reading, the deadly whiteness of a city fully illuminated and thus nullified. This is why Galip cannot stand classical detective novels: "When the puzzle was solved at the end, while the second realm which had been under wraps was illuminated, the first one would now sink into the darkness of oblivion" (191). Galip tells his wife that the only detective novel worth reading would be one whose author did not know who the murderer was.

The Black Book, which is just such a novel, is full of visionaries and paranoiacs who believe that they know the source and the nature of the crime polluting the city. One after the other of the novel's many fanatics of authenticity characterize Istanbul as the site of a Westernization conspiracy that makes it impossible for its citizens to be themselves, to lead lives unscripted by "hidden hands." Involved in self-destructive, paradoxical quests for uniqueness, for identities that are not imitations, they seek the purity they desire in an escape from the city. The speed with which goods, fashions, and styles circulate in the networks of Istanbul, the short memory, insatiability, and manipulability of its anonymous crowds, that is, the very characteristics that make Istanbul a metropolis, also make it the scene of the betrayal of cultural identity, the perfect instrument for the infiltration of the inauthentic and the foreign.

Rüya's former husband, for instance, who claims to have thwarted "a thousand-year-old conspiracy by refusing to be someone other than himself" believes that "Istanbul was the touchstone: let alone live there, even setting one foot in Istanbul was to surrender, to admit defeat" (112). He is sure that the students in the city's gloomy missionary schools are given liquids that destroy national consciousness. In a "pure white dream" he sees himself in "a pure white Cadillac" with Muhammad's two grandchildren, dressed in white, making disgusted faces for their grandfather's approval as they go through the streets polluted with posters, ads, movies, and whorehouses.

The prince in Galip's story states that "the most significant historical dimension" in his memoirs is his diagnosis of the city's disintegration into an imitation: "Hadn't he observed with his own eyes, before secluding himself in his lodge, that Istanbul streets were changing with every passing day in imitation of an imaginary city in a nonexistent foreign country? Didn't he know that the unfortunate underprivileged that crowded the streets transformed their garb by observing Occidental travelers and studying photographs of foreigners that fell in their hands?" (373–74). During a fifteen-year-old battle to rid himself, and thus the country he is to rule, of every possible form of imitation or repetition, of every thought, gesture, or style that originates elsewhere, he never sets foot in Istanbul. What remains after his death is another unreal scene of sterile whiteness: "There was a dreamlike whiteness in the bare rooms, . . . all recollections had faded, memory had frozen, and all sound, smell, objects having retreated, time itself had come to a stop" (178).

The destructiveness of this longing for a world of whiteness untainted with signs and secrets, free from the shadow of an original elsewhere, and proof against self-betrayal as well as foreign invasion is evident in the reference to "Field Marshal Fevzi Çakmak who, . . . fearing that the citizens might collaborate with the enemy, had conceived of blowing up all the bridges in the country, of pulling down all the minarets in order to rob the Russians of landmarks, and of evacuating Istanbul and proclaiming it a ghost town, thereby turning the city into a labyrinth where an occupying enemy would be lost" (164).

Accordingly, the task that *The Black Book* sets for itself is twofold. The mystery must remain unsolved, and the city should be protected from being reduced to a conspiracy that can only be thwarted by the purity of a blank page. On the other hand, for something like the conquest of the city to take place, the narrative must reveal something of the mystery, be energized by it, offer ways of participating in the power it exerts over the city. This necessitates the panoramic perspectives and aesthetic appropriations that I mentioned earlier as the means of locating the author in the heart of the city. *The Black Book* translates the defining aspects of urban life and the very precariousness of Istanbul's identity as a third-world metropolis into aesthetic principles that contain and subvert anxieties about authenticity, generating pleasure and authority out of the knowledge of urban realities.

The primary means of this translation is to turn the lack of singularity into the basic narrative technique of the novel. What Galip learns as he wanders through the streets in search of his wife is that "all Istanbul . . . was teeming with folks who were on the same trip!" (229). Pamuk's Istanbul is not a place of shocks and singular encounters, of love, either at first or last sight. Even, or perhaps especially, the heart of the city is not unique: "It occurred to him that, aside from this room in this flat which was a replica of itself as it was twenty-five years ago, there could be another room in a flat that replicated this place in another part of Istanbul" (226). Almost every place that Galip visits has already been visited and every sensation he receives from the city has been received by Jelal earlier, and by the time Galip gets around to having these experiences, we have already read about them in Jelal's columns. Whenever a secret seems to be on the verge of being revealed, it fades into a much larger pattern as only a small part of an endless network of relationships, conspiracies, and imitations. This creates a zoom effect by which the perspective becomes panoptical and the narrative is spatialized.

Epic catalogs are a stylistic tic in *The Black Book*. Its long sentences greedily collect mass-produced and discarded objects, piling them up like the waste that accumulates in every corner of the city.[5] Simply listing objects seems to produce an incantatory pleasure, constituting a rare instance in the Turkish novel of the aestheticization of consumption and excess instead of the customary moralistic hostility to them.[6] The sentences are also hopelessly periodic, and their subjects often get lost in a maze of clauses, like

---

[5] "Other things could be found on the repulsive basement floor that was encrusted with dirt a lot worse than manure: shells of pigeon eggs stolen by mice who went up the spouts to the upper stories, unlucky forks and odd socks that had slipped from flower-print tablecloths and sleepy bedsheets shaken out the windows and fallen into the petroleum-colored void, knives, dust cloths, cigarette butts, shards of glass and lightbulbs and mirrors, rusty bed springs, armless pink dolls that still batted their plastic eyelashes hopelessly yet stubbornly, pages of some compromising magazine and newsprint that had carefully been torn into tiny pieces, busted balls, soiled children's underpants, horrifying photographs that had been ripped to shreds . . ." (181).

[6] "[Aladdin] traversed the whole of Istanbul for years, inch by inch, store by store, to procure the oddest of merchandise (like the toy ballerinas who pirouetted as the magnetized mirror was brought close; the tricolored shoelaces; the plaster-of-Paris statuettes of Atatürk which had blue lightbulbs behind the pupils; the pencil sharpeners in the shape of Dutch windmills; the signs that said FOR RENT or IN THE NAME OF ALLAH THE COMPASSIONATE, THE MERCIFUL; the pine-flavored bubblegum which came with pictures of birds numbered from one to a hundred; the pink backgammon dice which could only be found at the Covered Bazaar; the transfer pictures of Tarzan and Admiral Barbarossa; the gadgets which were shoehorns on one end and bottle openers on the other; and the soccer hoods in the colors of the teams—he himself had worn a blue one the last ten years)" (38–39).

individuals in Istanbul's crooked streets. The characters in the novel do not change over time but multiply in space as doubles, disciples, and look-alikes.

To be at the heart of the city is to be an eye that can gaze at simultaneity. Pamuk has often expressed his fondness for the moment when the bluish light from television screens becomes visible through millions of windows, enabling him to feel that the city has a soul.[7] The same image is used in *The Black Book*: "By eight o'clock every evening, the bluish light from the TV sets would be flickering in the windows of all the buildings with the exception of the Heart-of-the-City Apartments" (199). These spatializing and aestheticizing techniques generate authority as well as pleasure because they display the narrative's ability to appropriate and provide a privileged view of urban structures and processes. Both Jelal and Galip get glimpses into focal points from which objects, images, fashions, and lifestyles radiate into the city. Aladdin's store, for instance, offers just such a glimpse of the mysterious rhythms by which the inhabitants of Istanbul go crazy over musical cigarette boxes one day and Japanese fountain pens the next. That the novel's emblem for art is the newspaper column rather than high literature becomes significant in this context. With secret messages for the disciples who read them everyday, Jelal's columns appropriate the city's anonymous crowds as networks of readers, making their writer another focal point. Jelal's family repeatedly accuses him of washing their dirty linen in his columns. This betrayal of privacy, the destruction of illusions of uniqueness, however, is the secret behind the writer's conquest of the city.

The deconstruction of uniqueness is also the process by which the novel clears Istanbul of the charge of inauthenticity. The problem of Westernization as imitation is contained, if not resolved, by the repeated demonstrations of the imitated nature of every identity. Istanbul is no different from any other city as a place where the people cannot be themselves. The division between the Eastern heritage and Western influence thus becomes a resource rather than a liability, generating further possibilities of textual stratifications, proliferations of mystery, and "coincidences of details." It is interesting to note, in this context, that the novel's plot is initiated as much by the visit of a group of BBC journalists to Istanbul as it is by Rüya's desertion. The journalists provoke a search for Jelal, in which both his murderer and Galip participate. The most "archetypal" journey in the city, a self-consciously Dantean and Joycean one, is also motivated by the journalists' presence. It is to them that Galip narrates his story of the prince over and

---

[7] Orhan Pamuk, "The Soul of the City," 44.

over, as a ritual confirmation of his authorship. A sort of complicity between them is evident in the woman journalist's going along with his impersonation of Jelal even though she recognizes him. Prophetic of the novel's international success, this aspect of the story seems to suggest that being a novelist of Istanbul today also involves making it readable for the globalized culture of the West.

Uncertain Boundaries

ANDREAS GAILUS

Form and Chance: The German Novella

A peculiar chiasmus: in the winter of 1794, Goethe was working on his *Wilhelm Meisters Lehrjahre* [*Wilhelm Meister's Apprenticeship*] and at the same time writing, for relaxation as it were, his novella cycle *Unterhaltungen deutscher Ausgewanderten* [*Conversations of German Refugees*].[1] While *Wilhelm Meister*, which continued the particularly German genre of the bildungsroman, was to become a model for the great English and French novels of the nineteenth century,[2] the *Unterhaltungen*, which drew on romance literary traditions, marked a departure from the novel tradition and inaugurated the novella's dominance in Germany.

The Limits of Symbolization (Goethe, Boccaccio)

The plot of the *Unterhaltungen* can be summarized briefly.[3] The German-French border at the Rhine, 1793: harried by French revolutionary troops, a German noble family takes leave of its property on the Rhine's western bank and seeks refuge in a country house east of the river. There their discussions about the revolution quickly lead to open argument and culminate in the departure of an old family friend. To prevent the group's dissolution, the refugees resolve to avoid political topics and to relate private stories instead. The strategy is effective. By narrating and discussing mysterious tales of the supernatural and of love, the refugees forget their political differences and find their way back to more polite modes of interaction. The collection ends with a long, deeply hermetic story, *Das Märchen* [*Fairy Tale*], without returning to the frame narrative.

What is the fundamental narrative conflict in Goethe's novella? I'll formulate my argument rather abstractly for now. The *Unterhaltungen* dramatize the disturbance of a system by a foreign body. At issue is the question of

---

[1] "After the burdens this pseudo-epic of a novel imposes on me, I find the little stories greatly enjoyable." Letter to Schiller, November 27, 1794, in Johann Wolfgang Goethe, *Sämtliche Werke*, ed. Karl Eibl, pt. 2 (Frankfurt on Main: Deutsche Klassiker Verlag, 1998), 4:45.

[2] See Franco Moretti, *The Way of the World. The Bildungsroman in European Culture* (London: Verso, 1987).

[3] The following section is a compressed version of my "Poetics of Containment: Goethe's *Conversations of German Refugees* and the Crisis of Representation," *Modern Philology* 100 (2003): 436–75.

how a certain order of discourse and interaction will react to the intrusion of a radically divergent element. Will the system master the disturbance and survive, whether by resisting it, integrating it, or by reorganizing its own structures? Or will the disturbance instead overwhelm the system and dissolve its borders? In other words, Goethe's *Unterhaltungen* may be said to narrate a moment of existential threat, a crisis in which the continued existence of an organized unity is at risk.

This problematic has served as a model for further production within the genre. The German-language novella of the long nineteenth century (1789–1914), I want to argue, is a *genre of crisis*. Novellas dramatize states of exception, moments in which the world- and identity-constitutive function inherent in traditional patterns of ordering and interpreting has become unstable. This involves an enormous amount of semantic variation: the crisis may be limited to the "system" of the individual and result either from the traumatic return of repressed signifiers from childhood (romanticism), from the dynamic of epiphanic experiences of creativity (Mörike), or from the mystical dissolution of identity-securing distinctions (Musil). It may also, however, appear as the disintegration of a collective system and be triggered by a pathological hyperfixation (Kleist, Storm), sexual desire (Gotthelf, Schnitzler), or the circulation of linguistic and monetary signs (Stifter, Keller). I shall come back to these differences; indeed, they will guide my description of the genre's internal differentiation. The issue at hand now, however, is to determine amidst these differences of content the semantic variations of a *single* problem that *all* novellas articulate. Novellas—and precisely this is the function of the crises of their plots—thematize the limits of (social, psychic, narrative) systems. More specifically, what novellas, from Goethe to Musil, repeatedly attempt to represent is a dysfunctional and asymbolic core at the heart of a functioning system, an excessive and traumatic element that threatens the unity of an organized whole from *within*.

Let us return to the *Unterhaltungen* to corroborate these abstract theses. Goethe's novella explicitly thematizes the relationship of crisis, genre, and limit. To maintain a system is to maintain boundaries, to demarcate the internal form from an external environment. "An outside begins," writes Jean Starobinski, "where the expansion of a structuring force ends or, to put it another way: an inside is constituted when a form asserts itself by defining its own boundaries."[4] This "boundary maintenance" is exactly what is

---

[4] Jean Starobinski, *Blessings in Disguise; or, The Morality of Evil*, trans. Arther Goldhammer [translation of *Le remède dans le mal: Critique et légitimation de l'artifice à l'âge des Lumières*] (Cambridge, Mass.: Harvard University Press, 1993), 203.

problematized in Goethe's novella. It is already indicated by the text's geographical localization in the border region between France and Germany. And it is made quite clear in the narrative's opening, which inverts the form-constitutive act of demarcation, thus allowing the novella's field of representation to coincide with a crisis in systemic self-maintenance. The first sentence of this first German novella is about a *border crossing*: "In the course of those unfortunate days, which had for Germany, for Europe, and indeed for the rest of the world the saddest of consequences, *when the Frankish army invaded our fatherland through a badly protected gap*, a noble family abandoned its possessions in those parts and fled to the other side of the Rhine."[5]

This sentence is programmatic. The invasion of the new and the alien (revolution) into the traditional and the familiar (fatherland) is not limited to the military arena, but is reproduced on the level of the beleaguered order itself, in the behavior of group members toward each other. What is at issue in the *Unterhaltungen* is not the damage done to external boundaries, but the disintegration of internal ones; not the threat represented by an outside enemy, but the weakening of that "structuring force" by which the system is individualized and constituted as a unified whole. Goethe's novella has to do with *traumas immanent to the system*, that is, with moments in which a system's operations turn against it and dismantle it from within.

This autodestruction occurs on two levels—one communicative, and one psychological. The communicative order of the group is founded on the rule of sociability, which charges individuals to use conversation as a means for producing commonalities, "whereby the one says that which the other was already thinking" (137). This implies "thresholds of thematization, for example, in reference to obscenities, religious feelings and confession, or matters over which there is general conflict."[6] And it is precisely these thresholds of communication that are breached. With political speech, the events in

---

[5] *Unterhaltungen deutscher Ausgewanderten*, in *Goethes Werke: Hamburger Ausgabe in 14 Bänden*, ed. Erich Trunz (Munich: Beck, 1981), 6:125, emphasis added. [Translator's note: A full English translation of the text, translated by Jan van Heurck in cooperation with Jane K. Brown, has been published as *Conversations of German Refugees*, in *Goethe's Collected Works* (New York: Suhrkamp Publishers, 1989), vol. 10. Because of the specificity of the language in the brief passages quoted here, I have translated them myself, adhering as closely as possible to the original syntax, and hereafter indicating the *Hamburger Ausgabe* page numbers parenthetically in the text. Unless otherwise indicated, further translations of cited material are also mine.]

[6] Niklas Luhmann, *Social Systems*, trans. John Bednarz Jr. with Dirk Baecker [from *Soziale Systeme* (Frankfurt on Main: Suhrkamp, 1984), 214] (Stanford, Calif.: Stanford University Press, 1995), 155.

France introduce into language a discourse that is incompatible with the rules of social communication. Just how menacing this revolutionary discourse is for the group's existence is made clear in an altercation between two of its members that culminates in veiled threats of murder. Their communication thus comes up against its own limit; beyond the threat of murder are to be found not words but acts, which would destroy the existence of the interlocutor and thereby the material basis for any communication.

The revolution foregrounds the novel danger of the self-destruction of the social through ideologized politics. Goethe, however, at the same time presents this social crisis as the result of a more deep-seated *psychological* crisis; and it is this further turn, with the new semantics of the subject it inaugurates, that retrospectively allows us to describe the *Unterhaltungen* as the point of departure for a genuinely *modern* tradition of the novella. Sociability is founded on the willingness of individuals to contain themselves. To speak in society means to speak with a view to the requirements of the *Other*; and it is precisely this psychic economy that collapses under the pressure of events. Courtesy gives way to aggression, and in place of tactful and agreeable conversation—"whereby the one says that which the other was already thinking"—comes "the irresistible urge to do harm to others" (130) and the "desire to maliciously wreak havoc on one's neighbor" (128). Conversation thus becomes the medium of a fundamentally *asocial* passion. It is the same dark passion that the Marquis de Sade celebrates in his works at the exact time as Goethe's *Unterhaltungen*: the passion for transgression, for destruction, for causing pain. One hundred and twenty years after Goethe and Sade, Freud would make this "irresistible urge to do harm to others" the core of his new theory of the subject. Aggression and sadism, according to Freud, are the externally directed manifestations of a drive to annihilate the self. There exists inherent in the psyche a need for self-dissolution, a drive to destroy one's own complexity and to return to the condition of mineral stasis.

Before I go on to demonstrate how this takes place in Goethe's text, I would like first to introduce a brief excursus on Freud. There are three aspects of Freud's theory that are of particular interest for the poetic of the novella I am proposing here: his model of trauma, his thesis of what lies "beyond the pleasure principle," and finally, encompassing both of them, the relationship between affect and meaning. As is well known, it was primarily neuroses resulting from war trauma that led Freud to postulate a "beyond" of his "pleasure principle." The traumatized soldiers had a tendency to repeat in their dreams the scenes of horror that had triggered the trauma. As these repetitions were accompanied by extremely intense attacks of fear, they contradicted Freud's previous theory, which held that dreams, like all other productions of the unconscious, were in the service of wish-fulfillment. Why then did the patients relive events that had caused them mental anguish? Freud's answer to this question involved nothing less than a new theory of the subject. The integrity of the mental apparatus, he writes in *Beyond the Pleasure Principle*, is based on the existence of an "envelope or membrane" that separates and protects the apparatus from its environment.[7] This shell has the task to "preserve the special modes of transformation of energy operating in [the mental apparatus] against the effects threatened by the enormous energies at work in the external world" (27). Trauma occurs when an external excitation is so strong that it breaks through the protective shield: "There is no longer any possibility of preventing the mental apparatus from being flooded with large amounts of stimulus, and another problem arises instead—the problem of mastering the amounts of stimulus which have broken in and of binding them, in the psychical sense, so that they can then be disposed of " (29).

Freud's description grants a central role to the economic dimension. Whatever the specific content of the traumatic event may be, from the subject's point of view it signifies an excess of stimulus that overwhelms his or her psycho-physical capacities. But such an economic account cannot be separated from a more strictly psychological one—for the psychic apparatus binds energies by connecting them to representations, and it is precisely this mechanism, that is, *the symbolization of affects*, that fails in cases of trauma. Trauma is beyond the pleasure principle because it comprises an affective surplus that resists being translated into representations and thereby integrated into the self-reproduction of the psychic system. In this way, affect becomes a psychic dud. Unbound and unsymbolized, it floats about in the psyche as pure stimulus, an internal alien element that by virtue of its enormous energetic charge is able to sunder the couplings of the psychic apparatus and destroy the system from within.

This is precisely what occurs in Goethe's work. The frame narrative of the *Unterhaltungen* dramatizes the revolution as a psychological and social trauma *avant la lettre*. As in Freud's model, the event in Goethe's text derives its impact from the *suddenness* with which it breaks through the symbolic protective shield of expectations and anxious anticipation. The enemy

---

[7] Sigmund Freud, *Beyond the Pleasure Principle* [*Jenseits des Lustprinzips*] (1920), in *The Standard Edition of the Complete Psychological Works of Sigmund Freud,* trans. James Strachey (London: Hogarth Press, 1955), vol. 18. Subsequent quotations from this edition are referenced by page number in the text.

troops force their way "through a badly protected gap"—as Goethe's quasi-Freudian metaphor has it—into the interior of the system. The *shock* this triggers results in the breakdown of everyday patterns of behavior, making the "conduct of any- and everyone peculiar and striking" (125). Luise, for instance, who while busy daydreaming about her beloved is caught off guard by news of the invasion, is "frightened out of her wits by the initial shock" and "even mistakes an old servant for her betrothed" (126). Notice how Goethe codes the revolution as the blank space of codification itself. For Luise, engrossed in erotic thoughts as she is, the military news is not significant information, but a meaningless alien element that cannot be integrated into her fantasies and thus provokes the reaction of fear, which involves "the mental apparatus . . . being flooded with large amounts of stimulus," thus leading to the collapse not only of the subject's own mental boundaries (Luise's "wits"), but of social distinctions and oppositions (private/public, noble/subordinate) as well. A similar mechanism can be read in the aggressive behavior of the group's members. Their inability to translate the trauma of the invasion into significance triggers a panicked feeling of helplessness that is abreacted outwardly, as "the irresistible urge to harm others," and tears apart the symbolic network of the society.

To summarize: Goethe narrates the revolution less as a specific historical event than as an unassimilable blank space of codification that causes the psychic and discursive structures of the old order to explode. With it, however, the novella genre enters a new phase in its development. With Goethe's *Unterhaltungen deutscher Ausgewanderten*, the novella is transformed into *that symbolic form which thematizes the boundaries of symbolization—it becomes a traumatic narrative genre.*

Now one might object that all this was already the case with the *Decameron*. Boccaccio famously describes in his "Introduzione" the plague's devastating effects on the social life of the city as both an existential *and* symbolic crisis. The plague not only endangers the inhabitants' lives, it also demonstrates that traditional religious and cosmological schemes no longer have explanatory force.[8] The plague triggers psychic and social anomies—but

---

[8] See also the various interpretations of the plague—as destined or divine punishment, as natural phenomenon, as test—that the narrator provides in the introduction: "There came the death-dealing pestilence, which, through the operation of the heavenly bodies or of our own iniquitous doings, being sent down upon mankind for our correction by the just wrath of God, had some years before appeared in the parts of the East and after having bereft these latter of an innumerable number of inhabitants, extending without cease from one place to another, had now unhappily spread towards the West." Giovanni Boccaccio, *Decameron*, trans. John Payne, rev. and

not among the narrators, who (and this is just what makes them the medium of a new form) remain rational and controlled in their affect throughout. Goethe's radicalization of Boccaccio's model consists in his pulling his narrators into the vortex of the narrated crisis, in effect making them its center. The plague now becomes a "plague of subjectivity," the major symptom of which—sadistic pleasure taken in the destruction of the other—endangers the group from within. This in turn makes the problem of the conflict's *resolvability* considerably more critical as well. Todorov has convincingly shown that the structural core of Boccaccio's novellas consists of violation— of custom, of social etiquette, of a law.[9] To this may be added that each transgression likewise provokes efforts to regulate it, and that in many of Boccaccio's novellas the actual narrative interest lies not in the violations per se, but in the "crafty solutions, the resourcefulness with which the sinners extricate themselves from the affair, that is to say, with the regulation of the case."[10] This enjoyment of the slick resolution, and with it the farcical character of so many of Boccaccio's novellas, disappears with the transition to Goethe. The subject of the modern novella is no longer a resolvable external problem but an unfathomable inner *mystery*, and the obstacle to be overcome by the novella's protagonist is the protagonist him- or herself, even (or especially) when this obstacle takes the form of an exterior resistance.

This has two consequences for the genre's structure and content: (1) the old European novella, which in its brevity resembled the anecdote, gives way following Goethe to a medium-length narrative with strong tendencies to the tragic; and (2) this new form becomes the vehicle of a new model of subjectivity. Whereas Boccaccio's protagonists deploy cunning and deceit to ensure their *self-preservation* and increase their enjoyment, the heroes of the modern novella are characterized by compulsive self-destructive tendencies.[11] Whether Kleist's Michael Kohlhaas or Storm's White Horse Rider, Hoffmann's Nathanael or Mann's Gustav von Aschenbach, Droste-Hülshoff's Friedrich Mergel or Zweig's Mirko Czentovic, these figures all act as if

---

ed. Charles Singleton (Berkeley: University of California Press, 1982), 8. On the nature of contingency in the *Decameron*, see Joachim Küpper, "Mittelalterliche Ordnung und rinascimentale Kontingenz," in *Kontingenz*, ed. Gerhard von Graevenitz and Odo Marquard, Poetik und Hermeneutik 17 (Munich: Wilhelm Fink Verlag, 1998), see esp. 206ff.

[9] Tzvetan Todorov, *Grammaire de Décaméron* (The Hague: Mouton, 1969), 77–78.

[10] Heinrich Bosse, "Geschichten," in *Literaturwissenschaft: Einführung in ein Sprachspiel*, ed. Heinrich Bosse and Ursula Renner (Freiburg: Rombach Verlag, 1999), 314.

[11] On the pathologization of modern novella protagonists as obsessive-compulsive, see Hannelore Schlaffer, *Poetik der Novella* (Stuttgart: Metzler, 1993), 57.

under the spell of a pathological fixation by which the external obstacle is understood as the symptom of an internal conflict, the other as the "phantom self" (Hoffmann). In short, the subject of the modern novella is "beyond the pleasure principle."

But let us get back to Goethe. The *Unterhaltungen* mark the transition from the traditional to the modern novella—a transition in that, despite having radicalized Boccaccio's example in the frame narrative, thereby opening a new anthropological and literary space for the genre, Goethe retracts this radicalization in the other novellas in the cycle and, moreover, explicitly works against it. Rather than providing detailed evidence for this here, I shall limit myself to two comments by way of summary. Goethe assigns the novellas in the *Unterhaltungen* a pragmatic-therapeutic function. The telling of stories serves to cushion the trauma of the invasion retroactively through literary symbolizations and to bind the released affects aesthetically. The symbolization does not happen directly, as an attempt to come to terms with the revolution in the narratives themselves, but by way of *displacing* the trauma from the world-historical and political level onto the level of private and familial stories. (The initial novellas have to do with ghosts and mysterious noises, that is, with phenomena that, like the invasion, involve a retreat from existing patterns of experience and interpretation.) While the shock of the invasion remains an embodied affect and is unconsciously abreacted, the mysterious ghost stories permit *a symbolization of the unsymbolizable,* through which the traumatic stimulus is bound in speech and used, by way of the communicative act of narration, in the reconstruction of the social order. With Goethe, the novella may thus be seen as a kind of homeopathy, healing the group's pathologies by repeating in a diluted and narrative-bound form the trauma that is their source.

A therapy of desire. But—and Goethe was no doubt aware of this—this therapy cannot unmake the nidus of the illness, the revolution and its consequences. Thus the *Unterhaltungen* begin by resuscitating the old European tradition of the novella, but they end without returning to the frame narrative and in a completely different genre: the programmatically titled and deeply hermetic *Märchen.* Goethe's text dramatizes both the downfall of good society, which had constituted the public of the traditional novella,[12] and the emergence of a new form of literary communication. In place of the traditional novella's pragmatic model, which assigns norm-establishing

---

[12] Ibid., 16.

power to the oral narration and discussion of stories, came the classical model of an *aesthetic* communication, in which mute and affect-controlled readers were to eavesdrop on the enigmatic utterances of great poets. It is hardly accidental that Goethe's novella was published together with Schiller's essay "On the Aesthetic Education of Man," whose plea for an autonomous art removed from political life was put into narrative practice by the *Unterhaltungen*.[13]

At the core of this conception of autonomy stands an understanding of the work of art as inscrutable symbol. The *Märchen*, according to Humboldt in a letter to Goethe, can be understood only by readers who are disposed "to love form for its own sake. All others will necessarily reduce the pitch of the *Märchen* to that of an allegory."[14] Here Humboldt is implicitly addressing *the* fundamental opposition in classical poetry: on the one side, allegory, which can be decoded and is therefore "rhetorical and conventional," and on the other side, the symbol, whose infinite readability enables a "vital and immediate revelation of the unfathomable."[15] It is in precisely this sense that the *Märchen* is symbolic: "I admit it was a difficult task," writes Goethe to Humboldt, "to be both meaningful and meaningless at the same time."[16] And in a letter to Schiller he states that the *Märchen* was a "product of fantasy," by way of which the *Unterhaltungen* "flowed out into the infinite, as it were."[17] In this respect, however, the *Märchen* departs from the narrative field of the novellas. At their center, as we have seen, is the encounter with an event that has resisted interpretation. But whereas the novellas thematize the rupture of meaning by a traumatic event, the *Märchen* articulates an infinite meaning in which the "unfathomable"—the unity of mankind and nature, of signs and bodies—is revealed. In this way, the experience of contingency becomes the premonitory experience of transcendental meaning, and a genre demarcating the limits of humanization becomes the medium of a new religion of art.

---

[13] This reading is all the more plausible inasmuch as the *Unterhaltungen* appeared together with Schiller's *Ästhetische Briefe* [*Aesthetical Letters*] in the first volume of *Die Horen*, the literary journal they edited together.

[14] Humboldt to Goethe, February 9, 1796, in *Briefe an Goethe*, ed. Karl Robert Mandelkow (Hamburg: Wegner, 1965), 1:219.

[15] Johann Wolfgang Goethe, *Maximen und Reflexionen*, in *Goethes Werke*, 12:471 (no. 752).

[16] Goethe, Letter to Humboldt, May 27, 1796, in *Sämtliche Werke*, pt. 2, 4:188.

[17] Goethe, Letter to Schiller, August 17, 1795, in *Sämtliche Werke*, pt. 2, 4:106.

"A Story That Has No place in History"

The following fact is, as far as I can tell, uncontested: beginning in 1800, which is to say, immediately after the publication of the *Unterhaltungen*, there was an explosion of middle-length prose works in Germany. This avalanche of texts was accompanied by theoretical reflections that attempted to define the novella in terms of genre poetics, looking first at Boccaccio, but then increasingly turning their attention to contemporary productions. The term *novella*, which was practically unknown before 1800, became in a relatively short time a household word; and the genre "achieve[d] overwhelming dominance of the literary scene in Germany from the 1820s on."[18] Note: the novella, not the novel.

How to explain this development? Why was Goethe's revival of a genre that was practically unknown in Germany seized upon so quickly? When a text that is essentially a by-product (and one of Goethe's more modest works) finds such enormous resonance, then one might well suppose that it articulates a problem considered urgent by others at the time. What I earlier called, rather abstractly, a breach of system can now be discussed more accurately in terms of the novella's polemic relationship to a specific historical discourse. Indications of this antagonism can already be found in the first poetological considerations of the genre around 1800, which without exception emphasize the discontinuity in the novella's relationship to *grand histoire*. Friedrich Schlegel defines the novella as "a story . . . that strictly speaking has no place in history";[19] his brother August Wilhelm speaks of a "story outside of history";[20] and Friedrich Schleiermacher defines the novella narrative as "an event plucked out of history."[21] Precisely this tension between history (the system) and event (the alien element) also lies at the center of Goethe's famous "definition" of the genre as "an unheard-of event that has already occurred."[22] "Unheard-of": that is, (a) never-before heard, new; (b) unusual, singular; and (c) scandalous. Goethe's semantically

---

[18] Martin Swales, *The German Novelle* (Princeton, N.J.: Princeton University Press, 1977), 5.

[19] Friedrich Schlegel, "Nachricht von den poetischen Werken des Johannes Boccaccio" (1801), in *Theorie und Kritik der deutschen Novelle von Wieland bis Musil,* ed. Karl Konrad Polheim (Tübingen: M. Niemeyer, 1970), 12.

[20] August Wilhelm Schlegel, *Vorlesungen über die schöne Literatur und Kunst* (1803–4), in Polheim, *Theorie und Kritik,* 21.

[21] Friedrich Schleiermacher, *Ästhetik* (1819), in Polheim, *Theorie und Kritik,* 22.

[22] "For what is a novella other than an unheard-of event that has already occurred." "Gespräche mit Eckermann (29 January 1827)," in *Goethes Werke,* 6:744.

compressed formula thus defines the novella as that literary form that thematizes the problem of symbolically integrating the new and the irregular. Central to the novella is the narratability of the new as a singular case, as "a case (*casus*) without precedent which is . . . not yet subsumed by law or canonical narrative."[23]

Why the narratability of novelty should have been such a problem in 1800 becomes clearer once we consider the transformation in the semantics of time and history that was being instituted in this period. As Reinhart Koselleck has demonstrated, a new and intrinsically complex concept of history was formed at the end of the eighteenth century.[24] On the one hand, the unity of history was emphasized; one spoke now of History with a capital *H*, of universal history and the history of humankind, and understood thereby a global process in which all local events and developments were encompassed. On the other hand, this unity was grounded in a concept of time as the medium of transformation; past, present, and future now were thematized above all in terms of their radical *difference*, as change. The decisive point, which Koselleck does not pursue, is that the identity of these two aspects of the concept of history—unity and change—is thoroughly problematic. In and of itself, the emphasis on change tends to imply the destabilization of the present: "Our epoch," according to Humboldt, "appears to lead us out of one period, which is passing, into another, which is no less different."[25] Koselleck speaks aptly of the growing difference between the space of experience and the horizon of expectations. Rapid transformation renders traditional experiences valueless and makes the future appear indeterminate and open. The perception of the present as a period of transition and breaking point lends it the aura of a new and absolute beginning, but it also makes it appear uncertain, alien, and threatening. It is this threat that is intercepted, as "progress," through the secondary modeling of the transformation. By linking past and future, the concept of progress integrates the ephemeral present into a meaningful context. The new is integrated in

---

[23] David Wellbery, "Afterword," in *Goethe's Collected Works*, ed. David Wellbery (New York: Suhrkamp, 1988), 11:294.

[24] Reinhart Koselleck, *Futures Past: On the Semantics of Historical Time*, trans. Keith Tribe [from *Vergangene Zukunft* (Frankfurt on Main: Suhrkamp, 1979)] (Cambridge, Mass.: MIT Press, 1985); Koselleck, "Geschichte," in *Geschichtliche Grundbegriffe*, ed. Otto Brunner, W. Conze, R. Koselleck (Stuttgart: Klett Verlag, 1975), 2:617ff.

[25] Wilhelm von Humboldt, *Das achtzehnte Jahrhundert*, in *Werke*, ed. Andreas Flitner and Klaus Giel (Darmstadt: Wissenschaftliche Buchgesellschaft, 1960), 1:398 (cited in Koselleck, *Futures Past*, 252).

narrative and symbolically domesticated by being reinterpreted as the telos of past events and as the sign of a tendency to improvement. "In an age of profound and pervasive change," writes Christian Meier, "this idea provided orientation for vast numbers of people. It gave meaning to their lives: the oppressive sense of impermanence, instability, and contingency was transformed into a sense of progress."[26]

Against this background, the emergence of the German novella may be understood as a reaction not only to the transformation of social structures (which occurred much more vehemently in England and France anyway) but above all to the specifically German semantic domestication of this transformation through the historicist conception of progress. Whereas the period's dominant, teleological genres, the bildungsroman and historiography, intercepted that "oppressive sense of impermanence" through models of continuous development, the novella intensified the sense of transitoriness by dealing with unheard-of events that resisted all attempts at integration and signaled the boundary of teleological schemata of meaning. Thus the novella diverts attention precisely to that aspect of social transformation that the semantics of progress were developed in order to repress: that its difference is meaningless.

This goes hand in hand with the turn away from the idea of a subjectivity that vouchsafes the unity of history. Seen structurally, the new appears at first to be nothing but variation and irritation, that is, a *deviation* from already established structures. Models oriented to continuity can permit deviations only insofar as they are compatible with existing structures. The irritation must be assimilable by the system; it must lead to a rebuilding of the system, not its destruction. Models of progress articulate the new only in diluted form—as innovation. This is *one* side of the historicist domestication of historical change. The *other* side results from the tendency of teleological discourse to attribute agency to transformation. Progress is ascribed to a subject; and history is described as the self-unfolding of a dynamic individual—whether that means a concrete human being, as in the bildungsroman; the whole of humanity, as in Kant and Schiller; or the Spirit, as in Humboldt and Hegel. Change is thus divested of its threatening strangeness. The new is no longer a foreign power confronting the subject from without but its next level of development. From the point of view of the present, however, this development is still something new and therefore

---

[26] Christian Meier, *The Greek Discovery of Politics*, trans. David McKlintock [from *Die Entstehung des Politischen bei den Griechen* (Frankfurt on Main: Suhrkamp, 1980)] (Cambridge, Mass.: Harvard University Press, 1990), 190.

indicative of the future. The new thus gets narrated twice in teleological texts: once as the other of the subject, as an event beyond intentional control (an unconscious action or accident), and once again when the event is considered retrospectively as a necessary step in a subjective process of development, one that culminates precisely in the subject's capacity to understand its necessity—that is, in the capacity to narrate it as a meaningful history. In the context of the model of progress, the new is nothing other than meaning on the way to its own self-knowledge.

The novella breaks with this hermeneutic model. In providing a narrative of irritations unassimilable by a given system, it distances itself from the developmental model and engages the "oppressive feeling" of change in earnest. In the unheard-of event, the new takes on existential features: the deviation from the status quo is intensified and becomes a threat; and the irritation, rather than heightening the complexity of the system as an innovation, turns against the system and destroys its structures. This is the source of the novella's specific temporality as well. On the one hand, the unheard-of event is sudden and momentary; surging past the given horizon of expectations, it crashes down on the subject with shocklike violence. On the other hand, the problematic character of the unheard-of event opens up a temporal horizon defined by the intensive seeking out of resolutions. The momentary shock inaugurates a *crisis phase*. "Crisis," writes Reinhart Koselleck, is a "processural concept that . . . moves toward a decision. It indicates that segment of time in which the decision is due, but is not yet made."[27]

It follows that the time of crisis is always both finite and object-oriented, limited and forward-moving. It is object-oriented because the decision is unavoidable, and finite because the crisis is accompanied by the certainty that it cannot (and should not) last forever. This gives the crisis the structure of *finite progress*: it runs its course unstoppably to the end. Seen in this light, important features of the novella's structure and content can be explained. First of all, the novelistic narrative presents itself explicitly as an isolated and limited interruption: it is "an event plucked out of history" (Schleiermacher) that contradicts the "connectedness of nations, or of times, or . . . the advance of humanity and circumstances of its education" (Friedrich Schlegel).[28] This finds its structural precipitate in the narrative framing so typical for novellas, which has the function of indicating the context—everyday life, progress, *grande histoire*—to which the story can be contrasted as a crisislike

---

[27] Reinhart Koselleck, "Krise" in *Geschichtliche Grundbegriffe*, 3:619.
[28] Friedrich Schlegel, "Nachricht von den poetischen Werken des Johannes Boccaccio" (1801), in Polheim, *Theorie und Kritik,* 12.

interruption. Second, the processural character of the crisis explains the significance of narrative length for the genre. The novella's medium length is neither arbitrary nor conventional, but a representational necessity: the torrential dynamic of the crisis can neither be unfolded in three pages nor be supported for three hundred. And last, it should come as no surprise that the narrational drive toward the end should so frequently climax in the ending par excellence: death, a topic German novellas thematized almost obsessively. (One need think only of Kleist, the Romantics, Storm, and Meyer, as well as Mann, Musil, Schnitzler, and Kafka.) Heidegger would have had a field day with this genre, for more than any other literary form, the novella emplots human Being as a Being unto Death.

As far-fetched as the reference to Heidegger may seem, it is thoroughly systematic in its significance. For the novella not only arose out of a polemical differentiation from dominant, contemporary, teleological genres; it also "anticipated" later philosophical critiques of modernity. Even the trope of death is hardly a conventional theme. Much more than that, it articulates in rarefied form the novella's insistence on the subject's finitude, which finds narrative expression in the above-mentioned temporal structure of finite progress. But death is not the only theme linking the novella with certain philosophical traditions that began in the nineteenth century and have found in Heidegger their most eloquent spokesman. The interest in states of exception and unattainable events—the novella's two other important constants—can be found in the so-called dark thinkers of the bourgeoisie, who had only contempt and scorn left over for modernity's optimism for progress. As is well known, the philosophical ennobling of the *exception* begins with Kierkegaard, gets taken up by Nietzsche, and comes into full force during the Weimar Republic. Benjamin, Schmitt, Bloch, Jünger, and Heidegger of course, raised the exception to a central concept in the struggle against "the flat and-so-forth of bourgeois stability."[29] "In the exception," writes Carl Schmitt in his 1922 book, *Political Theology*, "the power of real life breaks through the crust of a mechanism that has become torpid by repetition."[30] Schmitt's "crust" is related to the Freudian concept of a "shell"

---

[29] Rüdiger Safranski, *Martin Heidegger: Between Good and Evil*, trans. Ewald Osers [from *Ein Meister aus Deutschland: Heidegger und seine Zeit* (Munich, 1994)] (Cambridge, Mass.: Harvard University Press, 1998), 173. See all of chapter 10 of Safranski's book for an excellent discussion of the Weimar fascination with "the moment."

[30] Carl Schmitt, *Political Theology: Four Chapters on the Concept of Sovereignty*, trans. Charles Schwab [from *Politische Theologie* (Munich: Duncker and Humblot, 1922)] (Cambridge, Mass.: MIT Press, 1985), 15.

that functions as a "protective shield" for the mental apparatus against the overwhelming stimulating energies of the outside world. But for Schmitt, whose book appeared two years after Freud's *Beyond the Pleasure Principle*, the traumatic breach of this crust is now the moment of truth. As with Kierkegaard and Nietzsche before him, and Benjamin and Heidegger later on, Schmitt likewise sought historical truth not in a temporal continuum (in the everyday world depicted in the novel or the historiographic notion of progress), but rather in the abrupt incursion of the absolutely other, in the unheard-of event.

Blind Spot (the Case History, the Bildungsroman, Romanticism, Freud)

"If I am worth no more, at least I am different," writes Rousseau at the beginning of his *Confessions* (1770),[31] thus spelling out the threefold imperative that the new semantics of individuality imposes upon the subject: to be unique, to observe one's own particularity, and to be able to narrate it as an continuous life story. A few years later, and with explicit reference to Rousseau, the first psychological journal ever published appeared in Germany, Karl Philipp Moritz's *Magazin für Erfahrungsseelenkunde* [Magazine for Empirical Psychology] (1783–93).[32] While the *Confessions* still stood in the tradition of biography as the exemplary life history of an extraordinary person, Moritz popularized the method of autobiographical self-observation and made it the keystone of a new science of the human—now no longer understood as a member of a race, but as a self, formed by way of his or her unique life history. To this corresponded the invention of a genre that was to represent the life of the individual in all its deviations, detours, and idiosyncrasies: the psychological case history. Moritz's case histories thematize the individual as an "unheard-of event," as "a case (*casus*) without precedent which is . . . not yet subsumed by law or canonical narrative."

At the center of Moritz's genetic approach is the discovery of childhood as the birthplace of the individual. The task of psychological self-observation is "to trace back the earliest threads of the wondrous fabric of our thoughts," and, proceeding from this core of identity, to reconstruct the

---

[31] Jean-Jacques Rousseau, *Collected Writings*, ed. Roger D. Masters and Christopher Kelly (Hanover, N.H.: University Press of New England, 1990), 5:5.

[32] For a detailed discussion of Moritz's project, see my "A Case of Individuality: Karl Philipp Moritz and the *Magazine for Empirical Psychology*," *New German Critique* 79 (2000): 67–106.

individual's development as a case history.[33] But the objective of absolute historical transparency proves to be utopian. First of all, there is the limit of what can be remembered. In looking back on the "earliest years of child-hood" one runs up against "an impenetrable curtain" (Moritz, 4:195) that marks the ultimate blind spot of every self-observation: the inscrutable mystery of the subject's own biological origin. Second, it appears that precisely at its origin the self is inextricably involved with the speech of the other. What the self experiences and what it hears, "genuinely sensory impressions" and "other people's stories," are indistinguishable, so that the psychic origin of the individual remains as reflexively inaccessible as the biological. For if it is true that "our earliest memories from childhood . . . always get mixed in imperceptibly with [our subsequent ideas] and orient them in directions they otherwise would never have taken" (Moritz 4:195), then the "I" that remembers cannot be distinguished absolutely from the "I" that is remembered; and then the unconscious throws its shadow "imperceptibly" over every attempt at self-enlightenment. As a direct result of its demand for absolute transparency, the self-observation that passes itself off as neutral produces the "highest degree of self-delusion" (Moritz, 7:224).

The bildungsroman, which was developing around the same time, seems at first to present an answer to this problem. Here, the observational function is split, and in such a way that the secondary observer (the narrator) renders visible exactly what the primary observer (the protagonist) cannot see. "The novel makes manifest the problem of latency, of 'the unconscious,' of 'living a lie,' or of incommunicability. . . . The character is represented as lacking self-knowledge, as wanting to know him or herself, but being inca-pable of doing so. And that is precisely what permits a reader to identify with this character, that is, to learn from the novel, drawing conclusions about him or herself."[34] But that is not all. The bildungsroman at the same time presents a model that makes the self-obscurity it represents seem sur-mountable. The biography is told as a developmental narrative at the end of which the hero achieves insight into the latent wishes and motives that have been driving him or her from the start. Seen in this light *Bildung*, or educa-tion, consists in the evolution from primary to secondary observation, from a subjective and imaginary to an objective and symbolic point of view. Indeed, the bildungsroman ends at the precise moment when this process is

---

[33] Karl Philipp Moritz, *Gnothi Seauthon oder Magazin zur Erfahrungsseelenkunde* (1783–93) (Nördlingen: Franz Greno, 1986), 4:197.

[34] Niklas Luhmann, "Weltkunst," in *Unbeobachtbare Welt: Über Kunst und Architektur*, ed. Niklas Luhmann, Frederick D. Bunsen, and Dirk Baecker (Bielefeld: C. Haux, 1990), 33–34.

completed, and the hero—who up to this point has been unconsciously *creating* the story of his life—reflects on it through narrative. In this way, the end of the novel returns to its beginning. The hero now sees what the narrator was able to see from the start; narration and narrated contents converge in a moment of utter self-transparency.[35]

The romantic novella deconstructs this model. The unheard-of event is exactly that blind spot on which the pedagogical ideal of complete self-transparency founders. By making the unassimilable foreignness of the subject the narrative motor of their stories, authors like Tieck, Hoffmann, and Arnim developed a literary form that in terms of the historical semantics of the individual erected a bridge, so to speak, between the eighteenth and the twentieth centuries. On the one hand, romantic novellas radicalized doubts that had first surfaced during the evolution of the psychological case study but then were repressed by the bildungsroman. On the other hand, they "anticipated" insights that, one hundred years after Moritz's first attempt at human psychology, would lead in Freud's work to a new theory and practice of subjectivity. I shall demonstrate this now in two novellas, Tieck's *Der blonde Eckbert* [*Blond Eckbert*] and E.T.A. Hoffmann's *Das Fräulein von Scuderi* [*Mademoiselle de Scuderi*], and in a footnote to Freud.

Tieck knew Moritz: he attended his lectures on aesthetics and mythology[36] and possessed a complete edition of the *Magazin*.[37] Not only can his novella be traced back to Moritz, it simultaneously inaugurated the romantic obsession with origins. Berta and Eckbert, a childless couple, live in a castle in the Harz Mountains. When his old friend Walter comes for a visit, Eckbert, impelled by an "irresistible urge to tell all," convinces his wife to recount the story of her childhood.[38] This begins with Berta's running away from her parents and encountering an old woman who lives in an isolated forest hut with a talking bird and a dog. Berta follows the old woman, lives with her for some years, but finally runs away, abandoning the dog. A short time afterward, she meets Eckbert and marries him. After telling her story, Berta discovers with horror that Walter knows the name of the dog, a detail

---

[35] See Dietrich Schwanitz, *Systemtheorie und Literatur* (Opladen: Westdeutscher Verlag, 1990), chap. 4.

[36] Hans Joachim Schrimpf, *Karl Philipp Moritz* (Stuttgart: Metzler, 1980), 19.

[37] Ulrich Hubert, *Karl Philipp Moritz und die Anfänge der Romantik* (Frankfurt on Main: Athenäum, 1971), 51.

[38] Ludwig Tieck, *Der blonde Eckbert* (1797), in *Die Märchen aus dem Phantasus: Dramen* (Darmstadt: Wissenschaftliche Buchgesellschaft, 1964), 9. Subsequent quotations from this edition are referenced by page number in the text.

she herself could no longer remember. Berta immediately falls ill on the spot and dies, while Eckbert, driven by paranoia, murders Walter "without knowing what he was doing" (23). Years later, Eckbert befriends another man, named Hugo, once again entrusts the new friend with his innermost secrets, and again reacts to the self-disclosure with paranoia. Convinced of having seen Walter's and Hugo's faces dissolve into one another, he goes wandering half-mad through the woods, where he meets an old woman who reveals to him that she had impersonated Walter and Hugo, and that Berta was his half-sister: "Why have I always sensed this horrible thought?" Eckbert cries out. "Because in your youth you once heard your father speak of it; his wife would not allow him to raise this daughter, for he had fathered her with another woman" (26). At this, Eckbert goes insane.

Tieck centers the whole tale around the impossibility of authorial control and the suicidal fixation on origins. Berta's story introduces the theme of the blind spot. Walter's naming of the dog transforms Berta from the assumed subject of self-observation into the object of an other's gaze. In this way Walter effects the dissolution of a subjectivity based on the phantasm of absolute authorial control: Berta falls ill and dies. But Berta's biography does not only entail a blind spot; it is itself the blind spot around which Eckbert's subjectivity is formed. This becomes clear when the narrator introduces Berta's story with a reflection on Eckbert's "irresistible urge to tell all, to reveal his innermost being to his friend" (9). In other words, Eckbert's "innermost being" is localized outside him, in Berta's life: the intimate is the extimate.[39] The novella's conclusion dramatizes the self's encounter with its extimate center as the encounter with its (non-)origin. At the very moment when Eckbert is confronted by a knowledge that (as foreboding and unconscious fixation) had determined his object choice and hence his life, his psychic universe breaks down. The lifting of the "inscrutable curtain" (Moritz, 4:195) that reveals Eckbert's "primary foundations" (197), leads to his complete disintegration. Absolute self-observation coincides with the dissolution of the self.

Moritz had discovered childhood as the individual's place of origin, but in doing so he ran up against the limits of individual self-transparency and the *unconscious* origin of the subject in "other people's narration." Tieck

---

[39] The concept of the extimate (*extimité*) was developed by Lacan in order to describe the rather unusual psychological topography of the subject, whose absolute interiority—the unconscious—is the effect of intersubjective relations. See Jacques Lacan, *The Ethics of Psychoanalysis, 1959–1960*, trans. Dennis Porter, bk. 7 of *The Seminars of Jacques Lacan* (New York: Norton, 1992), 139.

pushes this "insistence of the letter in the unconscious" (Lacan) into the center of his novella. Eckbert's secret is the family secret of his father's forbidden affair, which he had heard in "other people's narration," but not understood, and which had determined his life "unnoticeably." It is an "enigmatic signifier," with which the child identifies and which, inasmuch as it is developed into a phantasmatic scene of origins, will determine his wishes and object choices.[40] *Der blonde Eckbert* thus has to do not simply with the subject's *biological* origin as an inaccessible blind spot in his or her own self-observation; rather, Tieck's novella narrates the birth of the *individual* out of the anti-spirit of the enigmatic—and in this sense, meaningless— signifier. At his core, in that which makes him a unique "other," the individual is the effect of the "unheard-of event" of an identification that cannot be accessed reflexively.

Der blonde Eckbert appeared in 1797, a year after Goethe's *Wilhelm Meister* and at the same time as his *Unterhaltungen*. The very first romantic novella, Tieck's *Eckbert* delivers a polemical answer to the bildungsroman and represents an intensification of the classical treatment of the subject's "other" side (*Unterhaltungen*). Furthermore, it marks the end of an Enlightenment project that both the bildungsroman and, at the same time though by other means, Goethe's novella, had attempted to continue: the project of human autonomy. This autonomy is paradigmatically resisted by the so-called accident of birth. Lessing, in *Nathan der Weise,* comments: "A man, like you remains not just where birth / has chanced to cast him, or, if he remains there / does it from insight, choice, from grounds of preference."[41] The Enlightenment was intended to replace the accident of biological birth—one's parents, body, social environment, instilled values—with a spiritual rebirth under the sign of liberty. Even Kant still described the awakening of reason as a rebirth that overcomes the scandal of the first birth—the self's beginning—in favor of a fresh start entirely of one's own making. Beginning with *Der blonde Eckbert*, romantic novellas departed from this program by telling stories about human beings determined by their contingent beginnings.

For example, take E.T.A. Hoffmann's *Das Fräulein von Scuderi*. Paris, circa 1680: a number of nobles are discovered murdered shortly after having

---

[40] On the concept of the "enigmatic signifier," see Jean Laplanche, *New Foundations for Psychoanalysis*, trans. David Macey [translation of *Nouveaux fondements pour la psychanalyse*], chap. 3.

[41] Gotthold Ephraiim Lessing, *Nathan the Wise*, trans. William Taylor (London: Cassell and Co., 1893).

purchased expensive jewelry at the shop of Cardillac, the city's most famous goldsmith. Madame de Scuderi uncovers the truth. It is Cardillac who is murdering his customers. Why? Because when his mother was carrying him, she had lusted after an aristocrat and his costly jewel necklace. During their first embrace, just as Cardillac's mother was about to touch the necklace, the aristocrat collapsed, dead. In time, the mother recovers from the shock, but not her unborn child. Hence Cardillac's whole life has been determined by an unquenchable obsession with jewels, which at first enabled him to become the best goldsmith of his time but in the end makes him compulsively murder his clients.

Hoffmann's novella portrays a character whose life course was already determined before his birth. The aristocrat's death has the status of a traumatic primal scene that fixed Cardillac's biography before he even existed as a subject. Hoffmann pushes the discourse on the accidental birth to the extreme. Cardillac's personality is the symptom of an accidental prenatal event, his biography the permanent repetition of a contingent encounter. In this way, the Enlightenment critique on the accident of birth becomes the romantic theorem of the *contingency of the individual*.

A hundred years after Moritz's *Magazin*, and seventy years after Hoffmann's final publications in his lifetime, the semantics of the individual sketched out between late-Enlightenment case studies and romantic novellas receives theoretical expression in Freud's work. Moritz's thesis about childhood as the origin of the individual; his interest in dreams and slips of the tongue; the romantic model of traumatic sexuality; incest, repetitions, and primal scenes; and above all, the nontransparency of the self to itself— all of these are also foundational theorems of psychoanalysis. Freud's relationship to romantic literature has been analyzed frequently, not least with regard to his superb reading of Hoffmann's novella *The Sandman*. Much less noted, in contrast, is the genre-specific dimension of this relationship. This is all the more astonishing inasmuch as Freud himself pointed to the similarity between the psychoanalytical case study and the novella. It "still strikes me myself as strange," he writes in his first case-study publication, the *Studien über Hysterie* [*Studies on Hysteria*], "that the case histories I write should read like short stories [*wie Novellen zu lesen sind*] and that, as one might say, they lack the serious stamp of science."[42]

What are the features of this family resemblance between the (psychoanalytic) case study and the novella? In the first place, the case serves both

---

[42] Sigmund Freud, "Case History 5: Fräulein Elisabeth von R.," in *Standard Edition*, 2:160. See also Freud's comments in "Fragments of an Analysis of a Case of Hysteria" (1905), *SE*, 7:59.

genres as a selection criterion. Both novellas and case studies limit the scope of representation to events marked explicitly as deviations. Case studies depict symptoms of illness; novellas deal with unheard-of events. And while case studies pass over any information not pertinent to the case at hand, the novella, unlike its polar opposite, the novel, focuses on the representation of a crisis that interrupts the course of everyday life. Second, psychoanalytical case studies and romantic novellas have the same problem to tackle. "What many find most seductive in psychoanalysis," writes John Forrester, "is its promise to give an account of the divergences, the detours, the idiosyncrasies of the individual's life."[43] This conception of the individual as deviation was exactly what motivated Moritz's invention of the case study and its transformation in the romantic novella. Like (psychoanalytic) case studies, novellas treat the individual as "a case without precedent." Third, I would like to argue that the tension so crucial for the novella—between event and context, frame and story, trangression and regulation—returns in the case study as a tension between narration (story) and discussion (discourse), symptom and medical evaluation, the patient's speech and the analyst's interpretation. Indeed, does not the very idea of a "talking cure," that turn to conversation as therapy on which the discipline of psychoanalysis was founded, have its precursor in the novella, a genre that more than any other emphasizes and dramatizes the performative function of speech? It is perhaps no accident that Berta Pappenheim, the patient (Anna O.) to whom Freud owed the concept of the talking cure, was herself a writer of novellas.

On the other hand, what are the differences between the fictional genre and the psychoanalytical one? Psychoanalysis, it seems to me, provides an albeit precarious response to the problem of self-observation, a response that avoids the suppression of this problem in the bildungsroman no less than its hypostasization in romantic novellas. On the one hand—and this is what distinguishes psychoanalysis from the bildungsroman (and from Hegel's philosophy)—Freud emphasized the nontransparency of the analyst, who, no different from the patient, possesses an unconscious. The analyst for Freud is *not* an omniscient narrator standing outside time, but a subject in a labyrinthine and unpredictable process fraught with false starts, surprising associations, and vague intuitions. On the other hand—and this is what differentiates psychoanalysis from romanticism—the analyst's unconscious is the medium of dynamic self-enlightenment. The analyst, Freud writes, "must turn his own unconscious like a receptive organ towards the transmitting

---

[43] John Forrester, "If *p*, Then What?" *History of the Human Sciences* 9 (1996): 10.

unconscious of the patient. He must adjust himself to the patient as a telephone receiver is adjusted to the transmitting microphone."[44] Freud's theory of transference and countertransference bypasses the problem of self-observation by "unselfing" the observer. The feelings and realizations set free in the analytic dynamic originate not in the patient's or the analyst's self but in the space of potential that exists *between* the unconscious of both. In this ghost conversation, the analyst momentarily suspends his scientific neutrality and allows himself to be affected and contaminated by the patient.

This brings us back to the novella. Unconscious infection through the speech of the other is a typical feature of modern novellas, which, in stark contrast to the old European novella, generally dramatize the act of narration or of speech as a threat that contaminates and or seduces. Against this background, Freud's conception of the analytical conversation appears to be a precarious balancing act. For while, on the one hand, he opens himself up to the dynamic of unconscious transmissions, on the other, he attributes a therapeutic function to the communication resulting from it. Freud's theory of transference is an attempt to reanimate the therapeutic function of speech under the conditions of a modern semantics of a subject who is nontransparent to him or herself. The "unheard-of event" of psychoanalysis is not the past trauma of subject formation that analysis brings to light but the emergence—for which the therapeutic process painstakingly paves the way, yet which is nonetheless necessarily sudden and unforeseen—of a new psychic structure that allows the patient to accept the unassimilable foreignness of his origin: the fact that he was begun. Tradition has a name for this: *amor fati*—which in light of all of the above could be translated as "love for the blind spot."

Contingency (Kleist)

The foundation of historical representation, writes Wilhelm von Humboldt, "is the recognition of the true form, the discovery of that which is necessary, the bracketing out of that which is accidental [*Zufällig*]."[45] *Zufall* (chance, accident, coincidence, or happenstance) is "bracketed out" because, though real, it is not necessary and therefore thwarts the very project of historiogra-

---

[44] Freud, "Recommendations to Physicians Practising Psycho-analysis" ["Ratschläge für den Arzt bei der psychoanalytischen Behandlung"] (1912), in *Standard Edition*, 12:115.

[45] Wilhelm von Humboldt, "Über die Aufgabe des Geschichtschreibers" (1821), in *Werke*, 1:591.

phy: to prove that the past is not an aggregate of unconnected events but a continuous process that becomes conscious of itself through historiographic reflection. With the bildungsroman matters are different. It comes with a claim to register the small and inconspicuous accidents of which a life is made and validates itself precisely in this construal of contingency as realistic and authentic. "He who sets store in such faithful representation," writes Karl Philipp Moritz in 1786 in the foreword to the second part of *Anton Reiser*, the first psychological novel in German, "will not take exception to what in the beginning may seem insignificant and unimportant, but rather will consider that this artificially woven fabric of a human life consists of an endless quantity of trifles, which in being woven all together become extremely important, however insignificant each may seem on its own."[46] This concurs with the new understanding of the novelistic hero. Instead of courageously and persistently pursuing a clearly defined goal as the old heroes had done, the new hero is meant to learn to be open to the unforeseeable, to avoid rigid fixations, and to regard any apparently unimportant and accidental event as an opportunity. Goethe's conception, voiced by the protagonist of his bildungsroman, "that while chance may be allowed to play its games, it must always be guided and directed by people's fundamental beliefs,"[47] puts this new program in a nutshell. The bildungsroman, and the same may be said for the realist novel, domesticates contingency by rendering it a necessary complement to human freedom. Chance is no longer an irrational power that must be "bracketed out" but rather a field of possibilities to be grasped and used by the individual.

But this is just why chance may now occur only in the restricted form of *lucky coincidence*. The hero and the world, intention and accident, what is one's own and what is other, are mediated dialectically: on the one hand, the hero suffers the resistance of the world in the form of uncontrollable accidents and learns through this confrontation with the other to surrender his fantasies of omnipotence; on the other hand, he is rewarded for his self-limitation in being granted, at the end, a "happiness"[48] that is all the greater for having come about accidentally—unforeseeably, unintentionally. Chance in the bildungsroman is by no means the absolute other of the subject but rather a medium of self-discovery and a stimulus for the enrichment of the

---

[46] Karl Philipp Moritz, *Anton Reiser*, in *Werke*, ed. Horst Günther (Frankfurt on Main: Insel Verlag, 1981), 1:120.

[47] *Wilhelm Meisters Lehrjahre*, in *Sämtliche Werke*, 7:308.

[48] Ibid., 610.

senses. To put it in terms of systems theory: chance may be characterized as an environmental irritation that is assimilated by the system (the subject) and used as stimulus for the construction of its own complexity.

The radicality of chance in the novella registers clearly against this background. What the philosophy of history "brackets out" and the novel "guides" is shifted in the novella to the very center of the form: here, chance is a foreign power that thwarts the characters' designs and frustrates the meaning of intentional actions. Modernity, according to the editors of a recent essay collection devoted to the concept of contingency, "has developed genres of its own based on isolated contingencies and their problematic rationalization: the picaresque novel and the novella."[49] Whereas the bildungsroman construes contingency as something with which the hero and the reader both must come to terms, contingency in the novella is a *factum brutum* of which all calculation and rationalization run afoul. Contingency in the novella is in fact the form's blind spot, a "blank space of codification," unsymbolizable and utterly irreducible to any meaning.[50]

No author of novellas and stories has endowed chance, accident, and coincidence with as much power as has Heinrich von Kleist. The Marchese enters "by chance" the room in which the old and sick beggar woman has settled;[51] while hunting, the Elector of Saxony happens by coincidence upon Michael Kohlhaas, as he is being transferred to Brandenburg (*Michael Kohlhaas*, 2:79); Nicolo "coincidentally" dresses up for a masked ball like Colino, Elvire's deceased lover ("The Foundling," 2:212); and Jeronimo is freed from his prison by an earthquake just as he was about to surrender himself "to death, with a piece of rope that chance had left him" ("The Earthquake in Chile," 2:145). The coincidence always sets off a chain of events, which, stepped up by further coincidences, culminate in the story's violent conclusion. "The Marchese, overwrought with horror," in the end sets both himself and his castle on fire (2:198); the Elector of Saxony returns to Dresden, "torn in body and soul"; after Elvire dies "from the consequences of a high fever, to which she succumbed as a result of the incident" (2:214), her husband Piachi, beside himself with fury and grief, smashes Nicolo's "brains against the wall" (2:214); Jeronimo finally is knocked down,

---

[49] Gerhard von Graevenitz and Odo Marquard, "Vorwort," in *Kontingenz*, xv.

[50] Joachim Küpper, "Mittelalterliche Ordnung und rinascimentale Kontingenz," in *Kontingenz*, 180–81.

[51] Heinrich von Kleist, "Das Bettelweib von Locarno," in *Sämtliche Werke und Briefe*, ed. Helmut Sembdner (Munich: Hanser Verlag, 1984), 2:196. Subsequent references to this and other stories in this collection are given in the text by volume and page number.

"with a monstrous blow of a cudgel" (2:158), by an enraged mob that holds him responsible for the earthquake.

Contingency is derived from the Latin *contingere*, literally "to touch together." This touching refers to an unforeseeable collision of at least two independent chains of events. Kleist has his own formula for this convergence. It is the phrase "Es traf sich, daß . . ." ("It just so happened that . . ."; literally: "It thus *met itself*, that"), which appears twenty-two times in his stories alone. Understood as a signal, this phrase sharpens our perception of a dimension of contingency that is constitutive of narrative texts.[52] Every narrative develops out of the intersection of two axes: a chronological axis, which orders the narrated—hence actualized—events in a sequence, and an anachronic axis, which consists of the virtual space of potential, though unnarrated, events. The Kleistian "Es traf sich, daß . . ." makes this second axis visible. It points to the potential of narrated events to be otherwise, and thus to the fact that every element of a narrative is created by selection from a field of discrete possibilities and is the result of a contingent choice. "Contingency," writes David Wellbery, "is always a selection, an actualization that draws on a reservoir of other, nonactualized possibilities, a throw of the dice, an intersection. Without this selection there would be no events to concatenate in narrative series, but the selection itself—the fact that this, and not something else, happens—belongs to no chronological pattern."[53]

Kleist's play with contingency destabilizes the narrative medium in two directions. In the one, it underscores the performative and constructivist character of language. By selecting and concatenating discrete elements, a narrative in fact actualizes a new world: it is not a mimetic depiction but an event, an emergence of the new. In the other direction, the (textual) world thus constructed loses all stability. As Roland Barthes has pointed out, we tend to read stories as temporally organized causal sequences, as if a given event were the cause of the following one. Kleist's "Es traf sich, daß . . ." marks a break with this linear model. His formula underscores the internal complexity of events. It demonstrates that events are not homogenous parts in a series but rather temporally fixed constellations issuing from the collision of heterogenous sequences of action. But inasmuch as any individual event is the momentary outcome of the clash of heterogeneous forces, the

---

[52] See, here and below, David Wellbery, "Contingency," in *Neverending Stories: Toward a Critical Narratology*, ed. Ann Fehn, Ingeborg Hoesterey, and Maria Tatar (Princeton, N.J.: Princeton University Press, 1992), 237–57; on Kleist, 242–50.

[53] Ibid., 249.

reality actualized through concatenation of these events loses all appearance of solidity and logical necessity. Hence the enormous instability of Kleist's narratives, which careen in fits and starts from one accident to the next, projecting the image of a reality in constant flux and lacking any hold. Kleist's best-known metaphor for this logical groundlessness is the earthquake. "Das Erdbeben in Chile" ["The Earthquake in Chile"] is an ontological tremor, one that convulses all of Kleistian space.

By way of a "fortunate coincidence," Jeronimo manages to see Josephe again after her father has banished her to a convent and to "make of the convent garden a stage for his unlimited joy" (first coincidence; 2:144); Josephe gives birth just as the ceremonial procession on Corpus Christi is taking place (second coincidence; 2:145); faced with a death sentence and beside himself with despair, Jeronimo decides to "give himself up to death with a piece of rope that chance had left him" (third coincidence; 2:145); just as he is about to hang himself, an earthquake devastates the city (fourth coincidence; 2:145) and the collapsing walls of the prison create an "fortuitous vault" through which Jeronimo escapes (fifth coincidence; 2:146); reunited, Josephe, Jeronimo, and their son Philipp encounter an aristocratic family, Don Fernando and Donna Elvire, who also have a newborn, Juan (sixth coincidence; 2:150); the families decide to go to mass together, but Donna Elvire being injured, Josephe takes Juan and goes arm in arm with Don Fernando, while Jeronimo, with Philipp in his arms, accompanies a distant relation, Donna Costanze, to church; during the service the enraged mob recognizes Jeronimo and murders him, Donna Costanze, and Juan, on the assumption that they are Josephe and her child; and so, as if by a miracle, Josephe's real son Philipp survives the massacre and is adopted by Don Fernando (seventh coincidence; 2:155ff.); "and when Don Fernando compared Philipp with Juan and the way he had received both, he almost had the feeling he should be happy" (2:159).

In summarizing it becomes evident that coincidence occurs here with such frequency that it takes on a *structure-bearing* role. The same may be said more or less for all of Kleist's novellas. For Kleist, coincidence never occurs in isolation, as a temporary suspension of the narrative order; rather, it is combined with others into *series of coincidences* that determine the plot and endow the text with narrative coherence. Coincidence thus creates a kind of order—albeit a paradoxical one inasmuch as the narrative continuity established through repetition culminates, in the violence of the ending, in the destruction of all orders internal to the diegesis. Kleist's novellas portray a world whose modus operandi is coincidence, accident, and chance, a world that is a continuous plunge into groundlessness, from one contingent case to another. "With Kleist," writes László Földenyi, "the world as a whole is a violent fall: singular and contingent."[54]

This lapsarian structure of the world determines the fundamental moral problematic confronting all of Kleist's protagonists. They must, to use Deleuze's formulation, show themselves "worthy of the event" befalling them; and that means affirming it in both its contingency and its necessity. The event is contingent because it could have happened otherwise, and is necessary because it nevertheless happened the way it did. It is a brute fact, a naked truth, the idiocy of the real; it is the concrete historical situation into which the characters have been thrown and within which they must make sense of their lives. Hardly any of Kleist's protagonists prove themselves up to the task. They react to the concussive breakdown of their intentional world with narcissistic fantasies of an absolute other who has staged the occurrences for their sake. In this way, they teleologize the event in retrospect and transform the threatening actuality of the real into a reassuring sign of God. Having escaped the earthquake, "[Jeronimo and Josephe] were very moved when they thought of how much misery the world would have to suffer so that they should be happy!" (2:150).

Only once did Kleist create a character who proved to be "worthy of the event." In "Die Verlobung in St. Domingo" ["The Betrothal in St. Domingo"], Toni, the mulatto woman, finds herself in a bind. Just after she spends a night of love with Gustav, the foreign white man, her black stepfather, Congo Hoango, shows up with his troops outside the house in order to capture and kill Gustav and his company. Under pressure of the double threat (either she loses her lover by handing him over or she is herself executed as a traitor), she happens on a potential way out.

> In this unspeakable fear she *chanced to glimpse* a rope, hanging, heaven knows by what *accident*, off the wall beam. *God himself,* she supposed, as she hauled it [him] down, had directed it there to save her and the foreigner. She bound up the boy, tying multiple knots . . . ; and once she had pulled the ends taut and secured them to the bed frame: happy to *have seized control of the moment*, she kissed him on the lips and hurried off to Hoango, who was already rattling up the stairs. (2:185; emphasis added)

Toni's action is meaningful, but this meaning is neither intentional nor transcendent by nature. It is not purely intentional because her idea for the

---

[54] László F. Földenyi, *Heinrich von Kleist: Im Netz der Wörter*, trans. from the Hungarian by Akos Doma (Munich: Matthes and Seitz, 1999), 536.

action comes from her contingent surroundings: the inspiration itself is a co-incidence, dependent on the existence of the rope that, in Kleist's exact notation, she *chanced to glimpse* (literally: "that *fell* into her eyes"). Nor is it transcendent, because Toni, in contrast to Kleist's other protagonists, does not read this accident as a sign from God, but as an opportunity that has befallen her, and which she can choose to seize or not. In short, she reads the accident as something she first has to *invest* with meaning. Hence, the tearing down of the rope takes on the significance of the destruction of transcendence. The text indicates this through the double reference of the gendered pronoun *ihn*, which means "him" as well as "it," and thus refers to both the rope and God: "*God* himself, she supposed, as she hauled it/him down." By hauling down the rope, the text suggests, Toni is hauling God into the immanence of her innerworldly agency. As a consequence, however, the meaning of her action depends on the interpretation of others. The rope is a human sign, a message that must be deciphered and may therefore always be misunderstood as well. Toni's speculations are based precisely on this polyvalency of the sign inasmuch as she makes the success of her plan dependent on Hoango's and Gustav's divergent interpretations of the rope: for Hoango it is a sign of racial loyalty, for Gustav a sign of love.

This scene represents, it seems to me, the only genuinely utopian moment in Kleist's work. Toni's action is a *free utterance*, in terms both of morality and of speech. Under pressure of a mortal danger, she makes use of the chance composition of her surroundings for an action whose meaning is ungrounded in convention or rule and is therefore absolutely new and contingent. Toni proves herself to be "worthy of the event" by investing it with a meaning that is itself an event. However—and here again we find Kleist's unrelenting insistence on the instability of a world experienced only as meaning—Toni's action is an *event* of communication that has neither ontological nor pragmatic support; it does not rest on deployed conventions. Its communicative meaning is therefore ephemeral and dependent on the comprehension of an other, without whose congenial interpretation it will expire like a communicative shooting star. But congeniality is something Gustav is entirely lacking; like all of Kleist's male protagonists, he wants certainty and so cannot cope with Toni's radical relinquishing of transcendence and unambiguousness. Incapable of unbinding the rope from its conventional meaning, of comprehending it as an "unheard-of event," Gustav assumes he has been betrayed and at the end of the story executes Toni by shooting her.

Of course, the role of chance, accident, and coincidence in the novella does not necessarily appear as a "hostile principle." It can also take the form of a lyrical epiphany, as in Mörike's novella *Mozart auf der Reise nach Prag*

[*Mozart's Journey to Prague*] (1855), which in many ways anticipates Proust's conception of *memoire involuntaire*. But the itinerary of novella narration is always determined by a power external to the protagonists' subjective intentions and narrative plans. In a century intoxicated by the myth of practicability, novellas tell of an irrevocable foreignness in the midst of reality, of an inaccessible contingency upon which the fantasy of total control runs aground. So it is hardly an accident that in Thomas Mann's great farewell to the passing world, his novella *Tod in Venedig* [*Death in Venice*] (1912), it is an accident that at a key moment determines what happens. Summoning his last reserves of willpower, Gustav Aschenbach decides to leave Venice, only to discover at the train station that his luggage has been sent accidentally to Como rather than to Munich. And so, glad in his heart of hearts over the chance turn of events, he returns to his hotel and abandons himself to his demise: "*Pas de chance*, Monsieur, the Swiss elevator man said, smiling, as they went up."[55] *Pas de chance*: with Mann, accident is not simply the other of rationality, but the medium of another, nonintentional rationality that drives the subject with inexorable necessity toward self-destruction. *Zufall*—accident, chance, coincidence—has now become a form of what lies "beyond" the pleasure principle.

The Anti-novella (Stifter)

With these words, he looked into the scope, but though his eye was, through practice, much sharper than that of the girls, still, he saw nothing other than what they had seen: a tremendous tower rising up with beautiful clarity from the edge of the woods without a roof, and with black burn marks; only it seemed to him as if a quite delicate, blue layer of haze still hovered over the ruin. It was an uncanny thought that in this moment the place was perhas full of the tremendous turmoil of war, and deeds were being done there that could break the human heart; but in the great scale of the world and the woods the tower itself was only a point. There was absolutely nothing to make one aware of [*ward man gar nichts inne*] the tumult of war, and only the smiling, beautiful stillness hung in the sky and over the whole barren wasteland.[56]

---

[55] Thomas Mann, *Death in Venice, Tonio Kröger, and Other Writings*, ed. Frederick A. Lubich (New York: Continuum, 1999), 129.

[56] Adalbert Stifter, *Der Hochwald*, in *Werke und Briefe*, ed. Alfred Doppler and Wolfgang Frühwald (Stuttgart: Kohlhammer, 1980), 1:306.

Stifter's early novella *Der Hochwald* (*The Alpine Forest*) takes place during the Thirty Years' War. In order to protect his daughters Clarissa and Johanna from the approaching Swedish troops, Baron von Wittinghausen entrusts them to the care of Gregor, a hunter who on the Baron's behalf has built a forest lodge far off in the mountains. The girls pass several quiet and happy months there, writing, playing music, and getting to know the natural world around them under Gregor's fatherly tutelage; and at regular intervals, equipped with a spyglass, they climb to the peak of a mountain to observe the landscape and their castle. Nothing in their world but the seasons seems to change, until one day, quite unexpectedly, Ronald, Clarissa's former beloved, now a supporter of the Swedes, turns up. Clarissa and Ronald decide to marry, and Ronald sets off again, having promised to stave off a Swedish regiment attack on the castle. Not long after, the girls look through their spyglass to find the scene described above. Anxious and alarmed, they return to the castle, which has been burned down to its foundations, and discover there that Ronald and their father have both been killed. Alone, unmarried, the sisters live out the rest of their lives in the castle ruins.

This passage marks a turning point in Stifter's novella. The castle's destruction signifies the end of the idyllic fusion of nature and culture figured in the girls' respite in the forest. This idyll found its most visible expression in their view from the mountain: on the one hand, because the view itself, as a medium, was grounded in the harmonious complementarity of technological and natural vision, the telescope and the eye; on the other, because it evoked an image of a world in which nature and culture, proximity and distance, the familiar (the castle) and the foreign (the forest) were seamlessly fused. By framing reality as a homogeneous sensory continuum, the gaze projected the phantasm of a world untouched and contained in itself, "as if there were no outside, no people other than those here, who love one another and learn to be innocent from the innocence of the forest."[57]

This explains the enormous force of attraction that the mountain exerts on the girls. At regular intervals, they climb it in order to see in the imaginary mirror of the landscape their desire for stillness and eventlessness fulfilled. Ascending the mountain in this way becomes a ritual of self-pacification that makes life in the forest seem permanently suspended in a single, timeless moment. This all comes to an abrupt end in the above-cited scene. If reality formerly appeared as a hermetically sealed system without temporal or spatial differentiation, then this new view through the spyglass

---

[57] Ibid., 292.

reveals the traces of a destructive external force. In other words, the passage is less the account of a specific event—the castle's destruction—than of *time's forcible entry into a supposedly eventless space.* It deals with the traumatic fall into history, doubly connoted by the polysemy of "innocence," both as the ontogenetic fall from paradise into world history and as the phylogenetic fall from childhood into sexuality.

This precipitous confrontation of edenic innocence and traumatic history is typical of Stifter's novellas. Equally typical is their *resistance* to the very upheavals they register. In the passage cited above, such resistance is articulated in a peculiar turning of the text against its own content; note how the last lines return to the prospect of the panorama and suggest (in the indicative!) the existence of a timeless idyll whose destruction the view through the telescope had earlier disclosed. That wishing seems to talk reality away, as it were, is confirmed by the sentence's uneven semantics. *Internalization* means to grasp something, after all, to understand it in terms of its inner truth; the same *cannot* be claimed for the naked eye's significantly less precise vision as compared with that of the telescope.

Freud described the dynamic articulated here with the concept of disavowal (*Verleugnung*). In disavowing, an item of reality is both registered and rejected, shunted off into a region where the subject "sait bien, mais quand même."[58] Syntactic ambivalence—even Stifter joins the sentence's two contradictory parts with a *but*—is the linguistic symptom of a mental conflict: disavowal is "a mode of defence which consists in the subject's refusing to recognise the reality of a traumatic perception."[59] The logic of this conflict, which Freud later formulated as a "splitting of the ego in the process of defence," governs Stifter's texts, too. The conflict between wish and perception, fantasy and knowledge, permeates all of Stifter's novellas, where it is articulated as a *splitting of the text*: on the one hand are Stifter's many positive constructs, such as nature, religion, morality, and tradition, which promise the coherence of meaning and stability; on the other hand, Stifter's novellas register with seismographic precision the "traumatic perceptions" and upheavals that elude this fixation of meaning. The greatness of Stifter's work consists paradoxically in his inability to put this tension to rest. More specifically, in Stifter's work, it is not only traumatic perceptions that take on the character of a symptom, but the images of homeostatic tranquillity

---

[58] Octave Mannoni, "Je sais bien, mais quand même . . . ," in *Clefs pour l'imaginaire ou l'autre scène* (Paris: Editions du Seuil, 1969), 9–33.

[59] Jean Laplanche and J.-B. Pontalis, "Disavowal," in *The Language of Psychoanalysis*, trans. Donald Nicholson-Smith (London: Karnac Books, 1988), 118.

themselves. Stifter's conservative idylls are phantasmatic defensive reactions against the terrifying experience of historical upheaval.

Nowhere does Stifter formulate his project of eventlessness more clearly than in his well-known foreword to his novella collection *Bunte Steine* [*Colorful Stones*]. "It was once remarked against me," he begins brashly, "how ordinary my characters always are. If that is true, then I am now in a position to offer readers something yet pettier and more insignificant."[60] Naturally, his apparent modesty conceals an immodest attempt at revaluing values. Stifter is interested in proving that what seems insignificant is the truly significant, that what is small is in truth great and earth-shaking. To that end, he calls on a mode of thinking that is fundamentally antithetical to his own: the materialism of his time, which accosts phenomena with experiments and slide rules in order to expose them as the effects of universal forces and laws. According to Stifter, the cultural preference for the monumental and the singular thus loses its legitimacy. Truth comes in the form of repetition: it is the "higher law," the rule, and is most clearly apprehensible in the most quotidian of acts and the most unspectacular of phenomena. Hence Stifter's programmatic turn away from the aesthetics of the sublime and of epic forms, as well as from the Hegelian historiographic concept of the "great individual": "But regardless how powerful or vaunted the tragic and epic forms may appear or what excellent levers they may be for art, . . . it is always the ordinary and everyday and innumerably recurring human actions in which this law rests squarely as the center of gravity" (*Bunte Steine*, 14).

Stifter's break with the tradition of the novella could not have been more clearly formulated. He explicitly devalues the phenomenal field of abruptness, crisis, and trauma that has been at the center of the genre since Boccaccio, and with even greater insistence since Goethe, and replaces it with an emphasis on continuity and repetition. Stifter cultivates a poetics of the anti-novella, oriented toward "maxims of slowness, care, and gentle growth."[61] The novellas' titles, based on the least suitable objects imaginable (stones), make clear just how radical this process of deceleration is meant to be.[62] Stifter's *Bunte Steine* is an immodest attempt to uncouple the novella genre from the field of historical time and to bind it to the *longue durée* of geological time. The vanishing point of Stifter's homeostatic paradise is the timeless and eventless realm of the anorganic.

---

[60] Adalbert Stifter, *Bunte Steine*, in *Werke und Briefe*, 2:9.

[61] Schlaffer, *Poetik der Novelle*, 269.

[62] The novellas are titled "Granite," "Limestone," "Tourmaline," "Quartz," "Mica," and "Rock Milk."

But as already indicated, this programmatic exit out of history fails, and Stifter's novellas remain bound to the genre's modern tradition despite their author's intentions. This is already demonstrated in Stifter's ambivalent turn to geologic time, which on the one hand is directed against the novella-specific poetics of the unheard-of event, while at the same time continuing that poetics' opposition to the semantics of progress, albeit by other means. Where the former reveals a layer of time and events *underneath* the homogeneous time of progress, Stifter oversteps the semantics of progress in the opposite direction through the macroscopic expansion of the temporal dimensions and the deceleration of time to the point of its quasi-suspension in the anorganic. Stifter's relation to the genre's modern tradition—that is, to the novella as a traumatic narrative form—becomes even clearer against the background of his novels. Like his novellas, Stifter's novels also represent attempts at the mastery of fear. But with the novels, fear is mastered in that its cause—temporal change—is not even admitted to begin with. The principal vocation of Heinrich, the protagonist of Stifter's novel *Der Nachsommer* (*Indian Summer*), is the collecting and cataloging of things and events—that is, the annihilation of time through its conversion into spatial or logical juxtaposition.[63]

The novellas are different. Their action is triggered by a frightening trauma that as absent cause remains virtually present and determines all subsequent events. In *Der Hochwald*, for instance, two events represent "the determining perspective of history, although they never manifest themselves on the functional level of plot":[64] the war and the seduction of the child Clarissa by a considerably older Ronald. Each event is reported only indirectly in character descriptions, yet they motivate all of the actions along the narrative axis, so that these are divested of all independent meaning and become the *signs of an absent cause*. With Stifter, the narrated present is fundamentally caught in the spell of a traumatic past: it is the symptom of a fear that goes on trembling in the images of harmonic tranquillity by whose ritual invocation the past is meant to be silenced. The idealization of undifferentiated, ahistorical nature, which the girls in *Der Hochwald* employ to banish their fears for their father's life and of the breakdown of their world, is just such a defense symptom. What applies to the idylls of *Der Hochwald* applies to all of Stifter's positive constructs. Stifter's novellas undermine a programmatic

---

[63] On this, see Hannelore Schlaffer and Heinz Schlaffer, *Studien zum ästhetischen Historismus* (Frankfurt on Main: Suhrkamp, 1975), 112–21.

[64] Reinhold Schardt, "Narrative Verfahren," in *Einführung in die Literaturwissenschaft*, ed. Miltos Pechlivanos et al. (Stuttgart: Reclam, 1995), 52–65.

distinction, which they themselves introduce, between "natural" homogeneity and "cultural" trauma by demonstrating that the supposedly originary homogeneity is itself already a phantasmatic reaction to its own loss. Stifter's tradition is an *invented tradition*, his untouched nature is a *verbal construct*, and his authorities are wish figures proceeding from *the fear of the dissolution of all binding norms*.

Albrecht Koschorke has spoken of an "congealment of fear" in late Stifter.[65] On closer examination, one might find this dynamic already present in the mineralogical poetic of *Bunte Steine*. The attempt to disengage the genre of the novella from the field of historical time and to bind it to the extreme *longue durée* of geological time is caught in the spell of a fear of progress that can only be experienced as catastrophe. Stifter's homeostatic paradise of eventlessness is an expression of the same longing that motivates Freud's death drive: the desire to reverse the course of evolution from the inanimate to the animate, that is, the entire course of history, and to return to the mineral repose of the anorganic. *Bunte Steine* is truly a conservative work, but in a much more radical way than has generally been thought.

Why Germany?

The novella in Germany, the novel in England and France. Why this bifurcation? And why did the *Unterhaltungen*, that disrespectfully received minor work of Goethe's, initiate the dominance of the novella genre in Germany, while the universally esteemed *Wilhelm Meister*, despite its long-term ideological influence (the discourse of *Bildung*, of education), did not cause the novel to take off in a similar fashion? I have so far explained the success of the German novella in terms of discursive history, as a polemical reaction to the idealist semantics of progress. In conclusion, I want to add a few considerations to this overview that, taking the aforementioned opposition between the novel and the novella as its point of departure, link the novella's success to Germany's political history.

We shall begin with the novel. Franco Moretti has shown how closely the novel's symbolic form is bound to the political reality of the nation-state:

---

[65] Albrecht Koschorke, "Der Text ohne Bedeutung oder die Erstarrung der Angst: Zu Stifters letzter Erzählung 'Der fromme Spruch,'" *Deutsche Vierteljahrsschrift für Literaturwissenschaft und Geistesgeschichte*, 61, no. 4 (1987): 676–719.

spatially, inasmuch as the abstract geography of the nation-state is given imaginary form by the novel;[66] politically, inasmuch as the novel's turn to everyday life assumes a state monopoly on power and the absence of severe ideological conflicts;[67] and stylistically, inasmuch as "the rich and varied national languages of the novel, loaded with local particularities and idioms,"[68] represent and bind the cultural and linguistic heterogeneity of the nation state. Finally, in narrating its protagonist's life course as a *career*, the novel provides models for the consitution of personal identity under the modern conditions of a functionally differentiated capitalist society. The privileged site of this career is the *metropolis*, which in gathering into the narrowest of spaces heterogeneous classes, practices, and forms of life, models the possibilities and dangers inherent in a biography increasingly less determined by the circumstances of birth or tradition.

This outline puts forth an *initial* answer to the question "Why Germany?," which is that the success of the German novella resulted from Germany's late development as a nation-state. The corresponding argumentation would then go something like this: whereas in England and France, in the wake of state sovereignty and advanced industrialization, a public political culture developed that self-confidently took form in the world-embracing novel, Germany, which was divided into territorial states, compensated for its political heterogeneity with a homogeneous religion of culture that found expression on the one hand in the discourse of education,[69] and on the other, in a nonpolitical popular ideology (*Volksideologie*). The latter, in particular, is articulated in the novella, whose tendency to adopt traditional, simple narrative forms (sagas, legends, fairy tales) is evidence of a thoroughly antimodernist impulse.

The weakness of this explanation consists in its inability to recognize in the novella anything more than the literary expression of a universal German misery. This is owing not least to the moralizing semantics of cultural-political *lateness*, which projects precisely that historiographical mix of norm and fact that calls the novella into question. So let us shift into a kind of argumental reverse gear and, taking up Franco Moretti's suggestions,

---

[66] Franco Moretti, *Atlas of the European Novel, 1800–1900* (London: Verso, 1998).

[67] Franco Moretti, *The Way of the World;* and Franco Moretti, "The Moment of Truth," in *Signs Taken for Wonders*, trans. Susan Fischer et al. (London: Verso, 1988), 249–62.

[68] Franco Moretti, "The Moment of Truth," 252.

[69] See Aleida Assmann, *Arbeit am nationalen Gedächtnis: Eine kurze Geschichte der deutschen Bildungsidee* (Frankfurt on Main: Campus, 1993).

approach the question of the novella in space (why Germany?) by examining the representation of space in the novella (which Germany?). We can outline the following spaces in the novella:

A. Nature: mountains (Stifter, *Bunte Steine*; Büchner, *Lenz*), steppes (Stifter, *Brigitta*), the sea (Storm, "Der Schimmelreiter" ["White Horse Rider"]), forests (Tieck, *Der blonde Eckbert*);

B. Country: Keller's Seldwyla (*Die Leute von Seldwyla* [*The People of Seldwyla*]), the provincial countryside in Droste-Hülshoff (*Die Judenbuche* [*The Jews' Beech-Tree*]) and Gotthelf (*Die schwarze Spinne* [*The Black Spider*]);

C. Exotic places: Venice (Mann, *Der Tod in Venedig*), Haiti (Kleist, "Die Verlobung in St. Domingo"), Goethe's gypsies ("Novelle");

D. War zones: religious wars (Meyer's novellas; Stifter, *Der Hochwald*; Keller, *Ursula*), revolutionary wars (Goethe, *Unterhaltungen*), Kleist's border conflict between Brandenburg and Saxony (*Michael Kohlhaas*), political upheaval (Arnim, *Isabella von Ägypten* [*Isabella of Egypt*]);

E. Traveling: Mörike (*Mozart auf der Reise nach Prag*), Chamisso (*Peter Schlemihl*), Eichendorff (*Aus dem Leben eines Taugenichts* [*From the Life of a Good-for-Nothing*]); and

F. Carnivalesque underworld: Tieck ("Liebeszauber" ["The Magic of Love"]), Grillparzer ("Der arme Spielmann" ["The Poor Fiddler"]), Schnitzler (*Traumnovelle* [*Dream Story*]), even Kafka ("Die Verwandlung" ["The Metamorphosis"]).

The list speaks volumes. Novellas take place either in a border zone—between nature and culture (a), Europe and its other (c), antagonistic religions, ideologies, or political powers (d)—or in a kind of *no-man's-land far away from the center* (a, b, e). Even the occasional urban novellas (f) yield to this pattern inasmuch as the city's everyday appearance serves merely as a foil for an obscure underworld (topos: carnival) in which the real action takes place.[70] The novella is then quite literally a *border genre, where the*

---

[70] The ending of Schnitzler's *Traumnovelle*, seen in this light, is structurally identical with that of Kafka's "Verwandlung": if in the one "the new day" begins, following the night's confusion, with "a triumphant ray of light" [Schnitzler, *Traumnovelle* (Stuttgart: Reclam, 1961), 103; last page of the story)], in the other, on the morning following Gregor's death, the Samsa family rides the tram, which "was filled with warm sunshine." Franz Kafka, *Kafka's "The Metamorphosis" and Other Writings*, ed. Helmuth Kiesel (New York: Continuum, 2002), 46. [Franz Kafka, "Die Verwandlung," in *Gesammelte Werke in zwölf Bänden*, ed. Hans-Gerd Koch (Frankfurt on Main: Fischer Taschenbuch Verlag, 1994), 1:157.]

border is at the same time the site of a conflict between incompatible forces. The Germany of the novella is not a homogeneous unity, but an unstable force field; it is the site of a tragic conflict in which the periphery (nature, countryside, exotic places) triumphs over the center, the state of exception (war, carnival) over the status quo. This suggests that we should read the border geography of the novella as a symbolic answer to the political geography of prenational Germany. Franco Moretti points out: "But where the state is unsettled and weak, culture tends fatally to 'fill the void': dismissing the novelistic everyday as a realm of vast appearances. This worldview finds its centre not just in politics, but in a tragic version of political struggle. In the notion of conflict as something which must inevitably lead to a crisis, and of *crisis as the moment of truth.*"[71]

True. The problem is just that Moretti's remark is taken from an essay on modern *tragedy*, which along with the novella governed the literary scene of nineteenth-century Germany. Now it is unlikely, despite all the similarities between the novella and the tragedy, that two genres would fulfill the same symbolic function. What then is the difference between the novella and the tragedy? It seems to me, the difference has to do with the nature of the represented conflict. The novella's conflict does not take place, as tragedic conflict does, between two identifiable forces, but rather between a (historical) world of forms and a (extrahistorical) formless power. The "other side" of the novella's protagonist is not an enemy representing an oppositional system of values, but the protagonist's (or the collective's) inaccessible *internal* other side, the blind spot.[72]

If these considerations are correct, then the novella's geographical spaces function above all as surfaces for the projection of a problem *immanent to the system.* To be more precise: they serve to externalize a tension that the system can no longer bind and thus must project onto the world outside as a conflict. This corresponds to the self-destructive craving for liminality characteristic of so many novella protagonists: one need only think of Aschenbach's connection to Venice, Hauke Hain's compulsive relationship to the sea ("Der Schimmelreiter"), Fridolin's "painfully-yearning excitement" that compels him into a carnivalesque world of the night (*Traumnovelle*); or, to

---

[71] Franco Moretti, "The Moment of Truth," 253.

[72] Which is why, unlike in a tragedy, the conflict of a novella does not have to end tragically. It can also be resolved with a compromise, whether through renunciation or the sublimating process of self-education (Goethe, Stifter), through ironization and the turn to the comic (Keller), or through a perverse happy ending that institutionalizes the violent conflict and suspends it permanently (Kleist, "Die Marquise von O . . .").

mention a non-German-language example, Marlow's wish to explore those parts of Africa yet uncharted by cartographic knowledge. Venice, the sea, carnival, Africa—these are, to put it another way—geographical ciphers for the system's *need for self-dissolution*. Consequently, novella spaces are both historically and superhistorically significant: historically insofar as they denote the other side of a specific cultural system (Venice/Tadzio = Europa/heterosexuality; the sea = mathematics; carnival = marriage; colony = empire), and superhistorically because they are phantasms providing the system's self-destructive dynamic with geographic form. The boundary of the novella is the desire (*desiderio*), projected into space, for the absolute dissolution of both boundaries and form.

Is this desire characteristically German? One would like to say yes, in view of Germany's twentieth-century history, and to see in the combination of projection and self-destructive expansion, which characterizes the novella's narrative form, the cultural anticipation of a fatal political dynamic. But it is doubtful whether such an approach—a reading in the mode of ideological criticism—can do justice to the problem. The fascination with excess and the dissolution of boundaries, with resolution and shock, is a trait of both right-wing and left-wing intellectuals; and the question of the other side of a symbolically coded world is at the center of modern philosophy, from Kierkegaard through Nietzsche to Husserl, Heidegger, and Wittgenstein. Let us leave the matter of the novella's moral and political categorization to those who enjoy imagining themselves on the "right" side. Regardless of which mode of interpretation one chooses, this much should be clear: the German novella of the nineteenth century is neither a moment in the decline of the novel nor a cultural sign of political tardiness, but rather an independent and profoundly *modern* symbolic form.

Translated by W. Martin

FRANCIS MULHERN

Inconceivable History: Storytelling as Hyperphasia and Disavowal

It is an old commonplace that modernist art is, among other things, reflexive, drawn more or less strongly to explore the material element of its existence—pigment, say, or language. With the so-called linguistic turn in the human sciences, and specifically the literary criticism of the past forty years, the commonplace has rejuvenated itself and pressed its interpretive claims with corresponding energy and confidence across an ever-wider field of literary history. Thus it is that in recent decades Joseph Conrad too has come to be read as yet another exemplary modern, as questioning of his medium, with its delphic promises of sincerity and truth, as of human motives. There is a good deal to explore here, as Edward Said has shown, in an early and distinguished contribution to this critical discussion.[1] However, there is also an attendant danger, which poststructuralist criticism typically fails to perceive or, therefore, to avert. The interpretive appeal to language, conceived just so abstractly, settles rather little. The more often and more widely it is reiterated, the less it explains. The critical adepts of unfixity bear a certain resemblance to Molière's doctor, who, faced with the infinite creativity of hypochondria, could see only "lungs, lungs." There is always a better account: better because more closely specified, more historical, that is, and materialist. The undoubted crisis in Conrad's work is in one sense inevitably linguistic—after all, it is writing, which is done in language—but its dynamics and characteristic textual figures emerge from a quite specific cultural and institutional context of literary practice. Conrad was not merely "a worker in prose" or a maker of "art," as he was prone to say.[2] He was not, · indeed, a teller of "tales," however insistently his subtitles lodge that claim on his behalf. The longer and shorter printed narratives that constitute his literary achievement belong, inescapably, to the world of the *novel*. That is the locus of Conrad's crisis as a writer, which worked itself out in a distinctive and paradoxical literary practice. The characteristic forms and strategies of his narratives (including the shorter fictions, which in this perspective are

---

[1] Edward Said, "Conrad: The Presentation of Narrative," in his *The World, the Text and the Critic* (Cambridge, Mass.: Harvard University Press, 1983), 90–110.

[2] Preface to *The Nigger of the "Narcissus"* (1897), edited and introduced by Cedric Watts (London: Penguin, 1988), xlviii–xlix.

not different in kind) are shaped by an impulse to abolish the novelistic, or at least outwit it.

For the younger Thomas Mann, the novel, or "literature," was the cultural epitome of modernity, as distinct from poetry and music, which sheltered the superior values of tradition.[3] Walter Benjamin, in a classic essay, likewise emphasized the essential modernity of the novel, defining it by contrast with the anterior narrative form of the oral "tale." The storyteller, he writes,

> takes what he tells from experience—his own or that reported by others.
> And he in turn makes it the experience of those who are listening to his tale.
> The novelist has isolated himself. The birthplace of the novel is the solitary
> individual, who is no longer able to express himself by giving examples of his
> most important concerns, is himself uncounseled, and cannot counsel others.
> To write a novel means to carry the incommensurable to extremes in the
> representation of human life.[4]

This is manifestly relevant to Conrad, but, paradoxically, perhaps too close, for critical purposes, to his own constant theme of isolation: with only a little alteration, he might have written these sentences himself, or put them in the mouth of his best-known fictional storyteller, Charley Marlow. It will be more helpful to develop Benjamin's insight in other, less psychologistic terms. Two general historical conditions detach the novel irrevocably from the world of the tale. The first is institutional, involving a change in the *social relations* of narration. Storytelling as a form presupposes a basic community of values binding teller and audience: shared intuitions of what is interesting, intelligible, pleasing or repugnant, fitting or not. Indeed, being oral, it depends on the actual co-presence of the two: the moral affinity is confirmed in time and space. Novelistic narrative, in contrast, is mediated as printed text for the market. Both the physical and the cultural supports of the tale fall away. Writing is temporally prior to reading, which, like writing, is now privatized, and practically variable in a way that listening is not. The audience is not only privatized; unknowable to the writer at work, it is also, in principle, unknown in its cultural disposition. Thus, the social relationship that grounds and is

---

[3] Thomas Mann, *Reflections of a Nonpolitical Man* (1918), translated by Walter D. Morris (New York: Frederick Ungar, 1983).

[4] Walter Benjamin, "The Storyteller: Reflection on the Works of Nikolai Leskov," in his *Illuminations*, edited and introduced by Hannah Arendt, translated by Harry Zohn (London: Fontana/Collins, 1973), 87.

fertilized by the tale is canceled; in a technical term from linguistics, novelistic communication lacks the long-familiar "phatic" guarantee.[5]

The second condition is strictly cultural. The shared values that stabilize the tale as institution may or may not be officially sanctioned, but they are in any case *customary*, matters of inherited common sense and virtue, whose continuing authority is itself a positive value. This is the world of "wisdom," from which the novel takes its leave, irreverently even if not in revolt. The tonal dominant in novelistic culture, which has always been predominantly realist, is contrastingly *critical* and *secular*. As Mann understood, the novel is the prose of "civilization" and the Enlightenment. Its cosmology is godless, even where its ethics remain scriptural. Ordinary believers may recoil from lewd representations, but far from entertaining miracles and evidence of inspiration in their fictional reading, they feel cheated by the intrusion of even purely mundane improbability. Dispositions that find easy articulation in poetry are inhibited in the culture of the novel, for which the currency and prestige of the human sciences are a historical given, welcome or not. Pragmatically at least, what finally counts as valid is some idea of rational knowledge.

These twin features of the novelistic were the discursive conditions of Conrad's literary practice. But, as any of his readers will know, they figure in the works themselves as negative terms in his characteristic thematics. Isolation, as Conrad imagines it over and over again, is a destructive condition whose outcomes are disgrace, corruption, madness, and death. Its avatars are Jim (*Lord Jim*); the Capataz and Decoud (*Nostromo*); Stevie, Verloc, and Winnie (*The Secret Agent*); and of course Kurtz (*Heart of Darkness*). None survives. Modern knowledges, and their associated norms of inquiry, have a recurring part in these human disasters, appearing at the same time trivial and mischievous, and in no case equal to the moral realities they affect to explain. There is already an appearance of paradox in this, and it is not dispelled by the recollection of the historical materials on which Conrad set his themes to work. "Exotic" or not, his fictional worlds are figures of the defining sites and crises of historical modernity: colonialism and the global thrust of capitalism, class struggle, the swelling of the metropolis, the revolutionary threat to Europe's old regimes. For this alone, he would merit a prominent

---

[5] The phatic function of communication, in Roman Jakobson's classic definition, consists in monitoring and confirming the integrity of the communicative medium—as when, in a telephone conversation, a speaker says "Yes, . . . yes," meaning not "I agree" or "It is so" but "I can hear you." In the expanded sense invoked in this essay, the phatic function bears also on the *social* conditions of the communicative act.

place in the canon of the modern novel. But there the paradox returns, and it is not merely that this novelist of modernity was a conservative disaffected from the new moral ecology he explored—there is nothing remarkable in that. It is that he was profoundly at odds with the conditions of his own writing practice, the novelistic itself. His "task," as he struggles "to make you *see*," is to resolve that paradox—or rather, to manage it, for resolution proper is hardly attainable. The labor of containment is the central process of his writing, the effective substance of his rhetoric.

Two related propensities, so strong they might even be termed compulsions, shape and texture Conrad's narratives. The first, here called *hyperphasia*, seeks primarily to restore the communicative guarantee that the novelistic is constitutionally unable to underwrite. Its further function is to regulate the flow of modern knowledges and the historical pressure that drives them. In this respect, hyperphatic anxiety serves the interest of the second compulsion, that splitting of knowledge and belief that Freud termed *disavowal*.[6]

Telling Tales, or Hyperphasia

In 1897, with three novels and a number of stories to his credit, Conrad returned to work on the novel that was to round off a "Malayan trilogy": *Almayer's Folly*, *An Outcast of the Islands*, and, now, *The Rescuer* or *Rescue*. He did so under pressure. His attempts to escape from what he himself already called 'Conradese' had not been successful; *The Sisters* was left as a fragment, and no magazine could be found to take a shorter work, *The Return*. Depending on writing for his income, Conrad could not afford to be disdainful of popular taste; his simple purpose was to make the novel "good enough for a magazine—readable in a word."[7] Yet this entailed his engaging with romantic-sexual material that had already proved intractable in *The Return*. ("There are things I *must* leave alone.")[8] And he also resented his vulnerability to the literary market, describing the book as "an infamous potboiler." *The Rescue*, and Conrad with it, passed into crisis. He became aware

---

[6] See "Fetishism" (1927), in *On Sexuality*, The Pelican Freud Library (London: Penguin, 1977), 7:351–57. For a discussion of disavowal as a process in culture generally, see Octave Mannoni, "Sì, lo so, ma comunque . . . ," in his *La funzione dell' immaginario* (Bari: Laterza Editori, 1972), 5–29.

[7] Letter to Edward Garnett, quoted in Ian Watt, *Conrad in the Nineteenth Century* (London: Chatto and Windus, 1980), 128.

[8] Ibid., 128.

"how mysteriously independent of myself is my power of expression," and was soon severely blocked: "I sit down religiously every morning, I sit down for eight hours every day—and the sitting down is all. In the course of that working day of 8 hours I write 3 sentences which I erase before leaving the table in despair."[9]

The path to redemption was at once institutional and rhetorical. Over the same period of months, Conrad had formed a strong relationship with *Blackwood's Edinburgh Magazine*, a prestigious and rather conservative monthly, which now began to publish the stories he was writing as a relief from the torments of *The Rescue*. The first of these, *Youth*, saw the adoption of a new formal device: narration at one remove, or secondary narration, through the instance of a character, Marlow. The new association with *Blackwood's* was providential: the magazine paid well and valued continuing relationships with authors. Conrad expressed his "unspeakable relief" at writing "for *Maga* instead of for 'the market.'" More than this, he could now sense an audience, a community of understanding: "One was in decent company there and had a good sort of public. There isn't a single club and messroom and man-of-war in the British Seas and Dominions which hasn't its copy of Maga."[10] The invention of Marlow secured this imagined community and gave it objective cultural currency.

To dwell on the obvious element of nostalgia in this would be to underestimate the force and generality of the desire it accommodates. There is more than one thing to say about the strategic value of secondary narration in Conrad. To begin with, it is crucial to recognize that Marlow is not a personified narrator like the earlier Gilbert Markham, who delivers Anne Brontë's *Tenant of Wildfell Hall*, or Holden Caulfield in *Catcher in the Rye*. He is himself narrated, held in a primary discourse whose point of enunciation is itself normally personified, however minimally. (Even in *Lord Jim*, where the primary narration is not attributed to a character, the occasional use of frequentative verbs carries an anthropomorphic suggestion: the narrating instance "knows" Marlow of old.) These narrating characters and their fellows—sailors, lawyers, accountants, well-traveled men of affairs—are the respectful, infinitely patient audience for Marlow's stories, the audience Conrad believed he had found in *Blackwood's*. In their first publishing context, then, the Marlow narratives invent a community talking to itself. The sense of their second and definitive context—that of book publishing—is still more striking. The random, anonymous readers of the novels and

---

[9] Ibid., 128, 130.
[10] Ibid., 131.

shorter fictions are drawn into narratives of a man telling stories, in the controlling perspective of an audience whose objective cultural-institutional coordinates are quite different from their own. The novel-reading public is refashioned by the thing in its hands as the listening community of the tale.

———

The meaning of this paradoxical narrative rhetoric emerges more distinctly in comparison with the work of another turn-of-the-century writer of fiction, Sholom Rabinowitz. Born, like Conrad, in the Ukraine and only two years younger than him, Rabinowitz turned to writing a little earlier, in the 1880s, under a pseudonym that is in itself a miniaturized version of his writing— Sholom Aleichem. The heartland of this fiction is the *shtetl*, the village world of East European Jewry, in a period when its deeply traditionalist culture was straining under the antithetical pressures of official persecution and enlightenment. The big city is Odessa, and the wider world is itself a local affair:

> I doubt if the Dreyfus case made such a stir anywhere as it did in Kasrilevke.
> Paris, they say, seethed like a boiling vat. The papers carried streamers, generals shot themselves, and small boys ran like mad in the streets, threw their caps in the air, and shouted wildly, "Long live Dreyfus!" or "Long live Esterhazy!" Meanwhile the Jews were insulted and beaten, as always. But the anguish and the pain that Kasrilevke underwent, Paris will not experience till Judgement Day.[11]

Inevitably, since the events come to the villagers second- or thirdhand, in the oral reports of Zeidel, the only newspaper-reader among them, and acquire their force in the excited talk that follows, talk is the model as well as the main diegetic substance of Sholom Aleichem's texts, as the opening of "Dreyfus of Kasrilevke" already suggests. They begin suddenly, often importunately, and nearly always in, or as, a speech situation. "The Pot" is a monologue, one of many such records of a one-sided conversation: "Rabbi! A question's what I want to ask you. I don't know if you know me or if you don't know me. Yente's who I am, Yente the dairy-vendor" (71). In the stories proper, the main narrator is usually personified, or at least assumes the grammatical signs of personality and the rhetorical licence of informal conversation.

———

[11] "Dreyfus in Kasrilevke," in *The Best of Sholom Aleichem*, edited by Irving Howe and Ruth R. Wisse (New York: Touchstone, 1980), 111. Subsequent quotations from this edition will be referenced in the text by page number.

These texts are devoted to an ambiguous art of the *fragment*. Read in a cluster, they appear as so many random samples from the continuous conversation of Kasrilevke and the many places like it. In this, Sholom Aleichem is bardic, the remembrancer of a common world. But his humor is often that of the gallows, and fragments can also testify to disintegration. The Tevye sequence (which found mass audiences in the later twentieth century in a stage and film adaptation, *Fiddler on the Roof*) narrates the breakdown of *shtetl* culture. Or rather, Tevye narrates it, in successive encounters with a character whose "vocation" is writing books, one Sholom Aleichem. All these encounters end with explicit partings, routine at first but, by the end, historic. They last meet after a pogrom ("Get Thee Out"), on a train, and Tevye does not know where next year will find him. Tevye's parting words always include reference to books, about which he is ambivalent. He is not sure that he wants to be recorded in print, and on one occasion, when he has told the story of his daughters' marriages, positively forbids it. "Write me often," he says, in the closing lines of "Chava"; letters, like the shared writing of the scriptures, are sustaining. But "don't forget what I asked you. Be silent as the grave concerning this. Don't put what I told you into a book. And if you should write, write about someone else, not about me. Forget about me. As it is written: '*And he was forgotten—*' No more Tevye the Dairyman!" (178).

The irony of these words, and of the entire sequence, illuminates and undermines Sholom Aleichem's practice as a writer, including the wishful fiction of his pseudonym. His texts bear a strong resemblance to Conrad's in their effort to capture speech and its typical genres as the moral substance of social relationships. Here too, the inscribed position of reading is that of an initiated listener. The writer's signature itself certifies the communal bond: *sholem aleichem* is purely phatic, a customary greeting inviting the specular response *aleichem sholem*. However, Tevye's story of his family troubles, and his injunction against repeating it in print, throw this symbolic settlement into disorder and self-contradiction. Chava has forgotten her faith and must now be forgotten. Sholom Aleichem must likewise forget her story, if he is to keep faith with Tevye. But to do so would be to thwart the basic commitment of his writing, which is to saving the speech-world of the *shtetl* for literate posterity. Either way, fidelity entails a breach of faith. The bond cannot endure. "Greetings to you, Mr. Sholom Aleichem," says Tevye, opening the last story of the sequence, "heartiest greetings"—a humorous extreme of hyperphasia. There is reason for concern: "I've been expecting you for a long time and wondering why I didn't see you any more" (179). Sholom Aleichem has been traveling "all over the world"; Tevye and his family, having been driven from their villages, are traveling too, to a destination still unknown to them. As in all the stories, Tevye's last word to the writer called Greetings is "goodbye."

———

Two circumstances, one collective and the other individual, might be said to moderate the phatic crisis in Sholom Aleichem's case. The first is that he wrote in Yiddish, which, to a far greater extent than any of its neighboring European vernaculars, could claim to be the medium of a common culture. (Isaac Deutscher, a Polish Jew from a later generation, wrote compellingly about this.)[12] For as long as there were Yiddish readers, the speech-world of Kasrilevke would not quite perish. Second, he accepted the historical probability of that loss; his nostalgia and occasional sentimentality were, in a way, a measure of his realism. Conrad was differently placed, in both respects. He clung to English with fierce, obscure commitment. It had adopted him, he wrote in *A Personal Record*: "if I had not written in English I would not have written at all."[13] But it was hardly clear, at this point in the history of an already multinational language, to what moral family, what community of sentiment, he thus belonged. Like Spanish or Portuguese, English was the common birthright of widely scattered, mutually alien speech-communities. Moreover, his fictions, unlike those of Sholom Aleichem, did not record and reflect on the life of an inherited world. They imagined an adoptive culture in the perspective of a grateful, devoted outsider compulsively drawn to the great transforming agencies at work in it. There is little nostalgia in Conrad. He was fascinated by the defining historical forces of his time. But that is not to say that he could quite believe in them, in either sense of that term. These were the uncertainties that shaped his narrative hyperphasia.

One characteristic effect of hyperphasia is quantitative: envisaged as a short story, *Lord Jim* grew into a long novel.[14] The elaboration is everything. Jim's history is quickly related. A young English seaman is drawn to "the East," where he joins the *Patna*, which has been chartered to carry two hundred Muslim pilgrims on their way to Mecca. The craft is unseaworthy, and after an accident, seems in danger of foundering. The captain and his cronies decide to abandon ship, and Jim follows. The *Patna* is saved by a

———

[12] Isaac Deutscher, *The Non-Jewish Jew and Other Essays* (London: Oxford University Press, 1968).

[13] Said, "Conrad," 98, 99.

[14] *Lord Jim* (1900) (London: Penguin, 1957). For this and other novels later discussed, references are given in the text, by page number.

French naval vessel. An official inquiry is ordered, and Jim, facing the proceedings alone, is stripped of his mariner's licence. In disgrace, above all in his own eyes, he takes refuge in one job after another, moving on when word of the *Patna* episode catches up with him. Eventually, he finds a kind of redemption in the remote upriver district of Patusan, in Dutch East Borneo, becoming the guarantor of peace and security for the local population, who acknowledge him as *Tuan* (Lord) Jim. But his nemesis arrives in the form of a boatload of outlaw raiders. A phase of armed confrontation ends in confusion and violent death. The locals' suspicions fall, mistakenly, on Jim, who finally, in effect, gives himself up for execution.

The story of *Lord Jim* is simpler still. A ship's captain named Marlow attends the inquiry. He is gripped by the *Patna* events but above all by Jim, whom he befriends. He takes pains, over a lengthy period, to gather a complete account of the episode, and in later years seizes any opportunity to disclose all that he has seen and heard and tried to make out about Jim. What the novel narrates, for 90 percent of its extent and all but four of its forty-five chapters, is Marlow's discourse on Jim, spoken for the greater part in an after-dinner gathering, and concluded in personal correspondence with one of that party. What Marlow narrates is a sequence of spoken encounters: the testimony given at the inquiry; then a lengthy interview with Jim; conversations with Captain Brierly, who is badly disturbed by the scandal, and then with his chief officer, who gives his account of the hours before Brierly's suicide; next with a French naval colleague who reports the later stage of the *Patna*'s voyage; and finally with Gentleman Brown, the "ruffian" who triggers the final catastrophe and survives to give his own version of it. Another conversation, with the sea-going entrepreneur Chester, yields the story of a partner, Robinson, as this emerges from the untraceable conversations of others—what "they say" about him. *Lord Jim* is not, strictly speaking, what Conrad claimed in his sub title, *A Tale*. It is a novel about a tale about other tales (about others still). Although Jim has been the protagonist of an intensely dramatic action, the primary narrator of *Lord Jim* catches sight of him only in the least romantic phase of his career, as a water-clerk soliciting business for a ship's chandler. That is appropriate, in a novel where nearly all that actually happens is talk.

Talk, for Conrad, is the linguistic site of solidarity, but here the talk is of a failure of solidarity and of normative identity—of "character." In its most abstract formulation, the moral drama is that of heroism pursued, forfeited, and at last regained. The heroic code supports Jim's account of himself, as both Marlow and the anonymous narrator agree. His sea-going "vocation" was animated by "a course of light holiday literature" (11), as was his life's finale: "And that's the end [Marlow says]. He passes away under a cloud, forgotten, unforgiven and excessively romantic. Not in the wildest days of his boyish visions could he have seen the alluring shape of such an extraordinary success! For it may very well be that in the short moment of his last proud and unflinching glance, he had beheld the face of that opportunity, which, like an Eastern bride, had come veiled to him" (313). For one moment, Marlow himself seems to honor Jim's code, or at least to acknowledge its attractions: "I was aggrieved at him, as though he had cheated me—me!—of a splendid opportunity to keep up the illusion of my beginning, as though he had robbed our common life of the last spark of its glamour" (103).

However, the burden of his obsessive questioning lies closer to home. Jim was "one of us": Marlow reiterates this proposition over and again as concession or as affirmation, compassionately or in disbelief. "There he stood, clean-limbed, clean-faced, firm on his feet, as promising a boy as the sun ever shone on; and looking at him, knowing all he knew and a little more too, I was as angry as though I had detected him trying to get something out of me by false pretenses. He had no business to look so sound. I thought to myself—well, if this sort can go wrong like that . . ." (36). Worse, Marlow confesses, for all his experience, he would have misjudged Jim himself: "I liked his appearance: I knew his appearance: he came from the right place; he was one of us. . . . I would have trusted the deck to that youngster on the strength of a single glance, and gone to sleep with both eyes—and, by Jove! it wouldn't have been safe. There are depths of horror in that thought" (36, 38). The horror is internal and communal. What Jim has put in question is "us."

"We" are, in the first place, the practitioners of "the craft," the merchant marine, and the keepers of its "honour" (40). Brierly, the "complacent," "self-satisfied" paragon of the Blue Star Line, leads the inquiry and is destroyed by what it discloses—though not so much to him as to others. The horror, for him, is not what happened on the *Patna*, but the "shame" of the official investigation. "Why eat all that dirt?" he protests; and why make "us," therefore, do the same? (54). The disaster lies in the scandal, "this infernal publicity": "there he sits while all these confounded natives, serangs, lascars, quartermasters, are giving evidence that's enough to burn a man to ashes with shame" (56). Brierly, frustrated in his wish that Jim should simply disappear, dispatches himself. The news of his death, conveyed to his "people"—who are acquainted with Jim's—goes unacknowledged.

Brierly's particular fear of scandal, and the terms in which he evokes the inquiry, suggest that "we" are not, or not finally, the community of "the craft"—which also includes some of those with whom he disgustedly refuses affinity. "We," as a later, contrastive reference to "one of us" reveals, are the category of "white men." But only a category, not a community, for which far more intimate conditions of affiliation must be satisfied. Marlow is unfailingly sensitive to national and racial difference. Much of the time, this is the dominant note in his characterology, a sufficient sign of personality and a leading clue to conduct. The master of the *Patna*, obese and with "a bullet head," is a German-turned"Flensborg or Stettin Australian" whose defiant threat to the authorities is "I vill an Amerigan citizen begome" (37). Personal nationality is marked, in the case of the French lieutenant, with an insistence beyond its apparent relevance. The only nationality for which special terms apply is the English. Of course, there is no room to doubt that Jim, Brierly, Marlow, and the rest are English. But what is the more notable then is how their nationality is indexed. "Home"—a recurring term—for Brierly and Jim is "Essex" or, as Marlow once says, facetiously, "the land uprising above the white cliffs of Dover" (70). "The British Isles," "Great Britain," and the national specification "Scot" each appear once, as symbols in the sentimental history of another German, Stein. The "English" language is named on a half-dozen occasions. But Marlow never applies that adjective to himself or his compatriots, or names the country they come from. We might settle for interpreting this as a case of the ideological gesture that Roland Barthes called "exnomination"—the dominant term in a system, *qua* dominant, is unmarked—were it not that normative Englishness is elsewhere ironized.[15] "Englishmen" and "the English" are identified as such only twice in the novel, the first time by the Flensborg or Stettin Australian who is chiefly responsible for Jim's disgrace—"You Englishmen are all rogues" (37)—and the second time by the outlaw Gentleman Brown and the treacherous Cornelius, the renegades who will bring about their compatriot's death:

> "What is he? Where does he come from?" inquired Brown. "What sort of man is he? Is he an Englishman?"
> "Yes, yes, he's an Englishman. I am an Englishman too. From Malacca." (277)

Brown's first three questions are also Marlow's; the fourth is the question he avoids, even suppressing the noun from his vocabulary. Cornelius's

---

[15] Roland Barthes, *Mythologies*, translated by Annette Lavers (London: Jonathan Cape, 1972), 138.

answers dramatize the aporia that Marlow can scarcely outwit, for all his show of subtlety. Indeed, he utters the thought metaphorically when he reflects that Jim "looked as genuine as a new sovereign, but there was some infernal alloy in him" (40)—some mixing of metals that weakens the mettle and debases the currency of England and Empire. This, in a discourse so finely attuned to the bloodlines of nation and race, suggests the unspeakable dilemma: Jim is an Englishman—but, having acted as he did, how can he be? Marlow likes to imagine that Jim at last succeeded in Patusan where he had failed on the *Patna*, creating a virtual Pax Britannica for the "native-ruled" district, and that his death was a moment of heroic fulfilment. "He is one of us. . . . Was I so very wrong after all?" (311). The locals, including his lover, would not disagree. As they see it, Jim has betrayed them, as they feared he would. "They never could understand" the "exact relation" between Gentleman Brown and "their own white man" (311)—the split figure of the imperial Englishman.

Marlow too cannot, or will not, understand. "It seemed to me," he says, as he recalls his first evening with Jim, that "I was being made to comprehend the Inconceivable—and I know of nothing to compare with the discomfort of such a sensation" (75). Here is a scene of trauma. It is coercive, and its sense is non-sense: rational disclosure of something that lies beyond imagining. Marlow's defense is his rhetoric. "Why these vapourings?" he asks in an irritable moment, referring to Jim. This question applies to his own monologue, and the answer is that the alternative would be an intolerable acknowledgment. Marlow's narrative strategy is in large part one of protraction, an exhausting proliferation of the telling in relation to the putative action of the tale. His rationale, which exploits the ambiguous semantics of his proprietary term "Inconceivable," is philosophical. Threatened by the encroachment of rational inquiry on a reality that he finds morally unimaginable, he affects a higher curiosity whose paradoxical terminus is the validation of mystery. He and his kind profess a "faith invulnerable to the strength of facts" or "the solicitation of ideas" (38). Marlow's prolix monologue is a filibuster, a process designed to delay conclusion. His narrative quest for Jim's reality has the appearance of curiosity but is antithetical in motivation: compelled by the suggestions of an image that no logos can be permitted to translate, it exemplifies the opaque, pseudo-cognitive syndrome of fascination.

———

The same compulsions drive Conrad's next Marlow narrative, *Heart of Darkness*, registering more graphically in a shorter work of simpler formal design.[16] The scene of narration, which is said to confirm a "bond," is a fully realized social occasion—a sailing party—and wholly contains the sailor's narrative, thus leaving the unnamed primary narrator to close the novel. Marlow's story of his journey, via Brussels, to West Africa and so up the Congo River to its farthest navigable point, itself yields elements of a third narrative, the assorted reports, comments and fragments of overheard conversation that are the legend of Kurtz—whom eventually he meets, thereafter joining the ranks of his own legend-bearing characters. Now, he wishes to account for his response to what he has seen, and "the kind of light"—"No, not very clear"—that it "seemed to throw on everything about me" (32).

This is a more anxious Marlow, and a more anxious audience. All three narrative planes show a greater or lesser weakening of phatic guarantees. The motives sustaining the talk of Kurtz are at every point questionable—envious, spiteful, self-deceiving, or naive. Marlow's own contributions to the legend, on his return to Brussels, are, in calculated effect, lies. The literary remains of Kurtz's career are either defective or misleading as acts of communication. The letters from the Intended, which Marlow returns in a sealed packet, record the intimate history of an illusion; the text of Kurtz's "vast plan," once shorn of its murderous postscript, is their public counterpart. Whereas his main informants in *Lord Jim* are, for all their moral inequalities, men of his own "craft," seamen, here they are so many once-met acquaintances on a journey from a company bureau in Brussels to a remote colonial outpost in Africa—to which he has been drawn by recollection of a boyish whim. Even the "bond" so confidently affirmed in the opening paragraphs of the novel is not perfectly secure. Marlow, the first narrator observes, is not free from "the weakness of many tellers of tales who seem so often unaware of what their audience would best like to hear" (32). Some time later, in midnarration, Marlow invokes the cognitive value of the "bond": "Of course, in this you fellers see more than I could then. You see me, whom you know . . ." The circumstantial reality is less reassuring. According to the narrator, "It had become so pitch dark that we listeners could hardly see one another. For a long time already, [Marlow], sitting apart, had been no more to us than a voice. There was not a word from anybody. The others might have been asleep." With this phatic fading comes interpretive anxiety: "The others might have been asleep, but I was awake. I listened, on the watch for the sentence, for the word, that would give me the clue to the faint uneasiness inspired by this narrative that seemed to shape itself without

---

[16] *Heart of Darkness* (1902), edited and introduced by Paul O'Prey (London: Penguin, 1983).

human lips in the heavy night-air of the river" (58). He might have been reading a novel.

The intensified hyperphasia that distinguishes *Heart of Darkness* from *Lord Jim* coincides with a shift in the terms of representation, from the earlier novel to the later. We can say that Marlow's obsessive meditation on the person of Jim is a displacement of attention from the system of social relations—imperialism—that shaped his projects and their outcomes. But we must then accept the corollary, which is that this is indeed so; the displacement has occurred; *Lord Jim* is centrally a novel of character. *Heart of Darkness* is not wholly different in this respect. Kurtz, the visionary "extremist" is Jim composed in another key; the "sordid buccaneers" of the Eldorado Exploring Expedition are functional equivalents of Gentleman Brown and his crew. Marlow is, as usual, much concerned with "character." Yet now, unmistakably, Conrad extends his field of vision to encompass the impersonal relations of "the new forces at work" (43) in European and African history, to probe the logic of the "fantastic invasion."

That European activity in the Congo amounts to an "invasion" is established beyond doubt. The pages in which Marlow narrates the cumulative discovery of his journey from Brussels to the Central Station, never less than sardonic, rise steadily toward a pitch of unrestrained, generalized denunciation. The summary judgment on the "explorers" illustrates the manner: "To tear treasure out of the bowels of the land was their desire, with no more moral purpose at the back of it than there is in burglars breaking into a safe" (61). Yet the same passage, with its ambiguous second clause, reminds us that, for all his straining after universal truths, Marlow's indictment may not be strictly general. The burglars of West and Central Africa are named— they are France and Belgium—and Marlow has already distinguished them and other colonial powers from one that is not quite named. Looking around the waiting room at the company's premises, he pauses at a map of Africa. "There was a vast amount of red," he notes, "good to see at any time, because one knows that some real work is done in there," as well as "a deuce of a lot of blue, a little green, smears of orange, and, on the East Coast, a purple patch, to show where the jolly pioneers of progress drink the jolly lager-beer" (36). The punctual turn to the idiom of the smoking room ("a deuce of a lot") and its associated cultural standards ("the jolly lager-beer" signifying German-ness) confirms the identification of Britain as a special case.

It would be easy to make too much of this claim to exceptionality. Marlow does not return to it. Perhaps the fate of Kurtz, who as an imperialist with a "redeeming idea" embodies an unstated will to emulate the British, must be taken as definitive in implication. The principal narrator's last words may suggest as much: ". . . the tranquil waterway [the Thames] leading to the uttermost ends of the earth flowed sombre under an overcast sky—seemed to lead into the heart of an immense darkness" (121). But only *seemed*: the hesitation is characteristic, and scarcely avoidable, given the main purpose of Marlow's tale, which is to reflect "a kind of light"—in some sense, to explain. "The conquest of the earth, which mostly means the taking it away from those who have a different complexion or slightly flatter noses than ourselves is not a pretty thing," Marlow declares—"when you look into it too much." And then: "What redeems it is the idea only" (32). Forced by circumstance to "look into it," or at least *at* it, Marlow becomes captivated by "the idea." He wonders first whether Kurtz will succeed, and, later, why he has failed, but this pair of questions is already a substitute for curiosity. In *Heart of Darkness* as in *Lord Jim*, Marlow's fascination is a means of keeping knowledge at a distance. He knows the basic reason for Kurtz's presence at the Inner Station: the company is "run for profit" (39). But as he narrates the journey upriver, the terms of his discourse shift, cynicism and indignation making way for an anxious meditation on the forest and its peoples, in their symbiotic relations. This world is "incomprehensible," "mysterious"; it overwhelms the mind and yet, in an animistic turn, comes to seem the controlling mind in the situation. The "stillness" is that of "an implacable force brooding over an inscrutable intention" (66). This is the force that "found [Kurtz] out early and had taken on him a terrible vengeance for the fantastic invasion" (97). Indeed, it is still more fantastic, for it finally takes over the attributes of the invaders: it is "the heart of a *conquering* darkness" (116, emphasis added). History mutates into nature and then into spirit, which envelops the invaders in its darkness—which at last overcomes the "flicker" of civilization on the Thames itself. Marlow has undertaken "amongst other things not to disclose any trade secrets" (36), and he does not do so. "The conquest of the earth, . . . when you look into it"— *really* look into it, in his preferred manner—is not what it seems, either to its complacent advocates or to its anti-imperialist critics.

Indeed, it may not be happening at all. The thought is certainly hyperbolic, but it is not, in textual fact, perverse. Secondary narration has a dual function in Conrad's narratives. It serves his compulsive hyperphasia, reconstituting, in the imaginary space of the novel, the contrasting conditions of enunciation of an older, unalienated narrative institution, the tale. In doing so, it symbolically restores the moral bond on which successful communication depends. In its other function, its role is apparently the contrary, qualifying narrative knowledge-claims and, at the limit of implication, querying the reality of the situations they putatively disclose. Formally speaking, the ultimate arbiter of fictional reality is the primary narrator, the substance, personified or not, that says *fiat*: let the world be and be thus. Only this instance can discriminate among the conflicting claims and evaluations of characters. Insofar as this authority is weakened, problems of interpretation deepen, and reading becomes less secure. Conrad's primary narrators are ill-placed to arbitrate, because they know little or nothing of what they now report at one remove. Secondary narrators may in their turn depend heavily on the reports of others—and they on others still. Marlow has rather little direct authority for what he reports of Kurtz's actions, and discloses little, in fact, of what he has heard from the man in person. The narrative organization is recursive ("I say that he said that he said . . .") and, in fictional effect, tantalizing; there is no formal guarantee that these things have happened, or happened quite thus. The more important point, for Marlow, is that they defy comprehension: much of his utterance is not narrative at all, but an elaboration of this theme. In the novels themselves, empirical uncertainty and interpretive bafflement are the twin modalities of the unshakeable conviction that these stories, and the larger history they instantiate, are *unbelievable*. Conrad, as a novelist, has been brought to know something, but cannot accept what he knows or that he knows it. His novels find their form in the struggle to contain an unbearable acknowledgment. Secondary narration is a strategy for accommodating this compulsive splitting of knowledge and belief. The brilliant, opaque protagonists of *Lord Jim* and *Heart of Darkness* who so fascinate Marlow are fetishes in the psychoanalytic sense, prized images of empire that allow him to look, indeed to gaze, without seeing. Here, at work in the plane of collective rather than personal history, is the process of "disavowal."

"Inconceivable History," or Disavowal

If the first paradox in Conrad is that his distinctive formal contribution to modern narrative originated in an impulse to undo the typical conditions of the novelistic as such, the second is that Anglophone culture in the twentieth century owed its first, still compelling, visions of contemporary history to a writer so alienated that his novels cannot credit its reality. In the first decade of the new century, he wrote about colonialism (*Lord Jim* and *Heart of Darkness*), the politics of capitalist development in the Americas (*Nostromo*), revolutionary conspirators and their official adversaries in Eastern Europe (*Under Western Eyes*) and the West (*The Secret Agent*). His work registered the impact of trade-union militancy (*The Nigger of the 'Narcissus'*), the sexual panic that flared in the persecution of Oscar Wilde (*Typhoon*), and the new, scientific claimants to authority in human affairs. And all this he confronted not merely with distaste—which was manifest, and often violent—but in disbelief. Contemporary history, as the teacher of languages judges in the case of Russia (*Under Western Eyes*), is "inconceivable."

The labor of disavowal, which thus becomes a condition of possibility of fictioning the present, is borne by the device of secondary narration. *Nostromo* illustrates the practice on its grandest scale, with more than a dozen narrators offering their disparate answers to the implicit conundrum of the novel: who or what makes history? Overhanging these narrative conjectures, as the mountains physically overhang the life of Sulaco, is the anonymous popular legend of the treasure of the Azuera peninsula, and an implied answer that puts the question in its place: history is made by not-history, by brute nature. *Under Western Eyes* illustrates another rhetorical stratagem. Opening the first chapter of the novel, the reader is immediately addressed by an unattributed first-person pronoun, which therefore may be read as marking an authorial guarantee. A few sentences pass before the *I* is occupied by its character, the English teacher of languages who narrates the text. Such irony supplements the work of secondary narration and sometimes overtakes it as Conrad's leading device, assisting darker, more extreme instances of disavowal.

———

"Irony," today, circulates too widely and too fluently in cultural commentary to specify any of the diverse textual processes it names. There is good reason, once again, to approach Conrad's practice indirectly, by way of a contrastive detour through the writing of another master-ironist of the early twentieth century, James Joyce. Here are the opening lines of *A Portrait of the Artist as a Young Man*: "Once upon a time and a very good time it was there was a moocow coming down along the road and this moocow that was coming down along the road met a nicens little boy named baby tuckoo."[17] In a common reading that sees this novel as dramatizing the growth of a personality, critical emphasis falls on the diction of the passage—the baby-talk of *moocow*, the ill-formed *nicens*—and its naive syntax. In this way, free indirect style renders early childhood. Yet the opening words set these features in a different light. The novel begins with, or as, the beginning of a story,

---

[17] *A Portrait of the Artist as a Young Man* (1916) (London: Jonathan Cape, 1968), 7.

conventional in form and ambiguous in provenance: the language of the telling may mark Stephen's childish effort at reiteration, or equally Simon's sentimental view of how a father speaks in a nursery. It is impossible to resolve this or any more interesting uncertainty in the novel, because there is no narrative exterior, no textually given authority to which the issue might be referred. *A Portrait* is already another of its own kind, a "Once upon a time . . ." thing. In the beginning was the word, Joyce leaves us to consider, but not the first word. In the beginning there was the already-uttered, or genre—and before the story has ended, another genre has impressed itself on the baby talk: Catholic liturgy, in the crucial instance of the Nicene Creed. The course of Stephen's inner life is a journey in discourse of various kinds and degrees, from schoolboy argot and saloon-bar gentility to the formal heights of philosophy. He is drawn to the obscure recesses of this symbolic universe—what, he wonders, is *smugging*?—but finds no alternative sense there. When he sins, he does so in the terms of the hell-fire sermon. "Another life," as he first grasps it, commits him to obsessive ritual observance and initiates him, word-perfect, into the commonplaces of Irish devotionalism: "His day began with an heroic offering of its every moment of thought or action for the intentions of the sovereign pontiff and with an early mass" (150)—and so on for page after cruelly accurate page.

Even the release into art is deceptive. Here is Stephen on the way to the college, his mind working freely as he goes:

> The rainladen trees of the avenue evoked in him, as always, memories of the girls and women in the plays of Gerhart Hauptmann; and the memory of their pale sorrows and the fragrance falling from the wet branches mingled in a mood of quiet joy. His morning walk across the city had begun, and he foreknew that as he passed the sloblands of Fairview he would think of the cloistral silverveined prose of Newman, that as he walked along the North Strand Road, glancing idly at the windows of the provision shops, he would recall the dark humour of Guido Cavalcanti and smile, that as he went by Baird's stonecutting works in Talbot Place the spirit of Ibsen would blow through him like a keen wind, a spirit of wayward boyish beauty . . . (179)

The discursive order he now inhabits is that of artistic autonomy, which the narrative reduces to a self-contradictory posture. Evocation turns mechanical; associative processes are foreknown; idle glances and even smiles are already scripted. The dispositions thought proper to the artistic calling emerge as a version of the everyday paralysis. Spontaneity of mind is just the higher commonplace. *A Portrait* holds Stephen at a distance from himself to the end. His mother is preparing his "new secondhand clothes," he records in his penultimate journal entry, anticipating in this small semantic disturbance the graver ambiguity to come: "Welcome, O life! I go to encounter for the millionth time the reality of experience and to forge in the smithy of my soul the uncreated conscience of my race" (252). Stephen's intended sense of "forge" is *shape*, as his heroic metaphor makes plain, but he cannot suppress—or even see—its other meaning, to *counterfeit*, or utter false coin.

If Joyce's irony is evidently directed at Stephen, its final implication concerns the relationship between the novel and its readers. *A Portrait* develops the Flaubertian critique of the bourgeois commonplace to the point of questioning the bohemian artist who thinks to expose and reject it; in doing so, it suspends the familiar contract between novelist and reader. This irony—unlike that of Joyce's English contemporary Arnold Bennett, for example—is not local or temporary in its incidence; it is pervasive and sustained, disqualifying given angles of vision and norms of judgment without ever validating more secure alternatives. It is art that reveals not the artist-figure (who, as Joyce's title suggests, is just another subject for genre painting), but what it reveals is open to more than one evaluation. The notorious "detachment" of the artist detaches the reader, with opposite subjective effects.

Conrad's irony functions differently. One strategic goal of his novels and stories, on the contrary, is to strengthen the bond between text and reader, to reinvent conditions of utterance for which, indeed, "commonplace" would be an exact and positive description. Of course, his secondary narration has paradoxical implications, symbolically binding audiences but at the same time complicating the knowledge-value of the stories they hear. At a certain extreme, the paradox reverses its terms, now generating extended irony. That extreme is reached in *Heart of Darkness*, as Marlow, back in Brussels, makes his visit to the Intended. At this point, his narration modulates from report, which has dominated throughout, to scenic presentation and a relatively spare exchange of direct speech. A short excerpt give the sense of this rhetorical shift:

> "And of all this," she went on, mournfully, "of all his promise, and all of his greatness, of his generous mind, of his noble heart, nothing remains—nothing but a memory."
>
> "We shall always remember him," I said, hastily.
>
> "No!" she cried. "It is impossible that such a life should be sacrificed to leave nothing—but sorrow. You know what vast plans he had. I knew of them too—I could not perhaps understand—but others knew of them. Something must remain. His words, at least, have not died."

"His words will remain," I said.

"And his example," she whispered to herself. "Men looked up to him—his goodness shone in every act. His example—"

"True," I said; "his example, too. Yes, his example. I forgot that."
(119–20, 121)

The irony of this scene has no bearing on issues of knowledge and evaluation in the plane of the text-reader relationship; it is strictly objective, inhering in the given reality of the situation. Marlow knows what the Intended does not, and also what she believes to have been the case. She, confident in what she believes, cannot imagine that Marlow might have grounds to believe otherwise. He conveys his truthful evaluation in words he knows she will translate into her illusion, which will thus persist as the authorized version. His tale, on this occasion, is a masterpiece of noncommunication. Dramatic irony is thus a necessary supplement to secondary narration in Conrad: it is the form assumed by his narrative hyperphasia in those moments where he imagines the final loss of shared belief, the snapping of the bond.

———

In *Heart of Darkness* that moment is an episode in a narrative whose scene of enunciation, by contrast, seems to promise phatic security. But ambiguity enters immediately, in the person of Marlow's host: "On the whole river there was nothing that looked half so nautical. He resembled a pilot, which to the seaman is trustworthiness personified" (27). He *looked*, he *resembled*; it was "difficult to realize" the fact. He is "the Director of Companies," and "his work" lies not seaward "but behind him, within the brooding gloom" of London. These uncertainties, like the following evocations of the city's reversible history—first as colonial outpost, then as colonizing center—qualify the easy contrast Marlow will shortly assert, between Britain's empire and the others. Even so, however, the marking of the city seems emphatic, as if registering the pressure of a further meaning. London may or may not be Brussels, but it is indisputably "the biggest, and the greatest town on earth" (27). Its constant index is "gloom": "a mournful gloom," "the gloom to the west." At sunset, "the sun sank low, and from glowing white changed to a dull red without rays and without heat, as if about to go out suddenly, stricken to death by the touch of that gloom brooding over a crowd of men. . . . [T]he place of the monstrous town was still marked ominously on the sky, a brooding gloom in sunshine, a lurid glare under the stars" (28–29). London, the type of the modern metropolis, is a site of cosmic disorder.

This is the universe of *The Secret Agent*, a place of unnumbered meta-morphoses, where the law of noncontradiction has fallen into abeyance.[18] Even its best-adapted creatures may become disoriented at times: late in the action, Ossipon, the lecherous *anarchisant* student of moral pathology, "[feels] himself losing his footing in this treacherous affair" (225)—and for once, most readers will sympathize. This London is not merely the prototypical modern city; it is, with Paris, a cradle of the novel. Indeed, with its atomized social relations, secularized mores, and disenchanted knowledges, it actually *is* the novelistic. Hence the desperate rhetoric of *The Secret Agent*: whereas the Marlow narratives simulate the moral conditions of the tale on the objective ground of the novel, this "simple tale" pursues the immanent logic of modernity, dramatizing the moral extremities of a novelized world.

There is no Marlow-figure to tell the story of how the pornographer and anarchist Verloc, under pressure from the foreign embassy for which he spies, induces his autistic brother-in-law to bomb the Greenwich Observatory; how Stevie stumbles and blows himself to pieces; how the police investigations go forward dubiously motivated and at cross-purposes; how Verloc's wife, Winnie, discovering that her husband has destroyed the brother-son who has been everything to her, murders him; and how at last, betrayed a second time—by Ossipon—she takes her own life. Secondary narratives play a familiar but now subordinate part in the organization of the text, which is given as an impersonal narration addressed, so to speak, to no one in particular. Two kinds of scene predominate.

The first is the solitary walk through the streets. None of these journeys is socially transparent, or benign in motivation or outcome. Verloc has been summoned to the embassy and is anxious lest any of his political associates should happen upon him. Chief Inspector Heat, of the Special Crimes branch, patrols here and there, monitoring the anarchist demimonde. The Assistant Commissioner, with his private interest in the outcome of the Greenwich investigation, descends into cosmopolitan Soho, dressed for the part and eluding his own uniformed officers as if a criminal himself. For the Professor, the supreme technician of terror, walking the streets is a political activity, an occasion for resentful fantasies and a show of defiance: the police are aware (he says) that he is a walking bomb. The few companionate journeys in the narrative are only apparently exceptional. Watching Verloc and Stevie leave home together, Winnie wishfully imagines them as father and son; in fact, they are on the first leg of their deceptive route to Greenwich. Deep family loyalty prompts Winnie and Stevie to accompany their mother

---

[18] *The Secret Agent* (1907) (London: Penguin, 1963).

to South London; but the occasion of the journey is her voluntary self-exile from the Verloc household, and the conversations that occur in the course of the trip will, in one available reading of events, lead to their deaths.

Conversations, normally duologues indoors, make up a second scenic group. Heat and his superior assess the Greenwich case with mutual resentment in a conversation that taps little of the inner speech on either side. Heat's main concern is his occasional informant Verloc, whom he proposes to safeguard by framing a vulnerable parolee, Michaelis—who, it happens, is the counterpart object of the Assistant Commissioner's concern, being the protégé of his wife's valued acquaintance, a great society hostess. It irritates the Assistant Commissioner that he must "take so much on trust" in his isolated position of command. His own superior, Sir Ethelred, in contrast, is too distracted by his plan to nationalize the fisheries to pay close attention to the creatures who inhabit the "slimy aquarium" of Soho. Ossipon and the Professor, in a matching discussion, fail to penetrate the enigma of the day's news, even though Ossipon immediately suspects a provocation and the Professor has supplied Verloc with the bomb. Knowing little of him or his household, in reality, they cannot correctly infer his role in the event, much less that the luckless bomber was someone else—and something else again. The household itself, supposedly a focus of intimate feeling and political solidarity, conforms to the rule of alienation. Conversation is sparse, unless the usual anarchists—grotesques all—turn up to talk at or past one another, while Verloc inhabits his double identity, Winnie gets on with things, and Stevie sits on the far side of an open door, lost in his drawing. What Stevie draws is in one aspect an expressive figure, in another a diagram: ". . . circles, circles; innumerable circles, concentric, eccentric; a coruscating whirl of circles that by their tangled multitude of repeated curves, uniformity of form, and confusion of intersecting lines suggested a rendering of cosmic chaos, the symbolism of a mad art attempting the inconceivable" (45–46). Here, in stylized form, is the noncommunicating world of *The Secret Agent*, which will eventually mean the death of Winnie and, through this, the loss of the last social bond.

"The inconceivable" in this case is the identity—perhaps even the fact— of "the secret agent." The distinction implied in the singular form of the noun is not self-evident in a world where everyone acts clandestinely, whether for love (Winnie and her mother) or gain (Verloc) or *raison d'état* (Vladimir) or social advantage (the Assistant Commissioner) or professional convenience (Heat) or self-styled revolutionary ends (the Professor). All are secret agents in a way, and even a "realistic" short list leaves three obvious candidates, Vladimir, Verloc, and the Professor, and a fourth who cannot be discounted, namely, Stevie. And if the identity of the secret agent remains ambiguous, it is because the narrative remains undecided about "his" motivation. *Who?* depends on *why?* or *how?*—questions to which the novel entertains two answers that, although compatible as accounts of an uncontroversial record of events, are antithetical in final historical implication.

The more strongly emphasized of the two explanations is, so to speak, "externalist" in kind, and begins with Vladimir, who seeks to further the domestic priorities of his own state in the contrasting political environment of Britain, using a local agent to organize an unlawful event that takes two innocent lives. Here Conrad reiterates the great theme of English conservatism, elaborated from Edmund Burke's *Reflections on the Revolution in France*. The states of continental Europe are characteristically rigid, intrusive apparatuses of rule that shape a correspondingly doctrinaire and extremist reflex in their political opponents; their defining types are secret police and terrorists. In Britain, in contrast, where civil society enjoys greater autonomy and where political rule is less formal and more flexible, an evolved liberal constitution grounds more reasonable terms of political engagement. This is shared wisdom in *The Secret Agent*. Vladimir finds England "absurd" in "its sentimental regard for individual liberty" (33). The Professor, who like all Verloc's revolutionary associates is "European," thinks the country is "dangerous, with her idealistic conception of legality," and adds: "The social spirit of this people is wrapped up in scrupulous prejudices, and that is fatal to our work" (67). Winnie embodies that spirit. On first hearing of the explosion, she comments: "I call it silly. . . . We ain't downtrodden slaves here" (168)—and specifically, as she has protested on another occasion, "not German slaves . . . , thank God" (57). Revolutionary activity is "not our business," she maintains; and the Assistant Commissioner, concluding his investigation and satisfying official interest in the events, agrees that it has been a foreign affair. What matters now "is the clearing out of this country of all the foreign political spies, police, and that sort of—of—dogs" (185). Every anarchist can be accounted or; it remains only "to do away with the *agent provocateur* to make everything safe" (186).

However, neither judgment can be taken as dependable. Winnie is not an exhibit for the Professor's gallery of English "prejudices"; fully aware, as she repeatedly says, that "things do not stand being looked into," she is a self-conscious pragmatist, in politics as in her marriage. The Assistant Commissioner, whose curiosity is his temperamental vice, not a professional principle, cannot hear the ambiguity in his confident report of his findings: "We could have gone further; only we stopped at the limits of our territory" (186). He means that he has observed diplomatic protocol, not intruding into sovereign space of the embassy. But in his words may be read the suggestion that he has not even entered "our" territory—that he has not looked inward, into England, and seen there the evidence for an alternative, "internalist" explanation of events. Yet the narrative leaves no doubt of this, or that Stevie, instrument and victim of the Greenwich plot, may be the incendiary reality misrecognized as "the secret agent."

Like the anarchists whose non-conversation he overhears, Stevie is an isolate. It is precisely this that defines his condition: what he lacks is not so much ordinary intelligence or feeling as his sister's pragmatism, the "common sense" that might moderate the reach of his curiosity and his compassion, which is extraordinary. Like the Professor, he "lacks the great social virtue of resignation" (69). Moreover, he has already shown himself ready to take violent measures against perceived wrong-doing—as when he launches a firework attack on his employer outraged by stories of the oppression of others (18). That episode of terroristic virtue suggests the inference to be drawn from a later episode, which in fact provides the only direct evidence of his disposition in the approach to the bombing attempt. Arrived at his mother's place of exile, Stevie falls into conversation with the cab driver, who details the drudgery of his working life and the poverty of his family. "Bad! Bad!" he exclaims, as "convulsive sympathy" surges in him. "Poor! Poor!" Then, a little later, as he and Winnie set out for home: "Bad world for poor people" (143). It occurs to him that the police might help. "The police aren't for that," is Winnie's half-distracted reply. Stevie is suddenly angry. "What are they for then, Winn? What are they for? Tell me." Then Winnie breaches the rule by which she lives: "Don't you know what the police are for, Stevie? They are there so that them as have nothing shouldn't take anything away from them who have" (144). With that, the explosive formula is complete. Compassion, inciting curiosity, leads to terror. The cab driver and Winnie have primed Verloc's instrument. In due course, the bomb will arrive, and not from Soho but from a "little country station" in Kent (89), the Garden of England. Foreigners have little to do with it.

———

This doubling of interpretive possibilities marks the crisis of political perception on which disavowal must do its work, somehow recuperating an unbearable anxiety within the terms of the accepted narrative. The radical ambiguation of the event is itself rendered suspect, resting as it does on an opposition of national types that may after all be groundless. England's political culture stands in favorable contrast with that of continental Europe, but who may confidently distinguish their corresponding human types? Vladimir, whose spontaneous "guttural" intonation is "startling even to Mr Verloc's experience of cosmopolitan slums," can produce "an amazingly genuine English accent" (29, 38). His adversary, the Assistant Commissioner, is English but has been shaped by his time in a tropical colony and has a taste for "foreign" disguise and for Soho, that "denationalizing" milieu whose restaurants, with their "fraudulent cookery," deprive patrons of "all their national and private characteristics" (125). Verloc is English-born, but his father was French. Even Winnie is indeterminate: if her mother's boast is to be credited, she too is partly French. Of course, these complications resolve nothing: their point is the further ambiguity they generate. Like Marlow's prolixity, they serve to fend off the threat of disenchantment.

Only the Professor is exempt from this drama of nationality: he has no proper name to place him, and his origins are unmarked. In fact, he largely escapes the semantic organization of the text as a whole, by virtue of his sheer abstraction. His pure hatred of the existing order entails no corresponding solidarity with either the masses, who are "an odious multitude," or the revolutionaries, whom he despises. Whereas Stevie embodies unmoderated compassion, the Professor affects pure cerebration; and unlike his political associates, he is formidably skilled, and incorruptible. His politics are socially meaningless, consisting in the pursuit of an ideal detonator; he is an aesthete of the revolution. If there is something fetishistic in the Professor's technical obsession, there is something the same in his place in the novel, which is disproportionate to his limited narrative function—making the bomb. Underemployed and abstract, he appears at once marginal and central, a figure whose purpose is simply to be present. The novel's closing vision is of him, not anyone who has acted with real consequence or suffered commensurate harm. The Professor is, in effect, a rhetorically simpler version of Jim or Kurtz, in a story with no equivalent protagonist. Like them, he is an object of fascination, a character in whom Conrad can at once register and obscure his perception of historical danger.

The Professor, like Jim and Kurtz, is centrally defined by his relationship with a local population. They are visible, self-consciously paternalist functionaries in their respective colonial systems; he, in contrast, is secretive and malevolent, an anonymous member of the crowd—"unsuspected and deadly, like a pest in the street full of men" (249). Yet he is hardly the alien aggressor the simile implies. No one in this world is transparent, or secure in his or her social being; and "the street" and its "men" are already in the grip of a protean disorder. The morning sun works its alchemy in reverse in the streets of the West End, "old gold" turning to "copper" and then "rust."

The numbering of the houses has fallen inexplicably out of series. The friezes in the Silenus Restaurant depict a medieval outdoor scene, but the music comes from a mechanical piano. The bomb plot destroys a family, which in much conservative thought, is the very model of social order. But that family has had reality only in Winnie's dreams—Verloc habitually takes his meals "as if in a public place." Stevie's lethal compassion is fired by the social misery of another family, and his own history embodies a record of familial decline: bullied in his early years by a violent father, he has grown up in his mother's boardinghouse, an interior no longer quite a home, if not yet its opposite, a hotel. Verloc looks from his bedroom window at "that enormity of cold, black, wet, muddy, inhospitable accumulation of bricks, slates, and stones, things in themselves unlovely and unfriendly to man" (54). The South London night, as Winnie's mother leaves for a solitary life as the tenant of a charitable foundation, is "sinister, noisy, hopeless and rowdy" (133). The cumulative force of these indications is irresistible. The modern city, acme of gregariousness, is the vanishing point of solidarity. If Conrad's "perfect terrorist" is a figure for the inconceivable social revolutionary, his London figures the inconceivability of lasting social order. The secret agent, now, is not a person at all, but the history that has created "the street full of men."

Coda: Jim in Ameriga

In the symbolic geography of *The Secret Agent*, poised as it is on the Greenwich meridian, danger comes from the East. The events of the decade following its appearance lent substance to Conrad's imaginings. By the end of 1918, the old regimes of the Romanovs, the Hapsburgs, and the Hohenzollerns lay in ruins, crippled by four years of warfare, then felled by revolutionary attacks—the work of insurgent crowds, be it said, not the feckless caricatures who inhabit Verloc's parlor. These transformations resonated throughout Europe, as inspiration or menace, not exempting England, the heartland of liberalism and "resignation." The subtler dangers of territories farther east (and south), the colonial settings of *Lord Jim* and *Heart of Darkness*, were a threat of another, politically less tangible kind. At the same time, however, Conrad's narratives discern the portents taking shape in the opposite quarter, in a country now salient in "the West." The New World is no more reassuring than what survives of the Old. The German-Australian who has abandoned the *Patna* sees it as a place where not even English justice can pursue him: in his own damning words, he "vill an Amerigan citizen begome." The Professor commends the United States as "fertile ground for us": "They have more character over there, and their character is essentially anarchistic. . . . The great Republic has the root of the destructive matter in her. . . . Excellent" (67). And the "root" is being transplanted abroad: the financial power behind the silver mines in *Nostromo* is the U.S. banker Holroyd. Here again, historical experience gave body to Conrad's apprehensions. The Great War brought a first involvement in European politics for the country that now boasted the world's largest economy; henceforward, the tendencies of developed capitalism would be construed simply as "Americanization." However, while Conrad and European writers of younger generations could not but try to evaluate the cultural promise or threat of American capitalism, there were others, across the Atlantic, to whom that mighty reality appeared in the form of an intimate historical enigma—as if the very idea of capitalism in America were finally unimaginable. F. Scott Fitzgerald was one such, producing, in *The Great Gatsby*, a truly Conradian *envoi* for "the American century."

———

The story begins with the ambitions of a Middle Western farmer's son, Jimmy Gatz, and continues with his transformation—through the fortunes of patronage and war, then bootlegging and fraud—into the rich, flamboyant Jay Gatsby of West Egg, Long Island, the host of any parasite's dreams. The motive for his great displays of hospitality is in truth unsociably private. He hopes to recapture his lost love, Daisy, who has come to live directly across the bay, in the more prestigious East Egg, with her husband, Tom. The parties themselves accomplish little, but with the help of his neighbor, Nick Carraway, who is Daisy's cousin, he succeeds, or nearly. His romance intersects disastrously with Tom's current sexual intrigue; misidentified as the driver in a hit-and-run accident in which Tom's lover, Myrtle, dies, he too dies, shot by her distraught husband. His funeral is a dismal, ill-attended affair; Tom and Daisy, the real authors of Myrtle's destruction, slip away from the area; Nick returns to the Middle West to muse on the significance of his summer in the East, at length delivering the monologue that is the exclusive textual substance of *The Great Gatsby*.

There is so much of *Lord Jim* in the novel, both as imagined action and as narration—so much, too, of *Heart of Darkness* and, in another way, *The Secret Agent*—that it is worth emphasizing the respect in which Nick's situation differs from Marlow's. He does not speak: his medium, as he immediately declares, is writing for print—"this book."[19] The implied audience, likewise, is largely unmarked, taking discernible form just once, in the educated face-tiousness of "that delayed Teutonic migration known as the Great War" (9). His Ivy League background and its later social echoes seem no more than circumstantial. He frequents the Yale Club, but only to dine and use the library. The "investments and securities" that he finds there are the matter of the books he reads; the fellowship of the club—an enabling value for Marlow—appears only negatively, in the shape of the usual "few rioters" (57). None of this suggests the hyperphasia that motivates the resort to secondary narration in Conrad. *Gatsby* is a novel at peace with its institutional conditions of existence. And yet, for all that, its crowning stylistic achievement is to fashion itself in a medium to which it has no access, that of speech. The Carraway figure is a simulated voice—something to return to, in a narrative whose supreme object of desire, Daisy, is normally represented as that and little more.

It is of course a normative, WASP voice—only the Jewish gambler, Wolf-shiem, and assorted plebeian characters, including Gatsby's father, have their words marked down by the old device of pseudo-phonetic transcription (as in "Oggsford" for Oxford). And one locution identifies it more closely. Nick is writing from his hometown, "*this* Middle Western city" (8)—a context-dependent form of words that invokes a preferred audience and aligns it in the symbolic space of the narrative, whose poles are East and West. This axis is a biographical constant for the main characters. Like Nick and Gatsby, Tom, Daisy, and her friend Jordan all come from points west; ambition of various kinds has drawn them, as if naturally, eastward, to New York. For Nick, as he looks back from the Middle West, this geography is a moral emblem. The journey east is one into danger, the "valley of ashes" that lies between the Eggs and the City, surmounted by a *deus absconditus* in the form of a huge, unseeing pair of spectacles advertising the optometrist Dr. Eckleburg. There is nothing in the narrative to motivate this unreal landscape; in this sense it is not even symbolic, rather a simple allegorical figure of spiritual exhaustion. "I see now," Nick concludes, "that this has been a story of the West, after all—Tom and Gatsby, Daisy and Jordan and I, were all Westerners, and perhaps we possessed some deficiency in common which made us subtly unadaptable to Eastern life" (167). But what has he "seen"? Why is the East thus, and in what way does the West differ? Nick is convinced that he has learned something; his story, like Marlow's, is rich in

---

[19] *The Great Gatsby* (1925), introduced by Tony Tanner (London: Penguin, 1990), 8.

philosophical generalization. He has had "privileged glimpses into the human heart" (8), and specifically into the hearts of Americans; these are the substance of his avowed learning. What he has actually seen is something quite different.

Compared with ordinary life in New York as it presents itself to Nick, the valley of ashes is a mere curiosity. The visible world as a whole is phantasmagoric. Natural objects seem artificial: a dog's fur is "a weather-proof coat" (30), and in West Egg the leaves proliferate "just as things grow in fast movies" (9). Artifacts are liable to the reverse transformation, Daisy's living room appearing as a windy seascape. In this world, objects come to animate life—"a hundred pairs of golden and silver slippers shuffled the shining dust" (144)—and are even spoken to: " 'No thanks,' said [Jordan] to the four cocktails just in from the pantry. 'I'm absolutely in training' " (16). Gatsby's parties, where drinks "float . . . through the twilight" and even the moon rises "out of a caterer's basket" (44), intensify such phenomena and confirm a morally ominous but also mysterious connection with wealth and theater. Turkeys, emblematic of the nation, are "bewitched to a dark gold" (41). Representations multiply and distract, as an actress is "erroneous[ly]" identified as "Gilda Gray's understudy from the Follies" (42). Such logics of substitutability extend to personal relations, one guest arriving "always with four girls . . . never quite the same ones in physical person, but . . . so identical one with another that it inevitably seemed they had been there before" (62).

Deceiving and disordering in its effects, the phantasmagoria is nevertheless regular in its forms, whose underlying process is unveiled just once, in a single passage: "Every Friday five crates of oranges and lemons arrived from a fruiterer in New York—every Monday these same oranges and lemons left [Gatsby's] back door in a pyramid of pulpless halves. There was a machine in the kitchen which could extract the juice of two hundred oranges in half an hour if a little button was pressed two hundred times by a butler's thumb" (41). The careful sequencing of this passage, and its regular mismatching of grammatical and real agencies, divulge the secret of the floating cocktails. The phenomenal world of West Egg now appears in relation to an objective system of goods, markets, and (occluded) labor. *The Great Gatsby* offers a brilliant visualization of what Marx explained as "the fetishism of commodities":

> A commodity appears at first sight as an extremely obvious, trivial thing. But its analysis brings out that it is a very strange thing, abounding in metaphysical subtleties and theological niceties. So far as it is a use-value, there is nothing mysterious about it, whether we consider it from the point of view that

by its properties it satisfies human needs, or that it first takes on these properties as the product of human labour. It is absolutely clear that, by his labour, man changes the forms of the material of nature in such a way as to make them useful to him. . . . The mysterious character of the commodity-form [or the use-value produced for exchange] consists . . . simply in the fact that the commodity reflects the social characteristics of men's own labour as objective characteristics of the products of labour themselves, as the social-natural properties of these things. . . . It is nothing but the definite social relation between men themselves which assumes here, for them, the fantastic form of a relation between things. . . . I call this the fetishism which attaches itself to the products of labour as soon as they are produced as commodities, and is therefore inseparable from the production of commodities.[20]

However, the commodified object-world of the novel is not commensurable with its relatively few indications of labor. Domestics, small farmers, mechanics, and fisher folk cannot account for its characteristic accessories—the opulent food and drink, the telephones, the automobiles, and the vast wealth. When Nick describes Daisy as being "appalled by West Egg, this unprecedented 'place' that Broadway had begotten upon a Long Island fishing village," he is in effect joining her in disavowal of American economic reality. Yet he cannot do otherwise, for to acknowledge it would be to accept that there is no final, anthropological difference between East and West, that one is the product and necessary function of the other. American capitalism is a systemic unity, and its human token, in the novel, is none other than the young man from the hinge of the agricultural and industrial economies—a Middle Western hardware business—who has come east to learn about finance. But Nick cannot accept the material reality of his home region. His preferred image of it might be a Hollywood set. "That's my Middle West," he says, thinking back to his college days "—not the wheat or the prairies or the lost Swede towns, but the thrilling returning trains of my youth, and the street lamps and sleigh bells in the frosty dark and the shadows of holly wreaths thrown by lighted windows on the snow" (167). The alternative to radical disenchantment is his story of "the great Gatsby."

Curiosity about the secrets of money is overcome by fascination with the enigmatic figure who lives next door. Gatsby, like Kurtz, is before all else a rumor. "They say he's a nephew or a cousin of Kaiser Wilhelm's," Myrtle's sister reports: "That's where all his money comes from" (35). According to another source, "Somebody told me they thought he killed a man once" (45).

---

[20] Karl Marx, *Capital*, translated by Ben Fowkes (Harmondsworth: Penguin, 1976), 163–65.

A third informant can confirm that he had spied for the enemy during the war—"I heard that from a man who knew all about him, grew up with him in Germany." Gatsby has more than one version of himself and seems to acknowledge the essentially rumorous quality of his existence when he mistakenly assumes, on his first encounter with Nick, that his neighbor already knows who he is. The truth, as he later discloses it to Nick, in fact confirms the validity of the rags-to-riches story it seems to travesty, renewing mystification where another success story—that of the Carraways—might dispel it. Gatsby has received his social training from a multimillionaire whose fortune had grown from silver and other metals speculation; his shady professional skills he owes to Wolfshiem, the man who fixed the World Series. In other words, wealth comes from the earth and proliferates in the hands of speculators and tricksters: the secret of money is safe. Nick distills Gatsby into a psychological essence: uniquely, in a human landscape where anticlimax appears to be an inexorable general law, Gatsby has "an extraordinary gift for hope, a romantic readiness such as I have never found in any other person and which it is not likely I shall ever find again" (8). His story, it may be, epitomizes a peculiarly American striving for a future that is always already past. In the ultimate reduction, Nick's Gatsby becomes a self-fashioned work of art: "If personality is an unbroken series of successful gestures, then there was something gorgeous about him, some heightened sensitivity to the promises of life" (8). Like Kurtz, he has been driven by "his Platonic conception of himself"; like Jim, "he turned out all right at the end" (8). Like both, he embodies opacity as revelation; his role is to fascinate. The decisive function of Fitzgerald's personification, as of Conrad's, is disavowal of an intolerable apprehension—here, that of capitalism itself. And thus, Freud converges with Marx in the space of a shared metaphor. Nick's Gatsby is his fetishistic defense against the reality of a fetishistic society. Only the image of Gatsby the illimitable enables him to recompose his relations with the West he must not know, "that vast obscurity beyond the city, where the dark fields of the republic [roll] on under the night" (171). And likewise only by this means, perhaps, could Fitzgerald imagine Nick's account of himself, this monodrama of bourgeois conscience, and embody it in a speaking voice that, for all the evidence to the contrary, is not, like cousin Daisy's, "full of money."

JOHN BRENKMAN

Innovation: Notes on Nihilism and the Aesthetics of the Novel

Can we define innovation in the novel? It obviously has something to do with modernism and postmodernism. The idea of modernism implies innovation: Make it new. *Il faut être absolument moderne.* The idea of *post*modernism—after, beyond, newer than the new—also implies innovation. A bad start on definitions.

Opposing ways out of this confusion have been proposed by Peter Bürger, Fredric Jameson, and Jean-François Lyotard. According to Bürger's *Theory of the Avant-Garde*, the early twentieth-century avant-gardes were genuinely innovative because they challenged the separation of art and life, until modernism institutionalized innovation and thereby killed it. He answers the confusion with a historical paradox: earlier artists made it new, newer artists do not. After futurism and surrealism, twentieth-century art is the afterglow or half-life of a failed project. Bürger mounts a principled defense of this position. But that is the problem, for to evaluate our era's art on the basis of the principle of fusing art and life assumes that the intellectual-aesthetic powers of the contemporary critic have somehow escaped the intellectual-aesthetic fate of contemporary artists. It is doubtful.

Jameson arrives at a similar embarrassment in *Postmodernism, or, The Cultural Logic of Late Capitalism*, starting out from the perspective that realism, modernism, and postmodernism correspond to the phases of capitalism, respectively: industrial, imperialist, and global (or developing, developed, and "late"). He preserves both the later Lukács's understanding of realism: the realist novel represents, despite ideological refractions, the total class structure of society, as well as Adorno's understanding of modernism: the modernist work represents, negatively, the individual's estranged relation to the (now hidden) truth of the social totality. Jameson then looks to adduce the comparable relation between late capitalism and postmodern art. As consumer society drives individuals ever further into the privatized world of commodities and as globalization disperses economic exploitation beyond anyone's tangible grasp, art begins to lose its very ability to *represent*. Insofar as postmodernism merely relishes the loss of representation, it is the symptom (the "cultural dominant") of this historical process. Can there then be a postmodern art that matches the knowledge embodied in Lukács's realism and the negative protest of Adorno's modernism? In answering that question, Jameson puts himself as literary critic in a position as awkward as Bürger's: rather than criticizing his society *through* the literature it produces, he calls for a literature that would represent the society he already, in theory, knows: "the new political art (if it is possible at all) will have to hold to the truth of postmodernism, that is to say to its fundamental object—the world space of multinational capital—at the same time as it achieves a breakthrough to some unimaginable new mode of representing this last."[1] Critics have frequently stimulated new artistic movements by denouncing the limitations of existing ones, but Jameson's call for the missing aesthetic of "global cognitive mapping" is epochal in scope. It is deduced from his theoretical premise about the nature of late capitalism and its "cultural dominant." Is the missing aesthetic a utopian-critical hypothesis or the alibi of the original premise? The issue is at best undecidable.

Lyotard, in contrast to Bürger and Jameson, sees permanent avant-garde revolution everywhere, right up through postmodernism: genuine art continually negates what came before. He revives the spirit of early-twentieth-century formalism's account of the avant-garde's defamiliarization of conventions and breaks with tradition. Art pursues "the unpresentable" and "dissension"—on principle. Since artworks do eventually become understood by a public (that is, become "institutionalized" in Bürger's sense), Lyotard solves the innovation puzzle with a purely logical rather than historical paradox: every genuine artwork is postmodern before it is modern, the *post*modern always *precedes* the modern.

Reliance on a singular principle or logic of artistic innovation leads to impasse, impasses that are all the more striking in these three theorists because their work is otherwise filled with interpretive insights and guided by deeply thought-out historical and aesthetic perspectives. This fact underscores how troublesome, and seductive, the keywords *avant-garde, modernism,* and *postmodernism* truly are. Meanwhile, journalistic as well as scholarly literary criticism now dispenses with the complexity and contradictoriness of aesthetic trends and typically divides the past century of literature into a "modern" and a "postmodern" half. Before the divide, literature affirms the self, aesthetic unity, and Enlightenment; afterward, it does not. The modern is foundationalist, totalizing, and universalist; the postmodern is not. An era of criticism that began under the inspiration of Derrida, Barthes, and de Man by excoriating binary oppositions and sneering at linear narratives today uses a half-dozen binaries and two periods to sum up all of twentieth-century art.

---

[1] Fredric Jameson, *Postmodernism, or, The Cultural Logic of Late Capitalism* (Durham, N.C.: Duke University Press, 1991), 54.

The modernist/postmodernist plot thoroughly distorts the history of the novel and the state of contemporary world fiction. Our era's fiction does not fall into two symmetrical halves; it unfurls in dizzying spirals of modern epics and language experiments, surrealisms and realisms, colonialist adventures and postcolonial tragedies, male mythologies and feminist rewritings, fictional autobiographies and documentary novels, not to mention the steady flow of romances, detective stories, and science fiction.

The reigning view of the novel tells, instead, a tidy little story: in the beginning was realism (naive nineteenth-century representations of vulgar social reality); in the middle was modernism; in the end, postmodernism. Antirealism becomes the defining feature of twentieth-century fiction: modernism supersedes realistic representations with stream-of-consciousness and formalistic rigor, and then postmodernism fractures or deconstructs representation, consciousness, and form. Accordingly, innovation removes the novel ever farther from realism.

But is any of this true?

The most important developments and innovations in recent fiction have come from novelists like Christa Wolf, Toni Morrison, Günter Grass, Milan Kundera, Norman Mailer, Carlos Fuentes, Salman Rushdie, Orhan Pamuk, and Nadine Gordimer. The imperatives of realism—to illuminate individual life histories in the flow of collective histories, to represent how time and impersonal forces move through individual experience and intimate relationships, to assess the boundaries of moral action—are manifest across these writers' diverse projects and varied styles. The realist imperative is ingrained in the very innovations that get labeled "modernist" or "postmodernist." Take Morrison. She incorporates reconstructed folk narratives, disjointed narrative voices, and layered temporalities not in order to overthrow realism but to get at the shape of experiences belonging to very precise times and places: a segregated community in northern Ohio in the early 1960s on the cusp of its awareness of the civil rights movement in *Song of Solomon*; an isolated community of escaped slaves in southern Ohio in the 1850s under the regime of the Fugitive Slave Law in *Beloved*; the streets and apartments of 1920s Harlem in the grip of migration and renaissance in *Jazz*; a black township in Oklahoma in the 1970s whose century-long memories and mythologies are torn apart by incoming fragments of Vietnam, the counterculture, and Black Power in *Paradise*.

My thesis, then: realism and innovation are a double imperative in the contemporary novel. To rethink what is meant by innovation in light of this thesis will require a skeptical reconsideration, though not a wholesale rejection, of all the other keywords in the discussion: *modernism, postmodernism, avant-garde, modernity*. I will return to these terms intermittently as I try to measure contemporary theory against the artistic achievements of the contemporary novel.

First, though, it is necessary to clarify how I understand the realist imperative of the novel. Forget the commonplace that what makes a novel realistic is its intent to mirror a stable reality. That idea has never been more than a caricature of the aesthetic of nineteenth-century realism. It helped justify the twentieth-century novel's new points of departure; it seemed to explain the stakes, for example, when the author of *Dubliners* undertook to write *Ulysses*. But realism never was a mirror, and reality was hardly more stable in the nineteenth century than today. When Stendhal famously said that a novel is a mirror moving down a roadway, his metaphor had nothing to do with picturing a stable reality. On the contrary, it evoked the upheaval, mobility, and uncertainty of social life and called upon the novel to find the artistic means of referring to that unstable reality.

Novels do not reproduce reality; they refer to it, with deep awareness of its elusiveness. Novelists are also atuned to the myriad other discourses that refer to reality, whether to flee it or master it: the discourses of romance, myth, religion, ideology, science. Novels thus make reference to reality by making reference to other discourses. That was Mikhail Bakhtin's great insight. There are only angles on reality. The perspectivalism that modern thought thinks it inherited from Nietzsche has been the vocation of the novel since its modern rebirth in Rabelais, Cervantes, and Grimmelshausen. (That Nietzsche disdained the novel as an empiricist illusion of the modern herd mentality is another story, a very intriguing one.) Even the most private perspectives intersect with shared ones, whether those of classes or sects, scientists or ideologues, parties or subcultures, believers or infidels. The novel is charged with disclosing the individual's fateful encounters at those crossroads. Its vocation ultimately arises perhaps from its impossible dual allegiance to skepticism and imagination; the novelist invents worlds to unmask the world. Yeats was as unreceptive to the novel as Nietzsche, and probably for the same reasons, but the calling he attributed to art in general surely fits the novel's demystifying, questioning, fabricating, perspectival habits: against the rhetorician's deceptions and the sentimentalist's self-deceptions, the novel "is but a vision of reality."

————

"To name the unnamable, to point at frauds, to take sides, start arguments, shape the world and stop it from going to sleep."[2] Salman Rushdie gives these

---

[2] Salman Rushdie, *The Satanic Verses* (New York: Viking, 1988), 97.

words to the satirical poet Baal of Jahilia, who lends them back to define the aesthetic of *The Satanic Verses*. The novel invents in order to question, fantasizes in order to expose, disputes in order to designate . . . unnamable reality.

"*I saw no God, nor heard any, in a finite organical perception; but my senses discovered the infinite in every thing.*"[3] William Blake gives these words to the prophet Isaiah, and one of Rushdie's protagonists reads them in his lover's "long-unopened copy" of *The Marriage of Heaven and Hell*. Isaiah is explaining to the enthralled Blake that he never in fact *heard* God; rather, his own righteous indignation *was* the voice of God. The biblical revelation was humanly inspired; the prophet was a poet. Isaiah's words too lend themselves to Rushdie's aesthetic. The satanic-satyric-satirical inversion of a sacred text is a poetic reimagining of the religious imagination.

The challenge posed to readers of *The Satanic Verses* is that its realist imperative is borne on the wings of worldly satire and sacred parody. Moreover, the novel mixes several distinct discourses, each with a purpose of its own:

- a fantastic tale of metamorphosis to signify the simultaneity of incommensurate worlds in the migrant's experience, and in the postimperial metropolis;
- a Dickensian satire to expose the seething wounds of urban life in Thatcherite England;
- a parody of the sacred text of the Quran to interrogate the paradox that today's religious fundamentalisms, far from being a return to pristine beliefs and traditions, are an utterly contemporary form of mass politics; and
- a tragicomic tale of rivalry, madness, and revenge to unfold the inner torment of two privileged expatriates, the novel's protagonists, Saladin Chamcha (the Anglophilic toady who impersonates a thousand voices in commercials) and Gibreel Farishta (the movie star who plays numberless deities in Indian "theologicals").

The Quranic parody takes up the novel's second and sixth chapters, "Mahound" and "Return to Jahilia." Raucous, irreverent, and profound, it is looped into the Saladin-Gibreel story with a simple premise and complex effects. Gibreel has always been filled with religious imaginings, from Ovid's tales of Jovian and human metamorphoses to the reincarnations and multiple gods of Hinduism, and he is captivated by Islam's primary, and dueling,

---

[3] Ibid., 304.

angels: Shaitan, the fallen angel, and Gibreel, the voice emitting Allah's truth to Mohammed. The cinematic "portrayer of gods" begins dreaming he *is* the angel Gibreel, and the dream slowly bleeds into his waking life and becomes delusion. The two chapters of parody are his dreams, an oneiric retelling of how Mahound (Mohammed) converts, with negotiations and threats, the polytheistic people of Jahilia (Mecca). That is the simple premise: Gibreel dreams the parody of the Quran.

As a literary feat, however, the parodic chapters abjure psychological realism. Even the dreams of a psychotic could not unfold in a prose so luminous and allusive and penetrating—not to mention in the same style as the rest of the novel. The dream device serves another purpose in *The Satanic Verses*; it links, loosely but richly, an array of altered states of consciousness: dreams, psychotic delusions, mystical visions, the Prophet's receiving the Recitation, the hysteria of crowds, the mass appeal of cinematic fantasias. Gibreel's dream is in the tradition of Lucian's satires, an occasion to throw the divine and profane, realities and fantasies, into a large bag and shake them up into an exuberant rearrangement that questions all manner of secular and sacred certainties.

The Quran's episode of the satanic verses is the weak knee of that textual monolith. Islamic tradition reckons that an allusion in the Quran to some demonic tampering with the Prophet's receptivity to Gibreel's Recitation—"Never have We sent a single prophet or apostle before you with whose wishes Satan did not tamper"[4]—refers to another episode in which Mohammed apparently rescinds his offer to grant legitimacy to three goddesses worshiped by the people of Mecca, whom he is trying to convert. If the Prophet was deceived by satanic verses once, why not twice? Often? Always?

According to the Quran, the goddesses Al-Lat, Al-Uzzah, and Manat "are but names . . . invented . . . vain conjectures . . . whims of [the unbelievers'] own souls."[5] Every monotheism hews to its own divinely revealed truth by accusing other religions of being the work of the human imagination. Monotheists were the first religious skeptics. That's what the Quran's episode of the satanic verses is all about: fallible man created the goddesses, and the Prophet himself is fallible. With that, the Quran opens the way to parody. To explain the flawed Recitation, Salman Rushdie invents Salman the Persian, Mahound's scribe. As the tranced prophet repeats the verses he hears from the angel Gibreel, Salman writes them down but makes devilish

---

[4] The Koran, "Pilgrimage" (22:52), trans. N. J. Dawood (New York: Penguin, 1974).
[5] The Koran, "The Star" (53:22).

changes in the text because he suspects that Mahound climbs Mount Cone and induces an imaginary Gibreel to tell him what he wants to hear and then is a bit too distracted to remember exactly what he dictates to Salman. It is a reversal worthy of Blake's Isaiah: "I saw no God, nor heard any."

Rushdie, however, does not share Blake's apocalypticism. He has a novelist's eye for mundane dramas underneath the heroics. As Gibreel Farishta dreams Salman the Persian's travesties and betrayals, he himself becomes a paranoid angel whose demonic adversary is Saladin Chamcha. Saladin too is infected by angel-devil scenarios and blames his troubles on Gibreel, the cinematic angel whose stardom and erotic conquests mock him with everything he himself lacks. He hatches an Iago-like plot to drive Gibreel into a jealous frenzy against his lover Allie Cone (yes, Cone, whose 27,000-foot ascent of Mount Everest to see the face of God is reversed in Saladin and Gibreel's 27,000-foot fall from an exploding airliner into the living inferno and waking nightmare of the Thatcherite metropolis at the beginning of the novel).

There is indeed an apocalyptic conflagration, an urban riot in which both demonized immigrants and police provocateurs are the arsonists. Saladin's wife Pamela and her lover Jumpy Joshi perish. Gibreel walks through the fires of Brickhall blowing an angelic trumpet, convinced he is creating the flames, and he saves Saladin from a burning building: "so that on a night when the city is at war, a night heavy with enmity and rage, there is this small redeeming victory for love."[6]

That edifying, reassuring denouement is short-lived. To use Rushdie's beloved *Arabian Nights* idiom, *it was so and it was not*. A few months later, back in Bombay, Gibreel's Saladin-induced jealousy is still raging, and he murders Allie and kills himself. The small victory of love saves only Saladin—the false self, the coward, the evildoer. "In spite of all his wrongdoing, weakness, guilt—in spite of his humanity—he was getting another chance. There was no accounting for one's good fortune, that was plain."[7] Reconciled with his dying father, inheriting a fortune, and reunited with his secret lover Zeenat Vakil, Saladin is led away from the final carnage by Zeenat, who is filled with dubious plans to reconcile him with India and transform him into a political activist. There the story stops.

"In spite of his humanity." Here we touch on the true mainspring of this novel. It took me more than one reading to see the centrality of the Saladin-Gibreel story and the puzzle posed by Saladin's survival. When *The Satanic*

---

[6] *The Satanic Verses*, 468.

[7] Ibid., 547.

Verses was honored as the first selection of the Ayotollah's Book Club, the author was terrorized and vilified (and not only by Islamic fundamentalists), and the novel itself became the most famous unread book on the planet. Those who did read it were unavoidably preoccupied by the Mahound chapters. Blasphemy was denounced in the name of revealed truth, in the name of multicultural sensitivity, in the name of anti-ethnocentrism, and, implausibly, in the name of Marxism. Or it got an understandably muted defense on the grounds that the satirical romp through the Quran is Gibreel's dream and psychosis.

But the genius of this novel lies in the moral questioning that interweaves the Quranic parody and the mundane revenge tragedy. Rushdie tempers the apocalyptic possibilities of Blake's enlarged senses with Kant's enlarged mentality, the capacity "to put ourselves in thought in the place of everyone else."[8] Or, more precisely, with the novelistic version of the enlarged mentality: the web of perspectives, identifications, and empathies by which the "standpoint of others" is made palpable—and more stubbornly plural and unreconciled than Kantian universalism would wish. Unlike the monotheist who rejects all other religions as mere human creations, the novelistic parodist—puncturing, inverting, desacralizing sacred texts—affirms a human-all-too-human creativity, including humanity's prodigious invention of its many gods, angelic voices and burning bushes, redeemers, miracles, and taboos.

Saladin's metamorphosis into a goat incarnates his dehumanization at the hands of immigration cops and so expresses, unambiguously, Rushdie's satirical social commentary on British racism, but Saladin recovers from his metamorphosis only when envy causes him to imagine that Gibreel is the source of all his suffering: "Mr Saladin Chamcha himself, apparently restored to his old shape, mother-naked but of entirely human aspect and proportions, *humanized*—is there any option but to conclude?—by the fearsome concentration of his hate."[9] He is ready for revenge. Is his "falsity of self" the source of his evildoing?

No! Let's rather say an even harder thing: that evil may not be as far beneath our surfaces as we like to say it is.—That, in fact, we fall towards it *naturally*, that is, *not against our natures*.—And that Saladin Chamcha set out to destroy Gibreel Farishta because, finally, it proved easy to do; the true appeal

---

[8] Immanuel Kant, *Critique of Judgement*, trans. J. H. Bernard (New York: Hafner, 1966), 140 (sec. 40).

[9] *The Satanic Verses*, 294.

of being evil being the seductive ease with which one may embark upon that road.[10]

The brutalized being recovers his humanity in concentrated rage; suddenly humanized, he slides effortlessly into the banality of evil. Is our humanity forever caught in this vacillation? The novel asks that question in each of its intertwined tales. It asks it of Saladin and Gibreel, of the brutalized crowds that rise up in rage and burn their own neighbors, of prophets who conquer infidels, of visionaries large and small who dream of leading a revolt of the masses. The novel does not furnish an answer. It tries to make the question stick, most uncomfortably in the survival of Saladin, the story's least heroic character.

Salman Rushdie yokes together exuberant imagination and tragic realism as few other writers in our time. That is the form-giving innovation of his writing. To what does it give form? The answer lies I think in Rushdie's own cultural formation—a *Bildung* rare and yet resonant with the unsettled world of our time. Rushdie was brought up in the monotheism of Islam, but his imagination was quickened by the polytheism of Hinduism; he was torn from his beloved India by sectarianism and partition; ill-adapted to Pakistan, he adopted England to nurture his intellectual curiosity and artistic ambitions.

Monotheism and polytheism have ancient histories and modern avatars, East and West. Max Weber located the origins of capitalism in the ascetic monotheism of Protestantism and then saw the ultimate destiny of the West in the secular polytheism of our world of technical, economic, and bureaucratic rationalities, which dissolve all supreme values and leave only the plurality of human projects and aims. Rushdie's sensibility has traversed, is traversed by, the harsh monotheism and luxuriant polytheism of the Indian subcontinent and the profane polytheism of the West endlessly rocking between rationalism and nihilism: it is the experience of that unnamable reality that his novels shape and name.

———

Isn't *The Satanic Verses* an example of metafiction? And, if so, does that not make it quintessentially postmodernist? It is worth dissecting the term *metafiction* and the claim that it epitomizes postmodernism. Many American critics consider Thomas Pynchon the representative practitioner of

---

[10] Ibid., 427.

metafiction. In keeping with the modernist/postmodernist plot, they define fictions-about-fiction as a final break with the suppositions of realism. Metafiction defamiliarizes all mimetic conventions and lays bare the devices of fiction-making.

Pynchon's solipsistic heroes vainly search for meaning in a world of paranoically total order and conspiratorial power, rendering the realist hero's quest absurd and debunking the modernist hero's rich inner life. The narrative whips back and forth between the hero's paranoia and the system's conspiracy until it reaches its comic-apocalyptic finale. According to such readings, *The Crying of Lot 49* or *Gravity's Rainbow* is a philosophical fable of fractured consciousness and totalitarian terror told as self-conscious fabulation. I find such readings persuasive, but I do not find the fable very compelling and therefore do not find Pynchon's novels themselves very persuasive.

There are two problems. The first comes to light in Pynchon's readers themselves. What they claim to value, even identify with, is the Pychonesque hero's inability to secure a grasp of himself or of the sinister world that keeps undoing his search for meaning, identity, knowledge—and that is clearly the theme of the novels. But the enjoyment that his most avid readers exhibit demonstrates just the opposite: the novels furnish the initiate with a completely ordered view and encyclopedic knowledge of the world of the novels themselves. Pynchon readers are fans; the novels are the arcane but unmysterious knowledge of a literary lodge. Hence the second problem. What makes Pynchon's novels unpersuasive to anyone except a fan is that their diagnosis of our society and culture is very thin. In *The Crying of Lot 49*, for example, the historical and social references are potentially rich: Los Angeles and Southern California, real estate speculation, the new partnership of science and capital, right-wing extremism, Hollywood, suburbia, and the automobile and freeways. And yet the themes of solipsism and paranoia are not enough to organize all these elements into a social commentary.

But is it a social commentary? Am I not responding to the novel's social content rather than its metafictionality? Am I not looking for referentiality instead of textual reflexivity? Yes. But not because I am misreading the text. I want now to turn the tables on the theorists of metafiction by reclassifying Pynchon's writing. Consider its stylistic features: an improbable premise enabling satirical commentary, learnedness, the oscillation between lyrical and grotesque, philosophical and scatological styles, the heterogeneity of social types, lists and inventories, the stylized voice (drugged, frenetic, parodic), the juxtaposition of different types of discourse. *The Crying of Lot 49* and

Gravity's Rainbow are instances of Menippean satire, the genre that, as Bakhtin and Northrop Frye have both shown, has accompanied the main lines of development of the novel at least since *Gargantua and Pantagruel* and *Tristram Shandy*. Thomas Pynchon writes Menippean satire, bad Menippean satire.

I am not making this genre argument just to badmouth Pynchon. By reclassifying his writing we can see the resemblance to other Menippean satirists, many of whom he has influenced. For Menippean satire is a significant trend in contemporary writing. Among its most effective practitioners are Günter Grass, Orhan Pamuk, and Salman Rushdie. Rushdie pays hommage in *The Satanic Verses* to one of the ancient originators of the form, Apuleius, "Moroccan priest, AD 120–180 approx., colonial of an earlier Empire,"[11] whose *Golden Ass* furnishes the model for Saladin's transformation into a goat. Rushdie and others succeed where Pynchon fails precisely because of the relevance and depth of *their* social diagnoses. The Menippean satire is a mode of social commentary, not pure metatextuality. Pynchon's philosophical preoccupations are part of the form's tendency to present, in Frye's words, "a vision of the world in terms of a single intellectual pattern." Though paranoia is a single intellectual pattern par excellence, it is insufficient to the task of diagnosing American society.

Linda Hutcheon, in *A Poetics of Postmodernism*, introduces the hybrid category of "historiographic metafiction" with reference to E. L. Doctorow and others in an effort to link metafictional reflexivity and political consciousness. Her effort draws too close a connection between politics and parodic mimesis-breaking devices, as though the disruption of literary conventions were intrinsically a challenge to inequalities of gender, race, and class. The axiom that literary experiment and radical political consciousness are organically linked is an avant-gardist inheritance. The programmatic ambitions of the historical avant-gardes and Russian Formalism's fertile idea of defamilarization have bequeathed to criticism the assumption that the innovative artwork makes a radical break with previous art, ideally with all previous art. This assumption has exhausted its critical power. The fatigue shows in critics' repetitive use of words like *rupture, disruption, deconstruction, undoing, dismantling,* and *overturning* to describe all manner of stylistic trends.

When contemporary criticism equates innovation with form-breaking, it typically projects, as in its characterization of nineteenth-century realism, a caricature of the forms supposedly being broken (unified text, monologism, stable mimesis, integrated consciousness, and so on). However, innovation

---

[11] Ibid., 243.

is not in essence form-breaking, because innovative artworks are form-*making* and actively create conventions. Startling formal inventions can seldom be explained by their break with literary tradition or assault on readers' expectations.

In a penetrating analysis of *Ulysses*, Franco Moretti shows in *Modern Epic* that Joyce's innovation of stream-of-consciousness was neither the first nor most radical attempt among writers of the period, but it is the one that survives. "And it survives because the selection process does not reward novelty as such . . . , but *novelty that is able to solve problems.* Moving beyond the horizon of expectations of the period, in itself, is of little interest. Constructing *a new perceptual and symbolic horizon*: this is indeed a comprehensible undertaking, and one with clear social value."[12] Every formal invention in Moretti's account is a cluster of existential, formal, and historical imperatives and possibilities that the writer wrings into a stylistic transformation. Its actual effects on readers and writers are in turn affected by later literary and social history. Nothing in Bürger's idea of modernism as institutionalization or in Lyotard's of postmodernism as unpresentability and dissension approaches the subtlety of such an analysis.

Add to this the fact that novelistic innovation is not always a matter of formal invention. Novelists also resuscitate older forms, as with Menippean satire in Grass, Rushdie, and Pamuk, and infuse them with new intentions. Milan Kundera develops the persuasive thesis in *The Art of the Novel* and *Testaments Betrayed* that several twentieth-century innovators—Kafka, Musil, Broch, Gombrowicz, and, today, Fuentes, Rushdie, and himself— reach back to the novel before the nineteenth century and find in Cervantes, Rabelais, Sterne, and Diderot formal and technical possibilities that answer to their own imperatives in a way the aesthetic of the nineteenth-century realists could not. "The point of this rehabilitation . . . is not a return to this or that retro style; nor is it a simple-minded rejection of the nineteenth-century novel; the point of the rehabilitation is more general: to *redefine* and *broaden* the very notion of the novel; to resist the *reduction* worked by the nineteenth century's aesthetic of the novel; to give the novel its *entire* historical experience for a grounding."[13]

Kundera's account of the spiraling history of the novel provides a rich alternative to the idea that twentieth-century literature is a series of breaks

---

[12] Franco Moretti, *Modern Epic: The World System from Goethe to García Márquez*, trans. Quintin Hoare (New York: Verso, 1996), 178.

[13] Milan Kundera, *Testaments Betrayed: An Essay in Nine Parts*, trans. Linda Asher (New York: HarperCollins, 1995), 75.

with tradition or that it was innovative only in its avant-gardist moments. He also eschews the modernist/postmodernist plot, breaching the great divide by identifying a continuity that runs from Kafka to Rushdie, while leaving open the inquiry into other strands that would bring out other continuities and conflicts in the 'past century of the novel. Such an inquiry rejects the search for a single principle of artistic innovation or a single aesthetic that would be the cipher of society as a whole.

Once innovation in the novel is seen to include both formal innovations and renovated forms, the concept of innovation no longer fits the avant-gardist and formalist account of making-it-new. Nonetheless, there is experimental fiction, and this strand too has to be included in any account of the history and aesthetics of novelistic innovation. Moreover, there is no doubt that newness is an intrinsic part of modern aesthetic experience. To rethink what newness is requires, then, a conception that will include formal invention, renovation, and experiment—and at the same time recognize the persistence of the realist imperative.

Innovations produced by experimental fiction profoundly influence the development of the novel without necessarily being part of vanguard political-artistic movements and without constituting *the* source or epitome of innovation. Without Borges, Beckett, Cortázar, and Calvino the contemporary novel would not be what it is. Their experimentalism does not reject or break with novelistic traditions so much as it interrogates them. These writers analyze the art of the novel novelistically, probing its techniques, means of representation, and forms.

Beckett's *Texts for Nothing*, published in 1958, the same year as *The Unnamable*, contains thirteen short texts each of which limns the outer boundary of some aspect of storytelling. In "Text for Nothing 4," it is the relation of author and character that Beckett x-rays. Creating characters is so essential to making a novel that it might define the genre, as it does for Kundera: "NOVEL. The great prose form in which an author thoroughly explores, by means of experimental selves (characters), some great themes of existence."[14] Although the methods of creating character are infinite (at least in the sense that, historically speaking, they have not yet proved to be finite), the process seems to oscillate between two poles. Novelists sometimes stress

---

[14] Milan Kundera, *The Art of the Novel*, trans. Linda Asher (New York: Harper and Row, 1988), 142.

a sense of identification—as when Flaubert says, "Madame Bovary, c'est moi"—as though the writer's own subjectivity "goes into" the making of a character. At other times writers testify that their characters are hardly known to them until the novel takes shape or that characters acquire a "will of their own" in the course of the writing, as though their acts and speech emanate from within themselves.

Identification and estrangement, projection and autonomy—Beckett's experimental text exposes this oscillation by reversing the relation between author and character. The nameless first-person narrator denounces the author's invention of him. The author is reduced to *he*, like a third-person character, while the character, in the role of the speaking *I*, protests, "If at least he would dignify me with the third person, like his other figments":

> Where would I go, if I could go, who would I be, if I could be, what would I say, if I had a voice, who says this, saying it's me? Answer simply, someone answer simply. It's the same old stranger as ever, for whom alone accusative I exist, in the pit of my inexistence, of his, of ours, there's a simple answer. It's not with thinking he'll find me, but what is he to do, living and bewildered, yes, living, say what he may. Forget me, know me not, yes, that would be the wisest, none better able than he. Why this sudden affability after such desertion, it's easy to understand, that's what he says, but he doesn't understand. I'm not in his head, nowhere in his old body, and yet I'm there, for him I'm there, with him, hence all the confusion. That should have been enough for him, to have found me absent, but it's not, he wants me there, with a form and a world, like him, in spite of him, me who am everything, like him who is nothing. And when he feels me void of existence it's of his he would have me void, and vice versa, mad, mad, he's mad. . . . He thinks words fail him, he thinks because words fail him he's on his way to my speechlessness, to being speechless with my speechlessness, he would like it to be my fault that words fail him. He tells his story every five minutes, saying it is not his, there's cleverness for you. He would like it to be my fault that he has no story, of course he has no story, that's no reason for trying to foist one on me.[15]

Identification ("he wants me there, with a form and a world, like him . . ."). *Estrangement* ("It's the same old stranger as ever, for whom alone accusative I exist, in the pit of my inexistence . . ."). *Projection* ("He would like it to be my fault that he has no story . . ."). *Autonomy* ("Forget me, know me not, yes, that would be the wisest").

---

[15] Samuel Beckett, *Stories and Texts for Nothing* (New York: Grove Press, 1967), 91–92.

To reveal these contradictory moments inherent in creating character, Beckett experiments with the linguistic possibilites latent in what structuralism called "shifters." "He wants me there": *me* refers to the object of the action in the *énoncé* (the narrated event) but at the same time indicates the subject of the *énonciation* (the speech event), while *he* refers to the subject of the *énoncé* but is an object of the *énonciation*. The shifters keep straight the relation between the speaker and everyone else in the tale. Literary convention permits us to respond to a first-person narrator *as though* (that is why it is a convention) he chooses his own words while we remain perfectly aware that the actual subject of the linguistic act is the author. By twisting the narrator-writer relation one more turn, making the narrator the writer and the writer the character, Beckett does not deconstruct this literary artifice so much as exploit its ability to disclose the emptiness around which his own novels churn: the writer's desire for his own project to wear itself out in speechlessness is endlessly thwarted, while the characters—who are without being or speech—keep speaking and existing.

In Beckett's aesthetic, words and figments deconceal a void they cannot stop concealing in words and figments; the sense of predicament is made to pervade the elemental workings of language and storytelling. This aesthetic has influenced novelists as diverse as Carlos Fuentes and Paul Auster, Kazuo Ishiguro and Raymond Carver, without creating imitators. Therein lies the rich, twofold legacy of experimental fiction: it brings to light means and techniques of expression that prove indispensible to other novelists' work, while challenging those novelists' most intimate relation to the practice of writing.

Borges, Cortázar, and Calvino have similarly stirred wonder and alarm in the world of literature. Borges's mastery of textual paradox is well known, but just as significant perhaps is his fascination with the labyrinth as a metaphor for the workings of narrative; allusions to the Arab world abound in his stories, and he takes the intertwining structure of *The Thousand and One Nights* as a model for his minimalist marvels. The arabesque structure also organizes Calvino's *If on a winter's night a traveler*, a novel of permuting stories that is at the same time a work of narrative theory as playful as Roland Barthes's *S/Z*. Cortázar, like Beckett, picks up his linguistic needle and treads the story line back through itself, as in "The Night Face Up," the story of a man knocked unconscious in a motorcycle accident who awakes from surgery having dreamed he is an ancient Indian hunted down for sacrifice only to discover that he is in fact lying on the sacrificial altar and "that the marvelous dream had been the other, absurd as all dreams are—a dream in which he was going through the strange avenues of an astonishing city, with green and red lights that burned without fire or smoke, on an enormous metal insect that whirred away between his legs."[16] It is not hard to imagine how the narrative labyrinths of Borges and Calvino or the oneiric loop-the-loop of Cortázar might well have found their way to Rushdie's gargantuan satirical arabesque.

I couched my description of Beckett's prose in structuralist terms, not because they necessarily provide the best linguistic account, but rather because of the affinity between structuralism and literary experiment. Since early in the twentieth century, writers and theorists alike have discovered ways of alienating language—creatively as well as analytically—from its embeddedness in everyday speech and social discourses. The connection was overt in the case of Russian formalism and the early avant-gardes and, later, with Barthes and the *nouveau roman*. Leaving aside Bakhtin's formidable challenge to structuralist procedure, the very capacity to alienate *langage* into *langue* is a definitive achievement of twentieth-century thought and literature. It is an enabling alienation. Formalism is an intrinsic possibility of twentieth-century literature, linguistics, and criticism.

Having said that, I do not think that formalism can explain formalism. The estrangement of language from its concrete uses is the continuation of a process inaugurated in Western culture as far back as the Renaissance, namely, the separation of artistic materials and techniques from their birthplace in ritual and religion and their foster home in theology and metaphysics. T. W. Adorno, elaborating on Max Weber, called this complex tendency "aesthetic rationality." I stress that it is a tendency because it was not a punctual event historically and, more important, is ongoing, first, because the artistic process never fully separates itself from nonartistic imperatives and, second, because every realized artwork sets itself back into the heterogeneous world from which its creation separated it. Beckett's work underscores this last point: his writing alienates the techniques of storytelling to an extreme, not in order to produce a pure form but to interrogate the being and the void of literary creativity.

———

Modernity is the vexing term behind the debate over postmodernism. As much as the debate has enlivened philosophy and social theory since the mid-1980s, it bogs down in efforts to define modernity by means of some intrinsic

———

[16] Julio Cortázar, *End of the Game and Other Stories*, trans. Paul Blackburn (New York: Pantheon, 1967), 76.

norm or substantive characteristic. There is irony in this, since almost all parties to the debate begin with the idea that modernity is postmetaphysical culture in the sense that modern society does not cohere through some shared mythology or religion as premodern societies do. Modernity is a world without an essence.

In 1915, Georg Lukács introduced *The Theory of the Novel* with a poignant description of the distance between the worlds of modern Europeans and ancient Greeks:

> The circle whose closed nature was the transcendental essence of their life has, for us, been broken; we cannot breathe in a closed world. We have invented the productivity of the spirit: that is why the primaeval images have irrevocably lost their objective self-evidence for us, and our thinking follows the endless path of an approximation that is never fully accomplished. We have invented the creation of forms: and that is why everything that falls from our weary and despairing hands must always be incomplete. . . .
>
> Our world has become infinitely large and each of its corners is richer in gifts and dangers than the world of the Greeks, but such wealth cancels out the positive meaning—the totality—upon which their life was based.[17]

Lukács took Greek culture as the counterpoint to modernity, following a tradition of enlightened German thought that runs from Goethe and Schiller to Weber and Freud, in order specifically to account for the fact that the modern novel inherits its form from ancient epic but at the same time *creates* form in a no longer "rounded world."[18] Lukács interprets modern aesthetic rationality in these postmetaphysical terms: "Art . . . has thus become independent: it is no longer a copy, for all the models are gone; it is a created totality, for the natural unity of the metaphysical spheres has been destroyed."[19] He then advances the thesis that has resonated in novel theory ever since: "The novel form is, like no other, an expression of this transcendental homelessness. . . . The novel is the epic of a world that has been abandoned by God."[20]

Lukács soon turned away from the consequences of nihilism originally explored in *The Theory of the Novel*, saying later that the book "was written

---

[17] Georg Lukács, *The Theory of the Novel*, trans. Anna Bostock (Cambridge, Mass.: MIT Press, 1971), 33–34.

[18] Ibid., 33.

[19] Ibid., 37.

[20] Ibid., 41, 88.

[in 1914–15] in a mood of permanent despair over the state of the world."[21] The October Revolution dissipated that despair in 1917. Marxism furnished Lukács with a new interpretation of modernity: capitalism is but the first phase of the modern productivity of the spirit, creating unlimited wealth with its means of production and at the same time alienating and impoverishing man with its relations of production. And Leninism furnished him with a substitute for the lost metaphysical roundness: proletarian class-consciousness, imputed to the masses but firmly possessed by the Leninist party, is a standpoint from which society in its alienated totality can be known and its transformation into a new, integrated whole envisioned. Armed with an ideology to replace myth and religion, Lukács then reread novelistic realism: the novel's artistically created totality does reflect the world's totality, like ancient epic, while transcendence, in the modern guise of utopian expectation, resides in the Future rather than with the gods. For this later Lukács, the novel's cognitive mapping is the hedge against nihilism.

I am a partisan of the early Lukács. The despair that motivated him to write *The Theory of the Novel* does not attenuate his insights. On the contrary, it enabled him to begin thinking through the relation between nihilism and the aesthetics of the novel. Since modern society lacks myth, religion, or theology to bind its members together, since it leaves values and ideals to the individual's inner psychological world, the outside world is unable "to find either the form of a totality for itself as a whole, or any form of coherence for its own relationship to its elements and their relationship to one another: in other words, *the outside world cannot be represented.* Both the parts and the whole of such an outside world defy any forms of directly sensuous representation."[22] Lacking intrinsic meanings and purposes, the social totality cannot be represented in its human dimension; it does, to be sure, attain lifeless representation in the empirical and statistical discourse of the social sciences, which, as Lukács learned from Max Weber, separate fact from value. But how can the parts and whole of outside reality attain a living human representation? How can they be represented "sensuously," that is, artistically, in image and story? "They acquire life only when they can be related either to the life-experiencing interiority of the individual lost in their labyrinth, or to the observing and creative eye of the artist's subjectivity: when they become objects of mood or reflexion."[23] Romanticism epitomized

---

[21] Ibid., 12.

[22] Ibid., 79 (my emphasis).

[23] Ibid.

the latter course; the novel realized the former. The outside world is made apparent in novelistic representation, according to Lukács, only in the jagged, contradictory, contrapuntual resistances that the protagonist encounters as he attempts to realize his own meanings and purposes. The "inner form of the novel" allows social reality to be, to use one of his favorite words, *glimpsed.* The novel is not a cipher, mirror, or cognitive map of totality. *The outside world cannot be represented.* That is why we have novels.

The novel's inner form belongs to the nihilism of modernity. The later Lukács looked to Marxism to overcome nihilism; the early Lukács faced nihilism, but he approached it in nostalgic counterpoint to Greek antiquity. Is it possible to face nihilism without looking to overcome it? to understand it without nostalgia for a lost world of meaning and purpose? to interpret the nihilism of modern culture as something to be embraced in philosophy and politics, not transcended?

I am going to suggest the direction of that effort by taking up a few themes in Heidegger that are relevant to aesthetic innovation in the novel, beginning with how he rethinks what newness is in art. Heidegger makes a breakthrough in aesthetic theory when he shifts the focus away from form in itself in accounting for the demand for newness implicit in aesthetic judgment. Kant inaugurated modern aesthetics by arguing that the judgment "this is beautiful" does not result from measuring an artwork's form against an existing standard; on the contrary, we always have to derive the "rule"—what makes this beautiful—from the particular artwork. The beautiful appears unexpectedly, gratuitously, unprecedently. Heidegger rethinks the origin of this unprecedentedness. He attributes it to the power of the artwork to make an "entity" present for the first time, to show the hitherto concealed "truth" of a being. The artwork is an event rather than mere form or representation. The god in ancient Athens does not exist before it is made present in the temple hewn from stone. The truth of the peasant's shoes, the essence of their usefulness in the world and experience of the peasant, comes into being only in Van Gogh's painting. Restated in less grand terms, the artwork lets something appear—lets something be seen, heard, told—*for the first time.*

An aesthetic judgment that intrinsically demands newness is a decidedly *modern* experience, yet Heidegger's elegant examples in "The Origin of the Work of Art" conjure up premodern worlds: the ancient dwellings of the gods, the rounded world of the peasant.[24] What is behind Heidegger's hesitation? Gianni Vattimo sheds light on this question. According to him, there is an ambivalence in Heidegger's project of overcoming metaphysics and of understanding Being without recourse to some transcendental realm where Being (Platonic Ideas, God, Supreme Values) resides. On the one hand, this task seems to go against the grain of modern nihilism, which for Heidegger stems from modern technology's "reduction of Being to values"[25] as it turns the earth and human beings themselves—that is, the whole of beings—into material for production and objects of calculation. Here Heidegger associates modernity and technology with metaphysics, Man's long-standing endeavor to reduce Being to a being (in the sense, for example, that theology reduces Being to the entity God the Father or the Creator). On the other hand, the nihilism of technology seems to be the "planetary event" that, like Heidegger's own philosophical project, *is* overcoming metaphysics, which is why, Vattimo argues, the later Heidegger keeps looking for a way to distinguish techno-calculative thinking from the philosopher's "meditative" thinking and yet not set them in antagonistic opposition to one another.

Giving a Marxian twist to Heidegger, Vattimo says that nihilism is "the reduction of Being to exchange-value";[26] then, giving a Heideggerian twist to Marx, he says that this reduction cannot be reversed: the dream of revolutionizing society into a realm of use-values and unalienated labor is mythic. Philosophy's new bearings must, Vattimo argues, give up the desire to rescue Being from its dissolution in exchange-values. Nihilism "reaches its extreme form . . . by consuming Being in value. This is the event that finally makes it possible, and necessary, for philosophy today to recognize that nihilism is our (only) chance."[27]

Novelists long ago jumped into the abyss where philosophers hesitated to leap. Kundera suggests that Heidegger missed something in not seeing that "the founder of the Modern Era is not only Descartes," who initiated modern philosophy's "forgetting of Being," but also Cervantes, "with [whom] a great European art took shape that is nothing other than the investigation of this forgotten being." And precisely as regards the "great existential themes

---

[24] Martin Heidegger, "The Origin of the Work of Art," in *Poetry, Language, Thought*, trans. Albert Hofstader (New York: Harper and Row, 1971), 17–87.

[25] Gianni Vattimo, "An Apology for Nihilism," in *The End of Modernity: Nihilism and Hermeneutics in Modern Culture*, trans. Jon R. Snyder (Baltimore: Johns Hopkins University Press, 1988), 20.

[26] Ibid., 21.

[27] Ibid., 23.

Heidegger analyzes in *Being and Time*—considering them to have been neglected by all earlier European philosophy,"

> with Cervantes and his contemporaries, [the novel] inquires into the nature
> of adventure; with Richardson, it begins to examine "what happens inside,"
> to unmask the secret life of feelings; with Balzac, it discovers man's rooted-
> ness in history; with Flaubert, it explores the *terra* previously *incognita* of the
> everyday; with Tolstoy, it focuses on the intrusion of the irrational in human
> behavior and decisions. It probes time: the elusive past with Proust, the elu-
> sive present with Joyce. With Thomas Mann, it examines the role of the
> myths from the remote past that control our present actions. Et cetera. Et
> cetera.[28]

Kundera in effect turns the theme of the "forgetting of Being (*Sein*)" against the later Heidegger's anti-Humanism, loaded up as it is with listening for the footstep of the disappearing gods, and takes it back to Heidegger's earlier analysis of *Dasein* (human existence) to affirm the pluralistic lowercase humanism and messy individualism of the novel.

Earlier I hijacked Heidegger's idiom in saying that the aesthetic of Beckett's *Texts for Nothing* lies in the venturing of words and figments to deconceal the void they conceal. Beckett pushes Heideggerian aesthetics farther than Heidegger himself. Heidegger wrenches a premodern, perhaps antimodern attitude from his own radically modern aesthetics. In the Van Gogh interpretation, the painting deconceals the truth of "equipment," that is, the pure use-value of the peasant's shoes as they bind the rural lifeworld to the earth it husbands. (I note in passing the marvelous deflation of this interpretation by the art historian Meyer Schapiro, who demonstrates that the painter was actually portraying his own very urban boots lying on the floor of his Parisian studio!) Heidegger values modern art insofar as it reappropriates the fading echoes of a meaning-endowed World. In the same vein, his extraordinary interpretation of Hölderin and Rilke puts poetry outside the reduction of Being to exchange-value: "Their song does not solicit anything to be produced."[29]

Things are different with the novel. The novel in its origins is liberated from the expectation that a meaning-imbued world could inspire and nourish its form-making, yet its primary imperative is to refer to the world, render

---

[28] Kundera, *The Art of the Novel*, 4–5.
[29] Heidegger, "What Are Poets For?" in *Poetry, Language, Thought*, 138.

it artistically, represent it sensuously (according to the various idioms of modern aesthetics).

Moreover, its very coming into the world is attended by a nihilistic midwife. The novel is commodity form and artistic form wrapped in one, the first type of artwork in which the object the artist creates (the novel) is indissociable from the object manufactured to be sold (the book). In making that argument about "print capitalism" in *Imagined Communities*, Benedict Anderson shows, though it is probably not his exact intention, how the novel confounds the use-value/exchange-value distinction developed by Marx and implicit in Heidegger.[30] The novel enters the world as "use-value" and "exchange-value" at the same time. Its public always manifests itself at once as a readership and a market. Its aesthetic validity cannot therefore lie purely in negating exchange-value, since "the reduction of Being to exchange-value" enables the creation of the artistic form itself. The art of the novel is not some pure countermovement to nihilism and reification, which helps explain the antipathy toward the whole genre shared by Heidegger, Adorno, and the historical avant-gardes.

The novel thrives on the impurity of its forms. And as the scope of Beckett's influence—extending to minimalists and Menippeans, postcolonial fabulators and trailer-park realists—attests, the novel also thrives on the plurality of its practitioners' lifeworlds and intentions. Impure forms and plural uses do not sit well with fundamental ontology, or neo-Marxism. Heidegger and Adorno both cast the poet's purposes as *in essence* at odds with the engineer's, the scientist's, and the entrepreneur's. Peter Sloterdijk knocks the props from under this philosophical distinction. Starting from the claim that "everyone today can easily observe the increasing role of the artificial in the existential universes of modern times," he argues that the philosophical tradition has always been unsettled by the artificial, because "one cannot say in a language of Being what machines, sign-systems, and artworks are 'by nature.' It seems to be in their nature to break with what nature typically is."[31] From this perspective, "inventors, artists, and entrepreneurs" share in the spirit of modernity; their projects are "an unwinding of the void":[32] "Nature and Being have lost their ontological monopoly: they have found themselves

---

[30] Cf. Benedict Anderson, *Imagined Communities: Reflections on the Origins and Spread of Nationalism*, rev. ed. (New York: Verso, 1991), 37 ff.

[31] Peter Sloterdijk, *L'heure du crime et le temps de l'oeuvre d'art*, trans. Olivier Mannoni (Paris: Calmann-Lévy, 2000), 29–30. (I have translated from this French translation of Sloterdijk's German text.)

[32] Ibid., 34.

challenged and replaced by a series of artificial creations coming from the void and by the emergence of a postnatural world issuing from the will. . . . Nihilism, as known to us now, represents but the flip-side of creativity and the faculty of willing—and what modernity would accept being denied its birthright to a creative life and projects born of the will?"[33]

Contemporary thought keeps returning to the nihilism of modernity, perhaps because its "essence" must forever escape our grasp. I have returned to Lukács's theory of the novel ninety years later because it captures better than most later theories the relation between innovation and nihilism in the novel. Kundera returns to the early Heidegger to affirm that novelistic explorations of human existence embody the "wisdom of uncertainty" better than philosophy does; Sloterdijk and Vattimo return to the later Heidegger in search of an "accomplished nihilism" that can assert values without needing a supreme value and judge meanings without hearing the voice of God. In a sense, we keep reinventing the wheel that Max Weber invented a little before Lukács and Heidegger, with tools supplied by Nietzsche: modernity inaugurates a world of projects without a metaphysical compass, a world at once nihilistic and polytheistic. "The strength of permanent modernity," writes Sloterdijk, "lies in the impossibility of exhausting the void."[34]

———

How, then, do we understand innovation in the novel? The modern aesthetic imperative to innovate seems to combine two forces that are difficult to distinguish except hypothetically: on the one hand, innovation is art as will-to-power (making-it-new, a project, the unwinding of the void); on the other hand, innovation is a crisis-ridden search for the means of expressing the relentlessly changing reality of a world devoid of meaning (exploration, experiment, glimpse, deconcealing). My refusal to privilege any one aspect of novelistic innovation—formal invention, the rediscovery of early forms, or experimental writing—is meant to acknowledge this perpetual ambivalence in the source of innovation. Aesthetic judgment—valuation—cannot rely on the newness of forms as such because their newness can only be judged in relation to what it is they "glimpse" or "deconceal." Nor can aesthetic judgment and criticism anchor in the supposition that genuine art is inherently antagonistic to technology, reification, or commodification; the novel befuddles the very attempt to separate artistic value and exchange-

———

[33] Ibid., 36–37.
[34] Ibid., 40.

value because its artistic form *is* its commodity form, its readership *is* a market.

Literary criticism has to learn to pursue all its essential activities—understanding, judging, and valuing—without a metaphysical compass. Historical analysis and social criticism face a similar predicament. Two images come to mind to suggest what is at stake. The first involves the stars, the second junk.

"Happy are those ages when the starry sky is the map of all possible paths—ages whose paths are illuminated by the light of the stars."[35] Thus begins Lukács's meditation on the rounded world of the ancients. We too have the stars, but our scientific knowledge contradicts, and alters, our perception of them; the stars are not simultaneous in the sky, since the lights arriving to our eyes come from stars "separated by incalculable epochs."[36] This image is the basis of the extraordinary passage with which Carlos Fuentes concludes *The Death of Artemio Cruz*. The passage I am about to quote is in the second person—*you* is Artemio Cruz. Who is speaking? The voice is indeterminately the protagonist's own conscience, the author's sometimes aggressive taunting of his protagonist, and the lost voice of the individuals and masses whom the protagonist has crushed in his relentless pursuit of power. The amalgamated voice addresses Artemio Cruz, the seventy-year-old man lying on his deathbed and the adventurous thirteen-year-old boy staring at the sky six decades earlier:

> The light you view is ancient, not that which in the now of star-time is racing away from the star: you have baptized the star with your stare. Dead in origin, it will still be alive in your eyes. Lost, calcined, fountain of light that now has no place of birth yet will nevertheless go on traveling toward the eyes of a boy who will live in the night of a different time, another time. Time that fills itself with vitality, with actions, ideas, but that remains always the inexorable flux between the past's first landmark and the future's last signpost. Time that will exist only in the reconstruction of isolated memory, in the flight of isolated desire. Time that, once it loses the opportunity to live, is forever wasted.[37]

What makes this image of temporality pertinent to our reflection is that it is a condensation of Fuentes' novel's entire structure. The significant chapters

---

[35] Lukács, *The Theory of the Novel*, 29.

[36] Carlos Fuentes, *The Death of Artemio Cruz*, trans. Sam Hileman (New York: Farrar, Straus, and Giroux, 1964), 302.

[37] Ibid., 302–3.

in Artemio Cruz's life are told in extended third-person narratives, each titled by the date of the central episode and presented out of chronological order (1941: July 6; 1919: May 26; 1913: December 4; 1924: June 3; etc.). In chronological order, they narrate an individual life that stays in step with each political victor in twentieth-century Mexican history; in their achronological order, they ramify the second-person fragments of "conscience" and first-person fragments of the dying man's final interior monologue. This structuring principle transforms the linear history of modern Mexico into a fractured star-time whose separated moments reach the corrupt old man as though simultaneously; conversely, it transforms the man's dying self-perception into the continual echo of all those who were defeated and lost in the ruling party's rise to total power and illegitimate wealth. The novel finds form without the guidance of the starry sky's constellations. Rather, the "inexorable flux" of memory and desire gives the novel its form—and at the same time its force as social commentary.

The second image is of junk. Sloterdijk likens our attempt to understand contemporary history to contemplating a metropolis today: the city is a site of ceaseless inventions, projects, investments, and at the same time it is layer upon layer of the ambiguous achievements, detritus, and garbage of past projects. History cannot be deciphered via any of the metaphysical schemes: not by the discredited myths of progress, rationalist or avant-gardist; not by Schelling's reassuring idea that everything that exists bears witness to past human freedom; not by the utopian expectation that the new society is gestating in the womb of the old; not by the hope of mastering the creativity-nihilism of modernity. Historical understanding and social criticism have to peer into the present's stratified temporality and judge what to save in the midst of the relentless launching of new, unmasterable projects.

So, junk and the stars—both images suggest the nihilism and polytheism of the modern world, a world made of creativity and debris, an unsheltered world unguided by transcendent values. These images also suggest that human history is unmastered time, indeed the temporality of nonmastery. Once again my argument has spiraled back to the early Lukács, for was not *that*—the temporality of nonmastery—his very definition of the novel? He came to see it as his untenable despair; we are beginning to see it as our only chance.

———

Important as the philosophical reflection on modernity is, it is not sufficient to explain modernity. Modernity as nihilism has to be matched by another, more historical and sociological sense of modernity. The empirical face of modernity is *modernization*, and its salient features can be readily identified: industrialization, urbanization, and the emergence of the masses. The concept of modernity will lapse back into fruitless abstraction unless we recognize that there is no model modernity. Modernization has befallen and transformed Nigeria and Mexico, France and Russia, Indonesia and China, but they do not experience modernity in the same way. The economic-political regime that directs—or forces—modernization has historically been as varied as liberal capitalism, state-socialism, Western colonialism, and communist imperialism, and today includes postcolonial democracies and dictatorships, postcommunist nationalisms, and even Islamic fundamentalism. Yet almost inevitably the novel emerges in this process as an important literary genre, responding to the experience of crisis and transformation. The challenge faced by novel theory is to establish a cogent, open field of inquiry into *comparative modernities.*

Consider Fuentes and Chinua Achebe. Measured by their impact on the literature of their respective continents and on world literature, they are unquestionably innovators in the contemporary novel. And yet *The Death of Artemio Cruz* and *Things Fall Apart*, published in 1962 and 1958, respectively, cannot possibly be lumped together as regards their style, form, or purpose. Add to this, if evidence is still needed that the modernist/postmodernist plot falsifies the history of twentieth-century fiction, the fact that 1958 also saw the appearance of Beckett's *Texts for Nothing* and *The Unnamable* and the American publication of Nabokov's *Lolita*. Achebe does not, like Fuentes, draw lessons from Joyce and Faulkner; he shares none of Beckett's or Nabokov's textual playfulness. What then makes *Things Fall Apart* such an extraordinary achievement? Paul Valéry gave a succinct formula for the goal of criticism: "to discover which problem the author posed himself (knowingly or not) and to find whether he solved it or not." So, what problem does Achebe pose for himself?

He sets out to chronicle how the Igbo people and their culture underwent the inaugural catastrophe of colonization with the arrival of British missionaries, armed forces, and administrators. His chronicle has to be written against the grain of British chronicles. At the very end of the story, Achebe signals, with restrained irony, his work's contentiousness: the District Commissioner intends to write a memoir, *The Pacification of the Primitive Tribes of the Lower Niger*, and chronicle—"Perhaps not a whole chapter but a reasonable paragraph, at any rate. . . . One must be firm in cutting out details"[38]—the curious story of Okonkwo's suicide. As Achebe explains in

---

[38] Chinua Achebe, *Things Fall Apart* (London: Heinemann, 1958), 148.

the recently published lectures *Home and Exile*, he wrote his novel against the massive tradition of British literature on Africa, exemplified for him by Joyce Cary's *Mister Johnson*, which happened to be the school assignment that prompted him and his classmates to their first intellectual rebellion against falsehoods about their own people. As a "beginning of the reclamation of the African story,"[39] *Things Fall Apart* wryly avoids direct encounter with Europe's storytellers; instead, the colonizers' garrulousness is boiled to the District Commissioner's one ignorant paragraph about the rich and tragic story the reader has just finished.

To create that story Achebe, like every historical novelist, faces the problem of reconstructing a world and experience he knows only indirectly. His distance and bond have a specific shape. In *Home and Exile* he tells of his family's return in 1935, when he was five, to his father's native town of Ogidi; a Christian convert and missionary, the father had left in 1904. Achebe recalls the many "conversations and disagreements" during visits from his father's friends and largely non-Christian family, from which "I learned much of what I know and have come to value about my history and culture," including the traditional society's cosmology and gods.[40] Okonkwo, the tragic protagonist of *Things Fall Apart*, belongs to Achebe's grandfather's or great-grandfather's generation, while the story of Okonkwo's son Nwoye has the broad outlines of Achebe's own father's religious conversion and estrangement from the cosmological patrimony. The young novelist bridges the historical gap by melding narrative forms that no one before him had imagined could be put together: the wisdom narratives of African proverbs and folktales; the story line of Greek tragedy; the discourse of Western ethnography; and the psychological realism of a son's rejection of his father's world.

The ethnographic discourse reflects, I think, Achebe's own estrangement (by religion, schooling, and language) from the ancestral world of sixty or seventy years before, yet it also enables him to explore and convey the life-world of the Igbo, the fabric of their practices—farm and household, bride bargaining and marriage, meals and medicines, oracles and ceremonies, meetings and markets—all of which are told in the ethnographer's mixed idiom of observer and participant. For example: "The land of the living was not far removed from the domain of ancestors. There was coming and going between them, especially at festivals and also when an old man died, because an old man was very close to the ancestors. A man's life from birth to

---

[39] Chinua Achebe, *Home and Exile* (New York: Oxford University Press, 2000), 72.
[40] Ibid., 11.

death was a series of transition rites which brought him nearer and nearer to his ancestors."[41]

Beyond ethnographic recording, Achebe uses the grammar of Igbo practices and symbols as the expressive vehicle of his psychological realism. Okonkwo's inner life is explored in the community's proverbial and sacred languages. For example: "He had been cast out of his clan like a fish on to a dry, sandy beach, panting. Clearly his personal god or *chi* was not made for great things. A man could not rise beyond the destiny of his *chi*. The saying of the elders was not true—that if a man said yea his *chi* also affirmed. Here was a man whose *chi* said nay despite his own affirmation."[42] All the actions that determine Okonkwo's destiny are likewise endowed with significance in the clan's symbolic world; they are offenses against the Mother Earth: he kills Ikemefuna, the young captive whom he has raised as a son, even though warned not to participate in the oracle-mandated sacrifice; he beats his wife during the Week of Peace; his gun explodes during Ezeudu's funeral, killing the dead man's son; and his own suicide is "an abomination . . . an offence against the Earth"[43] that prevents his burial.

Like the heroes of Greek tragedy, Okonkwo overvalues an essential communal value; his hard-earned masculinity as a wrestler, warrior, and farmer— intensified by the fear of being like his weak and lazy father—drives him to devalue and ultimately violate the clan's equally important feminine values. His fate, in that sense, is fully comprehended within his people's cosmology. But the rounded world of the villages of Umuofia faces another kind of force and violence that their symbolic order cannot comprehend—"the centre cannot hold; / Mere anarchy is loosed upon the world." The white man's courthouse and church tear at the communal fabric, until Okonkwo, shaken by his son's conversion and humiliated after he and five other leaders are taken before the District Commissioner's tribunal in handcuffs, finally rises up in rage and beheads the Commissioner's messenger. His action is questioned by the others, and Okonkwo, now knowing his clan "would not go to war,"[44] hangs himself.

Though Okonkwo has the role of ancient tragic hero, his actions propel his son Nwoye into living a modern drama. In Nwoye's eyes, the killing of Ikemefuna, who had become his closest companion and brother, remains

---

[41] Achebe, *Things Fall Apart*, 85.
[42] Ibid., 92.
[43] Ibid., 147.
[44] Ibid., 144.

incomprehensible. He does not find help in interpreting it through the communal cosmology, but suffers it as a wounding alienation: "As soon as his father walked in, that night, Nwoye knew that Ikemefuna had been killed, and something gave way inside him, like the snapping of a tightened bow."[45] It reminds him of the chill he felt when he "heard that twins were put in earthenware pots and thrown away in the forest."[46] When the missionaries first approach the people of Umuofia, the father laughs off "the mad logic of the Trinity,"[47] but the son is attracted to the new stories and symbols because they give meaning to his own inexplicable wound: "The hymn about brothers who sat in darkness and in fear seemed to answer a vague and persistent question that haunted his young soul—the question of the twins crying in the bush and the question of Ikemefuna who was killed. He felt a relief within as the hymn poured into his parched soul."[48] Nwoye soon joins the missionaries, and Okonkwo repudiates him.

Nwoye embodies the looming dissolution. In the words of one of the leaders, "All our gods are weeping. . . . Our dead fathers are weeping. . . . The sons of Umuofia . . . have broken the clan and gone their several ways."[49] Nwoye is also the figure in the story who links the writer—symbolically and autobiographically—to the broken history of the Igbo. Achebe honors the son's rebellion and at the same time exposes his complicity in the devastation. The novelist's vision of reality holds the two stories in one. "There is no story that is not true," says one of the characters reflecting on a murky old tale of "albinos" massacring a village in revenge for a killing. "The world has no end, and what is good among one people is an abomination among others."[50]

The aesthetic value of *Things Fall Apart* lies in its artistic solution to the problem it poses itself: to affirm Okonkwo's story *and* Nwoye's, without letting either one negate the other, in order to bestow their contrary truths on "the reclamation of the story of Africa." The emergence of the Nigerian novel on the eve of independence gave Achebe's artistic achievement its moral-political value as well; *Things Fall Apart* expressed how a people divided against themselves by their forced march into modernity might gather themselves together, understanding their history even as they saw that it

---

[45] Ibid., 43.
[46] Ibid.
[47] Ibid., 104.
[48] Ibid.
[49] Ibid., 143.
[50] Ibid., 99.

could not be undone. Achebe is today painfully aware how difficult that project has proved to be in forty years of independent Nigeria, making all the sharper his recollection in *Home and Exile* that his own commitment to the uniqueness of the individual and the relativity of every community's beliefs—a commitment that is necessary to the building of democracy and that Western liberals mistakenly proclaim a unique feature of Western modernity—was something he learned from Igbo tradition itself.

Achebe peers into the debris strewn by British imperialism and the novelties, salvaging from the living and remembered fragments of the Igbo cosmos values to affirm on the unlighted path of Nigerian modernity; neither a sentimentalist nor a rhetorician, the novelist does not offer a reassuring ledger of good and evil but reveals how they unfold in the experience of a tragic elder losing all he holds dear and a rebellious youth seeking uncertain redemption in the dissolution of tribal bonds. Like Rushdie, Achebe pulls on the contradictory threads of his own education and cultural formation—his *Bildung*—with its unique mix of languages and myths, of monotheism and polytheism, to weave from that skein of disparate discourses some new artistic form. *Things Fall Apart* weaves its "created totality" from African wisdom narratives, Greek tragedy, Western ethnography, and psychological realism; *The Satanic Verses* weaves its from social satire, Quranic parody, Aupeleian-Hindu-cinematic metamorphoses, and a comic revenge tragedy.

Innovations in the novel are a response to the unprecedented experiences and situations of human life in its varied modernities. The innovations themselves are therefore varied—in the artistic problems and solutions the novelists pose for themselves, in the imperatives that drive their creativity, and in the forms they wrest from the contradictory materials of their society and culture. When the early Lukács declared that modernity is "richer in gifts and dangers" than the ancient world, his own *Bildung*, like that of other classically educated Europeans in 1915, taught him to revere the ancient world of the Greeks and to find in his image of that lost world the measure of modernity. Rushdie and Achebe's learning has taught them to revere other worlds and seek other images to measure their modernities.

Novelists often do face the anguish and wisdom of uncertainty with suppler tools than philosophers. The postmodernism debate in philosophy has been plagued by the problem of knowing how to hold the gifts and dangers of modernity in a single conceptual glance. The modern era inaugurated the possibilities of Enlightenment, democracy, and collective responsibility for the future, *and* it gave rise to racism, slavery, colonialism, and the Holocaust. The impulse to attribute all the catastrophes of the modern era to antimodernity is no more convincing, though it is far less reckless, than the view that the catastrophes are the inevitable consequence of modernity and Enlightenment. Both views seek a philosophical anchor for a world without essence, as though the abyss were not bottomless, as though politics and art were not, of all human practices, the richest in gifts *and* dangers.

ESPEN AARSETH

Narrative Literature in the Turing Universe

> It's text. You READ it.
> No buttons. No links. No hyper-crap. Just because we
> got a grant to publish things in electronic format don't
> you go thinking that we're all charmed to pieces by this
> digital incursion.
> —JOHN McDAID, *Uncle Buddy's Phantom Funhouse*

Novels of Silicon

Jorge Luis Borges' short story "The Book of Sand" tells of a mysterious book, a monstrous volume of innumerable pages, without beginning or end. Page numbers make no sense, as page 999 is next to 40,514. The book is written in many different, strange languages, and the same page is never opened twice. The protagonist, having spent months in obsessive isolation trying to study this impossible object, finally gives up and decides to destroy it. But how? He could burn it, but a book of infinite pages might burn forever and therefore suffocate the earth with smoke. Finally he hides it on a random shelf in the National Library in Buenos Aires, a sure way to make a book disappear.

Some years ago, a joke started circulating on the World Wide Web: A web page proclaimed:

> You have reached
> the very last page
> of the Internet.
> We hope you have
> enjoyed your browsing.
> Enjoy the rest of your
> life.

This Web joke seems to make the inverse point of Borges' story: Just as Borges' book could never exist as a bound volume in the real world, the real World Wide Web cannot have a finite number of pages. Even at a given moment, dynamically generated pages make the number potentially infinite. In mathematical terms, "The Book of Sand" and the Web are the same, or at least equally infinite. But the Web exists, unlike its truly last page or Borges' monstrous book. As if to further prove Borges' point, there are now several dozen self-proclaimed "last pages of the Internet," any one of which may or may not be the original one.

Borges' story does not of course tell us anything about the Internet and the Web. Its allegory of the Web is accidental, an open text that touches something fundamental about writing that our new communication technologies have yet to make clear to us. But it does pose certain fundamental and strangely practical questions: What are the consequences of an infinite text? How does one read a book that never yields the same page twice? And, we may add, what are the consequences, if any, for literary theory and practice?

Digital writing has been with us for several decades now. Its impact on the publishing industry has been vast, and, as with Mark Twain's pioneering use of the typewriter a century before, literary authors have been quick to adopt this technological innovation. But have they changed their style or habits because of this new tool? Have writing and literature changed? It is probably far too early to answer this question reliably. After Gutenberg's invention, it took at least fifty years for books to develop and mature into something more than simulated manuscripts. Culture changes slowly, and we should expect a similar inertia now. But while we wait for another twenty to thirty years to pass, there are certain clues that can feed our speculative and very early analysis.

This essay will examine some of the efforts to create digital literature. The focus will be on narrative writing and its limits, with special attention to the idea of the novel. Are the parameters and perimeters of the novel medium-specific, or can novels exist happily in any medium? Clearly, novels need not exist only on paper but may thrive equally well as sound recordings, played back on cassette, CD, or MP3. In Ray Bradbury's *Fahrenheit 451*, novels were memorized and recounted by humans. And e-books, digital reading devices, are clear proof that computers can, in principle, provide an alternative medium to paper, although it remains to be seen whether they will be as successful as the paper versions, or even audio books. So far, the reading public has not been convinced. And how will the novel be influenced by the potentially much more advanced interface and rich functionality of the computer? Will it remain unchanged, give birth to a new literary breed, or perhaps to many? A number of problems arise, however, when we want to address what digital novels are, and could become.

First of all, there is the computer itself.

From the Book *to* E-book

The invention of the printing press in the fifteenth century did not change writers' methods and habits, or their technical infrastructure of pen, ink, and paper. Its wake provided authors with a distribution network and a market, but the creative process did not change, at least not materially. With the birth of the printing industry, the institutional and economic changes in the fifteenth and sixteenth centuries were profound, and undoubtedly this provided a "creative" turn as well as a professionalization and an industrialization of the "business" of writing.

However, the individual act of putting pen to paper was unaffected by Gutenberg's new media technology. Paper was invented in China around A.D. 100–200. After slowly traveling West on the Silk Road for centuries, the art of papermaking arrived in Europe a full millennium later. It remained, along with ink, the most supportive technology for writers until the 1870s. With the inventions of the typewriter, carbon copy, and the photocopier, however, the individual writer's situation was improved dramatically, while the printing industry still relied on slow evolution of the old methods. The personal computer and "desktop" revolution of the 1980s, on the other hand, changed both the writing, editing, and reproduction aspects of the industry, while the distribution, the market, and the material formats prevailed unchanged. Slowly, however, on-screen text and digital network distribution became alternatives to paper printing and distribution, and a decade ago the World Wide Web emerged as the heir apparent of the printing press and the publishing industry. But throughout, from Cervantes to Tom Clancy, a novel is a novel, at least materially. The printed, codex-format novel has shown remarkable stability and enjoyed a stable success through five hundred years.

Lately, however, the material foundation of the novel, printed paper, has been challenged by a new representational technology: digital text. In addition, a new distribution mechanism has challenged the traditional channels for selling and buying literary merchandise. But so far the economic, ergonomic and cultural conditions are not sufficiently evolved to make the digital media channels better alternatives to the good, old, printed book. Probably the most crucial missing aspect is a commercial infrastructure that will make professional writers embrace the distribution system with the same enthusiasm they welcomed the word processor. Ironically, the efficiency and low cost of digital distribution are the largest factors working against the inevitable transition from paper to digital literature. Illegal copying and distribution of copyrighted material are notoriously hard to avoid with today's technology, and until this problem is solved, the publishing industry will continue to use the expensive, but safer paper medium long past its technical sell-by date. Paper books were never safe from copying, however. With digital scanning and copying, and optical character recognition, protecting any kind of medium from piracy has become even more illusory than it used to be.

Given that printed paper sooner or later will be replaced by digital alternatives, it seems reasonable to expect that novels will migrate to some future form of computer screen. While print may never be completely gone, I predict that it will be dethroned in a mass-market sense, much as clay and stone inscriptions have been, although they are still in use for special purposes.

As the success of audio books (on tape or CD) has shown, there is nothing inherently paper-dependent, or even visual, about literary texts. Perhaps the preferred format of the future will be polymedial: a digitally encoded text that can be reproduced visually (with large print for the weak-sighted) or aurally, by the same reading device. The first generation of "e-book" readers of the late 1990s were not successful, because there was hardly any impetus for buying an expensive, single-purpose reading device (a severely impaired computer) with a limited library and a less than obvious future. For now, we should consider these pioneering but stunted gadgets as nothing more than proof of concept. But, given time, there is no reason why the computer should not overtake the printed codex as the chief literary medium.

Even a very primitive digital reading surface such as that of the PalmPilot, with a resolution of 160×160 pixels, or around 32×14 letters, affords enjoyable reading experiences. Reading a PalmPilot in bed, for instance, is considerably more comfortable than reading a thousand-page, brick-sized, two-pound book. But the crucial factor, perhaps not surprisingly, is the quality of the literary text being read. Just as bad print and cheap pulp did not stop readers from enjoying their favorite hacks in the past, the interface of the computer screen is certainly good enough for reading, if there is no better, lighter, or cheaper alternative within reach. Computers are already competing with TV as a medium for projecting moving pictures, so the much less demanding form of the black-and-white text (or the sound of the author's voice) will also find a digital home, especially given the increasingly better screens and new inventions such as the thin plastic sheets known as "digital ink."

Given this evolution from paper to digital, the main question becomes: Will the novel stay itself, or will it change to accommodate and exploit the possibilities afforded by the computer? And what can the computer bring to the literary equation? There is already substantial evidence that the novel *could* stay itself in a digital incarnation. But the computer offers a wealth of representational techniques that could potentially revolutionize literary communication. In the rest of this essay, some of these possibilities will be considered. But first, let us try to discover what is really different about the digital computer.

What's new, UNIVAC?

> If there is no software, there is only a heating device.
> —Niels Ole Finnemann

Myths and exaggerated claims about the computer have been with us since the middle of the past century, if not longer. The ideology of the "electronic brain" has been extremely pervasive—a collective dream that is hard to resist, because even the harshest critics are dependent on the infrastructure this technology provides. Technological determinism and the promise of the "new" make it hard to see the novelty that is actually there, beneath the layers of false claims and futuristic nonsense.

It is much too lazy of us to declare the computer revolutionary, and leave it at that. "The computer revolution" is the current culmination of a long line of communicatory *evolution*. Many, if not most, of the features of modern computing are simply more efficient forms of techniques and methods invented long ago. "The computer" is shorthand for a set of technologies that enhance the communicative traditions and practices of human culture, from accounting and archiving to personal correspondence, acts of government, public discourse, and aesthetic forms of expression. Civilization, and especially urban societies, have evolved in symbiotic parallel with writing and the inventions of new communication technologies. The computer represents the latest stage in a long process of social development, and is not, as some seem to think, a complete and radical break with what has gone before. There were calculating machines, information retrieval systems, and super-fast global communication long before the "Universal, Automatic Computer" (UNIVAC), and the fact that a new technology eventually would improve these important methods and operations should not surprise us.[1] Strong, specific needs in human society made "the computer revolution" happen, along with

---

[1] The UNIVAC, built by J. Presper Eckert and John Mauchly in 1951, was a "universal" machine designed to "handle both business and scientific problems" (Ceruzzi 1998, 18). Unlike previous computers, it did not rely on punched cards but used electromagnetic storage to feed its processor.

a number of other innovations. The claim that the computer will "revolution-ize" the very society that created it is therefore hard to believe. So far, it seems to have strengthened it, while at the same time made it more complex, just as the previous communication technologies did. And this holds true also for the field of writing and literature, and for art in general.

However, the digital media afforded by the computer must be new in some way. We should expect some unintended aesthetic consequences of such a formidable material change. There must be some element not seen before, some principle that is different enough to make a real difference, and not just an improvement. Let this be our working assumption. If we can pinpoint this novelty, we will be in a much better position to answer the question of what the computer will mean for literature and art.

Within the humanities, several attempts have been made to frame the principles of digital media. Computer semiotics, a recent branch of semiotic theory and analysis, was quick to claim that the computer is a "semiotic ma-chine," but did not offer substantial arguments to back up this claim.[2] The best work from this tradition, Peter Bøgh Andersen's *A Theory of Computer Semiotics* (1990), attempts to analyze the modern windows/mouse/icons in-terface as a new kind of semiotic system. Unfortunately, the idea of a special computer-sign type ignores the fact that the computer can be made to use all kinds of sign systems and consequently cannot be said to have one of its own. "The sign" seems to be the wrong level of investigation for a theory of computer mediation.

Recently, Lev Manovich (2001, 29–48) outlined five "principles of new media": numerical representation, modularity, automation, variability, and transcoding. According to Manovich, the last three are dependent on the first two. In other words, numerical representation and modularity are at the heart of "new" or "computer" media and determine what Manovich calls "new media objects." Representation seems like a good candidate for what the computer does, but is the method of representation essentially numeri-cal? Binary digits (bits) can represent numbers, but they are not numbers in themselves. Rather, as Niels Ole Finnemann (1999, 9) has pointed out, they constitute a binary *alphabet*, where the two "letters," unlike the numbers "1" and "0," are without a fixed semantic value. The binary notation system used in digital computing and the binary number system is not the same thing. In the binary notation system of the computer, the digits can repre-sent anything, including operations, whereas this is not the case in binary mathematics, as Finnemann notes. In relation to Manovich's argument, this

---

[2] See Aarseth 1997, 24–41 for a longer discussion of the problems of computer semiotics.

seems to make sense. Numerical representation is much older than computer representation (it is as old as writing), so it is not a principle exclusive to computing, whereas computer representation does not have to be linked to a numerical value. A digital code, say "101," could represent a color, a letter, an instruction for a "universal" (Turing) machine, or it could identify a member of any arbitrary set. As Finnemann claims, the binary notation has more in common with finite alphabets than with number systems. And the binary codes used by computers only make sense as part of a sequence of such codes, unlike, again, a binary number, which would have the same value in any system. As a subprinciple of numeric representation, Manovich mentions algorithmic manipulation: "In short, *media becomes programmable*" (2001, 27). Programmability which is also mentioned under the fifth principle (transcoding) but, strangely, not under the third (automation), might deserve to rank separately among the basic principles, but unfortunately the concept is not explored or related to the others.

Manovich's second main principle, modularity, tries to grasp the organization of the elements of the "new media objects": they are stored as separate, independent components, to be assembled at run-time by the program that displays them. Again, however, modularity seems to be a principle covering too many nondigital phenomena (Peter Cook's *plug-in city*, inspired by the automobile industry, springs to mind), while not covering all the digital ones—an HTML page with links and formatting, or an SMS message—so the primacy of this principle is less than apparent. Is the principle of modularity not at work in any industrial process, starting with the types, lines, pages, and folded sheets of printing? Clearly Manovich is on to something important, but the exact nature of the phenomenon remains elusive.

Finnemann (1999) also tries to frame the principles of digital media and comes up with three: representation in the mechanical (binary) alphabet, algorithmic syntax/formalisms, and interface. The first two clearly correspond to the first principle (and subprinciple) of Manovich and might be adopted by us as obvious candidates for what computers are all about, at least on a low, technical level. Finnemann's third term, *interface*, like Manovich's use of the word, seems to become too unwieldy. In both cases the concept seems to be synonymous with the computer program and its functions. Perhaps in both cases the problem is that low- and high-level principles are mixed: mechanical representation and programmed algorithms are not on the same level as interface (if we for a moment accept the concept as meaningful) or automation.

Is it possible to adopt only Finnemann and Manovich's first two principles, and leave it at that? Perhaps instead we should turn to Alan Turing, whose 1936 paper, "On Computable Numbers," for the first time suggested the radical principle of the universal machine: that program and data were interchangeable and manipulable. A machine could be coded in software, and the code would be able to act on itself and transform itself. There was no essential difference between program code and data. From this simple but extremely powerful principle, all the rest would follow, for example the "bootstrapping" methods where a program would compile another program that might compile a machine-readable version that could be run by the computer hardware.

But even if we can explain the "how" of the digital computer, we still need to understand the "what." What is the digital computer doing, that has not been done before? Or better, for what universal purpose is the universal machine being used? The short answer, and the high-level principle, is *simulation*. Simulation should here be understood as dynamic modeling in general, rather than the faithful mapping of "real" phenomena: we may simulate a dragon in a computer game, and even if no real-world counterpart exists, the dragon is still a simulated dragon and not a fictional dragon.

It is too easy to think of simulation as some obscure, scientific practice or as a far-out, perverted corner of computer science. Simulation is often incorrectly identified with 3D environments and so-called virtual reality, but it should not be tied to a specific visual or perceptual paradigm. Much more than an epistemology for certain computer applications, the method is at the core of all computing, from artificial reality research to distributed number crunching. In the former, human thought processes are simulated; in the latter the software models the real-world relationships of the distributed hardware. When programming complex systems—say, a control system for a factory—the real-world components are first simulated in software and then gradually replaced by real, mechanical parts. The core control component, however, having been used to test the validity of the simulated operation, then becomes the real core of the real system: a simulation taking control of the real world.

In short, the digital computer simulates: it simulates natural phenomena, human behavior, mechanical processes, business transactions, complex organizations, and not least, it simulates other computers. Every program (even the famous "Hello, World!" from introductory programming courses) contains some kind of model of some aspect of the world, and this model is a simulation that maps the real-world phenomena and their important relationships. My bank simulates me by my personal record: if I overdraw my account frequently, it will change its model of me. Surgeons use CAT-scanning and 3D-techniques to simulate bodies in preparation for difficult operations. My laptop uses a white screen and black dots to simulate writing on paper. My Nintendo® Game Boy simulates car races and weird monsters. A database entry or a meteorological computer model is a simulation of the object being represented. An autopilot is a simulation of a real pilot, capable of taking off and landing aircraft. When I print a document, the word processor builds a model of the finished product and sends this to the printer for realization. From the start, digital computers were used as simulations of human computers, taking over their tedious tasks while providing their masters with more interesting ones.

The drive for modeling, automation, and simulation is an old one, but Turing's universal machine is the first technology that lets us simulate the physical models and tools as well as the processes and phenomena they represented. The implications for the humanities and aesthetics, including literature and literary studies, are significant. But will digital simulation affect the novel, or just its physical stratum?

Simulation as Metaphor: The Virtual Imagination

Since simulation is a form of representation, we should take special care to avoid confusing it with other forms of representation. A picture is not a simulation, but it could be *the result* of a simulation, say a computer-generated projection of what a person would look like earlier or later in life. If we simply equate all forms of representation with simulations, then the concept would be useless. A simulation involves a mechanical transition between states in a dynamic system, from S' to S'', and consists of the rules or operations for reaching state S'' given state S'. Simulations are not so much representations of objects as representations of processes and dynamic relationships (control systems).

A close relation to simulation (especially for humanists) is translation, and at first it might seem difficult to distinguish between them. For instance, a Swedish translation of a poem by Rilke could easily be described as a simulation of the original poem. However, the crucial difference between simulation and translation is that the simulation is primarily a process involving transitions between multiple states and producing multiple texts, whereas translation produces primarily a single resulting text, the process of which is relatively unimportant.

Although the difference between a simulative process that produces texts and a representational text (a fiction) that produces readings is significant, there is a third alternative relationship between texts and simulations, and that is the texts that describe simulations and use them as fictional elements. Literary fascination with simulations is a central theme, especially in contemporary science fiction, where writers since L. Frank Baum have imagined technological devices that would generate virtual places, objects, or beings. Perhaps the first full-blown version of this virtual imagination is Ray Bradbury's "The Veldt" (1951), in which a "nursery" lets children imagine a fantasy landscape, which it then simulates:

> He stepped into Africa. How many times in the last year had he opened this door and found Wonderland, Alice, the Mock Turtle, or Aladdin and his Magical Lamp, or Jack Pumpkinhead of Oz, or Dr. Doolittle, or the cow jumping over a very real-appearing moon—all the delightful contraptions of a make-believe world. How often had he seen Pegasus flying in the sky ceiling, or seen fountains of red fireworks, or heard angel voices singing. But now, is yellow hot Africa, this bake oven with murder in the heat.

The children in Bradbury's story, worried that their parents will turn off their fantasy simulator, trap them in the veldt/nursery where the lions, suddenly real, kill them. This story can be read as yet another example of media panic: as a conflict between the necessity of the real and the seductive corruption of the imagination, a theme found in countless fictions from *Don Quixote* onward. But it could also be interpreted as a conflict between the amoral openness of the simulator (especially when it is being controlled by children) and the closed, controlling fiction of narrative, here represented by a reference to a tale from *The Thousand and One Nights*:

> George Hadley stood on the African grassland alone. The lions looked up from their feeding, watching him. The only flaw to the illusion was the open door through which he could see his wife, far down the dark hall, like a framed picture, eating her dinner abstractedly.
> "Go away," he said to the lions.
> They did not go.
> He knew the principle of the room exactly. You sent out your thoughts. Whatever you thought would appear. "Let's have Aladdin and his lamp," he snapped. The veldtland remained; the lions remained.
> "Come on, room! I demand Aladdin!" he said.
> Nothing happened. The lions mumbled in their baked pelts.

Since the publication of Bradbury's story, science fiction has tackled this theme countless times, perhaps most notably in the *Star Trek* TV series, where the crew of the starship *Enterprise* often are trapped in the simulated surroundings of alien races. Often potentially deadly, these traps are usually escaped when protagonists discover the nature of their artificiality and resist their seductive tropes. Vernor Vinge's novella "True Names" (1981) describes a simulated landscape where subversive computer superusers ("warlocks") hide their true identities and fight the Government for control of "The Other Plane," the global communication networks. Vinge's "modem society" is clearly inspired by his own experiences with computer games and e-mail communities in the late 1970s, and he correctly envisioned the identity games that were starting to take place in the various Internet media. In the movie *Tron* (David Lisberger, 1982) two hackers are translated from the physical world into the virtual space of a computer, where they must fight for survival, as gladiators inside a computer game, against the evil schemes of the "Master Computer Program."

In the second of the *Star Trek* TV series, from the late 1980s, the *Enterprise* is outfitted with a "nursery" of its own, called "the Holodeck." Here, the crew members (and the *Star Trek* TV audience) can escape the sterile, futuristic surroundings of the spaceship and engage any narrative setting by programming the simulator. Virtual actors on the Holodeck are mentally and physically indistinguishable from real humans but can only exist within the Holodeck room. This room can generate a seemingly boundless illusion of open landscapes, where the artificial intelligence of the virtual actors makes the illusion perfect. However, the needs and desires of the human users create problems that can only be solved by outside intervention: the Holodeck is a dangerous, futile, and ultimately false paradise.

Through all these narratives of the virtual runs the theme of the simulator as a technology of corruption and destabilization. Especially in the hands of the common people or children it becomes a forbidden fruit that gives its users a narrative position they should not be allowed to hold. The world of endless possibilities is one without narrative and authorial control and cannot be allowed to survive within a narrative universe. Even in the dystopian universes of Philip K. Dick, where various alternative realities constantly compete for the main character's sense of reality, entropy usually results. In Dick's novel *Time Out of Joint* (1959) the simulated reality breaks down to reveal its own construction: objects in the false but realistic environment are slowly being replaced by their names written on pieces of paper.

The most influential novelist to address the virtual is undoubtedly William Gibson, whose "cyberspace" novels, *Neuromancer* (1984), *Count Zero* (1986), and *Mona Lisa Overdrive* (1988), have evoked a technological longing for the kind of technological immersion he describes. Despite the irony of his futuristic vision, hackers, programmers, and computer scientists dream of making his fictional technologies real, and countless writers and filmmakers since Gibson have contributed to the collective dreaming. In Gibson's dystopian future, global, supernational corporations control the world. These companies proliferate in the immaterial cybernetic networks, while the social structures of society are in decay. Gibson presents us with two unconnected versions of the virtual: the *matrix,* where disembodied workers process data in an endless, three-dimensional "consensual hallucination"; and *Simstim,* a leisure technology that lets its users experience any situation and emotion with fantastic accuracy through direct neural stimulation. Through this technology, anyone can "become" someone else by experiencing the same sensory and mental states as the other person.

While there is little hope in Gibson's world, the seductions of the virtual worlds are never presented as acceptable alternatives to the real one. The realm of the virtual belongs to the artificial subject, the "artificial intelligences" (AIs) that are fundamentally alien. Later science fiction authors, such as Neal Stephenson (*Snow Crash,* 1992) depict a utopian, optimistic version of Gibson's bleak future. Stephenson's virtual world, "the Metaverse" is a better alternative to the world of flesh, a place for the rich and computer-literate, the global elite.

Perhaps the most ambitious literary implementation of the virtual imagination so far is Tad Williams's *Otherland* novels (1996–2001), a cycle of four novels (*City of Golden Shadow, River of Blue Fire, Mountain of Black Glass, Sea of Silver Light*) that is centered on a massive and secret simulation system, where a "brotherhood" of decadent billionaires are trying to achieve immortality by migrating into the system they have funded. Instead of one simulated landscape, the Otherland system consists of numerous, very different worlds; there is at least one world for every participant in the project. The simulation technology is so good that users are unable to feel their real bodies and connections, and virtual death in the simulation means bodily death in reality. A number of children fall into mysterious comas, and this seems somehow connected to the Otherland simulation technology.

The novels follow a number of characters in their search for the truth about the system, its rules, and its purpose. These persons are relatives or friends of the comatose children, and they become unable to log out of the system as they move deeper and deeper into it, from world to world. The span of worlds is very impressive (and often deliberately confusing), from ancient Homeric Greece or mythological Egypt, via Oz, to World War I and the Mars of early science fiction. One of the main characters suffers from memory loss and later discovers that he is already disconnected from his dead body in the real world. Another character, a boy who suffers from a terminal illness, is killed in a battle in one of the virtual worlds and is later resurrected by the simulation to live on in the virtual world only, where he can still meet his parents and friends and have a social life.

Although the conspiracy to produce the simulation technology is clearly evil in a grand and traditional way, Williams does not portray the technology itself as sharing the values of its owners. The breakdown of the simulated worlds, brought about by a psychopathic serial killer who works for one of the owners, is ultimately countered by the successful protagonists, who save the day and defeat the wicked brotherhood and their psychopathic minion. In the end, the advanced simulation system, built by hired hackers and designers who are unaware of the evil scheme of their employers, is delivered from the hands of evil and can be used for good. A central theme running through the *Otherland* cycle is that the artificial life produced by the complex simulations has value and that destroying it is an act of evil, just as in the real world. Although not new, this respect for the virtual life, whether indigenous or converted from the real world, represents an ideological break with the traditional virtual imagination, where the virtual and artificial were always somehow linked to alien or flawed subject positions. Although the plots and narrative structures of the *Otherland* virtual worlds are shown to be clichés, the characters within them are not. Ironically, while these aspects of Williams's fiction are among the most original and moving, his "artificial" characters are also the least simulation-like. In real simulations/computer games the characters are often the weakest point, while unexpected event sequences and emergent behavior are typically what make them interesting.

The virtual imagination, whether dystopian (Bradbury, Gibson) or utopian (Vinge, Williams), has to privilege narrative requirements that make the fictional portrayal of simulations ultimately quite different from the real thing. As in the TV series *Max Headroom* from the 1980s, where a real actor with makeup *simulated* a computer-animated simulation of the main (nonvirtual) character, the virtual characters in *Otherland* are just as real as the real ones. We might conclude that the virtual subject position is unreachable, or nonexistent, at least for fiction, since virtual subjects, like Hal in Stanley Kubrick's *2001*, or the neural network Helen in Richard Powers's *Galatea 2.2*, seem just as real or imaginary as other fictional subjects. As Mary Ann Buckles (1985) points out in her pioneering study of the first adventure game, *characterization* seems to be one crucial area where simulations so far clearly fail to emulate narrative fictions. Two decades later, her observation still holds. And while fiction seems to succeed in employing the theme of simulation for its own purposes, such as worlds in conflict, or existential issues, it must do so by completely disregarding the methods of simulation.

Stories from the Dungeon

In 1974, two game creators and enthusiasts, Gary Gygax and Dave Arneson, invented a new, collective mode of narrative play, called role-playing games. Their system, inspired by military strategy board games and fantasy fiction like J.R.R Tolkien's *The Lord of the Rings*, was called Dungeons and Dragons (D&D). It focused on exploration of a fantasy landscape, where players controlled single characters and the goal was to enhance their character's skills. The game itself was little more than a book of rules and was played by dice according to a fairly complex system. A "Dungeon Master" (DM) acted as both referee and narrator, and would make up the landscapes and events, as well as enforce the rules. The DM would present the players with choices and narrate the outcome of battles and explorations. The characters had names and numeric values ("levels") representing their skill levels. "Experience points" gained by fighting would improve these levels as the game progressed. Games could take a whole day or go on for weeks and months or even years. Because the players invested time and energy in building their characters, they would keep them through the game sessions and grow fond of them.

The games are interactions between the players and the DM, and a skilled DM will be highly admired by the players. The DM has to plan a game carefully, and at the same time be flexible enough to accommodate the players' creative solutions to the game's challenges. The original D&D rules were open enough to allow several different styles of play, from combat-oriented gaming to more peaceful explorations. The role-playing game incorporates both simulation and narrative, in a hybrid form that depends equally on the rules and the creativity of the participants. No two games of D&D will ever be alike, and while the stories produced during play would seem bland and derivative to a nonplayer, the pleasure experienced by the players in the gaming situation will be equal to that of any highly trained aficionado in pursuit of his or her favorite aesthetic activity.

The improvised, collective narrative, to be savored in the moment of creation rather than after, is a form quite different from other kinds of narratives. It has most in common with traditional oral storytelling, but the vital ingredients of simulation and direct player intervention make it crucially different from this mode as well. The game aspect and the narrative aspect are in balance, and as we shall see, the form is not easily translated to other media. Inspired by Dungeons and Dragons, computer game designers have created many types of games based on Gygax and Arneson's design. The computer is perfect for one of D&D's components—rule-based simulation—but, unfortunately, quite unsuited for the other—improvisational storytelling.

The ultimate goal, a computer game that is also a compelling story is, at least at the time of writing, the holy grail of the computer-game industry, and has been for more than fifteen years. However, as Selmer Bringsjord and others have pointed out, this goal cannot be reached without also reaching the goals of artificial intelligence, which would produce a machine capable of successfully simulating a human Dungeon Master. Given the fundamental lack of success in simulating human intelligence, however, we should not expect high-quality improvised stories from games in the foreseeable future. Instead, what we do have are highly directed plot lines for the players to follow, structures also known as "quests." A quest is not a story, but it structures the players' behavior into a corridor of possible events and actions as they move forward toward the fulfillment of a usually heroic goal. The game-quests are of course thematically and historically related to the quests of romantic medieval literature, but they lack the narrative closure of the latter, and also their tragic dimension. Ontologically the two forms are very different: one is controlled by temporal narration of past events, whereas the other is controlled by strategic decisions in a spatial labyrinth. Time in games is governed by the social act of playing, whereas time in narratives is controlled by the storyteller. If narratives structure time, these games structure space.

The quest itself is not a narrative structure.[3] What determines narrativity is how narrow the quest corridor is. In chess, the quest is simply to take down your opponent's king, which can be achieved in an almost infinite number of ways. In certain games, however, the quest corridor is so narrow that only one sequence of actions will solve the quest. These games, often called "interactive fictions" are really stories masquerading as games, because their spatial structures usually produce very linear, temporal event sequences. Their "interactivity," then, is certainly not evident from their narrative structure.

The first of these story games is generally considered to be William Crowther and Donald Woods's Adventure. This was a fantasy cave simulation programmed by Crowther, who was inspired by the Dungeons and Dragons game and by exploring a cave in Kentucky in 1972. Crowther made a first version of the game around 1974 as a present to his daughters, and it

---

[3] For an excellent discussion of quests, see Tronstad 2001.

was enhanced and rereleased by Woods in 1976. The game used text for input and output, and contained short prose descriptions like this: "You are in a splendid chamber thirty feet high. The walls are frozen rivers of orange stone. An awkward canyon and a good passage exit from east and west sides of the chamber." Puzzles, mazes, and the occasional monster dominated the game, and the players would have to map their progress carefully or risk getting lost in the labyrinth. Playing the game to the end might take weeks, but once the game was completely solved there would be little reason to play it again, unlike most other game types. The storylike quest structure, while entertaining, leaves no curiosity about what the game could offer on a second playing. Instead, it would seem that, like literature, film, or the arts, it would stimulate a wish for similar experiences. And so a new entertainment genre was born. The first adventure game gave rise to a large number of text adventures, but in the second half of the 1980s the textual format was popularly overtaken by graphical games, and the genre died out commercially. It was just as if the nineteenth-century novel would be completely replaced by film and television by 1920, and only a few experimental amateurs would continue to write books. The literary ambitions of those who continue to make textual adventure games are quite strong, but the hybrid combination of gaming and storytelling seems to attract little critical or popular attention.

By the late 1970s, another literary game genre appeared, but this time on paper: the Choose-Your-Own-Adventure books. This was a genre inspired by, and very similar to, the computer adventure games, a clear testimony to the flexibility and versatility of the old codex format, which could, in this case, simulate a computer program. In these literary adventures, often cast as detective stories, players had to choose between numbered fragments and move through the story-labyrinth in search of the solution to the mystery. Some of these books used dice to introduce a random element, whereas others relied solely on the player's choice.

The adventure game structure is very much alive still, in the form of 3D labyrinth action games such as Doom, Half-Life, and Max Payne, where the literary interface of the simulation has been replaced by a visual, almost cinematic one. Increasingly more complex graphics and detailed scenographies still manage to attract players, while the game structures remain largely unchanged from the first adventures. In terms of content, the games are more or less the same, still limited by the lack of intelligent characters and replayability.

The conflict between narrative and simulation is perhaps best illustrated by the surprising defection of game designer Robyn Miller from the game industry in 1998. With his brother Rand, Miller is arguably one of the most successful game creators ever. Their visually stunning best-selling game Myst (1993) is universally lauded as an important milestone of the genre. Myst is set in a world of beautiful islands, where the player must discover what has happened to the family who lived there. There are no characters in the game, except for a few video clips in which the main characters address the player. Despite its mausoleic feel, Myst was immensely popular. It sold more than six million copies and remained on the sales charts for five years. However, shortly after the publication of the sequel, Riven, which took four years to make, Robyn Miller announced that he wanted to tell linear stories in another medium: film. He had grown increasingly frustrated with the limits of storytelling and character development afforded by gamelike environments and was especially unhappy with the need to accommodate players who wanted freedom to choose what to do next. The rules and spatial structures of the game environment clearly cannot compensate for the lack of an intelligent human narrator or the players' need for autonomy. And while games like Myst have a great advantage over novels and films in presenting a believable world to the spectators, they are at a disadvantage when it comes to exploiting that world for narrative purposes.

Quite early in the history of adventure games, however, a new genre appeared that would dramatically change the way players behaved and viewed their roles in games. In 1978, two students at Essex University in England, Roy Trubshaw and Richard Bartle, started to develop what they called a Multi-User Dungeon (MUD), an adventure game where many players could interact in the same simulated landscape. Like the original D&D, this game had questing and increasing one's character's skills and abilities as the main goals. Users with special privileges, called wizards, would supervise the game play and enforce good behavior. Unlike D&D, however, there were no Dungeon Masters to control narrative gaming, so the quests were permanent and mechanical.

Because they required a network or modem connection to be played, MUDs did not become a popular game genre for several years but developed slowly on the mainly academic Internet in the 1980s. In the early 1990s, purely social versions developed, where the role playing did not involve points or quests. These were used for chatting, flirting, and more serious activities like teaching. At the same time, game MUDs proliferated, and there are now more than 1,700 MUDs available on the Internet.[4]

In the late 1990s, graphical MUDs appeared, and the most popular of these, such as the Korean offering, Lineage: The Blood Pledge, is played by

---

[4] http://www.mudconnector.com/.

two million to four million Koreans, with three hundred thousand to four hundred thousand people online in the same simulated world at the same time. The fantasies of Vinge and Gibson seem to have come very close to reality. Given environments where thousands of players interact, the traditional structures of narrative, which never worked well even for single-player games, seem to become even more inadequate. Players obviously enjoy the questing, level building, and role playing these games afford, but their worldview is focused on the social and strategic status of their character, not on the way in which their actions might fit some well-formed dramatic structure. These games are vast collective experiments, a technological avant-garde that combines the social and the aesthetic in an unprecedented way. Living and playing in these worlds have artistic and even literary qualities, since the communication with others takes place through verbal messages, but these dialogic forms are not therefore the reinvention of older literary genres. Instead, they should be seen as a new mode of communication, a new intersection between the social, the ludic, the aesthetic, and the simulated. The emotions and gestures are direct and immediate, produced for the moment (and not for the page or the stage). Even so, the tropes and strategies are carefully developed through weeks and months and years of collective playing. It would be a mistake not to see the emergence of a literary form in these practices, but it would be equally wrong to subsume it under existing literary genres, such as the novel or the stage play. The current academic drive to dress simulations and games up as a new kind of "emergent" narrative seems to be an ideological attempt to make traditional, humanist media theory (the narrative paradigm) matter. It is costly to maintain (narratology would have to be rewritten), and does not seem to pay off in the form of useful insights. One simply cannot theorize games into becoming literature or cinema, whatever the short-term ideological benefits.

Computer game quests, like the real-world equivalents of growing up, finding love, getting a satisfying job, taking revenge, or going to war, are highly structured processes that, unlike narratives, do not come with preset orders and endings. Their aesthetic attraction and main quality is the in medias res of influentiable uncertainty, the feeling of partial control that may actually lead to situations and events that are unique to the participant. In terms of creativity, this comes closer to writing than reading. This is also why game sequences seldom make sense as interesting stories. As the saying goes, "you had to be there!" An individual's raw emotions, strategies, and ambitions usually do not make interesting reading but need additional structure in the form of crafted narrative in order to produce empathy and become interesting for others. A reader of narrative fiction or experimental antinarratives is struggling to understand, whereas a writer or player is struggling to control. Why should the two modes ever meet?

Hypernovels: The Next Best Thing?

A "simulation novel," that is, a technical simulation that also, somehow, is a novel, would probably be too unlike our idea of what novels are to function as a category. Movies could be a case in point: while many movies have literary or even novelistic qualities, they are an independent media genre, in a way that an audio novel is not. The same goes for the mature comic books called "graphic novels." While these are closer relatives to novels than movies are, because of their central use of verbal elements and material-temporal format, they are still considered a separate genre. Unlike the audio novel, they use visual conventions and elements that constitute an autonomous artistic form, rather than just a visually "enhanced" novel, such as the illustrated volumes of Victorian literature. The same would probably hold for "novels" that tried to use simulation or other digital methods as a central component. The unwritten requirement for "novelness" or literariness in general seems to be that the verbal component must dominate.

Although the modes of simulation and narration may never merge into anything that resembles novels, digital media afford a simpler structure that might better serve and renew literary narrative genres. In 1945, an article called "As We May Think" was published in the *Atlantic Monthly*. The author was the leading American scientist Vannevar Bush, and in the article he presented a vision of how information could be structured via "trails" that would organize knowledge patterns between documents and publications. He described this as a mechanical microfilm machine called the "Memex" and hoped it would cope with the problems of information deluge already experienced in the sciences. Twenty years later, when computers finally could be used for composing documents as well as storing them, pioneers like Ted Nelson, Douglas Engelbart, and others started to develop and implement Bush's dream. While Engelbart developed actual systems and laid the foundations for the modern interface, Nelson thought up a system called *hypertext*, that would, ideally, allow for better, more flexible ways of writing and reading.

Hypertext is a deceptively simple concept. Fundamentally, it is a way to structure information (typically text and illustrations) in fragments, with connections directing the reader to other fragments. The fragments (nodes) and connections (links) have semantic value, and the reader's "path" through the fragments creates a personal reading experience, which depends on the reading order of the fragments. A hypertext can be shaped like a labyrinth, but other, more hierarchical structures are equally possible. Clearly, the hypertext is not an indigenous computer genre but one that can be found throughout the history of writing, from the Chinese oracular text *I Ching* (1000 B.C.) to the encyclopedias of the Enlightenment. Texts have always had need to refer the reader to other sections of themselves or to other texts, and digital hypertext merely makes this structure much more convenient to organize and use. The Choose-Your-Own-Adventure books mentioned earlier are excellent examples of hypertext in print codex form.

However, the idea that hypertext is merely a continuation of a long, predigital tradition does not fit well with the need to proclaim it as a revolution of writing. Therefore, hypertext has been mystified as a technology that would produce new, better ways of thinking. The ability to write like the mind works, a romantic ideal introduced by Bush in his 1945 article, has since been dismissed by psychologists.[5] Bush wanted readers to link between documents and form "trails," a kind of superdocument, while Nelson wanted to free writing within a document from its sequentiality. The idea that the "tyranny" of linear text would be abolished by the perhaps less than liberatory structure of the labyrinth is undoubtedly wishful thinking. Nevertheless, the hypertext structure can be used very effectively for certain types of knowledge organization, such as complex instructional manuals, where the reader needs access to specific information and has no need for long, linear arguments. Also the network structures afforded by hypertext linking are superb for representing phenomena like social relationships. But what about fiction?

For a demonstration of an early prototype in 1969, supported by IBM, Nelson wanted to make a hypertext version of Vladimir Nabokov's novel *Pale Fire,* which is shaped as a 999-line poem with the rest of the text in footnotes. To Nelson, this novel, with its multiple connections between two levels, was a natural hypertext that would illustrate his ideas perfectly. IBM, however, felt that this was "too far out." The radical flexibility afforded by hypertext, that is, the ability to represent both strict, closed hierarchies; impenetrable labyrinths; and open, decentered networks, should make it a perfect tool for experiments with literary form. A combination of the three divergent figures of hierarchy, labyrinth, and network seems almost like too

---

[5] See "The 'Homeopathic Fallacy' in Learning from Hypertext," by Jean McKendree, Will Reader, and Nick Hammon, *interactions* (Association for Computing Machinery) 2 no. 3 (July 1995): 74–82.

much of a challenge, and so far the experiments with hypertext structure have yet to produce an emergent, successful literary genre. This may still happen, of course, but the development of a transparent material standard, like that of print, would seem to be an important, still missing foundation.[6]

Nelson's pioneering ideals were hard to implement, and his solutions, the global networking system Xanadu among them, is still not completed. Meanwhile, others applied his ideas and built simpler, more pragmatic systems, the most famous of which is Tim Berners-Lee's World Wide Web, started in the late 1980s. What began as an attempt to revolutionize writing and augment the human intellect (Engelbart) seems to have become not so much a new cognitive tool as a hyperefficient, flexible, multimedia distribution system. Nelson's early vision of "nonlinear writing" has been overshadowed by the more obvious virtues of instant access to billions of different texts. The notion of hypertext as a more "spatial" form of text seems to have been negated by the brute, alphabetical power of search engines like Google. The traditional library of books, shelves, and Dewey decimals is far more spatial than the World Wide Web, and although three-dimensional interfaces to the Web do exist, they have yet to prove themselves useful.

It would be a mistake to equate the Web with hypertext, however. Before the Web, there were a number of hypertext systems in use, and some of those were made to create literature. In the early 1980s, classics scholar and programmer J. David Bolter and novelist Michael Joyce, inspired by artificial intelligence research and early adventure games, programmed a system for "serious . . . interactive fiction." In collaboration with the computer scientist John B. Smith, they created Storyspace, a hypertext editor and reader that would become the most influential system for fictional hypertext, later taken over by Mark Bernstein, chief editor and developer at the hyperfiction publishing house Eastgate Press.

It is interesting to note that Storyspace, as the name indicates, was created to accommodate adventure games as well as node-link structures. In a paper from 1987, which reads as a manifesto for a literary poetics of hypertext, Bolter and Joyce explain the mechanics behind Storyspace: "Each link carries with it a condition statement (specified by the author), which must be satisfied in order for that link to be followed. At present Storyspace recognizes two kinds of conditions. The link may require that the reader match a string (answer a question) before proceeding. The link may also require that the reader already have visited a particular episode before proceeding.

---

[6] Meanwhile, there are a large number of literary experiments available on the Internet. For a very useful overview, see http://directory.eliterature.org/.

Figure 1. *afternoon* / "No, I say"

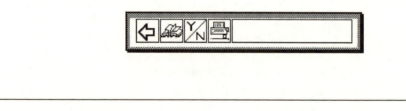

From "afternoon, a story" by Michael Joyce, Eastgate Systems, Watertown, MA, USA, 1990.
http://www.eastgate.com/

The author can also specify Boolean combinations of these conditions"
(1987, 44). Rather than relying on the simple node-link structure, Storyspace allowed a simple form of conditional, adventure-gamelike programming. But writers seldom used this feature. Perhaps the link provided such
a powerful structure in itself that the additional power of conditional linking and querying simply became too much, or perhaps those writers who
wanted the extra power were better served by more complete programming
environments, such as HyperCard or Macromedia Director. In any case,
Storyspace's conditionality became a tool for controlling the reader's access
to "episodes" and was not used for simulation (ibid., 41–50).

Joyce used Storyspace to create a branching fiction called *afternoon, a*
story (1987–93). This became the classic, inaugural work of hypertext literature, quickly defining a genre of its own. In *afternoon*, the main character,
Peter, has witnessed a car accident, in which his estranged wife and son may
or may not have died. The episodes weave in and out of Peter's day and
form an Escher-like structure in which he tries to find out what has happened. The narration in each episode is calm and conventional, but the arbitrary sequences of links create a difficult labyrinth where sometimes new

paths will open only the second or third time you pass a node. The reader is lost, and will have the uncanny conviction that the real continuation of the "story" is somewhere out of reach. Reading *afternoon* quickly becomes a question of logistics: how does one proceed to uncover the entire text? This is a question that readers of codex-based literature, no matter how experimental, never had to ask. As with adventure games, one viable strategy when reading *afternoon* is to draw maps of the possible directions. This might have created a ludic atmosphere, but there is no discernible indication of scoring, winning, or mastering, so the writing and the cognitive process of discovering meaning stay in focus.

As Bolter and Joyce point out in their early paper (1987), Storyspace fictions like *afternoon* become a means to continue the "tradition of experimental literature" from James Joyce to Philip Sollers. And *afternoon,* recently included in Norton's *Anthology of Postmodern Literature,* has eminently succeeded in reaching this goal. It is being read, taught in universities, and discussed by literary theorists. The question becomes whether it succeeds as a *genre-breaking* or *genre-inaugurating* novel. This is still too early to say. Many Storyspace hyperfictions have followed *afternoon* since its publication in 1990, but none has so far reached the same position of importance or influence, with the possible exception of Shelley Jackson's *Patchwork Girl* (1995).

In *Patchwork Girl,* Jackson rewrites the Frankenstein myth, using a number of literary sources, and stitches together a complex textual body of her own, cutting and pasting together Mary Shelley's original text with, among many others, L. Frank Baum's *The Patchwork Girl of Oz* (1913). The resulting hypercorpus, with the bits and pieces from the older texts (de-)forming a new and grotesque one, is unsettling and disorienting, but also elegant and compelling. The opening is an ironic comment on itself as a hypertext project: "I am Buried here. You can resurrect me, but only piecemeal. If you want to see the whole, you will have to sew me together yourself" ("Graveyard"). Clearly, Jackson's defamiliarization scheme is the perfect celebration of hyperliterary strategies, but one cannot help wondering whether this tour de force does more for hypertext than hypertext does for it. The heretical, unanswerable question becomes, what would this novel be like in codex form, or in some other topological structure? What would be lost?

Always fragmented, hypertext fictions sometimes seem to subvert themselves with their user-unfriendliness. In *Patchwork Girl,* however, the strong metafictional metaphor of patching outweighs this Luddite autosubversion: in a technopoetic naturalization process, reversing the uncanny subject position (or trajectory) of a body in fragments, postmodernist poetics subsumes the hypertext labyrinth by allegorizing it.

FIGURE 2. *PATCHWORK GIRL* / "AM I MARY"

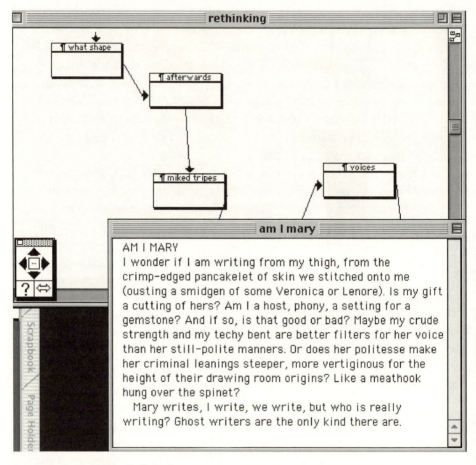

From *"Patchwork Girl"* by Shelley Jackson, Eastgate Systems, Watertown, MA, USA, 1996.
http://www.eastgate.com/

An often-overlooked experiment from the early days of digital literature is John McDaid's *Uncle Buddy's Phantom Funhouse* (1992), an elaborate mixed-media production (a "hypermedia novel," which Amazon.com lists, elliptically, as "audio cassette") that consists of HyperCard stacks (digital files), some pages of annotated proofs, and taped music (hence Amazon's mistake). McDaid's repertoire is more than fiction or even hyperfiction: his stacks even contain programming code (in the HyperCard scripting language) that also functions as literature. Central but missing in *Funhouse* is Arthur "Buddy" Newkirk himself, McDaid's alter ego. The materials in the boxed novel all belong to him, and like the John Barth short story the title

FIGURE 3. THE "HOUSE" OF *UNCLE BUDDY'S PHANTOM FUNHOUSE*

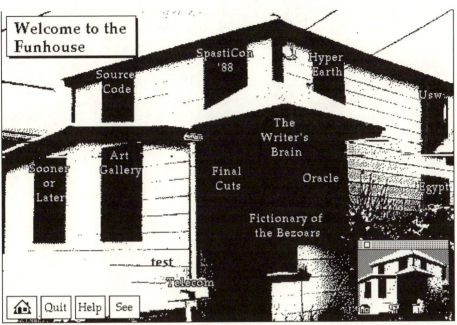

From "Uncle Buddy's Phantom Funhouse" by John McDaid, Eastgate Systems, Watertown, MA, USA, 1993. http://www.eastgate.com/

alludes to, the reader finds him- or herself lost in the "funhouse" of "Uncle Buddy's" material and digital relics. This of course begs the question, for whom is the funhouse fun?

The exploration of *Funhouse* has no obvious beginning. Do you want to listen to the tapes, read the proofs, or open one of the seventeen digital HyperCard stacks? One of the stacks, called "READ ME FIRST," contains a letter from a law firm, giving you possession of the documents. Clicking acceptance, you move to the stack "House," which is a menu with links to most of the other stacks. The "House" seems to be the table of contents, but it does not indicate what we should start with. "Source Code," for instance, turns out to be a "HyperMag of Hacker Poets." "Sooner or Later" is a screenplay, written by Newkirk in 1982. All the stacks present us with different interfaces, different types of material, and different perspectives on Arthur Newkirk's life. Some are his notes, some are made by his friends, and one, "Egypt," is password-protected. Once obtained, the password gives access to "Aunty Em's Haunt House," which contains flipside versions of all the stacks in the *Funhouse*, with names like "The Writher's Pain." This stack is written by Emily Keane, a friend of Newkirk's, and, guessing from the title of Newkirk's album, "Emily and the Time Machine," she is perhaps more than just a friend. Here we also find a newspaper front page with a story about a car accident in which an Arthur Newkirk, age twenty-two, is killed. So that was how he died, you think, until you realize that according to the date on the newspaper, the accident took place in 1979, while most of the Newkirk material is from the 1980s. Either the newspaper is false, or the rest of material is made up. This makes *Funhouse* into what Douglas Hofstadter (1979) calls a "strange loop," because the audio tapes featuring the voice of Newkirk/McDaid clearly document that Emily Keane could not have made up the entire Newkirk corpus by her fictional self.

In a long e-mail message, Emily reveals that it is her father, an almost famous author, who died in 1979. Emily claims to have taken his place and kept his death a secret from his readers. However, the voice of Emily in this passage is also the voice of the novel, commenting on itself:

> The author who was my father, the father who was my author. I broke my feet to fill his shoes, and they have healed that way . . . stronger than natural bone can. I'm not sure I can find my way back, or even *who the I is that might be looking.*
>
> The novel has a life of its own. It tells me what to do, what to record, what to be, how to feed it. Nothing will satiate it. Nothing will ever bring it to closure. (Italics mine)

Did Emily forge the newspaper story and invent Arthur Newkirk? Or did Newkirk invent Emily Keane, and her rewriting of him? Is it up to us to decide?

As with *Patchwork Girl* (although the two are very dissimilar), in *Funhouse* we uncover a postmodernist, ontological breakdown, both in the fiction and in the technical design.[7] The play on the interface, the jokes, the lack of a central perspective, and even the lack of a subversion of it, take this work's subversive meditation on its own medium even further than *Patchwork Girl* does. Unlike *Patchwork Girl* and *afternoon*, *Funhouse* is not really a subversive *narrative*, it is rather a work that is fictional without using storytelling as a central

---

[7] For longer analyses of *Uncle Buddy's Phantom Funhouse*, see Stuart Moulthrop, "Toward a Paradigm for Reading Hypertexts: Making Nothing Happen in Hypermedia Fiction," in *The Hypertext / Hypermedia Handbook,* ed. E. Berk and J. Devlin (New York: McGraw-Hill, 1991), 65–78; and Anja Rau, "Wreader's Digest—How to Appreciate Hyperfiction," *Journal of Digital Information* 1 no. 7 (2000): http://jodi.ecs.soton.ac.uk/Articles/v01/i07/Rau/.

strategy. We uncover Uncle Buddy's life and times through his music, his academic papers, his notes, his e-mail, and so forth: a large unorganized heap of documents in various genres. Clearly, HyperCard facilitates the easy mix of genres and styles, and adds a few tricks of its own, but in the end, Uncle Buddy exists through the words of the fiction. *Funhouse* is "wordware," a literary work that uses words for poetic rather than navigational purposes.

Again, however, the heretical question can be asked: Is the effect achieved through a hypertext poetics, or is hypertext (in this case HyperCard) illuminated by the metafictional poetics? (And can there be a hypertext poetics, or is that no more meaningful than a "codex poetics"?) The question might be unanswerable, but given the strong, self-consciously avant-garde flavor of most hypertext writing, perhaps it is not unreasonably suspicious. If the standard perspectives and vocabularies of literary theory had proved insufficient to discuss these novels, then that would have indicated the revolutionary quality of something we could call hypertext poetics, or perhaps even digital poetics. However, as playful and inventive as these texts are, they are still very much part of a tradition that, unlike computer games, literary theory can embrace without too much rewiring.

Conclusion: The More It Changes

After several decades of practice and theory, digital storytelling now has a history. We can ask critical questions and start to expect useful answers. This essay has not been an attempt to trace this history in detail. Several important chapters and authors have been omitted. Among these are computer-generated stories. I have not discussed these quite interesting experiments here, because I do not see them as pertinent to the question of the digital *novel*.[8] Unlike computer-generated poetry, which is currently a proliferating literary genre, the "automated novelists" (story-writing computer programs), briefly popular around 1975–85, have yet to produce anything worthwhile. They still may, but the chances seem slim.

Other genres of digital narrative, such as the highly popular options provided by games like Will Wright's *The Sims* (2000), which allow users to take snapshots of the action and add text to create long stories on the Web, are what we might call digital folk-art novels. Game players use the game simulation to produce images around which they develop elaborate stories.[9] But

---

[8] Instead, see Aarseth 1997.

[9] http://thesims.ea.com/us/exchange/index.html.

illustrated novels are of course not new, and while the Web and digitally produced pictures make it easier to create them, it does not follow that they will change the novel in significant ways. Much like the typewriter and the word processor, the Web's potential for multimedia writing is not going to change the novel.

Instead of asking *how* the novel will change, perhaps we should ask *why* the novel should change. The novel is a verbal system that channels words from a creator to a reader and could exist happily on most readable surfaces or audio formats. We can perhaps best define novels by their production process, where the words are assembled and balanced by a creative mind, before they are packed up and sent out into the world. We should expect changes to take place within those limitations, the same way a first-person shooter game is defined by the limits of the eye and hand, as Ernest Adams pointed out in a lecture at the Game Developers' Conference in San Jose, California, in 2002. Does the mechanism of simulation and automation have a useful role within the novel's limits? So far, the answer seems to be no. We should look forward to new and facinating ways in which novels will exploit the possibilities of computers and computer networks, but we should not expect them to take over and dominate this brave new world.

References

Aarseth, Espen (1997). *Cybertext: Perspectives on Ergodic Literature.* Baltimore: Johns Hopkins University Press.

Andersen, Peter Bøgh (1990). *A Theory of Computer Semiotics: Semiotic Approaches to Construction and Assessment of Computer Systems.* Cambridge: Cambridge University Press.

Bolter, J. David, and Michael Joyce (1987). "Hypertext and Creative Writing." *Proceedings from Hypertext '87*, 41–50. New York: Association of Computing Machinery.

Bradbury, Ray (1951). "The Veldt." http://www.veddma.com/veddma/Veldt.htm.

Bringsjord, Selmer (2001). "Is It Possible to Build Dramatically Compelling Interactive Digital Entertainment?" *Game Studies* 1, no. 1. http://gamestudies.org/0101/bringsjord/.

Buckles, Mary Ann (1985). "Interactive Fiction: The Storygame 'Adventure.'" Ph.D. dissertation, University of California–San Diego.

Ceruzzi, Paul E. (1998). *A History of Modern Computing.* Cambridge, Mass.: MIT Press.

Finnemann, Niels Ole (1999). "Hypertext and the Representational Capacities of the Binary Alphabet," ISBN: 87-7725-260-8. http://www.hum.au.dk/ckulturf/pages/publications/nof/hrc.pdf.

Hofstadter, Douglas (1979). *Gödel, Escher and Bach*. New York: Basic Books.

Jackson, Shelley (1995). *Patchwork Girl*. Cambridge, Mass.: Eastgate Systems.

Joyce, Michael (1990). *afternoon, a story*. Cambridge, Mass.: Eastgate Systems.

Manovich, Lev (2001). *The Language of New Media*. Cambridge, Mass.: MIT Press.

McDaid, John (1992). *Uncle Buddy's Phantom Funhouse*. Cambridge, Mass.: Eastgate Systems.

Nelson, Theodor Holm (1965). "A File Structure for the Complex, the Changing, and the Indeterminate." *Proceedings of the 20th National Conference*. New York: Association of Computing Machinery.

Tronstad, Ragnhild (2001). "Semiotic and Non-semiotic MUD Performance." Paper presented at the COSIGN conference, Amsterdam, September, 11. http://www.kinonet.com/conferences/cosign2001/pdfs/Tronstad.pdf.

Turing, Alan (1936). "On Computable Numbers, with an Application to the Entscheidungsproblem." *Proc. Lond. Math. Soc.* (2) 42 (1936–37): 230–65; correction, ibid. 43 (1937): 544–46. Also available at http://www.abelard.org/turpap2/tp2-ie.asp.

Wright, Will (2000). *The Sims*. Maxis Software.

A Century of Experiments

ANDREINA LAVAGETTO

The Notebooks of Malte Laurids Brigge
(Rainer Maria Rilke, 1910)

After the *New Poems* (1907 and 1908) and *The Notebooks of Malte Laurids Brigge* (1910), Rainer Maria Rilke found that he had to justify to many readers the sudden shift in his writing to a dry, terse, harshly "objective" style that depicted even sordid and painful aspects of reality.[1] This change alienated his most enthusiastic readers and friends, who had loved the intimist and ornamental Jugendstil of *Mir zu Feier* or the neoromantic pathos of *Book of Hours*. From the start his admirers and detractors alike used exclusively negative categories to describe the *Notebooks*: the minute, pervasive anguish of the atmosphere; the naked story of suffering, decay, solitude, and death. Rilke's mosaic of journal entries resisted any attempt at linear reading, taking to the extreme a trend that had already emerged in the *New Poems*. In sharp, lucid writing he insisted on the horrid, deformed faces of the world: bodies covered with infected sores; children disfigured by alienation and misery; discarded, spectral objects bearing the viscous residue of a bygone life. Rilke himself contributed to a negative reading of the novel through his letters, which provide a commentary on the protagonist's destiny of failure and death, and the work's formal arrange-

---

[1] My observations are indebted to the following works: Paul De Man, *Allegories of Reading: Figural Language in Rousseau, Nietzsche, Rilke, and Proust* (New Haven, Conn.: Yale University Press, 1979), 28–63; Ulrich Fülleborn, "Form und Sinn der *Aufzeichnungen des Malte Laurids Brigge*: Rilkes Prosabuch und der Moderne Roman," in *Unterscheidung und Bewahrung: Festschrift für Hermann Kunisch zum 60. Geburtstag 27. Oktober 1961,* ed. Hermann Kunisch, Klaus Lazarowicz, and Wolfgang Kron (Berlin: De Gruyter, 1961), 147–69; Alberto Destro, "Rainer Maria Rilke: *I Quaderni di Malte Laurids Brigge,*" in *Il romanzo tedesco del Novecento: Dai Budenbrooks alle nuove forme sperimentali,* ed. Giuliano Baioni et al. (Turin: G. Einaudi, 1973); and Manfred Koch, *"Mnemotechnik des Schönen": Studien zur poetischen Erinnerung in Romantik und Symbolismus* (Tübingen: M. Niemeyer, 1988), 203–53. In-text citations refer to Rainer Maria Rilke, *Sämtliche Werke,* ed. Ernst Zinn and Ruth Sieber-Rilke (Frankfurt on Main: Insel Verlag, 1955), 7 vols. The text of *Die Aufzeichnungen des Malte Laurids Brigge* is in vol. 6: 709–978. [Translator's note: The most authoritative English translation is M. D. Herder Norton, trans. *The Notebooks of Malte Laurids Brigge* (New York: Norton, 1964). The Stephen Mitchell translation (New York: Random House, 1982) has the advantage of the same entry markers as the German. Unless otherwise indicated, translations of Rilke's letters are by the translator of the present essay.]

ment into a disconnected series of disparate, arbitrarily chosen journal entries.[2]

The letters on the *Notebooks* describe a double rupture: fracturing the unity of the individual and fate, and of closed, linear narrative. Believers in the aesthetic religion that Rilke had prophesized in his youthful work were sorely disappointed: gone was the emphatic promise of salvation through artistic beauty on which the poet had built his complicity with his readers. At the same time this rupture ushered the *Notebooks* into the history of modern prose. Critics agree that the *Notebooks* is one of the great avant-garde novels of the German language. Indeed, it precedes chronologically the experimental dissolution of epic form that was marked, in Austria and Germany, by the works of Kafka, Musil, Broch, and Benn, and parallels the great modern epics of Joyce and Proust.

Brigge's journal entries are arranged in sequences that no longer comply with nineteenth-century standards of narrative continuity, space-time coherence, and plot development. Instead they are prose fragments in which a fluidly sketched subject records the only experience of the world still possible: the definitive emancipation of the real, in its late bourgeois urban manifestations, from the subject, who can only experience the real as violence and alienation. Exposed to the harsh life of the Parisian metropolis, the young Danish aristocrat, the last of his line, starts to write in order to fight his fears. His first entries are still reminiscent of the canonical diary; they narrate the burden of days spent in places of misery and woe: streets, hospitals, soup-kitchens, parks. The first sequence of short entries stands in contrast to the long segment in which Brigge begins to remember. In the subsequent entries, the everyday chronicle starts to alternate with memories of childhood on the Danish estates of Ulsgaard and Urnekloster, the traditional residences of the ancestral families. The fragmentary autobiographical passages are interwoven with cultural memories: entries on music and the theater focused, respectively, on the unnamed Beethoven and Ibsen. "Materials" begin their incursion into the novel and accrete with the writing process. There is still a narrative frame-story (that is, memory) holding together the portraits in the Urnekloster gallery, the Cluny tapestries, the lace, the *mise en*

---

[2] Among the many letters, see in particular the letters to Clara Rilke of October 19, 1907, in Rilke, *Briefe aus den Jahren 1906 bis 1907*, ed. Carl Sieber and Ruth Sieber-Rilke (Leipzig: Insel-Verlag, 1930), 393–95, and of September 8, 1908, in idem, *Briefe aus den Jahren 1907 bis 1914* (Leipzig: Insel-Verlag, 1939), 49–52; to Manon zu Solms-Lauch of April 11, 1910, in idem, *Briefe aus den Jahren 1907 bis 1914*, 97–101; to Witold Humelwicz of November 13, 1925, in idem, *Briefe aus Muzot, 1921 bis 1926* (Leipzig: Insel-Verlag, 1935), 369–77.

abîme of the Marquis of Belmare, and the Nikolai Kuzmitch and medical student episodes. The "green book" introduces the episodes of Grishka Otrepyov and Charles the Bold. But the historical material is completely emancipated in the long disquisition on Charles the Mad and Pope John XXII. By the time of the entries on the Roman theater at Orange (in Provence), the tragic art of modernity, Sappho, and the parable of the prodigal son, Brigge has completely disappeared from the writing, which breaks off at the peak of its autonomy.

The *Notebooks* thus appears to be a web of motifs connected by the author's imagination, a kaleidoscope of heterogeneous material. As in the *New Poems*, "things" that are exquisite or horrendous, magnificent or repugnant, are arranged according to a horizontal and metonymic compositional principle that Paul de Man has classified as "the interesting":[3] once all differences between the canons of the ugly and the beautiful have collapsed, every object has the same seductive power (the blue hydrangea and the leprous king, the morgue and the meridian angel). Rilke's novel is closely connected to his great twin volume of lyrics: both the doleful stations of the *Notebooks* and the shining gallery of the *New Poems* are sustained by the effort to "see" the things of the world in their simple, bare evidence, indifferent to human desires to possess them. But the supremacy of *das Ding*, which is so exalted and triumphant in the splendid poems, gives way to suffering in the prose. It is in this transition from one mode of "objective speaking" to another that we should seek the true role of the novel in Rilke's poetics.

For the moment let us remain at the level of exterior observation. The crescendo toward the narrator's final dissolution in a flood of material holds the key to the work's intention: to provide a formal analogue to the fragmentation of experience in late bourgeois society. This interpretation would seem to be confirmed by the nature of the materials. Derived from visibly remote sources, they enter Brigge's pages through a contradictory diction: faithful to the source and radically elliptical.[4] Entire passages are almost literal quotations, but they evade understanding by alluding to events that have been cleverly expunged; the reader has to either constantly fill in the

---

[3] De Man, *Allegories of Reading*, 30–31.

[4] The sources of Rilke's Danish and northern German references have been reconstructed by F. Lüning, "Einflüsse auf Rilkes *Malte Laurids Brigge* von Haseldorf und Dänischen Buchveröffentlichungen," in *Kunst in Schleswig-Holstein 1959*, ed. E. Schlee (Flensburg: Christian Wolff, 1959), 53–76. On his sources as a whole, see B. von Witzleben, "Quellenstudien zu Rilkes *Die Aufzeichnungen des Malte Laurids Brigge*," in *Materialien zu Rainer Maria Rilkes* Die Aufzeichnungen des Malte Laurids Brigge, ed. Hartmut Engelhardt (Frankfurt on Main: Suhrkamp, 1974), 280–302.

meaning or accept, as Rilke suggests, the "tension of animosity." Meaning is thus posited as an entity that is gradually eroded until it crumbles. The structure of the novel seems to reproduce this eclipse of meaning. In the way that it records this crisis, in this paradoxical narrative about the impossibility of narration, *The Notebooks of Malte Laurids Brigge* appears to join the other great experimental novels of the era.

But this is not the case. The *Notebooks* ended up becoming a great modern novel by an eccentric route. As important studies have noted, it developed from a unique premise.[5] It did not grow out of a reflection on the fate of narrative. Nor did it not join the enterprise of destroying the old form to achieve the new. Nor did it experiment with essayistic digression (Musil), stream of consciousness (Joyce), remembrance (Proust), or parable (Kafka) to project a narrative that would answer the new era's metaphysical questions. Without *pars destruens*, experiments, or excavating the past, Rilke departed from a void and arrived at a radically modern narrative. He was not, in fact, a novelist. He did not have a talent for the epic or the urge to lend narrative shape to the real (on the contrary: for him prose is the most unnatural form). Rather, he was a great poet and, like Gottfried Benn and Stefan George, the author of lyric sequences. He came to the *Notebooks* with considerable experience under his belt: the *Book of Hours*, the *Book of Images*, and the coeval *New Poems*; a tested and multiform repertory of motifs; an "associative imagination" so well exercised it could move almost by itself, sure and nimble;[6] a secure habit of capturing complex, changing phenomena in short, compact compositions that structured even the smallest details of syntax, vocabulary, and sound; and an unfailing rhythmic sense. This lyrical background makes it possible to describe Brigge's notebook entries in positive terms; they can be seen not as shards and remnants of a lost unity, but as brief self-contained prose units with a regular internal beat: prose poems in the tradition of Baudelaire, who is quoted at length at a crucial point in the *Notebooks*. By the same token, the order in which they appear is hardly casual or arbitrary, corresponding instead to the associative and rhythmic principle of the lyric sequence. The lyrical rather than epic genesis of the *Notebooks* explains the unique but loose order hidden beneath its apparent lack of structure.

---

[5] See Fülleborn, "Form und Sinn"; Walter Seifert, *Das Epische Werk Rainer Maria Rilkes* (Bonn: H. Bouvier, 1969); and Anthony R. Stephens, *Rilkes* Malte Laurids Brigge: *Strukturanalyse des erzählerischen Bewusstseins* (Bern: Herbert Lang; Frankfurt on Main: Peter Lang, 1974). For an interesting Italian study, see Destro, "Rainer Maria Rilke."

[6] Fülleborn, "Form und Sinn," 154.

The rhetorical skeleton of the *Notebooks* is a principle to which Rilke remained faithful throughout his life, especially in his poetry: his most important critics call it the law of complementarity. Following the *"sainte loi du contraste"* still described in one of the late poetry collections, *Vergers* (2:528), figures and motifs in Rilke's text tend to evoke their opposites, which posit themselves as a "reversal" and thus a necessary completion. The unit thereby constituted is not static but rather a dynamic whole in which the two parts are mutually illuminating, both giving and receiving physiognomy. Through its interaction with "the other part," in compliance with the *"ordres complementaires"* (2:529), each figure attains the fullness of its function.

This mechanism can be observed on various levels in the *Notebooks*. The entire temporal structure, for example, is articulated in terms of two complementary dimensions: the Parisian present narrated in the first seven entries is succeeded, in the eighth, by the past Danish childhood. The contrast is clear: the distressing fragmentation of the modern versus the coherence of the past; the "improper" death of the anonymous city crowds versus the authentic ritual death of the chamberlain. The present "calls" to the past to be its complement. From the eighth entry onward, the novel alternates between everyday chronicle and past remembrance. Only when Brigge starts to connect the two temporal dimensions and moves in the fluid new space of *"Vollzähligkeit, in der nichts fehlt"* (6:723) does he gain the possibility of understanding: his perception of himself, and the city broadens to include the positive along with the negative aspects; childhood begins to disinter itself from beneath the rigid pall of fear and to connect to adulthood. Through the tension of complementarity, the two time frames illuminate and give sense to each other.

The historic material also implies a clear framework of complementary relations. The single episodes (as Walter Seifert and Alberto Destro have shown) connect and interact according to a law of polarity that frees them from the gratuitousness of anecdote and structures them in meaningful units. But the *Notebooks* is shaped mainly by the complementarity of absence and presence: at the moment the dog runs toward an absent Ingeborg, toward the void left by Ingeborg—who is both dead and alive—the totality of Ingeborg appears in a sort of epiphany to the family gathered for tea (6:790–92). The nauseating ruins of the wall left after the demolition, from which Brigge flees in horror, evokes the house when it was still whole, filled with the squalid, miserable life of infinite anonymous existences (6:749–51). The Schulin family's castle was destroyed in a fire, but it is from that void that the castle's presence derives, so strong and overwhelming that it lives in the characters' every gesture (6:836–41). When in the city that momentarily sleeps, the noise tormenting Brigge subsides and he "hears" the even more terrifying silence, he grasps the full violence of the reality around him. The ancient family home at Urnekloster consists of absences: dead relatives and ancestors, deserted rooms, dark staircases, abandoned gardens, silences. But in their complicity the elderly Count Brahe and the child Erik experience a complete dimension because they do not distinguish between the living and the dead, between the living and ghosts, between the living and the unborn (6:729–41).

The constant central figure in the *Notebooks'* prose is absence, the concave form, the void. Like the *New Poems*, these elements trigger the totalizing movement, the reversal that produces totality (critics have referred to it as the *Umschlag*, the "reversal," and the *Umkehrung*). It is only through tension with its opposite, upon its return from negativity, so to speak, that each phenomenon acquires authentic form. The figure affirmed at the end of the process, in the totalization, is more strong, intense, and full. It is the sign and promise of a better existence.

Needless to say, many years after the *New Poems* and the *Notebooks*, at the end of a long, hard journey, the *Duino Elegies* would be the poem about the human passage on Earth and its attainment, through pain and death, of an *"überzähliges Dasein"* (1:720) that affirms the magnificence of being in the world (1:710) because it is filled with the bitter awareness of exile and transience. In the *Elegies* and the coeval *Sonnets to Orpheus*, this lament would be reversed into the Orphic celebration of existence.

Rilke's philosophy of art is difficult to locate in an era marked by Nietzsche's legacy and dominated by *Sprachskepsis*. Since the time of the *Book of Poverty and Death* (1903), his imposing poetic opus had addressed the great existential themes of death, suffering, and unfulfilled love. In Rilke's universe human beings are frail, ephemeral creatures debilitated by their awareness of death. Exiled from the "open" world of children, they are not at home anywhere and are always in the act of bidding farewell. In verses that have become celebrated, he names the great task of existence before which the human soul has always failed:

> Nicht sind die Leiden erkannt,
> nicht ist die Liebe gelernt,
> und was im Tod uns entfernt,
> ist nicht entschleiert (*Sonnets to Orpheus*, 1:743).[7]

---

[7] "We do not understand / grief, nor love's phases, / and what death keeps concealed / is not unveiled." *Sonnets to Orpheus*, trans. C. F. MacIntyre (Berkeley: University of California Press, 1960), 39.

In a 1915 letter to Lotte Hepner, Rilke wrote that the central idea of the *Notebooks* is: "Only *this*, by every means and every example this: *this*, how can we live if the elements of this life are wholly incomprehensible? How can we live if we are always inadequate in love, uncertain in making decisions, inept in facing death?"[8]

Yet at the very moment it establishes the metaphysical separation between nature and conscience, Rilke's text promises salvation: it is where the malaise of existence, in a single act, is affirmed and configured as something that can be overcome. To dismiss this thought by comparing it with the most banal positions of the fin-de-siècle aesthetic movement would be an oversimplification.

In Rilke's spiritual biography, the primary experience is quite visibly the happiness of poetic creation. "To say" the things of the world is his earliest instinct, unabated from the time of his youth. Rilke's identity is formed by his absolute awareness of his extraordinary linguistic and musical talent. His supple, rich, and fluid language appropriates all material with facility and virtuosity, transforming it into euphony and figurative order. From the start this gives him such a sense of omnipotence as to overshadow any feelings of existential pain or misery. The self experienced in the act of creation and returned, mirrorlike, by the poetic text (perfect, happy, coherent), competes with the self experienced in contact with the real. From the beginning Rilke posits the universe of sounds and figures as more authentic than the material universe. His youthful work is about nothing other than the euphoria derived from an unlimited expressive faculty; it celebrates its mastery in a diction that is absolutely self-referential.[9] As the poet's subjectivity steadily overflows into verse, singing its interior world, it takes on the tone and gesture of prophecy. In the poetic text Rilke captures a glimpse of the place where meaning is founded and constituted; emphatically, he becomes the voice of a religion of art that promises redemption from suffering. His first lyric collections and the writings that accompany them—essays, reviews, diaries, and letters until at least 1903—are filled with the pathos of a man who is announcing salvation.

Rilke quickly intuited the dangers inherent to the intimistic, aestheticizing abstraction of his poetry. He realized that an art which—by emphatically foregrounding the signifier—refused to deal with the material, the relentless otherness of nature, and the solidity of history and culture would be

---

[8] Letter of November 8, 1915, in Rilke, *Briefe in zwei Bänden*, ed. Horst Nalewski (Frankfurt on Main, Insel, 1991), 1:599–600.

[9] See De Man, *Allegories of Reading*, 36–40.

constantly bordering on kitsch. The poet who, intoxicated by his own power, transforms things into pure functions of his voice and becomes a prophet of the senses is inevitably a dilettante. Rilke thus embarked on the harsh road of self-discipline. In 1902, this led him to Paris to study with Rodin. Dozens of letters attest to the difficulties of the young poet's early years in Paris (the basis for the biographical and psychological material of the *Notebooks*) and how he was transformed by the ruthless severity of life at Rodin's Meudon studio. Rilke learned the ethos of obscure and thankless daily labor. He trained his eyes to see the forms of the real in their independence from human perception. He studied their simple manifestation of themselves and their inaccessible presence in space. From Rodin's teaching he developed the poetic practice of *sachliches Sagen*: a "speaking" that respects the mysterious autonomy of things and restores their pure evidence. The experiment succeeded magnificently. The danger of sentimentalism and kitsch seemed to have been averted. His new art was lofty, masterly poetry that was not even remotely dilettantish—and Rilke knew it.

But the rhetoric of his work contradicted its programmatic assumptions. The language of the *New Poems* shattered the same obstacles that it had posited. It appeared to gaze at *das Ding* and reinstate its coarse *Sachlichkeit*, but in truth it does something else. It does indeed gaze, but the only real thing it captures is the rhetorical game of totalization. It chooses those "things" that in figural logic can attain totality through integration with their opposite. His virtuosity is such that a broad range of objects, events, and thoughts enter into the *New Poems*. He achieves his greatest success where the challenge is greatest, where negativity is reversed into positivity. The text produces a figural order that is posited as an *exemplum* of unity, coherence, and totality by contrast with the separateness, fragmentation, and partiality of the real. The text constitutes the very sense that reality denies.

When Rilke completed the *New Poems* (1908), he entered a period of grave discomfort, fear, and anxiety over the fate of his poetry. When commenting on the *Sachlichkeit* poetic in the ensuing months and years, Rilke spoke of pride, voracity, and violence. In long epistolary confessions, he admitted that despite his agenda of asceticism and an ethics of respect, he had again given into his old instinct to possess things and violate them through the force and skill of his rhetorical instruments.[10] Rather than ushering in a time of security and happiness, his extraordinary achievement led to an

---

[10] See the letters to Marie Taxis of August 30, 1910, and to Magda von Hattingberg of February 17, 1914.

interminable, tormented period of crisis that would not end until 1922, when he wrote the *Duino Elegies* and the *Sonnets to Orpheus*.

The *Notebooks* is usually seen as the work of crisis, composed mainly between 1908 and 1910. It was indeed the first act of Rilke's suffering through a work as if it were a disease. But his suffering could not be explained (only) by the waning of the inspiration and amazing, extended concentration that had accompanied the *New Poems*. Nor can it be explained by the exhausting attempt to restore psychological and historical material to writing. Or even less by a generic need for change. The poetic adventure that began with the *Notebooks* can perhaps be read as Rilke's decision to submit to an extreme test his faith—ineradicable because it is constitutive—in the redemptive, regenerative powers of poetry. Faced by the paradoxical failure of his most perfect work—revealed to him by the Cézanne paintings at the Salon d'Automne in October 1907—Rilke radicalized his experiment: he took the path of extreme negativity, addressed the themes of raw existential pain, and told the story of the dissolution and death of Malte Laurids Brigge. But he did so through a rhetorical fabric that constantly proposed the reversal of the negative into the positive.

In the *Notebooks* and in all the great works that followed, Rilke preserved his faith in the sense that is generated by the play of signifiers and—aware of all his weaknesses—tried to give them the dignity of a philosophical project. This is where he differs from the other great poets and novelists of the modern. He does not respect the boundaries of a dimension of being that is irremediably "other" with respect to the human. He does not admit the inscrutability and relentlessness of the laws that govern the real. From the lucid notion of pain he arrives at an "ontodicea" that the poet bespeaks in celebrating the totality of existence.[11]

This is how we might interpret Rilke when, in the 1915 letter to Lotte Hepner, he describes his sense of the *Notebooks* "as an empty form, a negative all of whose cavities and furrows are suffering, dejection and painful awareness, but whose cast, if it were possible to construct one (like the positive figure one gets in bronze) might be happiness, approval—precise and certain bliss.[12]

Translated by Michael F. Moore

---

[11] Fülleborn, "Form und Sinn," 169.
[12] Rilke, *Briefe in zwei Bänden*, 65.

MYRA JEHLEN

The Making of Americans
(Gertrude Stein, 1925)

The Making of Americans *(written 1903–12, published 1925) is subtitled*
Being a History of a Family's Progress *and began as an epic of the formation*
of an American character out of the process of immigrants striving to make
new lives in the New World. Over the course of writing the novel, Gertrude
Stein gradually redefined it so that it had little to do with history and still less
with process. It became an exposition of a variety of psychological modes of be-
ing she strove to describe at what she considered their most basic levels of defi-
nition, which lay in nature rather than in history and culture.

No one reads *The Making of Americans*. Edmund Wilson devoted a whole
chapter of *Axel's Castle* (1931) to Gertrude Stein having himself only a partial notion of the work she considered her most important. "I confess," he
wrote impenitently, "that I have not read it all through, and I do not know
whether it is possible to do so."[1] Stein's major role on the literary scene apparently did not depend on her writing, or anyway not on its being successfully read. Wilson recognized and even celebrated her project of representing the workings of mind and the basic elements of character, but her
writing just did not communicate.

Paul Bowles could not make sense of it either. He met Gertrude Stein at
about the time Wilson published his study and, having been invited to dinner and promised an introduction to the Paris avant-garde, tried to read the
book, without success. Later he told an interviewer he was sure Stein knew
full well her experimental work could not be read. "She was pulling people's
leg when she would say, 'You've read *The Making of Americans*?' And the
person says, 'Oh, yes!' And then she would say, 'What do you think about
the change of style on page 161?' And, of course, the person wouldn't be
able to answer. And then she'd say, 'Sorry, it doesn't matter.' But what she
was saying really was, 'I knew you hadn't read it.' Because it's unreadable,
and she knew that."[2] Concerning Stein's comparison of *The Making of*

---

[1] Edmund Wilson, *Axel's Castle: A Study of the Imaginative Literature of 1870–1930* (1931; The
Modern Library Edition, New York, 1996), 271.

[2] "Desultory Correspondence: An Interview with Paul Bowles on Gertrude Stein," *Modern
Fiction Studies* 42, no. 3 (Fall 1996): 633, 642.

Americans to *Ulysses* and *A la recherche du temps perdu*, Bowles said no, they did not compare because you could read the other two and not hers. "You can't read the damn thing."

A critical reading of the purportedly unreadable is not impossible nor even unusual, but it runs the risk of being itself unreadable, and very boring. Criticism is best done in the presence of the work, and because *The Making of Americans* is not a work the reader is likely to have in mind, here is a complete paragraph taken from near the end, when Gertrude Stein was in full command of her style:

> In beginning his living David Hersland was of course a very little one and he was then quite interesting to some. In beginning his living he was of course not remembering anything and there were some who later remembered about him then. In beginning his living he was of course completely a very small one, he was beginning living and he was then going on in being living and he then went on being in living and he was then not such a very little one. He was then in being one beginning being in living a very little one. Then he was going on being in living and always more and more then he was coming to be not such a very little one. He was in beginning being living a completely small one. As I was saying he was a younger one, he came to be living after Martha and after Alfred Hersland had each of them been sometime living. Mr. Hersland had always intended to have three children and as I was saying there had been two and these two had not gone on being living and so David Hersland came to be living and sometime later in some way he heard this thing when he was still quite a young one and he had it in him then to be certain that being living is a very queer thing, he being one being living and yet it was only because two others had not been ones going on being living. It was to him then that he was certain then that being living is a queer thing. As I said of him in a way he was needing it that every moment he was one being being living by realising then that he was one needing then being one being living. He was in a way then as I was saying needing to be certain that he realised in him every minute in being living needing being being living. He certainly was one for sometime going on being living. He went on for sometime being one going on being living. As I was saying he could have it in him to be feeling that it was a very queer thing to one being living. He was one that could be realising very much and very often that he was needing being one being living. He was one needing to be understanding every minute in being living what meaning there was to him in his needing to be to him one being being living. He certainly then could have it in him to be going on being living. He certainly could have it in him to feel it to be a

queer thing to be one being living. He was one then as I was saying who was a very little one in beginning being living, he was then one beginning being living, he was then a very small one, he was the youngest of the three Hersland children, he was quite pleasant to the Hersland family then, all his living he was not unpleasant to any one of them the Hersland family, this is to be now quite a complete history of him.[3]

The first response this should inspire—or perhaps the second, after impatience—is that Edmund Wilson and Paul Bowles exaggerated: the writing does make sense. In the same interview, Bowles recalls Stein insisting it did. "Well, yes, she used to say that people thought she wrote for the sound but she really wrote for the meaning, for the sense." He thinks she was joking; everybody saw "it didn't make sense. But she said, 'Yes it does. You have to read it carefully and it does make sense. That's why it's written.' That intrigued a lot of people because they didn't believe a word of it. I can see why. You cannot find a sense. She said, 'It's right there. You just have to work at it'" (633).

Let us work at it. The passage is from the penultimate of the five sections of the book, entitled "David Hersland" after the hero who is modeled on Stein's brother, Leo. The reason David Hersland comes to think "being living is a very queer thing," is drawn from life: Gertrude Stein and her brother were conceived only after the deaths of two siblings and in order to make up a planned complement. The feeling Stein assigns her character, a vertiginous sense of fortuity, is one she and her brother had discussed. But we do not need a biographical gloss to understand what is going on. As a baby, David Hersland is, of course, mostly unself-conscious, but starting to grow up, he hears the story of his birth from which he concludes that just being alive is "a very queer thing." This explained, the narrative returns to describing him as a pleasant little boy bidding to become a pleasant man.

If you pay attention and go slowly, then, the passage appears eminently readable. Yet the original and the paraphrase feel wildly incommensurate. Why? It is true that a great deal gets lost with any paraphrase, even of a passage in Balzac; and this has been a very summary paraphrase. We can try again with a single sentence: "He was then in being one beginning being in living a very little one." An evident paraphrase would be, "He was a small child at the start of his life." But from up close, it becomes apparent that this

---

[3] Cited from the Dalkey Archive edition of *The Making of Americans* (Illinois State University Press, Normal, 1995), 743, which is a facsimile reprint of the original edition corrected by Gertrude Stein and Alice B. Toklas and published in 1925.

will not do: the paraphrase identifies David Hersland, at the point of start-ing life, as a small child, while the Stein sentence says nothing about his be-ing a child but only that he was, at the point of starting life, very little. In fact, this passage about his childhood nowhere casts him as a child. For all that he is "completely a very small one," he is, from the start, just as com-pletely David Hersland.

In the same way, the sentence "In beginning his living he was of course not remembering anything and there were some who later remembered about him then" does not tell us that he failed to recall his early childhood but rather that *while* a small child he did not go about remembering things. This distinction—between having at one time not been able to remember, and at one time not having engaged in the activity of remembering—is essential to the whole enterprise of the passage, which is to evoke a complete, once-and-for-all David Hersland, not a David Hersland in process. The passage's David Hersland is never an oblivious infant out of, say, *Great Expectations*.

At issue, obviously, is a concept of identity and of its relation to time. At this point one needs to read even more closely and not assume what seems logical, namely that, since David Hersland was always fully himself, time is immaterial to his character. For in fact the passage shows him changing over time and in response to experience. He is not born thinking life a queer thing but draws this conclusion on learning how he came to be conceived. Yet, all the while doing and thinking different things at different times, he is in each thing and time, wholly himself, never a contingent being. After hear-ing about the circumstances of his birth, David Hersland "had it in him then to be certain that living is a very queer thing." What David Hersland has in him he holds autonomously. Although, when he is small, his family is his en-tire world, he does not have relations with it so much as reactions to it that he incorporates into a being whose capacity for permutation does not pre-clude his being already complete. He is who he is, who he is, who he is.

He is so totally self-defined, so completely himself, that he does not trans-late and permits only a backhanded paraphrase filled with stipulations about what Stein is *not* saying, a paraphrase like a photographic negative. Sen-tences with virtually nothing to say—like "He went on for sometime being one going on being living"—are rendered nonetheless opaque by counterin-tuition. This sentence says nothing more than life goes on: "He went on for sometime." The continuation, ". . . being one going on being living" seems to add nothing but unintelligibility. And in fact, tied in knots that twist back on themselves, this continuation is of the essence of what makes *The Making of Americans* unreadable. "He went on for sometime being one who is going on being living" turns out to be a brilliant and perverse sentence. It starts off like a sentence in any novel; the protagonist of "He went on for sometime" is just moving down the path of life presumably toward some new event. Then, "being" rises up in the middle of the path, and the sentence stops and marches in place: "being one who is going on being living." At this point, one realizes that "sometime" is not a temporal estimate but a Bergsonian duration, and that David Hersland is engaged in neither progress nor process but simply in enduring. He is "going on" not toward something but *as* something; and the something is not substantive—he is not going on being happy or sad, a shoemaker or a cuckold—but categorical: being alive. Every impulse and tenet of a normal sentence of the sort that might advance the plot of *Great Expectations*—"He went on for sometime working at the forge," or, for that matter, "He went on for sometime doing nothing"— Stein's sentence denies. In fact, it culls half its meaning from the denial of a reader's expectation that "going on" engages time and space, or at least one of them. This "going on" is an engagement with oneself. For David Hersland, being is an activity; he is not doing something, he is doing *being*. To make being into doing, the phrase "going on being living" has multiplied three participles to produce an ungrammatical monster, a self-referential transitive verb: "Going on being living" is the active, transitive form of being. Being is doing being.

Fine. Only, this degree of self-reference comes about at catastrophic cost to the realm that ordinary ways of being and acting combine to produce: the realm of events, biography and history, conversation, war and peace, commerce. The realm, in a word, of the novel. Gertrude Stein's sentences and paragraphs pit themselves against the demands of the novel. Telling their story, they refute the novel's traditional story of persons defined by how they relate, or do not, to other persons. Stein's account of David Hersland wrestles to the ground the almost irresistible implication of storytelling, that relatives breed relations and relations a relative sort of character. Gertrude Stein brought into her construction of characters an idea taken from her earlier studies in psychology, that people fell into groups, kinds, or natures. David Hersland absorbs the information about his birth into his nature, and it becomes part of him absolutely: end of story. There will be more to tell about the ramifications of David Hersland, of course, but these ramifications will not amount to a story in the usual sense, for mostly nothing will happen, just be; and when something does happen, as when "sometime later in some way he heard this thing," it is not treated as an event but folded out of process into being. The image of folding is Stein's in her description of how her famous literary portraits, rather than unrolling a sequential exposition of what she knew about the person, instead rolled him or her, regardless of time and space, into the undivided wholeness of a text that then "was" the person and "folded itself up inside itself like you might fold a thing up to be another thing which is that thing inside in that thing."[4]

The trouble is that a novel cannot and does not fold up, it unfolds. Stein began doing portraits at the same time as she was writing *The Making of Americans*, whose philosophy of character visibly evolves in that direction. Circumstances obfuscate rather than define characters. "Of course," she wrote, "as I was saying" and "certainly" to assure us that nothing of moment is happening when something happens. Against the always threatening takeover of events (actions, plot), Stein deployed her familiar bulwarks: the gerund, a verb form that doubles as a noun and that, even as a verb, goes nowhere in an eternal present, along with reiteration ad infinitum of phrases looping back and forth in sentences that are sequential yet synchronic.

Not surprisingly, writing *The Making of Americans* persuaded Stein that she did not want to write novels. She later recalled this with exceptional clarity:

> When I first began writing although I felt very strongly that something that made that some one be some one was something I must use as being them, I naturally began to describe them as they were doing anything. In short I wrote a story as a story, that is the way I began, and slowly I realized this confusion, a real confusion, that in writing a story one had to be remembering, and that novels are soothing because so many people one may say everybody can remember almost anything. It is this element of remembering that makes novels so soothing. But and that was the thing that I was gradually finding out listening and talking at the same time that is realizing the existence of living being actually existing did not have in it any element of remembering and so the time of existing was the same as in the novels that were soothing. As I say all novels are soothing because they make anything happen as they can happen that is by remembering anything. But and I kept wondering as I talked and listened all at once, I wondered is there any way of making what I know come out as I know it, come out not as remembering. I found this very exciting. And I began to make portraits. ("Portraits and Repetition," 297)

She had found that novels were not the way to describe "the existence of living." This was a rather momentous finding, given that the novel is widely considered to have come into its own when Jane Austen and some of her

---

[4] "Portraits and Repetition," from *Lectures in America*, in *Gertrude Stein: Writings 1932–1946* (Library of America, New York, 1998), 308.

colleagues discovered the opposite, that the novel was particularly adept at telling what it feels like to go about in one's person. But for Stein, what it feels like to be oneself had to do not with going about but with being there, in a permanent *here* of the mind. In her portrait of Matisse, the painter *is* his sense of certainty about his painting, while the process by which he arrived at it is not essential to him. Mabel Dodge, whose portrait emerges from the depiction of an Italian villa, is equally a matter of being *in situ*. These portraits are still-lifes in which even movement has achieved an absolute value and become another pictorial feature. "As I say," Stein explained later referring to all her Americans, "the American thing is the vitality of movement, so that there need be nothing against which the movement shows as movement" (292). In the ordinary physics of novels where characters grow and events happen through their interactions, movement is by definition relative. But in Stein's view of selfhood, relative measurements are an abdication. By representing life as a passage through time (by "remembering" life), novels, if we take her perspective, blur individual identities, which as Steinian "natures" define themselves in self-sufficient, end-stopped moments. Instead of playing out a *sic transit*, individuals, in such moments, co-opt time for their own transcendent use—as does David Hersland when he translates the historical contingency of his birth into a principle of his being.

Yet the subject of *The Making of Americans*—how the Americans emerged as a distinct sort of people from immigrants coming into their own in the New World—seems defined expressly as an exercise in remembering. Its development through the histories of two families, the Eastern Dehnings and the Western Herslands (the latter based on Stein's family) promises an American *Forsyte Saga*. But, although the reader can trace a series of striking events—births, marriges, deaths, affairs both romantic and business—when the novel comes to an end or just stops, the categorical banality of its last observation, that families live on only so long as some of its members remain alive, does not feel inappropriate. Banality ("of course," "as I was saying," "certainly") is what this book is about: all the types of being expressing themselves in typical behavior. Emerson, to whom Stein seems finally closer than to William James, famously asked what we would know besides "the meal in the firkin; the milk in the pan; . . . the glance of the eye, the form and gait of the body."[5] This was in his lecture "The American Scholar," where he called on his compatriots to forge a national identity by letting go of history and each one attending to himself. One could show a resemblance between

---

[5] "The American Scholar," in *Emerson: Essays and Lectures* (Library of America, New York, 1983), 69.

Stein's style and Emerson's, obdurate as hers is and limpid his, at least apparently. Both styles avoid the implied unfreedom of having one sentence necessarily launch the next. Reading Emerson aloud, the voice falls at the end of sentences that also can often be rearranged without damage to their overall sense. On the contrary, a progressive dynamic is perhaps the novel's most important structure.

In sum, *The Making of Americans* goes head to head with the novel as most everyone until that time knew it. Stein began writing it in 1903 and concluded, at 925 pages, in 1911. Marcel Proust was writing *A la recherche du temps perdu* at the same time, 1906–12, but the first volume did not appear until 1913. *Ulysses* was published in 1922, the same year as *The Waste Land*, but *The Making of Americans* not until 1925. It was, of this group, stylistically the most radical, though politically the most conservative.[6] Morally and ideologically people of the center, its characters would be appalled by the ways of Bloom, let alone by Swann. David Hersland is self-directed not in dissent but in fulfillment of a cardinal American belief.

The Making of Americans overturns the tradition of the novel without any of the animus of *La Nausée*, which wants to indict the novel's whole culture. Alain Robbe-Grillet's "anti-novels" are closer descendants, but they too have an insurgent ambition Stein lacked. In her effort to capture the experience of being, of "actually existing," her quarrel with literary convention was not political but philosophical. Her style becomes unreadable when she pressed it to the logical conclusion of her metaphysics. From the eighteenth century onward, the novel had been telling stories about life as it is lived. *The Making of Americans* says that a novel instead ought to portray life as it *is*. This is very rigorous and inspiring, but *The Making of Americans* was a Pyrrhic victory; Gertrude Stein wrote no other novels.

---

[6] Gertrude Stein was generally politically conservative. Probably most relevant here would be the views she expressed in a series of articles for the *Saturday Evening Post* in opposition to the New Deal. The articles are entitled "Money," "More about Money," "Still More about Money," "All about Money," and "My Last about Money" (June–October 1936). The first begins: "Is money money . . . ? Everybody who earns it and spends it every day in order to live knows that money is money, anybody who votes it to be gathered in as taxes knows money is not money." And the last concludes: "One thing is sure until there are rich again everybody will be poor and there will be more than ever of everybody who is even poorer. That is sure and certain." In *Paris France (1939)* she summed up: "I cannot write too much upon how necessary it is to be completely conservative that is particularly traditional in order to be free." Last citation from Richard Bridgman, *Gertrude Stein in Pieces* (Oxford University Press, New York 1970).

ANN BANFIELD

Mrs. Dalloway
(Virginia Woolf, 1925)

Virginia Woolf made it clear on numerous occasions that she wished to "discover" a novelistic form that was an adequate vehicle for what Lytton Strachey called the "modern point of view."[1] The word *discover*, not simply *create*, is in keeping with her conviction that "modern fiction" aimed at a modern reality, one the novels of, say, Arnold Bennett, was incapable of capturing. Far from wishing to "tell stories," she thought of her art in quasi-scientific terms, perhaps marked, like Clarissa Dalloway, by her early reading of the Victorian physicist John Tyndall, friend of Woolf's father. In reshaping the novel, Woolf chose a model from the visual arts. Modernism, she intuited, was initially a movement in painting. That pictorial model was derived from the theories of her friend, the critic and artist Roger Fry, introducer into England of the painters that his 1910 exposition made known as the "postimpressionists." In Fry's theory, impressionism had carried to its logical conclusion the analysis of sense-appearances but had in the process dissolved the unity of the picture space. It was Cézanne who, benefiting from impressionism's "researches," had given its "vision" a "design." That form Fry did not entirely conceive as imposed on vision's findings; it was at least partly discovered underlying appearances, as Tyndall found in nature the form of the crystal or "the web of relations . . . experiments reveal to us."[2]

But how reconceive the "transformations" (again, Fry's term) of vision by design for a language art? Woolf's literary experiments recapitulated the art history Fry interpreted. After *The Voyage Out*'s (1915) tentative explorations, she had retreated to what years later she called "my exercise in the conventional style," *Night and Day* (1919). But alongside that exercise there were what she describes as "treats I allowed myself" when she had "done" her exercise. "I shall never forget the day I wrote the *Mark on the Wall* [1917]—all in a flash" (Bell, 2:42). The experimental play she treated herself to took the form of short stories, an apprenticeship other modern novelists practiced. "The *Unwritten Novel* was the great discovery," she pronounces of one story in the summer of 1917; it "showed me how I could embody all my deposit of

[1] Quentin Bell, *Virginia Woolf: A Biography* (San Diego: Harcourt Brace Jovanovich, 1972), 2:43. Hereafter cited parenthetically in the text.
[2] *Lectures on Light: Delivered in the United States in 1872–3* (New York: D. Appleton, 1873), 31.

experience in a shape that fitted it . . . *Jacob's Room* . . . *Mrs. Dalloway* etc."
(ibid.). These little fictions were not "stories" in the conventional sense; they
were moments, collections of impressions. Their impressionism consisted in
the thought experiment of imagining the world from another perspective in
time and space. For "there were other points of view."[3] "An Unwritten
Novel" speculates about "the knowledge of each face"[4] opposite the narrator
on a train, inventing the inner life of the woman across the compartment, as
Woolf would do in "Mr. Bennett and Mrs. Brown," the essay that counterposes her concept of the novel and its modern "reality" to the novels of Bennett, who had used the word *impressionist* disparagingly of Woolf. These
hypothetical viewpoints were the substitute for "the descriptions of reality"
as conceived by "the masculine point of view" ("An Unwritten Novel," 48).
In "place of . . . those real standard things" (47–48), like Sunday luncheons,
there was "a mark on the wall," "something definite, something real" (50)
with the solidity of a chest of drawers, of "the impersonal world which is a
proof of some existence other than ours" (p. 51). They are not simply the
substitution of private worlds for a reassuring world of social reality and
rules—"Whitaker's Almanack," "the Table of Precedency" (50); privacy is
put in contact with a world empty of the human. From the furniture, via
wood, the thought moves to trees, growing "without paying any attention to
us" (51). "Where was I? What has it all been about? A tree? A river? The
Downs? Whitaker's Almanack" (52). For the stories' impressionism consists
also in a style of free association, of the mind's wanderings, which supplies "a
new form for a new novel. Suppose one thing should open out of another—
as in An Unwritten Novel—only not for 10 pages but 200 or so . . . no scaf-
folding; scarcely a brick to be seen; all crepuscular."[5] Woolf was sensitive,
however, to Fry's criticism of impressionism. Planning *Jacob's Room* (1922),
she had pronounced "the unity . . . yet to discover . . . I must still grope & experiment" (*Diary*, 2:14; Jan. 26, 1920). She worried that the reviewers would
find *Mrs. Dalloway* "disjointed because of the mad scenes not connected with
the Dalloway scenes" (*Diary*, 2:323; Dec. 13, 1924).

Mrs. Dalloway had in fact begun in a short story, "Mrs. Dalloway in Bond
Street," a draft of the novel's opening. A comparison shows what besides

---

[3] *Mrs. Dalloway* (1925) (San Diego: Harcourt Brace Jovanovich, 1953), 197. Hereafter cited
parenthetically in the text.

[4] "An Unwritten Novel," in *A Haunted House and Other Stories* (1944) (Harmondsworth:
Penguin, 1973), 14. Hereafter cited parenthetically in the text.

[5] *The Diary of Virginia Woolf*, ed. Anne Olivier Bell, assisted by Andrew McNeillie (New
York: Harcourt Brace Jovanovich, 1978), 2:13–14. Jan. 26, 1920. Hereafter cited parenthetically in
the text.

length transformed impressionist story into postimpressionist novel. The first person of "An Unwritten Novel" and "The Mark on the Wall" disappears. The representation of Clarissa Dalloway's consciousness—in the story condensed in brief interior monologues, as is also the dialogue between her and Hugh Whitbread—are in the novel rendered in represented speech and thought (free indirect style). Not only are Clarissa's thoughts expanded in a use of this novelistic style for the representation of consciousness; the number of points of view is radically multiplied, as Monet multiplied the perspectives on Rouen cathedral. "I can bring innumerable other characters to her support," Woolf wrote of the Clarissa character (*Diary*, 2:272; Oct. 15, 1923). This is what Auerbach would call Woolf's "multipersonal style."[6] That multiplication of point of view would also explode each character, scattering the "shower of ideas" that "The Mark on the Wall" had spoken of, like the shot that scattered the rooks, a favorite metaphor.

The problem of unity caused by a radically impressionist technique required more than the explosion of the single point of view; the scattered ideas had to "settle," as the essay "Modern Fiction" would put it, into a Monday or a Tuesday, just as, Tyndall writes, "natural bodies have showered upon them, in the white light of the sun, the sum total of all possible colors, and their action is limited to the sifting of that total" (*Lectures on Light*, 29). Woolf's formulation suggests the design takes a temporal order. Here she may have benefited from the two models of Proust and Joyce, both of whom she was reading while writing *Mrs. Dalloway*. The novel borrows *Ulysses'* unity of time and place, the geography of a city. To give her June day a historical depth, Woolf uses what she calls a "tunnelling process" that "took me a year's groping to discover"; it gives "the past by instalments," making *Mrs. Dalloway* a kind of *Le temps retrouvé*—Proust's last volume also ends in a party reassembling the major characters—*A la recherche* compressed in one volume without the backing of the earlier volumes. Woolf called this "tunnelling process" in 1923 her "prime discovery so far" (*Diary*, 2:272; Oct. 15, 1923). That process had not been used in *Jacob's Room*, and it may have been her reading of Proust that triggered the "discovery." Nonetheless, the process is not his, nor its role in the design. She had earlier elaborated "about The Hours, & my discovery; how I dig out beautiful caves behind my characters"; the point was "that the caves shall connect, & each comes to daylight at the present moment" (*Dairy*, 2:263; Aug. 30, 1923). The technique is usually understood as the substitution of a subjective reality for

---

[6] Erich Auerbach, *Mimesis: The Representation of Reality in Western Literature* (Princeton, N.J.: Princeton University Press, 1953).

an objective one, but that is a half-truth. Each subjectivity thinks its own thoughts, but they contain references to times and places in the thoughts of other subjectivities that have thereby an independent existence—perhaps that is the reason for the Platonic word *caves*. The overlap is not necessarily apparent to the fictive thinker, although Clarissa has such intimations. With Peter Walsh and Sally Seton "she shared her past; the garden; the trees; old Joseph Breitkopf singing Brahms without any voice; the drawing-room wallpaper; the smell of the mats. A part of this Sally must always be; Peter must always be" (277). "Odd affinities she had with people she had never spoken to" (231). If the party brings Clarissa together with those she had, it is the novel's style that connects her to those she had not. Its ability to shift point of view and follow the mind's non sequiturs establishes relations between points of view and builds up a common past independent of the individual mind—it is this that the chiming of the hours in public time signals. The caves also interconnect via an impersonal past beyond human memory and a geography—not simply that of peopled London—on whose map also exists spaces empty of human presence. What is most important is not the moments of communication between two subjectivities, the thing that "permeated" that Clarissa lacked, that "broke up surfaces and rippled the cold contact of man and woman, of women together" (46). It is rather the knowledge, not possessed by any character, despite intimations of it, that there do exist hidden affinities. It is conventional to speak of the novel's impersonal knowledge in terms of the "omniscient narrator," but Woolf would have objected to the personification of a body of knowledge inherent in this theological notion. Writing in *Moments of Being* about her "philosophy" "that the whole world is a work of art," she resists the idea of a god in this creation: "there is no Shakespeare, there is no Beethoven; certainly and emphatically there is no God."[7] This "world seen without a self," as Woolf would call it in *The Waves*,[8] would assume a separate structural position to which she assigns the term *interludes* in the two novels that follow *Mrs. Dalloway*: the "Time Passes" section in *To the Lighthouse* (1927) and the chapter openings in *The Waves* (1930).

A literary design with the logical form of a knowledge larger than any individual's also structures a social vision. This is apparent in the scene early in the novel of the motor car passing through London carrying—"But nobody knew whose face had been seen. Was it the Prince of Wales's, the Queen's,

---

[7] *Moments of Being: Unpublished Autobiographical Writings*, ed. Jeanne Schulkind (Sussex: The University Press, 1976), 72.

[8] *The Waves* (New York: Harcourt Brace Jovanovich, 1931), 287.

the Prime Minister's?" (20). The event is registered by many minds, not only the major characters but ones created for the nonce by a proper name— Edgar J. Watkiss, Sir John Buckhurst, Moll Pratt, Sarah Bletchley, and Mr. Bowley—as later for the skywriting plane. They cohere in the crowd: the car "ruffl[es] the faces on both sides of the street with the same dark breath of veneration whether for Queen, Prince or Prime Minister nobody knew" (23). "All heads were inclined the same way" (25). An identical reverence moves the guests at Clarissa's party; without their being aware of the emotion shared with the street, they "felt to the marrow of their bones, this majesty passing; this symbol of what they all stood for, English society . . . a sort of stir and rustle rippled through every one, openly: the Prime Minister!" (262). Their "affinity" is shown to have consequences (like the "economic consequences of the peace" which for Keynes do their work beyond the personalities who created the Versaillles treaty). At the personal level, the emotion in each breast, although treated with gentle humor, is not presented as ridiculous or sinister. They "seemed ready to attend their Sovereign, if need be, to the cannon's mouth, as their ancestors had done before them" (26). But there is another level from which it is assessed. Everywhere the novel reminds us of the "prying and insidious . . . fingers of the European War" (129). It is especially Septimus Warren Smith who bears often silent witness to another viewpoint. Septimus hears Edgar J. Watkiss pronounce "The Proime Minister's kyar." His eyes, we read, "had that look of apprehension in them which makes complete strangers apprehensive" (20). Something has put him out of step with those inclined the same way, despite the fact that he "was one of the first to volunteer" (130). If "in the trenches" there occurs "the change which Mr. Brewer desired when he advised football" (130), we almost hear the voice of Samuel Beckett's Lucky, after another European war, countering "in spite of the strides of physical culture the practice of sports such as football running cycling swimming flying floating riding gliding conating camogie skating tennis of all kinds dying flying sports of all sorts . . . the dead loss per head."[9] For Septimus, suffering what Sir William Bradshaw diagnoses as "the deferred effects of shell-shock" (279) that lead to his suicide, has felt against the current the ripple effect of the motor car, "so trifling in single instances that no mathematical instrument, though capable of transmitting shocks in China, could register the vibration; yet in its fulness rather formidable and in its common appeal emotional; for in all the hat shops and tailors' shops strangers looked at each other and thought of the

---

[9] Samuel Beckett, *Waiting for Godot* (New York: Grove Press, 1954), 29.

dead; of Empire. In a public house in a back street a Colonial insulted the House of Windsor which led to words, broken beer glasses, and a general shindy" (25–26). The medium through which this power sends its waves is the same through which the "the ring after ring of sound" (56) of Big Ben and St. Margaret's tolls the hours. The metaphor of the waves denotes the same system of relations that the interconnected caves do.

If the social is a system of minds thinking in unison, with one put out of step (Peter Walsh, with all his criticism of empire, is moved by the same swell of patriotism as the crowd), it is also a conflict of points of view. Against the crowd's assent, there is one thoroughly negative point of view in the novel, that of "the odious" (193) Doris Kilman: "she talked too about the war. After all, there were people who did not think the English invariably right" (197). Clarissa's hatred of her (266) is scarcely counterbalanced by Woolf's portrait. Unlike in Arnold Bennett, no authorial voice decides the conflict, imposes one viewpoint; it eschews conversion, "a Goddess even now engaged—in the heat and sands of India, the mud and swamp of Africa, the purlieus of London," "loving to impress, to impose, adoring her own features stamped on the face of the populace" (151)—and whose missionary Kilman is, along with Sir William Bradshaw. Recording the postwar moment, that of the triumph of Britain, the defeat of the pacifist movement Bloomsbury had been a part of, *Mrs. Dalloway* counterposes the gaping crowd, one bearer of future possibility, to the unformed young, to Clarissa's daughter Elizabeth, to the young woman Peter Walsh follows, who passed Gordon's statue without a glance, "Gordon whom as a boy he had worshipped" (77), Gordon whose eminence Lytton Strachey reduced in *Eminent Victorians* (1918). Their viewpoints are scarcely revealed; the caves that contain their past have no depth yet. Elizabeth—between Kilman, "Elizabeth's seducer" (66), and Clarissa, who acknowledges the conflict as "real" (266)—exposed in the streets, floats in its currents, undecided. "She liked the geniality, sisterhood, motherhood, brotherhood of this uproar" (209), a "pioneer"—"no Dalloway came down the Strand daily" (208)—but does not yet partake in it.

Without one being privileged, the different viewpoints are measured with respect to some reality—the war, for instance, or class conflict. This is the work of a style that moves beyond the moment to another time, "when London is a grass-grown path and all those hurrying along the pavement this Wednesday morning are but bones with a few wedding rings" (23), beyond the here to another place, beyond "one little point of view" (255) to other minds and beyond them to another world, external to this one, where the car, "the enduring symbol of the state" would "be known to curious antiquaries, sifting the ruins of time" (23). Among the style's tools are the epic similes. Their force is universalizing: they interconnect the caves not only among themselves but relate them to a larger world both social and natural, to a history longer than the human life or indeed human life on earth. A particular character or situation is compared to an indefinite—"So before a battle begins, the horses paw the ground" (66); "like a Queen whose guards have fallen asleep" (65); "as a cloud crosses the sun" (73); "like the smoke from a cottage chimney" (125); "like a woman who had slipped off her print dress" (245); or "just as happens on a terrace in the moonlight, when one person begins to feel ashamed that he is already bored, and yet as the other sits silent, . . . moves his foot, clears his throat, notices some iron scroll on a table leg, stirs a leaf, but says nothing—so Peter Walsh did now" (63).

So, hearing "trumpets (the unemployed) blaring," Elizabeth is left wandering the streets as the text, analogically, imagines a truth contrary to fact; instead of people marching, "had they been dying," still that "uproar" would have risen to "whoever was watching" the dying, "consolatory, indifferent" (209). "It was not conscious," the text continues of the uproar, which partakes of a quality of the style itself. "There was no recognition in it of one fortune, or fate, and for that very reason even to those dazed with watching for the last shivers of consciousness on the faces of the dying, consoling. Forgetfulness in people might wound, their ingratitude corrode, but this voice, pouring endlessly, year in year out, would take whatever it might be; this vow; this van; this life; this procession, would wrap them all about and carry them on, as in the rough stream of a glacier the ice holds a splinter of bone, a blue petal, some oak trees, and rolls them on" (209–10). The analogy of the glacier, straight out of Woolf's girlhood reading of Tyndall, author of *The Glaciers of the Alps*, yields a vision of historical time in which forces running against the tide of empire, counter to the "boys in uniform, carrying guns, march[ing] with their eyes ahead of them" (76), are washed clean of Kilman's personal rancor; the protest of the anonymous unemployed gives postwar hope that contrasts with the docile reverence of the earlier crowd, who "had heard the voice of authority; the spirit of religion was abroad with her eyes bandaged tight and her lips gaping wide" (20). For it is only "for thirty seconds" that heads "inclined the same way" (25); the gaping faces cowed by "majesty" in the next second might blast the trumpets of the unemployed. Connected by the forces that confront it, that sometimes it worships, with disastrous consequences, and other times it opposes, the crowd, like the young, can list either way; "still untouched" (54), the moment, the individual, remains contingent, as when Peter Walsh, "because nobody yet knew he was in London," feels "the strangeness of standing alone, alive, unknown, at half-past eleven in Trafalgar Square" (77–78). But once caught in the frozen river of history, the moment of June, like the bone or petal, is forever in its place in the series; there, were the glacier to reach him, would Peter Walsh sit in his embarrassment forever, the chance lost.

If any attempt to sway the reading in one direction instead of the other seems tainted by the very spirit of conversion, the text nonetheless absolves the voices contaminated with *ressentiment*—Kilman's, "embittered," "her soul rusted with that grievance sticking in it" (16) or Clarissa's, with the indifference of privilege—and draws out conclusions immanent in their bias. So it is that Clarissa's continual confusion of the Armenians and the Albanians (181) does not simply condemn the insouciance of her class nor expose her husband's committee work in their behalf. Instead, strangely her unmoved reiteration of "the Armenians" allows the text to record the bare facts. "Hunted out of existence, maimed, frozen, the victims of cruelty and injustice (she had heard Richard say so over and over again)—no, she could feel nothing for the Albanians, or was it the Armenians?" (182). In this great work of modernism is one of the rare references in contemporary literature to that genocide; it wraps its mourning in the indifference of a Mayfair hostess, unconscious tool of the author, like the "consolatory" indifference Woolf attributes to the uproar of the London streets, and like Lucky's "the dead loss per head," an outcry disguised in the language of bureaucracy and barely heard in the stream of words. Behind the viewpoint is the fact, one of those that Wittgenstein's *Tractatus*, coming out of the war a few years before *Mrs. Dalloway*, said made up the totality of the world. There are alternative futures contained in the combination of fact and viewpoint making up its accumulation of retrospect, the novel suggests, without offering either hope or despair. All lies in the relation between the crowd and the new generation; struck together, what change will they produce? Such is the modernity of *Mrs. Dalloway*'s realism, "entre deux guerres."

JOSÉ LUIZ PASSOS

Macunaíma
(Mário de Andrade, 1928)

In 1928, when Mário de Andrade (1893–1945) published *Macunaíma. The Hero without Any Character*, he was already the author of four volumes of poetry, a collection of stories, a modernist poetics, and a first novel, published the year before. Brazilian prose fiction had only a recent history, having been inaugurated little more than eighty years earlier, and it assumed its characteristic national tendency from the romantic indianism of José de Alencar.[1] In the midnineteenth century, Brazilian romanticism had initiated a mode of treating national material in the novel; Brazilian modernism—contemporary with the European avant-garde of the 1920s—would appropriate from the earlier romantic generation a similar standard of aesthetic intentionality: aiming to renew itself in formal opposition to Europe by sounding its own national identity through the sophisticated incorporation of themes drawn from folklore and popular culture. The romantic Brazilian novel, above all in its indianist slant, devoted itself to securing for the young nation—independent from Portugal since 1822—an apparent mythical depth, expressed through legend and "foundational fictions."[2] In the two works that most succeeded at this operation, José de Alencar's novels *O Guarani* (1857) and *Iracema* (1865), the heroes are subjected to a transformation of identity that culminates in the symbolic or actual extinction of the protagonists through a full conversion of indigenous elements to Christian civilization, as represented by interracial marriage or, in an ultimate act, by an altruistically redemptive death. Three fundamental elements of romantic indianism would resurface in the composition of *Macunaíma*: the use of indigenous legends, myths, and fables in the making of the modernist intrigue; the mixing of this traditional repertoire with historical arguments and facts

---

[1] The relationship between nineteenth-century Brazilian fiction and the possible literary models for the "American novel," primarily Sir Walter Scott, Chateaubriand, and James Fenimore Cooper, appears to be an anxious one from the perspective of the most important Brazilian romantic prosaicist; for his own words, see J. M. de Alencar, *Como e porque sou romancista*, in *Obra completa* (Rio de Janeiro, 1958), 1:148–50.

[2] See D. Sommer, *Foundational Fictions: The National Romances of Latin America* (Berkeley: University of California Press, 1991), 138–71, and R. R. Mautner Wasserman, *Exotic Nations: Literature and Cultural Identity in the United States and Brazil, 1830–1930* (Ithaca, N.Y.: Cornell University Press, 1994), 186–219.

concerning the formation of the Brazilian nation; and finally, the insistence on the use of a new language, based on an adherence to a lexicon and, in many cases, syntax belonging to indigenous and popular culture. In this sense, the uncertainties inherent in the representation of a hybrid culture and the desire to define a modern Brazilian language—distinct from Lusitanian Portuguese—as well the persistence of themes associated with transformation and death, can be counted among the objectives that Andrade inherited from the nineteenth century that are clearly present in this novel that is at once encyclopedic, nationalist, and experimental.[3] Nevertheless, the two fundamental achievements of the romantic Brazilian novel would be inverted in Andrade's work though modernist parody: the composition and detailed examination of specific social spaces and types would be dissolved by the ambitious simultaneous representation of all possible Brazilian times and spaces; and the creation of the virtuous hero, who ought to internally combine the purity of a primitive culture and the nobility of Christian values, would be subverted by the modern hero, marked by a combination of often grotesquely contradictory psychological and biophysical traits.

Modernist production in Brazil, at least in its initial and most profoundly transgressive phase, seems to indicate a change in the regional and political organization of the national literary system: the federal capital—at the time situated in Rio de Janeiro—began to lose its exclusive role as productive center and disseminator of literary movements; and, in various senses, Brazilian modernism owes its existence to the accelerated growth of the coffee economy. Between 1890 and 1930, São Paulo was responsible for an intense modernization of the Brazilian agricultural economy, resulting in part from the use of foreign labor. Agricultural diversification, urbanization, and the beginning of modern industrialization on a national scale, initially financed by the coffee economy, permitted the city of São Paulo, already by the early 1920s to become the youngest—and perhaps the only—modern Brazilian metropolis. This accelerated process of social and economic change, associated with the strong presence of immigration, confronted the intellectual and proprietary elite of São Paulo with an apparent contradiction—asking them to assume the role of agents of progress and, concomitantly, to deal with what were, in fact, traditional aspects within the

---

[3] In an open letter to the poet Alberto de Oliveira, published in 1925 in the modernist journal *Estética*, Andrade effects an essential revision of the significance of romanticism within Brazilian cultural development. This letter makes clear the deliberate link between Brazilian romanticism and modernism proposed by the author of *Macunaíma*. See M. de Andrade, "*Carta a Alberto Oliveira*," in *Estética*, ed. P. Dantas (Rio de Janeiro, 1974), 332–39.

sort of social organization that this modernization implied. In other words, we should not lose sight of the fact that this surge in economic development and intellectual renewal was instigated and propped up by an essentially agricultural national economy, generating preindustrial products for external markets. The originality of Brazilian modernism resides, in large part, in the elaboration of aesthetic responses to the impasses generated by that contradictory modernization. The contrast of the archaic with the modern, through the coexistence of relations, values, and symbols of distinct sociocultural origins, would profoundly mark the artistic production of the Brazilian modernist movement and would be converted, above all in *Macunaíma*, into a principle of literary composition clearly dependent on a parody of high culture.

Based on a considerable collection of ethnographic and linguistic data, *Macunaíma* was composed primarily on the basis of the fables gathered by the German anthropologist Theodor Koch-Grünberg between 1911 and 1913, published in Germany during the 1920s.[4] Mário de Andrade found in this collection of fables and myths of the Amazonian tribes Taulipang and Arecuná a burlesque and contradictory semigod, "without any moral or psychological character" that the writer judged "somewhat suited to our epoch."[5] Divided into seventeen small chapters and a brief epilogue, the novel is faithfully based on a combination of the adventures of various indigenous entities, especially those of the indigenous "trickster" Macunaíma, who would be transformed by Andrade into an egoistic, lazy, self-interested, lying, and often perverse, but also happy, valiant, tender, and exceptionally enchanting hero.[6]

---

[4] Andrade based his writing principally on the ethnographic accounts collected in the second volume of T. Koch-Grünberg's *Von Roroima zum Orinoco, Ergebnisse einer Reise in Nordbrailien und Venezuela in den Jahren 1911–1913*, 5 vols. (Berlin, 1917–28). The various historical and literary sources used in *Macunaíma* were traced in the pioneering work of M. Cavalcanti Proença, *Roteiro de Macunaíma*, 5th ed. (Rio de Janeiro, 1978) and, subsequently, in the scrupulous study of the marginalia and library of the author, by T. Porto Ancona Lopez, *Macunaíma, a margem e o texto* (São Paulo, 1974).

[5] M. de Andrade, *71 cartas de Mário de Andrade*, ed. L. Fernandes (Rio de Janeiro, 1963), 31.

[6] The derivative relationship of the modernist hero Macunaíma to the eponymous character of indigenous legends is delineated in the critical edition of the novel: Mário de Andrade, *Macunaíma o herói sem nenhum caráter*, ed. T. Porto Ancona Lopez, 2nd ed. (Paris: Association Archives de la Littérature Latino-Américaine, 1988), 311–39.

Although the novel is characterized by the constant presence of countless legends and fables interpolated throughout the principal plot line, the narrative has a linear progression. The unity of the plot is guaranteed by exclusive attention to the exploits of the hero: Macunaíma, born "deep-dyed black" ["*preto retinto*"] among a tribe of Indians from the northern Amazon, sets off with two brothers on a journey without a specified end after having caused the death of his mother.[7] On the way, his union with the Amazonian Ci, the Mother of the Forest, converts him into the Emperor of the Virgin Forest. After the premature death of their son, Ci decides to go to heaven transformed into a star and presents the hero with the stone *muiraquitã*—as a source of luck and remembrance of the couple's amorous affair. The hero loses the stone in one of his escapes after affronting more than one mythical entity and later receives the message that it lies in São Paulo in the hands of the parsimonious Peruvian huckster Venceslau Pietro Pietra, the giant Piaimã, a cannibal. On his way to São Paulo, Macunaíma whitens his skin after having bathed in a fount of magical waters, transforming himself as well as his two brothers into a racial synthesis of Brazilian culture—"one blond one red another black."[8] The three head off to São Paulo, and the giant becomes the principal opponent of the hero, who refuses to marry one of the daughters of Vei, the sun, forsaking the opportunity to become the true son and unrivaled hero of the civilizations of the tropics.[9] In his various attempts to vanquish Venceslau Pietro Pietra—and also in the course of dealings with other characters in the city—the hero dies twice and, in both cases, is revived by one of his brothers. Finally, Macunaíma manages to kill his adversary through a combination of malicious and puerile games. With the *muiraquitã* retaken, the three brothers return to Uraricoera, their land of origin, where the jealousy and egoism of the hero result in the death of his brothers and of his companion. Macunaíma ends up living alone, accompanied only by a parrot who listens to and repeats his tales. Finally, the sun Vei avenges herself for the hero's betrayal in refusing to marry one of her daughters and sets up the scenario for his death: compelled by Vei's heat and seduced by a vision of Uiara, a sort of sweet water mermaid, he dives into a lake where he is dismembered by piranhas, again losing his amulet, the stone *muiraquitã*.

---

[7] Andrade, *Macunaíma o herói sem nenhum caráter*, ch. 1.

[8] Ibid., ch. 5.

[9] Whereas the Luso-Brazilian term for sun, *sol*, is masculine, the term *vei*, which signifies the sun in the Taulipangue language, is feminine in gender [Einaudi editorial note].

This brief plot summary of the novel makes clear Andrade's adherence to the legendary character of the materials on which he based his own making of a modernist hero.[10] The plot line progresses rapidly, accompanied by the perpetual state of displacement and change of a hero capable of transforming others—and himself—into diverse objects and animals. In the final chapter, when Macunaíma emerges from the water, recomposing the body mutilated during his struggle with the beasts that sought to avenge the sun Vei, the hero tries, unsuccessfully, to make sense of his ungoverned existence. Searching for one of his legs and for the present from his beloved Ci, without ever finding them, the hero—not for the first time—gives up on life, and the modernist fable closes a few pages later, having consummated the various prefigurations of Macunaíma's death and having brought the hero closer to that destiny common to the hybrid protagonists that Brazilian literature had already buried:

> The hero could hold out no longer, stopped. He crossed his arms with so heroic a despair that everything dilated in space in order to contain the silence of that grief . . .
>
> Then Macunaíma found no more sense in staying on this earth. Capei shimmered so new there in the *gupiara* of the sky. Macunaíma considered half-undecided still, uncertain whether he would rather live in the heavens or on the island of Marajó. For a moment he even thought of living in the city of Stone with the energetic Delmiro Gouveio, but then his spirit sagged. To live there as he had lived would be impossible. This senselessness was why he no longer found any pleasure in living on Earth. . . . All that had been his existence despite so many affairs so much play so much illusion so much suffering so much heroism, after all was no more letting oneself live; and stopping in Delmiro's city or on the island of Marajó, places on this earth, would require some reason. And he did not have the courage for any reasoning. He decided:
>
> "What how! . . . When *urubu* is out of luck the one below shits on the one above, this world doesn't suit me anymore and I'm going to heaven!"
>
> He would go to heaven to live with his *marvada*. He would be the beautiful but useless sparkle of an extra constellation. It didn't matter that he would be a useless sparkle, no, at least he would be the same as all those relatives, of all those parents of the living from his native land, mothers fathers

---

[10] Based on the morphological analysis proposed by V. Propp, H. de Campos elucidates the structural correspondence between the novel and its mythical matrices in *Morfologia do Macunaíma* (São Paulo, 1973).

brothers sisters brothers-in-law sisters-in-law, all those acquaintances living now off the useless shine/sparkle of the stars.

He planted a seed of the tortoise tree [*cipó matamatá*], son-of-the-moon,[11] and while the tree grew he grabbed onto a sharp stone [*itá*][12] and wrote on the flagstone[13] that had been a turtle[14] in an earlier age:

I DID NOT COME TO THE WORLD TO BE A STONE[15]

Macunaíma renounces life and goes to heaven, transformed into a constellation. The conclusion of Andrade's novel transforms the theme of moral redemption or Christian conversion, typical of the nineteenth-century romantic novel, into a correlative motif that would mark Brazilian fiction of the twentieth century: the connection between language, identity, and death.

Macunaíma was a hero without a cause, accommodating, rebellious, hedonistic, and in various ways solitary by choice. His death is less a punishment than an issue of his own internal conviction. For the hero, death represents both rest and a role as guide for future generations. In a conclusion that fuses elements of indigenous mythology with Christian symbolism, Macunaíma ascends to the heavens by renouncing both the option of returning to tradition—going to live on the island of Marajó—and that of gambling on modernity—returning to São Paulo, the city of Stone. The heavens and the metropolis form an antinomic pair, opposing the uselessness of the shining of the stars and the pragmatic organization of urban life that disenchanted Macunaíma, undoing any pleasure he might have had in living on earth. The island of Marajó would be the possibility of a return to an original legendary space, but Macunaíma opts to go to heaven and is transformed by the Father of Mutum—in fact, the constellation of the Cruzeiro do Sul—into Ursa Major. The image of the stars' useless shining translates the ideal of the purely static, of contemplation that opposes itself to the mechanical rhythm of the modern metropolis. The allegory of his conversion into a constellation essentially

---

[11] [Translator's note: *Matamatá* derives from the Tupi *matama'ta* and designates a bearded tortoise of the Chelonia family that lives in the still waters and lakes of the Amazon; here it refers to an Amazonian tree that Machado de Assis called *cipó filho da luna* [son of the moon]. Cf. Andrade, *Macunaíma: O herói sem nenhum caráter*, 453.]

[12] [Translator's note: This term, again derived from Tupi-Guarani and recognizable to the Brazilian reader, designates a rock or metal that is especially associated with death, polished to a shine and used to decorate funeral urns.]

[13] [Translator's note: The term can also mean gravestone.]

[14] [Translator's note: The term *jabuti* can mean both land turtle and separating ground or gin, for detaching seed from cotton.]

[15] *Macunaíma*, ch. 17.

represents the hero's maxim, "Ai! . . . what laziness! . . . ," associated with the idea of creative indolence, which functions throughout the narrative by interrupting the agitated construction of the protagonist's actions and undermining his engagement to any absolute principle or collective value. The constant prefigurations of the hero's death and his gradual degeneration, decay, and mutilation contrast with the sublime and cathartic character of the denouement, as if this finale were a matter of expurgation of the guilt of both worlds now inhabited by the hero, historical and mythical. Macunaíma's decision apparently favors useless and resigned isolation, but, in fact, this can be understood, if only in part, as a redemptive communion with memory, whose contribution would be precisely the antidote against the perversities of that intemperate and anonymous life that had initially enchanted the hero in the modern metropolis. His encounter with the degraded elements of Western civilization had already been glamorized in the so-called Letter to the Icamiabas—chapter 9 of the novel and the highest point of Brazilian modernism's experimental prose—in which the hero finds, in the grotesque character of the modern city, in the Old World, traces equivalent to his own natural disposition: "disorganized pornography," to use the author's own words; the compulsion to pursue easy gain; and a constant state of infirmity.[16] Insofar as Macunaíma is transformed by his visit to São Paulo, the transcendental conclusion of the hero's life can be taken as the beginning of a tropical critique of Latino-American modernity, realized through primitivist parody.

———

The encounter with difference and diversity characterizes not only this hero, impatient to collate the ambivalent traces inherent in his own self-definition, but also the mode by which Andrade organizes the narrative material of his novel. Several of the precursors of *Macunaíma* had already confronted a similar set of motivations at both formal and thematic levels. As already indicated, José de Alencar's *O Guarani* and *Iracema*, for example, also take part in this obsessive search for a foundational Brazilian legend or novel, which would find in the encounter of cultures the origins of a new language and of a new hero, defined, finally, by the intervention of conversion and death. In the spirit of nationalist experimentalism, Andrade himself had already composed a book of poems, *Clã do Jaboti* (1926), and a novel formed in the sentimental

---

[16] M. de Andrade, *Prefácios para Macunaíma*, in M. Batista Rossetti, Y. Soares de Lima, and T. Porto Ancona Lopez, eds., *Brasil: 1° tempo modernista—1917/29: Documentação* (São Paulo, 1972), 290.

tradition, *Amar, verbo intransitivo* (1927). The former testifies to the geographical and cultural extension of the themes treated by the author, who renounces an exclusive reliance on São Paulo and incorporates regional legends and themes in his poetry. In the 1927 novel, however, we find the first expansive expression of Mário de Andrade's efforts to "write Brazilian" by adopting a significantly oral diction and popular syntax.[17] *Macunaíma* consummates this project of systematizing the Brazilian language in view of generating a new artistic language capable of dealing with national reality. This novel is fabricated in an impossible, truly encyclopedic language. It gathers lexical and syntactical elements of various Brazilian regions, interweaving legends and popular sayings not only at the level of content, but also of style, through the incorporation of various linguistic and cultural registers that conform to an apparent unity of national culture.[18] In direct contrast with the prevailing standards of the romantic through the premodernist novel, which dictated the verisimilitude and homogeneity of the subject matter, *Macunaíma* presents a linguistic pan-regionalism that draws from the operation of *bricolage* that is inherent in manifestations of folklore and popular culture the elements necessary to the creation of a hero and a kind of speech that would transcend particularities.[19]

In composing his modernist hero, Andrade's choice of the "trickster" from among the various profiles offered by indigenous mythology results in

---

[17] In the unpublished postscript to *Amar, verbo intransitivo*, Andrade had insisted on the "necessity of employing lexical brasilianisms, not only in their exact sense, but rather already in a translated, metaphorical sense, as I did," with a view to the "future formation of a Brazilian literary language and grammar" (M. de Andrade, *Amar, verbo intransitivo: Idílio*, 16th ed. [Belo Horizonte, 1989], 151–52). Immediately following, in annotations for a preface that was likewise never published, the author would affirm that "Amar, Verbo Intransitivo + Clan do Jaboti = Macunaíma" (M. de Andrade, *Prefácios para Macunaíma*, 295).

[18] Concerning the author's efforts toward a Brazilian grammar that might go so far as to systematize national linguistic expression at the literary level, see J. M. Barbosa Gomes, *Mário de Andrade e a revolução da linguagem: A gramatiquinha da fala brasileira* (São Paulo, 1979); and E. Pimentel Pinto, *A gramatiquinha de Mário de Andrade: Texto e contexto* (São Paulo, 1990).

[19] One of the great difficulties in translating *Macunaíma* into any foreign language lies in the fact that the novel itself was constructed through a great effort at internal translation within the Portuguese language spoken in Brazil in its various dialects. This difficulty is particularly notable in the frequent enumerations that the narrative uses to describe the hero's surroundings: in these cases, short lists of substantives, undifferentiated by punctuation, comprise names of animals, plants, or geographical particularities. In many cases, the enumerations have a single referent, provoking, through the representation of multiple regional variations of the same term, an effect of lexical saturation that deregionalizes the scenario in which Macunaíma finds himself, rendering him present in various places in Brazil at the same time and situating him in a "degeographied" space, as the author himself used to say.

an inversion of the models and values generally associated with the characterization of the hero in the Western epic tradition.[20] Like the coyote of Navaho mythology and the picaro of the Spanish Renaissance novel, Macunaíma is a knavish hero; he represents the chaotic and subversive element in the cosmos, averse to hierarchies and to the regular character of work. His sagacious and reveling ingenuity together with his refusal to compromise with rules in general constitute both his subjectivist tendency and his lack of character, which can be well understood simultaneously as a lack of homogenous characteristics that might define his identity and as an indifference to Western moral values.

Mário de Andrade's experiment bore fruit. In the regionalism of the social novel of the 1930s—the movement that immediately follows the publication of *Macunaíma*—the exploration of linguistic and cultural particularities, albeit from a more traditional narrative perspective, forms the foundation of the search for a new national literary aesthetic. Subsequently, in the hands of perhaps the most notable Brazilian writer of the twentieth century, João Guimarães Rosa, the theme of the hybrid protagonist, hesitating between two cultures, would regain its experimental character in the tale "Meu tio, o Iauarête" (1961). In this work, a mestizo narrator, a hunter of jaguars, weaves a long monologue that seeks to seduce his hearer in order to subjugate him; in the end, the narrator transforms himself through language into a jaguar and compels his interlocutor to kill him. In the novels *Maíra* (1976), by Darcy Ribeiro, and *A expedição Montaigne* (1982), by Antonio Callado, we find the theme of linguistic experimentalism that explores the limits of novelistic form in order to narrate the misadventures of two acculturated Indians, who, after their conversion to Western values, head toward dissolution.[21] In all these texts, among others, we find the true legacy

---

[20] G. de Mello e Souza, in *O tupi e o alaúde: Uma interpretação de Macunaíma* (São Paulo, 1979), suggestively proposes that diverse forms of popular musical culture were incorporated in *Macunaíma* in order to compose a narrative that would mimeticize and parody the tradition of Arthurian romance and the quest for the Holy Grail. On the use and redefinition of epic in modernity, see F. Moretti, *Opere mondo: Saggio sulla forma epica dal "Faust" a "Cent'anni di solitudine"* (Turin, 1994). Comparisons approximating *Macunaíma* and European modernism are rare, although necessary. The connections between Andrade's novel and James Joyce's *Ulysses*, Virginia Woolf's *Orlando*, and Robert Musil's *Der Mann Ohne Eigenschaften* are evident; for an attempt at a partial comparison of the heroes Macunaíma and Leopold Bloom, see J. L. Passos, "Prefiguração musical em *Ulysses* e *Macunaíma*," in *Ruínas de linhas puras: Quatro ensaios em torno a "Macunaíma"* (São Paulo, 1998), 71–97.

[21] A comparative analysis of the three of the most important novels of Brazilian neo-indianism written between 1967 and 1982 can be found in J. L. Passos, "A figura, o réquiem e a cerveja: Três visões de um Brasil entre Darcy Ribeiro e Antônio Callado," *Revista de Crítica Literária Latinoamericana* 24, no. 49 (1997): 217–30.

of *Macunaíma*: the combination of the motifs of hybrid language, identity, and death as a solution for the most ancient desire of youthful Brazilian literature: to certify that its "impure speech"[22] was capable of expressing the ineffable and responding with beauty to the question that never seems to exhaust itself: after all, who are we, who live in two worlds?

Translated by Sharon Lubkemann Allen

[22] Andrade, "Epilogue" to *Macunaíma*.

SEAMUS DEANE

Finnegans Wake
(James Joyce, 1939)

Finnegans Wake is not a historical novel in any of the troubled senses of that
term, yet few works of fiction include more references to history, and few
versions of history assign to events such a tightly woven narrative pattern of
repetition with variation. The interfusion of Irish history with world history
and of world history with global myth is produced by an astonishing inter-
mingling of words and sounds in sequences that are brilliantly devised but
sometimes seem as though they are illuminatingly derived. These make the
Wake an etymological inferno. As a consequence of the Fall in the "garden
of idem" (263.20–21), words have lost their transparency and become
opaque, obscurely related to one another across various languages, producing wild broods and breedings of meaning through miscegeneation and ultimately, in falling further into the pit of writing, "sinscript" (421.18), have
reached the point where individual letters can generate different meanings
according to the typographical position they assume on the page.[1] Adam's
race is damned because of that first fall, and the subsequent court cases on
the crime constitute a core element of the history of a narrative that, by its
nature, must be postlapsarian and must be the one central story, endlessly
diversified. The accent in which the story is told can alter the "original
sinse" (239.2), especially if it is an Irish accent; but diacritical signs are also a
form of accent, and they too increase the range and inflect the musics of
meaning, especially if they are, like Irish or Hebrew, elaborate in their acci-
dence and syntax.

The *Wake* is also an epic and a mock epic, a myth and a near-myth, a
novel full of names but without characters (although the central names—
HCE and ALP—are not just initials, and therefore beginnings, but also
characters of an alphabet). The Fall separated signifier and signified, but it
also produced the false traumatic memory of the time, or the timelessness,
in which these two were happily married, before concupiscence and the
appalling large population of world-symbols that were thereby randomly
produced. The book is also an act of vengeance on the world of *Dubliners*

---

[1] James Joyce, *Finnegans Wake* (London: Faber and Faber), 1939. All quotations are from this
edition and are cited parenthetically in the text by page and line number.

and of *Portrait of the Artist as a Young Man*. Those works were immersed in the difficulties of finding speech, a language of one's own, which was also the difficulty of telling one's own story, the history that had left one bereft of the capacity either to tell it or to be silent about it. Joyce's response to this aspect of the Irish experience of colonialism is not a matter of finding one's voice or language, having somehow mislaid it. Nor is it entirely a matter of recovering a lost agency, the power of speaking or writing. To have undergone domination has at least the merit of exposing to the dominated the fragility of those fundamentals upon which systems of power rest, among them the identification of established power with the natural order. An attendant seduction is the idea of a realm of individual, autonomous freedom. Stephen Dedalus, for instance, engages in a contest between the belief that there is a unique language of the self to be discovered and the realization that he is spoken by the languages that he inherits, all the more so in virtue of his desire to escape from them. The fact that these include the "native" Irish he can no longer read or speak and the "foreign" English that has become native to him intensifies the contest beyond the possibility of resolution. However, his vain and vainglorious search does reveal the covert intimacies between political hypocrisy—the rationale of "civilization" that sanctions barbaric practices, for instance—and the forgery involved in the artist's creation of the "real." The critique of this provides one of the languages of the modern novel, from Conrad to Céline. But the language of the novel is only one among many in the *Wake*, the novel of language.

Yet the *Wake* is not a novel, and it is not not a novel either. The most novel idea in it is that there is no such thing as a novel story. All stories are the same story. It is perhaps the fiction in which anthropology first becomes a form of literature, the golden bough that grew from the grey trunk of nineteenth-century realism or naturalism. But this new form of writing demands a new form of reading. The dream-language of the *Wake* is freely associative and highly controlled; it is fallen language suffused with a prelapsarian nostalgia that is itself a consequence of the Fall. The figure of ALP (Eve, Ireland, Helen, Anna Livia) is praised for what she has done for us, but we need to listen carefully and to hear and look carefully to see all the nuances of this achievement or accident, if there is any durable distinction between the two: "How bootifull and how truetowife of her, when strengly forebidden, to steal our historic presents from the past propheticals so as to will make us all lordy heirs and ladymaidesses of a pretty nice kettle of fruit. She is livving in our midst of debt and laffing through all plores for us (her birth is uncontrollable), with a naperon for her mask and her sabboes kickin arias (so sair! so solly!) if yous ask me and I saack you" (11.29–35).

Such a text also challenges the process of printing and the procedures of proofreading. When is an "error" a mistake? Can any editor, proofreader, reader, or professional interpreter be trusted to know and then to say what the text should say, how it should be read? Perhaps only the disturbed sage (Le Sage) is detective enough to lift the roof off the house, the lid off the box and show what is going on or release all the previously pent-up possibilities, although they open to and derive from the same base—"sesameseed" (95.15). ". . . (I should like to ask that Shedlock Homes person who is out for removing the roofs of our criminal classics by what *deductio ad domunum* he hopes *de tacto* to detect anything unless he happens of himself, *movibile tectu*, to have a slade off) . . ." (165.32–36).

It may be the case, as Ford Madox Ford, one of the *Wake*'s most discerning early readers and defenders, said in May 1939: "To get a full joy out of Mr. Joyce's polychromatic fugal effects of language, one must have been brought up in either jesuit or high Anglican neighbourhoods or in any one of the vast territories that lie between those two extremes."[2] Even if people reared in such vicinities could be expected to savor all the effects Joyce produces from his agglomerations of what is said to be sixty-five languages, does this exile from such pleasures all those not so formed and educated? In one sense, the question is absurd, but it does immediately serve to remind us that the *Wake*, so widely considered to be ambitiously global in its form and medium, is the most untranslatable of works. A translation of it, in any accepted sense of the word, is inconceivable. This is perhaps an indication of its universality, even if that be of the Esperanto kind. Equally, it may indicate its inaccessibility. But neither need be true, although both can be. The work unquestionably has English as its base language, but it cannot be translated into English. This is not quite to say that as a text it poses impossible problems; rather it poses problems that no previous text had fully realized. Central to these issues of untranslatability, of the error-free text, of interpretive limit, of the one story that is all stories, of the original language that is always inevitably a mediated language, the history that is myth, the myth that is rewritten over and over as history, is Joyce's consciousness of the double bind within all of them.

Perhaps only Proust rivals Joyce in the sheer weight and abundance of the corrections and insertions he added to the margins of proofs and typescripts or appended to the galleys of his epic, *A la recherche du temps perdu*.

---

[2] Ford Madox Ford, *Letters*, ed. R. Ludwig (Princeton, N.J.: Princeton University Press, 1965), 321.

Both share the determination to exploit to the fullest the momentary experience in which and through which a whole world can be apprehended. From the famous opening line of Proust's work, with its shadings of the past tense, we switch from the worlds of sleep to those of wakefulness, until memory comes to draw the protagonist "out of the abyss of not-being . . . in a flash I would traverse centuries of civilization, and out of a blurred glimpse of oil-lamps, then of shirts with turned-down collars, would gradually piece together the original components of my ego."[3] The word *wake* enfolds and implies several tenses too, refering to death and reawakening of course, and also to the tracks or traces of what is left behind, the various kinds of aftermath. But whereas in Proust the function of memory is to reconstitute the subject and to observe the processes by which that subject apprehends and comprehends an enormously detailed world, in the *Wake* the subject is generic, a plural, whose history is a form of "stolentelling," plagiarisms of what others have written, not individuated to the point where all memory becomes a refined retrieval of the self. This, after all, is the sequel to *Ulysses*, the novel in which the self surrendered the illusion of its autonomy and yielded priority of narration to the systems of language that had created it.

There is a chiasmic rhythm in Joyce's fiction whereby it moves (in *Dubliners*) from accounts of generic people dominated and paralyzed by their circumstances to the story of the formation of the heroic artist-self who (almost) converts an alien world to his own desire (*Portrait* and the first twelve episodes of *Ulysses*) and back to the narratives in which generic figures, the formations of historical and political forces, again take precedence, though on a larger scale—Molly Bloom, HCE, ALP, Shem, and Shaun. The intense moments of personal epiphany, ultimately private in their associations, give way to the epiphanic moment in which a whole pattern or system is discerned and represented. The exposure of the implacably determining nature of the "system" is always paradoxical since it is vouchsafed in some sense to an "individual" whose perception of the self's nullity denies the all-pervasiveness of the system that cancels the self's independence.

Joyce claimed in a letter that he was "quite content to go down to posterity as a scissors and paste man for that seems to me a harsh but not unjust description."[4] Certainly, *Portrait*, *Ulysses*, and the *Wake* are, in varying ratios, made up of collages of quotation and reference. Joyce's *Notebooks*,

---

[3] Proust, *Remembrance of Things Past*, trans. C. K. Scott Moncrieff and Terence Kilmartin (Harmondsworth: Penguin, 1989), 6.

[4] *Letters of James Joyce*, ed. S. Gilbert (New York, Viking, 1966), 1:297.

recently edited, confirm that the collection of quotations and citations from myriad sources was fundamental to the structural formation of his last epic work. There is, however, a difference between the various strategies of quotation that we find in his earlier fiction and what we find in the *Wake*. Reference to, and acknowledgment of, quotation from earlier authorities is a conventional feature of traditional epic. Scattered, fragmented and echoic quotations and references are regularly found in early-modernist works, particularly in the "epic" forms associated with Eliot and Pound. In fact, the idea of a work composed entirely of a medley of quotations was by no means remarkable by the 1920s, when Joyce began to write the *Wake*. For example, Brahms's *German Requiem* (first performed in 1868) has a themed selection of biblical quotations that are repeated through an exhaustive series of orchestral and choral variations. Even though the biblical sources are canonical, they have been recomposed into a meditation on consolation in suffering that is essentially a constellation of quotations. This is as different formally from a Beethoven Mass as the *Wake* is from a novel by Balzac or Scott. In a sense, this is a new kind of plagiarism; a text not one's own is adapted to a new purpose, although in Brahms's case the purpose could hardly be said to be alien to the spirit that informed the Psalms or the Gospels from which the excerpts are taken.

The *Wake* is recognizably a modernist and recognizably an epic work in its indebtedness to other sources, although its range of reference is much wider and more miscellaneous than even Pound's *Cantos*. But the dissonances between the grandeur of the past and the squalor of the present, so central in Pound and Eliot, are not exploited by Joyce nor do they even seem to be of interest to him. The Fall into modernity from an Edenic past located variously by authors enagaged in melancholy polemics about the mass culture of the day is not a topic in the *Wake*. In it, all history and all language is a consequence of the Fall or of the idea of a Fall. Such a governing idea has produced a corresponding series of stories coherent with it and with each other, told in all the languages of the world that are really the one language. "The hundredlettered name again, last word of perfect language" (424.23–24), the peal of thunder that inaugurated the world is the last word of a perfect language because it provokes the first word of fallen language.

It is important that it is a name, the special class of noun that both individuates and makes generic, enacting thereby a movement, through comic mutation, that is central to the *Wake*. A variant of the name is the title—of a person, a nation, a race or community, or of a work of art, a popular song, a city, or a street. There are long listings of "titles" of books that never existed, culminating in one, almost four pages in length, that is an alternative title for the *Wake* itself (104–7). Names and titles move in the same sphere as phrases that sometimes aspire to that status and, as such, are often quotations that have become a form of nomenclature (for example, "felix culpa"). Such phrases regularly appear in various disguises, as do common clichés, especially those associated with journalism, bureaucracy, and political speeches. Words in the *Wake* often aspire to the condition of names, but once they achieve that, they disintegrate again into the syllables from which they were composed. The text is full of collection points for names—for instance, the travels and travails of Shem's letter through the universe of Dublin is a catalog of them (420.17–36 and 421.1–14) and the endless verbal inventories and listings are controlled by various numerical combinations (the central one is 1132). Everything is fixed into protean patterns, including the patterns of printing and typography. "The proteiform graph itself is a ployhedron of scripture" (107.8). Yet the patterns fluctuate, sometimes hardening into clear shape, sometimes deliquescing into a chaotic slurry of syllables and letters.

In all of his fiction, Joyce challenges the techniques he masters. Symbolism, realism, naturalism, allegory—all modes of representation are tested to the point of failure, because the reiterative features that make them successful also make them dully ritualized. The glamour of his reference systems and plagiarisms fade into the banality of the quotidian. Banality dominates by force of repetition of the same, until the mold of routine is fully formed and all moves within its apparently preordained system. Repetition is form. Form reveals monotony and sameness by the very diversity of its powers of instantiation. The *Wake* requires us to recognize that the novel, as a form, cannot escape the double bind of sameness and difference and that boredom is the mother of invention—and also its child.

DECLAN KIBERD

Molloy, Malone Dies, and *The Unnamable*
(Samuel Beckett, 1951–1953)

The writings of Samuel Beckett are characterized by a buoyancy of form and a tremendous sadness of content. He saw this as an Irish, no less than a human, condition: "When you are in the last ditch with your back to the wall, there is nothing left to do but sing."[1] His tramps and vagabonds are really latter-day versions of the Gaelic bards or *filí*, possessed of a mandarin training and self-image but cast out onto the highways as mendicants after the collapse of the old Gaelic aristocracy. Men who had once been given fields and farms as a recompense for their praise-poems by affluent chieftains now found themselves treated by the new order as little better than beggars.

When an admirer told Beckett that his tramps were strange beings who talked as if they had doctorates, he replied: "How do you know that they hadn't?"[2] The dented bowler hats and shabby-genteel clothes suggest better, far-off, palmy days. "You should have been a poet," says Didi to Gogo in *Waiting for Godot,* only to be told "I was. . . . Isn't that obvious?" as poor Gogo gestures helplessly toward his rags.[3] The Gaelic *filí* composed their quatrains as they lay on pallets in blacked-out rooms: "A voice comes to one in the dark. Imagine."[4] The dark protected them from distraction and recalled ancient druidic links between art and sorcery. Some poets even placed stones on their bellies or in their hands to assist concentration: "To one on his back in the dark. This he can tell by the pressure on his hinds parts and by how the dark changes when he shuts his eyes and again when he opens them again. Only a small part of what is said can be verified. As for example when he hears, you are on your back in the dark. Then he must acknowledge the truth of what is said."[5] The theme for the bardic disquisition was set overnight: each *file* worked on it all day, until night fell and lights were brought in and the words written down.

In Beckett's trilogy, all these indicators are present—Molloy's stones, Moran's homework, Malone's *pensum,* the writing task that had to be dis-

---

[1] Cited by Deirdre Bair, *Samuel Beckett: A Biography* (London, 1978), 282.
[2] Quoted in Vivian Mercier, *Beckett/Beckett* (London, 1977), 46.
[3] Samuel Beckett, *Waiting for Godot* (London, 1965), 12.
[4] Samuel Beckett, *Company* (London, 1982), 7.
[5] Ibid.

charged by each of the speakers of the trilogy for the approval of an over-master (the chief *ollamh* or professor of the bardic school): "Strange notion . . . that of a task to be performed before one can be at rest."[6] A liter-ature produced in this manner exists in the interstices between speech and writing. If as speech the monologues of the various Ms can seem somewhat writerly, then their writing also possesses many of the qualities of a speaking voice that issues from unconscious depths of the person. While speech is clarified in the articulation by tone and emphasis, writing must be more precise—but, even then, such a writerly tendency toward exactitude can in-sert itself back into the oral mode. This is the import of those paragraphs in which a seemingly bold rhetorical claim ("The silence was absolute") is scaled sown ("Profound in any case") to something much more honest ("All things considered, it was a solemn moment").[7] The oral tradition of the bards persists, however, in the love of catalogs and lists, a device much fa-vored by those bards who feared that their cultural artifacts must be tabu-lated if only to conserve the memory of those things that might soon be obliterated in fact. Hence those repeated inventories of their few remaining possessions made by each of Beckett's near-demented soliloquists.

The methods of the *filí* are also reflected in the looseness of the overall narrative structure of Beckett's prose works, as opposed to the obsessive, finicky precision of their constituent parts. What Hugh Kenner has called a technique of chaos in the macrocosm, order in the microcosm[8] exactly re-peats the modalities of the bardic lyric, whose quatrains "were individually well-wrought, but often with only a vague, formal connection between them."[9] The effect of Beckett's text is to install the reader in a universe that no sooner seems to assume a definite shape than it dissolves. Many of the greatest Gaelic lyrics are broken and gapped because scholars have never felt able to reconstitute their quatrains into a coherent, comprehensible se-quence. And this provides a vital clue to students of Beckett's art: each frag-ment can never be a synecdoche, pointing back to a lost sense of wholeness, for Gaelic culture never knew that security and pleasure. What is achieved, rather, is a rigor without radiance, for the reader can only relax with the mi-crocosm, knowing that it would be impossible to infer from it a whole of which it might never have constituted a part anyway. For Beckett, the Gaelic tradition seemed postulated on a void, with every text an utterance in the

---

6 Samuel Beckett, *Molloy: Malone Dies: The Unnamable* (London, 1959), 313.

7 Ibid., 159.

8 Hugh Kenner, *A Reader's Guide to Samuel Beckett* (London, 1973), 98, 100.

9 David Greene, lecture on "Bardic Poetry," Trinity College, Dublin, March 11, 1967.

face of imminent annihilation, every list an inventory of shreds from a culture verging on extinction. Its bards seemed to build structures without an overall purpose in a land that remained largely unmapped and decentered, a world that was both very ancient and oddly like Beckett's own. For the tramps of his narratives were images of a now-rootless Anglo-Irish Protestant upper class, as *deraciné* as once the *filí* had been.

Out of the collapse of the old Gaelic order the *filí* produced a literature of sumptuous destitution, one that seemed to grow fat on its denial of past pleasures and former glories. They proclaimed the death of a whole order, but in stanzas of such awesome (if fragmented) power as to rebut the very thesis: "I can't go on . . . I'll go on."[10] They were in fact the first discoverers of the modern artistic world of ruined dandies and alienated intellectuals: and they offered to do something rather strange—both to die and in the very act of dying to narrate an account of their own passing, just like the protagonist of *Malone Dies*. *An file ar leaba a bháis* (the poet on his deathbed) became, as a motif, the very sign of their culture's vitality, for any system that could imagine itself from its outset to its conclusion was in no real danger of extinction.[11] Each tradition lived on in the very lament for its passing, even as the account of the collapse of one code became the master-narrative of its successor. It was out of a similar set of paradoxes that Beckett constructed his trilogy, a work based on the old joke that dying may be hard but never quite as hard as trying to write a novel. To write a text in which one might chronicle one's own demise—a thing necessarily impossible because the pencil would fall from enfeebled hands even as the attempt to write a final sentence was made—becomes his immediate and immodest ambition. Although this appears a unique experiment in the history of modernism, within the traditions of Gaelic culture it has many precedents.

Gaelic culture in most parts of Ireland had been all but erased by the 1920s, when the young Beckett took pen in hand, but it had not been replaced by any sophisticated kind of English-language culture (at least not in the home in which he grew to young manhood).[12] No wonder that he set up shop in the void: "no notion who I was saying what you were saying whose skull you were clapped up in whose moan you had . . ."[13] For over four

---

[10] Beckett, *Molloy: Malone Dies: The Unnamable*, 253.

[11] See Breandán Ó Buachalla, 'Canóin na Creille," in *Nua-Léamha: Gnéithe de Chultúr, Stair agus Polaitíocht na hÉireann 1600–1900*, ed. Máirín Ní Dhonnchadha (Dublin, 1996), 153ff.; and Sarah McKibben, "Lamenting the Language: On the Metaphor of Dying Irish," M. Phil. dissertation, University College, Dublin, 1997, passim.

[12] Mercier, *Beckett/Beckett*, 37.

[13] Samuel Beckett, "That Time," in *The Complete Dramatic Works of Samuel Beckett* (London, 1986), 388–95.

hundred years Irish writers had turned death into a career move, realizing that it was "the sense of an ending" that gave their work its crisis-driven sense of modernity: and what Beckett did was simply to splice that tradition with the last-ditch confessional mode of the modernist psychological novel. The object of British colonial policy in Ireland, wrote Friedrich Engels in a famous letter to Karl Marx, was to make the Irish feel like strangers in their own country, or, in other words, to turn that place into Bohemia, a place in which all denizens feel themselves estranged.[14] The sudden change of language from Irish to English, experienced in most counties within a single generation of the midnineteenth century, had left the people "living without key in a superbly coded environment,"[15] just like those Beckettian tramps who seek to improvise some meaning out of a blasted, decontextualized setting.

This fish-out-the-water state provides most of the comedy in Beckett's text, for nothing (literally) is funnier than unhappiness: but it is also the basis for his monologues. If the comedy of manners describes a made society, then the tragedy of private soliloquy must make do to account for a society still in the making. The short story or extended anecdote is better fitted to describe the wanderers and outcasts of a submerged people than are the more stable amenities of the novel form.[16] Hence, what Beckett produced was most often a collection of microstories in the disguise of an experimental novel (for much the same reason that Dublin is an agglomeration of villages that got bolted together but still not a place that manages to convey the impression of a centrally planned city).

For the protagonists of Beckett's stories, freedom cannot be won in a fallen society, and so it must be won from it. The key moments in his texts, as in Joyce's *Ulysses* or (for that matter) Melville's *Moby-Dick* are not social epiphanies but personal confessions, made by a puritan writer who sees his art as a stain on the silence. If there has to be a stain, he seems to suggest, it should be as brief as possible on the route back to pure silence, hence the increasing minimalism of his pieces. Making a little go a long way is an old Puritan-Protestant tradition: and the Protestant values of Beckett's upbringing and education may lie behind his love of monologue, or what Kenner has called "the issueless Protestant confrontation with conscience."[17] If Joyce remained obsessed by the Roman Catholic faith that he rejected, then Yeats and Beckett both aestheticized elements of their families' Protestantism,

---

[14] Quoted by Nicholas Mansergh, *The Irish Question: 1840–1921* (London, 1966), 88–89.

[15] Vincent Buckley, *Memory Ireland* (London, 1983), 98.

[16] See Frank O'Connor, *The Lonely Voice* (London, 1967), passim.

[17] Kenner, *A Reader's Guide to Samuel Beckett*, 134.

crossing it with an "Eastern" mysticism that always proved highly attractive to youths in revolt against the overrationalism (as they saw it) of their teachers' theology.[18] Both Yeats and Beckett turned east, if not for an explanation, then at least for a moving expression of human bafflement in the face of creation. Many of Yeats's later poems emphasize the word *nothing* as a positive value, just like the Beckettian protagonist who rejoices in the fact that there is nothing to be done.

In Beckett's trilogy, *Molloy*, *Malone Dies*, and *The Unnamable* (1951–53), the linear plot of the Western novel makes way for a structure that is the artistic equivalent of meditation and for a narrative that is the artistic equivalent of confession. Beckett reported that he conceived *Molloy* on the day when he realized his past foolishness in not writing out of personal experience and when he admitted his stupidity in refusing to accept the dark side as "the commanding side of my personality."[19] That might be an inadvertent summary of the plot of *Molloy*, which chronicles the attempt by the prim Catholic Moran to confront the primeval Molloy within, to locate the panting anti-self that struggles to emerge, depriving Moran of his illusions of property, industry, and religious belief. Whereas the uncovering of that anti-self was for Yeats an artistic imperative, it had for Beckett all the confessional qualities of a religious testimony, a point made clear when the writer insists that he has no desire to "give way to literature."[20]

Molloy contains a parody of the Roman Catholic confession and substitutes for its perceived formulaic insincerity the muscular summons to confessional testimony. By the end, however even such testifying is exposed as self-defeating, since the self-reliance preached by the Protestant can result only in the death of the Old Testament God, as man listens instead to those inner voices that require "no vengeful deity" to make themselves heard.[21] That voice can liberate Molloy, unchain his innermost self—the needlepoint of the mystic—and allow him to expiate the sins of the past through confessing them. Moreover, the man who "once found it painful not to understand" can now accept even the incomprehensible patterns of dancing bees. Part of his comfort is the knowledge that the bees are an impermeable and closed system of their own, and that he will never be tempted to offload responsibility for himself onto them: "And I would never do to my bees the wrong

---

[18] Harvey Cox, *Turning East* (Boston, 1987), passim.
[19] Bair, *Samuel Beckett*, 198.
[20] Beckett, *Molloy: Malone Dies: The Unnamable*, 152.
[21] Ibid., 168.

I had done my God to whom I had been taught to ascribe my angers, fears, desires, and even my body."[22]

All forms of authority throughout the trilogy induce irresponsibility. Moran's son loses his way, when accompanied by his father, who insists on binding him to a rope, but he survives very well when left free on his own. Each protagonist of the trilogy discovers, like Murphy in Beckett's earlier novel of 1938, that he cannot resign his fate to an exterior godhead, since in each case the individual is "the prior system." Instead, as in Buddhist practice, the godhead is increasingly ironized by jokes or else courted in expectant silences: and, while all this is going on, the protagonists try to reach that pinpoint at which the mystic knows both darkness and illumination. There is an "Eastern" aspect to all this, as is clear in the Buddha-like postures adopted by the protagonists in the knees-and-elbow position, in the desire of the adept to please the master with a wisdom that can never be fully put into words, and in the attempt to cure all desire by ablating it. But—although Beckett gleaned much Eastern wisdom from his study of Schopenhauer— there is no strict necessity to posit a direct influence from Eastern philosophy. After all, the mystic moments so attained were central to the Protestantism of Martin Luther in its pristine stage: what is enacted is nothing other than the search embarked on by countless mystics. Even the noted prayer meetings of Quakers were marked by long silences designed for meditation during which the godhead might be wooed to announce itself.[23]

The voice that speaks in the last fifty pages of *The Unnamable* may be the voice of God, provided that this is not understood as a traditional godhead so much as a core of selfhood toward which all of Beckett's mystics move. Beckett was interested in studying the mind of God and said once that poetry is prayer. He is one of those rare writers who have captured the mystery of being in the world. He did this in a language that was completely devoid of pretence or of the accretions of institutional discourse. Most other Irish novelists have dealt only with the social effects of religious practice, but Beckett was that rare and wonderful thing: a genuinely religious writer who could explore spiritual practices in a literary form.

He may also have been the first truly Irish author, in the sense of one who purged himself of all factitious elements of "Irishness" in his early novelistic deconstruction of the stage-Irish stereotype in *Murphy*. There he used the novel form in order to explode a hoary theatrical prototype, submitting the

---

[22] Ibid., 170.
[23] Max Weber, *The Protestant Ethic and the Spirit of Capitalism* (London, 1985), 148ff.

cliché to the sort of psychological analysis that the novel makes possible. His embrace of French in the subsequent decade may be explained as a rejection of the wit-and-wordplay tradition routinely expected of Irish performers in English from Swift to Joyce. Instead, he preferred to return to a much older Irish tradition of the *filí*. For all their hip cosmopolitanism and post-Protestant spirituality, Beckett's prose masterpieces may ultimately take their place among the major contributions to the literature of the Gaelic revival. For at the center of that Gaelic world of Cuchulain, Maeve, and the Tain he found "no theme": and for him "no theme" was quite irresistible.

BEATRIZ SARLO

Hopscotch
(Julio Cortázar, 1963)

Published in 1963, *Hopscotch* quickly became the novel that everyone in
Argentina and Latin America recognized as the narrative experiment that
brought Latin American literature up to date. It was among the undisputed
best sellers of the famous Boom, even before the Boom was established as a
strategy for a large-scale capture of literary markets. While it may appear today that what was innovative about *Hopscotch* is exhausted, during the
1960s it was the paradigm for a revolution in literature. In many respects
it was.

The first printed reviews about *Hopscotch*, published in Buenos Aires by
a current-events magazine, were disconcerted by the radical innovation that
the novel appeared to convey to its audience. Just a few months later, *Hopscotch* quickly became the book everybody was waiting for. It connected
perfectly with the feeling of the times: sexual liberation, questioning of authority, even, like the Beatles shortly thereafter, a touch of orientalism. This
is what *Hopscotch* invoked in its young readers. But the novel also appealed
to informed readers who had established a relationship with avant-garde traditions. Above all, *Hopscotch* was what it set out to be: a criticism of the realist, naturalist, pan-psychological and social literature that was still being
written in Latin America according to more or less familiar guidelines.

The book's popularity was not entirely predictable, because it was the result of a combination of elements that had not come together in that way before. But it was enormously opportune. In just a few years' time it stirred
up, and still does today, virtual mountains of articles, essays, theses, and
polemics. Adored by the public and respected by writers, it was translated
practically all over the world. It is part of the first contingent of books that
started the process of internationalization of Latin American literature.

Hopscotch is an experimental novel linked to the European avant-garde,
especially to surrealism and pataphysics (the science of imaginary solutions),
but it also has distinctly Argentine roots. In 1948, Julio Cortázar wrote the
only comprehensive critical notes on a great novel by Leopoldo Marechal,
Adán Buenosayres. *Hopscotch* is clearly related to this gigantic work by
Marechal, which contains a little of everything from Dante's *Vita nuova* to a
parody of the 1920s avant-garde of which Borges had been a part. Like
Marechal, Cortázar was engaged in two quests. The first was religious for

Marechal and metaphysical for Cortázar. The second was for both a hypothesis about the exhaustion of the novelistic form and solutions to the problems posed by conventions of realist representation. Cortázar prizes the comedy and parody in Marechal's solution; we shall soon see which routes Cortázar chose.

The first extraordinary feature of *Hopscotch* is that it offers the reader two approaches. Under the heading, "Table of Instructions," the novel's chapters are ordered according to a sequence that does not correspond to the consecutive numbers that identify them. A reader who follows the "Table of Instructions," will read the novel in an order established by the author that joins sequences and chapters differently than one who chooses to read them in the customary manner, by the numbers. Cortázar invites the reader to decide between these two reading strategies, which, among other effects, keeps the novel's outcome up in the air. As Umberto Eco would have said during those years, this is an "open work," where the fortuitous plays a fundamental role. Once the reader's freedom to undertake one or another reading has been recognized, the alternative of itineraries other than those proposed becomes clear. Starting with the "Table of Instructions," the novel invites one to imagine other possible orders, especially on the subsequent readings that are almost inevitable, owing to the novelty that chance brings to bear on what is traditionally called a plot.

The second special characteristic is that the novel is divided into three major sections connected by the movements of its main character, Horacio Oliveira. "From the Other Side" corresponds to the chapters in which the action takes place in Paris (to put it simply, in a way that does not reflect the complexity of spatial crossings); "From This Side" corresponds, with the same qualification, to the episodes in Buenos Aires; and "From Diverse Sides" includes the chapters that, according to Cortázar, "the reader will skip without regrets" if he or she elects not to read them. Thus, if one reads as outlined in the Table of Instructions, the reading incorporates the "expendable chapters," but if one reads consecutively, the reading may end before those chapters and include only one of the endings (because there are at least two possible endings). It is also possible to read only the "expendable" chapters to gather from them all the intertextual clues that the novel hides from us. Moreover, Cortázar introduces them to reinforce the impression that *Hopscotch* was written in several voices.

From the first page, this organization reveals that *Hopscotch* does not obey a conventional narrative temporality. But more important, it highlights its intention to interrupt the continuity of the accounts, inserting fragments of essays and quotes between more narrative passages. In this sense, the novel reflects the avant-garde principles of collage. It is composed like an extensive score that can be played using several possible itineraries that lead to fragments of a different discursive nature, breaking all illusions of stylistic or authorial homogeneity. In this sense, *Hopscotch* is a spatial and musical novel whose subject matter is presented, developed, or lost, only to be found again, transformed.

Cortázar deliberately avoided a unifying narrative principle that would develop the plot as it evolved in time. However one might read it, the plot of *Hopscotch* is interrupted for several reasons: its end bifurcates in at least two directions; the order of reading can alter the linear logic; an oneiric web links Buenos Aires and Paris; and quotations from other texts stop the flow of a continuous narrative. The reading never settles in one area (not in Buenos Aires, Paris, or in the "expendable" texts). It hops from any one of these three areas to any of the others, impeding the plot and starting back up again from another past time or place, and especially when the register changes—from narration to argumentation about literature or aesthetics, from quotes from a vast repertoire of European or American authors to news in dailies and journals, from serious and sometimes poetic texts to humorous passages. Cortázar uses the quotes to facilitate reading. The quotes work as passwords or samples from an imaginary library so that the reader is always aware of the novel's aesthetic framework. In fact, the quotes and fragments supply many keys to the ideas that Cortázar contemplated in composing his work. Long literary disquisitions are attributed to the writer Morelli, an imaginary character, who to his friends epitomizes the writer who has broken with the rules of realism and conventional forms of the novel.

It is precisely to Morelli that the following passage applies: "Morelli had come up with a list of acknowledgments that he never included in his published work. He left several names: Jelly Roll Morton, Robert Musil, Dasetz Teitaro Suzuki, Raymond Roussel, Kurt Schwitters, Vieira da Silva, Akutagawa, Anton Webern, Greta Garbo, José Lezama Lima, Buñuel, Louis Armstrong, Borges, Michaux, Dino Buzzatti, Max Ernst, Pevsner, Gilgamesh, Garcilaso, Arcimboldo, René Clair, Piero di Cosimo, Wallace Stevens, Izak Dineson. The names Rimbaud, Picasso, Chaplin, Alban Berg and others had been crossed out with a very fine line, as if they were too obvious to list, but in the end all of them must have been too obvious to list because Morelli did not decide to include them in any of the volumes."[1] But Cortázar does include them, giving us clues to interpreting his novel. In fact, each one of

---

[1] Julio Cortázar, *Hopscotch*, trans. Gregory Rabassa (New York: Pantheon Books, 1966), chap. 60. Subsequent quotations are referenced in the text.

those names is linked to the web that comprises *Hopscotch*: jazz, dadaist collages, contemporary music, surrealism, film, poetry. Let us examine some of their purposes.

One of *Hopscotch*'s most famous sequences, that of the *discada* (listening to records), is constructed around jazz. A group of friends—a kind of avant-garde, bohemian gang—get together to listen to music and drink. With tremendous technical dexterity, Cortázar combines events having to do with the plot, conflicts between characters, stories about the past, commentaries about the music being listened to, voices in the first and third person, and free indirect dialogues and discourses. We have, then, a plethora of perfectly articulated proceedings in a masterful scene in which one experiences a kind of narration that evokes the cinematographic master shot, accompanied by a sort of conceptual background music constructed from remembered strains of the sounds of the great jazz musicians that the characters listen to, in apparent disorder, and that Oliveira discusses in a tone that is critical and poetic at the same time.

The mention of Kurt Schwitters refers directly to collage as a visual medium, implying the transfer of this technique to literature, and pays homage to dada as a movement that, like Alfred Jarry's pataphysics, underlines the lack of meaning and absurdity that corrode all pretensions of creating full meanings. Nonetheless, Cortázar's homage does not imply that *Hopscotch* is an impossible dadaist novel. On the contrary, *Hopscotch* criticizes and also affirms the possibility of knowledge and of capturing experience.

The coexistence in Morelli's list of rationalist artists like Webern and Berg alongside surrealists like Max Ernst and Buñuel and explorers of aesthetic and epistemological frontiers like Michaux and Roussel is also significant. Surrealism clearly influenced *Hopscotch*. The movements of Oliveira and la Maga, his lover, evoke those of André Breton's *Nadja*. There is certainly a good bit of *Nadja* in Cortázar's novel, from the close attention to certain streets, bridges, and houses in Paris to its search for a privileged experience of knowledge through passion and clairvoyance. As in *Nadja*, the characters of Oliveira and la Maga move along random routes. They run into each other without planning to, they travel streets in which they discover things that the ordinary gaze misses. This mysterious attraction that the surrealists called "objective chance" guides the drifting of both characters, who are moved by forces that in la Maga are completely natural, deep, and unconscious and that in Oliveira struggle against the reason that tries to interpret them.

The mention of *Nadja* and the intensity of the relationship between Oliveira and la Maga would lead one to conclude that *Hopscotch* is a love story. Although it is not appropriate to apply that formula to such a complex novel, the observation is not completely unjust. Oliveira seeks in la Maga, Pola, and Talita an absolute that of course he does not find. Nonetheless, in those oscillations of his desire he discovers that the passionate impulse that overwhelms reason and leads one beyond the limits of consciousness is one possible road to another basic search: that of a global grasping of the real, free from the compartmentalization of intellectual perception and science. In this regard, Oliveira's restlessness is metaphysical. He subjects what the novel calls "Western reason" to criticism, reason that works by dividing and analyzing its object. Oliveira opposes this reason in long soliloquies with a kind of knowledge, often linked to the *satori*, that is instantaneous rather than discursive and immediate. His search takes him through eroticism, degradation, and madness. The novel explores these alternatives in some of its most memorable passages.

The romantic encounters between la Maga and Pola create a poetic environment that is achieved through a linguistic representation of the erotic. How does sexuality fit into phonetic and semantic material? Cortázar gives an experimental reply to this question. The erotic language of *Hopscotch* de- and re-articulates fragments of words, moving syllables and inventing new words with sounds that evoke sexual contact; the marks of sex on the body; and the humors, orifices, and material noises of the physical encounter:

> As soon as he began to amalate the noeme, the clemise began to smother her and they fell into hydromuries, into savage ambonies, into exasperating sustales. Each time that he tried to relamate the hairincops, he became entangled in a whining grimate and had to face up to envulsioning the novalisk, feeling how little by little the arnees would spejune, were becoming peltronated, redoblated, until they were stretched out like the ergomanine trimalciate which drops a few filures of cariaconce. And it was still only the beginning, because right away she tordled her hurgales, allowing him gently to bring up his orfelunes. No sooner had they cofeathered than something like a ulucord encrestored them, extrajuxted them, and paramoved them, suddenly it was the clinon, the sterfurous convulcant of matericks, the slobberdigging raimouth of the orgumion. (chap. 68)

This language of love strengthens the exceptional, extraordinary nature of true passion, something that the novel states repeatedly, attributing to eroticism a potential for knowledge. There is no doubt that Cortázar, a meticulous reader of Bataille, belongs to a tradition that groups sexual climax together with the religious and death.

The second road, degradation, is the one Oliveira travels in the celebrated episode with the Parisian *clocharde*: a night of drunkenness and masturbation, curiosity and voyeurism beneath the bridges of the Seine. Dirt, bad smells and oily, viscous substances are the ingredients of a sexual encounter between the old drunk, aptly named Emmanuelle, and Oliveira. The experience of degradation also has its absurd version in the episode of the pathetic pianist, Berthe Trepat (the pianist's surname contains the word *death*, *trépas* in French). Oliveira is practically the sole audience member at her ridiculous concert, and later he accompanies her to her house in the rain, consoling the melancholy and embracing the madness of a worn-out old woman. An incomprehensible impulse of mercy sets him adrift, and his intelligence, perceptiveness, and will desert him, leaving him to suffer a sought-out humiliation through an unforeseen event.

The third route is that of madness. The second part of this novel takes place in Buenos Aires. Oliveira has returned to sink into the most banal everyday existence, on one hand, and to encounter, on the other, his friend Traveler, with whom he creates a triangle whose third vertex is Talita, Traveler's wife. This is not an ordinary adulterous triangle, which might have been a blunder worthy of a psychological novel, but rather a construct in which each man acts as the double of the other and the woman acts as the ghost of la Maga. Oliveira's return also implies an acceptance of stupidity and madness. In fact, there is an insane asylum, there are mad people, and on one memorable night, Oliveira calls on madness as yet another way to overcome the aporias of reason that in Paris he had criticized, but only partially, without fully giving himself over, mind and body, to irrevocable risk.

Madness and the absurd are the great paths traveled by Oliveira upon his return to Buenos Aires. In the manner of the pataphysicists, Oliveira creates a network of exceptions to the rules that regulate "normal" life at the same time that he sinks thoroughly into the triviality of linguistic clichés and a foreseeable sentimentality. He escapes this submersion in banality through madness (treated as a kind of ultimate lucidity) and the absurd, represented in another of *Hopscotch*'s many scenes that are good enough to be included in an anthology: the episode that features the plank connecting the windows of two houses across the street from each other.

For no reason, without any objective need, purely as an act, Talita crosses the plank from one end to the other. Oliveira is at one end and Traveler is at the other. Both men look at the woman, speak to her, prompt her, and claim her. Naturally, she represents something different to each of them. She is the double without being aware of her duality. The men are doubles who are conscious of the mirror that unites them in a relationship that synthesizes the River Plate cult of friendship and also of the duel and the challenge. The plank represents at the same time separation and a bridge, the tension between them and the recognition that the Other is out there beyond each of the subjects, not only as a spatial fracture but also as a representation of an insuperable existential abyss. The absurdity of the plank as the image of a bridge that is as impossible as it is useless is demonstrated in the comic content of the scene: a kind of parody of the communication that everyone desires but that is, at the same time, unachievable.

The plank/bridge; the specular doubles; the yearning for an erotic plenitude that is never fulfilled because relationships are inevitably fractured by the hiatus between the subjects; and the loss of reason only to find, beyond reason, the figure (hopscotch, the mandala) that allows some totalization: all of these are the nostalgic themes of *Hopscotch*. We are dealing with a typically modern nostalgia for a totality that has been lost as a result of technical civilization, epistemological pigeon-holing imposed by science, and the instrumentality of personal relationships. Thus *Hopscotch* proposes a psychological and moral utopia, inverting Oliveira's failure. The flip side of its formal experimentation is also a novel with characters and episodes that is enormously readable, quotable, and perhaps without intending to be, emblematic of its period.

Translated by Linda Phillips

URSULA K. HEISE

Gravity's Rainbow
(Thomas Pynchon, 1973)

Thomas Pynchon's *Gravity's Rainbow* (1973) is one of the very few American novels written after World War II to have risen to the status of literary "classic." Its sprawling plot and hundreds of characters, abundant historical detail and innovative narrative technique have made it the object of intense academic scrutiny, while its blend of high literary forms with elements of film, television, music, comic strip, and science fiction has also appealed to a popular audience. Thematically, *Gravity's Rainbow* focuses on twentieth-century technologies and their functions in social control and resistance, from the military technologies that evolved during World War II and the Cold War all the way to the synthesization of polymers and the use of drugs to modify the human body; it explores how these technologies alter common-sense perceptions of history and causality, and how they are re-structuring modernist conceptions of identity and individuality. These thematic concerns translate into a narrative structure that defies not only any notion of causally connected plot—a category that had already been put in question by many high-modernist novels of the early twentieth century—but also challenges plausible character construction as a foundation of literary storytelling, which had remained in place as a crucial narrative dimension in most modernist texts. *Gravity's Rainbow* shares with other American novels of the 1960s and 1970s a pronounced self-awareness of its textuality and its strategies of narrative construction; yet it avoids the monodimensional focus on procedures of writing and reading that made other texts of the period gradually recede in importance as American fiction returned to more representational modes of narration in the 1980s and 1990s. In its exploration of the technological "posthuman"—that is, the ways in which modern technologies are reshaping individual and collective human identities—*Gravity's Rainbow* has retained enduring significance for a period of rapid technoscientific development.

Pynchon's novel is set in Europe at the end of World War II. Its central strand of plot follows the movements of an American G.I., Tyrone Slothrop, who is stationed in London during the *Blitzkrieg* of late 1944 and is then transferred to southern France, where he eventually breaks away from his military unit and makes his way alone, first to Switzerland and then into the postwar German "zone." Germany functions in the novel as both a "holy center" and a wasteland where Western civilization has attained some of its highest achievements but has also sunk to its lowest moral depths; through the collapse of its political, social, and cultural structures at the end of the war, *Gravity's Rainbow* implies, the underlying foundations of both European and North American society might reveal themselves with greater clarity than at more ordinary historical moments. At the same time, the devastation of the German zone can be understood to mark a turning point in history, a ground zero from which new ideological possibilities can emerge. This ambiguous territory is described with an inextricable mix of historically accurate detail (regarding the German development of V-2 missiles, for instance), bits of legend (such as the witches' celebration atop mount Brocken, familiar from *Faust*), and wild invention (for example, the existence of an SS unit consisting of black soldiers from the German colony of Namibia). But the narrative also fuses 1940s Europe with 1960s America: quite a few aspects of the postwar landscape—drug smuggling and drug use, racial confrontation, sexual experimentation, and allusions to environmentalist discourse, for example—are more reminiscent of the U.S. counterculture of the 1960s than of Germany in 1945. These blends of discourses and periods ensure that *Gravity's Rainbow* cannot be misread as a novel about World War II: its more fundamental concerns lie in the way social domination and resistance in the second half of the twentieth century take shape under the influence of technological development.

This connection between technology and control first emerges by way of an idiosyncrasy in Tyrone Slothrop's sexual behavior: a colleague of his discovers that a map which Slothrop keeps of his multiple erotic encounters in London during the *Blitzkrieg* corresponds point for point to the map of V-2 missile impacts, predating them by between a few hours and ten days. As this discovery is communicated to his superiors, Slothrop turns into a focus of attention for various branches of the military and secret services, since the apparent predictive power of his behavior might provide a means of access to German military strategy. In the investigation, it turns out that Slothrop might have been subjected to certain physical conditioning procedures in his childhood, and he is transferred to the Riviera for secret testing and observation. But during his stay in France, Slothrop becomes aware of the scrutiny he is subject to and resolves to set out on his own to uncover the riddle of his childhood and identity. The novel hints that his initial escape from close military supervision might still have formed part of his superiors' plan, suggesting that even what he decides of his own volition might be controlled by someone else. As he travels through Switzerland and Germany, though, the secret services lose his track, and Slothrop begins an odyssey that crisscrosses German territory and leads him again and again to the construction sites of the rockets that are mysteriously linked to his own body—sites that also bring him in contact with a large number of other characters who haunt the postwar zone and are all attracted to the same places for a variety of pragmatic or quasi-religious reasons.

Gravity's Rainbow, then, starts out on a grotesque inflection of what is nevertheless a clearly recognizable genre pattern: that of the spy novel, in which the hero as well as a number of more or less camouflaged institutions of power hunt after a secret that might be of crucial military importance. Slothrop's evolution from a helpless victim to an accomplished master spy who skillfully deceives and evades his pursuers by repeatedly changing his identity fits this pattern well, and he gradually becomes a detective of sorts in search of the mysteries of his own past. But after Slothrop enters Germany, the structuring force of this genre model gradually weakens: he encounters so many characters that seem in one way or another connected to rocket development and to his own history, and finds such an abundance of clues that nonetheless never add up to any definitive conclusion, that the plot by and by disintegrates. Faced with a profusion of signs that seem to indicate some overarching historical connection, but unable to determine its precise shape, Slothrop as well as a range of other characters in the novel periodically succumb to visions of paranoia: they develop the firm conviction that a conspiratorial network of international business corporations, in cahoots with national governments, is in total control of all the apparently random events of the twentieth century, from the outbreak of two world wars all the way to the idiosyncrasies of their own lives. So Slothrop, as a small child, might have been sold by his father for experiments to a chemical corporation that conditioned him to react sexually to a newly invented polymer, Imipolex G, that might also form part of the structure of the V-2 missiles. The same corporate network would also have triggered both World War I and World War II so as to accelerate research and development of certain technologies that required financial expenditures justifiable only in terms of vital threats to the well-being of entire nations. Indeed, some characters go further than that, imagining even the multinational corporations to be ultimately subject to military, chemical, and pharmaceutical technologies whose evolutionary logic has become self-propelling; historical agency, in this view, would have been transferred from human individuals and institutions to technologies that develop according to parameters no longer under human control at all.

But this vision of the total reign of the inanimate over the animate, already a central theme in Pynchon's earlier novel *V.*, is never definitively confirmed

by the text in its entirety. The characters who have such visions of total coherence are notoriously unreliable: they are often unstable in their personal
attachments, addicted to drugs, and prone to a variety of psychological
obsessions. Moreover, they themselves alternate between visions of conspiratorial coherence and despair over utter randomness: their paranoid convictions repeatedly give way to intervals during which they are unable to
perceive anything but pure chance, coincidence, and arbitrariness around
them. This indeterminacy persists throughout *Gravity's Rainbow*, and even
those characters who toward the beginning attempt to discover what underlying truth really shapes their world end up losing their way in their own investigations. As the narrative progresses, it becomes increasingly difficult for
both characters and readers to construct any plot pattern or underlying
meaning for the phenomena they are confronted with. This indeterminacy is
not settled or clarified even by the ending of the novel: quite literally, *Gravity's Rainbow* is a novel whose plot gradually vanishes, disintegrating into a
multitude of episodes and characters that might or might not be connected
with each other.

Complex mechanisms of narrative embedding and disembedding further
contribute to this fundamental indeterminacy in the novel, which many of
its critics consider paradigmatically postmodernist. The very first scene, for
example, which describes the arrival and impact of a V-2 missile and thereby
seems to establish the novel's wartime reality, turns out to have taken place
only in a minor character's dream. The last scene takes place in a movie theater in Los Angeles that is about to be hit by a bomb, suggesting that perhaps the entire preceding narrative describes the contents of a film about to
be interrupted rather than the novelistic "real world." Some scenes that
seem to form part of the narrative reality are later put in question by other
characters in such a way that it is very difficult for readers to be sure, in
many episodes, whether what is being described takes place in the empirical
world that surrounds the characters, or whether it occurs in an embedded
narrative or a character's thoughts or dreams. As British critic Tony Tanner
has poignantly phrased it, it is often difficult to be certain whether a particular event takes place "in a bombed-out building or a bombed-out mind."[1]

In a high-modernist novel, such ambiguity, even as it might weaken the
hold of material or social reality on the narrative, would typically have served
to articulate the workings of an individual mind, the alternative reality constantly being constructed and reconstructed by human consciousness. Not so

---

[1] Tony Tanner, "*V.* & V-2." In Edward Mendelson, ed., *Pynchon: A Collection of Critical Essays*
(Englewood Cliffs, N.J.: Prentice-Hall, 1978), 51.

in *Gravity's Rainbow*, where character construction is as susceptible to indeterminacy and self-contradiction as the organization of the plot. The identity
of the protagonist Tyrone Slothrop, for example, disintegrates and vanishes
along with the spy novel plot; this gradual fragmentation begins when his
military identification papers are taken away from him on the Côte d'Azur
and continues as he assumes a variety of different disguises to elude the secret services and army branches that are searching for him, still in keeping
with the spy plot. But once he enters Germany, Slothrop also begins to take
on identities that are more difficult to reconcile with this genre: he smug-
gles drugs from the Soviet to the American zone in the disguise of a comic
strip character, Rocketman, and during a carnival celebration in a German
town is forced to slip into a pig costume and temporarily to take on the role
of a quasi-mythological Pig Hero. As his attempts to gain access to forged
identity papers fail and his hope of returning to the United States falters,
his own sense of identity also begins to weaken: his capacity for memory
and anticipation becomes more and more limited to a narrow slice of present, and toward the end he seems to become physically dispersed in space
to the point where his own friends are no longer able to recognize him as a
human person.

Slothrop's transformation from a recognizable literary character into a
mere figure of spatial dispersal is accompanied by a profusion of characters
whose names, kinship relations, and biographies echo and contrast with
each other in such a way that they come to seem parts of a semantic mosaic
rather than psychologically plausible human beings. Certain patterns of
dominating and dominated figures, black-skinned and white-skinned ones,
pairs of siblings and of parents and children repeat themselves in different
versions again and again and gradually redirect the reader's attention from
the details of individual figures to more general patterns of connection between groups of characters—connections that, once again, can be construed
as manifestations of an underlying coherence or as random coincidences. As
a consequence, psychological realism or the exploration of the workings of
the human mind cannot be called upon to explain the ambiguities and in-
congruities in the functioning of this novelistic world. On the contrary, character construction in *Gravity's Rainbow* is itself subject to the same overarching questions of narrative coherence, plausibility, and meaning that apply
to the plot.

Such difficulties in explaining the novel either by appealing to the principles of nineteenth-century social realism or high-modernist psychological
analysis are not in and of themselves surprising: many novels published in the
United States during the 1960s and 1970s quite explicitly rejected either

form of mimesis and foregrounded instead the linguistic, narrative, and ideological mechanisms by means of which fictional worlds come to appear credible or implausible. *Gravity's Rainbow* participates in this self-referential exploration of textuality in that readers who attempt to make sense of its fractured plot or to understand its disintegrating characters are inevitably led to reflect on their own procedures for establishing meaning in narrative. But this focus on textuality is not an end in itself; rather, the interrogation of narrative method in Pynchon's novel does lead back to broader cognitive and epistemological questions. The use of film as a theme and a metaphor, for example, foregrounds how a sequence of separate images, when displayed with sufficient speed, leads the viewer to perceive continuous motion; the persistence of this motif in *Gravity's Rainbow* points not only to the self-conscious question of how we might be able to construe a continuous sequence out of the increasingly disconnected episodes the novel offers us, but also, given its setting, how we come to perceive historical development and coherence in a particular series of events in the past and present. Similarly, repeated discussions between a Pavlovian behaviorist, Pointsman, and a statistician, Roger Mexico, about the nature of causality are clearly intended to alert the reader to the question of causal coherence in the plot, but beyond the novel itself also to questions of historical causality and agency. Along the same lines, the breaks and gaps in the novel's character construction lead readers to reflect not only on basic conventions of psychological plausibility in narrative but also on the ways in which traditional notions of individuality might have to be rethought in an age when bodies and minds are constantly being reshaped in the interaction with chemical substances and machines of various sorts. As *Gravity's Rainbow* questions both nineteenth- and early-twentieth-century conventions of narrative, in other words, it also foregrounds how these conventions have shaped common-sense notions of the "real" and the "plausible" far beyond literary texts.

With its interest in science and technology, its exploration of what constitutes historical understanding in a technological age, its skepticism vis-à-vis conventional notions of the self, and its self-referential foregrounding of textuality, *Gravity's Rainbow* represents much of what is characteristic of postmodernist narrative in the United States. Its breadth of invention and depth of historical and textual allusion has given rise to types of academic exegesis and popular fan culture that are in some ways comparable to those that have arisen around James Joyce's novels *Ulysses* and *Finnegans Wake*. The influence of *Gravity's Rainbow* extends from the domain of "high literature" to those sectors of American art and literature that seek to perpetuate some of the ideas of 1960s counterculture, and has manifested itself quite specifically in the genre of science fiction. Several of the novelists who attained prominence in the 1980s with the rise of "cyberpunk," which was centrally concerned with how computer technologies, biotechnology, and innovative pharmaceuticals are transforming individuals and communities, have explicitly referred to Pynchon as one of their models. This genealogy has led a younger generation of American readers back to Pynchon's fiction of the 1960s and early 1970s. *Gravity's Rainbow*, therefore, has established important connections to both the high literary sphere and some sectors of mass culture: its focus on twentieth-century technology with the determinisms and indeterminacies it generates has made it a culture as well as a counterculture classic.

Contributors

ESPEN AARSETH, Principal Researcher, Center for Computer Games Research, IT University of Copenhagen, and Professor II in Media and Communication Studies, University of Oslo

ROGER ALLEN, Professor of Arabic and Comparative Literature, University of Pennsylvania

APRIL ALLISTON, Professor of Comparative Literature, Princeton University

BENEDICT ANDERSON, Aaron L. Binenkorb Professor of International Studies, Emeritus, Cornell University

PERRY ANDERSON, Professor of History, University of California, Los Angeles

NANCY ARMSTRONG, Nancy Duke Lewis Professor of English, Comparative Literature, and Modern Culture and Media, Brown University

MIEKE BAL, Academy Professor, Royal Netherlands Academy of Arts and Sciences, and Professor of the Theory of Literature, University of Amsterdam

ANN BANFIELD, Professor of English, University of California, Berkeley

PIERGIORGIO BELLOCCHIO, journalist and essayist, Piacenza (Italy)

HOMI BHABHA, Anne F. Rothenberg Professor of English and American Literature, and Director of the Harvard Humanities Center, Harvard University

JOHN BRENKMAN, Distinguished Professor of English and Comparative Literature, CUNY Graduate Center and Baruch College

A. S. BYATT, writer, London

MARGARET COHEN, Professor of Comparative Literature, French, and Italian, and Director of the Center for the Study of the Novel, Stanford University

VALENTINE CUNNINGHAM, Professor of English Language and Literature, University of Oxford

SEAMUS DEANE, Keough Professor of Irish Studies, University of Notre Dame

THOMAS DIPIERO, Professor of French and of Visual and Cultural Studies, University of Rochester (New York)

IAN DUNCAN, Professor of English, University of California, Berkeley

UMBERTO ECO, Professor of Semiotics, University of Bologna

ERNEST EMENYONU, Professor of Africana Studies, University of Michigan–Flint

NATHALIE FERRAND, Senior Research Fellow, Centre Nationale de la Recherche Scientifique, Montpellier (France)

PHILIP FISHER, Reid Professor of English and Harvard College Professor, Harvard University

AMBROSIO FORNET, writer and publisher, Havana

Ernesto Franco, Editorial Director, Einaudi (Turin)

Massimo Fusillo, Professor of Literary Criticism and Comparative Literature, University of L'Aquila (Italy)

Andreas Gailus, Associate Professor of German, University of Minnesota

Simon Gikandi, Professor of English, Princeton University

Michal Peled Ginsburg, Professor of French and Comparative Literature, Northwestern University

Hans Ulrich Gumbrecht, Albert Guérard Professor in Literature, Stanford University

Ursula K. Heise, Associate Professor of English and Comparative Literature, Stanford University

Sibel Irzik, Professor of Comparative Literature, Cultural Studies Program, Sabanci University (Istanbul)

Fredric Jameson, Director of the Institute for Critical Theory, Duke University

Myra Jehlen, Board of Governors Professor of Literature, Rutgers University

Declan Kiberd, Professor of Anglo-Irish Literature and Drama, University College Dublin

Abdelfattah Kilito, Professor of Literature, Mohammed V University, Rabat-Agdal (Morocco)

Thomas Lahusen, Canada Research Chair in History, Arts, and Culture, University of Toronto

Andreina Lavagetto, Associate Professor of European and Postcolonial Studies, Ca' Foscari University of Venice

Leo Ou-fan Lee, Professor of Chinese Literature, Emeritus, Harvard University, and Professor of Humanities, Chinese University of Hong Kong

Peter Madsen, Professor of Comparative Literature, University of Copenhagen

Edoarda Masi, Professor of Chinese Literature, Oriental University Institute, Naples

Juliet Mitchell, Professor of Psychoanalysis and Gender Studies, University of Cambridge

Francis Mulhern, Professor of Critical Studies, Middlesex University, London

Lorri G. Nandrea, Assistant Professor of English, University of Wisconsin–Stevens Point

Ardis L. Nelson, Professor of Hispanic Literature and Cinema, East Tennessee State University

Francesco Orlando, Professor of Romance Literatures and Languages, University of Pisa

José Miguel Oviedo, Professor of Spanish American Literature, Emeritus, University of Pennsylvania

JOSÉ LUIZ PASSOS, Associate Professor of Spanish and Portuguese, University of California, Berkeley

THOMAS PAVEL, Gordon J. Laing Distinguished Service Professor of Romance Languages and Literatures and Social Thought, University of Chicago

FRANCISCO RICO, Professor of Medieval Literature, Autonomous University of Barcelona

BRUCE ROBBINS, Professor of English and Comparative Literature, Columbia University

BEATRIZ SARLO, Researcher, National Council for Scientific and Technological Research, Buenos Aires

KLAUS R. SCHERPE, Professor of German and Cultural Studies, Humboldt–University of Berlin

SYLVIE THOREL-CAILLETEAU, Professor of French Literature, Université Charles de Gaulle-Lille 3 (France)

PAOLO TORTONESE, Professor of French Literature, University of Savoie (Chambéry, France)

LUISA VILLA, Professor of English Literature, University of Genoa

GEOFFREY WINTHROP-YOUNG, Associate Professor of German, University of British Columbia

ALEX WOLOCH, Associate Professor of English, Stanford University

Author Index

Works Cited Index